ATTACK AND COUNTERATTACK
The Texas-Mexican Frontier, 1842

THIS BOOK IS PUBLISHED WITH THE ASSISTANCE OF THE

Dan Danciger Publication Fund

ATTACK
AND
COUNTER-
ATTACK

The Texas-Mexican Frontier, 1842

By JOSEPH MILTON NANCE

UNIVERSITY OF TEXAS PRESS · AUSTIN

Library of Congress Catalog Card No. 62–9789

Copyright © 1964 Joseph Milton Nance
Printed in the United States of America

TO

JERRY, JOE, AND JIM

PREFACE

This is the second in a series of three books covering the story of the Texas-Mexican frontier from 1836 to 1845. The first was published in 1963 under the title of *After San Jacinto: The Texas Mexican Frontier, 1836–1841*. The current book covers the story for the year 1842, commencing with the Vasquez raid upon San Antonio and concluding with the return of the Somervell expedition from the Río Grande after it had captured and levied requisitions upon Laredo and Guerrero.

The southern and southwestern frontier of Texas remained in an unsettled and tense condition throughout the year 1842. The gains made between 1839 and 1841 in the settlement and development of southern and western Texas were partly lost during that year owing to continued raids along the frontier by Texan and Mexican freebooters, and to the actual assembling and marching of armies. Settlements receded eastward and a number of immigrants even left Texas for greater safety and more favorable political conditions under which to conduct their businesses as farmers, merchants, traders, or speculators. In the spring of 1842 there was another runaway scrape, as settlers in some quarters hurriedly fled eastward, but the flight was by no means on the same scale as that in the spring of 1836.

Heretofore little has been written concerning the frontier of Texas in 1842. Texas histories have given a good picture of the Texan Santa Fé expedition of 1841 and there are frequent, if incomplete and garbled, accounts of the Texan Mier expedition of late December 1842, but few indeed are the accounts of what occurred between these two forays. Yet 1842 proved to be the most crucial year in the frontier relations of Texas since the days of San Jacinto. An effort is made in the following account to fill this void in the history of Texas-Mexican frontier relations.

Twice during the year San Antonio was occupied by Mexican troops. Goliad and Refugio were also occupied in the spring of 1842, but high water prevented enemy troops in the fall from making another assault upon the Texas settlements along the lower Nueces, San Antonio, and Guadalupe rivers. Each time the Texans rallied quickly to contain and to repel the Mexican invaders. During the year the Houston administration was provoked into going through the motions of planning three retaliatory expeditions against Mexico, but only one of these actually descended upon some of the settlements of northern Mexico. The remnants of a proposed Texan army for invading Mexico, made up largely of men recruited in the United States, was attacked in the vicinity of the lower Nueces River by Mexican troops on July 7. In September the Texans fought a significant engagement with a division of the Mexican army at Salado Creek near San Antonio and later in the fall marched against the Mexican Río Grande settlements.

In this study I have attempted to bring to light the full story of the situation on the southern and southwestern frontier of Texas during the year 1842. The materials I have used are found for the most part in manuscript and newspaper collections in the Latin American and Eugene C. Barker Texas History libraries of The University of Texas, in the Texas State Archives, in the General Land Office in Austin, in the Rosenberg Library at Galveston, in the National Archives in Washington, in the New York Public Library, New York, and in transcripts from the Public Records Office in London, the National Archives of Mexico, the State Archives of Coahuila at Saltillo, and the archives of Béxar, Laredo, and Matamoros.

Grateful acknowledgment is due to the custodians of these collections for courteous and considerate assistance, and especially to the late Miss Harriet Smither, long-time state archivist; Miss Winnie Allen, retired archivist, The University of Texas Library; Mr. Chester Kielman, director of The University of Texas Archives; the late Mr. E. R. Dabney, former custodian of the Newspaper Collection, The University of Texas Library; Miss Llerena Friend, librarian, Eugene C. Barker Texas History Center, The University of Texas Library; Mr. James M. Day, director, Texas State Archives; Mrs. Mildred Stevenson, reference librarian, Rosenberg Library; Mr. Robert W. Hill, keeper of manuscripts, The New York Public Library; and Mrs. Lavelle Castle of the Cushing Memorial Library of Texas A & M University. I am also much indebted to my wife, Mrs. Eleanor Hanover Nance, for the preparation of the maps.

JOSEPH MILTON NANCE

College Station, Texas

CONTENTS

ILLUSTRATIONS

Following page 338

MAPS

ATTACK AND COUNTERATTACK

The Texas-Mexican Frontier, 1842

Prologue

THE INTERNAL political and economic difficulties in Mexico, coupled with the memories and rumors of the savage fighting qualities of *los Tejanos diablos* operated strongly after San Jacinto to help Texas maintain its independence. Although those who occupied responsible leadership in the Mexican government always felt compelled publicly, for political effect at home, to agitate periodically for a war against Texas, privately they often expressed the view that Texas was forever lost to Mexico.

Following the battle of San Jacinto, the Texan army came to be made up principally of volunteers from the United States, who had arrived to assist the Texans in winning their independence and who were disappointed when they learned that the Mexican troops had evacuated Texas. Stationed upon the lower southern frontier around Victoria, Goliad, and San Patricio, the men of the army became restless and unruly from inactivity. Finally, in May 1837, President Sam Houston, who understood well the necessity of leaving Mexico alone, ordered most of the men in the army to be furloughed to relieve the financial strain upon the treasury and to forestall any unauthorized attack upon Mexico, which might cause that country to renew its efforts to subjugate Texas.[1]

As long as Mexico talked of renewing the war to reconquer Texas and encouraged the Indians and disgruntled Mexicans in Texas to attack the Texas frontiersmen, it was no easy task for Houston to maintain a defensive policy that even Lamar knew was correct in regard to Mexico. The eager adventurers from the United States and the Texan frontiersmen who had suffered much during the revolution could see little advantage to a defensive policy which did not provide adequate

[1] A comprehensive study of frontier defense during the early days of the Republic of Texas will be found in Joseph Milton Nance, *After San Jacinto: The Texas-Mexican Frontier, 1836–1841*.

3

security to life and property from Mexican brigands, lawless Texas freebooters, and hostile Indians who roamed the frontier. In answer to the repeated threats of an invasion from Mexico, each successive Texas president, at one time or other, for political effect at home and abroad, talked of administering a severe retribution to any hostile Mexican force that might be so bold as to cross to the Texan side of the Río Grande, and at times was even provoked into boasting of conducting vigorous offensive operations against the enemy's country.

After the disbandment of the army in the late spring of 1837, the defense of the Republic came to rest upon a poorly organized militia, upon a series of ranger companies of short term enlistment, upon small "Minute Men" companies formed in the frontier counties, and upon a limited infantry and cavalry force enrolled for three years.

On the basis of a law enacted by the Texan Congress in December 1836, Texas claimed the Río Grande as her boundary, and Mexico, while refusing to recognize the loss of Texas, was successful in keeping Texas from exercising its jurisdiction beyond the Nueces, even though her own authority could not be made effective over the area north of the Río Grande. As time passed, Mexico doubtless realized she could never reconquer Texas, and directed her energies toward preventing the new republic to the north from annexing significant portions of the states of Tamaulipas and Coahuila. Thus, the area between the Nueces (the historic boundary of Texas) and the Río Grande became a sort of no-man's land which was traversed at great risk to life and property.

By the spring of 1838 enterprising Texans commenced a profitable smuggling trade with the Mexican inhabitants along the Río Grande, a trade which was to expand during the French blockade of the Mexican coast in late 1838 and early 1839, and which persisted thereafter in spite of many handicaps. The frontier trade was complicated by the activities of the so-called Texan "cowboys" who robbed the Mexican ranches in the vicinity of the Sal Colorado, the Nueces, and the San Antonio rivers of their cattle and other livestock, and penetrated even to the Río Grande to get more. Their only excuse was that those whom they robbed were Mexicans; that the war had not ended; that the Mexican army in its retreat from Texas had carried off cattle and horses without remuneration as provided for in the treaty of Velasco (which, of course, had not been ratified by the Mexican government); and that their actions were only retaliatory. The "cowboys," however, were not always too careful about whose cattle they drove off, often stealing stock belonging to their fellow citizens for sale eastward.

4

While the Texas raiders forced the abandonment of many of the Mexican ranches between the Nueces and the Río Grande, Mexican gangs also penetrated the area and sometimes even crossed the Nueces to drive away cattle and horses. Mexican brigands and Texan cutthroats infested the frontier, robbed the traders, despoiling them of their money and goods, and sometimes killed them in cold blood. Both governments sought unsuccessfully to exterminate the "gangs"; yet, each accused the other of abetting them.

Meanwhile the Federalist wars in Mexico which helped to secure Texas from Mexican attack, also helped to create ill-will between the two nations. It was difficult for Mexico to realize that the Texans who participated in the Federalist wars from 1838 to 1840 did so as private parties and not as representatives of the Texan government. The motives of the Texans in aiding the Federalists were varied and not always altruistic, and those who fought in the Federalist service, in the long run, probably did more harm than good to that cause. The most significant result, however, was to intensify the bitterness on both sides of the border, to destroy confidence, and to adversely affect Texas-Mexican border relations for many years to come.

The acrimony of the presidential election in 1841 between the Houston and Lamar factions carried over into the Sixth Congress where an effort was made by each side to blame the other for the country's woes —woes which emanated largely from a nearly bankrupt treasury, a defenseless frontier, a frustrated foreign policy, and a feeling of utter hopelessness and despair on the part of many persons throughout a country affected by the depression. Many resented the wasteful expenditures of the Lamar administration, the sending of the army to Santa Fé, and the renting of the navy to Yucatán, believing that the latter two actions could only further antagonize Mexico. The persistence of marauders on the frontier, and the failure of the Sixth Congress, before its adjournment early in February 1842, to make adequate provision for frontier defense were very disheartening. To the inhabitants of the southern and southwestern border, peace and security for themselves and for their possessions seemed far away.

By 1842 the frontiersmen were desperate for survival, and their methods were likely to be unorthodox and not according to law. The depression following the panic of 1837 was not over; poor roads and transportation restricted markets; and money and credit were extremely short or nonexistent. Yet, before the hardy western farmer and cattleman could be expected to abandon the labor and improvements he had made he could be counted on to support any project that had a prospect of giving the security he so badly needed for his home and his family, and of bringing an improvement in his financial position. Men continued to talk about arriving at their own solution of the problem of defense through the creation of self-constituted military companies formed from among the local citizenry re-enforced by recruits from abroad. Many of the westerners assumed that the Mexicans and their government were the principal source of their misfortune. Quite a number of latecomers to Texas who had not become deeply rooted in their adopted land for various reasons, some of which no doubt were connected with their unwillingness to settle down to a monotonous grind of hard work, were willing to join any leader in any enterprise that offered adventure and easy gain. The idea of making a visit to Mexico appealed to many of them. Others said that they were tired of hearing of Mexican invasion threats, and that Mexico should be castigated for making them. Then, as news of the failure of the Santa Fé expedition was confirmed and reports trickled in of the mistreatment of its members, there was a slow realization in Texas that the members of Lamar's ill-starred expedition awaited an uncertain fate in Mexican dungeons whose horrors were well known to more than one Texan. Men began to talk boldly, and foolishly, of taking matters into their own hands and of marching immediately into Mexico to effect a release of the Texan prisoners and to punish Mexico severely. At the same time rumors began to reach Texas that Mexico was again preparing to invade Texas, causing a feeling among more thoughtful men in Texas that Lamar's rash policy might have so revealed the weakness of the Texas government as to encourage Mexico to make another effort to subjugate her recalcitrant province. The situation on the frontier was daily becoming more ominous.

"It is believed here," President Houston wrote his private secretary on February 15, 1842, shortly after his arrival in Houston, "and I do not doubt the truth of the assertion, that Santa Anna intends, and will if he can, send a large force, and station it upon the Río Grande," from which cavalry parties will be sent out to "annoy" and "assail all frontier points." The predatory incursions may be expected to "bear off such goods and citizens, as they may think will do us greatest injury. If this should not be done within one year, I'll answer, that we shall have peace upon our Río Grande border!"[2]

[2] Sam Houston to Washington D. Miller, Houston, February 15, 1842, in Amelia W. Williams and Eugene C. Barker (eds.), *The Writings of Sam Houston, 1813–1863*, II, 484–485; hereafter cited as *Writings of Sam Houston*.

Prologue

Lamar's poor judgment in sending out the Santa Fé expedition in the summer of 1841 unleashed a chain of events that brought the first significant body of Mexican troops into Texas since the battle of San Jacinto and made the year 1842 not only the most exciting one in the frontier history of Texas since that decisive action, but also the turning point in Texas-Mexican relations.

Late in the fall of 1841 General Mariano Arista, commanding on the northern frontier of Mexico, called upon the Mexicans to forget their differences at home and to turn their united efforts to chastising the real enemy. "In Texas," he declared, "there is a field open to gather fresh and glorious laurels that . . . false aspirations, . . . calumny and envy cannot wither. In Texas you can find a field in which to display your warlike ardor without the pain and mortification of knowing that the blood you shed and the tears you occasion are from your brethren."[3] In preparation for an advance into Texas, Arista ordered Captain José Manuel González in December to recruit two hundred men from the Third Regiment of Cavalry, the Presidial Company (*Defensores*) of Camargo, and the Auxiliaries of La Bahía under Lieutenant Norverto Galán and have them ready to enter Texas on January 9 in a surprise attack upon Corpus Christi, Goliad, and Refugio.[4] Later González was instructed to commence his march from Camargo on February 1, simultaneous with General Rafael Vasquez's march from Lampazos for San Antonio.[5] Lieutenant Colonel Manuel Savariego, who was familiar with the coastal area lying between the Río Grande and the Nueces, was to command the march into Texas by the lower route. When the time to march arrived, however, Savariego was unable to go on account of family affairs, and the command fell to Captain Ramón Valera of the Third Regiment of Cavalry, who was accorded the brevet rank of Lieutenant Colonel.[6]

From Monterey, the military headquarters for Tamaulipas, Arista issued an address on January 9, 1842, to the inhabitants of the "Department of Texas," carefully pointing out the hopelessness of their struggle

---

[3] Quoted in *Telegraph and Texas Register* (Houston), October 17, 1841.

[4] El General Mariano Arista al Ministro de Guerra, Deciembre 29 de 1841, Archivo Historico Militar de Mexico, cited in Frederick C. Chabot, *Corpus Christi and Lipantitlán*, p. 15.

[5] Fredrick C. Chabot, *Corpus Christi and Lipantitlán*, p. 16.

[6] El General Mariano Arista al General Rafael Vasquez, Monterey, Enero 8 de 1842; El General Mariano Arista al Ministro de Guerra, Enero 9 de 1842, cited in *ibid.*, pp. 15–16.

7

for independence and promising amnesty and protection to all who refrained from taking up of arms during his contemplated invasion. At the same time he warned that while his country held out "the olive branch and concord" with one hand, she would direct with the other "the sword of justice against the obstinate."[7]

With these announcements Mexico commenced strengthening her northern garrisons and making preparations for renewing the Texas campaign. However, thoughtful persons in Texas believed Mexico would not be so foolish as to launch an invasion in the spring or summer, by troops brought from the interior of Mexico, as they would be so susceptible to disease when brought down from the tablelands that they would be wholly unfit in a short time to endure a campaign during those seasons of the year. The Mexicans, it was reasoned, would surely wait until fall to commence a full-scale campaign in Texas. No one, however, could say with certainty.

[7] Mariano Arista, general de division y en gefe del cuerpo de ejército de Norte de la republica mexicana, á los que habitan el departamento de Téjas, Cuartel general en Monterey, Enero 9 de 1842, *El Cosmopolita* (Mexico City), March 30, 1842.

CHAPTER ONE

The Vasquez Raid

As THE MEXICAN PREPARATIONS for an invasion continued along the Río Grande, news of these activities, during the fall of 1841 and the succeeding winter, began to trickle into San Antonio, a frontier town with an estimated population of two thousand inhabitants, nine-tenths of whom were Mexicans and the remainder Anglo-Texans, thus fulfilling Samuel A. Maverick's assertion in 1838 that at San Antonio they knew exactly what was going on beyond the Río Grande and "would know to a certainty (and to the very day) when any force would be brought against the country."[1] Through a few friendly Mexican women of the town the Texans learned that preparations were rapidly being made in Mexico for sending another army into Texas. "Sometimes," recorded Mrs. Mary A. Maverick, "friendly-minded Mexicans dropped in to warn us and even to entreat us not to remain and be butchered, for they felt sure the invading army would be vindictive and cruel."[2]

The commander of the Army of the North, General Mariano Arista, was reported to have ordered the collection of a fifteen- to twenty-days' supply of provisions in the frontier towns for the presidial companies.[3] At Mexico City it was reported on February 5 that an expedition of 400 to 500 men, including 300 select dragoons had probably already left the Department of Tamaulipas for Béxar,[4] and, later referring to these same men, the *Vera Cruz Censor*[5] reported the expedition had left Tampico for San Antonio about the last of February. At the same time it was announced that in Nuevo León 2,110 auxiliaries had been organ-

[1] Rena Maverick Green (ed.), *Samuel Maverick, Texan, 1803–1870: A Collection of Letters, Journals and Memoirs*, p. 65.

[2] *Ibid.*, p. 151; Rena Maverick Green (ed.), *Memoirs of Mary A. Maverick: Arranged by Mary A. Maverick and Her Son George Madison Maverick*, p. 60. See also *Telegraph and Texas Register*, March 9, 1842.

[3] *El Cosmopolita*, Jan. 1, 1842.

[4] *Ibid.*, Feb. 5, 1842.

[5] Quoted in *Telegraph and Texas Register*, April 6, 1842.

ized, of whom 810 were infantrymen and the remainder cavalry.⁶ A considerable number of militiamen were reported concentrating at Mier, but in Texas it was believed these rancheros were wholly unprepared for a long march, and that their assembling was evidence of the apprehension the authorities in northern Mexico held that the Texans might attempt to revenge the outrages inflicted upon the Santa Fé prisoners by attacking some of the Mexican frontier towns.⁷

A citizen of Laredo and prominent leader in the Federalist revolutionary disturbances of 1838–1840, José María González, was arrested and taken to Monterey, arriving there on March 12, to stand trial on a charge of "being in intercourse with our insolent enemies the Texan adventurers and of having given them opportune information of the march our troops undertook against the city of Béxar," declared *El Centinela*.⁸ Apprehensions among the Texans at San Antonio were further stimulated when a number of Mexicans under the lead of Antonio Pérez, a well-known enemy of Texas, secretly left town to join the invader on the Río Grande. An old canonically deposed priest of the town, Refugio de la Garza,⁹ was reported to have received letters from lead-

⁶ *El Cosmopolita*, Feb. 5, 1842.

⁷ *Telegraph and Texas Register*, Feb. 23, 1842.

⁸ *El Centinela* quoted in *El Cosmopolita*, March 26, 1842; see also John H. Brown, *History of Texas, from 1685 to 1892*, II, 211. Juan N. Seguin, then in San Antonio, later testified in the court-martial trial of the ex-Federalist leader, José María González, that González had informed the people of San Antonio of Vasquez's intended march on Béxar. His testimony, however, seems to have been based upon hearsay. "Information derived from José María González and Juan Ramos," in Charles Adams Gulick and Others (eds.), *The Papers of Mirabeau Buonaparte Lamar*, VI, 119; hereafter cited as *Lamar Papers*.

⁹ Béxar [County] Committee of Safety to Col. Andrew J. Neil[l] and Citizens of Seguin, Gonz[ale]s County, San Antonio, Feb. 27, 1842, in Domestic Correspondence (Texas), 1835–1846, ms. Positive proof of Padre Garza's traitorous correspondence with the Mexican authorities was not obtained, reported Maverick, until after the padre's escape (Green [ed.], *Samuel Maverick*, p. 151). We find that in 1840 this same Garza had been arrested on August 6 on suspicion of corresponding with the enemy. "The Parish Priest of San Antonio, Refugio de la Garza," reported the *Austin City Gazette*, August 12, 1840, "has been discovered corresponding with the enemy. A package by him to Gen. Arista was lately intercepted, he was arrested and brought into town on Sunday evening last. He has acknowledged that the communication was in his handwriting. He left town this morning for San Antonio, in charge of Mr. Van Ness, by whom he will be handed to the civil authorities of Béxar County." That he was returned to San Antonio over the protest of the Secretary of State is quite evident from the following brief letter to the Secretary of War:

On yesterday [wrote the Secretary of State] you did me the honor to ask my

ing officers in the Mexican army, saying that a large Mexican force composed of infantry and artillery would be in San Antonio between the 4th and 15th of March. Another local priest, Padre Michael Calvo, showed Wilson I. Riddle, an Irish-Catholic merchant, a letter from Mexico which convinced him that an invasion was imminent.[10] Seeking to raise money to meet his financial obligations to Ogden and Howard by bringing in sheep from Mexico, Mayor Juan N. Seguin, who had been absent from the city in July and August 1841, on a visit to Mexico, returned to the city early in 1842, from where he wrote General Vasquez, commanding on the Río Grande frontier, requesting a passport to enable him to enter Mexico to purchase a drove of sheep. The tenor of Vasquez's reply, reported Seguin, caused him "to apprehend that an expedition was preparing against Texas, for the following month of March."[11]

As mayor of San Antonio, Seguin lost no time in calling a special session of the Board of Aldermen, and laying before it Vasquez's communication, stating that in his opinion San Antonio might soon expect the approach of a Mexican force. Colonel Seguin wrote President Houston on January 30 concerning his suspicions of an invasion and the matter was referred by Houston to the Secretary of War and Marine, George W. Hockley, who informed Seguin a few days later, "I regret exceedingly the impoverished condition of our country renders it almost helpless, and that we must depend upon the patriotism of those who

council, as to what disposition you ought to make of the prisoner Padre García [Garza] sent to you by the Military Commander at San Antonio. I then advised you, to keep him in close confinement until the arrival of the President. You have just informed me, that you had resolved to send him immediately back and direct him to be turned over to the civil authorities. Under ordinary circumstances I should interpose no objection to the course; but as we have reason to believe that, the prisoner is one of many concerned with him in a treasonable correspondence with the enemy, and that it is so well known, that, even its notoriety is offered as an excuse, and apology for the treason. I am therefore of the opinion that strong measures ought to be resorted to, and must therefore respectfully reiterate the opinion I had the honor to express on yesterday.

[Secretary of State] to B. T. Archer, Department of State, Aug. 10, 1840, in State Department, (Texas), Department of State Letterbook, no. 1, Nov. 1836–Jan. 1842), ms., p. 184; hereafter cited as State Department Letterbook, no. 1. See also, Ralph F. Bayard, *Lone-Star Vanguard: The Catholic Re-occupation of Texas, 1838–1848*, pp. 133–137.

[10] John Henry Brown, *Indian Wars and Pioneers of Texas*, pp. 643–644.

[11] Juan N. Seguin, *Personal Memoirs of Juan N. Seguin; from the Year 1834 to the Retreat of General Woll from the City of San Antonio in 1842*, p. 22; hereafter cited as Seguin, *Memoirs*.

are willing to defend it. I hope you will be enabled to rally a few about you upon whom you can depend in case the threatened advance shall be made, and rest assured that all assistance will be given by this Department, which its limited means will allow."[12]

A few days later Don José María García of Laredo reached San Antonio, and his report precluded "all possible doubts as to the near approach of Vasquez to San Antonio."[13] About the middle of February Henry L. Kinney, frontier trader and rancher in the Corpus Christi area, notified the President by special courier that an invasion was to take place early in March. Kinney says he captured three of Valera's spies himself without letting his men know of it, for fear that they would become alarmed at the invasion.[14]

In the various meetings held at San Antonio to determine a course of action, Mayor Seguin, already under suspicion by some of having tipped-off the Mexican officials concerning the fitting out of the Texan Santa Fé expedition the summer before, expressed his "candid opinion as to the impossibility of defending San Antonio," and declared that, as for himself, he intended "to retire to his ranch, and thence to Seguin, in case the Mexican forces should take possession of San Antonio."[15] The Anglo-Texan element, however, met and unanimously elected John C. Hays, a well-known Indian fighter, to lead them and authorized him to establish martial law in the town.

John Coffee Hays, son of Harmon A. and Elizabeth Cage Hays, was born at Little Cedar Lick, Wilson County, Tennessee, January 28, 1817, and died at his home near Piedmont, Alameda County, California, April 28, 1883. He was one of a family of eight children, and was from the same section of Tennessee as the McCullochs, Sam Houston, and Andrew Jackson, and was "the same adaptable sort of person." It is said that Jackson purchased the Hermitage from Hays' grandfather, John Hays, who served with Jackson in some of his Indian wars, and who built Fort Haysboro. John C. Hays' father also fought with Jackson,

---

[12] George W. Hockley to Col. Juan N. Seguin, Department of War & Marine, Austin 3d February 1[842? torn], in Juan N. Seguin Papers, ms.

[13] Seguin, *Memoirs*, p 23.

[14] "Information derived from Col. Kinney, Corpus Christi, 184—?" in *Lamar Papers*, IV, pt. I, pp. 213–214. Kinney does not say what he did with the Mexicans whom he captured, or what he learned from them other than that a movement against the frontier of Texas was intended.

[15] Seguin, *Memoirs*, p. 23.

and named his son for General John Coffee, one of Jackson's trusted officers. Having been orphaned when scarcely twelve years old, John C. Hays was forced to leave school at the age of fifteen. He went to Mississippi, where he learned to be a surveyor. Shortly after the battle of San Jacinto he arrived in Texas bearing a letter of introduction from President Andrew Jackson addressed to Sam Houston. He found employment for a while as a surveyor, and became noted as a gentleman of much ability and energy and of "the purest character." On November 7, 1837, he was appointed chief justice of the frontier county of Victoria by President Houston, but by 1840 had come to devote most of his time to the duties of a frontier ranger. He exhibited great daring in the battle of Plum Creek against the Comanches in 1840. He was placed by President Lamar, and later by Houston, in charge of the ranger force at San Antonio. Weighing only 160 pounds in 1842, he was described as a "small, boyish looking youngster," five-feet ten-inches tall, with "not a particle of beard" on his homely, weather-beaten, and darkly-tanned face. Possessing hazel eyes, beautiful jet-black hair, a wide forehead, large mouth, a Roman nose, and "a thoughtful, care-worn expression, amounting to a frown, always upon his face," "Jack," as he was commonly called, was known for his quiet, unobtruding nature, which some attributed to shyness. Yet, by 1842, he had become noted for his bravery, daring, and courage; and was a terror to un-friendly Indians, robbers, freebooters, and other lawless groups along the southwestern frontier. His rigid discipline, his exact justice to the men under him, and his treatment of each comrade in arms as in all respects his equal, when not on duty, are probably the reasons why the rangers, one and all, were "so willing, without a murmur, to live on parched corn, ride 70 or 80 miles without dismounting for five minutes at a time," and to fight Mexicans or Indians in any manner of condition or arms he deemed necessary. John S. Ford, a Texas ranger who knew Hays intimately, wrote, "The fame of Colonel Hays rested on a sub-stantial basis; it was acquired by hard fighting, by suffering privations, and by the exhibition of high qualities adorning a citizen and a soldier. His campaigns against the Indians and Mexicans making descents upon Texas, and the success of his operations, rendered him one of the most famous Rangers in the world. . . . He was lenient to the point of erring. . . . He was almost idolized by many. He was modest and retiring; any expression of admiration of his acts would cause him to blush like a woman. . . . He knew how to conduct marches requiring toilsome en-

13

durance, and to prevent his men from becoming despondent. . . . He was cool, self-possessed, and brave; a good shot."[16]

Hays forthwith took command at San Antonio and prepared to defend the place. He proceeded at once to establish martial law. Some of the men erected breastworks in the streets[17] and commenced fortifying one corner of the public square. The artillery pieces were mounted. A number of citizens and merchants subscribed considerable sums of money and goods to pay spies and to provision the volunteers.[18] At Austin the President's private secretary reported on the 23rd of February that Colonel John D. Anderson of Bastrop; Judge George W. Terrell, the Attorney General; and others had returned to the capital some three or four days before from San Antonio, where "they were feasted, feted and fandangoed in fine style." The report of an invasion in that quarter, he concluded, was generally considered "as all humbug."[19] This conclusion on the part of nonresidents was not borne out by the actions of the inhabitants of San Antonio.

On February 21 the Béxar County Committee of Safety, consisting of William B. Jaques,[20] John Madley, William Elliot, and Samuel A.

[16] John S. Ford, "Memoirs." See also *Jack Hays: The Intrepid Texas Ranger,* pp. 1–63; Walter Prescott Webb, *The Texas Rangers,* pp. 32–34, 67–123; Elizabeth H. West, "John Coffee Hays," *Dictionary of American Biography,* VIII, 463; John W. Lockhart quoted in Mrs. Jonnie Lockhart Wallis and Laurance L. Hill, *Sixty Years on the Brazos: The Life and Letters of Dr. John Washington Lockhart, 1824–1900,* p. 117; Cornelius Van Ness and Others to Gen. M. B. Lamar, San Antonio, Feb. 15, 1840, in *Lamar Papers,* V, 409–410; Z[enos] N. Morrell, *Flowers and Fruits in the Wilderness: or Forty-Six Years in Texas and Two Winters in Honduras,* pp. 168–169; "Jack Hays and His Men," in *The Texas Democrat* Dec. 16, 1846; J. D. Affleck, "History of John C. Hays," Pts. I and II, ts.; J. Frost, *The Mexican War and Its Warriors: . . .,* p. 304, has a picture of Hays at age 29; Stephen B. Oates (ed.), *Rip Ford's Texas,* pp. 61–69, 107–109; Walter P. Webb, "The Texas Rangers," in Eugene C. Barker (ed.), *Texas History for High Schools and Colleges,* pp. 592–598; James Kimmins Greer, *Colonel Jack Hays: Texas Frontier Leader and California Builder.*

[17] Seguin, *Memoirs,* p. 23.

[18] See Resolution of the City Council, June 21, 1842, in San Antonio, "Journal A: Records of the City of San Antonio," June 21, 1842, ts.; W. D. Miller to Sam Houston, Austin, March 6, 1842 (Private), no. 7, in Washington D. Miller Papers 1833–1860 (Texas), ms. copy.

[19] W. D. Miller to Sam Houston, Austin, February 23, 1842 (Private), no. 3, in Miller Papers (Texas), ms. copy.

[20] William B. Jaques was born in New Jersey about 1799. Prior to coming to Texas, he lived in Mexico a number of years and operated a stagecoach between Mexico City and Vera Cruz. It is said that he befriended Stephen F. Austin when

Maverick, dispatched Damacio and Farías (San Antonio Mexicans who had joined the Texan cause) to Presidio del Río Grande and San Fernando, Mexican military posts upon or near the Río Grande, to gather information about the impending invasion. Just beyond the Nueces River on the 23rd Damacio and Farias met Agatón Quiñones, the celebrated Río Grande robber, who, saying that his orders were to prevent all communication with the Río Grande, pre-emptorily seized and detained them one day and then ordered them to return.[21] They returned to San Antonio on the night of the 26th. Thereupon, other spies were dispatched, including Mike Chevallie and James Dunn,[22] and a call was sent to Gonzales for one hundred men to re-enforce those at San Antonio. Being a small community, Seguin[23] was not requested for assistance at this time. The citizens there, however, learning of the requests for help being sent to other points, reported through their leader, Andrew Neill, that they were desirous of rendering aid to the people of San Antonio in case of an attack.

We understand [said Neill] that an express went yesterday morning to Gonzales for aid. Why not give us the news also? And we can render some aid and forward the express to the next settlement. A company will leave this [place] on one or two hours notice for Béxar on foot at any time, so that we

---

Austin was released from prison in Mexico in 1835. Sometime in 1837, it seems Jaques came to Texas and settled at Brazoria from which place he applied in September 1837 for a passport to go to the United States for the purpose of bringing out his family (Edmund Andrews to Secretary of State, Brazoria, Sept. 22, 1837, in State Department (Texas), Department of State Letterbook, Home Letters, II, ms., p. 92). Jaques again entered Texas as an agent for the mercantile firm of Jaques and Browning of Grand Gulf, Mississippi. In the summer of the following year he brought his wife, the former Catherine Louise Browne, and two little daughters to San Antonio and settled on Commerce Street. Green (ed.), *Memoirs of Mary A. Maverick*, p. 25; Walter Prescott Webb and H. Bailey Carroll, (eds.), *The Handbook of Texas*, I, 905; hereafter cited as *Handbook of Texas*.

[21] *Austin City Gazette*, March 2, 1842; William B. Jaques, John Madley, William Elliot, S. A. Maverick, Béxar [County] Committee of Safety, to Col. Andrew J. Neil[l] and Citizens of Seguin, Gonz[ale]s County, San Antonio, Feb. 27, 1842, in Domestic Correspondence, (Texas), 1835–1846, ms.

[22] Chevallie had been with Hays in the attack on the Mexican marauding force under Ignacio García near Laredo in April 1841 (*Jack Hays: The Intrepid Texas Ranger*, p. 6). During the Civil War James Dunn was killed in 1864 at Las Rucias on the Lower Río Grande (Brown, *Indian Wars and Pioneers of Texas*, p. 270).

[23] Two families had settled in the new town of Seguin by March 23, 1840. [Samuel] Augustus Maverick to Mary A. Maverick, Gonzales, March 23, 1840, in Green (ed.), *Samuel Maverick*, p. 129.

may be relied upon when you send for us by giving us the true situation of your affairs, and we will not encumber ourselves unnecessarily by horses or anything else but arms, and can march through in a night.[24]

This communication reached San Antonio the night of the 26th.

Dunn and Chevallie were ambushed on the Nueces and captured.[25] The story of their capture is an interesting one. Approaching the Nueces, they discovered two Mexicans, and rode forward to capture them or give them fight. As they drew near to them, they discovered another and another until, within gunshot, five Mexicans stood before them.

Nothing daunted, however, they rode up, when they discovered the whole thicket was alive with yellow skins and that they were in the midst of the Mexican army. Gen[eral] Bravo ordered them to approach him and give up their arms. Chevalia [Chevallie] rode up and taking a pistol from his belt, he in an instant cocked and presented it to the breast of the Mexican general, saying, "If I surrender it shall be upon my own terms. You may order your men to fire, but I shall not die unavenged." Bravo, either disliking his own awkward position or being unwilling to shed blood, replied that his prisoner might dictate his own terms.

Chevallie then said he asked for his companion and himself the treatment due prisoners of war. But Chevallie "refused to withdraw his aim until the Mexican general had taken out his cross and sworn in the presence of his whole army that the lives of the captives should be spared, and [that] they should be kindly treated."[26]

Captain Hays next dispatched his favorite Mexican servant, Antonio Coy, who fell into the Mexican trap near the Río Frio and was not only captured but roughly treated for his known adherence to the Texan cause.[27] After waiting a reasonable length of time and having received no report from any of these spies—Dunn, Chevallie, or Coy— by the time the Gonzales men arrived, Hays on the evening of March 2 dispatched Alsey S. Miller and Benjamin McCulloch, whose father had fought under General Andrew Jackson in the Creek Indian War.

[24] A. Neill to C. Van Ness, Ed. Dwyer, and Samuel A. Maverick, Seguin, Feb. 26, 1842, in *ibid.*, pp. 151–152.

[25] Many years later Dunn petitioned the Legislature of the State of Texas for compensation for a horse, saddle, gun, and pistols taken from him by the Mexicans during the invasion in the spring of 1842. James Dunn to the Legislature of the State of Texas, Béxar County, Nov. 23, 1859, Memorials and Petitions (Texas), ms.

[26] *Civilian and Galveston Gazette*, April 16, 1842.

[27] James T. DeShields, "Jack Hays: Famous Texas Ranger," in *The American Home Journal*, June, 1906.

Both men had only recently arrived with the Gonzales troops. After pointing out to Hays the desirability of having a picket stationed at the crossing of the Medina to guard against surprise, McCulloch and his companion "proceeded to the Honda, and secreting . . . [themselves] in the chaparral, actually counted the men of the Vasquez 'expedition' as they leisurely marched by."[28] Supposing that San Antonio would not be surrendered to any force of that size, Miller and McCulloch then pushed on as far as the Nueces, and satisfying themselves that no reserves were on hand to follow the cavalry, returned by way of the mountains north of San Antonio to find, as they drew within sight of Béxar, that the Mexican flag floated over the dome of the cathedral of San Fernando and that Hays had withdrawn his forces from the town.[29] They joined Hays on the 6th at Flores Rancho,[30] opposite Seguin.

The inhabitants of San Antonio did not waste time in accepting the offer of aid from the citizens of Seguin. In an appeal to them on February 27, the Béxar County Committee of Safety wrote,

The only fact that we can vouch for, justifying these apprehensions is this —we have not for many weeks past seen anyone or received any letter that we could believe in; and it seems that very rigorous measures have been adopted to prevent our people and all others from coming home,—and from this state of things—it is inferred that something important (perhaps a war on us) is intended. The statements of the old priest are therefore listened to and give our people much uneasiness, and have in fact depopulated our town.

Our population is so reduced & our means of supplying provisions so limited (as to corn for horses &c) that we were obliged to ask our Guadalupe friends for only one hundred men for the present. We write also to Austin (to Capt. [George M.] Dolson) requesting our Travis neighbors to be ready to hear us, & help us if necessary. We beg to use the same freedom with you; but in case you see very few can come from about Gonzales, you will do us a kindness to get a few to come over immediately in order to keep our spirits up & prevent the necessity of our families moving eastward for want of strength.[31]

[28] Victor M. Rose, *The Life and Services of Gen. Ben. McCulloch*, p. 66.
[29] W. D. Miller to Sam Houston, Austin, March 9, 1842 (Private), no. 9, in Miller Papers (Texas), ms. copy.
[30] DeShields, "Jack Hays," in *The American Home Journal*, June, 1906.
[31] William B. Jaques, John Madley, William Elliot, and S. A. Maverick, Béxar [County] Committee of Safety, to Col. Andrew J. Neil[l] and Citizens of Seguin, Gonz[ale]s County, San Antonio, Feb. 27, 1842, in Domestic Correspondence, (Texas), 1835–1846, ms.

By February 27 three-fourths of the families had fled eastward from the town of San Antonio, and others were preparing to leave. Many of the Mexican families, including the family of Juan N. Seguín, the mayor,[32] sought refuge at the ranches in the area. Late in the evening of the 27th an urgent call was sent from San Antonio asking Captain Andrew Neill[33] at Seguin to send men and four or more wagons at once, as "the American families & property [are] to leave here tomorrow or next day at farthest" since new reports were that the enemy would probably arrive on the 4th of March.[34] The American women agreed to leave temporarily, and on March 1 the so-called "Runaway of '42" commenced. Those leaving on March 1, after hasty preparations, included Mrs. William Elliot, with three children and two servants; Mrs. William B. Jaques, with two children and one servant; Mrs. John Bradley, with six children and seven or eight servants; Freeman W. Douglas, an invalid gentleman; Pierre Gautier,[35] a French merchant, with wife and child; William and Andrew L. Adams, brothers of Mrs. Maverick; Judge and Mrs. Anderson Hutchinson in their fine carriage, with driver; and Samuel A. Maverick, with wife, three children, five slaves (Griffin, Wiley, Granville, Jinny, and Rachael), and several Negro children. Bradley, Jaques, Riddle, and Elliot[36] remained behind to

[32] W. D. Miller to Sam Houston, Austin, March 6, 1842 (Private), no. 7, in Miller Papers (Texas), ms. copy.

[33] Sometimes spelled "Neil." Andrew J. Neill, born at Lough Fergus Farm, County of Ayr, North Britain, was about thirty years old in 1842. He came to Texas in 1836 with Captain Felix Huston; served as district attorney for the Second Judicial District in 1843–1844; and was practicing law in San Antonio in September 1842, when he was made a prisoner by General Adrián Woll. D. W. C. Baker (comp.), *A Texas Scrap-Book: Made Up of the History, Biography, and Miscellany of Texas and Its People*, p. 638; Charles Elliot to Gen. Adrián Woll, Galveston, Oct. 18, 1842, in Ephraim D. Adams, (ed.), "Correspondence from the British Archives Concerning Texas," *Quarterly of the Texas State Historical Association*, XV (1911–1912), 349–350. For an interesting biographical sketch of Neill see Willie Mae Weinert, "Colonel Andrew Neill," in *Seguin Enterprise*, July 22, 1938.

[34] Edward Dyer, Acting for the Committee of Safety, San Ant[oni]o de Béjar, to Capt. A. Neil[l] 8 o'c[loc]k Even[in]g, Monday, February [27?], 1842, in Domestic Correspondence (Texas), 1835–1846, ms. A postscript to this letter written by John Madley reads, "Send four Waggons & others if it is in your power. *We are ready Come.*"

[35] Pierre Gautier came to San Antonio with his wife and child about December 1840 to engage in the Mexican trade. Green (ed.), *Samuel Maverick*, p. 136.

[36] John Bradley, uncle to Mrs. Samuel A. Maverick, brought his family to San Antonio on January 29, 1841. He was captured by Gen. Adrián Woll in September 1842, and spent some time in Mexican prisons. In the summer of 1844, after his

pack up and forward such other of their goods as were most valuable. Mrs. James Campbell and Mrs. ——— Moore remained behind a few days, and then hurriedly left shortly before Vasquez's entry, but never succeeded in overtaking the advance American party. Mrs. Wilson I. Riddle, the proud mother of a two weeks old baby daughter (Sarah Elizabeth), however, could not move. She was later taken eastward in a buggy behind a fleet horse by James W. Robinson, business partner of her husband and owner of the old mill above and on the edge of the

---

release from prison, he was taken sick with a fever while out electioneering for a seat in Congress, and died September 24, 1844. Green (ed.), *Memoirs of Mary A. Maverick*, pp. 54, 84; Green (ed.), *Samuel Maverick*, p. 136.

Wilson Irwin Riddle was born near Dublin, Ireland, in 1811. His parents came to the United States in 1819 and settled in Howard County, Pennsylvania. When about twenty years of age young Riddle went to Nashville, Tennessee, where he worked as a clerk in a mercantile house; he later was in business for himself at Pulaski, Tennessee, for five years. From there he went to New Orleans, joined Fisher & Miller's colonizing enterprise, and moved to Texas in 1839. In May 1841 he settled at San Antonio and entered the mercantile business on Commerce Street. (Edward W. Heusinger, *A Chronology of Events in San Antonio: being a Concise History of the City, Year by Year from the Beginning of Its Establishment to the End of the First Half of the Twentieth Century*, p. 22, says Riddle's establishment was "on the north side of Main Street where the Aztec Building now stands.") Between his coming to Texas and the Vasquez raid, he made two trips to Tennessee in 1840 and 1841. On the latter occasion on April 26, 1841, he married Miss Elizabeth Menefee of Pulaski. During the Vasquez raid Riddle's property was appropriated by the Mexicans or destroyed. He was among the San Antonians captured by General Adrián Woll in September, 1842, and carried into captivity. After his return from Mexico, he settled on a ranch eighteen miles from San Antonio, where he died on September 12, 1847, as a result of the exposure and hardships suffered during his imprisonment in Mexico. Brown, *Indian Wars and Pioneers of Texas*, pp. 643–644; Green (ed.), *Memoirs of Mrs. Mary A. Maverick*, p. 54.

William Elliot was born in 1799 in Ireland. Prior to his going to Mexico in 1820, he served some time as an apprentice to a mercantile house in Dublin. For a number of years in Mexico he engaged in merchandising and mining. In 1836 he was in business in Matamoros. He came to San Antonio in August 1839 with his wife and two children. Later a third child was born. At San Antonio, Elliot bought a house on the west side of Soledad Street, opposite the north end of the Samuel A. Maverick garden, and formed a partnership for a short time in a mercantile business with Edward Dwyer. Elliot was a successful trader and a thrifty businessman until his death in New Orleans on May 12, 1847, while on a business trip for his firm. Mrs. Elliot, whom he married in 1835, was the former Miss Eleanor Connally of New Orleans. She died at San Antonio on August 27, 1885. Brown, *Indian Wars and Pioneers of Texas*, p. 510; Green (ed.), *Memoirs of Mrs. Mary A. Maverick*, p. 25; *Handbook of Texas*, I, 557.

city.[37] Before leaving, the Mavericks buried a few articles under a store-room floor and left a chest of drawers containing a few keepsakes (books, silver, Mrs. Maverick's wedding dress, and other treasured articles) in the care of Mrs. Jesusa Soto, who begged that it be sent "to her in the night-time so that none of her neighbors should know."[38] By the time the enemy forces arrived, all the Anglo-Texans not absolutely needed for the defense of the town had fled eastward.

The Runaway of '42 had its humorous as well as its melancholy side. Some were afoot, others in wagons, carriages, and carts, or on horse-back. Granville drove the Maverick's woodcart, "drawn by two horses, which carried Jinny, Rachael, and quite a number of children white and black." The cart also carried their necessary clothing, bedding, and provisions. Sometimes the children rode in front of the riders on horseback. Maverick probably rode "Mex" (Mexico), a horse that he had bought from his brother-in-law William Adams, who had obtained it in San Antonio and ridden it to Tuscaloosa, Alabama, and back. Agatha, the Maverick's baby, rode in the lap of its mother. "Mrs. Elliott had a good large carryall; Mrs. Bradley a fine wagon and some riding horses," and often rode on horseback with the Mavericks. At times, it seemed like a frolic with gay gallops ahead, with laughter and banter while those who had ridden ahead waited for the caravan to come up. "The weather was charming," reported Mrs. Maverick, "the grass green and the whole earth in bloom."[39]

The first day the refugees traveled about five miles and encamped

[37] Petition of James W. Robinson to the City Council, March 19, 1840, in San Antonio, "Journal A, Records of the City of San Antonio," April 2, 1840, ts. James W. Robinson, a native of Ohio, came to Texas in 1824. He served as a delegate from Nacogdoches to the Consultation in 1835 and later as lieutenant governor of the Provisional Government. In the battle of San Jacinto he served as a private in Captain William H. Smith's cavalry company, and upon the organization of constitutional government in 1836 was appointed district judge of the Fourth Judicial District. Robinson was wounded in the Council House Fight in San Antonio on March 19, 1840. In September 1842 he was captured at San Antonio by General Adrián Woll and held prisoner in Mexico until released by Santa Anna to attempt to bring about a reconciliation between Texas and Mexico. Robinson moved to California in 1849, and there served as a district attorney from 1853–1855, in 1854 as school commissioner, and became interested in the promotion of a railroad from El Paso to California. He died in California in October 1857. [Elizabeth LeNoir Jennett], *Biographical Directory of the Texan Conventions and Congresses,* pp. 160–161; *Handbook of Texas,* II, 490.

[38] Green (ed.), *Samuel Maverick,* pp. 153–157.

[39] *Ibid.*

on the west bank of the Salado. During the night a light rain fell, and some of the women and children found protection under several small tents, while the men who were not taking their turn at standing guard sought sleep rolled in their blankets before the campfire. Once during the night it rained so hard that Maverick took refuge under Judge Hutchinson's carriage, in which Mrs. Hutchinson was sleeping. While he was lying awake, reports Mrs. Maverick,

Judge Hutchinson came up, opened the door, and remarking to Mrs. Hutchinson that he had just been relieved from guard and was wet and cold, was proceeding to enter the carriage, when Mrs. Hutchinson said in rather discouraging tones: "What makes you such a fool as to stand guard? You know you can't see ten feet."

"Well, my love, can't I come in?"

"No, my dear, you can't, you are damp and would give me a bad cold."

The judge resignedly closed the door and retired to the camp-fire, where he smoked his pipe, ruminating over the cruelty of his young second wife, or possibly over his own unwisdom in mentioning the fact that he was wet before he had gotten fairly in.[40]

The next day the refugees traveled eighteen miles to the Cíbolo and four miles farther to the Santa Clara and camped. Here they were met by Ben McCulloch, Alsey Miller, and several other volunteers on their way to San Antonio. McCulloch's party encamped with them and maintained a guard all night. "They were," said Mrs. Maverick, "as witty and lively as could be and we all sat late around the fire enjoying their jokes and 'yarns'." The next morning as the men who were headed west to meet the enemy were about to leave, they told the women that "Indians had been seen lurking in the neighborhood," and that they had stayed to give the party their protection during the night. On the 3rd the Runaway party advanced twelve miles to Flores Rancho, opposite Seguin on the Guadalupe, where they were met by Major Michael Erskine, who had bought the old De la Baume Ranch in 1840 on the Guadalupe River near the Capote Hills, about twelve miles east of Seguin, in Gonzales County. Major Erskine, a friend of Bradley's, accompanied the Runaways the remaining mile to Seguin and assisted them in crossing the Guadalupe. The party remained at Seguin during the night, but on the 4th proceeded the twelve miles to Erskine's place, after Maverick, the Adamses and a number of other men, who had come from the Lavaca and Gonzales, turned west to the defense of San Antonio.

[40] *Ibid.*, p. 154; Green (ed.), *Memoirs of Mary A. Maverick*, p. 62.

In the meantime, at San Antonio and throughout the western country, amid the excitement, there seems to have been a great deal of fore-
boding of doom, part of which, no doubt, was designed to whip up
hatred and war sentiment against Mexico. An early version of the yellow
press in Texas, the *Alarm Bell of the West*,[41] was hastily run-off on an
Austin press exuberating sentiment in favor of military action against
Mexico and at the same time strongly denouncing the Administration.

Arriving in Austin on March 2 from Seguin, Chief Justice John Hemphill, "the John Marshall of Texas," reported that on the previous morning fifteen men left Seguin for San Antonio, and that fifty more were encamped on the Geronimo that night on their way to Béxar.[42] A copy of
Arista's proclamation of January 9, apparently brought to Austin by
Judge Hemphill, appeared in the *Austin City Gazette* on March 2 and
gave added stimulus to the talk of a Mexican invasion. Attorney General George W. Terrell left Austin on the morning of the 3rd to make a
personal inspection of "the true state of things and the cause of alarm"
at San Antonio,[43] a report of which he intended upon his return to
incorporate in a dispatch to the President.

From San Antonio on March 3 Neill wrote to Seguin and Gonzales
urging the inhabitants on the Guadalupe not to leave, as they would be
warned in sufficient time. "We have been fortifying during the night,"
he wrote, and "troops are arriving regularly from the east, so that we
believe ourselves able to defend the place. . . . We do not believe that it

[41] No issue of the *Alarm Bell of the West* is known to exist. Judging from
Washington D. Miller's comment, however, it was apparently a very anti-Admin-
istration publication. Miller wrote President Houston, "I send you the 'Alarm Bell
of the West,' which I beg you to preserve for me with the utmost care. Read the
tissue of vile falsehoods contained in the editorial columns. It is equal to the Texas
Sentinel revived: every line a libel." W. D. Miller to Sam Houston, Austin,
March 9, 1842 (Private), no. 9, in Miller Papers (Texas), ms. copy. The *Morning
Star* (Houston) of February 3, 1842, carries this interesting notice:

Alarm Bell of the West. A newspaper having this startling title, came to hand
Tuesday evening with our exchange papers from Austin. It is dated San Antonio, Jan. 22nd, and has for its motto the memorable words "remember the
Alamo." It is a spirited sheet, and breathes nothing but war and vengeance, and
as usual this theme has rendered it truly eloquent and even poetic. We can only
say if it never sounds a false alarm, we bid it "God speed."

[42] "Postscript: Important from the West," in *Austin City Gazette*, March 2,
1842; Affleck, "John C. Hays," pt. I, 205.
[43] W. D. Miller to Sam Houston, Austin, March 2, 1842 (Private), no. 5, in
Miller Papers (Texas), ms. copy.

is a regular invasion," but only a band of ladrones.[44] By this time many of the Mexicans had left San Antonio, and the American families and goods were being made secure.

Captain Daniel Boone Friar of the newly projected town of Cuero, near Cuero Creek, reached San Antonio on the morning of the 4th with about twenty-five men from the lower Guadalupe; and in the afternoon Captain Callahan of Seguin, one of the few men saved at Fannin's massacre, appeared with a company made up of men from the Lavaca, Gonzales, and Seguin areas. On March 1 upon the receipt of the news on the Lavaca of the expected attack upon San Antonio, the youthful John Henry Brown, sergeant of a volunteer company of Minute Men formed in that area in the summer of 1841, had started west with four other young men. At Gonzales and Seguin they united with others, and by the time they had reached the Cíbolo their company amounted to about forty men.[45] At the Cíbolo they chose James H. Callahan captain and, as we have seen, reached San Antonio on the evening of March 4, where they found great excitement. Scouts were out, but had not returned as ordered. All was doubt. In order to effect a better organization among those who were there, an election of officers was held. Hays was unanimously chosen commander of all the Texan forces at San Antonio, and Duncan C. Ogden succeeded him as captain of the San Antonio company. Andrew Neill was named quartermaster. Supplies and provisions were obtained from such merchants as Jaques, Riddle, Elliot, Callaghan, Peacock, and Patton, and receipted for by Neill.[46] The com-

[44] A. Neill to the People of Seguin and Gonzales, March 4, 1842, with Postscript dated Friday, ten o'clock P.M. by John C. Hays, Commander, in Affleck, "John C. Hays," pt. I, 203–205; *Telegraph and Texas Register*, March 16, 1842. Neill's letter is probably misdated, as March 3 was on Friday.

[45] John Henry Brown, "Autobiography," ms.; DeShields, "Jack Hays," in *The American Home Journal*, June, 1906. DeShields says there were thirty-six men in the unit.

[46] The following military supplies and provisions were furnished: 62.5 kegs of powder, ½ dozen percussion caps, 1 dozen caps, 512 dozen flints, 130 bars of lead, 2 bags of buckshot, 1 hogshead of corn, 1 cask of salt, 175 pounds of nails, 25 bushels of meal, 475 pounds of sugar, ½ barrel of flour, ½ of a 75 pound box of tobacco, and 5 pounds of coffee. See Papers of A. Neill [Q]uarte[r Master at San Antonio] in March 1842 Vouchers &c No. 4, in Army Papers (Texas), ms.; A. Neill, Com[missariat] & Q[uarte]r M[aste]r to Mr. [Bryan] Callaghan, March 4, 1842, in *ibid*; Request of H. Clay Davis, Q. Sergt. approved by John C. Hays to Riddle to let Capt. William H. Patton's Company have 5 bushels of meal, dated San Antonio, March 4, 1842, in *ibid*; Receipt to Mr. Jacques dated March 4, 1842, and signed by A. Neill, Com[missariat] & Q[uarter] M[aster], for "one keg 25 lbs.

panies at San Antonio at this time were those of Duncan C. Ogden, largely men from the San Antonio area, formerly under Captain Hays; of Captain French Smith,[47] known as Company A; of Daniel B. Friar, the men from the Cuero settlement; of Captain William H. Patton, a small unit; and of James H. Callahan, the men from the Lavaca and other parts of Texas who had formed themselves into a company before their arrival at San Antonio. In all, they totalled approximately 107 men.[48] Elsewhere men stood ready to march to the point of attack should the Mexicans make a move against the Texas frontier.[49]

Spies, scouts, and reconnaissance parties had been kept out by the Texans at Béxar, but apparently very little information had been obtained until Friday night, March 3, when two Texan spies were fired at and pursued near the Medina. Four others were hailed and chased from near the Leona on the evening of the 4th, but all succeeded in returning to town safely.[50] McCulloch and Miller had not returned by sundown of the 4th, and as night descended the situation looked grim, for the men had great confidence in these two men. Was it a robber band or Indians lurking in the area, or was Béxar about to receive a visit

---

rifle powder, $25.00; ½ doz. rifle caps percussion, $6.00; 1 doz. com[mon] per [cussion] caps, $9.00; 1 doz. flints, $.38; 130 bars lead, $32.50; two bags buckshot, $12.50; 500 flints, $10.00; 1 hogshead corn, $18.00; 1 cask salt Rec'd one Blue Buckett, $1.50; Rec'd ½ Box 75 lbs. tobacco, $75.00," in *ibid.*

[47] See Captain French Smith's requisition for rifle powder, corn, and meal, dated San Antonio, March 4, 1842, and approved by John C. Hays, commanding. Army Papers (Texas), ms. John H. Jenkins of Bastrop has left the following description of Smith's conduct in the battle of Plum Creek against the Comanches in 1840:

> One instance of the hardness and cruelty of some men, even though not savage in form and color, was shown us on this raid. As was often the case some squaws were marching in Indian ranks, and one of them had been shot, and lay breathing her last—almost dead as we came by. French Smith with most inhuman and unmanly cruelty, sprang upon her, stamped her and then cut her body through with a lance. He was from the Guadelupe; indeed I do not believe there was a single man from Bastrop, who would have stooped to so brutal a deed.

John H. Jenkins, Sr., "Personal Reminiscences of Texas History Relating to Bastrop County, 1828–1847, as dictated to his daughter-in-law, Mrs. Emma Holmes Jenkins of Bastrop, Texas," ts.

[48] Brown, *Indian Wars and Pioneers of Texas*, p. 601.

[49] "Report of a Committee appointed by a Meeting of the Citizens of Western Texas on rumor that Mexicans were invading the state, March 1842," Thomas J. Rusk Papers, ms.

[50] See report of John C. Haight, commander, dated San Antonio, March 4, 1842, in W. Eugene Hollon and Ruth Lapham Butler (eds.), *William Bollaert's Texas*, p. 33; hereafter cited, *Bollaert's Texas.*

from the Mexican army? No one knew, but Hays was determined to find out, if he could. A new party of scouts, this time consisting of seven or eight men, left at dark to collect information about the enemy, as it was reported that Goliad, on the north bank of the San Antonio River, ninety miles below San Antonio, had fallen to a small invading force on March 3. The reconnaissance party was composed of Isaac N. Mitchell, Kendrick Arnold (a free Negro),[51] William Morrison, Stewart Foley, Joshua Threadgill, John Henry Brown, and two others.[52] In the chaparral, four miles west of San Antonio, they were fired upon from ambush by a Mexican picket guard. Leaving the road they moved on and soon on the bluff of the León Creek about eight miles from town, they discovered the enemy camp covering about one hundred acres of ground, illuminated by a hundred and fifty camp fires. They estimated the Mexican force at approximately 1,400 and returned to San Antonio about daylight to report.[53]

In the meantime, while the scouting party was out, frantic appeals for aid were sent eastward. "Times are getting warm," wrote G. H. Harrison. "San Antonio will be protected or another Alamo affair will take place."[54] "Communicate with the Committee on the Colorado," hastily scribbled French Strother Gray, a lawyer, to the Committee of Vigilance at Gonzales. "Tell them to raise all the force they can and we will endeavor to sustain ourselves until they can reenforce us."[55] John H. Moore from Fayette County informed the Committee of Safety (Vigilance) at Gonzales that his unit was leaving for Seguin and would "there await for the reinforcements of this county. Tomorrow night we shall expect your reinforcements."[56] With Moore was a company of

---

[51] *Handbook of Texas*, I, 71; see also Harold Schoen, "The Free Negro in the Republic of Texas," *Southwestern Historical Quarterly*, XXXIX (1935–1936), 292–308; XL (1936–1937), 26–34, 85–113, 169–199, 267–289.

[52] John Henry Brown, *History of Texas, from 1685 to 1892*, II, 212 n; *To Arms! To Arms! Texians!!* Broadside.

[53] See report of F. S. Gray, by order of John C. Hays, Col. Commanding, Béxar, March 5, 1842, in *Bollaert's Texas*, p. 33.

[54] Note by G. H. Harrison appended to A. Neill to the People of Seguin and Gonzales, March 4, 1842, in Affleck, "John C. Hays," pt. I, 203–204.

[55] F. S. Gray to the Committee of Vigilance at Gonzales, Béxar, March 5, 1842, in Affleck, "John C. Hays," pt. I, 203–205. See also, Brown, *History of Texas*, II, 212.

[56] John H. Moore to Gentlemen of the Committee of Safety of Gonzales, n.p., n.d., in *Telegraph and Texas Register*, March 16, 1842. John H. Moore lived nine miles below LaGrange.

volunteers under Captain Nicholas M. Dawson.[57] General Greenberry
H. Harrison, editor of the *Weekly Texian* (Austin), was sent from Austin by Secretary of War Hockley to Seguin on the 5th presumably with
orders to Colonel Moore.[58]

Early on the morning of the 5th Hays dispatched once more the
scouting party that had been out during the night to watch the Mexican
approach to the town. The only addition to the party was "Keno" Elli-
son, making nine in all.[59] It found the Mexican army advancing. Exchanging an occasional shot with the Mexicans, the Texan scouts circled
the enemy forces, and as they regained the Presidio Road, about two
miles from town, they noticed a white flag approaching. Two of their
number, Arnold and Mitchell, advanced to meet it. The bearer of the
flag identified himself as José María Carrasco, and said he wished to
speak to Van Ness and Morris, whom he had met last summer in
Mexico.[60] He bore a letter from General Rafael Vasquez to Cornelius
Van Ness, which was later conveyed by D. C. Ogden to the War Department at Austin.[61] He informed them that General Vasquez, in command of a regular army unit, demanded the surrender of the town,
promising complete protection and immunity to those who would not
resist his occupation. Colonel Carrasco was blindfolded and conducted
by the spy detail to the Ranger headquarters, where the demands and
promises were repeated. He told the Texans that Chevallie and Dunn

[57] Men known to have been members of Dawson's Company during the Vasquez
raid were William L. Adkins, Richard A. Barclay, Henry W. Baylor, John R. Baylor,
Hiram Ferrill, William However, A. S. Kennedy, David Smith Kornegay, Dr. A. P.
Manley, A. D. L. Moore, S. G. Norvell, Henry P. Redfield, John A. Redfield,
Peter V. Shaw, John O. Snelling, James Sorrells, James C. Toney, Fredric[k] Vogle,
Joshua Robert Wade, William Wyatt Wade, John Williams, and Leiper Willoughby.
See Houston Wade Papers, ms.

[58] George W. Hockley to General [Sam Houston], Department of War and Navy,
Austin, March 16, 1842, in Harriet Smither (ed.), *Journals of the Sixth Congress of
the Republic of Texas*, III, 17–18. The author has been unable to locate the "express" sent to Seguin, and it is only presumed that it was an order to Colonel Moore
informing him of the movement of re-enforcements and the course to be pursued in
meeting the threat to the frontier.

[59] Brown, *History of Texas*, II, 213; Affleck "John C. Hays," pt. I, 206; *To Arms!
To Arms! Texians!!* Broadside.

[60] John D. Morris to Dear Brother [Richard Morris? Galveston]. Seguin, March 8,
1842, in *Telegraph and Texas Register*, March 16, 1842.

[61] W. D. Miller to Sam Houston, Austin, March 7, 1842 (Private), no. 9, in
Miller Papers (Texas), ms. copy; *To Arms! To Arms! Texians!!* Broadside; *Telegraph
and Texas Register*, March 16, 1842.

were prisoners in the Mexican camp where they would be well treated for the Mexicans intended, according to Arista's proclamation, to conduct the campaign upon the highest principles of civilized warfare.

Thus early on the morning of March 5[62] General Vasquez,[63] who had been driven from north of the Leona by Hays in the summer of 1841, and for the past year or so had been stationed at or near Lampazos in command of a small contingent of regular troops, appeared suddenly, after a march of nine days from the Río Grande, in the vicinity of San Antonio with approximately 700 artillerymen, infantrymen, rancheros, and Indian warriors, and halted about two miles from town.[64] William B. Jaques, who was in San Antonio at the time and who was a prisoner of the Mexicans for a brief period, described their force as consisting of 450 cavalry, including Mexican volunteers from Béxar, two companies of infantry, 25 artillerymen, and 30 Caddo Indians, commanded by Vicente Córdova—"three women, two boys, eight young men—the balance old warriors, good for nothing and badly armed." The whole force was very poorly mounted. "The regular troops were forced here," it was said, "under the pretext that they were to go [on] a campaign against the Comanches. The balance were our western Mexican robbers."[65]

[62] John Henry Brown in his *History of Texas*, II, 212–214, gives the date of Vasquez's capture of San Antonio as March 6 instead of the 5th. This has caused many historians using secondary sources to be misled in their dates for certain other events of this period in Texas history.

[63] Rafael Vasquez, a native-born Mexican, commenced his military career as a captain of patriots of the Hacienda de Cienega de Mata, February 20, 1827, served in the Trigarante Army, and was promoted through the various ranks to general of brigade. He commanded a brigade of cavalry in 1834 against Chilapa, and was in the Texas campaign of 1835. During the Federalist uprising of 1838–1840, he fought on the side of the Centralists and in the battle of Saltillo in 1840 sought to draw the Texans under Colonel S. W. Jordan into an ambush. He later served as commandant general of Jalisco in 1851–1852. Alberto M. Carreño (ed.), *Jefes del ejército mexicano en 1847: biografías de generals de división y de brigade y de coronels del ejército mexicano pro fines del año de 1847*, pp. 219–220; *Telegraph and Texas Register*, March 16, 1842; *Civilian and Galveston Gazette*, March 12, 1842.

[64] *Telegraph and Texas Register*, March 16, and April 27, 1842.

[65] *Ibid.*, March 30, 1842. See also *Ibid.*, March 16, 1842; G. W. Terrell, Attorney General and Acting Secretary of State to ———, Washington, Oct. 15, 1842, in William Carey Crane, *Life and Select Literary Remains of Sam Houston of Texas*, pp. 144–147; H. Yoakum, *History of Texas from Its First Settlement in 1685 to Its Annexation to the United States in 1846*, II, 349, and other sources give the number of Vasquez's troops as approximately seven hundred, but General Mariano Arista, reporting to the commandant general at Chihuahua, gives it as five hundred

At the time the Texan force in San Antonio numbered a little over one hundred men mostly from Gonzales, under the command of Captain John C. ("Jack") Hays; and Hays had no intentions of becoming a Mexican prisoner.[66] He asked for a suspension of hostilities until the Texans could consider the lenient terms of the Mexican general. After a short parley, a truce was agreed to until 2 P.M. It was then 10 A.M. Carrasco was now re-escorted to his command.

The Texans hoped that re-enforcements might come in from the Colorado, but as the period of truce waned, only Captain George M. Dolson and a small party from the Colorado entered Béxar, and they stated that no other re-enforcements were near.[67]

In a hastily assembled consultation of war over which Hays presided, the various alternatives were discussed. The Béxar citizens to a man favored defending the town to the last extremity, but the volunteers from Gonzales, with the exception of three or four, voted in opposition, and declared that the rangers and volunteers should retreat to the

---

(*Voto de Son*, April 15, 1842, cited in Hubert Howe Bancroft, *History of Texas and the North Mexican States*, II, 348 n.). The Minister of War and Marine, however, in reporting to the Mexican Congress in January 1844 said that Vasquez's force scarcely numbered three hundred men, but this writer presumes that by this he meant "regular" troops ("Ministerio de Guerra y Marina. Memoria del Secretario de estado y del Despacho de guerra y marina, leida a las camaras del Congreso nacional de la Republica Mexicana, en enero de 1844," in *Diario del Gobierno* (Mexico City), May 15, 1844).

[66] Justin H. Smith, *The War with Mexico*, I, 258. Brown, *History of Texas*, II, 212, says the Texans numbered 107. William B. Jaques is alleged to have reported the combined Texan forces at 158, of whom only 60 were from Béxar (*Telegraph and Texas Register*, March 30, 1842). Two weeks earlier another informant had told the *Telegraph* (March 16, 1842) that when he left Béxar on the 5th, Hays had 120 men, about 40 of whom were from Béxar. John D. Morris to Brother [Richard Morris? Galveston], Seguin, March 8, 1842, says Hays had 120 Americans in his command at the time of Vasquez's entry (*Telegraph and Texas Register*, March 16, 1842). W. D. Miller to Sam Houston, Austin, March 6, 1842 (Private), no. 7, in Miller Papers, ms. copy, says the report from San Antonio was that companies from Gonzales and Fayette counties had arrived there, making in all about 150 men for the defense of the place. Others, he said, were en route from the Guadalupe and the Colorado. On the 9th he revised his estimate and said he had learned that the Texan force did not exceed 115, perhaps 100 of whom were from Gonzales (W. D. Miller to Sam Houston, Austin, March 9, 1842 (Private), no. 9, in Miller Papers (Texas) ms. copy). Vasquez is said to have reported the Texans at Béxar as 260 strong (*Telegraph and Texas Register*, April 27, 1842).

[67] *To Arms! To Arms! Texians!!* Broadside.

Guadalupe.[68] The overwhelming majority favored retreat. The position taken by the Gonzales men, reported Lieutenant Colonel of Militia John D. Morris three days later, "was probably a prudent one, for we had no means of ascertaining the number of troops coming against us."[69]

Preparations were now made for the retreat. Colonel Morris, a San Antonio lawyer then serving as district attorney for the Fourth Judicial District,[70] and Cornelius Van Ness,[71] congressman and former district attorney, were sent to Vasquez's headquarters to inform him that the Texans had determined to withdraw from the town and, in fact, had already commenced their march. The two commissioners were cordially received by the Mexican officers, and were "invited most particularly to remain in the camp during the afternoon, which we," reported Morris, "determined to do in order to acquire accurate information, if possible, in relation to their movements, forces [and equipment]."[72] They re-

[68] *Telegraph and Texas Register,* March 30, 1842. Brown, *History of Texas,* II, 213, declares that when the men were paraded, they voted 54–53 in favor of retreating; but this assertion is not borne out by other accounts. Affleck, "John C. Hays," pt. I, 207, states that the Texans held a council of war and with one exception it was unanimously agreed that they should fight; therefore, as it had been understood that a unanimous vote would be required to defend the place, they determined to retreat. A "Council of War" usually included only the officers, and it is my conclusion that this is what is meant, and that Brown, learning that the decision to remain was lost by one vote, interpreted it to mean a majority of one of the total number.

[69] John D. Morris to Dear Brother [Richard Morris? Galveston], Seguin, March 8, 1842, in *Telegraph and Texas Register,* March 16, 1842.

[70] Hobart Huson, *District Judges of Refugio County,* p. 16.

[71] Cornelius Van Ness was born at Burlington, Vermont, in 1803, the son of Cornelius P. Van Ness, governor of Vermont. Young Cornelius served as secretary of legation under his father, while the latter was the United States minister to Spain from 1829 to 1837. He returned to the United States from Spain in 1836, and came to Texas in 1837 to practice law at San Antonio where he was appointed district attorney of the Fourth Judicial District in December 1837. In 1838 he was joined in San Antonio by his brother George Van Ness. Cornelius Van Ness served Béxar County in the Third, Fourth, Fifth, and Sixth Congresses of Texas, 1838–1842. On May 2, 1842, while out riding a few miles below Béxar with James W. Robinson, he was accidentally killed when Robinson's horse suddenly started and threw his master's yager on the pommel of the saddle with such violence that it went off. Samuel A. Maverick Memoirs, May 13, 1842, in Green (ed.), *Samuel Maverick:* p. 162; *Handbook of Texas,* II, 831–832. *Telegraph and Texas Register,* May 18, 1842, contains an obituary on Van Ness.

[72] John D. Morris to Dear Brother [Richard Morris? Galveston], Seguin, March 8, 1842, in *Telegraph and Texas Register,* March 16, 1842.

ported that the whole Mexican force was mustered in their presence, and that it consisted of about 700 men—400 regular cavalry; 200 rancheros, partly from the Río Grande, *"but principally of our own Mexican citizens"*;[73] 70 infantrymen; and 30 Caddo Indians. Calixto Bravo was "colonel commanding," and Carrasco, aide-de-camp to General Vasquez. Later, Captain D. C. Ogden went into Vasquez's line with a flag of truce and saw Van Ness, Chevallie, and Morris.[74]

In the meantime, while Van Ness and Morris, both ex-commissioners to General Arista's headquarters,[75] conferred at Vasquez's quarters, the defenders of Béxar dismantled the six-pound cannon, collected what military equipment they could take with them, and prepared to retire to the Guadalupe River and send for assistance. Those who had mercantile establishments sought to salvage what they could by secreting some of the more valuable items that they could not take off immediately. Three citizens of San Antonio, Dr. Launcelot Smithers,[76] John McRhea, and John McDonald, lacking horses, declined joining the retreat and were left sitting upon the walls of the Alamo.[77] After knocking in the heads of 327 kegs of powder and dumping the kegs into the San Antonio River, the Anglo-Texans evacuated the town by way of the east side, without firing a shot.

Before withdrawing, John Twohig,[78] a merchant engaged in the

[73] Zambrano, Antonio Pérez, and others. W. D. Miller to Sam Houston, Austin, March 9, 1842 (Private), no. 9, in Miller Papers (Texas), ms. copy.

[74] George W. Hockley to Sam Houston, Department of War and Marine, March 7, 1842, in Texas Congress, Congressional Papers, ms., Sixth Congress.

[75] See Joseph Milton Nance, *After San Jacinto: The Texas-Mexican Frontier, 1836–1841*, pp. 432–443.

[76] Launcelot Smithers served as city treasurer of San Antonio, January 8, 1839–January 8, 1840, and was elected mayor pro tempore on August 19, 1841, succeeding Mayor Pro Tempore Francois Guilbeau, resigned, who had served as mayor since July 2, 1841, during Juan N. Seguin's absence in Mexico. Smithers served as mayor till September 7, 1841, when Seguin returned to resume the duties of that office. San Antonio, "Journal A, Records of the City of San Antonio," Jan. 8, 1839; July 2 and Sept. 7, 1841, ts.

[77] Brown, an eye witness to the leaving of the three men, reported erroneously that they had subsequently been slain by the Vasquez raiders (*History of Texas*, II, 214). Actually, the men were killed during the Woll campaign in September by a party under Lieutenant Manuel Carbajal. See the account in Chapter 15.

[78] John Twohig was born in Cork, Ireland, in April 1809, and died at San Antonio, Texas, October, 1891. At the age of fifteen he ran away from home, served for a while as an apprentice seaman on a British vessel, and was afterwards employed in the coastwise trade between Boston and New Orleans. Late in 1841 he came to San Antonio with a stock of goods and opened a store on the

Mexican trade, attached several slow-burning matches to a number of kegs of powder left in his storehouse. Aided and abetted by some of the disloyal San Antonio Mexicans, Vasquez's troops took over the town and began to loot the abandoned stores, warehouses, and homes. In the midst of their activities, the kegs of powder exploded, killing a number of would-be looters.[79] As one of the Texans was leaving the town, he met a Mexican officer, who evinced some exultation, which was not in every way acceptable to the Texan, who thereupon inquired, " 'What he was doing there?' The response was, 'It is none of your business.' This reply," it was reported, "not being sufficiently conciliatory, its author had the misfortune to receive a leaden rebuke for his incivility in the region of the olfactories, extending even to one of his auricular appendages. The effect was to facilitate his movements most wonderfully. He retreated faster than he had advanced. He was away in a twinkling."[80] Another Texan, believing himself the object of some unfavorable comments from a party of Mexicans surrounding a doorway on the street through which he was passing, "let go with his rifle, and either the powder or the lead, or both together, produced another rapid migration of the dusky revilers from that post of danger."[81]

southeast corner of Commerce and Plaza Mayor. Boyce House, *City of Flaming Adventure, The Chronicle of San Antonio*, pp. 114–115; Heusinger, *A Chronology of Events in San Antonio*, p. 22.

[79] Brown, *History of Texas*, II, 213–215.

[80] W. D. Miller to Sam Houston, Austin, March 9, 1842 (Private), no. 9, in Miller Papers (Texas), ms. copy.

[81] *Ibid.*

CHAPTER TWO

The Withdrawal of Texan Military Forces
from San Antonio

CROSSING THE POWDER-HOUSE[1] ridge and creek, with a brass six-pounder drawn by oxen, and leaving "another with a small mortar to fall into the hands of the enemy,"[2] the Rangers and their followers descended the long slope towards Salado Creek on the Seguin road, six miles from San Antonio, and encamped for the night at the Sulphur Springs on the Cíbolo (Buffalo), a tributary of the San Antonio River. Here they were joined at a late hour by the two commissioners who had been retained by Vasquez until night, when, after having been treated with great kindness and hospitality, they were escorted out of the enemy's lines and turned loose.[3] Their report that the Mexican force under Vasquez numbered upwards of seven hundred men, including approximately one hundred infantry, was apparently the first reliable information that the Texans had had on the size of the invading forces.

[1] The Powder House, which lay about one thousand yards southeast of the Alamo between the Gonzales and Goliad roads, was built by Lieutenant Colonel Antonio Cordero y Bustamante between 1807 and 1810. Cordero served as Spanish governor of Texas between 1805 and 1810. Antonio Menchaca, *Memoirs*, in Yanaguana Society *Publications*, II, [13]; Ralph W. Steen and Frances Donecker, *Our Texas*, p. 410.

[2] Thomas W. Bell, *A Narrative of the Capture and Subsequent Sufferings of the Mier Prisoners in Mexico, Captured in the Cause of Texas, Dec. 26th, 1842 and Liberated Sept. 16th, 1844*, p. 7. See also *Telegraph and Texas Register*, March 16, 1842; Ministerio de Guerra y Marina: Memoria del Secretario de estado y del despacho de guerra y marina, leida a las camaras del Congreso nacional de la República Méxicana, en enero de 1844, in *Diario del Gobierno*, May 15, 1844, pp. 57–58. The Minister of War and Marine stated that Vasquez found two pieces of artillery and other effects of war at San Antonio.

[3] John D. Morris to Dear Brother [Richard Morris? Galveston], Seguin, March 8, 1842, in *Telegraph and Texas Register*, March 16, 1842; H. Yoakum, *History of Texas from Its First Settlement in 1685 to Its Annexation to the United States in 1846*, II, 349; W. D. Miller to Sam Houston, Austin, March 9, 1842 (Private), no. 9, in Washington D. Miller Papers, 1833–1860 (Texas), ms. copy.

During the retreat from San Antonio, several Mexican scouting parties appeared on the Texan right, but stayed at a considerable distance. As the Texans descended the slope toward Salado Creek, a body of Mexican cavalry approached on the right at half a mile distance, at the edge of the timber on the creek, and waved their hats in defiance. Captain Ogden galloped down the Texan line, calling for forty of the best-mounted men to follow him in an attack upon the enemy cavalry. The men responded with alacrity. Among them were Stewart Foley, William Morrison, Henry Clay Davis, Calvin Turner, Isaac N. Mitchell, C. C. DeWitt, Andrew Neill, and other frontier rangers. As the Texans charged, the Mexican cavalry fled, but not before Calvin Turner, a boy from Seguin, tumbled a Mexican from his saddle and led his victim's horse back in triumph. During the charge, Neill and several other Texans were severely injured by thorns piercing their legs.[4]

From the Cíbolo, John Henry Brown, later a Texas historian, hurried home to get a fresh horse and returned by way of King's Ranch to Gonzales. In the meantime, a considerable number of young men had come in. Being without an officer, they assembled and unanimously elected Brown their captain and then proceeded on to San Antonio only to find that the invader had precipitantly fled.[5]

Colonel John H. Moore and the Fayette County men, organized into two companies under Captains Thomas J. Rabb and Nicholas M. Dawson, hurried forward to assist in repelling the invader.

While encamped that night on the Cíbolo, Hays sent a courier to Austin with dispatches to the government. Ambrosio Rodríquez was selected for this assignment, and Benjamin Highsmith carried the news of the capture of San Antonio to LaGrange. Captain Samuel Highsmith conveyed the news on the same evening to Seguin and beyond to Major Erskine's on the Guadalupe, to the ladies of the Runaway, arriving at the latter place before daylight on the morning of the 6th. The captain lost no time in arousing the people at the farm. At 3 o'clock in the morning, Captain Highsmith rapped loudly on the door of the blacksmith shop and when the women answered,

called out in a solemn and dismal voice, "Ladies San Antonio has fallen." It was startling news indeed and, the night being very dark and cold, we were seized with a vague sense of terror [reported Mrs. Maverick]. Mrs. Jacquez

[4] John Henry Brown, *History of Texas, from 1685 to 1892*, II, 214; J. D. Affleck, "History of John C. Hays," ts., pt. I, 208.
[5] John Henry Brown, "Autobiography," ms.

[Jaques] lighted a candle and commenced weeping hysterically; Mrs. Elliott fell upon her knees and ran over her beads oftener than once,[6] and the other member [Mrs. Maverick] of the matinee [except the Hutchisons who had gone eastward the day before[7]] took a shaking ague and could not speak for the chattering of her teeth. The children waked and cried; the negroes came in with sad and anxious looks, and we were in fact seized with a genuine "panic."[8]

Soon all were aroused. The Gautier family, who had taken up living quarters in the shed, adjoining the shop where the other three women and their children were staying, joined in the excitement. Gautier learned from Highsmith that the Anglo-Texans had fallen back in good order with their cannon, expecting Vasquez to be re-enforced shortly by a large contingent. Highsmith said that the Texans planned to retreat to Seguin, collect re-enforcements, and launch an attack or make a stand, depending on future developments. March 6 was a miserable day at the Capote Farm (Erskine's). All day rumors came; couriers passed in haste, and the ladies were informed, reported Mrs. Maverick,

That an army of 30,000 Mexicans had cut our forces up, and was marching directly towards Capote farm presumably intending to cross the Guadalupe at this point.

During the excitement in the morning Mrs. Jacquez [Jaques] buried her money, and Mrs. Elliott constructed three bustles, for herself and her two servantwomen, and in the bustles she deposited her gold doubloons. We then prepared and recited what we should say to the Mexican officers upon their arrival. After dinner we all went out to the public road and sat down on a log, all in a row, and watched to see them approach, whilst the invalid Mr. Douglas, wearing his comical long red silk smoking cap, tried to cheer and amuse us with his jokes and witticisms. Soon towards the fateful west was seen an approaching horseman urging his tired steed with whip and spur—"A Courier!" cried Douglas, "Now we shall know all." Sure enough it was my dear brother Andrew [Adams] come to set us at ease about the personal safety of our absent husbands, as he had a better horse than they;

[6] See Leonie Rummel Weyand and Houston Wade, *An Early History of Fayette County*, p. 145.

[7] Judge and Mrs. Anderson Hutchinson, accompanied by General Terrell, Harrison, and others, reached Austin in their carriage on the evening of the 7th, and left there the next morning for the lower Colorado, having lost their pianoforte and nearly all of their clothing which was taken with Jaques. W. D. Miller to Sam Houston, Austin, March 9, 1842, (Private), no. 9, in Miller Papers (Texas), ms. copy.

[8] Rena Maverick Green (ed.), *Samuel Maverick: Texan, 1803–1870: A Collection of Letters, Journals and Memoirs*, pp. 155–156.

for our husbands appreciated our anxiety, and had sent him forward as their avant-courier, and before dark Mr. Maverick and Mr. Elliott came, followed soon afterwards by Mr. Bradley and Mr. Jacques [Jaques],[9]

who had effected his escape from Béxar, where the Mexican officials seemed to have had little objection to the Anglo-Americans' leaving, if they so desired, as long as they left their property behind.

Hays advised that the party at the Capote Farm be moved to Gonzales, while he with some three hundred men[10] who had rendezvoused at Seguin attempted to retake San Antonio, he being now satisfied with the reports brought in by McCulloch and Miller that no additional forces were sustaining Vasquez. One of his immediate objectives became, if possible, "to capture and drive off the caballada of the enemy."[11] The day after leaving San Antonio Hays moved his camp to El Rancho Flores on the west bank of the Guadalupe, opposite Seguin and seventeen miles south of the present city of New Braunfels, where he was able to obtain meat and limited supplies of corn. The Flores Rancho, reported an agent of the German colonization company, had a

spacious yard . . . enclosed according to Mexican custom with a palisade of mesquite trees rammed into the ground, which were further connected with strips of raw oxhides. Several clumsy Mexican carts with disk-like solid wooden wheels stood near the entrance. A little farther on, sheep and goats were roaming about, a rather strange sight in Texas. The one-story home and the various outhouses were made partly of logs lying horizontally over each other, and partly of logs standing perpendicular, the crevices of which were filled with clay. These were built securely to withstand successfully Indian attacks, which in times prior to the founding of New Braunfels, were not improbable, since there were no settlements north of the Guadalupe.

Behind the buildings, is a large fenced-in field. On the other side close to the ranch flows the Guadalupe, forming here a rushing little waterfall. The river with its abundant, crystal clear, rapidly flowing water, shaded by beautiful cottonwood and other trees of the bottoms, presents a most pleasing view. The proximity of the river, the excellent farming land, and the unlimited pasturage with its tender grass on which thousands of cattle could find an abundance of nourishment, are natural advantages, which combine to make this ranch a valuable piece of property.[12]

[9] *Ibid.*

[10] John D. Morris to Dear Brother [Richard Morris? Galveston], Seguin, March 8, 1842, in *Telegraph and Texas Register*, March 16, 1842.

[11] W. D. Miller to Sam Houston, Austin, March 9, 1842 (Private), no. 9, in Miller Papers (Texas), ms. copy.

[12] Ferdinand Roemer, *Texas with Particular Reference to German Immigration*

Here at Flores Rancho the rangers learned that practically all the inhabitants of the Guadalupe Valley had fled eastward as best they could in wagons and carts, and on foot. Homes were deserted; possessions were left behind; and stock was turned out to roam at large. There was desolation amidst plenty. King's Ranch, lying between the Capote Farm and Gonzales, was deserted by its owners. "The corn crib was full, the smokehouse well supplied, and chickens and hogs moved about as usual —but on the front door a notice was posted: 'To all refugees, welcome, help yourselves to what you need. Also to all marchers to repel the invaders, take what you want, but leave the remainder to the next comers'."[13] Great losses were suffered by those who fled the frontier. William and Andrew Adams,[14] living on the San Marcos, sent their Negroes eastward, each with a Runaway family, and headed to join Caldwell and McCulloch for an advance against the enemy. While they were absent, "some wanton passerby left their fences down, and their hogs were killed and stolen—their cattle strayed off and to finish it all a flood came in May, swept away their bottom fences, and broke them up."[15]

Colonel John H. Moore with a company of Fayette County men arrived at Seguin on the 5th, where news of Hays' evacuation of San Antonio reached him that night. He was anxious to advance upon Béxar as soon as re-enforcements came in from the Colorado. Moore had 140 men on Tuesday, the 8th.[16] He expected to have 300 men on Wednesday and to be able to attack the Mexicans in San Antonio on that day, for

---

and the Physical Appearance of the Country Described through Personal Observation, p. 145.

[13] Green (ed.), *Samuel Maverick,* p. 158.

[14] William and Andrew Adams were brothers of Mrs. Samuel A. Maverick. The former established himself as a merchant in San Antonio in 1837 at the age of 22. Launcelot Smithers served as clerk to William Adams' mercantile establishment, and sold large quantities on credit to Mexicans in Coahuila, who though wealthy, never paid, and "after eighteen months merchandizing" William Adams was forced to close up without realizing the capital invested, and left San Antonio on Feb. 1, 1839, for Tuscaloosa, Alabama to bring out his Negroes to try farming, returning with his brother Andrew in October 1839. Rena Maverick Green (ed.), *Memoirs of Mary A. Maverick: Arranged by Mary A. Maverick and Her Son George Madison Maverick,* pp. 21–22.

[15] Green (ed.), *Samuel Maverick,* pp. 157–158.

[16] John D. Morris to Dear Brother [Richard Morris? Galveston], Seguin, March 8, 1842, in *Telegraph and Texas Register,* March 16, 1842.

the Texans, by then, were convinced that no additional forces from the Río Grande were near.[17]

As Captain Hays withdrew, the Mexicans entered Béxar by the west end and took possession of the town, hoisted their national flag, set up a civil government, and proclaimed the Mexican laws to be in force. At first, especially after the explosion at Twohig's place of business, private property was scrupulously respected, and sentinels were placed for its protection. Most of the remaining Anglo-Texans had left with the rangers. During the occupation the Mexican citizens of San Antonio held a public meeting in which they were reported to have agreed unanimously to take up arms against Texas, but when a paper was produced for them to affix their signatures to, many refused to do so.[18] Copies of Arista's proclamation of January 9 were distributed, but this was not the first appearance of this document in San Antonio. "From the Nueces river," recorded Seguin, "Vasquez forwarded a proclamation by Arista, to the inhabitants of Texas. I received at my ranch a bundle of those proclamations, which I transmitted at once to the Corporation of San Antonio."[19] Why these should have been sent to Seguin at his ranch is difficult to explain, unless there was yet some hope among the Mexican officers that Seguin would throw in with their plans.

The opinion of many of the Anglo-Americans at San Antonio was that Seguin was in secret correspondence with the Mexicans. Some thought (perhaps erroneously) that he had tipped-off the Mexican officials on the fitting out of the Santa Fé expedition. Vasquez is reported to have said this was the case and is also said to have exhibited as proof a letter from Colonel Seguin which he took from his pocket but which he did not permit anyone to read.[20] When Chevallie, then a prisoner in Vasquez's camp, asked to be allowed to see it, as he was familiar with Seguin's handwriting, Vasquez refused and cut short the interview. Actually, if Seguin were really in secret, traitorous correspondence with the Mexican officials, why should Vasquez wish to expose that fact to the Texans? Only while Seguin enjoyed the confidence of the Texans

---

[17] *Telegraph and Texas Register*, March 16, 1842.

[18] *Ibid.*, March 30, 1842, report by William B. Jaques.

[19] Seguin, *Memoirs*, p. 23.

[20] Mrs. Mary A. Maverick in her memoirs reports this charge against Seguin without an effort to show how news of a fitting out of the Santa Fé expedition might have become known to the Mexican officers in many other ways. Green (ed.), *Memoirs of Mary A. Maverick*, p. 59; Seguin, *Memoirs*, p. 23.

would he have been useful in imparting valuable information to the Mexican government; hence, if he were supplying important information to the Mexicans, why were they so anxious to inform the Texans of his treason? His imputed correspondence with General Vasquez, coupled with the fact that he had refused to help defend his homeland, having run off to his ranch, which seemed rather peculiar for a man who had shown so much bravery in 1836 when the outlook was more dismal, gave an opportunity to his enemies, like Goodman, to discredit him. The Mexican officers who occupied San Antonio declared that Seguin was working in their favor. Furthermore, the San Antonio Americans became even more convinced of Seguin's treasonable conduct when, upon Vasquez's retreat, he did not follow Judge Hemphill's advice to arrest and bring to trial those San Antonio Mexicans who had taken up arms in favor of the Mexicans. Mayor Seguin's failure in this respect was due, he claimed, to his going with the Texan party in pursuit of Vasquez.[21] Altogether, it would seem that Seguin's explanation of the whole affair bears some credence, but leaves much unexplained.

As to my reputed treason with Vasquez, when we consider that Don Antonio Navarro and I [recorded Seguin] were only Mexicans of note, in Western Texas, who had taken a prominent part in the war, the interest the Mexican General had in causing us to be distrusted, will be seen. Mr. Navarro was then [as a member of the Santa Fé Expedition] a prisoner; I alone remained; and if they were able to make the Texans distrust me, they gained a point. This is proved by the fact, that, since I withdrew from the service, there was never seen a regiment of Mexican-Texans. The rumor, that I was a traitor, was seized with avidity by my enemies in San Antonio. Some envied my military position, as held by a Mexican; others found me an obstacle to the accomplishment of their villainous plans.[22]

It would seem, however, that Seguin, trying to do business with both sides, lost the confidence of both.

[21] Seguin, *Memoirs*, p. 24.
[22] Ibid., p. 30.

38

CHAPTER THREE

The Mexican Advance along the Lower Route

As VASQUEZ ENTERED Texas by the middle route, another and smaller Mexican force under Lieutenant Colonel Ramón Valera, subject to Vasquez's orders if needed, began its march from Mier on February 19, and, after some delay caused by the rainy season and swollen streams, reached the height of Casa Blanca, south of the Nueces, on the morning of the 28th with a force of 2 captains, 2 lieutenants, 1 ensign, 16 sergeants, 16 corporals, a bugler, 120 men from the Third Regiment of Cavalry, and a few others to serve as spies or explorers because of their knowledge of the terrain.[1] Valera was joined by Agatón Quiñones and the First Company of Explorers, numbering 50 men.[2] He carried with him 150 copies of Arista's proclamation of January 9 to the inhabitants of Texas.

The scarcity of horses was a hindrance to the Mexican activities along the lower route. By the time they reached Casa Blanca, three-fourths of Valera's horses, which were practically useless from the start (especially those from Reinosa), were in a most deplorable condition, made unfit for use by traversing eighteen leagues of sandy desert devoid of water. The men were now forced to dismount and carry their saddles and harness. After crossing the Nueces, they continued the march. Two days were required to make a distance of twelve leagues; so Valera detached Captain Miguel Aznar and one other officer with 40 men at the Arroyo Blanco on the 2nd of March, mounted the men on the

[1] Ramón Valera al Gen. Mariano Arista, en el campo en las legunas de Santa Rosa, Marzo 12 de 1842, quoted in El General Mariano Arista al Ministro de Guerra, Monterey, Marzo 27 de 1842, in Frederick C. Chabot, *Corpus Christi and Lipantitlán*, pp. 17–21; Ministerio de guerra y marina. Memoria del Secretaría de estado y del despacho Mexicana, en enero de 1844, in *Diario del Gobierno*, May 15, 1844.

[2] El General Mariano Arista al Ministro de Guerra, Febrero 21 de 1842, cited in Chabot, *Corpus Christi and Lipantitlán*, p. 16.

best horses, and ordered them to push ahead rapidly to seize the Villa de Goliad while there was still a chance for a surprise attack.[3]

Shortly before dawn of March 3 Captain Aznar took up a position in an oak grove about a half mile from Goliad, and sent Lieutenant Norverto Galán, in charge of the Auxiliaries of La Bahía, with fifteen men to occupy a position between the town and the San Antonio River to prevent anyone from escaping. At dawn he divided the remainder of his force into four small parties, with one party of ten men being retained under his immediate command, and the other three groups placed under sergeants, with instructions to prevent the inhabitants of the settlement from moving from one house to another or escaping from the town and carrying news of the presence of the Mexican force to Guadalupe-Victoria, ten leagues away, where the enemy could quickly assemble a superior force.

At the agreed signal, Aznar advanced to the church, "which was strong and well built and defended to advantage." The citizens of Goliad who had taken refuge in the church and nearby houses refused to open the doors of their establishments, but soon realizing that each place was individually surrounded, finally agreed to a parley, except for three men in an adobe house. These, however, after reading a copy of Arista's proclamation and after Aznar's personal guarantee for the safety of their persons, gave themselves up. The four or five Anglo-Texans who did not surrender made their escape and reached Victoria at daylight Friday morning.[4] Having taken possession of the town, the captain asked for bread and meat for his men, "promising to pay for them in course of time," he later reported. The Mexican soldiers then drove ten beeves out of town for the remainder of their force. A reconnoitering party was sent in the direction of Victoria, and copies of the proclamation were sent "by mail" to the other side of the San Antonio River. Then after a peaceful occupation of Goliad all day, Aznar united his force and informed the local inhabitants that he was proceeding to Guadalupe-Victoria, and feigning a movement in the direction of the Espíritu Santo Mission, countermarched to the Arroyo del

[3] Miguel Aznar al Lt.-Col. Ramón Valera, en el campo en Arroyo del Mugerero, Marzo 4 de 1842, quoted in El General Mariano Arista al Ministro de Guerra, Monterey, Marzo 27 de 1842, in Chabot, *Corpus Christi and Lipantitlán*, pp. 21–22.

[4] James D. Owen to ———, Victoria, Friday, March 4, 1842, in *Telegraph and Texas Register*, March 16, 1842. This was a copy of the letter brought from Velasco to Galveston by Mr. Frankland of the firm of Frankland & Co. James D. Owen was a brother of Colonel Clark L. Owen.

Mugerero, one of General Fillisola's old camp sites in the campaign of '36, to rejoin Lieutenant Colonel Valera at midnight.

Valera ordered Captain Aznar the following day to surprise the Mission del Refugio. Marching at night with fifty-five men, Aznar reached the vicinity of the town at dawn. Although the inhabitants were said to have numbered four or five times those of Goliad, and although they were better armed and were supported by a detachment of ten Texas rangers, they surrendered without a fight.[5] Among those surrendering was Captain Hamlett Ferguson, who had just arrived in town. Again, as at Goliad, Aznar read to them Arista's proclamation of the 9th of January. At Refugio he learned that a party of Lipans, who of late had been cooperating with the Texans, had arrived the night before from the Río Grande country (with a number of horses and mules they had taken) and were occupying an abandoned house nearby. Captain Aznar attacked them at once. Those who resisted were killed, and the two who attempted to escape were captured and executed "at once for daring to fight our troops," he reported.[6] Among the dead were the son-in-law and the nephew of Castro, the chief of the Lipan tribe. On the first was found a passport or safe conduct granted by the Texan authorities. The leader of the Lipan party was killed by José Sandoval. From the Indians the Mexicans took forty-two horses and mules, said to have been stolen on the Río Grande, which were distributed among those soldiers who were on foot.[7] Each Indian was relieved of his gun, pike, bow, and arrows.

The Mexican force remained at Refugio during the day, requisitioned food, and late in the afternoon continued its march in the direction of the Aranzazu (Aransas) River, and then cut to the Nueces road to join Valera, driving off a considerable number of cattle as they had done in the Goliad area.[8] Valera, having received in the meantime no response from General Vasquez to the communication he had sent him upon his arrival in the vicinity of the Nueces, made plans to withdraw from Texas. His horses being in a deplorable condition,[9] he began to

---

[5] Miguel Aznar al Lt.-Col. Ramón Valera, en el campo en Arroyo de Aranzazu, Marzo 6 de 1842, in Valera al Arista, en el campo en las legunas de Santa Rosa, Marzo 12 de 1842, quoted in El General Mariano Arista al Ministro de Guerra, Monterey, Marzo 27 de 1842, in Chabot, *Corpus Christi and Lipantitlán*, pp. 22–23.

[6] *Ibid.*

[7] *Ibid.*, increased to forty-two in Valera's report.

[8] George L. Rives, *The United States and Mexico, 1821–1848*, I, 485.

[9] W. J. E. Heard to [William Menefee and Major George Sutherland], Victoria,

fall back toward the Nueces, making short marches, with his rear protected by Captain Aznar whose horses were in better condition than those of the others. On the night of the 5th Captain Ferguson effected his escape from Refugio, probably after the Mexicans withdrew, and made his way to Victoria, which place he reached late in the afternoon on the 6th with an exaggerated tale of 300 Mexican troops having captured him. He reported that they had told him of having 800 men beyond the Nueces, that 3,000 had gone to San Antonio, and that they had a total force of 14,000 this side of the Río Grande. They had also said that they had six vessels on the way to the Texas coast loaded with provisions for the army, and that the army was going to Copano to receive the supplies. The rumors grew. A Mr. Cleveland reached Houston at 12 o'clock on Wednesday night, March 9, with the news from Victoria. He repeated Captain Ferguson's account of the size of the enemy forces and the anticipated arrival of six supply ships at Copano.[10] Mr. Adcock of Houston came in from below Columbus to Houston on the morning of the 11th with an account of a three-pronged invasion force, consisting of a division each under Generals Arista, Vasquez, and Bravo, representing 10,000 to 20,000 troops, having already crossed the Río Grande.[11]

In the meantime, while Aznar advanced against Refugio, José María González had been sent in the direction of San Patricio. However, after having gone a short distance from Valera's camp, González's spies reported that a small party of Texans was on the Nueces. This was the reconnaissance party of W. J. Cairns which had gone up the river from Corpus Christi about March 1.[12] González immediately dispatched ten men under Sergeant Eulalio Palacios of the *defensores* to the river to cut off their retreat. About midnight the Mexicans came upon the Texans, sleeping on the bank of the river about thirty miles above Corpus Christi. In the ensuing skirmish at daylight Pedro Flores was

---

March 6, first published in the *Morning Star* (Houston) and later reproduced in the *Telegraph and Texas Register,* March 16, 1842; see also A. C. Allen to Col. James Morgan and Genl. Moseley Baker, Houston, March 9, 1842, in James Morgan Papers, 1841–1845, ms.

[10] *Bollaert's Texas,* p. 29.

[11] Anson Jones to Dr. [Ashbel] Smith, Houston, March 11, 1842, in Ashbel Smith Papers, 1838–1842, ms.

[12] A more detailed treatment of Captain W. J. Cairns' scouting activities on the frontier late in 1841 and early spring of 1842 may be found in Joseph Milton Nance, *After San Jacinto: The Texas-Mexican Frontier, 1836–1841,* pp. 486–487, 497–498, 537.

wounded, but four Texans were reported killed, one taken prisoner (S. Marvin), and two (Wells and Ewen Cameron) effected their escape. Among those Texans killed were Colonel Cairns, who, after being mortally wounded, killed a Mexican,[13] William Snodgrass, A. T. Miles, and a man named White. The Mexicans captured eight horses, six mounts, three rifles, a gun, three pistols, a rifle of sixteen shots, and a sword, all of which, except for the horses, were distributed among the troops under González.[14] Cameron succeeded in making his way on the 8th to the trading post at Corpus Christi, where he reported all lost but himself. Hasty preparations were made to defend the post. González, meanwhile, fell back toward the Nueces where he met Valera on March 7.

Captain John Wade of the sloop *Washington* reported at Galveston on March 7 that on the return from his cruise along the Mexican coast from Brazos Santiago to the Alvarado he had touched at Corpus Christi and found the place guarded by fifty Americans and twenty-eight Karankawa Indians, who were expecting an attack from two to three hundred Mexicans, whom they were confident they could repel.

Before withdrawing his force from the Texas settlements, Valera sent Captain Aznar at dawn on March 8 with thirty men to reconnoitre the right bank of the Nueces to the bay and to approach to the vicinity of Kinney's and Aubrey's trading post at Corpus Christi to see if any of the San Patricio detachment of Texans was there. The Mexicans, however, made no attempt to molest the settlers in the area. During the day of the 8th the Anglo-Texans at the post considered it wise to make an effort to communicate with the Mexican party. A Mexican officer came in and stated that a large invading force would cross the Río Grande in the fall.[15] The officer extended an invitation for several of the Texans to come out and visit their camp. He stated that their visit was for friendly purposes and that the killing of Cairns and his men was in violation of their commander's orders.[16] It was then agreed that Kinney,

[13] Letter from Captain Clark L. Owen reported in *Morning Star* (Houston), March 24, 1842; *Telegraph and Texas Register*, March 30, 1842.

[14] José María González al Ramón Valera, en el campo en El Paso de Piedra, Marzo 7 de 1842, in Ramón Valera al Mariano Arista, Marzo 12 de 1842, quoted in El General Mariano Arista al Ministro de Guerra, Monterey, Marzo 27 de 1842, in Chabot, *Corpus Christi and Lipantitlán*, pp. 23–24; W. B. Goodman, "A Statement of Facts," Washington, Feb. 10, 1843, in Washington D. Miller Papers, 1833–1860 (Texas), ms.

[15] *Telegraph and Texas Register*, March 16 and 30, 1842.

[16] *Ibid.*

Aubrey, Goodman, and F. Belden, as interpreter, should go to the Mexican camp, some five miles out.

Upon arrival at the camp, the Texans received a friendly reception, were handed copies of Arista's proclamation, and found Marvin a prisoner. The Mexicans asked leave to go unmolested to the trading post for water. It was agreed that they could do so on condition they released Marvin and restored Cameron's horse and equipment, all of which was promptly agreed to.[17]

The Mexicans then began their march toward the Río Grande, but soon ran into an unexpected situation. The Lipans, having learned of the fate of their tribesmen at Refugio, assembled a war party of three hundred braves composed of Lipans and Taraucachues [Karankawas?], and Mescaleros, whom the Mexicans alleged worked as allies to the Texans, and struck out after Valera's party. The Indians were well armed with guns and good ammunition. They fell upon the Mexicans below the Nueces between 2 and 3 P.M. on the 10th and for a brief period the situation of the Mexicans was precarious. The Mexican *caballada* and *vaqueros* were stampeded. Finally, the Mexicans rallied and beat off the Indian assault, putting them "to full flight" and causing "considerable loss" to them. In this affray Valera's troops suffered fifteen wounded, including Lieutenant Rafael Sáenz of the *defensores* of Camargo, and the loss of the stolen horses, and cattle, in addition to having sixteen horses seriously wounded.

The citizens of Victoria were awakened on the morning of Friday, March 4, with the news that the evening before forty-one Mexicans had captured Goliad. When the news of the Mexican invasion reached Texana, Col. Clark L. Owen sent expresses throughout Victoria and adjoining Jackson counties to rally the militiamen and volunteers, as well as to give warning to the people. He made hasty preparations to start toward Victoria on the following morning—the 5th[18] to aid in blocking the invader until the Texans to the eastward could come to his relief. Upon his arrival at Victoria, Colonel Owen found a number of men assembled for the defense of the place, and determined not to return to their homes until they had inflicted a severe retribution upon the Mexicans for their recent outrages. Sunday morning, the 6th, he left Victoria

[17] Goodman, "A Statement of Facts," Washington, Feb. 10, 1843, in Miller Papers (Texas), ms.

[18] Clark L. Owen to ———, Texana, March 4, 1842, in *Telegraph and Texas Register*, March 16, 1842. Copy of this letter was brought to Galveston by Mr. Frankland from Velasco.

for Goliad with a company of about sixty men, leaving behind twenty
men who had arrived under Captain William J. E. Heard,[19] but in consequence of the arrival of an express from San Antonio shortly after he
had departed from Victoria, stating that an invading force was within
three miles of that place, a courier was dispatched to overtake Owen,
requesting that he return at once to Victoria. Those who remained at
Victoria were badly armed and in great confusion. They sent out urgent
appeals for help, and prepared to fall back toward the Lavaca if conditions did not improve in another twenty-four hours. At Matagorda
the volunteers were reported organized on the 3rd and ready to move
forward as soon as they could learn where the foe was to be found.[20] In
all, five companies, totaling 256 officers and men, were organized under
Colonel Owen. By the 8th he had 150 men under arms in Victoria, and
60 men from Matagorda were expected to arrive on the 9th. The muster
rolls of these companies describe them as "volunteers companies" and
show their term of enlistment, except for two of the companies, as extending from March 6 to June 6, 1842. The companies were those of
Captain Lafayette Ward, 55 officers and men from Jackson County;
Captain John M. Smith, 25 officers and men from Victoria County;
Captain John Rugeley, 37 officers and men from Matagorda County;
Captain Albert C. Horton, 40 officers and men from Matagorda; and
Captain John S. Menefee, 60 officers and men from Texana.[21] The companies of Captain Rugeley and Captain Horton were permitted to return home on April 13, but the men were told to be in readiness for call
at any time. Captain John P. Gill's Company of 97 men, including
ex-president M. B. Lamar, which had been mustered at Columbia on
March 20, after the withdrawal of the Mexicans, was retained on duty
on the southern frontier until June 20.[22]

A Mexican supply ship apparently from New Orleans or some other
United States gulf port en route to a Mexican port anchored off St.
Joseph Island across from Aransas Bay. News of the vessel being in
the vicinity was carried by a friendly Mexican to a party of French

[19] W. J. E. Heard to [Citizens of Columbus?], Victoria, March 6, 1842, in *Tele-graph and Texas Register*, March 16, 1842.
[20] *Telegraph and Texas Register*, March 16, 1842.
[21] The Muster Rolls for these companies are found in the Archives Division of the Texas State Library in Austin. They are filed under the head of "Militia Rolls" and thereunder alphabetically by captain's name. See muster rolls in the Appendix.
[22] See Muster Roll of Captain John P. Gill's Company of mounted volunteers in the Appendix.

emigrants who had recently settled near Aransas Bay. The informer reported that the Mexican vessel was in charge of a captain and six soldiers. A small party set out for the island immediately, and guided by the Mexican came in sight of the vessel about sunset. Waiting until late at night, they rowed in a small skiff alongside the vessel. Two sentinels were on deck. These they shot, and then jumped on board. Before the men below deck could prepare for defense, the boarding party slammed the hatch shut and set sail for Dekrow's [Deckrow's] Landing, arriving there safely a day or two later with their prize.[23] The ship yielded 350 muskets, 4,000 pounds of powder, 30 barrels of flour, some sugar and coffee, and $3,000 in specie.

[23] *Telegraph and Texas Register*, March 23, 1842.

CHAPTER FOUR

The Withdrawal of Vasquez

BEFORE THE TEXANS could rally to the support of Colonel Clark L. Owen, near Goliad, and Captain Hays, on the Guadalupe, General Vasquez, after occupying San Antonio for two days, evacuated the town and commenced the withdrawal of his small predatory force towards the Río Grande as unexpectedly as he had entered Texas. One will find in contemporary writings and newspaper reports that Vasquez withdrew precipitately, but the more carefully considered accounts indicate that his retreat was orderly and not unusual. Although the Texans were beginning to rally and head for the frontier, their forces were not sufficiently concentrated in the San Antonio area to represent a serious threat to his position until three days after his withdrawal from the town. Should he have remained several days longer his small force not only might have had to fight, but would most likely have been routed. He began his withdrawal on Monday morning (March 7) and on Wednesday was twenty-six miles from Béxar.[1] From his conversation with some of the Mexican officers, William B. Jaques reported that he believed the Mexican government had no intention of making "a regular invasion." While in San Antonio, he wrote, the troops labored under a continual alarm about being attacked by "Americans," and they certainly had no idea of attacking Austin, nor would they have ventured to Béxar if it had not been for the encouragement given by a vast majority of the Mexican inhabitants of that place.[2]

Before retreating, the Mexicans collected in San Antonio all the valuables they could carry off, and appropriated all available carts and wagons they could find in which to carry away their loot. The actual plundering of San Antonio is reported to have been carried out by the

[1] W. D. Miller to Sam Houston, Austin, March 13, 1842 (Private), no. 11, in Washington D. Miller Papers, 1833–1860 (Texas), ms. copy.

[2] Information derived from a letter of William B. Jaques to George M. Dolson and Others of Austin, in *Telegraph and Texas Register*, March 30, 1842.

soldiers and the San Antonio Mexicans who left with them, and was not done by order of the officers; yet, the latter were responsible for the performance of the soldiers under their command.[3] The Mexicans at Béxar who supported the enemy cause paid dearly for their treachery, being compelled to forsake and forfeit their homes after a brief triumph of only three days; when they left they were determined to take as much valuable property with them as they could lay their hands on, no matter to whom it belonged. Typical of the plundering was the removal from the Maverick home of a beautiful sandpapered and oil-rubbed walnut mantel-piece which was pried out of the wall and carted off as some rare piece of wood. Mrs. Hutchinson's piano, too heavy to move in a hurry, was chopped open with an axe. County and municipal records and papers were captured, lost, or destroyed.[4] The home of William B. Jaques was burned.[5] Everything of value was stripped from the American homes.[6] The retreating forces and citizenry carried off 132 mule-loads of plunder and a dozen carts of goods, as well as several Mexican families.[7] Although Chevallie and Dunn were released, ——— Whit-

[3] W. D. Miller to Sam Houston, March 9 and 13, 1842 (Private), nos. 9 and 11, in Miller Papers (Texas), ms copy; H. Yoakum, *History of Texas from Its First Settlement in 1685 to Its Annexation to the United States in 1846*, II, 350. The copy of the proclamation by the Secretary of War and Navy, George W. Hockley, dated Austin, March 12, 1842, in *Telegraph and Texas Register*, March 23, 1842, begins "The Mexicans have left Béxar, and have plundered it. They were evidently a marauding party, commanded by regular officers."

[4] John D. Morris to Dear Brother [Richard Morris? Galveston], Seguin, March 8, 1842, in *Telegraph and Texas Register*, March 16, 1842; San Antonio, "Journal A, Records of the City of San Antonio," August 13, 1842, ts.

[5] *Handbook of Texas*, I, 905.

[6] Rena Maverick Green (ed.), *Samuel Maverick, Texan, 1803–1870: A Collection of Letters, Journals and Memoirs*, p. 159.

[7] *Telegraph and Texas Register*, March 30, 1842, The Mexican newspapers sought to defend the honor of the portion of the army that invaded Texas and the good name of the country against the charges made in newspapers in the United States involving the plundering of San Antonio. The goods seized, declared the *Semanario Politico de Nuevo-León* (quoted in *El Cosmopolita*, May 14, 1842),

were those abandoned on the field but whoever would complain as he could at that time, giving proof of seizure, had his property respected in the full sense of the word, since General Vasquez himself ordered guards to be placed at all the stores, imposing the death penalty upon whoever ventured to take the slightest thing from them. This conduct, so worthy and in conformance with the instructions which said commanding officer carried to protect the property rights of those who did not take up arms, was strictly observed the entire time that the Mexican force was in Béxar. . . . If they did not claim the effects of which we speak, it may

aker and another young man from the Colorado, who had been captured in the neighborhood of San Antonio while out as spies, were carried off.[8] Loaded down with baggage, the Mexicans retreated slowly toward the Río Grande, progressing at only eight miles a day.[9] At Austin, the successor to the belligerent *Alarm Bell of the West*, the *Anti-Quaker*, upon receipt of the news of the retirement of the invaders, quacked in its first and only issue, that the plunderers of Béxar "are no doubt well satisfied that they met with *nothing worse than merchandise*."[10] Judging from his reports, Vasquez reached Presidio del Río Grande on March 15.[11] He is said to have written that upon his "arrival on the banks of the river [Río Grande], his horses were so exhausted that, had his men been attacked, not more than 40 would have been able to join in the charge."[12] The reason he was not molested in his retreat, commented the editor of the *Telegraph*, was "that he ran away so fast that the Texans could not catch him."[13] No wonder his horses were ridden down.

As the Mexicans retired from San Antonio, a reconnaissance party

---

be inferred with little difficulty that they belonged to the enemy who was put to flight, refusing the guarantees that were offered them.

It was this property that was distributed among the Mexican soldiers. The distribution of this property was as given in the accompanying table, plus goods valued at 115 pesos and 6 reales which were given to citizens of Béxar and to the Caddo Indians and spies aiding the Mexican army. The total value of the goods seized was given by Vasquez as 2,540 pesos. See, Relacion de los efectos de botin de guerra que se repartieron de orden del general D. Rafael Vasquez, Cuerpo de Ejército del Norte, 2ª Division, Ríogrande, Marzo 15 de 1842. [Signed by:] José María Carrasco [and approved by:] Vasquez, in *Semanario Politico de Nuevo-León*, quoted in *El Cosmopolita*, May 14, 1842.

[8] W. D. Miller to Sam Houston, Austin, March 13, 1842 (Private), no. 11, in Miller Papers (Texas), ms. copy.

[9] Houston to the Editor of the Galveston Advertiser [?], Houston, Texas, March 17, 1842, in *Writings of Sam Houston*, II, 509.

[10] *Anti-Quaker* (Austin), March 12, 1842, cited in the *Morning Star* (Houston) from which the *Telegraph and Texas Register*, March 23, 1842, quotes.

[11] Citing as its source Monterey newspapers, the *New Orleans Bulletin* reported that General Vasquez had written an account of his expedition in a letter, dated March 11 on the banks of the Río Grande. From this it would seem that the Mexican army made the return trip in five days, which was doubtful but not impossible. But if it took Vasquez two days or more to cover twenty-six miles, as we have noted, it is not likely that he reached the Río Grande on the 11th.

[12] *Telegraph and Texas Register*, April 27, 1842.

[13] *Ibid.*

REPORT OF DISTRIBUTION OF GOODS SEIZED AMONG TROOPS OF VASQUEZ'S ARMY[a]

Corps	Goods	Value	Pesos	Reales
Artillery	Guinea lace, 29 pieces	@ 9 pesos/piece	261	0
Light Infantry	Drill cloth, 20 pieces	@ 11 pesos/piece	220	0
	Linen cloth, 1 piece	@ 10 pesos/piece	10	0
12th Regiment of Light Infantry	Wide tablecloth, 1 piece	@ 7 pesos/piece	7	0
	Narrow tablecloth, 1 piece	@ 5 pesos/piece	5	0
	Small cloth, 1 piece	@ 2 pesos 2 reales/piece	2	2
6th Regiment Infantry	Guinea lace, 1 piece	@ 9 pesos/piece	9	0
	Wide tablecloth, 16 pieces	@ 7 pesos/piece	112	0
	Indian cloth, 4 pieces	@ 5 pesos/piece	20	0
	Narrow tablecloth, 10 pieces	@ 5 pesos/piece	50	0
	Woolen blanket cloth, 2 pieces	@ 5 pesos/piece	10	0
	Small cloth, 3 pieces	@ 2 pesos 2 reales/piece	6	6
1st Regiment of Cavalry	Wide tablecloth, 33 pieces	@ 7 pesos/piece	231	0
	Drill cloth, 1 piece	@ 11 pesos/piece	11	0
	Narrow tablecloth, 20 pieces	@ 5 pesos/piece	100	0
2nd Regiment of Cavalry	Wide tablecloth, 8 pieces	@ 7 pesos/piece	56	0
	Narrow, tablecloth, 9 pieces	@ 5 pesos/piece	40 [45]	0
	Small cloth, 1 piece	@ 2 pesos 2 reales/piece	2	2
6th Regiment of Cavalry	Wide tablecloth, 20 pieces	@ 7 pesos/piece	91 [140]	0
	Drill cloth, 9 pieces	@ 5 pesos/piece	45	0
	Indian cloth, 8 pieces	@ 5 pesos/piece	40	0
	Woolen blanket cloth, 4 pieces	@ 5 pesos/piece	20	0
	Narrow tablecloth, 6 pieces	@ 2 pesos 2 reales/piece	13	4
Presidial Cavalry from Laredo	Wide tablecloth, 20 pieces	@ 10 pesos/piece	140 [200]	0
	Drill cloth, 5 pieces	@ 5 pesos/piece	25	0
Presidial Cavalry from Río Grande	Wide tablecloth, 7 pieces	@ 7 pesos/piece	140 [49]	0

Unit	Item	Price		
	Woolen blanket cloth, 10 pieces	@ 5 pesos/piece	50	0
	Indian cloth, 5 pieces	@ 5 pesos/piece	25	0
	Handkerchief cloth, 1 piece	@ 2 pesos 2 reales/piece	2	2
Cavalry from Agua Verde	Wide tablecloth, 7 pieces	@ 7 pesos/piece	147 [49]	0
	Woolen blanket cloth, 7 pieces	@ 5 pesos/piece	35	0
	Handkerchief cloth, 8 pieces	@ 2 pesos 2 reales/piece	18	0
	Indian cloth, 3 pieces	@ 5 pesos/piece	15	0
Defensores from Tamaulipas	Wide tablecloth, 15 pieces	@ 7 pesos/piece	105	0
	Woolen blanket cloth, 12 pieces	@ 5 pesos/piece	60	0
	Indian cloth, 10 pieces	@ 5 pesos/piece	50	0
	Handkerchief cloth, 6 pieces	@ 2 pesos 2 reales/piece	13	4
1st Cavalry Defenders of Río Grande	Wide tablecloth, 15 pieces	@ 7 pesos/piece	105	0
3rd Cavalry Defenders of Río Grande	Woolen blanket cloth, 5 pieces	@ 5 pesos/piece	25	0
	Indian cloth, 4 pieces	@ 5 pesos/piece	20	0
	Handkerchief cloth, 4 pieces	@ 2 pesos 2 reales/piece	9	0
Cavalry of Explorers from Calvillo	Wide tablecloth, 15 pieces	@ 7 pesos/piece	105	0
	Indian cloth, 1 piece	@ 5 pesos/piece	5	0
	Narrow tablecloth, 6 pieces	@ 5 pesos/piece	30	0
	Handkerchief cloth, 3 pieces	@ 2 pesos 2 reales/piece	6	6
		TOTAL	2,491 [2,416]	26 [26]
		or	2,494 [2,419]	2 [2]

a The effects of the Béxar traitors were valued in this report at 2,540 pesos. They were distributed to the corps, 2,424 [pesos]; and the rest of 115 pesos, 6 reales, to the citizens of Béxar, Cad[d]ós and spies, without other effects of dry goods [small wares] which were distributed in proportion. Relación de los efectos de botin de guerra que se repartieron de orden del general D. Rafael Vasquez, Cuerpo de Ejército del Norte, 2ª Division, Ríogrande, Marzo 15 de 1842. [Signed by:] José María Carrasco and approved by: Vasquez, in Semanario Político de Nuevo-León, quoted in El Cosmopolita, May 14, 1842, p. 1, cols. 2–4. In addition to a minor variance of 2 reales between the amount mentioned as distributed and the total valuation, this report also contains a difference of 45 pesos, 4 reales (or 6 reales) between these totals and the sum of the figures given in the itemization of the distribution. If mathematical discrepancies in the original figures of the itemization are corrected, this difference becomes 120 pesos, 4 reales (or 6 reales).

under Calixto Bravo encountered on the right bank of the Medina[14] a band of Waco and Tahuacano Indians, who apparently were on a predatory expedition into the Texas settlements. The Indians were caught in the open prairie, "moving stealthily down the stream," and the Mexican commander ordered a surprise attack, which resulted in the killing of some eight or ten Indians by the Mexican spearmen before the band could escape to the brush without resistance, so surprised were they.[15]

In retreat, Vasquez was followed beyond the Nueces by Captain Hays, accompanied by Juan N. Seguin, Captain Manuel Flores, Lieutenant Ambrosio Rodríquez, Matías Curbier, and other San Antonio Mexicans. Hays, however, lacked sufficient strength to risk an attack upon the superior Mexican force; so he fell back to the Nueces, eventually returning to San Antonio. Upon the return of Seguin to San Antonio, General Burleson, who had arrived upon the scene and been elected to command the Texan troops in the area, refused to establish a court of inquiry to investigate his conduct; however, Seguin discovered at Béxar so much hostility against him for his presumedly traitorous conduct, that he found it necessary to retire to his ranch. He received jointly with Colonel William H. Patton a commission from General Burleson "to forage for provisions in the lower ranchos" for the army.

At Béxar, Benjamin F. Highsmith, who had gone to San Antonio with Captain H. M. Childress, learned through Juan Cantú that Seguin was at the Calaveras' Ranch, thirty miles down the river. He applied to Captain Childress for twenty-five men to go and capture him. Permission being granted, Highsmith, guided by Cantú, set out for the Calaveras' Ranch to apprehend Seguin, under whom he had marched in the Federalist campaign of 1840. The party reached the ranch at night and surrounded it. The owner, Calaveras, was called out and asked if Seguin were there.

He said, "No."

"You lie," said Cantú, and proposed then and there to hang him.

A rope was produced, put around his neck, and he was drawn up, but was told he would be let down when he told where Seguin was. Calaveras, however, persisted in his first statement that Seguin was not there, and that he

[14] Ministerio de guerra y marina. Memoria del Secretario de estado y del despacho de guerra y marina, leida a las camaras del Congreso nacional de la Republica Mexicana, en enero de 1844, in *Diario del Gobierno*, May 15, 1844.

[15] *Morning Star* (Houston), Jan. 3, 1843.

did not know where he was. He was drawn up three times, but finally released and left nearly dead. No doubt Seguin had been there, but was gone,

concluded Sowell who interviewed Highsmith many years later. Highsmith and his men returned to San Antonio, where they were soon disbanded by order of Captain Childress.[16]

For several weeks Seguin remained in hiding, going first from one ranch to another; but, tiring of this, he attempted, with friends and relatives, to fortify his own rancho. He tendered his resignation as mayor of San Antonio on April 18 because of "the disorderly state in which this unhappy county finds itself at the present time."[17] On April 30, Seguin learned that Captain James W. Scott was bringing his company down the San Antonio River, "burning the ranchos on their way." The inhabitants of the lower ranches now called upon Seguin and his followers for aid against Scott. "With those in my house," said Seguin, "and others to the number of 100, I started to lend them aid. I proceeded, observing the movements of Scott, from the junction of the Medina to Pajaritos. At that place we dispersed, and I returned to my wretched life. In those days I could not go to San Antonio without peril of my life." Finally, Seguin decided to seek asylum in Mexico, the country he had fought against for so long.[18]

Juan Nepomuceno Seguin, son of Erasmo Seguin, was a native-born Texan who served as captain of a company of Mexican soldiers under Sam Houston in the battle of San Jacinto and later as a lieutenant colonel of the Second Regiment of Cavalry stationed at San Antonio. He represented Béxar County in the Senate of the Third and Fourth Congresses, and was elected mayor of San Antonio on January 4, 1841. After the Mexican withdrawal from Texas in 1836, Seguin found his *rancho* some thirty-three miles from San Antonio, despoiled, with large quantities of his livestock having been driven off by the "cattle raiders" on the frontier. "What little had been spared by the retreating enemy," he recorded, "had been wasted by our own army; ruin and misery met me on my return to my unpretending home." He found some of the newly ar-

---

[16] A. J. Sowell, *Early Settlers and Indian Fighters of Southwest Texas*, p. 14.

[17] Juan N. Seguin al Juez del Condado de Béxar, April 18, 1842, in San Antonio, "Journal A, Records of the City of San Antonio," p. 103. One of the Harris County companies in the Vasquez campaign was that of Captain M. B. Skerrett, later commanded by Captain James W. Scott. See Petition of James R. Burt to the Legislature of the State of Texas, San Antonio, Jan. 11, 1856 (two petitions, each 1 p.), in Memorials and Petitions (Texas), ms.; *Handbook of Texas*, II, 582.

[18] Seguin, *Memoirs*, pp. 24–27.

rived officers and men from the United States jealous of the large tracts of land owned by native Mexican families on the southwestern frontier. He accused John W. Smith, his successor as mayor of San Antonio, of joining the conspiracy against him.

In his memoirs, Seguin has recorded,

I have been the object of the hatred and passionate attacks of some few disorganizers, who, for a time, ruled, as master, over the poor and oppressed population of San Antonio. Happy-like, [Harpy-like?] ready to pounce on every thing that attracted the notice of their rapacious avarice, I was an obstacle to the execution of their vile designs. They, therefore, leagued together to exasperate and ruin me; spread against me malignant calumnies, and made use of odious machinations to sully my honor, and tarnish my well earned reputation.

A victim of the wickedness of a few men, whose imposture was favored by their origin and recent domination over the country; a foreigner in my native land; could I be expected stoically to endure their outrages and insults? Crushed by sorrow, convinced that my death alone would satisfy my enemies, I sought for a shelter amongst those whom I had fought; I separated from my country, parents, family, relatives and friends, and what was more, from the institutions, on behalf of which I had drawn my sword, with an earnest wish to see Texas free and happy. . . . I served Mexico; I served her loyally and faithfully; I was compelled to fight my own countrymen, but I was never guilty of the barbarous and unworthy deeds which I am accused by my enemies.[19]

Upon Seguin's arrival at Laredo, the military commander there had him placed in prison until he could communicate with Arista. Receiving information of Seguin's arrival on the frontier, Arista ordered him to be sent to Monterey, where he was held a prisoner until Santa Anna could be heard from. Santa Anna ordered Seguin to report to Mexico City, but upon the request of General Arista, the order was cancelled on condition Seguin would return to Texas with a company of "explorers" to attack its citizens and thus vindicate himself.[20] Arista sent him to Presidio del Río Grande to join General Adrían Woll's command, then preparing to invade Texas. At Santa Anna's request, Woll permitted Seguin to accompany his expedition, but refused to give him a command until he should prove worthy of it.[21]

[19] *Ibid.*, pp. iii–iv, 18.
[20] *Ibid.*, p. 27.
[21] *Ibid.*

CHAPTER FIVE

Texans Rally To Defend the Frontier

THE NEWS OF the near approach of the Mexicans upon San Antonio was carried to Austin by Ambrosio Rodríquez, who arrived at the capital early on the morning of the 6th with a report from Captain Hays to the Secretary of War. He reported that a large Mexican force had already reached the León, but that their precise number and intentions had not been ascertained, because nearly every spy that had been dispatched to reconnoitre the country had been cut off.[1] About three hours after the arrival of Rodríquez, J. D. Generes, "a young gentleman of the highest respectability," came as an express rider from San Antonio, having set out late the day before.[2] He reported that at the time he left some five hundred of the enemy had arrived near the town and were in view of observers stationed on top of the church. He declared that it had been pretty well ascertained that re-enforcements for the invading army were close at hand, and that it was believed the attack would be made by about two thousand men.

In the interval between the arrival of Rodríquez and the coming of Generes, the Secretary of War, George W. Hockley, ordered out a battalion of Colonel Henry Jones' regiment, which, with the men in town, would constitute a force of sufficient strength to defend Austin against a large marauding party, which he supposed the Mexican force

[1] W. D. Miller to Sam Houston, Austin, March 6, 1842 (Private), no. 7, in Washington D. Miller Papers, 1833–1860 (Texas), ms. copy.

[2] *Ibid.* Miller gave the name as "Generes," while Gerald Boerner, "Austin, 1836–1877," ms., p. 14, gives the name as "Genners," and says that he escaped from San Antonio at sunrise and reached Austin about dusk of the same day. I follow Miller's account, for the latter was making reports at this time almost daily to the President. In a sense, he was the "eyes and ears" of the President in the west after Houston left Austin, and was making his reports at the President's special request. Record of Executive Documents from the 10th December 1838 to the 14th December 1841, ms., p. 94, gives the name as J. D. Generis.

represented.[3] If the enemy force now approaching San Antonio was not checked, reported Hockley, a large force might be sent by Mexico against Austin to destroy the Archives while another might go to the right in an effort to cut off communications between the capital and the rest of Texas. The battalion of Jones' regiment promptly appeared in Austin, and the whole regiment was ordered to be concentrated there as soon as the men were able to rally. Generals Alexander Somervell of Fort Bend County and Edwin Morehouse at Houston were directed by Hockley[4] to hold their brigades in readiness until further orders. These militia groups were to muster and await further instructions from the Secretary of War. They were told that if it should be necessary for them to move, *"they must furnish their own arms and ammunition"* as the War Department had none available in Austin.

Upon Hays' withdrawal from Béxar, he sent Captain Duncan C. Ogden to Austin with dispatches to the War Department asking for re-enforcements, saying, "they only wanted 300 soldiers to whip the enemy from Béxar."[5] Ogden reached Austin Sunday evening in company with Robert S. Neighbors and Captain George M. Dolson to report the capture of San Antonio,[6] and there the news was published in a broadside "Extra" issued from the "Gazette Office, Half-past 10 o'clock, Mond[ay] Morn, [March 7, 1842]." A hastily inserted line, dated "Monday Morning, 6 o'clock," read, "An express has just arrived with information that Goliad has fallen, but no particulars." When questioned as to the number of Mexicans, Neighbors replied, there was " 'a d—d sight of them'."[7] Dolson estimated the invading force at twenty thousand.[8] Secretary of War Hockley sent a special courier from Austin on March 6 in the person of John Green, Jr.,[9] to the President at Gal-

[3] George W. Hockley to [Sam Houston], Department of War & Navy, March 6, 1842, in Harriet Smither (ed.), *Journals of the Sixth Congress of the Republic of Texas*, III, 15–16.

[4] George W. Hockley to Sam Houston, Depatrment [*sic*] of War and Marine, June 23, 1842, in *ibid.*, pp. 107–112; *Telegraph and Texas Register*, July 6, 1842; *Morning Star* (Houston), July 5, 1842.

[5] Quoted in the *Civilian and Galveston Gazette*, March 12, 1842.

[6] John Green, Jr., to Captain [George M.] Dolson, Austin, March 16, 1842, in *Austin City Gazette*, March 30, 1842.

[7] *Ibid.*

[8] A. C. Allen to Col. James Morgan and Genl. Moseley Baker, Houston, March 9, 1842, in James Morgan Papers, 1841–1845, ms.

[9] See Debt Certificate, War Department (Republic of Texas), to John Green, Jr., for carrying express to Galveston from Austin [marked:] Paid, April 1, 1842, in

veston. Green returned to Austin on the 15th with communications from the President to the various departments.[10] The news of the fall of Béxar was published in Houston on March 11 from an express "from Austin dated Monday last." From Houston the published news was conveyed by the steamer *Dayton* to Galveston, reaching the latter place on the 12th, where it was given publicity in an extra of the *Civilian and Galveston Gazette* of the 12th. From Galveston the news was carried by the steamer *New York* to New Orleans where it was published in the afternoon of March 15 in an extra of the *Daily Picayune* whose headlines shrieked, "Texas Invaded!!! Fourteen Thousand Mexican Troops in Texas!!" and in the *New Orleans Bee* of March 16.

Dr. Levi Jones, J. C. Watrous, and Joseph C. Megginson, representing the Galveston committee of vigilance, as commissioners seeking men and supplies in the United States, were passengers on the *New York*. Shortly after their arrival it was announced they had taken rooms at the St. Charles Exchange Hotel, where they would be happy to confer with such friends as might desire to become better acquainted with the situation and prosperity of Texas. As evidence of the needs of Texas, they came armed with a copy of a hastily written letter the committee of vigilance at Galveston had requested of Colonel Alden A. M. Jackson of the Fourth Regiment of Texas Militia as to what articles were most desired. Jackson reported a great need throughout the entire country for arms and ammunition of every description. "We are sadly in want of light or flying artillery, horseman's pistols and equipments for cavalry, blankets, knapsacks, cartridge boxes, tents and other camp equipage, muskets and bayonets, Spanish saddle trees, flints, caps, bowie knives, cutlasses and boarding pikes, and in fact many more accessories which need hardly be enumerated." Urgently needed for the defenses of Galveston were three hundred eighteen-pound cannon balls and fifty stand of grape and cannister for eighteen-pounders.[11]

In reporting the renewal of hostilities in Texas, the editor of the *Bee* commented,

---

Army Papers (Texas), ms.; George M. Dolson to John Green, Austin, March 17, 1842, in *Austin City Gazette*, March 30, 1842.

[10] George W. Hockley to General [Houston], Department of War and Navy, Austin, March 16, 1842, in Smither (ed.), *Journals of the Sixth Congress*, III, 17–18.

[11] *New Orleans Bee*, March 16, 1842; Alden A. M. Jackson to [Committee of Vigilance], Galveston, March 12, 1842, in *ibid.*, March 17, 1842.

The supine and pacific policy of Texas has at length invited the Mexican to invade the Republic. We apprehend that the Texians, among other qualities, have inherited a large portion of the *diplomatic* spirit of the United States. The actual incursions of the enemy could alone arouse them to take that stand, which had they taken a year ago, would have made Mexico the theatre of the war instead of Texas. . . . The persuasion of gunpowder can alone reach the understandings of such a people as Mexico; and it is the only argument that the United States should use in the matter of her citizens now held in degrading cruel bondage by that inflated Republic.

If the United States cannot go to war, he said, then it was time to join the banner of a sister republic. The standard of the Texan army should be decorated with a miniature of the cathedral of Mexico City so that every man could see it "the last thing in the evening and the first in the morning, to keep the end of his exertions continually in his mind; for not until the Texian banner is planted in the public square before the palace of Santa Anna should the war be terminated."[12]

Lightning-like the news of the invasion of Texas spread throughout the city of New Orleans, and "men gazed upon each other in astonishment." On the 17th an appeal "To the Citizens of New Orleans and the Valley of the Mississippi," dated the day before, appeared in the *Daily Picayune* over the signature of Jones and Megginson. They announced,

The fate of Texas is at this moment suspended on the issue of the contest now waging on the banks of the Colorado. The forces of ruthless and perfidious Mexico are suddenly precipitated on the country in numbers to render certain the repetition of the scenes of 1836, with aggravated horrors. The people, though taken by surprise, are rallying *en masse* with enthusiasm unexampled, to the rescue. They are fully resolved not again to lay down their arms until they extort the acknowledgment of their independence in the heart of the Mexican capital.

The commissioners stated they had been sent by the committee of vigilance of Galveston to represent as they believed "the feelings of the whole of Texas," and to solicit "contributions of useful materials as that condition demands." There were those persons in Texas and in the United States who believed that once an invasion of Mexico had begun, the Texans should not stop with the mere recognition of Texan independence, but should institute certain reforms in Mexico.

[12] *New Orleans Bee*, March 16, 1846; see also, *Daily Picayune*, March 16 and 17, 1842; James Love, John S. Sydnor, Jonas Butler, and George B. Innis, Committee [of Vigilance, Galveston] to Messrs. [J. C.] Watrous, [Levi] Jones, and [Joseph C.] Megginson, Galveston, March [12], 1842, in *New Orleans Bee*, March 17, 1842.

Later, when it became known that the Mexican invasion had fizzled, the Galveston correspondent of the *Daily Picayune*[13] wrote, "we are all wide awake, and determined to make one *powerful* and *united* effort to burst asunder the chains of civil and religious despotism by which our brethren in Mexico have long been bound. The days of the reign of the Catholic priesthood in Mexico are numbered."

On the 24th of March the news of the fall of San Antonio appeared in an Extra of the *Arkansas Gazette* whose report was based upon that of the *New Orleans Bee*, and two days later the story was published in the *Ohio Statesman-Extra*, Columbus, March 26, 5 o'clock P.M. The postmaster at Washington, Arkansas, may have been a strong friend of Texas or a lover of the "tall tale," or he may simply have been endowed with a peculiar sense of humor, for on a waybill of April 1 to Memphis, he penciled the following notation: "News of undoubted authority reached here last night, that the city of Austin was taken, and 1354 Texians were killed in two hours." This, commented the editor of the *Picayune*, "is the most extensive and successful first of April falsehoods we have heard of."[14]

As the news of the seizure of Béxar, Goliad, and Refugio spread eastward across Texas and into the United States, it caused a great "uprore."[15] It fired the imagination of the people and recalled to mind the trying, ruthless, bloody experiences of '36. It was rumored that the Mexicans were invading the country with an army of twelve to fourteen thousand. "From high authority—Thomas M. Duk[e], Judge Tolbert & others," word reached Brazoria that the Texan spies and friendly Mexicans at the Texan camp thirty-five miles from Victoria had reported fifteen hundred Mexican troops at San Patricio and nine thousand in their rear on the west bank of the Nueces, and reports were abroad, and believed by some, that twelve thousand troops were advancing upon Béxar.[16] Others estimated the Mexican force to be from fourteen to twenty thousand strong. "Although it is generally said Mexicans are not men of military talent," wrote Albert Wickes from Galveston, "they have certainly planned this expedition admirably and with great secrecy. . . . Nearly all our frontier towns are taken and the people

[13] *Daily Picayune*, March 29, 1842.

[14] *Ibid.*, April 14, 1842.

[15] James F. Perry to Eliza M. Perry, Peach Point, near Brazoria, Texas, March [19], 1842, in James F. Perry Papers, ms.

[16] James T. Caldwell to J. F. Perry, Sunday, A.M., March 20, 1842, in *ibid.*, ms; *Daily Picayune*, March 25, 1842.

falling back. The citizens throughout this portion of the country are turning out almost *en masse*. We shall try to meet them west of the Colorado."[17] Texans on visitation or business in the United States, friends and relatives in the United States of persons who had settled in the Republic, and those who were imbued with thoughts of the superiority of the Anglo-Saxon race became quite concerned with what seemed to be an effort by Mexico to subdue Texas. A great many of these, including the usual adventurer, prepared to go to the aid of Texas. Guy M. Bryan, nephew of Stephen F. Austin, withdrew from Kenyon College when he heard of the invasion, and started for home; but en route he learned of the Mexican withdrawal and returned to school.[18] And in Texas, Albert Wickes wrote his father, "I have made nothing in the country and have not one single personal interest at stake and did intend leaving for N[ew] O[rleans] or Mobile in a few days, but at this stage of affairs nothing can induce me to leave."[19]

Men left their work in the fields of Texas, saddled their horses, took up their rifles, and headed for San Antonio, Victoria, and other points along the southern and western frontier. All Texas was in a ferment and expected the enemy, several thousand strong, to make an effort to subjugate them or expel them beyond the Sabine, for Santa Anna, having once failed in the country, surely would not come a second time without being well prepared. Accustomed to forays of Indians and robbers, each ranger in the volunteer companies kept always in readiness "a good horse, saddle, bridle, and arms, and a supply of coffee, salt, sugar and other provisions" to start on fifteen minutes warning in pursuit of the marauders.[20] Preparations for a three months' campaign rarely required more than six hours, for after all, catching horses, running fifty bullets, parching and grinding half a bushel of corn for cold flour, and collecting one's long gun, pistols, bowie knife, a couple of blankets, and an extra shirt or pair of pantaloons, were the only preparations necessary. To these supplies might be added, if the occa-

---

[17] A[lbert] Wickes to George Wickes, Cairo, Green County, New York [dated:] Galveston, March 11, 1842, in Houston Wade Papers, ms. copy. Albert Wickes, son of George Wickes, was born December 9, 1816, and died February 26, 1847. He is buried in the Episcopal-Masonic Cemetery, Houston, Texas.

[18] Guy M. Bryan to James F. Perry, Gambier, Ohio, April 19, 1842, in Perry Papers, ms.

[19] A[lbert] Wickes to George Wickes, Cairo, Green County, New York, [dated:] Galveston, March 11, 1842, in Wade Papers, ms. copy.

[20] Rena Maverick Green (ed.), *Memoirs of Mary A. Maverick: Arranged by Mary A. Maverick and Her Son George Madison Maverick*, p. 28.

sion permitted, such items as coffee, salt, and sugar. Since Congress had refused to appropriate money for the maintenance of an army, only untrained and infuriated volunteers, without coordinated leadership, stood between the Texans and the Mexican army of invasion.[21] Within a few days, two to three thousand volunteers "well armed and equipped by voluntary contribution" were reported marching toward San Antonio.[22] "It would astonish you," wrote Joseph Eve, the United States chargé d'affaires in Texas, "to see the Patriotism, liberality, [and] alacrity with which all classes of men here join the Army in the hour of alarm and danger. This government has not a dollar in the treasury, without credit to borrow at home or abroad, with not a regular soldier belonging to the nation yet when the news reached . . . [Galveston] that San Antonio had been taken $12,000 was raised in one night by voluntary donations for the use of the army."[23] "Men who have neither goods or money to appropriate," reported Albert Wickes at Galveston, "are selling property to the highest bidder, the proceeds to be applied in the same way. And even ladies are selling their Jewelry to purchase ammunition."[24]

In Montgomery County, where some of the farmers were unable to leave their farms, they fitted out young and idle men with full military equipment; and in other instances a number of ladies, it was reported, "had urged their husbands and brothers to go to the war, and had voluntarily taken their place . . . in ploughing, planting, etc."[25] At Houston the merchants threw open their stores and contributed whatever articles were required for the soldiers. Powder, lead, clothing, flour, and other necessities were offered free of charge. On the 14th and 15th in this bayou city all was "bustle and hurry of busy preparations for war. . . . The clang of arms, the beating of drums, the neighing of steeds, and the hoarse words of command," wrote the editor of

[21] R. Mills to J. F. Perry, Brazoria, March 20 [1842] in Perry Papers, ms.

[22] Joseph Eve to James Franklin Ballinger, Galveston, April 26, 1842, in Joseph Milton Nance (ed.), "A Letter Book of Joseph Eve, United States Chargé d'Affaires to Texas," *Southwestern Historical Quarterly*, XLIII (1939–1940), 486–492; *Daily Picayune*, March 17, 1842.

[23] Joseph Eve to John J. Crittenden, Galveston, April 3, 1842, in Nance (ed.), "A Letter Book of Joseph Eve," in *Southwestern Historical Quarterly*, XLIII (1939–1940), 369–374.

[24] A[lbert] Wickes to George Wickes, Esq., Cairo, Green County, New York [dated:] Galveston, March 11, 1842, in Wade Papers, ms. copy.

[25] *Telegraph and Texas Register*, March 23, 1842. See also *Daily Picayune,* March 29, 1842.

the *Telegraph and Texas Register*,[26] "resounded from all quarters [of
the city]. It was cheering to every patriot to behold the martial spirit
and noble enthusiasm that everywhere prevailed. The militia and soldiers belonging to the independent companies turned out almost to a
man, and seemed willing and ready to obey any call that might be made
—to meet the emergency." Some of them left immediately (on the 11th)
for the west, and men prepared to march from Galveston the same day
or the next.[27]

Great alarm was felt, for this sudden invasion had caught the Texans
wholly unprepared. Although there had been rumors of invasion for
some time, these had been considered just like so many countless others
that had preceded them, and no one really paid much attention to them
except those who were "beating up" for a "hot war" with Mexico.

The messenger reached us late Saturday evening [March 4], [wrote the Reverend Z. N. Morrell of Gonzales] and, after a little consultation, it was decided that families, flocks and herds must start east, early Monday morning,
everything of course was thrown into confusion. Sunday morning's sun arose,
and instead of shining upon our people on their way to the baptism, furnished
them light by which to make their preparation to retreat before the invading
Mexicans. My little blacksmith shop was very soon surrounded with wagons,
needing repairs for the journey. More wagon wheels were repaired on that
Sunday than ever I witnessed at one little shop on any day before or since.
Wagons were loaded on Sunday night, and Monday morning a boy from
every family that had one was detailed to go out on horseback and drive in
all the stock of every description for miles around. The bleating and lowing
of the herd reminded us of the roving shepherd patriarchs. By one o'clock
Monday everything was in motion for the Colorado Valley.[28]

But as the men hurried to the front, not all the women and children
fled eastward. Spartan-like, some stayed to protect their homes, stock,
and personal belongings. "I would not allow in my house any man,"
declared one woman, "who would not hurry to help the afflicted homeland as soon as it was in distress. We have helped to establish our freedom; we form a part of the state. Our lives and those of our children

26 March 16, 1842.
27 A[lbert] Wickes to George Wickes, Cairo, Green County, New York [dated:]
Galveston, March 11, 1842, in Wade Papers, ms. copy; *Daily Picayune*, March 16,
1842.
28 Z[enos] N. Morrell, *Flowers and Fruits in the Wilderness*, p. 159. Morrell was a
frontier Baptist preacher.

depend on its maintenance—could any single one then, without losing his honor stay behind to protect house and home?"[29]

In Washington County a company of some thirty-six men was enrolled on March 11 under Captain Samuel Bogart and prepared to join General Edward Burleson's command then on its way to San Antonio from Austin.[30] When word of the invasion reached Richmond, Fort Bend County, there was considerable excitement. Young men and old came forward to volunteer their services. When the Reverend E. A. Briggs, a native of Massachusetts, who had arrived in Texas the year before and settled at Richmond to preach and teach school, found a majority of his students preparing to join the company being formed, he declared, "Well, boys, if you are all going to war I had as well go, too." So saying, he, too, joined the volunteer company.[31]

Wild were the rumors that ran through Southwest Texas. The committee of safety of Matagorda called upon the citizens of the eastern counties to help repel the large Mexican forces now invading the country. The committee reported as many as nine thousand Mexican troops entering the country via the Matagorda Road and another twelve thousand along the San Antonio road. "If there is not a prompt turnout by the Middle and Eastern counties," it said, "the enemy will ravage and overrun our country."[32]

A Mexican servant who had left Rancho del Coleto on March 18 reported to General Ampudia at Matamoros four days later that many families had fled from the Victoria vicinity to the interior of Texas, taking with them everything they could carry; that some armed Texans had assembled at the Rincón del Oso; and that "the Texans . . . intercepted the mail sent by the Mexican officer who had surprised La Bahía," and threatened to shoot him if he did not tell them all he knew about the Mexican invasion. The courier was reported to have given so grossly exaggerated an estimate of the size of the invading force that the Texans no longer considered themselves safe on the Guadalupe and at Victoria, and had been hastily evacuated. The Texans, he said, soon

[29] Max Freund (trans. and ed.), *Gustav Dresel's Houston Journal: Adventures in North America and Texas, 1837–1841*, p. 81.

[30] Muster Roll of Captain [Samuel] Bogart's Company of the Army of the Republic of Texas from the Eleventh day of March 1842, to the fourth day of May 1842, mustered into the service for the term of three months, in Militia Rolls (Texas), ms. The names appear in two columns. In the right hand column there are 36 names, and in the left hand column the 3 additional names appear.

[31] A. J. Sowell, *Early Settlers and Indian Fighters of Southwest Texas*, p. 343.

[32] *Civilian [and Galveston Gazette]—Extra*, Monday, March 21, 1842. Broadside.

learned of Valera's withdrawal, and volunteers quickly assembled at the frontier points and advanced to the Rincón del Oso, five leagues below Goliad. Between March 12 and March 15 over four hundred Texans concentrated at the aforesaid point, according to the Mexican refugee, not for the purpose of defending the frontier but to engage in an offensive war, to attack the settlements on the Río Bravo. When he left Texas, he reported, they were reconnoitring south of the Nueces. They had big fat horses in good condition.[33]

The news of the capture of San Antonio reached Austin on March 6. The mayor, Asa Brigham,[34] Treasurer of the Republic and a member of the Convention of 1836, immediately appointed a committee of vigilance and called out the Travis Guards,[35] who had first been organized in March 1840 from among the young men of the city. The committee consisted of the chairman, Major Samuel Whiting, editor of the *Austin City Gazette* and supporter of Sam Houston until the "Archive War"; innkeeper Richard Bullock; W. W. Thompson; Moses Johnson; Joshua Holden; Barry Gillespie; Jacob M. Harrell, one of the first settlers of Austin; H. B. Hill; and Dr. S. G. Haynie. At a full meeting of the committee on the evening of March 6 resolutions were adopt-

[33] Mariano Arista to the Minister of War, Monterey, March 31, 1842, with two enclosures, in Frederick C. Chabot, *Corpus Christi and Lipantitlán*, pp. 24–25.

[34] Asa Brigham was born in Massachusetts in 1790, and came to Texas from Louisiana in April 1830. He served as alcalde of the Municipality of Brazoria in 1835, and was one of the four delegates from Brazoria to the Convention of 1836 at Washington-on-the-Brazos where he signed the Texas Declaration of Independence. He served almost continuously as Treasurer of the Republic from 1836 to April 12, 1840, when he was suspended from office because of his inability to account for $37,000 of the public money and for his failure to dismiss the chief clerk, a Mr. Johnson, his brother-in-law, who was suspected of speculating with public funds. He was reappointed Treasurer on December 31, 1841, by President Houston. Brigham died at Washington, Texas, on July 2, 1844. *Colorado Gazette and Advertiser* (Matagorda), April 17, 1841; Mirabeau B. Lamar to Asa Brigham, Austin, April 12, 1840, in *Lamar Papers*, III, 369, 436 n; Ashbel Smith to Col. [Barnard E.] Bee, May 22, 1840, in Ashbel Smith Papers, 1838–1842, ms.; *Handbook of Texas*, I, 216; John Nathan Cravens, *James Harper Starr: Financier of the Republic of Texas*, pp. 69–70.

[35] On March 1, 1840, the young men of the City of Austin enrolled themselves into a volunteer military company known as the Travis Guards. The Guards were incorporated by an act of Congress, approved January 23, 1841, and included among their members James M. Ogden, R. F. Brenham, and others. The organization was modeled after the Milam Guards of the city of Houston. *Austin City Gazette*, March 4, 1840; H. P. N. Gammel (ed.), *Laws of Texas*, II, 516; *Handbook of Texas*, II, 797.

ed requesting the Secretary of War to place the city under martial law and to call into "actual service every person capable of bearing arms —and that none be permitted to leave without a permit from the Secretary of War, and then only in case of emergency, or of rendering sufficient protection to emigrating families."[36] It was recommended that "all the families of the city and vicinity . . . leave as soon as possible for a safer section of the country." Although the city since its establishment had lived constantly under the threat of Indian raids, the danger now was regarded as more imminent and serious. The Secretary of War, George W. Hockley, in Austin at the time, quickly proclaimed martial law in the city; closed all saloons and grog shops, prohibiting the further sale of spirituous liquors; and declared that no person was to leave town without receiving permission from either Colonel Thomas W. Ward, commissioner of the General Land Office, or the Secretary of War.[37] Hockley pointed out that the size of the forces of the enemy at Béxar and Goliad had been ascertained and that there was no cause for alarm or panic. It was reported late Tuesday evening that the number of Mexicans who had crossed the Nueces did not exceed 750 men. In the meantime, in anticipation of an effort by the invader to seize the nation's capital or by some enthusiastic patriot to burn them to prevent their falling into the hands of the enemy, the public records of the Republic, including the invaluable land-office papers, were buried in the ground under the different offices,[38] leaving sufficient papers in the pigeon holes to deceive the enemy. This method of seeking to preserve the public records seemed

[36] "Arrangements Entered into by the Citizens of Austin, with Reference to the Approach of the Mexicans, Austin, March 6, 1842," in Smither (ed.), *Journals of the Sixth Congress*, III, 14–15; or *To Arms! To Arms! Texians!! Arrangements entered into by the Citizens of Austin, with reference to the approach of the Mexicans; and the latest information from the West of the Invading Army.* [*Austin City*] *Gazette* Office, Half-past 10 o'clock, Mond[ay] Morn[ing] [March 7, 1842], Broadside. Contains proclamation of Asa Brigham, mayor, appointing a Committee of Vigilence [*sic*], of which Major Samuel Whiting was chairman, and a report of the committee meeting held on the evening of the 6th including its recommendations that the families leave.

[37] George W. Hockley's Proclamation of Martial Law, dated: Department of War & Navy, March 7, 1842, may be found in Smither (ed.), *Journals of the Sixth Congress*, III, 17; also printed as a broadside by the *Austin City Gazette* Office [March 7, 1842]; and in *The Houstonian Extra*, March 15, [1842], 11 o'clock A.M., Broadside.

[38] George W. Hockley to [Sam Houston], Department of War & Navy, March 7, 1842, in Smither (ed.), *Journals of the Sixth Congress*, III, 16–17.

to the local citizens, in their efforts to forestall a complete abandonment of the frontier city of Austin as the capital, far preferable to their removal eastward· Washington D. Miller, private secretary to the President, forwarded to the President "a number of packages containing your public and private correspondence and the regular series of your messages to Congress, &c in their original rough state. They have *not* all been recorded," he wrote. "I have to request of you, therefore, very particularly, to *preserve* them with great care in order that at some future day they may be recorded. The reason why I send them to you will be apparent. It is to provide, under a certain contingency against their destruction. There is no concert of action for defence if the necessity should arise."[39] As an afterthought, just before the mail left, Miller appended a brief note to his letter, ending with a short paragraph which showed his well-considered appraisal of the "seat of government" issue: "Until the true character of the invasion now reported is better known, and turns out to be formidable, I hope the removal of the archives may not be ordered. If an order to that effect should be premature, you can well appreciate the consequences." On the following day, Miller wrote in great haste to the President: "The truth has at last come upon us. . . . A regular invasion has commenced. This place will be sustained as far as possible at every hazard."[40] It "shall be defended to the knife," Hockley wrote by the same mail.[41]

Acting Quartermaster General Jacob Snively was ordered by the Secretary of War to make available immediately rations of beef and bread for two weeks for three hundred men expected to rendezvous at Austin,[42] where Colonel Jones' regiment was being concentrated. Hockley, a former clerk in the United States War Department and a devoted friend of President Houston for twenty years, wrote that he was organizing spies to mount that evening, March 6, "in all directions towards the point of danger."[43] He believed that the Mexican attack on Béxar

[39] W. D. Miller to Sam Houston, Austin, March 6, 1842 (Private), no. 7, in Miller Papers (Texas), ms. copy.

[40] W. D. Miller to Sam Houston, Austin, March 7, 1842 (Private), no. 8, in *ibid.*, ms. copy.

[41] George W. Hockley to the President of the Republic, Department of War and Navy, March 7, 1842, in Smither (ed.), *Journals of the Sixth Congress*, III, 16–17.

[42] Special Order No. 134, issued by George W. Hockley, Department of War and Navy, Austin, March 6, 1842, in Army Papers (Texas), ms.; George W. Hockley to Ashbel Smith, Galveston, December 15, 1842, in Smith Papers, ms.

[43] George W. Hockley to Sam Houston, Department of War & Navy, March 6, 1842, and March 7, 1842, in Smither (ed.), *Journals of the Sixth Congress*, III,

was only a feint to divert attention from their real objective—an attack upon Austin from above. Flacco and a small band of Lipans were sent with the spies, and Castro remained in Austin. For lack of complete and accurate reports from the vicinity of San Antonio, Hockley was handicapped in deciding what should be done to meet the invading force. However, he used the *"best information"* available; as he said, "I have NONE strictly military for my guide."[44] Austin was soon nearly deserted of all families. Miller reported on the 9th that "Bullock and Thompson, both members of the committee of Vigilance and Safety left today with bag and baggage—even to their stock of provisions." John G. Chalmers, for a while Secretary of the Treasury in the Lamar administration, and the Scott and Stickney families also left on the 9th. "There is an universal Hegira" continued Miller, and "the upper part of the valley . . . is breaking up rapidly."[45]

Three companies of infantrymen were immediately formed at Austin, numbering in all about 125 men. The Travis Guards under Captain Matthew P. Woodhouse,[46] chief clerk of the General Land Office, had about 30 men; the company under Captain George M. Dolson, about 50; and that under Captain Thomas Green, to which Washington D. Miller was attached, also contained about 50 men. These three companies, plus about 100 mounted men from Bastrop under Captain James H. Gillespie, comprised the First Battalion of Colonel Henry Jones' Fourth Regiment of Texas Militia.[47] A great deal "of marching and countermarching—drilling and watching, and eating heartily and talking largely," was done. Many avowed their eagerness to march to the front—to carry the campaign into Mexico and revel in the palaces of

15–16. See also Harriet Smither (ed.), "Diary of Adolphus Sterne," in *Southwestern Historical Quarterly*, XXXIII (1929–1930), 168, 232–233.

[44] George W. Hockley to [Sam Houston], Department of War & Navy, March 7, 1842, in Smither (ed.), *Journals of the Sixth Congress*, III, 16–17.

[45] W. D. Miller to Sam Houston, Austin, March 9, 1842 (Private), no. 9, in Miller Papers (Texas), ms. copy.

[46] After the Vasquez raid, Captain M. P. Woodhouse of the Travis Guards was succeeded in command by Joseph Daniels. Captain J. Daniels Receipt for Clothing and Camp Equipage, Travis Guards, dated: Houston, June 18, 1842, in Matthew P. Woodhouse Papers, ms.

[47] W. D. Miller to Sam Houston, Austin, March 9, 1842 (Private), no. 9, in Miller Papers, ms. copy; Muster Roll of James H. Gillespie's Company of Volunteers in the Vasquez Campaign will be found in the Militia Rolls (Texas), ms. and is reproduced in the Appendix of this book, with notations from Frank Brown, "Annals of Travis County and of the City of Austin," IX, pp. 12–13.

the Montezuma. But, "as usual," reported Miller, "there are many *gentlemen*, so called—par excellence, 'big bugs'—in this community at this time who are very garrulous in prognosticating results and doing the windword of the war, both present and to come, and who are every where else but in the ranks. What a despicable race!"[48] Some felt that they could be more useful as "agents of the government," soliciting funds in the United States in their former home towns, "than in any other way," and were anxious to secure appointments to enable them to leave the frontier at once.[49]

Guards were posted day and night at Austin. The three brass six-pound cannon purchased in Springfield, Massachusetts, the year before,[50] were taken from the arsenal and mounted on President's Hill, near the White House, and in the fort on Capitol Hill. The city became a bristling fortress. Scouts constantly ranged the country between Austin and the Guadalupe River in the direction of Seguin and San Antonio. There lurked the apprehension that a third division of the Mexican army might descend upon Austin from the mountains, but on the 9th Flacco and the Texan scouts who had gone west as far as the Llano returned to report that they had seen no signs of Mexicans in that direction. Early the next morning (Thursday), however, near panic developed when the Nashville mail carrier came in on foot, having had his horse shot from under him by the Indians about twenty-three miles from Austin. One of the Indians he had killed.[51] At first, it was felt that the Indians might be in collusion with the Mexicans, but investigation soon convinced the people of Austin that there was no connection.

Meanwhile, at Bastrop the little signal cannon sounded the alarm and called the men together. General Burleson took a considerable force

[48] W. D. Miller to Sam Houston, Austin, March 9, 1842 (Private), no. 9, in Miller Papers (Texas), ms. copy.

[49] A. D. Coombs to Anson Jones, City of Austin, March 9, 1842, in Domestic Correspondence (Texas), ms.

[50] In the fall of 1840 six brass six-pounders were purchased in Springfield, Massachusetts, and landed at Galveston. Two were assigned to the Houston Artillery Company under Captain J. Moreland, and the other four taken to Austin, where one was released to the Santa Fé expedition. David Ross, Clerk, Ordnance Dept., to Branch T. Archer, Ordnance Department, Sept. 8, 1841, in Smither (ed.), *Journals of the Sixth Congress*, III, 402–403. The three newly acquired artillery pieces and the Twin Sisters were in battery at the arsenal for the defense of the capital city.

[51] W. D. Miller to Sam Houston, Austin, March 10, 1842 (Private), in Miller Papers (Texas), ms. copy.

and headed for Austin.[52] On the evening of the 7th Dunn and Chevallie reached Austin to report that Vasquez's forces in their opinion were not the vanguard of an invading army. They suggested that the Colorado men march directly to San Antonio. Upon the receipt of this information, General Burleson, the Vice President, dispatched a messenger to Bastrop advising the citizens to discontinue their preparations for removing families, and ordering the troops assembled there to proceed at once directly to Béxar.[53] In a few days the First Battalion of Colonel Jones' regiment arrived at Austin from Bastrop, and was detained there to protect the capital. Upon the arrival of the Second Battalion of the regiment, the First was relieved, except for three companies, and marched toward Béxar.[54] Hamson D. Berry hauled the artillery and ordinance stores from Austin to San Antonio under contract.[55] "Retrenchment and reform" were blamed by the Secretary of War for the poor defense of the frontier. Had the old system been in effect and the old frontier station maintained on the San Marcos, "one battalion should have moved *instantly* upon Béxar, checked and engaged the enemy," while another fell back for the protection of Austin.[56]

While the upper Colorado men were rendezvousing at Gonzales, in the vicinity of which many immigrants had settled in recent months, and at Seguin, the men from Columbia were preparing to leave on the 7th. "We are incredulous here still," wrote R. M. Forbes from Columbia, "but are determined to act in spite of incredulity—To me it seems strange that we have nothing from Van Ness or Morris."[57]

Rumors began to reach Houston on March 6 and 7 that a party of some eight to nine hundred Mexicans, reported by some to be a marauding party and by others the vanguard of a Mexican invading army,

[52] John H. Jenkins, Sr., "Personal Reminiscences of Texas History Relating to Bastrop County, 1828–1847, as Dictated to his Daughter-in-law, Mrs. Emma Holmes Jenkins of Bastrop, Texas," p. 104. Jenkins was a member of Captain James H. Gillespie's company of volunteers.

[53] *Telegraph and Texas Register*, March 16, 1842.

[54] George W. Hockley to Ashbel Smith, Galveston, Dec. 15, 1842, in Smith Papers, ms.

[55] Republic of Texas to Hamson D. Berry, San Antonio, April 8, 1842, for Hauling artillery & ordinance stores from the city of Austin to San Antonio 18 days @ $6 per day as per contract with G. W. Terrell & B. Gillespie. [$30 paid in advance on the $108] Paid. Army Papers (Texas), ms.

[56] George W. Hockley to Ashbel Smith, Galveston, Dec. 15, 1842, in Smith Papers, ms.

[57] R. M. Forbes to Francis Moore, Jr., and A. Wynns, Columbia, March 6, 1842, in *Telegraph and Texas Register*, March 16, 1842.

were in the vicinity of San Antonio.⁵⁸ On the 8th General Edwin Morehouse arrived in Houston confirming the reports; and on the 9th John
Green, Jr., the dispatch rider from Austin, arrived with expresses from
the Secretary of War bringing news of the fall of San Antonio on the
preceding Saturday afternoon, March 5.⁵⁹ Three to five hundred men
planned to leave Houston as soon as possible for the frontier. It was
rumored that Van Ness, Morris, and John W. Smith—spies sent out by
the Texans at San Antonio—had *"gone over to the Mexicans."* The situation looked serious.

As soon as unofficial reports of an invasion reached President Houston
at Galveston on March 8, Colonel Alden A. M. Jackson of that city was
ordered to prepare one company of local militia to march at a moment's
notice "with eight day's provision, one hundred rounds of ammunition,
knapsacks, haversacks, one blanket and change of linen or one shirt,
each,"⁶⁰ and to bring his whole regiment to a state of perfect organization. From China Grove, George W. Scott wrote to Colonel Morgan at
New Washington that he and Colonel Amasa Turner planned to leave
for the west in about ten days and would like to attach themselves to
Morgan's unit "so as to form a company of horsemen with the privileges
that we old Texians have so as not to lie in camp."⁶¹

The town of Galveston, boasting a population of some 2,800, was
thrown into great excitement. "We are glad," commented the editor of
the *Houstonian*, "to find that the official organ of the president [*The
Civilian and Galveston Gazette*] is at length awake and calling out vigorously 'TO ARMS! SAN ANTONIO TAKEN!!' "⁶² A large public meeting was
held in Galveston, Wednesday evening, March 9, at the Merchants Exchange to receive the report of a committee appointed to confer with
the President. John S. Sydnor, commission merchant and real-estate

⁵⁸ A. C. Allen to Col. James Morgan and Genl. Moseley Baker, Houston, March 9,
1842, in Morgan Papers, ms.

⁵⁹ *Ibid.*

⁶⁰ Houston to Col. A. A. M. Jackson, Galveston, March 8, 1842, in *Writings of
Sam Houston*, II, 488–489; Executive Record of the Second Term of General Sam
Houston's Administration of the Government of Texas, December 1841–December
1844, ms., pp. 48–49. Similar orders were sent to General Edwin Morehouse at
Houston. Houston to Gen. Edwin Morehouse, Galveston, March 10, 1842, in
Writings of Sam Houston, II, 491; *Daily Picayune*, March 29, 1842.

⁶¹ G[eorge] W. Scott to Col. James Morgan [at New Washington], China,
March 11, 1842, in Morgan Papers, ms.

⁶² *The Houstonian Extra*, March 9, 1842, quoted in *Bollaert's Texas*, p. 28. See
also J. O. Dyer, "Historical Notes of Galveston," ms., p. 75.

promoter, was called to preside over the meeting and Hamilton Stuart, founder of the *Civilian and Galveston Gazette* in 1838, and Andrew J. Yates, publisher of the *Galveston Daily Advertiser*, were appointed secretaries.[63] George William Brown, who had only recently moved to Galveston from Virginia, presented the resolutions from the committee and read a copy of the letter that the committee had sent to the President and the latter's reply thereto. The reading of Houston's reply was "received with considerable hissing on the part of the audience."[64] The resolutions called for the enrollment and equipment of two hundred men for immediate service; for the appointment of a committee of two persons to request the President to name General Albert S. Johnston major general to command the forces for the defense of the Republic; for the appointment of a committee to solicit from the public contributions "to the amount of five hundred dollars for the purchase of ammunition,"[65] to request the President to order the brig *Wharton* to be prepared for sea; for a request that the President designate a committee to procure the arms requested by William H. Jack at Brazoria for the outfit of his command; and for the naming of a committee of vigilance to meet daily. The assemblage was addressed by James Love, a staunch supporter of Lamar, who used his home in Galveston frequently as a rallying place for the political opponents of Houston. George W. Brown and Colonel Henry N. Potter also addressed the group "with great effect, and the whole spirit of the meeting was characterized by a determination to act promptly" in the defense of the country, "whether sanctioned or opposed by the Executive."[66] The resolutions being adopted, the committees were appointed, and the meeting adjourned to the next day at noon. The committee of vigilance consisted of James Love, chairman, John S. Sydnor, Jonas Butler, and George B. Innes.

The public meeting at Galveston, however, resumed the next morning (Thursday) at 10 o'clock instead of at noon as scheduled. James Love started the discussion by offering a resolution requesting the President to order the *Wharton* outfitted for sea. On motion of Colonel Henry N. Potter an express just received from Captain William J. E. Heard at Victoria was read, and on the motion of Secretary Yates the chairman designated the committee appointed the evening before to call upon the President to request the outfitting of the *Wharton* and to

[63] *Bollaert's Texas*, pp. 29–30.
[64] *Ibid.*, p. 30.
[65] *Ibid.*
[66] *Ibid.*, p. 31.

convey to him Captain Heard's express. The committee of vigilance was now requested to make arrangements to send a committee by the *New York* to New Orleans to secure aid.[67] The meeting then adjourned to 1 P.M. to permit contacting the President and obtaining his reply to the various requests made of him.

The committee of vigilance, as previously noted, selected three commissioners (Jones, Megginson, and Watrous) to go up the Mississippi Valley to make an appeal to the people there for aid in the form of men, money, and supplies. During the dark days of the revolution the western frontiersmen in the United States had responded nobly to the Texan call for assistance, and it was hoped they would do so again.

At 1 o'clock the meeting was again convened, and Colonel Love announced that an express had just come in to the President reporting that Béxar had been abandoned by the Anglo-Americans to a Mexican force under General Vasquez and that the President was now engaged in the preparation of a proclamation to be issued that evening.[68] Upon Love's motion, the committee of vigilance was requested "to have all the horses on the island driven up and those [individuals] who were about to depart for the army ... supplied."[69]

In the meantime, Colonel Jackson had received orders on the 9th from Brigadier General Morehouse "to execute such orders as may be directed to you in a moment's notice."[70] On the 10th, Jackson, commanding the Fourth Regiment, Second Brigade, Texas Militia, ordered all companies composing Beats 1, 2, 3, and 4, including volunteers, to muster in their respective beats the next day (March 11) at 9 A.M. The companies comprising Beats 5 and 6 (Bolivar and Edward's Point) were to muster immediately upon receipt of the order.[71] On the 10th Jackson himself received direct orders from the President to have the fort at the east end of the island placed in an efficient state of defense, and to "prepare at least thirty rounds of fixed ammunition for the 18-pounders and the same number for the 24-pounders."[72] Three hundred and forty muskets were ordered retained at Galveston for the defense of the city,

[67] *Ibid.*, pp. 31, 135.

[68] *Ibid.*, p. 32.

[69] *Ibid.*

[70] E. Morehouse to Col. A. A. M. Jackson, Headquarters, 2d Brigade, Houston, March 9, 1842, in *ibid.*

[71] Order No. 7 issued by Alden A. M. Jackson, Col. Commanding, Headquarters, 4th Reg't., 2d Brigade, Texas Militia, Galveston, March 10, 1842, in *ibid.*, pp. 32–33.

[72] Houston to Col. Alden A. M. Jackson, Galveston, March 10, 1842, in *Writings of Sam Houston*, II, 494–495.

and all other arms were to be forwarded by steamboat at once to Houston for the use of the troops being fitted out there.[73] The Reverend Thomas O. Summers, formerly of the Baltimore Conference, now stationed at Galveston and Houston, consented to become chaplain for the army.[74] Generals M. B. Lamar and Albert Sidney Johnston, with about one hundred men equipped with Jenks' patent rifles, headed toward the frontier at once, while others left the island by steamer for Houston on the 11th.[75]

A general call to arms was issued by the President on March 10, ordering all who were "subject to military duty . . . to be in readiness to repair, to the scene of action, at the call of the authorities of the country." The colonel of each county was instructed to divide the county into "company beats" and permit the election of captains and lesser officers. The members of each company were to be divided into three classes, according to the class in which the men drew. The colonels were authorized to accept "efficient substitutes" for men subject to the draft. If the President should call the company into active service, each man was to report "with good arms, eight days' provisions, and one hundred rounds of ammunition," and be prepared for three months' service from the time of his reporting at army headquarters.[76] This proclamation was followed by another the next day warning against "the odious practice of indiscriminate impressment of private property, without authority from the government." Such seizures in the past had too often been "merely sanctioned by private will, . . . stimulated by cupidity and dishonesty."[77]

General Edwin Morehouse at Houston, commanding the Second Brigade, issued a general order to the men in his district to hold them-

[73] Houston to Gail Borden, Jr., Galveston, March 10, 1842, in *ibid.*, II, 493–494.
[74] *Daily Picayune*, March 31, 1842.
[75] *Ibid.*, March 16, 1842; *Bollaert's Texas*, p. 34; *Civilian and Galveston Gazette*, March 15, 1842. Proclamation of E. Morehouse, Brig. General, 2d Brigade T.M., City of Houston, March 13, 1842, in Galveston Hussar Cavalry Company Papers, 1842, ms.
[76] Executive Records of the Second Term of General Sam Houston's Administration of the Government of Texas, December 1841–December 1844, ms., No. 40, p. 46. See also *ibid.*, p. 51; "Proclamation to the Citizens of Texas, Galveston, March 10, 1842," in *Telegraph and Texas Register*, March 16, 1842; *Austin City Gazette*, March 30, 1842; Sam Houston to the Citizens of Texas, City of Houston, March 14, 1842, in *Writings of Sam Houston*, II, 490–491, 503.
[77] "Proclamation to the Army and Citizens of Texas, Galveston, March 11, 1842, in *Telegraph and Texas Register*, March 16, 1842.

selves in readiness to march at a moment's notice. At Lynchburg on the 10th the citizens met and organized their militia unit and declared that as far as possible they would furnish their own arms and ammunition.[78] In explaining to Captain De Roll why he could not aid in fitting out a company, the President was constrained to add, "I have not *one dollar* at my disposition either to purchase horses or the equipments necessary for *one man*."[79] The day after issuing the general call to arms the President informed the Texan consul at New Orleans of the conditions upon which the government would receive "emigrants" from the United States. Each emigrant, he wrote, should bring with him

a good rifle or musket, with a cartouch box, or shot pouch and powder horn, with at least one hundred rounds of ammunition, a good knapsack and six months' clothing, and enter service for six months subject to the laws of Texas. They must be landed for the present at some point west of the Brazos, with eight days' provisions. No less than fifty-six men in companies well organized will be received, and on landing each commandant will report to the secretary of war for orders.[80]

It was necessary that all "emigrants" to Texas at this time should come prepared and equipped with the above articles, and persons not so armed were to be rejected. Later it was ordered that all volunteer armed "emigrants" be landed at some point on the coast west of the Colorado River so as to be in the rear of the enemy if he should advance from Béxar to the Colorado. Such a maneuver would slow up the advance of the invading army and afford time for the Texan troops to be made ready for the field.[81] As an additional precautionary step for meeting the invader, the navy was alerted for further orders, since it was generally believed that any formidable land operation by the enemy would of necessity have to be sustained by sea.

It was reported and believed by many individuals at Galveston that three Mexican transports were headed for the coast at Paso Cavallo

---

[78] Proceedings of a Meeting of the Citizens of Lynchburg [Texas], March 10, 1842, William Garfield, Ch[ai]r[man] and Capt. William Wood, Secretary, in *Telegraph and Texas Register*, March 16, 1842.

[79] Houston to Captain De Roll, Executive Department, City of Houston, March 15, 1842, in *Writings of Sam Houston*, II, 503–504.

[80] Houston to P. Edmunds, Galveston, March 11, 1842, in *ibid.*, IV, 80–81. See also Houston to John S. Sydnor, Chairman of the Committee of Vigilance [of Galveston], Galveston, March 11, *ibid.*, IV, 79–80.

[81] Houston to Col. William Christy, City of Houston, March 20, 1842, in *ibid.*, IV, 85.

(separating Matagorda Island from Matagorda Peninsula) with troops, arms, ammunition, and provisions.[82] At the public meeting at the Exchange in Galveston on Thursday night, March 10, it was decided to seek permission of the President to fit out the *Wharton* by private subscription, the government being without money, and to send an expedition by sea along the coast in search of Mexican supply ships and troop transports. Three thousand dollars was "raised on the spot." The President approved the fitting out of the *Lafitte* and himself contributed $100 toward that purpose.

A considerable amount was paid in cash, and the balance in provisions, munitions, and other available property. Those who had neither money nor supplies, tendered property of every description. Houses, lots, horses, cows and calves, Durham bulls, negroes, rifles, wood, pictures, coal, head-rights, and almost every thing else in the catalogue of this world's goods which were put up at auction by the chairman of the meeting, and sold to the highest bidder.[83]

If a man had two rifles, he gave one. Within two weeks time, about $12,000 in provisions, munitions of war, and money had been contributed by the citizens of Galveston.[84] The women moulded bullets and made cartridges. Work was commenced on the *Wharton* to make her seaworthy, but it was days before she could safely leave port.

In preparing an expedition to go down the coast, Lieutenant John Wade, commander of the Galveston Coast Guards, was issued 150 muskets, 150 cutlasses, one long brass gun from the steamship *Zavala*, and four other cannon, either six- or nine-pounders, one American ensign and five boarding pikes.[85] At the time he ordered out the *Lafitte*, the President addressed a letter to Commodore Edwin Moore to apprise him of the invasion. "I anticipate warm work, and if so," declared Houston, "I wish the Navy now very much, so as to throw it in the rear of the enemy, and attack them. It will embarrass them more than anything else

[82] *Bollaert's Texas*, p. 27.
[83] *Daily Picayune*, March 16, 1842; see also *Bollaert's Texas*, p. 29.
[84] *Writings of Sam Houston*, II, 500 n.
[85] Houston to Gail Borden, Jr., Collector of Customs, Galveston [dated:] Galveston, March 10, 1842, and [Houston] to John Wade, Galveston, March 11, 1842, in Executive Record . . . Second Houston Administration, pp. 48, 50–51; also [Houston] to Captain John Clark, Galveston, March 12, 1842, in *ibid.*, p. 51; Houston to James E. Haviland, City of Galveston, March 11, 1842, in *Writings of Sam Houston*, II, 496; Same to John Clark, Galveston, March 12, 1842, *ibid.*, II, 499–500.

can do. I wish to cut off all supplies which they may expect by sea, and if they have any war vessels, I hope you may seize upon them in the course of the spring. . . . Make haste."[86] Moore received this communication by way of the United States revenue cutter *Woodbury*.

Preparations for the defense of Galveston went forward rapidly during the next few days. The district court, in session at the time, adjourned and Chief Justice Richard Morris and members of the bar quickly joined the various military units being formed. An eyewitness account of the "intense excitement" caused at Galveston by receipt of the news of the invasion has been left by William Bollaert, an English subject, world traveler, adventurer, and writer, who arrived in Galveston on February 20, 1842, and remained in Texas until the eve of annexation. Bollaert recorded in his diary:

> The Chief Justice Morris, who a few hours before sat gravely on the bench, was in the saddle and accoutred for war. The "gentlemen of the bar," busy raising companies of volunteers. The worthy chief clerk, Mr. [Thomas] Bates, booted and spurred, looked the bold dragoon. Public meetings called, which were attended to suffocation. Money, clothes, provisions, etc., [were] liberally subscribed. Many sold their lots of land, some their Negroes, others their very houses, horses, oxen, etc., so as to raise funds for the various purposes that might be required.[87]

Among the contributions received were large quantities of liquor; but the Coast Guard unanimously voted to sell the liquor and invest its proceeds in more essential equipment and suggested that all other military companies do likewise.[88] The crew of the *Lafitte*, however, did not choose to do so.

By the 12th news confirming the Mexican seizure of San Antonio reached Galveston, where it was reported that 500 of their troops had already entered that place and that 3,000 more could be expected at an early date.[89] At 11 o'clock on Sunday, the 13th, additional news was brought to the island from Houston by the steamer *Edward Burleson*, giving General Vasquez's force as 50 lancers, 350 cavalry, 100 infantry, 30 mounted Caddo Indians, and about 550 rancheros, and Madame Rumor, rude jade that she is, gave the distortion that all the Mexicans at Béxar had joined the invaders, that their force in Texas amounted to

[86] Houston to Edwin W. Moore, Galveston, March 11, 1842, in *ibid.*, II, 497–498.
[87] *Bollaert's Texas*, p. 34.
[88] *Civilian and Galveston Gazette*, March 15, 1842.
[89] *Bollaert's Texas*, p. 27; *New Orleans Bee*, March 16, 1842.

15,000 and that General Burleson was rapidly increasing his army of 7,000 at Gonzales to meet the enemy.

Among the several military and naval units at Galveston during this period of excitement were the Galveston Artillery Company, the Galveston Guards of which there is no complete list, the Coast Guards (or Galveston Vedettes), the Fusileers, and the local militia units under Colonel Alden A. M. Jackson, commanding the Fourth Regiment of the Second Brigade of Texas Militia. The Galveston Artillery Company had been organized on September 13, 1840, for the defense of the island against an anticipated Mexican naval attack. It was incorporated by an act of Congress, approved January 30, 1841.[90] However, it was not until some time later, October 26, 1842, that the Company adopted a constitution. Its constitution shows less the character of a social club than the constitutions of the Milam Guards of Houston formed in 1838 and the Travis Guards of Austin organized in 1840.[91] In 1842 the Galveston Artillery Company was commanded by Captain John Howe. During the excitement in the spring of 1842 the Galveston Guards, whose organization dated back to 1840, remained on the island to protect the women and children, and the Vedettes were stationed along the coast to give communication from San Luis to Galveston every six hours.[92]

Upon receipt of the news of the Mexican attack on San Antonio, a number of volunteers at Galveston quickly assembled, and took passage on the steamer *Dayton* for Houston on March 11, intending to mount themselves and head west. En route the twenty-seven men organized themselves into a military unit known as the Galveston Hussar Cavalry Company.[93] Seven others planned to join them at Richmond on the Brazos. Upon their arrival in Houston, an election of company officers was held on the 12th, and H. N. Potter was chosen captain.[94] Potter was

[90] Galveston Artillery Company, *The Charter and Constitution of the Galveston Artillery Company, Organized Sept. 13th, 1840.*

[91] Milam Guards (Houston), *Constitution and By-Laws of the Milam Guards: Established August, 1838*; Travis Guards (Austin), *Constitution and By-Laws of the Travis Guards: Adopted March First, 1840.*

[92] "Galveston Artillery Company," ts.

[93] Minutes of a Meeting Aboard the Steam-Boat *Dayton*, March 11, 1842, signed by B. L. Coles, Chairman, and George Levie, Secretary, in Galveston Hussar Cavalry Company Papers, 1842, ms. A list of the original members of the Galveston Hussar Cavalry Company will be found in the Appendix of this work.

[94] Report of an Election for Company Officers for Galveston Hussars, Head Quarters, Houston, March 12, 1842, in Galveston Hussar Cavalry Company Papers, 1842, ms. Pledge of J. S. Harrison, *et al.*, to Join the Galveston Hussars at Richmond,

then issued a commission by Brigadier General Edwin Morehouse, and thus the Hussars became a part of the Second Brigade of the Texas Militia.[95] The Hussars were equipped with Jenks' patent carbines (or rifles), which they had obtained at Galveston, and were supplied with lead, camp equipment, and coffee, sugar salt, and bacon by the Houston committee of vigilance.[96]

On the 13th Potter received orders to parade his company on the Courthouse Square in Houston at 12 o'clock noon "in order to repair to camp to be in readiness to march tomorrow morning."[97] Upon being paraded, the Hussars received orders to commence their march westward early on the morning of the 14th for San Felipe, where they were to await further orders.[98]

The Fusileers, an infantry company, was formed at Galveston on January 18, 1842, by a group meeting at the First Baptist Church, seeking to provide additional protection to the city. The organization seems to have been comparable to the Milam Guards and the Travis Guards, but lost its identity as a separate organization late in 1843 or early 1844, when it combined with the Galveston Artillery Company. The Fusileers were equipped with rather queer looking breech-loading weapons called by the boys *"fusees,"* considered to be superior guns. The Coast Guards, whose organization dated back to late 1839 or early 1840, and the Fusileers[99] made arrangements to equip the *Lafitte* for a cruise at sea

n. p., n. d., in *ibid.*, ms.; E. Morehouse to Capt. [H. N.] Potter, Houston, March 13, 1842, in *ibid.*, ms.

[95] Captain's Commission Issued to H. N. Potter by E. Morehouse, Brig. General, 2d Brigade T.M., City of Houston, March 13th, 1842, in *ibid.*, ms.; Proclamation of E. Morehouse, Brig. General, 2d Brigade T.M., City of Houston, March 13, 1842, *ibid.*, ms.

[96] Receipt Given to A. Sidney Johnston for Thirty-Seven Jenks Patent Carbines, Galveston, March 11, 1842, [and signed by:] H. N. Potter, Capt. Galv^n Hussars, in *ibid.*, ms.; Requisition of the Galveston Hussars, [dated:] Head-Quarters, Houston, Mar. 12/42 [and signed:] H. N. Potter, Capt. Galveston Hussars, in *ibid.*, ms. On February 7, 1842, the Secretary of War and Navy assigned to the custody of General Albert Sidney Johnston 100 Jenks Patent Rifles. G. W. Hockley, Sec'y of War and Navy, to [Collector of Customs, Galveston], Ordnance Department, [Austin], February 7, 1842, in *ibid.*, ms.

[97] C. W. Adams, Lt. Col., to [Captain H. N. Potter], Head Quarters, Houston, March 13, 1842, in *ibid.*, ms.

[98] E. Morehouse, Brig.-Genl., to Capt. [H. N.] Potter, Houston, March 13, 1842, in *ibid.*, ms.

[99] A list of the Galveston Fusileers of March 10, 1842, will be found in the Appendix to this work.

to intercept any Mexican transports that might be headed toward Texas and to give confidence to the inhabitants down the coast.

The small steamer *Lafitte,* the schooner *Santa Anna,* renamed the *Borden,* and the sloop *Washington,* which had returned to Galveston on March 7 after a cruise along the Mexican coast in a futile effort to carry a message to Commodore Moore of the Texan fleet, sailed from Galveston on Monday morning, March 14,[100] for the west[101] in search of Mexican troops and supply transports along the coast from Galveston to Aransas and Copano Bay and beyond, as might be thought necessary. The expedition sailed with instructions to intercept and seize contraband goods, whether under neutral or Mexican colors, and to send all prizes to Galveston for trial and adjudication. On board were fifty Fusileers under Captain A. Swingle, and the Galveston Coast Guard, supplemented by volunteers, amounting to one hundred men under Captain John Wade, who were to land at one of the western ports.[102] The *Borden,* a revenue cutter with one gun, was commanded by Captain L. M. Hitchcock, and the *Washington* by Captain James D. Boylan. The next day Captain John Clark of the *Archer* was authorized by the President, if he should fall in with the *Lafitte* and *Washington,* to take charge of the expedition of the Coast Guards, as this was the desire of the officers who had been appointed to command that expedition.[103] Clark was an old hand with ships, having held several commands in the Colombian navy under Simón Bolívar during the revolution in Venezuela. Captain Wade, a printer by profession who worked on the *Telegraph and Texas Register* and had been one of the five men in charge of the "Twin Sisters" during the battle of San Jacinto, commanded the *Lafitte* and the expedition.[104] His second in command was Captain James Haviland.

[100] *Bollaert's Texas,* p. 36 n; *Daily Picayune* (New Orleans), March 16, 1842; *Telegraph and Texas Register,* March 23, 1842.

[101] William Bollaert, "Arrival in Texas in 1842, and Cruise of the Lafitte," in *Coburn's United Service Magazine,* November 1846, pp. 341–355.

[102] The *Lafitte* carried for subsistence "2 barrels of coarse bread; 2 bbls. of fine bread; a half bbl. of sugar; 2/3 of a sack of coffee; 1 bbl. of pork; 4 lbs. of tea; 1 sack of salt; 30 lbs. of tobacco; 1 box of tallow candles; 20 lbs. of soap; 5 gals. of vinegar, and 1 gal. of lamp oil." Ben C. Stuart, "Early Galveston Military Companies, 1839–1901," ms., pp. 9–10.

[103] Sam Houston Dixon and Louis Wiltz Kemp, *The Heroes of San Jacinto,* pp. 85–86; Sam Houston to John Wade, Galveston, March 4, 1842, and Same to Captain John Clark, Galveston, March 12, 1842, in *Writings of Sam Houston,* II, 499–500.

[104] Sam Houston to Captain John Clark, Galveston, March 12, 1842, in *Writings of Sam Houston,* II, 499–500.

The Fusileers were dressed in modest uniforms and armed with patent rifles, having bayonets. The Coast Guards wore red woolen shirts, white trousers, and straw hats. They were armed with muskets, pistols, pikes, and boarding swords, but "there was no scarcity of hatchets, tomahawks, and Bowie knives for close quarters, if necessary."[105] The *Lafitte* carried a long brass piece in the bow and two iron carronades on either side. The ships were well supplied with ammunition, provisions, and sundry other comforts including the "Pig Tail," or what was more commonly known as "Honey Dew" plug tobacco and cigars. The President was opposed to all the movements of the people, with the exception of this one expedition; of it he heartily approved, but ordered that no man should leave the island who could not return immediately to it in case of an emergency.

Having issued several proclamations, President Houston finally at the solicitation of Colonel Alden A. M. Jackson and Charles Frankland of the British firm of Frankland & Co. assented on Sunday morning to the fitting out of the brig of war *Wharton* and the steamer *Zavala* "on condition that they should be fitted out by the citizens."[106] Frankland & Co. immediately offered to fit out the *Zavala* at the company's expense. The *Zavala* was to be placed near the mouth of the harbor. After making his decision to allow the *Wharton* to go out, President Houston hurriedly left Galveston at 10 o'clock, Sunday, the 13th, for the city of Houston, where he was awaited with great anxiety. "He goes cool and collected, as would seem from exterior appearances," wrote a correspondent of the *Bee*, "whilst at the same time, those who are intimate with him can but perceive that eruptions equal to Mount Vesuvius are at work in him. His health is firm, his spirits good," and he is possessed of an immovable determination "to heap vengence on the perfidious Mexicans."[107] "Every eye is turned towards the Old Chief in his emergency," wrote Anson Jones, the Secretary of State, to Ashbel Smith. "I hope the result of the present campaign will be such as to settle the long delayed question with Mexico," but in his diary under date of March 10 Jones reports he went from Galveston to Houston, "where every thing was *booh!* Mexicans & war. Staid untill Tuesd[ay] 15th; rode over to Burleigh. War ended."[108]

[105] Bollaert, "Arrival in Texas in 1842, and Cruise of the Lafitte," *Coburn's United Service Magazine,* November 1846, pp. 341–355.
[106] *Civilian and Galveston Gazette,* March 15, 1842.
[107] *New Orleans Bee,* March 16, 1842.
[108] Anson Jones to Doct. Ashbel Smith, Houston, March 14, 1842, in Smith

The President reached Houston on Sunday evening, the 13th, and on the following day issued a brief circular "To the Citizens of Texas," saying,

Let the troops be organized and wait for orders to march to any point where they may be required by the President. He will have the earliest intelligence from camp. The whole force of the enemy now in Texas cannot exceed 800 or 1,000 men and that of Texas now in camp and on the march West of the Brazos must be 3500 or 4000 men. If the enemy do not retreat, they will be taken prisoners or slain.[109]

On the 14th in response to Captain De Roll's request to impress private property including horses, for the use of his company preparing to go to the west the President wrote that he had "no power to impress horses, unless in the case of extreme danger to the country," and that he was not presently aware that such danger existed to justify impressment.[110] The President hoped to avoid one of the greatest evils that had plagued the country in 1835 and 1836: the promiscuous seizure of private property by irresponsible persons ostensibly, but not always, for public purposes. Furthermore, Houston abhorred the thought of self-constituted companies marching to the frontier without authorization from the government for any purpose. Consequently, finding General Morehouse's troops properly organized according to the President's instructions of March 10, and not yet aware that the enemy was in retreat, Houston ordered Morehouse to commence his march immediately to join the army under General Alexander Somervell, and started an express at once to General Somervell to apprise him of the march of the troops from Harris County so as to enable him to give orders as to the proper point of destination.[111]

Papers, ms.; Anson Jones, Diaries, ms., Memorandum Book, No. 3, March 10, 1842. Smith embarked from Galveston on March 12[?] 1842 for New Orleans and New York on his way to Europe to exchange ratification of the three treaties that had been made with Great Britain, to solicit British mediation between Texas and Mexico, to seek recognition of Texas independence by Spain; *etc*. See Anson Jones to Ashbel Smith, Galveston, March 9, 1842, in George P. Garrison (ed.), *Diplomatic Correspondence of Texas*, in *Annual Report of The American Historical Association*, 1908, III, 948–950.

[109] Sam Houston to the Citizens of Texas, Executive Department, City of Houston, March 14, 1842, in *Writings of Sam Houston*, II, 503, and also in *ibid.*, IV, 81.

[110] Sam Houston to Captain De Roll, Executive Department, City of Houston, March 15, 1842, in *ibid.*, II, 502–503.

[111] Sam Houston to Brigadier General E. Morehouse, Executive Department, City of Houston, March 15, 1842, in *ibid.*, II, 503.

In the meantime, Houston was contacted by representatives of the committee of vigilance and safety of the city of Houston with reference to conducting offensive operations against Mexico. Houston's reply was brief, decisive as to the present needs of the country, and noncommittal as to the future plans of the executive.[112] The enemy needed to be expelled. The question of offensive operations could wait.

Dissatisfied with the reply they received, the committee of vigilance and safety, headed by John D. Andrews, hastily called a meeting of the citizens of Harris County at the courthouse for the afternoon of March 15. The meeting took place at the courthouse with Barnard E. Bee as its elected chairman and J. W. Pitkin, secretary. Houston's reply to the committee of vigilance, dated March 15, was read and discussed, after which a number of questions were framed for presentation to the President.[113] First, would he "approve of and permit the prosecution of immediate offensive hostilities against Mexico under the Texian flag, provided men and means for the purpose . . . [could] be procured from abroad free from charge upon the Texas Government?" Second, for the promotion of such an object, would he "order the officers and men now in the field, to concentrate at such point or points as in his judgment . . . [would] best promote the furtherance of such design?" Thirdly, would he "clothe with legal authority, one or more agents to be sent abroad to solicit and to co-operate with the people of Texas in the enterprise?" Fourthly, would he "issue letters of marque and reprisal, for capturing all Mexican property on the high seas?" And, lastly, would he "issue orders to our naval commanders to harrass the commerce, and seize all vessels which they may find under the Mexican flag, until our independence shall be acknowledged by Mexico?" We make these interrogatories, said the committee, because the Mexican government now holds in servile slavery a large number of our citizens "in violation of a solemn treaty of capitulation, guaranteeing to them their liberty and a safe return to their homes, their families and friends. The armies of Mexico are now seizing our western towns, ravaging our farms, and despoiling our property, and have proclaimed to "the world that they have taken up arms against us, never to lay them down until they have subjugated us

[112] Sam Houston to the Committee of Vigilance, Houston, Executive Department, City of Houston, March 15, 1842, in *ibid.*, II, 504.

[113] Houston Committee of Vigilance, [Report of Public Meeting beginning:] "At a large meeting of the citizens of Harris County, assembled at the Court House this afternoon, in pursuance of a call from the Committee of Vigilance and Safety. . . . Houston City, March 15, 1842." Broadside.

to their authority. They have made frequent incursions upon our frontiers, carrying off our defenseless citizens, and by a mock-trial condemning them to ignominous death, or serville chains." Now is the time for Texans to act. "Our planters, merchants, and mechanics, have buckled on their armor and gone forth to battle, and wish not to return untill they have secured permanent peace to their country. Our business in all branches is broken up," they continued; "all the avenues to prosperity and successful enterprise are closed; and under these circumstances it would cost but little additional sacrifice to prosecute to a successful termination. . . . A Crisis in our affairs seems to be at hand, and we must have peace at all hazards, or the spirits of our people will succomb to the difficulties in which we are menaced."[114] The committee of safety then proceeded to appoint, with the approval of the President, Stephen P. Andrews to go to New Orleans and other points in the United States to solicit aid to conduct the war against Mexico.[115] Similar agents, J. C. Watrous, Dr. Levi Jones, and J. C. Megginson,[116] had been appointed by the committee of vigilance at Galveston. Houston instructed Andrews to have any supplies that might be contributed landed, at least for the present, at Galveston to the care of Gail Borden. "I wish you most *hearty* success," wrote the President.

At the entrance of the Mexican forces into Texas, the "Outs," who were in opposition to the Administration, formed themselves into a violent "War Party." "Their motive was to get a large number of volunteers from the U. States . . . that soon (as they said) they might revel in the 'Halls of Montezuma'."[117] The "War Party" had great popular appeal at Galveston, Houston, and in the west, and "to its standards rushed those who knew but imperfectly the real state of affairs, who had but

[114] *Morning Star* quoted in *Telegraph and Texas Register,* March 16, 1842. See also *Morning Star,* March 19, 1842; *Bollaert's Texas,* p. 52; Houston Committee of Vigilance, [Report], Broadside; *The Houstonian Extra,* March 15, [1842,] 11 o'clock A.M., Broadside; Sam Houston to John S. Sydnor, Chairman of the Committee of Vigilance, etc., dated: Galveston, March 11, 1842, in *Writings of Sam Houston,* IV, 79–80.

[115] *Telegraph and Texas Register,* May 4, 1842; Sam Houston to S. P. Andrews, Executive Department, City of Houston, March 17, 1842, in *Writings of Sam Houston,* IV, 81–82. Andrews was back at Galveston by May 10, and certainly was not one of those to whom the President referred in his proclamation of April 25 against the agents of certain "Committees of Vigilance and Safety."

[116] Ashbel Smith to Anson Jones, New Orleans, March 16, 1842, in State Department (Texas), Foreign Letters 1842–1844, ms., pp. 77–78, *Civilian and Galveston Gazette,* Sept. 10, 1842.

[117] *Bollaert's Texas,* pp. 37, 52.

little else to do or who fond of an adventurous roving life, preferred following the drum to the plough. However, those citizens who were established on their plantations and farms, thought with Houston, that it would be quite time enough to turn out, when the enemy had arrived within rifle shot."[118] At Paso Cavallo on April 17 Bollaert found a group of men who "roughly commented on" Houston's passive measures, but "generally appeared to think that he and his party knew the true position of Texas, and the 'Old Sam,' as they familiarly called him, knew how to get Texas out of the 'scrape'."[119]

To the questions propounded to him by the Houston committee of vigilance and safety the President replied on the 15th in a characteristic manner and in substance as he had earlier in this day: "Let us expel the enemy, and then we will know what is needful, and what we can do. Time will enable us to be a judge of our situation."[120] No more sage advice could have been given. "Old Sam" was at the helm, and while he may have had ideas as to what *should* be done, he knew what *could* be done, and more particularly what *could not* be carried out under conditions then existing in the Republic. He was not to be stampeded into rash action.

In the meantime, as the naval expedition headed down the coast, Bollaert dedicated a song to the Galveston Coast Guards, calling them "Red Rovers," their sea uniform being red shirts.

> Red Rovers, Red Rovers, huzzah!
> Red Rovers, Red Rovers, huzzah!
> By sea or by land, we are ready—our band,
> Red Rovers, Red Rovers, huzzah!
>
> In the gloom of the night when billows are dashing,
> And our path is lit up by the fierce lightning's ray
> To guard our dear coast—to repel the invader
> Is the joy of the Red Rover—the rover so gay.
> Red Rovers, &c.
>
> In battle for glory and our bright rising star,
> O what joy in each breast when we meet the base foe;
> And the fame of our actions will resound—aye, afar,
> And many will envy the Red Rover in War.
> Red Rovers, &c.

[118] *Ibid.*, pp. 57–58.

[119] *Ibid.*, pp. 63, 63 n.

[120] Houston to the Committee of Vigilance, Houston, Executive Department, City of Houston, March 15, 1842, in *Writings of Sam Houston*, II, 504.

Texans Rally To Defend the Frontier

> Then our cruise being over, our coast free from harm
> And anchored in port—there are other alarms;
> But they are of love's joys—the enduring caress:
> By the girl of his heart—the Red Rover is blest.
> Red Rovers, &c.[121]

It was presumed at Galveston that if the sea expedition failed to encounter the Mexican vessels headed for Texas either at Copano or Corpus Christi, it might land at the mouth of the Río Grande. As it was, the expedition followed the coast,[122] and on the night of March 15 crossed Paso Cavallo Bar and anchored at Deckrow's Landing. The next morning the Fusileers went on shore to exercise, while the crew of the *Lafitte* drilled and exercised with musket and boarding pike. "All took to soldiering very kindly," wrote one of the volunteers, "but there was a fear that they might kill one another in their anxiety to attack."[123] There were a number of foreigners in the expedition, some of whom were not adept English scholars. The recently arrived French emigrants at Matagorda under the leadership of Baron Ernest Philabeaucourt were "all for aiding, abetting, and assisting in the struggle."[124] At Deckrow's Point Captain Wade was informed that a small sloop, supposedly laden with provisions for the Mexican army, was ashore on St. Joseph Island.

On Thursday, the 17th, the expedition headed again down the coast and late in the afternoon, after hailing an American brig loaded with lumber which they had at first thought to be a Mexican vessel, crossed the bar at Aransas Pass, and discovered, apparently under suspicious circumstances, a small craft on shore on St. Joseph Island off Espíritu Santo Inlet (San Bernardo Bay) with a Union Jack flying at half mast. Captain Wade sent Lieutenant Haviland and four men ashore in a small boat to examine the vessel. Their boat was capsized in the first breaker, and after "struggling in imminent peril of their lives for more than a half hour," they effected a landing. They discovered the vessel to be the

[121] Bollaert, "Arrival in Texas in 1842, and Cruise of the Lafitte," *Coburn's United Service Magazine*, November 1846, pp. 341–355.

[122] *Telegraph and Texas Register*, March 23, 1842.

[123] Bollaert, "Arrival in Texas in 1842, and Cruise of the Lafitte," *Coburn's United Service Magazine*, November 1846, pp. 341–355.

[124] *Ibid.* The Baron Ernest Philabeaucourt had landed in March 1842, at Matagorda Bay, with his family and twenty emigrants with the intention of going to San Antonio when news of Vasquez's raid arrived and upset their plans. See also *Daily Picayune*, April 8, 1842.

Panther, fourteen days out of New Orleans, bound for Aransas with a cargo of flour, potatoes, and tobacco. She had run ashore while attempting to enter the narrow, shoally pass. The vessel and cargo were taken as a prize. The *Lafitte* then bore off toward Aransas Pass, and came to anchor for the night. The *Borden* came up the next morning, and the expedition continued toward Live Oak Point and came to anchor at 10 A.M. At this place lived James Power, one of the promoters of the Power and Hewetson Colony, who received the Coast Guardsmen and Fusileers most hospitably, providing them with fresh meat, milk, and fish. While the vessels took on fresh water, the men went on shore to do some washing of clothes, fishing, "oystering," and "gunning." They took up temporary quarters in several vacant buildings. The cloudy, wintry weather gone, the expedition resumed its course at 10 A.M. on Saturday, March 19, under refreshing southerly breezes and at 2 P.M. arrived off Copano. Captain Wade went ashore, where he found mostly women and children, practically all of the able-bodied men having gone west to repel the invader. He learned that three hundred volunteers had a few days since passed through the Mission Refugio on their way westward. Returning to his ship, Wade continued the expedition to Black Point, at the junction of the Aransas River with Copano Bay which place they reached around 5 P.M. His object was to cut and take on wood for the *Lafitte.* The countersign at night was "Pork." The 20th and 21st were spent cutting mesquite for the steamer. In the meantime, an express was sent to Refugio with the expectation of securing the cooperation of Colonel Clark L. Owen in an effort to take Brazos Santiago, the seaport of Matamoros.

The courier returned on the 21st with a reply from Owen to the effect that his army numbered only four hundred men, that the men were rapidly returning to their homes in view of the President's proclamation of the 17th issued through the public press and of the orders of the 18th to General Morehouse for the men to return to the cultivation of their fields now that the enemy had retreated, and that he could not keep them together. Shortly thereafter a party from the interior arrived with information that on March 7 a Mexican unit had surprised a company of Texans near San Patricio, killing Cairns, Snodgrass, Wells, Willis, and four Lipans.[125] It was also reported that on the 8th these Mexicans had appeared before Corpus Christi, and distributed Arista's proclamation.

[125] Bollaert, "Arrival in Texas in 1842, and Cruise of the Lafitte," *Coburn's United Service Magazine,* November 1846, pp. 341–355.

Early on the morning of the 22nd the *Lafitte* returned to Live Oak Point, arriving there at noon, where it again took on water. In the meantime, Private J. C. Stephens was given a court-martial "for unsoldierlike conduct, for having declared if eight or ten men would join him they would take their arms and leave camp," forcibly if it were required, "and go where they pleased."[126] Being found guilty, he was ordered to receive a public reprimand. The next morning, Captain Wade, in the *Lafitte*, accompanied by the *Washington*, headed for Corpus Christi, which they reached in the middle of the afternoon. There they learned further details about the killing of Cairns, whose party for some time past had performed military duty for Kinney and Aubrey at their fortified log trading post. Cairns' party had gone off in the direction of San Patricio where it was surprised and its members murdered, except for Ewen Cameron and Wells who effected their escape.

On the 24th Captain Wade returned to Live Oak Point, where he met the *Borden* coming down the bay in pursuit of a Mexican spy on one of the islands. A Mexican by the name of Incarnación had it seems been taken at a hut. Near the point of capture were several beeves, one of which the Texans tried to lasso and kill with the idea of having fresh meat aboard ship. The animal proved to be too wild; so the Mexican prisoner suggested to his captors that, being a first rate herdsman, he should be allowed to try his hand at roping the animal. Pointing to the fine mule saddled near the hut, he said if they would let him have the mule and lasso, he would soon catch the "beef." "This was immediately acceded to, when the wily Mexican, after pretending for some time to catch the 'beef,' got far out into the prairie and when at good starting distance, galloped off as fast as he could, leaving his former captors in no very good humor."[127] It was this Mexican that the *Borden* hoped to recapture.

It having become apparent by the 28th that there were no Mexican transports on the Texas coast, it was determined to leave most of the Fusileers at Lamar, opposite Live Oak Point, to remain for a few days awaiting more information from the army. If there was then no need for them, they were to return to Galveston by land. The Coast Guard and the remainder of the Fusileers prepared to return at once in the ships to Galveston. At 4 P.M. the vessels were brought up inside the bar for the night. The next morning they got under way at an early hour, and at 5

---

[126] Stuart, "Early Galveston Military Companies, 1839–1901," pp. 10–11.
[127] *Ibid.*

P.M. came to anchor off San Luis, where they received Houston's proclamation announcing a blockade of Mexican ports. Early Wednesday morning, March 30, the *Lafitte* reached the eastern end of Galveston Island, where it found the *Wharton* and the *Zavala*, the former waiting for a fair wind to go out cruising, and the latter preparing to serve as a guard ship.

On March 10, the day the general call to arms was sent out to the people of Texas, Brigadier General Alexander Somervell,[128] who had been elected to the rank of brigadier general in November, 1839, was ordered by the President to report to army headquarters to take command of the troops being assembled to repel the invader. "I am glad Somervell has the command of the Army," wrote Guy M. Bryan, who had served as an orderly under Somervell for a short period after the battle of San Jacinto. "He is prudent, brave and humane. O! that I could be in Texas under him. I have no doubt [I] could get an appointment that would enable me to *make* or *unmake* a name."[129] Those who knew Somervell liked him. He was a man of high character and good judgment.

Since there was no regular army, or army corps, in Texas, the President, in appointing Somervell, acted under that clause of the Constitution which permitted him to call out the militia to repel an invasion and to maintain domestic order. Evidently this was the second step in the process of ordering a brigade of militia into active service, for Houston was adverse to calling troops out en masse until he could ascertain the intention of the Mexican force and its size. It was necessary that corn be produced for use next winter and it would, therefore, be inadvisable to draw the farmers from their crops unnecessarily. "Every report," he

[128] Alexander Somervell was born in Maryland, June 11, 1796. At the age of twenty-one he moved to Louisiana and engaged in business, finally making his way to Texas in 1832, where he received a grant of land in Austin's second colony. On April 8, 1836, he was elected a lieutenant colonel in the First Regiment of Texas Volunteers, and participated in the battle of San Jacinto. In June 1836, he was discharged from the army to become Secretary of War in President Burnet's cabinet. Between October 3, 1836, and May 4, 1838, he served as Senator in the First and Second Congresses from the district comprising the counties of Colorado and Austin. Afterwards he moved to Fort Bend County, and on November 12, 1839, was elected brigadier general of the First Brigade. Dixon and Kemp, *Heroes of San Jacinto*, p. 126; Nance (ed.), "A Letter Book of Joseph Eve," in *Southwestern Historical Quarterly*, XLIII (1939–1940), 486 n.

[129] Guy M. Bryan to James F. Perry, Gambier, Ohio, April 19, 1842, in Perry Papers, ms.

wrote, "will be sent in to excite the public mind. *Heroes must be made to the West,* and there are so many pretenders that the United States cannot furnish supplies of glory," so they flock to Texas to seek it under the cloak of Texas patriotism.[130]

In response to a petition from a group of citizens of Galveston requesting the appointment of General Albert Sidney Johnston[131] as major general to command the forces to be raised for the defense of the Republic, the President replied that he did not possess authority to appoint a commander for volunteers troops.

I find [he said] in an act passed the 24th of January, 1839, it is provided that all officers shall be elected by the people.

If there were a regular army, or corps, in Texas, the President would have the right to nominate and the Senate to confirm the officers of such army or corps; but the people alone have the right to create by election the officers, where the privilege is granted to them by law.

If the power of appointment of commander is delegated to the President, other than the officers elected by those subject to militia duty, it is not within my knowledge.[132]

Such a reply on the part of the President is interesting in the light of future developments. At this time the President had in mind the probable necessity of having to call out the militia or volunteers in sufficient numbers to constitute a brigade, and had merely designated one of the elected officers to command the troops already assembling and to receive the orders of the government. He refused to recognize the right of the militiamen to choose *new* officers. Furthermore, it is doubtful if a

[130] Houston to Anson Jones, City of Houston, Buffalo Bayou, Tuesday, March 14, 1842, in *Writings of Sam Houston,* II, 502. See also Same to George W. Hockley, Secretary of War, Galveston, March 10, 1842 (Private), *ibid.,* IV, 76–77.

[131] Albert Sidney Johnston had seen service as a second lieutenant in the United States Army before coming to Texas in 1834. While in Texas he accused Houston of "using vituperative language" against him. He later returned to the United States, but after a few months there, again headed for Texas in the late summer of 1840 upon learning from a friend that a movement against Mexico was contemplated by Lamar. A. Sidney Johnston to Gen. Sam Houston, City of Austin, Jan. 5, 1840, and Sam Houston to Samuel M. Williams, Hall of Representatives, Jan. 7, 1840, in William Preston Johnston, *The Life of Gen. Albert Sidney Johnston: Embracing His Services in the Armies of the United States, the Republic of Texas, and the Confederate States,* pp. 121–122; A. S. Johnston to M. B. Lamar, Galveston Bay, Aug. 6, 1840, in *Lamar Papers,* III, 427.

[132] Houston to a Committee at Galveston, March 10, 1842, in *Writings of Sam Houston,* IV, 77–79; see also *Civilian and Galveston Gazette,* April 16, 1842.

relatively unknown man like Johnston, no matter how good he might be, would have inspired confidence in the soldiers as much as a person such as General Thomas J. Rusk or General Edward Burleson, whose fame had already been identified with the memorable events of the country's history.[133]

With such an understanding of the limitations of his authority, the President appointed Somervell to the command, and instructed him to report to the Secretary of War for further orders. In the meantime, Somervell was to proceed with the organization of the troops according to the militia laws[134] of the Republic and maintain subordination and discipline at all times.

You will maintain [wrote the President] the strictest discipline in camp. Have no music in camp unless you are ready to attack the enemy. Have the troops always under arms one hour before day, and let them remain in that position until the day fairly opens. Let your picket guards be posted at least three miles from the army, when your position will admit of it. Keep a sufficient number on camp guard. Do not dispense with patrols. If a man is taken asleep at his post, or on guard, let him be shot.[135]

If Somervell thought it advisable to attack the enemy after having ascertained his position and strength, he was authorized to do so at night, for "their surprise will be terrific." But, if he should find the enemy too strong for an attack, he was ordered to fall back, and "I shall be with you," wrote the President.

Since the volunteers who had assembled at Houston were anxious to join the army on the frontier, the President instructed Brigadier General Morehouse, who commanded the Harris County troops, to let them go immediately to the west with orders to report to General Somervell, who had been appointed to command the army assembling on the western frontier.[136] Colonel Moseley Baker, Colonel Barnard E. Bee, and Captain A. C. Allen prepared to leave Houston on the 17th. But on the

---

[133] *Red-Lander* quoted in the *Civilian and Galveston Gazette,* April 16, 1842.

[134] "An Act to Complete the Organization of the Militia, Approved January 18, 1841," by acting President David G. Burnet, in Gammel (ed.), *Laws of Texas,* II, 497–498, 579–580.

[135] Houston to Brig.-Gen. Alexander Somervell, Galveston, March 10, 1842, in *Writings of Sam Houston,* II, 492–493.

[136] Houston to Brig.-Gen. E. Morehouse, City of Houston, March 15, 1842, in *ibid.,* II, 503; see *The Houstonian Extra,* March 15, [1842], 11 o'clock A.M., Broadside. A. C. Allen to Col. James Morgan, New Washington, [dated:] Houston, March 16, 1842, in Morgan Papers, ms.

17th, when it became evident that the immediate danger from the invading force had passed, the remainder of the Harris County troops were instructed to return to their homes in accordance with the general orders sent out by the Secretary of War on March 12, disbanding all troops, except a small force to be maintained upon the frontier for the preservation of order and to act as a spy company.[137] At that time it was estimated that one thousand men were on the march west of the Colorado, and it was the hope of those on the Guadalupe that they would be able to cut off the Mexican retreat.[138] Over at Nacogdoches a committee appointed by a meeting of citizens let it be known through a series of resolutions that they stood ready "to march at a moments warning to the Western frontier . . . to meet the enemy upon our borders. . . . We are not now as we were then surrounded by a set of faithless and perfidious Indians. That enemy is now gone and every man can repair to the field without that constant apprehension which was then entertained of the massacre during his absence of his family."[139] The committee recommended that copies of its resolutions be sent to the adjoining counties and to the Red River district, and that a committee of correspondence, consisting of three persons, be created "for the purpose of obtaining and circulating as early as possible information relative to the movements of the enemy."

By the end of the month the Milam Guards and many of the unmounted volunteers from the counties east of the Brazos were returning home,[140] but Colonel Bee proceeded to San Antonio to get a better understanding of the situation, supposing that San Antonio would be the scene of military activity. In this he was disappointed. He found that volunteers on the way to the front had turned back, and others who

[137] By the end of the month, nearly all of the Harris County troops that had headed for the frontier had returned to Houston. A. Jones to Col. William H. Daingerfield, Houston, March 31, 1842, in *Writings of Sam Houston*, III, 16 n–17 n.

[138] W. D. Miller to Sam Houston, Austin, March 13, 1842 (Private), no. 11, in Miller Papers (Texas), ms. copy.

[139] "Report of a Committee appointed by a Meeting of Citizens of Eastern Texas on rumor that Mexicans were invading the state, etc. [March 1842]," in Thomas J. Rusk Papers, ms. This report is unsigned but is in Thomas J. Rusk's handwriting and apparently was framed six days after the receipt of news at Nacogdoches of Vasquez's retreat.

[140] *Telegraph and Texas Register*, March 30, 1842. The Milam Guards returned to Houston Sunday evening, March 27, 1842, "in good order and fine spirits." They had gone as far as Columbus on the Colorado and returned "in obedience to the order of the President." *Ibid.*

had arrived at Béxar were drifting homeward,[141] despite all efforts to keep up the impression that a strong invading force of at least ten thousand men was on its way to Texas. All public property, including arms, and private property impressed into the public service during the emergency, was to be forthwith returned. The impressment of private property often led to frauds being practiced upon the citizenry to the detriment of the country.[142] Farmers were advised to return to the cultivation of their fields, but to hold themselves in readiness for further service if necessary.[143] Texas was in no position at this time to invade Mexico, and neither was Houston so ready as his predecessor to engage in an offensive war. He was quite aware that any successful invading expedition from Texas needed to be strong, well equipped, and well disciplined. It was estimated at the time that it would require 120 days to raise and equip such an army of invasion. There was a shortage of corn and other food crops, especially on the frontier; so, in the meantime, farmers and mechanics were ordered to return to their homes to await further instructions from the government. This was necessary, especially in a society where almost every man was in turn farmer, cattle herder, and soldier against the ever threatening Mexican or hostile Indian.

Shortly after the news of the invasion was received in Austin, Secretary of War Hockley learned of Vice President Edward Burleson's intention to lead a force for the relief of San Antonio, supposedly on his "own hook," since the Secretary had no power to authorize him to command such an expedition. Feeling that he had no authority to detain him either, he "not being immediately under my command and anxious to go to San Antonio," Hockley reported, "I thought it best to send him there."[144] "General Burleson," wrote Joseph Waples, a clerk in the State

[141] Barnard E. Bee to James Morgan, San Antonio, March 29, 1842, in Morgan Papers, ms.

[142] Houston to Brig.-Gen. E. Morehouse, City of Houston, March 17, 1842, in *Writings of Sam Houston*, II, 506–507; and Same to Same, Executive Department, City of Houston, March 18, 1842, in *ibid.*, II, 511.

[143] Proclamation of George W. Hockley, Secretary of War and Navy, Department of War and Navy, Austin, March 12, 1842, published in the *Austin City Gazette* and reprinted in *Telegraph and Texas Register*, March 23, 1842; Houston to Brig.-Gen. A. Somervell, City of Houston, March 18, 1842 (two letters), and Houston to Brig.-Gen. Edwin Morehouse, City of Houston, March 18, 1842, in *Writings of Sam Houston*, II, 509–511; Houston to Major I. W. Burton, Executive Department, City of Houston, March 17, 1842, in *ibid.*, II, 507.

[144] George W. Hockley to General [Houston], Department of War and Navy, Austin, March 16, 1842, in Smither (ed.), *Journals of the Sixth Congress*, III, 17–18.

Department at Austin, "is about to start for . . . Béxar, determined, as the ball is in motion to keep it rolling to some purpose,"[145] and as the troops marched from Austin, they vowed not to return until they had retaliated upon the Mexicans, "by giving them a small trucer on the Río Grande—the President's proclamation to the contrary notwithstanding. . . . It's the only measure they can now adopt," wrote Long from Austin, "on which to hang a hope to relieve them and the section of the country in which they live, from its embarrassed situation, and as a last resort they will, I have no doubt, make the effort."[146] "The West is entirely broken up for this year," declared Miller, "and all anxious for war. A great deal of impatience is evinced on the subject."[147] "The Mexicans thought, perhaps, that they could repeat the villainies perpetrated at Refugio, and escape with impunity—but they are mistaken," reported the editor of the *Morning Star*.[148] "They have roused the ire of thousands of daring spirits, who are fired with just indignation, and thirst for vengeance. The towns of Texas are scarcely worth plundering; but those of Mexico will afford a rich harvest. The troops that are pursuing the retreating foe, are determined to retaliate with an iron rigor, and will soon compel the suppliant enemy, to make ample amends for the injury inflicted." "So sure and so determined are they [the Texans] in conquering and capturing the Mexico [Mexicans?]," wrote James Morgan, ". . . all h—ll can't keep them from going into the City of Mexico once they are armed up again."[149]

Burleson was considered "warm for the Río Grande" and in favor of prosecuting vigorously the war with Mexico until a lasting peace could be achieved. Accordingly, accompanied by Judge Terrell and Barry Gillespie, he left Austin Friday morning (the 11th) for San Antonio with "about three companies of horse," being those of Captain James H. Gillespie, Captain H. M. Childress, and one raised by Colonel Louis P. Cooke, together with some volunteers.[150] Captain Thomas Green re-

[145] Quoted in Herbert Pickens Gambrell, *Anson Jones: The Last President of Texas*, p. 238.

[146] J. M. Long to Matthew P. Woodhouse, City of Austin, May 21, 1842, in Woodhouse Papers, ms.

[147] W. D. Miller to Sam Houston, Austin, March 17, 1842 (Private), no. 13, in Miller Papers (Texas), ms. copy.

[148] Quoted in the *Telegraph and Texas Register*, March 23, 1842.

[149] J. Morgan to Genl. Saml. Swartwout, New Washington, Galveston Bay, Texas, Jany 27th 1842, in Morgan Papers, ms.

[150] W. D. Miller to Sam Houston, Austin, March 13, 1842 (Private), no. 11, in Miller Papers (Texas), ms. copy; *Telegraph and Texas Register*, March 16, 1842;

linquished the command of his company so that he could leave for Béxar, too; and Washington D. Miller was elected captain to succeed him.[151] The next morning there appeared at Austin the "first and last" edition of the *Anti-Quaker*, which seemed to be "a new edition of the 'Alarm Bell'," whipping up the wind for a descent upon the Río Grande and vengeance.[152]

Although Burleson went to San Antonio under his own authority, Hockley dispatched under his command a brass six-pounder from the park of artillery recently purchased in the United States. Upon his arrival at San Antonio, Burleson claimed, or most likely assumed, that the Secretary of War had asked him to take command of the troops there.[153]

The tide of war at any rate [Miller wrote the President two days after Burleson left Austin] is moving westward, and cannot be arrested until retribution has been taken for the injury consequent upon the fall of Béxar. At what time or place that will be had it is not now possible or important to say. It is considered enough that the war has begun—it will be prosecuted in the best way and with the utmost efficiency in our power. Let us impel the ball until our independence is established freely and finally upon a basis too solid for the entire strength of all Mexico to shake.[154]

Upon Burleson's advance from Austin, Colonel Jones remained behind in command of three companies—the Travis Guards, under Captain Woodhouse, numbering about thirty men; and two companies of about fifty men each under Captain George M. Dolson and Captain

---

George W. Hockley to [Sam Houston], Austin, March 16, 1842, in Smither (ed.), *Journals of the Sixth Congress*, III, 17–18.

[151] A copy of the roster of Captain Washington D. Miller's company [March 11, 1842] will be found in the Appendix to this book.

[152] *Morning Star*, March 22, 1842. No issue of the *Anti-Quaker* has been found. The issue mentioned by the *Morning Star* was dated March 12, 1842. Thomas W. Streeter, *Bibliography of Texas*, II, 505.

[153] Edward Burleson, "To the Public" [Address of General Burleson to his "Fellow-Citizens of Texas"] dated April 6, 1842, in Smither (ed.), *Journals of the Sixth Congress*, II, 43–47. See also Burleson, *To The Public* [being an address of General Edward Burleson to his "Fellow-Citizens of Texas":] dated April 6, 1842; followed by a letter from him to Brigadier General Somerville [*i.e.* Somervell] and Somervell's reply, both dated San Antonio, March 31, 1842; and ending with Burleson's address disbanding the volunteers under his command, dated Alamo, San Antonio de Béxar, April 2, 1842, Broadside; *Telegraph and Texas Register*, April 20, 1842.

[154] W. D. Miller to Sam Houston, Austin, March 13, 1842 (Private), no. 11, in Miller Papers (Texas), ms. copy.

Washington D. Miller, respectively, were left at the barracks in the capital where they performed light duty and expected to be furloughed in a day or two.

Houston's order for the removal of the national archives[155] reached Austin on the evening of the 15th, and to say that it created quite a commotion west of the Brazos would be an understatement. People were soon saying they would much rather take their rifles to oppose removal of the archives than to fight Mexicans.[156] Colonel Jones ordered Captain Woodhouse of the Travis Guards to permit no additional transfers from his command "until further orders,"[157] and to "station a guard during the day upon the streets of the outskirts of the city, so as to prevent the leaving of waggons or horsemen either by the Eastern or South Eastern road, or indeed by any other route if possible to prevent. All such attempting to leave will be stopped and reported to Head Quarters, unless in the possession of a written permit signed by the Col. of the Reg[imen]t."[158] This order was, of course, designed to prevent the removal of the archives. Secretary of War George W. Hockley countered with a "Special Order," declaring that no orders issued by commanding officers under martial law would be obeyed unless approved by the Secretary of War.[159] That night (the 16th) messengers were dispatched to San Antonio and southward down the Colorado Valley to apprise the western settlers and the men at San Antonio, principally from the west, of the order for the removal of the archives, and to arouse them to help resist the fulfillment of the President's order.[160] The next day, March 17, the Secretary of War furloughed the Travis Guards; although permitted to return to their respective private occupations, the men were instructed to "hold themselves in readiness to resume military duties should their services be required."[161]

[155] Houston to George W. Hockley, Galveston, March 10, 1842, in Smither (ed.), *Journals of the Sixth Congress*, III, 17.

[156] W. D. Miller to Sam Houston, Austin, March 13, 1842 (Private), no. 11, Postscript, Wednesday Evening, March 16, 1842, in Miller Papers (Texas), ms. copy.

[157] Henry Jones, Col. Commanding 4th Regt., T.M., to Captain [Matthew P.] Woodhouse, Head Quarters, March 16, 1842, in Woodhouse Papers, ms.

[158] Henry Jones, Col. Com[manding] to [Captain Matthew P. Woodhouse], [Austin], n. d., in *ibid.*

[159] Special Order No. 146, Department of War & Navy, Austin, March 16, 1842, copy in Woodhouse Papers, ms.

[160] W. D. Miller to Sam Houston, Austin, March 17, 1842 (Private), no. 13, in Miller Papers (Texas), ms. copy.

[161] Special Order No. 147, issued by George W. Hockley, Secretary of War &

The "Archives War" was on! It was not long after this that the citizens of Austin gained possession of the government munitions stored at the arsenal. They first applied to the officer-in-charge of the arsenal for a quantity of powder and lead, alleging that they needed it for defense of the city against the Indians, but he refused to let them have any without a requisition from the War Department. The citizens returned to the arsenal in the evening, but their request was again denied. They then surrounded the officer, took possession of his keys and helped themselves to what arms and ammunition they desired. "The next day they supplied each citizen with a portion of what was thus obtained. They also took away with them [from the arsenal] a howitzer, caisson, ammunition," and other supplies and "placed them under a shed near the corner of Congress Avenue and Pecan Street" to be used for defense and in assembling the people.[162]

Meanwhile, when the re-enforcements from Austin reached San Antonio on the evening of March 15, the enemy had already fled. By this time volunteers from other parts of the Republic, particularly from west of the Trinity and from the lower settlements on the Guadalupe and Colorado, had begun to arrive in San Antonio in such numbers that those in favor of crossing the Río Grande estimated that more than thirty-five hundred volunteers had assembled.[163] Actually only one-fifth of that number were there;[164] and most of these were ill-equipped and ill-prepared for an immediate invasion of Mexico, a majority of the men having come prepared for a campaign of only a few weeks. In spite of the general enthusiasm among the men for an immediate descent upon the Río Grande, by the 19th some of them had begun to return home.

Marine, Department of War & Marine, Austin, March 17, copy in Woodhouse Papers, ms.

[162] Boerner, "Austin," pp. 17–18.

[163] It was reported in Houston on the 23rd of March that a gentleman from Gonzales estimated the number of men under arms west of the Brazos at not less than 6,000. About 3,500 of these were on the upper route towards Béxar, and between 2,000 and 3,000 on the lower route towards Goliad. All of the men, it was said, were from the counties west of the Brazos, except about 900 from Harris, Montgomery, and adjoining counties. *Telegraph and Texas Register*, March 23, 1842.

[164] Colonel Barry Gillespie and James Nicholson, of Bastrop, arrived in Austin on the morning of March 17 from Béxar. They reported about 700 men at Béxar when they left, and that most of them were anxious to go to the Río Grande. W. D. Miller to Sam Houston, Austin, March 17, 1842 (Private), no. 13, in Miller Papers (Texas), ms. copy.

They did not feel much apprehension of a general invasion at this season, and on second thought they found that they were not themselves prepared to make one.[165]

As soon as news of the Mexican withdrawal reached Austin, Secretary Hockley issued a proclamation on the 12th announcing the Mexican retreat and urging the citizens to remain safely at their homes, as sufficient forces had been sent to punish the enemy upon his retirement. He urged all those liable to militia service to hold themselves in readiness, for the enemy emboldened by his recent successes might soon return with a regular invading army.[166] Houston instructed Somervell to conform to the order of the Secretary of War on the 12th, "unless you are perfectly assured that the enemy are advancing in force into the country," in which event he was to meet and defeat them. "Some," he said, "may have a disposition to go to the Río Grande . . . without orders and in a tumultuous mass, and in parties without concert or orders. This will expose them to every disaster that can arise from insubordination. Let any who may proceed without your orders call to mind the fate of Johnson, Grant and indeed, all the disasters of the Spring of 1836."[167]

A consultation of the officers at San Antonio was held on March 15 after the arrival of the troops from Austin, and the consensus of opinion was that the Mexicans had already crossed to their side of the Río Grande. Since no one in San Antonio possessed orders authorizing them to cross the boundary and Burleson had explicit orders from the War Department, stating that "in no event" was he to cross the Río Grande, it was decided to halt until Burleson could ascertain the views of the President on the subject of entering the enemy's territory. Burleson was of the opinion that as much of the fighting as possible should take place on the enemy's soil and both armies should be subsisted upon the enemy's country.[168] General Albert Sydney Johnston, who had hastened

[165] James F. Perry to Eliza M. Perry, Peach Point, near Brazoria, Texas, March [19] 1842, and R. Mills to J. F. Perry, Brazoria, March 20 [1842], in Perry Papers, ms.

[166] Proclamation of George W. Hockley, Secretary of War and Navy, Department of War and Navy, Austin, March 12, 1842, published in the *Austin City Gazette—Extra*, March 12, 1842, and reproduced in the *Telegraph and Texas Register*, March 23, 1842.

[167] Houston to Brigadier General A. Somervell, Executive Department, City of Houston, March 18, 1842, in *Writings of Sam Houston*, II, 509–510.

[168] Edward Burleson to Fellow Citizens of Texas, April 6, 1842, in *Telegraph and Texas Register*, April 20, 1842; *Writings of Sam Houston*, III, 43–45; Ed Kilman

from Galveston to San Antonio, complained, "The war, after great preparations on the part of the enemy, is upon us without the slightest effort being made by us."[169] For a long time Johnston had been a strong advocate of an aggressive military policy toward Mexico. It has been claimed that Johnston, whose name had been used against Houston in the presidential election of 1841, had started for the rendezvous in anticipation of being chosen to command the volunteers. "It was understood," wrote Johnston's son years later, "that Burleson concurred in the intention of the volunteers to choose him [Johnston] as their commander. It was probably this fact," he continued rather erroneously, "that led to their discharge by the Executive."[170]

Two days later, March 17, much to the chagrin of the Burlesonites, Somervell, the senior brigadier general on the western frontier, arrived at San Antonio to take command of the army in the field in accordance with President's orders of the 10th. Burleson yielded the command in obedience to the executive's orders, but the men and officers, numbering some seven hundred, refused to recognize Somervell as their commander, claiming the right as volunteers to elect their own officers.[171] Thereupon, an election of officers was held by the men, and Burleson, (who had cited Somervell for great bravery in 1835[172]) was chosen without opposition to command the troops. Later, while defending the right of volunteers in Texas to elect their own commander, Burleson said, and no doubt truthfully, that the office was unsolicited on his part.[173]

Following the election of Burleson, Somervell retired from San Antonio, leaving Burleson in command, but without orders. Permission was

and Lou W. Kemp, *Texas Musketeers: Stories of Early Texas Battles and Their Heroes*, p. 302.

[169] Johnston, *Life of General Albert Sydney Johnston*, p. 124.

[170] *Ibid.*

[171] Anson Jones to William H. Daingerfield, Houston, March 31, 1842, in *Writings of Sam Houston*, III, 16 n.

[172] In the "Grass Fight" with the Mexicans, November 26, 1835, near San Antonio, Lieutenant Colonel Alexander Somervell had distinguished himself with great bravery. Edward Burleson, Commander-in-Chief of the Volunteer Army, to the Provisional Government. Army Papers (Texas), ms.; copy in State Department (Texas), State Department Records, Book 3, ms., pp. 202–204; Gammel (ed.), *Laws of Texas*, I, 611, 613.

[173] Edward Burleson to Brigadier-General A. Somervell, San Antonio de Béxar, March 31, 1842, in *Telegraph and Texas Register*, April 20, 1842.

then solicited by Burleson and others of the War Department to invade the enemy's country.[174]

Feeling that his request might not be granted and not wishing to see the nucleus of an army for offensive operation against Mexico broken up, Burleson penned a letter from San Antonio on March 18, the day after Somervell's arrival on the frontier, to President Houston, saying:

I am hear and have bin and am so concedered yet at the head of the troops assembled at this place amounting at present to about Eight hundred and since commencing this letter have received information from Clark L. Owen by Express that he is encamped west of Victry [Victoria] with four hundred more and troopes are coming Hourly.

He reported that there was a general desire on the part of the men to go west, "even across the Río grande," and "Your Presouts [*sic*] hear at this time," he informed Houston, "I think would be of vast importance to the Country. The men heare are in high health and as vicious as vipers."[175] Describing the conduct of the men and their newly elected general on this occasion, Somervell informed the Secretary of State as follows:

I have no doubt political intrigue has been at work, with the view to block out the next President. It is a rough concern, and no glory that can be won in the field will ever polish it. I think there is a move for the Vice-Presidency also. The hobby on which they ride is, invasion of Mexico, to give peace and happiness to poor suffering Texas, and thereby achieve immortal glory for themselves.[176]

While awaiting an answer to his request to lead an attack against Mexico, Burleson set about organizing his force. He appointed John W. Smith assistant quartermaster,[177] effective March 30, 1842, and author-

---

[174] W. D. Miller to Sam Houston, Austin, March 17, 1842 (Private), no. 13, in *Miller Papers* (Texas), ms. copy.

[175] Edward Burleson to Genl. [Sam] Houston, Sanantonio, March 18th, 1842, original ms. in Autograph Collection, 1808–1921, Containing Signatures and Letters of Eminent Men of Texas and the United States, ms., p. 38.

[176] A. Somervell to Anson Jones, San Antonio, March 25, 1842, in Anson Jones, *Memoranda and Official Correspondence Relating to the Republic of Texas, Its History and Annexation—Including a Brief Autobiography of the Author*, pp. 172–173. See also Houston to Brig.-Gen. A. Somervell, City of Houston, March 25, 1842, in *Writings of Sam Houston*, IV, 85–86.

[177] Edward Burleson to John W. Smith, Headquarters, San Antonio de Béxar, March 30, 1842, in *Army Papers* (Texas), ms., copy of original belonging to

ized Colonel John Caldwell to seize the horses of every man who "leaves camp with the intention of returning home without permission . . . for the purpose of mounting those of your command who are on foot."[178] Major Andrew Neill was permitted to leave Burleson's camp at San Antonio to attach himself to the command of General Albert Sydney Johnston.[179] While at San Antonio, reported John H. Jenkins from Bastrop, the men "lived by foraging on the Mexican citizens of the place," even destroying many of Juan N. Seguin's hogs, which had something to do with his turning to the Mexican side.[180] Three Mexican spies were captured on the frontier, two of whom, at Burleson's order, were hung near Goliad.[181]

In the meantime, the spies which Captain Hays had sent out to follow the retreating enemy returned to San Antonio to report that they had seen the Mexicans cross the Río Grande. Later, failing to receive a favorable reply from the President to his communication, but learning by rumor that General Somervell had returned to San Antonio with new instructions, Burleson sent Thomas Jefferson Green to him on the 31st with a note, saying, "having understood from general rumor (not having been officially informed of the same)" that he had returned to San Antonio to take command of the army under the President's order, he wished to invite him to his camp at 12 o'clock the next day, at which time he would cheerfully surrender the command to him. Somervell declined this offer, saying that he was "as willing as any person that volunteers should exercise the right they claim of electing their own

---

Mahuldale Burleson Owen, given to the Texas State Library by Mrs. Emma Kyle Burleson, granddaughter of General Edward Burleson.

[178] Edward Burleson to Col. John Caldwell, Headquarters, San Antonio, March 20, 1842, in *ibid.*, ms.

[179] Edward Burleson, Com[mandin]g forces [at] Béxar to [Major Andrew Neill], Head Quarters [San Antonio], March 20, 1842, in *ibid.*, ms. Captain Andrew Neill was appointed by George W. Hockley, Secretary of War, July 20, 1838, to go to Galveston Island to relieve Lieutenant Colonel Lysander Wells and to remain in command at the island until Captain George T. Howard recovered from his illness and was able to resume his command (George W. Hockley to Capt. A. Neill, Department of War, July 20, 1838, in *ibid.*, ms.). Neill, however, soon applied for a promotion, but the Secretary of War, not being prepared to make promotions at the time, accepted Neill's resignation from the service (George W. Hockley to Capt. A. Neill, Department of War, August 2, 1838, in *ibid.*, ms.).

[180] Jenkins, "Reminiscences," ms., p. 104.

[181] Bollaert, "Arrival in Texas in 1842, and Cruise of the Lafitte," *Coburn's United Service Magazine*, November 1846, pp. 341–355.

officers," and since the troops claimed the right of choosing their commander, he was unwilling again to subject himself to "the mortification of their refusal" to obey his orders.[182] The President's new instructions advised General Somervell that if the volunteers at San Antonio persisted in their determination not to organize under him, they "must depend upon their own resources," as they would not receive any recognition or support from the government.[183]

Finally, on April 2, Burleson disbanded the companies under his command, leaving to the men the privilege of returning to their homes or enlisting under General Somervell. Before letting the men go, however, Burleson made it clear that he was not responsible for their disbandment nor did he approve of it.

For you, soldiers, [he said] I will bear witness, that if you have not chased the barbarian enemy to his hiding place, and chastised him for his insolence and outrage, it is no fault of mine. If the President has thought fit, by a different course of policy, to disband a force which, by this time, might have been strong enough to have blead the enemy to his heart's core, I beg you to recollect that he is the constitutional 'Commander-in-Chief of the Army and Navy' and he alone is responsible for it.[184]

On April 6 an address to the citizens of Texas, believed by the *Galveston Civilian* to "benefit neither Gen. Burleson or the country,"[185] was issued over Burleson's name in which Burleson's conduct was defended. A few short excerpts from the address will illustrate its tenor:

I feel no hesitancy [he said] in believing that if my orders had permitted me to cross the Río Grande and retaliate upon our enemy his often repeated outrages, by this time 1,000 brave men would have been west of said river, inflicting a chastizement upon him which would have resulted in an honorable peace. But President Houston says that "120 days will be necessary before we can make a move against the enemy." His order put a finishing stroke to

[182] Edward Burleson, Commanding, to Brig.-Gen. A. Somervell, San Antonio de Béxar, March 31, 1842, and A. Somervell to Gen. E. Burleson, San Antonio, March 31, 1842, in Smither (ed.), *Journals of the Sixth Congress*, III, 45; *Telegraph and Texas Register*, April 20, 1842.

[183] Houston to Brig.-Gen. A. Somervell, City of Houston, March 25, 1842, in *Writings of Sam Houston*, IV, 85–86.

[184] Address of Edward Burleson to Citizen Volunteer Soldiers, Alamo, San Antonio de Béxar, April 2, 1842, in Smither (ed.), *Journals of the Sixth Congress*, III, 46–47; also printed in *Telegraph and Texas Register*, April 20, 1842.

[185] *Civilian and Galveston Gazette*, April 23, 1842.

all our present prospects of redress. Whether this plan can be executed under the burning rays of an August sun, yet remains to be seen. . . .

If any ask why it is that the Vice-President is in the field? my answer is that I love my country more than I fear the executive's displeasure. I did not stop to estimate the weight and dignity of my civic honors when that country was invaded and her capital threatened; but, with my often tried and devoted neighbors, rushed to her rescue, prepared to spill my last drop of blood defending the President's household. . . .

I still believe it of vital importance to the prosperity of Texas, that the campaign should have been made upon the valley of the Río Grande, so that both armies may be subsisted upon our enemies, for let us await the invasion of a large Mexican force, and though we may and will meet, and conquer them, even victory will be defeat to our pillaged citizens whose cattle must be eaten and whose fields must produce thistle instead of corn. We all recollect, that in 1836, the glory of our conquest was the starvation of our women and children—such glory I hope never again to witness. For one, I am free to admit that seven years' patient endurance of insult and injury—of outrage and oppression from our Mexican enemy makes me exceedingly anxious to end this war. A total disregard of all the laws of civilized warfare since the summer of 1835, has not only characterized his course, but even the friendly remonstrance of other nations has tightened our chains. What patriotic Texian can, in good temper recur to the murder of Col. Johnson, while under the sacred protection of a flag of truce, which the most savage Indian will respect? Can the plunder of our western towns, the abduction and murder of our best citizens, teach us greater patience. Or lives there a man deserving of the name of Texian, who does not feel self-reproach at the dying voice of the lamented Dimmitt, and the clanking of servile chains upon the brave Cooke and his compatriots, now menial scavengers of the dung-hills of the Mexican tyrant.[186]

Thus, Burleson not only defended his own conduct but criticized that of Mexico and evinced much asperity

towards the "Old Chief" [Houston]. Thus the Vice President of the Republic [wrote one of the President's close friends] has set himself up in opposition to the Executive of the Nation—a thing of which I believe not even the annals of Mexico can furnish a parallel. . . . [Burleson] has been made a tool—a "Cat's paw," to be wielded by the hands of others to the prejudice of the Administration. Not one syllable of his address did he write himself. But that will be explained when you learn that Thomas Jefferson Green, *et*

[186] Address of Edward Burleson to the Public, April 6, 1842, in *Telegraph and Texas Register,* April 20, 1842; Edward Burleson *To the Public,* Broadside; the address and letters are reprinted in Smither (ed.), *Journals of the Sixth Congress,* III, 43–47.

id omne genus, have been near his person. You can from this fact alone determine the rest. The object is to thwart the plans of the Executive, render him unpopular, and *make capital for the next* presidency! Oh! My Country! to be thus the unhappy victim of intrigue and design![187]

A few days after the publication of the Vice President's address, its "purported author" received a polite reprimand for his participation in the disobedience of orders at San Antonio. After requesting Burleson to use his influence to suppress the seditious acts of certain individuals in prohibiting the removal of the national archives from Austin, on the exposed western frontier, Houston warned, "if our friends in the United States find that the orders of government are to be disregarded and every man is to become a leader, or dictator, 'on his own hook,' our hopes will be short-lived; and even those who have rushed to aid us, by the first impulse, will soon withdraw from a cause which is not sustained by reason and law, and whose foundation is not order, subordination and civil rule."[188]

[187] W. D. Miller to William H. Daingerfield, Houston, April 13, 1842, in W. D. Miller Papers (Hardin-Simmons), ms. "Gen. B.," said the Galveston *Civilian,* "is one of our best men—unpretending, brave, and persevering as a soldier, and as devoted to the public interest as a man can be—but it unfortunately happens that, through the officiousness of bad advisers, he is some times tempted into the public prints, where he is much less at home than on the field of battle. He has no great capacity in his own for composition," being an extremely poor student of English, "and in this instance has unluckily availed himself of the assistance of some one much less capable than himself." *Civilian and Galveston Gazette,* April 23, 1842. "I think he [Burleson] is too illiterate for a public man, more especially to the office which he assumes," wrote a friend of Houston's during the election campaign of 1841. Thomas William Ward to Gen. Thomas J. Rusk, Sept. 15, 1841, in Rusk Papers, ms.

[188] Houston to Edward Burleson, City of Houston, April 11, 1842, in Smither (ed.), *Journals of the Sixth Congress,* III, 32–34; see also Same to Same, City of Houston, May 12, 1842, in *Writings of Sam Houston,* IV, 100–101.

CHAPTER SIX

Houston Assumes the Offensive
To Appease Texans

AS REPORTS CONTINUED to come in from the frontier regarding the size, nature, and retreat of the predatory Vasquez expedition, President Houston began to realize more and more that his predictions earlier in the year of Mexico congregating a large force upon the Río Grande from which to send into Texas parties of cavalry to annoy and injure the Texans were being fulfilled. Rumors from the Nueces had it that there were four hundred Mexicans at the Santa Gertrudis Ranch "catching and breaking horses of the enemy."[1] The senior editor of the *Galveston Daily Advertiser* and a strong advocate of public education, A. J. Yates, who had lately visited the ranch of Aubrey and Kinney, reported "he had a full and free conversation with the enterprising proprietors of that place, and with several other gentlemen resident there, and from them had learned that as far as they had been able to obtain information, the immediate invasion of Texas by a large force under Arista was intended."[2] Captain Valera, who visited the Rancho with copies of Arista's proclamation, had reported it was Arista's intention to enter the country with fourteen thousand men, to take possession of San Antonio and Victoria, and to establish himself in those places this spring and "pursue his operations through the remainder of Texas the following season. That his intention was to leave unmolested those who continued in the peaceable cultivation of their lands or the ordinary pursuits of business, and that his object was offensive only towards those whom he found arrayed in arms to impede his progress."[3]

[1] A. Jones to Col. William H. Daingerfield, Houston, March 31, 1842, in *Writings of Sam Houston*, III, 16 n–17 n.

[2] *Telegraph and Texas Register*, April 13, 1842, basing its information upon Yates' report found in the *Galveston Daily Advertiser*, April 4, 1842.

[3] *Ibid.*

While the President expected further incursions to be made by the enemy, the inhabitants in the western part of the Republic were noisily clamoring for permission to carry the war to the enemy beyond the Río Grande. Let the tocsin be sounded! Five thousand volunteers, it was said, with the cooperation of the navy could wring a peace from Mexico. The people of the west were anxious that the recent invasion of their homes and the threat to their future safety should not go unpunished. The President's own private secretary, Washington D. Miller, wrote urging that permission to invade Mexican territory be granted. The west was anxious for war. "Let them go," he said.[4] Soon thereafter we find the President himself writing, "1200 men can whip a Cavalliardo[5] of Mexicans. 'Tis so.' "[6]

On March 16, George Van Ness, one of the Santa Fé prisoners recently released by Santa Anna, arrived in Houston with a report that the Mexicans were making formidable preparations for an invasion, thus further stimulating the desire for action on the part of Texas.[7] He reported seeing ten thousand soldiers in San Luis Potosí, fifty wagons loaded with arms, and three hundred mule packs of ammunition assembled for a campaign.[8] Houston's ire toward the Mexican government was further increased by Santa Anna's new "pompous declaration," which reached Texas before the excitement attending the Vasquez invasion had subsided. This latest perfidy and trickery of President Santa Anna, wherein he tried to appear indignantly virtuous before the world, grew out of his receipt of a letter from General James Hamilton.

In 1839 the Texas agents who had been negotiating with the Mexican government for an acknowledgment of the Republic's independence got the idea from a Mexican named Juan Vitalba in New Orleans, who claimed to be the secret agent of the Mexican government, that Mexico might be bribed into according recognition of Texas independence. Much correspondence between the agents of the two governments followed, but nothing was accomplished. Later, availing themselves of what they believed to be an opportunity again to try their hand at brib-

---

[4] W. D. Miller to Sam Houston, March 27, 1842, in Washington D. Miller Papers, 1833–1860 (Texas), ms. copy.

[5] A *caballada* means a number of horses.

[6] Sam Houston to Ashbel Smith, n.d. [April? 1842], in *Writings of Sam Houston*, III, 14.

[7] Sam Houston to Brigadier-General A. Somervell, Executive Department, City of Houston, March 16, 1842, in *Writings of Sam Houston*, II, 505.

[8] A. C. Allen to Col. James Morgan, New Washington, [dated:] Houston, March 16, 1842, in James Morgan Papers, 1841–1845, ms.

ery, Colonel Barnard E. Bee[9] and Hamilton, although no longer agents of the Texas government, wrote Santa Anna on the subject. Lacking a means of direct communication with the Mexican authorities, however, Hamilton, in his desperate bid to regain prestige and influence in the affairs of Texas, resorted to trickery to get his letter delivered. He requested Sir Richard Pakenham, the British minister to Mexico, to transmit to Santa Anna "a sealed packet describing it as merely a personal letter 'of a confidential character'."[10] In his letter, marked "confidential," Hamilton proposed that if a treaty of peace and limitations could be made Texas would pay five million dollars. The five million dollars, he said, "I can place in London for this object within three weeks after receipt of the agreement together with two hundred thousand dollars, which will be secretly placed at the disposal of the Agents of the Mexican Government."[11] Santa Anna, assuming a role of self-righteousness, informed Hamilton that his offer of a bribe was "an insult and an infamy unworthy of a gentleman,"[12] and that Mexico would continue the war

[9] Born in Charleston, South Carolina, in 1787, Barnard E. Bee studied law; played a prominent role in the South Carolina nullification controversy; came to Texas in 1836 where he joined the army. Shortly after Houston's first inauguration as President of Texas, when Santa Anna was released from his Texas prison and sent under escort to Washington, D.C., to visit President Andrew Jackson, Bee, George W. Hockley, and William H. Patton constituted the escort. Bee countersigned a draft drawn by Santa Anna on a Vera Cruz bank, which draft the self-styled "Napoleon of the West" repudiated upon his return to Mexico, but Bee made it good in New Orleans and was later re-imbursed by the government of the Republic of Texas. For a while Bee served as Secretary of War under President Houston, and later as Secretary of State under Lamar, and afterwards as Texan diplomatic agent to the United States. He opposed the annexation of Texas to the United States. Bee returned to South Carolina and died there in 1853. Bee County, Texas, is named after him. Mrs. I. C. Madray, *A History of Bee County: with Some Brief Sketches About Men and Events in Adjoining Counties*, pp. 9–10.

[10] E. D. Adams, *British Interests and Activities in Texas, 1836–1846*, p. 80.

[11] James Hamilton to Santa Anna, on board the steamer *Forth*, on its voyage between Havana and New Orleans, from England, Jan. 13, 1842 (confidential), and Barnard E. Bee to Santa Anna, Dec. 27, 1841, in *Niles' Weekly Register*, LXII (March 26, 1842), 49–50; *Austin City Gazette*, March 30, 1842; *Telegraph and Texas Register*, March 23, 1842. See also H. Yoakum, *History of Texas from Its First Settlement in 1685 to Its Annexation to the United States in 1846*, II, 357.

[12] Santa Anna to James Hamilton, Feb. 18, 1842, and Santa Anna to Barnard E. Bee, Feb. 6, 1842, in *Niles' Weekly Register*, LXII (March 26, 1842), 50; *Austin City Gazette*, March 30, 1842; *Telegraph and Texas Register*, March 23, 1842. A lengthy extract from James Hamilton's reply to Santa Anna's letter of February 18 will be found in [George Folsom], *Mexico in 1842: A Description of the Country, Its Natural and Political Features; with a Sketch of its History, Brought Down to*

until she planted her eagle standard on the banks of the Sabine. Hamilton's proposal afforded Santa Anna an opportunity to destroy the bad impression made among his countrymen by his previous conduct in Texas when he had readily bartered that province for his life. Privately, "Santa Anna was only amused at Hamilton's cleverness in getting this bribe before him, and related the matter to Pakenham as a joke."[13]

Having answered Hamilton's letter, Santa Anna proceeded to give wide publicity to the correspondence in Mexico, the United States, and Europe. It first appeared in the newspapers of the City of Mexico on February 18, 1842, and later was widely reprinted. Seeing the correspondence in print, President Houston penned a lengthy letter to Santa Anna on March 21, criticizing the pretensions of the Mexican dictator. After reviewing the relations between Texas and Mexico since 1836 and disclaiming any official responsibility for the correspondence which had ensued between private citizens of Texas and the President of Mexico, he boastfully declared,

In the war which will be conducted by Texas against Mexico, . . . we will march across the Río Grande, and, believe me, Sir, ere the banner of Mexico shall triumphantly float upon the banks of the Sabine, the Texian standard of the single star, borne by the Anglo-Saxon race, shall display its bright folds in Liberty's triumph, on the isthmus of Darien.[14]

This bombastic brag likewise was widely circulated in the United States and Europe, and was published in Spanish in Yucatán, from where copies found their way into Mexico. Four days before, however, Houston, having received news of the Mexican evacuation of San Antonio, through the medium of the press in Texas, had already indicated to the people a change in his policy towards Mexico.[15] On March 17, the very day that Somervell arrived at San Antonio and partly in response to public pressure from various quarters, Houston informed one of the leading Texas newspapers that "war shall now be waged against Mexico, nor will we lay our arms aside until we have secured recognition of our independence. Until then I will never rest satisfied, nor will

the Present Year, to Which is Added, an Account of Texas and Yucatán; and of the Santa Fé Expedition, pp. 227–230. Hamilton's reply was dated "Charleston, S.C., March 21st, 1842."

[13] Adams, *British Interests and Activities in Texas*, p. 80.

[14] Houston to Antonio Lopez de Santa Anna, President of Mexico, City of Houston, March 21, 1842, in *Writings of Sam Houston*, II, 513–527; *Telegraph and Texas Register*, March 30, 1842.

[15] *Telegraph and Texas Register*, March 16, 1842.

the people of Texas. We invoke the God of Armies."[16] The tide of war, at any rate, was moving westward and could not be arrested, it was believed, until retribution had been taken for the injury committed in the sack of the western towns. "At what time or place that will be had it is not now possible or important to say. It is considered enough that the war has begun," wrote the President's private secretary. "It will be prosecuted in the best way and with the utmost efficiency in our power. Let us impel the ball until our independence is established fully and finally upon a basis too solid for the entire strength of all Mexico to shake."[17]

In adopting this new attitude in the Republic's relations with Mexico, Houston was aware of the many pitfalls ahead, but he was resolved to pursue a policy which he believed would prove most beneficial to the welfare of Texas and promote political quiet and stability at home. The late Mexican incursion, the popular clamor at home for revenge, and the boastfulness of Santa Anna, all in the brief space of two weeks, caused the President to change his opinions as outlined to George William Brown and others in order to meet the new situation. Two weeks before he had written in respect to the demand of "the people of Galveston" for offensive war against Mexico:

But months—if not years—would be required to present an army before the City of Mexico. . . . I have apprehended that the expressions of public meetings in Texas will be of no advantage to our suffering countrymen [the Santa Fé prisoners], but rather calculated to aggravate their sufferings. The language and epithets applied to the authorities who have the control of the prisoners, as well as those applied to the nation in general, cannot fail to excite corresponding resentment, which, in all probability will be an excuse for maltreatment, if not cruelty towards our friends. . . . Any reliance placed upon a plan of . . . [foreign aid], would in my opinion, prove abortive for the want of cohesion in the military leaders who would bring into camp their several commands. In this time of universal depression and pecuniary distress it would be utterly impossible to realize, from private contributions, the necessary aids in money and the indispensable munitions of war. Less than five thousand troops need not attempt the invasion of Mexico, with any hope of success; and for this force (an invading army) less than two and a half million dollars would not be an adequate supply. To defend a country requires comparatively but little means—to invade a nation requires every-

[16] Houston to the Editor of the *Galveston Advertiser* [?], Houston, Texas, March 17, 1842, in *Writings of Sam Houston*, II, 509; Postscript to Houston's letter to I. W. Burton, March 17, 1842, in *ibid.*, IV, 100–101.

[17] W. D. Miller to Sam Houston, Austin, March 13, 1842 (Private), no. 11, in Miller Papers (Texas), ms. copy.

thing. To conquer Mexicans in Texas is one thing—to battle with Mexicans in Mexico is a different kind of warfare.

The true interest of Texas is to maintain peace with all nations and to cultivate the soil. The first will enable her citizens to prosecute the latter; and if she should be invaded, the husbandman could be easily converted into the soldier. . . . The President of the Republic of Texas has no power to lend the flag of Texas to any nation, association, or enterprise not recognized by the constitution of the country.[18]

"I hope to God," wrote Anson Jones, a member of the Cabinet, "the President will act with promptness and energy and follow up the *Manifesto* by *deeds* corresponding to the *words* of that instrument. I want to see in the course of six weeks Matamoros, Tampico, and Vera Cruz in our power and a formidable army in the valley of the Río Grande threatening all Northern Mexico, and even Mexico herself. Then, I think, we may *negotiate* and settle the matter in short order."[19] Even though the invading force may by now have been captured or driven from the country, declared the editor of the *Telegraph and Texas Register*,

Texas should not rest satisfied. Her soldiers have been called to the field, and we trust, the sword will not be sheathed until her wrongs are fully avenged. We rejoice to learn that the President has determined to avenge the insult thus inflicted by our enemy. . . . Let our standard be once more borne to this Rubicon [Río Grande] of Texas, and the event will be no longer doubtful. Offensive war is the result, and our brave troops would soon be found wending their way towards the towering heights of the Sierra Madre. Here they could mark out a new boundary for our Republic, and dictate terms of peace that might be heard. We are not of the number who believe that the conquest of Mexico is at hand. Years must pass by, ere the resources of Texas even joined with those of our sister states, will permit this great work. Mexico has yet 8,000,000 of people, and cowardly, despicable as they are, the final effort that is to sustain her existence as a nation will be tremendous.—Crippled as Mexico is, she yet has a giant's strength, and the power that conquers must be mighty. We do not wish to advocate measures that are at this time to strike at her vitality; but merely by annoying her, and if necessary, severing a still larger portion of her territory, to humble her arrogance and

[18] Houston to George William Brown and Others, March 3, 1842, in *Writings of Sam Houston*, IV, 73–76; *Telegraph and Texas Register*, March 16, 1842. Brown came to Texas in 1842 for his health and was anxious to join an expedition against Mexico.

[19] A. Jones to Col. William H. Daingerfield, Houston, March 31, 1842, in *Writings of Sam Houston*, III, 16 n–17 n.

extort from her fears, an unwilling peace. This we think can be done with out exhausting our own resources. . . . The young men of our country, who are idle, are sufficient for the purpose. . . . Having the harbor of Matamoros in our possession, we could collect supplies of provisions, and military stores, and receive foreign troops at this point, and complete the necessary arrangements to carry on the campaign into the interior of the country.[20]

The western itch lay deep in the soul of the Anglo-Texas frontiersmen. A week later this same editor was belittling the "giant's strength" of the Mexican Republic. "It was the intelligence, the energy and the valor of Europeans or men of European descent," he said, "that sustained and directed them" in the days of her independence movement; "but these are gone, and the destinies of this wretched nation, are now in the hands of a miserable mongrel race, inferior even to negroes. . . . The miscreant [Santa Anna] who is now at the helm of government unites in his character, the lowest vices of the negro, with perfidy and cowardice of the Mexican. Mexico has nothing to hope from his virtues—Texas nothing to fear from his depravity."[21] "The people of Laredo, Mier and Camargo have suffered so much from the depredations of the Indians and our western cow-boys, that they are almost driven to despair and long for a change that will afford them protection," declared Dr. Francis Moore. "It is believed that most of them would cheerfully yield obedience to our government, if a sufficient force could be sent west of the Río Grande to give them confidence."[22]

In the meantime, however, the sloop *Phoenix* arrived at Galveston on the 23rd having left Corpus Christi on the morning of the 22nd. It dispelled the rumor that a large Mexican force was on the Santa Gertrudis,[23] near the Nueces. The *Lafitte*, it was presumed, since she had not been heard from for several days, had proceeded to the Brazos Santiago. However, on March 31 the *Lafitte* returned to Galveston with most of the Galvestonians on board—"all safe." The volunteers had gone only as far as Copano. "We regret," said the editor of the *Telegraph and Texas Register*, "that they did not visit the Brazos Santiago, [for] the very sight of a Texian Steamer in that port would have created an alarm at Matamoros, probably as injurious to Mexico as the late alarm at the West has been to Texas." The troops on the *Lafitte*, it was believed, could have captured the customhouse at Brazos de Santiago. "We

[20] March 16, 1842.
[21] *Telegraph and Texas Register*, March 23, 1842.
[22] *Ibid.*, May 4, 1842.
[23] *Ibid.*, March 30, 1842.

hope," continued the editor of the *Telegraph*, "the citizens of Galveston will not permit their warlike ardor thus to 'flash-in the pan,' but will again beat up for volunteers and send the *Lafitte* and the *Zavala* down the coast."[24] With the two companies of volunteers from Houston and Galveston and the recently arrived volunteers from Mobile, it was believed that serious damage could be done to the Mexican coast. Possibly Matamoros, with its garrison estimated at only three hundred soldiers, could be captured.

The President's comprehension of the difficulties to be encountered in conducting a successful war against Mexico is clearly apparent in a letter written to his private secretary the day after he issued a statement to the press declaring his policy to be "war."

War does not press upon us, [he said] and if it did, the government must move in its own orbit. We will be in no hurry, and one thing is true, that few *wise men* are hasty in *great business!* Weak men and silly ones are hasty; *wisdom is the result of reflection!* The people of Texas may rest assured that *I will never cease to war upon Mexico, until Independence is secured, or the nation is conquered!* Texas can't be conquered. No time until the present, has justified the resolution of carrying war into Mexico. I will now press the figure and trust to a brave people. Our cause is holy, and all we have to do now, is to act with wisdom, discretion, and valor!

You will rejoice, no doubt, at this determination, but, my dear Miller, you have only looked upon the lights of the picture! Remember the lights have their shades! When you contemplate all difficulties, and cast an eye upon the perspective, you will perceive, many objects, which a careless observer would not discover.

I will watch every thing.[25]

Having determined that Mexico should ultimately be invaded, the President began "coolly and deliberately" to execute his plans for raising and equipping an army without calling Congress in special session, believing that he could "not trust their wisdom in our present attitude," for he did "not wish bad made worse." Congress' failure at its last session to enact sensible, constructive legislation for frontier defense had been very discouraging to the President.[26] Accordingly, General Somer-

---

[24] *Ibid.*, April 6, 1842

[25] Houston to Washington D. Miller, City of Houston, March 17, 1842, in *Writings of Sam Houston*, II, 507–508.

[26] Houston to William H. Daingerfield, Lynchburg, April 1, 1842, *ibid.*, III, 14–16; Washington D. Miller to Ashbel Smith, Houston, Texas, April 6, 1842 (Private), in E. W. Winkler, *Manuscript Letters and Documents of Early Texians, 1821–1845*, pp. 257–263.

vell was instructed to defend the country from an invading force, and to enforce strict obedience to orders.[27] From those who wished to join the army, Somervell was to enlist two hundred men, *"well prepared* to pass the summer in service to range the frontier." Should he, however, be unable to secure the services of so many, he was to have organized two companies of fifty-six men each, "with orders to report to the President regularly." Colonel Hays' services were to be secured, if possible, to command this corps, whose chief objective would be "to range and spy from San Antonio to Corpus Christi, and Westward" during the next few months while an invading force was collected. "I repeat," wrote Houston, "that Texas *at this time is not in a situation* to invade Mexico; nor will she be before one hundred and twenty days."

Subsequently learning, however, that a considerable number of volunteers were on the frontier, at Béxar and Victoria, "damning the President" and anxious to advance against the enemy, Houston modified his orders to General Somervell to permit him to cross the Río Grande if his forces were "sufficient in strength and organization." If Somervell should attempt to invade Mexico, he was to enter the "country by the way of Laredo, or the most eligible crossing," taking such towns above Matamoros as he thought proper. By the time the towns of Guerrero (Reveilla), Mier, Camargo, and Reinosa had fallen, the President hoped to be able to cooperate by sea in an attack upon Matamoros.[28] Somervell was cautioned, however, against advancing upon Matamoros with an inadequate force, as it was very unlikely that any cooperation

[27] Houston to Brig. Gen. A. Somervell, City of Houston, March 18, 1842, in *Writings of Sam Houston*, II, 509–511. Two letters of the same date.

[28] You would be amused and miserably provoked at some of our "Heroes," [Houston wrote]. It has been reported by rumor (for that has been the only official) that Burleson was at San Antonio with 1500 men & Clark L. Owen with 1000 at Victoria, all burning with revenge to cross the Río Grande and "damning the President" that he would not let them go on. Oh, they were snorting!

In their fury I sent an order to Genl Somerville to march as many as wished to cross the Río Grande to take Reveilla, Mier, Camargo, and Rhinosa and by that time it might be possible to co-operate by sea, and then Matamoros would be an object. Well, the last news is that Burleson has at San Antonio about 600, and about 100 are under the immortal Genl [Albert Sidney] Johns[t]on of the Cherokee War. All as I suppose are "on their own hook." Genl Somerville was the only officer that I could by law order to the command—Genl of the 1st Brigade and Lieut. Brigadier! Somebody will be taken down a button or two!

Sam Houston to William H. Daingerfield, Lynchburg, April 1, 1842 (Private), in *ibid.*, III, 14–16. See also Sam Houston to General A. Somervell, Executive Department, City of Houston, March 22, 1842, in *ibid.*, II, 530–531.

could be expected by sea. Matamoros[29] was the chief military post on the lower Río Grande against which all the "would-be-generals" in Texas wanted to march forthwith. For some time among a segment of the population in Texas there had been a "foolish passion to take Matamoros without means."[30] "Until the upper towns on the Río Grande are taken and the stock driven in," advised the President, "it will not be wise to advance upon Matamoros. There should be system and cooperation in all important movements."[31] Houston was moving coolly, deliberately, and cautiously in the execution of his plan. He had no intention of letting Somervell or anyone else make more than a show of strength on the frontier to deter any further Mexican raids. At the same time he wanted Somervell, a dependable officer who knew how to obey orders, to command the "hot-heads." The plans of Burleson, Green, Johnston, and others for an invasion had to be thwarted, indirectly if possible without stigma to the Administration, in the interest of the country.

You will [continued the President in his orders to Somervell] be governed by the rules of humane and civilized warfare. Let no outrage be committed upon the peaceful inhabitants. Whatever stock and other property you can obtain from the enemy, you will have driven into Texas—taking good care not to weaken the force at your disposition. . . . There is always danger in sending out small detachments in an enemy's country. . . . You will not fail, if the campaign is prosecuted, to move as soon as practicable. . . . Should you cross the Río Grande do not permit yourself to be unprepared. You will prosecute your operations with caution, quickness and energy. By surprising the enemy, you will gain every advantage. Strike into them and they will flee before you: but do not let this supposition throw you off your guard.[32]

As an afterthought the President dispatched a second letter to Somervell on the 22nd, saying, "I hope you will find no sedition in camp, as no one has a shadow of a right to your rank or command. You command

---

[29] Matamoros was formally established as a city in 1823, created from a group of scattered ranch settlements known as the Congregación de Refugio, since 1796. Two years later work was begun on the port of Matamoros, and within a short time the city became one of the most important and strategic settlements on Mexico's northern frontier.

[30] Yoakum, *History of Texas*, I, 389.

[31] Sam Houston to Gen. A. Somervell, Executive Department, City of Houston, March 22, 1842, in *Writings of Sam Houston*, II, 531–532.

[32] Sam Houston to Brig.-Gen. A. Somervell, City of Houston, March 22, 1842, in *ibid.*, II, 530–531.

the first brigade—your brigade is in the field, and you have the orders of the President."[33] Although the First Brigade of the Texas Militia, comprising the militiamen of Brazoria, Fort Bend, Austin, and Washington counties, east of the Brazos, and having been under the command of Brigadier General Somervell since 1839, was now technically called into service, it was hoped that the volunteers at San Antonio would enlist in his brigade under his leadership.[34] When the men, however, refused to do so, they were presumed to be "on their own hook" and were eventually disbanded by Burleson, who himself had failed to obtain permission to lead them across the Río Grande. Many of the seven hundred men, all of whom were under the command of General Burleson, except one hundred volunteers under Albert Sidney Johnston, returned home, and most of those who remained did not care to serve under General Somervell.[35] Somervell instructed Captain Eli Chandler of Old Franklin in Robertson County, on April 9, to raise all the men he could for "the campaign." The recruits were to be enlisted for not less than three nor more than five months, and were to be organized into companies of fifty-six men, rank and file, under officers of their own choice. Provisions and munitions were to be furnished the men by the government upon their reporting at Béxar "mounted and equipped for service."[36] Late in April it was reported that about one hundred soldiers, apparently unorganized, remained at San Antonio awaiting the volunteers that were soon expected to start for the Río Grande.[37] Immense herds of cattle were said to be pastured in the valley of the San Antonio sufficient to afford meat for a large army for many months. However, the efforts to recruit a force failed.

As Somervell's "supposed" army disintegrated, Captain Hays, with a small company of rangers, remained upon the frontier as a corps of observation with headquarters at San Antonio,[38] and Captain Jesse Stiff

[33] Same to Same, City of Houston, March 22, 1842, in *ibid.*, II, 531–532.
[34] H. P. N. Gammel (ed.), *Laws* of Texas, II, 497–498, 579–580.
[35] John Henry Brown, *Indian Wars and Pioneers of Texas*, pp. 47–48.
[36] A. Somervell, Gen. 1st Brigade, T. M., to Capt. Eli Chandler, San Antonio, April 9, 1842, in Army Papers (Texas), ms.
[37] *Telegraph and Texas Register*, May 4, 1842.
[38] Hays was assisted by a small group of men under Captain Humphrey Bogart (Muster Roll, Captain Humphrey Bogart's Company, April–May 1842, in Texas Rangers, Muster Rolls 1830–1860, ms.). One G. Teas Elley of Hays' Company was taken prisoner by the Mexicans on June 1, 1842, and held in capativity until March 24, 1844. G. Teas Elley to the Congress of the Republic of Texas [undated], in Memorials and Petitions (Texas), ms.

commanded a small company of Fannin County Guards, enrolled for twelve months and stationed thirty-five miles from the settlements on the northwestern frontier in the late spring of 1842.[39] Somervell, himself, did not stay long at San Antonio, but on Saturday, April 30, returned to the seat of government at Houston to report in person to the War Department. On May 16 he was appointed collector of customs for the Port of Calhoun, on Matagorda Island, Matagorda Bay, where he entered upon the duties of his office on June 9.[40]

One company could not efficiently supervise the long frontier between San Antonio and Corpus Christi; so the President, on April 20, instructed Captain Ephraim W. McLean,[41] who had earlier commanded a detachment of troops in the Corpus Christi area, to raise a company of

[39] Muster Roll of Captain Jesse Stiff's Company of Fannin County Guards, April 22–May 19, 1842, in Texas Rangers, Muster Rolls 1830–1860, ms.

[40] Sam Houston to A. Somervell, City of Houston, May 16, 1842, in *Writings of Sam Houston*, III, 50; W. D. Miller, Private Secretary of the President, to Anson Jones, Houston, April 12, 1842, in Anson Jones, *Memoranda and Official Correspondence Relating to the Republic of Texas, Its History and Annexation—Including a Brief Autobiography of the author*, p. 187; Gammel (ed.), *Laws of Texas*, II, 511–513, 976; *Telegraph and Texas Register*, April 24, 1844; G. W. Hockley, Secretary of War & Marine, to Sam Houston, Dept. of War & Marine, June 23, 1842, in Harriet Smither (ed.), *Journals of the Sixth Congress of the Republic of Texas*, III, 109; A. Somervell to James F. Perry, Matagorda, June 28, 1842, in James F. Perry Papers, ms. From his post as customs collecter Somervell reported: "I find it very lonesome . . . at the Pass where I am obliged by the law to remain." *Ibid.* The ports of Lavaca and Matagorda were discontinued January 21, 1841, and the Port of Calhoun was established at the town of Calhoun on Matagorda Island. The Port of Calhoun was the port of entry for the area lying between the mouth of the San Antonio River and Cedar Lake. Deputy collectors were stationed at Matagorda and Linnville. In February 1844, Congress ordered the removal of the customhouse from Port Calhoun to Port Cavallo.

[41] Ephraim W. McLean was born in Christian County, Kentucky, in 1816, and died in Galveston, Texas, on January 31, 1896. As a youth he moved to Indiana, thence to Missouri, and late in 1835 started for Texas by way of Arkansas. He arrived in Texas with a herd of horses shortly after the battle of San Jacinto. He purchased the schooner *Columbus*, ninety-six tons, which he operated in the coastwise trade between Velasco and New Orleans, until the vessel was wrecked on the bar at the mouth of the Brazos in 1837. He then organized a company to look for a lost silver mine in the Washita Mountains. The expedition was gone seven months, and turned out to be a failure. In 1839 McLean joined the Rangers, and in 1840 was placed in command of a company and dispatched to the Corpus Christi area. "Upon his arrival he found not a solitary building there, but one small house had been commenced. Kinney and Aubrey, traders, and Simon L. Jones were about the only Americans there." *Galveston Daily News*, Feb. 1 and Oct. 18, 1896.

fifty-six men to serve as a corps of observation for six months pending the opening of the campaign against the enemy. McLean was given to understand that plundering upon the frontier was not to be permitted.[42] Later when Adjutant General James Davis was appointed commander of the southwestern frontier, McLean was instructed to report to him for orders. Unfortunately, however, "for the want of means, the order was not executed,"[43] as McLean found it impossible to recruit volunteers who had no hopes of receiving pay from a bankrupt treasury. In the meantime, Captain Hays was assisted by a company of fifty-two friendly Lipans organized under two chiefs, Flacco and Colonel John, who operated at times in conjunction with the Texas captain and at other times directly under orders from the War Department. The government was in arrears of pay to these friendly redskins.[44] In spite of the efforts to afford protection, a sense of insecurity and uncertainty hung over the western frontier, and many families began to move eastward. Yet, "for nearly two months past there had not been a single company of Mexican soldiers east of the Río Grande. The whole country had been left entirely unprotected."[45]

[42] Houston to Capt. Ephraim McLean, City of Houston, April 20, 1842, in *Writings of Sam Houston*, III, 34; Houston to Maj. James K. McCrearey, Houston, April 10, 1842, in *ibid*, IV, 89.

[43] Houston to Capt. Ephraim McLean, City of Houston, May 5, 1842, in *ibid.*, III, 44, Houston to the Senate, City of Houston, July 18, 1842, in *ibid*, III, 105–106.

[44] G. W. Hockley to Sam Houston, Depatrment [*sic*] of War and Marine, June 23, 1842, in Smither (ed.), *Journals of the Sixth Congress*, III, 107–112.

[45] *Telegraph and Texas Register*, May 4, 1842.

CHAPTER SEVEN

Preparing the Navy for Offensive Operations

HAVING DECLARED his intention of unfurling the single star of the Republic upon the Isthmus of Darien, the President proclaimed a blockade of the east coast of Mexico, from Tabasco to the Brazos de Santiago, to prevent the several vesssels which had been constructed in England and the United States for the Mexican navy from reaching their destination, as well as to cut off the enemy ports from foreign trade and commerce. The Texan consul at New Orleans reported that the Mexicans had bought the steamer *Natchez* and intended to use it for the purpose of blockading Galveston harbor.[1] Privateers were commissioned,[2] and plans were laid for collecting at the mouth of the Nueces a force for the invasion of northern Mexico.

Immediately upon receipt of the notice of the blockade, the French corvette *Brilliante* appeared at Galveston to learn all the details concerning it, and while there on June 15 the British brig of war *Victor* appeared off the bar and paid a visit to the island, where its captain received assurances from President Houston, then at Galveston, that the West Indian steamers would not be molested by the Texan cruisers.[3] Although the President received the British officer sent ashore to make inquiries about the blockade very kindly, "a ruffian-like volunteer from the states insulted him."

[1] By the President of the Republic of Texas, A Proclamation of Blockade, March 26, 1842, *Writings of Sam Houston*, II, 537–538; H. Yoakum, *History of Texas from Its First Settlement in 1685 to Its Annexation to the United States in 1846*, II, 355; the proclamation will also be found in the *Telegraph and Texas Register*, March 30, 1842; Sam Houston to Brigadier General Alexander Somervell, Executive Department, City of Houston, March 25, 1842 (Private), *Writings of Sam Houston*, IV, 85–86.

[2] "The government," wrote the President's private secretary, "will grant letters of marque and reprisal . . . to annoy the commerce of her enemy." W. D. Miller to Ashbel Smith, Houston, Texas, April 6, 1842 (Private), in Ashbel Smith Papers, 1838–1842, ms.

[3] *Bollaert's Texas*, pp. 99–101.

117

Since the inauguration of Houston, the Texan navy had not been inactive. It was, one might say, almost in exile. President Houston had no use for the naval alliance with Yucatán made during the Lamar administration, and repudiated it soon after taking office in December 1841. On December 15, three days after taking office, and two days after Commodore Edwin W. Moore had sailed from Galveston, Houston ordered the navy to return to Galveston to await further orders,[4] but Moore ignored the order when it reached him outside the Laguna de Términos bar at the port of Carmen on March 10.[5] With the commencement of what seemed to be another Mexican campaign against Texas, Houston became more conciliatory toward Moore, and dispatched from Galveston the eighteen-gun brig of war *Wharton* to Sisal to inform Commodore Moore of the proclamation concerning the blockade.[6] Houston ordered that Moore's small fleet, now re-enforced by the *Wharton*, commence enforcement of the blockade.

During the ensuing weeks, Moore took several prizes off the Mexican coast between Vera Cruz and Tuxpan.[7] Among those taken were the *Dolorita* and the *Dos Amigos*, both of Matamoros, but of little value.[8] The Mexican schooner *Progreso*, operating between Vera Cruz and Matamoros, was captured on February 6 in sight of Vera Cruz and sent to Galveston, where a portion of its cargo of flour and sugar was sold at auction. The flour was sold, without opposing bids, for $1.00 per sack of 220 pounds, to the local committee appointed to secure supplies for the Texan volunteers. "We can very well afford to carry on war while the enemy furnishes us with supplies upon such liberal terms," declared the *Galveston Civilian*,[9] and it might have been added, at the expense of their Yucatecan friends, who under the naval agreement, were to share equally in the prizes taken.[10]

---

[4] George W. Hockley to Commodore E. W. Moore, Department of War and Navy, December 15, 1841, in E. W. Moore, *To the People of Texas: An Appeal in Vindication of His Conduct of the Navy*, p. 43.

[5] Alex Dienst, "The Navy of the Republic of Texas," in *Quarterly of the Texas State Historical Association*, XIII (1909–1910), 37.

[6] Jim Dan Hill, *The Texas Navy: in Forgotten Battles and Shirtsleeve Diplomacy*, p. 156.

[7] Dienst, "The Navy of the Republic of Texas," in *Quarterly of the Texas State Historical Association*, XIII (1909–1910), 37.

[8] Report of the Secretary of War & Marine, Houston, June 23, 1842, in *Telegraph and Texas Register*, July 6, 1842; Hill, *The Texas Navy*, pp. 155–156.

[9] Quoted in the *Telegraph and Texas Register*, March 30, 1842.

[10] Hill, *The Texas Navy*, pp. 145, 153.

Somewhat to the disgust of Commodore Moore, Houston directed on May 3 that the *Progreso,* now in the hands of new owners, "be permitted to pass the blockade . . . and to *enter any one* of said [Mexican] ports without hindrance or molestation by the navy of this Republic."[11] Taking advantage of this passport, the *Progreso* sailed under Mexican colors from New Orleans, with four hundred kegs of powder, while Moore was there.

Thus, while there were businessmen and merchants in the United States who did not hesitate to sell and convey supplies for cash or on sound credit to either side in the Texas-Mexican war, those engaged in the cause of Texas did what they could to break up the trade in contraband with Mexico. While cruising some twenty miles off the mouth of the Mississippi on June 1 the sloop *Washington,* still registered under the United States flag, whose captain had obtained a privateer's commission from the government of Texas,[12] captured the schooner *Mary Elizabeth* of New York laden with 315 sacks of corn, two days after the latter had cleared the port of New Orleans for Tabasco. Concealed on board was a quantity of powder and lead not mentioned in the ship's manifest.[13] The captain was a Bayonnese, the supercargo was "Felice Tormento," and there were two Spaniards or Mexicans on board whose names appeared on the ship's list as "Henry Townsend" and "John Wilson." "Her papers appeared to show that she belonged to a Mr. Power of New York," reported an eye-witness, "but we have an idea that Mr. Power is a Mexican in Tabasco." According to the ship's papers, the *Mary Elizabeth* had been dispatched by Schmidt & Co. of New Orleans and consigned to Lobache & Co. Under these suspicious circumstances the vessel was sent to Galveston as a prize in charge of Lieutenant James D. Boylan and three others. Another privateer, the *Frolic,* chased a Mexican privateer into neutral waters off the Mississippi.[14]

The New Orleans merchants protested vigorously this interference with their Mexican trade. "It is a notorious fact," wrote the collector of

---

[11] George W. Hockley to Com. E. W. Moore, Dept. of War and Marine, Galveston, May 3, 1842, in Dienst, "The Navy of the Republic of Texas," in *Quarterly of the Texas State Historical Association,* XIII (1909–1910), 89.

[12] *Bollaert's Texas,* pp. 88–89.

[13] Thomas Gibbon Morgan, Collector, to Walter Forward, Secretary of the [U.S.] Treasury, Collector's Office, New Orleans, June 23, 1842, in Domestic Correspondence (Texas), ms. copy; *Bollaert's Texas,* pp. 88–89.

[14] *Bollaert's Texas,* p. 102.

customs at New Orleans, "that the Texian Government has not at this time and has not for more than a month had a single vessel of war cruising on the coast of Mexico, and the merchants of this city engaged in the Mexican trade complain with great cause of this interruption of their business—under the pretext that their vessels intended to force or evade a blockade, which has no real existence."[15]

While Moore patrolled off the coast of Mexico and Yucatán, he received word by the *San Bernard*,[16] which had been ordered to Galveston with dispatches and reports, that the President wished to see him. The fleet needed to be refitted, especially the key vessels, the *Austin*, the *Zavala*, and the heavy-gun brig *Archer*. The latter, although only recently put in commission, was badly in need of repairs, and the *Zavala*, at anchor at Galveston, was unseaworthy. Moore was to send his vessels to New Orleans at once for repairs, refitting, and provisioning. "Orders will be given that every exertion will be used to fit out the vessels instantly, and if possible," wrote Hockley, they will be ready by the time you join them at New Orleans.[17] The fleet was to be used, in part, to assist in transporting the volunteers from the United States ports to points along the Texas coast,[18] as well as in blockading the Mexican coast and in conducting a possible amphibious operation against the enemy.

Moore sailed on April 25 for Galveston from the east coast of Yucatán where he had been cooperating with the Yucatecan navy under Commodore James D. Boylan, formerly of the Texas navy, and collecting $8,000 a month rent from that rebel state for the assistance it received from the Texan navy. He reached Galveston on May 1,[19] and the following day began his conferences with the President at Houston. On May 3, the Secretary of War and Marine issued fresh orders to Moore. He was to proceed at once to New Orleans and outfit his vessels, after which he was to "proceed to Mobile for the purpose of receiving such supplies as

[15] Thomas Gibbon Morgan, Collector, to Walter Forward, Secretary of the [U.S.] Treasury, Collector's Office, New Orleans, June 23, 1842, in Domestic Correspondence (Texas), ms. copy.

[16] The *San Bernard* was commanded by Downing H. Crisp, the son of a commander in the British navy. *Writings of Sam Houston*, III, 362.

[17] George W. Hockley to E. W. Moore, April 14, 1842, in Moore, *To the People of Texas*, pp. 50–51.

[18] W. D. Miller to William H. Daingerfield, Houston, April 13, 1842, Miller Papers (Hardin-Simmons), ms.

[19] E. W. Moore to George W. Hockley, May 1, 1842, in Moore, *To the People of Texas*, pp. 60–61.

will be furnished by our Consul at that place," and then enforce the blockade against Mexico[20] and stand ready to assist in convoying all transports of volunteers from Mobile or New Orleans to Corpus Christi or other points along the Texas coast.[21]

Upon returning to the fleet[22] at Galveston, Moore found that his officers had resigned almost to a man, for they had not been paid since May a year ago. He assembled them and, after explaining the financial situation of the government and his new orders, appealed to their patriotism to resume their ranks. The officers withdrew their resignations, and the fleet, except for the *Wharton* and *San Bernard*, left at Galveston to protect the coast, was soon (May 8) underway to New Orleans. Eventually the *Wharton* proceeded to New Orleans, where she arrived on June 6 with only nine men before the mast, most of her enlisted personnel having vanished by desertion or expiration of enlistments.[23]

The *Wharton* was described as unseaworthy, but her commander, J. T. K. Lothrop, brought instructions from Hockley for Moore to proceed with the squadron "with the *utmost possible despatch* to enforce the blockade of the Mexican ports" in accordance with the Executive's proclamation.[24] The lack of money and the poor credit of the government, resulting from large unpaid debts, handicapped the outfitting of the fleet. By June 1 the schooners *San Antonio* and *San Bernard* had been provisioned at Mobile, thanks to the efforts of the patriotic citizens of that Gulf port; and the *Austin* had been sufficiently overhauled to be ready for immediate sea duty. Money, however, was still needed to pay for provisions and repair bills at New Orleans and to pay the two hundred and thirty officers and men who had been shipped for the four vessels; so, Moore dispatched the *San Antonio* under Lieutenant William Seegar early in June to Yucatán to collect $8,000 with the hope of

[20] George W. Hockley to E. W. Moore, May 3, 1842, in *ibid.*, p. 63.

[21] *Ibid.*, W. D. Miller to William H. Daingerfield, Houston, April 13, 1842, in Washington D. Miller Papers (Hardin-Simmons), ms.

[22] The fleet at that time consisted of the flagship *Austin*; the brig *Wharton*, eighteen guns; the brig *Archer*, eighteen guns; the *Potomac* (fit only as a receiving ship); the schooners *San Antonio* and *San Bernard*; and the useless steamer *Zavala*. The brig *Jim Bowie* seems to have been laid up at Galveston as unseaworthy. See G. W. Terrell to Ashbel Smith, Houston, Aug. 20, 1842, in George P. Garrison (ed.), *Diplomatic Correspondence of Texas*, in *Annual Report of the American Historical Association*, 1908, III, 1004–1006.

[23] Hill, *The Texas Navy*, p. 162.

[24] Moore, *To the People of Texas*, p. 71.

121

being able to get the whole fleet to sea against the common enemy. The *Austin* and the brig *Wharton,* at New Orleans, were expected to be ready for sea about July 7 or 8. By that time it was hoped that the *San Antonio* would have returned from its mission, and the squadron could proceed to sea to enforce the blockade or to carry out some other assignment. The *San Antonio* rejoined the fleet at New Orleans on July 1.

In the meantime, knowing that the rent from Yucatán would not meet his obligations and learning that Congress was to meet late in June, Moore repaired to Houston to lobby for the navy, reaching Galveston on June 30[25] and Houston on July 2. He remarked to an Englishman that the fleet would be ready before it was positively wanted.[26] The Congress appropriated $15,000 for reconditioning the *Zavala,* which had recently been beached at Galveston to prevent it from sinking in the harbor; $25,000 for provisioning the navy; $28,231 for the back pay of officers and men; and $29,428.50 for future payrolls.[27] Although Houston, the "Talleyrand of the Brazos,"[28] signed the appropriation bill, he refused to issue exchequer bills, claiming that there were already too many of these in circulation at half their face value. Finally, after Moore threatened to "disband the navy and leave the vessels to rot in a foreign port, as officers and men could not be kept aboard without rations,"[29] Houston agreed on July 30 to issue $18,812 in exchequer bills; but, at the time these were handed to Moore, he was also given a packet of "sealed orders" to be opened upon his arrival at New Orleans, but before he had spent any of the money.[30] When Moore reached New Orleans on July 31, he found that the "sealed orders" prohibited him from spending the exchequer bills which had been handed him in Texas. He was to place them in the hands of only such merchants, ship handlers, and other individuals who might be willing to extend credit for an indefinite length of time and "who were willing to hold a corresponding value of the exchequer bills as collateral."[31]

The Commodore's new purchasing power was not enough to get the fleet to sea. Among the sealed orders was a new proclamation of block-

---

[25] *Bollaert's Texas,* p. 106.
[26] *Ibid.*
[27] H. P. N. Gammel (ed.), *Laws of Texas,* II, 813.
[28] Marquis James, *The Raven: A Biography of Sam Houston,* p. 338, quoting Lamar.
[29] Moore, *To the People of Texas,* p. 83.
[30] Hill, *The Texas Navy,* p. 167.
[31] *Ibid.*

ade of the Mexican ports, which was to be in force three days after its publication by Moore in the New Orleans newspapers. The previous proclamation of blockade (March 26) had been suspended until the vessels necessary for its effectual enforcement could be refitted. In the wake of the collapse of Davis' command on the Nueces and the disbandment of the volunteers from the United States, many of the vociferous, disgruntled adventurers returning to the United States by way of New Orleans denounced Texas and Texas policies in unsavory terms. Under these circumstances Texan naval recruiting in the Crescent City practically came to a standstill, and desertions increased. The blockade was lifted before the fleet was ever able to put to sea.

In giving Moore and the navy the runaround President Houston was probably influenced by several factors. To begin with, his first administration had been embarrassed by the insubordination of the Navy Department. Furthermore, the new navy was a creation of the Lamar administration and its commodore owed his appointment to the President's greatest political enemy. During the last presidential election Houston had denounced the outgoing administration for meddling in Mexican politics and he certainly did not approve of the leasing of the Texas navy to the Yucatán rebels, thereby increasing the animosity of Mexico towards Texas. His motto seems to have been to "let sleeping dogs lie." The recent defiance of orders by Commodore Moore had not improved the situation. The Vasquez raid caused the President to swallow his pride temporarily and to prepare on all fronts to repel the Mexican invasion; but when it developed that the "invasion" was nothing more than an abortive raid, not likely to be repeated soon, Houston's apparent friendliness toward the navy subsided. The financial problem was the core of the whole matter. Texas was in no position to wage a full-scale war against Mexico. Yet, the "War Party" was for "keeping up the excitement and 'go ahead' even to the 'Halls of the Montezumas',"[32] and Houston was compelled to continue his plans for an expedition, knowing that it could not be successfully launched. He would quietly see that it was of sufficient strength, well supplied, properly disciplined, and properly led, before he would let it go. He knew his opponents too well to believe that this could ever happen.

In the meantime, Ashbel Smith, in New Orleans on his way to England as the Texan diplomatic agent, discussed with Saligny, the French chargé d'affaires to Texas, the propriety of the French government's

[32] *Bollaert's Texas,* p. 76.

sending a war vessel to the neighborhood of Galveston to look after the interests of the French merchants and their commerce in case the Mexicans should make a descent on Galveston by sea. The suggestion seemed to strike favorably the French chargé d'affaires, who was preparing to return to the Republic after his differences with Texas over innkeeper Bullock's pigs had ended.[33]

When the British government was told of the declaration of a blockade of the Mexican coast by the Texas president, Lord Aberdeen informed the Republic's chargé d'affaires in London that an efficient blockade of the Mexican ports by Texas would be recognized by his government, but that such a blockade would be likely to interfere with British commerce and to lead to misunderstanding, however carefully conducted.[34] The announcement of the blockade in England caused Mexican bonds to decline on the exchange. In England the Mexican and South American Association presented a memorial to Lord Aberdeen on June 3, denouncing the legality of the blockade. Generally speaking, however, the official announcement of the blockade in London "excited a lively sensation," reported Smith, and has "been productive thus far of the happiest effect."[35] Needless to say, the blockade did not sit well with the merchants of the United States nor with those of the leading European countries, whose governments protested that it was not a legal blockade according to international law. In conformance to one of the treaties signed with Texas in 1840, wherein Great Britain agreed to mediate between Texas and Mexico, the British government, together with that of the United States, was able to bring about a suspension of the blockade. As early as June 3 William Kennedy expressed the opinion that a suspension "might reasonably be conceded by the Government of Texas" until Great Britain and the other powers should have an oppor-

---

[33] Ashbel Smith to Anson Jones, New Orleans, March 16, 1842, in State Department (Texas), Foreign Letters, 1842–1844, ms. copy, pp. 77–78. Adding to the difficulties between Richard Bullock, innkeeper at Austin, and Alphonse de Saligny, the French minister, over the nonpayment of rent, was the killing of a number of pigs by the servant of the French minister, who discovered them entering the stable of his master to consume the corn intended for the horses. The full story of this incident and related complications resulting in de Saligny's demanding his passports and temporarily leaving Texas, are told in Stanley Siegel, *A Political History of the Texas Republic, 1836–1845*, pp. 160–162.

[34] Ashbel Smith to Anson Jones, Legation of Texas, London, June 3, 1842, in Garrison (ed.), *Diplomatic Correspondence of Texas*, 1908, III, 959–961.

[35] *Ibid.*

124

tunity to act.[36] The exchange of ratification of the three treaties between Texas and Great Britain was finally effected on July 28, the delay having been caused by the desire of Great Britain to appear completely neutral in regard to Texas-Mexican relations.

Englishmen in Texas, like Charles Power, and others were anxious for the difficulties between Texas and Mexico to be adjusted on an amicable basis. Such a settlement, wrote Power from Galveston to Sir Robert Peel, would promote "British interests, . . . and so raise up a Country which will afford our British Manufacturers a considerable market for her products as well as the raw material without being so dependent on the United States; whereas if something is not done I much fear from the financial state of matters here, that Texas may be lost to British enterprise and at least become annexed to the United States," for the people of Texas are of the conviction that their limited financial resources will not enable them long to cope with energy against Mexico and that they must eventually be forced into seeking annexation to their northern neighbor.[37] "The popular feeling" in Texas, wrote William Kennedy, "is undoubtedly swaying strongly towards annexation to the United States. And if this feeling is to be allayed, Great Britain must interpose her Mediation with effect for an *early* settlement of the differences between Mexico and Texas. To a young Country the threat of invasion is hardly less injurious than invasion itself. Mexico *can never conquer Texas*, and the sooner the present dubious condition of affairs is terminated the better for both."[38] At the same time, Power called upon Saligny, the French chargé d'affaires in Texas, to use his influence to awaken France to the desirability of maintaining the independence of Texas. And to Peel he wrote,

You know enough of the composition of the [American] people to know and feel that the European Govts. ought not to allow the race to travel beyond

[36] William Kennedy to Aberdeen, Monday [June 3, 1842], ¼ past 3 p.m., in Ephraim D. Adams (ed.), "Correspondence from the British Archives Concerning Texas," in *Quarterly of the Texas State Historical Association*, XV (1911–1912), 297; Aberdeen to Charles Elliot, Foreign Office, July 1, 1842, in *ibid.*, XV (1911–1912), 312–314; Garrison (ed.), *Diplomatic Correspondence of Texas*, 1908, III, 1014.

[37] Charles Power to Robert Peel, Galveston, Texas, June 20, 1842, in Adams (ed.), "Correspondence from the British Archives Concerning Texas," in *Quarterly of the Texas State Historical Association*, XV (1911–1912), 301–302.

[38] William Kennedy to Aberdeen, Austin, Texas, Jan. 28, 1842, in *ibid.*, XV (1911–1912), 257–258.

its present limits, for travel they will with their energy and the sooner some arrangement of Mediation for this Country [Texas], with a guarantee of those powers (United States, France, and England), in mediating a peace with Mexico the better. By this means the onward march may be arrested some 50 or 60 years and a good and lucrative trade carried on by them in the introduction of their manufactures

even to the extent of smuggling goods from Texas with her low tariffs into northern Mexico and the western states of the United States. "Every day," he declared, "is bringing the U. States in competition with us in manufactures of every description, and latterly the improvement is astonishing. The possession then of this Market, would afford them increased stimulus to the export of their products and drive us completely out of Market."[39]

While Texas prepared for an invasion of northern Mexico, and expected to use its navy upon the Gulf to harass Mexican commerce and towns, and to facilitate its own military operations, disturbing news concerning Mexico's efforts to rebuild a navy began to reach Texas. True, one of the schooners built at New York for the Mexican government was said to be still lying at anchor on March 2 in the harbor at Vera Cruz where it had been since early February when Commodore Moore in the *Austin*, accompanied by the *San Bernard*, had looked into that harbor. The schooner was still in possession of the American crew that had taken her out, Mexico having not yet fully paid for the vessel; however, it was expected that she would do so within a few days.[40] A second schooner had been lost on the Florida reef on her way out from New York.[41] The English steamer recently purchased from Captain Cobb was also in the harbor at Vera Cruz, but she was pictured as an inefficient vessel of about twenty-five years of age. One of her guns was described as of such caliber and weight that if fired would probably shatter the vessel itself.[42] Thus, during the spring and early summer, the units of the Texas navy, under contract to Yucatán, cruising off the coast of Yucatán and Mexico, were able to keep the Gulf clear of Mexican cruisers and to hold their steam frigate useless, for the Mexican

[39] Charles Power to Robert Peel, Galveston, Texas, June 20, 1842, in *ibid.*, XV (1911–1912), 301–302.
[40] *Telegraph and Texas Register*, March 30, 1842; Hill, *The Texas Navy*, p. 153.
[41] Dienst, "The Navy of the Republic of Texas," in *Quarterly of the Texas State Historical Association*, XIII (1909–1910), 36.
[42] *Telegraph and Texas Register*, March 30, 1842.

naval units dared not venture out from under the protecting guns of the Castle of San Juan de Úlloa.[43]

In April 1842 it became known that the Mexican government had contracted with the English firm of Lizardi and Company for two steam war vessels for its navy. Both were being built secretly in England. One, the *Guadaloupe*, of 775 tons and with 180 horsepower engines, was being constructed in the shipyards of John Laird at Liverpool on the river Mersey. It was an iron steamship with watertight compartments, and upon its delivery was probably one of the first iron men-of-war in the western hemisphere. The *Guadaloupe* mounted two long sixty-eight-pounders—one fore and one aft on swivels—and four twelve-pounders. It was expected to sail for the Mexican coast in June with an English crew under the command of Edward Philips Charleswood of the British Royal Navy.[44]

The other vessel being constructed in England was the *Montezuma*, a wooden steam frigate of modern design, 1,111 tons with two engines of 140 horsepower each. It was being built by Greens and Wigrams at the East India Docks on the Thames just below London. It was to be armed with one sixty-eight-pounder, two long thirty-twos, four thirty-two-pound carronades, and a small nine-pounder. The *Montezuma* was expected to sail about the same time as the *Guadaloupe* and to be manned likewise by an English crew under the command of a British naval officer by the name of Richard F. Cleaveland.[45]

[43] Report of the Secretary of War and Marine, Department of War and Marine, June 23, 1842, in *ibid.*, July 6, 1842.

[44] W. Pringle to Ashbel Smith, [London], July 8, 1842, Ashbel Smith to [Lord Aberdeen]. Legation of Texas, Sept. 17, 1842, in Garrison (ed.), *Diplomatic Correspondence of Texas*, 1908, III, 995, 1020–1021. Ashbel Smith to Col. James Morgan, London, June 9, 1842, in James Morgan Papers, 1841–1845, ms. Edward Philips Charleswood was commissioned a lieutenant in the Royal Navy, January 19, 1838, and assigned to the *Bellona* (72 guns) stationed at Plymouth, and was promoted to rank of commander, November 5, 1840. He joined the *Pembroke* (60 guns) as captain on March 1, 1858, and retired as captain, July 1, 1864. According to the Navy Lists, Public Records Office, London, England, he was in continuous service of the British Navy from 1838 to his retirement. At least his name appears every year in the Navy Lists. B. Harding to J. M. Nance, Public Records Office, London, March 26, 1963.

[45] Richard F. Cleaveland was commissioned a lieutenant in the British navy, October 14, 1834, and is first shown attached to a ship in the Navy Lists, Public Records Office, London, England, on July 25, 1837, when he joined the *Edinburgh* (74 guns) of the Lisbon Station. On July 29, 1839, he was promoted to the rank of commander. He was last entered in the Navy Lists in 1842. *Ibid.*

By April 1842, the construction of the two vessels in England was well advanced. It was rumored that they would sail with their guns mounted, and that the British officers had been given long leaves of absence from the Royal Navy. The vessels were expected to sail in late June and to reach the Gulf of Mexico about August 1. The *Guadaloupe* sailed on July 7 as a merchant vessel bound for La Coruña and Havana, but actually for Vera Cruz.[46] The *Montezuma* sailed from Gravesend on Thursday, September 27, having been delayed some six weeks because of the protest of the Texan agent in London against the fitting out from a neutral power of an armed vessel to war against his country. The *Montezuma* was finally given permission by the Lords of the Treasury to sail after its great guns and their carriages and the military stores connected with them were relanded and its crew reduced to that of a merchant ship of comparable size. It still had concealed on board, however, at the time of sailing a considerable quantity of ammunition and small arms.[47]

The British government observed a policy of strict neutrality in the war between Texas and Mexico, but sought to protect her rights under international law. She might not have been so cognizant of her rights and duties under international law, however, had it not been for the repeated protests of the Texan representative in England, Dr. Ashbel Smith, whose insistence caused the government to give its attention to the fitting out of the ships.

"So long as the Steam vessels in question," declared Lord Aberdeen, "are in the eye of English law, private property and unarmed, although they may be surmised, or even known, to be destined for the use of the Mexican Government, the British Government has no right to interfere with them; nor were the Vessels destined for the use of the Texian, instead of the Mexican Government, would the conduct of Great Britain be altered in any particular."[48] The government, it was contended, had no connection with the building of the vessels; and under British law such vessels could be built in England to be sold to anybody like other merchant vessels. Sailors were privileged to go where they pleased and

[46] [William] Pringle to Ashbel Smith, [London], July 8, 1842, in Garrison (ed.), *Diplomatic Correspondence of Texas*, 1908, III, 995.

[47] Ashbel Smith to Anson Jones, London, Oct. 3, 1842, in *ibid.*, 1908, III, 1023–1024.

[48] Aberdeen to Charles Elliot, Foreign Office, July 16, 1842, in Adams (ed.), "Correspondence from the British Archives Concerning Texas," in *Quarterly of the Texas State Historical Association*, XV (1911–1912), 322–324.

to enter whatever service they so desired, but officers could not.[49] Ordnance and munitions of war could be exported from England but not in a condition to be used on a vessel offensively. Ashbel Smith was able to cause a limited delay in the sailing of the vessels for the Mexican service, to have the royal naval commanders warned that if they entered the Mexican naval service they would have to terminate their relation with the British navy, to have the size of the English crews reduced to merchant-ship equivalents, and to prevent the guns of the vessels being mounted in English ports.[50] Privately Smith wrote, "It has been generally believed in America that England is assisting Mexico. After the most careful inquiry, I do not discover any ground for such an opinion, though I am well aware that Mexico possesses the sympathies of this country."[51]

General James Hamilton left England for Boston shortly before the *Montezuma* sailed from England on September 27 bound for Vera Cruz. His concern for Texas was great. Upon his arrival at Boston he requested the Texan chargé d'affaires, James Reily in Washington, to meet him in New York, where he wished to learn if Paixhan guns had been forwarded to Texas from the United States and to get a firsthand report on the munitions-of-war situation in Texas, for he felt that Texas was likely "to have warm work before many months."[52]

The *Guadaloupe* and *Montezuma* reached Vera Cruz in November 1842, and their guns were then mounted. By that time the British government had issued orders for all British officers and seamen in the Mexican service to return home. Before Christmas the two new additions to the Mexican navy had joined the Mexican fleet off Yucatán, consisting of *Yucateco* (brig), *Iman* (brig), *Aguila* (schooner), *Campechano* (schooner), *Regenerador* (armed merchant steamer) plus several supply ships and troop transports.[53]

At the time of the Vasquez raid the United States was involved in

[49] Ashbel Smith to Anson Jones, Legation of Texas, London, July 3, 1842, in Garrison (ed.), *Diplomatic Correspondence of Texas,* 1908, III, 971–976.

[50] Peel stated in the British House of Commons on August 2, 1842, that application had been made to permit the vessels to be manned by British seamen, but that permission to do so had not been granted. Ashbel Smith to Anson Jones, Legation of Texas, Paris, Aug. 13, 1842, in *ibid.*, 1908, III, 1001–1002.

[51] Ashbel Smith to Col. James Morgan, London, June 9, 1842, in Morgan Papers, ms.

[52] J. Hamilton to Anson Jones, Boston, Oct. 5, 1842 (Private), in Garrison (ed.), *Diplomatic Correspondence of Texas,* 1908, III, 1025.

[53] Hill, *The Texas Navy,* p. 173.

diplomatic efforts to effect the release of the Santa Fé prisoners, many of whom were citizens of the United States. In view of the developments between Mexico and Texas in March, the Texan chargé d'affaires in Washington, James Reily, assumed the responsibility of suggesting that the United States mediate the difficulties between the two countries. President John Tyler and his Cabinet approved the suggestion, and General Waddy Thompson, the United States minister to Mexico, was accordingly instructed to offer the mediation of his government to end the war. Thompson, however, found the Mexican government hostile to the suggestion and infuriated at the United States for the aid being given Texas by its citizens. Strong diplomatic notes were exchanged between the two countries. Bocanegra, the Mexican minister of foreign relations, accused the United States of not adhering closely to the international rules governing neutrality. The United States, he said, had permitted the continued hostility and aggression of its citizens against Mexican territory. He firmly refused to consider the American offer of mediation, and gave every indication that Mexico intended to reconquer Texas. He assumed that Texas was still a part of Mexico, and that immigration into it from the United States was a violation of Mexican law.[54]

The United States decided that it did not wish to jeopardize the successful conclusion of the Webster-Ashburton negotiations then in progress between the United States and England by antagonizing England with strong demands upon Mexico in favor of mediation. Consequently, the proposition of mediation was not pushed vigorously.

After the exchange of ratification of the several treaties[55] with Great Britain at the end of July 1842, Dr. Ashbel Smith, the newly appointed Texan chargé d'affaires to England, went to France in the midst of his

[54] Daniel Webster to Waddy Thompson, Washington, June 22, 1842, William R. Manning (ed.), *Diplomatic Correspondence of the United States: Inter-American Affairs*, Vol. 8, pp. 108–110; James Reily to Anson Jones, Legation of Texas, Washington, June 24, 1842, Garrison (ed.), *Diplomatic Correspondence of Texas*, 1907, I, 563–566; Thomas M. Marshall, "Diplomatic Relations of Texas and the United States, 1839–1843," *Quarterly of the Texas State Historical Association*, XV (1911–1912), 281–283; George L. Rives, *The United States and Mexico, 1821–1848*, I, 507–513.

[55] Three treaties were signed with Great Britain in November 1840. These were (1) treaty of commerce and navigation; (2) treaty providing for British mediation with Mexico; and (3) treaty for the suppression of the slave trade. The exchange of ratification of these treaties took place on July 28, 1842. Joseph William Schmitz, *Texan Statecraft, 1836–1845*, p. 150.

controversy with England over the construction and fitting out in British ports of steamers for the Mexican navy. His instructions from Texas were to secure the assistance of England and France to act in concert with the United States in mediating the difficulties between Texas and Mexico and in bringing the "war of pillage and assassination upon our defenceless citizens" to a close.[56] Guizot, the French premier, indicated a readiness to cooperate with Great Britain and the United States, but believed the latter would be unwilling to join in a triple representation because of its strained relations with Mexico.[57] At London, however, Smith found that Lord Aberdeen, Secretary of Foreign Affairs in the Peel Ministry, did not favor the plan for triple mediation and refused to cooperate with France and the United States on the matter, believing the effort useless unless all were prepared to enforce peace on Texas and Mexico, and such a step the British government was not ready to take.[58] The British government had already transmitted instructions to its Minister at Mexico, Pakenham, to work unilaterally for mediation. For some time Pakenham's enthusiasm and confidence regarding Texas had been unbounded, but Hamilton's trickery in getting him to pass a personal letter "of a confidential character" to Santa Anna, which was everything but a personal letter, not only angered him, but made him mistrustful of Texan agents in the future. To him the unauthorized Texas Santa Fé expedition seemed to be a conspiracy to overthrow the government of New Mexico, and Houston's declaration of a blockade of the Mexican coast seemed preposterous. Addington, the Undersecretary of Foreign Affairs, informed Pakenham that Lord Aberdeen had expressed the view "that perhaps the *sole* mediation of England promises quite as much as the 'triple interposition' proposed."[59] Relations between the United States and Mexico were quite strained as evidenced by the recent exchange of notes between the two countries, and the Mexican feeling toward France, since the bombardment of Vera Cruz

[56] Anson Jones to Ashbel Smith, City of Houston, June 7, 1842, in Garrison (ed.), *Diplomatic Correspondence of Texas*, 1908, III, 963–965.

[57] Ashbel Smith to Francois P. G. Guizot, Legation of Texas, Paris, Aug. 15, 1842 (copy); Same to Anson Jones, Legation of Texas, Paris, Aug. 15, 1842; Same to Same, Legation of Texas, London, Aug. 31, 1842, in *ibid.*, 1908, III, 1387–1388; see also, *ibid.*, 1908, III, 1383–1384, 1385–1387.

[58] Ashbel Smith to Albert T. Burnley, Paris, Nov. 20, 1842, in Smith Papers, ms. copy.

[59] Ashbel Smith to Anson Jones, Legation of Texas, London, Aug. 31, 1842, in Garrison (ed.), *Diplomatic Correspondence of Texas*, 1908, III, 959–961. See also Same to Same, Legation of Texas, June 3, 1842, in *ibid.*, III, 1385–1387.

in 1839, could not be regarded as very friendly. Britain declined to join with the United States in an effort to mediate the Texan-Mexican affair. Great Britain was jealous of her favored position in Mexico, and was apparently afraid that "triple mediation" might break down Mexico's hostility toward the United States and France and endanger the veritable monopoly of trade which her subjects enjoyed. Mexican recognition of Texas independence might lessen in some quarters in the United States opposition to the annexation of Texas, which envisaged annexation as meaning also the annexation of a war with Mexico.

Pakenham presented an offer of mediation by Great Britain to the Mexican government, but late in August 1842, Santa Anna rejected emphatically any mediation based on the independence of Texas.[60] The Mexican situation was a difficult and rather hopeless one. Santa Anna's government was a purely military one, and such a government could not exist long without an excuse. The war against Texas furnished a good pretext for keeping up the large army on which his powers rested. A war against Texas had great popular appeal and no man at the head of affairs in Mexico, however disinterested or enlightened, could remain in power for long if he entertained the question of recognizing the independence of Texas. The financial embarrassments of Texas and recent difficulties concerning the volunteers from the United States were known in Mexico, and the Mexicans, it was said, "believed the present to be a favorable opportunity to reconquer the country."[61] It was reported in England that Mexico was determined to prosecute the war efficiently against Texas and to commence hostilities early next spring. Indeed, the reconquest of Texas, if the attempt were made with energy, seemed far from an impossibility even to Pakenham.

[60] Ashbel Smith to Anson Jones, Legation of Texas, London, Oct. 17, 1842, in *ibid.*, 1908, III, 1026–1029.
[61] *Ibid.*

CHAPTER EIGHT

Recruitment of Men and Supplies
from the United States

SINCE IT WAS NECESSARY, wrote the President, "to look to our 'Uncle Sam' for our great business in the work of invasion,"[1] agents were dispatched to various points in Louisiana, Tennessee, the Carolinas, Alabama, Kentucky, Illinois, and elsewhere to recruit men, money, and munitions for such an enterprise. William H. Daingerfield, a Virginian, recently senator from Béxar, and Secretary of the Treasury, was dispatched as "special commissioner" to New Orleans "for the purpose of giving proper direction" to such aid as the citizens of the United States might wish to render to Texas in her contest with Mexico.[2] He was, however, "to have it *noticed* and *impressed* upon the public that 'self created' agents, said to be of Texas, are no agents, but imposters."[3] When, toward the end of April, Daingerfield ascended the river to Nashville to pursue an affair of love, Colonel Barry Gillespie was appointed "general agent" of Texas to New Orleans to have charge of all transactions in the Mississippi Valley having to do with the furnishing of troops and aid to Texas in her present crisis.[4] Abner S. Lipscomb, former circuit judge and chief justice of the Supreme Court of Alabama for eleven years before coming to Texas, where he served as Secretary of State under Lamar, was named "General Agent of Texas for the State of Alabama"; however, the Texan consul at Mobile, General Walter Smith,

---

[1] Houston to William H. Daingerfield, Lynchburg, April 1, 1842, (Private), in *Writings of Sam Houston*, III, 14–15.

[2] Houston to William H. Daingerfield, Executive Department, City of Houston, March 25, 1842, in *ibid.*, IV, 86–87.

[3] Houston to William H. Daingerfield, City of Houston, April 10, 1842, in *ibid.*, III, 21–22.

[4] Houston to Col. Barry Gillespie, Executive Department, City of Galveston, April 30, 1842, in *ibid.*, III, 41–42.

was to act in that capacity until Lipscomb could arrive.[5] Colonel Lewis M. H. Washington, who had served on the staff of Colonel James W. Fannin, left his plantation on the Trinity to offer his services to the government and was dispatched by the President early in April to New Orleans to recruit volunteers[6] and lay plans for acquiring steamers or securing their use for conveying men to Texas or against Matamoros. He was authorized to act or spend funds received without waiting for orders from the Secretary of War.

Major General John C. Pickens, commanding the Third Division of Alabama state militia, was informed that if he could bring one thousand emigrants to Texas by the last of June or July 10 he would be accorded the rank of brigadier general and be subject to the orders of only the President or the Secretary of War. He would need, he was told, at least ten wagons for his command. He, too, was informed that his men must be "completely armed, munitioned, clothed, and provisioned for six months," but that it would only be necessary to bring two months' provisions with the command. It was suggested that he bring equipment for one hundred cavalry. His men were to be landed at Copano. If he should be unable to raise the full force by the time suggested, he was urged to bring half of them, and leave behind instructions for the second regiment to follow as soon as it could be raised and organized.[7] Also, in Alabama, the services of Colonel Martin A. Lea at Mobile, brother-in-law to President Houston, were enlisted.[8]

Major Nicholas Cruger, who had important friends and family connections at Charleston, was detached from military service at Galveston Island and sent to South Carolina "to raise funds and men to an unlimited extent for the army of Texas"; the volunteers so raised were to serve under his immediate command.[9] In case Cruger should be unable

[5] Houston to General Walter Smith, City of Galveston, Texas, April 30, 1842, in *ibid.*, IV, 90–91; III, 40 n–41 n.

[6] Houston to William H. Daingerfield, Lynchburg, April 1, 1842 (Private), and A. Jones to William H. Daingerfield, Houston, March 31, 1842, in *ibid.*, III, 14–16, 16n–17n; Houston to Col. H. Washington, Galveston, May 1, 1842 (Private), in *ibid.*, IV, 91–92.

[7] Houston to General [John C.] Pickens, City of Galveston, May 1, 1842, (Private), in *ibid.*, IV, 92; Military State Register (Alabama), ms.

[8] Houston to Col. Martin A. Lea, City of Galveston, May 2, 1842, (Private), in *Writings of Sam Houston*, IV, 93.

[9] Col. Alden A. M. Jackson to Major Nicholas Cruger, Headquarters 2nd Regt., 2nd Brigade, Galveston, April 29, 1842, in Army Papers (Texas), ms; Sam Houston to Major N. Cruger, Galveston, April 30, 1842, in *ibid.* Upon his return to Texas

to "raise means sufficient to carry out the expedition now intended, which I have fully explained to you," Houston wrote, you are authorized "to promise and guarantee the reembursement of any funds, that you may be able to raise from influential individuals out of the very first military chest the army may possess."[10] The private expenses of the agents sent to the United States were to be deducted from funds that they might raise.

To facilitate recruiting in the United States and cooperation from local citizens, President Houston issued a lengthy "proclamation to all Texans" on April 14,[11] setting forth the causes for taking up arms against Mexico, and the organization and discipline of the army to be raised. "Repeated aggressions upon our liberties," he began "—the late insult offered by a Mexican force advancing upon Béxar—and the perfidy and cruelty exercised towards the Santa Fé prisoners, all demand of us to assume a new attitude—to retaliate our injuries and to secure our independence." In adopting this new course which the Texan government finds itself compelled to pursue, he continued,

neither passion nor prejudice has been cast into the scale. Reason urged by necessity and sanctioned by patriotism, induces its adoption. We have sought to avoid war, because we have experienced its calamities. We have desired peace, because its influences are mild and beneficial. We wish to become husbandmen and farmers, and we are not emulous of warlike distinction. Our desires, however, have been set at naught, and we are enforced to the execution of our purposes.

Until the late events alluded to, a partial peace had existed for the last six years. . . . We had hoped that her [Mexico's] unfound prejudices and national animosity towards the Anglo-American race would have died away, [but] her vanity knows no bounds, and her stupidity can only be corrected by inflicting upon her tyrannic rulers the severest punishment.

And like a great United States president of the twentieth century in reference to another power, Houston carefully distinguished between the government of Mexico and the people of Mexico.

Major Cruger was promoted to the rank of colonel on June 10, 1842, and assigned to President Houston's staff as an aide-de-camp. George W. Hockley to Col. [Nicholas] Cruger, Dept. of War and Marine, Houston, June 10, 1842, in *ibid.*

[10] Houston to Major N. Cruger, Galveston, April 30, 1842, in *ibid.*; also in *Writings of Sam Houston*, III, 42–43.

[11] Address of the President of the Republic to the People of Texas, Executive Department, City of Houston, April 14th, 1842, in *Telegraph and Texas Register*, April 20, 1842.

It is not the peaceful citizens of Mexico upon whom we are to make war [he declared]. It is to be made upon the self-created authorities of the country —upon those who have usurped the rights of the people and become their oppressors. Oppression has broken down the spirit of the community. Liberty among them is but a name; and the term *Republic* is used only to sanctify the ends of extortion.

Mexicans experience more debasement under their present authorities than they did under the vice-royalty of Spain. Their armies are maintained by exactions. Under the name of volunteers they are impressed and driven in chains, like cattle to the market, for the purpose of filling the ranks of the army. They are not in a situation to resist these acts of outrage; for they are deprived of the use of private arms. Millions sigh in secret and desire the return of the happiness and protection which they enjoyed anterior to the revolution of 1812. If they had power, they would fain throw off the yoke which now galls their necks. A people under such circumstances would rejoice at an opportunity to cast aside their manacles and enjoy the privileges of self-government. They would hail the people of Texas as friends to liberty —friends to order—friends to equal rights, and enemies to the tyrants of the Mexican people. Their dictator proclaims that he will subdue Texas. He cannot do it. He is well aware of this truth; yet he has the power to molest our frontier and depredate upon our border citizens. We can no longer submit to these annoyances. We have the means and we will use them to prevent the evils with which he would visit us.

Thus is Texas compelled to make war; a war not of aggression, but one which the civilized world will justify—one that is due to ourselves—one to which Mexico has provoked our exertions—one to be conducted upon the most exalted principles—not directed against the nationality of Mexico—not opposed to its religion, but a war upon its despots and oppressors.

The President asserted his belief that the war could very easily be financed by the sale of public land, an idea which he was to reject less than three months later. However, at this time (April, 1842) he recognized the deplorable financial condition of the country;

yet, [he said] Texas possesses boundless wealth. Her hundred and fifty million acres yet vacant and unappropriated, lying in a region the most delightful— blessed by the influence of a genial climate and the redundancy and variety of its productions—all unite to render it the most inviting portion of the globe. Watered by beautiful rivulets and navigable streams, with a soil of unequalled fertility, Texas, with these advantages, and when her lands are brought into market, will possess the means to compensate those who may render aid in her present circumstances.

He blamed the last session of Congress for not providing for the sale of

136

the Cherokee lands, which, he claimed, would have brought millions of dollars into the treasury and

would have sustained the country in every emergency—prevented all burthens of taxation, and induced an enterprising, wealthy and intelligent emigration from the United States and from Europe. But that, like every other measure recommended by the Executive, which had for its object the defence or protection of the country, met with an unfavorable reception by the Honorable Congress, which left him in a most unenviable situation. He is responsible for the performance of certain duties under the constitution, and yet denied the requisite means for their execution.

He called for the immediate organization throughout the Republic of volunteer companies of fifty-six men each, who were to remain at home until called into service. In the meantime, he declared, "all troops who may attempt to visit the frontier, under the name of volunteers, and depredate 'upon their own hook' *will not meet with the sanction of the government;* because they will be acting in violation of the laws."

The people of Austin and the Upper Colorado who were so bitter against the President's order for the removal of the archives from Austin, believing the execution of the order as equivalent to the abandonment of the seat of government, its reoccupation by the savages, and the ruination of the western country, were said now to think less harshly toward the President since his proclamation of warring unceasingly against Mexico until independence had been secured or Texas conquered.[12] Although by March 26, when the Secretary of War and Marine left Austin, "the better part of the citizens of Austin" were said to have left the place, the few families who remained were determined to resist a removal of the archives at all hazards.

The Texan consuls Alexander H. McGuffy at Cincinnati, John Brower at New York, General Walter Smith at Mobile, and P. Edmunds at New Orleans were quite active in taking up contributions and supplies for Texas.[13] James Reed of James Reed and Company was named receiving

[12] W. D. Miller to Ashbel Smith, Houston, April 6, 1842 (Private), in Ashbel Smith Papers, 1838–1842, ms.

[13] Houston to Walter Smith, Galveston, April 30, 1842 (Private), in *Writings of Sam Houston,* IV, 90–91; Same to Same, Houston, May 12, 1842 (Private), and Same to John Darrington, May 12, 1842 (Private), in *ibid.,* IV, 102–105. Smith's resignation of the consulship at Mobile was accepted in October. See Anson Jones to Gen. Walter Smith, Dept. of State, Washington, Oct. 5, 1842, copy in Consular Correspondence (Texas), 1838–1875, ms.; Alexander H. McGuffy to James S. Mayfield, Texan Consulate, Cincinnati, Sept. 14, 1842, and Same to Anson Jones,

and disbursing agent at New Orleans for the Texas government.[14] It was reported at Houston on March 30 that the citizens of Mobile had chartered a steamboat and fitted out two companies of soldiers amounting to two hundred men to join the army of Texas.[15] These were expected to reach Galveston in a few days. Colonel M. E. Holliday at Parkersburg, Virginia, offered his services to raise and bring volunteers to Texas.[16]

Let Texas, suggested the New Orleans *Commercial Bulletin*,[17] call to "her standard the thousands of impatient daring, and ambitious spirits in the South West, by whom a march to the city of Montezuma would be embraced as an adventure full of fun and frolic, and holding forth the rewards of opulence and glory." In the same tone the *New Orleans Bee*[18] declared, "Texas has drawn the sword in earnest—let her melt the scabbard into bullets. The eager hand of destiny has drawn the curtain" that reveals to the gaze a prize richer than a poet's dream. "Who will not take a part in the great contest now so vigorously begun? An empire is the prize and the world for spectator!" The Mexican consul at New Orleans, Francisco de Arrangoiz, reported to his government that the *New Orleans Bee* of March 28 had asserted that the late Mexican invasion of Texas was nothing more than a pretext to carry out the abolition of slavery; that the Vasquez expedition took place at the instigation of England and was financially supported by that government; that in case of a war between England and the United States, Mexico would declare also against the United States and would arm the Indians and Negroes of the southern states.[19] The *Bee* may not have been entirely wrong, for

Consulate of the Republic of Texas, Cincinnati, March 31, 1843, in *ibid*. P. Edmunds was appointed Texan consul at New Orleans in February 1842 (*Telegraph and Texas Register*, Feb. 9, 1842); Anson Jones to William Bryan, Department of State, Austin, Feb. 7, 1842, in Consular Correspondence (Texas), 1838–1875, ms. copy.

[14] P. Edmunds to W. D. Miller, New Orleans, May 3–10, 1842, in Washington D. Miller Papers, 1833–1860 (Texas), ms.

[15] *Morning Star* quoted in *Telegraph and Texas Register*, March 30, 1842.

[16] Houston to Col. M. E. Holliday (Private), Houston, Texas, May 6, 1842, in *Writings of Sam Houston*, IV, 93–94; M. E. Holliday to Sam Houston, Parkersburg, Va., April 10, 1842, has not been found.

[17] March 17, 1842.

[18] March 31, 1842.

[19] F. de Arrangoiz ál Ministro de relaciónes exteriores y gobernación, Mexico, Consulado de la Republica Mexicana en Nueva Orleans, E. U., New Orleans, March 28, 1842, in "Relaciónes Exteriores Reseñas Politicas, 1841–1842. Estados Unidos 1842," Barker Transcripts, from the Archivo de la Secretaría, ms.

the informal talks between Lord Ashburton and Webster to settle the multiple differences between Great Britain and the United States had not yet begun; and Ashbel Smith, on his way to England at this time, was assured by M. de Saligny in New Orleans that the latter had been informed in a manner not admitting of doubt, that England was "sustaining Mexico at this time."[20] Although the Texan Secretary of State, Anson Jones, declared he could not believe such reports concerning England, he informed Smith that he had received from various quarters "assurances of the most positive character that England has been instrumental in inducing the move which Santa Anna is now making" in Mexico in reference to Texas.[21]

If England had anything to do with the recent Mexican raid in Texas, which is more than doubtful, the Ministry must have taken an inventory of its Mexican policy following the receipt of General James Hamilton's confidential letter from South Carolina. Upon the arrival at Charleston of the news of Vasquez's invasion, Hamilton hastily dispatched a letter to Lord Aberdeen[22] telling him that Santa Anna's threat to invade Texas had been carried out

by Genl. Aristo [Vasquez] at the head of 14,000 men. I have no doubt, [he continued], Aristo will be crushed before he reaches the Colorado. If he is not, I shall claim my privileges of citizenship in Texas, and strike as hard and as heavy as I can. The Star of Empire will travel West, and no Man can tell *where* we shall *stop*. Nothing can exceed the infatuation of this people, apparently doomed, or the Union and enthusiasm of the People of Texas. In any event be assured we will take care of English interest.

The news of the Mexican invasion reached Washington on March 24, through a New Orleans newspaper of the 16th of the month. Daniel Webster, the Secretary of State, at once contacted President Tyler on the subject of restraining the Indians along the Southwestern frontier, and later assured James Reily, the Texan representative in Washington, that the United States government would see that the Indians kept within their proper territories. "I feel satisfied," reported Reily to his

[20] Ashbel Smith to Anson Jones, New Orleans, March 15, 1842, in State Department (Texas), Foreign Letters, 1842–1844, ms., pp. 75–77.

[21] Anson Jones to Ashbel Smith, Dept. of State, Houston, April 4, 1842, in State Department (Texas), Foreign Letters, 1842–1844, ms.

[22] J. Hamilton to Aberdeen, Charleston, March 25, 1842 (Private and Confidential) Per Halifax Steamer, in Ephraim D. Adams, (ed.), "Correspondence from the British Archives Concerning Texas," in *Quarterly of the Texas State Historical Association*, XV (1911–1912), 261–263.

government, "that it will be done, and that Texas in her struggle can have the aid of all her gallant sons, both in the east and along the Red River line, since the United States will save their homes and property from the depredations of the savages. The Government here will likewise take means to defend the lives, liberty, and property of her citizens on Galveston Island."[23]

In carrying through on this policy, Major General Edmund P. Gaines hurriedly left Washington for the Southwestern frontier of the United States three days after the news of the fall of San Antonio arrived, even though his leave of absence had not yet expired. Brigadier General Zachary Taylor was in immediate command of the United States troops along the northern and eastern Texas frontier. Under the apprehension that the Indians west of Arkansas and Missouri might during the Texas-Mexican contest take the warpath against each other or do violence to the inhabitants of the frontier, the Tyler administration ordered immediately to Fort Towson on Red River an additional eight hundred infantry and four hundred dragoons to re-enforce eight hundred troops already there. Taylor was instructed to take every means in his power to prevent the Indians from crossing the boundary between the United States and Texas on any pretext whatever, and he was especially charged to afford adequate protection and security to the inhabitants of the frontier,[24] and to station any force he could spare at the points that would enable it most effectually to deter any Indians from crossing into Texas. The United States had a military force of two thousand men immediately on the boundary line.[25] Instructions were also sent to the several Indian agents of the United States among the Cherokees, Creeks, Choctaws, and Chickasaws to urge watchfulness on

[23] James Reily to Anson Jones, Washington, March 25, 1842, in George P. Garrison (ed.), *Diplomatic Correspondence of Texas,* in *Annual Report of the American Historical Association,* 1907, I, 546. See also Daniel Webster to James Reily, Department of State, Washington, April 7, 1842, in *ibid.,* 1907, I, 550–551, and in United States Congress, *Senate Executive Documents,* 32nd Congress, 2nd Session, Vol. III, no. 14, p. 74.

[24] *Daily Picayune* (New Orleans) quoted in *Telegraph and Texas Register,* April 27, 1842; J. C. Spencer to Brigadier General Z. Taylor, Fort Gibson, Western Territory [dated:] War Dept., March 26, 1842, in *ibid.,* May 11, 1842; and in U. S. Congress, *Senate Executive Documents,* 32nd Congress, 2nd Session, Vol. III, no. 14, p. 75; J. C. Spencer to Daniel Webster, War Department, March 26, 1842, in *ibid.*

[25] J. C. Spencer to Daniel Webster, Department of War, July 30, 1842, in *ibid.,* pp. 81–82.

their part to prevent the United States Indians' crossing over into Texas. That there might be difficulties with the border Indians could well be expected in view of the repeated outrages committed by certain Texans upon them. Not only had their boats upon Red River been destroyed by the Texans, but Texans had shot across the river into the Choctaw country killing an Indian woman, crossed over in an attempt to steal Negroes belonging to the tribe, had kidnapped several free Negroes, and had also killed several Indians and Negroes in the United States and committed other depredations.[26] In New Orleans it was reported that Spencer, son of J. C. Spencer, the United States Secretary of War, had arrived there on the evening of March 19, post haste from Washington with dispatches to be delivered in person to President Houston, and had departed on the *New York* the following evening for Texas, having for some mysterious reason, reported the *Bee,* applied to the Mexican consul in New Orleans "for a passport to travel through Texas." The consul refused to issue him one, but countersigned the credentials that had been given him by the government of the United States.[27]

Major James R. O'Neal of the Texas Militia had no more tact or regard for the efforts of the United States to keep its Indians quiet and in a peaceful state than to appeal to the chiefs of the Choctaws and Chickasaws to cross into Texas and join him in a campaign against the wild Indians about the first of July next.[28] When informed of Major O'Neal's conduct, the Texan government hastened to assure the United States that the Major's action "was wholly unknown and unauthorized by the authorities of the government of Texas," and met "the President's decided disapprobation."[29] The district attorney was ordered to make an

[26] Extract of a letter from a Choctaw to P. P. Pitchlynn, Choctaw Nation, Feb. 9, 1842, and P. P. Pitchlynn to John C. Spencer, Washington City, March 25, 1842, in *ibid.,* pp. 76–78. Spencer was the United States Secretary of War and Pitchlynn was the delegate in Washington from the Choctaw Nation.

[27] *New Orleans Bee,* March 21, 1842.

[28] James R. O'Neil, Major 2d Battalion, 4th Regt., and 4th Brigade, Texas Militia, to the Chiefs and Principal Officials of the Choctaw and Chickasaw Nations [June? 1842]; A. M. M. Upshaw C[hickasaw] A[gent] to Col. Issac Abberson, Chief of Chickasaw District C[hickasaw] N[ation], near Fort Towson, July 5, 1842; A. M. M. Upshaw, C. A. to T. H. Crawford, Commissioner of Indian Affairs, near Fort Towson, July 6, 1842; J. C. Spencer to Daniel Webster, Department of War, July 30, 1842; and Joseph Eve to G. W. Terrell, Acting Secretary of State of the Republic of Texas, Legation of the United States, Galveston, Sept. 5, 1842; all in U. S. Congress, *Senate Executive Documents,* 32nd Congress, 2nd Session, Vol. III, no. 14, pp. 81–85.

[29] Joseph Waples, Acting Secretary of State, to Joseph Eve, Chargé d'Affaires of

inquiry into O'Neal's conduct in this matter and to take such measures for his punishment as the law required.[30] In reporting the results of his investigation, the district attorney made no mention of O'Neal, but was "gratified . . . to state that the participators, generally speaking, in these outrages [upon the United States Indians], are not citizens of the republic, but are fugitives from other countries—reckless and dangerous men" and that he would do what he could to bring them to a speedy and impartial trial. In the meantime, he accused the United States Indian agents of exciting the Indians to take revenge for any depredations that the citizens of Texas might commit on them.[31] Thus the main thing gained for Texas by raising the question of Indian depredations was to stimulate the United States to make a show of force on the frontier of Texas while Texas was directing her attention toward an invasion of northern Mexico. Surely this must have given some confidence to the Texan frontiersman along the Red River while his government's attention was distracted in another direction.

In April 1842 Henry A. Wise, representative from Virginia in the United States Congress, pictured Texas, guided by her single star, marching on to her enemy's capital.[32] More than one friend of Texas hoped that war would break out between the United States and Mexico. In his book, *Mexico in 1842*[33] published in New York in 1842, George Folsom declared that since a force of two to three thousand men seemed sufficient to revolutionize Mexico, eight to ten thousand well-equipped troops might at any moment be able to lay "the whole people . . . under contribution."

Under such circumstances, [he declared] it would be fortunate for the people of Mexico, if some Anglo-Saxon leader, imbued with the true spirit of free institutions, should carry the standard of federalism to the gates of the capital,

---

the United States, Department of State, Texas, Houston, Sept. 9, 1842, in *ibid.*, pp. 85–86.

[30] Same to Jesse Benton, District Attorney of Seventh Judicial District, Department of State, Houston, Sept. 9, 1842, in *ibid.*, p. 87.

[31] Jesse Benton to Anson Jones, Secretary of State [n.d.], in Isaac Van Zandt to Daniel Webster, Legation of Texas, Washington, Feb. 3, 1843 (extract), in *ibid.* pp. 105–106.

[32] United States Congress, *Congressional Globe*, 27th Congress, 2nd Session, p. 422.

[33] [George Folsom], *Mexico in 1842: A Description of the Country, Its Natural and Political Features; with a Sketch of Its History Brought Down to the Present Year. To Which Is Added, an Account of Texas and Yucatán; and of the Santa Fé Expedition*, pp. 26–28.

and plant it as the emblem of substantial reform on the walls of that noble city, there to wave in triumph while the blessings of peace and prosperity, under a popular and well established government, should be extended throughout the borders of a land so richly endowed by nature with all that is requisite to human comfort and happiness.

From New York John S. Bartlett wrote Colonel Morgan that at last the event he had always predicted was about to take place: "An invasion of Mexico by Texas. The Río Grande once passed and *Mexico* becomes sooner or later *Texas*." Texas, he thought, would need cavalry as well as infantry to conduct a successful invasion of Mexico, but there would be no problem in getting mounted troops if Texas would promise to grant each man who came mounted one hundred acres of land at the end of the war. It was only inevitable, he concluded, that "the Spanish Moorish race must give way to the Anglo-Saxon blood, who go not only with the hardihood and vigor of the north but with the light of modern science among an ignorant, benighted and worn out people."[34]

The outfitting of the Santa Fé expedition and the several alarms of Indian and Mexican marauders upon the western frontier had by the summer of 1842 practically depleted the Texan Ordnance Department, except for 395 muskets, 581 kegs of powder, and 837 pounds of lead.[35] The President reported that there was no beef available for troops west of the Colorado. "The late flurry has destroyed it," and he accused "the prudence, wisdom and subordination of Neddy, good Neddy Burleson" of being the culprit.[36]

A law passed by Congress in January 1842, had brought the treasury notes down to only 2 per cent of par,[37] and as a means now of bolstering the finances of the nation an effort was made to raise a loan of up to one million dollars in the United States, at the very time William Kennedy, the English consul general in Texas, was reporting commercial and monetary affairs in the United States as "deplorable." "In New Orleans," he reported, "the banks . . . are sustained in a course of virtual insolvency by the apprehensions of the traders and planters, who are anxious to

---

[34] John S. Bartlett to Col. James Morgan, New Washington, [dated:] New York, April 9, 1842, in James Morgan Papers, 1841–1845, ms.

[35] G. W. Hockley, Secretary of War & Marine, to Sam Houston, Dept. of War and Marine, June 23, 1842, in Harriet Smither (ed.), *Journals of the Sixth Congress of the Republic of Texas*, III, 107–112.

[36] Houston to William H. Daingerfield, City of Houston, April 10, 1842, in *Writings of Sam Houston*, III, 22–23.

[37] Justin H. Smith, *The Annexation of Texas*, p. 40.

procrastinate the evil day."[38] For the purpose of raising a loan for Texas William H. Daingerfield, then in New Orleans, was appointed on May 17 a commissioner under an unrepealed law of Congress, dated January 22, 1839,[39] to negotiate such a loan and to hurry on the tide of emigration to tear from the grasp of an imbecile enemy the mingled wreath of laurel and olive. Three weeks later, the President sent Anson Jones, the Secretary of State, to New Orleans as a commissioner to conclude this loan for one million dollars.[40] The purpose, said the President, is to

take the war out of our territory and give the enemy an active employment within his own, by occasionally presenting within the border of his, a calm, bold, and menacing front. The meaning of this is seldom mistaken or disregarded. It is addressed to the head, as well as to the heart, and carries a weight, and importance alone, almost entitled to respect, and always, so treated. The adoption of such a policy, fortified by energy and determination, is calculated to thrill the enemy with concern for his own safety, and inspire him with fearful apprehensions for the future, as well as the present.[41]

As for the loan, even should it be raised, both Houston and Daingerfield were agreed that it could not be used except as authorized by Congress.

We must hold to the Constitution and let the blame or harm of obedience fall where it should do. No appropriations have been made for the expenditure of one dollar, but for so much in Exchequer of Gold & Silver! [declared

[38] William Kennedy to the Earl of Aberdeen, Galveston, Texas, Jan. 10, 1842, in Adams (ed.), "Correspondence from the British Archives Concerning Texas, 1837–1848," in *Quarterly of the Texas State Historical Association*, XV (1911–1912), 252–256.

[39] Houston to William H. Daingerfield, May 17, 1842, in *Writings of Sam Houston*, III, 54; An Enclosure in the Letter of Houston to William Henry Daingerfield of March 12, 1842, in Sam Houston, Unpublished Houston Correspondence, 1842, ms., III. The interest on the loan was not to exceed 8½ per cent per year, and as security the Texas government would put up from 500,000 to 1,000,000 acres of land, depending on the location of the land.

[40] Houston to Anson Jones, Executive Department, City of Houston, June 5, 1842, in *Writings of Sam Houston*, III, 63; Same to Same, Executive Department, City of Houston, June 10, 1842, in *ibid.*, III, 66.

[41] W. D. Miller to William H. Daingerfield, Houston, April 13, 1842, in Washington D. Miller Papers (Hardin-Simmons), ms. See also Same to Same, Houston, April 9, 1842, in *ibid.*; Houston to William Henry Daingerfield, Executive Department, City of Houston, March 25, 1842, in *Writings of Sam Houston*, IV, 86–87; Same to Dr. John O'Bannon, Houston, Texas, May 6, 1842 (Private), in *ibid.*, IV, 94–95; Same to Colonel H. R. A. Wigginton, Houston, Texas, May 13, 1842 (Private), in *ibid.*, IV, 107–108.

the President] "Defence will justify extreme measures, and would, in my opinion, if we were hard pressed any, and everything to save the country. We are invading Mexico and not defending ourselves against invasion. Were I to take any course not authorized by the constitution, no matter what the result might be in favor of Texas, it would furnish an excuse, or a supposed justification, for the gross and mean violations which have been perpetrated by fools and scoundrels.[42]

Without a dollar in the Treasury with which to purchase food, clothing, arms, and munitions of war, Texas embarked upon a plan to invade Mexico, depending exclusively upon aid furnished by citizens of the United States and by contributions from her own people. While the President's plans were described as "well devised," by his private secretary, that individual hastened to inform Daingerfield, then in the United States, that the maturity of those plans would depend upon the assistance that could be received from the United States. Any compensation to the "emigrants" for expenses and services would have to come from the enemy, who should be made to pay the cost of the Texan invasion.[43] "Our army abroad will find rich and plentiful subsistence. This one thing," wrote Miller, "is a matter of very great moment, and will prove itself so, to us all on both sides of the Río Grande."[44] "The harvest is rich and inviting," declared the President.[45] Constantly the agents in the United States were reminded of "the *absolute necessity* of requiring all who embark in the cause of Texas to come well prepared. Men thrown upon the country will ruin us. Starvation must ensue, to be

[42] Houston to William H. Daingerfield, Lynchburg, April 1, 1842 (Private), *ibid.*, III, 14–16.

[43] Houston to Washington D. Miller, City of Houston, March 17, 1842, in *ibid.*, II, 507–508; Same to William H. Daingerfield, Executive Department, City of Houston, March 25, 1842, in *ibid.*, II, 536; Same to Same, Executive Department, City of Houston, May 17, 1842, in *ibid.*, III, 54; Same to Anson Jones, Executive Department, City of Houston, June 5, 1842, in *ibid.*, III, 63; Same to Col. L. B. Franks, Houston, Texas, May 21, 1842, in *ibid.*, III, 55–56; Same to Col. M. E. Holliday, Houston, Texas, May 6, 1842 (Private), in *ibid.*, IV, 93–94; Same to Maj. Charles H. Goldsborough, Houston, Texas, May 10, 1842 (Private), in *ibid.*, IV, 97–98; Same to William S. Johnston, Houston, Texas, May 10, 1842 (Private), in *ibid.*, IV, 99.

[44] W. D. Miller to William H. Daingerfield, Houston, April 9, 1842, in Miller Papers (Hardin-Simmons), ms. See also Same to Same, Houston, April 13, 1842, in *ibid.*

[45] Houston to Col. M. E. Holliday, Houston, Texas, May 6, 1842 (Private), in *Writings of Sam Houston*, IV, 93–94; Same to Dr. John O'Bannon, Houston, Texas, May 6, 1842 (Private), in *ibid.*, IV, 94–95. O'Bannon was a resident of Missouri.

succeeded by a sedition and discontent. Receive none who cannot come well equipped and provisioned for a campaign of six months."[46] Without ample provisions of pilot bread, flour, bacon, sugar, and coffee "all is smoke." Care was to be exercised to "assure all persons, Emigrants, that we do not want them here unless they are prepared, and with . . . arms and munitions of war" and "six months provisions and clothing. If they come unprepared we *will,* and *must be ruined.* They will only add to confusion, and confound everything in Texas. We have too many agitators here and I wish that we were without them."[47] A depot was established at New Orleans for collecting supplies "*such* as will not *waste*" to be forwarded to Texas.[48]

As far as the public in the United States was concerned, the news of the invasion added fresh fuel to the flame of excitement which had already been kindled by the account of the failure of the Santa Fé expedition and the brutal treatment of the prisoners. Enthusiastic meetings in behalf of Texas were held at New York, Philadelphia, Louisville, Cincinnati, Memphis, Savannah, Augusta, Mobile, New Orleans, and elsewhere. Committees were appointed to raise money, and small numbers of "emigrants" were enrolled and started from New Orleans and other points. A large and enthusiastic meeting was held on the evening of March 17 at Banks' Arcade in New Orleans on the subject of the invasion of Texas and the treatment of the Santa Fé prisoners. J. M. Wadsworth opened the meeting and explained briefly its object. General Henry S. Foote of Mississippi, who had recently been in Texas gathering information for his history of that republic, was called to the chair, and resolutions were drafted in favor of the Texan cause and a committee of five was appointed to take up contributions. Four days later, March 22, S. P. Andrews, formerly an attorney-at-law in New Orleans, arrived on the steamer *Neptune,* as a commissioner appointed by the Houston committee of vigilance to solicit aid for the Texan cause. By March 30 John J. B. Hoxey, former aide-de-camp to General Thomas J. Rusk, had raised

[46] Houston to Col. [Lewis M.] H. Washington, Houston, Texas, May 22, 1842, in *ibid.,* III, 56–57; see also Same to Mr. Lumsden, Galveston, May 18, 1842, in *ibid.,* III, 55.

[47] Houston to William H. Daingerfield, City of Houston, April 8, 1842, in *ibid.,* III, 20–21. See also Same to Same, City of Houston, March 25, 1842, in *ibid.,* II, 536; Same to William Scott Haynes, Houston, Texas, May 6, 1842 (Private), in *ibid.,* IV, 95–96.

[48] Houston to William H. Daingerfield, City of Houston, April 10, 1842, in *ibid.,* III, 22–23; see also Same to Col. John Darrington, Houston, Texas, May 12, 1842 (Private), in *ibid.,* IV, 102–103.

$2,000 and twenty men in Georgia, and was prepared to start soon for Texas with a company to be landed at some port as far west as possible. He wrote ahead that he would need some horses and hoped General Rusk would help him secure a commission in the army.[49] Mrs. Sarah Barnes of Mobile was said to have given $200 to aid the committee there in fitting out volunteers for Texas.[50] A public meeting was held on the courthouse lawn in Philadelphia on May 2 at which three thousand persons attended to express "the warmest enthusiasm in favor of Texas." Among the speakers addressing the crowd was the Reverend William L. McCalla, who had visited portions of Texas two years before and recently had published a book describing Texas and his adventures there.[51] At Baltimore a performance was scheduled at the Front Street Theater by the eccentric actor Junius Brutus Booth who, it was alleged, contributed his services to impersonate Shylock for the purpose of obtaining funds to fit out a body of volunteers for the Texas service.[52] While donations were being taken up at a meeting at Fort Pickering, Shelby County, Tennessee, a young lady "took from her neck a string of coral beads, which she presented to the auctioneer" to be sold and its sale price contributed to the "Texas fund." The beads were readily sold and then returned to the auctioneer to be resold—this procedure being continued for at least a dozen times until the final purchaser presented them to the fair donor who objected to their return. "Keep it, then," replied the purchaser, "as a memorial of what it has done, and wear it in memory of your departed friends!"[53] The sentiment at Augusta, Georgia, was that the war in Texas was one in which the people of the United States had a right to take sides, since it was a war "in which liberty, law and civilization" were arraigned against "despotism, misrule and barbarism." "It is upon our borders—we cannot get rid of the interest we have in the result," declared the *Charleston Mercury*. "We have a right to interfere from the mere character and position of the contest—we have

[49] John J. B. Hoxey to General [Thomas J.] Rusk, March 30, 1842, in Thomas J. Rusk Papers, ms.; *New Orleans Bee*, March 17, 1842. For the meeting at New Orleans, see the *Daily Picayune*, March 18, 1842; and for the arrival of S. P. Andrews, *ibid.*, March 23, 1842.

[50] *Morning Star*, March 31, 1842.

[51] *Telegraph and Texas Register*, April 27, 1842. McCalla's book, published at Philadelphia in 1841, was entitled *Adventures in Texas, Chiefly in the Spring and Summer of 1840: with a Discussion of Comparative Character, Political, Religious and Moral*.

[52] *Telegraph and Texas Register*, May 4, 1842.

[53] Quoted from the *Fort Pickering Eagle* in *ibid.*

a more distinct right, from the faithless conduct of the Mexican Government towards ours. We say again, let the Government of the United States vindicate her position."[54] At Charleston about two hundred volunteers were preparing, it was said, to embark for Texas, and a Mr. Aristides Welch had presented equipment sufficient for 1,500 men to the government of Texas.[55]

A meeting of citizens was held at Memphis on March 24 "for the purpose of expressing their sympathy for their brethren of Texas, whom they then believed were about to be overwhelmed by the ravenous brutes of Santa Anna." Colonel F. S. Latham, editor of the Memphis *American Eagle*, was selected chairman of the meeting. A committee of ten was appointed to solicit contributions and some $300 in cash and munitions were subscribed on the spot, part of which was paid down. Following several addresses, it was proposed to form a company for a "Texian Wolf Hunt," for which some fifteen to twenty men, including Colonel Latham, volunteered.

Tennesseans, [began the rousing report of the meeting] the wolves of Mexico have made a ferocious and brutal descent on the fertile plains of Texas. So blood thirsty and numerous are the herds, that they attack and devour our very brethren, our mothers, friends, and the beautiful helpless women! The *river towns* are doing *their duty*. Will our *country* friends hold back? Come in! Join us in the chase! Bring your guns! If you can't come, *send* your guns— your *contributions*! Send them to our care—or to the *Wolf Hunt Committee* at Memphis. The chivalry of Kentucky will soon pour down her bright legions! Will *Tennesseans* falter! By the middle of next week, at farthest, the company will leave here for New Orleans. Come, country boys! join us in exterminating the butchering brutes of wolves now laying desolate in blood and plunder, the homes of our brethren! The cries of their distresses have already reached us! The blood of our relatives cries aloud from the crimson plain! Shall we refuse to aid? Tennesseans! is this appeal from your brothers made to you in *vain*! No![56]

The response was immediate. On April 1 the *Queen of the West* reached New Orleans with a company of volunteer Tennessee Wolf Hunters under Captain Augustus Williams.[57]

An address of the Texan agents published in Louisville announced that the Texans intended to visit Mexico in the fall, and that then all

[54] *Charleston Mercury* quoted in *ibid.*
[55] *Telegraph and Texas Register,* May 4, 1842.
[56] Reported in *ibid.,* April 20, 1842.
[57] *Daily Picayune,* April 2, 1842.

who were in Texas would have an opportunity to take part in the conquest of that "pays d'or, where the golden chandelier, images, and furniture of one church are estimated to be worth five million dollars."[58] One of Memucan Hunt's friends from Washington County, Mississippi, wrote that he was looking for an opportunity to make a fortune, and inquired for information as to, first, what could be done in the field of medicine in Texas, and, second, what opportunities might there be presented to him in case of prosecution of the war into Mexico. Finally, in desperation, he asked, "Can any other business be successfully carried on [in Texas] without capital?"[59] At Philadelphia a speaker informed a meeting of friends of Texas, "Emigrate to Texas! It abounds in game of all kinds. You will find plenty of employment for as many rifles and muskets as you can get there. You will no doubt go farther. There are many richly endowed institutions in Mexico that sadly need professors. Go, then, to Mexico, and teach the young idea how to shoot."[60] After the speaker had taken his seat, his audience voted that the invasion of Texas was an "unwarranted aggression" by Mexico, and, promising Texas all lawful aid possible, appointed a committee to raise money to finance "emigrants."[61]

"Great excitement has prevailed in this country [wrote Guy M. Bryan from Kenyon College, Gambier, Ohio] in behalf of Texas. We have thousands of well wishers here, but not so many efficient friends. All *'talk'* in our behalf but not so many act. I do not mean to disparage the friends of Texas, [he informed Moses Austin Bryan] but simply to state . . . that our friends here, Yes the *majority* of them, even if they have the ability never have gone nor *never will* go farther than to talk.

Well aware that many patriotic friends of liberty had gone to Texas during the revolution and the present disturbance and that many others, who had not visited or emigrated to Texas, had contributed freely of money and means to the Texas cause and defended her from the "base and slanderous charges . . . [of] 'pretended' friends," he believed that in the event of war with Mexico "Texas . . . must go into it with the *expectation and determination* to beat the enemy herself, without the aid of an extraneous force from abroad." If aid was given, it should be re-

[58] *Anti-Slavery Standard*, April 21, 1842.
[59] H. Houghton to Gen. M. Hunt, Washington Co., Miss., July 5, 1842, in Memucan Hunt Papers, ms.
[60] *Washington Globe*, May 5, 1842.
[61] *Philadelphia Public Ledger*, April 4, 1842.

ceived "gratefully," "but let us not expect it; *but be prepared to fight—* to conquer. The *volunteers* who *are now* or *may come in [to] Texas* to aid us in battling against the mymudores of Mexico, should be well treated and no cause of offence . . . should be given them for on their report depends [to] no inconsiderable extent our *future success* in this country in raising new money" and supplies, he cautioned.[62] Neither did James Morgan look forward with enthusiasm to having tens of thousands of volunteers from the United States join the Texans in their fight with Mexico. "God forbid they should come," he wrote Samuel Swartwout. "I say furth[er] [it] would be like the locusts of Egypt."[63]

At Mobile and New Orleans, where several vessels belonging to the Texas navy were being provisioned and fitted out, the patriotic citizens were generous in their contributions. At Mobile "one thousand dollars were collected in ten days and one hundred men volunteered to emigrate." Another meeting at Mobile on Monday night, May 16, at the Corinthian in behalf of the Texan cause was addressed by Colonel Megginson and General Smith, the Texan consul, as well as G. F. Lindsay and Percy Walker of that city. A collection was taken up, and provision was made to hold another meeting as soon as Commodore Moore and Colonel Lewis M. H. Washington should arrive in the city. Augusta gave a thousand dollars. In New York the Texan consul, John S. Brower, received almost enough in donations to purchase five Paixhan guns.[64] Ex-governor Hiram G. Runnels of Mississippi was appointed at a large meeting of citizens of Jackson a member of a committee to receive donations in behalf of the Texas cause and to determine how they might be used most advantageously. "With the generous chivalry of a Lafayette," Runnels came in person to Texas in April to ascertain in what manner aid could be most effectually rendered."[65] In the excitement over the raid, New Orleans offered to contribute $14,000 and 1,000 emigrants; Mobile, $14,000 and 500 emigrants; Tuscaloosa, $4,000 and 100 emigrants; Natchez, $6,000 and 225 emigrants; and Columbia, Georgia,

---

[62] Guy M. Bryan to Moses Austin Bryan, Kenyon, April 25, 1842, in Guy Morrison Bryan Papers, ms.

[63] J. Morgan to Genl. Saml. Swartwout, New Washington, Galveston Bay, Texas, Jany 27th, 1842, in Morgan Papers, ms.

[64] *Telegraph and Texas Register*, April 27, 1842; *Daily Picayune*, May 21, 1842.

[65] *Ibid.*, April 27, 1842. Later in the year Runnels moved to Texas and became a Brazos-bottom planter. Z. T. Fulmore, *The History and Geography of Texas as Told in County Names*, p. 239.

$885.[66] Such was the ready response in the United States, especially in the South and West, to the Texas call for aid, based upon exaggerated reports from Texas that 9,000 Mexicans had been seen beyond the Nueces and 12,000 more were on their march to San Antonio.[67] William Kennedy, the British consul at Galveston, was able to report to his government that the success he had attained in Texas in allaying the excitement in favor of immediate annexation to the United States had now been undone. The position of the question of annexation, he wrote, "is now materially altered by the Mexican invasion," and "I am reluctant to hazard an opinion as to the probable result of the invasion, but I greatly fear it will eventually prove as injurious to English interests, as it will be *temporarily* detrimental to Texas, and *permanently* injurious to Mexico."[68]

When it became known that the invasion had turned out to be nothing more than a mere raid and that the Mexican troops had recrossed the Río Grande, enthusiasm throughout the United States cooled as quickly as it had flared up, and nothing further was heard on the subject until the Woll invasion in September. "These infamous rumors" from Texas of a large scale Mexican invasion, "when corrected," reported the Texan consul at New Orleans, "made Texas ridiculous here and destroyed the ardor of most of her best friends. But worst of all," he continued, "after some of . . . [the] agitators [in Texas] had carried the humbug as far as they could and found they could not succeed in making some *one* a great man, they turn round and write private letters here, abusing the Pres[iden]t and charging the whole failure to him."[69] In time the various committees in the United States suspended their activities and returned the contributions on hand to the donors, and the volunteers were in most cases disbanded ere they could sail. Sometimes, however, as individuals or organized groups, they came on. Typical of those who were disappointed with the failure of Mexico to push its invasion of

[66] *Philadelphia Public Ledger*, June 14, 1842; *New Orleans Bee*, April 1, 6, 9, and 20, 1842.

[67] P. Edmunds to W. D. Miller, New Orleans, May 3–10, 1842, in Miller Papers (Texas), ms.

[68] William Kennedy to Aberdeen, On Board the Roseins, Liverpool, April 20, 1842 (Private), in Adams (ed.), "Correspondence from the British Archives Concerning Texas," in *Quarterly of the Texas State Historical Association*, XV (1911–1912), 264–265.

[69] P. Edmunds to W. D. Miller, New Orleans, May 3–10, 1842, in Miller Papers (Texas), ms.

Texas with the first cries of "wolf," were the troops who had quickly turned out at Natchez under Captain Walter Hickey and those from the vicinity of Holly Springs in northern Mississippi under Captain W. G. Wilson. Fifty volunteers under Captain Wilson reached New Orleans on Thursday night, April 7, on the way to Texas. They encamped on the square opposite the charred ruins of the recently burned St. Charles theatre. "They appeared greatly disappointed and dissatisfied with the prospects presented here," reported the editor of the *Daily Picayune*, "and both captain and men spoke determinedly of immediately returning home."[70] Wilson was a son of George Wilson, the oldest newspaper editor in Tennessee, and a graduate of Nashville University. Wilson explained in a letter to the editor of the *Picayune* why he and some of his men would not go forward to Texas. "Please, do us the justice to state that we arrived here under the impression that Texas was overrun with Mexicans, and that a portion of us were so situated that we were scarcely justified in leaving our homes under different circumstances. That portion of us will return. We go back with the kindest feelings towards Texas, and with our interest in her cause unabated. We leave with our companions all that we think likely to be of service to her, and hope to rejoin them ourselves under more favorable circumstances."[71] The emigrants from Natchez under Captain Hickey disclaimed being dissatisfied, and declared their intention of proceeding to Texas.[72]

Late in May, the President of Texas in a rage admonished Colonel Barry Gillespie, the Texan agent at New Orleans, to adhere strictly to the instructions which had been issued previously to him in regard to recruiting and sending volunteers from the United States.

Starvation will beget insubordination, [wrote the President] and the ruin of our country will be the wretched sequel. For God's sake and your country's good, see, then, that every man that departs for Texas with any designs to participate in our struggle, is well supplied with six month's provisions, good clothing, and military equipment necessary for the campaign, and see, moreover, that none land at Galveston under any circumstances. . . . Water has given out at that point.[73]

[70] *Daily Picayune*, April 9 and 10, 1842.
[71] W. G. Wilson to Editors of the *Picayune*, New Orleans, April 10, 1842, in *Daily Picayune*, April 10, 1842.
[72] *Daily Picayune*, April 12, 1842.
[73] Houston to Barry Gillespie, City of Houston, Texas, May 22, 1842 (Private), in *Writings of Sam Houston*, IV, 113–114.

Gillespie, who had the management and supervision of Texan affairs in the valley of the Mississippi, was "in *no case* . . . [to] furnish any emigrant, or company of emigrants with anything whatever in the way of equipment. It is expected and required that they come *fully* prepared themselves even to the simple matter of a single flint,"[74] for, as the President wrote Daingerfield in New Orleans, "I feel confident that we will have no invasion 'sub rosa',", and will need all the provisions we can get.[75] A week later to Colonel Lewis M. H. Washington, who was in New Orleans supervising the forwarding of volunteers, Houston stated, "Texas is in a most deplorable condition. The introduction of emigrants contrary to orders, without supplies, has reduced us to our present calamitous condition. Why were not abundant supplies sent with them?" he queried. "Orders were sent by every steamer to command or suggest the imperative duty; and as often as infraction was committed, some promise of supplies, or apology for the fact, was rendered. I wish no violations of orders, there is no excuse."[76]

The President's determination to invade Mexico was approved in public meetings at Crockett,[77] Galveston, and other places.

The mass of people [asserted the *Civilian and Galveston Gazette*] have . . . confidence in his prudence, discernment, and watchfulness of the public interest. A few persons may cavil because he has not attempted to bring about an immediate crisis in our affairs, but we know that he is using every endeavor to husband and augment the resources and auxiliaries of the country, and believe that all the delay complained of will tell in the increased strength and energy of such final movements as are in contemplation.[78]

The present condition of the country justified drastic action.

As it is, we cannot deny that the country is overwhelmingly embarrassed, [wrote the editor of the *Austin City Gazette*] and all things seem to wear a most gloomy and drooping aspect. . . . It is owing . . . solely to the policy which, for a series of years, Mexico has thought proper to pursue towards Texas. Powerless in the way of re-conquering us, she has not been generous and magnanimous enough to appreciate our forbearance towards her; and

---

[74] *Ibid.*
[75] Houston to William H. Daingerfield, City of Houston, April 10, 1842, in *ibid.*, III, 21–22.
[76] Houston to Col. [Lewis M.] H. Washington, City of Houston, May 31, 1842, in *ibid.*, III, 62–63.
[77] *Telegraph and Texas Register*, April 27, 1842.
[78] April 16, 1842.

recognize, that we have established in the eyes of all civilized nations, our claim to independence. . . . She has wantonly exercised her power to molest and plunder our border towns; and, in the fullness of her bloated vanity, and boasted power, she has continually held out to the world her intention to invade and reconquer Texas. Here, then, is to be found the cause of all our difficulties—the source of heavy national debt—crippled commerce—neglected, if not parallyzed, husbandry; and an emigration; and it renders cautious and hesitating purchasers of improvements, and operations of every kind, in consequence of this continually threatened invasion. Our Mexican relations must be regarded as the great barrier to our immediate and unrivalled prosperity. . . . Being convinced as to the cause of our present evils, what, then is the remedy? [he asked]. It is an immediate invasion of the northern provinces of Mexico—carry "the war into Africa." The Río Grande should be the theater of every battle; and on the enemy should our men subsist, [until our rights are acknowledged.][79]

There were those in the west anxious to carry the war beyond the boundaries of Texas.

The President had his enemies, however, and there were many "arm chair" generals in Texas and "hot-headed westerners" who wished to start at once for Mexico, although the President had set as his goal 120 days for outfitting an invading army and was represented as being "firm in his determination to prosecute the war." Many believed that Houston intended "merely to humbug the people of Texas by ordering the campaign to be commenced in midsummer," and others openly asserted that he was opposed to offensive measures and had "resorted to this expedient to defeat the very object" he pretended to wish to carry into effect. "They say that he knows," reported the editor of the *Telegraph*, "that flesh and blood cannot endure the exposure incident to a campaign at this season, when the western prairies are parched and sere, and the beds of the streams as dry and dusty as roads, consequently, the people will refuse to march, and then he will cast the blame on them and say, 'I have called unto you and you would not come,' the fault therefore is your own."[80] Apparently there was a deep seated scheme on the part of a few leaders of the opposition to overturn the government, but fortunately it gained very little headway before it was exposed and nipped in the bud.

I could tell you something that would startle you [James Morgan at New Washington wrote his friend Swartwout in the United States]. It was the

[79] March 30, 1842.
[80] *Telegraph and Texas Register*, June 8, 1842.

disposition of a party to revolutionize this Country. Yes a party in the Country who had it in contemplation to abolish the Constitution—upsett the present Govt., [and embark upon] a new plan!! and what was most distinctly there were those at the head of it who had more or less influence & *Something at Stake*. When finding they could not rule & Gov[n] "Old Sam" . . . [they were] just ambitious enough to make anarchy & confusion [and] thro all into chaos rather than not have their own way—all to gratify, a malignant selfish ambition.[81]

A number of the western leaders talked of raising an army of volunteers and advancing immediately against the enemy, with or without orders from the War Department, for it was generally believed in the west that five hundred Texans could conquer the whole of the Río Grande villages below Presidio.[82] With that object in mind, several companies of "buckskin heroes" were organized in the west, composed chiefly of citizens of the depopulated counties, determined to wage war against Mexico until peace was secured. "These men are all prepared for a long campaign," reported the *Telegraph*,[83] "and as their equipments consist only of a rifle, a powder horn, bullet pouch and butcher knife, they can advance or retreat with ease, and will be equally formidable, whether on foot or on horseback."

Pursuant to previous notice, a large and respectable meeting of the citizens of Travis and Bastrop counties, plus a few individuals from other counties, assembled in Austin, Monday, April 11, 1842, to remonstrate against an executive order for the removal of the national archives. The meeting was presided over by Major Samuel Whiting. After the protest had been adopted and signed by three hundred persons attending the meeting, Colonel James S. Mayfield, who had served as Secretary of State during Lamar's administration, and was a bitter political opponent of President Houston, delivered an "eloquent" harangue to the assembled citizens. Upon concluding his speech, he offered a series of resolutions, which were unanimously adopted. Among the resolves was one declaring that

The citizens of Travis and Bastrop are firmly convinced, that the time is at hand when our war with Mexico (now of seven years' continuance) should be brought to a close; that a longer continuance of the war on our part, upon principles of defense, is ruinous to the people of Texas, both nationally and

[81] James Morgan to Saml. Swartwout, New Washington, Galveston Bay, Texas, June 23, 1842, in Morgan Papers, ms.
[82] *Telegraph and Texas Register,* April 13, 1842.
[83] April 6, 1842.

individually: public meetings are, therefore, requested to be held at the earliest possible period, in every county of the Republic, in furtherance of this object; and, to united public sentiment, a committee of five persons be appointed by the Chair [Major Samuel Whiting], to address the citizens of Texas upon said subject—recommending a plan by which unity and concert of action may be had; that said committee be instructed to submit a plan of organization, by which the volunteers and soldiers of the United States shall unite and co-operate with the volunteers of the country, at the most favorable point west of the Guadalupe River.[84]

It was also resolved that the policy of a defensive war was a suicidal one "destructive of the whole western settlements of the country, and the total ruin of each and every frontier settler thereof—as it is subsisting our army, and that of the enemy, upon our own country, when our support should be drawn from the enemy." It was further stipulated that the citizens of Bastrop and Travis counties would unite with the citizens of Galveston and Harris counties in their resolutions to conduct an offensive war against Mexico, and "the thanks of the nation are due to the citizens of said counties for setting so bright an example of patriotism." A committee of correspondence, consisting of six men,[85] was set up to contact similar committees to be erected at other points in the Republic and in the United States. Plans were instituted for a convention to be held at Brazoria in May or early June.[86] June 1 was designated the day upon which the volunteers were to assemble in the west,[87] and a letter was addressed to President Houston requesting permission to commence their march to the Río Grande at that time under the leadership of General Burleson.[88] The "War Party" was strong in its invectives against the Executive "for not organizing *coute que coute* active warlike operations."[89]

Numerous resolutions were adopted at the Austin meeting. One of these praised Vice President Burleson for "flying to the protection of the capital upon the first news of the late invasion," for "his subsequent pa-

[84] Smither (ed.), *Journals of the Sixth Congress*, III, 39–40.
[85] Col. James S. Mayfield, L. C. Cunningham, Henry J. Jewett, Major Samuel Whiting, Col. Thomas Green, and T. Bissell composed the Committee of Correspondence. *Telegraph and Texas Register*, June 15, 1842; *Northern Standard*, Aug. 27, 1842; Smither (ed.), *Journals of the Sixth Congress*, III, 39–42.
[86] *Bollaert's Texas*, p. 83.
[87] Smither (ed.), *Journals of the Sixth Congress*, III, 39–40.
[88] *Telegraph and Texas Register*, April 27, 1842. I have not found a copy of the letter to Houston.
[89] *Bollaert's Texas*, p. 83.

triotic and self-denying course while in command at San Antonio" and for his address of April 6 to the people of Texas. Upon motion of Colonel Mark B. Lewis it was resolved

That the company now under the command of Captain George M. Dolson, which was organized for the protection of Austin and the frontier, be disbanded, and a spy company be substituted, to be composed of such of the citizens of Travis and Bastrop counties as may choose to enrol[l] themselves for that purpose; and that said company be commanded by a captain and one first and one second lieutenant, to be elected by the company.

It was further resolved that Colonel Henry Jones be requested "to superintend the raising and organizing the spy company in the counties of Bastrop and Travis, for the protection of the Seat of Government and the national archives."

In "a most impressive and eloquent speech," Dr. P. Walter Herbert of Fannin County assured the meeting "that under a secret organization in the Mississippi Valley of the United States, 12,000 volunteers were organizing for the invasion of Mexico, and only awaited the sanction of this Government, to enlist under her flag, and to take up the line of march." As soon as the deafening applause resulting from these remarks died out, General Thomas Jefferson Green presented three resolutions calling for "vengeance rather than redress," and declaring that 120 days "contemplated by General Houston for preparation to invade Mexico, is an unnecessary and dangerous delay,[90] more particularly, as that time would come under the burning rays of an August sun, when we have neither grass, water, nor the comforts of a well-appointed army in the midst of the sickly season; by that delay," he said, "we hazard losing the excitement in our favor in the United States." Green, who was usually defiant of constituted authority, declared in his third, and last, resolve that "the people of Western Texas, having little hope for President Houston's protection, . . . pledge themselves each to the other, to be ready at a minute's warning, to meet the enemy as far west of their homes as possible; and that, trusting in our proud hearts, unerring rifles, and the eternal justice of God, we solemnly believe, that let the day of battle come soon or late, a glorious triumph awaits us."[91]

[90] Green was entirely mistaken. The President's order to General Somervell of March 22, we have already noted, permitted an immediate descent upon the Río Grande towns if an adequate expedition could be formed at San Antonio from among the men rushing to that place. It was men like Green and others who prevented such an expedition from being made up.

[91] Smither (ed.), *Journals of the Sixth Congress*, III, 42.

Two days later, at a so-called meeting of citizens of Travis County, held at Nolan and O'Brian's room, Major Whiting was again called to the chair. The declared object of the meeting was to provide for the security of citizens' property from private depredations and the protection of the national archives, especially from any effort of the Executive to remove them from the city. A committee of vigilance and safety, consisting of the major, aldermen, and seventeen men was appointed by Chairman Whiting. The committee's principal duty seems to have been "to take the necessary measures for the examination of wagons leaving the city and give the proper certificates, &c."[92]

The impatience displayed in the west in favor of an immediate descent upon the Río Grande was not shared by more thoughtful men, and it was not long until news of the proceedings at Austin reached the President, along with reports that agents and commissions for agents to recruit troops and supplies in the United States had been sent east of the Sabine, where they were causing confusion and interference with the regular and specially appointed agents of the government. The impetuosity of such leaders could possibly bring disaster upon the country, but Houston believed that the people generally were behind his policy toward Mexico, and that "the excitement which is got up by speeches in the Towns is no index to the country, or even the people of the Towns," he wrote, "but the expression of a 'clique' who are committees, stocked and palmed, upon the people. They are now understood and will bear the *mark on the forehead!*"[93] Fortunately, the incendiaries, he believed, did not exceed twenty in number;

but they are composed of men who have some smartness, some means, and possess all the attributes of mischief. Unemployed in the acquisition of honest gains, they wish to produce a state of things in Texas, which will enable them to trample upon the rights of the people, and like Robespierre and Danton, cry out for "the will of the people," when in truth, they would, if it were in their power, reduce them to anarchy; and when the people would attempt to rise from its paroxysms, they would crush them to a condition of moral degradation. Who are these men? [asked the President] They are not men who have shared in the toils of the Revolution, nor have they stood shoulder to shoulder with those who have embraced the perils of a well fought field.

[92] [Proceedings of a Public Meeting of the Citizens of Travis County, held at Nolan & O'Brian's Room on Wednesday, the 13th of April, 1842], in *ibid.*, III, 47.
[93] Houston to William H. Daingerfield, Galveston, April 27, 1842, in *Writings of Sam Houston*, III, 37–40.

They are men who have no principle but self; and aside from that feel no affections.[94]

President Houston lost no time in issuing a proclamation, dated April 25, denouncing the agents of certain "Committees of Vigilance and Safety" who were collecting money, supplies, and offering "Commissions to gentlemen who were about to emigrate, as they say, by the authority of General A. Sidney Johnston, whom they represent as in the command of the Army of Texas."[95] Well might Houston be concerned, for the Galveston committee of vigilance had instructed its agents— Jones, Megginson, and Watrous—to inform all would be volunteers of

our poverty and our wants—tell them that we have nothing to promise them but the glory of the enterprise, and such advantages as may arise from the conquered territory. It is theirs if they unite with us and win it. They must come, if they come at all, prepared with arms, ammunition and provisions. . . . We believe the army will be commanded by Gen'l. Johnston, whose bravery, and military capacity, eminently fit him for that high and responsible stations.[96]

The promise of remuneration from the spoils of war, including possibly land; the indication of who might command the expedition; and the instruction to the commissioners to report directly to the committee of vigilance of Galveston seemed a clear indication that the constituted authorities of Texas were to be circumvented. Houston warned in his proclamation against making contributions to anyone except a properly appointed agent of the President, for the aid already contributed to such

infamous imposters . . . by our noble and generous friends, have not been reported to the government and are therefore, not available to the use of the cause for which they were designed. . . . It is further declared, [he said] that the war in which Texas is involved is a national war, and one of principle, which has for its object the recognition of our independence, and originating in and directed by the constitutional head of the nation; and that it is no marauding association which has for its object pillage and spoil.

[94] Houston to Col. Barry Gillespie, City of Houston, May 16, 1842, in *ibid.*, III, 51–52.
[95] "A Proclamation Concerning Self-Appointed Texas Agents," [dated:] Galveston, April 25, 1842, in Proclamations of the Presidents (Texas), ms.; *Telegraph and Texas Register*, May 4, 1842.
[96] James Love and Others, Committee [of Vigilance, Galveston] to Messrs. Watrous, Jones, and Megginson, Galveston, March 1842, *New Orleans Bee*, March 17, 1842.

The offer of commissions in the Army of Texas by such agents

are acts of audacity and impudence and without any semblance of authority,
[he declared.] General Johnston is a private citizen and holds no command
under the authority of government. The people of Texas are united in the
holy cause of liberty; and all the reports which the factions and seditions may
attempt to propagate for the purpose of embarrassing the government, will
recoil upon the heads of the malignant and imbecile few (if any there be) in
Texas, who may dare to raise a parricidal arm against their country.[97]

Needless to say, General Johnston was infuriated that it should be imputed that he had assumed authority to commission agents to go to the
United States, and he demanded that Dr. William C. Turner, "upon
whose representations," he said, "the proclamation was issued," clarify
the matter and set the President right. But all that Dr. Turner would
say was that

should any apprehension in regard to the statement that I made to the President of the Republic of Texas, concerning the appointing power as emanating
from Genl. Johns[t]on as proffered by the Texas commissioners in the U.
States, have a tendency to cast blame on them it was foreign from my design.
The only power that they seemed to convey was recommendation for promotion and my impression was that it was by the Government authority.[98]

Johnston sent Houston a copy of Turner's letter, and disavowed any
knowledge of the transactions alleged in the latter's proclamation and
asserted that it was quite untrue that he had anything to do with such
matters. "I have given no authority either verbally or in writing to grant
commissions, raise means, or to take any measures to raise troops in my
name," declared Johnston, and "I request" that the injustice done me by
your proclamation "may be remedied in such manner as may serve to
relieve me from imputations so injurious."[99]

Houston replied to the Johnston letter immediately, exonerating him

[97] "A Proclamation Concerning Self-Appointed Texas Agents" [dated:] Galveston,
April 25, 1842, in Proclamations of the Presidents (Texas), ms; *Telegraph and Texas
Register,* May 4, 1842.
[98] William C. Turner to Gen'l [A. S.] Johnston, Texas, April 27, 1842, in *Telegraph and Texas Register,* May 18, 1842.
[99] A. Sidney Johnston to Gen. Sam Houston, President of the Republic of Texas,
[dated:] City of Galveston, May 1, 1842, in *ibid.* See also A. Sidney Johnston to
the People of Texas, Galveston, May 6, 1842, in *ibid.* For J. C. Megginson's intem-
perate reply which degenerated into a strain of bitter invective against the Executive
rather than a defense of his part as an unauthorized agent, see *Civilian and Galveston Gazette,* September 10, 1842.

and declaring that the Turner letter "had no relevancy to the facts so far as you may be concerned." "Although my proclamation . . . did not implicate you as being concerned in the illegal and disorganizing acts of the agents spoken of, and was intended as a rebuke to such persons alone as were concerned in them—it gives me great pleasure to learn from yourself that you had no participancy in or knowledge of, such unpatriotic and mischievous acts of insubordination to the laws and constitution of the country."[100] Fortunately, the President was backed by that stable element of society, which had its roots firmly planted in the soil of Texas.

The great good sons of the solid yeomanry, the bones and sinew of the country, have begun to see things in the proper light and the "State is Safe." [Morgan informed Swartwout] The present Cal'd Session of Congress will develope much—you shall know all. We want no volunteers—nor invasion— our best policy is to let Mexico alone. . . . All the adjoining States on the Rio Grande are favorably friendly. . . . Then why quarrel with these people & maraud upon them. We cannot march an army to Mexico. It is preposterous to think of it, and a border warfare will be an injury to us. We are getting along very well. If our people can only be bright to believe it is best to let the Mexicans alone. Mexico cannot—will not invade us. If she does then we will show the world what we can do again! . . . and [since my visit with Houston at Galveston] I believe Old Sam is of same way thinking![101]

While the President's proclamation against unauthorized agents wrecked the plans of the "hot-heads," those in favor of immediate military action against Mexico were determined, if nothing more, to embarrass the Executive and force his acceptance of their point of view. Consequently, with some of the leading agitators at Galveston fresh from the recent meeting at Austin, it was determined to hold a large public meeting at Galveston on Tuesday, April 26, the day after the issuance of the President's proclamation and while Johnston was still frothing under the implications of it. The purpose of this meeting was to protest the course of action pursued by the Executive in respect to the proposed invasion of Mexico. The meeting was attended by citizens

[100] Sam Houston to Gen. A. S. Johnston, Galveston, May 2, 1842, in *Telegraph and Texas Register*, May 18, 1842; *Writings of Sam Houston*, III, 43–44; William Preston Johnston, *The Life of Gen. Albert Sidney Johnston: Embracing His Services in the Armies of the United States, the Republic of Texas, and the Confederate States*, pp. 125–126.
[101] James Morgan to Saml. Swartwout, New Washington, Galveston Bay, Texas, June 23, 1842, in Morgan Papers, ms.

from the Brazos, from the vicinity of San Jacinto, and from Galveston, as well as by the volunteers who were in the city.

Until the morning of the meeting fears had been entertained that a seditious spirit would be manifested, and that the President's policy would be soundly denounced. Three days before (April 23) General Burleson's "Address to the People of Texas" had been published in the city, adding fuel to the flame of discontent.[102] At the time of the publication of the address the editor of the *Civilian* commented that

Gen. B. . . . is some times tempted into the public prints, where he is much less at home than on the field of battle. He has no great confidence in his own capacity for composition, and in this instance has unluckily availed himself of the assistance of some one much less capable than himself. As far as the course of the President is concerned, in regard to the Commander of the Army, we believe that he has been guarded strictly by the constitution and laws, and, as relates to the other measures which have been taken, we think that he has acted with as much promptitude and efficiency as the circumstances would permit, or as promised to be advantageous to the country.

As for the proposed invasion of Mexico, the editor let it be known he was of the decided opinion "nothing should be attempted which there is not a reasonable prospect of accomplishing, or will not repay the trouble, when accomplished."

On the morning of the 26th and during the day, however, it was rumored that Houston was about to issue another proclamation—this time calling for supplies;[103] and that he was preparing to order the steamship *Zavala*, which had been laid up at Galveston since her first cruise in 1840,[104] fitted out to transport the volunteers then at Galveston

---

[102] *Civilian and Galveston Gazette,* April 23, 1842.

[103] A Proclamation Asking for Supplies for Troops, Galveston, April 26, 1842, in *Writings of Sam Houston,* III, 36–37.

[104] The *Zavala,* a sidewheeler, purchased by Texas in 1838, for $120,000, lost much of her copper on her first cruise and was tied up in the harbor at Galveston, where her bottom was supposed to have become considerably worm-eaten. While lying at her mooring she sprang a serious leak, and Lieutenant W. C. Brashear, in charge of a small caretaker party, was forced to run her aground in Galveston Bay in May 1842, to keep her from sinking. It was estimated in June 1842, that it would cost $15,000 to put her in complete repair, for which purpose it would be necessary to send her to the dry dock at New Orleans. Secretary of War and Marine Hockley recommended that instead of spending such a sum on the *Zavala* she be sold immediately at Galveston or in the United States, and that if a steamship were needed

to Corpus Christi, where the troops were being concentrated, it was hoped, for a prompt opening of the campaign.[105] "The people, ever ready to sustain the constituted authorities," reported the *Galveston Advertiser*, "rejoiced with this assurance, and the result was, a unanimity of feeling and assurance of a hearty cooperation with him on their part, such as could by no other means have been obtained."[106]

When the meeting assembled at the Merchant's Exchange in Galveston, the people were addressed by Colonel James Love, William H. Jack, Judge Abner S. Lipscomb, Colonel James S. Mayfield (a Lamar supporter and strong advocate for an immediate attack on Mexico), General James Davis, General Albert Sidney Johnston, John D. Morris of Béxar, and a Mr. Swett, after which a series of resolutions was presented by Colonel Love and Jack of Brazoria County and adopted unanimously by acclamation. The resolutions offered cooperation to the suffering west, pledged full assistance in chastising the common, merciless foe, and pledged the group "to discountenance all factious opposition calculated to embarrass its [the Government's] operations at a time like the present, when union alone is safety."[107] They tendered to the President their "prompt and united support on every measure based upon the prosecution of immediate war with Mexico, regarding that as the only means by which to effect the liberation of our countrymen, and the acknowledgement of our independence," and said they were glad to know that it was the intention of the Executive to take measures for the immediate invasion of the enemy's country.

Three days later, in reply to the resolutions, Houston assured the people of Galveston that the attack on Mexico would go forward backed by "all the means which may be within my control," and would take place "at the first moment that will promise success and renown to the cause

---

for the navy, the government should have a new one built. By the terms of a law of February 5, 1842, Congress sought to dispose of the *Zavala*, but the several attempts to do so ended in failure. Report of the Secretary of War and Marine, Houston, June 23, 1842, in *Telegraph and Texas Register*, July 6, 1842; Jim Dan Hill, *The Texas Navy: in Forgotten Battles and Shirtsleeve Diplomacy*, p. 160; *Telegraph and Texas Register*, May 25, 1842. The *Zavala* was broken up in 1844 and sold for scrap.

[105] *Telegraph and Texas Register*, May 4, 1842.

[106] Quoted in *ibid.*

[107] Report of the Meeting will be found in the *Telegraph and Texas Register*, May 4, 1842.

of our country and arms."[108] Privately, he hoped that an expedition against some of the Mexican ports might be carried out, for it would likely be more advantageous to Texas *than any other.* The spirit in Texas he felt was very strongly in favor of war, if it was for the purpose of defending Texas.[109]

[108] Houston to A. S. Lipscomb, and Others, Committee, Galveston, April 29, 1842, in *Writings of Sam Houston*, III, 40.

[109] Houston to William H. Daingerfield, Lynchburg, April 1, 1842 (Private), in *ibid.*, III, 14–16.

CHAPTER NINE

The Army on the Frontier

AFTER SOME DELAY, Corpus Christi, only two days' cavalry march from the Río Grande, was selected as the point of rendezvous for troops preparing to make a descent upon the relatively strong Mexican military post at Matamoros, located on the west bank of the river some twenty-five miles from its mouth. Troops landed at Corpus Christi and other western ports could reach the settlements on the Río Grande in short order, and once within the enemy's country, the army would be able to reap the harvests now ripening and thus supply itself with all the food it would need for a campaign. It was reported that the coastal route could be traversed with ease, as there were several small lakes along it that were never dry.[1] Furthermore, it was reliably reported that at almost any point within twenty to thirty miles of the coast fresh water could be had by digging wells ten to twelve feet deep. A dozen soldiers might sink a well in a few hours, that would afford water sufficient for a regiment. Thus, contrary to the assertions of Houston's critics, it seemed only reasonable to believe that the army might cross the lower Nueces country with as little difficulty in July, as in May or September.

An alternate route for launching an attack in summer upon northern Mexico lay through Béxar to Presidio del Río Grande by way of the upper road. Those who had resided for a long time in the west declared that there would be little difficulty in marching an army from San Antonio to the Río Grande, even in July or August, provided the upper Presidio road, skirting the high ridge extending from the sources of the San Antonio to near the Río Grande, be followed, as it furnished numerous excellent springs of water in the dry season. Traders from the Río Grande had long traveled this route at all seasons of the year.[2] This route would have the disadvantages of being longer; more inconvenient to the volunteers from the United States; less desirable for effective army-

[1] *Telegraph and Texas Register,* June 8, 1842.
[2] *Ibid.*

165

navy cooperation in an attack upon some vital point on the Mexican frontier; and more difficult to maintain supply lines and communications to; and as leading only to the relatively unimportant upper river towns. An attack upon Matamoros could be supported and sustained by sea. "What about the descent upon the coast?" queried the President of his friend Daingerfield. Whatever the plan of attack, he said, "We must be very secret. Our Editors will ruin Texas if they don't change their course."[3]

Accordingly, instructions were now sent to have the "emigrants" being recruited in the United States assembled at Corpus Christi between the 20th and 28th of July at the latest.[4] Texas was represented as determined, even if unaided by her friends in the United States "to battle alone . . . and never yield, until her Star is crimsoned and her last Banner shall be bathed in blood."[5] It would have been a tough job recruiting and outfitting an expedition under the most favorable conditions at Corpus Christi, much less under the handicaps confronting the government in 1842. Houston's Administration, without money and without credit, was in reality doing its best to collect some sort of a military force; and, although there were those who criticized the publicity that was given in the press and in official circles to the impending campaign, feeling that secrecy would have been the best policy, it is difficult to see how the government could have done otherwise since the plans were dependent upon the caprice of volunteers for their fulfillment. It was necessary to divulge the plans to a sufficient extent to inspire confidence. Besides, it was doubtful if Mexico, knowing the plans and even the time of the attack, would take them seriously, because of the nature of the country through which the Texans apparently intended to march in the midst of the summer; nor, if she took the Texans seriously, could she have placed herself in any better position of defense than she already was. "Instead," it was argued in the Texas press, "of imparting vigor to the national councils of that distracted country," such information "would but tend to weaken them, still more; especially, if publication

[3] Houston to William H. Daingerfield, City of Houston, April 9, 1842, in *Writings of Sam Houston*, III, 20–21.

[4] Houston to Gen. Leslie Combs, Houston, Texas, May 11, 1842, in *Writings of Sam Houston*, III, 47–48; Same to Col. Barry Gillespie, City of Houston, May 16, 1842, *ibid.*, III, 51–52; Same to Gen. [John C.] Pickens [of Alabama], City of Galveston, May 1, 1842 (Private), in *ibid.*, IV, 92; Same to Col. M. E. Holliday, Houston, Texas, May 6, 1842 (Private), in *ibid.*, IV, 93–94.

[5] Houston to Barry Gillespie, City of Houston, May 16, 1842, in *ibid.*, III, 51–52.

were made that the invading army would make common cause with the federal party against Santa Anna."[6] All that seemed to be needed in Texas was confidence in the Administration's leadership, for as G. M. Beard wrote, "If the people will give Old Sam his way he will bring Texas out at the big End of the Horn at last."[7]

Volunteers began to arrive from the United States on March 29 aboard the steamship *Neptune*.[8] The *Neptune* brought seventy volunteers from New Orleans, having left that port on Sunday the 27th "amid loud cheering from a multitude of spectators on the Levee." During the next few weeks other volunteers came on the *New York*, the *San Bernard*, and the *Tom Salmon* and other vessels.[9] Formerly employed in the carrying trade between United States ports and Mexican and Texan ports, the *Tom Salmon* was chartered by friends of Texas in Alabama to transport volunteers to Texas.

One hundred and fifty "armed emigrants" reached Galveston April 6 on the *New York*,[10] two days from New Orleans, and were described as being "remarkable for their gentlemanly deportment," and "an air of stern determined courage that indicates their object. They are but the advance guard of a gallant host that will, we trust," said the editor of the *Telegraph*, "ere long display the banner of the single Star beyond the Río Grande."[11] The day after their arrival they were treated to a battalion inspection of the units on Galveston Island consisting of the Fusileers, Coast Guards, Galveston Guards, and Artillery.[12] By April 21 Jeremiah Clemens, formerly a member of the Alabama House of Representatives, was reported on his way to Texas with a body of "emigrants."

It was reported at Houston on April 27 that 200 "emigrants" had

[6] *Telegraph and Texas Register*, April 27, 1842.

[7] G. M. Beard to Rev. J. C. Woolam, San Augustine, Texas, [dated:] Huntsville, June 8, 1842, in Littleton Fowler Papers, Feb. 9, 1841–Dec. 10, 1843, ms.

[8] F. Pinchard to James F. Perry, Galveston, March 29, 1842, in James F. Perry Papers, ms.; *Daily Picayune*, March 29, 1842; *Telegraph and Texas Register*, March 30, 1842, says the *Neptune* brought one hundred volunteers.

[9] *El Sol*, quoted in *El Cosmopolita*, June 25, 1842; José María de Bocanegra to the Minister of War, cited in Frederick C. Chabot, *Corpus Christi and Lipantitlán*, p. 28.

[10] John B. McMaster, *A History of the People of the United States, from the Revolution to the Civil War*, VII, 307; *Telegraph and Texas Register*, March 30, and June 8, 1842.

[11] *Telegraph and Texas Register*, April 13, 1842.

[12] *Bollaert's Texas*, p. 55.

sailed from Charleston, 100 from Baltimore, and that within the last few days 100 had arrived at Galveston from Alabama.[13] The *New Orleans Bee* reported another 640 "emigrants" from northern Alabama and the southern border of Tennessee on their march towards Memphis well armed and equipped.[14]

> Our rifles are ready,
>   And ready are we;
> Neither fear, care nor sorrow
>   In this company.
> Our rifles are ready
>   To welcome the foe,
> So away o'er the Sabine,
>   For Texas we go.
>
> For Texas, the land
>   Where the bright rising star
> Leads to beauty in peace,
>   And to glory in war.
> With aim never erring
>   We strike down the deer,—
> We chill the false heart
>   Of the Red Man with fear.
>
> The blood of the Saxon
>   Rolls full in the veins
> Of the lads that must lord
>   Over Mexico's plains—
> O'er the Plains where the breeze
>   Of the south woos the flowers,
> As we press those we love
>   In their sweet summer bowers.
>
> Our pledge to our loves!
>   When the battle is done,
> They shall share the broad lands
>   Which the rifle has won,—
> No tear on their cheeks—
>   Should we sleep with the dead,
> There are Rovers to follow

[13] *Telegraph and Texas Register*, April 27, 1842. Volunteers raised in the United States for the Texas campaign were designated "emigrants" as a means of getting around the United States neutrality laws.

[14] *Ibid.*, May 4, 1842, citing the *New Orleans Bee*.

Who will still "go-a-head"—
Who will still "go-a-head",
Where the bright, rising star
Leads to beauty in peace,
And to glory in war.[15]

In most cases the volunteers paid their own passage. Thomas Baldwin from New Orleans informed his uncle in Texas, James F. Perry, that "a Mr. John Massie who with some Hundred others visits Texas to help her out of her troubles with Mexico" go by the steamer *New York* whose captain "has behaved very badly making those young men pay him Eight Dollars each for Deck passage—when the *Neptune* carried men under the circumstances for four—there is not much patriotism to be found in the Capt[ain] of the *New York*."[16] Fifty or sixty of the volunteers who had gone to Texas had returned to New Orleans before May 10.[17]

Many of the men were landed at Galveston despite the President's orders that they were to disembark at Corpus Christi. Not all of those, however, who landed at Galveston were guilty of violating the Executive order, for those who had come early in response to the Texan plea for aid and landed prior to the issuance of the order on April 8 were not to be blamed, for the government itself had not completed its plans for the invasion.[18] Some of the volunteers who landed at Galveston moved later to Copano to participate in the preparations going forward at that point for the invasion. The newly arrived companies were described as being composed of as "fine looking fellows as ever bore the proud appellation of Americans. They were the real nobility of the Republic of our motherland," declared Miller,[19] as contrasted to the de-

---

[15] *Telegraph and Texas Register*, Feb. 3, 1841. These verses were written by William Kennedy, who had recently visited Texas, and upon his return to England had published a two volume history of Texas, entitled: *Texas: The Rise, Progress and Prospects of the Republic of Texas*. See also *Telegraph and Texas Register*, Dec. 4, 1839; *Bollaert's Texas*, p. 86.

[16] Thomas Baldwin to James F. Perry, New Orleans, April 3, 1842, in Perry Papers, ms.

[17] P. Edmunds to W. D. Miller, New Orleans, May 3–10, 1842, in Washington D. Miller Papers, 1833–1860 (Texas), ms.

[18] Houston to G. Earle Martin, Rodney, Mississippi [dated:] Houston, Texas, April 8, 1842, in *Writings of Sam Houston*, IV, 88.

[19] W. D. Miller to William H. Daingerfield, Houston, April 13, 1842, in Washington D. Miller Papers (Hardin-Simmons), m.s.; *Telegraph and Texas Register*, April 13, 1842.

scription given by the Mexican consul at New Orleans who pictured them as poverty-stricken wretches.[20]

Before going to Copano, some of the volunteers at Galveston, instead of proceeding down the coast in a vessel procured by the government, paid a visit to the city of Houston on April 8, with the intention of going from there by land. They were warmly received, but the government was too poor to provide them with horses and other equipment needed for going overland, a fact which caused them considerable dissatisfaction. They then determined to return to Galveston, and proceeded from there to the rendezvous point. As their boat was about to leave the wharf to return to Galveston, they were addressed by Dr. Branch T. Archer, and the President gave Captain Henry W. Allen of Claiborne County, Mississippi, and his Grand Gulf Volunteers a "parting bow."[21] Whereupon, they "very cordially and respectfully saluted them." The President then acknowledged "the compliment in a short address, which gave *very* great satisfaction to his truest friends as well as to the volunteers," reported Miller. "He promised them peril, glory and spoil—that they should stand with him shoulder to shoulder in the strife and clash of arms as comrades united in one cause, dear to humanity, liberty and constitutional government—the cause of Texas. He spoke like a hero, and every word was animation and delight. . . . It was," said Miller, "in the right time and the right spirit."[22] One Alabama company had backed out at the last minute, reported Stephen F. Minton upon arrival in Galveston with Captain Everett's men contrary to the advice of his parents, who had urged him to stick to his business in Selma, Alabama.[23] On Wednesday morning, April 26, President Houston addressed Captain Thomas Newton Wood's company of Alabama volunteers who had arrived at Galveston at sunrise three days before after seven days from Mobile on the schooner *William Penn*,[24] and had been mustered into

[20] Chabot, *Corpus Christi and Lipantitlán*, p. 28, referring to Bocanegra's report to the Minister of War, with New Orleans consular report no. 127 and enclosures.

[21] A[ndrew] J. Yeates to the Editors of the *Picayune*, Galveston, April 12, 1842, in *Daily Picayune*, April 15, 1842. The Muster Roll of Captain Allen's Company is reproduced in the Appendix of this work. Houston to Captain H. W. Allen, Houston, May 12, 1842, in *Writings of Sam Houston*, III, 48. A good biographical sketch of Henry Watkins Allen will be found in the *Writings of Sam Houston*, IV, 105 n–107 n.

[22] W. D. Miller to William H. Daingerfield, Houston, April 13, 1842, in Miller Papers (Hardin-Simmons), ms.

[23] Chabot, *Corpus Christi and Lipantitlán*, p. 39.

[24] *Telegraph and Texas Register*, May 4, 1842; *Daily Picayune*, April 28, 1842.

the Texas service at Galveston on April 23 by Major W. J. Mills, quartermaster of the Fourth Regiment of Texas Militia and inspecting and mustering officer. Wood's company of forty-four men were from Tuscaloosa and Eutaw, and had come "fully prepared for the duties of citizens of Texas with about three months provisions." Three hours after the arrival of the *William Penn*, the schooner *Floridian* entered port eleven days from Apalachicola with forty-two "emigrants" from Columbus, Georgia, under Captain John J. B. Hoxey.[25] One of the difficulties encountered at Galveston was the obtaining of certain needed supplies. To facilitate acquiring provisions immediately for the transportation of the troops to Corpus Christi, Houston, in a generous mood, gave his own personal note on the 26th for $75.00 for sixty days, but before the end of the day asked Gail Borden, collector of the port of Galveston, to lift his note and charge the bread, coffee, sugar, and other supplies obtained from H. H. Williams & Co. and Durst & Kuhn to naval appropriations.[26] Some two weeks later, May 13, the President again authorized the purchase on his own personal credit of $250.00 worth of sugar and coffee for the troops at Corpus Christi.[27]

The day after Houston's address to the Alabama volunteers, a large portion of the volunteers at Galveston sailed for Corpus Christi. "There will be no restraining the volunteers from going ahead," declared James Morgan; "they are almost uncontroulable now [May 17], such is their anxiety to get to Mexico."[28] Captain Hitchcock returning to Galveston from Corpus Christi on April 30, reported 300 volunteers in camp near the mouth of the Nueces.[29] A letter dated May 2 from Galveston, with considerable exaggeration, gave the number of troops at Corpus Christi at the end of April as 1,000 and at Victoria as 300. A group of "Missouri Invincibles," primarily from the St. Louis area, numbering 120, left St. Louis on May 2 on the steamer *Alton* and reached New Orleans on the

The Muster Roll of Captain Thomas N. Wood's Company is reproduced in the Appendix of this work.

[25] *Telegraph and Texas Register*, May 4, 1842; see Muster Roll, Appendix of this work.

[26] Note of Sam Houston, dated April 26, 1842, endorsed by Alden A. M. Jackson, Colonel Commanding, and Houston to G. Borden, Jr., Galveston, April 26, 1842, in *Writings of Sam Houston*, III, 36–37.

[27] Sam Houston to John S. Sydnor, City of Houston, May 13, 1842, in *ibid.*, III, 49.

[28] James Morgan to Saml. Swartwout, New Washington, Galveston Bay, Texas, May 17, 1842, in James Morgan Papers, 1841–1845, ms.

[29] *Telegraph and Texas Register*, May 4, 1842; *Daily Picayune*, May 2, 1842.

CONSOLIDATED RETURN OF THE STRENGTH OF VOLUNTEERS MUSTERED INTO SERVICE OF THE REPUBLIC OF TEXAS BY W. J. MILLS, MUSTERING AND INSPECTING OFFICER, WITH THE SUPPLIES IN THEIR POSSESSION*

Company	Captains	1st Lt.	2nd Lt.	3rd Lt.	Ensigns	Sergeants	Corporals	Privates	Swords	Pistols	Rifles	Muskets	Shotguns	Cartridge boxes	Powder flasks	Knapsacks	Pounds powder	Pounds lead	Flints	Haversacks	Canteens	Pounds bread or flour	Pounds pork or bacon	Pounds beef	Pounds coffee	Pounds sugar	Quarts salt	Barrels of potatoes	Remarks
D Capt. J. M. Allen	1	1	1			4	4	26	3	7		34		30		21	75	120	150	50	37	400	200	140	25	25	128		Embarked on board Schooner *Roridian,* April 2
E Capt. H. W. Allen	1	1	1	1	1	4	4	27	5	12	20	15		12	23	16	100	63	80	42	40	320	200		25	25			do
F Capt. John J. B. Hoxey	1	1	1			5	4	31	4	10	8	21	9	21	15	19	200	300	500	30	43	1300	900		80	160	100		do
G Capt. Thos. N. Wood	1	1	1	1		4	4	33	6	22	20	16	6	5	40	28	204	300	500		44	300	800		90	80		3	Quartered at Navy Yard, Galveston
Total	4	4	4	2	1	17	16	117	18	51	48	86	15	68	78	84	579	783	1230	122	164	2320	2100	140	220	290	228	3	

Galveston April 27, 1842
W. J. Mills, Inspecting & Mustering Officer

* Militia Rolls (Texas).

night of May 9 bound for Texas. Some 80 other "emigrants" were at this time at New Orleans awaiting transportation. It was expected that both groups would sail in a few days for Texas.[30] Another company, numbering 100, was reported on its way from Huntsville in northern Alabama prepared to settle west of the Nueces.[31] From Natchez, 53 volunteers reached Galveston on the *New York* on May 13, with provisions for ninety days. These were called the "Natchez Mustangs" and were under the command of Captain Walter Hickey.[32] By the time they were mustered into the Texas service on May 24 their number had been increased to 57.

In the meantime, other volunteers reached Galveston. Every steamboat and vessel from the United States brought in some "emigrants,"[33] and word was sent to Gillespie in the "Crescent City" to spread the word that the President wished to see all who were *fully prepared* to emigrate . . . *at the rendezvous at Corpus Christi between the 20th and 28th of July.*"[34] The *Neptune*, under Captain William Rollins, arrived on May 4 with some 30 to 40 "emigrants," and on the 20th this same vessel was again at Galveston with over 150 volunteers, part of whom belonged to the St. Louis Company under Captain Stevenson and the others to Captain Jeremiah Clemens' Alabama company.[35] The new arrivals reported that another 100 to 200 men were still at New Orleans awaiting transportation. Stevenson's men reached Galveston on or shortly before May 25, the date on which they were mustered into the service of Texas. After a few days Stevenson proceeded to Houston where he received on June 7 his appointment as captain, and at that time appointments were also issued to other officers at Galveston, including Captain Jeremiah Clemens.[36]

---

[30] P. Edmunds to W. D. Miller, New Orleans, May 3–10, 1842, in Miller Papers (Texas), ms.; *Telegraph and Texas Register,* May 18, 1842; *Daily Picayune,* May 10, 1842.

[31] *Daily Picayune,* May 10, 1842; *Telegraph and Texas Register,* May 18, 1842.

[32] *Telegraph and Texas Register,* May 18, 1842. See Muster Roll, Appendix of this work.

[33] *Bollaert's Texas,* pp. 55, 84.

[34] Sam Houston to Col. Barry Gillespie, City of Houston, May 16, 1842, in *Writings of Sam Houston,* III, 51–52.

[35] *Telegraph and Texas Register,* May 11 and 25, 1842.

[36] Houston to [George W. Hockley], Executive Department, City of Houston, June 7, 1842, in *Writings of Sam Houston,* III, 64. Alexander Stevenson served from April to August 16, 1842. See John C. Grosjean and Patrick Daugherty, in Miscellaneous Claim Papers (Texas), ms.

Captain Coffey reached New Orleans early in June with 49 "emigrants" raised in east Tennessee, who, because of the coon skin caps they wore, were said to belong to the order of Captain Davy Crockett. Coffey's men embarked on the steamship *Tom Salmon* from Mobile, partly financed by friends of Texas in Mobile.[37] So far, all the "emigrants," who had come to Texas had done so from the southern and western parts of the United States; none arrived from the eastern cities.[38]

The volunteers who remained at Galveston were soon in a starving condition for want of food and water, and had to be transferred to the bay shore to enable them to obtain sustenance. Wood's company was stationed at Cedar Point for a while.[39] The result was dissatisfaction, discontent, and disappointment on the part of those who had enlisted under the "lone star," and who "unfortunately not having Mexicans to fight with. . . . commenced fighting among themselves. Several serious difficulties have been the consequences," reported William Bollaert.[40] Eventually on June 17 James D. Boylan, who had brought in the prize *Mary Elizabeth,* was ordered to transfer the troops at Galveston to Live Oak Point, using for that purpose the brig *Retrieve* of Newburyport then in port which was seized by presidential order for transporting the troops.[41] Major James H. Cooke was to furnish the meat rations for the troops and Colonel Robert Mills, "the Duke of Brazoria,"[42] who com-

---

[37] *El Sol* quoted in *El Cosmopolita,* June 25, 1842.

[38] *Telegraph and Texas Register,* May 18, 1842.

[39] Houston to Captain of the "Mustang," Galveston, Texas, June 11, 1842, in *Writings of Sam Houston,* III, 67.

[40] *Bollaert's Texas,* p. 55.

[41] Houston to Col. [Lewis M.] H. Washington, Houston, Texas, May 22, 1842, in *Writings of Sam Houston,* III, 56–57; Same to Same, City of Houston, May 31, 1842, in *ibid.,* III, 62–63; Same to James D. Boylan, Galveston, Texas, June 17, 1842 in *ibid.,* III, 70; Thomas Gibbon Morgan, Collector [of Customs] to Walter Forward, Secretary of the Treasury, [dated:] Collector's Office, New Orleans, June 23, 1842, copy in Domestic Correspondence (Texas), 1835–1846, ms. Seizure of the *Retrieve* brought a protest from the United States chargé d'affaires in Texas, to which Houston replied, "I regret that any difficulty should have arisen as to the cruise. . . . All just remuneration will be made to the captain and owners, . . . [but] at this time the country has no means to meet the demand." Houston to Joseph Eve, Executive Department, City of Houston, July 30, 1842, in *Writings of Sam Houston,* III, 135.

[42] It is said that John L. Sleight was the one who conferred upon Mills the title of "Duke of Brazoria." Robert Mills was born in Logan County, Kentucky, in 1809, and educated at the University of Tennessee at Nashville. The son of a prominent,

manded the Navy Yard at Galveston, was to furnish military support, if necessary, in carrying out the order.

Aransas City, located on Live Oak Point, in what was then Refugio County, was developed in the fall of 1837 as a townsite by Colonel Henry L. Kinney and Colonel James Power. It was the most western coastal habitation north of the Nueces. Located at the end of the peninsula separating Copano Bay from Aransas Bay, Live Oak Point, formerly the site of a Spanish-Mexican fort called Aranzazu, was high and pleasantly situated with good water and an excellent growth of live oak. It was the site of a customhouse for Copano and Aransas bays for about a year until June 1839, when it was removed across Aransas Bay to the new townsite of Lamar on Copano Creek near the entrance to Copano Bay. Five companies—one each from St. Louis (Captain Stevenson), Natchez (Captain Hickey), Tuscaloosa (Captain Symmes), Huntsville (Captain Jeremiah Clemens), and Perry County, Alabama—were moved from the Galveston area on June 23 for Corpus Christi.[43] Upon being landed at Live Oak Point, the volunteers who had come from the United States inadequately supplied with food and equipment despite positive and repeated orders of the President, were compelled to subsist as best they could. Although occasionally limited supplies of coffee, sugar, and bacon were available, the men found it extremely difficult to obtain food other than beef, and, if we believe Houston's prejudiced statement, there was "no beef west of [the] Colorado." Captain Eli

wealthy, and successful planter, Robert sought to follow in his father's footsteps, opening at the age of eighteen a plantation in Madison Parish, Louisiana. After several successful years, he suffered such heavy losses as the result of a flood that he abandoned his plantation and removed to Texas in 1830, and settled at Brazoria. In Texas he engaged in merchandizing, and with his brother established the firm of R. & D. G. Mills, which for thirty years was a powerful business firm engaged in planting, trade, and commerce. In 1835 Robert Mills made valuable contributions toward outfitting the Texas navy and feeding and clothing the Texas army. By 1860 he owned four plantations in Brazoria, totally over 20,000 acres; two in Matagorda of 2,000 acres; one in Fort Bend County of 1,000 acres; and additional acreage in other places. In all, it is said, he owned 160,000 acres of land and 850 slaves. The Civil War cost him two to three millions of dollars in the depreciation of his properties, as well as the loss of some $850,000 in slave property; but still he was not broke. In 1867 many cotton firms failed, and so did the business establishment of R. & D. G. Mills, and the "Duke" lived in comparative poverty during his remaining years. See "Galveston Sketches," ts., pt. II, pp. 262–269.

[43] *Telegraph and Texas Register*, June 29, 1842; *Daily Picayune*, April 21 and July 8, 1842.

Chandler of Robertson County also commanded a company in Texas in May 1842, the only company raised in Texas that had reported to the War Department by May 13.[44]

In the weeks immediately following Valera's raid, several interesting developments had taken place on the lower Nueces frontier. A few days after the excitement from the raid began to die out, Colonel Kinney, B. Belden, and F. Belden made a trip to Matamoros, evidently for the purpose of reassuring the Mexican authorities of their peaceful intentions in spite of the Texas war talk.[45] After Kinney and his party had been gone a few days several parties of traders from the Río Grande arrived at the Aubrey and Kinney Rancho and stayed ten days, but suddenly left early in the morning of the day that Captain Jack R. Everett's company of Alabama volunteers landed in the evening.[46]

The first troops to arrive in the Corpus Christi area reached Black Point, an old Spanish landing at the point where the Aransas River empties into Copano Bay,[47] near the Rancho, early in April under Captain Everett where they subsisted upon beef furnished by the ranch. This first contingent consisted of 150 volunteers from New Orleans and Mobile, who left Galveston on April 4 on the *Colonel Hanson*.[48] Two other companies, newly arrived from the United States and commanded, respectively, by Captains John Ross and Augustus Williams, were dispatched to Black Point. Williams' company[49] of Tennessee volunteers was received into the service of Texas on April 7, and ordered to proceed in the transport schooner *Colonel Hanson* to Black Point, where the company was to disembark and march overland to the Rancho.[50]

[44] Sam Houston to Capt. Eli Chandler, Houston, Texas, May 13, 1842, in *Writings of Sam Houston*, III, 49–50; *Handbook of Texas*, I, 329.

[45] W. B. Goodman, "A Statement of Facts, Washington, Feby 10, 1843," in Miller Papers (Texas), ms.

[46] *Ibid.*

[47] Once owned by Philip Dimitt, Black Point was used as a landing depot for munitions and supplies for the northern Mexican Federalists, 1838–1840. The small community of Bayside occupies roughly the same site today. *Handbook of Texas*, I, 169–170.

[48] The Muster Roll of Captain Jack R. Everett's Company is reproduced in Appendix of this work; Goodman, "A Statement of Facts, Washington, Feby 10, 1843," in Miller Papers (Texas), ms.; *Daily Picayune*, April 9, 1842.

[49] The Muster Roll of Captain Augustus Williams' Company is reproduced in Appendix of this work.

[50] *Daily Picayune*, April 15, 1842. Augustus Williams brought a company of volunteers from Tennessee to Texas in 1842, and after the breakup of the intended expedition against Mexico, remained in Texas. He settled in Fayette County and

As the *Colonel Hanson* pulled away from the Galveston landing, a mighty shout arose from those on board, who expected soon to pay a visit to Mexico. Their provisions were to be sent by the sloop *Washington* to Black Point.[51] Williams, a North Carolinian by birth and brother of Robert H. Williams of Matagorda County (one of the Old Three Hundred), was instructed to report to Colonel Clark L. Owen,[52] who commanded a small group of men, consisting principally of Captain John P. Gill's mounted volunteers, totalling 97 men in all who had been mustered into service on March 20 and then stationed on the frontier in the Victoria-Corpus Christi area after the Vasquez invasion.[53] Williams' orders specifically stated that "so soon as a Regiment of Volunteers can be formed, they will be organized and proceed to an election of their own officers"—the detachments, however, were to hold themselves subject to further orders from the War Department.

represented it in the Ninth Congress, 1844–1845. After killing Aaron A. Gardinier, sheriff of Fayette County, in a duel fought in June 1845, over a political canvass, Williams moved to Goliad, where he represented that county in 1846 in the House of Representatives of the First Legislature of the State of Texas. Williams served as a member of the annexation convention of 1845. He died at Brownsville, Texas, in 1847. [Elizabeth LeNoir Jennett], *Biographical Directory of the Texan Conventions and Congresses*, p. 191; Frank Brown, "Annals of Travis County and of the City of Austin," XIII, 14.

[51] George W. Hockley to [Captain Augustus Williams], Department of War & Marine, April 7, 1842, in Harriet Smither (ed.), *Journals of the Sixth Congress of the Republic of Texas*, III, 77–78.

[52] Clark L. Owen has been described by Ben Stuart as "a brave, modest, unassuming Christian gentleman, a worthy scion of a worthy sire." He was born in Shelby County, Kentucky, in 1808, and gave up a mercantile business at New Castle, Kentucky, to come to Texas in March 1836, to aid in the cause of Texan independence. He joined the Texan army, and received an appointment as captain in May 1837. Owen served as senator from the district of Matagorda, Jackson, and Victoria, in the Sixth Congress. John Henry Brown, *History of Texas, from 1685 to 1892*, II, 240; Texas Congress, Congressional Papers, ms., Sixth Congress; Ben C. Stuart, "Texas Fighters and Frontier Rangers," ms., pp. 233–234; H. S. Thrall, *A Pictorial History of Texas*, p. 597.

[53] Special Order No. 3, Department of War & Marine, April 7, 1842, in Smither (ed.), *Journals of the Sixth Congress*, III, 77–78; a copy of the foregoing order will be found in Army Papers (Texas), ms.; Muster Roll of Captain John S. Menefee and 52 others, who served from March 6 to June 6, 1842 (commanded by Clark L. Owen, Colonel-Commanding) and Muster Roll of Captain John P. Gill's Mounted Volunteer Company enrolled at Columbia by Capt. John P. Gill (commanded by Clark L. Owen, Colonel-Commanding and serving from March 20–June 20, 1842) contains the names of 97 officers and privates. See Muster Rolls in Appendix of this work.

When Colonel Clark L. Owen arrived in Corpus Christi on April 24 to organize and drill the volunteers arriving at that place, he found the camp in great confusion, but did not have an opportunity to straighten matters out before he was relieved of his command on the following day by Major Thomas Casey, who had been appointed to the command on April 9 as "Volunteer Aid to the Executive," with the rank of "major."[54] Casey, formerly of Cahawba, Alabama, left Galveston on April 18 for the frontier to organize and drill the men at the encampment on the Nueces and to report their organization and strength to the War Department. He reached Corpus Christi on April 25 and found "every thing... in the utmost confusion."[55]

As soon as it was known in the camp that Casey had been ordered to relieve Owen of his command, a mutiny of the officers was called. The volunteers, it was said, had willingly consented to be commanded by Colonel Owen, "a gentleman who understands the Geography of the Country," and who "also has considerable experience in the field of battle," and who, therefore, was a man upon whom they were willing to depend. If they could not have him as their commander, they said, "we must rely upon our camp alone, for such officers as are necessary for the guide and direction of our companies." The men not only refused to come under Casey's command, but said they would do the same for anyone else who had so little knowledge of the country and was so totally unknown to them.[56] They were willing to accept any qualified appointed officer only until their number had been sufficiently increased to permit them to be organized into a regiment and then proceed to the election of their own officers in accordance with the orders of the Sec-

[54] George W. Hockley to Major Thomas Casey, Department of War & Marine, April 10, 1842, in Smither (ed.), *Journals of the Sixth Congress*, III, 78 (copy also in Army Papers (Texas), ms.); Same to Same, Department of War & Marine, April 29, 1842, in Chabot, *Corpus Christi and Lipantitlán*, p. 48; Proclamation of Sam Houston, dated City of Houston, April 9, 1842, in *Writings of Sam Houston*, III, 21; *Daily Picayune*, May 6, 1842.

[55] Thomas Casey, Major and Aide to the Executive, to Geo[rge] W. Hockley, Corpus Christi, April 27, 1842, in Smither (ed.), *Journals of the Sixth Congress*, III, 78–81.

[56] Augustus Williams and Others to Major [Thomas] Casey, Corpus Christi, April 23, 1842, in *ibid.*, III, 81; copy in Army Papers (Texas), ms. Those who signed with Williams were Capt. John Ross, Company A; 1st Lt. H. H. Brown, Company A; 2nd Lt. W. P. Moore, Company A; Capt. J. R. Everett, Company B; 1st Lt. E. S. Ratcliffe, Company B; 2nd Lt. Thomas Mills, Company B; Capt. William F. Scott, Company C; 1st Lt. John McBith, Company C; and 2nd Lt. Hugh O'Connor, Company C.

retary of War. Casey's principal difficulty seems to have resulted from the fact that he was relatively unknown to the men, for he was considered by the President to be a man of high character, a good soldier, and a sound officer.[57]

Being near the place where the officers had collected, Casey walked over to the group and "explained to them," he said, "that they were entirely mistaken as to the views and intentions of the [War] Department"; that his own commission was one in the staff and that he had been assigned to command "their organization and drill until such time as a sufficient number could be collected together to form a Regiment, when an election for . . . field officers would be held as . . . promised."[58] Acting as spokesman for the officers, Captain Williams, who had been chosen commander of the volunteers in the area "until such time as Col. Owen should arrive," informed Casey that they would reconsider the matter and would call and inform him of their determination. That afternoon Captain Everett called upon Major Casey to state that he had signed the protest upon a mistaken view of the issues, and that he now wished to say that he and Second Lieutenant M. Mills would obey the orders of the War Department, but that they were the only officers who would so acquiesce in this matter.

The next morning Captain Williams called upon Casey to tell him that, with the exception of Everett and Mills, the officers to a man refused to submit to his command. Colonel Owen, fearful of being involved in the disobedience of orders, instructed that the companies be paraded; and upon their being drawn up in formation, he turned his command over to Major Casey. Feeling that his continued presence in camp might tend to increase the difficulties, Owen retired to his home at Texana, after writing a note to his friend James Power at Live Oak Point requesting him to permit Mr. Fugitt, acting under orders of Major Williams, to procure at Live Oak Point ten head of beeves for which he would give a receipt. It was represented that the troops at Corpus Christi were destitute of subsistence and that beef was now their only reliance.[59]

Upon Owen's turning over the command of the troops, Major Casey

[57] Houston to James Davis, City of Houston, May 14, 1842, in Chabot, *Corpus Christi and Lipantitlán*, p. 46.

[58] Thomas Casey to George W. Hockley, Corpus Christi, April 27, 1842, in Smither (ed.), *Journals of the Sixth Congress*, III, 78–81.

[59] Clark L. Owen to Col. James Power, Corpus Christi (Camp Everitt), April 27, 1842, in Army Papers (Texas), ms.

ordered all the captains to report to his headquarters for instructions; however, only Captains Everett and Ross appeared and "expressed their willingness to comply, but [said] that they could not control their men." Williams refused to report his command. A little later in the day he again called upon Major Casey to state that he had been elected "major commanding" and that he would continue to act as such.[60]

On the morning of April 26, Casey, orally and in writing, informed Williams that his (Casey's) orders to relieve Colonel Owen of his command included Williams' Company of Tennessee volunteers who could not place themselves under the command of anyone else without direct mutiny. "Should you as their Captain," he wrote, "or any member of your Company fail to obey any order legally issued by me, as the commanding officer at this place, he will be instantly held answerable to the rules and articles of war, for such cases made and provided."[61] Casey concluded by telling Williams that in the afternoon he would publish an order to the troops, which he sincerely trusted would satisfy them and prevent any disagreeable consequences; and "I certainly hope and expect that Capt. Williams will exert his own influence, as he is bound to do, by the regulations to which he has voluntarily subjected himself, to put down every thing like insubordination amongst the men."

Captain Ross submitted his resignation to Major Casey on April 27, "reporting his company in a state of absolute mutiny—his life threatened by one of his company, and [said] that the man when arrested by him, . . . [was] forcibly released by the order of Capt. Williams."[62] During the afternoon of the 26th, as promised, Casey issued orders for the purpose of determining if the companies under Captains Everett and Ross would submit to the orders of their officers. No sooner were the orders read than Captain Williams

stepped forward and addressed the men in a most disorganizing manner, stating that he considered their rights infringed, and that should they yield in this, they would be called on to yield in every thing else; and that although

[60] Augustus Williams, Major Commanding, to Major Casey, April 25, 1842, in Smither (ed.), *Journals of the Sixth Congress*, III, 82; Thomas Casey to Captain Augus[tus] Williams, Camp at Corpus Christi, April 26, 1842, in *ibid.*, III, 82.
[61] Thomas Casey to Capt. Augus[tus] Williams, Camp at Corpus Christi, April 26, 1842, in *ibid.*, III, 82.
[62] Thomas Casey to George W. Hockley, Secretary of War & Marine, Corpus Christi, April 27, 1842, in *ibid.*, III, 78–81; copy also in Army Papers (Texas), ms.; *Telegraph and Texas Register*, May 11, 1842.

willing to resign the station to which they had elevated him, he was determined to carry out their wishes in all respects, and that therefore, he desired an expression of their opinion as to what course they would pursue. About two thirds [of the men] shouted hurrah for Williams. . . . So soon as he had finished [reported Casey], and being anxious to understand how many were disposed to continue in a state of subordination, I made a few remarks to the troops, explaining the views of the Department, its willingness to comply with its promises as regarded the election of officers—its absolute and undoubted right to pursue the course it had done in sending an officer to organize them; the nature of the offense they were committing &c., and desiring all who were willing and anxious to remain in a state of subordination to step to the front. Although as I have since learned [continued Casey in his report the next day], some were anxious to obey the orders, no one stepped forward, and I found myself alone, and unsupported—save by a few of the officers, and they through fear of losing popularity with their men, unwilling to take any decided or efficient steps. Under these circumstances, I was under the necessity of stating that I should take no farther control over them, unless they voluntarily reported themselves to me for duty, but that I should report the whole command in a state of mutiny and total disorganization.[63]

The chief offenders were Williams and Second Lieutenant W. P. Moore of Captain Ross' Company.

A curious letter, showing a general lack of discipline among the troops on the frontier, was written by William C. McKinstry, acting assistant quartermaster on May 15 from the "5th neigh of the Devil, Head-quarters of Mutineers," to Orderly Sergeant Josiah Walton Thompson, "Camp Nueces, Mexico." Thompson had served in the Seminole War in Florida. The letter commences,

Dear Thompson:

Appointed the Quarters of Major Casey Loyalists look out. Mutiny is hanging. Prepare to make your peace with God! What will poor Williams do in hell with the reumatiz [rheumatism] and Rover too, when he is roasted on one side[.] Who will turn him over on the other[?] You know he would die before he would turn himself and thus he would be half cooked, and the Devil likes his meat well done. Don't send any more unnecessary company for me as it is not convenient for me at present to wait upon them. When you send a man or men send some more. No persons from the camp have yet reported to me, and of course [I] could not call on them to do anything except please do this and please do that. . . . I can get along now untill I come myself. It is as

63 Thomas Casey to George W. Hockley, Corpus Christi, April 27, 1842, in Smither (ed.), *Journals of the Sixth Congress*, III, 78–81.

much as I feel able to do to guard the provisions, without standing guard over refractory men.[64]

During the troublesome days on the frontier, it was rumored, apparently without much serious consideration on the part of the President, that Houston himself was preparing to proceed to the southwestern frontier to take command of the army.[65] General Somervell arrived in Houston on May 2 to report in person to the President and the Secretary of War on the disbandment of the troops under his command at San Antonio. However, instead of appointing him to command the troops on the Nueces, the President, greatly displeased with the conduct of the volunteers, named James Davis acting adjutant general of the Texas Army on May 3 and sent him two days later to relieve Major Casey of his command.[66] Davis had been in Texas only a few months, having arrived in February from Mississippi, and had been selected late in April to replace Daingerfield at New Orleans as Texas agent.[67] The crisis in command on the Nueces caused a sudden change in the President's plans for Davis. His new instructions were to give strict attention to discipline and subordination; and, if there were any attempts to interfere with his command, he was to place the culprits "in confinement of the most rigid character, until further orders, or send them in irons to Houston." He was to give special attention to the comfort of his troops, to exclude ardent spirits and intoxicating liquors from the limits of his command which was to embrace the whole southwestern frontier from the San Antonio River to the Río Grande, and to establish martial law and proceed with a court-martial trial of offenders in the area.[68] At the same time Captain McLean's ranging company was

[64] Quoted in Chabot, *Corpus Christi and Lipantitlán*, p. 38.

[65] William Kennedy to Aberdeen, Gregory's Hotel, Arundel St., Haymarket, June 15, 1842, in Ephraim D. Adams (ed.), "Correspondence from the British Archives Concerning Texas," in *Quarterly of the Texas State Historical Association*, XV (1911–1912), 300.

[66] *Daily Picayune*, May 11, 1842; Proclamation Appointing James Davis as Acting Adjutant-General, Executive Department, City of Houston, May 3, 1842, in *Writings of Sam Houston*, III, 44. George W. Hockley, Secretary of War and Marine, to Major Thomas Casey, May 11, 1842 (copy), in Army Papers (Texas), ms.

[67] Barry Gillespie to Capt. James M. Ogden, May 2, 1842, in Chabot, *Corpus Christi and Lipantitlán*, p. 36; *Handbook of Texas*, I, 470; Houston to William H. Daingerfield, Galveston, April 27, 1842, in *Writings of Sam Houston*, III, 37–40.

[68] Sam Houston to James Davis, Executive Department, City of Houston, May 5, 1842, in *Writings of Sam Houston*, III, 45–46.

brought under General Davis' command.[69] On May 11 Secretary of War Hockley wrote Davis that two companies were being sent him by the *Prigo*, a schooner recently captured by the Texan navy, and that the squadron under Moore had left Galveston for New Orleans the day before to be refitted.[70]

The President saw in the insubordination down on the Nueces "the influence of Galveston." "My dear friend," he wrote Davis on May 14, "we are to have some trouble, but we must maintain order, and with it the country. . . . There is no particular show of excitement in this vast city [Houston]. They [the opposition] have for the present haulled off to refit and doubtless anew [renew] the action, as they hope, with more success. Defeat thus far has resulted to their plans."[71]

Remembering the disastrous folly which had prompted the attempt to advance on Matamoros in 1835, Houston specifically warned Davis that under no circumstances was an advance to the enemy's frontier to be made, unless ordered by the War Department; "and should any insubordinate attempt be made, or should have commenced, you will instantly communicate it to the War Department and suppress the sedition. The greatest, and every curse, which has befallen Texas, and every disaster and massacre," declared the President, "has resulted from a foolish passion to take Matamoros without means. When there are means for a successful attack, it shall be taken; and until then, any attempt would be destructive to Texas."[72]

On May 11 General Davis was ordered to have Captain Williams, a "self-made major," report forthwith in person to the War Department at Houston.[73] Upon his arrival in Houston, Williams admitted having held

[69] Sam Houston to Captain Ephraim McLain, City of Houston, May 5, 1842, in *ibid.*, III, 44–46; Smither (ed.), *Journals of the Sixth Congress*, III, 77–84.

[70] George W. Hockley to James Davis, May 11, 1842, in Chabot, *Corpus Christi and Lipantitlán*, p. 60.

[71] Sam Houston to Genl [James] Davis, City of Houston, May 14, 1842, in *ibid.*, pp. 46–47.

[72] Sam Houston to James Davis, City of Houston, May 5, 1842, in *Writings of Sam Houston*, III, 45–46.

[73] George W. Hockley, Secretary of War and Marine, to Major Thomas Casey, Department of War and Marine, May 11, 1842 (copy); Special Order No. 4, Department of War and Marine, May 11, 1842 (copy) by George W. Hockley ordering Williams to report at Houston; Special Order No. 10, Department of War and Marine, May 30, 1842 (copy), ordering Williams to report in person to the Department; Extract from letter of George W. Hockley, Secretary of War and Marine, to Major Thomas Casey, Department of War and Marine, May 11, 1842; all in Army Papers (Texas), ms. See also Houston to James Davis, City of Houston,

an election among the volunteers at Corpus Christi in violation of the orders of the government. He was accordingly summarily discharged from the service of the Republic on July 8 and interdicted from again entering it for having "committed mutiny."[74] At the same time, the War Department re-emphasized the necessity of obedience to orders and the enforcement of the same.

Since he had thus supposedly been deprived of his office of "captain" without being permitted a trial by a court-martial, and because the charges against him were considered "too trivial to notice," Congress unhesitatingly passed a bill requiring the President to restore Williams to his former rank of "captain" on the grounds that the law provided that no officer in the military or naval service of the Republic should be "deprived of his commission, unless by the sentence of a court martial."[75] This bill was vetoed by the President, who denied that this law applied to the Williams case, since it made reference "only to commissioned officer," and Williams had not been deprived of "his commission," nor had he been "deprived of any office which entitled him to a commission by our laws." The removal was based on the law of June 12, 1837, governing the army. It was impossible, declared Houston, to assemble

a court martial with any prospect of conviction, because a sufficient number of officers to constitute a court could not have been assembled, without including some officers who were equally culpable with Captain Williams, and involved in the same mutinous transaction. [Williams] had voluntarily abandoned the command of his company, and another gentleman had been elected to the command which he had voluntarily vacated. Whether Captain Williams was legally elected a Major in the Texas Service, is a question which it is not necessary to determine [declared the President]. He had of his own free will vacated the office of Captain of the Company which he commanded—another gentleman was elected to supply the vacancy thus created. . . . Does not the Honorable Congress perceive that this action of theirs must therefore involve

May 14, 1842, in Chabot, *Corpus Christi and Lipantitlán*, p. 46; Smither (ed.), *Journals of the Sixth Congress*, III, 82–83.

[74] Special Order No. 17, Department of War & Marine, July 8, 1842; and General Order No. 1, Department of War & Marine, July 8, 1842, in Smither (ed.), *Journals of the Sixth Congress*, III, 83–84; copy also in Army Papers (Texas), ms.

[75] H. P. N. Gammel (ed.), *Laws of Texas*, II, 609; Sam Houston to the House of Representatives, City of Houston, July 22, 1842, in Smither (ed.), *Journals of the Sixth Congress*, III, 175–176; "Joint Resolution for the relief of Captain Augustus Williams," passed over the President's veto, July 23, 1842, in Gammel (ed.), *Laws of Texas*, II, 820; *Telegraph and Texas Register*, July 27, 1842.

them in a most disagreeable dilemma? If it were unlawful for the Executive to remove Captain Williams, is it not equally so for the Honorable Congress to remove his successor? . . . Mr. Williams was not deprived of any commission, nor of any office which entitled him to a commission in our service—he was simply dismissed from the service, in which he held no commission—and this the Executive had the right to do. A court martial was not convened for his trial, for the reasons above given, nor was it necessary—the facts alleged against Mr. Williams were admitted. There was, therefore, no necessity for a court martial to ascertain those facts.

Nevertheless, upon the reading of the veto message, the bill re-enstating Williams was immediately and unanimously passed over the President's veto; whereupon the House adjourned *sine die.*[76] The bill then went to the Senate where, in the afternoon of the same day, it was re-enacted and the Senate likewise adjourned *sine die.*[77]

Although Congress restored Williams to his command of the company of Tennessee volunteers, it did not exempt him from trial by court-martial and punishment "for any mutinous or insubordinate conduct." Williams, however, received no orders from the government after July 8, and his estate, after his death at Brownsville in 1847, was ultimately paid $368.00, four months' captain's pay at $92.00 per month.[78]

By the time Davis reached the volunteers on the frontier, most of the men had been moved from the vicinity of the Aubrey and Kinney Rancho to Lipantitlán. The old Spanish presidio of San Miguel Lipantitlán was situated on the southwestern frontier on the south bank of the Nueces just below the Irish settlement of San Patricio (or Hibernia), where the Matamoros road to La Bahía del Espíritu Santo crossed the Nueces. The presidio is said to have been built in 1734, but having fallen into decay, was restored or built anew on or near the same site by the Mexicans in 1830 under orders of General Manuel de Mier y Terán, military commander and inspector of the Interior Provinces of the East stationed at Matamoros, "in order to wipe out the tribes of the Lipans."[79] The Texan Secretary of War considered that it

[76] *Morning Star,* July 26, 1842; Smither (ed.), *Journals of the Sixth Congress,* III, 175–177.

[77] Smither (ed.), *Journals of the Sixth Congress,* III, 96.

[78] Williams' claim for $386.00 was paid to Robert Williams, his administrator, April 15, 1854. Public Debt Papers (Texas), ms.

[79] Quoted in Leroy P. Graf, "Colonizing Projects in Texas South of the Nueces, 1820–1845," in *Southwestern Historical Quarterly,* L (1946–1947), 436, from Orozco y Berra Map Collection Seccion de Cartografia, Ministerio de Fomento, Mexico, D. F. The site of Old Fort Lipantitlán is 12.5 miles northwest of present

could be easily defended. It was protected on the north by a strip of bluff and Lake Lipantitlán; on the west there was a ravine, and on the south and east a palisade and moat, whose water came from Lipantitlán Creek.[80] One of the camp sites in the area was known as "Camp Williams" and another as "Camp Everitt."

The new location at Lipantitlán had several advantages over the previous point of rendezvous. The place could be more easily defended, and it was a more favorable location on account of the abundance of excellent water and grass in the vicinity for horses and cattle.[81] Some sickness, such as fever and inflamation, prevailed in the camp, however, and a number of the soldiers suffered from a lack of clothing, from sore feet for the want of shoes, and especially "great inconvenience for the want of tents."[82] When Davis reached the Nueces, he found the troops there also suffering "extensively and severely" from lack of food and medical supplies, and "almost in a state of mutiny, determined to break up in a few days."[83]

Lieutenant Ratcliff of the Mobile volunteers had been ordered by Williams on May 11 to take a schooner at Corpus Christi and proceed to St. Joseph Island to requisition twenty beeves.[84] A detachment of thirty men was sent under his command.[85] No one else was to be permitted to leave Captain Everett's camp. Fifty-one beeves were obtained east of the Colorado and driven to camp on the Nueces, and Sergeant

---

Banquette, Nueces County, Texas on the present Bluntzer estate. The fort was abandoned by General Filisola on May 31, 1836. He dismantled the fort and threw its two cannons into Lake Lipantitlán. In 1849 Nicholas Bluntzer bought the Fort Lipantitlán grant and established a ranch home near the old ruins, which he marked with a concrete block. The site of the old Fort now belongs to Paul Bluntzer of Corpus Christi. On June 26, 1938, the state of Texas dedicated a four acre tract surrounding the site of the old fortifications as the Bluntzer Memorial Park. It is now an out of the way place. Cyrus Tilloson, "Lipantitlán," *Frontier Times,* XXV (1947–1948), pp. 27–29.

[80] Tilloson, "Lipantitlán," in *Frontier Times,* XXV (1947–1948), 27–29.

[81] *Telegraph and Texas Register,* June 8, 1842; Chabot, *Corpus Christi and Lipantitlán,* pp. 52–53.

[82] *Telegraph and Texas Register,* June 8, 1842.

[83] Copy of an extract from a letter of James Davis to Sam Houston, Head Quarters Volunteers, Corpus Christi, June 21, 1842, in Army Papers (Texas), ms.

[84] Augustus Williams to E. S. Ratcliff, May 11, 1842, in Chabot, *Corpus Christi and Lipantitlán,* p. 44.

[85] Captain [John R.] Everett to J[osiah] Walton Thompson, Orderly Sergeant, Headquarters of the Texan Army, Camp Williams, May 15, 1842, in Chabot, *Corpus Christi and Lipantitlán,* p. 37.

Josiah W. Thompson, of Company B, nephew of Burton Walton of Augusta, Georgia, was under orders to scour the surrounding country for beeves.[86] By late June an effort was being made to obtain beeves from the Brazos area and farther eastward, where there was said to be plenty of animals available, which would have to be driven to the Nueces by men in the service of the Republic since there was no way of paying others to herd them west.[87] Owen recommended that before beeves be driven such long distances, an effort be made to draw them from the enemy upon the Little Colorado which was nearer and where animals could be had for the mere taking.[88]

The volunteers themselves were in a large measure to blame for the "starvation" on the Nueces and at Galveston. Many of them came to Texas in violation of positive orders to the effect that six months' provisions were to be brought with them. Yet, it is inconceivable that they could have come otherwise, for the bulkiness of supplies would have precluded their shipment without heavy costs to those who were in many instances contributing their all when they volunteered. Men who contributed their own powder, lead, and arms, and brought along a few personal belongings, as well as paid their own transportation could scarcely be expected to bring along a bulky commissary, particularly when so much had been said about being able to live off of the enemy once the campaign was under way. The funds contributed in the United States were in the aggregate never large, and the Texas government was without sufficient funds to feed and clothe the men who volunteered their services. Voluntary contributions were occasionally made for their support by men of means in Texas or friends of Texas in the United States, and even President Houston contributed money and credit on his own personal account to obtain items of necessity for the men in camp.[89]

Bodies of men, totalling some eighty-six in number, formed into self-

---

[86] David Murphree to [William? S.?] Hotchkiss, Acting Assistant Qr. Master, Corpus Christi, [dated:] Doct[or] Southerland's, Colorado, June 7, 1842, in *ibid.,* pp. 37–39.

[87] Clark L. Owen to James Davis, Texana, June 23, 1842, in *ibid.*

[88] Copy of an extract from a letter of James Davis to Sam Houston, Head Quarters Volunteers, Corpus Christi, June 21, 1842, in Army Papers (Texas), ms.; Houston to Col. [Lewis M.] H. Washington, Houston, Texas, May 22, 1842, in *Writings of Sam Houston,* III, 56–57.

[89] Sam Houston to James Davis, Galveston, June 15, 1842 (Private), in *Writings of Sam Houston,* IV, 119–121; Same to John S. Sydnor, City of Houston, May 13, 1842, in *ibid.,* III, 49.

constituted spy companies under Captain James P. Ownsby and others, including a thieving party from the Guadalupe, roamed the frontier as usual, without submitting to any authority,[90] and created unrest among the volunteers from the United States who had come with the expectation of looking to the enemy for their compensation. Privately, Captain Everett informed his orderly sergeant, "We will have our share of the spoils or die in the attempt should they be taken from the Mexicans."[91] When it was reported in Houston that Captain Ownsby was again the leader of a self-constituted company on the frontier, Houston wrote Davis:

If this is the fact, I direct that he, or any other, under similar circumstances, be seized and held in custody and safely guarded, until orders from the War Department may be given for their trial. There shall be subordination in the service. We cannot permit the rogues any longer to frequent our frontier. . . . We must punish them. You will have Captain McLean and Hays' command . . . put a stop to such atrocious villanies as have been practiced on our South Western frontier. . . . No man is to be with, or about the army, who is not subject to the regulations of the army,[92]

and "none [are] to draw rations, but such as belong to your command."[93] Captain Ephraim McLean's company and Captain John C. Hays' company were the only two independent spy companies authorized to operate on the southwestern frontier from Corpus Christi to San Antonio and westward. When Ownsby's small party came in, as they said, to join the Texan army, they were seized and held prisoners eight or ten days and when released found that most of their horses and blankets, which they no doubt had previously appropriated from some defenseless persons, were missing.[94] Another warning against ardent spirits was issued by a President known by many as "Big Drunk."

[90] George W. Hockley to James Davis, June 6, 1842, in Chabot, *Corpus Christi and Lipantitlán*, pp. 49–51; *Telegraph and Texas Register*, June 15, 1842.
[91] Captain [J. R.] Everett to J[osiah] Walton Thompson, Orderly Sergeant, Headquarters of the Texian Army, Camp Williams, May 15, 1842, in Chabot, *Corpus Christi and Lipantitlán*, p. 37.
[92] Sam Houston to James Davis, City of Houston, May 31, 1842 (Private), and Same to Same, City of Houston, June 6, 1842 (Private), in *Writings of Sam Houston*, IV, 115–117.
[93] Sam Houston to James Davis, Galveston, June 15, 1842, in *ibid.*, IV, 119–121.
[94] Goodman, "A Statement of Facts, Washington, Feby 10, 1843," in Miller Papers (Texas), ms.

"There can," he said, "no more be order and subordination in a camp where there is ardent spirits vended than in Bedlam, where madmen are associated all in one ward."

Finding the men on the lower Nueces disorganized and without food, General Davis began trying to form them into a well-organized military unit in accordance with the President's proclamation of April 14 to the people of Texas. David Murphree was named acting quartermaster for the Texan army and William C. McKinstry was made acting assistant quartermaster. William B. Goodman was placed in charge of the commissary.[95] Paul H. Earle was named surgeon and N. J. Moore, assistant surgeon. Major John J. B. Hoxey, elected commander of the First Battalion of Texas Volunteers, outlined in Battalion Order No. 1 of May 14 the daily routine. Upon the sounding of reveille at daybreak, each company was to form on its own parade ground for roll call. At sunrise, the "Surgeon's Call" would be sounded at which time the orderly sergeant of each company would conduct the sick to the surgeon. "Officers' Drill" was set for 8 A.M., followed by the mounting of the guard at 10 A.M., after which the "Company Drill" began at 10:30 A.M. At 3 P.M. there was another "Officers' Drill," followed by "Company Drill" at 5 P.M. "Retreat" was sounded at sunset and "Tatoo" at 8 P.M. At both "retreat" and "tatoo" roll call was to be taken and the proper reports made.[96] On June 6, J. M. Wells was appointed drill-master.[97] Martial law was established, but not strictly enforced. The quartermaster could obtain little more than beef for the troops and this from the few settlers in the vicinity without remuneration.[98] Consequently, the citizens of Refugio County, led by Michael Reilly, soon sent a petition to the President, bitterly complaining of the consumption of their cattle and their provisions, contrary to a general order issued by the President on March

[95] Chabot, *Corpus Christi and Lipantitlán,* pp. 35, 52; James Davis, Acting Adjutant General Texian Army, to Sam Houston, Head Quarters, Texian Army, Corpus Christi, May 20, 1842, in *ibid.,* pp. 54–55. Goodman relates some of the happening in the Corpus Christi area in 1841–1842 in "A Statement of Facts, Washington, Feby 10, 1843," in Miller Papers (Texas), ms.

[96] Battalion Order No. 1, Corpus Christi, May 14, 1842, [issued:] By order of Maj. Hoxey—J. B. Reaves, Acting Adjutant, copy in Chabot, *Corpus Christi and Lipantitlán,* pp. 36–37.

[97] Chabot, *Corpus Christi and Lipantitlán,* p. 37.

[98] Claim of John R. Baker, First Lieutenant in Colonel Clark L. Owen's Company, for $889.50 worth of beeves and corn furnished to General James Davis' command in 1842, dated October 23, 1850., in Public Debt Papers (Texas), ms.

11, 1842.[99] "Not only have all our beeves been taken," said the petitioners, "but our cows and young calves are impressed, and many of our families left without beef, the principal means of support."[100] Being rather disgusted with the whole situation, Acting Quartermaster Mc-Kinstry informed Sergeant Thompson on May 16 from "Hell's Depository," where he was guarding the meager supplies of the army, that he had requested permission of Major Williams to go to Mobile. He stated that he was leaving on a boat for Mobile, but expected to return on his horse in time for the campaign in Mexico.[101] The supply situation on the frontier was becoming desperate.

By May 26 the total force in the Corpus Christi-Lipantitlán area was reported near three hundred volunteers plus an additional eighty in the spy companies.[102] As soon as the six hundred infantry at Galveston and the three hundred cavalry expected in the next few days should arrive, the camp was to be moved eight miles below to Ochula Lake.[103] Whenever the expected re-enforcements reached camp, there would be a need for a considerable increase in provisions. At the present time, the consumption of beef, at the current ration allowance of three and a half pounds per man per day, was three beeves daily for the army; but since there were already complaints that this was not enough, it was expected that within a short time the ration allowance would have to be increased to four pounds per person. President Houston felt that an allowance of two pounds of beef with other rations was sufficient, but that three pounds of beef should be allowed when beef alone was available. "For God's sake," he wrote Davis on June 15, "and our beloved country's sake don't be afraid to do your duty and risk the consequences. Trust in God!"[104] On June 14 Acting Quartermaster Mc-Kinstry reported that he had on hand in camp 9 sacks of coffee (enough for 63 days), 8 barrels of sugar (sufficient for 41 days), and a limited

[99] "Proclamation to the Army and Citizens of Texas, Galveston, March 11, 1842," in *Writings of Sam Houston*, II, 496–497.
[100] Petition of Michael Reilly and Others, May 13, 1842, quoted in H. Yoakum, *History of Texas, from Its First Settlement in 1685 to Its Annexation to the United States in 1846*, II, 356.
[101] Chabot, *Corpus Christi and Lipantitlán*, p. 38.
[102] Clark L. Owen to ———, Corpus Christi, May 26, 1842, in Chabot, *Corpus Christi and Lipantitlán*, p. 35.
[103] *Ibid.*
[104] Sam Houston to James Davis, June 15, 1842, quoted in Chabot, *Corpus Christi and Lipantitlán*, p. 45.

amount of bacon, but a supply of beef for only two more days.[105] Lieutenant Ratcliff was ordered to Houston and Galveston to see if he could procure clothing and breadstuff for his company.[106] He carried letters from General Davis. Upon the receipt of Davis' communication, Secretary of War Hockley made plans to procure the *Lafitte* to transfer what supplies were available at Galveston to the western frontier,[107] and to obtain in New Orleans and elsewhere in the United States a camp forge, tools, and an armorer. Hockley informed Davis he was sending ten deer skins for the army's use, and pending the obtaining of shoes in New Orleans, the volunteers would have to make moccasins from the raw hides of the butchered beeves. About May 20 Captain J. M. Allen, a friend of Houston's, left Davis' camp at Corpus Christi as a dispatch bearer to the government and for the purpose of hurrying on the supplies from Galveston as well as to get clothes for General Davis and to attend to private business. At Galveston he obtained from the quartermaster stationery, shoes, flints, and other supplies which were forwarded on June 1 from that port aboard the *Phoenix* along with "the prisoners [deserters], dispatches, letters and newspapers."[108] However, stationery was in short supply, and most of the company records continued to be kept on coarse brown wrapping paper.[109] Captain Alexander Stevenson of the "Missouri Invincibles" was sent to New Orleans late in May to report to Colonel Lewis M. H. Washington and to receive and forward such stores as he might be able to procure for the Texan service.[110] A public meeting at Mobile was addressed on May 21 by Dr. Branch T. Archer, Commodore Moore of the Texas navy, and Colonel Lewis M. H. Washington. A large subscription was raised on this occasion.

As soon as the troops from Galveston arrived on the frontier, General Davis was to report the strength of the volunteers, excluding Colonel

[105] Chabot, *Corpus Christi and Lipantitlán*, p. 45.
[106] *Telegraph and Texas Register*, June 8, 1842.
[107] George W. Hockley to James Davis, June 6, 1842, in Chabot, *Corpus Christi and Lipantitlán*, pp. 49–50.
[108] Captain J. M. Allen to James Davis, Galveston, May 31, 1842, in *ibid.*, pp. 56–57.
[109] W. J. Mills, Quarter Master and Commissary, Texas Army, Galveston, to Gen'l. James Davis, May 30, 1842, in Chabot, *Corpus Christi and Lipantitlán*, pp. 45–46.
[110] George W. Hockley to [Captain Alexander Stevenson], Department of War and Marine, May 21, 1842, Special Order No. 7, in Army Papers (Texas), ms.; *Telegraph and Texas Register*, June 1, 1842.

Washington's two companies, to the War Department; and, if the number of troops justified, the Department would then order the election of field officers.[111] By the end of April, the United States chargé d'affaires reported five hundred volunteers had arrived at Galveston from the United States, eager to march against Mexico,[112] and on May 10 it was estimated there were fifteen hundred volunteers in the Texas service, including about six hundred from the United States.[113] If the number of recruits grew as in the past, it was thought that by the first of June the army would be sufficiently strong to march across the Río Grande. At Corpus Christi the army had a twelve-pounder, and Captain Allen at Galveston wrote on May 31 that he hoped to bring down in a few days four or five French artillerists.[114] The twelve-pounder seems to have been the one left by the Federalists in 1840 and kept at the Aubrey and Kinney Rancho. Major Nicholas Cruger was reported June 17 to be on his way to Galveston from South Carolina with at least one hundred men.[115] The men had not gotten off by the 20th. On the 19th one of the volunteers from Mobile shot a brother volunteer, and the next day, another row among the volunteers resulted in another shooting. In Houston late in June a man by the name of Gill, belonging to Lieutenant Colonel Clemens' company from Alabama, was shot by Rufus Goodenow of the St. Louis Volunteers, but upon examination before the mayor Goodenow was acquitted, having acted in self-defense. It was shown that Gill was "a desperate and dangerous character." "The sooner some of these men are sent off to fight the Mexicans," commented Bollaert, "the better."[116] On June 24 a poorly organized battalion of volunteers from the United States, described as "a queer set of fellows," sailed from Galveston for Corpus Christi.[117] About June 15 the *Phoenix* was

[111] Department of War, Special Order No. 13, June 7, 1842, quoted in Chabot, *Corpus Christi and Lipantitlán*, p. 36.

[112] Joseph Eve to James Franklin Ballinger, Galveston, April 26, 1842, in Joseph Milton Nance (ed.), "A Letter Book of Joseph Eve, United States Chargé d'Affaires to Texas," in *Southwestern Historical Quarterly*, XLIII (1939–1940), 486–492.

[113] Joseph Eve to Richard Southgate, Galveston, May 10, 1842, in *ibid.*, pp. 492–494; Same to James T. Morehead, Galveston, May 31, 1842, in *ibid.*, pp. 497–500.

[114] Captain J. M. Allen to James Davis, Galveston, May 31, 1842, in Chabot, *Corpus Christi and Lipantitlán*, pp. 56–57.

[115] *Bollaert's Texas*, p. 102.

[116] *Bollaert's Texas*, p. 102. I have taken the liberty to rearrange Bollaert's sentence so as to place "the better" after "to fight the Mexicans." See also *New Orleans Bee*, July 9, 1842.

[117] *Bollaert's Texas*, p. 104.

ordered to move all troops at Galveston, except those to be retained for the defense of that place, to Live Oak Point.[118]

The maximum number of United States volunteers to reach Texas in the spring and summer of 1842 was approximately 600, but the number of Texan volunteers was obviously greatly exaggerated by the United States diplomatic agent. The Texan Secretary of War reported on June 23 that the number of volunteers mustered into the Texas service amounted to 473, rank and file, of whom 253 were stationed at Lipantitlán, and the remaining 220 were en route from Galveston via water to join them. It was expected that Colonel Lewis M. H. Washington would arrive in about two weeks at Corpus Christi in the passenger steamer *Merchant*, which had been bought on the personal credit of Commodore Moore and other Texans for the Texas navy,[119] and with other transports bringing additional troops recruited in the United States. The Lipan chief, Castro, and his braves left Houston for Corpus Christi, to which point the Lipans and Tonkawas had been ordered for the purpose of accompanying the Texans in their march to the Río Grande. From the camp near Corpus Christi it was reported that the troops continued to be in good health and were generally contented;[120] but, were "spending their time in inglorious activity." Davis, however, after six weeks on the frontier, wrote, "my situation has been any thing but pleasant since my arrival at this place. I found the volunteers almost in a state of mutiny, determined to break up in a few days."[121] It was not judicious to have volunteers inactive; for as a foreign observer in Texas remarked, they add to the "plagues" of the country: "viz: lawyers, doctors, parsons, politicians, and mosquitos."[122]

As for local troops, a plan for a militia draft upon the different counties was prepared by the Secretary of War as General Order No. 1, issued at the city of Houston, May 25, supplemented five days later by an "After Order" making known that an acting assistant inspector general

[118] Sam Houston to Col. J[ames] Davis, Galveston, June 15, 1842, in *Corpus Christi and Lipantitlán*, pp. 58–59.

[119] Hill, *The Texas Navy*, p. 169; Alex Dienst, "The Navy of the Republic of Texas," *Quarterly of the Texas State Historical Association*, XIII (1909–1910), 13; *Daily Picayune*, July 8, 1842.

[120] *Telegraph and Texas Register*, June 29, 1842, gives the report of a gentleman who left the Texan camp on June 23 for Houston. See also the *Daily Picayune*, June 14, 1842.

[121] Copy of an extract from a letter of James Davis to Sam Houston, Head Quarters Volunteers, Corpus Christi, June 21, 1842, in Army Papers (Texas), ms.

[122] *Bollaert's Texas*, p. 104 n.

would be appointed to muster and inspect the troops in nineteen of the counties. The officers of the militia of the Republic of Texas were instructed to proceed immediately to organize and to discipline their respective brigades.[123] With the exception of the western counties of Béxar, Goliad, Refugio, San Patricio, and Travis, where the population could not stand a heavy draft, one-third of the eligible voters of each county were to be drafted for the proposed invasion, and company officers were notified to prepare up-to-date lists. It was announced that volunteers would be accepted in lieu of those to be drafted. Volunteer companies would have the right to choose their own officers. Cavalry companies were to consist of sixty men rank and file—one captain, two lieutenants, and three sergeants; whereas, infantry companies were to consist of fifty-six men rank and file—one captain, two lieutenants, four sergeants, and one musician. The requisition on the different counties was in proportion to their estimated population. The number and type of troops, place and time of muster and inspection were given as follows. The muster seems to have been generally carried out according to schedule.[124]

County	Number of men required			Time and place of muster and inspection
	Cavalry	Infantry	Total	
Austin	66	64	130	San Felipe, Thurs., June 16
Bastrop		128	128	Bastrop, Mon., July 11
Brazoria	66	64	130	Brazoria, Tues., June 21
Bowie	66		66	Boston, Mon., June 20
Colorado	00	04	130	Columbus, Thurs., July 7
Fannin		64	64	Warren, Tues., June 14
Fayette		128	128	LaGrange, Sat., July 11
Fort Bend	66	64	130	Richmond, Sat., June 18
Galveston		192	192	Galveston, Wed., June 15
Gonzales		128	128	Gonzales, Mon., July 4
Harris		256	256	Houston, Mon., June 20
Harrison (Panola)		128	128	Marshall, Fri., June 24
Houston	66		66	Crockett, Fri., July 1

[123] General Order No. 1, City of Houston, May 25, 1842, [signed:] By order of the Secretary of War and Marine—Memucan Hunt, Acting Inspector-General, T. M., in *Telegraph and Texas Register*, June 1, 1842; G. W. Hockley, Secretary of War & Marine, June 23, 1842, in Smither (ed.), *Journals of the Sixth Congress*, III, 108.

[124] General Order No. 1, City of Houston, May 25, 1842, [signed:] By order of the Secretary of War and Marine—Memucan Hunt, Acting Inspector-General, T.M., in *Telegraph and Texas Register*, June 1, 1842; After Order, Department of War and Marine, May 30, 1842, [signed:] Geo. W. Hockley, Secretary of War and Marine in *ibid*. The original of the latter is in Army Papers (Texas), ms.

Jackson		64	64	Texana, Tues., June 28
Jasper		128	128	Jasper, Thurs., July 7
Jefferson		64	64	Beaumont, Mon., July 11
Lamar		64	64	Paris, Thurs., June 16
Liberty	66	64	130	Liberty, Thurs., June 23
Matagorda[125]		128	128	Matagorda, Sat., June 25
Milam		64	64	Caldwell, Mon., July 11
Montgomery	132	128	260	Montgomery, Mon., June 27
Nacogdoches	66	128	194	Nacogdoches, Wed., June 29
Navasota (Brazos)		64	64	Boonville, Tues., July 5
Red River	66		66	Clarksville, Sat., June 18
Robertson	66		66	Franklin, Fri., July 8
Sabine		128	128	Milam, Mon., July 4
Shelby	66	64	130	Shelbyville, Mon., June 27
San Augustine	66	128	194	San Augustine, Fri., July 1
Victoria		64	64	Victoria, Fri., July 1
Washington	66	64	130	Mt. Vernon, Wed., July 13

The lists were drawn, and by the middle of June some four thousand militia men were awaiting orders to rendezvous, and Acting Inspector General Memucan Hunt and the newly appointed acting assistant inspector general of the militia of the Republic of Texas, Colonel Jacob Snively,[126] were preparing to carry out their duties.

All the volunteers [reported Judge Eve] are armed and equipped not at the expense of the government [but] by voluntary contributions. This City [Galveston] subscribed and paid about $75,000 for the benefit of the army. It is a Phenominan in the history of man to see a young nation just emerging from its cradle with a population of less than 100,000 souls without a dollar in its Treasury, not a regular soldier belonging to it, without credit sufficient to borrow a dollar at home or abroad, constantly at war with numerous of canibal Indians, and at the same time making offensive war upon a nation containing a population of eight millions. . . . The Texans are a bold, chiverous interprising people, they consider the mexicans a feeble, dastardly, supersticious priest riden race of mongrels, composed of Spanish, Indian and negro blood and are always willing to fight them or the Indians five to one.[127]

Down on the Nueces, General Davis reported that his men were anxious to advance and were growing restless from inactivity. To this the President replied,

[125] On inspection day, June 25th, the volunteers at Matagorda numbered 160, or 32 more than the number required. *Telegraph and Texas Register*, Aug. 3, 1842.

[126] George W. Hockley to Col. Jacob Snively, Department of War and Marine, Houston, June 8, 1842, in Army Papers (Texas), ms.

[127] Joseph Eve to Richard Southgate, Galveston, Texas, May 10, 1842, in Nance (ed.), "A Letter Book of Joseph Eve," in *Southwestern Historical Quarterly*, XLIII (1939–1940), 492–494.

My dear Sir, you have no idea of the pain you inflict on me, when you suggest to me the anxiety of the men to advance upon the enemy. . . . They will find that they are very young in service, and I fear—greatly fear—that we have again to see reenacted the scenes of Grant, Johnson and others, before our people will reflect. My heart is truly sick when I hear that men think seriously of doing *so-and-so*. Travis thought *so-and-so*, and so did Fannin. . . . When I want a movement made, I will order it. . . . How can men with naked feet talk of Matamoros, Monterey, and other places? This is all done by "thinking." Colonel Washington, and agents on whom I relied for obedience of orders, "thought" that if they could get men here, all was right; and Colonel Gillespie is commended for assuming the generous responsibility of taking upon himself to send them contrary to orders. . . . This is *generosity*—this is what comes of the assumption of "responsibility" in the face of orders reiterated by every boat. . . . The consequence will be that Texas will "whip herself" without the assistance of Mexico. . . . Do the best you can.

Truly thy friend,

SAM HOUSTON[128]

Anticipating the need of financial support for calling out the militia, or reviving the army, for an invasion of Mexico, Houston, contrary to the advice of his Secretary of State, issued a proclamation on May 24 for a special session of Congress to convene at the city of Houston on June 27.[129] Only Congress could authorize the raising of an army and its use, along with that of the navy, in an offensive war. As for the militia, some doubt existed as to whether or not it could be constitutionally employed in conducting an invasion of foreign territory,[130] or for any purpose "except [to] suppress insurrection or to repel invasion." It was believed that the only method by which Texas could carry on an offensive war with Mexico was by the aid of volunteers. "If we had the necessary resources," wrote the editor of the *Telegraph and Texas Register*, "Congress could authorize a regular army to be formed subject to the orders of the government, to conduct the war; but as the national treasury is empty, and

[128] Quoted in Marquis James, *The Raven: A Biography of Sam Houston*, p. 325.
[129] A Proclamation Calling a Special Session of Congress, May 24, 1842, in *Writings of Sam Houston*, III, 58; Endorsement of Anson Jones on letter from Sam Houston dated, July 19, 1842, in *ibid.*, III, 111–112. Jones wrote,

I deemed the called session useless and pernicious. The President convened it contrary to my advices and for the purpose of making capital for himself. The result has been, as I expected, a mere quarrel between him and Congress about the seat of Government, and the "war policy," by which the country has been injured and disgraced. As the President "has made his bed, so he must lie." I will have nothing to do with such petty squabbles.

[130] *Telegraph and Texas Register*, June 15, 1842.

196

the people are scarcely able to endure the taxes requisite to sustain the civil departments of government, the President will be compelled to regulate his plans, so that the war may be conducted solely by voluntary aid."[131] After having put forth a considerable amount of effort to obtain voluntary aid during the past two months in which he had planned offensive war against Mexico, the President at the last moment decided to take Congress into his confidence and cloak his plans with a semblance of legality.

The "War Party" was strong for invading Mexico with whatever forces there were in the country. Some of them were saying that they wished to "go the whole animal horns and all," and added, "Let us prepare for an invasion of Mexico in the fall—we will have 20,000 men in the field. Our brethern in the states," they asserted, "are burning with desire to assist us and fix our boundary along the mountains [Sierra Madre]."[132] Houston was so worried by the "War Party," that it was being whispered that his most intimate friends were having much difficulty in persuading him to retain the presidency. During the late presidential election campaign, one of the stories told about General Houston was that

some of his most violent opponents declared that it would be well if the General could be "got out of the way." A stout fellow in a hunting dress leaning upon a long rifle begged to know what it was required to do with the General. When he was informed "it was to shoot him," the hunter said that he would shoot him or any other man if he were paid for it. His price was demanded— It was $1,500. The dollars were not forthcoming. The hunter sloped [disappeared suddenly], and General Houston opened the Extraordinary [Session of] Congress.[133]

On the appointed date the special session of the Sixth Congress began to assemble in Houston, a city of two thousand population.[134] The old capitol building, since the removal of the government to Austin, had been converted into a hotel, and the proprietor saw no need to turn out paying guests to accommodate the penniless government. The Senate first met in the Masonic Hall in Kessler's Arcade but on the 29th began meeting at the Odd Fellows' Hall. On the first day, June 27, only three members—J. A. Greer of San Augustine (president pro tempore), Oli-

---

[131] *Ibid.*
[132] Quoted in *Bollaert's Texas,* p. 104.
[133] *Bollaert's Texas,* pp. 104–105.
[134] *Ibid.,* p. 110 n.

ver Jones of Austin, Colorado, and Fort Bend counties, and Francis Moore, Jr., of Galveston, Harris, and Liberty counties—put in appearance. William H. Jack of Brazoria was reported to be in town, but too ill to attend. The House of Representatives met in the new Presbyterian Church, and a quorum had gathered by the first afternoon. A committee was then appointed to notify the Senate that the House was ready to proceed with business, but the Senate was unable to obtain a quorum until the 29th, and then only by adjourning to the room of William H. Jack, who was still ill, for the purpose of forming a quorum of ten. The House was then informed that the Senate was ready to proceed to business. President Houston, being duly informed that Congress was now ready to receive any communications that he might have to offer, addressed a joint session of the Congress at the Presbyterian Church.[135]

In his message the President reviewed the incidents that had transpired since the last meeting of Congress, and reminded Congress that it was "indispensable that protection be given to the frontiers." He stated he had invited "emigrants" from the United States with a view to affording protection to the advance settlements of the country, and that "so far as he had power, and even beyond the means afforded him, by the government, he . . . [had] proceeded in the organization of the militia, so as to place them in the best possible condition to prosecute the war, should the Honorable Congress deem it necessary or expedient to adopt such a course." Houston pointed out that up until this time the immigrants had been supported almost entirely by private contributions, but that such a policy could no longer be continued without government assistance. Congress was reminded that the time for the general rendezvous had been designated between July 20–28, and it was now imperative the Congress make known immediately whether or not an invasion would be sanctioned, so that the forces of the "emigrants"

[135] The Senate was unable to muster a quorum on June 30, July 1, 2, 3 (Sunday), and 4. A quorum was achieved on the 5th only after the sergeant-at-arms was dispatched to bring in an absent member—Ludovic Colquhoun from Béxar. Again on the 6th of July the sergeant-at-arms had to be sent out to round up absent members; on the 7th there was no quorum; on the 8th there was a quorum at the start of the day's session; on the 9th the sergeant-at-arms was again sent to bring in a quorum; the 10th was Sunday; from the 11th to the 14th, inclusive, and from the 16th to the 23rd, when Congress adjourned, a quorum was present. Smither (ed.), *Journals of the Sixth Congress*, III, *passim*. Joseph Waples to Anson Jones, Houston, July 3, 1842, in Anson Jones, *Memoranda and Official Correspondence Relating to the Republic of Texas, Its History and Annexation—Including a Brief Autobiography of the Author*, pp. 192–193.

and the militia might be coordinated in a successful campaign. If, however, Congress should not favor an invasion of Mexico, he suggested that at least adequate provisions be made for defense of the frontier. The President, however, did not take the responsibility of advising an invasion of Mexico, but simply placed the matter squarely before Congress.

Also, in his message, the President pointed out the need of an adequate revenue for paying the costs of government, supporting and maintaining a navy, and keeping efficient officers, some of whom had already retired for lack of payment of their salaries. The national debt was estimated to exceed twelve million dollars, and had increased nearly fourfold during his predecessor's administration, while the public credit had fallen to zero.[136] The last Congress, in effect, repealed the direct tax laws and withheld appropriations for the transportation of the mails which embarrassed the administration in receiving correct and speedy official information regarding the conditions on the frontier and other sections of the country at a time when the nation was threatened with invasion. The suspension of the mails had prevented the distribution of the laws and journals of the last session of Congress. Because of the unsettled condition of the frontier and the exposed position of the city of Austin, formerly the town of Waterloo, founded by Jacob M. Harrell in 1835, the President urged that the seat of government be transferred to some point more "convenient for the speedy and efficient transaction of the public business." According to Houston, the seat of government should be in the more settled area of the country nearer the coast for

---

[136] The public debt of Texas at the end of Lamar's administration stood at nearly seven and one-half million dollars, having "increased nearly four-fold, and the public credit had fallen to zero; by his savagism as displayed in the extermination creed, the Indians had been driven to the highest degree of exasperation; the balance of trade was heavily on the debit side." Hubert Howe Bancroft, *History of Texas and the North Mexican States*, II, 341–342; A. K. Christian, "Mirabeau Buonaparte Lamar," in *Southwestern Historical Quarterly*, XXIII (1919–1920), 246 n. The Lamar administration, 1838–1841, spent ten times as much money as the second Houston administration, 1841–1844. *Ibid.*, XXIII (1919–1920), 245 n. The unfavorable balance of trade is revealed by the following table.

	Imports	Exports
Year ending Sept. 30, 1838	$1,740,376.87	$183,323.00
Year ending Sept. 1, 1839	1,506,897.67	274,518.09
Year ending Sept. 1, 1840	1,378,568.98	220,401.15
	$4,625,843.52	$678,242.24

the convenience of administration and ready access to communication
with foreign powers. As for himself, he no doubt preferred the city of
Houston to the city of Austin, which had been selected as the permanent
seat of government in April 1839, largely as the result of Lamar's influence.[137] As has been noted, at the time of the Vasquez raid President
Houston had sought to remove the national archives under the emer-
gency-powers clause of the Constitution, only to be frustrated by the
citizens of Austin who exerted force to prevent the removal of the public
papers. His suggestion now that Congress define the offence of insurrection so as to enable the administration to deal more effectively with acts
of a treasonable nature probably cost the President some of the support
in the west which he had lost with his first attempt to remove the archives but had largely regained by his publicly declared intention of
prosecuting vigorously the war against Mexico until Texas independence should be recognized or Texas conquered.[138] The next day Houston
returned to Galveston, but on July 1, was again back at the temporary
capital.[139]

Apparently, the President's message was well received, for the
Morning Star[140] reported that "all parties appear to be well pleased with
the [President's] message and . . . a general disposition is manifested
by the members present to carry out so far as practicable, the policy
suggested." The message was described as "judicious, temporate, and
conciliatory."[141] The public eagerly awaited the decision of Congress on
the war issue. A crisis in the affairs of the country had been reached.
Many reluctantly seemed to be swinging to the view that although,
since San Jacinto, Texas had gone out of its way to avoid trouble with
Mexico and to secure by peaceful means recognition of her independence, now, in the early summer of 1842, Texas must demand "recognition" and "respect" for her rights as a nation at the point of the bayonet,
"instead of begging it by sending ministers." "Let the rifles be our passports," declared Francis Moore of the *Telegraph*, "and when asked for

[137] Christian, "Mirabeau Buonaparte Lamar," in *Southwestern Historical Quarterly*, XXIII (1919–1920), 265.
[138] Houston to the Senate and House of Representatives, City of Houston, June
27, 1842, in *Writings of Sam Houston*, III, 74–83; and *Telegraph and Texas Register*, June 29, 1842; Washington D. Miller to Ashbel Smith, Houston, Texas, April
6, 1842 (Private), in E. W. Winkler (ed.), *Manuscript Letters and Documents of
Early Texians, 1821–1845*, pp. 257–263.
[139] *Bollaert's Texas*, p. 106.
[140] June 30, 1842.
[141] *Bollaert's Texas*, p. 107.

our credentials, show them the cannon's mouth." Let's "go to the banks of the Río Grande, and if need, pass onward."[142]

In the meantime, while the "War Congress" was at work on the President's recommendation, the latter moved "coolly and deliberately in the execution of his plans." The agents in the United States were constantly urged to hurry on the tide of "emigration." A letter apparently from Texas to Barry Gillespie, the Texan general agent at New Orleans, which found its way into the *New Orleans Sun*, declared,

If there are volunteers who may come [to Texas], they will soon see the result of their agreement. The time for receiving auxiliaries from the United States draws to an end. If we do not receive any, Texas will go to war as a young giant with only one arm and unaided. The brilliant rays of the lone star will soon be reflected in the rapid current of the Río Grande. We have raised the standard of glory and will soon march toward the west sustained by strong arms and brave hearts. Let those come soon who wish to participate in the perils and triumphs of military life. The camp for adventurers and enterprising persons is open to our brothers from all countries, the same as to our citizens. Mexican tyranny has ridiculed, has challenged the courage and the power of the inhabitants of the great Mississippi Valley. Do you not wish to meet the champions of these [manly characteristics] on the burning plains of the distant southwest? Will the Americans waiver at sight of the battlefield, when Americans struggled for liberty and the spread of morality and learning? Tell them that they may come then, that they may participate in the perils and fruits of the spoils of war. You know what the conditions are; then let them be fulfilled; the result depends on proper preparations.[143]

By mid-June it was "so dry at the West" that the prairies were so parched and seared that the corn on almost every plantation west of the Guadalupe was destroyed. No longer were there any serious apprehensions of a Mexican attack upon the Texan position, for the country between the Nueces and Río Grande had become like a desert and the water courses had dried up, so that it was considered impossible for Mexican troops to march to the Nueces, and equally so for Texan troops to move from the latter river to the Río Grande. The drought, it was said, had "completely closed all intercourse between the two countries."[144]

[142] *Telegraph and Texas Register,* July 13, 1842.
[143] ——— Al Sr. Barry Gellispie [*sic*] agente general de Téjas en Nueva-Orleans (translated into Spanish and reproduced without date) in *El Cosmopolita,* June 25, 1842.
[144] *Telegraph and Texas Register,* June 15, 1842.

By the end of the month conditions at the camp on the Nueces were in a deplorable state, even though occasionally reports came in to the more settled areas of Texas that the troops were "now well supplied with coffee, sugar, beef" and other necessities "and are generally healthy." Many of the men were dissatisfied with their camp, their food, the brackish water which they were forced to drink, and general inactivity. All seemed to want to command, few to obey. Military exercises were usually nonexistent. A sullen torpor pervaded both men and officers. Men were allowed in camp without being attached to any command. Gambling and the sale of liquor brought additional problems. The general found it impossible to carry out his orders to exclude all ardent spirits and intoxicating liquors from the limits of his command.[145] Under these conditions, Major Hoxey informed the Secretary of War that "Feeling that I can be of no service to the Republic of Texas under the circumstances existing now in camp, I have the honor of hereby tendering my resignation."[146] Although Hoxey sent in his resignation, we find that he was still on active duty on July 6, when he was ordered by Davis to arrest two men in the vicinity of the camp, who had refused to obey any orders.[147]

It was believed that had steps been taken in late April or early May to make a movement against either Matamoros or Camargo by the combined forces at San Antonio and on the Nueces the spirits of the men would have been kept up and the capture of either place would have furnished a secure rallying point for the forces on their way from the United States.[148] If nothing more, a gigantic and very profitable cattle raid could have been pulled, for it was estimated that there were 300,000 head of cattle pastured between Camargo and Matamoros on the Texas side of the Río Grande. These cattle have hitherto, reported the *Telegraph and Texas Register,*

been protected by Col. Vil[l]areal with only 70 or 80 Mexican cavalry. These would fall an easy prey to our soldiers, and as cattle are worth at least $3 a head, these if captured, and driven east of San Antonio, would be clear gain to the national wealth of $900,000. The capture of these [continued the

[145] Houston to Adjut.-Gen. James Davis, City of Houston, May 31, 1842 (Private), in *Writings of Sam Houston,* IV, 115–116; Same to Same, Galveston, June 15, 1842, in *ibid.,* III, 68–69.

[146] Quoted in Chabot, *Corpus Christi and Lipantitlán,* p. 61.

[147] *Ibid.* The two men—B. Rummey and F. Fontleroy—belonged to Captain H. W. Allen's Company E.

[148] *Telegraph and Texas Register,* April 20, 1842.

editor] might be stigmatised as *"Cow stealing,"* but it should be recollected that *war* is but a species of robbery, and he who is the most successful in *stealing* away the resources of his opponent gains the vantage ground.[149]

The inactivity and discontent in camp soon led to desertion fomented to a large extent by Captain Augustus Williams, and after him, by Second Lieutenant Hugh O'Connor of the Tennessee Company, John J. B. Hoxey, and other officers and men.[150] Through failure to take strong, effective measures leading to the punishment of those who were found guilty of insubordination and desertion, Davis was partly responsible for the lack of discipline in his command. "Disobedience of orders is mutiny—mutiny should be punished with death," declared the President and the Secretary of War.[151] Davis failed to obey his instructions to report all deserters and dischargees to the War Department. Some of the men even marched off with arms to San Antonio without permission,[152] and the Galveston Invincibles, numbering some 150 men, left

[149] *Ibid.*

[150] Houston to the House of Representatives, City of Houston, July 22, 1842, in *Writings of Sam Houston*, III, 114–116. When Williams left to report at Houston, some of his men also left. On the back of a document dated "La Panteclan, July 2, 1842" are listed the following deserters from the First Battalion of Texas Volunteers:

Company A: Privates: C. A. Allen, Jeremiah Babcock, John Marcks, David Hulse, George Byington.

Company B: D. D. Donaldson, ———— Cohens [A. L. Rowen], James [H.] Marsh, M. DeValla, J. P. Johns[t]on, D. Ensminger, and Frank Hopkin.

Company C: Hugh O'Connor, 2d Lt.; John Shelton, 2d Sgt.; Sam[1] B. King, 3d Sgt.; Fred B. Gull, 4th Sgt.; R. Cochran, 1st Corp.; William Peoples, 3d Corp.; John Riley, 4th Corp.; William H. Crawford; G. E. Dyson, I. C. Davis; John Kirksey; I. Mosely; James McMahan; A. M. McCashin; Govan Pain; Ruluff Peck; John Richardson; James N. Runnells, David K. Ross; Richard Sneed; Thomas Sisk.

Company E: Robert Hackett, 3d Sgt.; R. Lamberson, 2d Corp., ———— [D.] Hubbard; I. Allen; ———— Bradley; W. Hays; and B. W. Rummey, 1st Sgt.

Company F: Privates John B. Arnold, G. W. Gordon, R. W. Atkinson, and P. W. Clayton.

Chabot, *Corpus Christi and Lipantitlán*, pp. 51–52; James Davis, Acting Adjutant General, to Sam Houston, Camp Lipantitlán, July 3, 1842, in Army Papers (Texas), ms.

[151] General Order No. 1, July 8, 1842, in Smither (ed.), *Journals of the Sixth Congress*, III, 84.

[152] Lt. E. S. Ratcliff of Captain Everett's Company B (Alabama Volunteers) admitted to Colonel Snively "having in his possession a public horse which he reports as lost," and "having a public saddle which he sold." When questioned by

203

Corpus Christi about June 1.[153] Many returned to the United States.[154] "The Yankees are beginning to leave for the north," recorded Christian Friedrich Duerr, a merchant at Houston. "A speedy passage to them."[155]

Not all desertions were at Corpus Christi. Some took place from the post at Galveston.[156] On June 28 the *Civilian and Galveston Gazette* promised to publish the names of all deserters, and the Houston *Telegraph* declared, "the poor fellows probably became homesick and wish to see their mammas."[157]

Apparently those who went to San Antonio did not do so for the purpose of protecting the place, for we find Thomas H. O'S. Addicks arriving in Houston on Monday, June 13, with a petition to the President signed by many citizens of San Antonio, praying for protection.[158]

We regret [said the editor of the *Morning Star*] that the government has not the means to station a company of soldiers near that city to protect the citizens not only from the marauding Mexicans, but even from our own volunteers. We have been informed that some thieving volunteers, lately drove off nearly a thousand head of cattle towards the Colorado, belonging to citizens of Béxar. Messrs. Navarro, Flores, Erasmo Seguin, and others, who have ever been faithful to our cause, have suffered greatly. Shame to the men who claim the name of soldiers, and act the part of theives [sic], by robbing their own countrymen!

About the same time down on the Nueces, Davis found it necessary, because some of the volunteers were entering fields and houses, pillaging

---

Colonel Snively, Ratcliff indicated a willingness to pay for the horse and saddle by a draft on Mobile. George W. Hockley, Secretary of War & Marine, to Sam Houston, June 8, 1842, in Sam Houston, Unpublished Correspondence, 1842, ms., III. The body of a soldier, supposedly belonging to Captain Scott's company of volunteers, was discovered at the Cavasso, six miles above La Bahía. The indications were that he had been murdered by a party of Mexicans disguised as Indians. When discovered, his body was sticking full of arrows. *Daily Picayune,* June 24, 1842.

[153] The Galveston Invincibles were commanded by Captain J. M. Allen. Chabot in *Corpus Christi and Lipantitlán,* p. 32, gives a return of the company signed by Lt. E. T. Fox, showing 42 men (32 privates), 39 muskets, 37 cartridge boxes, 5 flints, 2 kegs of powder, 3 rifles, and 45 haversacks. See Muster Rolls in Appendix of this work.

[154] Brown, *History of Texas,* II, 218; *Telegraph and Texas Register,* August 31, 1842.

[155] Christian Friedrich Duerr, Diary, June 6, 1842, ms.

[156] *Telegraph and Texas Register,* June 29, 1842.

[157] *Ibid.*

[158] Quoted in *ibid.,* June 15, 1842.

and committing other injuries, such as "tearing away the roofs and other fixtures," to issue a general order against the destruction of private property.[159]

By July 7 the forces on the lower Nueces had been reduced through desertion and other causes already indicated, to 192 men, and even these were ill-rewarded for their devotion to the cause of Texas.

Joseph F. Smith, returning from Corpus Christi, reported on June 24 that he found the "camp disorderly and disaffected." "The soldiers are constantly intoxicated," he wrote, "and will be so while the camp remains where it is; for every citizen is a whisky pedlar. Court-martials are in session every day and convict, but are unable to enforce their penalties."[160] Quartermaster Goodman was ordered by Davis to board and search diligently for ardent spirits every vessel entering the port of Corpus Christi and to take possession of any spirits that he might find.[161] Houston advised that "if any one attempts to introduce whiskey or spirits into your neighborhood, shave their heads, and bathe them in salt water to prevent their taking cold."[162] I. Sullivan was sentenced to two days at hard labor for refusing to obey orders. Third Sergeant Robert Hackett of Company E ("Mississippi Guards") was reduced to the rank of private for refusing to remove his "shack" from ground laid off for military purposes. For leaving camp without permission, James A. Reynolds of Company C was sentenced by court-martial to five days at hard labor. William Tracy of Captain Augustus Williams' Company also went AWOL, and, upon being brought back from Captain Ewen Cameron's camp, was sentenced to ride the cannon from 8:00 until 10:00 o'clock the following morning. Although accused of disorderly conduct —abusing and cursing Quartermaster Goodman, ——— McDermott was permitted to go unpunished;[163] but sleeping on sentinel duty was a more serious infraction of regulations and William Wright of Company A was sentenced to cut wood for twenty-four hours. Others like Alvin White, James Bennett, and W. B. Council were tried for selling liquor. Although Davis sought to maintain order and subordination among his

159 Chabot, *Corpus Christi and Lipantitlán*, p. 49.
160 Joseph F. Smith to Anson Jones, Refugio County, June 24, 1842 [endorsed:] Joseph Smith, June 29th, 1842. Rec'd 12th July [1842], Domestic Correspondence (Texas), 1835–1846, ms.
161 James Davis to William B. Goodman, Corpus Christi, June 29, 1842, in Chabot, *Corpus Christi and Lipantitlán*, p. 48.
162 Quoted in Chabot, *Corpus Christi and Lipantitlán*, pp. 48–49.
163 *Ibid.*

men it was believed that only a man like General Andrew Jackson could have enforced obedience, "for the citizens do all they can to bring his order into contempt."[164]

Difficulties developed with peaceful Mexican traders who came in to trade at the Kinney Rancho. Mention has already been made of the Río Grande traders who left the Rancho on the day the first volunteers landed in the area. As they departed, they promised to return in twenty-five days. In twenty-six days the same party of traders, with their number increased, returned, but Major Augustus Williams, who had assumed command of the Anglo-American volunteers in the area, ordered them seized, made prisoners, and permitted them to be stripped of their property, which was then divided among the volunteers. Upon his arrival on the frontier, Davis ordered the traders, approximately twenty in number, held under arrest, and referred the case of the traders to President Houston.[165] Learning of their arrest, President Houston instructed Davis to free them and to restore their goods and property, including horses, and, after allowing them to trade at the Rancho in all things except munitions of war and arms, to have Captain McLean furnish them a protecting convoy to the Río Grande. In the end, however, the President left the question of regulating trade on the frontier to Davis' discretion. Some of the troops on the Nueces refused to obey the orders for the release of the traders and their property, and the President's order was only partially carried out. The traders were released, but their property was not restored to them. Whereupon, Davis was instructed to issue dishonorable discharges to the ringleaders in the ranks and to order the officers to report in person to the Secretary of War at Houston.[166] When McLean was called upon to return to the

---

[164] Joseph F. Smith to Anson Jones, Refugio County, June 24, 1842 [endorsed:] Joseph Smith, June 29, 1842. Rec'd 12th July [1842], Domestic Correspondence (Texas), 1835–1846, ms.

[165] James Davis to Sam Houston, Head Quarters, Texian Army, Corpus Christi, May 20, 1842, in Chabot, *Corpus Christi and Lipantitlán*, pp. 54–55; *Daily Picayune*, June 14, 1842.

[166] Houston to Colonel James Davis, Acting Adjutant General, Texas Army, [dated:] New Washington, May 26, 1842, in *Writings of Sam Houston*, III, 61–62; Same to Same, Galveston, Texas, June 15, 1842, in *ibid.*, III, 68–69; Houston to W. P. Aubrey, New Washington, May 26, 1842, in *ibid.*, III, 60–61; *Telegraph and Texas Register*, June 1, 1842; Capt. J. M. Allen to James Davis, Galveston, May 31, 1842, in Chabot, *Corpus Christi and Lipantitlán*, p. 56. The tempestuous volunteers from the United States were eager for action, and disciplining them was no easy matter.

I envy no man the command of volunteers [wrote William Jefferson Jones]

Texas camp to effect the President's wishes in respect to the traders, he informed Davis in great disgust, "I have been in readiness and willing at any time to discharge any duty to forward the desires of the executive or yourself but every thing appears to work backwards. To be called upon 25 or 30 mi. from camp to return and wait the movements of committees to carry into effect the orders of the executive is more than I am willing to stand any longer. I shall discharge my men and let them return home or elsewhere."[167] Ultimately, the traders recovered two-thirds of their property and left for the Río Grande under an escort provided by Captain Everett, which was to accompany them as far west as might be deemed necessary for their protection. In issuing orders to Everett, Davis said, you will cultivate "an intercourse of the most friendly character; and in parting with them, you will say when the Texians' army crosses the Río Grande it will not be for the purpose of making war and plundering peaceable citizens, but against Santa Anna and his rule."[168] Two of the soldiers who had assisted in capturing the Mexican traders, however, took two of their horses with saddles, blankets, and other equipment and absconded eastward; but since they were known, it was thought they would soon be apprehended.[169]

The chief disturbing element at Corpus Christi, reported Smith, emanates from the activities of Colonel Henry L. Kinney and W. P. Aubrey, partners in large ranch interests and mercantile trade, "whose acts and assertions have been treasonable ever since they have been here." Smith believed that too much confidence was placed in them by the President and General Davis, who permitted Mexicans to trade freely at the ranch "in all things . . . [except] munitions of war and arms."[170]

---

when in the settlements and not on active duty—I had a hard task to perform but I never tired. I have had to command my men *singly* and *alone*. I have had no help from the subordinate officers. I had to walk to Bastrop myself to get my men to follow me. I have had their murmurings to silence—their discontents to allay and their patriotism to arouse to get them along—I have cursed them—I have shamed them and I have done all that *man* could do to make soldiers of them.

W. Jefferson Jones to M. B. Lamar, Camp on Wilbarger's Prairie [endorsed:] Waterloo, April 15, 1839, in *Lamar Papers*, II, 530–531.

[167] E. McLean to James Davis, June 8, 1842, in Chabot, *Corpus Christi and Lipantitlán*, pp. 57–58.

[168] James Davis to Capt. John R. Everett, Head Quarters, Corpus Christi, June 11, 1842, quoted in *ibid.* p. 58.

[169] *Telegraph and Texas Register*, July 6, 1842; Goodman, "A Statement of Facts," Washington, Feby 10, 1843, in Miller Papers (Texas), ms.

[170] Joseph F. Smith to Anson Jones, Refugio County, June 24, 1842 [endorsed:]

Attack and Counterattack

The first Americans west of the Nueces had established themselves at Corpus Christi at the mouth of the Nueces in 1839, and engaged in trade—some of it contraband in nature. When Henry Lawrence Kinney settled in the Corpus Christi area in 1839, the country was not entirely new to him. He had made a trip to it as early as 1832, "when he visited the Irish colony at San Patricio and became a good friend of *empresarios* McMullen and McGloin and formed desirable contacts with a number of Mexican rancheros."[171] On January 4, 1840, Colonel Kinney purchased from Captain Enrique de Villareal, with the approval of the governor of Tamaulipas, ten leagues of land extending from the Oso to the Nueces River. On the west bank of the Nueces he established Kinney's Ranch and Trading Post in a commanding position on the corner of a high bluff, and associated with him William P. Aubrey. Together they conducted a profitable trade in leaf tobacco, domestic cotton, and calicos with northern Mexico. Kinney seems to have been in almost constant written and oral communication with the Mexican officers, "even going beyond the Río Grande, at his pleasure, in safety."

In all the marauding expeditions to this country [reported Smith] their persons and property were religiously respected. The officers would call and drink with them in mutual friendship, which was giving the enemy "aid and comfort"; and so popular were they in Mexico, that they had prisoners released at will and Dimitt captured from interest as he interfered with their friendship. When the Mexicans paid us a visit in the spring, the officers called on Kinney as usual, and asked where Capt. Carnes and his men were. He told them that they were on the Nueces river below San Patricia, but he says, that he made them promise they would not molest them; the party, five in number, were surprised and all killed but one. But notwithstanding all these acts of treason, it seems that our march to the Río Grande is to be governed by the information of these men, whose every act has proved they would sell their "God for thirty pieces of silver."[172]

According to reports from the Río Grande late in May Colonel Kinney was under guard at Monterey.[173]

Joseph Smith, June 29th, 1842. Rec'd 12th July [1842], Domestic Correspondence (Texas), 1835–1846, ms. See also Houston to W. P. Aubrey, New Washington, May 26, 1842, in *Writings of Sam Houston*, III, 60–61; Same to Col. James Davis, New Washington, May 26, 1842, in *ibid.*, III, 61–62.

[171] Coleman McCampbell, *Saga of a Frontier Seaport*, p. 24.

[172] Joseph F. Smith to Anson Jones, Refugio County, June 24, 1842, in Domestic Correspondence (Texas), 1835–1846, ms.

[173] *Telegraph and Texas Register*, June 1, 1842.

208

Arriving in New Orleans from a trip to Mexico where he had successfully concluded the settlement of an important claim against the Mexican government, Stewart Newell, former United States consul for the
port of Velasco,[174] wrote Anson Jones that he was surprised to learn

that direct communications were kept up between Arista and certain men in
Texas who profess friendship for Texas; and when I have mentioned it here,
I was told that the same men gave information to Texas of the Mexican movements, and that if I should name my impressions, or *what* I consider as proofs
of their treachery, it would not be available, so confidently are they believed
to be true to Texas; this being the case renders it useless for me to detail the
circumstances that led me to conclusions of their guilt, and the names of the
persons; but when I see you we will speak upon the subject.[175]

Three years later, the situation had not changed significantly. In the
words of Lieutenant Richard H. Wilson, Adjutant of the English Infantry, Corpus Christi was considered "the most murderous, thieving,
gambling, God-forsaken hole in the Lone Star or out of it."[176] In August
1845, Colonel Ethan Allen Hitchcock of the United States Army described Corpus Christi as a very small village whose "inhabitants were
smugglers and lawless persons to whom war was prosperity and 'satisfaction.' . . . Kinney seems to have a government of his own here, and to
be alternately the friend and foe of Mexicans, Texans, Americans, and
Indians, sometimes defying them and meeting them with force and
sometimes bribing and wheedling them. He lives by smuggling goods
across the line."[177] A few days later Colonel Hitchcock jotted down in
his diary, "Colonel Kinney's position here is an extraordinary one. While
an object of suspicion to both Texans and Mexicans, he seems to be regarded as a man of power by both sides and capable of serving both

[174] R. A. Irion to Alcée la Branche, Department of State, City of Houston, Dec.
1, 1837, in George P. Garrison (ed.), *Diplomatic Correspondence of Texas,* in *Annual Report of the American Historical Association,* 1907, I, 272.

[175] Stewart Newell to Anson Jones, New Orleans, July 8, 1842, in Jones, *Memoranda and Official Correspondence Relating to the Republic of Texas,* p. 198.
Similar and more detailed information was given by Newell in a letter he wrote to
Houston in June, and to Anson Jones in another letter he said, "I had reference to
officers or to citizens, and particularly to McKinney or Williams." Same to Same,
City Hotel, New Orleans, June 28, 1842, in Jones, *Memoranda and Official Correspondence Relating to the Republic of Texas,* p. 197.

[176] Quoted in Coleman McCampbell, *Texas Seaport: The Story of the Growth of
Corpus Christi and the Coastal Bend Area,* p. 27.

[177] W. A. Croffut (ed.), *Fifty Years in Camp and Field: Diary of Major General
Ethan Allen Hitchcock,* pp. 195–197.

sides. He seems to have no concealments, but frankly declares that the Texans have no right to go (or claim) to the Río Grande."[178] Kinney and Aubrey contended that Texas had never extended its conquests west of the Nueces and that the area west of the river, including Corpus Christi, belonged to the state of Tamaulipas. Aubrey claimed to be a British subject; and Kinney (a young Irishman) to the Mexicans professed to be a British subject too, and to the Texans, a citizen of the United States.[179] Both claimed immunity from the payment of import duties.

[178] *Ibid.*, p. 198.

[179] H. L. Kinney was born in Wyoming Valley, Pennsylvania, June 3, 1814. He moved to Illinois in 1830, and while there fought in the Black Hawk War and afterwards served in the Seminole War. Then for a brief period he operated as a trader in Havana. His proposed marriage to Daniel Webster's daughter, Julia, in 1837, met with a decided, "no." McCampbell, *Saga of a Frontier Seaport*, pp. 4, 124–125; McCampbell, *Texas Seaport*, p. [23]; Coleman McCampbell, "Colonel Kinney's Romance with Daniel Webster's Daughter," *Crystal Reflector* (Corpus Christi), June 1939; Claude Moore Fuess, *Daniel Webster*, II, 64–65; Howard Louis Conrad, *Nathaniel J. Brown: Biographical Sketch and Reminiscences of a Noted Pioneer*, pp. 14–15.

CHAPTER TEN

The Failure of the Republic's Efforts To Fit Out an Invading Army

AFTER THE RETREAT of General Vasquez, excitement in the United States began to die down, and men and money came in ever decreasing quantities, and by the middle of June the editor of the *Telegraph and Texas Register* was induced to believe from the tenor of United States newspapers that the excitement against Mexico had almost completely subsided.[1] Occasionally, however, there were reports of large groups of volunteers preparing to enter Texas in the near future. General Pickens of Alabama, it was said, was preparing to bring out in September eight hundred "emigrants" well supplied with clothing, rifles, and other necessary articles for settling that section of the country adjoining the Río Grande.[2] However, thoughtful men in the United States were beginning to wonder if the Texans and their government really knew what the situation was and if the reports from Texas, so numerous and conflicting, could be relied upon. The feeling of the average citizen in the United States came to be somewhat like that expressed by a gentleman from one of the middle states who wrote,

Though peace honorably and judiciously preserved is better than war, still the vague and changeable aspect which your nation has assumed in our journals, has given her a kind of braggadocia air, which has rendered us somewhat sceptical as to her real grievances; or her prowess and patriotism in combatting the foes of freedom. At first, a disciplined army of 14,000 men were marching upon her western borders, inflamed by hopes of spoil and revenge; and the friends of liberty were loudly called upon to shield her from the wrathful arms of the tyrants, to throw themselves into the deadly breach for her defence; but soon this mighty host dwindled to a mere marauding

[1] *Telegraph and Texas Register*, June 22, 1842.
[2] *Ibid.*, July 6, 1842.

211

party, which in one of their predatory forays had infringed upon the western limits of Texas. Then came the busy note of preparation, the clangor of arms— we heard that the tide of invasion was soon to be rolled back upon the invader, and that the hand-writing proclaiming her final dismemberment and downfall, was more palpable than the ominous signals which greeted Belchazza in his palace. We already saw, in imagination another chain which held the human family in bondage, severed, and the Anglo-Saxon banner floating in triumph on the battlements of the ancient city of Montezuma! But the tide of war is changed, and the ploughshare and pruning hook have again driven their officious defenders, the spear and the sword, back into retirement. Perhaps all these conclusions have not been warranted by the authorized acts of the Texian government, yet this has been the feeling, to a great extent, which has pervaded the United States.[3]

Failure of the Republic to maintain order on the frontier and to afford proper protection to the inhabitants from Indians, robbers, brigands, and Mexican raiders operated to discourage immigration from the United States. Those who would have come to establish homes, cultivate the soil, and engage in business stopped to weigh the disadvantages of the unsettled political and economic conditions in Texas, and often turned to the frontier in the United States rather than run the risk of being caught in a Mexican invasion. In his effort to float a loan of a million dollars in New Orleans, the Texan agent, Colonel William H. Daingerfield, obtained not a dollar. The hurried trip of Anson Jones, the Secretary of State, to New Orleans resulted in the promise of a loan, but no money was forthcoming.[4] The United States was just beginning to recover from the tremendous economic dislocations brought about by the Panic of 1837. "You can form no idea of the extreme depression and hopeless pecuniary embarrassment of the citizens of this country," wrote Daingerfield from New Orleans. "Their condition is in every way much worse than that of Texas."[5] From New York Samuel Swartwout, prominent land speculator in Texas, wrote that he was glad to see volunteers going to Texas for this meant settlers for the land and defenders for the country.

[3] *Ibid.*

[4] Anson Jones, *Memoranda and Official Correspondence Relating to the Republic of Texas, Its History and Annexation—Including a Brief Autobiography of the Author*, p. 203; Herbert Pickens Gambrell, *Anson Jones: the Last President of Texas*, pp. 250–251.

[5] William H. Daingerfield to Anson Jones, New Orleans, April 15, 1842, in Jones, *Memoranda and Official Correspondence Relating to the Republic of Texas*, pp. 201–203.

Money you will not get, I presume, much of [he informed Morgan]. There is none in y[ou]r or this country. All you can do is to procure powder & ball & fire away at nothing! For d—m the Mexicans c[oul]d not procure in all the Tyrant's dominions [enough men] to venture as far as the Brazos. I believe you are safe enough. Texas like Mississippi is d—d, and altho[ugh] you may get a few volunteers to join your army, men of property will avoid you.[6]

By the middle of July provisions and equipment to the value of approximately $500 had been received at Galveston from friends in the United States; the Augusta Committee (Georgia) had forwarded money to the amount of $927.44 to the Texan consul at New Orleans;[7] from the Tampa Bay area some 1,300 cartouche boxes and other supplies had been received at New Orleans;[8] and Robert Sanderson of New Orleans had contributed ten barrels of beef.[9] Unrecorded amounts of lead, powder, and other supplies came overland from the southwestern part of the United States, but in no sense were such contributions large enough to fit out an invading army.[10] The contributions from citizens of the Republic were likewise niggardly. Such meager contributions to a bankrupt "campaign chest" could scarcely be expected to intimidate the enemy or satisfy the adventurers who came from the United States to participate in an invasion of Mexico. It was estimated that to pay, equip, and provision a mounted company of twelve officers and fifty-five privates would cost between $54,465.92 and $73,665.92, depending upon whether or not one or two sets of horses were lost by negligence or stampedes caused by the enemy. However, at the rate of exchange current in Texas at the time the maximum cost per company was estimated at $147,331.84.[11]

[6] Samuel Swartwout to Col. James Morgan, Mount Savage Iron Works, Maryland, April 15, 1842, in James Morgan Papers, 1841–1845, ms.

[7] Sam Houston to the House of Representatives, City of Houston, *Writings of Sam Houston*, III, 102–103; Harriet Smither (ed.), *Journals of the Sixth Congress of the Republic of Texas*, III, 157; Executive Records of the Second Term of General Sam Houston's Administration of the Government of Texas, December 1841–December 1844, ms., pp. 118–120.

[8] Edmunds to W. D. Miller, New Orleans, May 3–10, 1842, in Washington D. Miller Papers, 1833–1860 (Texas), ms.

[9] Report of William H. Daingerfield, Washington, Dec. 7, 1842, in Smither (ed.), *Journals of the Sixth Congress*, III, 158.

[10] Ten kegs of powder and several kegs of lead, subscribed by the citizens of Natchitoches, reached Nacogdoches on April 19, 1842, for use against Mexico. Harriet Smither (ed.), "Diary of Adolphus Sterne," in *Southwestern Historical Quarterly*, XXXIII (1929–1930), 239.

[11] J. Snively to Sam Houston, Washington, Dec. 27, 1842, in Army Papers

In Europe and elsewhere the financial standing of the Republic was lowered as a result of the failure of the Santa Fé expedition, which revealed an apparent inability of Texas to occupy the territory claimed by it. Conditions were so unstable in the Republic that foreign promoters of immigration societies and friendly capitalists in the United States were wary about risking investments in a country which was without money, credit, a regular standing army, and was constantly threatened by Mexico and harassed by the Indians.[12] In England misrepresentations concerning Texas were put out by Mexican bondholders and persons engaged in speculative colonizing enterprises in British colonial possessions who wished to discourage emigration to Texas. The diplomatic and consular agents of Mexico carried on a bitter campaign against Texas abroad, and the propaganda put out by British merchants engaged in the Mexican trade adversely affected British emigration and may have had some influence upon emigration from other areas.[13] On the other hand, the continental European colonizing agents were active in laying their plans and in encouraging emigrants to go to Texas. Armand Ducos and Alexandre Bourgeois were at New Orleans in June on their way to France to make arrangements for sending emigrants to their two grants, one of which bordered upon the lower Río Grande; Henri Castro was active in France soliciting settlers for the grant awarded him west of San Antonio, while Henry F. Fisher and Burchard Miller were preparing to colonize the San Saba Valley with immigrants from Germany. In the meantime, English settlers arrived at Galveston on June 16,[14] to locate on the William Kennedy grant.

From San Augustine it was reported that the customhouse for that district was closed and no duties were being collected. "The people all along the line from the Red River to the mouth of the Sabine," reported

(Texas), ms.; William C. Binkley, *The Expansionist Movement in Texas, 1836–1850*, p. 96. A law of February 4, 1841, allowed $6,832 for the maintenance of a company of fifty-six volunteer minute men for four months. The same number of regulars of an army would have cost one-third less. G. W. Hockley, Secretary of War & Marine, to Sam Houston, Dept. of War & Marine, June 23, 1842, in Smither (ed.), *Journals of the Sixth Congress*, III, 109–110.

[12] *New Orleans Courier*, Jan. 22, 1842; Ashbel Smith to Anson Jones, March 31, 1843, in George P. Garrison (ed.), *Diplomatic Correspondence of Texas*, in *Annual Report of the American Historical Association*, 1908, III, 1429.

[13] Ashbel Smith to Anson Jones, Legation of Texas, London, July 3, 1842, in *ibid.*, 1908, III, 471–476; Arthur Akin to Ashbel Smith, London, July 1, 1842, in *ibid.*, 1908, III, 992.

[14] *Bollaert's Texas*, pp. 100–101.

the *Telegraph and Texas Register*,[15] "openly defy the collectors and bring in their goods from the United States, with as little hindrance as they would meet with in transporting them from one county to another." It should be added that, in the opinion of many historians, the old southwestern border was the roughest in United States history and that law and order had never been firmly established and sustained in that area.

Rumors spread through the United States by the abolitionists and those who were opposed to annexation often discouraged persons from going to Texas. Occasionally discontented elements in Texas were accused of originating such rumors, and Vice President Burleson's letter to the people of Texas, April 6, did not help matters. In fact, the *New Orleans Bee* of April 25 strongly implied on the basis of Houston's published address to the people of Texas of April 4 and Burleson's of the 6th that the plans of Texas to invade Mexico were all "hum-bug," and the Texan consul in that city found it necessary "to appear publicly in vindication of a course which," he said, "I had hoped would have remained secret."[16]

In your synopsis of news from Texas in this morning's paper, [began Consul Edmunds] I see much to discourage emigrants who are on their way to . . . [Texas]. Your course towards us heretofore has evidenced your interest and anxiety for our success; and I can well imagine your feelings and disappointment, when from "*private* sources," Gen. Houston's address to the people of Texas, you infer he will give the invasion of Mexico the "go by," and not move in the matter until the meeting of the ensuing Congress. . . . You say "His Excellency is in favor of procrastinating that measure (invasion) until the meeting of Congress. We infer from what we gather from the news, as well through the press as *private sources*, that Mr. Houston (as Santa Anna designates his Excellency) is not in high favor with the people of Texas, and that the *brandy*

---

15 Dec. 14, 1842.

16 Consul P. Edmunds sent a copy of his letter to the Editors of the *Bee*, Consulate of Texas, New Orleans, April 25, 1842, to the Texan Secretary of State; and, also, a letter addressed to Dr. Francis Moore of the *Telegraph and Texas Register*, "for perusal and judgment" by the Secretary and the Attorney General with the privilege of altering "the style of it so as to make it read well and forcibly, but under no circumstances change the substance of what I have said, because they are truths. . . . Add as much as you choose," wrote Edmunds. Jones was requested, if he so desired, to hand the letter to Dr. Moore for publication; or, if it were thought best, he was instructed to destroy it. P. Edmunds to Anson Jones, New Orleans, April 26, 1842, and Same to Same, New Orleans, April 27, 1842 in Consular Correspondence (Texas), 1838–1875, ms. P. Edmunds to W. D. Miller, New Orleans, May 3–10, 1842, in Miller Papers (Texas), ms.; *New Orleans Bee*, April 25 and 29, 1842.

bottle has well nigh used up the faculties, locomotive and reflective, of the Hero of San Jacinto. The President seems to cherish a moral enmity to the most prominent men in Texas—hence the confusion and failure of the expedition which it was expected would cross the Río Grande."

Edmunds quickly assured the editor that the President in no way contemplated postponing the expedition until the meeting of Congress.

The invasion will be made, and that speedily. [he declared] The departure of emigrants from this point in a short time, will *practically* give the correction to all impressions that may be made against His Excellency of a prejudicial character, in reference to promptness of action. So far as confidence on the part of the *people* is concerned, it is useless for me to assert his pre-eminence. . . . "The most prominent men in Texas" may for all I know consider themselves objects of his "mortal hatred." But whatever "prominency" consists in self-estimation, or the congregated confidence of the people, are matters which require no discussion. They speak for themselves. Perhaps some "prominent" man, has in a private way led you to believe the "brandy bottle" has used up General Houston's faculties. If so, I pronounce the author guilty of willful misrepresentation and an enemy to Texas. I *know* General Houston does not indulge in intemperance, and I further know he has not even tasted anything of an intoxicating character since September, 1841. Temperance, prudence and consistency characterize his private and public conduct; and it seems because he does not wrecklessly keep pace with some few steam warriors in Texas, proclaim to the world the manner, time and place of attack on Mexico, he is to be abused by "prominent men" there, and the whole scheme and plan of operation defeated here. [Under these circumstances, Edmunds said] I am forced to . . . proclaim to all interested in behalf of Texas, that the invasion of Mexico will be commenced in a short time, and that we ask all the aid we can get concentrated at this point [New Orleans] as soon as possible. . . . Let none, therefore, listen to rumors, but rush to our aid.[17]

The editors of the *Bee*, however, were still convinced that Houston's address to the people of Texas of April 4 was an unwise publication, and would do much to discourage those resolute spirits in the United States joining the standard of Texas in a campaign against Mexico. On June 10 the *Daily Picayune* published an exceedingly favorable description of General Houston which appeared in the Fort Pickering *American Eagle* and had been written by its editor, F. S. Latham, who had gone to Texas in charge of a company of volunteers. Latham wrote,

---

[17] P. Edmunds, Texas Consul, to the Editors of the *Bee*, Consulate of Texas, New Orleans, April 25, 1842, *New Orleans Bee*, April 29, 1842; also in *Telegraph and Texas Register*, May 18, 1842.

The Failure of the Invading Army

Much to my surprise, and contrary to every opinion I had formed from the remarks of others respecting him, my first visit and intercourse with Gen. Houston left [a] far different and more agreeable impression on my mind in his favor, than what I anticipated. Instead of finding him a dissipated, testy debauche in appearance, nothing is further from the truth. I found him a very dignified, affable and courteous gentleman, remarkably kind and affable in his address, and as free in appearance and in fact from dissipation as any man living. He is said to be a new and reclaimed man in this respect since his last elevation to the Presidency, being totally abstemious; without, however, as has been reported, having taken any public pledge of teetotalism. He is a large, noble specimen of physical humanity, dresses very genteelly, and is most certainly a perfect gentleman, as well as in many respects a *great man*.

I visited Texas, from political association and other causes not entirely unmingled with prejudice, with a very bad opinion of Gen. Houston. But that opinion is changed—totally changed. He doubtless has his faults. But he is a gentleman so different in character to that which has been reputed to be his, that I could scarcely believe him to be that man.[18]

The private sources in New Orleans attempting to discredit Houston and his Mexican policy received encouragement from Albert Sidney Johnston and his supporters.

I am almost tempted here to tell you what I really think of some of the agitators in Texas, but I won't do it. [Edmunds wrote Anson Jones] I could also describe a swaggering upstart now in power [Edward Burleson], but this also must pass. . . . Dont show Genl Houston the copy of the Bee I now send you. It will excite him and this is unnecessary. . . . What a villianous and slanderous article it is. Dont you know, Bullet's best friends in Texas are the Genl's worst enemies? If you do not, I do. Bullet [Albert Sidney Johnston] and all the rest are from Kentucky. I suppose you comprehend this. . . . I wish I could see you for a few hours and tell you what I really think of some great men at home, and a swaggering sycophant abroad. But silence must be observed until the struggle is over.[19]

Then two weeks later to Miller, the President's private secretary, he confided, "I knew you would condemn my card in the Bee. . . . What else," he asked, "could I do when the dam[d] rascals were slandering the 'Old Chief'. . . . I have been informed the Pres[iden]t of these United States will demand my recall, because of the cards in the Bee and Bulletin. Who would have thought I ever would have become a McLeod almost?

[18] *Daily Picayune*, June 10, 1842.
[19] P. Edmunds to Anson Jones, New Orleans, April 27, 1842, in Consular Correspondence (Texas), 1838–1875, ms.

Had I not better go far enough to get in jail for patriotism? What think you?"[20]

Feeling that he had overstepped the bounds of propriety under the neutrality laws of the United States, Edmunds asked for permission to return to Texas for a week as soon as Washington's troops got off from New Orleans.[21] On May 30, he was granted a leave of absence for three weeks to visit Galveston, and was authorized to appoint a vice consul to administer the duties of the consulship during his absence.[22] Upon his return to Texas during the summer, Edmunds informed Houston of his intention of resigning his position at New Orleans as Texan consul; whereupon, the President appointed William Bryan to fill the position. Bryan took over the seals and papers of the office on September 5.[23]

Certain individuals at Galveston, Mr. Alsbury being among them, started a rumor in the United States to the effect that the people and the President "were at open rupture in regard to the war." At Galveston[24] a group of citizens—including James Love (the brother-in-law of the United States chargé d'affaires in Texas), who once referred to His Excellency as "a bloated mass of corruption,"[25] threatened "to put the President aboard a vessel and send him to the United States." Some of the local opposition newspapers, especially the *Galveston Times*, the *Morning Star* (Houston), and the Houston *Telegraph*, were pursuing an

[20] P. Edmunds to W. D. Miller, New Orleans, May 3–10, 1842, in Miller Papers (Texas), ms. *New Orleans Bulletin* of May 10, 1842, carried an extract of Edmunds' letter to John Lyde Wilson, ex-governor of South Carolina.

[21] P. Edmunds to Anson Jones, New Orleans, April 27, 1842, in Consular Correspondence (Texas), 1838–1875, ms.; P. Edmunds to W. D. Miller, New Orleans, May 3–10, 1842, in Miller Papers (Texas), ms.

[22] Anson Jones to P. Edmunds, Department of State, Houston, May 30, 1842 (copy), in Consular Correspondence (Texas), 1838–1875, ms.

[23] Joseph Waples, Acting Secretary of State, to P. Edmunds, Department of State, Houston, Aug. 18 [1842] and William Bryan to Anson Jones, Consulate of the Republic of Texas, New Orleans, Sept. 7, 1842; in *ibid.*; *Telegraph and Texas Register*, Aug. 24, 1842.

[24] "Now, Mr. Speaker, where is Galveston?" asked "Three-Legged-Willie" (R. M. Williamson) in the House of Representatives of the Sixth Congress. "Sir," he answered, "it is a little sandy spot situated away out in the Gulf of Mexico, where the pelican lays her eggs and the sea gull screams, once the stamping ground of Lafitte and his pirates, and now inhabited by the lordliest set of d—d rascals that my two blue eyes ever blazed on." Mrs. Jonnie Lockhart Wallis and Laurance L. Hill, *Sixty Years on the Brazos: The Life and Letters of Dr. John Washington Lockhart, 1824–1900*, p. 64.

[25] James Love to Gen. M. B. Lamar, Galveston, April 14, 1840, in *Lamar Papers*, III, 371–372.

"infamous course . . . in villifying and abusing the country, its institutions, and character, and misrepresenting the actions of the Gov[ernmen]t. The falsehoods uttered and circulated through these vile channels . . . [and] the licenciousness of this portion of the newspaper press," wrote Jones, "gives cause of deepest mortification to every friend of decency and good order here, and leads them frequently even to doubt whether this licenciousness is not a greater curse to the country than the liberty of the press is a blessing."[26] "I fear that my country suffers more from the great number of incompetent advisers, directors, and leaders, or would be great men, that her present situation has called into existence than from any other cause," wrote Guy M. Bryan.[27]

"The late uproar, and excitement in this country," reported James Morgan from New Washington, "has put a stop to everything and Old Sam has been so much excited all the time and there was such a disposition by a certain party here to put him down and thwart all his plans and measures, he became Snarlish as a half starved dog."[28]

We have to labor against wind and tide here—dissention at home, and private letters from "influential men" as some would have it. [wrote Consul Edmunds from New Orleans] We may succeed—and we may not. . . . But really I believe no help can be had from this country hereafter unless something is done now. Genl. Houston's enemies say he cannot be pushed into an invasion altho he declares his views to that effect publicly. I trust he will now correct these enemies, by proving by his acts, they have lied. If the invasion once commences then thousands will come [from the United States]. I tell you, most people here believe it will all turn out nothing. This being the case ought not something to be done at once?[29]

From the want of other objects to occupy their time and attention, [declared Mrs. Houstoun, an English visitor to Texas in 1843] a large proportion of the people amuse themselves by abusing . . . [President Houston] both in his public and private capacity. . . . Every instance of adversity, and every deficiency of dollars, is attributed at once to the President's mismanagement

[26] Anson Jones to Ashbel Smith, Dept. of State, Washington, Feb. 16, 1843, in Garrison (ed.), *Diplomatic Correspondence of Texas*, 1908, III, 1514–1516; see also Houston to William H. Daingerfield, City of Houston, April 19, 1842, in *Writings of Sam Houston*, III, 20–21.

[27] Guy M. Bryan's postscript to the letter of Stephen S. Perry to James F. Perry, Kenyon, June 6, 1842, in James F. Perry Papers, ms.; *Handbook of Texas*, I, 233.

[28] James Morgan to Saml. Swartwout, New Washington, Galveston Bay, Texas, May 17,1842, in Morgan Papers, ms.

[29] P. Edmunds to Anson Jones, New Orleans, April 27, 1842, in Consular Correspondence (Texas), 1838–1875, ms.

or cupidity. The latter charge is so strange, and so utterly unfounded, that it finds but few believers. [Among the other causes of complaint against him, the principal one is his avowed dislike of going to war,] which in common with all people who have but little to lose, is a favourite pastime with the Texans. The advice of the President to his countrymen—"stay at home, gentlemen, look after your flocks and herds, and sow corn,"—meets but little sympathy from his fellow-citizens. Another cause of his unpopularity with the fighting party, is his opposition to the existence of a navy in Texas . . . contending that they have no use for ships and that the support of a navy is a useless incumbrance to the republic. [Another object of his special enmity is] American sympathizers and *loafers*. . . . No persons are so much to be feared [as these]. They are people who go about in search of promiscuous plunder, and it matters nothing to them, whether friend or enemy falls a victim to their rapacity. If nothing is to be made of the Mexicans, they turn upon the Texans in search of prey.[30]

The people were accused of driving Houston into a renewal of the war with Mexico, and the President was pictured as "parading the streets of Galveston like a mad man, raving and swearing against all who advocated war."[31] "Among other conversations," recorded Bollaert, who called upon the President on July 7, "he c—d[32] the Volunteers, who, to get them out of the way, he had allowed to go down the coast—and was fearful [now] that they would bring on a fight on the frontier and then if they were all killed, why then he would be blamed for it."[33]

Jones, Secretary of State, privately believed "the President must certainly be running 'mad,' but he was obliged to seem publicly"[34] to support the President's plans for invasion. In April Jones seems to have been trying to avoid committing himself too much in favor of the war policy, but by June his public support of the President's policy to invade Mexico was being re-enforced by private expressions of enthusiasm for the campaign. On June 20, 1842, Jones upon his return from New Orleans where he had made a contract with Alexandre Bourgeois d'Orvanne to loan Texas one million dollars, recorded in his *Diary*,

[30] Mrs. [M. C.] Houstoun, *Texas and the Gulf of Mexico: or Yachting in the New World*, II, 162–164.
[31] P. Edmunds to Anson Jones, New Orleans, April 12, 1842, in Jones, *Memoranda and Official Correspondence Relating to the Republic of Texas*, pp. 188–189.
[32] Cursed.
[33] *Bollaert's Texas*, p. 108.
[34] Endorsement on letter of W. D. Miller to Anson Jones, Houston, April 12, 1842, in Jones, *Memoranda and Official Correspondence Relating to the Republic of Texas*, p. 187.

We must fight with Mexico. Another San Jacinto on the Río Grande will secure to Texas nationality and Independence. The Anglo-Saxons once precipitated beyond the Río Grande no one can predict their limits, or their point
of stop. If Mexico is wise she will invoke with us the interference of the
United States, France and England to mediate.[35]

The extreme pressure in the money market in the United States and a
most unusual destruction of confidence among the commercial community following the Panic of 1837 forestalled the Texans in obtaining
appreciable supplies of provisions and munitions in the United States as
gifts or on credit. Furthermore, Bourgeois d'Orvanne was unable to raise
the million-dollar loan in Europe. If conditions in the United States
and Europe were bad in 1842, they were not much better in Texas.
Galveston in 1842 was pictured as "one of the most dull and dreary
places on the face of the earth. The citizens," wrote General Morehouse,
"have assumed the right to obey or disobey an order from the government as best may suit their particular fancy."[36] In the summer of 1842
one of the nation's leading newspapers reluctantly admitted: "A general
gloom seems to rest over every section of the Republic, and doubt and
sorrow are depicted on almost every brow."[37] The market for Texas lands
had collapsed by 1842. Exchequer bills were circulating at 70 per cent
discount.[38] "Texas lands will not sell for anything," wrote Henry Smith.
"There seems to be no property here now that would answer in the place
of money except good work Mules or Negroes at a fair price."[39] At
Nacogdoches, Adolphus Sterne recorded in his diary on February 5 and
March 18, 1842, "Grog Shops all Shutt up *no* Cash Credit very sick";
and "times have never been so hard in Texas, like they are now. I have
never known the want of two bits until now,—!!!!!"[40] "That the monetary
affairs of Texas are at present in a more deranged situation than at any
former period of our history," wrote the editor of the *Austin City Gazette*,[41] "none can deny—the merchant has already felt the shock; the

[35] Anson Jones, Diaries, Monday, June 20, 1842, ms.
[36] Gen. E. Morehouse to Anson Jones, Galveston, Dec. 28, 1842, in Jones, *Memoranda and Official Correspondence Relating to the Republic of Texas*, pp. 199–200.
[37] Quoted in William Ransom Hogan, *The Texas Republic: A Social and Economic History*, p. 291.
[38] *Bollaert's Texas*, p. 124.
[39] Henry Smith to James Power, Jan., 1842 (copy), Henry Smith, 1822–1846,
ms.
[40] Harriet Smither (ed.), "Diary of Adolphus Sterne," in *Southwestern Historical
Quarterly*, XXXIII (1929–1930), 160, 231.
[41] July 15, 1840.

farmer, the mechanic and the laborer are all suffering; none have escaped. All classes unite in raising one universal shout of 'Hard times! Hard Times!!'" "Postponed the [auction] Sale—thier [*sic*] being no money!!!!!!" recorded Sterne at Nacogdoches, and within a short space of time we find other entries in his diary depicting a lack of prosperity: [Wed., July 21, 1841] "weather hot—every body in Town drunk, nothing doing; idleness Root of all evils. . . ." [Sept. 5, 1841] "I candidly believe we are in a state of *collapse* so that nothing in the shape of Legislation can save us from a governmental as well as individual Bankruptcy. . . . Our government is, like most of the People comprising it—*not able to pay the Honest Labourer for his work.* . . ." [March 9, 1842] "Times getting worse & worse every day. Ten dollars now as much an object as one Hundred were some few years ago, how the People of this Country can get the necessaries of life till next fall God only knows."[42] "Trade," recorded Bollaert in his diary, "is at a low ebb, and credit still lower—yet with all this, 'Texas will go ahead'."[43] The financial crisis in New Orleans was increasing.[44] From Austin, "the dullest and most deserted of cities,"[45] J. M. Long wrote that he was going down to town,

or rather down where the town *used for to be* [to get the mail]. Everything [here] is however going on pretty smoothyly & nothing to do, no money to spend and nothing to spend it for. We are lords of all we survey. Every fellow does as he pleases, and no person dare make him afraid. I am luxurating—have plenty of good liquor—a plenty to eat—a plenty [of] time to sleep—play cards etc. I have also become during these hard times to be a considerable ladies man. I have necessarilly, owing to the scarcity of beaus, had it forced on me, and I go it—hark from the tomb—we have about twenty odd women here—old and young—all of whom want beaus—and you may judge, five or six see sights.[46]

Six weeks after General Burleson disbanded the volunteers at San Antonio, a report from there said, "Business is at a stand and the gloom of desolation seems to rest over the devoted city. Poor Béxar, her history

---

[42] Smither (ed.), "Diary of Adolphus Sterne," in *Southwestern Historical Quarterly,* XXXI (1927–1928), 184; XXXII (1928–1929), 166, 174; XXXIII (1929–1930), 167; XXXIV (1930–1931), 72.

[43] *Bollaert's Texas,* p. 61.

[44] *Ibid.,* p. 106.

[45] G. H. Harrison to W. D. Miller, City of Austin, May 20, 1842, in Miller Papers, 1833–1860 (Texas), ms.

[46] J. M. Long to Matthew P. Woodhouse, City of Austin, May 2, 1842, in Matthew P. Woodhouse Papers, ms.

is replete with disaster and misfortune."[47] "The Western country from the Colorado to the San Antonio has been almost totally devastated by our own troops," wrote Miller from Houston.[48] Some of the western settlers had returned to the United States to await more propitious times.[49] Only ten or fifteen American families had returned to Béxar after Vasquez's withdrawal, and the Mexican sympathizers were confident that another invasion would take place. By May 13 it was reported that the only Americans at San Antonio were a few men who had important business interests to look after or who were in the ranger force under Captain Hays. Many of the Mexican families had also left Béxar— some for the Guadalupe and some to join the enemy.[50] The Mexicans residing on the San Antonio below Goliad were viewed with great suspicion by the Anglo-Americans. It was believed that they, especially those living in the vicinity of Carlos Rancho, twenty miles below Goliad, where the road from Victoria to Mission Refugio crossed the San Antonio River, held regular communication with the hostile Mexicans on the Río Grande and that they were leagued with the bandits under Savariego and Agatón. It was reported that they had "frequently threatened to drive every American from the San Antonio river, and had lately procured forty or fifty good rifles from the deserters" and that little doubt existed but that they were "waiting for a favorable moment to join the [Mexican] army."[51] The remnant of the weak, destitute Carrizo tribe, numbering now only about fifty to sixty warriors, appeared to be making common cause with the "renegade" Mexicans. These Indians were reported recently to have stolen a number of horses near Goliad.[52]

The City Council at San Antonio resolved on May 23 that the mayor, John W. Smith, should proceed immediately to organize and send out a patrol of ten men to pass up and down the San Antonio River for the purpose of keeping order and reporting to the authorities of the city any matters of importance that might occur, the patrol to be renewed weekly until otherwise ordered.[53] During the months just past, the Lipans and

[47] *Telegraph and Texas Register,* June 15, 1842.
[48] W. D. Miller to William H. Daingerfield, Houston, April 13, 1842, in Washington D. Miller Papers (Hardin-Simmons), ms.
[49] *Bollaert's Texas,* p. 61.
[50] *Telegraph and Texas Register,* May 18, 1842.
[51] *Telegraph and Texas Register,* July 13, 1842.
[52] *Ibid.*
[53] San Antonio, "Journal A: Records of the City of San Antonio," ms., p. 105.

Tonkawas were frequently employed by Captain Hays as scouts against the Mexicans, and they sometimes proceeded with the Texans beyond the Nueces, as reports, later proven false, continually reached the settlements, through Mexican spies, of the advance of the enemy. Early in the summer a deputation from the Lipan camp on the San Marcos, consisting of Castro, Flacco, Colonel John, and several warriors, proceeded by way of Austin to Houston to lay their claims for pay against the government, some of their claims being of long standing.[54] Anton Lockmar, direct from San Antonio with letters from John Bradley and John W. Smith, reached the Colorado near LaGrange on May 13, with a report that all the Americans had again left Béxar, and that seven to eight hundred Mexican troops were said to be ten miles below the town on the San Antonio River, and would likely seize the place since the troops had disbanded and gone home. Francisco Rada and others were reported captured by the Mexicans thirty miles below San Antonio near Calaveras (Calvillo) Rancho. About twenty men under Hays, who had gone west, had overstayed their appointed time, and fears were entertained for their safety. Cornelius Van Ness had been accidentally shot and killed by James Robinson.[55]

News of the Mexican force in the vicinity of Béxar created great excitement in Austin, but no one dared to go out to confirm the report. However, a company of fifty or sixty from Bastrop went out, and learned that there "were no Mexicans there except the citizens who were herding their cattle either to take care of them or to drive them beyond the Río Grande."[56] The report was that no organized Mexican forces had been in the area of Béxar since the retreat of Vasquez and that Hays was on the Medina with his spies.[57] The rumor that the Colorado boys who had gone west in search of the Mexican force near San Antonio, not finding the enemy, had plundered several Mexican ranches in that vicinity and had driven off many cattle and horses was soon proved to be false. "These volunteers," declared the *Telegraph*,[58] "so far from

[54] George W. Hockley to Sam Houston, Department of War and Marine, [Houston], June 23, 1842, in *Telegraph and Texas Register*, July 6, 1842.

[55] Rena Maverick Green (ed.), *Memoirs of Mary A. Maverick: Arranged by Mary A. Maverick and Her Son George Madison Maverick*, p. 66; Rena Maverick Green (ed.), *Samuel Maverick, Texan, 1803–1870: A Collection of Letters, Journals and Memoirs*, p. 162.

[56] G. H. Harrison to W. D. Miller, City of Austin, May 20, 1842, in Miller Papers (Texas), ms.

[57] *Telegraph and Texas Register*, May 25 and June 15, 1842.

[58] *Ibid.*, June 1 and 15, 1842.

plundering the unfortunate Mexicans, actually rescued a large number of cattle from a *thieving party from the Guadalupe,* and drove them back to their owners." Colonel James Latham, just arrived from Béxar and Austin, declared in Houston that only three or four individuals had been engaged in the nefarious business of stealing.[59] " 'The Colorado boys' have ever been ranked among the bravest soldiers of Texas, and we are glad to find," continued the editor of the *Telegraph,* "that they still verify the old maxim—that *'The brave are never base'.*"

The mail system was deplorably insufficient. Poor roads, a depleted treasury, and the uncertainty of travel were the chief causes for the break-down of the postal system. During the summer of 1842 "the mails were totally suspended."[60] Houston in a message to Congress in 1842 called attention to the virtual nonexistence of a dependable postal service to keep the government officials informed of events and to promote greater efficiency in administration. At Nacogdoches Postmaster Sterne privately recorded on August 1: ". . . have a serious Idea of resigning my Postmastership it is a loss to me, every day, and the government is so destitute of means that the Establishment can not be kept up as it ought to be—it is the *beginning of the End*—God grant it may not be—but!!!"[61] On December 8 he gives further insight into the condition of the mail: "The western mail arrived last night, . . . the Boy having rode two days in the rain so that the whole Contents were so mangled, and mixed up that it looked more like mush than anything else, so that nothing can be read to find out to whom the documents belong or where they came from."[62]

Economic and political conditions were at so low an ebb in the Republic in 1842 that most Texans believed they could not possibly get any worse and might, in the course of time, improve. It was under such conditions as these that President Houston proposed to launch an invasion of Mexico. These same conditions doomed his plans to hopeless failure.

As the time scheduled for opening the invasion approached, Captain Benjamin McCulloch, who had served in the House of Representatives

[59] *Ibid.*

[60] *Telegraph and Texas Register,* May 31, 1843; W. L. Newsom, "The Postal System of the Republic of Texas," in *Southwestern Historical Quarterly, XX* (1916–1917), 103–131.

[61] Smither (ed.), "Diary of Adolphus Sterne," in *Southwestern Historical Quarterly,* XXIV (1930–1931), 72.

[62] *Ibid.,* XXXIV (1930–1931), 347.

of the Fourth Congress, was instructed to raise a cavalry company of from fifty-six to sixty-five first-class rangers, carefully selected as to equipment, subordination, and stamina to withstand active and arduous duty. This company was to serve as a special scouting party unattached to any particular regiment.

You will . . . take care [wrote the President] that your command is not disgraced by that most dangerous and most odious of all vices—the lust of plunder. See that you have gentlemen, and not robbers as your associates. . . . Plunder will not be allowed. The enemy must support the war; but even the enemy must be treated as the honor of our race and our national name will demand.[63]

As noted earlier in this chapter, an executive proclamation of April 14 called for the raising of volunteer companies according to law and authorized their formation into battalions and regiments. Each volunteer company was to consist of such citizens as could "best leave their homes" and whose absence would "not injuriously affect the agricultural interest of the country." The men were to elect their own officers, and upon organization were forthwith to file with the Secretary of War a muster roll of the company and a report on the condition and character of their arms. The President would then accept or reject the tender of their services. Those selected would be permitted to remain at home until the country should need their services.[64] In line with these recommendations, the company and regimental officers throughout the Republic began to check the county organizations under their command and to call for volunteers or to draft men to bring the local militia units, especially those of the First Class, up to required strength.[65] The Lipan chief, Castro, and his party left Houston on Wednesday, June 22, for the west to unite his tribe with the Tonkawas and move to Corpus Christi to accompany the Texan army to the Río Grande. The Lipans seemed delighted and eager to renew hostilities against their old enemies—the Mexicans.[66] Flacco, a young chief, was given a note by the Government

[63] Houston to Capt. Benjamin McCulloch, City of Houston, June 18, 1842, in *Writings of Sam Houston*, III, 71–73.

[64] *Telegraph and Texas Register*, April 20, 1842.

[65] Smither (ed.), "Diary of Adolphus Sterne," in *Southwestern Historical Quarterly*, XXXIII (1929–1930), 323–324; George W. Hockley, Secretary of War & Marine, to Sam Houston, Department of War & Marine, June 23, 1842, in Smither (ed.), *Journals of the Sixth Congress*, III, 108–109.

[66] *Telegraph and Texas Register*, June 29, 1842.

authorizing him to command a company of Lipans. Proudly considering himself now a "Texian Captain," he declared, "Me no fight like Indians any longer, and steal horses. Me Texian officer and fight like Texians. Me kill Mexicans and no steal."[67]

What was needed more than anything else, reported the Secretary of War, was a regular soldiery, for, though,

the brave yeomanry of our country are always ready to obey its call, . . . they cannot be expected to leap into the saddle, or to march with their rifle, in the instant. They have families, and very correctly make themselves sure of their safety, previously to taking the field. They are scattered and time is required for them to concentrate. The regular soldier has no other duty to perform but to obey his orders, and his profession devotes him to the service of his country, and the sacrifice of his life if necessary in its defence.[68]

Besides, the cost of maintaining regular troops was about one-third less than that for "Minute-Men," as authorized by the law of February 4, 1841.

The fitting out of the Santa Fé expedition by the last administration and the several alarms of the approach of Indians upon Austin had by late June woefully depleted the military supplies in the arsenal at Austin, the only arsenal in Texas, leaving but 395 muskets, 581 kegs of powder of all kinds, and 837 pounds of lead. The two pieces of brass cannon remaining at Austin, with the "Twin Sisters," together with ammunition for them and the small arms, together with their appointments and ammunition in the Ordnance Department, were ordered to San Felipe in charge of the captain of ordnance in readiness for transportation to any point that might be designated in opening the contemplated campaign. The carriages and train for the artillery pieces needed some repairs, which could not be completed at Austin for "the want of means"; harness had been ordered from New Orleans; caissons, port-fires, and other necessary items were deficient. The armorer remained at Austin in charge of the other public property at the arsenal.[69]

[67] Quoted in *ibid.*, June 1, 1842.

[68] "Report of the Secretary of War and Marine, Department of War and Marine, [George W. Hockley to Sam Houston], June 23, 1842," in *Telegraph and Texas Register*, July 6, 1842; Texas War Department, *Report of the Secretary of War and Marine* [George W. Hockley], *Printed by Order of the House of Representatives.*

[69] George W. Hockley to Sam Houston, Secretary of War and Marine, June 23, 1842, in *Telegraph and Texas Register*, July 6, 1842.

The artillery that had been at San Antonio during the late alarm had been removed to Gonzales. This included the brass six-pounder at Béxar at the time of the Vasquez invasion which was removed when the Texans evacuated the place, and the piece of like calibre from the park of artillery recently acquired in the United States and sent to San Antonio from Austin during the late alarm. Both pieces were still at Gonzales late in June.[70]

[70] *Ibid.*

CHAPTER ELEVEN

The Battle of Lipantitlán

WHILE PREPARATIONS were going forward in Texas for an offensive operation against Mexico, great uneasiness prevailed along the northern
Mexican frontier in consequence of a report being circulated that the
Texans were coming in force. Following Vasquez's withdrawal, Mexico
made feverish preparations for defense from an attack which she expected to follow quickly, judging by all the bluster in Texas and from
the reports of her agents at New Orleans and in Texas. At Matamoros on
March 22 General Pedro de Ampudia was informed by Francisco
Carlos, described as a servant who had left Rancho del Coleto four
days before, that upon the advance of the Mexican forces against Goliad
and Guadalupe-Victoria, the inhabitants at those two places and along
the Guadalupe had begun to flee eastward toward the Colorado taking
with them their cattle and supplies. A few days later, however, when
news came in from the Nueces that only a small Mexican force had invaded the Texas frontier, everything changed. Men with arms began to
assemble. Volunteers came from all directions to fill the defense line.
From March 12 to 15, over four hundred Texans had assembled in
Rincón del Oso, five leagues below Goliad, not to defend Texas but to
commence offensive action against the settlements on the Río Grande.[1]
By the time he left the Texas frontier, declared Carlos, the Texans were
sending their patrols beyond the Nueces toward the Agua Dulce. In
April 1842 it was rumored at Matamoros that a Texan force, supported
by a thousand Lipan Indian allies, who had recently killed several
Mexicans, was advancing toward the Río Grande for the purpose of

---

[1] *El Provisional de Matamoros*, April 15, 1842, quoted in *El Cosmopolita*, May
7, 1842; *Daily Picayune*, June 15, 1842. It was reported that Colonel Enrique
Villareal, who had commanded a ranging company on the Sal Colorado during the
past year, had retreated across the Río Grande, and had left his ranch exposed to
the depredations of the Texan cowboys, who, it was said, had reduced his stock
within the past year, from several thousand to a few hundred head. *Telegraph and
Texas Register*, May 4, 1842.

robbing the ranches along the left bank of their cattle and other stock and thus depriving the Mexican army of the resources it would need in carrying out its work in Texas; and possibly occupying Matamoros, if but temporarily.[2] The announcement of the Texan blockade in the government press at Mexico City was accompanied by the usual blustering denunciations, derision, and contempt, and orders were issued by "the hero of Panuco" for repelling any aggression beyond the Río Grande by the "insolent Texans." As a result, the greatest alarm prevailed in Matamoros. General Ampudia, who commanded about one thousand effective men at Matamoros, ordered the streets barricaded; and feverish preparations were made to fortify the public square.[3] The old ditch that had been dug about the square the year before was reopened.[4] Arista was ordered to move his headquarters from Monterey to Mier, and troops were reported "on the march to the frontier from various points of the interior" to supplement the militia called out from the small towns along the Río Grande.[5]

Notwithstanding these military preparations, there were numerous celebrations and demonstrations of joy at the "glorious" victory gained over Texas in the recent campaign. In the midst of these rejoicings a large party of Comanches crossed the Río Grande, near Camargo, about the middle of March and "penetrated into the centre of the department of Nuevo León, killing the defenceless inhabitants and devastating the country wherever they went, and finally succeeded in making their escape with a quantity of plunder, without the loss of a man."[6] Six weeks later the excitement at Matamoros had subsided as the Texan threat seemed to wane.[7]

It was reported in Texas that Colonel Kinney, accompanied by "two other Texian renegades," had arrived at Matamoros, having been sent for by General Arista. At Matamoros, it was said, Coloney Kinney told

[2] D. W. Smith to Daniel Webster, Matamoros, April 20, 1842 (No. 185), Consular Dispatches (United States), 1837–1848 (Matamoros), ms.

[3] *Telegraph and Texas Register*, June 1, 1842.

[4] D. W. Smith to Daniel Webster, Matamoros, May 30, 1842 (No. 186), Consular Dispatches (United States), 1837–1848 (Matamoros), ms.

[5] Same to Same, Matamoros, April 20, 1842 (No. 185), in *ibid.*

[6] Extract from the Mexican correspondence of the *New Orleans Bulletin,* dated Tampico, March 21, [1842], quoted in *Telegraph and Texas Register,* May 11, 1842. See also *Daily Picayune,* March 17, 1842.

[7] *New Orleans Picayune,* April 28, 1842.

the Mexican authorities that he had had "a narrow escape from a party of Texians, who pursued him as far as Laguna."[8]

No doubt, too, Mexican officials were aware of the proposal of President Houston and his Secretary of State, Anson Jones, to establish alternate colonies of French, English, and Belgians along the lower reaches of the Río Grande, and of the contracts which had been signed to that end in February and June 1842. They also were alert to the efforts being made to recruit volunteers in the United States, under the name of "emigrants," for the proposed Texan army of invasion. As the volunteers streamed into Texas, the Mexican government officially protested on several occasions to the United States "against the continued hostilities and aggressions of the citizens of those States against the Mexican territory" [Texas] and against the numerous public meetings held at various points in the United States to recruit men and supplies in violation of the principles of the law of nations for a campaign to be fitted out from Texas against a friendly power with whom the United States had treaties of amity.[9] Bocanegra, the Mexican Minister of Foreign Affairs, first wrote the United States Secretary of State, Daniel Webster, on May 12, that from the beginning of the revolt in Texas,

the Mexican Republic has received nothing but severe injuries and inflictions from the citizens of the United States—the Mexican Government speaks only of the citizens of the United States, as it still flatters itself with the belief, that it is not the Government of the country which has promoted the insurrection in Texas, which has favoured the usurpation of its territory, and has supplied the rebels with ammunition, arms, vessels, money, and recruits; but that these aggressions have proceeded from private individuals [without respect for the obligations of nations, treaties, or the policy of the Washington Administration. The success of the Texans in their insurrection has been due to] the aid and . . . efficient sympathies of citizens of the United States, who have publicly raised forces in their cities and towns, have fitted out vessels in their ports, and laden them with munitions of war, and have marched to commit hostilities against a friendly nation, under the eyes, and with the knowledge of the authorities, to whom are entrusted the fulfilment of the laws [of the United States]. It is worthy of remark, that no sooner does the Mexican Gov-

---

[8] *Telegraph and Texas Register,* May 18, 1842.

[9] José María de Bocanegra to Daniel Webster, Secretary of State of the United States [dated:] National Palace, Mexico, May 31, 1842; Circular directed to the Mexican diplomatic and consular agents in Europe and America by the Minister of Exterior Relations and Government, May 31, 1842, copies of both in *ibid.,* July 20, 1842.

ernment, in the exercise of its rights which it cannot and does not desire to renounce prepare means to recover a possession usurped from it, than the whole population in the United States especially in the Southern States, is in commotion, and in the most public manner, a large portion of them is turned upon Texas, in order to prevent the rebels from being subjected by the Mexican arms, and brought back to proper obedience.

He protested vigorously against the aggression of citizens of the United States, declaring that the Government of Mexico would consider a continuation of these conditions as violations of the treaty of amity between the two countries and creating a dangerous situation.[10]

Less than three weeks later, before Webster had even received the communication of May 12, Bocanegra addressed another communication to the American Secretary of State, calling attention to his protest of May 12 from which he had expected "a pleasing change in the state of affairs," but the continuation of those acts against which his Government had protested, prompted him again to call attention to the tolerance shown by the Mexican nation to a friendly power whose citizens cast themselves into the role of being its enemies. He went on to say that he had been under

the impression that the Washington Government would not protect openly, secretly or in any manner whatever, the scandalous usurpation of an acknowledged part of National territory, . . . [but he regretted] to find, by acts patent to all the world, that the same Government of the United States, and the subaltern and local authorities, observe a conduct openly contrary to the most sacred principles of the law of nations. . . ; sufficient proof of this being found in the fact that the most clamorous public meetings are permitted to be held at various points in those States; arms are recruited, a growing number of volunteers are engaging themselves in the enterprise, and preparation is made to contribute aid when and where possible to the Texans, and to the invasion of a neighboring and friendly Republic.[11]

A continuation of this situation, he threatened, would be considered "a positive act of hostility" against the Mexican Republic.

Bocanegra's letter, protesting "the permitted interference by American Citizens in behalf of Texas in the war with Mexico," gave great offense to President Tyler and a large segment of the United States Con-

[10] José María de Bocanegra to Daniel Webster, Mexico, May 12, 1842, William R. Manning (ed.), *Diplomatic Correspondence of the United States: Inter-American Affairs*, Vol. 8, pp. 487–489.

[11] Same to Same, Mexico, May 31, 1842, *ibid.*, Vol. 8, pp. 489–490; *Telegraph and Texas Register*, July 20, 1842.

gress.[12] The United States considered the letter insolent and insulting, and Secretary of State Webster instructed General Thompson to so inform Bocanegra, who had by-passed Thompson by sending his May 12 communication to Webster through Velásquez de León, at New York, who informed the United States Department of State by a letter accompanying Bocanegra's that he had been appointed chargé d'affaires of the Republic of Mexico to the United States, "although he had not yet presented his credentials." Thompson was also to point out that the United States, animated by a desire for amicable relations, had not failed to maintain in Mexico a diplomatic mission of the highest rank; whereas, Mexico for a long time had had no representative near the government of the United States. The Mexican complaint was rejected as unwarranted and illogical. Webster carefully analyzed the situation as follows:

Mr. de Bocanegra's complaint is two fold; first, that citizens of the United States have supplied the rebels in Texas with ammunition, arms, vessels, money and recruits; have publicly raised forces in their cities and fitted out vessels in their ports, loaded them with munitions of war and marched to commit hostilities against a friendly nation, under the eye and with the knowledge of the authorities. In all this Mr de Bocanegra appears to forget that while the United States are at peace with Mexico, they are also at peace with Texas; that both stand on the same footing of friendly nations; that since 1837 the United States has regarded Texas as an Independent sovereignty, as much as Mexico; and that trade and commerce with citizens of a government at war with Mexico cannot, on that account, be regarded as an intercourse by which assistance and succor are given to Mexican rebels. The whole current of Mr de Bocanegra's remarks runs in the same direction, as if the Independence of Texas had not been acknowledged; it was acknowledged in 1837 against the remonstrance and protest of Mexico; and most of the acts of any importance of which Mr de Bocanegra complains, flows necessarily from that recognition. He speaks of Texas as still "an integral part of the territory of the Mexican Republic"; but he cannot but understand that the United States do not so regard it. The real complaint of Mexico, therefore, is in substance neither more nor less than a complaint against the recognition of Texan Independence. It may be thought rather late to repeat that complaint, and not quite just to confine it to the United States, to the exemption of England, France and Belgium, unless the United States having been the first to acknowledge the independence of Mexico herself, are to be blamed for setting

---

[12] [J. P.] Henderson to Ashbel Smith, Philadelphia, July 18, 1842, in Ashbel Smith Papers, 1838–1842, ms.

an example for the recognition of that of Texas. . . . Acknowledging Texas to be an independent Nation, the government of the United States of course allows and encourages lawful trade and commerce between the two countries. If articles of contraband of war be found mingled with this commerce while Mexico and Texas are belligerent States, Mexico has the right to intercept the transit of such articles to her enemy. This is the common right of all belligerents and belongs to Mexico in the same extent as to other nations. But Mr de Bocanegra is quite well aware that it is not the practice of nations to undertake to prohibit their own subjects, by previous laws, from trafficking in articles contraband of war. Such trade is carried on at the risk of those engaged in it, under the liabilities and penalties prescribed by the Law of Nations or by particular treaties. If it be true, therefore, that citizens of the United States have been engaged in commerce by which Texas, an enemy of Mexico, has been supplied with arms and munitions of war, the Government of the United States, nevertheless, was not bound to prevent it without a manifest departure from the principles of neutrality, and is in no way answerable for the consequences. The treaty of the 5th of April, 1831, between the United States and Mexico itself shows, most clearly, how little foundation there is for the complaint of trading with Texas, if Texas is to be regarded as a public enemy of Mexico. The 16th article declares "It shall likewise be lawful for the aforesaid citizens respectively to sail with their vessels and merchandize before mentioned and to trade with the same liberty and security from the places, ports and havens of those who are enemies of both or either party, without any opposition or disturbance whatsoever." . . .

The 18th article enumerates those commodities which shall be regarded as contraband of war; but neither that article nor any other imposes on either nation any duty of preventing, by previous regulation, commerce in such articles. Such commerce is left to its ordinary fate, according to the law of nations. . . .

There can be no doubt at all that for the last six years, the trade in articles contraband of war, between the United States and Mexico, has been greater than between the United States and Texas. It is probably greater at the present moment. Why has not Texas a right to complain of this? For no reason, certainly, but because the permission to trade, or the actual trading by the citizens of a government in articles contraband of war, is not a breach of neutrality.

After mentioning that two vessels of war had recently been fitted out from New York "for the use of the government of Mexico and well understood as intended to be employed against Texas," Webster pointed out how these had been permitted to sail. "It appeared to be a case of great doubt," he said; "but Mexico was allowed the benefit of that doubt, and the vessels left the United States with the whole or a part of their armament actually on board."[13]

With respect to that portion of Bocanegra's complaint of emigration from the United States to Texas, Webster asked,

And how does Mr. de Bocanegra suppose that the Government of the United States can prevent, or is bound to undertake to prevent, the people from thus going to Texas? This is emigration, the same emigration, though not under the same circumstances, which Mexico invited to Texas before the revolution. These persons, so far as is known to the government of the United States, repair to Texas, not as citizens of the United States, but as ceasing to be such citizens, and as changing at the same time their allegiance and their domicile. Should they return, after having entered into the service of a foreign state, still claiming to be citizens of the United States, it will be for the authorities of the United States government to determine how far they have violated the municipal laws of the country, and what penalties they have incurred. The Government of the United States does not maintain and never has maintained the doctrine of the perpetuity of natural allegiance. And surely Mexico maintains no such doctrine; because her actually existing government, like that of the United States, is founded on the principal that men may throw off the obligations of that allegiance to which they are born. . . .

In her great struggle against Spain for her own independence, did she [Mexico] not open her arms wide to receive all who would come to her, from any part of the world? And did not multitudes flock to her new-raised standard of liberty, from the United States, from England, Ireland, France and Italy, many of whom distinguished themselves in her service both by sea and land? She does not appear to have supposed that the governments of these persons, thus coming to unite their fate with hers, were, by allowing the emigration, even pending a civil war, furnishing just cause of offence to Spain. Even in her military operations against Texas, Mexico employed many foreign emigrants; and it may be thought remarkable that in those very operations, not long before the battle of San Jacinto, a native citizen of the United States held high command in her service and performed feats of no mean significance to Texas. . . . May we not ask, then, how she can reconcile her present complaints, with her own practice?

Webster flatly refuted the charges made by Bocanegra, reiterated the desire of the United States for continued peace with Mexico, and stated that if war came the responsibility would rest with Mexico.

[13] Daniel Webster to Waddy Thompson, Washington, July 8, 1842, Manning (ed.), *Diplomatic Correspondence of the United States: Inter-American Affairs*, Vol. 8, pp. 110–120.

What was of more immediate concern to the Mexican military commanders on the northern frontier than the Texan threat were the devastating raids of the Comanches and Lipans along the Río Grande.
In April a party of some three hundred Comanches swept down the
eastern bank of the Río Grande from Laredo nearly to the coast, laying
waste the whole country, capturing and carrying off several women and
children. Most of the Mexican families abandoned the ranches east of
the Río Grande and moved west of the river.[14]

Arista hoped to have 10,000 troops placed at his disposal by the War
Department for the defense of the northern frontier, but early in April
lamented that out of the 684 recruits which had arrived from the departments of Jalisco and Guanajuato only 98 were fit for duty. "Their
unfitness is so apparent," Arista is alleged to have informed the Secretary of War, "that it cannot be believed that they were ever seen by the
government officers; otherwise, it is inconceivable that such a multitude
of deaf, dumb, lame and blind, should have been forwarded at the
public expense. Indeed, they were afflicted with such other classes of
infirmities, that it appears that they must have been turned out of some
of the hospitals as incurable subjects."[15] Apparently Santa Anna was not
too anxious to share his limited resources with a general who was often
reported in the press as being dissatisfied with Santa Anna's conduct of
the government and who was likely at the first favorable opportunity to
rise in revolt against the "Napoleon of the West."[16] It was even reported
from Matamoros that Santa Anna disapproved of the late demonstration
against Béxar, and had "sent orders to Gen. Woll to go immediately to
Monterey, and assume command of the Brigade placed under Gen.
Vasquez, for the protection of the frontier."[17] It was not long, in any
case, before General Arista was succeeded by General Isidro Reyes as
commandant of the Army of the North.[18]

[14] *Telegraph and Texas Register,* May 4, 1842.
[15] Quoted in *Telegraph and Texas Register,* May 4, 1842, from the *New Orleans
Bulletin* of April 19, 1842, which carried an extract from Arista's report to the
Secretary of War concerning the 10,000 re-enforcements that he was to receive.
[16] *Telegraph and Texas Register,* May 11, 1842.
[17] *Ibid.*
[18] Arista, in announcing his surrender of the command of the Army of the North,
said that during the three years in which he had commanded, union and tranquility
had been promoted on the frontier and many evils oppressing the towns had been
corrected. The fatigue of his duties, he asserted with tongue in cheek, had impaired
his health to the extent of requiring him to retire. For this reason he announced
he was delivering his command of the Army Corps of the North to his immediate

The Battle of Lipantitlán

Arista and his successor, Reyes, in May, 1842, along with General Pedro de Ampudia; Colonel Antonio Canales; Colonel Cayetano Montero; Jesús Cárdenas, prefect of the Northern District of the Department of Tamaulipas, and a host of lesser officers sought to organize the defenses of the northern frontier and to inspire enthusiasm and courage among the inhabitants of Matamoros and the other river towns to defend Matamoros against "that mob of adventurers who come against it with all the hate which arises from class inferiority, with all the vehemence that inspires in vile hearts the criminal desire to rob, and with all the ferocity which cowardice is in the habit of engendering."[19] In an appeal to the inhabitants of Tamaulipas to volunteer for the defense of the frontier against the "perfidious" and "ungrateful" Texans now advancing upon Matamoros to wage a war of "devastation," General Ampudia urged Mexicans to hasten forward to join the ranks of those who would soon battle the "abominable enemy." "I call upon you for the honor of the nation and for our own well-being not to lose time in enlisting in the common defense and in coming to participate in the present event preparing for us."[20] The response to the call for volunteers to man the defenses of Matamoros was overwhelming. Even young robust boys and old men too decrepit to do much fighting at all offered their services. The civilized Indians from the disbanded ancient mission posts in the suburbs and outskirts of the Villa de Reinosa were recruited as guides and spies. Eighteen of these Indians reached Matamoros on April 13, and, after being provided with tobacco and rations, joined the Mexican troops under Savariego that left the next day to take up a picket position on the Arroyo Colorado, a small tidal creek twelve leagues from Matamoros and one hundred and twenty-five miles below Corpus Christi.[21] The First Battalion of the Seventh Regiment of Infantry left Santa Ana de Tamaulipas on April 17 to re-enforce the garrison at Matamoros, and it was reported in Galveston and New Orleans early in

---

subordinate, D. Isidro Reyes. General Reyes announced his assumption of the command on June 2. El General de division Mariano Arista á los habitantes de los departamentos de Tamaulipas, Nuevo León y Coahuila, Monterey, Mayo 28 de 1842, and El ciudadano Isidro Reyes, general de brigada y en gefe del cuerpo de ejército del Norte, á sus companeros de armas, Cuartel general en el Saltillo, Junio 2 de 1842, in *El Cosmopolita*, June 25, 1842; *Bollaert's Texas*, p. 106.

[19] *El Provisional de Matamoros*, April 15, 1842, quoted in *El Cosmopolita*, May 7, 1842.

[20] Pedro de Ampudia, *El General Comandante de las armas á los habitantes de Tamaulipas*, Matamoros, Abril 17 de 1842, Broadside.

[21] *Ibid.*; *Telegraph and Texas Register*, June 1, 1842.

May that General Canales was on the Río Grande with 400 men and had received orders to march with a force of 750 men to Corpus Christi to "destroy the Ranch of Aubrey & Kinney, in compliance with a request of a large number of merchants in Matamoros, who had represented that the contraband trade carried on at that point was a serious detriment to Matamoros."[22]

By the end of May there were nearly 2,500 soldiers in Matamoros, and about as many more quartered in the small towns on the Río Grande above the city.[23] In all, the Mexican force on the frontier was estimated not to exceed 5,000 men. The excitement at Matamoros, however, began to die out as the weeks passed and no blockade materialized. By the end of May the alarm about an invasion from Texas had altogether subsided, and before the end of the month the barricades in the streets were removed.[24] Toward the middle of June the Texan spies from the Río Grande were reporting they doubted that the whole Mexican force exceeded 3,000 men, and that the majority of these were "rancheros," who were "unwilling to fight."[25] It was believed that the accounts of a large force being collected for an invasion of Texas were simply rumors sent abroad to intimidate the Texans and to discourage a Texan army from marching into Mexico.

It was not long after the excitement at Matamoros had died down before it was again being reported at Santa Ana de Tamaulipas, at Matamoros, at Camargo, and at other points in northern Mexico that adventurers under the disguise of "peaceful colonists" were leaving New Orleans every fifteen days by steamboat for Galveston, and it was believed by "persons of sound judgment" that "something" was intended against the Mexican frontier.[26] Nevertheless, in spite of the renewed excitement in northern Mexico, two weeks later, about July 1, three Americans recently from Matamoros by way of Corpus Christi reported only four to five hundred soldiers at Matamoros, and declared the reports being sent to New Orleans that large bodies of troops were collected at Mier and Matamoros were mere falsehoods intended to discourage the Texans from attacking those places.[27]

[22] *El Cosmopolita*, May 7, 1842; *New Orleans Bee*, May 6, 1842.
[23] D. W. Smith to Daniel Webster, Matamoros, May 30, 1842, (No. 186), in Consular Dispatches (United States), 1837–1848 (Matamoros), ms.
[24] *Ibid.*
[25] *Telegraph and Texas Register*, June 22, 1842.
[26] *El Cosmopolita*, June 22, 1842.
[27] *Telegraph and Texas Register*, July 6, 1842.

Traders recently from Aubrey's and Kinney's post at the mouth of the Nueces reported in Mexico the assembling of a Texan military force on the lower Nueces.[28] On June 5 Brigadier General Isidro Reyes, who had been named general in chief *ad interim* of the Army Corps of the North, was instructed by President Santa Anna to order General Adrián Woll to prepare his brigade for a second attack upon San Antonio which place served as a sort of headquarters, he said, for the enemy, who, if permitted, would unite their forces there from which they could detach units to attack "some of our flanks."[29] Then on June 10 Santa Anna announced to Congress his intention of vigorously prosecuting the war against Texas without intermission and at whatever sacrifices until Mexican arms and rights had triumphed. And in assuming command of the Army Corps of the North at Saltillo on June 2, General Reyes informed the troops he would be on the frontier in a few days to share with them the privations and fatigues of a campaign. "In Texas," he declared, "are unfading laurels; there the national Honor is found. You will know how to wear the first and how to preserve unscathed the second."[30]

By mid-June the concentration of a Texan expedition on the lower Nueces frontier came to be recognized in northern Mexico as imposing a serious threat to the security of the frontier; but as this matter soon resolved itself, there is no indication that the execution of the decision to launch a second attack against San Antonio was impeded by the developments in the vicinity of Corpus Christi. In the meantime, reconnaissance parties from Camargo informed Colonel Canales on June 19 that five hundred Texan volunteers were encamped on the Escondido, a fresh water lake emptying through a small stream into the Santa Gertrudis, about forty leagues from the Río Bravo, on the road to the Nueces, with fifty horses and one cannon. Other volunteers were reported at Galveston, awaiting transfer to the frontier. Actually, the Texan force in the vicinity of Lipantitlán had not advanced southward, but had for some weeks been sending their spy companies as far south as the Agua Dulce, forty-five leagues to the northeast of Camargo.[31]

[28] President's Message to Congress, June 10, 1842, in *ibid.*, June 11, 1842.

[29] Ministerio de guerra y marina. Memoria del Secretario de estado y del despacho de guerra y marina, leida a las camaras del Congreso nacional de la Republica Mexicana, en enero de 1844, in *Diario del Gobierno*, May 15, 1844.

[30] El ciudadano Isidro Reyes, general de brigada y en gefe del cuerpo de ejército del Norte, á sus companeros de armas, Cuartel general en el Saltillo, Junio 2 de 1842, in *El Cosmopolita*, June 25, 1842.

[31] Isidro Reyes al Ministerio de guerra y marina, Junio 30 de 1842, no. 498, in

Having relayed this information to the Supreme Government, Reyes ordered Colonel Cayetano Montero with the Second Battalion of the Fourth Regiment of infantry and the Seventh Cavalry of the regular army with one field piece, a four-pounder, and Colonel Canales, commandant of the Villas del Norte, with his auxiliaries from Camargo, Reinosa, Mier, and Guerrero to meet him at El Rancho de la Coma, situated three or four miles southwesterly from "La Sal del Rey," commonly called "El Sal del Rey," and then hurried to Matamoros to check its defenses. The aforementioned river towns not only equipped their respective squadrons, but the authorities of those towns also joined the expedition. From Reinosa and its vicinity there came 160 rancheros.

On June 23 Canales' so-called militiamen, badly armed and equipped,[32] camped on the left bank of the Río Grande along with the squadrons from Camargo. Colonel Montero left Mier on June 23 and camped that afternoon at the Rancho de Garcitas, one and a half leagues distant. The crossing of the Río Bravo required five hours owing to the fact that only three canoes were available for the purpose. The following day (June 24) at the Charco Salado one soldier deserted. On June 25 Canales joined Montero's unit. Two days later, Canales and Montero were at the Agua Nueva and remained there through the 28th. On the 29th at Grangenito, beyond the Agua Nueva, the Mier and Guerrero squadrons came up. The combined forces included 462 rancheros and 185 men of the regular army. At this point, Canales said, 108 local auxiliaries had to return home because their horses had become useless. There being no water near Grangenito, the march continued at 4 P.M. toward Texas across the Wild Horse Desert, or El Desierto de los Muertos, a barren, sandy ridge lying between El Sal del Rey and Los Olmos. Captain Blas Cabazos and three others were sent ahead as spies, and to serve as an advance picket guard to intercept any Texan spies operating along the road in that direction.[33] The march was

---

Frederick C. Chabot, *Corpus Christi and Lipantitlán*, p. 28; Cayetano Montero á Isidro Reyes, Camargo, Julio 15 de 1842, in *ibid.*, p. 63; Isidro Reyes al Ministerio de guerra y marina, Cuerpo de ejército del Norte, Cuartel general de Matamoros, Julio 11 de 1842 (no. 532), in *El Cosmopolita*, July 27, 1842.

[32] *Telegraph and Texas Register*, May 4, 1842.

[33] Antonio Canales á Isidro Reyes, Camargo, Julio 17 de 1842, in Chabot, *Corpus Christi and Lipantitlán*, pp. 64–66; Antonio Canales al Sr. general en gefe del cuerpo del ejército del Norte, D. Isidro Reyes, [dated:] Cuerpo de ejército del Norte.—General en gefe. Núm. 1, Comandancia de las Villas del Norte, Lipantitlán, Julio 7 de 1842—a las once de la noche, and Cayetano Montero al Sr. general en gefe de ejército del Norte, D. Isidro Reyes, [dated:] Cuerpo del ejército del Norte.

continued until 11 o'clock at night, when the Palo Blanco and water were reached. After a short rest, the march was resumed at 6 o'clock in the morning. At noon the Mexican troops again halted. The next day, July 1, after going six leagues, they reached the Paso de Santa Cruz on the Arroyo de Concepción, a tributary of Los Olmos Creek. The men were now without meat, and their horses were worn down. Here they rested two days, awaiting fresh horses and a report from their spies.

On the 3rd, 160 horses were brought in and the camp was moved to the Los Patricios where there was an ample supply of good water. The Mexican army remained here on July 4. During the morning, according to Montero's report, some of their spies returned from the vicinity of the Escondido to report that the Texan camp was not there, but at Lipantitlán,[34] near the Nueces and thirteen leagues west of the Kinney Rancho, and that the Texans, numbering 400 infantry and 50 cavalry, had left their cannon at Laguna Madre, adjoining Corpus Christi Bay. They declared that their spy unit would very much liked to have proceeded to the Rancho to get the cannon, but that it was unable to do so, having had nothing to eat for the past three days; so the spies had returned to their camp on the Agua Dulce. The Mexican army commenced its march forward within half an hour of receiving the report of its spies. On the evening of the 5th the army reached La Trinidad, a tributary of the Santa Gertrudis, where it was met by additional spies who confirmed the earlier report of the location of the Texan army at Lipantitlán. At La Rosita two deer were killed, which, of course, was quite inadequate for some 539 men. On the morning of the 6th at about 10:30 o'clock Canales and Montero camped at Los Presenos, southwest of Casa Blanca and some eight leagues from Lipantitlán, which location and adjacent terrain were well known to Canales who previously as a Federalist leader had fitted out several expeditions from that area. Here the two Mexican colonels made their final plans for a surprise attack against the Texans at dawn the next day—July 7.

—General en gefe. Núm. 2, Sección ausiliar de la primera brigada, Lipantitlán, Julio 7 de 1842—a las once de la mañana, in *El Cosmopolita*, July 27, 1842.

[34] Montero's and Canales' reports vary in detail, but often the former gives more information. Canales said they were met at the Arroyo de Concepción by two spies returning, and that the army moved forward within half an hour of receiving the report of the spies. Montero says some spies returned to the Mexican camp at Los Patricios. Cayetano Montero á Antonio Canales, Camargo, Julio 15 de 1842; Antonio Canales á Isidro Reyes, Camargo, Julio 17 de 1842, both quoted in Chabot, *Corpus Christi and Lipantitlán*, pp. 64–66.

It was hoped that the Texans could be cut-off from the woods, for as Canales expressed it—"in the woods they were brave and quick; but in the open they tremble and are cowardly." The Mexican troops were divided into three columns. One column consisted of 130 men of the Second Battalion, Fourth Regiment, and 60 unmounted auxiliaries (rancheros) from the squadrons of Reinosa and Guerrero under the command of Colonel Ponciano Eguren. A second column under Colonel Cristobal Ramírez was made up of the 105 men of the squadron from Mier mounted and supported by the light cannon. The squadron from Camargo, consisting of 80 men under its commander Matías Ramírez, comprised the third column. A reserve unit was formed with 42 men from the Seventh Cavalry and 40 men from the squadrons of Camargo and Reinosa.

At 3 o'clock in the afternoon of the 6th, the march was resumed. At Las Motas de Agua Dulce, five leagues from the Texan camp, the Mexicans left in camp the horse herd, tired mules, and a portion of their equipment under a small guard; and at 8 o'clock at night continued their march with 457 men, their cannon, and four loads of supplies for the guns. At 2 o'clock on the morning of the 7th a halt was called at a half league from the Texan camp.

In the meantime, reports filtered into Texas of the concentrating of a Mexican force in the lower Río Grande valley between Mier and Matamoros for an attack upon Texas by the lower route, possibly upon General Davis' position.[35] The latest report, as given by three Americans and a Mexican who reached Corpus Christi about June 20 from Reinosa, was that the Mexicans had a force of nearly 1,000 at Matamoros,[36] Apparently the Mexican authorities were aware of the deplorable condition of the weak, insubordinate force which had been assembling on the Nueces during the last several weeks, for it was only after Davis' command had been weakened by desertions that Mexico decided to remove this potential threat to her northern frontier. Finally, on June 26, Campbell of Refugio reached Houston with dispatches from General Davis and a letter from Captain Owen reporting the discovery by the Texan spies on the Santa Gertrudis of a Mexican military unit advancing toward the Nueces "in great numbers." This report caused the President, on July 2, to call upon "the Citizens of Texas West of the Red River" to turn out at once to defend the country from an enemy force estimated at

[35] Paul S. Taylor, *An American-Mexican Frontier, Nueces County, Texas,* pp. 20–21.

[36] *Telegraph and Texas Register,* July 6, 1842.

from 8,000 to 12,000. "All our citizens must now repair to camp—there is now no excuse for delinquency," he declared, "and if men will do their duty our army will be as numerous as theirs. . . . Those who do not defend the country cannot share the soil;[37] let all the citizens act promptly and the Enemy will be expelled. . . . The man does not deserve liberty who will not defend it. Repair to the camps immediately. Let no excuse detain you."[38] Major John C. ("Colonel Jack") Hays and Captain José Antonio Menchaca,[39] a descendant of one of the Canary Island families of San Antonio, each received orders to raise a company of men to scout between the San Antonio River and the Río Grande,[40] and commissioners were dispatched to treat with all the hostile Indian tribes on the frontier.

Since Campbell had reported that the supply of beef was low at the Texan camp, there being only six beeves in camp when he left it, and that the citizens west of the Colorado had contributed so liberally in the past that they scarcely had a sufficient supply for their own consumption, efforts were made to secure beeves from the Colorado and Brazos where several of the planters who owned large herds of cattle offered to supply the army if the Government would furnish men to drive the animals into camp.[41]

In the meantime, Davis prepared to concentrate the available Texan forces and defend his position. On July 5 he sent a dispatch to Lieutenant Colonel Jeremiah R. Clemens, in command of the troops at Live Oak Point, to move a portion of his forces to Lipantitlán; but Clemens, after consultation with his officers, found them unanimously opposed to moving until the pleasure of the President could be known, as "we be-

---

[37] The Constitution of the Republic declared that "All persons who shall leave the country for the purpose of evading a participation in the present struggle, or shall refuse to participate in it, or shall give aid or assistance to the present enemy, shall forfeit all rights of citizenship, and such lands as they may hold in the republic." H. P. N. Gammel (ed.), *Laws of Texas,* I, 1079.

[38] Houston to the Citizens of Texas West of Red River, Sabine, July 2, 1842, in *Writings of Sam Houston,* III, 84–85.

[39] Antonio Menchaca "served as an alderman of San Antonio for several terms and became mayor *pro tem* on July 20, 1838, succeeding William Henry Daingerfield who had resigned." He was a personal friend of Manuel Flores, but when the latter persisted in his efforts to create discord and rebellion, Menchaca broke with him. *Writings of Sam Houston,* III, 107 n.

[40] Houston to the Senate, City of Houston, July 18, 1842, in *ibid.,* III, 105–106; Harriet Smither (ed.), *Journals of the Sixth Congress of the Republic of Texas,* III, 72–73.

[41] *Telegraph and Texas Register,* July 13, 1842.

lieve," he wrote, "that orders have been transmitted to you by the Executive to join us at this place." Furthermore, "I cannot consent to a division of the battalion" and, lastly, "because provisions are so scarce that we would suffer greatly if we were to join you before a supply had been received."[42]

By the time he received this disappointing news from Clemens, Davis' position was apparently becoming more untenable by the hour. Consequently, he quickly dispatched another courier to Clemens apprising him that the enemy was approaching and that he felt it necessary to fall back because of the small number in his command and the extreme shortage of provisions. He urged Clemens, whose command exceeded 250 men, to come to his relief as he fell back toward Live Oak Point with the expectation of meeting him on the Chiltipín.[43] Clemens immediately responded that he was entirely dependent upon supplies from the country adjacent to Lamar, and that none of the beeves could be driven to the relief of Davis' men. Beeves at Lamar, he said, could not be driven or brought across the bay alive. He would, however, endeavor to effect a junction with Davis about half way between the two camps.[44]

Colonel Clemens wasted no time in making preparations to meet General Davis. Two officers were sent forward on the 8th to select a camp site in the neighborhood of water about one day's march from Live Oak Point. A small detachment was sent ahead under Captain Murphree, who in cooperation with Colonel Clark L. Owen, was to collect and drive out a two-days supply of beef to the camp on the Chiltipín.[45] Clemens wrote Davis he would begin his march on the 9th, with approximately 230 to 235 effective men, and hoped to be able to effect a junction with the latter's forces at some point on the Chiltipín.

We have no pack horses or baggage wagons, and nothing short of the danger to your command would justify a removal of the men.

If the Mexicans are indeed advancing in the force represented to you, I beg

---

[42] J. Clemens to Gen. J[ames] Davis, Live Oak Point, July 6, 1842, in Army Papers (Texas), ms.; copy also in *Telegraph and Texas Register*, July 20, 1842. For a biographical sketch of Jeremiah R. Clemens see *Writings of Sam Houston,* IV, 117–118.

[43] *Telegraph and Texas Register*, July 20, 1842.

[44] See Jeremiah Clemens to Gen. James Davis, Live Oak Point, July 8, 1842 [endorsed: no. 5], copy in Army Papers (Texas) ms. I have not found Davis' letter of about July 7 to Clemens.

[45] *Telegraph and Texas Register*, July 20, 1842.

to suggest the propriety of selecting the most eligible ground for giving battle on the Chiltipín. Send a guide to us, with directions when to join you, and let us know on which bank of the Chiltipín you are encamped. We will be with you as soon as the distance can be marched after we hear from you. . . . If there is water within 16 or 18 miles of this place, I will encamp there tomorrow night and await further advices. . . .

Notwithstanding all the disadvantages under which we are laboring you may calculate certainly upon our assistance whenever and wherever it is needed. My men are in the highest spirits and look forward to a *battle* as to certain *victory*. A better body of troops was never brought into the field and with God's high will we shall teach the horde of plunderers who are now advancing into the country a lesson by which their children may profit.[46]

Down on the Nueces, the Texan camp was still beset by desertions. On July 2 Lieutenant Hugh O'Connor of the Tennessee Company left camp with some of the volunteers. He had for some time been operating upon the Tennessee Company, which, reported Davis, "has ever been a curse to the battalion," and a bad effect upon other disaffected persons in the camp.[47]

I did not attempt to prevent them by force [from deserting, continued Davis] as I have become perfectly satisfied the disaffected would continue to desert until the whole of them left camp. . . . [They] were communicating their poison to those disposed to do their duty, and I was willing they should go in a body, which they did under the hisses of those that remained. I did not consent to the movement, and ordered Lt. O'Connor to consider himself under arrest and confine himself to his quarters . . . [which, of course, was not obeyed]. I am informed he stole our bugle and had it with him.

Davis reported that his ammunition was nearly exhausted and that he was short of arms.

At his position at Lipantitlán Davis found that a superior Mexican force was upon him before aid could arrive. The Mexican force was reported to have already passed the Arroyo Colorado, a salt lagoon about a hundred yards wide and three or four feet deep, and was rapidly nearing the Nueces. Davis' spies, operating in the vicinity of the Agua Dulce, reported on the evening of July 6 the advance of Colonels Ca-

---

[46] Jeremiah Clemens to Gen. James Davis, Live Oak Point, July 8, 1842 [endorsed: no. 5], copy in Army Papers (Texas), ms.

[47] James Davis to Sam Houston, Head Quarters, Texian Volunteers, Camp Lipantitlán, July 3, 1842, copy in *ibid.* Houston to Acting Adjutant-General James Davis, Executive Department, City of Houston, July 10, 1842, in *Writings of Sam Houston*, III, 99–100.

nales and Montero with an estimated force of 200 regulars and 500 volunteers or rancheros, of whom 500 were cavalry. Actually, the Mexicans outnumbered the Texans about three to one.

What was the size of the Texan army? The Secretary of War reported on June 23 the number of volunteers mustered into service as 473, rank and file, of whom 253 were stationed at Lipantitlán, and the remaining 220 were en route from Galveston by water to join them.[48] The volunteers who only a few days before had reached Aransas from Galveston were ordered by Davis to join him at once.[49] Other volunteers under Colonel Washington were expected to arrive in about two weeks from the United States in the steamboat *Merchant* and other transports. These, however, numbering 293, left New Orleans on July 2 under Colonel Jackson aboard the *Mary Elizabeth* and the *Merchant*.[50] As for local troops, up-to-date lists had been drawn in accordance to the Executive Order of April 14, and the men were awaiting orders to rendezvous. Down on the Nueces, however, Davis' command had been reduced by July 7, through desertions and other causes already indicated, to 192 (although estimated by Montero at 400[51]) men organized into a battalion of six companies under Major John J. B. Hoxey, whose resignation had not yet been accepted. William H. Hughes acted as adjutant and J. M. Wells served as muster master to the battalion. The command included Company "A" from New Orleans under Captain H. H. Brower, assisted by Lieutenants W. P. Moore and G. C. Work; Company "B" from Mobile under Lieutenant N. H. Birmingham; Company "C" from Memphis and "E" from Mississippi, commanded by Captain H. W. Allen, assisted by Lieutenant J. W. Field; Company "D" from Galveston and vicinity, commanded by Lieutenant E. T. Fox; Company "F" from Georgia under Captain William R. Shivers, assisted by Lieutenant

[48] G. W. Hockley, Secretary of War and Marine, to Sam Houston, Department of War and Marine, [Houston], June 23, 1842, in *Writings of Sam Houston*, III, 107–112; *Telegraph and Texas Register*, July 6, 1842.

[49] *Telegraph and Texas Register*, July 13, 1842.

[50] Bocanegra al Ministro de Guerra, Augusto 9 de 1842, in Chabot, *Corpus Christi and Lipantitlán*, p. 29. The Mexican government claimed that the *Mary Elizabeth*, in spite of the ruling of the Admiralty Court at New Orleans, had not been returned to her rightful owners, but was taken by Colonel Jackson and his volunteers.

[51] Cayetano Montero al D. Isidro Reyes, Cuerpo del ejército del Norte, sección auxiliar de la primera brigada, Lipantitlán, Julio 7 de 1842, a las once de la mañana [mañana del 8 de Julio?] in *El Cosmopolita*, July 27, 1842.

Thomas Y. Redel; and a company of mounted gunmen under Captain Ewen Cameron.[52]

The Texan camp was on a small hill (sometimes described as being in the prairie) to the right of the Nueces River, whose high banks protected it for at least five hundred yards on the northwest, north, and northeast. The camp appeared to be nestled in an arc of the river. Destitute of cannon and unprotected by any form of works at his front, General Davis decided to abandon his camp late in the afternoon upon the approach of the Mexicans, and withdrew two hundred yards to a secure position upon the second bluff of the river. In this position his right wing was protected by the river and a small strip of timbered area. The men's tents, largely made of brush, were left standing and their fires burning in the open prairie in order to deceive the enemy while the Texans prepared to avail themselves of the advantages of a night attack should the Mexicans descend upon their camp during the darkness. Some of the Texans would not believe that the Mexicans were coming and neglected to remove their cooking utensils and blankets from their old position.

"Canales, distrustful of the deceitful quiet of their noiseless tents, and apprehensive of an ambuscade, permitted the night to wear off without any attempt to molest them,"[53] later claiming in his report that he had sought to surprise the Texan forces at dawn, but because his guides of the Camargo cavalry, which had been assigned the task of enveloping the Texan camp, got lost, the Texans became aware of the presence of the Mexican force at dawn. Canales' plan was to cut the Texans off from the timber by having his troops occupy all the space along the woods, thus preventing all retreat for the enemy and forcing him to fight from

[52] James Davis to Col. G. W. Hockley, Secretary of War and Marine, Head Quarters, Texian Volunteers, Camp Lipanticlán [sic], July 7, 1842, in Texas Congress, *Journals of the House of Representatives of the Seventh Congress of the Republic of Texas convened at Washington on the 14th of November, 1842*, Appendix, pp. 14–15.

[53] William Preston Stapp, *The Prisoners of Perote: Containing a Journal Kept by the Author who was Captured by the Mexicans, at Mier, December 25, 1842, and Released from Perote, May 16, 1844*, pp. 17–18 (parts of this journal first appeared in print in the *Texas National Register* (Washington), June 19, 1845. See also H. Yoakum, *History of Texas from Its First Settlement in 1685 to Its Annexation to the United States in 1846*, II, 361. William Preston Stapp was the son of Elijah Stapp and Nancy Shannon Stapp. Elijah Stapp, who was the father of ten children, was postmaster at La Baca [Lavaca], Jackson County, in 1840. Stapp's information on Santa Anna and his description of life in Mexico are plagiarized from Brantz Mayer's *Mexico: As It Was and As It Is*, published the year before.

the open prairie. As already noted, the Mexicans commenced their final advance from the Agua Dulce at 8 o'clock at night on July 6, approaching the Texan camp from the west. At 2 A.M. they halted. Shortly before daylight columns one and three, commanded respectively by Colonels Eguren and Matías Ramírez, sought to take up positions to the north and northwest of the Texan camp. Their guides apparently got lost in the dark; and instead of reaching the points assigned, they proceeded south, passing to the left of the Texans, very close to them but unobserved. Colonels Canales and Montero accompanied the second column under Colonel Cristobal Ramírez and the reserve cavalry unit toward the front of the Texan camp and within gunshot distance of it.

Canales and Montero reported that their men waited an hour for the infantry to open fire, as instructed, when the frontal units were to charge simultaneously; but as we have seen, the infantry went too far south. With the approach of daylight, the Anglo-Texans began to stir. Several of them, with thoughts of breakfast, remembered the provisions and cooking utensils they had left in their old camp, and returned to their camp to bring off the necessary items. About this time one of their comrades came out from behind the protecting bank of the river with a light and, discovering the Mexicans, sounded the alarm. At this moment, reported Canales, the Mexican infantry appeared on the Texans' right (when it should have been on their left) defiling before the front of their line where they were easily seen. Except for the Camargo squadron, momentarily lost, the entire Mexican force, aided by the fire of artillery so disposed as to rake the encampment, assaulted the Texan camp, but with no other injury than to scatter a few blankets and knock about a few camp kettles. Flushed like a covey of quail, the few Texans who had returned to their camp of the day before, succeeded in reaching their comrades in safety near the river, but in so doing disclosed the position of the main body of Texans. Had the Camargo squadron been at its assigned position at the edge of the timbered area on the northeast, it might have been able to cut these men off; but certainly Canales had been momentarily fooled as to the location of the main Texan force under Davis.

Canales now quickly reversed his order of battle, and bore down upon Davis and his men with as much fury as he had previously descended upon their empty camp. Holding their fire until the charging Camargo cavalry squadron was within fifty to sixty yards of their position, a portion of the Texans opened fire with a murderous volley, emptying a number of saddles. This checked the advance, and the vanguard began to fall back toward the main body. The Mexican infantry, supported by the ranchero cavalry from Reinosa and a part of that from Guerrero, now dismounted, advanced toward the Texan line. The Texans were quite amused to notice that "the Mexicans, when in the act of firing their guns, . . . did not take aim, but pointed the guns towards [the Texans] and just as they were about to fire turned their faces away, as if they were afraid to look in the direction they wished to shoot."[54]

One bold fellow [it was reported] came running some twenty or thirty steps in advance of his company and bro't his musket to a level pointing it at a soldier; but while turning his head before firing, the musket rose to an angle of about 45 degrees and the ball did not even touch the tops of the trees over the ravine; before he could run back to his company after this gallant exploit, he was shot in the knee by one of our soldiers, and two or three ran out and dragged him into camp. It was afterwards ascertained that he was an orderly sergeant belonging to one of the companies from Matamoros, and was regarded by the Mexicans as a veteran.[55]

The Mexican infantry and dismounted cavalry, too, quickly retraced their steps (although Canales says they pursued the enemy into the woods[56]). A brisk firing on both sides was kept up for a few minutes, but the distance was too great to produce results. Soon the Texans ceased firing, but dared not leave the protection of the ravine and the woods. The Mexican troops remained at a respectful distance.

Finally, about mid-afternoon, the lone Mexican artillery piece—a four-pounder brought by Colonel Montero from Camargo—protected by fifty cavalrymen was advanced to a position of about two hundred and fifty yards to the left of the Texans with a view to raking their line. At this moment, a Texan by the name of Ferguson with a lucky shot from a large rifle inflicted a mortal wound upon the officer commanding the detachment. Montero and Canales both reported that the cannon was disabled almost from the first shot, when it broke from its carriage, and that an effort to secure it with thongs failing, it had to be withdrawn from the field of battle at 4 o'clock. Whatever may have happened, the fact remains that after twenty minutes of fighting, the Mexican force, affected by what Texans described as "buck ague,"[57] withdrew, leaving

---

[54] *Telegraph and Texas Register*, Aug. 3, 1842.

[55] *Ibid.*

[56] Col. Antonio Canales á Gen. Isidro Reyes, Comandancia de las Villas del Norte, Lipantitlán, Julio 7 de 1842, in *El Cosmopolita*, July 27, 1842.

[57] Panic of men in battle was referred to as "buck ague."

three of their number dead upon the field. Ensign José María Delgado of the Third Company, Seventh Regiment of Cavalry, later testified that Colonel Montero ordered the infantry to pursue the Texans into the woods, but that the commander of the Defensores, Matías Ramírez, came forward and declared he would not permit his troops to be shot by the enemy in the forest.[58]

In this brief encounter the Texans reported only one man slightly wounded, but the Mexican accounts claimed twenty-two killed[59] and an undetermined number of dead in the woods whose bodies they were unable to count.[60] Canales reported that the Texans fled into the woods in the direction of Mesquital de Brazada at the entrance of the Rincón de la Cerda, where it was reported, he said, another two hundred Texans had disembarked.[61] The abandoned Texas camp had, of course, been overrun by the Mexicans. Davis lost his official papers, and the Texan force lost its park of equipment, a number of blankets and camp kettles, five barrels of powder, eleven rifles, forty-two pistols of various calibres, thirteen useful muskets and two useless ones, some "filthy" clothes, two flags and one standard.[62] The spoils of the Texan camp

---

[58] Adrián Woll al Ministro de Guerra y Marina, Mayo 12 de 1843, no. 253, enclosing 89 sheets of "sumaria" against Montero and Canales, ff. 25–26, in Chabot, *Corpus Christi and Lipantitlán*, p. 69.

[59] Adjutant-General James Davis to G. W. Hockley, Secretary of War, Camp Lipanticlán [*sic*], July 7, 1842, Texas Congress, *Journals of the House of Representatives of the Seventh Congress of the Republic of Texas*, Appendix, pp. 14–15; *Telegraph and Texas Register*, July 20, 1842; Isidro Reyes al Ministro de guerra y marina, Cuerpo de ejército del Norte, Cuartel general en Matamoros, Julio 11 de 1842 (no. 532), in *El Cosmopolita*, July 27, 1842.

[60] Antonio Canales al Sr. general en gefe del cuerpo del ejército del Norte, D. Isidro Reyes, [dated:] Cuerpo de ejército del Norte.—General en gefe. Núm. 1, Comandancia de las Villas del Norte, Lipantitlán, Julio 7 de 1842,—a las once de la noche, and Cayetano Montero al Sr. general en gefe de ejército del Norte. D. Isidro Reyes, [dated:] Cuerpo del ejército del Norte.—General en gefe. Núm. 2, Sección ausiliar de la primera brigada, Lipantitlán, Julio 7 de 1842—a las once de la mañana, in *El Cosmopolita*, July 27, 1842, and July 23, 1842; *Telegraph and Texas Register*, Aug. 31, 1842.

[61] Antonio Canales á Isidro Reyes, Camargo, Julio 17 de 1842, no. 1, in Chabot, *Corpus Christi and Lipantitlán*, pp. 64–66.

[62] According to the testimony given later by Andres Mena, the flags and standard were not taken in action, but were found in the deserted camp. One flag was a tricolor of red, white, and blue worsted with a white star sewed to the blue band. The other flag was made of purple silk (or taffeta) with a gold fringe. On it was an inscription in gold lettering which read, according to one witness: "Galveston Invincibles—Texas Independence," or according to another witness: "Galveston In-

were distributed among the Mexican troops. The flags and standard were sent under the care of Captain Gabriel Treviño of the Second Company of Auxiliaries from Reinosa, (who had presented them to General Reyes in the name of his Company) to the Minister of War to be given to the President. They were placed on public exhibition in Mexico City on July 22, where the city was illuminated at night and there was great rejoicing, "while Santa Anna in person reviewed and harangued the troops."[63]

The Mexicans reported their losses as one corporal and two soldiers of the Second Battalion, Fourth Regiment, killed; and one corporal killed and two sergeants wounded of the Reinosa squadron.[64] The Texans found three Mexicans left dead on the field, and the trails indicated that many were dragged off. Davis' official report estimated thirty Mexicans killed and wounded.[65] The overthrow of this hostile Texan force of four hundred men, reported Canales, would have been

vincibles: Our Independence." *Telegraph and Texas Register*, Aug. 31, 1842. According to Mrs. Farrel D. Minor of Beaumont, Texas, who saw the flag in 1907 on display in the Artillery Museum in Mexico City, it was a small banner of a brownish color with a single star in the center. Above the star were the words, "Our Independence," and beneath it, "Galveston Invincibles." Ben C. Stuart, "Early Galveston Military Companies, 1839–1901," ms., p. 5.

The standard was represented by the Mexicans as being a cavalry flag. It was of white silk with a purple silk fringe. On each side was an oval shape in the middle of the white. Painted in the oval on one side was the picture of a dragon on horseback, and in the oval on the other side were painted three columns, each with figures holding the words: "Wisdom," "Justice," and "Union." Chabot, *Corpus Christi and Lipantitlán*, p. 72.

[63] *El Cosmopolita*, July 23, 1842; *New Orleans Bee*, Aug. 20, 1842.

[64] Corporal Severiano Narváez of the 2nd Bat., 4th Regt., killed; Juan José Maya and Matilde Martínez, both soldiers, of the 2nd. Bat., 4th Regt., wounded. It was reported in *El Cosmopolita*, Sept. 21, 1842, that the two soldiers of the 4th Regiment of Infantry were taken prisoners by the Texans in the skirmish at Lipantitlán, and that the one who was not wounded had been beheaded by order of General James Davis. Corporal Alejandro Smaldera of the Reinosa Squadron was killed and 2nd Sergeants Laureno Casares and José María Villegas of the Reinosa Squadron, wounded—the latter so gravely that he died the following day.

[65] James Davis to Col. G. W. Hockley, Secretary of War and Marine, Head Quarters, Texian Volunteers, Camp Lipanticlán [sic], July 7, 1842, Texas Congress, *Journal of the House of Representatives of the Seventh Congress*, Appendix, pp. 14–15; *Telegraph and Texas Register*, Aug. 17, 1842, reported the Mexican force under Canales at Lipantitlán on July 7 lost a lieutenant colonel and thirty men. William Bollaert, reporting the news at Houston, says six or eight Mexicans were killed, twenty wounded, and some were taken prisoner. *Bollaert's Texas*, p. 121.

complete, "if those banditti who call themselves 'invincibles,' according to the motto on one of their flags had not fled like cowards into the forest to save themselves, thereby misleading our guide, and escaping from our troops."[66] Canales was apologetic that the number of Texans, dead, wounded, or even prisoners, had not amounted to the full number of their force; but, he explained, "the obscurity of night completely misled us and we were not able to accomplish it."[67] Canales, Montero, Reyes, and others hailed the action as a triumph for Mexican arms and the forerunner of greater successes to be achieved in the field against the Texan usurpers and invaders of Mexican territory. In appreciation for their bravery and the glory which they added to the name of Mexico, Canales, Montero, and eleven other officers in the expedition against the Texans at Lipantitlán were awarded the Cross of Distinction.[68] The captured standard bearing the words "Galveston Invincibles" belonged to a company from Galveston which had returned home several weeks before. The flag, reported the editor of the *Telegraph,* had been left in the possession of a soldier "as a piece of waste cloth and if it had not been captured with the old camp kettles by these heroes would soon have been made a dish cloth, instead of the splendid trophy of a *Mexican* victory." Most likely, the returnees were ashamed to carry it back home as their fortitude had oozed away.

Canales wished to proceed to Corpus Christi or near there, but as his men had been without food for three days, and, since it was doubtful if supplies could be obtained there, he decided to turn back. Even the Texan camp failed to yield much in the way of provisions, except a little coffee, sugar, and a small quantity of meat so lean that his men, notwithstanding their hunger, would not touch it. The total provisions obtained from the camp was not enough for a single company. Since no cattle were to be found in the area between Lipantitlán and Camargo, reported Canales, it was necessary to return the troops to Camargo as

[66] Isidro Reyes ál Ministro de guerra y marina, Cuerpo de ejército del Norte, Cuartel general en Matamoros, Julio 11 de 1842 (no. 532), in *El Cosmopolita,* July 27, 1842; for additional information see also *ibid.,* July 23, 1842.

[67] Lic. [Antonio] Canales á Isidro Reyes, Comandancia de las Villas del Norte, Lipantitlán, Julio 7 de 1842, in *El Cosmopolita,* July 27, 1842; Francisco Mejía á José Ygnacio Gutiérrez, Saltillo, July 25, 1842, in H. R. Wagner Manuscript Collection, ms. Canales' report was written from near Lipantitlán at 11 P.M. following the battle.

[68] Ministro de Guerra á Isidro Reyes, Julio 22 de 1842, in Chabot, *Corpus Christi and Lipantitlán,* p. 73; see also, *Telegraph and Texas Register,* Aug. 31, 1842.

soon as possible; so the return march began from the vicinity of Lipantitlán on the morning of July 8.

Cameron's "cowboys" and veterans of the Federalist wars, like John T. Price, acquitted themselves well on this occasion, and Cameron further "endeared" himself to Canales, for which he was later to pay with his life. It was, however, a lucky stroke for the Anglo-Texans that the Mexicans did not press their attack, for Davis' command was practically without ammunition and arms. On July 3, four days before the attack, Davis had written to the President that his supply of ammunition had been exhausted and his command had no arms.[69] The deserters, who had been permitted to march off in open daylight in defiance of the general's authority without any restraint whatsoever being imposed, had taken their guns and ammunition with them. Before receiving news of the engagement, the President had written Davis, in part, as follows:

> You were required, from the first order giving you command, up to this date, never to permit the introduction of liquor within the limits of your command, but to have all destroyed. You were commanded to report all deserters—neither of these orders has been obeyed. My orders for the restoration of stolen property were not executed. . . . I positively require the name of every deserter since you assumed command at Corpus Christi. I require the execution of every order. . . . The Secretary of War has ordered that the deserters be returned to you. You know what constitutes the offence of desertion. You know the penalty and the mode of insuring it to the culprit. The law has prescribed it. I expect it to be executed.[70]

If Davis had accepted Cameron's advice, he would not have been surprised at Lipantitlán.[71] Cameron, who had seen service in Captain

[69] Houston to Acting Adjutant-General James Davis, City of Houston, July 10, 1842, in *Writings of Sam Houston*, III, 99–100.

[70] *Ibid.*

[71] Ewen Cameron, who came to Texas about the time of the Revolution, had been born in Scotland about 1807, and had served in the Texan army almost continuously, with the exception of a few months, as a "Permanent Volunteer" for varying periods of enlistment from April 29, 1836, to Jan. 10, 1839. He saw service under Captain Clark L. Owen, Captain G. C. Briscoe, and Major George W. Bonnell, who later lost his life on the Río Grande as a member of the Mier expedition. Travis Bounty No. 186; Muster Rolls—Bounty File Peter Goss; Robertson 2–651; Bounty Certificate No. 4241, Survey No. 32 San Patricio County; Béxar Bounty No. 1068, in General Land Office Records (Texas), ms.; Hobart Huson, "Iron Men: A History of the Republic of the Río Grande and the Federalist War in Northern Mexico," ms., p. 77.

Price's Company during the Federalist wars, had repeatedly warned Davis that "it would not do to trust Mexicans there, whether they were friends, traders, or what—he understood their character well."[72]

[72] "James Wilkinson's Account of the Cow-Boys," in *Lamar Papers*, VI, 117.

CHAPTER TWELVE

The "War Bill"

WHILE GENERAL DAVIS was readying his men for the expected attack, the "War Session" of the Sixth Congress began its consideration of that portion of the President's message pertaining to offensive operations against Mexico. A joint resolution declaring it the policy of Texas to carry on an offensive war with Mexico was offered in the House of Representatives on June 30 by Archibald Wynns of Harris County and referred to the Committee on Military Affairs,[1] which reported on the afternoon of the 4th (despite the holiday) in favor of prosecuting such a war.[2] The majority of the Committee, consisting of Isaac Van Zandt, William E. ("Fiery") Jones, John W. Dancy, Charles H. Raymond, and William L. Hunter, reported that in view of the

melancholy state of things, the majority of the committee sincerely believe and . . . submit it to the House of Representatives, as the deep, deep, conviction of their mind that the only course left . . . *is an appeal to arms, and to the God of Battles.* They believe that the time has arrived, when the causes not only justify, but demand . . . a prompt, speedy, and efficient prosecution of offensive war. . . . Its prosecution will require but little more means, than to maintain a sufficient force at home to protect us from their incursions.

The Committee spoke of the advantages of fighting on the enemy's soil, and of the thousands of volunteers who would flock to Texas from the United States to rally "around the standard of the Single Star, and lighted by its rays, follow it to victory and to freedom." It pointed out how easily the war could be financed through the sale of the public domain, and "voluntary contributions of arms, ammunition, provisions,

---

[1] Harriet Smither (ed.), *Journals of the Sixth Congress of the Republic of Texas,* III, 113.

[2] Joseph Waples to Anson Jones, Houston, July 3, 1842, in Anson Jones, *Memoranda and Official Correspondence Relating to the Republic of Texas, Its History and Annexation—Including a Brief Autobiography of the Author,* pp. 192–193.

255

and the equipments necessary to the prosecution of a war." The latter, they declared, "could undoubtedly be obtained . . . [in] sufficient amount to equip and sustain an army in their advance to the scene of action." It was even possible that patriotic citizens would donate "land of unquestioned title, lying within the settled portion of the Republic, and therefore not only of prospective, but actual value . . . to [help] defray [the] necessary expenses of the war."[3] The Committee reported a bill to authorize offensive war against Mexico as a substitute for the Joint Resolution referred to them. The reasons given for their action were (1) the utter hopelessness of trying to adjust amicably through negotiation or the mediation of any friendly power the existing difficulties between the Republic and Mexico; (2) Mexico's refusal to acknowledge the independence of Texas, which Texas had shown to the world she was capable of maintaining; (3) Mexico's recommencement of "active hostilities by harrassing and plundering our frontier"; and (4) the detainment "in a slavish captivity [of] our fellow-citizens of the Santa Fé Expedition, contrary to the rules of warfare as recognized by the rules of civilized nations."

When the "War bill" came up for debate in the House on the 7th, 8th, and 9th there was great oratory in favor of the measure. The speech of "Fiery" Jones of Gonzales was "worthy of the days of '76 and was received with rapturous applause by all parties."[4] Mayfield, Wynns, Cooke, and Van Zandt also spoke strongly in favor of the bill, some, however, with suggestions for changes.

This only is evident, [declared the *Morning Star*[5]] the friends of the bill act with unfaultering unanimity, and meet all the artifices and indirect attacks of their opponents with the most unblenching firmness and *sang froid*—no arts or wiles or threats can drive them from their position. They are ever found in solid phalanx ready and willing to meet opposition from whatever quarter it may come. This singular unanimity and concert of action, gives a vast advantage, and is hailed by the friends of the measure, as the sure harbinger of ultimate success.

[3] "Majority Committee Report, House of Representatives, City of Houston, Committee Room, July 4, 1842," in Smither (ed.), *Journals of the Sixth Congress*, III, 119–127; *Telegraph and Texas Register*, July 6, 1842; Texas Congress, House of Representatives, *Report of Majority of Military Committee, July 4, 1842*. The bill shown in the reconstructed journals of the Sixth Congress, is the final bill as amended, rather than the actual report of the Committee. In describing the bill reported by the Committee on Military Affairs I have kept this fact in mind.
[4] *Morning Star*, July 9, 1842. None of the speeches have been found.
[5] *Ibid.*

On the 8th the House authorized the President to command the army in person, after beating down a proposal by Cooke, supported by Mayfield, to insert "provided he be the choice of the assembled troops."[6] Robinson of Brazoria County sought unsuccessfully to strike out that section of the bill authorizing the use of the militia in offensive war. Mayfield then offered a substitute bill, which was rejected.[7] After a few minor changes, the "War bill" passed the House on July 12 by a vote of 21 to 14,[8] with James H. Kuykendall, who opposed the bill, going so far as to resign his seat in the House upon learning that many of his constituents were in its favor.[9] The vote on the bill was strictly along sectional lines, with the southwestern, western, and frontier eastern counties voting for the bill, and the eastern and interior counties, with the exception of Harris and Montgomery, voting against it. Shelby County divided its vote. With the exception of Washington County, west of the Brazos, and the two counties of Brazoria and Fort Bend, astride the Brazos River, all counties west of the Brazos voted for the "War bill," as did the frontier counties of Lamar, Harrison, Panola, Brazos, Robertson, and Houston east of the Brazos. Harris and Montgomery counties supported the bill, while the representatives from Sabine, Austin, and Fannin counties either were not present or did not vote and the same may be said for one of the delegates from Béxar and Galveston.

The House bill reached the Senate on July 12 where it was referred to the Committee on Military Affairs, and the majority report of the Committee was made the following day. The attack on the bill was led by James Webb from the senatorial district embracing the counties of Bastrop, Fayette, Gonzales, and Travis, whom Houston regarded "as one of the most corrupt men in the Republic or any other."[10] Webb objected to the "War bill" on the grounds that (1) no definite date had been set for calling out the volunteers or for the commencement of operations; (2) no time limit had been set for the calling out of the militiamen; (3) the President should not take command of the army in the field, but a commander should be chosen; (4) no restriction had been placed on the amount of money to be raised by the sale or hypothecation of the public lands; (5) there was no specific authorization for the expenditure of the funds obtained; and (6) the President was not made

[6] Smither (ed.), *Journals of the Sixth Congress,* III, 144.
[7] Mayfield's substitute bill has not been found.
[8] Smither (ed.), *Journals of the Sixth Congress,* III, 149.
[9] *Telegraph and Texas Register,* July 13, 1842.
[10] Smither (ed.), *Journals of the Sixth Congress,* III, 7 n.

accountable for either the raising or the expenditure of the funds from
the public treasury for the conduct of the war that was authorized.[11]
Webb's assault upon the bill represented, in part, the animosity of the
west and of the Lamar supporters to Houston. Webb moved to strike
out that portion of the third section of the bill which authorized President Sam Houston to take command of the army in person, and proposed to insert a clause requiring President Houston to "immediately
order an election for a Major General, at which election, all persons
within the Republic subject to military duty shall be entitled to vote;
and the Major General, when elected, shall take command of the Army
raised under the provisions of this act; and if in said election, the President Sam Houston should be chosen by the voters as the Commander,
he is hereby authorized to take command of said army in person."[12] His
motion was defeated. Only Colquhoun, Webb, and Kindred H. Muse of
Nacogdoches voted for it. Muse had unsuccessfully sought to amend
Webb's motion by attaching to it the words, "provided he resign his
station as President of the Nation."[13]

Senator Ludovic Colquhoun from Béxar concurred in Webb's sentiment against the bill, except that he wanted it to be known that he objected to the President's taking command of the army in person "because
of his inefficiency and inability to command an army with advantage to
the country."[14] William H. Jack of Brazoria, John A. Greer of San Augustine, president pro tempore of the Senate, and Francis Moore, Jr.,
editor of the *Telegraph and Texas Register* and representing the District of Harris, Galveston, and Liberty, entered their protest on July 18,
mainly on the grounds that they were opposed to the use of the militia
in offensive war, believing it a violation of Article II, Section 6, of the
Constitution, which states that Congress shall have the power "to call
out the militia to execute the law, to suppress insurrections, and repel
invasion."[15] While holding to this interpretation of the Constitution,
however, Dr. Moore declared in the *Telegraph* that "so desirous are we
that the Executive should be sustained in the position he has assumed
and enabled to carry on offensive war effectively, . . . we are unwilling

[11] James Webb's Protest was dated July 15, 1842, the day that the "War bill"
passed the Senate, and will be found published in the *Telegraph and Texas Register,* July 27, 1842; and in Smither (ed.), *Journals of the Sixth Congress,* III, 60–62.
[12] *Ibid.,* III, 53–54.
[13] *Ibid.*
[14] *Telegraph and Texas Register,* July 27, 1842.
[15] *Ibid.*

to agitate the question, and sincerely hope every patriot will aid as freely and cheerfully in carrying out the draft as if there was not the shadow of doubt as to the constitutionality of the measure."[16] Some of the Senators most enthusiastic for war were among the bitterest opponents of the "War bill" and the use of militiamen in offensive war.

Two changes in the House bill were recommended by the Senate Military Affairs Committee. One was to permit the President to sell as well as to hypothecate the public domain, and the other was to set a limit of ten million acres upon the amount of land to be sold or hypothecated. Both of these proposed amendments were adopted, and the bill passed the Senate on July 15 by a vote of 7 to 4 with John A. Greer (San Augustine), William H. Jack (Brazoria), Francis Moore, Jr. (Harris, Galveston, and Liberty), and Kindred H. Muse (Nacogdoches and Houston)[17] voting against it. On the 18th the House of Representatives concurred in the Senate amendments to the bill and sent it to the President for his approval. At the same time, the House adopted the Senate substitute joint resolution for the relief of Captain Augustus Williams, and passed the joint resolution extending thanks to the volunteers from the United States. Upon the final passage of the "War bill" in the House, Robert M. Williamson (Washington) and James S. Mayfield (Nacogdoches) announced that they would enter their protests at a later date. Williamson's protest, if made, has not been found but Mayfield read his protest in the House on July 21.

Never losing an opportunity to embarrass the administration, Mayfield, Secretary of State under Lamar, "availed himself of the opportunity, as he generally does on almost all occasions," declared the editor of the *Galveston Civilian and Gazette*,[18] "to make a great many remarks not particularly complimentary to the Executive, and in my humble opinion entirely irrelevant and uncalled for."

In the present attitude of our country [declared Mayfield] it appears to me that nothing else but a declaration of war on our part, can redeem the country from obliquy [obloquy], ransom our fellow-citizens from disgraceful servitude and confinement; for the sin of bearing our national standard on an errand of peace; maintain the integrity of our soil, and extort an acknowledgment of our Independence. . . . I came with alacrity and zeal to fulfil my duties to the country in this house; harboring with all confidence the

[16] *Ibid.*, July 20, 1842.

[17] Smither (ed.), *Journals of the Sixth Congress*, III, 69. The "War bill" is printed in the *Telegraph and Texas Register*, July 20, 1842.

[18] July 24, 1842; see also *Telegraph and Texas Register*, August 3, 1842.

hope, that warlike measures would be adopted, and the field fully opened to our patriotism and chivalry. But measures have taken a dubious if not a dangerous turn; the public will has not been declared and all the power of this Nation is resigned to the discretion of the President, the true issue has not been presented, and Congress has behaved rather as an auxiliary than an independent branch of the Government. . . .

The unholy union of political power in the same hands is to be found in an act entitled "an act to authorize offensive measures against Mexico and for other purposes" passed at our present session.

If the passage of that act were an exercise of the power of this body "to declare war" it should have my most cordial approbation and strongest support. . . . Has Congress declared that we shall engage in war with Mexico? No! But it has decided that with the concurrence of the Executive we shall have war. Now the power of declaring war is not a power to be exercised jointly by the Congress and the Executive, but it is a power confided solely to Congress, and if they do not exercise that power in an unequivocal manner it cannot be exercised at all. . . . If the judgment of the President dictates war, will that war result from the discretion of the President or the will of Congress? Plainly the former. So I [continued Mayfield] record my protest against this bill, *because it avoids the duty we ought to have performed,* and because it confers a power of which no agency can divest this body, because it leaves to the President a power inconsistent with his office, and divests Congress of a power that cannot be bestowed.—"Congress shall have power to declare war," and do all things necessary to carry that power in effect; but does this mean that it may break down the partitions the Constitution has established, and destroy its necessary distinctions?[19]

It was not that Mayfield objected to offensive war against Mexico, but that he thought Congress was acting too much as an auxiliary to the executive power; instead of forthrightly declaring war, as it had the authority to do, it was leaving the ultimate decision to the President by permitting him to "direct the commencement of operations at such time and in such manner as he in his judgment may deem compatible with the public interests." Using the same line of reasoning, Mayfield also raised constitutional objections to that section of the "War bill" giving the President authority to hypothecate a portion of the public domain, for that would, he thought, make him an agent of Congress and subject him to its control. Concluding with a venomous tirade against the President, Mayfield declared, "I believe that a war is the only refuge we have from the evils which assail us; but this bill commits unconsti-

[19] *Telegraph and Texas Register,* Aug. 3, 1842; also Smither (ed.), *Journals of the Sixth Congress,* III, 164–167.

tutionally vast powers to the President, which he would not execute if he could avoid, for he has lulled and deceived the people by open promises of war, while his secret machinations were at work to dismay the public hope and chill the general enthusiasm to avert war if he could, and leave the people to submission and despair."

The "War bill" passed Congress on July 18, five days after the news of the Texan victory at Lipantitlán reached Houston. The bill did not formally declare war, but "authorized and required" the President "to call for and accept the services of volunteers to form an army for the prosecution of offensive war against Mexico" at such time as he might "deem compatible with the public interest." Should the number of volunteers not be sufficient, the President was to call out the militia, "not to exceed for offensive operations, one third of the whole population capable of bearing arms, including those who may have volunteered." If, however, there should be an invasion from Mexico, the President could "order out so much of the militia . . . as he may deem necessary to repel such invasion." The President was authorized to take command of the army "in person," and to keep the navy at sea in active service against the enemy, irrespective of any law to the contrary now in force. Any volunteer or drafted man who served an enlistment of six months was to receive a land grant of 640 acres, and the President was empowered to appoint suitable agents in the counties and elsewhere

to receive contributions of land, money, provisions and equipment necessary for the prosecution of an offensive war, . . . to employ all the available resources of the Republic not otherwise specially appropriated by law, [and] . . . to hypothecate or sell any portion of the public domain not exceeding ten millions of acres for the purpose of raising funds for the prosecution of the war, upon such terms and in such manner as he in his judgment may deem proper.[20]

Many of the would-be "conquistadores" and frontiersmen, tired of the Mexican raids, applauded the sweeping provisions of the bill and seemed surprised when the President received the bill in silence. When it was rumored in Houston that he might return the bill with a veto, dire threats were made by persons in less responsible positions. The Acting Inspector General of the Republic, Memucan Hunt, made a direct personal appeal to President Houston, saying

[20] "A bill to be entitled an Act to authorize offensive war against Mexico and for other purposes," in *Telegraph and Texas Register*, July 20, 1842; and Smither (ed.), *Journals of the Sixth Congress*, III, 125–127.

The Bill presented for your consideration and signature opens to yourself a field for glory which has had no parallel since Napoleon crossed the Alps. . . . Call upon the choicest spirits of the land to rally to your banner. Challenge to the field your leading personal and political adversaries . . . and . . . you will find yourself at the head of an army which no Mexican force can withstand . . . the idol of both camp and country.

The opposite course—the veto of the bill—whilst it brings despair and desperation to a large and gallant portion of the country will disarm . . . your friends and sharpen the weapons of your enemies. . . . You stand before the world committed to an offensive war "to the knife." . . . Indeed I conscientiously believe that if you veto this bill there will not be another assemblage of congress in sufficient numbers to form a quorum and legislate under the present constitution.[21]

The editor of the *Civilian and Galveston Gazette* prophesied that the bill would be vetoed, "and if so," he declared, "it will elevate Gen. Houston so far above all his enemies that henceforward he will be invulnerable to the shafts so lavishly aimed at him. His refusal to accept the almost unlimited power vested in him by the provisions of this Bill will evince his superior strength of mind in refusing what his enemies have so loudly declared was his only object and desire—the complete control of the purse and sword."[22]

Since the "War bill" made no provision for length of service and provided no definite financial means for equipping such an expedition, the President, whom, it was said, "the whirlpools—and quicksands never deprive of reason or jostle in the least,"[23] unhesitatingly vetoed it. He had, in the first place, never intended that there should be an invasion of Mexico. Writing from Philadelphia four days before Houston sent his veto message to Congress, James Pinckney Henderson, former Texan minister to England and France, informed Ashbel Smith at New York that Houston had written him "a short time before I left home that he would not consent under any circumstances to an invasion."[24] While believing that the country should vigorously defend itself at all times against any invasion from Mexico, Houston felt that the Republic's resources precluded offensive operations and that the soundest policy was

[21] Memucan Hunt to Sam Houston, July 21, 1842, quoted in Marquis James, *The Raven: A Biography of Sam Houston,* p. 326.
[22] July 24, 1842.
[23] H. F. Gillett to D[octor] Ashbel Smith, Washington, Texas, Nov. 25, 1842, in Ashbel Smith Papers, 1838–1842, ms.
[24] [J. P.] Henderson to Ashbel Smith, Philadelphia, July 18, 1842, in *ibid.,* ms.

not to provoke Mexico into a renewal of the Texas campaign. General
Houston, recorded Bollaert,[25]

is kept well informed from Mexico and acts accordingly. He is aware of their
inability to do anything. The late affair [at Lipantitlán] was of a marauding
character. It would be preferable could peace be obtained—even at this date,
[declared Bollaert, who was interested in the English colonization program
in Texas] by acknowledging a certain quota of Mexico's debt to England.
This peace would facilitate all sorts of operations. Why not someone sent to
Mexico à la coon to negotiate. . . . Offensive war would irritate and do no
good. Defensive—when and if the marauders come they will be hung as sure
as 2 and 3 make five.

Years later, a well-known Texas ranger, John S. Ford, recollected that
it was

the opinion of gentlemen who had opportunities to know the truth, that a
long conference between Gen. Houston and the Hon. Kenneth L. Anderson
[Speaker of the House of Representatives] caused him to change his views.
Col. Anderson convinced him of the inability of Texas to furnish capital to
defray the expenses of an army prosecuting a war upon foreign territory.
The danger of the war degenerating into a robbing expedition was placed in
bold relief. The disgrace arising from such hostile movements was dwelt
upon. Events had not been favorable to Texas, and a false move would damage the reputation of her people for chivalry and hightoned sense of honor.[26]

Speaker Anderson may have thought that Houston would succumb to
the demands of the Texan "War Hawks" and that he should try to con-
vince him that his original policy of peace with Mexico, unless necessary to repel an attack, was the best for Texas. It is doubtful if Houston
needed much convincing, but how to stem the popular tide for war
evinced in Congress created a major problem. The utter impossibility of
fitting out an expedition composed of a large element of undisciplined
volunteers from the United States and without adequate financial support had become quite clear to him and to all thoughtful persons. An
aggressive campaign against Mexico seemed out of the question; yet,
Texans could claim, after the repulse of Canales and Montero, that they
could defend the frontier against Mexican attacks.

In a closely reasoned veto message[27] the President declared that five

[25] *Bollaert's Texas*, p. 121.
[26] John S. Ford, "Memoirs," ms., II, 250.
[27] Sam Houston, *Veto Message of the President of the Republic of Texas to the
Bill "Authorizing Offensive War Against Mexico and for Other Purposes"*; [Sam

thousand men would be needed for at least one year's service, and that the mere setting aside of ten million acres of land and giving him authority "to employ all the available resources of the Republic not otherwise specially appropriated by law" would not furnish means for conducting the war. The land was practically valueless and no ready sale of it could be expected when land under existing laws could be obtained "by occupancy alone." Furthermore, there were hundreds of thousands of acres of Texas land scrip afloat in the United States, at a price not exceeding twenty-five dollars for six hundred and forty acres. Also, it would be difficult to sell the land when it had not been surveyed, and, too, that section of the bill intended to give each volunteer or drafted militiaman six hundred and forty acres would be a drawback to ready sales.

The authority to call out the militia for an offensive war was doubtful. "In the prosecution of an offensive war," the President reminded Congress, "there should be no question as to the right of the government to command the services of its citizens. Unfortunately, at the very outset, the question arises: Has Congress the power, by the constitution, to order a draft, and compel the citizens of the Republic to march beyond our limits in a war of invasion? If this power exists, it is not to be found among the enumerated powers expressly delegated by the constitution to the Congress; and to me it is clear that no such power has been delegated but is expressly reserved to the people. If Congress does not possess such power, then such a law would be unconstitutional."

The meager results of the efforts to get up an expedition may have caused President Houston to take this opportunity to wiggle out of a difficult situation, and to await the outcome of Waddy Thompson's negotiations in Mexico upon the proposition of the United States government suggesting that Mexico discontinue its war with Texas and permit United States mediation in its difficulties with that country. "I feel confident," reported the United States chargé d'affaires in Texas, "that the President will as well from inclination as from necessity, postpone all aggressive military operations against Mexico, untill the results of Mr. Thompson's negotiations . . . shall be made known."[28] Furthermore,

---

Houston] to the House of Representatives, Executive Department, City of Houston, July 22, 1842, in Smither (ed.), *Journals of the Sixth Congress*, III, 168–174; *Writings of Sam Houston*, III, 116–124; *Telegraph and Texas Register*, July 27, 1842.

[28] Joseph Eve to Daniel Webster, Legation of the United States, Galveston, Aug. 22, 1842, in "Correspondence and Reports of American Agents and Others in Texas, 1836–1845," Justin H. Smith, "Transcripts," Vol. V., ms. News of the intentions of

England had only recently recognized the independence of Texas and was committed to interceding with Mexico in behalf of Texas.

Many persons in Texas believed that "Old Sam" was the only man in the country at that time who could extricate the nation from its pressing difficulties. The Administration, however, could not go it alone. To do so would require the full cooperation of all citizens, and this was made more clearly evident in the ensuing months by the United States Senate's rejection of certain key features of the Treaty of Amity, Commerce, and Navigation which had been signed in Washington on July 13, 1842. Isaac Van Zandt, the Texan representative in Washington, reported that "the day after" the Foreign Relations Committee of the United States Senate reported on the treaty "the news of our internal commotions, our dissensions and civil discords, coupled with our disasters, reached here, in all their glowing and exaggerated enormities, and, like a withering sirocco, blasted every effort of our friends, and paralyzed every movement in behalf of our treaty."[29]

The veto of the "War bill" in Texas caused considerable criticism of the President and his policy, but he remained firm in his purpose and the "War Party" was somewhat "perplexed to know what to be at,"[30] but only for a brief spell. They lived on excitement and loved it. Soon they were again crying vociferously for an invasion of Mexico. "On to the halls of Montezuma" became their chant. Anything to embarrass the Administration caught their attention and made them rant.

The President labored at his desk in Houston through the heat of the day and at night could be seen through the windows of the executive mansion, pacing the floor, while in the streets hotheaded critics talked of his assassination.[31] Bitter words were exchanged between General Hunt and the President over the veto and the efforts of the former to get approved his accounts for service as Acting Inspector General of the Republic which he had agreed to perform "without cost to the Govern-

---

the United States to attempt diplomatic intervention in the Texas-Mexican dispute reached Texas just prior to the passage of the War bill.

[29] Dudley G. Wooten (ed.), *A Comprehensive History of Texas, 1685 to 1897*, I, 409; H. Yoakum, *History of Texas from Its First Settlement in 1685 to Its Annexation to the United States in 1846*, II, 394. See also Isaac Van Zandt to Anson Jones, Legation of Texas, Washington City, Jan. 25, 1842, and Same to Same, Washington [City], March 13, 1842, in George P. Garrison (ed.), *Diplomatic Correspondence of Texas*, in *Annual Report of the American Historical Association, 1908*, II, 115–118, 132–138.

[30] *Bollaert's Texas*, p. 124.

[31] *Houston: A History and Guide*, pp. 58–59.

ment,"[32] and for which Houston now refused to give his approval. Having recently toured the different counties to organize the militia preparatory to offensive operations against Mexico, Hunt was indignant over the veto, and resigned his office in disgust.[33] Largely, however, as the result of the efforts of mutual friends, George W. Terrell and Henry K. Hardy, the differences between the President and Hunt were settled amicably,[34] even to the extent that the President offered Hunt, who two months before had challenged Lamar to a duel,[35] the office of Secretary of War and Marine. This office the latter graciously declined. Having his hopes of war with Mexico shattered, Hunt prepared to return to the United States to engage in trade in New Orleans, but before he could leave Texas the Mexicans again raided San Antonio and he rushed to Béxar to help defend the frontier and to participate in a campaign against Mexico.[36]

Learning of the forthcoming presidential veto, members of the House of Representatives from the southern and western parts of the Republic drew up the draft of a letter addressed to the Speaker resigning their seats in the House.[37]

This step [declared the draft letter] is the result of mature deliberation, [and] we assume this last and positive stand, convinced that we cannot render our country any service, however little, to ameliorate the present condition [of our western frontier.] The Executive, after having beguiled us into the most ridiculous position in our course upon offensive measures against a common enemy who have continued to prey upon the vitality of [the] nation and the very life blood and property of our constituency, now mocks us with the most rankling odiums. But notwithstanding all these distresses and contamilies [calamities?] we would endure them with a patriotic cheerfulness if we could see in futurity the hope of remedy, but we cannot even gleam [glean?] this scanty hope from among the probabilities in reason. The West

---

[32] Sam Houston to Memucan Hunt, City of Houston, July 28, 1842, in *Writings of Sam Houston*, IV, 131–132.

[33] J. Morgan to Doctor Ashbel Smith, New Washington, Galveston Bay, Texas, Augt. 20, 1842, in Ashbel Smith Papers, ms.

[34] Henry K. Hardy to Gen. M. Hunt, Houston, Sept. 8, 1842, and Same to Same, Houston, Texas, Sept. 11, 1842, in Memucan Hunt Papers, ms.

[35] *Telegraph and Texas Register*, Sept. 7, 1842.

[36] A. P. Walden to George Morgan, New Orleans [dated]: Houston, Sept. 15, 1842, and William B. Hawkins to Memucan Hunt, Nashville, Nov. 17, 1842, in Hunt Papers, ms.

[37] An unsigned copy of a letter addressed to "The Speaker of the House of Rep [resentatives], City of Houston, July 22, 1842," in Washington D. Miller Papers (Texas), ms.

& Southwestern frontiers which we here so hopelessly represent is [are?] now the scene of open and ruthless warfare. We can only aid it by our individual arms and we solemnly and humbly conceive it our imperative duty [it was said] to retire at once to our homes and the post of danger which we have here so signally and hopelessly failed to avert.

This letter was never signed and presented to the Speaker, probably because the promoters of the idea sensed that public opinion was against them, and that little could be accomplished by resigning their seats the day before Congress adjourned. By staying, they might be able to embarrass the administration more without running the risk of discrediting themselves.

As a whole, the people were doubtless satisfied with the veto,[38] even in the west. Before Congress met it was reported in some circles among men who kept in touch with public affairs that popular opinion was "against invading Mexico" and that it was pretty well ascertained that Congress would "not advise or direct it. So the 'Old Chief' will have it his own way—fortunately for the country," wrote Henderson.[39] Writing to Van Zandt, a member of Congress, Peter Swanson reported more than two weeks before the convening of the special session that "in Consulting with the people, they all appear to speak their Sentiments in accordance with my own feelings, that is to Defend [our] own Side of the Riogrande . . . and then if not successful we can not blame our Members for defeats in the field."[40] From New York Samuel Swartwout commented to James Morgan that " 'Old Sam' never did a wiser or better thing than to stop the war with Mexico. It was all d—d nonsense. . . . I think Mexico will soon be *forced* by England, France & the U. States to acknowledge yʳ. Independence, when your war expenses will cease, & you can all swagger away without danger of being killed or wounded."[41]

From the Hermitage, ex-President Andrew Jackson wrote Houston expressing his approval of the veto.

I approve your veto fully [he said]. To make offensive war without ample means both in money and men would be the hight [sic] of folly and madness, and must result in defeat and disgrace. To invade a country with

[38] *Civilian and Galveston Gazette*, July 27, 1842.
[39] [J. P.] Henderson to Ashbel Smith, Philadelphia, July 18, 1842, in Ashbel Smith Papers, ms.
[40] Peter Swanson to Isaac Van Zan[d]t, June 10, 1842, in Isaac Van Zandt Papers, 1839–1843, ms.
[41] Samuel Swartwout to James Morgan, New York, Dec. 6, 1842, in James Morgan Papers, 1841–1845, ms.

drafted militia for a limited time, without a regular army enlisted and for and during the war, would be the hight of folly, and lead to the destruction of the army attempting it, and the disgrace of the general leading it.

If you had not vetoed the bill, it would have lead to the destruction of your country and disgrace of all concerned in the invasion of Mexico, as the attempt under your present situation must have inevitably failed, and placed you in a situation from which you could not have successfully defended Texas from being reconquered by the power of Mexico.

Your true policy is to act upon the defensive, and husband all your means for this purpose, and be at all times prepared to meet and destroy any invading army or marauding party of Mexicans, and in carrying on this defensive war, to pursue the enemy to their strong holds, and destroy them and make reprisals. . . . Foster your commerce and revenues, and prepare for defense and the protection of your republic—that is, as appears to me your true policy.[42]

Writing on May 26, Joel R. Poinsett, former United States minister to Mexico, expressed himself in a similar vein. Texas, he said, should maintain a "defensive attitude, strengthening itself as much as possible at home and abroad, and suffering Mexico to forget its existence, which with their usual apathy, if unmolested, they would soon do."[43] As time passed an invasion by Mexico would become less probable, and in the meanwhile Texas would wax stronger and stronger.

Nevertheless, the veto stirred up a storm of indignation among some of the would-be volunteers in the proposed invasion, and many westerners were vociferously dissatisfied.[44] Some cursed the President and called him a "traitor" leagued with Santa Anna to destroy the government. Some lauded his course of action, while others, astonished, held their peace. One of the President's close friends had named his eldest son "Houston," hoping "that the name would be a credit to the country and probably to the child but after a strict trial," he wrote, "I am now under the conviction that he is not the Honest patriot I thook [sic] him to be; . . . therefore, after mature consideration, I have thought proper to change the name of my son to that of an Honest man . . . 'Hunt'."[45]

When asked how Texas stood in public esteem in the United States,

[42] Andrew Jackson to Samuel Houston, Hermitage, Aug. 17, 1842, in *Writings of Sam Houston*, III, 124 n.

[43] Yoakum, *History of Texas*, II, 361 n.

[44] *Ibid.*, II, 362; Francis R. Lubbock, *Six Decades in Texas: or Memoirs of Francis Richard Lubbock*, p. 145.

[45] John M. Leon to Mrs. Gordon, Clarksville, Red River [dated:] Galveston, Aug. 27, 1842, in Army Papers (Texas), ms.

John P. Davie, just returned to Galveston from a visit to Norfolk, Virginia, replied, "I would say d—— low." He declared he would "leave in a very big hurry" if it would not mean making too great a financial sacrifice at that time. "Since my return to Galveston," continued Davie, "I have got so completely disgusted at the way things are managed, that I intend to turn as much as I possibly can into cash by next summer, and pull up stakes for some part of the states, unless there is a great change for the better."[46]

Many regarded the late special session of Congress and its principal enactment—the "War bill"—as a mere struggle between the President and Congress, in the deranged state of national finances, as to who should bear the responsibility for the policy to be pursued against Mexico; and the general opinion seemed to be that Congress, by concentrating all the power relating to offensive war in the hands of the President, hoped to make him accountable for the failure of an enterprise which it believed could not succeed under the near bankrupt condition of the Republic's treasury. It was felt that the ultimate defeat of the bill by veto was due to its friends having "rashly ventured to load it down with a section"; namely, the use of the militia in offensive warfare, which "many of the most intelligent and strenuous advocates for offensive war considered unconstitutional."[47]

The President, at least, editorialized H. Stuart in the *Civilian and Galveston Gazette*,[48]

had the prudence to reject powers highly tempting and dangerous to an ambitious man, and has given an example of devotion to the Constitution and respect for the reserved rights of the citizens, which should not be lost on those who may succeed him, and which should act as a salutary rebuke upon those who, in Congress, may be willing to transcend their own powers and ask the Executive to surpass his, to gratify their own spleen, divest themselves of a wholesome responsibility, or obey the call of a transitory popular excitement.

"The *Outs* . . . lived on excitement only, and violent opposition to the Executive,"[49] and Vasquez's entry and the distribution of Arista's proclamation had fired their imagination and throughout the land people had "construed General H——'s conduct as *treason*, . . . but within the

[46] John P. Davie to Matthew P. Woodhouse, Galveston, Aug. 1, 1842, in *ibid.*, ms.
[47] *Telegraph and Texas Register*, July 27, 1842.
[48] July 27, 1842.
[49] *Bollaert's Texas*, pp. 129–130.

last few days," recorded Bollaert, "all must see that the Executive was *right*. Party spirit may now—seeing. . . [the negotiations going on by foreign powers for mediation of the Texan-Mexican dispute]—even try to thwart them and throw obstacles in the way of the well-being of the country."

It must be remembered, however, that the country was neither united in favor of war, nor prepared to wage it. More was needed than bluster and oratory. But why, it might be asked, did Houston seem so strongly disposed to retaliate upon Mexico? He stormed and blustered like many "indignant" western politicians. He talked war; he proclaimed a block-ade of Mexican ports; he ordered the navy to recondition and enforce the blockade; he sought to recruit a strong expeditionary force of Anglo-Americans to attack northern Mexico; he called Congress in special session and gave every impression in his message to it that he favored an energetic prosecution of the war, and in the end vetoed the bill authorizing offensive operations against the national enemy. What else could he do? He had to seem to appease the vociferous demands of his countrymen whose views of the nation's problems lacked maturity of judgment. He believed that armed intervention in Mexico would be suicidal considering the limited financial and manpower resources of the Republic. On the other hand, the country had been invaded and there was a possibility that Mexico might launch a determined campaign at any time to subdue Texas. He could not afford to sit idly by and do nothing. The country must be prepared for an invasion, and though he hoped to avoid war, he could not afford to create at home or abroad a feeling of weakness or reluctance to meet any Mexican challenge. Even though he did not want to carry the war into Mexico, "would it not be much better for the morale of the Texans and for the confusion of the enemy if this reluctance were concealed"?[50] Would not those foreign countries interested in the peaceful development of both Texas and Mexico be aroused to an effort to help solve for once and all the cleavage between Mexico and her former province of Texas? Throughout both of his administrations Houston was consistently opposed to an armed invasion of Mexico, but he stood ready to support an invasion if forced to do so by circumstances. The failure of Mexico to follow up Vasquez's entry into Texas with a determination to subdue Texas handicapped recruiting efforts in the United States and gave Houston a good excuse to abandon his plans for a campaign which he never really wanted. The

[50] Joseph William Schmitz, *Texan Statecraft, 1836–1845*, p. 175.

southern and western frontiersmen of the country, however, were not satisfied, and Houston still found it necessary to appear to please them by a Mexican campaign "if . . . ." Too, the announcement of another effort to get up a campaign, as shall be noted in the following chapter, would keep the pressure on interested major powers to endeavor to bring about mediation of the differences between Mexico and Texas. In time, Houston grew in stature in the estimation of his fellow countrymen. "There was some little excitement caused by the veto, which has pretty much died away," reported James Morgan, "and 'Old Sam' is more popular than ever I believe."[51]

On the same day that the "War bill" passed Congress, July 18, President Houston recommended to the Senate that, in view of the "spirit of utter insubordination and mutiny," "disrespect and disobedience," which had from the first characterized the actions of the foreign volunteers stationed upon the western frontier, destroying every hope of their usefulness and harmony, the use of such troops be discontinued.

It is therefore, submitted to the honorable Congress [he said] whether it would not be more politic to rely upon our own militia, and furlough or discharge those who will no longer yield obedience to the laws and rules of war enacted for their government?
I despair of reformation and will not be accessory, through the Department of War, of tantalizing the hopes and expectations of our citizens, who have hoped for succor from volunteer aid from the United States. They are expensive as they have heretofore proved useless to our country.[52]

A request of this nature to Congress clearly indicated that the President desired the legislature to pull the executive's chestnuts out of the fire. The President, on his own initiative, had instituted a recruiting program in the United States to get "emigrants" to carry the war to the enemy, and now he sought to avoid the responsibility of putting an end to an unfruitful policy. His accusations were only, in part, true, and did not go unchallenged. Jeremiah Clemens of Alabama, who had served with distinction during the last four years in the legislature of his native state and who had come to Texas as a lieutenant colonel in command of two hundred volunteers, made a heated defense of the foreign volunteers. The "galling bitterness" of your message, he wrote Houston, its "slander" and "injurious imputations" comes at a time

---

[51] James Morgan to Ashbel Smith, Aug. 20, 1842, in Ashbel Smith Papers, ms.
[52] Houston to the Senate, City of Houston, July 18, 1842, in Smither (ed.), *Journals of the Sixth Congress*, III, 77.

when you were fresh from the perusal of a despatch containing the intelligence that a portion of those "Foreign Volunteers" had nobly repulsed and driven back a Mexican force more than three times their number and saved the western country from the ravages of a remorseless foe. For these services . . . [you have] offered them a *rich* return—wanton, unprovoked, unmanly insult, added to gross injury and injustice. They will have reason to remember your gratitude and strong inducements to return a second time if they should again be needed.[53]

Clemens declared that most of the men complied with the President's proclamation and brought at least the quantities of provisions and ammunition required, and that some brought ten times the amount. That the quantity of supplies brought was grossly exaggerated was obviously well-known to Clemens, who left no loop-hole in his line of reasoning by asserting,

But even if it were true [as charged by Houston], those conditions were waived by receiving and mustering them [the emigrants] into the service of the Republic—and from that date on you lost all right to complain of any deficiencies that might have existed. It is not true, as you have stated, that the conduct of the volunteers has been marked from the first, by utter disregard for the rules and articles of war. With a few individual exceptions, a more obedient, orderly, well conducted soldiery never were in, the employment of any Government. . . . Yet, for the purpose of excusing your own vacillating and contradictory course, you have not hesitated to pen the vilest calumnies upon the characters and conduct of the gallant men who had left their own fire-sides to battle for yours—who, without even the hope of pay, have endured hardships and undergone privations from which the hardiest might well be excused for shirking.

As for the foreign volunteers being "expensive" and "useless," their defender exclaimed,

Expensive indeed!. In what way? at what time? and for what article has the Government of Texas expended one dollar for the benefit of the volunteers? You [he wrote the President] did not furnish them with a tent cloth, a baggage wagon, or a pack horse. You did not supply them with a blanket, a shoe, a frying-pan, camp kettle, canteen, tin cup, or any cooking utensil or article of clothing. You did not give them an ounce of bread or a pound

[53] Jeremiah Clemens to Gen. Sam Houston, Galveston, Aug. 6, 1842, in Army Papers (Texas), ms.; copy in Sam Houston, Unpublished Correspondence, 1842, ms., III; copy in *Wetumpka Argus* (Wetumpka, Alabama), Sept. 21, 1842; also in *Telegraph and Texas Register*, Sept. 7, 1842.

of bacon; not a particle of sugar, coffee, beans, rice or any thing but a few head of beef cattle,

and even then the second battalion had to feed on the "carcase of a dog."

Likewise, Colonel Latham, who had recently visited Texas with the company of Tennessee "Wolf Hunters," having returned to his editorial work on the *Fort Pickering Eagle*, declared in his paper on August 12:

President Houston, after all the fuss he has made, and war sounding proclamations he has issued, has vetoed the bill passed by the Texian Congress, "to authorize offensive war against Mexico." We understand his principal reason was the impossibility to raise funds necessary for the purpose. He ought to have known this before he duped volunteers to go to Texas, only to be starved back home. We are inclined to believe, however, that President Houston relied greatly on many thousand volunteers and dollars flocking to the Texian Standard. This failing, all his hopes failed, and hence he concluded to knock the *offensive* war on the head.[54]

The failure of the "War bill" by no means implied the cessation of hostilities against Mexico. In response to the request of the House of Representatives on June 30 for information relative to the number, description, equipment, movement, and subsistence for troops required to prosecute the contemplated campaign, the President, on July 15, submitted his estimates on the expenses of four companies of cavalry for six months and made no mention of a campaign. The following day estimates for the navy were sent to Congress.[55] There was no regular force for frontier defense, for the want of means for their support. In emergencies a few small companies had been raised to operate for a few days. Captain McLean had been ordered to keep a spy company west of the lower San Antonio River, but for the lack of funds the order had not been executed for any reasonable length of time. Major Hays and Captain Menchaca had orders to raise companies and keep an eye on the country between the San Antonio and the Río Grande.[56] The day follow-

[54] *Fort Pickering Eagle* quoted in the *Telegraph and Texas Register*, Sept. 21, 1842.

[55] Houston to the House of Representatives, City of Houston, July 15, 1842; Same to Same, July 16, 1842, in *Writings of Sam Houston*, III, 101–103.

[56] Houston to the Senate, Executive Department, City of Houston, July 18, 1842, in Texas Congress, Congressional Papers, Sixth Congress, no. 2619, ms.; Executive Records, of the Second Term of General Sam Houston's Administration of the Government of Texas, December 1841–December 1844, p. 121, ms.; *Morning Star*, Aug. 6, 1842; *Telegraph and Texas Register*, Aug. 10, 1842.

ing receipt of the President's veto of the "War bill" Congress adjourned after rushing through a joint resolution, permitting the Executive to enlist one company of volunteers to range the Trinity-Navasota frontier "provided they equip themselves, at their own expense, for a tour of not less than two months." Out of the $20,000 appropriated earlier in the year for frontier defense, Congress set aside $250 to be used to procure supplies for the company. For defense of the southwestern frontier, the President was authorized to recruit two companies and to expend $2,000 of the $20,000 previously appropriated.[57] On July 14 a bill from the House reached the Senate declaring the office of major general vacant and fixing a date for an election to fill the vacancy.[58] In the Senate the bill was referred to the Committee on Military Affairs, headed by Jones. The Committee reported a substitute bill for that of the House, which was read, discussed, and adopted. The House bill has not been found. The substitute bill, however, recognized the existence of a vacancy in the office of major general of militia due to the resignation of Felix Huston and his removal from the Republic to New Orleans. It required the President to order the holding of an election for major general of militia on Monday, September 1, next, and changed the term of the office from two to four years.[59] By an act, approved July 23, Congress provided that the officers, seamen, and marines of the navy be paid at the same rate as those in the United States, including rations and perquisites.[60] By another law the President was authorized to survey and sell 400,000 acres of the Cherokee Lands[61] for, according to press reports, the special support of the navy and the fitting out of two additional warships to enable Texas to maintain her supremacy upon the Gulf and to annoy the enemy's coastal towns and commerce. Finally, before adjourning on July 23, Congress re-instated Williams to his rank in the Texan volunteer service, and the House enacted the Senate bill requiring the President to hold an election for major general of the Texas militia on September 1. While the act pertaining to Williams received

[57] "Joint Resolution for Frontier Protection," approved July 23, 1842, in H. P. N. Gammel (ed.), *Laws of Texas*, II, 816.

[58] Smither (ed.), *Journals of the Sixth Congress*, III, 56.

[59] *Ibid.*, III, 56 n, 57.

[60] "Joint Resolution Making Appropriations for the Support of the Navy" approved July 23, 1842, in Gammel (ed.), *Laws of Texas*, II, 813–814; *Telegraph and Texas Register*, July 13, 1842.

[61] "An Act to Provide for the Survey and Sale of a Portion of the Territory Formerly Occupied by the Cherokee Indians," approved July 23, 1842, in Gammel (ed.), *Laws of Texas*, II, 814–815; *Civilian and Galveston Gazette*, July 27, 1842.

an executive veto, as we have seen, which was overridden by Congress, the act pertaining to the selection of a major general was pocket-vetoed.

No sooner had Congress enacted the law pertaining to the election of a major general than General Albert Sidney Johnston announced his candidacy for that office, and according to Johnston's son, with a considerable degree of exaggeration, "would have been chosen almost by acclamation,"[62] but since President Houston forgot to sanction the measure by his signature, "until *too late*," the act was a nullity.[63] Thus Johnston seems to have announced "a *little too* soon!" Shortly afterwards Johnston left the country for Kentucky. Congress adjourned without declaring war; but, according to Houston, did "as much as can be had of the willing kind. I do sincerely hope," he continued, "that it may and will go on. It is the kind of war that the country can sustain . . . though, as Fullenvyder said, it 'will be a d—d dight squeeze,' if we get on tolerably well for some time to come."[64]

The day after the battle of Lipantitlán, Davis and his men began to fall back towards Live Oak Point, to take up position on the Chiltipín

---

[62] William Preston Johnston, *The Life of Gen. Albert Sidney Johnston: Embracing His Services in the Armies of the United States, the Republic of Texas, and the Confederate States*, p. 127.

[63] J. Morgan to Doctor Ashbel Smith, New Washington, Galveston Bay, Texas, Augt. 20, 1842, in Ashbel Smith Papers, ms.

[64] Houston to Anson Jones, City of Houston, Aug. 2, 1842, in Jones, *Memoranda and Official Correspondence of the Republic of Texas*, pp. 185–186. Peter H. Fullinwider was a German immigrant who received a grant of land in Stephen F. Austin's Colony.

On March 20, 1854, State Comptroller James B. Shaw issued a statement showing the expenses incurred by the Republic in protecting her frontier against the Indians during the years 1837–1844, inclusive. Yoakum, *History of Texas*, II, p. 282.

1837	Houston's first term	$ 20,000
1838		170,000
		$190,000
1839		$1,430,000
1840	Lamar's term	1,027,319
1841		95,000
		$2,552,319
1842	Houston's second term	$20,000
1843		66,950
1844		17,142
		$104,092

from which they were removed to Lamar, arriving there on July 15,[65] where their destitute condition of the last few days was relieved by adequate supplies of beef, coffee, and other provisions. Here they found the troops under Lieutenant Colonel Clemens.[66] Captain Cameron with some fifty mounted rangers took up a position at Refugio. Davis wasted no time in turning his command over to Clemens[67] and in hurrying to Houston to report to the President. A few days later an "odd and mischivious [*sic*] fellow sought to drive the troops out of the country." Knowing "how rudely the citizens had been treated by the troops—at Corpus Christi, Live Oak Point, and Lamar," he circulated a rumor that 7,000 Mexican troops were on their way to attack Davis' command, and were expected to arrive in about twenty-four hours.[68] Upon the receipt of this report in camp, narrated Quartermaster Goodman, the "self stiled Col. C. gave orders to start [their retreat] the next day."[69] There ensued a mad scramble to get-off. All available wagons, mules, horses, and oxen were pressed into service, leaving the citizens with their wives and children in a helpless condition. First, Clemens crossed his men from Lamar to a shallow lagoon in a ferry boat; marched a part of his command across the lagoon; drove the oxen and wagons into a bog; broke an ox's neck; and camped for the night with a part of his men on one side of the water and the balance on the opposite side. During the day the command got lost in the prairie and spent three days in getting to Carlos Rancho on the San Antonio, a distance of some twenty-five miles. Thence, the men proceeded eastward to Victoria. In the semi-illiterate writing of Goodman we have a graphic picture of the hasty flight: "This, the last of the Immortal self stiled Col. Clements covering his retreat with a wagon, an Ox, bogg down, leaving the farr west covered with

---

[65] W. B. Goodman, "A Statement of Facts, Washington, Feby 10, 1843," in Miller Papers (Texas), ms.

[66] *Ibid.*

[67] *Civilian and Galveston Gazette,* July 24, 1842.

[68] Goodman, "A Statement of Facts, Washington, Feby 10, 1843," in Miller Papers (Texas), ms. It was reported at Galveston that a considerable number of Mexicans, principally rancheros, believed to be from the party that had made the attack at Lipantitlán, were encamped on the Santa Gertrudis, and that at Matamoros the enemy had four to five thousand troops. *Civilian and Galveston Gazette,* July 24, 1842. The latter force was greatly exaggerated.

[69] Goodman, "A Statement of Facts, Washington, Feby 10, 1843," in W. D. Miller Papers (Texas), ms.

the Glory of his own shame flying before a fantom of his own imagination that Canales with his legions would soon be on him."[70]

Soon after the veto of the "War bill," the volunteers under General Davis were ordered disbanded, and Davis, himself, reached Houston on July 26 and retired "for the present from the service" on July 28,[71] under assurances of the President's approbation of the manner in which he had exercised the duties of his command.

"You accepted it [said the President] under the most discouraging circumstances. The men were disorganized. They have been mutinous. Their supplies were insufficient & the country without means to sustain you in your command. Desertion left you almost without men. You were attacked by more than treble your number of men, and tho' you were without defences, against the enemy's artillery, by your skill, and firmness you gallantly repulsed the assailants, with loss on their part, whilst you preserved your command from injury, or loss of life."

In the breakup and disbanding of the proposed expedition against Mexico not only was there dissatisfaction and disillusionment toward the government of Texas, but there was also sometimes bitterness among the participants themselves. Captain Hickey of the Natchez Volunteers and Captain Stevenson of the St. Louis Volunteers (Missouri Invincibles) had "hot words" about the use of a boat in which the volunteers were crossing from Live Oak Point on Corpus Christi Bay to Lamar. There was a challenge, and a duel took place at Lamar. At ten paces the two captains exchanged four shots. At the last fire Captain Hickey was dangerously wounded by his adversary, whose bullet passed through one thigh and lodged in the other, fracturing both bones.[72] "It must be a bitter reflection to every patriot," sadly commented the editor of the *Telegraph*, "that the gallant men upon whose prowess the country depends for defence, should, instead of displaying their courage in repelling the enemy, turn their arms against each

[70] *Ibid.*

[71] Houston to General James Davis, City of Houston, July 28, 1842, and Executive Approval of a Requisition to Pay General James Davis, Houston, July 28, 1842, in *Writings of Sam Houston*, III, 133–134. See also *Telegraph and Texas Register*, Aug. 3 and 31, 1842; J. Morgan to Doctor Ashbel Smith, New Washington, Galveston Bay, Augt. 20, 1842, in Ashbel Smith Papers, ms.

[72] *Civilian and Galveston Gazette*, July 24, 1842; *Telegraph and Texas Register*, Aug. 3, 1842. Captain Hickey was reported on August 10 to be rapidly recovering from his wound. *Ibid.*, Aug. 10, 1842.

other." For having participated in a duel, both the principals and their seconds, according to the laws of Texas, forfeited their rank in the service.[73]

A joint resolution of Congress extended thanks to the volunteers from the United States who had "so nobly and promptly come to our assistance in the present critical emergency of the Republic."[74] Many of the St. Louis Volunteers went to Egypt on the Colorado, from whence they were expected to go to Galveston to take passage for the United States. Captain Henry W. Allen's "Mississippi Guards" were discharged on August 25. Part of the men returned to the United States, but a few remained to make Texas their home.[75] By the end of August many of the volunteers from the United States had embarked for home; others had gone overland by way of the upper route through Nacogdoches and San Augustine; while still others were leaving as fast as funds could be raised to pay their passage[76]—"many disgusted and all disappointed."[77] Many of these happy-go-lucky young men who had come with high hopes of an easy, exciting, and highly remunerative campaign against Mexico were described now as being in a very destitute condition, wanting in clothing and other necessities.[78]

On leaving Galveston for the United States after resigning his commission early in August, Colonel Clemens assured the editor of the *Commercial Chronicle* (Galveston)[79] that he made a distinction between the "people" and "the Executive of Texas." He declared that he

[73] George W. Hockley to Alexander Stevenson, Department of War & Marine, Aug. 16, 1842, in Army Papers (Texas) ms. copy. Hockley accepted Stevenson's resignation as captain of the Missouri Invincibles. The writer has not found a copy of Stevenson's resignation.
[74] Smither (ed.), *Journals of the Sixth Congress*, III, 62–63, 74.
[75] *Writings of Sam Houston*, IV, 106 n.
[76] Joseph Eve to Daniel Webster, Legation of the United States, Galveston, Aug. 22, 1842 (vol. 2, no. 23), "Correspondence and Reports of American Agents and Others in Texas, 1836–1845," in Justin H. Smith, "Transcripts," Vol. V, ms.
[77] J. Morgan to Doctor Ashbel Smith, New Washington, Galveston Bay, Texas, Augt. 20, 1842, in Ashbel Smith Papers, ms. George L. McNair of the Mobile Greys published in New Orleans in October 1842, a broadsheet on the *Texian Campaign of 1842*, which was a disgruntled account of his tour of duty in Texas along the Nueces Frontier during the late spring and summer of 1842. See *Telegraph and Texas Register*, Oct. 26, 1842; Thomas W. Streeter, *Bibliography of Texas*, Part III, vol. II, pp. 383–384; copy also in Archivo General de la Secretaría de Relaciónes Exteriores, Mexico City, Mexico.
[78] *Telegraph and Texas Register*, Aug. 10, 1842.
[79] Reported in *ibid.*, Sept. 7, 1842.

had the warmest admiration for the spirit which seemed everywhere to animate the people and that it was certainly not their fault that the war was not vigorously prosecuted against Mexico. He did not blame "the people of Texas" for "the indignation inspired by the injuries which had been inflicted upon himself and his companions." Colonel Washington, who figured so prominently in the sending of volunteers from the United States to Galveston, was described as *"quite satisfied* with what he has done, and was rewarded to his *heart's content,* a la lode de Texas," reported James Morgan, "for his patriotism, and the cash expended in the cause! He has set down on his farm [in Liberty County] with pockets not quite so heavy as when he undertook his commission. I never saw a man more crest fallen."[80]

By the end of July Aubrey and his party of thirty to thirty-five guards had abandoned their combination trading-post and fort, with its one nine-pound field piece,[81] for Galveston, and only a widow remained at the old station of Aubrey and Kinney. As for Kinney, he was reported early in August to be under arrest at Matamoros, where he was accorded the liberty of the town but was prohibited from leaving.[82]

[80] J. Morgan to Doctor Ashbel Smith, New Washington, Galveston Bay, Texas, Augt. 20, 1842, in Ashbel Smith Papers, ms.
[81] *Telegraph and Texas Register,* July 30, Aug. 3, 1842.
[82] *Ibid.,* July 27, Aug. 3, 1842.

 CHAPTER THIRTEEN

Conditions on the Texas-Mexican Frontier During the Late Summer, 1842

As HAS BEEN NOTED, soon after the repulse of Canales at Lipantitlán by the remnants of a half-starved, poorly disciplined, volunteer Anglo-Texan army, the soldiers at that point, as well as other detachments in the neighborhood, were disbanded and returned to their homes. During the ensuing months the poverty-stricken Republic failed to set up an efficient, well-disciplined military organization to protect its southwestern frontier and to cope with future predatory incursions from Mexicans and Indians. At the end of the summer the frontier lay unprotected except for a few rangers stationed at San Antonio under the command of Captain John C. Hays, then only twenty-five years of age, and at Victoria under Colonel Clark L. Owen of Texana. Late in July 1842, Captain Hays made a hurried trip to the bayou-city, Houston, the temporary capital, to confer with the President, and while there, because of his youthful appearance and unbearded face, seems to have created some excitement among those who knew him only as "the veritable Jack Hays, the celebrated Indian fighter, the man whose name was sung with praise by all Texans."[1] As soon as he registered at the hotel, he was off to see the President and the Secretary of War. Preferring modesty to praise, he did not linger to be lionized, but as quickly as he could complete his business, headed for the frontier, staying only one night and a half day at the seat of government.

Hays was promoted to the rank of major and ordered to keep one hundred and fifty spies and mounted rangers stationed along the frontier between San Antonio and the Río Grande to cover the border settlements, to preserve order and suppress banditti groups operating in the area, to

[1] John W. Lockhart quoted in Mrs. Jonnie Lockhart Wallis and Laurance. L. Hill, *Sixty Years on the Brazos: The Life and Letters of Dr. John Washington Lockhart, 1824–1900*, p. 117.

watch the activities of the Mexicans along the Río Grande, and to challenge the predatory visitations of the country's foes. En route to San Antonio the young ranger major went through the Guadalupe counties seeking recruits, but found little enthusiasm for enlistment among the western settlers. His enlistments by early September scarcely totaled fifty men.[2] The indifference of the west, no doubt, discouraged aid from the eastern counties. Again poverty ruled.

Commenting upon the difficulty of recruiting for the ranger service, the Secretary of War said, "Those who had been most active and efficient for the past two years in that kind of service had either exhausted their subsistence in the purchase of horses, equipments, and supplies, expended in the public service, for they have not been remunerated, or were compelled to withdraw from it to attend to their respective vocations. Hence few men could be found at once able to mount and equip themselves and willing to enter a service which promised little else than fatigue and danger. Those who were willing to enlist were for the most part utterly destitute of means to fit themselves for the field; the government was equally so—it could neither furnish the means to equip and mount a force, nor sustain them for any length of time when in the field."[3] Although Hays could not increase his force, he was able to send out a few spies to watch the roads and river crossings, particularly those on the Nueces, to warn of the approach of any hostile force. If the enemy could be kept beyond the Río Grande, the entire southern frontier would be protected and access afforded to a gradually increasing supply of beef, mules, and horses on which to subsist, pack supplies, mount rangers, and work the crops. Hays' force could not be expected to withstand any serious challenge from south of the border, even though it has been said that the Texas ranger combined the fighting qualities of three races, being able, as Professor Walter P. Webb expresses it, to "ride like a Mexican, trail like an Indian, shoot like a Tennessean, and fight like the devil."[4]

As a result of the Mexican raid on San Antonio in March 1842, countless Indian forays along the fringe of civilization, and the abandonment of the capital by the President, his cabinet, and other officers, the western frontier was rapidly becoming depopulated.

[2] *Telegraph and Texas Register*, Sept. 7, 1842.
[3] Report of the Secretary of War, Nov. 12, 1842, in *Telegraph and Texas Register*, Jan. 4, 1843.
[4] Walter Prescott Webb, *The Texas Rangers*, p. 15.

Tranquillity again reigns on the western frontier, [wrote the editor of the *Telegraph*] but it is the tranquillity of desolation. The country from the Guadalupe to the Nueces, lately dotted over with many smiling farms, is now transformed into a silent desert, and most of the once happy settlers are wending their way with their wretched, starving families towards the more secure districts of middle Texas, again to depend upon charity for their daily bread. Many still turn imploring looks to the Government for aid in vain. They might as well expect a living voice to issue from the dull, cold marble, as to expect aid from this quarter. . . . The western pioneers may turn back for a season, but it is only to gain strength and then rush forward like the mountain torrent, bearing down whatever obstacles oppose them.[5]

"Poor Austin," moaned one of Lamar's correspondents, "has sadly changed since you saw it, as indeed, has all the Western part of the Country. We have now but a small population—no business—and are living under great privations,"[6] while many of our friends and relatives still languish in Mexican prisons. By the middle of June 1842, business at San Antonio was at a standstill and the gloom of desolation hovered over the city. Only ten or fifteen Americans remained in the place.[7] The crack of the rifle, the whirring of the deadly arrow, the taking of women and children into captivity, where they were subjected to all the horrors of hell, made the boldest tremble and ask themselves, "Will it pay to remain here longer?" "Many of the Citizens have so long borne the brunt of frontier troubles that they are truly War worn, and in means worn out," wrote P. Hansbrough Bell, adjutant general, while on an inspection tour of the frontier. "The West has constituted a chain of sentinels to the Republic until the relief-hour has arrived."[8] No Mexican troops had been seen east of the Río Grande for many weeks. Yet, the Mexicans at Béxar were confident that Colonel Seguin would soon visit San Antonio with a large detachment of Mexican troops.[9]

The citizens of Victoria County met at the City Hall, Victoria, on July 30, 1842, "to consult upon and adopt proper measures to protect themselves and property from the Mexican enemy."[10] The meeting was

[5] *Telegraph and Texas Register*, Aug. 31, 1842.

[6] James Webb to M. B. Lamar, Austin, May 4, 1843, in *Lamar Papers*, IV, pt. I, pp. 19–20.

[7] *Telegraph and Texas Register*, Sept. 7, 1842.

[8] P. Hansbrough Bell, Adjt-Gen. of Militia, to Branch T. Archer, Secretary of War and Navy, Victoria, Nov. 21, 1841, in *Lamar Papers*, II, 592–594.

[9] *Telegraph and Texas Register*, Sept. 7, 1842.

[10] Richard Roman, H[amilton] Ledbetter, James D. Owen, and Others to Sam Houston, Victoria, July 30, 1842, in *ibid.*, Aug. 24, 1842.

The Frontier during the Late Summer

presided over by James D. Owen. After the assemblage was called to order, William Van Norman and the Reverend William C. Blair explained the object of the meeting. A committee was then appointed to draft a preamble and resolutions, which were unanimously adopted and which read as follows:

Whereas, the movements of our Mexican enemy indicate in the most convincing manner, that the time has arrived when it is imperative on the western frontier to choose one of three alternatives to wit: —1st, of tame submission to their terms. 2d, the abandonment of our homes for a residence in Middle or Eastern Texas. 3dly, of making the utmost possible resistance to their incursions. And whereas the late veto message of our Executive, Sam Houston, renders all prospect of government aid hopeless; and whereas we still retain confidence in the existence of a sufficiency of patriotism in our fellow citizens, when properly called into requisition, to maintain inviolate from the sword of the enemy our homes and our sacred institutions—Therefore be it

Resolved, That our exposed situation be made known to our patriotic fellow citizens of the western and other portions of the Republic, and that our reliance for safety is in a well concerted plan of defence by citizens acting without aid from our government.

Resolved, That for the purpose of securing aid and concert of action on this subject, we appoint a committee of five persons, who shall communicate with the citizens of the neighboring counties, and earnestly solicit their aid and immediate co-operation against the aggressions of the enemy, by the adoption of such plans as their wisdom and justice may dictate; and to report as early as practicable to the Chairman of this meeting.

Resolved further, That the said Committee be required to address his Excellency the President, setting forth the reasons which have impelled us to the adoption of the foregoing measures; and that they shall specially make known our abiding devotion to the Laws and Constitution of the Republic.

Resolved further, That the Committee shall likewise petition the patriotic citizens of every section of the Republic, setting forth the dangers to which we are exposed, and soliciting such aid as may be in their power to extend.

Resolved, That we tender to the brave volunteers, officers and soldiers, who so promptly hastened to our relief when threatened by the invasion of a barbarous foe, our sincere thanks. And that we consider them entitled to the gratitude of our government and the friends of liberty throughout the Republic.

Resolved, That the thanks of the citizens of the county be tendered to Capt. Cameron, and his company for the efficient service they have rendered the west.

Resolved, That the editor of the Colorado Gazette, and other editors

283

friendly to the protection of the country, be requested to publish the fore-going proceedings.

Charles M. Creanor offered the following substitute resolution, which was rejected:

Resolved, That it is expedient that all citizens of Victoria County remove to the eastern side of the Colorado river.

After the adoption of these resolutions, the following were appointed a committee of correspondence: William Van Norman, Richard Roman, Hamilton Ledbetter, John McHenry, and A. S. Cunningham.

To this request of the citizens of Victoria, President Houston replied that he was fully cognizant of the condition of the western section of the Republic, and that he had always rendered such protection and assistance as his means and power would enable him to do.

My own purse would not sustain, even a single day, a force upon the frontier sufficient to give protection. The appropriation made by the first session of the last Congress would not suffice to sustain a single company upon the border. . . . We are in trouble, but that trouble has not been brought upon the country by the present administration [he gave them to understand]. It existed when the present Executive came into office. Our difficulties have not been increased, but are only the more manifest, because the evils produced by the last are fully disclosed in the poverty of our present condition. The present Executive has not hundreds to expend where the last had *millions.* . . . To those who apply the kind terms and epithets of *enemy* and *traitor* to me, I can only reply, "I have done as much for my country as you have, and have realized as little as you could have done from it."

If those who seek to create discontent or destroy confidence in the government and its officers, . . . would step forward and level their rifles against the Mexican enemy, when desired to do so by the President, it would have a tendency to give more protection to the frontier than all the abuse that can ever be directed against him. . . . Those who wish to embark in war against Mexico [he concluded] will find that the President has done everything in his power to give it forwardness. If the people wish to fight, they have its authority and besides the encouragement he has given to them, they have his sincere wishes for the most perfect success and glory in the proposed campaign.[11]

Thus did Houston attempt to throw the responsibility for frontier defense back upon his critics and political opponents.

[11] Sam Houston to Richard Roman, H. Ledbetter, James D. Owen and Others, City of Houston, Aug. 10, 1842, *Writings of Sam Houston,* III, 142–145; *Telegraph and Texas Register,* Aug. 24, 1842.

Naturally, the opposition was not happy with Houston's reply, but there was little that the westerners could do toward promoting offensive action against Mexico other than to follow the plan outlined by the President.

We have long been of the opinion [declared the editor of the *Telegraph*[12]] that the only method by which the western citizens could relieve themselves from impending difficulties, was by a firm, decided and energetic movement, like the one thus taken by the citizens of Victoria. "Heaven helps those who help themselves"; and if the western citizens had, at an earlier period united in their own defence and struck one effectual blow upon the dastardly enemy that violated their territory, we believe thousands would have nobly rushed to aid them in the glorious cause. Such, however, has been the apathy manifested, that we have been constrained to believe, that their inaction was lately owing to a want of ability on their part. We hope we have been mistaken.

Then, as if outlining the sequence of events that were soon to follow, and no doubt exerting great influence on the future conduct of the westerners in defense of the frontier, the editor wrote,

The Government too will doubtless lend its aid; but this will be, we fear, as it has been feeble as a broken reed. It is something, however, to have its authority; and such confidence may be inspired by the knowledge that the President has given his free assent to the measure. Those who really desire to aid in forwarding the measure, will have the consolation of knowing that they are acting by his authority. This is the more important at this time, for it will tend to dissipate the impression that has gone abroad, that the offer of England and the United States to mediate betwen Texas and Mexico, would impose upon our Government the necessity of suspending hostilities. We are now assured that the policy of the Executive will not be changed on this account, and that no orders will be given to suspend in the least degree his former orders. The land forces and the navy will be left free to prosecute the war, against Mexico, as vigorously as *their situation will warrant*. If, therefore, the citizens of the West have the ability and the inclination to commence the campaign, now is the appropriate season for prompt and decisive action, and no time should be lost in useless and unprofitable delay or in casting idle reproaches [like] he [Houston] is casting upon the former administration. A few more weeks only should elapse ere the question is finally determined. If the citizens of the West, after due deliberation and with a full knowledge of their own resources, decide for offensive measures, we believe the whole country will cheerfully co-operate with them; but if they shall determine otherwise, there will be but one alternative left. The country must resume its

[12] *Telegraph and Texas Register*, Aug. 31, 1842.

former defensive policy, and the people of the West will again be under the necessity of waiting with folded arms until some kind interposition of Providence shall decide their destiny.

Although the Victoria meeting did not formally recommend that people in the area move to the east side of the Colorado River for greater safety, many persons in the county did so for their own security. Early in August seven or eight Texan spies went down to the station of Aubrey & Kinney, but found that Aubrey and a part of his company had gone to Galveston and that the remaining settlers in San Patricio County, with the exception of a widow at the old station of Aubrey & Kinney at Corpus Christi, had removed to the east side of the Guadalupe.[13] In the evening after the arrival of the Texan spies at the trading post at Corpus Christi, about twenty-five Mexican soldiers came in, apparently to reconnoiter the place, and stopped at a short distance from the fort. While the Mexicans waited, as if undetermined whether to attack the fort or not, two of the Texans crept up near them and shot two of the company. The remainder fled instantly. It was presumed that they had been sent by Canales as spies.[14] The Texans immediately left the station and returned to Victoria. By August 10 all troops at Lamar were removed to Victoria, which now became the extreme frontier town in that quarter. All Texans and Anglo-Americans, including the families of Judge Robinson and Campbell, had moved to the east side of the Colorado, but about fifty Mexican families remained at Carlos Rancho, or New La Bahía, and were viewed with suspicion by the Anglo-Texans; yet, "they appear . . . to be inoffensive, and probably temporarize with both parties like the Mexicans at Béxar," it was said, "in order to maintain their homes undisturbed."[15] Many of the inhabitants along the Navidad were preparing to move their families east of the Brazos, where they might enjoy the blessings of security and peace.[16] Captain Ewen Cameron with approximately fifty rangers was encamped a few miles above Victoria, at the Paso del Gobernador (Governor's Pass) on the Guadalupe, and the citizens of that section of the frontier were represented as "preparing to organize themselves into a company to join any expedition that might be fitted out from the East; but so much un-

13 *Ibid.*
14 *Ibid.*
15 *Ibid.*, Aug. 24, 1842.
16 *Ibid.*, Aug. 3, 1842.

286

certainty and doubt existed . . . they hardly knew what course to pursue."[17]

By early September the settlers in the lower country around Victoria had determined to solve their own problems of defense and with remarkable unanimity had pledged themselves to sustain their ground. Their resolution "had a singular effect in restoring confidence, and strange to say, Victoria, that was recently almost entirely deserted," was again resounding to the busy hum of returning settlers.[18] It was reported in Houston on September 8 by a gentleman just arrived from Victoria that almost all of the houses that were recently vacant there were again occupied by the families who had returned and that even one or two new houses were under construction. "The farms around the village and along the Guadalupe are again exhibiting the evidences of cultivation," reported the editor of the *Telegraph*.

A bold and chivalrous leader, too, has at length sprung forth, who already by his valor and military skill promises to become the Bruce of the West [Captain Ewen Cameron], a soldier worthy of the most heroic of his Scottish ancestors. Unaided by government with even so much as an encouraging word, he has, with indefatigable zeal and the most indomitable energy, mustered a little band, determined to be the last in the retreat, and if necessary to form the rear-guard of the retiring settlers. . . . Encouraged by his gallant bearing and the assurances he gave, that while there was a single beef or morsel of bread on the western frontier for his soldiers, their good blades shall be unsheathed in its defence, [continued the editor of the Houston paper], the settlers resumed confidence.[19]

In the meantime, Cameron's band had grown from less than thirty men to seventy or eighty. Having resided for several years in the Mexican provinces adjoining the Río Grande, Cameron had become well acquainted with the roads and mountain passes, so that an expedition into the enemy's country, whenever his force should become sufficient in size to undertake one, could be conducted with a certainty of success.

Already talk of getting up an expedition against Mexico was underway in the east, where General Hunt is reported to have found, during his recent visit, great enthusiasm for an offensive war against Mexico.[20] This enthusiasm among certain elements of the population, and espe-

[17] *Ibid.*, Aug. 24, 1842.
[18] *Ibid.*, Sept. 14, 1842.
[19] *Ibid.*
[20] *Ibid.*, July 20, 1842.

cially among the adventurers from the United States, did not die out
with the collapse of the summer campaign, and there was talk of getting
up another expedition in the fall. On August 2 Captain B. Owen Payne,
with a company of twenty-one volunteers, reached Houston from New
York, after having arrived at New Orleans by water, and proceeding
thence by boat to Alexandria and from there marching overland into
Texas. Learning that the army at Lipantitlán had disbanded, Payne and
several enterprising citizens at Houston announced their intention of
raising a company of volunteers to join the western troops in an expedition against Mexico. Several of Jordan's "old soldiers" were in town
and willing to join such an enterprise, provided they could obtain the
arms and equipment necessary for the campaign. A few days after his
arrival, Payne was named captain of ordnance, succeeding Captain
David Ross, deceased,[21] and was thus made responsible for the meager
quantity of ordnance and ordnance stores at Houston.[22]

The people were most impetuous in their demands that the government establish order on the frontier and accord protection to life and
property, and Houston was determined to do something, although Congress had been irresponsible in its policy of frontier defense and in providing for an invasion of Mexico. There being no inclination on the part
of Mexico to accept the friendly offices of neutral powers to mediate,
Texas was inclined to establish an active and efficient blockade of Mexican ports and "to prosicute [*sic*] hostilities vigorously by land."[23] But
ever, "the first wish of the President's heart," declared the Acting Secretary of State, was "to bring about an amicable adjustment of the long
continued and profitless difficulties" between the two countries.[24]

Playing a shrewd game of politics at home and abroad, President

[21] *Ibid.*, Aug. 3 and 17, 1842. Payne's appointment was confirmed by the Senate
on December 14, 1842. E. W. Winkler (ed.), *Secret Journals of the Senate, Republic of Texas, 1836–1845,* pp. 231–232.

[22] Captain of Ordnance, B. Owen Payne, received the following ordnance and
ordnance supplies from Jacob Snively, Acting Quartermaster General: 33 Jenk's
Patent carbines, 57 muskets with bayonets, 243 bars of lead, 1 set harness (incomplete), 10 horse collars, 24 wipers (for carbines), 2 thumb vices, 1 pair brass bullet
molds, 17 screw drivers, 13 flint caps, 143 musket flints, 11 rifle flints, 2 bags of
small shot, 3 felling axes, 13 small blank books, and 2 broken kegs of powder.
Receipt of B. Owen Payne, Capt. of Ordnance, given to J. Snively, Acting Quartermaster Genl., Augt. 11, 1842, in Army Papers (Texas), ms.

[23] G. W. Terrell to Ashbel Smith, Department of State, Houston, Aug. 20, 1842,
in George P. Garrison (ed.), *Diplomatic Correspondence of Texas,* in *Annual
Report of the American Historical Association,* 1908, III, 1004–1006.

[24] *Ibid.*

Houston continued his plan for invading Mexico after the breakup of Davis' command near Lipantitlán. Having placed the responsibility for the bankrupt financial condition of the country squarely upon Congress, he was determined, he said, to perform to the best of his ability the duties of his office as prescribed by law, in spite of the fact that the called session of the Congress had adjourned in July without making adequate provision for frontier defense. Although the idea of recruiting volunteers in the United States was now given up, the President still indicated his willingness to receive any who might come to conduct a civilized and honorable warfare without permitting "the love of spoil to tarnish his escutcheon or renown."[25] Two days before General Davis was relieved of his command, the President outlined in a circular letter sent on July 26 to the senior militia officer in each county west of the Trinity plans for a campaign, designed "to produce to the enemy the most serious annoyance."[26] He proposed to raise nineteen companies of 66 men each, plus 100 Lipans and Tonkawas, making in all a total of 1,354 mounted men. These were to be equipped, he said, at their own expense, as the Government was to furnish "nothing but authority to march" and such supplies of ammunition as might be "needful for the campaign." The volunteers would be permitted to elect their own company officers and, at the point of general rendezvous, to choose the field officers for one regiment. As for compensation, "they must look to the valley of the Río Grande," the President declared. "The Government will claim no portion of the *spoils*. They will be divided among the victors. The Flag of Texas will accompany the expedition," he said. The latter announcement was of considerable importance. The government of the United States had formally announced, and the other nations with which Texas had treaties had intimated, that Mexico would be required to observe toward the soldiers of Texas captured during the war all the mercy and kindness due prisoners of war. In order to entitle them to such treatment, it would be necessary that the persons captured should be bona fide soldiers of Texas, fighting under the flag of Texas, and acting under the orders and authority of the government, and not mere marauders, or men fighting for plunder or revenge, without the sanction of law or the authority of a recognized government.

Houston proposed to raise the required number of volunteers west of

[25] Houston to Col. William Christy, New Orleans, dated City of Houston, August 15, 1842, in *Writings of Sam Houston*, IV, 134–135.

[26] G. W. Terrell to Ashbel Smith, Department of State, Houston, Aug. 20, 1842, in Garrison (ed.), *Diplomatic Correspondence of Texas*, 1908, III, 1004–1006.

the Trinity River, in order to conserve the food supplies in the western part of the country and prevent emigration from that area for want of supplies. The time for assembling was to be set by the President at some future date, but the rendezvous point on the western frontier for the troops was to be at the Sulphur Spring near the mouth of the Cíbolo, where "they will prepare the requisite amount of provisions from cattle contributed to sustain them till they reach the Río Grande." Because of its scarcity, grain was not to be fed the horses while going to the point of rendezvous or while the volunteers remained upon the Texas frontier.

The expedition, he declared, would be authorized to cross the Río Grande and make such reprisals upon Mexico "as civilized and honorable warfare will justify in our present relations with our common enemy." As soon as the troops were mustered in their respective counties and had elected their own officers, they were to report to the War Department for further orders. To prevent discontent from developing, the troops would be retained at the rendezvous point only long enough to permit them to be organized. Once across the Río Grande, they would be permitted to remain in the enemy's country until Texan independence was recognized, an armistice concluded, or it was deemed wise for the safety of the expedition to recross the river. The commander of the expedition, although enjoying great discretion in the field because of the detached nature of the army, would at all times be subject to the orders of the War Department. Two companies were to be raised from each of the following counties: Washington, Bastrop, Fayette, Montgomery, Jackson (including Victoria), and one each from Robertson, Milam, Austin, Fort Bend, Harris, Gonzales, Matagorda, Colorado (including Ward), and Béxar (including Hays and Menchaca).[27]

Although he desired to afford protection to the frontier and check emigration eastward, the President was aware that if he had sanctioned the "War bill" passed by Congress earlier in the month "threats of revolution would have been constant." "As it now stands," he informed Anson Jones, Secretary of State, "there can be no censure upon the Executive. All that has been desired is embraced in the project [for a campaign]; and for my country's sake, and for the credit of those who have been so anxious, I sincerely hope there will be volunteers enough to answer the design of a visit to the Río Grande. We will see!"[28] A

[27] Circular Letter Concerning the Campaign Against Mexico, City of Houston, July 26, 1842, in *Writings of Sam Houston*, III, 128–131; Sam Houston to Col. Joe L. Bennett, City of Houston, July 26, 1842, in *ibid.*, IV, 129–131.

[28] Houston to Anson Jones, City of Houston, Aug. 2, 1842, in *ibid.*, III, 137–138;

regular, formal invasion would, in Houston's estimation be not only difficult but impolitic. However, wrote Houston, "those who wish to embark in a war against Mexico will find that the President has done everything in his power to give it forwardness."

Colonel Owen was ordered to collect all the ammunition and other government supplies scattered along the Victoria-Refugio-Corpus Christi frontier from the breakup of the expedition under Davis' command.[29] A large quantity of various supplies was supposed to be in Victoria County.[30] In July Colonel John H. Moore was authorized to raise a corps of two hundred volunteers for the defense of the western frontier. "He is an old commander," commented the editor of the *Civilian and Galveston Gazette*,[31] "and never has been known to discharge a body of men until they have fought a battle." "If the Mexican force cannot be found on this side of the Río Grande," declared the *Telegraph and Texas Register*,[32] "these troops will pass that stream as readily as they would cross the little rivulets of the Cibolo." The naming of Moore was supposed to quiet the westerners and give them more confidence in the Houston policies. Men in the west were responding with considerable alacrity to the call for volunteers. Colonel James R. Cook of Washington County, it was announced in Houston on August 10,[33] had, upon receipt of the President's orders, "cheerfully commenced enlisting recruits, and had already engaged a large number to join his company. . . . many of the young men of Washington County," it was said, "had been long preparing for the campaign," and had obeyed the order with utmost promptness. For several weeks past citizens in the west had been preparing for the campaign, by fattening their horses, preparing buckskin clothing, and drying beef and venison. They were expecting to be called out by draft about August 1.[34] The Houston *Telegraph* emphasized that if a county furnished more volunteers than its assigned quota,

---

Same to Richard Roman, H. Ledbetter, and Others, City of Houston, Aug. 10, 1842, in *ibid.*, III, 142–145. Roman and Ledbetter had been members of a committee of six to draft the Victoria resolutions calling upon the Government and eastern counties for assistance. *Telegraph and Texas Register*, Aug. 24, 1842.

[29] Sam Houston to Col. C. L. Owen, Executive Department, City of Houston, Aug. 18, 1842, in *Writings of Sam Houston*, III, 146.

[30] [Sam Houston] to [M.C.] Hamilton, City of Houston, Sept. 20, 1842, in *ibid.*, III, 162–163.

[31] July 24, 1842.

[32] July 27, 1842.

[33] *Telegraph and Texas Register*, Aug. 10, 1842.

[34] *Ibid.*, Aug. 3, 1842.

they would be received and none would be restrained by the Executive.[35] Although it is expected, continued the editor of the *Telegraph* that a sufficient number of volunteers west of the Trinity and "troops from the United States" will turn out to capture the whole of the enemy's country east of the mountains, any volunteers from east of the Trinity who should like to join the expedition will be permitted to do so, "provided they can bring a supply of provisions so as not to forage upon the already suffering counties of the West." The impressment of horses, cattle, corn, or other articles will not be sanctioned.

Simultaneously with these preparations and apparently with the idea of distracting Mexico's attention from the assembling of troops on the Cíbolo by striking at one of her weakest points—the northwestern frontier—and at the same time administering retribution for the injuries and cruelties inflicted by the authorities in New Mexico upon the Santa Fé prisoners, Charles A. Warfield was authorized by the Secretary of War on August 16 to raise an expedition to raid New Mexico.[36] Warfield was given a colonel's commission and told that he might commission all subordinate officers with the assurance that his appointments would be confirmed by the government of Texas. He was told that during the war, or until further orders, his command would be considered as being in the Texas service, and that he had authority in the name of Texas, to levy contributions upon Mexican towns and capture Mexican property on condition that half of the spoils would be delivered to the Texas government. The other half of the spoils was to be distributed among the captors to supplement the public funds the Republic was expected to appropriate for the participants. Warfield was instructed to strive to conquer Santa Fé and such other towns as he might be able to take. All Mexican property was to be confiscated. After capturing Santa Fé, he was to await further instructions, and subsequent developments indicate that "the government had expected him to act immediately, for the purpose of attracting the attention of the New Mexicans while another Texan expedition was to cross the Río Grande in the Fall."[37] After oc-

[35] *Ibid.*

[36] George W. Hockley to Charles A. Warfield, Aug. 16, 1842, in U. S. Congress, *Senate Executive Documents*, 32nd Congress, 2nd Session, Vol. III, no. 14, pp. 117–118; *Telegraph and Texas Register*, May 3 and 17, 1843.

[37] William Campbell Binkley, "The Last Stage of Texan Military Operations Against Mexico, 1843," in *Southwestern Historical Quarterly*, XXII (1918–1919), 263. See also Anson Jones to Isaac Van Zandt, Department of State, Washington [Texas], June 8, 1843, in Garrison (ed.), *Diplomatic Correspondence of Texas*, II, 189. Warfield was acquainted with the country through which he would operate,

cupying Santa Fé, Warfield was to move down the river and join that force.

While these preparations were getting under way, the U.S. brig *Dolphin* touched at Galveston on July 30, six days from Vera Cruz, with news that the Santa Fé prisoners had been freed and would arrive at Galveston in a few days. The *Dolphin* also brought Mexican newspapers filled with reports of the forthcoming Mexican invasion of Texas.[38] On the 10th of August the U.S. brig *Boxer* arrived at Galveston from Vera Cruz, bringing Colonel William G. Cooke, Captain W. D. Houghton, and Dr. Richard F. Brenham of the recently released Santa Fé prisoners. Most of the Santa Fé men had their plans to return to Texas upset by the Mexican government's suddenly pressing all vessels at Vera Cruz into government service to transport troops to Yucatán. Finally, on August 21, "a Brig with a white flag at her fore and Mexican at her Pique came in" to Galveston with Colonel Hugh McLeod and 182 of the Santa Fé prisoners after a cruise of ten days.[39] Visitors who went aboard the vessel about dusk, after it had come to anchor three miles below town, found the men "little else than a sluggish moving mass of sun-burnt visages and ill-clothed. . . . The effluvia on board was unpleasant. . . . There were sundry reports of 'yellow fever' being on board. A Captain [John J.] Holliday had died on the passage. The men appeared well generally—some observed that 'they had had enough of such expeditions,' some 'that they were ready for another'."[40]

On August 20 Joseph Eve, the United States chargé d'affaires in Texas, received dispatches from his government directing him to express to the Texan government that it would be to its interest "to suspend any offensive military operations which may be in contemplation against Mexico" until the results of the negotiations to be undertaken by Waddy Thompson in Mexico should be known.[41] General Thompson had been commissioned United States envoy extraordinary and minister plenipotentiary to Mexico on February 10, 1842, with instructions on April 5

having lived for many years in New Mexico and traveled much over the southern Rocky Mountain region. His plan of raising a force of eight hundred to a thousand men in Texas and from the western frontier of the United States by May 15, 1843, soon melted away.

[38] *Bollaert's Texas*, pp. 125–126.

[39] *Ibid.*, pp. 130–131.

[40] *Ibid.*

[41] Joseph Eve to Joseph Waples, Legation of the United States, Galveston, August 12, 1842, Garrison (ed.), *Diplomatic Correspondence of Texas*, I, 581.

to demand the release of the Santa Fé prisoners who were citizens of the United States and to require that the Texan prisoners be treated as prisoners of war and be given treatment "according to the usage of modern times and civilized states."[42]

Joseph Eve, the United States chargé d'affaires, and Charles Elliot, the British chargé d'affaires in Texas, who had only recently arrived, solicited and obtained a joint conference on September 10 with President Houston.[43] The governments of their countries, it was pointed out, were both endeavoring to promote an amicable adjustment of the difficulties between Texas and Mexico. The Texan blockade of Mexican ports disturbed their governments greatly. While they did not deny the right of Texas to institute such a blockade, they believed it was not one that was conducted according to international law and that it would in the end lead to trouble. After listening to Eve's and Elliot's protest of the blockade in the name of their respective governments, Houston proposed to them (provided they were clothed with such powers) that "if they would immediately correspond with Genl Reyes and other Mexican Commanders on the Frontier, and obtain a cessation to the predatory warfare being carried on, that then he would withdraw the blockade, but while the Mexicans were annoying us," he said, "we were right in annoying and crippling their resources on the Gulf." The foreign agents, however, did not believe their instructions would permit them to correspond with Mexican military officers on such matters, but they told him "they would feel themselves authorized to write to the representatives of their Governments in Mexico, and request them to urge upon that Govt. the improper policy they were pursuing, at the same time they would inform their Govts. of having so written, and request them to instruct those Representatives to demand of the Mexican Govt. a cessation of its predatory incursions in this country, and the uncivilized warfare, it was carrying on."[44] Eve and Elliot declared that their governments were seeking through Pakenham and Thompson in Mexico to bring about an early recognition by Mexico of the independ-

[42] Daniel Webster to Waddy Thompson, Washington, April 5, 1842, William R. Manning (ed.), *Diplomatic Correspondence of the United States: Inter-American Affairs*, Vol. 8, pp. 105–108. See also Dudley G. Wooten (ed.), *A Comprehensive History of Texas, 1685 to 1897*, I, 383.

[43] Joseph Eve to Joseph Waples, Legation of the United States, Houston, Sept. 10, 1842, in Garrison (ed.), *Diplomatic Correspondence of Texas*, 1907, I, 605–606.

[44] Memorandum of Conference between Houston and Eve and Elliot, Sept. 10, 1842, in *ibid.*, I, 606–607; Joseph Waples to Joseph Eve, Department of State, Texas [dated:] Houston, Sept. 14, 1842, in *ibid.*, I, 608.

ence of Texas, and that if Texas kept up the blockade it was calculated to injure the commerce of her friends and would constitute an obstacle to their effort and would likely "dampen their ardor in the cause." Houston responded that in the light of these considerations and the inefficiency of the Texan blockade he would give the matter immediate consideration, and recommended that they put their request in writing to which he would give a prompt reply. This was done, and after a second interview, on the 11th, he assured them he would issue a proclamation on the 12th lifting the blockade, which he did.

The blockade had failed to accomplish its purpose and had only irritated the foreign merchants and their governments, particularly the English, who had a very profitable commerce with Mexico.[45] Furthermore, by September Houston seems to have concluded that it would be almost impossible to get together an adequate invading force. "I have used all my endeavors," he wrote Owen, "to get up an efficient force to give the whole country its independence and safety. If it has failed, the fault is not the government's; for all has been done that can be done by its officers. The want of will to do so, is not in the government, but must rest somewhere else."[46] Peace was believed inevitable, and no invasion was expected by the Texans at San Antonio.[47]

Early in September, Colonel Clark L. Owen of Texana and Major "Jack" Hays at San Antonio were instructed to look after the peace and safety of the frontier and to open it to traders from Mexico who were reported on their way to Texas, if the trade were likely to be advantageous to the people of the frontier. It was believed that reopening and encouraging a revival of trade between San Antonio and the Río Grande valley would give an opportunity to obtain reliable information about the movement and intention of Mexican troops. It was also thought that, since further predatory incursions would adversely affect any trade which might develop with the Río Grande Mexicans, they themselves would constantly exert pressure in favor of peace and would probably, said Houston, "let us know of anything which would interrupt their trade."[48]

[45] J. Morgan to Doctor Ashbel Smith, New Washington, Galveston Bay, Texas, Aug. 20, 1842, in Ashbel Smith Papers, 1838–1842, ms.

[46] Sam Houston to Clark L. Owen, City of Houston, Sept. 2, 1842, in *Writings of Sam Houston*, III, 152–153.

[47] E. W. Winkler (ed.), "The Béxar and Dawson Prisoners," in *Quarterly of the Texas State Historical Association*, XIII (1909–1910), 294.

[48] Houston to Clark L. Owen, City of Houston, Sept. 2, 1842, in *Writings of Sam*

Such was the situation when, on September 10, intelligence was received at San Antonio from two confidential Mexican spies that a force under General Adrián Woll, a Frenchman in the service of Mexico, was approaching the town which it expected to enter the next morning.[49]

Houston, III, 152–153; Same to Major John C. Hays, City of Houston, Sept. 14, 1842, in *ibid.,* IV, 144–146.

[49] John C. Hays to Secretary of War, Seguin, Sept. 12, 1842, in Texas Congress, *Journals of the House of Representatives of the Seventh Congress, convened at Washington, on the 14th November, 1842,* Appendix, p. 16.

CHAPTER FOURTEEN

The Mexicans Again Seize San Antonio

THE MEXICAN GOVERNMENT was determined that the repulse of Canales should be avenged and that the southwestern frontier of Texas should be kept in a state of constant excitement. There was nothing like waving the flag and keeping the Texas question before the eyes of the people to justify the tyranny practiced upon them by their rulers. After General Antonio López de Santa Anna had, through the use of force, reestablished himself on October 9, 1841, as provisional president, he had in accordance with the Bases of Tacubaya issued orders for the convocation of a Congress to frame a new constitution. Before the Congress convened, however, it was apparent that, in spite of Santa Anna's intimidations and interference in the elections, the Liberals (or Federalists) and not Santa Anna's followers would control the Congress and that they would write a constitution that would cut short the despotism that destroyed the liberties of the people.[1]

The very day that Congress met, therefore, Santa Anna presented to it the Texas issue. He notified Congress that measures had been taken to replenish the poverty-stricken treasury and to institute a prompt opening of a new campaign to restore the territory of Texas to the Supreme Government.[2] On June 10, 1842, the President declared,

My principal attention is directed and fixed on the territory of Texas, which has been usurped to the end of making possible other usurpations. The struggle [that has] commenced is vital to the Republic; and if she conserve the honorable name that she enjoys in the civilized world, it is necessary that employing her energy and consuming her resources, she combat without intermission and at cost of whatever sacrifices until her arms and her rights triumph. The army is preparing for this noble work, and on this day,

[1] Hubert Howe Bancroft, *History of Mexico*, V, 252–255.
[2] José María Tornel, Circular to the Governor and Commandant Generals of the Departments, Ministry of War and Marine, Mexico, July 6, 1842, in *El Cosmopolita*, July 20, 1842.

forever memorable, in which the national representation [legislature] assembles, it pleases me to make known to you the opinions of my government, the desires of the army and the interest of the people.[3]

It required more than this, however, to whip up excitement in Mexico for any administration, where public money had for years been so callously squandered by whatever party that happened to be in power.

To give you some idea of the Gaspillage [wastefulness] going on even at Vera Cruz, [reported the commander of H.M. Sloop *Comus*] I heard it repeated over and over again that the Battery erected against the [Texan] Schooner San Bernard was merely to draw money out of the Treasury, the Sand Bags cost nearly 7,000 Dollars, and [were] afterwards resold:—the Military and those employed pocketed nearly two thirds of the sum; it is in this manner the public Money is frittered away from one end of the Republic to the other.[4]

While instructions went out to launch another expedition against the Texas frontier, Santa Anna, finding his prestige waning, sought in other ways to beat the drums and call attention to the sacrifices and daring deeds he was supposed to have rendered the country which should ever be grateful to the military hero. The leg that he had lost four years earlier defending the homeland against the French was buried in September 1842, in an imposing public ceremony, and before the end of the month another monument was erected in commemoration of the defeat of the Spaniards under Barradas in 1829. Since Santa Anna had shared in the latter campaign, a medal was struck with a laudatory inscription about the dictator. Failing, however, to stem the rising tide of unpopularity, he finally decided to retire on October 26, 1842, to his estate at Manga de Clavo, leaving the government in the hands of Nicolás Bravo, as president of the council. The real executive though was the

---

[3] Message to Congress, June 10, 1842, in *ibid.*, June 11, 1842.

[4] Evan Nepean to Commander P. T. Douglas, H. M. Sloop "Comus," Jamaica, July 24, 1841 (confidential), in Ephraim D. Adams (ed.), "Correspondence from the British Archives Concerning Texas," in *Quarterly of the Texas State Historical Association*, XV (1911–1912), 240–243. See also James Webb to James S. Mayfield, Galveston, June 29, 1841, in George P. Garrison (ed.), *Diplomatic Correspondence of Texas*, in *Annual Report of the American Historical Association*, 1908, II, 751–752; James Webb to Richard Pakenham, On Board the Texan Schooner San Bernard, Harbor of Sacrificios, near Vera Cruz, June 1, 1841, in *ibid.*, 1908, II, 753–755.

minion of Santa Anna, José María Tornel, the Minister of War, under whose direction the Texas campaign had been launched.[5]

General Isidro Reyes, who had served since February 1842, as commandant general of the Department of Coahuila[6] and as second-in-command of the Army of the North, was made commander-in-chief of that army on May 28 upon the retirement of General Mariano Arista,[7] and was instructed by the President on June 5 to prepare General Woll's Division for a second attack upon San Antonio.[8] On the afternoon of June 27 Reyes reached Matamoros on his tour of inspection of the frontier defenses;[9] but, as we have already seen, his attention was temporarily diverted by the Texan army being assembled at Lipantitlán. After this difficulty was resolved, late in July an order was issued for the establishment of councils in the towns of northern Mexico to collect donations for continuing the war against Texas,[10] and with the reopening of trade on the frontier, Mexican spies in the person of traders began to infiltrate the western settlements of Texas. During July and August, the Mexican Army of the North, commanded by Major General Reyes, who had taken up his headquarters at San Fernando, recruited men and supplies for another raid into Texas.[11]

News of the outfitting and sailing of the Mexican steamers from England was creating "some little uneasiness at *Galveston*," reported James Morgan, and Commodore Moore was preparing to give them a warm

[5] Bancroft, *History of Mexico*, V, 253–254.

[6] *El Cosmopolita*, Feb. 26, 1842; Alberto M. Carreño (ed.), *Jefes del ejército mexicano en 1847; Biografías de Generals de Division y de coronels del ejército mexicano por fines del año de 1847*, pp. 129–130.

[7] *El Cosmopolita*, Feb. 26 and June 25, 1842; General Mariano Arista á los habitantes de los departamentos de Tamaulipas, Nuevo León and Coahuila, Monterey, Mayo 28 de 1842, in *ibid.*, June 25, 1842. On May 3, 1843, General Reyes was named governor and commandant general of the Department of Puebla by the Provisional President. See José María Tornel á Isidro Reyes, Ministerio de guerra y Marina, Mayo 3 de 1843, in *ibid.*, May 10, 1843.

[8] Ministerio de Guerra y Marina: Memoria del Secretario de estado y del despacho de guerra y marina, leida á las camaras del Congreso nacional de la Republica Mexicana, en enero de 1844, in *Diario del Gobierno*, May 15, 1843.

[9] *El Cosmopolita*, July 20, 1842; *Telegraph and Texas Register*, August 17, 1842.

[10] "Expediente sobre la creación de una junta patriotica en esta capital para colectar donativos para la guerra de Téjas, Julio 30 de 1842," ms.

[11] See Circular á los primeras authoridades politicas del departamento Nuevo-León, [issued by the office of] secretaría del gobierno del departamento, Monterey, 15 de Agosto de 1842 [and signed by] Santiago Vidaurri, s[ecreta]rio, quoted from *El Semanario* (Monterey) in *El Cosmopolita*, Sept. 3, 1842.

reception should they steam along the Texas coast. "But a navy at best," he continued, "is an unpopular armament in Mexico; and when the cost and *daily* expense of these steamers are felt by that poor degraded, miserable, imbecile nation, you will find it will soon abandon that mode of warfare, and let the steamers rot, and go to the d—l, as their former navy did."[12] Colonel William G. Cooke, just returned from imprisonment in Mexico as a Santa Fé prisoner, reported the assembling of a large military force in that country, but believed that Santa Anna had no intention of invading Texas, and, if he did so, could not possibly send more than fifteen thousand troops across the Río Grande.

Such an invasion, [declared Morgan] would be a blessing rather than a curse to Texas. The readiness and ease with which we would meet and annihilate such a force would serve to exalt us, and give confidence abroad of our ability to protect our country from any attempt on the part of Mexico to subjugate this country; and we should have immigrants from all quarters, and of the right kind too, sufficient to populate our wastelands, protect our frontiers, and soon bring our country into notice by the vast amount of our exports. . . . We are safe, depend on it.[13]

Santa Anna's first objective was to subjugate Yucatán and to concentrate a large force for his own protection. It was Morgan's opinion that he did not care "a fig for Texas anyway."

News of the Mexican preparation began to reach Texas. A letter from Matamoros dated July 2[14] reported General Woll on the Río Grande with about twelve hundred men, and stated that his scouting parties were being pushed almost as far as Béxar. One of Hays' rangers, William A. A. ("Bigfoot") Wallace[15] informed his leader late in August or early

---

[12] J. Morgan to Doctor Ashbel Smith, New Washington, Galveston Bay, Texas, August 20, 1842, in Ashbel Smith Papers, 1838–1842, ms.

[13] *Ibid.*

[14] *Telegraph and Texas Register*, August 17, 1842.

[15] William Alexander Anderson Wallace, descendant of the great Scotch Highland fighters William Wallace and Robert Bruce, was born in Lexington, Virginia, April 3, 1817, the third son in a family of nine children, and died January 7, 1899, near Devine, Texas. He came to Texas from Virginia with his uncle Blair and cousin James Paxton, arriving on October 5, 1837, at Galveston on the *Diadem*, seeking adventure and an opportunity to kill Mexicans to avenge the massacre of his eldest brother, Samuel, his cousin William, and a distant relative, Major B. C. Wallace, at Goliad as members of Fannin's command. Wallace was a magnificent physical specimen. In the prime of life he stood six feet two inches "in his moccasins" and weighed 240 pounds without surplus fat. "His giant stature and childlike heart, his drollery and whimsicalness endeared him to the frontier people. His inexhausti-

September that there were at least a dozen strange Mexicans in San Antonio who were not permanent residents of the place. Cristobal Rubio, a desperate villain who was wanted in San Antonio and Seguin for many crimes, was reported to have been in San Antonio as a spy for the Mexicans. He was believed to be in hiding at the Mission San Juan Capistrano, nine miles down the river. Hays, with twenty rangers, proceeded to the Mission to arrest Rubio and one of his confederates. As the large gates of the Mission compound swung open in response to Hays' order, Rubio, caught by surprise, sought to hide behind one of them. Perceiving, however, that it would be almost impossible for him to avoid detection, Rubio changed his mind and endeavored to escape across an *acequia* full of water, but fell and was captured. "His com-

---

ble fund of anecdotes and a quaint style of narrative, unspoiled by courses in English composition, made him welcome by every fireside." (Walter Prescott Webb, *The Texas Rangers*, p. 87.) A number of years after the Mexican war, Wharton J. Green, son of Thomas J. Green, visited San Antonio, Texas, and "Bigfoot" Wallace. Green has left this interesting description and philosophy of life of one of the most colorful figures in Texas history:

Uncouth in garb and oft in speech, his simple word was more than tantamount to hosts of sworn witnesses in rebuttal. Get drunk he would occasionally, it grieves me to say, but drunk or sober, he could not tell a lie, or act one either. Essentially peaceably by nature, there was not a blustering bully in all those parts who would venture to encroach upon his inherent rights. . . . He was as foreign to fear as to falsehood, avarice, or duplicity. . . . A distinguished legal friend of the place [San Antonio], Hon. John A. Wilcox, told me repeatedly that from extended correspondence with parties in Virginia he was absolutely convinced that "Old Bigfoot" had a fortune awaiting him in that State, ranging from fifty to a hundred thousand dollars, only requiring proof of identity and a few technical formalities to place him in possession and yet for the life of him, he could not induce the bull-headed old fool to go out and take it. Intimating that perhaps I could succeed better, I tried my powers of persuasion on old "Bigfoot" but with like result. Here is the purport of his reply: "Yes, I know it was there waiting for me to go and take it, long before Colonel Wilcox told me about it. Why don't I go and get it? Simply because I don't want it. What use would it be except to make me miserable? I'm tolerably well satisfied over yonder, beyond the Medina, by myself. My rifle and traps furnish all I need for meat, and the peltries my other little wants, such as powder, lead, coffee, salt, and a little dram when I run down here every month or two to see you town fellows. What more does a man require to make him happy? And yet you and Jack Wilcox, both my friends, would have me break up a life that suits me and take to one that I hate and despise. A big house, a big drunk, and a big fool all combined, with lots of pretended friends as long as the money held out. Wouldn't I be a pretty d—n fool to make the swap?"

Wharton J[ackson] Green, *Recollections and Reflections: An Auto[biography] of Half a Century and More*, pp. 129–130; see also [Doris] Shannon Garst, *Big Foot Wallace of the Texas Rangers*, pp. 3, 5, 23.

panion, known as the 'Ranchero,' another miscreant, equally as disreputable, was arrested at the same time, and both were securely bound," and led into San Antonio where the populace demanded their immediate execution.[16] Hays, however, informed the people that it was his intention to take the prisoners to Seguin where they had committed numerous outrages and turn them over to the people there. This announcement almost precipitated a fight between the people of San Antonio and the rangers. Although the crucial moment passed, some of the irate citizens swore that the prisoners should not reach their destination.

Hays placed the prisoners in charge of two of his most trusted men, John Lee and Escue; mounted the prisoners on horses; and late in the afternoon, "under lowering skies that threatened a storm," they started along the road for Seguin with the ranger company serving as an escort. After nightfall, Lee and Escue, with their prisoners, dropped back to the rear of the company and turned off to the right across the open prairie, while the escort, as previously arranged, proceeded a short distance down the road and returned to San Antonio.

About midnight Lee and Escue halted with their charges. Lee helped Rubio dismount from his pony, bound the prisoner's feet and rechecked the bindings of his hands, and sat down beside him with his gun cocked and at the ready, determined that Rubio should not escape. Escue plopped himself down to rest at a distance of several rods from Lee to prevent their staked horses from becoming entangled. Although securing his prisoner, Escue failed to guard him carefully. The "Ranchero" covered himself with his buffalo robe and appeared to fall fast asleep almost immediately. Escue tied the rope that secured the Mexican to his ankle and soon succumbed to the arms of Morpheus. The cunning "Ranchero" now quickly freed himself, crawled noiselessly to Escue's horse, untied him from the stake-rope which he proceeded to tie to the limb of a tree, and then led the horse beyond hearing before mounting and riding off.

Early the next morning Lee saw a band of horsemen approaching rapidly. He hallooed to Escue, who arose quickly from his slumbers to find both his prisoner and horse gone. The two rangers quickly sized up the situation. They believed that the approaching horsemen were citizens of Béxar who sought to take the prisoners they were escorting,

[16] J. D. Affleck, "History of John C. Hays," ts., pt. I, pp. 224–228. See also A. J. Sowell, *Early Settlers and Indian Fighters of Southwest Texas*, p. 58.

but as they drew nearer, they realized their error. It was a Mexican marauding band. There was little hope for Escue's escape on the broken-down pony which had been ridden by the "Ranchero," but the horse ridden by Rubio was of sound quality; so Lee "instantly came to a decision. He drew his pistol, shot Rubio through the heart, yelled to Escue to mount the pony from which the lifeless body of the desperado had fallen," and the two rangers hastily returned to San Antonio.[17] The marauding band, it was later believed, had come in on the flank of Woll's army, and the "Ranchero" had fallen in with it and had guided it towards the rangers' camp, hoping to rescue his confederate, Rubio.

Lee and Escue gave added confirmation to the rumor that those about to attack Béxar belonged to a robber band.

On Saturday, September 10, news from Austin reached Houston that three Mexican spies had been captured near the Guadalupe. When one of these was taken to a tree and a halter placed about his neck, he promised to confess, if his life be spared. On being released he made the startling confession that a party of fifty Mexicans from Béxar, including two American gamblers from San Antonio, had for some weeks been encamped in the thickets of the Cíbolo, raiding the vicinity of Austin, Gonzales, and Bastrop—raids which previously had been attributed to the Indians.[18] The suspicions of the Anglo-Texan element at Béxar were further increased late in the summer by the fact that all at once no ammunition could be bought in San Antonio by the American element; and, yet, the Mexicans seemed to be able to obtain it from the local Mexican traders. François Guilbeau, the French consul, "refused to give us or even supply us with ammunition," reported Andrew Neill, "although he was offered ample security that the large and exorbitant price put upon it should be paid by four of the best and wealthiest citizens of Béxar."[19] Being short of ammunition, Captain Hays dispatched

[17] Affleck, "John C. Hays," ts., pt. I, pp. 224–228.
[18] *Telegraph and Texas Register*, Sept. 14, 1842.
[19] A. Neill to Anson Jones, Secretary of State, Washington, Texas, Jan. 29, 1843, in Washington D. Miller Papers, 1833–1860, ms. This letter is printed in E. W. Winkler (ed.), "The Béxar and Dawson Prisoners," in *Quarterly of the Texas State Historical Association*, XIII (1909–1910), 313–320. François Guilbeau and his son, François Jr., came to San Antonio in 1839. The elder Guilbeau served in the armies of Napoleon and was awarded the cross of the Legion of Honor. The younger Guilbeau established what is said to have been the first bakery in San Antonio, and was the French consular agent. He is credited with saving the grapevines of his native land by sending to France plants of mustang grapes for grafting purposes.

Wallace and Nathan Mallon, also a ranger, to the government arsenal at Austin for powder, caps, and lead. At Austin the two rangers could obtain only a barrel of powder and small quantities of lead and caps. Wallace rolled the barrel of powder in his blanket and strapped it to the pommel of his saddle. Mallon did the same for the caps and lead, taking proper precautions to protect the caps.[20]

Late at night, Friday, September 9, Antonio Parez, a leader among the loyal Mexicans of San Antonio, warned John W. Smith,[21] the mayor, in confidence, of the approach of an estimated fifteen hundred Mexicans from the Río Grande. A short time past midnight the able-bodied Anglo-Americans were aroused from their slumbers and told that a large Mexican force was approaching the town. Hastily dressing, they assembled in the public square, "where we found," recorded Trueheart, "all bustle and confusion, some addressing [advising] one thing and some another, some wishing to remain and others to desert the town; at length it was agreed to call a meeting, to determine what was best to be done in the emergency of the case."[22]

In the meantime, a San Antonio Mexican was visited by two of his countrymen, known to be in the Mexican service. From them he learned of the approach of a sizable Mexican force. This intelligence the San

The younger Guilbeau served as mayor of San Antonio. Boyce House, *City of Flaming Adventure: The Chronicle of San Antonio,* p. 117.

[20] Sowell, *Early Settlers and Indian Fighters of Southwest Texas,* pp. 58–59.

[21] Affleck, "John C. Hays," ts., Pt. I, p. 228; Hutchinson's diary in Winkler (ed.), "The Béxar and Dawson Prisoners," in *Quarterly of the Texas State Historical Association,* XIII (1909–1910), 294; M. L. Crimmins, "John W. Smith: the Last Messenger from the Alamo and the First Mayor of San Antonio," *Southwestern Historical Quarterly,* LIV (1950–1951), 344–346. Following the resignation of Juan N. Seguin, Smith was elected mayor of San Antonio for the third time on April 25, 1842, and took the oath of office on April 27. He held that office to March 30, 1844 (San Antonio, "Journal A, Records of the City of San Antonio," ts., p. 103). John W. Smith came to Texas from Missouri in 1826, lived at Gonzales for a while before moving to San Antonio in 1830; participated in the siege of San Antonio in 1835; was chosen by Travis to carry the last dispatch from the Alamo; was clerk of Bexar County from July 3, 1837 to April 5, 1841 (*Handbook of Texas,* II, 625; Edward W. Heusinger, *A Chronology of Events in San Antonio: being a Concise History of the City Year by Year from the Beginning of its Establishment to the End of the First Half of the Twentieth Century.* p. [19]). While serving as senator from Béxar County, John W. Smith died on January 12, 1845, at Washington-on-the-Brazos (*Texas National Register,* Jan. 18, 1845).

[22] Frederick C. Chabot (ed.), *The Perote Prisoners: Being the Diary of James L. Trueheart Printed for the First Time Together with an Historical Introduction,* p. 91.

Antonian communicated to Antonio Menchaca who lost no time in making it known to Judge Hutchinson and Hays.[23]

Thus on the morning of the 10th, ere the called meeting could be held, it was known that the enemy would likely invest San Antonio that night. Great "tumult and confusion were created."[24] In consequence, the grand jury was discharged, and the District Court which had begun its sessions on September 5 and was in the midst of trying the case of *Shields Booker* v. *the City of San Antonio,* suspended its work. Dr. Booker, formerly of Brazoria and Dr. Anson Jones' assistant surgeon at San Jacinto, was suing the city for a fee of fifty pesos that the former mayor Juan N. Seguin had promised him.[25] His attorney was Samuel A. Maverick, a signer of the Declaration of Independence and congressman-elect, who, accompanied by his servant Griffin, J. Beale, Griffith Jones, and a Mr. Jackson, had left his family at Colonel John W. Dancy's[26] in Fayette County, opposite LaGrange on the Colorado, to return to the fall term of court at San Antonio.

Frantic preparations were now made for defending the town. The citizens, both Anglo-Texans and Mexicans, were quickly assembled at the courthouse by the ringing of the bell. The meeting was presided over by Judge Hutchinson. The two Mexican citizens, who had conveyed the intelligence of the approach of the Mexican army to Menchaca, now came forward and stated that by daylight the next morning the town would be in the hands of a large Mexican force, and that the Mexican population should evacuate the town by 12 noon this day. They urged the Americans to do likewise. However, the report of the approach of a Mexican army was generally discredited, although the two citizens declared that one of the enemy's spies had been in town

[23] George Cupples, "Eulogy on the Life and Character of the Hon. Samuel A. Maverick," in Rena Maverick Green (ed.), *Samuel Maverick, Texan, 1803–1870: A Collection of Letters, Journals and Memoirs,* p. 386.

[24] A. Hutchinson, F. S. Gray, William E. Jones, A. Neill, and [Wilson J.] Riddle to the Citizens of Gonzales County, San Antonio, Saturday 10 o'clock P.M. Sept. 10, 1842, in Texas Congress, *Journals of the House of Representatives of the Seventh Congress of the Republic of Texas, convened at Washington, on the 14th November 1842,* Appendix, pp. 18–19; W. A. Miskel to Dr. [Francis] Moore, Dec. 14, 1842, in *Telegraph and Texas Register,* Dec. 21, 1842. Miskel is reporting the facts relating to the seizure of San Antonio as they were related to him "by one of the citizens of that place, who made his escape in the fog."

[25] Herbert Pickens Gambrell, *Anson Jones: The Last President of Texas,* pp. 259–260.

[26] An excellent biographical sketch of Colonel John W. Dancy will be found in John Henry Brown, *Indian Wars and Pioneers of Texas,* pp. 484–486.

the night before and had informed them that a large Mexican force was within one day's march of Béxar and would enter the town that day or the next; they too advised that the Texans should flee. The Anglo-Texans decided to remain long enough at least to ascertain the true character of the approaching force, many believing it to be a band of robbers who wished to frighten them away so that they could pillage the town with impunity. In the meantime, spies would be sent out.

The able-bodied men were now organized into two small groups, one, consisting of approximately one hundred resident Mexicans under Salvador Flores;[27] and the other, of about seventy-five Anglo-Texans, under Chauncey Johnson.[28] Hays, who was placed in command of both groups, issued verbal orders for the defense of the town. The Mexican group, declaring its willingness to fight and die for Texas, was stationed in the old courthouse, and Johnson's men hurriedly fortified the Samuel

[27] Hutchinson's diary in Winkler (ed.), "The Béxar and Dawson Prisoners," *Quarterly of the Texas State Historical Association,* XIII (1909–1910), 294; Louis J. Wortham, *A History of Texas,* III, 97.

[28] Hutchinson's diary in Winkler (ed.), "The Béxar and Dawson Prisoners," *Quarterly of the Texas State Historical Association,* XIII (1909–1910), 294; W. A. Miskel to Dr. [Francis] Moore, Dec. 14, 1842, in *Telegraph and Texas Register,* Dec. 21, 1842, reported that the defenders of San Antonio consisted of 107 Mexicans and 87 Americans "well armed and determined." A. Hutchinson, F. S. Gray, William E. Jones, and Others to the Citizens of Gonzales County, San Antonio, Saturday, 10 o'clock P.M., Sept. 10, 1842, in Texas Congress, *Journals of the House of Representatives of the Seventh Congress,* Appendix, pp. 18–19, gives the number of Americans as "some 60" and the Mexicans "about 100." The "Muster Roll of the San Antonio Comp^y Capt. C. Johnson, taken at San Antonio, Septr 11th, 1842 [with later notes in the same hand and ink, and certified as authentic by A. Neill and D. C. Ogden, at Austin, Nov. 28, 1850]." in Militia Rolls (Texas), ms. The "Muster Roll" contains a list of fifty-two names, and the certification says, "this list contains a correct list of prisoners taken in San Antonio on the 11th day of Septr 1842 by Genl Adrián Woll. . . . so far as our recollections serve." The title of the "Muster Roll" would seem to imply that it was a complete list of Johnson's Company, but apparently was only a list of those taken prisoners. General Woll reported the enemy (Texan) force as consisting of 250 men ([Adrián Woll], *Expedición hecha en Téjas, por una parte de la Division del Cuerpo de Egército del Norte,* p. 9), but Hays says that the Americans numbered 75, and that Woll had captured (probably he meant "retained") fifty-three. J. C. Hays to the Citizens of Texas, San Antonio, Sept. 12, 1842, in Texas Congress *Journal of the House of Representatives of the Seventh Congress,* Appendix, pp. 21–22. Chauncey Johnson brought his family to San Antonio about October 1840. Green (ed.), *Samuel Maverick,* p. 136.

A. Maverick residence,[29] so located at the northwest corner of the old mission quadrangle (now Alamo Plaza) as to command the Government (Main or Public) Plaza. Two platoons of spies were sent out with instructions "to report by to-morrow at 10 A.M., if alive." The first of these was dispatched by the Mexicans who sent two commissioners, Domingo Bustillo and Ignacio Chávez, with two guides, one of whom was named Zavalla, to contact the approaching Mexican commander.[30] About 4 o'clock in the afternoon, Zavalla returned to report one hundred horses at a short distance north of the Presidio Road. He stated that since the commissioners had considered it the advance guard of a regular invading army, rather than a party of robbers, Bustillo and Chávez had continued on. The Texans, however, were still uncertain as to the nature of the force and its objective; and, therefore, continued to re-enforce their position on the square, and by dark had completed their work. With the exception of a small guard left at the fortified positions, the citizen volunteers went to their homes for the night with the understanding that if anything unusual developed they would assemble at a moment's notice.

As the two commissioners did not return by nightfall, the assumption gained strength that the approaching force was nothing more than another of those small marauding bands so commonly found ravaging the country between the Nueces and the Río Grande; for, it was argued, a regular army would not retain the commissioners as prisoners. About 7 o'clock in the evening Major Hays set out from the town with five men to reconnoiter the approaching hostile force, which from the best reports available seemed to be nothing more than a gang of robbers; although some of the inhabitants believed it another "foray" and estimated its size at from 1,300 to 3,000 men. As a further precautionary measure, a courier was dispatched shortly after 10 P.M. to the Guadalupe settlements to request that 110 men be sent immediately to San Antonio, and Gonzales County was asked to furnish from 50 to 100 men at once.[31] "Let there be no alarm. We have found from sad experience

---

[29] The Maverick residence was located at the corner of Commerce and Soledad Streets. Green (ed.), *Samuel Maverick*, p. 164; Charles Ramsdell, "Old England in Béxar," in *San Antonio Express*, Sept. 18, 1848.

[30] W. S. Miskel to Dr. [Francis] Moore, Dec. 14, 1842, *Telegraph and Texas Register*, Dec. 21, 1842.

[31] Hutchinson's Diary in Winkler (ed.), "The Béxar and Dawson Prisoners," *Quarterly of the Texas State Historical Association*, XIII, (1909–1910), 294 n.

the consequences of a false rumor. The only thing we recommend is to make preparations for removal," wrote the Citizens' Committee at San Antonio, "if on further information there shall be danger. We defend this point until compelled to fall back upon Seguin."[32]

Hays failed to encounter the enemy "on any public road," but during the night discovered that the enemy had come down through the mountains to the city, having left the main road. However, he did not discover the Mexican troops until he attempted to enter the town shortly before daylight on the 11th,[33] the anniversary of the Mexican victory over the Spanish troops attempting to re-establish Spain's authority over her lost colony. There surrounding the town was the Mexican army he had gone out to scout, and Hays' little band now found itself cut off from its comrades within the town. An effort to pass through the Mexican line for the purpose of entering the city failed.[34]

The Mexican raiding party consisted principally of the Second Division of the Army Corps of the North, under its commandant, Brigadier General Adrián Woll. Woll, a Frenchman, was born on December 2, 1795, in St. Germain-en-Laye, near Paris, and educated for the military profession. He served under the first Empire, and in 1815 was captain adjutant major in the 10th legion of the National Guard of the Seine.[35] Upon the restoration of the Bourbons in France, Woll went to New York and, thence, to Baltimore, Maryland, with letters of introduction to General Winfield Scott of the United States army, who befriended him. On July 3, 1816, at Baltimore he commenced his Mexican military career as a lieutenant colonel on the staff of General Francisco Xavier Mina to aid in the establishment of Mexican independence. With Mina he disembarked at Soto la Marina on April 15, 1817, but avoided Mina's fate and thus began a half century of active participation in Mexican military and political affairs, adhering from first to last to the fortunes of General Santa Anna. After the achievement of Mexican independ-

---

[32] A. Hutchinson and Others to the Citizens of Gonzales County, San Antonio, Saturday 10 o'clock P.M., Sept. 10, 1842, in Texas Congress, *Journal of the House of Representatives of the Seventh Congress*, Appendix, pp. 18–19.

[33] John C. Hays to the Secretary of War, Seguin, Sept. 12, 1842, in *ibid.*, Appendix, p. 16.

[34] *Ibid.*

[35] Gustave Vapereau, *Dictionnaire Universel des Contemporains: Contenant Toutes les Personnes Notables de la France et des Pays Etrangers*, p. 1849. See also, Joseph Milton Nance, "Adrián Woll: Frenchman in the Mexican Military Service," *New Mexico Historical Review*, XXXIII (1957–1958), 177–186.

ence he continued in the army, became a naturalized citizen of Mexico,[36] and married a Mexican.[37]

Commissioned a colonel in the Mexican army in 1828, Woll served as an aide-de-camp to Santa Anna in the siege and capture of Tampico from the Spaniards in 1829. For bravery displayed on that occasion, he was promoted to the rank of brigadier general in 1832 and awarded the Cross of Tampico.[38] Also, along with several other officers, he was commissioned by Santa Anna to conduct and place in the hands of the Supreme Government at Mexico City the flag taken from the Spaniards. In the same year he took part in the *pronunciamiento* against President Anastasio Bustamante which brought General M. Gómez Pedraza to the presidency of the republic. From Guadalajara he was detached with a small, well-organized force to proceed quickly to Colima, whose authorities had refused to aid the revolt. At Taxinastla Woll defeated Lieutenant Colonel Joaquín Solorzano and entered Colima on the 15th of November where he freed the prisoners and established in office persons loyal to the revolutionary movement before moving on to Morelia with his troops.[39] In 1835 Woll was made quartermaster general to the troops in Santa Anna's victorious campaign against the Federalist uprising under the pure-blooded Indian Juan Alvarez in the south and Francisco García in the state of Zacatecas.

As quartermaster of the army in the Texas campaign of 1836, Woll reached San Antonio de Béxar on March 8[40] and served under General Vicente Filisola, second in command of the army. Among the detachments sent out from San Antonio by Santa Anna after the fall of the Alamo were those of Generals Ramírez y Sesma and Woll which confronted the Texan troops under General Houston across the Colorado at Beason's Ferry, nearly opposite the site of the present town of Columbus. Arriving at the Atascosito Pass of the Colorado on April 5 and finding a part of Ramírez y Sesma's force already across but only one canoe available for crossing, Santa Anna ordered the regular battalion of

---

[36] Miguel Angel Peral, *Diccionario biográphico mexicano*, p. 870.

[37] Woll's son, according to John Henry Brown, was operating a hotel in Mexico City in 1869–1870. John Henry Brown, *History of Texas, from 1685 to 1892*, II, 67, 222 n.

[38] Heinrich August Pierer, *Universal-Lexikon der Gergangenheit und gegenwart oder Neuestes encyclopädisches wörterbuch der wissenschaften künste und Gewerbe*, XIX, 338.

[39] Peral, *Diccionario biográphico mexicano*, p. 870.

[40] Vito Alessio Robles, *Coahuila y Texas desde la consumación de la independencia hasta el tratado de paz de Guadalupe Hidalgo*, II, 140.

Aldama, under the direction of General Woll, to construct rafts to facilitate the crossing of the rest of the army under Filisola's direction while
he set out with the leading brigade for San Felipe, which he reached
on the morning of April 7. On April 26 General Filisola made Woll his
chief of staff. The next day "Deaf" Smith reached Filisola's camp with
dispatches from President Santa Anna concerning the latter's capture.
On the following day (April 28) Woll was dispatched to the Texan
army as an emissary under the pretext of learning the terms of the
armistice, but actually for the purpose of gaining information on the
strength, armament, and resources of the enemy.[41] Woll entered the
Texan camp on April 30 under a flag of truce and conferred freely with
the Mexican prisoners, but was retained because, as Santa Anna reported, the Texans "feared he would disclose the strength of the con-
querors,"[42] although the Texans tried to claim that he had been held
prisoner in order to protect his life from lawless persons. After a brief
period, the new commander in chief of the Texan army, General
Thomas J. Rusk, ordered him transferred as a prisoner to Velasco,
where he was eventually given a passport for his safe conduct, escorted to Goliad, and permitted to return to Mexico. Woll rejoined the
retreating Mexican army on June 12, the day that Filisola resigned his
command to General Juan José Andrade, who served as *ad interim*
commander of the troops until they could be placed under General
José Urrea as ordered by the Mexican government. Woll claimed in
1842 that during the Texas campaign of 1836 he had convinced Santa
Anna of the impropriety of the order to shoot James W. Fannin and his
men, but the order had departed and could not be recalled.[43]

For several years after the Texas revolution, while Santa Anna lived
in quiet seclusion in Mexico, Woll seems to have played a rather incon-
spicuous role in Mexican affairs, but he emerged eventually from the
struggles between the Centralists and Federalists as an important supporter of Santa Anna. Upon General Mariano Arista's renunciation of
the command of the Army of the North, General Isidro Reyes, who had
served as second in command of that army since February 1842, and as

[41] *Ibid.*, II, 165.

[42] Antonio Lopez de Santa Anna, *Manifesto Relative to his Operations in the Texas Campaign and His Capture* (translated by Carlos E. Castañeda, in *The Mexican Side of the Texas Revolution*), p. 85; William C. Binkley (ed.), *Official Correspondence of the Texan Revolution, 1835–1836*, II, 716–717.

[43] Hutchinson's diary in Winkler (ed.), "The Béxar and Dawson Prisoners," *Quarterly of the Texas State Historical Association*, XIII (1909–1910), 296.

commandant general of the Department of Coahuila, was made commander in chief on May 28 of that year and assumed his command at Saltillo on June 2.[44] At this time, Woll was appointed second in command of the Army Corps of the North and commandant general of the Department of Coahuila. Reyes' command included the departments of Tamaulipas, Nuevo León, and Coahuila.

On June 5 General Reyes was instructed by the President to prepare Woll's brigade for a second attack on San Antonio de Béxar,[45] westernmost outpost of the Republic of Texas, and to make a reconnaissance to the Guadalupe River and down its west bank to the Gonzales River.[46] Under no condition was his raid into Texas to last more than a month. The death penalty was decreed on August 24 for all military personnel who might desert from the army while on the march to the Texas frontier.[47]

Woll assembled his army at Presidio del Río Grande, and on August 24 the army began its march toward San Antonio de Béxar by heading in the direction of the Nogal Pass.[48] At this point the river was 350 feet wide. The next day the first of his dragoons commenced crossing the Río Grande in two small canoes. It required from the 25th through the 30th—six days—for General Woll to cross his army, which, according to the report of his quartermaster, Colonel José María Carrasco, consisted of 957 men, 12 wagons loaded with corn, 150 loads of provisions, 50 or more head of cattle, 2 pieces of artillery and an artillery train, 919 horses, and 213 mules.[49] During the afternoon of the 30th General Woll

[44] *El Cosmopolita,* June 25, 1842.

[45] Ministerio de Guerra y Marina: Memoria del secretaria de estado y del despacho de guerra y marina, leida a las camaras del Congreso nacional de la Republica Mexicana, en enero de 1844, in *Diario del Gobierno,* May 15, 1844.

[46] Adrián Woll ál Sr. general en gefe [Isidro Reyes], San Antonio de Béjar, a las 6 de la mañana del dia 20 de Septiembre de 1842, in Woll, *Expedición hecha en Téjas,* pp. 38–39.

[47] *El Latigo de Téjas* (Matamoros), Aug. 29, 1844.

[48] A lone pecan tree stood on the east side of the Río Grande near its bank. Kinto's Ranch was situated above the crossing. Samuel A. Maverick's Journal, Sept. 22, 1842, in Samuel Maverick Papers, ms.

[49] Adrián Woll to Isidro Reyes, [Presidio del] Río Grande, August 29, 1842, enclosing "Report showing the force that is . . . proceeding as the Texas expedition on August 29, 1842, Office of the Adjutant General, 2nd Division, Army Corps of the North," in Joseph Milton Nance (trans. and ed.), "Brigadier General Adrián Woll's Report of his Expedition into Texas in 1842," in *Southwestern Historical Quarterly,* LVIII (1954–1955), 525; "Itinerary of the first column of the Army of the Mexican Republic to Texas, commanded by Brigadier General D. Adrián Woll,

and the chiefs of division crossed over and the troops were inspected, and Woll, addressing his troops, announced the opening of "the second campaign against Texas."

To you [he said] is confided the honor of leading the van—you will prove yourself worthy of the mission and of the army to which you belong—great fatigue awaits you in traversing the numerous rivers and the vast solitary plains, which separate you from the enemy they protect. But your valor and your firmness will overcome all those obstacles—you will make yourself great as the desert is vast. In combat you will recollect the injuries committed by ingratitude to Mexican hospitality. *Be as Brass*—after triumph you will remember you are Mexicans—be generous—do not distrust fortune—she will be faithful to justice—victory will crown your heroic efforts and a generous country will reward your worthiness. Soldiers, let us march then upon the enemy.[50]

The next morning, after the troops had formed to begin their march, General Reyes, accompanied by General Woll, moved to the front of the line. At the center of it he read a proclamation to the soldiers, concluding with the following statement: "March, comrades, and in combat let your battle cry be *Santa-Anna*. This name, magic to Mexicans, will augment your military valor; it will make you superior to the privations and fatigues of the most honorable of campaigns, and will return you to the arms of your friends with your temples surrounded by laurel which shall never wither, neither [because of] time, nor foul party spirit."[51] Thereupon, Reyes retired across the Río Grande.

At six o'clock in the morning on the last day of August the march toward Béxar was commenced through a veritable trackless terrain, and

---

Commandant of the 2nd Division, drawn up by his Quartermaster, Brevet Colonel José María Carrasco, Captain of Sappers, San Antonio de Béxar, September 11, 1842, in *ibid.*, LVIII (1954–1955), 534–538. The report of the Ministry of War and Marine says Woll had 802 men of all arms (Memoria del Secretario de estado y del despacho de guerra y marina, leida a las camaras del Congreso nacional de la Republica mexicana, en enero de 1844, in *Diario del Gobierno*, May 15, 1844).

[50] Adrián Woll ál Sr. General en gefe [Isidro Reyes], Campo en la margen izquierda del Río Bravo, Agosto 30 de 1842, enclosing a copy of the Proclamation to the Troops of his Command, [dated:] en la margen izquierda del Río Bravo, Agosto 30 de 1842, in Woll, *Expedición hecha en Téjas*, pp. 5–6. The Proclamation will also be found in Texas Congress, *Journal of the House of Representatives of the Seventh Congress*, Appendix, pp. 23–24; *Telegraph and Texas Register*, Sept. 28, 1842; *El Cosmopolita*, Sept. 28, 1842.

[51] Proclamation to the Soldiers of the 2nd Division by General D. Isidro Reyes, Paso del Nogal, August 31, 1842, in *El Cosmopolita*, Sept. 28, 1842.

at noon the army camped on the Arroyo de la Cueva. Woll's route, depicted on the accompanying map, followed an old smuggling trail some twenty miles or more north of the Upper Presidio-La Pita Road which had been laid out shortly after 1800 as a more direct route from Presidio to San Antonio.[52] He skirted the high ridge extending from near the Río Grande to the headwaters of the San Antonio, for here were to be found numerous excellent springs of water even in the dry season. For many years thereafter the Woll route was the main road between San Antonio and the Río Grande, and was substantially the route followed by General John E. Wool in his march from San Antonio to the border in September 1846. Considerably straightened, Woll's road in its upper portion is the present Uvalde-San Antonio highway. After the Mexican War, in order to give protection to the Texas frontier from Indians, smugglers, and Mexican bandits, the United States War Department built several forts along the Woll road; namely, Fort Lincoln[53] on the Seco (July 7, 1849), Fort Inge on the Leona (March 13, 1849), and Fort Duncan on the Río Grande (March 27, 1849).

On the second day (September 1) the main army did not move, but waited for the company from the presidial regiment, whose horses had stampeded the night of the 30th; however, the *carretas* of corn, escorted by the *defensores* of Béxar continued their course, after leaving behind two days' rations for the cavalry. On the 2nd the division, having been joined by the presidial company, resumed its march, following a north-northeast course through a smooth prairie. By noon, however, the terrain became more difficult on account of forests and arroyos which lay across the route, and the main force halted at the Arroyo de Saladito.[54] Seguin and Carrasco now went forward with their men to open a road. The upper Nueces country through which Woll marched lies between the Medina and the Río Grande, and extends from the Edwards Plateau to the northern boundary of Webb County. Although cut by the Nueces and its numerous tributaries, as the accompanying map shows, the region is semi-arid; and mesquite, cat's claw, huajillo, and prickly pear on the prairie, live oak, pecan, and cypress along the rivers, and

[52] Ike Moore (ed.), *The Life and Diary of Reading W. Black: A History of Early Uvalde*, p. 7.

[53] Fort Clark, established June 19, 1852, on Las Moras Creek and the El Paso road partly replaced Fort Lincoln which had been established some three years earlier on the west bank of Seco Creek. *Handbook of Texas*, I, 622, 628.

[54] Nance (trans. and ed.), "Adrián Woll's Report of His Expedition into Texas in 1842," in *Southwestern Historical Quarterly*, LVIII (1954–1955), 536.

cedars in the hills and mountains are the important native plant life. The area abounded in deer, wild horses, black bear, civet cats, coyotes, javelinas, armadillos, jack rabbits, wild turkey, chaparral birds, quail, doves, rattlesnakes, and other forms of indigenous animal life. Between the Río Grande and Nueces the country was, without much exaggeration, described as all barren, but between the Nueces and San Antonio it was "described as a rolling prairie, pretty well wooded, and, after leaving the Medina, eminently beautiful and picturesque, covered at most seasons of the year with a luxuriant growth of grass, and abounding in game."[55]

Woll resumed his march on the 3rd toward the northeast across a smooth desert-like prairie cut by deep, narrow arroyos and covered in places with what the Mexicans described as "thick forests." Picoso Creek was bridged and crossed, but for all the other arroyos ramps were used to facilitate crossing them. The crossing of a barranca or arroyo was always accomplished after considerable digging, bridging, scraping, and shouldering of the wheels, with the usual accompaniment of whooping, swearing, and cracking of whips. In the early afternoon Woll camped at the Chaparrosa lagoons, and late in the afternoon made preparations to renew his march quickly the next morning at 4 o'clock. On the 4th he crossed a large hill, called the Divisadero (Divide),[56] and arrived at the Arroyo de Rancherías,[57] deep and rough, necessitating the use of ramps on both sides. At 4:30 P.M. the Nueces River was reached and crossed between the passages known as the Amoladeras and the Chicle, and at this time the crossing was renamed—the new name being "General Woll." The army rested on the 5th on the east bank of the Nueces.

The following day the Mexican army passed the head of Uvalde

[55] Report of George W. Hughes, Captain Topographical Engineers, Feb. 1, 1847, U.S. Congress, *Senate Executive Documents*, 31st Congress, 1st Session, Vol. III, no. 32 (serial no. 558), pp. 35–38.

[56] El Divisadero (the Divide) in the official Mexican reports apparently has reference to the rocky, sandy ridge, principally Sand Mountain today, in northwestern Zavala County lying between Turkey and Mustang (Arroyo de Rancherías) creeks and dividing the streams flowing directly into the Nueces from those emptying into Lake Espantosa. See maps for "Dimmit County, Texas," in U.S. Dept. of Agriculture, *Soil Survey*, Washington, D. C.: "Zavala County, Texas," in *ibid.;* "Southwest Texas," in U.S. Soil Survey, U.S. Department of Agriculture, *Field Operations of the Bureau of Soils*, 1911; United States Geological Survey, *Cline [Texas] Quadrangle," "Brackettville [Texas] Quadrangle,"* and *"Uvalde [Texas] Quadrangle,"* in U.S. Dept. of the Interior, *Geological Survey*.

[57] Mustang Creek today.

Cañon, and continuing along the edge of the *lomerío* de San Saba, crossed the Leona and camped on its eastern bank. Concerning the Leona, Captain George W. Hughes of the United States topographical engineers who traversed the same area in September four years later wrote, "I can scarcely allow myself to speak of the beautiful river, and its rich and lovely valley, for the language of truth, when applied to it, must necessarily assume the appearance of fiction."[58] In continuing his description of the region through which Woll passed, Hughes reported,

All the rivers between San Antonio and the Nueces, may be characterized as beautiful and noble streams of clear and excellent water, and many of them would afford an almost unlimited amount of water power. . . . I know of no country better adapted to manufacturers than western Texas, and there is perhaps no region in the world where wool can be grown at so low a rate, or where the necessaries of life may be produced so cheaply. . . . At almost every rod we startled up herds of deer, and flocks of partridges and wild turkeys. The reverse of the picture is, that it abounds with venomous reptiles, snakes, scorpions, centipedes, and tarantulas. . . .

It is melancholy, in traversing this rich and beautiful country, so eminently fitted for the support of human life, to find it but one vast solicitude, undisturbed save by some wary traveller or trader, who pursues his stealthy course at night, with the hope (often vain) of eluding the crafty savage, who looks out from his mountain home like an eagle from its eyrie, watching for his victim. But it requires only a slight effort of the imagination to fancy it peopled with an industrious and teeming population, its heights crowned with human habitations, its fertile valleys in cultivation, and its plains covered with bleating flocks and lowing herds.

At 6 o'clock the next morning, September 7, the Mexicans renewed their march, and at two leagues distance they passed the Frio. They encamped for the night on the left bank of the Sabinal. On the 8th they encamped on the east bank of the Arroyo Hondo, and on the following day the course was continued through a forest of mesquite in an east-northeast direction, leaving the lagoon of the Cuije (Quihi) on the left. After crossing the plain of Cuije, the army turned east, and reached the Medina at 5 o'clock in the afternoon. Early the next morning, September 10, Woll's troops were again in motion. At 2 o'clock in the afternoon they reached the Arroyo de León, about three leagues from San Antonio de Béxar, and rested until 7 o'clock. In the meantime, the spies which had

[58] Report of George W. Hughes, Captain Topographical Engineers, Feb. 1, 1847, U.S. Congress, *Senate Executive Documents,* 31st Congress, 1st Session, Vol. III, no. 32, pp. 35–38.

been sent out, returned, giving assurance that within the city there was no report of the expedition's approach. An order was issued against the pillage of homes and persons not in arms and it was declared that if any soldier or citizen should enter by force "any house or store with intent to rob, committing violence, [he] will be immediately shot without saving him by excuse or privilege wherever, and in order that no one may plead ignorance, this order shall be read," said Woll, "to the companies, morning and evening."⁵⁹

With the idea of investing the city of San Antonio that night, Woll renewed the march at 7 o'clock. Favored by the darkness, the Mexican army was to station itself around the city, take possession of all roads, and await the coming of day to enter the city. In this *interim* one of the scouts returned accompanied by four Mexican citizens of Béxar,⁶⁰ who informed Woll they came charged by the inhabitants to implore him not to enter the city, for if he did so they would be forced by the Texans, they stated, to join them in resisting the Mexican troops. Thus it was that Woll learned that the arrival of his troops was known to the inhabitants of Béxar, the knowledge of his presence in the vicinity having been made known to the San Antonians, he reported, by "the indiscretion of one of our spies with a woman."⁶¹ Up to that time there had been, as far as he knew, no notice of the army's approach, "nor even the least suspicion." This we know was not true. The four commissioners were placed under arrest. The baggage and provisions were left under a guard of fifty soldiers from the presidial companies, commanded by Captain Francisco Castañeda, and the army now moved forward rapidly with the object of throwing a tight ring about the city. At the edge of the cemetery⁶² it halted. Here the division entered into line on the

⁵⁹ "Orden general del 9 al 10 de Septiembre de 1842 [de General Adrián Woll ál Ejército de su mando]," in Woll, *Expedición hecha en Téjas*, p. 9; Texas Congress, *Journals of the House of Representatives of the Seventh Congress*, Appendix, pp. 22–23; ms. copy of the order is in Army Papers (Texas), ms.

⁶⁰ These four emissaries were Domingo Bustillo, Ignacio Chávez, and two guides, Zavalla having returned to San Antonio to report.

⁶¹ Adrián Woll ál Sr. general en gefe [Isidro Reyes], S. Antonio de Béjar, Septiembre 12 de 1842, in Woll, *Expedición hecha en Téjas*, pp. 12–17.

⁶² On our way to camp, [reported one of the men heading for Somervell's camp later] we visited the grave yard. It contained about an acre of ground enclosed with a wall of stone about six feet in height, except the Gateway, which is of sufficient height to admit a horse and a carriage, and is about two feet in thickness. The wall is extended about three feet above the gateway, with a square stone centrally fixed on the top with the date 1808 upon it, which was perhaps the time of its enclosure. In the centre of this enclosure there is a square pile of stone

left bank of the Arroyo de San Pedro, the infantry forming to the left of the road and the Santa Anna Regiment to the right with the two artillery pieces upon the road in battery formation. The San Pedro was within cannon shot of the center of the town. Several detachments of *defensores* from Béxar, from the Río Grande, and some detachments of the presidial soldiers were placed in the Alamo and at all points around the city, closing all roads. The passes, or streets, leading to the Alamo were guarded by Vicente Córdova and his Cherokees. The Santa Anna Battalion, commanded by Colonel Sebastián Moro del Moral, with one piece of artillery, was formed in a column, supported by a second battalion under Lieutenant Colonel Cayetano Montero composed of two squadrons of the Santa Anna Regiment of regular cavalry and the other artillery piece. By midnight the troops had been arranged and were resting upon their arms awaiting the coming of day. The prearranged signal to enter the city and seize the plaza was to be the firing of a cannon ball at daybreak. At the firing of the cannon, all stations were to beat reveille and apprehend all persons who should seek to flee the city. Colonel Moro del Moral's column was to enter and form in battle formation about the Plaza del Ayuntamiento,[63] while the renegade, Colonel Juan N. Seguin, was to occupy the Plaza de las Armas[64] with the remaining *defensores* of his corps.

At 4:30 A.M. the troops encircling the city filed in columns, by half companies, up to the edge of the first houses with General Woll, his staff, and the musicians of the Santa Anna Battalion in the lead. A dense fog obscured both men and horses. While the Mexicans awaited the coming of day, one of their spies reported that a redoubt and loophole openings had been made in the houses fronting the church and in others that formed the first block of the street leading to the Alamo. At 5:30 the fog persisted. Suddenly, as day approached, the Texans sounded reveille. Thinking that his own detachments had confused the order of the signals, and that the sharp notes of reveille came from his own stations, Woll ordered the cannon shot fired, and the musicians struck up the well-known dancing tune of "La Cachucha" as Moro del Moral's column

---

rudely thrown together, with a cross standing in the centre. Upon this pile of stone was a large collection of sculls. Also, human sculls were scattered promiscuously over the yard with various bones, sticking out of the earth.

Harvey Alexander Adams, "[Journal of an] Expedition Against the Southwest in 1842 and 1843," Nov. 1, 1842, ms.

[63] Civil or Government Plaza; sometimes known as the Plaza de las Islas.

[64] Military Plaza. Seguin, *Memoirs*, p. 27.

317

moved forward toward the plaza. Upon hearing the report of the cannon, many of the Texans who had gone to their homes during the night, rushed to join Johnson's Company at Maverick's corner. Only about sixty were able to reach the point of rendezvous, the others being cut off by the encircling troops. In the meantime, Woll and his staff, on horse, accompanied the skirmishers, but as the latter entered the square they turned right; whereas, in the dense fog, Woll and his staff failed to follow, but continued straight ahead, coming abreast of the vanguard. The Mexican troops moved on toward the middle of the plaza.

Although the Texans, at first, could not detect the enemy because of the mist and fog, Johnson ordered his small force to open fire in the direction of the music down the street toward Callaghan's house. Flores' Company of Texas-Mexicans likewise opened fire, but soon realizing (apparently before the Anglo-Texans did) that the enemy was the regular Mexican army, retreated,[65] much to the disgust of José Antonio Menchaca,[66] who cried out that their "d—d Mexican friends had retreated."[67] General Woll's infantry, supported by two pieces of artillery —a six- and a four-pounder—began a concentrated fire upon Maverick's corner, and made an effort to take the plaza but a withering fire from the small, determined band of Texans at the corner and from the flat roof of the Maverick house "threw his column into disorder and it retired . . . [to] shelter behind the eastern line of the military square,"[68] leaving a drummer, Antonio Piñeda of the Santa Anna Battalion, dead and several wounded in the plaza. The horses of the general and three of his staff were also wounded.

As the Mexican column recoiled before the fire of the Texans, whose

[65] W. A. Miskel to Dr. [Francis] Moore, Dec. 14, 1842, in *Telegraph and Texas Register*, Dec. 21, 1842. Miskel was one of those who had stood guard during the night at the fortified Maverick house.

[66] José Antonio Menchaca, son of Juan Mariano Menchaca and María Luz Guerra, was born in January 1800 at San Antonio. José married Teresa Ramón, daughter of Martin Ramón and his wife Ana Aguilar. James P. Newcomb, who knew José Antonio Menchaca, describes him as "physically a large man, not overly tall, but massive; his complexion fair, his eyes blue, his countenance strong and dignified; he bore the marks of a long line of Castilian ancestors." Quoted in Charles M. Barnes (comp.), *Antonio Menchaca Memoirs*, Yanaguana Society *Publications*, II, [11]; Frederick C. Chabot, *With the Makers of San Antonio*, p. 106.

[67] Hutchinson's diary in Winkler (ed.), "The Béxar and Dawson Prisoners," *Quarterly of the Texas State Historical Association*, XIII, (1909–1910), 295.

[68] *Ibid.*; see also Andrew Neill to Anson Jones, Jan. 29, 1843, Winkler (ed.), "The Béxar and Dawson Prisoners," *Quarterly of the Texas State Historical Association*, XIII (1909–1910), 296.

hurrahs were rending the early morning air, and Lieutenant Manuel de Frago abandoned his artillery, Woll, incensed by the "determined resistance" of the defenders of the town, sought to rally his troops behind the two cannon—one firing ball and the other canister. Captain Marcelo Torreblanca was dispatched with fifty men to occupy the belfry of the church on the west side of the plaza; Captain Ignacio Ruiz was ordered to establish his men in the houses in front of the enemy; and Captains Ildefonso Vega and Juan Garrido were ordered to take possession of a house on the right and left flanks respectively, which they succeeded in doing at once. On the roof of the Edward Dwyer house, on the southeast corner of the plaza, thirty-five Coushatta Indians were placed. Another detachment crossed the river and took up a position near the large pecan tree in front of the barracks.[69] Cavalry guarded the east bank. Soon from all sides of the plaza the Mexicans were able to direct a steady fire of small arms upon the Texan position. In the meantime, Seguin entered the Plaza de las Armas without opposition.[70] The joy of the Texans was but for a moment, reported Woll to his superior, for "the reproof appeared horrible, because at the same time that the fire broke upon them from all directions, the day dawned! Confined in a district of the town from which his firing was being extinguished, the encircled enemy was about to be put to the sword in his entrenchments, which our brave infantrymen were already touching, when at the sight of a white flag I ordered the firing to cease."[71]

In this and on other matters dealing with his encounter with the Texans during his invasion, to be mentioned later, Woll's report disagrees with the reports of the Texans. According to the latter, with the recoil of the Mexican skirmishers, Johnson had already ordered his son to open the front and back doors of the Maverick house preparatory to charging the enemy's cannon when suddenly a white flag was seen approaching, followed by Colonel Carrasco. The flag was received and Carrasco ex-

[69] George Cupples, "Eulogy on the Life and Character of the Hon. Samuel A. Maverick," in Green (ed.), *Samuel Maverick*, p. 387.

[70] Goodman, a bitter enemy of Seguin, who Seguin says was one of those at San Antonio who had made his continued living there highly undesirable after the Vasquez raid, now sent Juan Hernandez to Seguin begging forgiveness for what he had done. Hernandez came out of Goodman's shop and made the request of Seguin, who declared he had "no rancor against him"; whereupon, Goodman came out of hiding, surrendered himself, and was placed under the special charge of Captain Manuel Leal. Seguin, *Memoirs*, p. 28.

[71] Adrián Woll ál Sr. general en gefe [Isidro Reyes], S. Antonio de Béjar, Septiembre 12 de 1842, in Woll, *Expedición hecha en Téjas*, pp. 14–16.

plained that General Woll's army of two thousand troops was the vanguard of a large army, and that the Texans would be granted a half hour to treat for surrender. Whereupon, Colonel Johnson agreed to dispatch four commissioners (William E. Jones, Samuel A. Maverick, George Van Ness, and C. W. Peterson) to discuss the terms of surrender with General Woll.[72]

Making the best of a bad situation, for a number of Mexicans had been killed and wounded, the commissioners sought to explain that they did not know they were fighting a large Mexican army, but thought it to be only a handful of robbers. They explained then, as later, in an open letter written with the permission of General Woll to "the Authorities and People of Texas," and intended not to offend their captors, that had they "been aware of the approach of an invading force, we [they said] should have most certainly retreated from the place; because it would have been madness to attempt its defence."[73] The Texans contended that if Woll had not retained Bustillo and Chaves, who entered his camp under a flag of truce, they would have known it was a regular Mexican army and would not have resisted, but would most likely have fled.[74] With no other alternative, except to fight in a most hopeless situation, the commissioners now offered in behalf of their colleagues to surrender their arms provided they should be permitted to retire to their homes. To this request Woll said, "I replied that if they did not surrender at discretion they would be exterminated without exception."[75] General Woll then proceeded to explain that if it had not been for the loss of Mexican lives, he would have permitted the Texans to disperse after their surrender; but, nevertheless, he would see that they were accorded the treatment due gentlemen. The commissioners replied that they would have to consult with their comrades and requested permission to return to their lines. The request was granted, and the commis-

[72] William E. Jones and Others to the Authorities and People of Texas, San Antonio, September 11, 1842, in Texas Congress, *Journals of the House of Representatives of the Seventh Congress*, Appendix, pp. 20–21; C. W. Peterson to the Editor of the *Telegraph*, San Antonio, Sept. 12, 1842, in *Telegraph and Texas Register*, Sept. 21, 1842.

[73] William E. Jones and Others to the Authorities and People of Texas, San Antonio, Sunday, Sept. 11, 1842, in Texas Congress, *Journals of the House of Representatives of the Seventh Congress*, Appendix, pp. 20–21.

[74] W. A. Miskel to Dr. [Francis] Moore, Dec. 14, 1842, *Telegraph and Texas Register*, Dec. 21, 1842.

[75] Adrián Woll ál Sr. general en gefe [Isidro Reyes], S. Antonio de Béjar, Septiembre 12 de 1842, in Woll, *Expedición hecha en Téjas*, pp. 14–16.

sioners soon returned to announce that "they were resigned to their fate" and would surrender, trusting in the humanity and generosity of the Mexican government. It was now agreed that the Texans should surrender, as they termed it, "as prisoners of war," but as the Mexicans understood it, probably correctly, "with considerations of the most magnanimous Mexican nation." Woll reported that, "Moved by a spirit of humanity and in order that they might recognize Mexican generosity, I guaranteed them their lives."[76] The Texans were granted the privilege of retaining all personal belongings, except their arms and the flag which they had "dared to hoist" in view of the Mexican troops. In the meantime, while the terms of surrender were being arranged, the Texan flag was lowered and hidden under a pile of rocks, but was later found by the Mexicans and forwarded by Woll to General Reyes.[77] As Woll informed Judge Hutchinson, he was satisfied with the Texan explanation that they did not expect an invading army, because "he had rendered it impossible for us to discover his approach by opening for himself a road thro' the wilderness north of the Presidio road."[78]

The members of the Mexican company, which had shown so little desire to defend the town, were permitted to return to their homes, without being held as prisoners, and many of them later were observed by the Texans to be fraternizing with and cheering the invaders.

In spite of the promises in reference to the security of personal possessions, the prisoners were carefully searched and deprived of various items, including pen knives, pencils, razors, private papers, clothing, and other valuables, although a few of these were subsequently returned. Some of the men, like Maverick, threw their papers and other prized personal belongings over the fence to Mrs. William Elliot before the surrender took place.[79]

[76] *Ibid.* See also Andrew Neill to Anson Jones, Jan. 19, 1843, in Winkler (ed.), "The Béxar and Dawson Prisoners," *Quarterly of the Texas State Historical Association*, XIII (1909–1910), 296. It was stated many years later that Woll had orders, which he showed to an intimate friend of Maverick's in 1863, to put to death, as a rebel and traitor, every man taken with arms in hand. Cupples, "Eulogy on the Life and Character of the Hon. Samuel A. Maverick," in Green (ed.), *Samuel Maverick*, p. 387.

[77] Adrián Woll ál Sr. general en gefe [Isidro Reyes] S. Antonio de Béjar, Septiembre 12 de 1842, in Woll, *Expedición hecha en Téjas*, pp. 14–16. *El Cosmopolita*, Sept. 28, 1842.

[78] Hutchinson's diary in Winkler (ed.), "The Béxar and Dawson Prisoners," *Quarterly of the Texas State Historical Association*, XIII (1909–1910), 296.

[79] Green (ed.), *Samuel Maverick*, p. 197.

As each surrendered his arms, his name was recorded and opposite it was indicated the type of arm he had in hand. That evening another list was made, comprising the names of the prisoners, their professions, and birth places. Wilson I. Riddle,[80] a merchant, and Francis McKay, both of Béxar, were seized at their homes although they had not participated in the fight. Riddle and his wife, as the reader may recall, had sought refuge in Gonzales during the "Runaway" of the previous March.

There a friendly priest informed them that a large force would soon attack San Antonio. Wilson Riddle determined to go and help the Americans, and his brother John accompanied him, saying, "I cannot let my brother go without me."

They arrived in San Antonio at the moment Woll had the Americans surrounded at the Maverick home. Riddle explained to the Mexican officer, "We are not soldiers, we came to confer with the Americans."

Colonel Car[r]asco answered, "Well, there are your arms stacked against the wall—and you are not wearing that powder horn to drink milk out of!"[81]

Whereupon, the brothers were ordered held under arrest and were ultimately taken with the other prisoners into Mexico. Woll took 62 prisoners, although he credited himself with a victory over approximately 250 Texans, justifying the small number of prisoners taken by reporting, "Unfortunately a dense fog [mist] favored the escape of a great number of enemies, who by the rear of the houses, crossing the river and some large Indian cornfields, gained the forests at the time the others surrendered."[82] Actually, only eight Anglo-Texans escaped capture, among whom were W. A. Miskel and John W. Smith, the mayor, who, by going "round under the mountains," reached Seguin.[83] Ten of

[80] Wilson I. Riddle was a native of Ireland. He had been reared in Pennsylvania, later moving to Tennessee, from whence he came to Texas in 1839, and to San Antonio in 1841 to engage in trade. Chabot (ed.), *The Perote Prisoners*, p. 100; Green (ed.), *Samuel Maverick*, p. 140.

[81] Green (ed.), *Samuel Maverick*, p. 165.

[82] Adrián Woll ál Sr. general en gefe [Isidro Reyes], S. Antonio de Béjar, Septiembre 12 de 1842 in Woll, *Expedición hecha en Téjas*, pp. 14–16. See also Same to Same, S. Antonio de Béxar, Sept. 11, 1842, in *ibid.*, p. 9. The Mexican consul at New Orleans reported that he had received official documents by the schooners *Emblem* and *Creole*, dated Matamoros, Oct. 20, 1842, showing that Woll's command of 600 cavalry and 400 infantry had defeated 150 Texans entrenched on the public square. Seventy-eight of the Texans, he said, escaped and seventy-two surrendered at discretion. F. de Arrangoiz, Mexican Consul, to the Editors of the *Bee* [New Orleans], New Orleans, Nov. 9, 1842, reprinted in *Telegraph and Texas Register*, Nov. 30, 1842.

[83] John W. Smith to [Mathew Caldwell], n. d., in Z[enos] N. Morrell, *Flowers*

the prisoners were subsequently released by General Woll because of their youth, indisposition, or promises of loyalty in the future;[84] and, although their liberty was gained, their possessions were lost. Mrs. William Elliot, Mrs. William B. Jaques, and the other Anglo-American women who remained in the town were not molested.

Among the Texan prisoners were a number of men of considerable importance of that day: Judge Anderson Hutchinson of the Fourth Judicial District; James W. Robinson, a former lieutenant governor of the Republic; C. W. Peterson, the district attorney of the Fourth Judicial District; French S. Gray, the assistant district attorney; William E. Jones, lawyer and member of Congress; Samuel A. Maverick, lawyer, land speculator, and member of Congress; Andrew Neill, lawyer; James L. Trueheart, clerk of the district court; David Morgan, sworn interpreter to the district court; and others, including clients, aldermen, physicians, a few rangers, and several merchants or traders. The capture of these men put an end to civil government in San Antonio for eighteen months.[85]

---

and Fruits in the Wilderness: or Forty-Six Years in Texas and Two Winters in Honduras, p. 161; see also W. A. Miskel to Dr. [Francis] Moore, Dec. 14, 1842, in *Telegraph and Texas Register,* Dec. 21, 1842.

[84] Two merchants, Bryan Callaghan, an alderman, and Joseph McClelland, were released on the 13th and 14th, respectively, for not having taken up arms; Antonio Menchaca, who had frequently cooperated with Hays in defending the frontier, had been lamed by a stone detached by a cannon ball and he, too, was released on the 14th, being unable to travel; John S. Johnson, the youthful son of Chauncey Johnson, and another boy were freed on the 15th; and five Mexicans whose families and themselves had in the past been faithful to the Mexican government were freed upon their promise to be loyal in the future. Andrew Neill to Anson Jones, Jan. 29, 1843, in Hutchinson's diary in, Winkler (ed.), "The Béxar and Dawson Prisoners," *Quarterly of the Texas State Historical Association,* XIII (1909–1910), 295; Adrián Woll ál Sr. general en gefe [Isidro Reyes], S. Antonio de Béjar, Septiembre 12 de 1842, in Woll, *Expedición hecha en Téjas,* p. 19. Woll implies that all of the prisoners were released not later than September 12, but since the Texans were not released until the 13th, 14th, and 15th, the presumption is that his letter, while dated the 12th, was not written until later, possibly, for conveyance by Captain Posas or someone who went with him and the prisoners to Presidio del Río Grande. Woll's dispatch to the Minister of War and Marine, dated San Antonio, Texas, September 12, 1842, and published in the *Diario del Gobierno,* Oct. 22, 1842, and in the *Telegraph and Texas Register,* Nov. 30, 1842, shows 52 names of prisoners taken at Béxar. Woll's list of prisoners also appears in Nance (trans. and ed.), "Adrián Woll's Report of His Expedition into Texas in 1842," *Southwestern Historical Quarterly,* LVIII (1954–1955), 533. See Appendix A for a complete list.

[85] As a result of the disorganized state of affairs in Béxar County, there were no

323

The only casualties in the action of the 11th were a chicken rooster killed by the Mexicans near the Texan position, one Mexican killed and twenty-three wounded, and one set of artillery mules killed; the horses of three of Woll's aides-de-camp wounded, and the General's favorite horse was killed.[86] No Texans were killed. One (Antonio Menchaca)

elections held for local officers until March 23, 1844, when the chief justice of the county, David Morgan, who had returned from imprisonment in Mexico, ordered one to be held in accordance with a law of Congress approved by the President on January 14, 1842. At that time the following persons were elected: Edward Dwyer, mayor; William Elliot, treasurer; Martin Delgado, collector; and Rafael Garza, Ambrosio Rodríquez, Juan Antonio Urrutia, Antonio Menchaca, José M. Flores, James Goodman, Robert Lindsay, and Thomas Whitehead, aldermen. Dwyer, Garza, and Urrutia had been aldermen at the time of the Woll invasion. San Antonio "Journal A, Records of the City of San Antonio," ts., March 30, 1844, pp. 104, 120, 132.

[86] As for personnel, Woll reported his casualties as follows: 1 killed (Antonio Piñeda, a drummer) and 23 wounded (Lt. Antonio Villagra of the 1st Regiment of regular infantry, "who was slightly wounded in the corner of his left eye near the nose"; Guillermo Ortiz, surgeon, whose thigh was pierced by a rifle ball; José María Sánchez, drum major, 2nd Sgt. Bartolo Suárez, Col. Feliciano Martínez, Buglers Miguel García, and Miguel Rosales, and soldiers Basilio Rodríguez, Bruno Carbajal, Joaquín Arreaga, José Hernández, Candelario Jaso, Gregorio Guzmán, José María Becerril, Manuel Trinidad, José María Cantero, José María Ramírez, Alejandro Mendieta, José García, and Francisco Eulogio, all of the Santa Anna Battalion. In the artillery corps Estanislao Valle and Mariano Ramírez were wounded. A contract musician by the name of José María Gómez was also wounded. Contrary to the Texan reports, Woll reported that the wounds of most of the men were very slight. Adrián Woll ál Sr. general en gefe [Isidro Reyes], S. Antonio de Béjar, Septiembre 12 de 1842, in Woll, *Expedición hecha en Téjas*, pp. 14–16; "Report of the Office of Adjutant General, 2nd Division, Army Corps of the North, showing the dead and wounded which the division sustained in the taking of this plaza and the munitions consumed in it this day, General Headquarters in San Antonio de Béxar, September 11, 1842," enclosed in *ibid.*

The Texan accounts vary considerably in the number of Mexicans killed and wounded on this occasion. They were made at later dates by individuals whose information was based largely upon hearsay, and are, therefore, of questionable reliability. Woll's report, no doubt, minimized his losses. All the Texan reports mention a number of the wounded dying later, and this may account for the difference in the reports. James L. Trueheart, one of the Texan captives, has recorded in his diary that the Mexican losses were 10–12 killed and 25 wounded, all of whom later died except two who were crippled for life. Trueheart Diary in Chabot (ed.), *The Perote Prisoners*, p. 96. In her memoirs, Mrs. Samuel A. Maverick, who was not present at the time but was later a long-time resident of San Antonio, says the Texans killed 2 Mexicans and wounded 26, six of whom later died of their wounds. Rena Maverick Green (ed.), *Memoirs of Mary A. Maverick: Arranged by Mary A. Maverick and Her Son George Madison Maverick*, p. 68. William Small, who lived

324

was lamed by a stone detached by a cannon ball, and John Twohig, a merchant, received an injury from which he never fully recovered. Woll's first report gave the Texan losses as 5 killed and 3 wounded. The wounded, he said, "flung themselves into the river and escaped." In a subsequent report, dated September 17, Woll claimed that seven bodies of the enemy had been found in the forests from where they began their flight, and that he had ordered these identified, if possible, and buried. In New Orleans the Mexican consul publicly represented the Texan losses as amounting to several hundred killed and wounded. When this announcement reached Washington, D. C., it produced quite a sensation among the less informed.

The Texan prisoners were kept under close guard in the Maverick house from whence the principal resistance to the Mexicans had taken place. They supplied themselves through their own means or through the kindness of a few families at Béxar, and "received nothing from our captors," recorded Trueheart.[87] Many of their friends, accompanied each time by an officer, visited them. The prisoners were not allowed to communicate with friends on the outside, except in the presence of an officer. Among those who were kind to the prisoners were Mrs. William Elliot, Juan Antonio Chávez, Miguel Gostari, Victoriana, and others.[88]

---

eight miles below San Antonio, visited the city on Monday, the day after its surrender and was permitted to leave unmolested. His report made at that time and published in the *Telegraph and Texas Register*, Sept. 21, 1842, is the same as that given by Mrs. Maverick. Mrs. William Elliot, a close friend of Mrs. Maverick, was in San Antonio at the time Mr. Maverick and the others were captured. W. A. Miskel to Dr. [Francis] Moore, Dec. 14, 1842, in *Telegraph and Texas Register*, Dec. 21, 1842, reported that the Mexican casualties included 1 killed and 20 wounded, nine of whom later died. Another account says Woll lost 14 killed and 27 wounded (Cupples, "Eulogy on the Life and Character of the Hon. Samuel A. Maverick"; in Green [ed.], *Samuel Maverick*, pp. 381–395). Memucan Hunt, who was in San Antonio two or three weeks after the engagement, conversed with most of the Texan officers engaged in the repulse of Woll. He reported 6 enemy killed and 22 badly wounded (Memucan Hunt to Dr. Francis Moore, Jr., Houston, Oct. 17, 1842, in *Telegraph and Texas Register*, Oct. 26, 1842).

The reports about Texas casualties are found in Green (ed.), *Samuel Maverick*, p. 164; Adrián Woll ál Sr. general en gefe [Isidro Reyes], S. Antonio de Béjar, Septiembre 12 de 1842, in Woll, *Expedición hecha en Téjas*, pp. 14–16; Adrián Woll ál Sr. general en gefe [Isidro Reyes], Béjar, Septiembre 17 de 1842, in *ibid.*, p. 36; and Isaac Van Zandt to G. W. Terrell, Legation of Texas, Washington City, Dec. 7, 1842, Garrison (ed.), *Diplomatic Correspondence of Texas*, I, 618.

[87] Chabot (ed.), *The Perote Prisoners*, pp. 96–97.

[88] S. A. Maverick to Mary A. Maverick, San Fernando, 45 miles from the Presidio Río Grande Crossing, Oct. 6, 1842, in Green (ed.), *Samuel Maverick*, pp. 195–197.

Mrs. Elliot was permitted to visit the prisoners two or three times before they were marched out of the town, and on one of these occasions, Maverick slipped twenty gold doubloons (about $325) to her for Mrs. Maverick, who was at the time living at Colonel Dancy's in Fayette County, opposite LaGrange on the Colorado. The money was transmitted to her through John W. Smith.[89] On the last day when Mrs. Elliot saw Maverick before he was marched off to Mexico, he handed her his watch to give to his wife. B. C. Sánchez, a merchant at San Antonio, friend of the Mavericks, and presumed to be a native of Havana, was accused of "interfering in the affairs of the prisoners after they surrendered and when they had no power to defend or protect themselves."[90] He was among those visiting the prisoners, but by his conduct proved not to be their friend. Some enjoyed more vigorous punishment and less liberty, wrote Neill, as a result of his "identifying some of us and making us known to the Mexican officers who accompanied him in order that we might be more rigorously watched or dealt with."[91] Sánchez was accused of giving aid and counsel to the enemy, and of boarding some of the Mexican officers at his home without remuneration. After Woll's withdrawal, Sánchez suddenly found it wise to leave Texas. François Guilbeau, the French consul, was accused of failing to observe a strictly neutral position, for his having tendered to General Woll "previous to his even alighting from his horse" his store and everything within it.[92]

It was no surprise to the Texans to find among Woll's officers men who had formerly lived at San Antonio and elsewhere in the Republic and who had gone to Mexico, where some engaged in raids upon the Texan frontier. Among these were José María J. Carrasco of Victoria; Juan N. Seguin of San Antonio; Vicente Córdova formerly of Nacogdoches; and Antonio Pérez and Leandro Arriola, both formerly of San Antonio.

On the day of their surrender, sixteen of the Texan prisoners were permitted, they said, "through the kind permission of the Commanding General" to assure their friends that they were being "treated all the

---

[89] Green (ed.), *Samuel Maverick*, p. 166; Eleanor Elliot, to Mary A. Maverick, San Antonio de Béjar, Nov. 11, 1842, in *ibid.*, pp. 201–202; Chabot (ed.), *The Perote Prisoners*, p. 97. Mrs. William (Eleanor) Elliot was formerly Eleanor Connally of New Orleans. She married Elliot in 1835 and they came to San Antonio in 1839 with their two children (Mary and Billy). They lived in a house opposite the north end of the Maverick garden on the west side of Soledad Street.

[90] A. Neill to Anson Jones, Secretary of State, Washington, Texas, Jan. 29, 1843, in Miller Papers (Texas), ms.

[91] *Ibid.*

[92] *Ibid.*

leniency compatible with our condition as prisoners of war." An open letter was sent "To the Authorities and People of Texas," saying that fifty-three of the Anglo-Texans at Béxar had surrendered as "prisoners of war" to an "advanced division" of the Mexican army under General Woll, "an officer well known through the country for his magnaminity, gallantry and generosity." They declared they had been ignorant of the character and number of the invading force, believing the assaulting force to have been a robber band not exceeding three hundred men, and probably not more than one hundred. "Had we been aware of the approach of an invading force," they declared, "we should have most certainly retreated from the place, because it would have been madness to attempt its defence."[93] They said they had been told by General Woll that had they not fired upon the Mexican troops they would have been permitted to depart unmolested. They reported that the officers of the formal invading army into whose hands they had fallen were "determined to conduct the war upon the principles of the most honorable and chivalrous character," and that the Texan prisoners now requested that if any Mexican officer or soldier should fall into the hands of Texans, "through the casualties of war that they be treated with the respect due their rank and the humanity due to prisoners of war."

On the eve of their leaving San Antonio under a Mexican escort to the Río Grande, the prisoners were required to draft a letter "To the American Officers and Citizens," again urging the Anglo-Americans not to blame the citizens of Béxar for their catastrophe.

The undersigned, Americans, prisoners in the hands of the Mexican Army at this place, feel it to be a duty to recommend to all Americans, who may come here after our departure, to treat the Mexican population residing in this place with lenience and kindness. Up to the time of the unfortunate occurrence by which we were made prisoners nothing transpired to prejudice them in our estimation, and since our captivity they have been untiring in their kindness, supplying us in the most liberal manner with everything which could conduce in the least degree to our comfort.

We do hope, therefore, should this place again fall into the hands of Americans, that for *our* sake the Mexican population here will not be in any way disturbed or injured either in person or property.

This letter was signed by fifty-one of the prisoners, including John S.

[93] William E. Jones and Fifteen Others to the Authorities and People of Texas, San Antonio, Sept. 11, 1842, Texas Congress, *Journals of the House of Representatives of The Seventh Congress*, Appendix, pp. 20–21; *Telegraph and Texas Register*, Sept. 28, 1842.

Johnson, Joseph McClelland, and Bryan Callaghan, who were subsequently released. Those whose names do not appear on the list of signers were W. H. O'Phelan, Andrew Neill, Thomas Hancock, John Forester, and Antonio Menchaca.[94]

On the 13th one of the Mexican spies sent out from San Antonio on the 10th returned. He informed the Texans, then prisoners, that he had failed to meet with the enemy, but he could give no account of what had happened to his two comrades.[95] After signing on Thursday, the 15th, a document pledging not to escape between Béxar and the Río Grande,[96] the fifty-two captives were removed from the city at noon under a heavy guard of 125 men commanded by Captain Emeterio Posas, and held in camp on the edge of the prairie near the Alazán, about four miles from town preparatory to being sent, together with the wounded Mexicans under the care of Dr. Manuel Pizarza, to the Río Grande. Twenty-two[97] of the prisoners, including Maverick on his fine horse, were permitted to ride their own horses, but Neill's horse was taken from him and ridden by a Mexican soldier. Neill says he was forced to walk because he had refused to sign his name to one of the many documents drawn up for the prisoners' signatures to be sent into Texas or left behind respecting the prisoners' treatment.[98] Maverick's horse, however, proved too fine an animal for a lowly Texan prisoner to ride in Mexico; so it was taken from him at San Fernando de Agua Verde by Colonel Carrasco, who gave him in exchange "a little black, tender footed horse."[99]

As the prisoners passed Woll's quarters, on leaving the city, he shouted in English, from a window before the crowd that filled the square, to Judge Hutchinson that he had written, as he had promised, on

[94] William E. Jones and Others to the American Officers and Citizens, San Antonio, Sept. 14, 1842, in *Telegraph and Texas Register*, Sept. 28, 1842; C. W. Peterson to the Editor of the *Telegraph*, Sept. 12, 1842, in *ibid.*, Sept. 21, 1842; Green (ed.), *Samuel Maverick*, pp. 173–174; Samuel A. Maverick Papers, ms.; Waddy Thompson Papers, 1824–1848, ms. The copy in the Thompson Papers contains fifty-one names.

[95] Trueheart's diary in Chabot (ed.), *The Perote Prisoners*, p. 98.

[96] Trueheart's diary, Sept. 15, 1842, in *ibid.*, pp. 98–102.

[97] Miskel, who was not present at the time, reported later nineteen of the prisoners were mounted. W. A. Miskel to Dr. [Francis] Moore, Dec. 14, 1842, *Telegraph and Texas Register*, Dec. 21, 1842.

[98] A. Neill to Anson Jones, Secretary of State, Washington, Texas, Jan. 29, 1843, in Winkler (ed.), "The Béxar and Dawson Prisoners," *Quarterly of the Texas State Historical Association*, XIII (1909–1910), 313–320.

[99] Maverick, Diary, Oct. 7, 1842, in Maverick Papers, ms.

his behalf to General Reyes, and had sent along a confidential officer to see that the prisoners were well treated.[100] According to Hutchinson,[101] in turning the prisoners over to Captain Posas, Woll informed him, "I hope you will cause them to be treated with the considerations which international law requires; especially, those whose [names] are marked with an asterisk . . . being persons who merit a few privileges. Yet, this should not keep you from taking all means and precautions that you may judge expedient for their security, as you are the sole person responsible [for them] from the moment that you receive them."[102] He is also said to have promised that upon their arrival at Presidio del Río Grande they would be freed by General Reyes. However, it is not likely that Woll would have foolishly made a commitment for his superior. More than likely he said they would probably be released by Reyes upon their arrival at Río Grande and would soon be back home. Mrs. Alsbury went with the prisoners, and Francisco Ruiz, one of the native Mexicans of San Antonio, informed Maverick and Twohig before they left that he would do all he could to have them released as quickly as possible.[103]

Arriving at the camp site at the Alazán, the Texans were made to lie down and were told that they were not to move unless accompanied by a guard. A portion of their escort was sent back to Béxar. On the 16th the prisoners were started on the march shortly after sunrise. As they prepared to leave camp they heard the firing of the cannon salute in San Antonio in celebration of the anniversary of Mexican independence. Some of the prisoners who had good horses were deprived of them, and given others in their places.[104] Late that afternoon after a long, fatiguing march they reached the Medina at the Presidio Ford and pushed on up the river to Woll's crossing, where they crossed the river and encamped on an eminence on the west side of the river about three to four miles

[100] Trueheart's diary, Sept. 15, 1842, in Chabot (ed.), *The Perote Prisoners,* pp. 98–102; Hutchinson's diary, in Winkler (ed.), "The Béxar and Dawson Prisoners," *Quarterly of the Texas State Historical Association,* XIII (1909–1910), 296–297.

[101] Hutchinson's diary in Winkler (ed.), "The Béxar and Dawson Prisoners," *Quarterly of the Texas State Historical Association,* XIII (1909–1910), 296–297.

[102] Quoted in Adrián Woll to Isidro Reyes, Béxar, Sept. 15, 1842, in Nance (trans. and ed.), "Brigadier General Adrián Woll's Report of His Expedition into Texas in 1842," *Southwestern Historical Quarterly,* LVIII (1954–1955), 539–540.

[103] Eleanor Elliot to Mary A. Maverick, San Antonio de Béjar, Nov. 11, 1842, Green (ed.), *Samuel Maverick,* pp. 201–202.

[104] Trueheart's diary, Sept. 16, 1842, in Chabot (ed.), *The Perote Prisoners,* pp. 102–103.

above the Cañon Ford. In camp the prisoners that night discussed the desirability and the feasibility of effecting their escape during the night, but according to Hutchinson, several of the company were so "desirous to avail themselves of the opportunity of being taken into Mexico" that they were unwilling to attempt it.[105] Judge Hutchinson believed that if any ten had made the attempt to escape, they would have succeeded.

On the following day the march along the Upper Presidio Road was renewed at sunrise. During the day J. R. Cunningham, who for the past two days had been suffering from a high fever contracted at Houston which had assumed a congestive stage, fell from his horse, and being unable to ride farther was by order of Captain Posas placed in one of the carts with the Mexican wounded. Upon arrival at the Río Hondo, Booker and McKay, both physicians, requested of the Mexican commander permission to administer aid to Cunningham, but Captain Posas refused their request and would not let any of the Texans converse with or render assistance to him. A brief halt was made at the Hondo to permit the troops and prisoners to rest. Captain Luis Vidal, an aide-de-camp to General Woll and the superintending officer, finding Hutchinson exhausted, made a tent for him and "gave him of his rice and assured him of his friendship."[106] After a short rest, the guard and prisoners moved on, reaching the Río Seco about 8 o'clock at night, where they camped on the east bank[107] and the prisoners were forced to sleep in two lines with the soldiers camped on both sides of them.

The next morning was Sunday (the 18th). Cunningham appeared to be stronger. As preparations were being made to renew the march he was sitting beside the "road." He wished to ride on horseback, but his Texan friends advised against it and he rode once more in the cart. The Texans never saw their comrade again, for he died on the Leona.[108]

[105] Hutchinson's diary in Winkler (ed.), "The Béxar and Dawson Prisoners," *Quarterly of the Texas State Historical Association,* XIII (1909–1910), 296–297; see also Trueheart's diary, [Sept.] 16, 1842, in Chabot (ed.), *The Perote Prisoners,* pp. 102–103.

[106] Hutchinson's diary, in Winkler (ed.), "The Béxar and Dawson Prisoners," in *Quarterly of the Texas State Historical Association,* XIII (1909–1910), p. 297.

[107] Maverick, Diary, Sept. 17, 1842, in Maverick Papers, ms.

[108] It was later learned that Cunningham died the next day, September 19, and the body after being stripped of its clothing, was buried on the west side of the Leona "about a mile or a mile and a half from the creek on one side of the road made by Gen. Woll, a short distance from the terminus of the bottom as you ascend a slight hill," reported Trueheart. Some of the Texan prisoners, however, understood that the body was not buried, but only a few pieces of brush thrown over it.

Noon was spent at the Sabinal and a little after dark the prisoners and their escort reached the Río Frio and camped on the west side. After having proceeded four or five miles that morning, Trueheart suddenly remembered that he had left his money where he had slept the night before. He requested permission to return and look for it, and was permitted to do so under guard. He found the money under a bunch of grass where he had hidden it to keep from being robbed during the night. During the morning the prisoners crossed the Leona at a spot near where Seguin had camped to await the arrival of General Woll as the expedition moved into Texas. In the afternoon they crossed the Nueces, and camped at the Laguna Espantosa on the west side about three miles from the river.[109] Throughout the night Captain Posas, who may have been a little superstitious and restless about being so near the Haunted (Espantosa) Lake, seemed to be quite uneasy about the security of his prisoners, getting up "repeatedly during the night to see that everything was going on all right."[110] His restlessness, too, may have been caused by the rain which fell during the night. However, all went well.

On Tuesday, the 20th, the prisoners passed Chaparrosa Creek, a good location with fine grass, eighteen to twenty miles west of the Nueces, to camp among prickly pears on a small arroyo called the Saladito. The next day, having been compelled by a shower of rain to get up early to keep themselves and their blankets dry, they got started at an unusually early hour. About 9 o'clock the weather cleared, and it proved to be a beautiful day. Late in the afternoon they arrived in sight of the Río Grande, and were told by the commanding officer that they might either go down to the river or stop at watering holes nearby on Cueva Creek.[111] For the last two or three days, the Mexican soldiers had been amusing themselves by killing rattlesnakes which were found in great abundance in the area west of the Nueces, some of the snakes being of enormous size. One of the young officers offered a soldier a *real* to capture a snake

---

Cunningham's hat and blanket were delivered to the San Antonio prisoners at San Fernando. Trueheart's diary, Sept. 18, 1842, in Chabot (ed.), *The Perote Prisoners*, p. 104.

[109] Trueheart's diary, Sept. 19, 1842, in *ibid.*, pp. 104–105. Maverick says the lake was seven miles west of the Nueces, and that they camped at the head of it. See also Green (ed.), *Samuel Maverick*, p. 175.

[110] Trueheart's diary, Sept. 19, 1842, in Chabot, *The Perote Prisoners*, pp. 104–105.

[111] Trueheart's diary, Sept. 21, 1842, in *ibid.*, pp. 105–106.

by taking it by the back of the head. The soldier made the attempt. He stepped on the snake's tail and "was boldly walking up, when the snake, too quick for that, bit him through a hole in his old shoe."[112] His friends carried him to the river (Río Grande), where Dr. Booker lanced the wound, and among other things, poured salt into it. The soldier got better in a few days.

On the eighth day (September 23) after leaving San Antonio the prisoners and their escort crossed the Río Grande in two dugout canoes brought over from the west bank. In parties of eight or ten, each carrying his own baggage, the prisoners and their guard commenced crossing the river at the point where Woll had crossed late in August. While the men crossed in small parties, those waiting to cross rested under the shade of a large pecan tree. After most of the men had crossed over, the horses were driven into the water and forced to swim across.[113] Only two or three of the horses were drowned. By sunset nearly everything had been taken across, and camp was made on top of an adjacent hill in a sheep pen. Here they learned of the death of Cunningham. The next day the men were permitted to bathe in the river, which proved to be a source of great pleasure to them. Afterwards they marched to Presidio del Río Grande, a town of about one thousand inhabitants situated some three or four miles from the river. The old road from Monclova to San Antonio passed though the town. The town appeared to be a poor miserable place in fast decay; but, nevertheless, the Texans rested here until the 27th. They were quartered in an old house fronting on the plaza. A date on the structure showed that it had been built in 1776. All buildings were made of adobe. The guard which brought the prisoners was now ordered back to Texas to meet Woll, but upon arrival at the river learned that Woll was only a short distance away, so the guard returned to Presidio del Río Grande.[114]

On the 27th the prisoners were conducted to Nava, near the old Spanish mission of San Juan Bautista, and the next day to San Fernando de Agua Verde, headquarters at that time of General Isidro Reyes, who could be seen looking through a window of his quarters as the Texans entered the town.[115] Reyes later visited the Texans in their quarters.

[112] Maverick's diary, Sept. 21, 1842, in Maverick Papers, ms.

[113] Trueheart's diary, Sept. 23, 1842, in Chabot, *The Perote Prisoners*, pp. 106–107; Hutchinson's diary in Winkler (ed.), "The Béxar and Dawson Prisoners," *Quarterly of the Texas State Historical Association*, XIII (1909–1910), 298.

[114] Trueheart's diary, Sept. 27, 1842, in Chabot, *The Perote Prisoners*, p. 108.

[115] Unless otherwise indicated, the foregoing itinerary of the march of the San

San Fernando was situated about forty-five miles northwest of the Presidio del Río Grande, on a creek, often dry, named Agua Verde. In 1842 the town was about the size of San Antonio de Béxar. Doña Marina Rodríguez y Taylor furnished some of the Texan prisoners with food free of charge and coffee three times every day. She even purchased a horse for Judge Robinson when the prisoners left San Fernando.[116] From San Fernando Andrew Neill wrote his old friend Francisco Vidaurri y Villaseñor at Santa Rosa asking him to pay all, part, or at least the interest on the note Vidaurri, former vice president of the defunct Republic of the Río Grande, had given Samuel G. Powell, dated November 5, 1839, for he (Neill) was badly in need of money for himself and friends. Neill, who probably was Powell's lawyer, offered a receipt for the amount.[117] On the 4th of October the San Antonio prisoners were joined at San Fernando by Bradley, Faison, Manton, and seven others of the Dawson captives.[118] On the 6th, the day before the prisoners left San Fernando for Mexico City, one of them wrote that he had spent the preceding day with General Cela, and

taking every thing into consideration, passed a very agreeable time of it. We played chess during the afternoon, dined about seven o'clock—the dinner excellent, coffee, butter, &c. So far I have found the Mexican officers gentlemen, and the soldiers generally kind and disposed to make our situation as comfortable as possible.

I apprehend no violence to any of our party; on the contrary, I feel sanguine that under the peculiar circumstances under which we were taken at San Antonio, our captivity cannot be very long.

I should be more disposed to complain of my present disagreeable situation, were it not that others are here whose lot is perhaps even harder than mine. They have families living on the Colorado and Guadalupe, and were

Antonio prisoners to the Río Grande is based on Maverick, Diaries, Miscellaneous, 1829–1843, in Maverick Papers, ms.

116 James W. Robinson, Samuel A. Maverick [Andrew] Neill, C. Johnson, and George C. Hatch to Whom it May Concern, San Fernando, Oct. 6, 1842, in Green (ed.), *Samuel Maverick*, p. 198; Ellen [Eleanor] Elliot to Mrs. Samuel A. Maverick, San Antonio de Béjar, Nov. 14, 1842, in *ibid.*, pp. 202–204.

117 A. Neill to Francisco Vidaurri y Villaseñor in Santa Rosa, San Fernando, Oct. 3, 1842, in Domestic Correspondence (Texas), ms. The note was for upwards of $3,000.

118 S. A. Maverick to Mary A. Maverick, San Fernando 45 miles N.W. from the Presidio Río G[rande] Crossing, Oct. 6, 1842, in Green (ed.), *Samuel Maverick*, pp. 195–197. An account of the Dawson Massacre will be found in Chapter 16 of the present work.

in San Antonio only for a short time, attending court, where, but a day or two before they were to have returned, when they were captured. I, myself, intended leaving in two days at furtherest; the absence of a gentleman who held some papers, without which I could not conveniently leave, alone detained me.[119]

On October 7 forty-eight of the San Antonio prisoners and ten Dawson men were started on the road toward Mexico City. Maverick and twenty-two of the San Antonio men were permitted to ride. Van Ness, Fitzgerald, and Hancock were left behind with the expectation of being shot, being former Santa Fé prisoners reapprehended in arms against Mexico.[120]

[119] *Telegraph and Texas Register*, Nov. 23, 1842.
[120] Maverick, Diary, Oct. 7, 1842, in Maverick Papers, ms.

CHAPTER FIFTEEN

The Battle of Salado

Now LET US RETURN to Woll's activities at San Antonio and the efforts that were made in Texas to expel him. Hays, who had been cut off from San Antonio, received a note from one of the prisoners, sent by a messenger, stating that the Texans within the town had surrendered. All day on the 11th Major Hays hovered in the vicinity of the invading army which he estimated at 1,300 strong, capturing a Mexican, and at night withdrew to the Guadalupe, leaving spies behind; and, "if I can," he wrote the Secretary of War, "I will try and watch their approach to this river. All information will be reported every opportunity."[1]

From the captured Mexican it was learned that Woll intended to fortify the town and await re-enforcements which Hays believed were not then near at hand. Before reaching the Guadalupe, Hays sent out a call for troops to rendezvous quickly at Seguin to repel any scouting party the enemy might send out from San Antonio, and urgently requested that a "few well mounted men" join him as quickly as possible for the purpose of spying.[2] Seguin, the initial rendezvous point, had been laid off in 1838 under the direction of Joseph S. Martin at a site spotted by live-oak motts and numerous springs. It had long been a favorite camping place of the Indians, and the rangers from the settlements on their scouting trips had found it a good place to rest, on account of its excellent grass and water. Martin retained 25 per cent of the town lots and sold the remainder to a group of rangers from Gonzales,

[1] John C. Hays to the Secretary of War, Sept. 12, 1842, in Texas Congress, *Journals of the House of Representatives of the Seventh Congress of the Republic of Texas, convened at Washington on the 14th November 1842*, Appendix, p. 16; see also A. J. Sowell, *Early Settlers and Indian Fighters of Southwest Texas*, p. 59.

[2] John C. Hays to the Citizens of Texas, San Antonio, Sept. 12, 1842, in Texas Congress, *Journals of the House of Representatives of the Seventh Congress*, Appendix, pp. 21–22; J. D. Affleck, "History of John C. Hays," pt. I, p. 232, ts.; W. A. Miskel to Dr. [Francis] Moore, Dec. 14, 1842, in *Telegraph and Texas Register*, Dec. 21, 1842.

who were "with a single exception of Captain Mathew Caldwell's Company of Gonzales Rangers, or of Captain Callahan's Company of Minute Men."[3] The town was first named Walnut Springs, but a few months later was changed to Seguin, in honor of Juan N. Seguin, one of the heroes of the Texas Revolution.

Upon effecting his escape from San Antonio, Mayor John W. Smith[4] hastily sent a note to Colonel Mathew Caldwell[5] at Gonzales, who had commanded the advance guard on the Santa Fé expedition the year before and had only recently returned from imprisonment in Mexico.[6] Smith's communication reached Caldwell on Monday morning. As soon as the news of the fall of San Antonio reached Gonzales, on the left bank of the Guadalupe, the Texans in the vicinity quickly gathered what ammunition they could find and started for Seguin, leaving instructions behind for recruits from farther east to follow their trail. At Seguin the men obtained a few ears of corn, had it parched and ground, and mixed with sugar at the ratio of two pounds of sugar to ten ears of corn.

Meanwhile, Wallace and Mallon, en route back to San Antonio from Austin with their meager supplies of powder and lead, stopped at Antonio Navarro's rancho, and to their surprise found Rice and Johnston, two of Hays' rangers, "sitting on the ground while two Mexican women picked cactus spines out of their bare feet. Wallace reined up, laughing at their sad appearance: 'Hello, boys. What are you doing here?' "[7] Here, while the two arrivals from Austin obtained corn for their horses (the principal reason for their having come by this route), they learned

---

[3] Quoted in Charles Ramsdell, "Introduction to Seguin," *San Antonio Express Magazine*, Sept. 18, 1949, p. 5.

[4] It was Captain John W. Smith who piloted Captain Albert Martin's company into the Alamo on the night of March 1, 1836, and afterwards, as a courier, bore Travis' last dispatch, and, thus was spared the fate of the men of the Alamo. Smith represented Béxar County in the Texas Senate in 1842. Hubert Howe Bancroft, *History of Texas and the North Mexican States*, II, 209.

[5] In spite of what many historians and would-be-historians have attempted to make of it, Mathew Caldwell consistently spelled his name with one "t."

[6] Although the last of the Santa Fé men, except José Antonio Navarro, had been released in April, 1842, not all of them had yet reached Texas. Fourteen of them reached New Orleans on September 24 on the U.S. revenue cutter *Woodbury*. Commodore Moore of the Texan navy received them on board his ship and furnished them rations, and under the flag of Texas aboard the steam packet *Merchant* they took passage for Texas on Oct. 2, 1842. William Bryan to Anson Jones, Consulate of Texas, New Orleans, October 2, 1842, (Marked: Duplicate), in Consular Correspondence (Texas) 1838–1875, ms.

[7] Stanley Vestal, *Bigfoot Wallace*, p. 69.

of the fall of San Antonio and the hasty withdrawal of their comrades, whom the Mexican cavalry had chased through the prickly pear and chaparral. They were told that a force was being collected at Seguin to drive out the invader. Thereupon, Wallace and Mallon, anxious not to miss an opportunity to fight Mexicans, hurried on to Seguin, where they found the town full of men from Gonzales and surrounding places anxious to advance upon San Antonio. Hays, his lieutenant, Henry E. McCulloch, and others were glad to see the two rangers, even though they had been able to secure only one keg of powder and a small quantity of caps and lead in Austin.

News of the capture of San Antonio spread rapidly eastward from Seguin and Gonzales to Lavaca, the Colorado, and the Brazos. William Small,[8] a blacksmith who lived eight miles below Béxar and had lost a wagon and three or four yoke of oxen to foragers from the Mexican army or to bandits, brought the news to LaGrange, apparently arriving there shortly before the express rider from Béxar. "We are looking to-night for another express," wrote A. C. Allen of Houston who was passing through LaGrange on his way home when news of the invasion reached there.[9] He had visited San Antonio on Monday, September 12, and had been permitted to depart unmolested. He reported having seen the Mexicans, whom he described as "miserable wretches." Although he could give nothing as to the size of the enemy force, he reported that seven hundred of their cavalry were to leave by the St. Marks road for Gonzales and that a re-enforcement of one hundred men under Colonel Calixto Bravo had entered Béxar on Monday with an estimated $300,-000 in specie for payment of the troops.[10] At 3 o'clock on the morning of the 14th a dispatch from San Antonio, dated the 12th, reached La-Grange by way of Gonzales, giving accurate information on the size and strength of the invading army, and enclosing a copy of the letter written by a portion of the prisoners to the authorities and people of Texas, a copy of Hays' letter of the 12th, and a copy of Woll's proclamation of September 12 to the people of San Antonio.[11] A public meet-

[8] "Joint Resolution for the Relief of William Small," Jan. 21, 1840, in Harriet Smither (ed.), *Journals of the Fourth Congress of the Republic of Texas*, III, 254–255.

[9] A. C. Allen to Francis Moore, Jr., La Grange, Sept. 15, 1842, in *Telegraph and Texas Register*, Sept. 28, 1842.

[10] *Ibid.; Civilian and Galveston Gazette*, Sept. 24, 1842; Memucan Hunt to Francis Moore, editor of the *Telegraph*, Houston, dated Béxar, Jan. 8, 1843, *Morning Star*, (Houston), Jan. 17, 1843.

[11] J. W. Harrison, D. S. Kornegay, N. H. Dawson, A. A. Gardenier, and James

ing was called, and when it assembled, Joseph Shaw, referred to as an old man, was chosen chairman and John W. Harrison, secretary. A committee of three (Dr. Francis F. Wells, A. Vail, and George Hill) was appointed to inform the citizens of the proceedings of this meeting, wherein it was resolved that the volunteers of Fayette County should meet and organize at Black Jack Springs at 12 o'clock the following day (15th). Black Jack Springs was situated about ten miles southwest of LaGrange on the north side of the fertile Navidad prairie. To the north of the springs was post-oak timberland. At this time the citizens of LaGrange also appointed a committee of vigilance composed of G. W. Sinks, W. B. Merriwether, and B. F. Nabors. Troops east of Gonzales were instructed to rendezvous at Gonzales,[12] and it was hoped that three hundred men from Fayette County would be at Gonzales in three or four days,[13] ready to march west.

The next day a letter from Caldwell, dated the 14th from Seguin, was received. It warned of Antonio Pérez's march of 250 men from San Antonio on the lower road toward Gonzales. The men under Pérez were believed to be a portion of the 700 men mentioned by Small, and Caldwell felt that their object was to report on the assembling of any Texan force and to cover Woll's retreat.[14]

Twenty men residing on the Lavaca in Gonzales County, beyond the town of Gonzales, headed west almost immediately upon receipt of the news of the Mexican capture of San Antonio. Others left on the 15th. The latter stopped for the night at Peach Creek, which was on the rise and difficult to cross because of the late heavy rains.[15] On the 16th other

---

Hudson to the Citizens of San Felipe, La Grange, Sept. 14, 1842, Texas Congress, *Journals of the House of Representatives of the Seventh Congress*, Appendix, pp. 19–21; see also, William E. Jones and Fifteen Others to the Authorities and People of Texas, San Antonio, Sunday, Sept. 11, 1842, in *ibid.*, pp. 20–21; [Adrián Woll] El General 2º En Gefe del Cuerpo de Egército de Norte, ál Vecindario de esta ciudad, San Antonio de Béjar, Septiembre 12 de 1842, in Adrián Woll, *Expedición hecha en Téjas, por una parte de la Division del Cuerpo de Egército del Norte*, pp. 29–30.

[12] Citizens' Meeting at La Grange, Sept. 14, 1842, *Telegraph and Texas Register*, Sept. 21, 1842.

[13] A. C. Allen to Francis Moore, Jr., La Grange, Sept. 15, 1842, *Telegraph and Texas Register*, Sept. 28, 1842.

[14] *Ibid.*; see also *Telegraph and Texas Register*, Sept. 21, 1842.

[15] J[ohn] H[enry] B[rown] to the Editor of the Houston *Telegraph*, La Vaca River, Gonzales Co., Oct. 2, 1842, *Telegraph and Texas Register*, Nov. 2, 1842; a manuscript copy of this letter will be found in the John Henry Brown Papers, 1835–1872, ms., under title, "The Battle of Salado, Sept. 11, 1842."

Samuel Bogart

Henry L. Kinney

EDWARD BURLESON.

Jesse Billingsley

Edward Burleson

Samuel A. Maverick

Memucan Hunt

Morgan C. Hamilton

Peter Hansbrough Bell

From Dudley G. Wooten (ed.), *A Comprehensive History of Texas*, the Barker picture collection, and L. E. Daniell, *Personnel of the Texas State Government*; all courtesy Barker Texas History Center, The University of Texas.

Antonio Menchaca   Juan N. Seguin

Adrián Woll   José María Bocanegra

From Frederick C. Chabot, *With the Makers of San Antonio*, courtesy Barker Texas History Center; and Vicente Riva-Palacio, *Mexico á través de los siglos*, courtesy Latin-American Collection, The University of Texas.

Ben McCulloch

John Coffee Hays

From Samuel C. Reid, Jr., *The Scouting Expeditions of McCulloch's Texas Rangers*, courtesy Barker Texas History Center, The University of Texas.

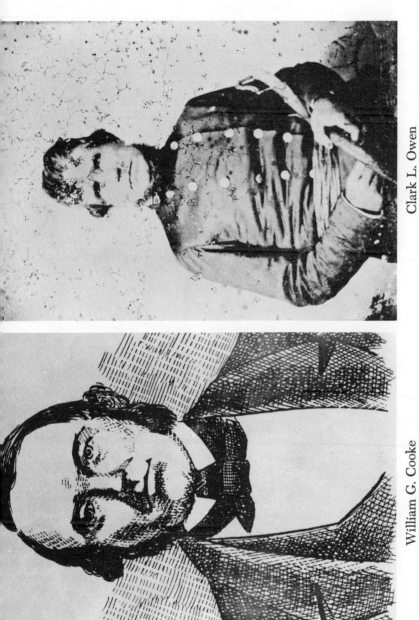

William G. Cooke

Clark L. Owen

From Z. T. Fulmore, *The History and Geography of Texas as Told in County Names*, courtesy Barker Texas History Center, The University of Texas; and the Archives picture collection, courtesy Texas State Archives.

A Lipan Warrior

"BIG-FOOT WALLACE"

William A. A. "Big-Foot" Wallace

From the Barker picture collection and William H. Emory, *Report of the United States*

San Fernando Cathedral, San Antonio

Somervell's army in the bogs of the Atascosa, by John Knott.

From Barker picture collection and Z. T. Fulmore, *The History and Geography of Texas as Told in County Names*; courtesy Barker Texas History Center, The University of Texas.

Bullock's Hotel, Austin, 1839.

From William S. Red, *A History of the Presbyterian Church in Texas*, courtesy Barker Texas History Center, The University of Texas.

Diorama of the Capitol of the Republic of Texas at Austin.

From William R. Hogan, *The Texas Republic*, courtesy Barker Texas History Center, The University of Texas.

View of Live Oak Point, Texas, taken in March 1842, on an expedition to Copano commanded by Captain John Wade, of the city of Galveston.

The City of Galveston.

From Mrs. Matilda C. F. Houstoun, *Texas and the Gulf of Mexico*, courtesy Barker Texas History Center, The University of Texas.

San Antonio de Béxar, 1840.

From Homer S. Thrall, *A Pictorial History of Texas*, courtesy Barker Texas History Center, The University of Texas.

Military Plaza, San Antonio, c. 1855.

From William H. Emory, *Report of the United States and Mexican Boundary Survey*, courtesy Barker Texas History Center, The University of Texas.

The Alamo, 1837.

Mission San José y San Miguel de Aguayo.

Courtesy Barker Texas History Center, The University of Texas.

Arroyo Secate, two miles below Laredo.

From William H. Emory, *Report of the United States and Mexican Boundary Survey,*

men joined them, and they swam the creek at daybreak. The Lavaca men entered Gonzales and learned that the Texans were rendezvousing on the Cíbolo, six miles above the crossing. They hurried forward over the muddy road. Without stopping their horses and permitting them to rest, they reached Seguin at 3 A.M. on the 17th, where they rested until sunrise. At 2 P.M. they reached the Texan camp, where they were informed of the murder of Dr. Smither, Rhea, and McDonald.[16]

Couriers rode day and night conveying the news of the fall of Béxar, and urging re-enforcements to hasten to the west with a plentiful supply of powder and lead. The poverty, hardships, and many trials which the inhabitants had undergone of late taught them to rely upon themselves, and gave them courage, vigor and determination to repel the many onslaughts of the enemy. The cry was "Get ready, men, as soon as possible to meet the enemy as near the Colorado as possible. Don't wait to organize into companies. Go as soon as you can get ready by ones, twos, tens, or twenties, as soon as the case may be."[17]

A company of volunteers was raised at Matagorda on September 12, by Captain A. C. Horton.[18] During the afternoon of the 14th two spies were dispatched from Victoria. They went as far as Goliad, but were unable to cross the San Antonio River then in flood. They reported seeing horses and several persons tied up in the abandoned town and many signs of mounted horsemen having passed in its vicinity. On Friday morning, September 16, word reached Victoria that the Mexicans had been in Goliad the night before. A man named Howard, who lived below Carlos Rancho reported seeing twelve to fifteen enemy soldiers at the rancho the evening of the 15th. He declared the Mexicans at the ranch were in high spirits and were giving fandangoes. He pretended to join them, and learned, he said, that the Mexicans had fifteen thousand troops on the east side of the Río Grande, and he had gathered that a thousand were to be in the rancho on the night of the 15th and as many more at Goliad. The roads in that area were muddy and the streams swollen, which would retard the movement of wagons and families fleeing before the invader, as well as hinder the advance of the

[16] The murder of these men will be discussed later in this chapter.

[17] John W. Lockhart, "Darkest Days in Texas," *Galveston Daily News*, March 26, 1893.

[18] Muster Rolls of Captain Albert C. Horton's company of Volunteers, commanded by A. C. Horton subject to direction of Genl. A. Somervell called into the service of the Republic of Texas on the 12th day of September 1842 [recruited at Matagorda], Militia Rolls (Texas), ms.

enemy's army. "We hope," said Owen, "to make a stand here [at Victoria] long enough to enable the families to get off," although the streams and roads were likely to be impassable for several days.[19]

By the 20th, Colonel Owen had 150 men at Victoria and other volunteers were arriving daily. The companies from Matagorda were expected hourly, and in a few days his force was expected to be augmented to some 300 or 400. Spies had been dispatched as far as the Nueces, some of whom had returned by the 20th to report seeing no large body of Mexicans. William L. Hunter,[20] former chief justice of Refugio County and member of Congress, and another man made a reconnaissance toward the old rancho of Kinney and Aubrey about September 15 and discovered a party of about 60 Mexicans there. The two Texans were pursued and Judge Hunter's companion was captured. Hunter reached Victoria safely, and a company of about 60 Texans was quickly formed to go to Corpus Christi to attack the Mexicans at the rancho. Before the Texans left Victoria, however, information was received that a large enemy force was approaching; so they delayed two days. When they did go down they found Kinney and Aubrey's rancho deserted except for two Mexicans, one of whom was a one-armed soldier. These they made prisoner and carried to Victoria.[21]

While General Woll was moving upon San Antonio by the upper route, General Ampudia, who had recently been named successively counsellor for Tamaulipas[22] and then commandant general of the Department of Tamaulipas,[23] sent five hundred men under Gougales to re-enforce Woll. These troops left Matamoros on August 26, but, after advancing ninety miles through inundated prairies, the men wading for

[19] James D. Owen to ———, Victoria, Friday 12 o'clock, Sept. 16, 1842, in Texas Congress, *Journals of the House of Representatives of the Seventh Congress,* Appendix, pp. 22–23.

[20] William L. Hunter was born in Virginia in 1811 and came to Texas in October 1835 with the New Orleans Greys; he participated in the siege of Béxar late in 1835 and served under James W. Fannin, but escaped the Goliad Massacre. In 1838 he was elected chief justice of Refugio County and represented that county in the Fourth, Sixth, and Seventh Congresses. In the Eighth Congress he represented the counties of Goliad, Refugio, and San Patricio in the Senate. He participated in the campaigns to repel Vasquez and Woll and took a prominent part in the Constitutional Convention of 1845. *Handbook of Texas,* I, 866.

[21] *Telegraph and Texas Register,* Oct. 5, 1842.

[22] *El Cosmopolita* (Mexico City), June 22, 1842. It was believed that he would not go to Mexico City, there being more important work for him in the north.

[23] Pedro de Ampudia, Comandante general interino del Departmento de Tamaulipas, á sus habitantes, Tampico, Sept. 12, 1842, *Gaceta de Tampico,* Sept. 28, 1842.

several days with the water up to their waists, abandoned their march upon learning of Woll's retreat. Upon their withdrawal, they were forced to abandon their four cannon twenty-five miles east of Matamoros, after having sent to Villareal's ranch for oxen to pull them from the bog. It was estimated in Matamoros that no less than two hundred of the Mexican soldiers in this expedition died from fatigue and starvation.[24] Around September 20th the lower Nueces was in flood and the water was reported to be the highest it had been in the last twenty years and it was considered impossible for a large body of troops to cross the river.[25] "Several showers of rain have fallen each successive day for about 14 days past," reported the editor of the *Telegraph* on August 31. "There has been a general deluge of rain in this section of the country 2 or 3 weeks," wrote A. C. Allen from LaGrange on September 15, "and the weather still looks very lowry [lowering?]. The creeks are all up."[26] The rains were general over the whole country, from Red River to San Antonio, and there was no indication that the weather would change for the better, as the showers seemed to be increasing rather than diminishing. Along the Colorado watershed the rainfall had been so heavy that the editor of the *Austin City Gazette* of September 7, had been led to declare, "The waters of the Colorado have not been so high as they are at the present time since 1839. The river is twenty feet above its usual low water mark."[27]

It is interesting to note that on the very day that General Woll captured San Antonio, Sunday, September 11, Adolphus Sterne at Nacogdoches, in east Texas, recorded in his diary, "we will soon be invaded by Mexico, probably to have three different divisions to attack us at the same time, Sabine, Galveston, and by land from Matamoros."[28] At this time the Mexican plans envisioned an attack along only one of the suspected routes, and they were "prevented by high water from arriving at Victoria."[29]

[24] Report of the Correspondent of the *Crescent City*, Matamoros, Nov. 1, 1842, copied in the *Telegraph and Texas Register*, Nov. 23, 1842.

[25] *Telegraph and Texas Register*, Oct. 5, 1842.

[26] A. C. Allen to Francis Moore, Jr., La Grange, Sept. 15, 1842, *Telegraph and Texas Register*, Sept. 28, 1842.

[27] *Telegraph and Texas Register*, Aug. 31 and Sept. 21, 1842; see also *Austin City Gazette*, Sept. 7, 1842.

[28] Harriet Smither (ed.), "Diary of Adolphus Sterne," in *Southwestern Historical Quarterly*, XXXIV (1930–1931), 163.

[29] Statement of A. C. Cunningham of Victoria in the Texas state constitutional convention of 1845. William F. Weeks, *Debates in the Texas Convention*, p. 410.

News of the fall of San Antonio reached Washington on Saturday evening, and within "half an hour every man and boy of 15 or over who was able to go was hard at work cleaning his gun," and braiding lariats with which to stake his horse. The women occupied themselves in getting scanty provisions ready and moulding bullets for the rifles of their sons and husbands.[30] Each volunteer furnished his own provisions, consisting usually of a few pounds of roasted ground coffee tied carefully in a little sack, a few pounds of raw bacon or jerked beef, and a peck or more of "cold flour."[31] The latter was a mixture of coarse corn meal parched brown, to which was usually added a small quantity of sugar; it was eaten cold as a substitute for bread, since that article could not be taken in sufficient quantity to last more than a day or so. By Sunday morning, soon after daylight, those who had worked the greater part of the night commenced to leave in small squads, and by Monday morning scarcely a man was to be seen in the streets, "even the Rev. W. M. Tryon headed for the frontier on Monday morning."[32]

Once again Texans belted on two, three, and sometimes even four pistols, a large bowie knife apiece, shouldered their rifles and, under various local leaders, headed in the direction of Béxar. The fighting men rallied in squads, and later formed themselves into companies. Soon the lonely plains of "western Texas" were "swarming with armed men, marching in bristling files to repell" the invading foe. The volunteers from Fayette County met and organized at Black Jack Springs on September 15 as instructed, and troops from the east assembled at Gonzales. Around Seguin a scarcity of horses existed because of a recent Indian raid in that area, and horses were now sold or traded at a premium to those who were anxious to go to the relief of San Antonio, for Texas was not without its share of "sunshine patriots." A stray horse which happened to be in town, was the cause of such a lively dispute that neither disputant was able to go at all. Caldwell and the Gonzales

[30] *Ibid.*

[31] "Cold flour" and "cole flour," as it was sometimes written, was made by sifting common ashes into a pot or kettle and "heated until the ashes boiled like plaster of paris; shelled corn was poured into the boiling ashes, and stirred until the grain could be broken between the fingers. It was then poured out into a sheet and sifted to separate the ashes from the corn. The corn was then ground . . . into meal, and it was ready for use. It was often eaten dry or stirred in water or made into mush, and its use was very common in the early days of Texas." John H. Reagan, *Memoirs with Special Reference to Secession and the Civil War*, p. 39 n.

[32] John W. Lockhart, "Darkest Days in Texas," *Galveston Daily News*, March 26, 1893.

men reached Seguin late Monday. During the night additional volunteers came in. The people of the town appeared to be very kind, but were very much imposed upon by some of the volunteers who showed "their patriotism by infringing upon the rights of the Citizens," by seizing whatever of their property—beeves, sheep, and corn, they assumed would be necessary to their campaign.[33] Caldwell made arrangements with young Antonio Navarro for a plentiful supply of beef, and Major Valentine Bennet of Gonzales, a soldier of the Revolution, former quartermaster of the Texas army, and recently returned Santa Fé prisoner, was soon busily butchering and drying meat on a scaffold for the accommodation of re-enforcements on their way.

By common consent Caldwell, "a rough fighter" known for his daring achievements on the Texas frontier, who had scarcely gotten home from a lengthy imprisonment in Mexico,[34] assumed the leadership of the group and on the morning of the 13th moved through the scattered growth of mesquite, interspersed here and there by live oaks and quite a sprinkling of prickly pear, to within twenty miles of San Antonio, where he encamped on the Cíbolo, above the Seguin and San Antonio road, to await re-enforcements and to afford protection to Gonzales should Woll move in that direction. The site selected by Caldwell was in relatively level country with a scattered growth of mesquite, with here and there an occasional live oak mott. The undergrowth was a specie of chaparral containing quite a number of cacti. The excellent grass of the region was almost its only redeeming feature. On the 14th he reported that his command numbered 125 men and that others were still coming on in small parties.[35] Only a few of the Cuero men had arrived—none from the Lavaca; but volunteers from Lavaca and others

[33] Harvey Alexander Adams, "[Journal of an] Expedition Against the Southwest in 1842 and 1843," Oct. 3, 1842, ms. Adams was born in Providence, Rhode Island, December 19, 1812. While he was a small child, his parents moved to Ohio, and upon reaching manhood he accompanied them on to Illinois. Arriving in Texas shortly after the battle of San Jacinto, he established himself at Houston, where he entered the carpenter's trade. From Houston, he hurried west in the fall of 1842 to help drive out General Woll, and at San Antonio enrolled in Samuel Bogart's Company. Neal B. Fox, "A Correlated Study-Unit of a Diary of the Expedition Against the Southwest, 1842–1843," ms., pp. v–vi.

[34] As one of the Santa Fé prisoners, Caldwell had been released as a prisoner in April 1842; he reached Houston the last week in August and immediately left with his son for Gonzales. *Telegraph and Texas Register*, Aug. 31, 1842; *Bollaert's Texas*, p. 130.

[35] Matthew Caldwell to Ezekiel Williams, Cibolo, Sept. 14, 1842, *Telegraph and Texas Register*, Sept. 21, 1842.

from Cuero were expected to arrive at any moment. His dispatch showed clearly the spirit that motivated him and the men under his command and is reminiscent of the stirring days of 1836. It breathed energy and heroic daring in every line. "My men are united and determined," he wrote, "and say the prisoners must be released." He hoped in a few days to be at "the walls of San Antonio." In the meantime, Caldwell cautioned the people in the western settlements not to panic, but to stay at home for the present, for in his opinion they had nothing to fear. As soon as his force doubled, he hoped to surround Béxar and open fire on the enemy troops. "We used to attack San Antonio with 200 men when the enemy numbered 1,500 or more and defeated them, and I am now determined," he declared, "to act under the old system. . . . The enemy must be whipped. We have them where we want them. . . . Hurry on! Hurry on! and lose no time. We fear nothing but God, and through him we fight our battles. Huzza! huzza for Texas!"[36]

A call was now made for ten of the best horses and lightest riders to go forward immediately to meet Captain Hays that night on the Salado. Hays, having returned to the vicinity of San Antonio on Monday, September 12, to watch the movements of the enemy, had sent back a special messenger requesting re-enforcements. Among the ten volunteers selected to assist the spy company was the Reverend Z. N. Morrell. As the volunteers neared the point of rendezvous selected by Major Hays, "a keen whistle was given," and was readily answered by Hays. With the new recruits, Hays' scouting party now consisted of thirteen men, whose commissary contained a very limited supply of "cold flour" (or *panola*). One spoonful of "cold flour" mixed with water constituted their breakfast. After breakfast, the spy company was divided into three sections. One detail was to remain in camp on the Salado; another was to approach San Antonio from the east to report on the movements of any Mexican troops toward the interior of the Republic; and the third group, under Major Hays was to head for the San Antonio River and seek to circle the city to see if any re-enforcements were arriving from Mexico.[37] During the day Hays encountered a party of Mexican cavalry and was forced to forego his plan to circle the town. The Mexican troops may have been a unit from Woll's forces in town, but most likely were the pickets from the presidial companies of Béxar (twenty-five men)

[36] *Ibid.*
[37] Z[enos] N. Morrell, *Flowers and Fruits in the Wilderness: or Forty-Six Years in Texas and Two Winters in Honduras*, p. 163.

and Laredo (thirty-one men) that entered San Antonio, September 13, conveying the funds for the payment of Woll's troops.[38]

On Thursday Hays made another effort to get the number and intention of the Mexicans, but again was repulsed, apparently by a Mexican unit out of San Antonio, and failed to reach the enemy's rear. Upon returning to the Salado he found about forty Mexican cavalrymen upon his trail, and, even though he was re-enforced by Morrell's patrol which had gone down the Salado that morning, the Texans found it necessary to beat a hasty retreat. Hays fell back before the advancing Mexicans until the pursuing cavalry was clear of the timber. Then, wheeling his little band of thirteen, he charged and the Mexicans fled. No one was injured.

The next morning, Friday, the spy company was sullen and mutinous. Around them was a plentiful supply of deer, turkey, rabbits, and other game, but their captain had issued strict orders against the firing of guns. From Monday to Friday the men had subsisted on coffee and a few spoonfuls of flour a day, and now their flour was exhausted. Some of the men were swearing "vengeance on the game at all hazards."[39] Hays requested the minister, Morrell, to make a speech to the men. Riding out in front of the men, Morrell sought to reason with them in a humorous vein:

Boys, [he said], when I left Colonel Caldwell's camp, I felt like I was forty years old. When I had starved one day, I felt like I was thirty-five. After that, on two spoonfuls a day, I felt like I was twenty-five; and this morning, when our cold flour and coffee are both out, I feel like I am only twenty-one years old, and ready for action. Our situation this morning is critical,—the Mexicans, we fear, have gone toward Gonzales; secrecy surely is the best policy; and we ought to report the situation, if possible, to Colonel Caldwell to-night.[40]

On Thursday, while reconnoitring along the Salado, Morrell's party

[38] Adrián Woll to Isidro Reyes, [Presidio del] Río Grande, August 29, 1842, enclosing a Report of the Adjutant General, 2nd Division, Army Corps of the North, dated August 29, 1842, with a note attached dated as late as September 13, 1842, in Joseph Milton Nance (trans. and ed.), "Brigadier General Adrián Woll's Report of His Expedition into Texas in 1842," in *Southwestern Historical Quarterly*, LVIII (1954–1955), 524–525. William Small reported from San Antonio that General Bravo [Colonel Calixto Bravo?] entered Béxar with 100 men on Sept. 13, with a "reported" $300,000 in specie to pay the troops. *Telegraph and Texas Register*, Sept. 21, 1842.
[39] Morrell, *Flowers and Fruits in the Wilderness*, p. 165.
[40] *Ibid.*

had discovered Seguin's trail leading in the direction of Gonzales, which they supposed had been made by two or three hundred Mexican cavalry. It was therefore urgent that additional information about the enemy be gathered and a report made to Colonel Caldwell. The men agreed to postpone their game hunting after it was understood that the spy company would again operate toward San Antonio during the day, and that night would report to Caldwell and get some game for supper. A few minutes later the Texans were off.

After going only a short distance from their camp, they met Henry E. McCulloch with thirteen men, thus increasing their number to twenty-seven. McCulloch reported that Caldwell had learned of the cavalry trail in the direction of Gonzales, and that the Mexican cavalry had turned back toward San Antonio. McCulloch's men had fresh meat hanging to their saddles, and nothing would do but that Hays' men should have breakfast. While the men ate, a reorganization of forces took place. Hays was elected captain, and McCulloch, lieutenant. That night the spy company encamped within five miles of Béxar, probably on the Salado, where fresh water could be had.

Before daylight Saturday morning the little band was astir. Hays detailed Morrell and three others to approach the town before daylight, while he and three others would make a third attempt to go around the city. McCulloch was ordered to watch the roads leading to Seguin and Gonzales. The morning was cool and pleasant, and the sky somewhat overcast by light, fleecy, velvety clouds floating in the south and east. Hays' effort to reach the rear of San Antonio this time proved successful, and he even succeeded in capturing a Mexican spy. Under the cover of darkness Morrell and his associates approached the old Lookout Tower or Powder House,[41] known in Spanish as "La Garita," standing on a high

---

[41] The Powder House was situated on a high eminence overlooking the surrounding country for some distance. It commanded a fine view of San Antonio, although situated three-quarters of a mile to the southeast of the city. The building was about sixteen feet square and was constructed of materials similar to those of the missions. Its walls were about two and a half feet thick, plastered on both sides. The walls were pierced with portholes, three on a side. Inside on one wall was a rough drawing of a cannon with two cannoniers in the rear of it, one of whom was shown applying a fuse to the touchhole. The building was three stories high with a parapet on the top, and a pinnacle at one corner raised a few feet above the parapet. The floors were supported by joists covered by a thick coat of concrete to form the thickness of a foot or more. Adjoining this building was another about ten feet square, which was probably used as a magazine. Harvey Alexander Adams, "[Journal of an] Expedition Against the Southwest in 1842 and 1843," Nov. 1, 1842, ms.

eminence overlooking the surrounding country and San Antonio in particular. The Powder House was a thousand yards from the Alamo and
three-fourths of a mile from the town. The Texans secreted themselves
nearby. Shortly after sunup a Mexican came out to get a yoke of oxen
feeding near them. The Texans captured him and his pony within six
hundred yards of the enemy and in full view of the invaders. Seeing the
Mexicans feverishly saddling their horses, the four Texans beat a hasty
retreat with their prisoner. In two hours they covered the twenty miles
to Caldwell's camp on the Cíbolo. There they found McCulloch and
Hays with the Mexican they had captured. The two trembling and sup-
plicating prisoners, one of whom was known to Mayor Smith, were
promised that they would not be harmed if they told the truth. They
both told the same story. From the information which the captives supplied, it was estimated that Woll's army consisted of 1,300 men plus 200
or 300 Indians and San Antonio Mexicans who had joined his force.[42]
Caldwell's command on the 16th numbered only 163 men.[43]

As the men came in from the east, they assembled beside the waters
of the Cíbolo. During the stay on the Cíbolo in the vicinity of its "beautiful hole of Blue water,"[44] the men were busy moulding bullets, cleaning rifles and pistols, grinding knives and bayonets, and packing wallets
preparatory to meeting the enemy. During the night of the 16th several
small groups of volunteers arrived; so that by the morning of the 17th
approximately 210 men were in camp.[45] A general organization was now
effected. At 4 P.M. the men were formed in a line to elect the general
officers. Colonel Mathew ("Old Paint") Caldwell of Gonzales, signer of
the Declaration of Independence and a captain in the Santa Fé expedition,[46] was enthusiastically chosen commander by the volunteers.

[42] Morrell, *Flowers and Fruits in the Wilderness*, p. 167.
[43] Rena Maverick Green (ed.), *Samuel Maverick, Texan, 1803–1870: A Collection of Letters, Journals and Memoirs*, p. 167.
[44] Adams, "[Journal of an] Expedition Against the Southwest," Oct. 4, 1842, ms.
[45] Thomas J. Green, *Journal of the Texian Expedition Against Mier*, p. 30, and
Memucan Hunt to Dr. Francis Moore, Jr., Houston, Oct. 17, 1842, *Telegraph and
Texas Register*, Oct. 26, 1842, give the number as 210. John Henry Brown, *History
of Texas, from 1685 to 1892*, II, 223, and Morrell, *Flowers and Fruits in the Wilderness*, p. 167, say 202; and Bancroft, *History of Texas and the North Mexican States*,
II, 357, gives it as 220. Caldwell in a dispatch dated September 17 at Salado, but
not sent until 10 A.M. of the 18th listed his force as 225 "strong." Mathew Caldwell to the Citizens of Gonzales, Salado, 2 miles above the Old San Antonio Crossing, Sept. 17, 1842, *Telegraph and Texas Register*, Oct. 5, 1842.
[46] *Morning Star*, Jan. 19, 1843; "Address Delivered at the Grave of Colonel
Mathew Caldwell by D. C. Van Derlip," *Telegraph and Texas Register*, Jan. 25,

Major John C. ("Jack") Hays was placed at the head of a scouting
party of forty-two of the best mounted men; Canah C. Colley was made
adjutant; Dr. Caleb S. Brown, of Gonzales, was selected to act as surgeon; and the Reverend Z. N. Morrell served as "physician . . . for the
soul."[47] The men were organized into companies under captains of their
own choice, among whom were Daniel B. Friar of Cuero with thirty-
five men; James Bird of Gonzales, assisted by James H. Callahan,[48] with
sixty men from Gonzales and Seguin; Adam Zumwalt, assisted by John
Henry Brown, with twenty-five men from the Lavaca;[49] and Ewen
Cameron from Victoria with forty "cowboys" from the Victoria vicinity.[50] Among the lieutenants were John R. Baker and Alfred Allee.

Caldwell now dispatched a youth named John Wilson from Bastrop,[51]
the son of John C. Wilson, eastward to urge on volunteers, and at sunset,
Saturday, September 17, the march for the forested valley of the Salado
began. About midnight, the Texans encamped on the east bank of Salado Creek adjacent to a ravine[52] two miles above the Old San Antonio
crossing[53] a mile below the present New Braunfels crossing in a well-
selected place six or seven miles northeast of San Antonio "on the site of
the present Fort Sam Houston" on what is now the Mahler farm on the
W. W. White Road along the Salado[54] and near the site of the battle of

---

1843. Caldwell was a participant in the Council House Fight, March 19, 1840, with
the Comanche chiefs. He had gone to the Council House unarmed. When the fight
began, he wrenched a gun from an Indian and killed him with it, and then beat
another to death with the butt end of the gun. During the melee he was shot
through the right leg by the first volley, he thought, of the Texas soldiers. After
breaking the stock of his gun, he fought with rocks, with his back to the Court
House wall. Green (ed.), *Samuel Maverick, Texan*, p. 110; Rena Maverick Green
(ed.), *Memoirs of Mrs. Mary A. Maverick: Arranged by Mary A. Maverick and
Her Son George Madison Maverick*, p. 34.
  [47] "I have," wrote Caldwell, "two physicians, one for the soul and one for the
body—Parson Morrell and Dr. C. S. Brown," Mathew Caldwell to Ezekiel Williams,
Cibolo, Sept. 14, 1842, *Telegraph and Texas Register*, Sept. 21, 1842.
  [48] L. W. Kemp, "James Hughes Callahan," in *Handbook of Texas*, I, p. 272; John
Henry Brown, *Indian Wars and Pioneers of Texas*, p. 601.
  [49] John Henry Brown, "Autobiography," ms.
  [50] Leonie Rummel Weyand and Houston Wade, *An Early History of Fayette
County*, p. 147; Brown, *History of Texas*, II, 222–228.
  [51] Sowell, *Early Settlers and Indian Fighters of Southwest Texas*, p. 817.
  [52] Green (ed.), *Samuel Maverick, Texan*, p. 168.
  [53] Mathew Caldwell to the Citizens of Gonzales, Salado, 2 miles above the old
San Antonio Crossing, Sept. 17, 1842, *Telegraph and Texas Register*, Oct. 5, 1842.
  [54] Edward W. Heusinger, *A Chronology of Events in San Antonio: being a Con-*

Rosalis of March 29, 1813. The Texans unsaddled their horses, put out a strong guard, and lay upon their arms. John W. Smith, whose long residence in San Antonio gave him an entrée that few other Anglo-Texans enjoyed, was sent into the city during the night as a spy. He slept in town that night. Just before day the moon went down. Soon afterward, the gray, and then the purple streaks of morning began to light up the eastern sky, and the stars, one by one, melted into the blue heaven. Gradually the surrounding objects became more and more distinct as the day approached. Smith returned at daybreak, stating that General Woll was still in town, but that the prisoners had been gone several days.[55] He reported that Woll had held a Council of War in which he was alleged to have told his fellow-officers he intended "to immortalize his name in Texas, or make it his grave yard." Many of his officers were not willing to adopt these as their sentiments. Some wanted to retreat; others wished to stay and fight. Smith reported that Woll's force consisted of 1,100 men ("and no more") and that he had no "prospect of reinforcements for some time to come."[56] It was reported, also, that the Mexicans had 200 yoke of oxen and 2,000 horses, mostly of an inferior quality.

At dawn, under the light morning sky, while a part of the Texans butchered several beeves, of which they had a plentiful supply, Caldwell carefully inspected the terrain, and being satisfied with his position, protected by a hill, the stream, and trees, he determined to make his stand in his present location. At this point the Salado was very straight, running almost due west to east for some distance. The timbered bottom was approximately eighty to one hundred yards wide. From the bottom on the north side the bank gently rose about eight feet to a level with the prairie valley which extended from four to eight hundred yards in width covered by a sparse growth of mesquite trees. The timber of the Salado bottom was rather dense, being principally pecan

---

cise *History of the City, Year by Year, from the Beginning of Its Establishment to the End of the First Half of the Twentieth Century,* p. 21; Anna Ellis, "Dawson Massacre Anniversary to See Unveiling of Memorial," *San Antonio Express,* Sept. 15, 1935; Mary Olivia Handy, *History of Fort Sam Houston,* p. 4; [Anonymous], *A History of the San Antonio Quartermaster Depot,* p. 5. Caldwell reported his camp as eight miles from San Antonio.

[55] J[ohn] H[enry] B[rown] to the Editor of the Houston *Telegraph,* La Vaca River, Gonzales Co., Oct. 2, 1842, *Telegraph and Texas Register,* Nov. 2, 1842.

[56] Mathew Caldwell to the Citizens of Gonzales, Salado, 2 miles from above the old San Antonio Crossing, Sept. 17th, 1842, in *ibid.,* Oct. 5, 1842.

and elm, with a thick undergrowth of various kinds. To the east and northeast of the Salado the terrain was generally level, interspersed here and there by clumps of mesquite and live oak, but very little of either. It afforded an excellent spot for cavalry to maneuver, and to that extent would be advantageous to the Mexicans; but the Texans would have the greater advantage of shooting into the open prairie from the protection of cover. West and southwest of the Salado toward San Antonio were some high hills and deep gullies or valleys whose generally black soil was covered with flint pebbles and a dense growth of mesquite thickets, prickly pear, and other chaparral. At the lower end of the Texan line a deep ravine 150 yards long ran into the Salado, and below this ravine the valley ceased, the high prairie at this point jutting abruptly up to the creek. A Texan guard unit of twenty men was assigned to occupy this ravine in case of an attack.

Caldwell's plan was to send Major Hays with a company of mounted men into the town to draw out the enemy. If the enemy could be decoyed out into the open prairie, the Texans, with their horses tied back in the timber and themselves protected by a natural embankment, could give him a warm reception, although outnumbered five to one.[57] About sunrise, before the men could get their breakfast, an order was issued for the men to fall in, and a committee started selecting the horses for the arduous task. Only 38 of the 202 horses among the Texans were deemed fit for the occasion. With Hays rode Henry E. McCulloch, "Bigfoot" Wallace, Richard A. Gillespie (later of Mexican War fame), Christopher ("Kit") B. Achlin,[58] Sam Luckie, Mike Chevallie, Creed

[57] On the morning of the battle Caldwell estimated that he had 225 men, and "that by the best information," he reported, "that I am able to get, the enemys number is about 1100 regular troops." Mrs. Samuel A. Maverick's brothers, William and Andrew Adams, who were with Caldwell on this occasion and reported the particulars of the battle, claimed that Caldwell had 225 men. Mathew Caldwell to the Secretary of War, Head Quarters of the Volunteer Army of Texas, Salado Creek, 8 miles from San Antonio, Sept. 18, 1842, Texas Congress, *Journals of the House of Representatives of the Seventh Congress*, Appendix, pp. 16–18; Green (ed.), *Samuel Maverick, Texan*, p. 167. The Mexican report was that Woll defeated 450 Texans in the battle of Salado. *El Cosmopolita*, October 8, 1842.

[58] Brown, *Indian Wars and Pioneers of Texas*, pp. 269–270, gives the name as "Christopher H. Acklin." *Bollaert's Texas*, p. 215, gives it as "Ackland," and Sowell, *Early Settlers and Indian Fighters of Southwest Texas*, pp. 23–24, gives it as "Kit Ackland." "Muster and Pay Roll of Company of Rangers commanded by Captain John C. Hays stationed at San Antonio de Béxar from the 27th day of June to the 28th day of October, A.D. 1844," Texas Rangers, Muster Rolls, 1830–1860, ms., and "Receipt Roll of Captain John C. Hays' Frontier Ranging Company, Feb. 25–

Taylor, Andrew Sowell, and others. Those who did not go with Hays returned to the task of preparing the meat for roasting and picking their defense positions.

In the meantime, having established his control over San Antonio, General Woll issued a proclamation to his troops announcing that on this day, September 11, anniversary of the defeat of the Spaniards at Tampico in 1829, "the enemy who in its delirium dared to hoist in our view the Texas flag . . . had to surrender at discretion. . . . As I announced to you on the banks of the Río Bravo del Norte," he continued, "fortune has been true to justice; our heroic efforts have settled it; our mission has begun, and with such flourish, no doubt it shall be fulfilled."[59] The next day he called on the inhabitants of Béxar for their cooperation, and assured them security of person and property as long as they did not perform any hostile act against the Mexican army.[60] After which Woll proceeded to re-establish Mexican law over the city and to appoint local officers according to Mexican custom, and to remove the local priest, a native Spaniard, who had been brought over by the new vicar general, John M. Odin, and to restore the native Catholic priest, Don Refugio de la Garza,[61] who had been removed by Odin because he had a large family of children. On the evening of the day (September 15) that the prisoners and Mexican wounded left San Antonio, Woll gave a ball for the Mexican ladies of Béxar, which is reported to have been well attended.[62] On the 16th the invaders celebrated Mexican independence day, but Woll seems to have been in error in asserting that this was the first such celebration in San Antonio

---

June 26, 1844," in Texas Rangers, Receipt Rolls 1830–1860, ms., both give the name as "C. B. Achlin." For a brief biographical sketch of Christopher B. Achlin, see John Holland Jenkins, III (ed.), *Recollections of Early Texas: The Memoirs of John Holland Jenkins*, p. [239].

[59] [Adrián Woll] El General 2º En Gefe del Cuerpo de Ejército del Norte y Comandante de la 2º Division á las Tropas de su Mando, Cuartel general en S. Antonio de Béjar, Septiembre 11 de 1842, in Woll, *Expedición hecha en Téjas*, p. 11; see also extract of Woll's letter to a "distinguished Merchant" of New Orleans, reprinted in *Diario del Gobierno*, May 14, 1843.

[60] [Adrián Woll] El General 2º En Gefe del Cuerpo de Egército de Norte, al Vecindario de esta ciudad, San Antonio de Béjar, Septiembre 12 de 1842, in Woll, *Expedición hecha en Téjas*, pp. 29–30; *El Provisional* (Matamoros), Oct. 14, 1842.

[61] Frederick C. Chabot (ed.), *The Perote Prisoners*, pp. 52–53.

[62] Trueheart's Diary, Sept. 26, 1842, in Chabot (ed.), *The Perote Prisoners*, p. 108.

in six years. Mrs. Maverick states that the date was also celebrated in 1840.[63] A cannon salute was fired, and Woll in another proclamation boasted, "from today henceforth it will be celebrated in this Department of Texas, unjustly usurped by the . . . colonists."[64]

While the Texans were rallying to drive out the Mexican army, Woll sent Colonel Seguin and Captain Francisco Herrera on the 12th with 150 cavalry from the presidials and *defensores* of Béxar to reconnoiter along the Gonzales road toward the Guadalupe as far as the town of Gonzales with the object of acquiring information on the movements and the points of gathering of the Texans.[65] All hostile enemy forces were to be driven out or captured, but the lives and property of peaceful residents were to be respected. Following instructions from the Supreme Government of Mexico, the scouting party was specifically ordered not to cross the Guadalupe. At the Cíbolo, Seguin divided his force, sending a portion up the creek and another down it, while with the main body he proceeded on the Gonzales road.[66] One of the parties was commanded by Lieutenant Manuel Carbajal, and presumably the other was commanded by a Captain Herrera.

At the Azufrosa (Sulphur Springs), two leagues beyond the Cíbolo, at the right of the road, the small reconnaissance party under Carbajal discovered three Texans and a Mexican. According to Seguin's report,[67] the Texans, who had gone to the springs to bathe in its sulphurous water

---

[63] Green (ed.), *Memoirs of Mary A. Maverick*, p. 53; El General [Woll] 2º en Gefe del Cuerpo de Ejército del Norte y comandante de la 2ª Division á las Tropas de su Mando, Cuartel general en San Antonio de Béjar, Septiembre 16 de 1842, in Woll, *Expedición hecha en Téjas*, p. 34.

[64] El General [Woll] 2º en Gefe del Cuerpo de Ejército del Norte y comandante de la 2ª Division á las Tropas de su Mando, Cuartel general en San Antonio de Béjar, Septiembre 16 de 1842, in Woll, *Expedición hecha en Téjas*, p. 34; *El Provisional*, Oct. 14, 1842.

[65] Trueheart Diary, Sept. 14, 1842, in Chabot (ed.), *The Perote Prisoners*, p. 99, says Seguin went out on the 14th, and Seguin in his *Memoirs*, p. 28, claims he had 200 men. Woll however, reported to his superior that he sent 150 cavalry. Seguin was encamped on the Cíbolo on the 14th, and returned to San Antonio on the 17th.

[66] Seguin, *Memoirs*, p. 28.

[67] Juan Nepomuceno Seguin á Adrián Woll, Campo sobre el arroyo del Cibolo, Septiembre 14 de 1842, copy in Adrián Woll al Sr. General en gefe [Isidro Reyes], Béjar, Septiembre 15, 1842, in Woll, *Expedición hecha en Téjas*, pp. 31–32; Seguin, *Memoirs*, p. 28.

for their health, ignored an order to surrender, elevated their guns, and started firing. They were soon killed by the Mexican troops. The Mexican surrendered without resistance.[68]

There has always been some doubt in Texas that Dr. Launcelot Smithers (a clerk to William Adams, brother-in-law of Samuel A. Maverick and one of Travis' messengers from the Alamo in 1836),[69] John McDonald (a half-brother of Bryan Callaghan whom Woll had released), and John McRhea really offered or intended to offer any resistance. It may be recalled that at the time of the Vasquez raid the preceding spring, these same three men, lacking horses, declined joining the Texas retreat from San Antonio and were left sitting upon the walls of the Alamo. It was reported and generally believed in Texas that Juan N. Seguin, who commanded the scouting party sent out from San Antonio by Woll, killed the three men at the Sulphur Springs. If the Mexican report is to be believed this is not true. There were no other eyewitness reports; yet Caldwell stated in a letter dated September 16, 1842, that "Col. Seguin has killed three sick men at the Sulphur Spring." Smithers was a decrepit old man and formerly the neighbor and friend of Seguin,[70] and it is not likely that Seguin would have killed him had he been present. The next day, however, when the two detachments joined the main body, Seguin appropriated Dr. Smithers' fine American horse with which he soon drove his family in a buggy to the Río Grande.

From the Cíbolo Seguin reported on the 14th that more than two-thirds of the unit's horses were worn out, but he said nothing about the probable waning of the courage of his men as they penetrated deeper and deeper into Texas.[71] Woll ordered that the tired horses be returned to San Antonio, and that the reconnaissance be continued as he had instructed.[72] On the 17th, Seguin and Herrera returned to San Antonio and reported seeing no enemy forces this side of the Guadalupe. Other

[68] Woll, *Expedición hecha en Téjas*, pp. 31–32; Green (ed.), *Samuel Maverick, Texan*, p. 167.

[69] Green (ed.), *Samuel Maverick, Texan*, p. 69; Trueheart's Diary, Sept. 15, 1842, in Chabot (ed.), *The Perote Prisoners*, pp. 99–102.

[70] *Telegraph and Texas Register*, Oct. 5, 1842.

[71] Juan Nepomuceno Seguin á Adrián Woll, Campo sobre el arroyo del Cibolo, Septiembre 14 de 1842, quoted in Adrián Woll ál Sr. general en gefe [Isidro Reyes], Béjar, Septiembre 15 de 1842, in Woll, *Expedición hecha en Tejas*, p. 31.

[72] Adrián Woll ál Sr. general en gefe [Isidro Reyes], Béjar, Septiembre 15 de 1842, *ibid.*

reports assured Woll that there were no enemy forces either at Goliad, Copano, or Corpus Christi.[73]

Accordingly, Woll, unknown to Caldwell, planned to evacuate San Antonio and Texas on the afternoon of the 18th and to return to general headquarters south of the Río Grande in conformance to General Reyes' orders that his expedition should not last longer than a month.[74] "Our mission had been fulfilled," he reported on the 20th, but did not bother to explain why he had planned to start his return march in the afternoon rather than early in the morning as was the case when entering Texas. Woll says that on the 17th he was secretly warned of several parties of enemy troops approaching San Antonio by the Seguin road. He could scarcely believe the news, as the scouts who had gone out regularly each day in that direction had detected no signs of enemy troops. During the morning and night of the 17th spies and guerrilla bands "were continually dispatched to the Salado," but always returned without seeing or "sensing" the presence of Texans.[75] The truth seems to have been that rumors of approaching Texan troops and the occasional appearance of their spies near the city caused small reconnaissance parties of Mexican soldiers to be wary of getting out of sight of San Antonio. As a precautionary measure, Woll had the horses and mules of the army quartered for the night in corrals in the center of the town, and the men held in readiness at their quarters for whatever the night might bring.

Scarcely had the Mexican outposts been withdrawn on the morning of the 18th and the reconnoitring parties, which had regularly gone out at dawn each morning in all directions, returned to report seeing nothing, when from the direction of the Alamo came the cry of "enemy," followed by a roll of the drum calling the troops to arms. Between the hours of nine and ten o'clock,[76] Hays' Company reached a point about

[73] Adrián Woll ál Sr. general en gefe [Isidro Reyes], San Antonio de Béjar, a las 6 de la mañana del dia 20 Septiembre de 1842, in *ibid.*, p. 33.

[74] Adrián Woll ál Sr. general en gefe [Isidro Reyes], Béjar, Septiembre 17, 1842, (no. 248), in *ibid.*, p. 35.

[75] Adrián Woll ál Sr. general en gefe [Isidro Reyes], San Antonio de Béjar, a las 6 de la mañana del dia 20 de Septiembre de 1842, in *ibid.* pp. 38–45.

[76] Caldwell's report says Hays was sent at 10 o'clock to entice the Mexicans out of San Antonio. Mathew Caldwell to the Secretary of War, Head Quarters of the Volunteer Army of Texas, Salado Creek, 8 miles from San Antonio, Sept. 18, 1842, Texas Congress, *Journals of the House of Representatives of the Seventh Congress,* Appendix, pp. 16–18. Although dated the 18th, it is clear from the information embodied in the letter that it was probably not completed until about the 24th.

a half mile from the Powder House and a mile from the town. The company halted, and Hays taking Lieutenant McCulloch and six others, went forward, leaving instructions for the remainder of his men to hold themselves in readiness for any emergency. Waving hats, shouting taunts, and cutting capers—Indian fashion—the seven rangers followed their intrepid leader, whose dark flashing eyes instilled confidence in his men. At a gallop the Texans approached the Alamo from the east along the row of large cottonwoods (*alamos americano*) bordering Alamo Avenue,[77] going down close to it and bantering the enemy for a fight. Quickly ordering his troops formed in front of their quarters, Woll mounted a horse and dashed off in the direction of the Alamo, where he found the Santa Anna Regiment saddling its horses. Accompanied by his aides, he advanced along the road toward Seguin, where in the distance he saw several Texans approaching. As the Texans drew to within less than a half mile of the Alamo, Woll sent Captain Perez with twenty-five cavalrymen, supported by sixty presidial soldiers under Captain Francisco Castañeda to meet the challenge. The Texans fled. Perez's cavalry, now re-enforced to 150 men, gave pursuit.

As Hays approached the main body of his company, he ordered, "Mount, and fall back." The Texans now moved off briskly in retreat across the mesquite-covered prairie toward Caldwell's position, where their comrades lay in eager expectation among the cottonwoods, cedars, mesquites, and live oaks of the creek bottom. For the first four miles the Texans kept out of reach of the Mexican cavalry without much difficulty, but not for long. Soon the fifty odd horses captured by Woll on the 11th started gaining on the Texan horses, considerably worn by the labor of the last week. McCulloch, commanding the rear guard, pressed close upon the heels of the foremost rangers. "The race was an earnest one," wrote a participant.[78] Hats, blankets, and overcoats were scattered in the wake of the retreating rangers. About midway between the Alamo and Caldwell's position, Augustus H. Jones' horse began to fail and it seemed as if the highly esteemed gentleman might be captured. Hays, mounted on his dark bay war-horse, noticing that his good friend would soon be in grave danger, threw the whole company behind Jones to afford him protection. The Mexican cavalry thundered on, now be-

---

[77] Charles I. Sellon to Marilla ———, San Antonio de Béxar, Sept. 6, 1846, ms., Illinois Historical Society Library, Springfield, Ill., reprinted in *Southwestern Historical Quarterly*, XLVII (1943–1944), 63.

[78] Morrell, *Flowers and Fruits in the Wilderness*, p. 168.

ginning to fire their *escopetas*[79] by elevation as they drew nearer to the retreating Texans, and dropped balls constantly among the little company as it beat a hasty retreat. From then on the rangers kept up a running fight with their pursuers, wheeling repeatedly to fire upon the Mexican cavalry in an effort to keep it from getting too near. As those on the creek witnessed their scouting party fleeing before the enemy, they ran their horses quickly into the timbered bottom and tied them, and every man was soon in position along the creek bank, anxiously awaiting a charge from the enemy. Closely pressed, Hays' men crossed the Salado two miles above the old crossing, or about a mile above their camp, and turned right, quickly entering the forested valley. The Mexican cavalry crossed the stream and followed close upon their heels, taking up a position "at different intervals on the ascent of the hill, which rises from the valley to a level with the high land,"[80] at a distance of about four hundred yards to the rear of Caldwell's men. In the meantime, Caldwell had gotten off another express, at 10 o'clock, at "full speed" to the citizens of Gonzales urging that volunteers come at once. "Let every man on his way come ahead as fast as possible," he wrote "—loose [*sic*] no time day or night, for now is the time to do something."[81]

Believing that now at last he had trapped the wolf in his den, Woll ordered Captain Castañeda to attack the Texans with 100 presidials, but the captain sent back word that the enemy was in an advantageous position and that he would need assistance.[82] Whereupon, Woll instructed Colonel Moro del Moral to leave half of his battalion to protect the plaza, and to march out with 200 infantrymen, 160 dragoons belonging to the Santa Anna Regiment, and the two pieces of artillery to

---

[79] An *escopeta* was a short, smooth bore, light "blunderbuss" used by the Mexican cavalry. William A. Wallace described it as a "short-bell-mouth, bull-doggish, looking musket, carrying a very heavy ball, which is 'death by the law' when it hits, but that is seldom," for it shoots with little accuracy, often being held above the head and fired at random in order to avoid the tremendous "kick" of the recoil. John C. Duval, *The Adventures of Big-Foot Wallace: The Texas Ranger and Hunter*, p. 173.

[80] "Battle of Salado, Sept. 18, 1842," in Brown Papers, 1835–1872, ms.; another account is given by John H. Jenkins, Sr., in his "Personal Reminiscences of Texas History Relating to Bastrop County, 1828–1847, as Dictated to his Daughter-in-law, Mrs. Emma Holmes Jenkins of Bastrop, Texas," ms.

[81] Mathew Caldwell to the Citizens of Gonzales, Salado, 2 miles above the old San Antonio Crossing, Sept. 17, 1842, *Telegraph and Texas Register*, Oct. 5, 1842.

[82] Seguin, *Memoirs*, p. 28.

support an attack upon the Texans.[83] Woll accompanied his troops. He estimated that Caldwell's men numbered 300, and saw that they had placed themselves in a highly advantageous position at a spring of water to await re-enforcements before attacking the Mexican army. He did not realize that Caldwell hoped to provoke the Mexicans to attack him on a field which he had selected for battle. On the other hand, Woll considered his San Antonio position a very precarious one with the assembling of Texan troops, and he believed that if he attacked Caldwell at once he might not only gain an easy victory and more prisoners, but might also sufficiently disrupt the Texan forces assembling on the frontier to enable him to make a safe retreat into Mexico. "Although my instructions forbid me attacking . . . [the enemy] in forests," he reported, "the case was so urgent that I decided to do so. To this end I inspected the terrain with thoroughness and crossing the Salado lower down, I formed two lines at the rearguard of the enemy."[84]

While Woll was moving the bulk of his army out to support an attack upon the Texans, the opposing forces on the Salado stood glaring at each other. In the meantime, Hays' men refreshed themselves and their horses with water. After a half hour's rest, Hays assembled his company and advanced toward the enemy cavalry. A skirmish ensued at long range, killing several Mexicans and severely wounding two of the Texans. Captain Castañeda urgently requested re-enforcements, and Woll immediately sent Seguin with orders "to attack at all hazard." The Mexican cavalry advanced to the attack, but the horses recoiled at the Texan fire, and those who lost their riders dashed back in great confusion. The unhorsed cavalrymen could scarcely run with their huge spurs on and were invariably killed by the Texans if they happened to be within rifle range. The rowels of the spurs were several inches in diameter, and the battleground before the end of the day was said to have looked as if a garden rake had been pulled over it. In the first charge, Seguin says he lost three killed and eight wounded; in the second, seven killed and fifteen wounded. He was preparing for a third charge when he was relieved of his command by Colonel Carrasco.[85]

---

[83] Altogether his force amounted to 900 to 1,000 men. Memucan Hunt to Dr. Francis Moore, Jr., Houston, Oct. 17, 1842, *Telegraph and Texas Register*, Oct. 26, 1842.

[84] Adrián Woll al Sr. general en gefe [Isidro Reyes], San Antonio de Béjar, a las 6 de la mañana del dia 20 de Septiembre de 1842, in Woll, *Expedición hecha en Téjas*, p. 41.

[85] Seguin, *Memoirs*, p. 28.

Woll, himself, having arrived upon the scene by this time, Seguin "returned to the side of the General" and made his report; whereupon, Woll ordered the firing to cease. From the time Hays had returned to Caldwell's camp to the arrival of Woll before the Texan position, there had been a lapse of some two to three hours, during which a sporadic skirmishing had been kept up, and many gallant acts performed on both sides.

The Mexican cavalry and small infantry force was re-enforced about 1 P.M. by the arrival of Woll with an additional 400 infantrymen, 40 Cherokees under Vicente Córdova, 100 volunteer citizens of San Antonio, 160 dragoons belonging to the Santa Anna Regiment, and two pieces of artillery.[86] He formed his men in two lines in the prairie at a distance of four hundred yards to the rear of the Texans. The first was composed of 200 infantrymen of the Santa Anna Battalion and one piece of artillery; the second was made up of the squadrons from the Santa Anna Regiment with the piece of the light brigade. On the left were the *defensores* of Béxar and the Río Grande, numbering approximately 80 men; and on his right Woll stationed the presidial soldiers under Captain Castañeda re-enforced by 25 men under Herrera. Woll did not attempt to cover the side of the forest and arroyo fronting Béxar, believing the Texans would not attempt to escape by that route.

As Woll's infantry joined his cavalry in the prairie and cut off the possibility of a retreat toward the east, Caldwell appeared in front of the Texan line with his sleeves rolled up and addressed his small army. He pointed out the sufferings he and others had endured in Mexican dungeons and the possibility of death if recaptured in arms against Mexico. He urged his men to make up their minds to fight it out, even if it required hand-to-hand combat, and he promised that the white flag would not be raised. "Now my boys," he is reported to have said, "keep cool and recollect for what we are fighting—it is for liberty and our insulted country."[87] He then asked the Rev. Morrell to address the men

[86] Mathew Caldwell to the Secretary of War, Head Quarters of the Volunteer Army of Texas, Salado Creek, 8 miles from San Antonio, Sept. 18, 1842, Texas Congress, *Journals of the House of Representatives of the Seventh Congress*, Appendix, pp. 16–18; Thomas Jefferson Green, *The Texan Expedition Against Mier*, p. 31. Caldwell's report shows Woll bringing out 100 more infantrymen than Woll reports using, but does not show the arrival of the 160 additional cavalrymen. Woll's report does not mention the 40 Cherokees or the volunteer citizens of San Antonio being used in the battle, although Córdova is mentioned.

[87] "The Battle of Salado, Sept. 18, 1842," in Brown Papers, 1834–1872, ms. John Henry Brown, living on the Lavaca, in company with other volunteers reached

briefly, which he did, concluding with the statement: "Let us shoot low, and my impression before God is that we shall win the fight."[88] Caldwell now sent his men forward to attack the Mexican cavalry, while Woll was still in the process of forming his men. The fighting which had begun around 11 o'clock in the morning and continued intermittently, now became more furious and lasted until 5 in the afternoon.

Ever careful to conceal the true size of their force, the Texan command seldom permitted more than 15 to 20 men to skirmish with the Mexicans at a time. Frequently a few bold, "mischievous fellows would go out and use many epithets," reported John Henry Brown, the noted Texas historian and a participant in the battle, to provoke the Mexicans to charge; "but their invariable answer would be: 'Come out you d—d cowards and fight like men.'"[89] The *defensores* and *presidiales* dismounted and prepared to meet Caldwell's men as they advanced, but the Texans halted a short distance from the arroyo. After both sides had waited for some time for the other to advance, Woll detached fifty infantrymen and ordered them to crawl, inch by inch, through the mesquite toward the Texan line. The Texans retreated to the arroyo, and Woll recalled his guerillas and sent a reconnoitring party to explore along the Seguin road to see if any Texas re-enforcements were near. The exploring party reported seeing no one in that direction, except an enemy horseman who escaped from the forest on a fleet mount. This "enemy horseman" was either Nathaniel W. Faison or Alsey S. Miller, Dawson's scouts, who reported that one of them was chased and almost captured by the Mexican cavalry.

It was growing late, when Woll, feeling that his rear was secure against attack, decided to storm the Texan position. His men were readied for the assault. One hundred and fifty infantrymen were held in reserve. His artillery now fired two rounds each, one cannon shooting grape and the other cannister, followed in succession by a lone cannon shot and the drums beating attack, the prearranged signal for beginning the general assault.

Caldwell's camp on the morning of the 17th and continued in the campaign until it closed, keeping a diary of the whole. Upon returning to the home of his mother on the Lavaca, he wrote a history of the campaign under date of "La Vaca River, Gonzales County, October 2d, 1842," and sent a transcript of his notes to the *Telegraph and Texas Register*, where they were published under date of November 2, 1842.

[88] Morrell, *Flowers and Fruits in the Wilderness*, p. 169.

[89] "The Battle of Salado, Sept. 18, 1842," in Brown Papers, 1834–1872, ms.

As the cannon fired, the Mexican infantry rushed forward in dense masses with great intrepidity, firing very rapidly by platoons. Protected by the embankment from the Mexican cannon, the Texans easily repulsed the several daring attacks of the invader, who fell back in confusion and disorder behind the battery on the elevated ground. The round shot from the Mexican cannon did little damage, except to bark the trees, since they usually crashed through the tree tops or struck the ground long before the balls reached the Texan line and ricochetted through the tall grass, spending their force before they bounced over the protecting banks. "After the fight commenced," the Texans "found it was such an easy-going affair," reported one of the participants no doubt with considerable exaggeration, that "after each charge was repulsed, and before the Mexicans slowly reformed and advanced again, [they] would descend into the ravine," while the cannon balls passed above them, "and take a lunch of boiled meat and hot coffee. They joked and sang and were very gay, and they wanted nothing better than to have the Mexicans come up and be shot—it seemed like child's play!"[90] The Texan marksmanship, the speed, continuity, and fury of their fire dropped the Mexican soldiers by the score, but the number of their comrades was great and the gaps were quickly closed as they pressed close to the Texans in the creek bottom. The fire of the Texans, however, caused their line to waver and the assaulting column to fall back in great disorder.

"Big Foot" Wallace was anxious to obtain a large pair of pants to replace the spare pair that had fallen into the hands of the Mexicans when they took possession of the ranger headquarters in San Antonio.

During a close charge by the Mexicans one daring fellow charged Wallace, and presenting his carbine at him, cried out, "Take that, you d—d cowthief," and fired in his face. The large ounce ball from the *escopeta* grazed Wallace's nose and almost blinded him with smoke. Big Foot fired but missed.

Henry Whalen, standing near, said, "D—n such shooting as that," and aiming his rifle, quickly sent a ball through the body of the Mexican, who fell against a mesquite tree and soon died.

During the next charge, one of the rangers said to Wallace, "Big Foot, yonder is a Mexican who has on a pair of pants large enough to fit you." The Mexican in question was at this time assisting some of the wounded back to the rear.

Wallace was a conspicuous figure during the fight. His dress, massive frame, and actions, while talking about the big Mexican, attracted the at-

[90] Green (ed.), *Samuel Maverick: Texan*, p. 168.

tention of General Caldwell, who rode up to him and said, "What command do you hold, sir?"

"None," says Wallace. "I am one of Jack Hays' rangers, and want that fellows breeches over yonder," at the same time pointing out his intended victim.[91]

However, when Wallace levelled his gun upon the intended victim and fired, he missed, and it was the unerring aim of Ben McCulloch who a few seconds later dropped the big Mexican. Ben stripped him of his trousers, which he presented to Wallace. The trousers were made of fine material, and Wallace wore them the following year while a prisoner in Mexico.

While the Mexicans made their frontal assault, Córdova led his band, largely Cherokees, below the Texan position on the creek and "reached a dry ravine where it entered the timbered bottom, at right angles with the corner of the creek." Here they were confronted with the Texan "guards" and Captain Cameron's Company. At intervals along the ravine were small thickets with open spaces in between. In the nearest open space to the bottom and about ninety yards to the right of my company, reported Brown, Córdova was in the act of firing when he was shot dead by a "yeager ball" sent the full ninety yards by John Lowe,[92] "who belonged to the adjoining company on our right and stood about thirty feet from me, while I was loading my gun. I watched the affair closely," continued Brown, "fearing that one of our men might fall from Córdova's fire. There could, at the instant, be no mistake about it. Others saw the same; but no one knew it was Córdova till his men were driven from the position by Lieut. John R. Baker of Cameron's Company, when old Vasquez, a New Madrid Spaniard in our command, recognized him,"[93] as did others later, like Augustus C. Allen of Houston, who had known him while a resident of Nacogdoches.[94] Thus ended

[91] Sowell, *Early Settlers and Indian Fighters of Southwest Texas*, pp. 59–60; see also [Doris] Shannon Garst, *Big-Foot Wallace of the Texas Rangers*, p. 90. Sowell says Wallace killed the Mexican.

[92] Sowell, *Early Settlers and Indian Fighters of Southwest Texas*, pp. 25, 422, says that Córdova was killed by Wilson Randle of Seguin, but I believe him to be in error since I have been unable to substantiate it from any other source, and I find that Sowell's account of this and other actions is full of errors.

[93] Brown, *Indian Wars and Pioneers of Texas*, pp. 56–57, 66–67. In another place in the foregoing citations Brown reports John Lowe "standing within three feet of where I [J. H. Brown] stood."

[94] *Telegraph and Texas Register*, Oct. 12, 1842.

the career of the Mexican agent from Nacogdoches who had fled from Texas in 1839. Fourteen Cherokees fell with him.[95]

The Mexican infantrymen fought bravely, and, according to their own general, "with an intrepidity without equal." As his columns recoiled before the Texan fire, Woll, supposing his men would be pursued by the Texans, lowered his artillery so as to rake the ground eighty to one hundred yards in front of the Texan position, hoping to hew down the hated rebellious colonial if he should venture out too far. Woll misjudged the Texan tactics, for Caldwell had ordered his men to act only on the defensive and not risk being led into a trap.[96]

During the excitement caused by Hays' feint on San Antonio, Stephen Jett, who resided on the Medina west of San Antonio, had been able to effect his escape from the town and had succeeded in reaching the Texan camp a little before General Woll arrived. He was the only Texan killed in the battle of Salado Creek.[97] Jett had tied his horse carelessly some distance from the horses of the other Texans; and, seeing some Indians who had come out with the Mexicans approach the animal, he ignored the orders of his captain, abandoned his post, and sought to save his horse. In the combat with the Indians, he killed three of them, but was finally killed and his horse carried off. His comrades, who witnessed the whole affair, might have gone to his assistance, but were forbidden to do so, as he had disobeyed orders. The next day his companions buried him in a shallow grave dug with bowie knives.

In the several assaults the Mexican losses had been heavy. "My brothers [William and Andrew Adams, who were with Caldwell] told me," wrote Mrs. Maverick, "it was a pleasure to our boys to shoot down those Mexicans, for they had broken up all our homes and taken many of our brave comrades into cruel captivity."[98] "Here, there, every where, we see the Mexicans tumble down like beeves," recorded Brown, "and

---

[95] *Ibid.*

[96] "The Battle of Salado, Sept. 18, 1842," in Brown Papers, 1834–1872, ms.

[97] Brown, *History of Texas*, II, 222–228; Morrell, *Flowers and Fruits in the Wilderness*, pp. 167–179; Colonel Caldwell's report of the battle, written at 7:00 P.M., Sunday, Sept. 18, 1842, may be found in the *Telegraph and Texas Register*, Sept. 28, 1842; Weyand and Wade, *An Early History of Fayette County*, p. 148; *Jack Hays: The Intrepid Texas Ranger*, p. 15; Mathew Caldwell, Col. Commanding Texas Volunteers, to the Secretary of War, Head Quarters of the Volunteer Army of Texas, Salado Creek, 8 miles from San Antonio, Sept. 18, 1842, Texas Congress, *Journals of the House of Representatives of the Seventh Congress*, Appendix, pp. 16–18.

[98] Green (ed.), *Samuel Maverick: Texan*, p. 168.

every such sight would give additional strength to the shouts of our band."[99] Although Woll reported he was preparing to lead 100 of the 150 infantrymen he had been holding in reserve to conclude the battle with the Texans, whose defense he represented as very languid and unstable, the fact is he was apparently on the verge of withdrawing from the field when a messenger arrived with information that a small group of Texans was advancing upon his rear along the Seguin road at a distance of approximately two miles. In his report to his superiors, he magnified the small group of 53 Texans to an estimated 150 to 200 men.[100] Realizing the critical position in which he was now placed, Woll determined to crush the threat to his rear by overwhelming odds. He hastily dispatched two squadrons of cavalry and the light artillery piece to meet the Texan re-enforcements. The cavalry squadrons were from the Santa Anna Regiment and were commanded respectively by Colonel Pedro Rangel and Captain José María Carrasco. The over-all commander was Lieutenant Colonel Cayetano Montero, commandant of the Santa Anna Regiment.[101]

[99] "The Battle of Salado, Sept. 18, 1842," in Brown Papers, 1834–1872, ms.

[100] Adrián Woll ál Sr. general en gefe [Isidro Reyes], San Antonio de Béjar, a las 6 de la mañana del dia 20 de Septiembre de 1842, in Woll. *Expedición hecha en Téjas,* p. 41; Same to Same, Béjar, Sept. 18, 1842, in *ibid.,* p. 36.

[101] Adrián Woll ál Sr. general en gefe [Isidro Reyes], Béjar, Septiembre 18 de 1842, in *ibid.,* p. 36; and Nance (trans. and ed.), "Brigadier General Adrián Woll's Report of His Expedition into Texas in 1842," in *Southwestern Historical Quarterly,* LVIII (1954–1955), 540–541.

 CHAPTER SIXTEEN

The Dawson Fight

CAPTAIN NICHOLAS MOSBY DAWSON, a veteran of San Jacinto, with a small group of men from Fayette County had started for San Antonio immediately upon learning of the call for assistance. En route from LaGrange, Dawson's party overtook some men headed west and was overtaken by others. At the Sandies Creek, the men, numbering about fifty-three, mostly from Fayette County, elected Dawson captain and hurried on.¹ Late in the afternoon of the 17th they had encamped for the night at Nash's creek when a courier, John Wilson, from Caldwell arrived to urge them forward for the attack scheduled the next day. Immediately the company resumed its march, and after riding all night, reached Seguin about daylight. The men crossed the Guadalupe near the town for the purpose of grazing their horses and making some coffee, the first time they had stopped long enough to do this since leaving home. Later in the morning as they were preparing to renew their march, Dawson dispatched Alsey S. Miller and Nathaniel W. Faison² to spy out the exact location of Caldwell's men, with instructions "to go ahead" on Caldwell's trail, and upon discovering his location one of them was to return to report to the company while the other proceeded into Caldwell's camp.³

On the trail, about four miles west of the "beautiful hole of Blue Water" of the Cíbolo, seven miles east of the Salado, Dawson's men met the spies returning early in the afternoon at half-speed to report

---

¹ E. Manton to Mrs. J. Sinks, LaGrange, Feb. 1, 1891, in Edward Manton Papers, 1818–1891, ts. Edward Manton was one of the Dawson Company. See Appendix B for a list of the men in Dawson's Company.

² A. A. Gardenier to the Editor of the *Telegraph*, LaGrange, Oct. 21, 1842, *Telegraph and Texas Register*, Nov. 16, 1842.

³ An account of the Dawson Fight as told by one of Dawson's men, a prisoner in Mexico, to the correspondent of the *Western Advocate*, City of Mexico, Jan. 27, 1843, reprinted in *ibid.*, May 3, 1843. Hereafter cited as A Dawson Prisoner's Report, City of Mexico, Jan. 27, 1843, *Telegraph and Texas Register*, May 3, 1843.

that a battle was already in progress on the Salado between the Texans and Mexicans; and that probably two hunderd Mexican cavalry were standing on a hill to the east, apparently being held in reserve to support the action on the creek as well as to afford protection to the Mexican rear. Miller and Faison said they had approached so near that the enemy had given chase and had almost succeeded in capturing one of them.[4] Realizing that he had only a small force, Dawson suggested the expediency and advisability of falling back to join Captain Jesse Billingsley, who was believed to be about four miles to the rear with approximately eighty men.[5] With a junction of the two forces, they might be able to force their way through to Caldwell's position. At first a majority of the men were in agreement with these sentiments, believing a forward advance under present circumstances too rash to consider. However, from the spies' report, it was understood that the battle on the Salado was closely drawn and that Texan success hung in the balance. So, while Dawson's men debated what to do, "the passionate addresses of Mr. [Joseph] Shaw, an aged gentleman from La Grange," caused them to disregard the suggestions of prudence, and to desire to rush on to the "rescue of their countrymen without considering that if Caldwell with his large force and selected position could not sustain himself against the enemy, this small corps could not encounter them with safety on the open prairie."[6] Finally, Dawson took a vote on whether the company should attempt to charge through or await the arrival of re-enforcements under Billingsley.[7] An overwhelming majority of the men favored pushing forward at once, and this being the sentiment, an order to advance was issued. The men now spurred their horses forward at a slow gallop, when suddenly between 3 and 4 P.M. they discovered a small body of enemy cavalry interposed between them and Caldwell's position on the Salado, five miles away. As they continued forward, they could make out what seemed to be two groups of troops. The Texan spies declared the unit to the left of the trail to

---

[4] A. A. Gardenier to the Editor of the *Telegraph*, LaGrange, Oct. 21, 1842, *Telegraph and Texas Register*, Nov. 16, 1842.

[5] *Ibid.*

[6] Memucan Hunt to Dr. Francis Moore, Jr., Houston, Oct. 17, 1842, *ibid.*, Oct. 19, 1842. Reaching Béxar after the Salado and Dawson fights, Hunt learned, presumably from a conversation he had with Gonsalvo Woods, that at first a majority of Dawson's men were opposed to the rash measure of marching upon the enemy until Shaw talked them into it.

[7] *Telegraph and Texas Register*, Oct. 12, 1842.

be the Mexicans, and the one to the right the Texans. Soon it was discovered that both forces were advancing in Dawson's direction, and were within one-half to three-fourths of a mile. Dawson now wheeled his men some one hundred yards to the right which brought his men to a small, sparse mesquite thicket, covering about two acres, spectacle shaped, in the midst of a large prairie.[8] In the distance could be heard the roar of guns. As the distance between Dawson's Company and the two oncoming groups shortened, the Fayette men suddenly realized that both advancing units were Mexicans, reported one of the Dawson prisoners later, and it was "then too late." Dawson's men quickly dismounted and tied their horses, as was customary in repelling an attack, and prepared for action. "Some of his men spoke of retreating . . . [but] Dawson raised his rifle and said that he would shoot the first man who said retreat or surrender."[9] One of these was Norman Woods, who remarked to Dawson as the Mexicans deployed around the Texans, "Captain, we are in a bad fix."

To which Dawson replied, drawing his pistol, "I'll shoot the first man who runs."[10]

Caught in the open prairie, Dawson sought to make the most of an uncomfortable situation. The ground selected for battle "was not [a] very propitious place for fighting," reported Harvey A. Adams, who visited the battlefield three weeks later.[11] The little band of Texans made its stand in "a small grove of tufted mesquit of not very large dimentions [*sic*],"[12] covering about two acres of ground within the con-

---

[8] A Dawson Prisoner's Report, City of Mexico, Jan. 27, 1843, *Telegraph and Texas Register*, May 3, 1843.

[9] Harvey Alexander Adams, "[Journal of an] Expedition Against the Southwest, in 1842 and 1843," Oct. 5, 1842, ms.

[10] Quoted by Paul R. Spellman to Houston Wade, San Antonio, Texas, Sept. 5, 1934, in Houston Wade Papers, ms. The Woods boys always resented any implication that any of them were opposed to fighting on this occasion.

[11] Adams, "[Journal of an] Expedition Against the Southwest," Oct. 4–5, 1842, ms.

[12] The site is at what is now the junction of Houston Street in San Antonio with the Missouri-Kansas-Texas Railroad. Boyce House, *City of Flaming Adventure: The Chronicle of San Antonio*, p. 96. A marker was erected in 1935 during the Texas centennial celebrations at the side of the Austin-San Antonio highway, a mile from Dawson's battleground, which was some distance to the right of the point where the Rittman Road crosses the Missouri-Kansas-Texas Railroad. Anna Ellis, "Dawson Massacre Anniversary to See Unveiling of Memorial," *San Antonio Express*, Sept. 15, 1935.

fines of the present Fort Sam Houston.[13] For a mile around the country was almost level, "but much higher, and out of view from the battle-field on the creek," a mile and a half away.[14] It was believed that if Dawson had gone sharply to the left of the main road, he would un-doubtedly have reached the Salado bottom "in safety, unobserved by the enemy," reported Adams. "But that dare me devil don't care which is characteristic of Texians," reported Adams, "led these brave spirits on to the slaughter, before the last extremity came."[15]

Within a few minutes after the Texans had dismounted, they were surrounded. Colonel Montero rode up with a small body of Mexican cavalry to the upper edge of the mott, raised a white flag, asked for a parley, and finally called upon the Texans to surrender to the Mexican government, but they "answered with scoffing and bantering."[16] Daw-son ordered the Mexicans off, but they were reluctant about going; so, he threatened to fire upon them. Whereupon, the Mexican unit rode around the mott at a gallop and joined the main body. As the Mexicans now formed for an attack, the Texans commenced firing, killing two soldiers.[17] The Mexicans fell back out of range, formed at a distance of about 350 to 400 yards from the Texans, lying concealed behind the clumps of mesquite, and then to the number of approximately four hundred cavalrymen under the command of Colonels Montero, Carras-co, and Pedro Rangel, advanced at a gallop in fine military order to within 70 yards of the Texan position, where every Texan bosom burned with a desire to obtain a good shot. In the distance, they heard the Mexicans firing upon Caldwell's men and the answering crack of the Texas rifles.[18] Dawson, who had formerly served in the regular army of the Republic and had been one of "Deaf" Smith's spies, now stepped from the ranks, and with a steady, deadly aim, dropped the advancing Mexican officer, and turning with a smile, said to his men, "that is the way I used to do."[19] Whereupon, his men opened a general

[13] Mary Olivia Handy, *History of Fort Sam Houston,* p. 4; [Anonymous], *A History of the San Antonio Quartermaster Depot,* p. 5.

[14] *Bollaert's Texas,* p. 215.

[15] Adams, "[Journal of an] Expedition Against the Southwest," Oct. 5, 1842, ms.

[16] Seguin, *Memoirs,* p. 29

[17] M. E. Manton to Mrs. J. Sinkes, LaGrange, Feb. 1, 1891, in Manton Papers, 1818–1891, ms. See also Seguin, *Memoirs,* p. 29.

[18] A. A. Gardenier to the Editor of the *Telegraph,* LaGrange, Oct. 21, 1842, *Telegraph and Texas Register,* Nov. 16, 1842.

[19] *Ibid.*

fire upon the advancing cavalrymen, and the enemy fled in great confusion, leaving several of their number dead and wounded on the field.
The Mexican cavalry retreated out of range of the hail of lead from
the Texan rifles, and its piece of artillery to the south (until now unobserved by the Texans) opened upon them a galling fire of grape and
cannister, dealing death among the horses at every discharge. Montero's
cavalry went to the right and Carrasco's and Rangel's to the left. Now
followed a general cross-fire from the whole Mexican force which lasted
for about three-quarters of an hour.

As the firing along the Salado died out, Caldwell's men heard "the
roar of artillery and rifles . . . in the rear of the Mexican army"; and, although "we understood at once," wrote Morrell, "that the engagement
was with reinforcements making their way to relieve us, by the time we
were up, and . . . [ready] to go to their assistance the firing ceased, and
we knew that the Mexicans were successful."[20] Near 5 o'clock in the
afternoon, as the battle raged, Captain Jesse Billingsley and John Caldwell, both prominent citizens of Bastrop County, with approximately 70
men from the Colorado, composed of the companies of Captain Childress of Bastrop and Captain Cooke of Austin,[21] reached the high
ground overlooking the valley of the Salado, where the little band
perched like eaglets on the heights of the Salado and eyed the contending squadrons in the vale below.[22] Their two scouts, Samuel H. Walker
and Cicero Rufus Perry, reported 150 infantrymen held in reserve at
the rear of the Mexican army, and stated that squads of their cavalry
were placed all around so as to cut off and intercept the Texan spies.[23]
As the Colorado men watched, they prayed that the LaGrange men,
four hours in advance of them on the road, had succeeded in uniting
with Caldwell's men, not realizing that Dawson's men were at that time
engaged in a death-struggle with Woll's men. Not knowing the general
lay of the terrain or the true position of Woll's men, and having no one
in his command who did, Captain Billingsley sent out spies to learn the
position of the enemy and to enter Caldwell's camp, while he fell back
with the company three miles. He deemed his unit too weak to force a

[20] Z[enos] N. Morrell, *Flowers and Fruits in the Wilderness: or Forty-Six Years
in Texas and Two Winters in Honduras*, p. 170.

[21] John Henry Brown, *Indian Wars and Pioneers of Texas*, p. 227.

[22] *The State Times* (Austin), July 26, 1856.

[23] Jesse Billingsley and John Caldwell to ———, Sunday, 9 o'clock at night, 18th
Sept. 1842, in *Telegraph and Texas Register*, Oct. 5, 1842; *The State Times* (Austin), July 26, 1856.

passage through the Mexican line, and he did not wish to risk an encounter with the Mexicans at this time. Colonel John H. Moore from LaGrange, who had been authorized in July to raise a corps of 200 volunteers,[24] and was just recovering from a severe case of inflammatory rheumatism, could not be expected to arrive until sometime the following day; however, shortly after 9 o'clock Billingsley was joined by 30 men under Colonel Joseph Washington E. Wallace, who had served as a lieutenant colonel in joint command of the Texan forces at the battle of Gonzales in the fall of 1835 and as an officer in the Plum Creek Fight with the Comanches in 1840. If Billingsley had realized the serious situation of the Mexican army, and if he and Dawson had been aware of their proximity to one another, the battle of Salado might have been as decisive in the annals of Texas history as that of San Jacinto, and the Dawson Fight part of a great victory instead of a "massacre." Such was not to be the case.

With their rifles, the Fayette men were able to keep the enemy cavalry at a respectful distance, but soon the cannon began to get the range, and the iron hail raking through the sparse mesquites created havoc among the small band of volunteers and their horses. Death in every shape stalked through their thinned ranks; yet, they fought with added fury. "The enemy lay in piles around the bodies of Slack, Cummins, Berry, and Maverick's large negro."[25] Through all this, Dawson moved up and down the line, visited every exposed situation, encouraging the young and inexperienced, and directing the old, urging the necessity of being cool, to reserve their fire and take careful aim.

In the position they had chosen Dawson's men did not have a chance. It was a duel between artillery and rifles of "long tau." Yet, the Texans lying behind the clumps of mesquite, put up a determined fight, and with a number of well directed shots, even at this great distance, brought some of the enemy down. Montero sent for more ammunition, but Woll angrily asked if his dragoons had not sabres or lances; however, ere the general's reply reached him, Montero had ordered an all out assault upon the Texan position. As the Mexican cavalry arrived at the edge of the mesquite mott, they dismounted, and, urged on by their officers, entered the grove, with sabres in hand to complete the job, reported Woll, "slashing as many enemies as they encountered."[26]

[24] *Civilian and Galveston Gazette,* July 24, 1842.
[25] H. G. Woods' account as related by A. A. Gardenier to the Editor of the *Telegraph,* LaGrange, Oct. 21, 1842, *Telegraph and Texas Register,* Nov. 16, 1842.
[26] Adrián Woll al Sr. General en gefe [Isidro Reyes], San Antonio de Béjar, a las

With eight or ten of their number dead, several wounded, and many of their horses killed or run off, Captain Dawson, severely wounded in the hip, sought to effect a surrender for his men. Near the middle of the action, he stood up and with a mackinaw blanket on his gun serving as a white flag, advanced toward the enemy through the "small timber . . . so terribly raked with cannon shot," but the Mexicans continued to fire, wounding him several times. Dawson dropped to the ground either from the effects of his wounds or to seek cover. He arose once more in an effort to surrender his men, but to no effect. Seeing that the enemy would give no quarter, he exhorted his men to sell their lives as dearly as possible—" 'let victory be purchased with blood,' were his last and dying words."[27]

> They come, they come, the ruthless band,
>   To enforce the tyrant's foul decree,
> To desolate this smiling land,
>   The dwelling of the fair and free:—
> Sons of the West, the hour has come
> Of victory or martyrdom.
>
> These field, which oft our brows bedew'd
>   Till bloom'd the desert with our toil,
> Shall be in blood more deep imbrued
>   Ere thraldom stains the Texian soil:
> When bleach our bones on every plain,
> Then wolves may greet Santa Anna's reign.
>
> Well shall the aspiring traitor learn
>   The cost of such a dreary sway—
> Behold yon warriors, few but stern,
>   Who front the invaders broad array:—
> True as the rifle to its aim
> Each heart is to the cause they claim.
>
> On, gallant souls, where glory calls,
>   And "*God* and *Freedom*" be the cry;
> Where one devoted patriot falls
>   An hundred ruffian slaves shall die;

---

6 de la mañana del dia 20 de Septiembre de 1842, in [Adrián Woll], *Expedición hecha en Téjas, por una parte de la Division del Cuerpo de Egército del Norte,* p. 42; *El Provisional* (Matamoros), Oct. 14, 1842.

[27] A. A. Gardenier to the Editor of the *Telegraph,* LaGrange, Oct. 21, 1842, *Telegraph and Texas Register,* Nov. 16, 1842.

And should they win one conquer'd rood,
'Tis with a slain battalion strew'd.

On, while heroic shades look down
    And view your kindred ranks with pride—
Your sires who fought with Washington,
    Your brethren who with Mina died;
"Shame not your race," they cry, "ye brave,
Preserve a home or find a grave."

Blest are the bowers no storms invade,
    Where plenty reigns and hearts are warm,
Blest are the Free whose swords have made
    Their dwellings safe from foes and harm,
But far more blest the valiant dead
Who die in honor's gory bed.[28]

Alsey S. Miller sought to get the flag received. He mounted a horse belonging to one of his companions, his own having torn loose during the excitement, and rode out of the grove with a white flag in full view of the whole enemy force, while his comrades cried out, "We surrender!" The flag was perforated with balls. Seeing that no quarter was to be given, he fled through the encircling enemy lines without arms.[29] Although many shots were fired at him, he escaped unhurt. One historian

[28] R. M. P[otter], "War Song of Texas," in *Telegraph and Texas Register,* Jan. 4, 1843.

[29] Memucan Hunt to Doctor [Francis Moore], Houston, Oct. 17, 1842, in *ibid.,* Oct. 26, 1842. During the battle the Mexicans set out in front of their ranks before Caldwell's men on the Salado two flags—one white and the other red. After the firing had continued for some time, Captain Ambrosio Martínez approached the Texas lines with the white flag, but as the left flank of the Mexican army kept up a fire on the Texans, the Texans continued to return the fire. (Editorial comment in *ibid.,* Oct. 26, 1842.) Hunt said

in the latter part of the battle of Salado, Gen. Woll passed through his Aid-de-Camp, Capt. Martínez, an interchange with Col. Caldwell under a flag of truce, but contrary to all usage in warfare allowed [the Indians and a portion of the Mexicans on] the left wing of his command to continue a steady fire upon our right. The just result was a total disregard of the truce by Col. Caldwell, and Capt. Martínez returned without reaching our lines [mortally] wounded.

As some of the San Antonio prisoners regarded Woll as an honorable man, it is difficult to appraise his conduct on this occasion. Possibly he was unaware of the reason for Caldwell's refusal of the white flag, and concluded that the Texans intended no quarter; this would account for the Mexicans' refusing Dawson's flag of surrender, since some of Dawson's men continued to fight, not knowing that their captain was trying to effect a surrender.

371

says that when Captain Dawson hoisted the "white flag" of surrender several of his men continued to fire and were put to death by the Mexicans.[30] Even after a part of the Texans had laid down their arms, the Mexican soldiers continued to kill them.[31]

The Mexican assault bore all before it. It was now hand to hand fighting with knife, sword, saber, and gun stock. "Now and then," narrated a participant, "a cry for quarter was heard from some soul as it took its flight into eternity."[32] In little over an hour's time, altogether, the fighting was over.[33] Many deeds of heroism were performed that afternoon by the Dawson men. Through the exertions of Colonel Carrasco, who exclaimed, "such men are too brave to die,"[34] and several other Mexican officers, a few of the Texan lives were spared, but Samuel A. Maverick's Negro slave, Griffin, of Herculean powers, who had fallen in with the Dawson men en route to San Antonio with the intent of passing himself off as a runaway slave and following Woll's army into Mexico to free or aid his master, fought furiously and, when he had broken the stock of his gun, jerked off the limb of a mesquite tree and used it as a club until he was killed, refusing quarter.[35] It was believed that the

[30] Hubert Howe Bancroft, *History of Texas and the North Mexican States*, II, 358.

[31] *Telegraph and Texas Register*, Oct. 26, 1842.

[32] A Dawson Prisoner's Report, City of México, Jan. 27, 1843, in *ibid.*, May 3, 1842.

[33] Memucan Hunt to Dr. [Francis Moore, Jr.], Houston, Oct. 17, 1842, in *ibid.*, Oct. 26, 1842. Woll reported that the fighting was over in a quarter of an hour. (Adrián Woll ál Sr. general en gefe [Isidro Reyes], San Antonio de Béjar, a las 6 de la mañana del dia 20 de Septiembre de 1842, Woll, *Expedición hecha en Téjas*, p. 42.) He probably meant a quarter of an hour after the launching of the last Mexican assault. The various Texan accounts, both by participants and by those who interviewed survivors, give the time around an hour or more.

[34] A. A. Gardenier to the Editor of the *Telegraph*, La Grange, Oct. 21, 1842, *Telegraph and Texas Register*, Nov. 16, 1842. Gardenier's account of the Dawson fight is based largely on Henry Gonzalvo Woods' account of the occurrences. Woods was one of the escapees.

[35] Griffin had accompanied Maverick to San Antonio late in August, 1842, and after Woll's capture of that place had hurried to the Colorado to tell Mrs. Maverick of the capture of her husband.

I called him to me [reported Mrs. Maverick] and talked to him about going out to San Antonio to pass himself for a "runaway," follow to Mexico, and do anything he could to free or even aid Mr. Maverick, and he could have his freedom. He answered that to do anything for his master would delight him, and he had been wanting to ask me to let him go—"as for freedom," he added, "I do not want any more than I have, master has always treated me more like a brother

Dawson men killed about thirty Mexicans, and wounded between sixty and seventy more. In all, thirty-six Texans were killed, fifteen taken prisoners, and two escaped.[36]

> How sleep the brave who sink to rest,
> By all their countrys' wishes blest,
> When Spring with dewy fingers cold
> Returns to deck their hallowed mould,
> She there shall dress a sweeter sod,
> Than Fancy's feet have ever trod.
>
> By Fairy hands their knell is rung,
> By forms unseen their dirge is sung,
> There *honor* comes a pilgrim gray
> To bless the turf that wraps their clay,
> And *freedom* shall awhile repair
> To dwell a weeping hermit there.[37]

Five of the prisoners were severely wounded, having been hacked with swords and lances, but recovered after great suffering. No one can imagine, let alone describe, the scene of the battleground. All of the Texans who had fallen were stripped of every article of clothing, and the captives lost all of their outer garments.[38] The prisoners' hands were

----

than a slave," and he choked up unable to say more. He took a gun, a good mule, some money, and made ready and started within a few hours—happy to think he might do something to help his master.

Rena Maverick Green (ed.), *Memoirs of Mrs. Mary A. Maverick: Arranged by Mary A Maverick and Her Son George Madison Maverick*, p. 167.

[36] *Telegraph and Texas Register*, Oct. 12, 1842; Woll reported 120 Texans killed; 15 taken prisoner, including 5 wounded; and two or three escaped. Adrián Woll to Isidro Reyes, Béxar, Sept. 18, 1842, in Joseph Milton Nance (trans. and ed.), "Brigadier General Adrián Woll's Report of His Expedition into Texas in 1842," *Southwestern Historical Quarterly*, LVIII (1954–1955), 540–541; also in *El Provisional* (Matamoros), Oct. 14, 1842. Colonel John H. Moore is reported to have counted forty-eight dead bodies of the gallant Fayette band, but a month later the editor of the *Civilian* after publishing Moore's statement, printed the names of those who had been killed and gave the total as thirty-five, which appears to be the correct figure. Moore did not reach the scene of Dawson's fight until after the crude burial of the men. *Civilian and Galveston Gazette*, Oct. 1, 1842.

[37] *Telegraph Extra*, Saturday, Sept. 24, 1842, quoted in *Telegraph and Texas Register*, Sept. 28, 1842, from poem by William Collins (1721–1759), "How Sleep the Brave."

[38] In San Antonio, Mrs. Elliot took a green blanket-coat off of her son and gave it to A. H. Morrell, the preacher's son, who had been captured. Morrell, *Flowers and Fruits in the Wilderness*, p. 173. Another account says the living were stripped of

tied behind their backs, and were in turn all tied together with a rawhide lariat. Each was carefully searched for money. Nathaniel Faison was apparently the only one who had any, and that being only about two dollars; but he had a ring on his finger which attracted the attention of a soldier. When asked to take it off, Faison claimed he could not get it off as he had often tried to do so at home; however, when "the Mexican soldier drew his knife and made signs that he would take the finger off, Faison made another trial at the ring and found that it came off very easily."[39] The prisoners were then marched to Béxar, which they reached about 10 P.M., and from there were carried into Mexico when Woll's army retreated. Faison was thoughtful enough to leave on the wall of the Texans' prison at San Antonio the names of his comrades still alive.[40]

One of the two men to escape was Henry Gonzalvo Woods, who early in the fight received a wound in the shoulder and saw Jerome B. Alexander[41] and Elam Scallon killed at his side. After his father, Zadock Woods, seventy years of age, had been killed, and his brother, Norman, had been seriously wounded, he sought to surrender, hoping to be able to remain with his brother and save him, although his brother urged him to try to escape and urged him to take care of Jane (Norman's wife) and the children. During the melee toward the end of the battle, Henry threw down his gun and shot pouch and advanced twenty paces toward an officer whom he mistook for Colonel Seguin, and in Spanish, which he spoke very well, asked for quarter for himself and all the Texans. The officer nodded and rode past him, after which he was attacked by four cavalrymen. Two of the men fired their guns without effect, while the guns of the other two merely snapped, whereupon, one of the Mexicans struck him over the head with his musket; another cut him over the head with his sword, and a third sought to spear him.[42] Seizing the

everything except shirt and pantaloons. A Dawson Prisoner's Report, City of México, Jan. 27, 1843, *Telegraph and Texas Register*, May 3, 1843.

[39] E. Manton to J. Sinks, La Grange, Feb. 1, 1891, in Manton Papers, 1818–1891, ms. In December 1845, N. W. Faison was County Clerk of Fayette County. Manton Papers, 1818–1891, ms.

[40] *Quarterly of the Texas State Historical Association*, VII (1903–1904), 81–83.

[41] Jerome B. Alexander was clerk of the third Judicial District Court, Fayette County, 1838–1839. *Ibid.*, VII (1903–1904), 81–83.

[42] A. A. Gardenier to the Editor of the *Telegraph*, La Grange, Oct. 21, 1842, in *Telegraph and Texas Register*, Nov. 16, 1842.

latter's lance as he dodged it, Woods jerked the Mexican to the ground, drove the lance through his heart, pulled it out, mounted the Mexican's horse, and made his escape, carrying the lance with him.[43] His boldness so astonished the other Mexican cavalrymen that they did nothing for the moment. Finally, one of them attempted to pursue him, but was kept at a distance by Woods' taking one of the pistols from the holsters on the saddle and pointing it at him. The Mexican soon broke off the pursuit and returned to his companions. His horse giving out soon thereafter, Woods dismounted and crawled into some high grass to await the coming of darkness.[44] He then backtracked along Dawson's trail for eight miles before exhaustion from the loss of blood forced him to hide in a clump of mesquite bushes. About 9 o'clock the next morning he heard the tramp of horses. Quickly hiding himself in the grass and mesquite, he lay motionless in eager expectation. Soon he heard men talking in English; among them was John Wilson from LaGrange on his way to the front with a party of volunteers. Woods, still in possession of the bloody lance, made his presence known, and they took care of him.[45]

The other escapee was as we have already noted, Alsey S. Miller. He was pursued in his flight by Antonio Pérez and other renegade Mexicans, formerly of San Antonio. His mount was soon winded, but luckily he was able to seize Edward T. Manton's fine horse which had escaped from the grove and came galloping by at just the right time. With a better mount, Miller soon outdistanced his pursuers and arrived safe at Seguin—bare-headed, badly sunburned, and with his horse covered

---

[43] Sowell, *Early Settlers and Indian Fighters of Southwest Texas,* p. 817.

[44] Another version of Woods' escape was related many years later by John H. Jenkins of Bastrop. According to Jenkins' account, Woods rode full speed for about two miles, when seeing two men, one of whom he mistook for Alsey S. Miller whom he had seen make a desperate run through the Mexican line, he sought to join them;

> when lo, they were two Mexicans, who immediately rushed upon him firing as they came. Seeing a pistol attached to the horn of his saddle, he [Woods] snatched it to fire, when he saw the cartridge fall to the ground, thus leaving him once more powerless to defend himself. They, however, did not know the pistol was empty, so he managed to 'bluff' them, until reaching a hollow and dismounting, he hid himself and *finally* made his escape.

Jenkins, "Personal Reminiscences of Texas History Relating to Bastrop County, 1828–1847, as Dictated to his Daughter-in-law, Mrs. Emma Holmes Jenkins of Bastrop," pp. 109–110. A slightly different wording appears in the edited version: John Holland Jenkins, III (ed.), *Recollections of Early Texas: The Memoirs of John Holland Jenkins,* pp. 98–99.

[45] Sowell, *Early Settlers and Indian Fighters of Southwest Texas,* p. 817.

with foam.[46] This was the first news to arrive eastward from the battle-field. For several days now, after the departure of the men from Gonzales, Seguin, and other points, wives, mothers, children, and other loved ones left behind anxiously watched and waited for a messenger from the scene of action. Once more the wives and mothers of the Guadalupe valley recalled the horrible scenes of the Alamo and Goliad, and every moment expected the messenger of death to dash up with the sad news of defeat and slaughter of loved ones. Eagerly they clustered around Miller to hear the latest news from the west. They heard him tell of the desparate fight put up by the Dawson men; how they had been surrounded and cut to pieces, and that he alone, as far as he knew, was the only survivor. He could not give any encouragement of the fate of Caldwell's men, but could only say that there was heavy firing in the direction of the Salado and that the Mexicans had them cut off from the rest of Texas.

About one hour of sundown (about 5:00), General Woll ordered his musicians to play "assembly," "which was executed," he reported, "with much sluggishness on the part of our brave men, who did not wish to let their spoils escape."[47] He assembled his troops in the prairie, and, mounting a cannon, praised the success of Mexican arms in glowing terms. While the Mexican soldiers shook their arms and shouted with joy, "Vive a Méjico," "Viva al ilustre General Santa Anna," and "Viva al General Woll," within sight and hearing of the Texans, the latter dared not risk an attack upon the enemy in the open prairie.[48] Toward sunset Woll ordered his musicians to play retreat and made preparations to return to San Antonio for the night. The wounded were collected and immediately dispatched to the city under the care of Doctor Montanari, where they were attended by the Mexican families of the place.[49]

---

[46] Brown, *History of Texas*, II, 226; Norman Woods to H. G. Woods, Molino del Rey, July 5, 1843, in L. U. Spellman (ed.) "Letters of the 'Dawson Men' from Perote Prison, Mexico, 1842–1843," *Southwestern Historical Quarterly*, XXXVIII (1934–1935), 257–259. Norman Woods claims that Colonel Carrasco ordered the prisoners to be executed, but that their lives were spared by an order given from General Woll. *Ibid.*

[47] Woll reported that the Texans now took advantage of the circumstances and the gathering obscurity of night to enter "farther into the woods, fleeing terrified far from the sight of our soldiers." Adrián Woll ál Sr. general en gefe [Isidro Reyes], San Antonio de Béjar, a las 6 de la mañana del dia 20 de Septiembre de 1842, in Woll, *Expedición hecha en Téjas*, p. 42.

[48] *Ibid.*

[49] Adams, "[Journal of an] Expedition Against the Southwest," Oct. 5, 1842, ms.

The roll was called, and while some proceeded to gather the spoils of the enemy, the remainder of the troops rested on their arms, maintaining the same positions they had occupied during the battle. At 10 P.M. Woll headed for San Antonio. His men had been without food all day, and were greatly fatigued by the time they began to enter the city at midnight amid the ringing of the church bells in celebration of a great victory, according to the Mexican accounts; but rather it was the tolling of the dead. The grand fandango scheduled for the evening in honor of victory, for which one of the Mexican officers had so sedulously collected a large sum of money that morning before the army marched out, was forgotten. In its place next morning there was held a mass funeral for those whose bodies had been brought in and the wounded who had died during the night.[50] The citizens of Béxar reported that on the day before Woll's army commenced its retreat on the 20th "not a cheerful face was to be seen, but sadness and gloom seemed to pervade the whole army as if some terrible calamity had occurred."[51] It was reported by Mr. Jones, who was in San Fernando during this time, that Woll hastily sent an express from Béxar to General Reyes at Presidio for reenforcements; but despite every exertion only forty or fifty men could be raised, and, there being an insufficient number of arms in town even for these, the men were disbanded.[52]

Woll reported the Texan losses as 120 killed by the Mexican cavalry, "60 corpses . . . stretched out in the forest," fifteen prisoners,[53] and an

[50] *Telegraph and Texas Register*, Oct. 26, 1842.
[51] *Ibid.*
[52] "Information of Mr. Jones from San Fernando," *ibid.*, Jan. 25, 1843. Jones, an American who had spent several years in northern Mexico, had been imprisoned by General Reyes at San Fernando. He effected his escape after the return of Woll's army and reached San Antonio on November 13 in a weakened, starved condition. Eleanor Elliot to Mary A. Maverick, San Antonio de Béjar, Nov. 14, 1842, in Green (ed.), *Samuel Maverick, Texan, 1803–1870: A Collection of Letters, Journals and Memoirs*, pp. 202–204.
[53] The 15 prisoners were from Dawson's Company, of whom 5 were wounded. The Mexican consul at New Orleans stated that on the basis of the official reports he had received Caldwell had 300 men and Dawson 150, of which 120 of the latter were killed and 15 taken prisoners. F. de Arrangoiz, Mexican Consul, to the Editors of the [*New Orleans*] *Bee*, New Orleans, Nov. 9, 1842, *Telegraph and Texas Register*, Nov. 30, 1842. A. J. Sowell reports that Thomas Galbreath told him of a man named Butler with eight men who heard the firing of the rangers and Mexicans on the west side of the Salado during the running fight from town, "and thinking it was the main body of Texans, and that they were engaged, crossed over there and were cut off by the [Mexican] cavalry and killed." Sowell, *Early Settlers and*

"immense number" of wounded, of which only five were picked up by the Mexican troops, the others having been carried off by their comrades. "In these short campaigns," summed up the Mexican consul in New Orleans, "the Texians have lost their arms, ammunition, horses, and more than six hundred men, killed, wounded, and prisoners—the latter being well treated."[54]

Woll's exaggerated report of 180 Texans killed[55] is contradicted by more reliable Texan accounts, for the Texans, we must remember, remained on the field after the battle. Reporting two hours after the battle and before the Mexicans had withdrawn from the field, Caldwell placed his losses at ten wounded, none killed.[56] These figures exclude Dawson's losses. The Texas historian, John Henry Brown, who was with Caldwell, has given the Texan losses as one killed (Stephen Jett of Medina) and eleven wounded, one mortally.[57] Brown also says Woll left 60 dead on the Salado battlefield, hauled away 44 dead and 150 wounded into San Antonio.[58] However, as to his own losses, Woll reported 29 killed, including Vicente Córdova, and 58 wounded.[59] Among the latter was the brother of Rafael Vasquez, Ensign Victores Manero,

---

Indian Fighters of Southwest Texas, pp. 316–317. The writer has no where found information in either Mexican or Texan source materials that could in any way substantiate this claim.

[54] F. de Arrangoiz, Mexican consul, to the Editors of the [*New Orleans*] *Bee*, New Orleans, Nov. 9, 1842, *Telegraph and Texas Register*, Nov. 30, 1842.

[55] Adrián Woll ál Sr. general en gefe [Isidro Reyes], San Antonio de Béjar, a las 6 de la mañana del dia 20 de Septiembre de 1842, in Woll, *Expedición hecha en Téjas*, pp. 38–45.

[56] Report of Mathew Caldwell, Sunday, Sept. 18 [1842], 7 o'clock P.M., *Telegraph and Texas Register*, Sept. 28, 1842. Among the wounded was Calvin Turner of Seguin, who had been hurt on the side of his head by a glancing shot from a musket ball. Sowell, *Early Settlers and Indian Fighters of Southwest Texas*, p. 422.

[57] "Battle of Salado, Sept. 18, 1842," in Brown Papers, 1835–1872, ms.

[58] *Ibid.*

[59] Adrián Woll ál Sr. general en gefe [Isidro Reyes], San Antonio de Béjar, a las 6 de la mañana del dia 20 de Septiembre de 1842, in Woll, *Expedición hecha en Téjas*, p. 43. These same figures were reported some sixteen months later by General Tornel, Minister of War and Marine, to the Mexican Congress. He gave the Texas losses as 200 killed and wounded. Ministerio de guerra y marina. Memoria del Secretario de estado y del despacho de guerra y marina, leida a las camaras del Congreso nacional de Republica Mexicana, en enero de 1844, *Diario del Gobierno* (Mexico City), May 15, 1844, pp. 57–58.

who died during the night of the 20th on the Medina.[60] Such losses, he admitted, were "great and deplorable," but understandable if his superiors could only know "how hard-fought have been the two battles in which a part of the Second Division covered itself with so much glory."[61] Memucan Hunt, who was in San Antonio shortly after the battle of Salado and met with most of the Texan officers engaged in the action, wrote, "It is a moderate estimate to state that sixty of the enemy were killed and about one hundred and twenty wounded while ten of our men were wounded, and that occasioned generally by unnecessary exposure."[62] Another visitor to the scene of battle, two and a half weeks after the action, reported 100 Mexicans killed on the battlefield, including those who crawled off toward the creek for water and died amidst the thick grass, brush, and along the water course, where they had sought to appease their burning thirst. He also tells us that approximately 100 Mexicans were wounded, 23 of whom died the next day in San Antonio,[63] and were buried in San Antonio, where the most seriously wounded were left to be taken care of by the local families when Woll began his retreat on the 20th.[64] Presumably, most, if not all, of these died within a few days, for it was soon reported in the Texas press that 48 wounded Mexicans from the engagements near the Sa-

[60] Adrián Woll ál Sr. general en gefe [Isidro Reyes], Campo sobre la margen izquierdo de río Medina, Septiembre 2 de 1842, in Woll, *Expedición hecha en Téjas*, p. 49; Report of A. C. Allen, in *Telegraph and Texas Register*, Oct. 12, 1842.

[61] Adrián Woll al Sr. general en gefe [Isidro Reyes], San Antonio de Bexar, a las seis de la mañana del dia de Septiembre 20 de 1842, in Woll, *Expedición hecha en Téjas*, p. 43. *El Cosmopolita* (Mexico City), Oct. 8, 1842, reported that Woll defeated 450 Texans at the Arroyo Salado, near Bexar, on September 18, 1842, leaving 120 corpses and taking 15 prisoners. The Minister of War in reporting to the Mexican Congress much later stated that the Texan losses amounted to 200 killed and wounded, and that their own losses were 29 killed and 58 wounded. Ministerio de guerra y marina. Memoria del Secretario de estado y del despacho de guerra y marina, leida a las camaras del Congreso nacional de la Republica Mexicana, en enero de 1844, *Diario del Gobierno* (Mexico City), May 15, 1844, pp. 57–58. James S. Mayfield reported the Mexican losses as 100 killed and over 200 wounded. James S. Mayfield to General E. Burleson, Camp Salado, Tuesday Morning, Sept. 20, 1842, *Telegraph and Texas Register*, Sept. 28, 1842.

[62] Memucan Hunt to Dr. Francis Moore, Jr., Houston, Oct. 17, 1842, *Telegraph and Texas Register*, Oct. 26, 1842.

[63] *The Telegraph and Texas Register*, Oct. 26, 1842, reports that the Mexicans brought into San Antonio more than 100 wounded of which at least 48 died by the next morning and were buried.

[64] Adams, "[Journal of an] Expedition Against the Southwest," Oct. 5, 1842, ms.

lado had died in the town. Later, at San Fernando Colonel Carrasco is alleged to have told the San Antonio prisoners that "there was a smaller portion of Mexicans wounded in this battle than in any other that took place, and a large proportion were killed. He said most of the Mexican soldiers in the battle were shot in the head or breast,"[65] thus testifying to the unerring aim of the Texas frontiersmen and the bravery of the Mexican soldiers. Carrasco praised very highly the bravery of Dawson's and Caldwell's men.

The Texans reported that the Mexicans carried off many of their dead and wounded, but, said Caldwell, left 60 dead and mortally wounded, most of whom died during the night; and, if they did not, the writer supposes they were either dispatched of their misery by the Texans the next day or left to die, for there are no reports of any wounded Mexicans being picked up by the Texans as prisoners. When morning came and Caldwell's men, in spite of the incessant rain which fell throughout the day, inspected both their own and Dawson's battle-grounds and witnessed the gruesome scene of the Dawson massacre, their animosity and exasperation knew no bounds, especially when they found their fellow-citizens stripped of every article of clothing and some of the bodies gashed over with wounds evidently inflicted after death.[66] They stripped the Mexican dead of all clothing and other valuables, including small denominations of silver coin carried in their ears.[67] The Texans did not bother to bury the enemy dead, but as best they could they sought to give burial in the "mott" to their own who had died defending their homes against a remorseless enemy. There were no dead bodies of Mexicans near where the Dawson men fell, "but the prairie was all covered with blood within rifle shot distance and showed that a very large number of wounded or dead Mexicans must have been carried off."[68] A year later the bones of the Mexicans were still bleaching in the sun at some distance around the "mott" and along the Salado.

[65] *Telegraph and Texas Register*, Jan. 25, 1843.
[66] Matthew Caldwell to the Secretary of War, Head Quarters of the Volunteer Army of Texas, Salado, 8 miles from San Antonio, Sept. 18, 1842, Texas Congress, *Journals of the House of Representatives of the Seventh Congress*, Appendix, pp. 16–18; Adams, "[Journal of an] Expedition Against the Southwest," Oct. 5, 1842; [Anonymous], "A Leaf from Memory: Scene of the Battle-Field of Salado, by an Old Texian," *Texas Almanac for 1860*, pp. 72–74; James S. Mayfield to Gen. E. Burleson, Camp Salado, Tuesday Morning, Sept. 20, 1842, *Telegraph and Texas Register*, Sept. 28, 1842.
[67] Stanley Vestal, *Big Foot Wallace*, pp. 74–75.
[68] *Civilian and Galveston Gazette*, Oct. 1, 1842.

The Dawson Fight

Jett was buried in a small grave dug with bowie knives, and the Dawson men were buried on the site where they had fought, in shallow graves over which were piled brush and stones to protect the remains from vultures and animals of prey. The bodies, however, were not buried "sufficiently to prevent the wolves and fowls from digging them up." Visitors to the scene a few weeks later found a skull or two,

many arms and legs . . . sticking out through the soil under the brush that had been put over the place to protect them. We saw several bones, [reported Adams, including] one entire leg from the hip down, which we interred under the rubbish as well as we could. Here, [he said] I picked up the entire sole of one of the feet of them that fell on that fatal spot. It bore evidence of great hardship to the owner, for it was pierced through with many thorns and the wearer was undoubtedly barefoot at this tragic time. I took on an idea at the time, that it and the leg were companions, and that they once belonged to Jerome Alexander who was the tallest man in the company. . . . I carried this *sole* until our company in conjunction with Capt. Hays, as spies went into *Guerrero*, Mexico, and on that occasion it was lost, having left my baggage with some of the Co[mpany] at the huts of the Caresa [Caresee] Indians at the crossing of the Río Grande.[69]

[69] Adams, "[Journal of an] Expedition Against the Southwest," Oct. 5, 1842, ms.

381

CHAPTER SEVENTEEN

Woll's Withdrawal from Texas

EARLY IN THE EVENING following the battle of Salado, Caldwell dashed off a brief report of the engagement to the people of Texas and sent it by special courier eastward, saying that his men had fought all day until the enemy retreated, carrying off their dead. In words worthy a Leonidas, he hastily scribbled, "The enemy are all around me on every side; but I fear them not. I will hold my position until I hear from re-inforcements. Come and help me—it is the most favorable opportunity I have ever seen. There are eleven hundred of the enemy. I can whip them on my own ground without help, but I cannot take prisoners. Why don't you come on? Huzza! huzza for Texas!"[1] In the meantime, Cald-well took all necessary precautions to avoid being taken by surprise if Woll should attempt to renew the battle. He kept out pickets and scout-ing parties to check upon Woll's activities, but the ex-Frenchman's ap-petite for battle had been satisfied. During the night, Caldwell was joined by the men from Bastrop and Travis counties under Captains Billingsley and Wallace, who were under the over-all command of Col-onel James S. Mayfield, one of Lamar's close friends. They reached the camp a little before daybreak on the 20th. Among the new arrivals was Samuel H. Walker, who was, from his first campaign in Texas, to become one of the most distinguished of Texas rangers before his death at Hua-mantla, Mexico, in 1847. In spite of the inclement weather, several small squads of Texan volunteers came in during the day following the battle. Early in the morning of the 20th the Texan scouts brought in a Mexican prisoner and reported that Woll was still holding his position at San Antonio. The prisoner revealed that General Ampudia was expected to re-enforce Woll with 1,500 men, who he said, were now near Goliad. Mayfield, having been in camp only a few hours, hastily penned a note

---

[1] Report of Mathew Caldwell, Sunday, Sept. 18, [1842] 7 o'clock p.m., in *Tele-graph and Texas Register*, Sept. 28, 1842; see also John Henry Brown, "Autobi-ography," ms.

to General Burleson, saying, "Arouse the country—let's chastize the
enemy and defend and save our families. More depends upon the lively
patriotism of the people than all the Government can give."[2]

Late in the evening of the 19th while the Mexican army rested in San
Antonio, its scouts reported that the Texans on the Salado were being
strengthened and that their scouting parties were appearing with increasing frequency near the outskirts of the town. So on the morning of
the 20th after having occupied the town ten days, Woll, concluding that
his mission had been fulfilled, hastily withdrew toward the Río Grande,
leaving behind the Béxar archives and court records, but taking what
wagons, yokes of oxen, and goods he could lay his hands on.[3] In reporting the retirement of the Mexican force, the British chargé d'affaires declared, "and it is satisfactory to observe that there had been no plunder,
and that all the supplies had been liberally purchased."[4] Such, also, was
the opinion and report of Major Mayfield who entered San Antonio
upon the heels of Woll's withdrawal.[5]

[2] J. S. Mayfield to Gen. E. Burleson, Camp Salado, Tuesday morning, Sept. 20,
1842, *Telegraph and Texas Register*, Sept. 28, 1842.

[3] Memucan Hunt to Francis Moore, Jr., Editor of the Telegraph, Houston, dated:
Béxar, Jan. 8, 1843, *Morning Star* (Houston), Jan. 17, 1843. On May 22, 1841,
Thomas H. O'S. Addicks, the clerk of Béxar County, forwarded to the Secretary of
State at Austin in accordance with instructions he had received from President
Lamar, "the Archives of the Military Authorities, Papers of the Old Customs House,
& Post Office of this city, and the Archives of the Department of the Political Chief,
all previous to our declaration of Independence." The papers were sent in the
wagons of Hendrick Arnold. Thomas H. O'S. Addicks, Clerk Bexar County, to James
S. Mayfield, Secretary of State, San Antonio, May 24, 1841, in Domestic Cor-
respondence (Texas), 1835–1846, ms.

[4] Charles Elliot to the Earl of Aberdeen, Oct. 17, 1842, Ephraim D. Adams (ed.),
British Diplomatic Correspondence Concerning the Republic of Texas, 1836–1846,
pp. 112–114.

[5] On October 18, 1842, James S. Mayfield arrived at Nacogdoches from San Antonio for the purpose of enlisting volunteers for an expedition to cross the Río
Grande. He reported that Woll had not taken the government records in San Antonio, and he further stated that "the Mexican troops behaved well, paid for all
they got, and that the wounded Texian prisoners who fell into their hands were well
treated." See Harriet Smither (ed.), "Diary of Adolphus Sterne," in *Southwestern
Historical Quarterly*, XXXIV (1930–1931), 262; Samuel Augustus Maverick, Diary,
Sept. 28, 1842, ms. On the other hand, Pearson Newcomb states that Woll "destroyed or removed many old and important records. One of the files removed contained the original boundary field notes of the town as set out in the Spanish grant."
Pearson Newcomb, *The Alamo City*, p. 19; Mrs. Mary A. Maverick, who was not
present, recorded under date of September 20, 1842, that "the Mexican citizens of
San Antonio who espoused the Mexican cause, with a guard of four hundred sol-

That he [Woll] did not come for the purpose of plunder [reported the *Telegraph and Texas Register*,[6]] is evident from the fact that, during his stay at Béxar, he did not permit one of his soldiers to take a single article of private property; and so scrupulous was he in this respect, that he even required his officers to pay for the teams that he took to convey away his wounded soldiers. He also remained in Béxar until the last company of soldiers had marched out, in order that he might prevent them from committing depredations. He required also the traders that accompanied him, to pay for every article of merchandize that they took away; and, it is said, that not less than fifteen thousand dollars in specie were paid out to the merchants of Béxar during his stay.

The day after the battle of Salado and previous to Woll's withdrawal, some two hundred families of San Antonio who had espoused the Mexican cause, took the occasion to leave under Woll's protection for Mexico, fearing to remain longer in Texas.[7] Among those leaving was the venerable old Erasmo Seguin, one of the truest friends Texas ever had, who went along hoping to persuade his eldest son, Juan N. Seguin, to leave the Mexican service and remain in Texas. The elder Seguin accompanied the fleeing Béxar citizens, who were protected by troops under his son's leadership, as far as the Medina River, from whence he returned to San Antonio, having failed to persuade his son to return with him. On his way back, Erasmo Seguin, worn and haggard with countenance of sorrow, was met near the Medina by the Texan troops who permitted him to pass unmolested to his home, now rendered desolate by the treachery and flight of his son.[8]

The plundering of San Antonio was the work of the Mexican families who fled under the cover of the Mexican army. They drove before them five hundred head of cattle and carried away as much plunder, in addition to their own private possessions of household furniture, utensils, and other moveable objects, as the 150 carts in their possession permitted.[9] Less than six months later many of them were to return to

---

diers, left San Antonio for Mexico, taking with them five hundred head of cattle and much plunder." Rena Maverick Green (ed.), *Memoirs of Mary A. Maverick, Arranged by Mary A. Maverick and Her Son George Madison Maverick*, pp. 74–75.

[6] Oct. 19, 1842.

[7] Rena Maverick Green (ed.), *Samuel Maverick, Texan, 1803–1870: A Collection of Letters, Journals and Memoirs*, p. 170, says they left on September 20 under a guard of 400 troops.

[8] *Telegraph and Texas Register*, Oct. 12, 1842.

[9] *Ibid.*, Oct. 19, 1842; Seguin, *Memoirs*, p. 29.

Béxar, saying that they had been "induced to accompany the Mexican army because Col. Seguin told them that they would all be massacred" by the Texan soldiers if they remained in San Antonio after Woll left.[10] Less than six years later Colonel Seguin himself was to rue the day he left Texas to serve Mexico.[11]

In their hasty departure, the Indians under Woll left behind at their camp site on the San Pedro above town a number of tents, moccasins, and other paraphernalia. With Woll went the Dawson prisoners. Bradley was furnished a horse by William Elliot and was otherwise well provided for by the Elliots and Jaques;[12] but the horse was taken from him.

About 10 o'clock on the morning of the 20th Caldwell learned of the enemy's retreat from Captain Menchaca, young Veramendi, and Rafael Calixto de la Garza, recently elected representative to the Seventh Congress from Béxar, who came out from the town.[13] Caldwell forthwith called a council of war composed of the officers in his command. His force at the time numbered 325 men, and 150 more, under Colonel John H. Moore, were expected hourly from LaGrange.[14]

In spite of the mud and a shortage of ammunition, coffee, salt, and tobacco, with no hope of obtaining fresh supplies in the western country, the council determined that the enemy should be pursued and attacked if a favorable opportunity were offered. So, incited by the desire to avenge their slaughtered countrymen, as well as by the hope of rescuing the unfortunate captives and wreaking vengeance upon a hated foe, the Texans, with Hays' company out in front, gave immediate pursuit. At noon the Texans paused at the head of the San Antonio River, anxiously hoping for re-enforcements; but, none arriving, they crossed the river above the town early in the afternoon and pushed on

[10] *Telegraph and Texas Register*, March 15, 1843.

[11] John A. Veatch, the American commander at Presidio del Río Grande on February 23, 1848, reported, "Our *Texian-Mexican* Seguin, presented himself a few days since, desiring permission to bring his family—which he thinks is in Saltillo—to this place. He says he will return to Texas and risk consiquences [*sic*]. He looks care worn & thread-bare. He is just from Queretaro and came by way of San Luis Potosí," John A. Veatch to Gen. M. B. Lamar, Presidio del Río Grande, Feb. 23, 1848, in *Lamar Papers*, IV, pt. I, pp. 193–194.

[12] Ellen Elliot to Mrs. Samuel A. Maverick, San Antonio de Béjar, Nov. 14, 1842, Green (ed.), *Samuel Maverick, Texan*, pp. 202–204; B. C. Sánchez to Same, San Antonio, Sept. 20, 1842, in *ibid.*, p. 105.

[13] *Telegraph and Texas Register*, Oct. 12, 1842.

[14] J. S. Mayfield to Gen. E. Burleson, Camp Salado, Tuesday morning, Sept. 20, 1842, *ibid.*, Sept. 28, 1842.

at a rapid gait. At midnight they camped near the bank of the Medina River, about two miles above the Presidio Road and approximately twenty-five miles from San Antonio. In the meantime, Judge Hemphill and Reverend Morrell, anxious to learn of the fate of the latter's son believed to have been with Captain Dawson, went into San Antonio where they learned from Mrs. Jaques and Mrs. Elliot that young Morrel was a prisoner.[15] The women reported that the Mexicans had robbed the Dawson men of their clothes, and that the Morrell boy, who had been lightly wounded on his left arm near the shoulder by a lance thrust, was in his shirt-sleeves. Mrs. Elliot, it was reported, had taken a green blanket-coat from her own son, and had put it on the Morrell youth. "This coat," young Morrell afterwards declared, "was the means of saving his life."[16]

The Mexican army, with Hays hovering upon its rear, encamped about six miles above the present site of Castroville and a short distance above what was known as the Cañon Ford.[17] That night, Hays with Benjamin McCulloch,[18] who, at the time the alarm was spread, had been

[15] J. D. Affleck, "History of John C. Hays," pt. I, p. 251; Z[enos] N. Morrell, *Flowers and Fruits in the Wilderness: or Forty-Six Years in Texas and Two Winters in Honduras*, p. 173.

[16] Morrell, *Flowers and Fruits in the Wilderness*, p. 173.

[17] Memucan Hunt to Dr. Francis Moore, Houston, Oct. 17, 1842, *Telegraph and Texas Register*, Oct. 26, 1842.

[18] Benjamin ("Ben") McCulloch was born in Rutherford County, Tennessee, on November 11, 1811, and during his youth often accompanied David Crockett on hunting trips. With the beginning of the Texas Revolution, McCulloch decided to cast his fortunes with the Texans. After the Battle of San Jacinto, he was made a first lieutenant on April 22, 1836, but soon returned to Tennessee to learn surveying, after which he settled at Gonzales and from 1838 to 1846 was noted on the frontier for his bravery. His military leadership was first noted in the Peach Creek fight with the Wacos and Comanches in March 1839, and in the Plum Creek fight against the Comanches the next year he served under Caldwell as a captain. He refused Lamar's invitation to participate in the Sante Fé expedition, but from July 11 to Dec. 18, 1841, he served as a minute man at Gonzales. It was Ben McCulloch and Alsey S. Miller who had counted the Vasquez men as they advanced, and had returned to San Antonio to find Captain Hays gone. McCulloch arrived too late to participate in the battle of the Salado, but he did participate in the pursuit of Woll, and served as a scout in the Somervell expedition. From June 1843 to Nov. 10, 1843, he served as a private in Hays' company; in 1844 he was a lieutenant in that company. He served twice in the Congress of the Republic and later in the State Legislature. He served as a Texas Ranger in the Mexican War. In September 1849 he went to California, where he became a peace officer. In the summer of 1851 he returned to Tennessee and from there went to Washington to seek a government ap-

visiting friends on the Colorado and had joined the volunteers on the frontier after the battle of Salado, were riding a short distance in advance of the other members of the company, when they suddenly discovered Woll's camp just ahead. Reining up short, they sat on their horses for a few minutes observing the camp, dimly outlined by the smoldering campfires. The moon shone brightly, and a galaxy of stars twinkled overhead. As the two Texans, whose courage may best be described as a complete absence of fear, peered through the darkness, the idea of entering Woll's camp presented itself. After a brief discussion of the dangers involved, they decided to attempt it. Dismounting, they tied their horses where their comrades could see them when they came up; and then proceeded to untie their Mexican blankets from behind their saddles. Wrapping these around their bodies and pulling their hats well down, the two Texans strode leisurely into the Mexican camp to observe and gather information about the condition and strength of the enemy. Some of the Mexicans were asleep; others were squatting around small fires roasting pieces of meat or boiling coffee, while nearby a woman or two pounded a few grains of corn into meal. Here and there sat a small group, talking and smoking. An air of tenseness pervaded the whole camp. As the Texans walked about the camp, a dog seemed to follow, but did not bark, probably being a San Antonio dog accustomed to Texans. Soon a child attracted the dog's attention much to the relief of the two spies. Completing their stroll through the camp, Hays and McCulloch slowly worked their way toward the point at which they had entered. On leaving the camp they passed too near a sentry and were hailed by "*¿Quien vive?*" ("Who goes there?") "Texians, damn you," responded Hays instantly, drawing his pistol. The night was bright, and McCulloch, who "at forty paces could drive a nail into a tree with the ball fire from his rifle,"[19] warned,

---

pointment. He was appointed United States marshal for the Eastern District of Texas, with headquarters at Galveston. McCulloch was a devoted follower of Sam Houston.

McCulloch was "a man of bold features, prominent forehead, straight nose, and deep-set blue eyes. . . . His face a mask and his features under such control as to give no clue to his feelings, or emotions, or intentions, it was as natural for Ben McCulloch to remain calm in danger as it was to breathe. Sudden emergencies served to quicken his faculties, rather than to confuse them. His courage may best be described as a complete absence of fear." Walter Prescott Webb, *The Texas Rangers*, p. 95; J. W. Wilbarger, *Indian Depradations in Texas*, pp. 287–290.

[19] Victor M. Rose, *The Life and Services of Gen. Ben McCulloch*, p. 54.

"Take care, Jack, or that fellow will shoot you."

But Hays responded, "He won't shoot. I judge by his voice that he is scared. You hold your gun on him while I will go up and take him prisoner."[20]

So saying, Hays advanced and disarmed the sentry, and the two rangers, with their captive, left the camp without creating a disturbance.[21]

From their reconnaissance Hays and McCulloch discovered that the Mexican cavalry horses were corralled at a short distance from the main camp, and McCulloch now suggested that an effort be made to capture or stampede the horses to prevent General Woll's army from moving the next day. Hays, however, vetoed this suggestion, saying that an attempt to take the horses would raise an alarm and the Mexican army, which still greatly outnumbered the Texan forces, might effect its escape. He recommended waiting until morning when the Texan force might be better consolidated or re-enforced, since volunteers were constantly arriving from the east; and then they might rout Woll's army and capture his cannon, horses, and wagon train, besides effecting a release of the Texan prisoners and capturing numerous Mexicans. With his companions, Hays now returned to Caldwell's camp on the river below to report.

The next morning the camp was divided on the question of attacking the Mexican army. After listening to the exploits of the two spies and their recommendations for an immediate descent upon the Mexican camp, some of the newcomers regarded the proposal as too chimerical and rash, alleging that it was merely an impractical idea of a few "wild boys." Many were in favor of awaiting the arrival of additional re-enforcements, which were known to be upon the road. Divided counsel resulted in nothing being done; so on the morning of the 21st Hays again went forward with his company to reconnoitre the enemy's position, and returned about 12 o'clock with four prisoners, stragglers from Woll's army.[22] These men were now securely bound to save guarding them closely, as a battle seemed to be impending and the guard wished to participate in it. Hays reported Woll to be encamped about eight miles

[20] The young chief of the Lipans once said of Hays, "Me and Red Wing not afraid to go to hell together. Captain Jack heap brave; not afraid to go to hell by himself." Webb, *The Texas Rangers*, p. 65.

[21] "Life and Adventures of Colonel John C. Hays, detailed by himself," from the Major John Caperton ms., quoted in Affleck, "John C. Hays," pt. I, pp. 252–253.

[22] John H. Jenkins, Sr., "Personal Reminiscences of Texas History Relating to Bastrop County, as Dictated to his Daughter-in-law, Mrs. Emma Holmes Jenkins of Bastrop, Texas," p. 110, gives the number of Mexican stragglers captured as five.

above. During the day two Texans were killed by a Mexican spy, who proved to be a San Antonio traitor.[23] Around 4 o'clock in the afternoon, 80 volunteers under Colonel John H. Moore, organized at LaGrange, and 20 from the Lavaca, unorganized, reached the Texan camp. The Texan forces, numbering 489 men, were now reorganized into two battalions. Caldwell was elected colonel; John H. Moore, a well-known Indian fighter, was chosen lieutenant colonel, and James S. Mayfield, major. Tom Green of Fayette County reached the Salado late that night with 70 men and encamped.[24] He expected to join Caldwell on the Medina the next morning at the latest, and Colonel Edward Burleson, the vice president of the Republic, had by this time reached the Cíbolo with other re-enforcements, estimated at 400 men,[25] and had sent out an urgent appeal to "Texian Soldiers." "Come on my brave citizens," he had written, "and let us retaliate for the loss of our brave men who have fallen fighting for us."[26]

During the night Caldwell moved his army up the Medina to the crossing, two miles beyond the present site of Castroville. Woll's camp on the opposite side of the river lay within two miles of the Texan camp,[27] but at midnight Hays reported that the Mexicans had fled. The Texans followed immediately, but the crossing of the river and the mud delayed them. Hays' rangers, having fanned out on both sides of the road, pressed rapidly forward, and in the middle of the afternoon (about 3 o'clock) came up with Woll's rearguard. A hasty exchange of shots followed, and Samuel H. Luckie, one of Hays' most dependable rangers, reeled in his saddle, and his horse bolted and ran a short distance before its rider fell from the frightened animal. Reverend Morrell went to Luckie's assistance, while a number of the rangers charged into a dry branch of Verde Creek, the direction from which the shot had come.[28] The Texans caught a glimpse of a fleeing Cherokee, who was

---

[23] "Battle of Salado, Sept. 18, 1842," in John Henry Brown Papers, 1835–1872, ms.; John Henry Brown, "Autobiography," ms.

[24] Tom Green of Fayette [County], Camp Salado, 12 o'clock [midnight, Sept. 21–22], Sept. 22, 1842, *Civilian and Galveston City Gazette*, Sept. 24, 1842.

[25] Colonel Edward Burleson was reported in the *Civilian and Galveston Gazette* as having 170 men on the Cíbolo, and was expected to be joined on Friday (the 23rd) by 150 Milam and Robertson counties men. *Ibid.*, Oct. 1, 1842.

[26] Edward Burleson to Texian Soldiers, Cibolo, Thursday, 22nd [Sept.] 1842, in *Telegraph and Texas Register*, Sept. 28, 1842.

[27] John W. Smith reported the Texan army was "within four miles of the———rascals." Report of John W. Smith of Béxar, 12 o'clock, 22nd Sept. 1842, *ibid.*

[28] Affleck, "John C. Hays," pt. I, pp. 254–256; Morrell, *Flowers and Fruits in the*

believed to have fired the shot. Luckie was shot through the right breast and lung, the ounce ball coming out at the point of his shoulder. Although given prompt medical attention, there seemed to be little hope for his recovery. He was carried to the Medina in a litter and from there taken to San Antonio in a cart, where for several days his life hung in the balance, but he recovered and lived until October 30, 1852, when he died at his home in San Antonio.[29]

The shooting of Luckie has sometimes been described as a case of mistaken identity. It was presumed the shot which wounded Luckie had been intended for Captain Hays, for whose head a Mexican general is said to have offered $500. Besides being a noble looking man, older and more mature in his features than Hays, Luckie was riding a more attractive horse that day than his captain. However, since there was a scattered fusillade when the Texans suddenly appeared at the rear of the Mexican army, it seems probable that Luckie was just unlucky at that particular moment.

Upon the initial exchange of shots, Hays' company quickly dismounted and formed for battle on or near the site where it had come upon the enemy, about a mile and a half in advance of Caldwell's main army which now comprised some 500 to 600 men.[30] Expecting an attack by the Mexican force, the Texans were ordered to fall back to a stronger position "three or four hundred yards into a dry creek or swag in the prairie, near the Hondo."[31] While Caldwell's men and the rangers waited half an hour in anticipation of an asault, Woll moved the bulk of his men rapidly forward, hoping to put the Arroyo Hondo between them and their pursuers. As the Mexican rearguard pulled back, the Texan spy company and main unit followed rapidly on its trail, soon overtaking it once more, about two miles further on. A part of Woll's army was discovered on a high ridge near the Arroyo Hondo, about fifty miles from San Antonio, where the new road, made by Woll when entering Texas, passed through a dense chaparral.

Wilderness, pp. 174–175; Memucan Hunt to Francis Moore, Jr., Houston, Oct. 17, 1842, in *Telegraph and Texas Register*, Oct. 26, 1842; John Henry Brown, *History of Texas, from 1685 to 1892*, II, p. 229. Samuel H. Luckie represented Béxar County in the House of Representatives of the Sixth Congress of the Republic in 1841–1842 and in the Senate of the Republic in 1845.

[29] [Elizabeth LeNoir Jennett], *Biographical Directory of the Texan Conventions and Congresses*, pp. 127–128; Jenkins, "Personal Reminiscences of Texas History," p. 110.

[30] Jenkin, "Personal Reminiscences of Texas History," p. 110.

[31] *Ibid.*

Deeming it imprudent to attack the enemy's rearguard which had the advantage of position, Hays halted out of range of the Mexican cannon and dispatched a courier to Colonel Caldwell, a mile and a half in the rear. Woll, noting that the Texans were unprepared for an immediate attack, started moving his army across the Hondo, "just below the mouth of Quihi Creek," and assumed a defensive position. On the east side of the river he placed a cannon manned by twenty artillerymen, supported by a group of infantrymen,[32] to afford protection to his men as they crossed the river. As the main army crossed, it formed in the flats on the west side where another cannon, facing eastward, commanded the approaches to the crossing and his cannon and rearguard on the opposite bank.[33] It was now a little past 4 o'clock in the afternoon.[34] Shortly after the appearance of the Texans once more upon his rear, an express reached Woll on the west bank, reporting that a party of Texans under Captain Hays was approaching some *carretas* which had stopped at a quarter of a league from the Mexican camp and had already taken several prisoners, including Don Refugio de la Garza, the parish priest of Béxar and chaplain of the Río Grande Company,[35] and seemed determined to make an assault on the Mexican's rearguard.

While the Mexican families, whom Woll's army had overtaken and found encamped on the east bank, scrambled to cross over immediately, Woll planned to support his rearguard. Greatly worried, since his division at this time numbered scarcely 500 men (he had sent two strong detachments forward as escorts for the wounded and prisoners), Woll fully realized the difficult situation confronting him. His successful retreat from Texas depended not only upon speed, but also upon maintaining his army intact. He, therefore, determined to recross the river

---

[32] Thomas W. Bell, *A Narrative of the Capture and Subsequent Sufferings of the Mier Prisoners in Mexico, Captured in the Cause of Texas, Dec. 26th, 1842 and Liberated Sept. 16th, 1844*, p. 11 (hereafter cited as Bell *Narrative*), says 400 men were in the rear guard, but this is doubtful, for it represents too large a proportion of Woll's diminished force and fails to answer the question of who was crossing to the west bank. Bell's narration of events that he did not personally witness is most inaccurate.

[33] Affleck, "John C. Hays," pt. I, pp. 254–256.

[34] A Dawson Prisoner's Report, City of Mexico, Jan. 27, 1843, *Telegraph and Texas Register*, May 3, 1843.

[35] Adrián Woll ál Sr. General en gefe [Isidro Reyes], Campo sobre el Río hondo, Septiembre 22 de 1842, in Adrián Woll, *Expedición hecha en Téjas, por una parte de la Division del Cuerpo de Egército del Norte*, pp. 49–51.

with 100 infantrymen (two companies) and 50 cavalry to protect the families and to save his cannon.

Quickly placing his camp on the west side under the command of Colonel Sebastián Moro del Moral, Woll crossed the river, and directed Captain Agatón Quinoñes to take the lead with his ten explorers to exchange shots with the enemy as soon as he could encounter them, with specific orders to retreat, drawing the enemy toward Woll.

In the meantime, Hays advanced with a few of his men to the enemy's rearguard and halted at a point a short distance above the future village of New Fountain, Medina County. While the men sat upon their horses eagerly awaiting word from Caldwell, they could hear the Mexicans up ahead crossing the river apparently in great panic, judging from the noise coming from officers giving commands, teamsters and artillery-men shouting and cursing, mules braying, supplemented by an occasional war whoop from the Mexicans' Indian allies, and the din of the rattle of wagon and cart wheels on the rocky bed of the Hondo. News of an impending fight, for it was said that the Hays' men were determined to attack at any cost whenever the enemy might again be overtaken, caused Caldwell's troops to rush forward, the colonel, himself, being among the foremost. A half hour or so of sunset approximately 150 of the fleetest horsemen of the Texan army had arrived near the crossing anxious to attack the Mexicans at once. Although the Texan forces the evening before were variously estimated from 450 to 650 strong (probably numbered somewhere between 560 and 600),[36] the men were now widely scattered and strung out by the rapid march during the day. Nevertheless, after some hesitation, Caldwell permitted Hays to make an attempt to take the Mexican cannon at a bend on the east side of the Hondo. Captain William M. Eastland was to support him with 100 of

[36] *Telegraph and Texas Register*, Oct. 12, 1842, reported Caldwell's force as numbering 450. On September 22, Thomas Green reported it as "600 strong," and on the same day Colonel Burleson reported it as 600 men. See Report of Thomas Green of Fayette [County,] Camp Salado, 12 o'clock, Sept. 22, 1842, in *ibid.*, Sept. 28, 1842, and *Civilian and Galveston City Gazette*, Oct. 1, 1842; Edward Burleson to Texian Soldiers, Cibolo, Thursday, 22nd Sept. [1842], *Telegraph and Texas Register*, Sept. 28, 1842. Mrs. Samuel A. Maverick reports that Caldwell had 650 men. Frederick C. Chabot (ed.), *The Perote Prisoners; Being the Diary of James L. True-heart Printed for the First Time Together with an Historical Introduction*, p. 56. Woll reported the Texans numbered more than 600 men. Adrián Woll ál Sr. general en gefe [Isidro Reyes], Campo sobre el Río hondo, Septiembre 22 de 1842, in Woll, *Expedición hecha en Téjas*, pp. 49–51; Jenkins, "Personal Reminiscences of Texas History," p. 110, says the Texan force numbered 500–600 men.

the best mounted of Caldwell's men then in the vicinity.[37] Eastland, reported a participant, formed his line, "but was ordered back into ranks," presumably by Colonel Moore.[38]

The Texans who were to make the assault on the cannon were hastily formed in line of battle, and Hays called for volunteers. The Reverend Morrell, anxious to liberate his son, whose capture he had confirmed in San Antonio, rode down the line, wearing his fur cap, pleading for the men to come forward. Halting at a suitable spot along the line, he waved his cap and shouted:

Boys,—You have come out here from one to two hundred miles from home, to hunt the elephant. He has been running from you for two days. We have got him in close quarters, just up the hill. We want forty men to join Hays' Company. With one hundred men, we can successfully charge and capture the cannon, and turn the grape shot the other way. The old fellow can't hurl his missiles of death at us more than two or three times before we will stop his breath. Besides, the prisoners . . .

and here he was interrupted by shouts along the line, "Come, boys, we will go with him."[39] Hays' Company was now quickly supplemented with volunteers, and after listening briefly to a few words of instruction from their leader the small group of 50 wild, reckless, picked fellows was ready for the desperate attack on the Mexican rear "in a narrow and serpentine defile" through the dense chaparral.[40] One of the participants in the charge has left this vivid description of the assault:

At length the shrill, clear voice of our captain sounded down the line— "Charge!" Away went the company up a gradual ascent in quick time. In a moment the cannon roared, but according to Mexican custom overshot us. The Texas yell followed the cannon's thunder, and so excited the Mexican infantry, placed in position to pour a fire down our lines that they overshot us; and by the time the artillery hurled its cannister the second time, shotguns and pistols were freely used by the Texans. Every man at the cannon was killed, as the company passed it.[41]

As the Texans bore down upon the cannon, some of its defenders momentarily sought protection under it to avoid the rush of *los diablos*

[37] Jenkins, "Personal Reminiscences of Texas History," p. 111.
[38] *Ibid.*
[39] Quoted in Morrell, *Flowers and Fruits in the Wilderness*, p. 175.
[40] Brown, *History of Texas*, II, 229.
[41] Morrell, *Flowers and Fruits in the Wilderness*, pp. 176–177.

Americanos, but as Kit Achlin passed, he leaned from his saddle with a pistol in hand to shoot between the spokes of the cannon wheels at the Mexicans cowering beneath the gun.[42] Benjamin F. Highsmith, who participated in the assault upon the cannon, halted his mount under a mesquite tree after the Mexicans had been killed and driven from the gun. While he sat upon his horse, a solid shot from the artillery piece across the arroyo struck the top of the tree and cut it off. The fragments falling upon him and his horse, badly frightened the latter, and "he wheeled and ran off with . . . limbs hanging all over him."[43]

In making his report the evening following the engagement at the Hondo, Woll declared the Texans charged with "great impetuosity, until the shots from our infantrymen and two cannon made them flee precipitantly, leaving a few horses dead and carrying away many wounded, among whom was a captain who, as I have learned, died upon reaching the place where the bulk of the enemy force was situated."[44] In the attack, the Mexicans lost five killed and several wounded. The Texans had four wounded, none killed, and one horse, that belonged to a youth named Harrell, killed in the charge upon the cannon.[45] Several baggage wagons and a part of the supplies of the Mexican army were captured.

The Texans captured the cannon, but held it only eight to ten minutes. The Mexican cannon on the west bank covered the one on the east bank in the hands of the Texans. Woll moved forward rapidly from the river to rally his men, and in so doing, it was reported, "threw . . . [the Mexican] women and children into the space between the cap-

---

[42] A. J. Sowell, *Early Settlers and Indian Fighters of Southwest Texas*, p. 27.

[43] *Ibid.*, pp. 27–28.

[44] Adrián Woll ál Sr. general en gefe [Isidro Reyes], Campo sobre el Río hondo, Septiembre 22 de 1842, in Woll, *Expedición hecha en Téjas*, pp. 49–51.

[45] Morrell exaggerated the number of Mexicans killed. The Texans wounded were Hurd ("Dutch") Perry, John Castleman, Archibald Gibson, who had a cheek bone shot off, and Colonel W. G. Cooke, who received a slight wound from grape shot. Brown, *History of Texas*, II, 229; "Battle of Salado, Sept. 18, 1842," in Brown Papers, 1835–1872, ms.; Leonie Rummel Weyand and Houston Wade, *An Early History of Fayette County*, p. 27; *Telegraph and Texas Register*, Oct. 5 and 12, 1842; Stanley Vestal, *Big Foot Wallace*, pp. 77–78. Sowell, *Early Settlers and Indian Fighters of Southwest Texas*, p. 28, also lists Anderson Harrell among the wounded, and reports Nick Wren's horse as killed under him within forty yards of the cannon. The report of John W. Smith of Béxar (mayor and ranger), dated 12 o'clock, Sept. 22, 1842, gives some interesting details of the pursuit of "the —— rascals." *Telegraph and Texas Register*, Sept. 22, 1842.

tured artillery and their main army."[46] It is possible that in the confusion and the forward movement of Woll's re-enforcements the families fleeing Béxar were unwillingly caught for a moment between the two lines. There was a dreadful pause. Amid the tumult—the firing of muskets and rifles, the shouts, shrieks, and screams of men, women, children, and bewildered animals—the Mexican infantry in good order advanced with grim determination, and Hays' men had to fall back. Caldwell now rode forward and finding the Mexicans drawn up in line of battle, ordered a halt to form his men.[47] Although a large segment of the main Texan army had arrived within three hundred paces[48] of the enemy's position, tied its horses in the woods, and then skirted the wooded area, eager to rally in the prairie to engage the enemy, a countermarch was ordered for the purpose, it was believed, of bringing the horses nearer, dismounting all the companies, and bringing the whole force into action.

We were now certain [narrated Jenkins later] that a fight was at hand, and already hearts beat fast, and eyes brightened in prospect of action and danger. There seemed [however] to be a strange want of discipline or system or harmony among the officers . . . who could not agree as to the proper line of policy, and stood discussing and debating questions, while the soldiers were all the time growing more perplexed and impatient.[49]

Finally when the Texans again reached their horses, Caldwell, it was reported, "thinking the sun too low to use the rifle to advantage, deferred the attack until morning."[50] Nevertheless, a few parting shots were exchanged at too great a distance for effectiveness.

The Texans failed to sustain their spy company's capture of the cannon because, it was said, "the balance of the Texians owing to a difficulty which arose among the officers [over] who should command,"[51]

---

[46] Green (ed.), *Samuel Maverick, Texan*, p. 171; see also *Telegraph and Texas Register*, Oct. 12, 1842.

[47] *Ibid.*

[48] Memucan Hunt to Dr. Francis Moore, Houston, Oct. 17, 1842, *ibid.*, Oct. 26, 1842.

[49] Jenkins, "Personal Reminiscences of Texas History," pp. 111–112.

[50] Memucan Hunt to Dr. Francis Moore, Houston, Oct. 17, 1842, *Telegraph and Texas Register*, Oct. 12, 1842.

[51] Joseph Eve to Richard M. Johnson, Galveston, Oct. 5, 1842, Joseph Milton Nance (ed.), "A Letter Book of Joseph Eve, United States Chargé d'Affaires to Texas," in *Southwestern Historical Quarterly*, XLIII (1939–1940), pp. 504–507; *Telegraph and Texas Register*, Oct. 5, 1842.

gave the enemy time to recover from the first shock, to permit him to charge upon Hays' small force and drive it from the cannon, and to take it and themselves safely across the river. Colonel John H. Moore, the ranking officer in the field at the time, although he had two days earlier accepted the status of second-in-command to Caldwell, now claimed the right to lead the men into battle; but Caldwell's men are alleged to have indicated that they would refuse to follow him. On the other hand, Mayfield's men indicated that they would follow none but their leader. Finally, Caldwell declared he would follow Moore or any other leader and take his men into battle with him.[52] About the same time,

Captain Billingsley understanding the situation, and knowing the value of prompt action, called out to the soldiers—"*Boys do you want to fight?*"

A loud "*Yes*" was the instant reply.

Then "*Follow Me!*" he called, and marched on, leading a considerable force. We were already approaching very near the Mexican infantry drawn up in line of battle, [reported Jenkins] and in two minutes the charge would have been made and the fight commenced. But at this juncture superior authority interfered.

Col. Caldwell galloping up, called out to Billingsley, asking, "*Where are you going?*"

"*To Fight!*" was the answer.

"*Counter march those men back to ranks*," Caldwell commanded, and we were forced to take our places back in the *standing* army, all worried and disgusted with what seemed to us then a cowardly hesitation and still seems a disgraceful confused proceeding without motive or design."[53]

Colonel Carrasco's comment later was that the Texans who fought at the Hondo "Were not fit to stand in the shoes of those who fought at the Salado."[54] In the end nothing was done. "Hays' gallant spirit was wounded by this unaccountable and ignominious scene and his feelings found utterance in tears—yes, tears of shame and rage," reported Mrs. Maverick.[55]

In his official report of the pursuit, Caldwell claimed that he was never able at any time to see the Mexican front. He assumed the blame for the failure, saying that

[52] Such is Chabot's account in *The Perote Prisoners*, pp. 56–58, based on Green (ed.), *Memoirs of Mary A. Maverick*, pp. 75, 170–172.

[53] Jenkins, "Personal Reminiscences of Texas History," pp. 111–112a.

[54] Chabot, (ed.), *The Perote Prisoners*, p. 114.

[55] Green (ed.), *Samuel Maverick, Texan*, p. 171.

owing to the boggy situation of the ground and tired horses, I failed to support him [Hays]. I then found General Woll with his command formed in the prairie, ready for action, and owing to the situation he had taken [protected by the stream and a narrow woodland that skirted it], I considered that I was not able to attack him, without suffering severe loss—nor was I able at any time, to force him to fight, only on his own ground, and owing to the situation of tired horses, tired men, and scarcity of ammunition, I deemed it prudent to fall back to San Antonio. I also had the best reasons to believe that General Woll had re-enforcements near at hand to cover his retreat.[56]

Night was coming on, and it was nearly dark before the Texans could be reformed. There they stood till dark, "suffering for water and tantalized almost to madness by the delay and the want of harmony among . . . [their] leaders."[57] The firing ceased. There were those who were anxious to charge the Mexican lines, but Benjamin McCulloch and others, after examining the enemy's position, advised that the attack be postponed until morning, probably for a better consolidation of the Texan forces. The Texans were now ordered to mount and march up the creek above the Mexican forces. En route, as they drew opposite the Mexican camp, the enemy, thinking it to be the intention of the Texans to cut off their retreat, fired upon Caldwell's men. The Texans were ordered to continue the march and were not permitted to stop and give battle. A half mile farther up the creek, the Texans were ordered to halt, dismount, and prepare to encamp. A guard was placed around the horses.[58] Between 9 and 10 o'clock, just as the moon was rising, one of the Dawson prisoners said later, he heard the sound of Texan rifles firing "on the west bank of the Honda," and almost at the same instant the cry, "Boys, come out of that."[59] His hopes for release soared, but the Texans were not there in force, and with Woll's artillery and army, he believed "four hundred men [Texans] would have fallen a sacrifice to rashness. . . . I then, as now thought that the Texans acted very prudently. Sacrifices already made were quite sufficient; and I must here bear testimony," con-

---

[56] Matthew Caldwell to the Secretary of War, Head Quarters of the Volunteer Army of Texas, Salado Creek, 8 miles from San Antonio, Sept. 18, 1842, Texas Congress, *Journal of the House of Representatives of the Seventh Congress*, Appendix, pp. 16–18. This report, begun on the 18th, was apparently not finished until about the 23rd of September.

[57] Jenkins, "Personal Reminiscences of Texas History," p. 112a.

[58] *Ibid.*

[59] A Dawson Prisoner's Report, City of Mexico, Jan. 27, 1843, *Telegraph and Texas Register*, May 3, 1843.

tinued the prisoner who seems to have had no rancor in his heart, "to the officer-like conduct of the brave Caldwell and his men. We were near them on the Salado, but they were not strong enough to venture out to our aid. They have my thanks for their good conduct."[60]

At 11 o'clock that night Woll's army, leaving behind many carts, wagons, and much baggage, fled noiselessly and unobserved by the Texans, being favored by the wet ground. Sometime after midnight it was ascertained that the enemy was again in retreat. Many of the Texans saddled their horses for pursuit, but no order was given for a forward movement.[61] Early the next morning the officers met in a council of war, and a majority decided in favor of discontinuing the pursuit. After breakfast, the men were assembled and the decision was announced by Colonel Mayfield. Colonel Mayfield, who represented Nacogdoches in the Fifth and Sixth Congresses, 1840–1842, and had made an unsuccessful speech the evening before, now made a longer one in favor of breaking off the pursuit because of the great dangers involved. According to the argument used by this future member of the Somervell Expedition, the Texans would be operating in enemy territory with a shortage of ammunition and other supplies; the Texans were outnumbered two to one; and their horses were worn down,[62] whereas the Mexican horses were relatively fresh. Caldwell then addressed the troops in much the same vein, giving it as his opinion that it would be imprudent to continue the pursuit as the enemy were much better acquainted with the country. He hoped that the men would agree with him and follow him in good order back to San Antonio.[63] In spite of all that Hays, Morrell, and others could do the contest was abandoned and the Texans broke off the pursuit at the Arroyo Hondo. Hays' company unanimously condemned the order to return, and for a while refused to obey it and held their ground; but, being too few in number, they ultimately yielded to the will of the majority. The order to retreat caused tears to stream down the manly cheeks of ex-Chief Justice[64] John Hemp-

[60] *Ibid.*

[61] Memucan Hunt to Dr. Francis Moore, Houston, Oct. 17, 1842, *Telegraph and Texas Register*, Oct. 26, 1842.

[62] "Our horses and men were jaded very much, and [we] gave up the chase," reported a member who was present. "We were entirely out of provisions, too, and returned home on what we could kill." John Henry Brown, "Autobiography," ms.

[63] Memucan Hunt to Dr. Francis Moore, Houston, Oct. 17, 1842, *Telegraph and Texas Register*, Oct. 26, 1842.

[64] John Hemphill to Anson Jones, City of Austin, Jan. 22, 1842, in Domestic Correspondence (Texas), 1835–1846, ms; Sam Houston to the House of Repre-

hill and the renowned warrior, Captain Ewen Cameron, and many others who had ridden hard and sacrificed much for the security of their country.[65] Many were loud in their complaints of Caldwell and openly reproached him. Their reproaches so annoyed him that "he went off by himself as a private soldier," during their retreat to San Antonio, "and on the bank of the Medina [that evening] he was seen sitting alone by a little camp fire that he had built with his own hands, roasting a piece of meat on the end of a stick, the only food that he could obtain!"[66]

The blame for the failure to continue the pursuit and engage the Mexicans in a general fight was cast principally upon Caldwell by those military leaders whose ambitions made them jealous of the "hero of the Salado." "Old Paint ought to have been left untrammeled as he had fought and won the battle of the Soldau [Salado]," recorded Harvey Adams in his diary, for he "would have captured Woll's entire army and rescued all the prisoners, if [he had been] left to his own choice, but that would have added too many Laurels to the brow of the old hero."[67] On learning of the repulse of the Mexicans at the Salado, President Houston not only congratulated Colonel Caldwell for the success achieved, but also expressed a hope that the Mexicans would be pursued and crushed before they crossed the Río Grande.[68] The President even gave Caldwell permission to cross the river in pursuit of the quarry if it could be done without too much danger to his command. "In battle," declared Houston, "let your men be fierce and terrible as the storm —in victory remember mercy, where it would not be abused. Do not suffer yourself or men to be surprised."[69] Later, however, when it was learned that the enemy had been allowed to withdraw without a serious attempt being made to annihilate his army, the President appeared to be a little annoyed. "A little Cast Steel," he wrote, "or steel without the soap, well applied would have prevented the Mexicans ever leaving Texas—but so the world wags!!!!"[70] "What a pity they did not reconnoiter the force at San Antonio—e're they hallowed wolf. This won't

sentatives, Executive Department, City of Austin, Jan. 22, 1842, in *Writings of Sam Houston*, II, 438.

[65] *Telegraph and Texas Register*, Oct. 26, 1842.

[66] *Ibid.*, Oct. 12, 1842.

[67] Harvey Alexander Adams, "[Journal of an] Expedition Against the Southwest in 1842 and 1843," Dec. 18, 1842, ms.

[68] Houston to Capt. Mathew Caldwell, City of Houston, Sept. 22, 1842, in *Writings of Sam Houston*, III, 166.

[69] *Ibid.*

[70] Houston to Thomas M. Bagby, Washington, Oct. 6, 1842, *ibid.*, III, 171–172.

make a Major General. My composure is not much startled. 1200 men can whip a Cavalliardo of Mexicans. 'Tis so!"[71]

Caldwell, as we have already seen, assumed the full responsibility for breaking off the pursuit for which act he was so severely criticized, but this does not mean that he was entirely to blame. Several factors probably accounted for the failure to make a general attack. One of these was the regard which he no doubt held for the safety of his own men. His experience as a Santa Fé prisoner, during which time he had suffered from an attack of small-pox, may have not only undermined his health but made him more cautious than usual on such occasions, knowing that he as well as others in his command had taken an oath, with their fingers crossed, no doubt, not to take up arms again against Mexico on penalty of death for so doing. Other factors in the decision may have been the lack of coordination and respect for a unified command by the several units of volunteers arriving on the frontier; the poor discipline among the Texan troops; the failure of the Texan pickets cast about the Mexican camp on the night of September 22 to inform Caldwell of the resumption of the march by the retreating Mexicans that night; the boggy nature of the ground due to recent rains; a scanty supply of ammunition; and the lack of provisions, equipment, and fresh horses on the part of the pursuers, whose mounts had been nearly worn down in reaching Béxar, while the horses of the Mexicans had been rested and recruited during their temporary occupation of the town. An important factor no doubt was the weariness of the men themselves. Many of the Colorado men had just arrived without stopping to rest or refresh themselves or their horses. Some had ridden three or four successive days and nights, and were so completely worn out that they had often on the way fallen asleep on their horses, and their companions had been obliged to keep a sharp look out to prevent them from dropping off or losing their guns. One soldier, who lagged in the rear of the army, was found by the rearguard fast asleep in the road, lying beside his horse. Both man and horse were sleeping as quietly together as if they were messmates. It appeared that the horse having become tired, had lain down, and the sleeping rider having been thrown off while the horse was in the act of lying down, had not even waked up, but had continued sleeping just where he had fallen. His rifle was found at a short distance, having been dropped just before he fell.[72]

[71] Houston to Ashbel Smith [Sept., 1842?] *ibid.*, III, 14.
[72] *Telegraph and Texas Register*, Oct. 19, 1842.

There was never much discipline among the buckskin republicans of the Texas frontier, and those who led them usually prevailed by sheer force of personality. Once again, to use the words of General Thomas J. Rusk in April, 1836, "the rock on which Texas has heretofore split begins to rear its cragged head above the foaming spray. I mean unhallowed ambition."[73]

Some of the troops [reported the *Telegraph and Texas Register*[74]] even before the army . . . left the Medina were murmuring, and wished to select a commander; this spirit doubtless contributed to discredit the plans of Col. Caldwell, who was unable at the Hondo, even to detail a small force to act as a reserve for the main army to rally upon in case the troops should be thrown into confusion by any stratagem of the enemy. Even the few men that were left to guard the prisoners went off and left them, so anxious were all to be in the fight; and after the camp was pitched and the army had taken up the position for the night, even the picquet guard left their posts and refused to do duty.

It must be acknowledged, reported Memucan Hunt after his trip to the west and conversation with many of the officers and men who participated in the campaign of September 1842, to drive out Woll,

from what I have heard that I am surprised at the threats of some men that they would return home for want of provisions—because their horses were broken down, and because the commander did not fight at this, that, or the other time or place, and the tameness too with which the great body of the men marched off under the order of retreat, as is stated, is a matter of surprise. I am informed that many of their murmurs could have been easily repressed by judicious conduct on the part of the officers, and when the enemy was nearly in sight, as was the case in this instant, the officers should have continued by night and day until he was overtaken, and should not have failed to have engaged the enemy until they had the most unequivocal proofs of his being too strong to be conquered, or that our own troops had not the disposition or courage to engage in fight.[75]

While Hunt seems to have been rather critical of the Texan officers and to have held them largely responsible for Woll's successful escape without placing the burden any more on Caldwell than the other officers, the

[73] Thomas J. Rusk, Secretary of War, to David G. Burnet, President of Texas, April 26, 1836, William C. Binkley (ed.), *Official Correspondence of the Texan Revolution, 1835–1836*, II, 643.

[74] Oct. 19, 1842.

[75] Memucan Hunt to Francis Moore, Jr., Houston, Oct. 17, 1842, *Telegraph and Texas Register*, Oct. 26, 1842.

editor of the *Civilian and Galveston Gazette*[76] seems to have summed up the situation most accurately: "From what we can gather, we incline to the belief that the escape of Woll was rather the result of circumstances, which could not be controlled by our volunteers without much risk and great exertion, than of any thing like culpable neglect or mismanagement." However, the humiliation and bitter vituperation to which Colonel Caldwell was subjected, preyed heavily upon the distinguished hero's conscience until his health, never fully recovered from his lengthy imprisonment and recent severe illness, was completely undermined. He died at his home in Gonzales on December 28, 1842, at the age of forty-three.[77]

As for Woll, the boldness of the Texan assault at the Hondo alarmed him greatly, and it was Carrasco's opinion that had the Texans charged the Mexican army at the Arroyo Hondo in full force, they would have readily defeated it.[78] Although Woll beat off the attack of the Texan vanguard momentarily, he was fully aware that the bulk of Caldwell's men, equaling his own in number, were close at hand and that at dawn he might find his forward movement cut off. Too, the priest Don Refugio de la Garza and three other Mexicans, owners of some of the *carretas* that had been captured by the Texans, had succeeded in effecting their escape during the confusion of the attack. Soon after Woll returned to his camp, they appeared before him, "still with the bindings on their arms," and told how the "barbarians had inhumanly maltreated" them.[79] The next morning as the Texans were breaking off the pursuit, a Mexican deserter entered their camp and reported that when the Texan vanguard came upon the Mexican army at the Hondo, the Mexican troops were so frightened that about two hundred fled from the ranks and dispersed in every direction, and that it was with great difficulty that Woll could compel the remainder to form in line of battle.[80] His men were anxious to leave at once, if not sooner; and an inci-

[76] Oct. 12, 1842.

[77] *Telegraph and Texas Register,* Jan. 25, 1843.

[78] "Information from Mr. Jones," *Telegraph and Texas Register,* Jan. 25, 1843.

[79] Adrián Woll ál Sr. general en gefe [Isidro Reyes], Campo sobre el Río hondo, Septiembre 22 de 1842, in Woll, *Expedición hecha en Téjas,* pp. 49–51. James L. Trueheart incorrectly reported in his diary under date of Sept. 27, 1842, that Pedro Garza was the one captured by the Texans, who released him when Woll threatened to shoot immediately the San Antonio prisoners, Chabot (ed.), *The Perote Prisoners,* p. 108.

[80] *Telegraph and Texas Register,* Oct. 12, 1842.

dent related by Woll in his official report of the engagement at the Hondo no doubt placed him in a similar frame of mind.

After having put the enemy to flight and returned to my Arroyo Hondo Camp [he wrote], "being yet on horseback and accompanied by my aides-de-camp, a Texan, Captain Hays, presented himself on horseback on the other side of the arroyo at the edge of the forest, and, taking off his hat, hailed me. He called me by my name and title, requesting that I approach to speak to him. Notwithstanding the remarks of my aides-de-camp who implored me not to believe these friendly demonstrations, I advanced; and, taking off my hat to reply to the salute, I had gone a distance of about 30 yards, which is the breadth of the arroyo, when two Texans hidden behind some trees aimed and discharged their rifles at me. Fate determined that they should not hit their mark, and the whistling balls passed over my head: then the aforesaid Hays projected himself precipitantly into the most dense [part] of the forest, defaming God and insulting me and calling me a coward. The specie was so rare that I could do no less than laugh to myself, asking my aides-de-camp what they thought of the wretched one and which of the two was the coward.[81]

Later in the evening, as we have already noted, some of the Texans went down to the river and fired upon the Mexican pickets on the other side. This was too much for the Mexicans, and by 11 o'clock they were fleeing toward the Río Grande. On the 27th the Mexican army encamped on the Saladito, and two days later it reached the left bank of the Río Grande at the Presidio Crossing, ten days after having commenced its march from San Antonio.[82] Accompanying the army were many families from Béxar, "bringing with them 200 carts containing their furniture, moveables, cattle, horses, and in fact everything." Other families arrived at San Fernando, including Peter Ford, a former resident of Béxar.[83] At 10 o'clock in the morning of October 1 Woll's army entered Presidio del Río Grande, where it was reported a few days later in the

[81] Adrián Woll ál Sr. general en gefe [Isidro Reyes], Campo sobre el Río hondo, Septiembre 22 de 1842, in Woll, *Expedición hecha en Téjas*, pp. 49–51. The writer has found no other account of such an incident having taken place.

[82] Adrián Woll ál Sr. general en gefe [Isidro Reyes], Campo sobre el Saladito, Septiembre 27, 1842; and Same to Same, [Presidio del] Río Grande, Octubre 1 de 1842, in *ibid.*, pp. 51–52; A Dawson Prisoner's Account, City of Mexico, Jan. 27, 1843, *Telegraph and Texas Register*, May 3, 1843; Address of General Woll to the Troops from the Camp on the right bank of the Rio Bravo del Norte, Sept. 30, 1842, *ibid.*, Nov. 30, 1842.

[83] Trueheart Diary, Sept. 28, 1842, in Chabot (ed.), *The Perote Prisoners*, p. 111.

official press in Mexico City that it had been received with great joy and hailed for its many victories.[84] This was the official version, but according to that of a Mr. Jones who had been at San Fernando about six months previous to Woll's leaving for Texas and was there after his return and until the 28th of October, Woll lost 302 men in the campaign and all of the numerous wagons, carts, and animals that he had pressed into the government service. As General Woll drew near to Presidio, declared Jones, General Reyes induced the citizens to form a procession and go out to meet him and accord him the honors of a victor. Reyes, himself, went forth in advance of the procession in a splendid carriage decked with garlands. Great was the disappointment of the populace when they found the troops all worn down with fatigue and completely dispirited. The faint exclamations of joy that arose to greet the returning soldiers, we are told, were quickly silenced by General Woll, who with blunt candor informed General Reyes that "there was no cause for rejoicing in this instance, for his army had gained no credit in the campaign in Texas."[85] Yet, in a proclamation to his troops Woll said, "Soldiers: today you are returning to your quarters without spoils of war and poor as some Spartans; but you are returning covered with glory and loaded with laurels. You have shown yourselves worthy sons of Mexico."[86] In appreciation for his "brilliant" Texas campaign, the Mexican government awarded Woll a "cross of honor" and soon made him commander in chief of the Army of the North.[87]

The wounded Dawson men were kept under guard at Presidio del Río Grande for two months, where they plotted to escape. They revealed their plans to a Frenchman, who told them that crossing the Río Grande at this season of low water would be easy. Thus encouraged, Milvern Harrell, his uncle Norman Woods, W. D. Patterson and John MacCredae perfected their plans. Noticing that their soldier-guards played cards a great deal and satisfying themselves that their guns were unloaded, the prisoners slipped out one bright moonlight night after the guard had passed the door of the house in which they were confined and ran around the house towards the river, stumbling over the rocks that littered the ground and falling several times as they ran along. Norman

[84] *El Cosmopolita* (Mexico City), Oct. 8, 1842.
[85] "Information from Mr. Jones," *Telegraph and Texas Register*, Jan. 25, 1843.
[86] Adrián Woll, El general 2° en gefe del cuerpo de ejército del Norte, á las tropas de su mando, Campo sobre la margen derecha del Río-bravo del Norte, Se[p]tiembre 30 de 1842, in Woll, *Expedición hecha en Téjas*, p. 53.
[87] *Diario del Gobierno* (Mexico City), May 14, 1843.

Woods, who had not yet fully recovered from his wounds, was easily recaptured. The other three, instead of going straight to the river, which was a mile or two away, ran up stream for some ten or twelve miles, and then cut toward the river, reaching it about daylight.[88]

Since Patterson was the oldest of the three, the others followed his advice. They now looked for a shoally place to cross, and selected, finally, a point where the river was narrow and "bent in towards the Texas side." A sandbar lay a short distance from the bank and a high bluff arose on the opposite side of the river. The three men waded out beyond the sandbar, when suddenly Patterson stepped into deep water and began to swim. He called to his companions to follow.

The water was icy cold, [narrated Harrell later] and we had been confined until we were weak. We had gone only a little distance when McReady called to us that he could go no further, and sank. Pattison and myself swam on. A general's coat that Pattison had tied around him had slipped off, and he asked me to get it for him. I turned back for the coat, and taking it by my teeth, swam after him. On nearing the Texas bank we got into a swift current, and were washed rapidly downstream. Pattison called out to me that he could go no further, but must drown, and sank almost immediately. By this time I was completely exhausted and was helpless in the current. Thinking every second would be my last, I was suddenly washed upon a rock in the river, and carried high upon it, the water being only about six inches over its surface. I stood up and straightened myself. It was sleeting now, and I was almost frozen. I decided that I could not reach the Texas side, and knowing that I would freeze where I was, I went back to the Mexican side of the river. There was a long smooth beach where I reached the bank, and I ran up and down it for some time to loosen my joints, which had become stiff from being in the water so long.

Then leaving the river and going up a hill to get my location, I saw a house in the distance, and went toward it. A Mexican, seeing me approaching, came down to meet me. When he drew nearer, I recognized him as a Mexican I had known at San Antonio, and with whom I had traded. He came up and taking off his overcoat threw it around me. I went up to the house with him where he had a big, bright fire burning in the chimney. He would not let me go near it, but would have me move up a little at a time. His wife brought in some hot coffee for me, and I thought it was the best I had ever tasted. After getting warm, I told them that I desired to lay down, as I was sleepy.

---

[88] Milvern Harrell's account of his attempt to escape is in the *Dallas Morning News*, June 16, 1907. See also, E. W. Winkler (ed.), "The Béxar and Dawson Prisoners," *Quarterly of the Texas State Historical Association*, XIII (1909–1910), pp. 299–300.

A bed was prepared, and I slept from about seven o'clock in the morning until two or three o'clock in the afternoon, and on awakening I saw four Mexican soldiers in the room. . . . Of course, they carried me back with them.[89]

Harrell, Norman Woods, another of the wounded Dawson men, Van Ness, Fitzgerald, and Hancock were in the prison at Saltillo when the Mier prisoners arrived at that place.

At daylight on the 23rd the Texans, estimating Woll to be now some fifteen miles in the lead, failed to renew their pursuit. The San Antonio prisoners, who had been sent on in advance, crossed the Río Grande on the 22nd, the day before the chagrined and wearied Texan volunteers, without much semblance of order, began to retrace their course to San Antonio. The Texan troops, however, were so exasperated on account of the conduct of the Mexicans that they determined almost to a man to make a campaign to the Río Grande and chastise the enemy there. On the way back, the Texans met General Edward Burleson at the Medina with approximately seventy or eighty men,[90] who returned with Caldwell's men. Burleson had been away on an Indian campaign at the time the Bastrop men left home to meet the Mexican invaders,[91] but when he learned of the fall of San Antonio he hurried to the front. All reached San Antonio on the 24th, where they found several hundred other volunteers. The following day a general meeting was held in front of the Alamo at which time a number of speeches were made, including one by Vice President Burleson. Standing in a window of the Alamo, Burleson addressed the crowd, estimated at about twelve hundred. He spoke in favor of carrying the war to the enemy, and recommended that all the men present return home and get fresh horses, clothing, provisions, arms, and ammunition and meet him at San Antonio a month later, on October 25. The aggressions and cruelties of the Mexicans, being fresh in the minds of these citizen-soldiers, many speeches were offered in favor of the expedition, including one by Mayfield which was full of fight, and the idea was embraced with enthusiasm, many declaring it to be "their intention to capture and kill the last surviving Mexican on this continent."[92] Burleson, and Thomas Jefferson Green, who had

[89] Milvern Harrell's account in the *Dallas Morning News*, June 16, 1907.
[90] *Telegraph and Texas Register*, Oct. 12, 1842.
[91] Jenkins, "Personal Reminiscences of Texas History," p. 112a.
[92] Adams, "[Journal of an] Expedition Against the Southwest," Oct. 2, 1842, ms. Edward Burleson severely criticized Mayfield for his cowardly talk on the 23rd and made reference to his boldness now that the enemy had fled. As a result Mayfield challenged Burleson to a duel, which the Vice President readily accepted; but before

also arrived, both labored under the impression that General Woll had retreated no farther than the Nueces to await re-enforcements before penetrating again into the settled area of Texas. At least, this was one way of encouraging volunteers to come on and of whipping up enthusiasm for marching south.[93] No patrols were sent out to see just how far Woll had retreated.

Now that Woll had fled, most of the volunteers headed for home, feeling about like Jack did when he let the bird go. En route they encountered men at the Guadalupe, the San Marcos, and elsewhere on the way to the frontier, but when these were informed of the Mexican withdrawal, they usually turned back; however, a few pushed on to San Antonio to "know the facts."[94] James R. Cook, of Washington County, sent back word from near Gonzales, urging the Washington County "boys" to disregard the reports of the Mexican retreat and to come on as fast as possible.[95] Some, no doubt, went home with the idea of returning as Burleson had suggested, but many were never seen this far west again. Others, however, remained at San Antonio and became the nucleus for the so-called Somervell and Mier expeditions. With the exception of José Antonio Navarro,[96] the last of the Santa Fé prisoners had

---

the duel could be fought, Mayfield was again beset by a cowardly feeling and concluding he had made a mistake swore out a warrant in Fayette County for the arrest of both Burleson and himself. There was no duel. Weyand and Wade, *History of Early Fayette County*, p. 27.

[93] Brown, *History of Texas*, II, 229–230; Joseph Eve to Richard M. Johnson, Galveston, Oct. 5, 1842, in Nance (ed.), "Letter Book of Joseph Eve, United States Chargé de Affaires to Texas," *Southwestern Historical Quarterly*, XLIII (1939–1940), 504–507; Same to John Tyler, Legation of the United States, Galveston, Oct. 11, 1842 (private), in *ibid.*, XLIV (1940–1941), 96–100; E. W. Winkler (ed.), "Sterling Brown Hendrick's Narrative of the Somervell Expedition to the Río Grande," *Southwestern Historical Quarterly*, XXIII (1919–1920), 115.

[94] Adams, "[Journal of an] Expedition Against the Southwest," Sept. 29, 1842, ms.

[95] See brief notes from (1) J. H. [R?] Cook of Washington on the road, near Gonzales, Sept. 23d [1842], 11 o'clock P.M., and (2) W. B. Meriwether and G. W. Sinks, LaGrange, Sept. 24th, 1842, 9 o'clock A.M., transmitting Cook's note eastward, *Telegraph and Texas Register*, Sept. 28, 1842.

[96] Prior to the revolution, Navarro represented Texas in the state legislature at Saltillo. He was one of two native-born Texans who signed the Texas Declaration of Independence and helped to frame the Constitution of 1836. These are the usual reasons assigned for Santa Anna's desire to punish Navarro, one of the commissioners to Santa Fé, by retaining him longer in a Mexican dungeon; but there also seems to have been another reason. Soto informed Lamar that his father and Santa Anna both were third lieutenants in General Joaquín de Arredondo's army in the battle of the Medina River in 1813, and that Santa Anna had wanted to marry José Antonio

been released on June 16, 1842, and many of them had returned to Texas anxious for revenge in spite of their pledge not to take up arms against Mexico in the future. Others, people who had held back for fear of endangering the lives of the Santa Fé prisoners, now came forward after the release of the prisoners to support a march to the Río Grande and beyond.

_____

Navarro's sister; but the family objected to the union because of the general bad character of Santa Anna, especially for his having robbed Arredondo's military chest by the use of forged orders. Santa Anna's cruelty to Navarro later as a Santa Fé prisoner was believed by Soto to have stemmed from this incident. "Information derived from Mr. Soto," *Lamar Papers*, VI, 118–119. For additional information on Santa Anna's illicit love affairs in San Antonio in 1813 and 1836, see "Statement by Captain Antonio Menchaca," *ibid.*, VI, 338.

CHAPTER EIGHTEEN

Defensive Preparations and the Clamor for Offensive Operations

UPON THE RECEIPT of intelligence that a new Mexican invading force had captured San Antonio, many of the families who up until then had remained along the western border could be seen fleeing from their homes toward the interior, leaving behind fine crops of unharvested corn and cotton.[1] The wildest apprehensions pervaded the public mind. Yet, in spite of incredible panic and uncertainty, committees of vigilance and public safety began to rally to the support of the President. Small groups of mounted men, with determined faces, could be seen winding their way toward San Antonio to drive out the hated *"pelados."*[2]

As soon as news of the invasion reached Houston on September 16, the President issued orders for all the effective force of the counties of Matagorda, Victoria, Brazoria, Fort Bend, Austin, Washington, Colorado, Fayette, Gonzales, and Bastrop to repair forthwith to the scene of action.[3] All militiamen were to assemble and muster at the usual points of rendezvous in their respective counties and elect company officers. Each commander was to report his muster roll to the War Department, and then proceed by the most direct route to Béxar. Those first to ar-

---

[1] Harvey Alexander Adams, "[Journal of an] Expedition Against the Southwest in 1842 and 1843," Sept. 30, 1842, ms.

[2] Some Texans often contemptuously applied the word *pelado*, meaning "poor" or "penniless," to all Mexicans.

[3] "Orders to the Country by M. C. Hamilton, Acting Secretary of War & Marine," Houston, Sept. 16, 1842, *Writings of Sam Houston*, VII, 6–7; Houston to M. C. Hamilton, Secretary of War, City of Houston, Sept. 16, 1842; *Writings of Sam Houston*, III, 159–160; *Morning Star* (Houston), Sept. 20, 1842; *Telegraph and Texas Register*, Sept. 21, 1842; C. W. Peterson to the Editor of the *Telegraph* [Sept. 12, 1842], *ibid.*; *Houstonian*, Sept. 20, 1842, announcing capture of San Antonio on September 11.

rive on the frontier were to annoy and harass the enemy until all the troops had arrived; at which time, the whole force would then organize into regiments, elect field officers in proportion to the number of men in the field, and move against the enemy.

If the enemy [should] evacuate and fall back, [wrote the President] "the troops are authorized and required to pursue them to any point in the Republic, or in Mexico, and chastise the marauders for their audacity. . . . More detailed instructions are considered unnecessary, [he continued] as it is presumed that every soldier will do his duty; and that the troops will call to their command an officer whose wisdom, discretion and valor may be relied upon.

The volunteers from Fayette, Gonzales, and Bastrop were to be marched by way of Austin to cooperate with the citizens of Travis County in defending the city of Austin and the archives of the government which had not been removed because of the refusal of the citizens, by force of arms, to permit the execution of the President's order of the previous spring for their transfer. The troops from Brazoria, Colorado, and Matagorda counties were to pass by Victoria en route to their destination so as to afford protection to the center as they converged upon San Antonio.[4] The troops of Harris, Montgomery, Brazos, Robertson, and Milam counties were to be held in readiness as a reserve, and throughout the Republic the militiamen were ordered to be ready for prompt action, if their services should be required. The two companies in the city of Houston and Harris County were ordered to San Antonio by the most direct route.[5] News of the fall of San Antonio reached Galveston on the afternoon of the 20th, and Judge Morris who was in the process of conducting the trial of a woman for the murder of her husband, dismissed court and placed the woman on bail, and the judge, lawyers, and principal officers of the court joined the army.[6] The enthusiasm and excitement at Galveston for war, especially offensive action, reported a visitor, was not as great as in the spring following the Vasquez raid.[7]

On September 22, three days after a severe hurricane had visited Galveston two companies were ordered from Galveston to sail around to Matagorda Bay on the *Lafitte*, if the services of that vessel could be

[4] Houston to Morgan C. Hamilton, City of Houston, Sept. 20, 1842, *Writings of Sam Houston*, III, 162.

[5] Sam Houston to Morgan C. Hamilton, City of Houston, Sept. 22, 1842, *ibid.*, III, 164.

[6] *Bollaert's Texas*, pp. 145, 148; *Civilian and Galveston Gazette*, Sept. 21, 1842.

[7] *Bollaert's Texas*, p. 150.

procured, and to land at the most advisable point, or "if . . . it would not be proper to land so far West," the troops were to be landed at the mouth of the Brazos.[8] Colonel Robert Mills was to prepare for use the guns near the point at the east end of Galveston Island, and two pieces of artillery were sent from Houston to the island. The hurricane and high tide had carried the platform supporting the battery of three guns towards the sea. On September 30, the day after Hockley's arrival at the island, the Coast Guards were sent to the point. Colonel Hockley contemplated erecting a good battery near the point and also "erecting at least one more at the Bayou below the town."[9] The three eighteen-pounders were now hauled up, the sand cleared away and the guns were made ready to be placed farther inland.[10]

Washington H. Secrest, who had served during the Revolution as a spy under "Deaf" Smith, was ordered to raise a spy company to be subject to the orders of the officer to be placed in charge of the troops.[11] O. R. Willis was appointed acting commissary of the army and ordered to proceed forthwith to headquarters, near San Antonio, and report to the commanding officer.[12] The next day a large quantity of powder and lead was sent from Houston by the government.[13]

Again the clang of arms rang through the city of Houston, and all was excitement and bustle. Soldiers were seen hurrying to and fro, and the hoarse note of the drum and the frequent report of rifles indicated that war was abroad in the land. At Houston no alarm or fear was displayed, but every countenance beamed with confidence and high hope. Several citizens offered to furnish horses to the volunteers who needed them, and the City Council "appropriated all the license taxes now due,

[8] Sam Houston to Morgan C. Hamilton, City of Houston, Sept. 22, 1842, *Writings of Sam Houston*, III, 164.

[9] *Bollaert's Texas*, p. 152.

[10] *Ibid.*, p. 151. In the fall of 1844 the battery at the east end of the island was again destroyed "by the action of the waters of the Gulf" in a short but severe gale. The guns and most of the shot were retrieved and removed along with the framework, but the battery had not been rebuilt by the end of 1844. M. C. Hamilton to Sam Houston, Washington, Nov. 30, 1844, Texas Congress, *Journals of the Ninth Congress of the Republic of Texas*, Appendix, pp. 28–31.

[11] Sam Houston to Washington H. Secrest, Executive Department, City of Houston, Sept. 22, 1842, *Writings of Sam Houston*, III, 165.

[12] M. C. Hamilton to O. R. Willis, Department of War and Marine, Sept. 23, 1842, in Army Papers (Texas), ms.

[13] *Morning Star* (Houston), Sept. 24, 1842, quoted in *Telegraph and Texas Register*, Sept. 28, 1842.

and one hundred dollars for the purpose of furnishing supplies and provisions for the army."[14]

As information about the occupation of San Antonio continued to pour in, the President sent a special messenger to Colonel Joseph L. Bennett with orders to march immediately to the western frontier all available drafted men of the Montgomery County regiment, without waiting for the concentration of the whole force of the country.[15] At this time Montgomery County comprised not only present Montgomery County but also Walker and Grimes counties and the major portion of San Jacinto County, making it one of the most populous counties in the country. Similar orders were sent to Colonel Jesse McCrocklin at Hickory Point in regard to the Washington County regiment. McCrocklin commanded the Second Regiment, First Brigade of the Militia of the Republic. In the end, two-thirds of the militiamen of Washington and Montgomery counties were ordered out, which caused "some complaints among the ladies," who were left at home alone to manage the affairs of the farms and households.[16]

As quickly as these two regiments could be mustered, they proceeded in the direction of San Antonio. On October 9 an advanced detachment of about sixty men belonging to Bennett's command passed through Washington, and the next day, Monday, the 10th, Colonel Bennett, himself, with some two hundred of his men bearing "a very large blood red flag, with the lone white star and the motto, Independence, emblazoned upon it,"[17] arrived at the temporary capital of the Republic. That afternoon before a crowd estimated at five hundred persons, President Houston, being requested to address the troops, "urged them to cross the Río Grande" with other forces to be found at San Antonio. He advised them to beware of Mexican promises and never in any instance place reliance in promises. Houston warned them of the fate of Fannin and told them that, however great the odds, "he hoped they would never surrender to Mexicans, but fight on to the last, even if

[14] *Ibid.*

[15] Houston to Morgan C. Hamilton, City of Houston, Sept. 22, 1842, *Writings of Sam Houston*, III, 164; John Henry Brown, *History of Texas from 1685 to 1892*, II, 233; H. Yoakum, *History of Texas from Its First Settlement in 1685 to Its Annexation to the United States in 1846*, II, 364.

[16] J. McCullough to Col. James Perry [at] Gulf Prairie, Nov. 15, 1842, at Mrs. Bell's in James F. Perry Papers, ms.; see also John M. Swisher, *The Swisher Memoirs*, p. 13.

[17] Adams, "[Journal of an] Expedition Against the Southwest," Nov. 7, 1842, ms.

there were but one Texian to a hundred Mexicans."[18] Houston's speech, we are told, was received with great applause, and the soldiers joyously proceeded on their way. The following day about one hundred more men belonging to the Montgomery troops passed through the capital, and it was expected that another two hundred men from Montgomery County might pass through Washington within the next few days.[19] Two hundred troops of Washington County, mustered at Captain Fuller's on October 17 under the command of Colonel McCrocklin, were soon on their way to Béxar. The Harris and Milam county troops were to march to San Antonio without delay by "the most direct and secure route." Captain Moseley Baker's company was paraded on the Courthouse square in Houston at noon, Wednesday, September 28. At that time the company was presented a "handsome flag" by Miss Tihnan, who made a "very interesting address on the occasion to which Captain Baker made a very eloquent and appropriate reply."[20] The next morning Baker headed west with his company, but en route was taken ill of fever and had to stop. His men, however, continued on to Camp Rocky, near Gonzales, under the command of Lieutenant Gardiner Smith.[21]

A "fine company" of about fifty men, partly from Cypress Creek and partly from Houston, commanded by Captain James H. Cocke, and known as the Border Guards, left Houston on October 2 for the west.[22] Two days later another company of about thirty men from the San Jacinto, under W. Curtis, started westward.[23] Colonel Colin DeBland headed toward San Antonio in October with a company of some sixty men from various counties, but they turned back at Seguin upon receipt of the news of the withdrawal of Woll.[24]

Upon his resignation as Secretary of War and Marine on September

[18] *Telegraph and Texas Register*, Oct. 12, 1842; see also Houston to Thomas M. Bagby, Washington, Oct. 6, 1842, *Writings of Sam Houston*, III, 171–172.

[19] *Telegraph and Texas Register*, Oct. 12, 1842.

[20] *Ibid.*, Oct. 5, 1842. Since Moseley Baker served as a brigadier general in the Texas Army in 1839 in a campaign against the Indians on the upper Brazos River, he often went under the title of "General Baker." *Handbook of Texas*, I, 100–101; *Telegraph and Texas Register*, Oct. 19, 1842.

[21] *Telegraph and Texas Register*, Oct. 19, 1842.

[22] James H. Cocke was later appointed collector of the Port of Galveston by President Houston, and was considered by the people of Galveston to have been a good appointment. *Ibid.*, May 10, 1843.

[23] *Ibid.*

[24] Adams, "[Journal of An] Expedition Against the Southwest," Oct. 14, 1842, ms.

1, "from no personal difference . . . between himself and the Executive, but purely as to political subjects connected with the public administration,"[25] Colonel George W. Hockley was appointed on September 22, 1842, acting colonel of ordnance and engineer for the port of Galveston by Morgan C. Hamilton, former chief clerk in the War Department and now the Acting Secretary of War and Marine. Hockley served in his new capacity from September 24, 1842, to January 10, 1843.[26]

The defense of Galveston was important not only for the protection of the citizens and property on the island, but also to prevent the enemy from cutting off "the principal and only certain source of revenue to the

[25] W. D. Miller to Ashbel Smith, Washington, Texas, Dec. 8, 1842, in Ashbel Smith Papers, 1838–1842, ms. See also M. C. Hamilton to Sam Houston, Department of War and Marine, Washington, Nov. 12, 1842, in Texas Congress, *Journals of the House of Representatives of the Seventh Congress of the Republic of Texas, convened at Washington on the 14th November 1842*, Appendix, pp. 30–38. Houston to Col. G. W. Hockley, City of Houston, Sept. 3, 1842, in *Writings of Sam Houston*, III, 153. In telling Dr. Ashbel Smith of his resignation, Hockley wrote,

You have, doubtless, learned ere this that I am no longer in the Cabinet. The whims, oddities and caprices of our singular friend, I could bear and have borne, but when prejudice against an important arm of the service (the Navy) usurps the place of reason, and all attempts for preparation and action wilfully defeated, and when the views (I will not say asinine (?)) of the president and his Secretary, Mr. Jones, [are] so widely [different from mine] that it becomes almost [like] submitting to dictation to carry them out, I thought it best to resign, and in doing so I took the liberty to give my views partly—much in full it may be too tactless—but whilst the truth was being told, 'twas well to give the whole—and in such language always respectful, as could not be misunderstood. This produced an invitation to dinner (in company with Judge Terrell, Atty Genl. who was privy to the whole matter) and for the purpose of obtaining a personal interview. This I declined until my resignation was accepted, which produced a long letter in reply to it. Upon perusing about two pages, I returned it to Judge Terrell to be handed back, with the message that I could not read it—the assertions contained in it not being founded upon fact, and that further intercourse would cease.

George W. Hockley to Ashbel Smith, Galveston, Dec. 15, 1842, in Ashbel Smith Papers, 1832–1842, ms.

[26] The position of Secretary of War and Marine was offered to General Memucan Hunt, who declined it. *Telegraph and Texas Register*, Sept. 7, 1842. Hamilton took over the duties of Secretary of War and Marine as Acting Secretary on September 3, 1842. Sam Houston to Col. G. W. Hockley, City of Houston, Sept. 3, 1842; and Same to M. C. Hamilton, Executive Department, City of Houston, Sept. 3, 1842, *Writings of Sam Houston*, III, 153–154; M. C. Hamilton to Sam Houston, Department of War and Marine, Washington, Nov. 12, 1842, Texas Congress, *Journals of the House of Representatives of the Seventh Congress*, Appendix, pp. 30–38. Houston to Asa Brigham, Executive Department, Washington, March 4, 1843, *Writings of Sam Houston*, III, 325–326.

Government."[27] Hockley reached Galveston on September 29 to superintend the improvement and repair of the fortifications of the city and
to attend the erection of new ones, if needed.[28] Upon arrival at the
island, he found that a hurricane had struck there the night of the 18th
(Sunday), doing much damage to the merchant ships and other property, but that no lives had been lost.[29] The Strand was a scene of devastation. Great damage had been done to the Exchange, the stores, the
wharfs, homes, and other property. The Protestant and Catholic
churches had been wrecked; the *San Bernard*, the brig *Atlantic*, and the
prize schooner *Mary Elizabeth* had been blown aground.

Brigadier General Alexander Somervell, who resided at Matagorda,
was called from his duty as collector of customs at Port Calhoun on the
east end of Matagorda Island and ordered to proceed to the western
frontier to assume the over-all command of the forces assembling in
the San Antonio neighborhood. Arriving at Columbus on his way to
the west to take command of the troops, Somervell, senior officer of the
western militia, found two to three hundred volunteers, including the
Milam Guards,[30] Moseley Baker's Border Guards, and Sidney Sherman's cavalry awaiting the arrival of General Burleson. By the 28th
news reached Columbus, on the west bank of the Colorado, that the
Mexican army had retreated,[31] and that many of those who had gone
to San Antonio were returning home, having driven out the enemy.
Captains William M. Ryon, and F. M. Gibson of Fort Bend County and
many of the men at Columbus, having arrived from the middle section
of the country were anxious to go forward in pursuit of the enemy
across the Río Grande and put an end to his threats. Frequent calls to
arms had sounded the death knell of many business enterprises in
Texas.

[27] M. C. Hamilton to Sam Houston, Department of War and Marine, Washington,
Nov. 12, 1842, Texas Congress, *Journals of the House of Representatives of the
Seventh Congress*, Appendix, pp. 30–38.

[28] *Civilian and Galveston City Gazette*, Oct. 1, 1842.

[29] *Telegraph and Texas Register*, Sept. 28, 1842; Charles Elliot to Aberdeen,
Galveston, Sept. 23, 1842, in Ephraim D. Adams (ed.), "Correspondence from the
British Archives Concerning Texas, 1837–1848," in *Quarterly of the Texas State
Historical Association*, XV (1911–1912), 339; Same to J. Bidwell, Galveston,
October 10, 1842, in *ibid.*, pp. 342–343; *Bollaert's Texas*, pp. 142–144.

[30] Francis R. Lubbock, *Six Decades in Texas: or Memoirs of Francis Richard
Lubbock*, pp. 90, 146.

[31] Adams, "[Journal of an] Expedition Against the Southwest," Sept. 29, 1842, ms.

We are glad to find [wrote the editor of the *Telegraph*] that our citizens are at length aroused to a true sense of duty, and are preparing to turn the tide of war from our own borders to those of the enemy. Large numbers of volunteers are preparing to cross the Río Grande, [he declared] and levy contributions upon the Mexican towns. This policy has been forced upon us by the enemy, and if carried out with proper prudence and energy, will do more towards securing our independence and enriching Texas, than any other that could be adopted.

Latest information from Matamoros gave the whole Mexican forces in the valley of the Río Grande, including Woll's army and the 2,000 troops at that place, as less than 5,000 men, in widely scattered detachments so far apart, that it would be difficult, if not impossible, to concentrate more than 2,000 at any other point than Matamoros.

These troops, too, are generally ill-armed and many of them are unfit for service [declared the editor of the *Telegraph*]. An army of a thousand Texians, therefore, could sweep the whole country from Chihuahua to the coast. Intelligent gentlemen who have visited Chihuahua, say that it could easily be captured by 500 or 800 Texians, and that a contribution of $200,000 specie, could be levied and collected with ease. From Monterrey and Saltillo, $100,000 could be levied also, and a proportional sum from other towns. In the valley of the Río Grande thousands of horses, cattle, sheep and goats, could be gathered and driven into the settlements. Thus could we [he said] extort from Mexico an amount of property greater and more valuable than the whole products of Texas have been for the last five years. Our citizens could not engage in a more lucrative business than in carrying on an offensive war with Mexico. . . . The army now in the field will soon be augmented by the bands of adventurous youths that are hurrying from every county of the Republic, and we trust it will not turn back until it has extorted from the Mexican provinces an ample indemnity for all the losses that Texas has sustained during the last seven years.[32]

The President, it was felt could aid the western settlers by calling out a small portion of the militia of the eastern counties, and stationing them on the Nueces or the Río Grande as an army of reserve for a few months, while the western troops, and such volunteers as would join them, marched into the eastern provinces of Mexico.

As news of Woll's retreat was carried eastward, General Somervell at Columbus disbanded the troops that he found there upon his arrival, presumably because they would not now be needed as Woll had

[32] *Telegraph and Texas Register,* Oct. 5, 1842.

abandoned San Antonio.[33] Many of the men returned home, but Thomas S. Lubbock, commanding N. O. Smith's company, marched on to Béxar while others awaited word from General Burleson. The two militia regiments also continued their march to San Antonio.

Before Somervell's arrival at Columbus, Thomas Jefferson Green (who had landed at Velasco in June 1836, with a small body of troops from the United States and frustrated by a display of force the immediate return of Santa Anna to Mexico) had gone after General Burleson, at his home some sixty miles away, to get him to lead the troops assembling at Béxar across the Río Grande. In the meantime, Somervell, having disbanded the troops at Columbus, proceeded to San Felipe de Austin, "an insignificant village of half a dozen log cabins on the west bank of the river" near a ferry crossing on the Brazos, twenty-six miles from Columbus.[34] From there he wrote the President, then preparing to move to the new seat of government at Washington, apprising him of the state of affairs and requesting further orders. In the interval, Green returned to Columbus on the third day, as promised, with General Burleson, who resided eleven miles below Bastrop.

The west was determined that the enemy should be chastised.[35] By the fall of 1842 the effects of the three Mexican marauding expeditions upon the frontier were becoming noticeable. In the first place, a sense of insecurity depressed the inhabitants and discouraged immigration; in the second place, drawing the able-bodied men from their homes to defend the frontier often placed the women and children at the mercy of the slaves and Indians; in the third place, the interruption of every

[33] Lubbock, *Six Decades in Texas*, p. 146; Adele B. Looscan, "Harris County, 1822–1845," in *Southwestern Historical Quarterly*, XIX (1915–1916), 51; B[uckley] B. Paddock (ed.), *A History of Central and Western Texas: compiled from Historical Data Supplied by Commercial Clubs, Individuals, and Other Authentic Sources*, I, 155.

[34] [Frederic Benjamin Page], *Prairiedom: Rambles and Scrambles in Texas or New Estremadura by a Suthron*, p. 100. San Felipe de Austin was founded in 1824 by Stephen F. Austin as the capital of his colony, but had been burned by the Mexicans in 1836. It had a solitary public-house kept by a Virginia Yankee, a very mean sort of a fellow, reported a traveller, who deserves, like Sancho, "to be tossed in a blanket for his sins. We paid an exhorbitant bill here for as wretched fare and accommodations as Texas anywhere affords in its solitary houses of entertainment for man and beast; . . . and we caution all wayfarers not to tarry long with 'mine host' of the inn of San Felipe." *Ibid.*, p. 101.

[35] Thomas W. Bell, *A Narrative of the Capture and Subsequent Sufferings of the Mier Prisoners in Mexico, Captured in the Cause of Texas, Dec. 26th, 1842 and Liberated Sept. 16th, 1844*, pp. 12–14.

417

variety of peaceful occupation, not only temporarily stopped agriculture and trade, but caused embarrassment for some time to come; and, finally, it increased the financial burden of the struggling community.[36] The maintenance of the friends who came to aid them had bankrupted and beggared many of the frontiersmen and others farther east; and often there had occurred "the odious practice of indiscriminate impressment of individual property, without authority from the government and merely sanctioned by *private will,* and often stimulated by cupidity and dishonesty."[37] Many of the western families sought safety in the eastern part of the Republic. "All the vacant Houses which were so only a few months ago," recorded Adolphus Sterne, "now having [*sic*] Tenants. It is one of the sure signs that our Western Country is breaking up. San Augustine will rise by the downfall of the Western Country but if we have peace with Mexico and People can live in Security on the western frontier—San Augustine will be an *indifferent sort* of village."[38] "Two or three more appearances or displays of the enemy on our western confines," wrote W. D. Miller from Washington, "would I am quite sure make this river, the Brazos, the frontier. Those sections of the country thus trembling under the battle axe of the enemy will not of course pay taxes, and no importations will be made from which to derive import revenue."[39]

Poor Austin! [wrote Joel Miner, a New England printer living in Austin] She [is] not "at herself" now, as they say in this refined "one-horse Republic!!" She has been undergoing a sort of depletion, preparatory to the ushering in of the millennium, which, as Joe Smith says, must take place soon, when the buffalo, bull-yearlings and Bollax McCarty . . . lie down together. Enough of this. Austin will one day be renovated—"recuperated," ramfri-generated;— she will rise like the "Ponus" from her ashes; altho' shorn of locks, she shall be renewed in her strength and be great. The h—ll you say! My prophetic soul says aye, and Dr. S. G. H. has dreamed a dream wherein it is all duly set forth and noted down—Sam Houston, H—ll, and hocus-pocus to the contrary

[36] By October 1842, the Texans, particularly those in the west, had since January been called from their homes twice to repulse the Indians, and three times to defend themselves against the Mexicans, not to mention the constant robberies committed upon them by Indians, Mexicans, and a few lawless Anglo-Americans.

[37] Proclamation to the Army and Citizens of Texas, Galveston, March 11, 1842, (by Sam Houston), *Austin City Gazette,* March 30, 1842.

[38] Harriet Smither (ed.), "Diary of Adolphus Sterne," in *Southwestern Historical Quarterly,* XXXV (1931–1932), 153.

[39] W. D. Miller to Ashbel Smith, Washington, Texas, Dec. 8, 1842, in Ashbel Smith Papers, 1838–1842, ms.

notwithstanding. Seriously, Woodhouse,[40] it does seem to me that we are God-forsaken and parish d—d, given over to bats, Boluxies and bad liquor. I for one, stand unaffected, like the little girl, who, upon being interrogated why she was crying, said, "Daddy's in jail, mother's drunk, the baby's b—sh—t, and she did not care a d—n." I have taken hope, the "lover's staff to lean upon," calculating largely upon the influence a successful campaign West will have upon the destiny of this place.[41]

In the summer of 1842, following its suspension after the Vasquez invasion, the *Weekly Texian*, a supporter of the Houston administration, was moved from Austin to Washington where it continued publication under the name of *Texian and Brazos Farmer*. The *Austin City Gazette* continued to be published until Woll's invasion so upset things at Austin that it suspended publication some time after September 7, 1842. It was "renewed" at Austin "as the *Western Advocate* in February, 1843, by George K. Teulon and others."[42] Now was the time to take up the cudgels against the Administration and fan the excitement for an invasion of Mexico. For this purpose the *Texas Times*, a strongly anti-Houston newspaper, was established by D. Davis and Ferdinand Pinckard at Galveston. It commenced publication on October 12, 1842, and continued to April 22, 1843, when it folded because the "War Party" and "Malcontents" could no longer afford to subsidize it.[43] The west blamed the President for its misfortunes and some persons there were saying without reserve that if they were compelled to abandon their homes, the President's blood should atone for it. Others, becoming convinced that no aid could or would be furnished by the government, were talking of taking matters into their own hands for self-preservation of both lives and property. A few of the westerners were no doubt like the occupant of a log cabin near Nashville, "a shiftless fellow, . . . [who] complained

[40] Matthew P. Woodhouse was appointed Acting Secretary of the Treasury on August 19, 1842. Sam Houston to M. P. Woodhouse, Executive Department, City of Houston, Aug. 19, 1842, Seymour V. Connor (ed.), *Texas Treasury Papers: Letters Received in the Treasury Department of the Republic of Texas, 1836–1846*, II, 830.

[41] J. Miner to [Matthew P.] Woodhouse, City of Austin ("Used to Was"), October 17, 1842, in Matthew P. Woodhouse Papers, ms.

[42] Thomas W. Streeter, *Bibliography of Texas*, II, 506. The *Telegraph and Texas Register* of September 21, 1842, refers to an issue of the *Austin Gazette* of September 7, 1842.

[43] Lota M. Spell, "Samuel Bangs: The First Printer in Texas," *Southwestern Historical Quarterly*, XXXV (1931–1932), 267–278; *Bollaert's Texas*, p. 168.

bitterly of his misfortunes and sufferings, and that, what with the Indians and the war of Independence, he was nearly ruined."

"Poor fellow!" exclaimed a traveler. "His stock of horses and cattle
remaining was only about five hundred head. What would the Irish and
German peasant say to this with his solitary cow and brace of pigs!"[44]
West of the Colorado, at the Big Mound and elsewhere, fine fields of
corn, cotton, and pumpkins were deserted,[45] but by mid-October the
"army Worm" had moved in and stripped sixty per cent of the cotton,
while continued violent rains had rendered the country and roads impassable for hauling out the little cotton already produced.[46]

From LaGrange on October 3, Burleson himself dispatched Colonel
William G. Cooke with a letter requesting the President to authorize
him to organize and lead an expedition across the Río Grande "to end
this war." He stated that "a large number of Citizens" had called upon
him to lead such an expedition in conformity to orders from the War
Department of September 16.

My answer has been [said Burleson] that on the 25th inst. a General rendezvous shall take place at Béxar at which time if it be the pleasure of the Troops
for me to command I will do so; if not I will serve in any other capacity. But
in the mean time I have proceeded to use my best exertions to get up the
expedition upon such plan as will insure success to our arms and security to
our frontier."[47]

He requested that Colonel Cooke be authorized to collect the government's artillery and munitions of war for the enterprise.

It is expected [concluded Burleson] that the expedition will cost the Government nothing, save much articles which ar[e] on hand and can be conveniently speared [spared]. A large number of our Troops are now concentrated at Béxar under experienced and gallant officers which is fortunate for
good order and discipline necessary in such an expedition. I shall repair to
Béxar in person so soon as the organization can be compleat upon the upper
Colorado. . . . Therefore let me beseech you in the name of our common
Country to urge forward this expedition by every legitimate means in your
power.

---

[44] [Page], *Prairiedom*, pp. 105–106.
[45] Adams, "[Journal of an] Expedition Against the Southwest," Sept. 30, 1842, ms.
[46] *Bollaert's Texas*, p. 156.
[47] Edward Burleson to Sam Houston, La Grange, Oct. 3, 1842, in Sam Houston,
Unpublished Correspondence, 1842, III, ms.

Without waiting to hear from the President, Burleson proceeded with Green to Columbus, where, on October 5, with the latter's aid, he addressed a letter "To the People of the Brazos and the East," calling for volunteers to meet him at San Antonio on the 25th, armed and equipped to cross the Río Grande to fight the Mexicans in their own country, unless he should meet them sooner.[48] The brave men of the Colorado and Guadalupe, declared Burleson, want the aid of their Brazos and other friends. "Fellow-Citizens, need I call upon your patriotism?" he asked. "Need I cite to you the bleeding condition of the West? Need I refer you to the repeated inroads and insults of our enemy? Or need I call to your notice the humiliation of the helpless women and children whose husbands and fathers are now toiling in foreign captivity? God forbid that your sense of justice and patriotism should need such an appeal."

Burleson declared that under an order of the War Department, issued September 16, the men would be permitted to elect their officers and complete their organization before they moved against the enemy. "This I have done," he said, "in my individual character, and if it be the pleasure of the troops when assembled that I shall lead them I will do so; if not, I will cheerfully serve in the ranks." While proceeding farther up the river with his recruiting activities Burleson soon learned that his rival, Somervell, had been named to command the troops to invade Mexico.[49] Thereupon, failing to carry out either of his promises, he returned home with disillusioned hopes to wait and attend his official duties in the Senate during the Called Session of Congress set to meet November 14 at Washington-on-the-Brazos. En route home Burleson stated at LaGrange on October 24 that four hundred men could be expected to turn out from Bastrop and Travis counties, and expressed the belief that there would be three thousand men at San Antonio by the 5th of November. "There will be," reported a westerner, "no difficulty with regard to the command—the West will be satisfied if the invasion is properly conducted, and will make no objections to any commander the President may appoint."[50] On the other hand, the editors of the *Telegraph and Texas Register* felt that after the experience of last March, the President should have appointed someone who had more of the

---

[48] Edward Burleson to the People of the Brazos and the East, Columbus, October 5, 1842, *Telegraph and Texas Register*, Oct. 12, 1842; *Civilian and Galveston Gazette*, Oct. 12, 1842.

[49] On October 24, 1842, Burleson passed through LaGrange headed for home. *Civilian and Galveston Gazette*, Nov. 2, 1842.

[50] *Ibid.*

confidence of the western troops. The reappointment of Somervell was considered a bad policy, although he was regarded as a good man.[51]

We hope [said the editors] that the prominent men of the West, will in this crisis, display a magnanimity worthy of the occasion. If Burleson, [John H.] Moore, Caldwell, Owen and others, who have won the esteem of their fellow citizens by repeated acts of valor, will cheerfully resign their claims to office, and willingly . . . consent to accept the humbler stations in the Army, they will gain more real glory than they could acquire by winning a battle. What is this *bauble* of office, that men should prefer it to serving their country? Let selfish aggrandisement and false ambition be laid aside, and all unite in carrying out the great objects contemplated in the expedition.[52]

On October 3, General Somervell, "an officer of good standing and considerable reputation,"[53] reported "Big-Foot" Wallace, received more detailed instructions stating that he was to "proceed to the most eligible point on the south western frontier of Texas," and unite under his command not only the two regiments of militia, under Colonels Bennett and McCrocklin, but also all volunteer troops who might be willing to submit to his orders. If, upon reaching the southwestern frontier, he believed that he could advance with success into the enemy's territory, he was to do so immediately.[54] Although Somervell was given permission to take one or two pieces of artillery from Gonzales, he was reminded by the President that

Our greatest dependence will be upon light troops, and the celerity of our movements. Hence the necessity of discipline and subordination. You will therefore receive no troops into service, but such as will be subordinate to your orders and the rules of war.

You will receive no troops, but such as will march across the Río Grande under your orders if required by you to do so. If you cross the Río Grande, you must suffer no surprise, but be always on the alert. . . . You will be con-

[51] *Telegraph and Texas Register*, Oct. 12, 1842.

[52] *Ibid.*

[53] John C. Duval, *The Adventures of Big-Foot Wallace: The Texas Ranger and Hunter*, p. 167.

[54] Houston to Brig.-Gen. A. Somervell, Washington, Oct. 3, 1842 (copy), in Domestic Correspondence (Texas), ms.; Texas Congress, *Journals of the House of Representatives of the Seventh Congress*, Appendix, pp. 3–4. These orders were very similar to those issued to Somervell on March 10, 1842; see also, *Telegraph and Texas Register*, Oct. 12, 1842. The *Telegraph and Texas Register*, Oct. 5, 1842, says the President left Houston "to-day and will probably reach Washington on Saturday next," October 8. The other officers of the Government had already left Houston for the capital.

trolled by the rules of the most civilized warfare, and you will find the advantage of exercising great humanity towards the common people. In battle let the enemy feel the fierceness of just resentment and retribution.

In as much as the volunteers at Béxar had not reported to the War Department in accordance with the Government's instructions of September 13,[55] Somervell was informed that he alone was responsible and would be the only one to receive the support and resources of the Government. He was warned by the President against poor discipline and insubordination as the two evils most likely to lead to ruin and disgrace. "A mob can do wonders in a sudden burst of patriotism or of passion, but cannot be depended on, as soldiers for a campaign."

Ten days later (October 13) additional orders were forwarded from Washington instructing General Somervell to proceed at once to San Antonio or, if he were already on his way to Washington, to arrive at the latter place as soon as possible. Since secrecy in the conduct of all his movements was essential, he was instructed to take up his position on the Cíbolo,[56] east of San Antonio, or elsewhere if deemed expedient, but he was cautioned that San Antonio would not be a proper place to recruit his army because of the likelihood of enemy spies in the town. He was especially warned to deny native Mexicans of San Antonio entrance to his camp.[57] However, "in direct violation of the most positive orders," Somervell, who had assisted in polling the army on deposing of General Sam Houston as its commander during the "Runaway Scrape of 1836,"

[55] The failure of the parties arriving on the frontier to report to the War Department was more the result of poor communication than insubordination and a lack of responsibility. Late in October 1842, Mr. Baldwin reported that "the object of the Government is not generally understood; the Colonels of Regiments have received no orders since the retreat of Woll, and do not know whether those they received previous [to] that time are to be obeyed." Recruiting, therefore, was hindered. *Telegraph and Texas Register*, Nov. 2, 1842; M. C. Hamilton to Sam Houston, Dept. of War and Marine, Washington, Nov. 12, 1842, in Texas Congress, *Journals of the House of Representatives of the Seventh Congress*, Appendix, pp. 30–38.

[56] The Cíbolo had a beautiful hole of blue water, "having a rich color imparted" to it, and in early October was "no doubt highly flavored by the *Carcas* of a dead horse in it, which rendered it unfit for use." The horse was doubtless a casualty of the Woll campaign. Adams, "[Journal of an] Expedition Against the Southwest," Oct. 4, 1842.

[57] M. C. Hamilton to Brig.-Gen. A. Somervell, Washington, Oct. 13, 1842, photostat in Army Papers (Texas), ms. Original in National Archives, Washington, D.C.

selected San Antonio de Béxar as the place of general rendezvous,[58] when it had been expected that under no circumstances would he have organized his command west of the Cíbolo and that his command would "operate almost exclusively west of the San Antonio." By the 14th of November, however, Somervell's headquarters had been moved to Camp León on León Creek, seven miles west of San Antonio.[59]

Now that a campaign against northern Mexico was contemplated, the coastal defenses of Texas would require attention in case the Mexicans with their newly acquired vessels should attempt a countermovement by sea. Word had been received that an expedition was to sail from Vera Cruz on October 17 for the Texas coast.[60] As early as the 15th vedettes were assigned to watch the coast,[61] and many persons were fleeing Galveston Island, fearing that it might be attacked.[62]

On October 23 Colonel Hockley ordered the Fourth Regiment of the Texas Militia in the Galveston district to be mustered into service on the 25th. Immediately an order went out from Colonel Alden A. M. Jackson to the commanders of the several volunteer and beat companies comprising the regiment to have their muster rolls brought up to date and their men assembled with arms and equipment for inspection at the appointed time.[63] Very little help could be expected from the Texas navy. The *San Antonio* had been dispatched to Yucatán on August 19 to collect the balance due for the use of the Texas navy, but had not been heard from and had probably been lost in the September gales on the gulf.[64] The *Austin* and *Wharton* were in New Orleans where they

[58] M. C. Hamilton to Brig.-Gen. A. Somervell, Washington, Nov. 19, 1842, photostat in Army Papers (Texas), ms. Original in National Archives, Washington, D. C. See also, Herbert Pickens Gambrell, *Anson Jones: the Last President of Texas*, p. 61.

[59] A. Somervell to Sam Houston, Head Quarters, South Western Army, Leon, 7 miles west of San Antonio de Béxar, Nov. 14, 1842, in Texas Congress, *Journals of the House of Representatives of the Seventh Congress*, Appendix, pp. 11–12.

[60] *Morning Star*, Nov. 10, 1842; *Telegraph and Texas Register*, Nov. 16, 1842.

[61] *Bollaert's Texas*, p. 155.

[62] *Ibid.*, p. 157.

[63] Alden A. M. Jackson, *Attention Head-Quarters, 4th Regiment, 2d Brigade, Texas Militia, Galveston, Oct. 23, 1842. Order No. 30.* [Text begins:] "In obedience to a special order of this date from Col. George W. Hockley, commanding on Galveston Island, this Regiment will be mustered into the service of the Republic on Tuesday, the 25th inst. . . ." [At end:] By order of Alden A. M. Jackson, Col. Commanding. C. G. Bryant, Act. Adj. [Galveston, 1842], Broadside.

[64] Sam Houston to the Senate and House of Representatives, Executive Department, Washington, Dec. 22, 1842 (Secret), *Writings of Sam Houston*, III, 241–248; Tom Henderson Wells, *Commodore Moore and the Texas Navy*, p. 122. Hous-

had been repaired and provisioned but could not leave for lack of funds to pay for crews, clothing, and other items. The *San Bernard*, which, like the *San Antonio*, had been completely fitted out in Mobile, was aground at Galveston as a result of the late storm. The brig *Archer* was at Galveston and had sustained but little injury in the recent hurricane, but the steamer *Zavala* was a hopeless wreck.

At nightfall, November 7, letters from Velasco reached Galveston reporting a rumor that a fleet of vessels accompanied by steamers had been seen off that port. "All the volunteers [at the island] obeyed the tocsin which was wrung at the Presbyterian Church." The different companies assembled under their respective officers and spent the greater part of the night in getting Colonel Hockley's fort on the east end of the island in order in case the enemy should show up. "Anxiously we watched the morning's dawn on the 8th," reported Bollaert.[65] "I accompanied Simpton, the Pilot, to the Beacon;" he continued, "he climbed to the top, waited there until it was broad daylight, but [there were] no signs of the enemy." Three days later, the *New York* came in with the news that a Mexican fleet composed of ten sails had left Vera Cruz for Yucatán, promising to come to Galveston after the rebellion there had been subdued.

By early December some progress had been made in strengthening the defenses of Galveston despite a 50 per cent decline in the revenue usually received at that port due to the apprehension of a Mexican attack by sea. The Republic's meager finances had been terribly crippled by the war scare,[66] and laborers and materials were difficult to obtain without money. "Retrenchment and reform," declared Hockley, have done their work; however, he hoped to complete the defenses of Galveston, such as they would be, in a short time. The defenses were to consist of "a platform at the entrance of the harbour, near the beacon, mounting four medium eighteen pounders and one pivot, long twelve, flanked on its right by three twenty-four pounders." At the old position, near the east end, would be mounted three twenty-four pounders for the protection of the town below. These were to be invested with field artillery consisting of the two six-pounders which he had brought with

---

ton reported that the *San Antonio* appears to have been ordered to Sisal on August 19. Wells says the *San Antonio* sailed from Galveston on August 27, 1842.

[65] *Bollaert's Texas*, pp. 157–158.

[66] W. D. Miller to Ashbel Smith, Washington, Dec. 8, 1842, in Ashbel Smith Papers, 1838–1842, ms.

him from the park lately purchased and three other pieces already mounted. The roads leading from the town to the beach were also being improved.⁶⁷ By the middle of November the War Department had issued from its stores for the defense of Galveston two six-pound brass field pieces, with their appointments, and a moderate supply of ammunition, fifty muskets, and fifty sabres.⁶⁸

⁶⁷ George W. Hockley to [Ashbel Smith], Galveston, Dec. 15, 1842, *ibid.*, ms.
⁶⁸ M. C. Hamilton to Sam Houston, Department of War and Marine, Washington, Nov. 12, 1842, in Texas Congress, *Journals of the House of Representatives of the Seventh Congress*, Appendix, pp. 30–38.

CHAPTER NINETEEN

Assembling of an Army at San Antonio

THE ANNOUNCEMENT of the formation of an expedition to visit the Río Grande met with ready enthusiasm in the western counties, and it was believed that at least two thousand men would be assembled at Béxar by October 25 for the campaign.[1] The western inhabitants, who had the means, were liberal in contributing to fit out the soldiers and in furnishing provisions for an army to expel the invaders and, later, in supporting the army while on the frontier. The Brazos planters displayed considerable liberality. Leonard W. Groce sent nearly every horse from his plantation near Hempstead, and even turned out the "Gin Mules" to aid in conveying men and ammunition to the scene of action.[2] W. A. Miskel, near San Felipe, made similar sacrifices. Many of the planters around Washington—J. M. Brown, J. D. Rodgers, J. Lockhart, J. K. T. Walton, and William Maxey, to mention a few—subscribed ten bales or less of cotton, in proportion to their means, for the purpose of procuring articles for the army.[3] As a whole, the western citizens, affluent or otherwise, did everything in their power to encourage the troops in camp, and many of them "turned out the last cow they had to furnish the soldiers with beef."[4]

En route to the frontier, the militiamen and volunteers, whether singly, in small groups, or in large units lived off the land and the kindness of the settlers, or the property and crops which the settlers had abandoned. At Seguin, a party of eleven "obtained a small beef of one of the Mexicans living at the place, who was very liberal under the circumstances."[5] After killing and dressing it, they gave the hide and half of the carcass to the former owner and proceeded to dry the remainder

[1] *Telegraph and Texas Register*, Oct. 19, 1842.

[2] *Ibid.*, Oct. 5, 1842.

[3] *Ibid.*

[4] *Ibid.*, Dec. 7, 1842.

[5] Harvey Alexander Adams, "[Journal of an] Expedition Against the Southwest in 1842 and 1843," Sept. 30 and Oct. 3, 1842, ms.

for their own use. The people of Seguin, reported Adams, appear to be very kind, but "they have been very much imposed upon by some of the Volunteers who show their patriotism by infringing upon the rights of Citizens. One of the Mexicans," he said, "that let us have the beef, had five head of his sheep killed by some of those calling themselves Volunteers."[6]

The object of the government in respect to the proposed campaign was not generally understood. The colonels of the regiments had received no orders since the retreat of Woll and were not sure whether the orders they had previously received were to be obeyed. "This uncertainty, in some counties favorable to the war," reported the editor of the *Telegraph*, "has prevented any movement on the part of the people."[7] The appointment of Somervell was considered by some thoughtful men to be in poor taste.

We regret that this appointment has been made, [wrote Francis Moore, a critic of the Houston administration] not because we dislike Gen. Somervell, for there are few citizens whom we esteem more highly; but we know the jealousy of the western troops; and the history of the last campaign should have convinced Gen. Houston, that this appointment is but the casting of a fire brand among inflamable materials. The appointment of this gentleman before, worthy although he is, did more than any other cause to break up the army. . . . Many of Gen. Houston's enemies will doubtless believe, that this second appointment is but an indication that he still secretly wishes to break up the present army, and thus defeat the contemplated campaign. [If this really were his object, declared Moore] still it would be the best policy for the western troops to receive at once the commander appointed, and cheerfully submit to his orders until some open demonstration of disposition to thwart their wishes should be made, as by this means all bickerings and jealousies would be for a season silenced, and that discipline and subordination, so essential to success, would be the more readily established.[8]

The appointment of a general to command should have caused greater adhesion at the front, than the election of an officer from among rival candidates, with its inevitable delays and the bickerings and dissentions which could destroy the army before it could render the least service. If the western troops would accept the appointment of Somervell, it was argued, they could secure the countenance and cooperation of the government, and by this means the whole effective force of the Republic

[6] *Ibid.*
[7] Nov. 2, 1842.
[8] *Telegraph and Texas Register,* Oct. 12, 1842.

might be brought into action, instead of merely the troops from the western counties. Unless the government sustained the western citizens, the militia of the eastern counties might refuse to aid in conducting the contemplated campaign, leaving the volunteers of the western and middle counties to contend singlehanded without the whole force of the Republic. This line of reasoning, no doubt, had great influence among the volunteers at San Antonio in causing them to accept Somervell, for to have done otherwise would have meant virtually giving up the idea of a campaign to the Río Grande. The expedition to the Río Grande was expected to be of advantage to the country, for it would mean hereafter that the war would be carried on there rather than in the inhabited area of Texas. "Our prospects politically," wrote Guy M. Bryan, "are rather gloomy—not that we fear Mexico, but the times are so hard and people so poor that our government has no means to do anything."[9]

While Brigadier General Somervell, commander of the First Brigade of the Texas Militia, was being ordered to the frontier to take command of the troops at San Antonio and its vicinity, those who remained at San Antonio after the hasty retreat of General Woll or arrived later in small groups or companies eager to advance to the Río Grande had many interesting experiences, only a few of which might be mentioned here. Some of the companies, like that of Hays, were organized under captains appointed by the President; but, most often, the captains and other officers were chosen by the men. Usually if the men arrived singly or in two's, three's, and other small units they affiliated with first one or the other of the companies already organized; but few companies at the end of September and early October seem to have been up to full strength. Some of the men were on their "own hook," unattached to any organization. By early October it was reported that four hundred and fifty troops had assembled at Béxar,[10] and, for the time being, were furnished with a plentiful supply of corn, potatoes, and beef by the Mexican families in the neighborhood.

As the troops assembled, rumors were afloat that the Mexicans were coming, and it was not definitely known whether Woll had crossed the Río Grande, or even retreated beyond the Nueces. At Gonzales John W. Smith reported that General Woll was on the Nueces and had been re-

[9] Guy M. Bryan to Rutherford B. Hayes, Peach Point, near Brazoria, Texas, Jan. 21, 1843, in E. W. Winkler (ed.), "The Bryan-Hayes Correspondence," *Southwestern Historical Quarterly*, XXV (1921–1922), 103–107.

[10] *Telegraph and Texas Register*, Oct. 12, 1842.

enforced by five hundred men, but was awaiting a further increment from the eastern provinces.[11] The Mexicans at Béxar were reported to have become quite insolent and were openly declaring that General Woll would soon come to their aid and assist them in moving their property toward the Río Grande. Smith said the Mexicans of San Antonio had "clandestinely driven their cattle about 25 or 30 miles westward towards the Río Grande." Rather than being considered an indication of their disloyalty, could it not have been their intention to prevent the Anglo-Texans in the vicinity consuming their stock for which there was little hope of remuneration?

Many of these rumors concerning Woll and a renewal of the Mexican invasion were the result of a pure case of jitters, but some of them may have stemmed from the desire to cause other would-be-volunteers to rush pell-mell to the frontier for its defense and to launch a campaign against northern Mexico.

The repeated rumors of hostile Mexicans and Indians being in the vicinity of Béxar kept the Texan camps in a state of extreme nervousness. For example, on the night of October 6 Captain Bogart stationed out three pickets: one, at the upper mission crossing of the San Antonio River; another, at a crossing of a *seco* (ditch) a few yards from the river; and, the third, about three hundred yards below on the same ditch.[12] The sentinels near the ford understood that the picket guard, five in number, was to go across the river; but, instead, the picket crossed the ditch. The picket had not been on duty more than two hours, when the men saw persons riding, which caused them to fire an alarm; then instead of waiting for orders or to be relieved, they came rushing into camp. As they dashed toward camp, the sentinel at the upper post fired on the picket as it came into camp. Fortunately no one was hurt.

A short time after this incident another sentinel fired and said that he saw an Indian, or some other person. Not long after this second fire [firing], another shot was heard from the Sentinel at the lower post, [and] report was made that he saw an Indian trying to steal a horse. But on examination he had shot the Capt[ai]n's horse, five of the shot entering the jaw and neck. It was a bad shot, [reported Adams] but I think the horse will recover. The wildest excitement originated from this great fit of imagination. The Captain had all [of] his men paraded under the bank of the *Saco* [*seco*—ditch] ready for action at every alarm, thinking it not impossible for us to be attacked, although it was in the night.

---

[11] *Ibid.,* Oct. 26, 1842.

[12] Adams, "[Journal of an] Expedition Against the Southwest," Oct. 7, 1842, ms.

The last report for that eventful evening was about a "gun that went off accidentally." During all the excitement, no lives were lost nor was any material damage done, except to the captain's horse.

On the night of the 10th of October there was some uneasiness in camp as the result of a report that Woll was on the Nueces, re-enforcing to renew the attack on San Antonio. It was rumored that several of his men, including Colonel Seguin and Antonio Pérez, had been seen in San Antonio on the 9th and 10th.[13] All the American families at Béxar were preparing to move to the interior, at least as far as Gonzales. Even some of the *weak-breed* in the camp were talking of starting home and many did, but volunteers were arriving daily. On October 12 five spies were dispatched from Bogart's company along Woll's trail to the Nueces. The next day fires were seen in the hills above San Antonio; so at dark Captain Bogart with five men headed in the direction of the fires, but toward morning it became so foggy that the men could not see more than a few rods in advance of them, which necessitated their return without making any discovery.[14] As the spies sent in the direction of the Nueces had not returned by the 16th, preparations were made to send a larger group, this time some fifteen to twenty men, to scout toward the west, but the next evening the scouts sent on the 12th returned loaded with spoils left in the wake of Woll's hasty retreat. Fifty miles west of San Antonio, beyond the Arroyo Hondo, they reported $800 to $1,000 worth of rubbish—broken carts, chairs, trunks, and such—strewn upon the road. Also, they said there were many broken-down horses, some of which they brought back with them.[15]

On October 17 General Thomas Jefferson Green, a troublemaker, visited the Texan camp, spending the night with Bogart's company. "He is an Office Seeker and my impression is," recorded Adams, "that it will be no go-he."[16] By the 18th some of Bogart's men headed for home having lost their enthusiasm for a campaign.[17] The rumors of Mexicans on the Nueces stemmed from an inadequate corps of observation on the

---

[13] *Ibid.*, Oct. 10, 1842. "Col. Seguin and Antonio Perez visited Bexar in the night about a forenight since and left the city the next morning. He probably came as a spy to learn the situation of the place, and it was only by accident that it was afterwards learned that he had entered the city." *Telegraph and Texas Register*, Oct. 26, 1842.

[14] Adams, "[Journal of an] Expedition Against the Southwest," Oct. 13, 1842, ms.

[15] *Ibid.*, Oct. 17, 1842.

[16] *Ibid.*

[17] *Ibid.*, Oct. 18, 1842.

frontier, but more especially from the western desire to invade Mexico. The persistence of the rumors of a Mexican force on the Nueces, however coupled with the fact that since the break-off of the pursuit of Woll at the Hondo the Texans had not bothered to send spies to watch the movements of the retreating Mexican army, caused Captain Bogart, on October 19, to send eight or ten men as far as the Nueces again to check on Woll. This small group of rangers returned a few days later to report that it had gone thirty miles beyond the Nueces and had found numerous carts, wagons, and articles of furniture, and plunder of almost every description, strewn along the route, indicating that the Béxar Mexicans and Woll's troops had fled precipitately and no doubt in great alarm.[18] The spy detail reported that the Mexicans had entirely disappeared. From this time onward spies were kept out at a proper distance from San Antonio to warn of the approach of an enemy force.

On Wednesday, October 26, an Apache chief and four Texans arrived at the Texan camp at San Antonio. The Texans were said to be commissioned by President Houston to make a treaty with the Apaches.[19]

They will go direct to Prosedia [Presidio] on the Río Grande [recorded Adams], to treat with a part of the tribe who are there; the same being ratified by the whole tribe. The Apache Chief was rigged out with horse, saddle, sword, hat, clothing and various articles given to him by Genl Sam Houston. The chief camped with us for two or three days and created no little sensation while with us. When he first made his appearance in camp he looked so ludicrous as to set the whole camp in a roar of Laughter. He was tall, athletic, and black as the ace of spades, [with] long coarse hair, streaming over his neck, and shoulders with some hawk feathers entwined therein, a stove pipe hat over a painted face which rivalled all description. The boys laughed until they cried. But the chief took it all in good part in the end and seemed to enjoy the fun as well as any of them. At first, however, he seemed to be shocked at the rude reception with which he was received at the hands of our boys. He undoubtedly wanted to inspire the boys with a sort of reverence for his chiefship, as he frequently called out: "Me big Chief Sam Houston. Me big Apache Chief."[20]

Captain Bogart ordered out several spies on the 27th to see if anything could be learned about the movement of the enemy. Captain

[18] *Telegraph and Texas Register*, Nov. 2, 1842.
[19] Proclamation appointing James Grant agent to the Lipan Indians, Executive Department, City of Houston, August 15, 1842, in *Writings of Sam Houston*, III, 146. The Lipan Indians, as they were often called, were a branch of the Apaches.
[20] Adams, "[Journal of an] Expedition Against the Southwest," Oct. 26, 1842, ms.

Hays sent out spies, too, along the Medina Road. Colonel Bennett and Harvey A. Adams rode three miles below camp and crossed the San Antonio River at Higginbotham's Mill; and thence by way of Mission San José on the La Bahía Road to the Salado, which they crossed and proceeded eastward for half a mile to a ridge from where they could scan the surrounding country for fires.[21] They remained at this point of observation until 7 P.M., and returned to camp about 11 A.M. the next day, where it was learned that none of the spies had made any discoveries.

On October 28 fifteen to twenty men, with a Mexican guide to lead them, were detailed to go about thirty miles southwest of San Antonio to the Medina to get a herd of public cattle reported to be in that area. A drove of horses, sheep, and goats was also reported to be in the same general area and a certain Mexican in the vicinity, they were told, would show them the location of the stock. A part of the men returned on the 30th without beeves, reporting that the Mexicans had tricked them, but the men from Harvey A. Adams' mess in Bogart's Company remained overnight and killed some game in the Medina area. On the 31st the remainder of the company returned with a few beeves and a small amount of plunder.[22]

On the 2nd of the following month a Mexican who had been taken prisoner, after being kept under guard for a couple of days, was released, but the roads leading to the Río Grande were closed and a strict watch over his movements was maintained. A white man suspected of being a Mexican spy arrived at San Antonio this same day, and the guards on the roads to the Río Grande were ordered to intercept him if he should attempt to return, "but he does not leave San Antonio today," recorded Adams.[23] On the night of the 5th the Mexicans or Indians stampeded and ran off forty head of horses belonging to Captain Bennett's Company. Most likely it was Mexicans, because two of the horses were found later tied in a thicket below the San José Mission with saddles, baggage, and *escopetas* on their backs. Twenty of the horses were recovered.[24]

From the latter part of October to the middle of November, volunteers poured into San Antonio from all parts of the country west of the Trinity. Many of them had been there before when General Burleson,

21 *Ibid.*, Oct. 27, 1842.
22 *Ibid.*, Oct. 29–31, 1842.
23 *Ibid.*, Nov. 2, 1842.
24 *Ibid.*, Nov. 6, 1842.

standing in a window of the Alamo, had addressed the twelve hundred[25] Texans who had rallied to the relief of San Antonio. None of these, however, had taken the trouble to report to the War Department in accordance with orders issued early in September. Some of them had very little interest in the Administration and its policy. All were eager to pursue the enemy and punish him in his own country, for they were tired of having to lay down the plow, and to discontinue the planting or the gathering of their crops in order to take up arms to defend their homes from predatory warfare. Since they hoped to put an end once for all to such disturbances, sentiment among a portion of the volunteers was strong for retaliation by an invasion of Mexico itself. Others looked forward to adventure, glory, and easy plunder. Although the regular session of Congress was not scheduled to meet until the first Monday in December, the President on October 15 issued a proclamation convening the legislative body three weeks earlier than the law required, and on November 14, the appointed day, congressmen began straggling into Washington-on-the-Brazos, the third seat of government in ten months. There was no quorum in the House until November 24 and in the Senate until November 30, and thereafter none in either house for many days. On the same day that Congress was asked to meet, an appeal was made to the governments of France, Britain, and the United States to use their influence with Mexico to arrest the clandestine war of pillage being waged against Texas.[26]

The call to arms was responded to with as much promptness as could be expected under the circumstances. The facilities for the transmission of intelligence and orders were, however, so limited as to render it next to impossible to bring about a prompt and uniform movement of the militia, when emergencies arose requiring their immediate action. The streams were all high from excessive rains, and added to this, reported the Acting Secretary of War on November 12,

it is proper to remark that not a single dollar has ever been placed at the disposition of the Department for 'Express purposes.' The consequence is, that not infrequently dispatches lie on the table forty-eight hours, and in some instances a week before an order can be procured. . . . Delays in forwarding communications, and the impassable condition of the streams for

[25] Guy M. Bryan to Rutherford B. Hayes, Peach Point, near Brazoria, Texas, Jan. 21, 1843, in Winkler (ed.), "The Bryan-Hayes Correspondence," *Southwestern Historical Quarterly*, XXV (1921–1922), 103–107.

[26] *Writings of Sam Houston*, III, pp. 179–184; Gambrell, *Anson Jones*, pp. 262–268.

some weeks past, have retarded the movement of troops, and the collection of supplies of beef, so that no reports have as yet been received of their readiness to march for the enemy's frontier.[27]

Many obstacles were encountered by troops going to Béxar. The weather was wretched; it rained often and mud and high water slowed the movement of troops. The streams were swollen and swift, and the Navasota, the Brazos, the Colorado, and the Blanco were approaching flood stage. As early as September 24, Miskel, dispatch bearer from the Salado to the City of Houston, reported "the prairies . . . completely flooded with water," and suggested that the troops from Harris County be mounted, as it would be "almost impossible for them to march on foot for some days."[28] The condition of high water and poor roads continued into the middle of November.[29] The prairies were trackless seas of water, and the roads had become wet and heavy. Major James D. Cocke marched from the city of Houston over miry roads in command of a company composed of Cypress Creek militiamen and volunteers from Houston, equipped with government arms and ammunition.[30] The bayou at Mrs. Wheaton's was very high and the troops were compelled to march by the Richmond route to San Felipe where there was a good ferry. About three hundred troops from Washington County were upon the road nearly three weeks in traveling from Fuller's place, the site of their county rendezvous, above Independence to San Antonio. They forded many streams and found it necessary to do a great deal of swimming, sometimes being pulled across the raging waters holding to the manes or tails of their horses. The swollen Colorado

[27] M. C. Hamilton to Sam Houston, Dept. of War and Marine, Washington, Nov. 12, 1842, in Texas Congress, *Journals of the House of Representatives of the Seventh Congress of the Republic of Texas, convened at Washington, on the 14th November 1842*, Appendix, pp. 32–33.

[28] *Telegraph and Texas Register*, Sept. 28, 1842.

[29] J. McCullough to Col. James Perry [at] Gulf Prairie, Nov. 15, 1842, at Mrs. Bell's in James F. Perry Papers, ms. Harvey A. Adams in his "[Journal of an] Expedition Against the Southwest" reported the weather at San Antonio on the following dates as follows: Oct. 8—"rain followed by a real Texas northern"; Oct. 18—"rain"; Oct. 19—"rained in torrents all day and half the night"; Oct. 20—"rained most of the day"; Oct. 21—"drisseling rain; dark and dreary; rained all day and night; cool southwest wind"; Oct. 22—"rained this morning"; Nov. 4—"drisseling rain most of the day and night and became hard"; Nov. 10–11—"drisseling rain, followed by a severe northern blowing a perfect gale"; Nov. 14—"heavy mist during the night"; Nov. 15—"looks like rain."

[30] Maj. J. D. Cocke to ———, Matamoros, Jan. 12, 1843, reprinted from the *New Orleans Bulletin* in the *Morning Star* (Houston), March 4 and 7, 1843.

delayed their crossing at LaGrange. The troops and volunteers that proceeded to the front by way of Austin found that the rampaging Colorado had washed away the ferryboat; the men were forced to swim their horses across the river by the side of little canoes.[31]

By October 15 there were about 650 Texan troops at Camp Rocky, near Gonzales, including some 300 from Montgomery County under the command of Colonel Bennett; about 100 at Béxar; and 150 at the old mill a few miles from Béxar. The troops were all reported to be in fine spirits and delighted to find that there was now a certainty that the campaign against Mexico would go forward. The troops at Gonzales and Béxar, it was said, were well supplied with beef and corn, but were in need of coffee, tobacco, lead, powder, flints, and percussion caps. Those at Gonzales, according to Lieutenant Smith, were short of percussion caps, moulds for musket balls, coffee, and other items.[32] Occasionally a tame or semi-wild beef was acquired from one of the neighboring ranches, but even these were scarce. Usually it was confiscated beef.

Beef! O' Beef! thou stay of Texas soldiers! [exclaimed one of the volunteers]. Thou bread of Life to the weary and hungry half-starved denison of the plains! And thou *Raw-hide*, how dost thou pinch up ones feet when dried and when thou getest well soaked three or four feet could be gathered within thy flabby folds. Boots and shoes have no comparison with thy contracting and expanding qualities. It is often said of thee, that thou art the salvation of Texas.[33]

When Somervell arrived upon the frontier it was necessary to issue special and general orders to protect private property, such as horses, cattle, corn, and cornfields.[34]

Colonel Bennett's Montgomery County militiamen, numbering between 250 and 300 men, reached San Antonio on November 3. Arriving also on that day were Captain Phillip H. Coe (40 men), Captain John Shelby McNeill (60 men), Captain John R. Baker (50 men), Captain

---

[31] Lucy A. Erath, "Memoirs of Major George Barnard Erath," *in Southwestern Historical Quarterly*, XXVII (1923–1924), 37.

[32] *Telegraph and Texas Register*, Oct. 26, 1842. Letter from Lt. Smith, dated Gonzales, Oct. 8, 1842, referred to in *Telegraph and Texas Register*, Oct. 19, 1842.

[33] Adams, "[Journal of an] Expedition Against the Southwest," Oct. 8, 1842, ms.

[34] A. Somervell, Special Order No. 1, Head Q[rs] So. Western Army, San Antonio, Nov[r] 6, 1842; A. Somervell, General Order No. 5, Head Q[rs] So. Western Army, San Antonio, Nov[r] 7, 1842, in "A Record Book of the General & Special Orders and Letters of the South Western Army," pp. [1], 3–4, ms.

William Ryon (46 men), and Captain William Bowen (full company).
Other troops arrived on the 4th, and on the 5th additional troops from
Washington County came in, and others "keep coming in hourly," re-
ported Adams. On the 10th a company of about thirty men from the
Lavaca reached Béxar.[35]

Somervell passed through Columbus on October 29 on his way to the
army. By the time he reached San Antonio on Friday night, November
4,[36] approximately 1,200 volunteers and drafted men had arrived, including a few recruits recently from Louisiana, Arkansas, and other
states, where the news of Woll's attack had produced quite a sensation,
especially since the Mexican consul at New Orleans had represented
"the loss of Texas as amounting to several hundred killed and
wounded."[37]

The number of volunteers from the United States was very small. The
would-be volunteers there had had their fill of Texan promises, and had
too often listened to the Texan cry of "wolf" and found no campaign
forthcoming. Too many had visited Texas for one reason or another and
had returned to the United States disillusioned. The stories of the land
promoters and would-be "Napoleons" had been too rosy. There may
have been other reasons, too. "Our good friends in New Orleans," recorded a newcomer to Texas, "have got some reports from Mexico that,
this time it is a 'regular invasion' and are not very anxious in coming

---

[35] Adams, "[Journal of an] Expedition Against the Southwest," Nov. 3–5, Nov.
10, 1842, ms.

[36] *Telegraph and Texas Register*, Nov. 2, 1842; A. Somervell to M. C. Hamilton,
Head Quarters, South Western Army, San Antonio de Béxar, Nov. 7, 1842, in Texas
Congress, *Journals of the House of Representatives of the Seventh Congress*, Ap-
pendix, pp. 10–11; Francis R. Lubbock, *Six Decades in Texas: or Memoirs of
Francis Richard Lubbock*, p. 146; A. Somervell to G. W. Hill, Secretary of War
and Marine, Washington, Feb. 1, 1843, in *Morning Star*, (Houston), Feb. 18, 1843;
Telegraph and Texas Register, Nov. 2, 1842.

[37] Isaac Van Zandt to G. W. Terrell, Legation of Texas, Washington City, Dec.
7, 1842, in George P. Garrison (ed.), *Diplomatic Correspondence of Texas*, 1907,
I, p. 618. If there ever were 1,200 men at San Antonio, as most accounts seem to
mention, after Somervell's arrival, he does not mention it in his reports. On November 7 he reported that volunteers were arriving daily from the east, and on the
14th he mentions "about eight hundred men" being present and anxious to advance
against the enemy. A. Somervell to M. C. Hamilton, Head Quarters, South Western
Army, San Antonio de Béxar, Nov. 7, 1842; Same to Sam Houston, Head Quarters,
South Western Army, Leon, 7 miles West of San Antonio de Béxar, Nov. 14, 1842,
in Texas Congress, *Journals of the House of Representatives of the Seventh Congress*, Appendix, pp. 10–11.

forward to assist us . . . . The folk in New Orleans are scared at the position of Texas, will send no goods," and then in a half-hearted way he apologized for them by saying, "probably their own affairs are in a bad way."[38] The men at San Antonio were almost exclusively from the counties west of the Trinity, except for a few volunteers from the counties further to the east or from the United States. They were stationed in some six or eight different camps within one to ten miles of the town. Most of the camps were in the vicinity of the moss-covered mission of Concepción two miles below San Antonio, from one of whose towers floated the Texan flag, at the San José Mission four miles below the town, and the mission of San Juan Capistrano seven miles below. Within the four or five acre enclosure of the San José Mission were a number of huts all occupied by Mexican families. Much of the outer wall had fallen or been torn down; yet, some of the parts remaining towered ten to fifteen feet high. The mission was described as being "such a filthy place," that some of the troops when they had the opportunity refused to take refuge in it from the inclement weather.[39] The outer walls of the mission of San Juan Capistrano, located seven miles below town, enclosed six or more acres and stood, except where they had been broken down by the ruthless hand of time, eight to ten feet high. The west and north walls were in fairly good condition. Inside the enclosure were quite a number of huts rudely built of wood or mesquite poles set in the ground and thatched with grass. Some were built of stone or adobe. Most of the huts were occupied by Mexican families.[40]

After a visit to Mission Concepción in 1840, a Texas soldier described it as follows:

On the opposite side of the [San Antonio] river, and perhaps two miles from Saint Hosea [José], I reached the Mission Conception. I found it more limited in its dimensions, more beautiful in its proportions, and in a complete state of preservation, though the walls that inclosed it were level with the ground, and its fortress and domiciles are overspread by moss and weeds and desolation. I rode into the door of the church and from among the images that adorn its lofty ceiling and echoing dome, the bats came screaming forth, as though man were a stranger to their dwelling.[41]

[38] *Bollaert's Texas*, pp. 156–157.
[39] Adams, "[Journal of an] Expedition Against the Southwest," Oct. 20, 1842, ms.
[40] Ibid., Oct. 10, 1842; Rena Maverick Green (ed.), *Memoirs of Mrs. Mary A. Maverick: Arranged by Mary A. Maverick and Her Son George Madison Maverick*, p. 25.
[41] *Austin City Gazette*, June 10, 1840.

On October 6, 1842, there were about 1,500 goats and sheep corralled at Mission Concepción.

The old missions were havens for thousands upon thousands of bats. In passing the mission of San José near dusk one's ears were saluted by a sound very similar to that of a heavy wind, produced by the wings of myriads of bats passing out in continuous streams from every door and window in the building. Quite a number of acres in the old mission area were irrigated. The early troops in the area found that the corn had been planted so thick in rows that it looked as if it had been sown. Cultivation was by a forked stick pulled by a yoke of oxen. Most of the corn was soon consumed by the volunteers and their horses. Just above the San Juan Mission there was a first rate saw mill and grist mill[42] with a pair of excellent mill stones. The grist mill furnished the troops with a fine grade of meal while the corn lasted; yet, there were a few sunshine patriots "who wished to put it to their private use."[43] By early November, when the troops began to arrive in considerable number, most of the corn in the vicinity of San Antonio had been gathered and consumed. About thirty-five miles away, at Seguin's ranch, there was said to be some three hundred bushels of cribbed corn, plenty of cattle, hogs, and chickens, and no one living at the place.[44] By this time, the soldiers in camp were almost destitute of coffee, sugar, salt, and tobacco—articles that were deemed indispensable for their welfare. It was reported in Houston that they had plenty of fresh beef but no bread stuff. The latter they cared not for, as they could be made quite contented with coffee, beef, salt, and a little tobacco. Subscriptions for such items were taken up in Houston and sent by wagon by way of Bastrop. Other articles were sent, from time to time, by couriers or special persons going west with a few pack horses.

Bogart's Company appropriated the large baptismal font from the deserted church at Mission Concepción and made soup in it. When the company moved its camp site the copper font was buried on "the plains of Béxar" about five or six miles below San Antonio on the north side of

---

[42] Higginbotham's Mill. Thomas Higginbotham, a carpenter by trade, came to San Antonio in 1839, and took the house opposite the Mavericks on the corner of Commerce Street and Main Plaza. His brother and sister settled in the country on the river below the San José Mission. Green (ed.), *Memoirs of Mrs. Mary A. Maverick*, p. 25

[43] Adams, "[Journal of an] Expedition Against the Southwest," Oct. 9, 1842, ms.

[44] *Ibid.*, Nov. 5, 1842.

the river.[45] For reasons of sanitation and because of the need of grass for the horses, the various units moved their camps every two or three days.[46]

Just who were the men who comprised the Somervell expedition? The volunteers and militiamen were of all ages, with varying degrees of military experience, social and political standing, leadership, and educational qualifications. There were several ministers of the gospel, many other churchmen, businessmen, small farmers, artisans, a few young boys, and quite a number of adventurers and soldiers of fortune. Many of them longed for new adventures in the mysterious west, that allured them with its strange fascination. Brave, honest, God-fearing, vigorous in mind and body, dependent on their own resources and their trusty rifles for food and defense, they looked forward with excitement to their forthcoming adventure. "Big-Foot" Wallace, a member of both the Somervell and Mier expeditions, has left a somewhat different picture of the men who assembled at San Antonio for the purpose of invading Mexico. Many of the drafted militia and volunteers may have fitted the first characterization; but, no doubt, quite a few—far too many—met Wallace's description:

A motley, mixed-up crowd we were, you may be certain—broken-down politicians from the "old States," that somehow had got on the wrong side of the fence, and been left out in the cold; renegades and refugees from justice, that had "left their country for their country's good," and adventurers of all sorts, ready for anything or any enterprise that afforded a reasonable prospect of excitement and plunder. Dare-devils they were all, and afraid of nothing under the sun (except a due-bill or a bailiff), and if they had been managed with skill and judgement, they would undoubtedly have accomplished all that was expected from the expedition.[47]

Soon after Somervell's arrival upon the frontier the business of organizing the troops got under way. The general staff officers were appointed by President Houston, and consisted of the following: Chief Justice

[45] *Ibid.*, Oct. 9, 1842.

[46] *Ibid., passim*; Memucan Hunt to Francis Moore, Jr., Editor of the *Telegraph*, Camp Leon, Southwestern Army, Nov. 16, 1842, *Telegraph and Texas Register*, Dec. 21, 1842; *ibid.*, Nov. 2, 1842; John Henry Brown, *History of Texas, from 1685 to 1892*, II, 235; Thomas J. Green, *Journal of the Texian Expedition Against Mier*, p. 41.

[47] John C. Duval, *Adventures of Big-Foot Wallace: The Texas Ranger and Hunter*, p. 167.

John Hemphill[48] acting adjutant-general of the forces of the Republic; Colonel William G. Cooke, recently returned Santa Fé prisoner, acting quartermaster general and chief of the subsistence department; E. H. Winfield and J. M. Alexander, assistant quartermaster generals; and Colonel James R. Cook, acting inspector general and mustering officer.

[48] Born in South Carolina on December 18, 1803, John Hemphill graduated from Jefferson College, Pennsylvania, in 1825, taught school for a while and then read law in Columbia, South Carolina. He served as a second lieutenant in the Seminole campaign in Florida in 1836. In the summer of 1838 he came to Texas and settled in Washington, which boasted a very able bar. "But a man of his talents, his thorough knowledge of law, his oratorical powers, and his bland and gentlemanly deportment," declared John Henry Brown, "could not remain undistinguished in any country." After six months in Texas, he was offered a place in Lamar's cabinet, but declined the appointment, saying that he preferred to pursue the law. On January 20, 1840, he was elected judge of the Fourth Judicial District, and thereby automatically became an associate justice of the Supreme Court. He participated in the Council House Fight in San Antonio in March, 1840. During 1840 and 1841 he participated as a private soldier in several campaigns against the Comanches. During December 1840, he was elected chief justice of the Supreme Court, and became known as the "John Marshall" of Texas. Hemphill was a member of the constitutional convention of 1845, and was appointed chief justice of the Supreme Court under the new state constitution, a position he held to 1858 when he resigned to accept election to the United States Senate; he was a leading advocate of secession and a representative of Texas in the Congress of the Confederate States of America until his death on January 4, 1862. Scrapbook, in John Henry Brown Papers, 1835–1872, ms.; James T. DeShields, *Border Wars of Texas: being an Authentic and Popular Account, in Chronological Order, of the Long and Bitter Conflict Waged Between Savage Indian Tribes and the Pioneer Settlers of Texas*, pp. 314–315; *Dictionary of American Biography*, VIII, 520–521.

William G. Cooke was born in Fredericksburg, Virginia, March 26, 1808. When he grew up he moved to New Orleans to engage in business, and when the Texas revolution broke out he joined the New Orleans Grays with the rank of lieutenant. He served as assistant inspector general under General Sam Houston in the battle of San Jacinto. In 1839 Lamar appointed him quartermaster general of the army, and the next year as a commissioner to deal with the Comanches. He was in the Council House Fight, March 19, 1840, and was later named by Lamar as one of the Santa Fé commissioners. As a member of that ill-fated expedition he was taken prisoner by the Mexicans. Upon his release, he returned to Texas, and married Miss Angela Navarro, daughter of Don Luciano Navarro, brother of Don José Antonio Navarro. In 1846 he became adjutant general under the state government. Cooke died at Seguin in December 1847. Cooke County is named after him. Harry Warren, "Col. William G. Cooke," *Quarterly of the Texas State Historical Association*, IX (1905–1906), 210–219; Allen F. Adams, "The Leader of the Volunteer Grays: the Life of William G. Cooke, 1808–1847," ms.; Frederick C. Chabot, *With the Makers of San Antonio*, p. 206; John Henry Brown, *Indian Wars and Pioneers of Texas*,

Brigadier General Alexander Somervell commanded the men in the field, and his staff consisted of Thomas Green, later John H. Herndon, brigade major; George T. Howard, later Jerome B. Robertson, and finally Robert H. Dunham, brigade inspector; Jesse Willie, judge advocate; Lieutenant Colonel Jesse L. McCrocklin, brigade paymaster; Cornelius McAnelly, brigade surgeon; George L. Hammeken,[49] interpreter and secretary to General Somervell; and Captain Peter H. Bell, aide-de-camp.[50]

On November 7 Somervell ordered the various detachments around San Antonio concentrated at the Mission of San José for the purpose of forming a permanent organization. At that time the Montgomery County boys, the largest unit on the southwestern frontier, were housed in the mission, where they had hoisted their flag upon the dome of the

---

p. 77 n; Commission of Appointment of William G. Cooke, Acting Quarter Master General of the Forces of the Republic, Washington, October 25, 1842, signed by Sam Houston, in Executive Records, of the Second Term of General Sam Houston's Administration of the Government of Texas, December 1841–December 1844; ms.; M. C. Hamilton to Col. William G. Cooke, Department of War and Marine, Washington, Oct. 25, 1842, in Army Papers (Texas), ms.

In connection with the appointments of Winfield, Alexander, and Cooke, see M. C. Hamilton to Brig.-Gen. A. Somervell, Washington, Oct. 19, 1842, in *Writings of Sam Houston*, III, 187–188; Brown, *History of Texas*, II, 234; William Preston Stapp, *The Prisoners of Perote: Containing a Journal Kept by the Author who was Captured by the Mexicans, at Mier, December 25, 1842, and Released from Perote, May 16, 1844*, p. 22; M. C. Hamilton to Col. William G. Cooke, Washington, Oct. 25, 1842, in Army Papers (Texas), ms.; Same to Same, Department of War and Marine, Washington, Oct. 26, 1842, Special Order No. 57, in *ibid.*; Same to Same, Dept. of War and Marine, Washington, Nov. 19, 1842, in *ibid.*; *Telegraph and Texas Register*, Oct. 26, 1842.

[49] George L. Hammeken, a relative of the Bryans, was living in Mexico in 1833, where he met Stephen F. Austin, who suggested that he settle in Texas. He came to Texas in October 1835, as the agent of a group of English bankers. In 1837 he translated Filisola's *Evacuation of Texas*, and in 1839 and 1841 served as secretary to Barnard E. Bee and James Webb, respectively, on their missions to Mexico. *Handbook of Texas*, I, 762; Guy M. Bryan to Rutherford B. Hayes, Peach Point, near Brazoria, Texas, Jan. 21, 1843, in Winkler (ed.), "The Bryan-Hayes Correspondence,"*Southwestern Historical Quarterly*, XXV (1921–1922), 103–107.

[50] A general break-down of the officers as constituted on November 16 after the first organization of the army was listed in Memucan Hunt to Francis Moore, Jr., Editor of the *Telegraph*, Camp Leon, Southwestern Army, Nov. 16, 1842, *Telegraph and Texas Register*, Dec. 21, 1842. He shows William Joel Bryan as Aide-de-Camp to General Somervell, but, subsequently, Bell was appointed to this position and served during the campaign.

church.[51] The work of organizing the troops was commenced under the direction of Colonel Hemphill. The 7th and 8th of November were spent effecting the organization of the men into companies, and the regimental organization was expected to be carried out on the 9th and 10th;[52] but was not actually completed until the 11th.[53] The volunteers were permitted to organize themselves under the Militia Law of January 18, 1841, which allowed the men to elect their own officers, who, in turn, would be subordinate to the commandant of the expedition and to the general staff officers. "After considerable *Hawing* and *Geeing*, packing and unpacking, to suit the caprice of two or three would-be officers, we repaired to camp," reported Adams, "where we remained for the night, to reflect on the scientific evolutions of the day, and the transitory scenes of life."[54] It was found "impossible to organize the troops in strict compliance with the orders from the Department of War and Marine," declared Hemphill. "The companies have been formed for some time, [and] an attachment between the officers and privates had arisen which it was impossible to disregard without endangering in the most serious manner, the existence of the Army, and defeating the objects of the campaign."[55] It was impossible to separate completely the drafted militiamen from the volunteers. Due to desertions and new arrivals, many of the companies underwent reorganization several times during the ensuing weeks, choosing new officers. While the men were being organized, preparations were made on November 8 and 9 for shoeing the horses for the arduous work ahead. Wood was gathered to burn into charcoal, and the shoeing was progressing slowly on the 10th in spite of a cold, drizzling rain, while other men collected the horses and mules left in the vicinity by General Woll.

The Texan forces at San Antonio on November 7 were reported as numbering about 1,200 men, of which about 200 were from Harris

[51] Adams, "[Journal of an] Expedition Against the Southwest," Nov. 7, 1842, ms. See also A. Somervell, General Order No. 1, Head Qrs So. Western Army, San Antonio, Novr 5, 1842, in "A Record Book of the General & Special Orders and Letters of the South Western Army," p. [1], ms.

[52] *Telegraph and Texas Register*, Nov. 23, 1842.

[53] Adams, "[Journal of an] Expedition Against the Southwest," Nov. 11, 1842, ms.

[54] *Ibid.*, Nov. 7, 1842. The law of Jan. 18, 1841, was republished in the *Telegraph and Texas Register*, May 11, 1842.

[55] John Hemphill, Acting Adjutant General, T. M., to M. C. Hamilton, Acting Secretary of War and Marine, Head Quarters, Camp Cooke, near Medina, Nov. 21, 1842, in Texas Congress, *Journals of the House of Representatives of the Seventh Congress*, Appendix, pp. 12–14.

County, 450 from Montgomery County, and 300 from Washington County.[56] The remainder were from the other counties west of the Trinity. These men were formed into one regiment and the skeleton of another, which, reported Somervell, we expect to fill up "in a short time. Re-enforcements are arriving daily."[57] Thirty men from the Lavaca came in on the 10th. The powder and lead had not yet arrived by November 14. The cannon from Gonzales was expected to be brought in on the 15th.

The First Regiment of the First Brigade was made up largely of the drafted militiamen, and was commanded by Colonel Joseph L. Bennett, assisted by Lieutenant Colonel R. J. Gillespie and other officers.[58] It contained six companies whose captains were William Barrett, William Bowen, M. G. McGuffin, Levi Manning, Richard Williams, and Z. Wilson, and there were a few men under Captain Israel Worsham, but it is not known if the latter constituted a regular company.[59] One report from the camp below the San Antonio on November 8 said that the men "were all in good spirits, and pleased with the officers appointed by the President."[60] Other reports, however, mentioned great dissatisfaction among the drafted troops, most of whom, it was said, were desirous to return to their families, "but the volunteers almost to a man" were determined to go to the Río Grande.[61]

The First Regiment of the Second Brigade, made up of volunteers,

[56] *Telegraph and Texas Register,* Nov. 2, 1842.

[57] A. Somervell to Sam Houston, Head Quarters, South Western Army, San Antonio de Béxar, Nov. 7, 1842, in Texas Congress, *Journals of the House of Representatives of the Seventh Congress,* Appendix, pp. 10–11; see also *Telegraph and Texas Register,* Nov. 23, 1842.

[58] Robert Smither, major; R. Oliver, adjutant; J. McCown, quartermaster; C. Heenon, surgeon; and L. G. Weaver, sergeant-major.

[59] For Captain William Barrett's Company, see Public Debt Papers (Texas), ms., of Andrew B. Hanna. Muster Roll of Captain William Bowen's Company, South Western Army, Adjutant General's Office, Austin, August 18, 1851, certified by H. S. Upshur, Actg. Adjt. Gen., and William Bowen, in Militia Rolls (Texas), ms. Bowen says the men actually entered service October 1 [1842] rather than Oct. 27, [1842]. For a list of men in McGuffin's Company, see "Captain M. G. McGuffin's Comp^y Discharges," [Somervell Expedition, 1842], Army Papers (Texas), ms. For Captain Levi Manning's Company, see Public Debt Papers (Texas), ms., of John McGinley and also Army Papers (Texas), ms. See also "Capt. R. Williams Company discharges Somervell Expedition, 1842, and Captain Israel Worshams' Company Discharges [Somervell Expedition, 1842], in Army Papers (Texas), ms. For Muster Rolls, see Appendix C of this work.

[60] *Telegraph and Texas Register,* Nov. 23, 1842.

[61] *Ibid.*

chose for their commanding officer Colonel James R. Cook of Washington County (who had been appointed acting inspector general and mustering officer); and as lesser officers they elected George Thomas Howard of San Antonio, lieutenant colonel; David Murphee of Victoria, major; Captain W. D. Houghton, adjutant; W. R. Cook, surgeon; William Needham, quartermaster; and Daniel J. Kiger, sergeant major. This brigade was made up of eleven companies whose captains were Phillip H. Coe of Washington County; E. Sterling C. Robertson of Washington County, who was then only twenty-two years old and had been assistant secretary to the Senate of the Sixth Congress; William S. Fisher of Washington County;[62] Isaac N. Mitchell of Lavaca (John Henry Brown was largely instrumental in raising this company and then having Mitchell, who later married Brown's cousin Mary A. Kerr, elected captain; Brown, himself, by his own choice, was elected first sergeant);[63] Clark L. Owen of Jackson County; Jerome B. Robertson, county treasurer of Fayette County, whose men were formerly commanded by William P. Rutledge; Gardiner Smith, whose illness caused the active command of the company to devolve upon First Lieutenant Thomas S. Lubbock;[64] Ewen Cameron with his Victoria "Cow Boys" (or, "Menslayers"); John Shelby McNiell of Brazoria County;[65] William M. Eastland of Fayette County; and William M. Ryon of Fort Bend County.[66] The county designations following the captain's name do not necessarily

[62] Brown, *History of Texas*, II, 233–234. See also A. Somervell, General Order No. 10, Head Qrs, Camp Hope, San Antonio River, Novr 10, 1842; A. Somervell, General Order No. 11, Head Quarters, Camp Hope, San Antonio River, Novr 11, 1842, in "A Record Book of the General & Special Orders and Letters of the South Western Army," pp. 7–10, ms.

[63] John Henry Brown "Autobiography," ms.

[64] Captain Gardiner Smith was left sick at Gonzales and his company was commanded by First Lieutenant Thomas S. Lubbock, with E. M. Haines as second lieutenant and Lewis B. Harris as first sergeant, Memucan Hunt to Francis Moore, Jr., Editor of the *Telegraph*, Camp Leon, Southwestern Army, Nov. 16, 1842, *Telegraph and Texas Register*, Dec. 21, 1842; Brown, *History of Texas*, II, 233–234.

[65] Moses Austin Bryan, brother of Guy M. Bryan, served as first lieutenant of the Brazoria company. Guy M. Bryan to Rutherford B. Hayes, Peach Point, near Brazoria, Texas, Jan. 21, 1843, in Winkler (ed.), "The Bryan-Hayes Correspondence," *Southwestern Historical Quarterly*, XXV (1921–1922), 103–107.

[66] M. C. Hamilton to Brig.-Gen. A. Somervell, Washington, Oct. 19, 1842, *Writings of Sam Houston*, III, 187–188; Brown, *History of Texas*, II, 234; Stapp, *Prisoners of Perote*, p. 22; Memucan Hunt to Francis Moore, Jr., Editor of the *Telegraph*, Camp Leon, South-Western Army, Nov. 16, 1842, *Telegraph and Texas Register*, Dec. 21, 1842.

mean that each man in the company was from that county, although this was generally the case.

These, however, were not all the companies at San Antonio at the time of the first organization. There was the regular ranger company under Major John C. Hays, which, at first, numbered only eighteen men. Its first lieutenant was Henry E. McCulloch, who had originally enrolled on September 12 as a member of Captain Albert C. Horton's company of volunteers.[67] Ephraim W. McLean served as second lieutenant under Hays, and James W. ("Smokey") Henderson as first sergeant. Re-enforcements were arriving daily, and evenutally Hays' company was built up to approximately sixty men.

Since it was contemplated that the Texan expedition should be assembled at some point other than San Antonio, Jack Hays, who had been promoted to the rank of major after the Woll invasion,[68] received instructions to establish martial law in Béxar County and to turn all straggling troops over to General Somervell, and if the latter moved his troops toward the Río Grande, Hays was to report to the general and act under his orders.[69] The establishment of martial law in the San Antonio area was necessitated by "the exposed situation of Béxar County, the confusion and disorder represented among the citizens, the civil officers, having been captured by the enemy or ceased to exercise the functions of their offices, and the facilities afforded the enemy for communication and observation, and to protect the driving of cattle, thence, to the Río Grande."[70] When Somervell selected San Antonio as his headquarters, Major Hays properly turned his instructions on the matter of martial law over to Somervell, the senior officer. Although Somervell instituted martial law in the area, it was not vigorously enforced.

Working with Hays' scouts was a small group of Lipans under the young Chief Flacco, who had sworn lasting hostility to the Mexicans for having intercepted and annihilated a party of Lipans en route to join the Apaches.[71] In recognition of his previous services to the Government of

[67] Muster Roll, Capt. Albert C. Horton's Company of Volunteers, subject to direction of Genl. A. Somervell, Sept. 12, 1842, enrolled Matagorda County, 12th Sept. 1842, in Militia Rolls (Texas), ms.

[68] J. D. Affleck, "History of John C. Hays," pt. I, p. 210.

[69] M. C. Hamilton to Brig.-Gen. A. Somervell, Department of War and Marine, Washington, Nov. 19, 1842, *Writings of Sam Houston*, III, 197–199.

[70] M. C. Hamilton to Sam Houston, Dept. of War and Marine, Washington, Nov. 12, 1842, in Texas Congress, *Journals of the House of Representatives of the Seventh Congress*, Appendix, p. 33.

[71] *Telegraph and Texas Register*, Jan. 11, 1843. The Lipans were the most

Texas, Flacco had been accorded the title of "Colonel" and presented with a full colonel's uniform, including a sword and a plumed hat. These he kept stored in a rawhide box and donned only on occasions of ceremony.[72] The Lipans were the easternmost division of the Apache family, but were friendly to the Texans, and often while boasting of their valor threatened to exterminate both Mexicans and Comanches. In 1840 they numbered about two hundred warriors and ranged the country between the Guadalupe and the Río Grande.[73] One of their principal camping spots in 1842 was at the springs at the head of the San Marcos River.

In San Antonio also was Captain Samuel Bogart's company which remained unattached to a brigade. Samuel Bogart[74] of Washington County had been one of "the first to appear in the rescue of Old *Paint* [Caldwell],"[75] and had stayed on at San Antonio after many of the volunteers had returned home following the withdrawal of General Woll. His company, also, numbered approximately sixty men. On November 7 Bogart's Company was accorded the privilege of acting as an independent spy company. On Sunday, November 13, his company was paraded at headquarters, Camp Hope, on the San Antonio River, and the horses were inspected, following which seventeen of the men were ordered to fall out and go into the Regiment, "but none of them would do so," reported Adams, "having sworn to stick together to the death and also having been the first volunteers" to appear on the frontier. General Somervell then ordered Bogart and his men to fall in under Major Hays, but Bogart thought that this was going back on the general's previous promise for his company to act as an independent spy company, and refused to do so, saying "that he would go on his own hook or go home with his company," unless he was given equal footing with Hays' Company.[76] Accordingly, the next morning Bogart led his

---

numerous of all the Apaches. The most formidable enemy of the Apaches for many decades had been the Comanches.

[72] Noah Smithwick, *The Evolution of a State*, pp. 221–224. See also A. Somervell, General Order No. 45, Head Quarters, Camp Murphree on the Atascoso, Nov[r] 26, 1842, in "A Record Book of the General & Special Orders and Letters of the South Western Army," pp. 31–33, ms.

[73] *Telegraph and Texas Register,* June 10, 1840.

[74] For a short biographical sketch of Samuel Bogart and his previous military career, see the *Southwestern Historical Quarterly*, XXIII (1919–1920), 117.

[75] Adams, "[Journal of an] Expedition Against the Southwest," Nov. 7, 1842.

[76] *Ibid.*, Nov. 13, 1842. See also A. Somervell, General Order No. 14, Head Quarters, Camp Hope, San Antonio River, Nov[r] 12, 1842, in "A Record Book of

men into San Antonio, where Somervell had gone, to confer personally with Somervell and succeeded in obtaining equal status with Hays, but not equality in rank. Hays had seniority and the blessing of General Somervell and was to head the spy organization of the army. Bogart finally agreed to march under Major Hays' orders, provided that when the spies went forward to reconnoitre they would be drawn equally from both companies and the spoils would be shared equally by all members of the two companies.[77] When the commanding officer of one company was out with the spies, the other was to command the remnants of the two companies left behind.[78]

Hays was ordered to move his command on November 14 by way of the Laredo road to the Medina, from there to proceed slowly up the bank of the Medina to where the Presidio road crossed the river, and to reconnoitre the country between the Medina and the Arroyo Hondo. If he thought it advisable, he was authorized to send scouts as far as the Río Frio in an effort to apprehend any and all persons who might be passing from or to the Río Grande settlements.[79]

News of the assembling of a large force at Béxar for an invasion of Mexico reached General Isidro Reyes, commander-in-chief of the Mexican Army of the North, and caused him to pen a stirring appeal to the Mexicans to rise to the defense of "the integrity of our territory from Texian vandalism, [and impose] an insuperable barrier to the immoral rapacity of the barbarous Pirates of the North."[80] He hastily assured the Supreme Government that if "the Knight errants of Texas should dare to invade the frontier . . . they will be exemplarily punished." In order

the General & Special Orders and Letters of the South Western Army," p. 13, ms.

[77] Adams, "[Journal of an] Expedition Against the Southwest," Nov. 14, 1842, ms. E. W. Winkler (ed.), "Sterling Brown Hendricks' Narrative of the Somervell Expedition to the Río Grande, 1842," *Southwestern Historical Quarterly*, XXIII (1919–1920), 117. See also A. Somervell, General Order No. 18, Head Quarters, Camp León, near San Antonio, Novr 13, 1842, in "A Record Book of the General & Special Orders and Letters of the South Western Army," pp. 14–16, ms.

[78] Adams, "[Journal of an] Expedition Against the Southwest," Nov. 16, 1842, ms.

[79] A. Somervell, General Order No. 18, Head Quarters, Camp León, near San Antonio, Novr 13, 1842, in "A Record Book of the General & Special Orders and Letters of the South Western Army," pp. 14–16, ms.

[80] Quoted from *El Nacional* (Jalapa), Dec. 15, 1842, in the *Morning Star* (Houston), Jan. 26, 1843; *Telegraph and Texas Register*, Feb. 1, 1843. In May 1844, Reyes was appointed Minister of War, succeeding General Tornel, who, according to C. M. Bustamante, Santa Anna thought was getting too rich. George L. Rives, *The United States and Mexico, 1821–1848*, I, 653.

to protect the frontier more effectively, Reyes established his headquarters and the troops under his immediate command at the Paso del
Aguila on December 2, from which point he could operate either upon
San Fernando or the Presidio del Río Grande. Reyes had two small detachments stationed at the crossings of the Nueces and outposts placed
at the crossings of the Río Grande to give warning of the enemy's approach.[81]

General Woll hurriedly left San Fernando for Monterey to seek
re-enforcements and on November 1 was reported to have taken up
position at Lampazos.[82] The whole Mexican force east of the mountains, it was estimated in Texas on the basis of reports from Matamoros,
would scarcely number three thousand men, of which some five hundred
were at Matamoros.

San Antonio de Béxar, called indiscriminately San Antonio, San Fernando de Béxar, and Béxar, was located on the eastern edge of the Edwards Plateau in the midst of a large fertile plain, surrounded by a chain
of low hills. In 1842 the town covered about one-half of a peninsula
formed by a horseshoelike bend of the beautiful San Antonio River,
which broke out of the hills (or mountains) in a series of springs about
three miles above the city and was never affected by high or low water.
The river was as clear as a crystal, and one could easily see the pebbles
at the bottom in thirty feet of water. The principal spring, at Camp
Cooke, gushed from the earth in a fountain several feet in diameter. On
the southern side of the town flowed San Pedro Creek.

As one approached from the east he crosssed the Salado, another
beautiful crystal stream, some six or seven miles from San Antonio, and
commenced ascending one or another of the several hills which overlook
the city. Arriving at the top of one of these, the traveler viewed a prospect whose beauty can scarcely be imagined: a fertile valley or basin
some ten or fifteen miles in diameter, girdled on the west and north by
an arc of mountains. Between the Salado and the city were scattered
hills, deep valleys, and a soil that was generally black, covered with flint
pebbles, and with dense thickets of mesquite, prickly pear, and other
prairie growth; here and there appeared large cultivated fields, where
in late summer could be seen growing corn, peaches, watermelons,

[81] Isidro Reyes to the Secretary of War and Marine, Head Quarters of the Army
of the North, Passo de Aguila, Dec. 5, 1842, from *Diario del Gobierno*, translated
in *Telegraph and Texas Register*, Feb. 1, 1843.
[82] *Telegraph and Texas Register*, Nov. 23, 1842.

muskmelons, figs, and wild grapes in abundance.[83] To the east and southeast the terrain was quite elevated and from there the town had the appearance of lying in a depressed plain. To the south and west the country seemed to flatten out, but on the north and northwest the hills rose gradually, culminating in low mountains in the distance. As the traveler drew nearer to the city, he came in sight of the missions and churches, lifting their spires into the air far above the surrounding objects and presenting a beautiful picture. Upon examination at close range, one found the walls of these buildings covered with mould, grass, moss, and vines, and parts of them crumbling with age and decay, and inhabited by thousands of bats.

San Antonio de Béxar had been founded by the Spaniards in 1718 as one of several military outposts to protect the northern frontier of New Spain from French and English encroachment. From 1773 to 1824 it was the capital of the province of Texas; but in 1824 under the new Mexican constitution Texas and Coahuila were joined in statehood, and San Antonio lost its importance as a capital, although it remained the chief Mexican stronghold in Texas and the center of local government until 1836. In 1840 San Antonio had an estimated population of two thousand (nine-tenths of whom were Mexican or part Mexican), scattered for a mile along the cool spring-fed river, whose "bosom of blue reflected a panoramic view of the firmament."[84] San Antonio was incorporated by an act of the Texas Congress approved January 4, 1842.[85]

As the volunteers approached San Antonio from the north, one of the first objects to strike their attention was the ruins of the old fortified mission of the Alamo, standing at the northeast corner of the town about two hundred yards from the opposite side of the river.[86] The Alamo was an immense, irregular stone edifice, once surrounded by a thick wall ten to fifteen feet high, enclosing about three acres of ground. The walls had been entirely battered down, and the main edifice itself was but a pile of ruins.[87] Visible were the remains of some twelve or fifteen apartments separated by stone walls several feet thick. Since 1836, the

[83] John W. Dancy, Diary, Aug. 5, 7, and 8, 1838, ms.; "Extracts from a Traveller's Journal," in *Morning Star* (Houston), May 13, 1839.

[84] John C. Reid, *Reid's Tramp, or a Journal of . . . Travel through Texas, New Mexico, Arizona, Sonora, and California*, pp. 61–62.

[85] H. P. N. Gammel (ed.), *Laws of Texas*, II, 704–706.

[86] Frank W. Johnson, *A History of Texas and Texans*, I, 441, contains R. M. Potter's description and diagram of the Alamo in 1841.

[87] "Sketches of Travel in Texas by the Editor of the American Eagle," *Telegraph and Texas Register*, Aug. 17, 1842.

damaged roof of the Alamo, which had fallen in in 1762, had undergone minor repairs and the fortification had been improved by the western rangers, and was not in quite as bad condition as when the troops of General Juan José Andrade left it in 1836.[88] In 1842 the Alamo was a short distance from the inhabited portion of the town, with "a mesquite thicket" and a few jacales intervening.[89] To the east, about six-tenths of a mile away, stood the old Powder House. Alamo Plaza contained nothing more than the convent, and some old broken-down walls and ruins. Numberless heaps of ruins within the town and its vicinity marked the places where houses had once stood. The town, built after the style of the ancient Moorish or Spanish towns, was oblong in form, and on the east extended into the bend of the river. There were no houses west of the San Pedro. The streets of the city, reported a soldier, are "unpaved, irregular, narrow and crooked. When wet they were excessively muddy—and owing to the great quantities of lime contained in it, it sticks to your feet with a tenacity, the like of which, I have never elsewhere seen"[90]

In the center of the town an oblong space of some sixteen acres was divided into two equal portions by a number of buildings, including the old, dilapidated[91] cathedral of San Fernando. The eastern portion of this space was known as the civil plaza (Plaza de las Islas or, sometimes, Plaza de Constitución), and the western, as the military plaza (Plaza de las Armas). The cathedral, with its three bells which rang every morning and evening for mass, fronted on the civil plaza with its rear touching upon military plaza.[92] Both plazas had been laid off in 1731. Around the whole extent of the two plazas was erected a continuous wall of mud and stone houses. From the exterior this row of houses, with their rough walls (about twenty feet high, dotted here and there by a door), their flat roofs (obscured by a parapet wall) and their port holes, resembled an impregnable fortification; "while on the interior with their plastered

[88] Juan José Andrade, *Documentos que pública sobre la Evacuación de la ciudad de San Antonio de Béjar del Departamento de Téjas a sus compatriotas.* This was Andrade's official report of the dismantling of the Alamo, the evacuation of San Antonio, and the retreat of the Mexican garrison out of Texas.

[89] W. P. Zuber, "The Escape of Rose from the Alamo," *Quarterly of the Texas State Historical Association,* V (1901–1902), 2–3.

[90] William A. McClintock, "Journal of a Trip through Texas and Northern Mexico in 1846–1847," *Southwestern Historical Quarterly,* XXXIV (1930–1931), 147.

[91] Dancy, Diary, Aug. 12, 1838, ms.

[92] Charles I. Sellon to Marilla ———, San Antonio de Béxar, Texas, Sept. 6, 1846, *Southwestern Historical Quarterly,* XLVII (1943–1944), 63.

fronts, large windows and spacious corridors they present[ed] at once an appearance of comfort, uniformity and security."⁹³ Not a solitary window in the exterior walls invoked the blessed breeze or even the sunlight. Even the better houses were clumsily built of stone and siliceous, pebbly cement, dug out of the earth. They were but one-story high with walls several feet thick and some twenty to twenty-five feet high, forming a parapet above the roof. The roof itself was made of thatched flags, rushes, palmetto, or cane, covered over several inches thick with a sort of sandy sub-cement and thus making the dwellings fire-proof. In some cases there were no windows—the front and back doors serving to supply both light and air. The ground, or dirt floor, and thick stone or adobe walls made the houses remarkably cool and pleasant in the hottest weather. The poorer buildings, wrote a visitor in 1840, "are for the most part miserable huts built of crooked musket logs stuck endwise into the ground, [and bound together with strips of raw oxhide] the crevices filled with clay, without windows, with dirt floors, and for the most part thatched with prairie grass, or bull rushes."⁹⁴ In his "rambles and scrambles" through Texas, Page described the huts of the masses in San Antonio as follows:

The frail cabins of the frail and imbecile occupants—half Mexican [Spaniard?], half Indian, and who are as idle and lazy as may well be—are indiscriminately made of adobes (unburnt brick), tapia, mud, and reeds, with thatched roofs, and now and then a buffalo-hide to fill up a crevice and keep out the sun [and water]. . . . They seldom have other than dirt floors, with deer or buffalo-skins spread out for carpets, and which serve the double purpose of bed and chairs; and where the indolent occupant spends most of his time, like the Turk in dreaming away his existence over his chocolate and cigarrito, in preference to coffee and the pipe. He knows no care but rejoices like the Persian at the rising, and the Swiss at setting sun. . . . Music and dancing, hunting and the chase, cards and love, make up their whole existence.⁹⁵

As has been indicated, the eastern, or civil square, was surrounded on three sides by one-story, mud or stone houses with flat roofs. The fourth

⁹³ *Austin City Gazette,* June 10, 1840.

⁹⁴ *Ibid.* See also Adams, "[Journal of an] Expedition Against the Southwest," Oct. 5, 1842, ms.; Amelia Williams, "A Critical Study of the Siege of the Alamo and the Personnel of Its Defenders," *Southwestern Historical Quarterly,* XXXVI (1932-1933), 266.

⁹⁵ [Frederic Benjamin Page], *Prairiedom: Rambles and Scrambles in Texas or New Estremadura by a Suthron,* pp. 127–128.

or western side was occupied by the old church of San Fernando built in Spanish style with a low tower above the entrance. Its turrets, belfrys, and massive, sombre walls made it an object of interest. A number of the houses were in themselves small fortresses with thick walls and few windows. Those surrounding the square and the church, which occupied the center of the town, were perforated by hundreds of musket and cannon shots. Often the effects of the shots had been nothing more than to knock off pieces of stucco from the stone walls which were three feet thick. The walls of the houses were raised as parapets, three or four feet above the roof. Only a few of the houses had windows, and even these were protected by strong iron bars. "I've seen the bars of these windows," wrote McClintock, "cut in two by cannon shot. Even the bells of the chapel have been broken, three or four at least, by shot —the stucco of the belfry is [as] full of holes as a honeycomb."[96]

The main street of San Antonio ran along the north side of the squares. The suburbs on the eastern bank of the beautiful blue-green waters of the San Antonio River, where a considerable portion of the population resided, reached on both sides of the road from the Alamo to the full extent of the city. *Acequias* conducting drinking water from the San Pedro Springs and the upper San Antonio River traversed the city. The river afforded delightful bathing at all seasons of the year, and at all hours of the day and night parties of both sexes could be seen enjoying this luxury. The ladies of the town wore loose robes while bathing in the river. The streets of the city were generally unpaved, and the place, as a whole, gave the impression of decay. There were no bridges across the San Antonio River or San Pedro Creek.[97] The inhabitants crossed on logs laid across the river.

In August 1842, it was said,[98] San Antonio contained a Mexican population of between fifteen hundred and two thousand inhabitants; whereas, before the revolution it had possessed a population of something like twice that number. The few American families who had resided

[96] McClintock, "Journal of a Trip through Texas and Northern Mexico," in *Southwestern Historical Quarterly*, XXXIV (1930–1931), 146.

[97] The City Council of San Antonio began consideration on September 9, 1841, of the construction of a permanent bridge across the San Antonio River for public use in the most suitable street, and on October 16 approved plans for a bridge presented by Roderick F. Higginbotham. San Antonio, "Journal A, Records of the City of San Antonio," Sept. 9 and Oct. 16, 1841, ms.

[98] "Sketches of Travel in Texas" by the Editor of the *American Eagle*, in *Telegraph and Texas Register*, Aug. 17, 1842.

there had all abandoned the place in consequence of the war difficulties, there being in late July and early August only twenty or thirty young Americans living there, and these were continually moving in and out as the chances of invasion ebbed and flowed.

The population of San Antonio [wrote a visitor] is divided into three classes. The third is the connecting link between the savages and the Mexicans, and are termed Rancheros (or herdsmen), a rude uncultivated, fearless race of beings, who spend the greater part of their lives in the saddle, hurding [*sic*] their cattle and horses, and in hunting deer and buffalo or pursuing mustangs, with which that country so fully abounds. Unused to comfort, and regardless alike of ease and danger they have a hardy, brigand, sunburnt appearance, especially when seen with a broad slouched hat, a red or striped shirt, deer skin trowsers [*sic*] and Indian mockasins [*sic*].

The second are a link between the Mexican and the Spaniard, or Castilian, and are somewhat more civilized, more superstitious, owing to the influence of the priest, and yet possessed of less bravery, less generosity and far less energy than the former. They reside in the city with but very scanty, visible means of support, and without the least effort to procure the comforts of life; still they vegitate, and appear to be perfectly independent and contented, [in their lazy, indolent state]. Their usual dress is a broad brim white hat, a roundabout, calico shirt, and wide trowsers [*sic*] with a red sash or girdle around the waist. At hour of day [daybreak] they go to mass, then loiter out the morning [sometimes cultivating the small gardens adjacent to the huts], sleep through the afternoon, and spend the night in gaming, dissipating and dancing—but they drink but little ardent liquor. Almost entirely uneducated completely cut off from all intercourse with the world . . . and therefore deprived of the common means of intelligence, they have no enterprise or public zeal, no curiosity, but little patriotism,—know nothing of government and laws, and seem incapable of feeling themselves, or appreciating in others those lofty aspirations which fire the brain, warm the heart, nerve the arm and burn in the bosom of a freeman. With apparent good nature, and much awkward courtesy, they are yet treacherous and deceptive, and can no more stand the frank honest gaze of a real white man, than a fox can the eye of a lion. The wives and daughters of the Rancheros are as rough and uncouth as their husbands and fathers, and disdain those light and polite amusements that generally amuse their sex. But the females of the second class are agreeable, handsome and fascinating, although not particularly accomplished. They dress plain and tastefully, and in a style best calculated to develop the elegant proportion of their persons. Generally poor, they of course wear but few costly jewels, yet with much good sense seem to consider their own natural charms (which border on the voluptousness) as the richest ornaments that can adorn a woman, and as those surest to attract the notice and secure the attention of the rougher portion of humanity. This class are the votaries of the Fandangoes for which San Antonio is so justly distinguished. . . .

The first class now reduced to but a limited number is composed of the direct lineal descendents [*sic*] of Spanish Dons and Castilian nobles, who though stript of the titles and prerogatives which they enjoyed under a royal government, yet retain their dignity, their loyalty, and their fortunes, and keeping aloof from the two degenerate and subordinate classes already described, and are content to live in ease and aristocratic retirement. While a bench or two, a *matato,* for grinding corn, a copper kettle, an earthen jar, and a few cow hides and Mexican blankets spread on a dirt floor with a shelf of clothes and a saddle and larreito, are the articles of furniture usually found in the thatched hovels and stone huts of the two first classes: the comfortable dwellings of the first [class] are supplied with most of the comforts and many articles of taste and elegance. In this class may be found gentlemen of education and talents, of polished manners and refined and hospitable feelings, and if the females in the second class are handsome and fascinating, those in the first class are splendid and irresistibly captivating. Having been educated in the city of Mexico, the United States, or Europe, they have with perhaps a few exceptions, travelled much, seen much of the world—and those superlative advantages with which nature has gifted them, have been cultivated, cherished, and embellished until they exceed in appearance, and equal in capacity, . . . [most women].[99]

Somervell took up his headquarters in San Antonio for approximately two weeks, and was accused of receiving "the hospitalities of those very individuals who just before had been foremost in entertaining General Woll."[100] Such accusations usually stemmed from the anti-Houston faction, however, and since there was much criticism of Somervell's appointment to head up the expedition, their accusations are probably not to be relied upon.

He was accused of attending the nightly fandangos held at various places in the city and of dancing with black-eyed *señoritas* to the tune of a fiddle or violin. One of the famous spots for dancing the cotillion and waltz was a house on the square near the church, managed by Doña Andrea Candelaria, "patroness of the fandango," who was described by Auguste Fretelliere in 1844 as "a Mexican woman in the forties, with black hair, . . . bright eyes, extraordinary activity, above all with the most agile of tongues."[101] Dancing took place in a long, narrow

[99] "Comanche Expedition, and a Glance at San Antonio, the Alamo, and the Dilapidated Missions [in 1840]," *Austin City Gazette,* June 10, 1840.
[100] Green, *Journal of the Texian Expedition Against Mier,* p. 41.
[101] Julia Nott Waugh, *Castro-Ville and Henry Castro, Empresario,* p. 93.

room, level with the ground, dimly lit by several wax candles fastened to the wall—a sort of combination gambling hall, pastry shop, and dance hall.

Conducted with much decorum and yet without such useless restraints as announcements, bows, and introductions, the Fandangoes were well calculated to afford rare sport for a company of young volunteers and so omnipotent was their influence over the ladies, and so terrible their appearance with pistols and bowie knives to drill brown skin gallants that the arrival of a single platoon was sufficient to clear the room of every soul of the latter, except a few who loafed around as silent and disinterested spectators.[102]

[The] belles and beauties of San Antonio looked like a band of Houries from fabled land of the east, or like an assemblage of young princesses of some royal house. They were all so young, so lovely, so splendid and so noble, and yet so very natural and unaffected—they smiled with such exquisite sweetness, laughed with such delight, and their voices possessed such melody, mein so artless, danced so divinely, and spoke broken english so prettily that more than . . . [one] of our troopers lost their hearts . . . and have nearly sighed themselves to death.[103]

While the violin or guitar players strummed a monotonous piece of music over and over again, the Mexicans and Anglo-Texans crowded around a few tables at which games of chance were being played. Monte, a game of cards, was the favorite, and gold and silver changed hands rapidly. Occasionally a loitering spectator or player, doffing his wide sombrero, would turn to one of the belles of San Antonio patiently waiting, dressed in their best apparel, on one of the benches at the end of the room and ask for a dance with the damsel with jet black braids and dark eyes flashing beneath drooping lashes. Then the lean, sinewy, and graceful gentleman-cowboy, soldier, and adventurer would glide skillfully over the floor with a brown, blunt-nosed *señorita* in a blue challis dress, to the twang of the guitar and jingle of silver spurs about high-heeled boots. The dance was not always a fandango, as one would suppose from the name, "but a peculiar contradance which moved in rather slow tempo, but despite its simplicity was not an unpleasant sight."[104] After the dance, the gentleman led his partner to a corner of the room where the proprietor of the fandango tended a bar,

[102] "Comanche Expedition, and a Glance at San Antonio, the Alamo, and the Dilapidated Missions [in 1840]," *Austin City Gazette*, June 10, 1840.
[103] *Austin City Gazette*, June 10, 1842.
[104] Ferdinand Roemer, *Texas with Particular Reference to German Immigration and the Physical Appearance of the Country Described through Observation*, p. 122.

and where the gentleman was expected to treat his partner to a glass of wine, or something stronger if desired or, should she prefer, she joined him in a smoke, or at the end of each set would take him by the arm and deliberately conduct him to a table near the gambling tables, for the selection of refreshments of the simplest kind, usually small cakes which were sold by an old Mexican woman. The girl selected a piece of pastry and her dancing partner would pay for it. In this manner the proprietor was re-imbursed and fandangoes were popularized. "However, as a rule the refreshments were not eaten by the girls, but tied in a cloth which evidently had been brought along for this purpose. Each new dance added another piece to the supply and at the end of the dance, all was carried home, which, after all," reported Roemer, the German colonization official, "was the real purpose for attending the dance."[105] At the end of the fandango, the dancers paid the fiddler, treated their partners, paired off by twos, and "silently though not very sentimentally striking," shuffled off "by the light of the stars to every quarter of the city."[106] Among the Mexican population of the city it was not uncommon to play and dance all night, and for a siesta to sleep away the greater portion of the ensuing day. "They sleep with the sun and wake with the moon," reported a traveler.[107]

Early in 1841 the Mavericks gave a party, at which "some natives remained so late in the morning that we had to ask them to go," wrote Mrs. Maverick in her memoirs. "One man of reputable standing carried off a roast chicken in his pocket, another a carving knife, and several others took off all the cake they could well conceal, which greatly disgusted Jinny Anderson, the cook. Griffin [our faithful slave] followed the man with the carving knife and took it away from him." A few months later when President Lamar visited San Antonio, a ball was given for him early in June. John D. Morris, the Adonis of the ball, escorted on that occasion Miss Arceneiga, who "on that warm evening wore a maroon cashmere with black plumes in her hair, and her haughty airs did not gain her any friends. Mrs. Yturri had a new silk, fitting her so tightly that she had to wear corsets for the first time in her life. She was very pretty, waltzed beautifully and was much sought as a partner. She was several times compelled to escape to her bedroom to take off the corset and 'catch her breath'."[108]

[105] *Ibid.*, p. 123.
[106] *Austin City Gazette*, June 10, 1840.
[107] [Page], *Prairiedom*, p. 44.
[108] Green (ed.), *Memoirs of Mrs. Mary A. Maverick*, p. 56.

Another form of amusement, in addition to the celebration of the numerous saints' days, was the regular Sunday cock-fight. As each man went to church on Sunday morning he staked his rooster out on the sidewalk in front of the saloon near the church, entered the cathedral of San Fernando and fervently offered up his prayers, including a secret one for a victory for his cock in the fight that was soon to ensue in the shadow of the belfry tower. Impatiently the benediction was awaited. No sooner were the religious services over than the betting commenced on the cocks soon to be pitted against one another in a fight to the death.

Instead of concentrating his forces, and organizing, drilling, and moulding them into a well disciplined unit, Somervell, contrary to orders, took up his headquarters in town for approximately two weeks, where his supposed fraternizing, or "feasting and fandangoing" with the suspected enemies of the Republic did not increase the average volunteer's respect for this unpopular commander. One month and one day from the time Somervell was ordered to think in terms of advancing to the Río Grande, he reached San Antonio, where, in view of Burleson's announcement, it was expected that the troops should concentrate at Béxar by October 25. Word had gone forth through the land that Somervell had orders to lead an expedition against northern Mexico. Even after Somervell arrived on the frontier it took a week to organize the forces there, and further delays were encountered by waiting for lead, powder, and the cannon from Gonzales. Finally, on November 12, the day after the organization of the force had been effected, the army was moved to the León, seven miles from town.[109]

The assembling of the Texan forces near San Antonio was accompanied by the usual amount of intrigue and disorder. "From the time of the first assembly of the troops," says Yoakum, "until their departure, there was much confusion arising out of a want of provisions and ammunition, but, above all, from the insubordination and ambitious pretensions of various persons in the army, who, feeling themselves competent to assume the direction of the entire force, and march them to victory over the whole of Mexico, were surprised and indignant that the command was not conferred on them."[110] Although regarded by

---

[109] A. Somervell, General Order No. 10, Head Q^{rs}, Camp Hope, San Antonio River, Novr 10, 1842, in "A Record Book of the General & Special Orders and Letters of the South Western Army," pp. 7–8, ms.

[110] H. Yoakum, *History of Texas*, II, 368.

many as "an officer of courage and ability,"[111] Somervell's indifference
and lack of interest in the campaign caused much murmuring and gave
encouragement to the ambitious malcontents. Popular sentiment was
in favor of making General Edward ("Ned") Burleson, Vice President
of the Republic, commander of the expedition. Consequently, some of
the volunteers, hoping to have their own commander or none, refused
to report to Somervell upon his arrival; yet, they were permitted to
remain in camp subsisting upon the meager supplies which should have
been reserved exclusively to more willing hands.[112] The dissension
among the volunteers was no more than could be expected in a country
where there was no union, harmony, or concert among the leaders; and
especially was difficulty to be expected in a new state infested with a
class of noisy, second-rate men, who were often in favor of rash and
extreme measures.[113] Burleson, the favorite of the west, was described
by the United States chargé d'affaires in Texas, Joseph Eve, as having
the support of "many of the most tallented, influential, and wealthy
Citizens," and, of course, the "war party" generally preferred his leadership. There was an atmosphere of impetuosity about these young
volunteers, many of whom had been friends and supporters of the
Lamar Administration. They had no patience with the dilly dallying
and crafty caution of the Houston regime. They desired revenge and
hoped to wring from Mexico a prompt and categorical acknowledgment
of Texan independence. Eve wrote President Tyler that the government of Texas might "be well compared to a ship upon a stormy sea
without sail or ballast where every mariner claims to be pilot, and where
it requires great firmness, prudence and tallents to save it from being
capsized by the waves of popular dissension, or strand[ed] upon the
beach by the Mexican bayonet."[114]

Pending the arrival of additional forces and the cannon there was
much lingering about San Antonio; and with only a minimum of drilling,

[111] Stapp, *Prisoners of Perote*, p. 22; see also Hubert Howe Bancroft, *History of Texas and the North Mexican States*, II, 359; Winkler (ed.), "Hendricks' Narrative," *Southwestern Historical Quarterly*, XXIII (1919–1920), 116–118.

[112] M. C. Hamilton to Brig.-Gen. A. Somervell, Department of War and Marine, Washington, Nov. 19, 1842, *Writings of Sam Houston*, III, 197–199.

[113] Gambrell, *Anson Jones*, p. 31.

[114] Joseph Eve to John Tyler, Legation of the United States, Galveston, Oct. 11, 1842 (Private), in Joseph Milton Nance (ed.), "A Letter Book of Joseph Eve, United States Chargé d'Affaires to Texas," *Southwestern Historical Quarterly*, XLIV (1940–1941), 96–100.

poorly organized and conducted without regularity, the men became restless and discontented. Moving camp every few days gave some training in operating as a unit and in movement on a trail. On other occasions the men were paraded on horseback and put "through several evolutions making sham charges and dismounting and trailing . . . arms on foot, at . . . full speed."[115] Some effort was made to drill the men "in marching, wheelings, extensions, the movements in line and column, from line into column and the reverse," and in how to deploy themselves in meeting cavalry.[116]

For the want of something to do the men in small groups visited the historic sites—the missions, the Alamo, the springs above town (where an effort had been made, several years before, to project a new town called Avoca) and the beautiful scenery about and above them, and other places of interest—sometimes they carved their names on the edifices, or broke or cut off pieces of beautiful carving as souvenirs. Bill Bates from San Augustine fixed a purchase to enable him to reach the two little images, representing angels, carved in bold relief on each side of the main entrance to the Alamo, and "with his hack knife cut off the two heads of these images and carried them away."[117] There were many souvenir hunters among the Texans on the frontier.[118] Other pieces of wood (carvings or otherwise) were taken from the Alamo and converted into pipes. Harvey Adams cut a picture of "the whole Alamo" on a large pipe, the wood having been taken from one of the two large

---

[115] Adams, "[Journal of an] Expedition Against the Southwest," Oct. 19, 1842, ms.

[116] A. Somervell, General Order No. 13, Head Quarters, Camp Hope, San Antonio River, Novr 12, 1842, in "A Record Book of the General & Special Orders and Letters of the South Western Army," p. 12, ms.

[117] Adams, "[Journal of an] Expedition Against the Southwest," Oct. 12, 1842, ms.

[118] We have lately seen several beautiful miniature monuments, urns, candlesticks, vases, pipes, and other articles carved from the rock composing the walls of the Alamo by Mr. Nangle. [wrote the editor of the *Telegraph* in January 1842] This gentleman with indefatigable industry, has devoted his whole time for the last two years to these pious labors . . . Among other specimen of sculpture that he had completed, is a small monument about six feet high, consisting of a square column supported on a small square pedestal, and terminated by an urn neatly carved. The four faces of the column are ornamented with beautiful devices of various kinds, and appropriate inscriptions. He has also a portion of the soil containing the ashes of the heroes of the Alamo, which he intends to enclose in the monument. Under the expectation that it will be purchased by Congress and placed in the Capitol, he has taken it to Austin, where it is now set up. *Telegraph and Texas Register*, Jan. 26, 1842.

statues lying prostrate on the ground in front of the Alamo, but which at one time had stood on each side of the front arch facing west.[119]

Other men were busily employed in gathering pecans in the nearby creek and river bottoms, which they sold in town for one dollar per bushel, and were thus able to procure coffee, salt, tobacco, and other items for themselves.[120] Captain Pierson went out from camp on his own hook on November 6, and on the 9th three of his men were cut off by the Comanches. One of the three effected his escape into San Antonio, but the fate of the other two was not known on the 10th.[121]

On October 24 a number of the men went into San Antonio. Among these were two young men of Bogart's company from Austin County, E. W. Stevenson and John Atkinson, who, reported Adams,

entered the house of Widdow Smith, said to be the widdow of Deaf Smith, . . . where they laid their hands on and took off three blankets, two of which were *Mexican* and one *Mackinaw*. These were taken off by those boys who call themselves Volunteers for the defence of their country & volunteer their services to steal this covering off the widows and orphans beds, from the Wife of a man who had suffered every privation that was possible for his Country in her hour of peril and died a martyr to patriotism.[122]

The next day Captain Bogart paraded his company, condemned the conduct of Stevenson and Atkinson, ordered the blankets returned to the owner by the two young men under guard, and requested their withdrawal from the company. The culprits returned home. Shortly after this Pierre Gautier and his family, citizens of France living in Béxar, were granted a letter of safe-conduct by General Somervell and permitted to leave for Brazoria County.[123]

As time passed the drafted men became weary with delay, which led to dissatisfaction and a desire to return home; but the volunteers, many of whom had come for glory and a good time, were impatient to go for-

[119] Adams, "[Journal of an] Expedition Against the Southwest," Oct. 12, 1842, ms.

[120] *Ibid.*, Oct. 20 [29th] 1842.

[121] *Ibid.*, Nov. 10, 1842.

[122] *Ibid.*, Oct. 24–25, 1842.

[123] Letter of Safeguard to Mr. Pierre Gautier and Family Given by Brigadier General A. Somervell at Head Quarters, Camp Hope, San Antonio River, Nov. 13, 1842, in Domestic Correspondence (Texas), 1835–1846, ms.; Copy in Domestic Correspondence (Texas), undated, ms., showing "By Command of The General John Hemphill Act'g Adjt Genl. Mr. Guatier's family consisted of himself, wife, two children, and four Mexican servants.

ward.[124] Daily men in "little parties of five or six" began to "slip out of the shuck" and return home.[125] The desertions increased when the rains and "northers" set in, for often the men camped in a "naked prairie" without shelter from the fury of the storm, except for their blankets which too often were thin and scanty. The units scattered their men to enable them to seek whatever protection they could from thickets or brush. If near one of the missions or the Alamo, the men took refuge therein against the elements. The men often stood or squatted near some tree or brush pile when it rained, and afterwards, exhausted, lay down upon the ground wrapped in their wet blankets before a roaring fire to dry and sleep. Occasionally a group of men would pool their blankets and, supplementing them with stretched beef hides, make a tent to keep their small baggage, guns, ammunition, and jerked beef dry; but, as for themselves, only a few of the men could get under the improvised tents at a time, while the rest were compelled to stand and take the inclement weather; but, even so, it was asserted, this was not too bad, for there was need for someone to watch the horses. But be this as it may, standing day or night to take nature's fierce blast of cold rain or piercing north wind, proved too much for more than one man. While there are very few reports of men being sick, and sickness was seldom given as a cause for returning home, desertion was a serious problem with which Somervell and the captains had to contend.

The material from which Somervell recruited his army was on the whole of an inferior grade. The sturdier and more reliable men gradually drifted homeward, leaving a rabble of adventurers and self-willed men unable or unwilling to subordinate their impetuous desires to the general good. Some good, capable, highly respectable men did remain with the force, but they were definitely in a minority by the time the Mier expedition was organized. However, fourteen Texas counties today bear the name of men in that expedition, showing that a number of the men were, or later became, prominent in public affairs.[126]

---

[124] "The Army," *Telegraph and Texas Register*, Nov. 23 and 30, 1842.

[125] *Ibid.*, Nov. 30, 1842; Adams, "[Journal of an] Expedition Against the Southwest," Oct. 1 and 11, 1842, ms. Alfred Hall and Allen Hall turned back before they even reached San Antonio, while William H. Francis and G. W. Cleveland returned from San Antonio. William H. Pearson became sick and returned eastward. For further information on desertion, see A. Somervell, General Order No. 12, Head Quarters, Camp Hope, San Antonio River, Novr 11, 1842, in "A Record Book of the General & Special Orders and Letters of the South Western Army," pp. 10–11, ms.

[126] The names of these men were Peter H. Bell, Ewen Cameron, William G. Cooke, William M. Eastland, George B. Erath, R. A. Gillespie, John C. Hays, John

On the 9th of November the men who had gone out five days earlier from Bogart's company succeeded in getting about eighty head of beef cattle, and the men who went from the Brazoria company got about the same number.

The men from the latter company, have from reports, [recorded Adams], acted very badly, having ventured to force the Mexican families from their homes, [causing them] to droop about in the woods and seek shelter wherever they could find it. Moreover to gratify their beastly lusts [they have] compelled the women and Girls to yield to their hellish desires, which their victims did under fear of punishment and death.[127]

A Mr. Jones, an American, who had spent twenty-nine days in prison with Samuel A. Maverick and others at San Fernando, reached San Antonio on November 13 in company with three Mexicans, explaining that they had escaped from General Woll, who had carried them away from San Antonio by force.[128] They stated that they had been fourteen days on the road from San Fernando, the last seven without anything to eat but pecans. Jones was in such a starved condition that he was taken into the home of the Elliots, where Mrs. Elliot reported she was "doing all in my power to get him strong as General Summerville is most anxious that he . . . accompany our troops to the Río Grande," where he knows the country and the people, having lived two years in northern Mexico. Jones and the Mexicans from the Río Grande informed Somervell that there were no troops at Presidio del Río Grande; and that at San Fernando there were approximately eight hundred men and at Santa Rita de Morelos about two hundred. No other troops were nearer than Monterey. The San Antonio prisoners, they said, had been marched toward Mexico City, except for Van Ness, Fitzgerald, and Hancock,

---

Hemphill, Memucan Hunt, Thomas S. Lubbock, Benjamin McCulloch, Elijah Sterling Clack Robertson, Alexander Somervell, and James C. Wilson.

[127] Adams, "[Journal of an] Expedition Against the Southwest," Nov. 9, 1842, ms.

[128] *Ibid.*, Nov. 14, 1842; Ellen Elliot to Mrs. Samuel A. Maverick, San Antonio de Bejar, Nov. 14, 1842, Rena Maverick Green (ed.), *Samuel Maverick, Texan, 1803–1870: A Collection of Letters, Journals and Memoirs*, pp. 202–204; A. Somervell to Sam Houston, Head Quarters, South Western Army, Leon, 7 miles West of San Antonio de Bexar, in Texas Congress, *Journal of the House of Representatives of the Seventh Congress*, Appendix, pp. 11–12. Somervell says that Jones and the three Mexicans came into the Texan camp on November 12, which may well be the case, since the Texan camp was seven miles west of San Antonio. However, he says they had been five days on the road from Presidio del Río Grande.

formerly Santa Fé prisoners, who were expected to be shot soon. Jones reported an abundance of provisions around Presidio del Río Grande and San Fernando. Jones and the Mexicans joined Hays' spy company and planned to head west with the expedition.

On the 14th of November most of the Texan troops were camped on the León, about seven miles from town, where they were protected by timber. Bogart's company, having gotten the matter of command of the spy company straightened out, headed west to join the army. Passing across a large level plain with scarcely any timber, they arrived at the forested valley of the León, seven miles from town. They crossed the León and encamped on a high tableland with thinly scattered timber, twelve miles from San Antonio.[129] The soil was loose and black, with an abundance of flint pebbles. The men in the army were all well and in fine spirits anxious to move west. The dissatisfied, it was thought, had gone home.[130] A picket guard was maintained throughout the day on a high hill, and at night both picket and camp guards were stationed out. After an early supper, the spy companies took up the line of march at dusk and camped at midnight on the Medina about one-half mile below the San Antonio-Laredo road. The Medina was filled only to the first of its two banks, and the top bank rose some thirty feet above the water. The river abounded in several kinds of fish, and the cypress, pecan, and cottonwood timber along its course afforded protection to an abundance of game—deer, turkey, bear, and various small animals. During the day hunting parties had brought into camp thirteen deer. Late in the afternoon of the next day, while reconnoitring in the vicinity of the camp, Major Hays spied three persons, Mexicans or Indians, but he could not determine which at the distance; so he returned to camp and called for fifteen to twenty volunteers with the best horses to go with him in pursuit. The men were promptly in the saddle and the trail was followed until darkness put an end to their pursuit and they returned to camp.[131] While out they came upon an American horse, but he was too wild, and it was so late in the afternoon that they failed to capture him.

On the 16th Bogart led out the spies. With fifteen men he crossed the Medina for reconnaissance. A heavy mist which had fallen during the night persisted throughout the morning. At 2 P.M. the spies found an

---

[129] Adams, "[Journal of an] Expedition Against the Southwest," Nov. 14, 1842, ms.

[130] *Ibid.*, Nov. 15, 1842.

[131] *Ibid.*

old English musket, which they brought in as a trophy.[132] November 17
arrived and brought with it "a most cutting north wind," which proved
as "uncomfortable to the men without blankets lying still in an open
prairie, as General S[omervell]'s luxurious indulgences in the city were
to those who had blankets."[133] At daybreak the men sought protection
under the bank of the river for themselves and their horses, and at
noon took refuge in a grove of timber one-half mile down the river. Back
in the main camp the men sought shelter in the forested valley of the
León. Many deer had been killed on the previous day, but the piercing
norther now caused even a greater number to lose their hides, under the
circumstances more important than the meat, to the versatile Texas
frontiersman. The hides were dressed for clothing, as many of the early
arrivals were scantily clad and without money to make purchases in
San Antonio from the meager supplies available. While out hunting for
a "buckskin" one of the men wandered too far from camp, and stayed
out all night. The next morning some of his friends were preparing to
go in search of him when he came into camp.[134]

Some of the men lacked shoes and adequate clothing for the late November weather. Sixty men from Harris County were reported to be in
dire need of shoes and coarse woolen pantaloons, and word was sent to
Houston that a little coffee and tobacco would be greatly appreciated
along with the other items. During the cold weather a rumor circulated
through the camp to the effect that the "General" would have been out
"that day" had he not stopped the night before to attend another fandango. Many of the volunteers began to believe that nothing would be
effected by the expedition, while others were more highly indignant at
not being provided with those absolute, indispensable munitions of war
—powder, lead, beef, and bread. Disorder and a rebellious sentiment
among the troops was "occasioned by the insubordinate tendencies of
some persons and the aspirations of others to the chief command."[135]
General Woll had carted off most of the available supplies in the vicinity
of San Antonio, and the "character of the service and the destitute condition of the Government" rendered it almost certain that little else than

---

[132] *Ibid.*, Nov. 16, 1842.

[133] *Ibid.*, Nov. 17, 1842; see also Green, *Journal of the Texian Expedition Against
Mier*, pp. 41–42; *Telegraph and Texas Register*, Dec. 21, 1842.

[134] Adams, "[Journal of an] Expedition Against the Southwest," Nov. 18, 1842,
ms.

[135] Bancroft, *History of Texas and the North Mexican States*, II, 359.

provisions would be furnished the troops.[136] So scarce was the supply of corn in the west that it was found necessary to specifically order that none should be fed to horses. Early in November, in reply to Cooke's request to Major Snively for definite information in regard to supplies of beef and other items for the troops, the Secretary of War declared "it was understood, generally and of course presumed to be by you that the Government had not the means to purchase a single ration, nor would contract liabilities with a promise of immediate or ultimate redemption, since she could make none with the remotest hope of a compliance on her part." It was understood at Washington, he asserted, that "ample supplies of Beef could be furnished and would be contributed by the citizens of the county [Béxar] for the contemplated expedition."[137] The duty then of the quartermaster general and his assistants, said Secretary Hamilton, "will simply be to collect, receive and receipt (to such as may wish receipts) for such cattle and other supplies as may be deemed necessary for the campaign, taking a full description of all cattle— marks and brands, with the net weight as near as practicable, but the *price, mode* and *time* of payment will in all cases be left for the future action of the Gov[ernmen]t." Less than two weeks later the Secretary in- structed the quartermaster general with the army to follow this same procedure of receipting for such "articles which you may find it neces- sary to purchase." "The department," he continued "has no means at its disposition, and therefore can not with propriety give a guarantee for the acceptance or payment of any drafts drawn upon it for supplies. Such as you absolutely require can surely be attained without money. If not, why the army must subsist upon what you can procure—Beef and Bread alone."[138]

The strictest regard to economy was to be had in the making of spurs and their distribution was to be limited to only such troops as had organized and reported to the commanding officer. As for ammunition, "the Government can . . . supply but little . . . under any circumstances,"

---

[136] M. C. Hamilton to Col. William G. Cooke, Washington, Oct. 25, 1842, Army Papers (Texas), ms.; Same to Brig.-Gen. A. Somervell, Washington, Nov. 9, 1842, *Writings of Sam Houston*, III, 193–194.

[137] M. C. Hamilton to Col. William G. Cooke, Dept. of War & Marine, Washing- ton, Nov. 7, 1842, in Army Papers (Texas)), ms.; for a typical request for reim- bursement later, see Petition of John and Esther Clark to the Legislature of the State of Texas, Jan. 11, 1848, in Memorials and Petitions (Texas), ms.

[138] M. C. Hamilton to Col. William G. Cooke, Department of War and Marine, Washington, Nov. 19, 1842, in Army Papers (Texas), ms.

declared Hamilton. "Not a single Keg of Rifle Powder remains on hand, and the amount of Lead in the public store at Galveston, though not correctly ascertained [since last spring], must be small," especially since Davis' volunteer army had been supplied out of the stores there.[139] "The Hon[orable] Secretary of War and Marine," wrote Snively to Colonel Cooke, the acting quartermaster general with the troops at San Antonio, "is not willing that Powder and Lead should be sent to the Army, until it is organized; and a requisition made by the Commanding Officer, for such Ordnance stores as he may require."[140] Two kegs of powder and a small quantity of lead were reported to be at Colonel William Pettus' on Mill Creek, where they had been left by someone on the way to assist in driving out Woll. Actually, however, this powder and lead were taken by two men, O. R. Willis,[141] acting commissary of the army, and a companion, on pack horses to San Antonio, arriving there on or about October 5.[142] "The precussion [*sic*] caps are here," wrote Snively from Washington, "but no Lead came with them. I see no probability of getting the caps to the Army. I will do all that I can to get them under way."[143]

The next day Hamilton wrote Somervell that sufficient supplies of ammunition had been sent by the War Department for the support of the expedition, but that the mistake had been made of forwarding them by various individuals, making it extremely doubtful if they would

[139] M. C. Hamilton to Col. William G. Cooke, Dept. of War & Marine, Washington, Nov. 7, 1842, in *ibid*.

[140] J. Snively to Col. William G. Cooke, Washington, Nov. 8, 1842, in *ibid*.

[141] O. R. Willis, the illegitimate son of Thomas Scurry and husband of Mrs. Mary A. Willis, died of diarrhea in the hospital in Mexico City about September 16, 1843. Willis had come to Texas because of "the old neighborhood affairs" around Rutherfords, Lauderdale, Tenn. He married on February 3, 1842, and a child (Cordelia Owen) was born, but died about September 15, 1844, at the age of eighteen months. Mrs. Willis later married Thomas W. Bell, one of the Mier prisoners. A. S. Thurmond to Mrs. Mary A. Willis, Rutherfords, Lauderdale, Tenn., [dated: Castle of Perota, Oct. 18, 1843], copy in No. 244, Records of the Probate Court, Fort Bend County, Texas; Same to Same, Castle of Perote in Mexico, July 7, 1844, in *ibid.*; William Ryon to Mrs. Mary A. Willis [Perote, July 7, 1844?], in *ibid.*; Affidavit of Mary A. Bell, County of Gibson, State of Tennessee, July 16, 1852, copy in *ibid*. See also M. C. Hamilton, Act⁵ Sec. War and Marine, to O. H. [R?] Willis, Esq., Department of War and Marine, Sept. 23, 1842. Army Papers (Texas), ms.

[142] Adams, "[Journal of an] Expedition Against the Southwest," Oct. 4 and 5, 1842, ms.

[143] J. Snively to Col. William G. Cooke, Washington, Nov. 8, 1842, in Army Papers (Texas), ms.

"ever reach Head Quarters." "It is scattered all over the Western Country," wrote Hamilton. "This is always the consequence when it is sent without requisitions, and by irresponsible individuals. It must," he continued, "be collected by the Quarter Masters, for the Government can supply no Rifle Powder, and but a small quantity of Lead, a few hundred pounds remains in the public stores at Galveston."[144] Ten days later Hamilton declared,

It is a matter of surprise as well as regret, that no reports[145] have been received from you relative to your progress and movements, when daily opportunities are offered you by men leaving your encampment for their homes. The department is ignorant, except from rumor of men in camp of their condition for service—the quantity of supplies on hand or the prospect of procuring them.

It has been represented that the whole number of men in camp will not exceed Six hundred; and that a part of them will not report, inasmuch as they do not understand clearly the character of your orders—that they are not disposed voluntarily to join the expedition of the force; and further, that supplies of both ammunition and provisions are insufficient. I am under the necessity of making the enquiry whether these rumors be true, because you have failed to keep the Department informed of the state of things:—Your orders were to neither *muster into service nor issue supplies of any kind to any but those who reported with a firm resolve to cross the Río Grande if required to do so.* Were they read and explained to the troops upon your arrival in camp? Or have any been mustered into service or retained in camp contrary to their inclinations and in violation of the orders of His Excellency the President and of the Department?

It was expected that those who were anxious to enter the enemies [sic] territory would be prepared to march immediately upon their organization, which should have been completed when they reported themselves. . . . Those who were not disposed to join the expedition should have departed instantly for their homes. It was not the design of the Government to keep an undisciplined and disorganized army stationed on the frontier merely for the

---

[144] M. C. Hamilton to Brig.-Gen. Alexander Somervell, Nov. 9, 1842, *Writings of Sam Houston*, III, 193–194.

[145] The Acting Secretary of War was not the only one failing to receive reports. Somervell himself wrote on November 14 that it had been ten days since his arrival in camp, and "I am in receipt of no communication from your Excellence nor from the Hon. Secretary of War and Marine." A. Somervell to Sam Houston, Head Quarters South Western Army, Leon, 7 miles West of San Antonio de Béxar, Nov. 14, 1842, in Texas Congress, *Journals of the House of Representatives of the Seventh Congress*, Appendix, pp. 10–11.

purpose of consuming the little substance remaining of a population already nearly reduced to starvation. . . .

Your communication of the 7th inst. has just been received; but it affords no information as to the probable number of men at your encampment—how they are supplied—when you can probably take up the line of march, or whether it will be practicable with the force which you are likely to have at your command, to carry out, at this advanced season of the year, the objects contemplated. *If it is,* you will see the necessity of prompt and energetic movement. *If it is not,* why it is hoped that you will see the propriety of disbanding the troops at once—they have now been on the frontier six weeks, and are seemingly as little prepared for the march as when they first arrived.[146]

Again it was repeated, "You will under no circumstances permit Liquor to be brought within the limits of your encampment, nor within the reach of the troops."[147]

Three days before the expedition marched from the vicinity of San Antonio, Hamilton at Washington dashed off a belated warning to the quartermaster general: "It would be well for you to *know exactly what you can supply and when it will be in camp,* and a statement of the same laid before the Commanding Officer for his information; for I am led to believe that you are depending upon uncertainties."[148] There was no ammunition at Washington, and as far as the Secretary knew there was none on the way to the army; "nor will it be possible," he said, "if I am correctly informed to raise supplies of Beef, Coffee, and other articles from this [Washington] and Montgomery counties and forward it to the army short of six weeks, if it can be done at all."

There seems little doubt as to the correctness of Hamilton's information, for by November 9 the troops at San Antonio were reported in a state of starvation for want of provisions. The food supply, especially meat, was somewhat improved by the hunters' successes, and by the seizure of beeves from some of the nearby ranches before the army was ready to move; but certain other essential items were exceedingly scarce. As late as the 14th Somervell informed the President, "our sup-

[146] M. C. Hamilton to Brig.-Gen. A. Somervell, Department of War & Marine, Washington, Nov. 19, 1842, *Writings of Sam Houston,* III, 197–199.

[147] Same to Same, Department of War and Marine, Washington, Nov. 21, 1842, in Texas Congress, *Journals of the House of Representatives of the Seventh Congress,* Appendix, pp. 9–10.

[148] M. C. Hamilton to Col. William G. Cooke, Dept. of War & Marine, Washington, Nov. 22, 1842, in Army Papers (Texas), ms.

plies of Powder and Lead which we very much need, have not yet come up—the Cannon from Gonzales will be here tomorrow."[149] Actually the cannon did not arrive until eight days later. On November 19 General Somervell ordered Quartermaster General Colonel William G. Cooke[150] (who had once before held that position between January 13 and August 18, 1840, until he succeeded Burleson in command of the First Regiment of Infantry), to procure for the use of the army five kegs of rifle powder, five hundred pounds of lead, and ten or twelve bushels of salt. Such supplies were to be acquired on the credit of the Government from private persons. On the 21st Cooke was ordered to send immediately all "Subsistence and Ordnance stores intended for the So[uth] Western Army" to Camp Cooke,[151] near the Medina. Every means having failed to supply the army with the necessary provisions and ammunition, impressment of certain necessary items found in the area was ordered, although this system of raising supplies had been prohibited by the President. To facilitate the prompt transfer of the supplies, Cooke was authorized to impress "a sufficient number of carts, mules, or oxen & cartmen."[152] Among those whose private property was seized by Henry Clay Davis,[153] one of the assistant quartermasters, was

---

[149] A. Somervell to Sam Houston, Head Quarters, South Western Army, Leon, 7 miles West of San Antonio de Béxar, Nov. 14, 1842, in Texas Congress, *Journals of the House of Representatives of the Seventh Congress*, Appendix, pp. 10–11; *Telegraph and Texas Register*, Oct. 19, 1842.

[150] For a biographical sketch of Colonel William G. Cooke, see Warren, "Col. William G. Cooke," *Quarterly of the Texas State Historical Association*, IX (1905–1906), 210–219.

[151] The Comanches taken prisoners at the Council House Fight, March 19, 1840, "were first removed to San José Mission, where a company of soldiers was stationed, and afterwards taken to Camp 'Cook,' named after W. G. Cook[e], at the head of the river, and strictly guarded for a time." Green (ed.), *Memoirs of Mary A. Maverick*, p. 37.

[152] Brig.-Gen. [A.] Somervell to the Quarter Master General, Head Qrs. So. Western Army, Camp Cooke, Near the Medina, Nov. 21, 1842 (order no. 28), Army Papers (Texas), ms. See also A. Somervell to Col. Wm. G. Cook, Act^g Q^r M. Genl, Head Quarters, So. Western Army, Camp Leon, Novr 19, 1842 (Special Order No. 5), in "A Record Book of the General & Special Orders and Letters of the South Western Army," pp. 21–22, ms.

[153] Henry Clay Davis had been a mounted volunteer and had participated in the Council House Fight in March 1840. During the engagement, "an Indian sprang up behind him, and, while trying to kill him with an arrow used as a dirk," Davis killed the Indian with one of the first lot of Colt revolvers ever brought to Texas. Davis is said to have quit the Mier expedition at the Carrizo Indian village on the

Francois Guilbeau,[154] a merchant and French consular agent at San Antonio. Davis' men were accused not only of defying the French flag, but also of threatening with their carbines the person of the French agent who sought to remonstrate against the impressment of his goods. From the French consul three sacks of salt, two hundred and nine pounds of lead, and six bushels of maize (corn) were taken, valued in all at $164.[155] Later when M. le Vte. de Cramayel, the French chargé d'affaires, protested to the Texan government about Davis' conduct, the government investigated the affair and then apologized; ordered the restoration of the property, if it could be located, and the punishment of the perpetrators according to the laws of Texas.[156] However, in June 1843, it was believed that Davis had been killed by the Indians while on his homeward march from the army the preceding December, and it was known that there was no record of the names of those who assisted in the execution of the order, or of the companies from which they were detailed; hence, it was impossible to identify them, and no one was punished. General Somervell, when summoned to Washington in June 1843, officially disavowed any responsibility for Davis' exceeding his

---

Río Grande (now Zapata) and to have gone to Mexico and kept under cover until the excitement growing out of that expedition blew over. He married into the wealthy Garza family of Camargo, and it is upon the land belonging to this family that Davis is said to have established Río Grande City. Davis established a large ranch east of the Río Grande, which was known as El Rancho Davis, or Davis' Landing. He built a fine, long, low, one story brick home upon his land in 1845. He later served in the Texas State Senate. He met an untimely death by the accidental discharge of his own gun while out hunting. Brown, *Indian Wars and Pioneers of Texas*, p. 77 n; Virgil N. Lott and Mercurio Martinez, *Kingdom of Zapata*, pp. 34–35.

154 M. Francois Guilbeau, Jr., son of Francois and Marguerite Louise Mortier Guilbeau, was born August 4, 1813, at Acenis, Brittany, and immigrated to Texas with his father, and the two of them went to San Antonio with William Elliot in 1839, where they engaged in the frontier trade. The son became the French consular agent at San Antonio. The elder Francois Guilbeau died in June 1845, at the age of seventy years. Francois Guilbeau, Jr., married Rosario Ramón on July 15, 1848. Frederick C. Chabot, *With the Makers of San Antonio*, pp. 263–264.

155 J. de Cramayel to Anson Jones, Galveston, March 1843; M. C. Hamilton to Anson Jones, Washington, June 27, 1843; A. Somervell to M. C. Hamilton, Washington, June 27, 1843, Garrison (ed.), *Diplomatic Correspondence of Texas*, 1908, III, pp. 1424–1426, 1453–1456.

156 Anson Jones to Andrew Neill, District Attorney, 2nd Judicial District, Department of State, Washington, June 20, 1843, in State Department (Texas), Department of State Letterbook, Home Letters, II (1842–1846), p. 66, ms.; A. Neill to Anson Jones, June 28, 1843, *ibid.*, p. 97.

orders.[157] In the end, the Republic paid the claim of $164 "for goods taken by order of General Somervell for the use of the Army."[158]

Colonel Cooke found it necessary to "press into service a few sacks of salt and some lead, while Captain Bogart, of Washington County, and . . . [Thomas Jefferson Green] became individually responsible for iron to shoe the barefooted horses."[159] Although there was a very limited quantity of corn, there was not enough to supply the army until it reached the enemy's country. Around the San José Mission during the middle of October there was an ample supply of corn, but as more men arrived and the encampment persisted, the supply dwindled quickly.[160] "Breadstuffs were out of the question, and so was everything else in the way of provisions except beef."[161] About three hundred beeves were collected with difficulty to be driven along with the army. The men often claimed that the confiscated beef always tasted better than other meat.[162]

Under these circumstances, 40 of Colonel Bennett's command deserted on November 16, but General Somervell ordered out a detachment from the regiment to arrest and bring them back.[163] This action, however, on the part of the general did not prevent a sizable segment of the army from deserting two days later. Many of the drafted militiamen from Montgomery and Washington counties deserted on the 18th and returned home in disgust. Discipline had become so poor in the army

---

[157] M. C. Hamilton to Anson Jones, Department of War and Marine, Washington, June 27, 1843, *ibid.*, pp. 95–96.

[158] Anson Jones to J. B. Miller, Secretary of the Treasury, [dated:] Department of State, Washington, Sept. 25, 1843, *ibid.*, p. 71.

[159] Green, *Journal of the Texian Expedition Against Mier*, p. 43.

[160] Adams, "[Journal of an] Expedition Against the Southwest," Oct. 9, 1842, ms.

[161] Lucy A. Erath (ed.), "Memoirs of George Bernard Erath," *Southwestern Historical Quarterly*, XXVII (1923–1924), 37.

[162] Adams, "[Journal of an] Expedition Against the Southwest," Oct. 15, 1842, ms.

[163] Memucan Hunt to Francis Moore, Jr., Editor of the *Telegraph*, Camp Leon, South-Western Army, Nov. 16, 1842, *Telegraph and Texas Register*, Dec. 21, 1842. See also A. Somervell to Col. Jos[eph] Bennett, H^d Q^rs So. Western Army, Camp on Leon, Novr 16, 1842; A. Somervell, General Order No. 24, H^d Q^rs, Camp Leon, Novr 16, 1842; A. Somervell to Capt. Bartlett Sims, Head Quarters, Camp Leon, Nov. 16, 1842; A. Somervell, General Order No. 26, Head Quarters, Camp Leon, Novr 16, 1842, in "A Record Book of the General & Special Orders and Letters of the South Western Army," pp. 17–21, ms.

and arrests so numerous that General Somervell on the morning of the 18th found it necessary to write Colonel Cooke as follows:

As it is under stood that a large portion of Col. Bennetts command are deserting this morning you are authorized in the event of your being likely to be overpowered by force to desist from taking prisoners, or if you have taken them to deliver them up.

I am anxious to avoid bloodshed as from what I can learn of the disposition of the army generally it will not be attended with beneficial results to the cause.[164]

Colonel Bennett and about 70 members of his Montgomery County militiamen remained, although the majority of the drafted men returned home.

Following the desertions on the 18th the little army, now reduced to approximately 760 men, was moved to a point near the Medina (hereafter called Camp Cooke) where it pitched camp at the crossing of the Presidio Road, some twenty miles west of San Antonio, to await the arrival of cannon and additional supplies. The artillery was expected to arrive from Gonzales in a day or two under the escort of Captain Eastland's company from Fayette County, but great difficulties had been encountered, according to Assistant Quartermaster Valentine Bennet.[165] From Gonzales Bennet wrote,

I have much trouble in geting [*sic*] the artillery from this place. Everything worked against me. The inhabitants would render no assistance at all. I am much indebted to Ca[p]t. Eastland's Company for their assistance in getting the cannon over the River. I could not get any harnesses at all. I have written to the Secretary of War to send on harness but have had no return.

There has been no arrival of any public property of any kind from the East.

The flooded streams west of San Antonio were another cause for delaying the march of the expedition.[166] In the meantime, Thomas Green of Fayette County went to Austin to aid Captain Mark B. Lewis in rais-

---

[164] A. Somervell to Col. William G. Cooke, San Antonio, Nov. 18, 1842, Army Papers (Texas), ms. See also M. C. Hamilton to Brig.-Gen. A. Somervell, Washington, Nov. 19, 1842, *Writings of Sam Houston*, III, 197–199; H. F. Gillett to Ashbel Smith, Washington, Texas, Nov. 25, 1842, in Ashbel Smith Papers, 1838–1842, ms.

[165] Memucan Hunt to Francis Moore, Jr., Editor of the *Telegraph*, Camp Leon, South-Western Army, Nov. 16, 1842, *Telegraph and Texas Register*, Dec. 21, 1842; V. Bennet to Wm. G. Cooke, [Gonzales, Nov. 1842], in Army Papers (Texas), ms.

[166] *Telegraph and Texas Register*, Dec. 7, 1842.

ing and bringing on a company from Travis County. During this time several small parties reached the Texan camp from various points in the west, but no full company had arrived between November 14 and December 16, when Captain Sims of Bastrop County came in with his command.[167] It was rumored in the west that three hundred troops were on the march from the east to join the army before Béxar, and the men at the front were highly pleased with the prospect of assistance from the eastern counties of the Republic.

At Camp Cooke, the Texans estimated that they were within five days' march of General Woll's retreating army. The men were anxious for a fight, and it was believed by some that had General Somervell moved promptly against the Mexican force he could have captured it.[168] Instead, however, the main body of the Texan army remained at the Presidio Crossing, southwest of San Antonio, for a week while Somervell was in town. These days were well spent. Ten to fifteen blacksmiths were busily at work shoeing horses and repairing arms. Others assisted by gathering wood which they burned to make charcoal to facilitate the shoeing of the horses. Other men killed beeves and dried the meat on stakes over fires, while the officers of the Second Regiment availed themselves of "every opportunity to drill and discipline the regiment."[169] Some of the men spent their time in hunting and fishing, making leather straps for the pack animals, cleaning guns, and in other ways preparing for the anticipated campaign. Many of the volunteers had left home during the warm days of September and early October with pantaloons too thin for the sharp weather of November. Since there was no regulation clothing furnished by the Government, they quickly

transferred the covering of many an unwary buck to their own legs. I never [recorded Green, a member of the expedition] saw deer so plentiful; many hundreds were killed, and the whole camp for several days had more the appearance of a tremendous tanyard than an army which expected in a few

[167] *Ibid.*, Dec. 21, 1842.

[168] Archibald Fitzgerald and George Van Ness, among Woll's prisoners, later reported that probably the whole Mexican army could have been captured after the firing of the first volley of an attacking Texan army. They stated that the Mexican officers and men had sought out the Texan prisoners, when they learned Somervell was advancing toward Presidio, "to know how they should surrender, and what to say to the Texians to save their lives." Green, *Journal of the Texian Expedition Against Mier*, p. 45.

[169] Memucan Hunt to Francis Moore, Jr., Editor of the *Telegraph*, Camp Leon, South-Western Army, Nov. 16, 1842, *Telegraph and Texas Register*, Dec. 21, 1842.

days to meet the national enemy upon his own soil. Indeed, the scene here presented was no bad illustration of the facility with which Texians . . . [could] accommodate themselves to unforeseen emergencies; and he who could not creep upon the most keen-sighted buck, and "ease him of his jacket," was not fit for a soldier; and many who could not or would not do it, returned home, as they said, "to get some warm clothing."[170]

However, experience proved that those who went home for "warm clothing," a "better horse," or a "better gun" almost invariably remained.

Each man was dressed according to his own tastes or means. Bob Waters of the Fort Bend company wore a cap which he made from the skin of a leopard cat he had killed in a Brazos canebrake. A number of the men painted "bloody mottoes" upon their caps, but Green records that he did not remember seeing a man with a "Liberty or death" motto who did not take the liberty of returning home a little too soon.[171] More than one man was dressed in homespun cloth, while others wore leather jackets and pantaloons, and a number of the men protected their bodies from the elements with deer and bear skins, buffalo hides, and wool blankets, many of which had been obtained from the Mexican trade or appropriated in San Antonio. Some of the men possessed shot-pouches made from the skin of an ounce or leopard cat. At night they slept on the ground in all kinds of weather, unprotected by tents, putting some brush or grass cut with their Bowie knives under their blankets, partly for softness, partly for warmth, and often to keep their blankets from soaking up water in case of rain. Each man was a hunter, able to live on the abundant game the country afforded. Every man was a natural-born guerrilla trained in the art of frontier warfare, and able and willing to live on the natives of Mexico, and, therefore, eager to be on his way.

Since, however, many of the discontented had gone home, morale among the men on the Medina was good during the week,[172] but this state of affairs was not to last. At this time all the men were in good health and fine spirits; yet, it was reported that at the time the army marched for the Río Grande it was in need of sixty pairs of coarse

[170] Green, *Journal of the Texian Expedition Against Mier*, pp. 45–46; Adams, "[Journal of an] Expedition Against the Southwest," Nov. 20, 1842, ms.

[171] Green, *Journal of the Texian Expedition Against Mier*, pp. 47–50.

[172] Adams, "[Journal of an] Expedition Against the Southwest," Nov. 20, 1842, ms.

475

woolen pantaloons, sixty pairs of shoes, and a little coffee and tobacco.[173] In spite of the fine spirit, two important things were lacking—discipline and adequate supplies for a sustained operation against the enemy. Valuable time had been lost in getting the expedition organized, and the season for effective operations was already far advanced before the army was ready to move on November 25.

About mid-morning of the 19th an order to move the spy camp was issued. Going down stream, the men failed to find a suitable crossing; so they returned up stream to a point two and a half miles above their former camp and crossed, making camp about three hundred yards from the river in a grove of live oaks. The cold and drizzle persisted; some of the men went to San Antonio for corn meal.[174] On the 21st the camp was moved four miles up stream to a grove of live oaks on a small stream fed by springs emptying into the Medina. The springs flowed from the base of a thirty-five to forty foot hill and the water was quite warm. Along the banks of the river and stream were numerous pecan, sycamore, cottonwood, and cypress trees.[175] While hunting on the 21st W. H. Woodward, a member of Bogart's company, killed a fat bear weighing three hundred pounds. There was much excitement upon its being brought into camp, and several men started out at once to try their luck, among whom were Joseph T. Marshall and H. Kuykendall. These two had scarcely been gone thirty minutes when Marshall was shot through the arm about five inches above the elbow, the ball passing between the bone and muscle, also through his coat flap on one side and through his pantaloons just above the navel. William Bates, belonging to the same company, had mistakenly shot Marshall, supposing him to be a bear, as he was creeping through the woods in a bending position. Bates went immediately for Dr. Cook who was at the camp of the Washington County company, six miles away. In the meantime, the wound was dressed by Humphrey, Adams, and others. Dr. Cook redressed the wound and after several days, the patient returned home accompanied by Elias Marshall,[176] who, according to Adams, had "a predisposition to be sick."[177]

The night of the 21st during the second watch an alarm was sounded.

[173] Report of Mr. Curtis in *Telegraph and Texas Register*, Dec. 21, 1842.
[174] Adams, "[Journal of an] Expedition Against the Southwest," Nov. 19, 1842, ms.
[175] *Ibid.*, Nov. 21, 1842.
[176] *Ibid.*, Nov. 21, 1842.
[177] *Ibid.*, Oct. 1, 1842.

Tom Middleton fired his gun, alleging that he saw someone whom he took to be an Indian, but it was later discovered that this was a ruse gotten up by certain ones to steal the bear meat which had been placed on a scaffold for barbecuing. The ruse failed, however, because some of the men did not fall in when parade orders were given. Suspecting some sort of trickery, a part of the mess stayed to guard the meat. "This was done," said Adams, "because this mess were stingy fellows, and would never divide anything with the company." Three days later another bear was killed and divided among all the messes in the two spy companies, except the mess which had killed the three hundred pound bear and was so stingy with it.[178]

Most of the volunteer companies had been included in the brigade under Colonel James R. Cook, but Captain Bartlett Sims'[179] company and a few other small groups remained unattached for a while; and after the ranks of McCrocklin's and Bennett's commands had been so thinned by desertion, an effort was made to reorganize them into a battalion. An election was ordered for "major." The candidates were Colonel Bennett and Captain Peter H. Bell. The first vote resulted in a tie, and in the second, Bell was elected,

but it bred an ulcer, which was not entirely cauterized during the campaign. Bennett was a brave old veteran, who had represented Montgomery County in the Third Congress, writhing under the fact that so many of his militia regiment had gone home against his wish; while Bell was a princely looking young man of dash, a soldier of San Jacinto, and [was] supported unanimously by those who knew him from Travis, Bastrop, Fayette and Washington. The result was that neither assumed the position.[180]

[178] *Ibid.*, Nov. 24, 1842.

[179] Bartlett Sims, one of Austin's Old Three Hundred colonists, received a large grant of land in 1824 in what is now Wharton County. Later moving to Bastrop, he surveyed much of the land in Austin's Little Colony. He represented Mina in the Convention of 1833 and the Consultation of 1835. He was captain in several expeditions against the Indians, participated in the siege of Béxar in 1835, and was a member of several of John H. Moore's expeditions and participated in the Battle of Brushy Creek. In 1843 Sims moved to Williamson County. William C. Binkley (ed.), *Official Correspondence of the Texan Revolution, 1835–1836*, I, 39, 78; Frank Brown, "Annals of Travis County and of the City of Austin," ms., IV, 19–20; Lester G. Bugbee, "The Old Three Hundred," *Quarterly of the Texas State Historical Association*, I (1897–1898), 116; *Handbook of Texas*, II, 614; Harry McCorry Henderson, *Colonel Jack Hays, Texas Ranger*, p. 50; Worth S. Ray, *Austin Colony Pioneers*, pp. 211, 307–308.

[180] Brown, *History of Texas*, II, 233–235. See also Memucan Hunt to Francis

The command of the so-called battalion devolved upon Captain Sims, the senior captain, whose health was very poor, as he was suffering from the effects of a recent severe attack of fever and was delayed in reaching San Antonio until November 16.

On November 21 the First Regiment (so-called since the dissolution of Colonel Bennett's command), commanded by Colonel James R. Cook, was composed of eleven companies commanded, respectively, by Captains E. S. C. Robertson (68),[181] Gardiner Smith (55), Phillip H. Coe (66), Samuel Bogart (59),[182] William S. Fisher (67), John Shelby McNeill (52), Ewen Cameron (56), Isaac N. Mitchell (40), Clark L. Owen (51), William Ryon of Fort Bend County (46),[183] and Jerome B. Robertson (78) (formerly commanded by William P. Rutledge of Clark L. Owen's Company).[184] Besides these there were the remnants of the companies belonging to Bennett's old command plus the men belonging to Sims' company (38) from Bastrop County. Exclusive of Bennett's, Ryon's, and Sims' men and the staff, there were 592 officers and privates. In addition, there were the men belonging to

---

Moore, Jr., Editor of the *Telegraph*, Camp León, South-Western Army, Nov. 16, 1842, in *Telegraph and Texas Register*, Dec. 21, 1842. For a while during Lamar's administration Hunt served as Secretary of the Navy.

[181] The roll of the company as drawn at its place of muster at Independence, October 17, 1842, shows 68 men of whom 44 were listed as AWOL, 8 were represented by substitutes, 2 transferred to another company, 1 promoted, and only 13 were present. At Camp Hope on November 20, 1842, the company was shown as having 56 men, including 2 on furlough, 4 substitutes, and 1 AWOL. See Muster Roll of Captain E. S. C. Robertson's Company D of the 2nd Regiment, 1st Brigade, Army of the Republic of Texas [Texas Militia], Commanded by Lt. Col. J. L. McCrocklin from the 17th day of October 1842 (when last mustered) to the 10th day of November 1842 (Mustered and inspected by James R. Cook, Nov. 20, 1842), Militia Rolls (Texas), ms.

[182] For a short biographical sketch of Samuel Bogart and his previous military career, see the *Southwestern Historical Quarterly*, XXIII (1919–1920), 117.

[183] Captain William Ryon arrived at the camp near San Antonio on November 3, 1842, with 46 men. Adams, "[Journal of an] Expedition Against the Southwest," Nov. 3, 1842, ms.

[184] John Hemphill, Acting Adjt.-General, T. M., to M. C. Hamilton, Head Quarters, Camp Cook, near Medina, Nov. 21, 1842, in Texas Congress, *Journal of the House of Representatives of the Seventh Congress*, Appendix, pp. 12–14. The number in parenthesis following the captains' names indicated the total number of commissioned and noncommissioned officers and privates in the companies. Ryon's company was "returned without certificates" and it was stated that its roll would not be forwarded until corrected. See Appendix C for Muster Rolls of the companies mustered at San Antonio for the Somervell expedition.

Major Hays' ranger company. Two muster rolls, one dated April 12 and the other September 12, of a company commanded by Captain Ewen Cameron, were forwarded by Adjutant General Hemphill along with his report of Somervell's command. There were no companies from east of the Trinity. Hemphill's report of the status of the expedition had not reached the Secretary of War's office by December 14.[185]

On November 21 the Acting Secretary of War and Marine, M. C. Hamilton, wrote Somervell to use all possible exertion to get his command under way without delay, "provided it has been determined to carry forward" and he was instructed "to move with as much celerity as practicable," for "it is worse than useless to remain on the frontier inactive. By this time," he declared, "the fact must be apparent whether you can prosecute the campaign with success or not." In case it were determined to disband the force, the ordnance and public stores of every kind were to be carefully collected by the quartermaster and moved eastward at least as far as the Guadalupe and safely stored so that they might not fall into the hands of the next marauding party visiting the western frontier.[186]

On the 22nd Major Hays was ordered to send out a detachment of spies to scout the country west of the Medina, but was told not to go beyond the Seco. He was especially ordered to follow the trail of two horses which had been discovered near the Cañon Ford of the Medina along Colonel Caldwell's old route. If Hays thought it to be advisable, he was also to dispatch scouts out along the old Presidio road.[187]

On the same day (November 22) all companies, detachments, and squads were ordered to report to army headquarters on the Medina by early morning of the 23rd, at the latest, preparatory to marching westward.[188] The cannon arrived on the 23rd and that afternoon the Texan army with the brass six-pounder and two hundred rounds of ammunition, drawn by oxen, moved forward and camped on the Medina just

---

[185] "Report of the Secretary of War & Marine to Sam Houston, Dec. 14, 1842, to be submitted to the House of Representatives in accordance to their resolution of December 13, 1842," in *ibid.*, pp. 10–11.

[186] M. C. Hamilton to Brig.-Gen. A. Somervell, Department of War & Marine, Washington, Nov. 21, 1842, in *ibid.*, pp. 9–10.

[187] A. Somervell, General Order No. 27, Head Quarters, Camp Cook, near Medina, Nov[r] 22, 1842, in "A Record Book of the General & Special Orders and Letters of the South Western Army," pp. 22–23, ms.

[188] A. Somervell, General Order No. 30, Head Quarters, Camp Cook, near Medina, Nov[r] 22, 1842, in *ibid.*, p. 24, ms.

below the spy companies.[189] The campsite was designated "Camp Howard." The Brazoria Company, under Captain Mitchell, came up at this time, and joined the regiment. William McQueen was ordered to enroll a company of artillerists from among those volunteers not yet mustered into service, but if the necessary number could not be obtained the deficiency was to be madeup from persons detailed from the command.[190] Colonel Cook was asked by Somervell to make a detailed report to him on the condition of arms, ammunition, and accoutrements belonging to the various companies of the regiment and to state the quantity of powder and lead necessary to supply the men with one hundred rounds each.[191] Similar reports were requested of Hays, Bogart, Sims, and Eastland for their respective companies. [192] On the 25th all ammunition was ordered to be apportioned equally among the privates in each separate company.[193]

On the 25th the order was issued to begin the march westward at 8 A.M. However, all commanders of detachments or squads not incorporated in the First Regiment or into what was now called the First Battalion of the Second Regiment (the remnants of Colonel Bennett's old command, consisting of the companies of Captain Sims and Captain Barrett, and the squads under Captains Eastland and Pierson) were ordered to remain at San Antonio until a full company could be formed. When such a company was formed, it was to march by the Laredo road to join the army.[194] The cannon, for which the army had waited so long, was returned to San Antonio, it being concluded that it would be too much of an impediment to the march.

The newspapers reported that the army could have begun its march a week or two sooner, but that the streams west of San Antonio were so high that they were impassable.[195] For several days the Río Frio was

189 Adams, "[Journal of an] Expedition Against the Southwest," Nov. 21, 1842, ms.

190 A. Somervell, General Order No. 30, Head Quarters, Camp Howard on the Medina, Novr 22, 1842, in "A Record Book of the General & Special Orders and Letters of the Southwestern Army," p. 25, ms.

191 A. Somervell, General Order No. 32, Head Quarters, Camp Howard, on the Medina, Novr 23, 1842, in *ibid.*, p. 25, ms.

192 A. Somervell, General Order No. 33, Head Quarters, Camp Howard, Novr 24, 1842, in *ibid.*, p. 26, ms.

193 A. Somervell, General Order No. 35, Head Quarters, Camp Howard, Novr 25, 1842, in *ibid.*, pp. 26–27, ms.

194 A. Somervell, General Order No. 36, [n. p., n. d.], in *ibid.*, pp. 27–28, ms.

195 *Telegraph and Texas Register*, Dec. 7, 1842.

four miles wide and the Nueces "at the crossing of the Presidio road had overflowed the country so as to fill the whole valley to the bordering hills," and the prairies were so wet and miry that they were almost impassable.[196] During the last two months or so the weather had been so inclement that even the Indians were compelled to discontinue their journey to the Waco Village where a conference had been scheduled for October 24.

The original plan was to attack San Fernando de Rosas situated thirty-eight miles west and slightly north of Presidio del Río Grande. San Fernando, a town about the size of San Antonio, was the military headquarters of General Isidro Reyes. Reports from Presidio del Río Grande of as late as November 7 (conveyed by the three Mexicans brought into the Texan camp on November 12) stated that there were no troops at Presidio and that although General Woll had gone to Monterey, his troops were still at San Fernando. The latest intelligence reported that Reyes had eight hundred men at San Fernando, and Vasquez, about two hundred at Morelos[197] Four hundred of these were reported to be cavalry and the remainder infantry, and all were pictured as "much dispirited by their late campaign, that they tremble at the name of a rifle." At San Fernando and Santa Rita de Morelos, six miles away, were seven pieces of artillery, the nightmare of all troops; but there were no cannon at Presidio. No other troops were said to be nearer than a small garrison of less than a hundred men at Laredo. Regular troops, of course, were at Matamoros. The prisoner's statements were confirmed by Jones, previously mentioned, who had been confined at San Fernando on suspicion of being a spy for Texas.[198] One thousand troops were reported to be at Monterey under General Pavón (who had been one of the Centralist leaders whom a handful of Texans had helped the Federalists defeat in the battle of Alcantro [Alamo], twelve miles beyond Mier, on October 3, 1839).[199] In the lower Río Grande

[196] *Ibid.*, Dec. 7, 1842; see also *ibid.*, Nov. 30, 1842.

[197] A correspondent of the *Crescent City* (New Orleans) in a letter dated Matamoros, November 1, 1842, placed Woll and Reyes at Lampazos, sixty miles from the Presidio del Río Grande, with 1,500 troops. *Telegraph and Texas Register*, Nov. 23, 1842. This information is doubtful. See Report of Mr. Jones, *ibid.*, Jan. 25, 1843, which says Woll was at Presidio on the 28th of October.

[198] A. Somervell to Sam Houston, Head Quarters, South Western Army, Leon, 7 miles west of San Antonio de Béxar, Nov. 14, 1842, in Texas Congress, *Journals of the House of Representatives of the Seventh Congress*, Appendix, pp. 11–12.

[199] Memucan Hunt to Francis Moore, Jr., Editor of the *Telegraph*, Camp Leon, South-Western Army, Nov. 16, 1842, *Telegraph and Texas Register*, Dec. 21, 1842.

area three hundred troops were reported to be at Matamoros, one hundred at the mouth of the river, and one hundred at Brazos de Santiago.[200] It was reported by the three Mexicans who had come in from the Río Grande that those who had left Béxar with General Woll two months before wished to return. Corn was said to be scarce and costly at Presidio, although abundant at La Nava, Peyotes, San Juan, Morelos, and San Fernando. In the meantime, realizing the weakness of the Mexican military position in the north, General Reyes, under date of November 17, transmitted the news of the assembling of the Texan force at Béxar to General Tornel, the Minister of War and Marine, who immediately took measures to re-enforce the line of the north,[201] but the Superior Government's action came too late.

[200] *Telegraph and Texas Register*, Nov. 23, 1842. The American consul at Matamoros reported on December 25, 1842, that General Ampudia, who commanded at that place, left there on December 24 with 600 troops under his command to join General Isidro Reyes to meet the Texan threat. I. D. Marks to Daniel Webster, Matamoros, Dec. 25, 1842, no. 2, Consular Dispatches (United States), 1837–1848 (Matamoros), ms.

[201] *El Cosmopolita*, Dec. 3, 1842.

CHAPTER TWENTY

The March of the Somervell Expedition
to Laredo

BY THE TIME THE Texan army was ready to advance it had been reduced to about seven hundred and fifty men, a number far short of the one thousand men which General Somervell considered necessary for an attack upon San Fernando. However, since only a few months before two to three hundred Comanches had carried fire and tomahawk among the settlements of northern Mexico almost to the very precincts of Monterey and had returned in safety to their lodges laden with the spoils of victory, could not three hundred western rangers do as much as these half-armed savages?[1] Consequently, with the unanimous consent of a council of war, composed of the field officers, general staff, brigade staff, and captains of the army, Somervell altered his plans in favor of marching against Laredo, which was not as heavily guarded as San Fernando.[2] Furthermore, a Mexican, who had recently arrived at Béxar from the Río Grande, had declared that the rains had scarcely affected the Río Grande and it was believed that the army could easily ford the river at Laredo. Should the ford prove unsafe, however, the troops could ascend the river about fifty miles, where there was an excellent ford and "an extensive settlement of wealthy Mexicans, and beef, corn and other necessary articles could be obtained in abundance."[3] Two days before General Somervell marched, the President was unaware of his intentions, but

it seems to me [wrote Houston] that, unless your information is better than mine, the Presidio is much out of the way. It may, however, be proper, as I do

---

[1] *Telegraph and Texas Register*, Sept. 7, 1842.

[2] Report of Brig.-Gen. Somervell to the Hon. G. W. Hill, Secretary of War and Marine, Washington, Feb. 1, 1843, *Morning Star* (Houston), Feb. 18, 1843; Texas Congress, *Journals of the Ninth Congress of the Republic of Texas*, Appendix, p. 70.

[3] *Telegraph and Texas Register*, Dec. 28, 1842.

not know your particular object, farther than to destroy the enemy to the greatest extent possible. It appears to me that Camargo would be the point at which you would be the least expected, and where the greatest impression could be made on the country. The most efficient force of the enemy will be at the Presidio. You will find the Cherokees and the warriors associated with them, the most efficient and dangerous enemy that you could encounter on the other side of the Río Grande. They are located in the neighborhood of the Presidio.[4]

Houston regarded the report of the spies concerning the abundance of supplies at Presidio as unreliable in view of the fact that Woll's army had been fitted out from that point and had fallen back to that place after its incursion into Texas.

On November 25, a "bright and beautiful morning," two days after the arrival of the artillery, which after all was not taken along, the so-called Southwestern Army of Operations, comprising a little over 750 men, each mounted and equipped with rifle, knife, pistols, and a hundred rounds of ammunition, moved out from the west bank of the Medina down the Presidio road, later turning in a southwest by south direction so as to strike the Laredo road "at or near a large mound about thirty miles from where the lower [del Presidio] Río Grande road crosses the Medina."[5] Accompanied by a few Lipans, the spy companies were out in front. Hays' company carried a new flag made by Mrs. Eleanor Elliot of San Antonio, bearing the following motto embroidered on it: "*We give* but ask *no quarter.*"[6] "Not a single instrument of military music accompanied the troops." There was neither trumpet, fife, nor drum "to awake the echoes of the morn with the inspiring reveille, or salute the drowsy ear at close of day with the animating strains of the tatoo."[7] There were no wagons and only a few pack animals. The

[4] Houston to Gen. A. Somervell, Washington, Nov. 23, 1842, *Writings of Sam Houston*, III, 201–202.

[5] E. W. Winkler (ed.), "Sterling Brown Hendricks' Narrative of the Somervell Expedition to the Rio Grande," *Southwestern Historical Quarterly*, XXIII (1919–1920), 118; see also Harvey Alexander Adams, "[Journal of an] Expedition Against the Southwest in 1842 and 1843," Nov. 23, 1842, ms.

[6] Eleanor Elliot to Mary A. Maverick, San Antonio de Béxar, Nov. 14, 1842 (postscript), in Rena Maverick Green (ed.), *Samuel Maverick, Texan 1803–1870: A Collection of Letters, Journals and Memoirs*, pp. 202–204.

[7] William Preston Stapp, *The Prisoners of Perote: Containing a Journal Kept by the Author Who Was Captured by the Mexicans, at Mier, December 25, 1842, and Released from Perote, May 16, 1844*, p. 23. Memucan Hunt says that the expedition left the Medina on November 24, but apparently it was not until the morning of the 25th that it got under way. Memucan Hunt to Francis Moore, Jr., Editor of

latter were often made possible by three or four men joining together
to outfit a pack mule. John Henry Brown, a member of the expedition, estimates that there were about two hundred pack mules.[8] Three
hundred beeves were driven along to furnish meat for the men. In
appearance, the army, as it moved along, resembled in many respects
the volunteer troops that followed Stephen F. Austin to San Antonio in
1835.

Buckskin breeches were the nearest approach to uniform and there was
wide diversity even there, some being new and soft and yellow, while others,
from long familiarity with rain and grease and dirt, had become hard and
black and shiny. Some having passed through the process of wetting and drying on the wearer while he sat upon the ground or upon a chunk before the
fire with his knees elevated at an angle of eighty-five degrees, had assumed
an advanced position at the knee length, exposing shins as guiltless of socks
as a Kansas senator's.

Boots being an unknown quantity, some wore shoes and some wore moccasins. Here a broad-brimmed sombrero overshadowed the military cap at its
side; there a tall "beegum" rode familiarly beside a coonskin cap, with the tail
hanging down. . . . Here a big American horse loomed above the nimble
Spanish pony ranged beside him; there a half-broke mustang pranced beside
a sober, methodical mule. Here a bulky roll of bedquilts jostled a pair of
"store" blankets; there the shaggy brown buffalo contrasted with the gaily
checkered counterpane on which the manufacturer had lavished all the skill

---

the *Telegraph*, dated Béxar, Jan. 8, 1843, *Morning Star* (Houston), Jan. 17, 1843.
John Henry Brown, in his *History of Texas, from 1685 to 1892*, II, 235, says the
expedition left San Antonio on November 22 and camped two nights and a day at
the Medina, then crossed the stream on the 24th.

By December 1, the army had a bugler in the person of Private Jackson of
Captain E. S. C. Robertson's Company. Where he obtained his "bugle" is not
explained in the accounts of the expedition. It may well have been a blowing horn
made from a cow's horn. With the appointment of Jackson as bugler, the army
was instructed as follows: at daybreak upon the first sound of the "bugle" the men
were to rise and prepare breakfast; upon the second call of the "bugle" the adjutant
was to march the details for guard duty from the regiment and battalion to the
parade ground (designated by a flag) where they were to be received by the
brigade major and turned over to the officer of the day; at the third sound of the
"bugle" the horses were to be collected; at the fourth call of the "bugle" the horses
were to be saddled and packed and the troops formed in the order of march; and
upon the fifth signal the army was to commence its march without "riotous and
disorderly noise and shouting." A. Somervell, General Order No. 52, Head Quarters,
Camp Río Frio, Decr 1, 1842, in "A Record Book of the General & Special Orders
and Letters of the South Western Army," pp. 37–40, ms.

[8]Brown, *History of Texas*, II, 235.

of dye and weave known to the art—mayhap it was part of the dowery a wife brought her husband on her wedding day, and surely the day-dreams she wove into its simple folds held in them no shadow of a presentiment that it might be his winding sheet. In lieu of a canteen, each man carried a Spanish gourd, a curious specimen of the gourd family, having two round bowls, each holding about a quart, connected by a short neck, apparently designed to adjust a strap about. A fantastic military array to a casual observer, but the one great purpose animating every heart clothed us in a uniform more perfect in our eyes than ever was donned by regulars on dress parade.[9]

The sights were often most amusing. One determined "Texian" was clad half-Mexican and rode a mule, an old saber strapped to the left side of the saddle, with pistols and cartridges for the musket-like gun in his raw cowhide belt. Another, restraining a high-strung mustang and nearly touching the ground with his feet, was wrapped in a widely colored motley blanket coat, below which was partially concealed a bowie knife. Strapped to the pommel of his saddle was a little leather bag with ammunition, and across the pommel lay the long, old, but re-liable rifle. Both his hands rested upon it. Each man carried a small supply of provisions in his saddlebag or portmanteau.

By pulling a feint in the direction of the Presidio road, General Som-ervell hoped to confuse the Béxar Mexicans who might be spying upon his movements and leave them with the impression that the Presidio Crossing of the Río Grande was the first objective. The expedition moved out from the Medina along the Presidio road for a few miles and then turned in a southerly direction for the Laredo road. As one mem-ber of the expedition recorded, "we moved in high spirits, and bright anticipations [that morning], proudly looking forward to the time when, face to face, we should meet our country's foe, and hurl his haughty insolence back to his teeth!"[10]

The largest portion of the Army [reported Thomas W. Bell, a volunteer] was composed of volunteers burning with anxiety to meet the enemy and exchange at least a few shots. Having joined the army merely for the sake of their country, they desired to achieve something that would at least erase the stigma cast upon her by the recent inroads of the Mexicans, and avenge in some manner the cruelties practised upon her citizens—also to capture citizens of

[9] Noah Smithwick, *The Evolution of a State*, pp. 109–110; see also Louis J. Wortham, *A History of Texas*, II, 365–366.

[10] Joseph D. McCutchan, Diary, ms.; see also *Telegraph and Texas Register*, Dec. 14, 1842.

Mexico to give in exchange for those taken by Gen. Wall [*sic*] at San Antonio.[11]

After proceeding seven or eight miles the army encamped at a water hole for the night.[12] The route had been across a terrain with a red cast, clothed with mesquite and now and then a grove of live oak or post oak.

The next morning, November 26, after traveling approximately eight miles, the guide took the wrong course that "led us across the proper road, where we were delayed for some time in great perplexity," said Adams, "waiting for Capt. Hays to find the right road." While the Texan army waited for Hays to make his reconnaissance, many of the men employed themselves in hunting bees, and as on the previous day, several trees were found to contain great quantities of honey. A few of the men cut a coon out of a tree, thus giving this side excursion the name of a "coon hunt." After some time it was decided to back track to the Atascosa.[13] Proceeding down it, the army camped on a high sand hill near the Atascosa, opposite Navarro's old ranch, having traveled sixteen miles during the day. The campsite was named "Camp Murphree." The horses were permitted to graze in the bottom below. During the early evening the men's spirits were drenched by a heavy rain which continued all night. Many of the men stood throughout the night by mesquite fires, finding it well nigh impossible to stay out of the water which covered the ground in every direction. Some sought to lie down on piles of mesquite brush. Most of the men were wet to the skin and their boots had begun to fill. Even tents made from blankets failed to keep out the pelting storm.

Crossing the Atascosa (Boggy) near the ranch the next morning, the army resumed its march. After four or five miles, it came to a sandy post-oak country where the horses, mules, and cattle had great difficulty in progressing through the quagmire. The men were forced to dismount and each to shift for himself in the poor, sandy prairie into which they had been led. The day was cold, wet, and gloomy. The whole country was inundated with water, and soon the expedition was in a boggy post-

[11] Thomas W. Bell, *A Narrative of the Capture and Subsequent Sufferings of the Mier Prisoners in Mexico, Captured in the Cause of Texas, Dec. 26th, 1842 and Liberated Sept. 16th, 1844*, p. 14.

[12] Adams, "[Journal of an] Expedition Against the Southwest," Nov. 25, 1842, ms.

[13] *Ibid.*, Nov. 26, 1842; A. Somervell, General Order No. 45, Head Quarters, Camp Murphree on the Atascoso, Nov[r] 26, 1842, in "A Record Book of the General & Special Orders and Letters of the South Western Army," pp. 31–33, ms.

oak woods, where the horses went to the girth at every step and the men, while supporting their animals and permitting them frequent rests, themselves often floundered knee deep in mud. To the eye the land had the appearance of firmness, and often it would support the weight of a man, but it would let the horses' feet through. Once an animal sank through the grass sod, the soft quicksand would soon worry it down. As far as the eye could see, men were scattered many miles apart over the woods in utter confusion, floundering in the seemingly bottomless morass. Sometimes in the worst places the legs of the horses went completely out of sight and the animals with bodies and noses upon the ground rested in perfect quietude, and looking longingly at their owners, so much as said, " 'You put me here, now get me out,' while the owner would be standing by giving utterance to all manner of curious oaths."[14] Under such circumstances, the horses became so deeply imbedded in the mire that it often became necessary for several men to help them out, and when the animals became exhausted from over-exertion, the only course left was "to roll the animal over and over until a firm standing place was obtained"; and let the poor creatures rest; after which they might travel on for another hundred yards and the process have to be repeated. "Some [of the horses] would be lying on their side, afraid to trust their legs under them, while the poor pack mules, with their little feet, stood the worst kind of chance. The coffee pots and frying pans would go one way and the *aparajos* and other camp appurtenances another."[15]

For the foregoing reasons, the region between La Parita Creek and the Presidio road, a distance of something like twenty-five miles, became known to the Texans as "the bogs of the Atascosa," or "the devil's eight leagues." The pack mules sank until their kyacks (packs) stayed their farther descent. A few men would then lift them up and start them on their way anew, while those, both horses and mules, which could not be extricated were promptly shot "to preserve them against the slow and lingering deaths that awaited them."[16] The cattle had to be

[14] Thomas J. Green, *Journal of the Texian Expedition Against Mier*, p. 53.

[15] Adams, "[Journal of an] Expedition Against the Southwest," Nov. 25, 1842, ms.; see also Green, *Journal of the Texian Expedition Against Mier*, p. 53.

[16] Stapp, *Prisoners of Perote*, p. 2. See also Bell, *Narrative*, p. 14; Adams, "[Journal of an] Expedition Against the Southwest," Nov. 27–28, 1842, ms.; Sidney S. Callender to John H. Brown, 994 Magazine St., New Orleans, June 2, 1886, in John Henry Brown Papers, 1835–1872, ms. Callender was a member of the Somervell expedition.

scattered and driven abreast to prevent too many of them from becoming mired. At intervals the men rested and cursed their leader for not having led them eight miles down the Atascosa below their previous encampment where they could have struck the Laredo road and avoided boggy ground. "Captain Hays . . . was the pilot and between him and General Somervell lies the blame!" shouted one of Bogart's officers.[17] The upshot of it was that the average citizen-soldier believed himself a better strategist than his general. "Never before in my life," reported Harvey Adams, "have I seen men on as equal a footing, as they were in this instance. Generals, Majors, Colonels, Captains and other *tall* men were brought down to the humiliating condition of being in mother earth as deep and as dependent as the lowest private."[18]

When night fell the men encamped upon a hillock, not exceeding a mile in circumference, appalled at their anticipations for the next day. They had traveled only five or six miles after entering the bog. During the night, while the rain fell in torrents drenching both man and beast and lightning flashed across the heavens, the horses broke through the ten to twelve inch crust of earth covering the hill. Few slept amid the tenor chorus of the surrounding swamp, and the "horrible" cry of the bellowing bullfrogs. Wolves, coyotes, and screech owls added their familiar howl and hoot to the dismal serenade. Toward morning the rain ceased, and soon after daylight a bridge of trees and brush was constructed across a piece of low-lying ground some fifty feet in breadth, upon which the expedition crossed safely during that and the ensuing day. At one and a half miles distant from the hillock on which they had camped, the spy company halted on the highest hill in all this country to make observations with the spy glass. Men, indistinguishable by the naked eye, could be seen two and a half miles ahead. After resting, the company circled the hill to keep out of the mess below and to get as near the Laredo road as possible. Thence, traveling about six miles through a rolling prairie country with red-colored hills and heavy black soil in the valleys, the advanced spy company camped under a large spreading mesquite tree on a high hill while the main body of spies encamped in the valley about one and a half miles distant. "Camp Boggy" was the designation given to army headquarters on the 28th. The main army was spread out on all sides as far as one could see through the spy glass, camping about in squads here and there. Large campfires were

[17] Winkler (ed.), "Hendricks' Narrative," *Southwestern Historical Quarterly,* XXIII (1919–1920), 118.
[18] Adams, "[Journal of an] Expedition Against the Southwest," Nov. 27, 1842, ms.

built and an effort was made to dry out and get warm. As the buckskin breeches began to dry, some of the men discovered that they shrank above their knees and in some cases became so tight as to be very uncomfortable. "All kinds of meetings were held, political, theatrical and comical."[19] For drinking water the men dug wells two to three feet deep in the hillsides with their large hack-knives.[20]

On the 29th the advanced spy unit under Hays waited for the arrival, at about 10 A.M., of the main spy company. Many men of the regiment were ahead of the spies. In the early afternoon the army began to concentrate, and Joseph Rogers was appointed "pack-master" to help reorganize the transportation of supplies. About mid-afternoon the army reached Pilot Knob, about fifty miles from the Texan camp on the Medina. To the left of Pilot Knob they came into the Laredo road,[21] as anciently and solidly packed down as the San Antonio road, and proceeded on it for five or six miles where the spy companies camped for the night in a low mesquite flat—the army some distance behind, on the Parita, a small inconsequential stream, five miles from Pilot Knob.

Although again upon solid ground after nearly three days in the bogs, many of the horses were now unfit for use, having been fatigued and injured in the morass. They "were ever afterwards unable thoughout the campaign," reported Somervell, "to make those quick marches essential to the accomplishment of the objects of the campaign."[22] This and subsequent events reduced the number and strength of the animals to such an extent that some of the men, who had been fortunate enough to possess tents, had to abandon them and thereafter sleep on the ground in the open air.[23] At this point on the Laredo road, approximately twenty of the men decided that they had had enough and returned home. While the army was preparing to encamp, Captain Bogart ordered Lieutenant Ephraim W. McLean of Captain Hays' command, in the latter's absence, to pitch his camp at a certain designated spot. McLean refused to

---

[19] Brown, *History of Texas*, II, 235.

[20] Adams, "[Journal of an] Expedition Against the Southwest," Nov. 28, 1842, ms.

[21] *Ibid.*, Nov. 29, 1842.

[22] Report of Brig.-Gen. A. Somervell to the Hon. G. W. Hill, Secretary of War and Marine, Washington, Feb. 1, 1843, in Texas Congress, *Journals of the Ninth Congress of the Republic of Texas*, Appendix, pp. 70–71; *Telegraph and Texas Register*, Feb. 22, 1843; Winkler (ed.), "Hendricks' Narrative," *Southwestern Historical Quarterly*, XXIII (1919–1920), 118.

[23] Adele B. Looscan (ed.), "Journal of Lewis Birdsall Harris," *Southwestern Historical Quarterly*, XXV (1921–1922), 193.

obey the order, and later in the evening when Hays returned an effort was made by Bogart, Hays, and Somervell to have some understanding in regard to the issuance of orders. General Somervell's support of Captain Hays in this matter angered Captain Bogart and his company to the point that they decided to return home the next day. "Our intentions," wrote Hendricks, "was now to quit the field and at once return home; for this purpose I was sent forward to offer General Somervell the resignations of the officers of the company and to ask discharges for the men."[24] Somervell rejected the request and Bogart and his men declined to leave without permission for fear of being branded deserters.

After passing through a rolling country covered with numerous varieties of cacti and thorny bushes, not exceeding four or five feet in height, late in the afternoon on November 30 the army crossed the San Miguel, fifteen miles beyond the Parita, and encamped one and a half miles from the stream on a gravelly hillside, where there was scarcely wood enough to make a fire or grass enough for their jaded horses. Bogart's men pushed on one mile farther to encamp for the night in a grove of trees in the prairie. After a hasty breakfast of soup the next morning, the spy company moved forward for ten to twelve miles, stopping just in sight of the Río Frio for an hour to noon it; after which the company crossed the swollen stream whose waters came mid-side to their horses. In the early afternoon of December 1, the army crossed the Frio,[25] while Bogart's company pushed forward, leaving the army eight miles behind, and halted for the night amid good grass, water, and wood on the banks of a small stream—Hays was in front by half a day's march.[26] Some of the men had tents, but most of the men merely "spread their blankets."

At the left of the Frio, after one crosses it going in a southwest direction, there was a large collection of stones irregularly placed in circular form with a beautiful lake of water south of them.

The wall [reported a member of Bogart's Company] looks as tho[ugh] it had been some ancient building or fortification, and reminded me of descriptions

[24] Winkler (ed.), "Hendricks' Narrative," *Southwestern Historical Quarterly*, XXIII (1919–1920), 120.

[25] An express rider from the army reached Washington around Dec. 10–12 and reported that the troops crossed the Frio on Nov. 29th, *Telegraph and Texas Register*, Dec. 14, 1842.

[26] Winkler (ed.), "Hendricks' Narrative," *Southwestern Historical Quarterly*, XXIII (1919–1920), 121; Adams, "[Journal of an] Expedition Against the Southwest," Nov. 30, Dec. 1, 1842, ms.

of scenery in some of the old countries where the nobles had their palatial residence, their parks and artificial lakes. I fancied, I could see the grand building with its inmates, busy with life and the tiny boat upon the artificial lake, freighted with merry songsters sailing over its smooth waters, where gentle Swains with arched pride delighted to sport, and silvery sided fishes leaping from their element into the air. I have no doubt but this place was inhabited once, but the lapse of time has bro[ugh]t it to decay. I did not have time to examine the place & therefore left it in its *lonliness*."[27]

Nothing of importance had transpired since the expedition had freed itself from the bog, except for a fruitless chase of a drove of mustangs by a few of the men, but this evening (December 1) while encamped in the midst of the chaparral within a few miles of the Nueces River, the southern boundary of Texas as recognized in Spanish and Mexican law, a number of the men suddenly became sick.[28] As the men had been living for some time, both in camp and upon the road, primarily upon beef, with an occasional meal of bread, anything that appeared eatable was seized with a rapacious appetite by many of them. Hence, when a root, looking like a turnip growing largely out of the ground except for a small tap root, and resembling somewhat in flavor the Irish potato, was found at this encampment, a number of men, influenced by the guide or some Mexicans, roasted and consumed a considerable quantity of it.[29] A majority of these men were soon "punished by a few hours of torturing sickness, some even with thoughts of death," but in the end no one died from the effects.[30]

On December 1 all soldiers on foot were placed under the command of Lance Corporal John Tanney, and directed to proceed henceforth at an early hour in the morning in advance of the army so as to speed up the movement of the troops. The foot soldiers were exempted from having to stand guard duty at night.[31] At noon, December 2, the army reached the spot where Hays had encamped the previous night and halted for refreshments. The prairie grass had caught from Hays' campfires after he had left that morning and had burned for some distance

[27] Adams, "[Journal of an] Expedition Against the Southwest," Dec. 1, 1842, ms.
[28] I. J. Cox, "The Southwest Boundary of Texas," *Quarterly of the Texas State Historical Association*, VI (1902–1903), 81–102.
[29] Adams, "[Journal of an] Expedition Against the Southwest," Dec. 2, 1842, ms.
[30] McCutchan, Diary, ms., p. 17; see also Adams, "[Journal of an] Expedition Against the Southwest," Dec. 2, 1842, ms.
[31] A. Somervell, General Order No. 51, Head Quarters, Camp Río Frio, Decr 1, 1842, in "A Record Book of the General & Special Orders and Letters of the South Western Army," p. 37, ms.

around. There was very little to eat, except a few grains of parched corn
and lean beef slaughtered, cooked, and swallowed in the same hour. At
night the army, having traveled about twenty miles during the day,
pitched camp on a small stream two miles from the Nueces, and let its
horses graze on the young curly mesquite grass which had begun to
spring up as a result of the recent rains in the western prairies. Numerous wild horses, cattle, deer, and turkey could be seen. Some of the men
from Bogart's company went in the direction of the mustangs to see if
any could be taken, but it was of no use, for the horses left with great
speed and were soon lost from sight in the distant prairie. The day had
been a serene and beautiful one. Low somber-looking hills surrounded
the camp on all sides, and "eternal desolation seemed to brood and
slumber upon their gloomy tops," though the army seems to have camped
in a garden spot surrounded by a desert. Here for the first time the
Texans beheld

vast ramparts and towers of prickly pear that seemed to form walls and mountains in their terrible array. From the midst of many of these banks of prickly
pear, young trees or saplings of the same nature were to be seen from twenty
to thirty feet in height. The whole country had a peculiar appearance, presenting a view of boundless extent and of unbroken grandeur. Yet there was
no beauty—it was a profound and cheerless desolation. Towards the north the
prairies stretched forth in broad perspective, and were only bound by the
mists and shadows that would rise like clouds upon the view.[32]

As the men weaved their way single file through the prickly pear, they
often threw their legs in front of them crosswise on the saddle, like
tailors, to protect them from the thorns. Except for the great Nueces
bottom, heavily timbered with elm, ash, pecan, and oak, from the
branches of which long festoons of moss waved gracefully in the breeze,
almost the only growth that could be seen besides the prickly pear and
Spanish daggers was the mesquite which grew on every little stream
and which was the Texans' only source of wood. The sun set in all its
majesty, and the night closed in calmness and beauty. The stars shone
forth, and by midnight not a cloud was to be seen above the horizon.
The air was cool and tranquil.

Hays' company halted on the west bank of the Nueces, while its

[32] Winkler (ed.), "Hendricks' Narrative," *Southwestern Historical Quarterly*,
XXIII (1919–1920), 122. See also Sidney S. Callender to John H. Brown, 994
Magazine St., New Orleans, June 2, 1886, in John Henry Brown Papers, 1835–
1872, ms.

leader, accompanied by Ben McCulloch on "Old Pike," another ranger, Chief Flacco and a fellow Lipan,[33] a deaf mute whose sense of sight was peculiarly acute, went forward toward Laredo under Somervell's orders to gather information concerning conditions on the Mexican frontier. About dark it was reported that several of the horses had started back on the Laredo road. Two of the men went out to bring their mounts close to quarters during the night. They had secured their mounts, and were in the act of returning when one of them said he saw an Indian, reported by Hendricks to have been a "wolf," creeping in the grass, "which so frightened their horses that they immediately threw their riders and dashed into camp."[34] "The men also hastened on to camp not being willing to risk Mr. Indian by themselves."[35] As a matter of precaution, a picket guard was placed out for the night, but the Texans were not molested.

From the leaves of the numerous maguey (dagger) plants growing in the area the Texans made rope and hobbles for their horses by roasting the leaves of the plant in the hot embers of the camp fires to separate the fibers, which they then twisted together. By unfolding the spines of the plant some obtained "a good *papyrus* from the inner folds by taking the lining from either side, and when dry and folded in a book become almost as white and as good as paper to write upon." Having no paper, Harvey A. Adams used this substitute to keep his notes on, until, at Laredo, he was able to secure enough paper to last him home.[36]

The Nueces was in flood, having overflowed its eastern bank about two miles to a depth of one to three feet. There were numerous sloughs, and in some places it was almost deep enough for swimming. The bottom lands were of a clayey, sticky nature when wet. On the west bank dry land approached the water's edge, the bank being just visible above the water. On December 3 Bogart's men swam their horses across the river and pulled their baggage (blankets and provisions) over on an

[33] Smithwick, *Evolution of a State*, p. 221; John Henry Brown, *Indian Wars and Pioneers of Texas*, p. 65. "Old Pike," captured by Ben McCulloch, was "a fast racer of rich chestnut color, sixteen hands high, faultless in disposition and one of the most sagacious horses ever known in the country [Texas]." *Ibid.* J. D. Affleck, "History of John C. Hays," pt. I, p. 288, says that "Luis, an Apache, who had been smuggled out of prison by the released Santa Fé prisoners and came to Texas with them the previous summer," also accompanied Hays.

[34] Winkler (ed.), "Hendricks' Narrative," *Southwestern Historical Quarterly,* XXIII (1919–1920), 121.

[35] Adams, "[Journal of an] Expedition Against the Southwest," Dec. 2, 1842, ms.

[36] *Ibid.,* Dec. 2 and 9, 1842.

improvised raft to which they had attached ropes. The men themselves swam across. The men were obliged to stand in the water three hours before all of their things were safely over. Only one horse was lost by the company. Its owner had tarried behind with five or six others seeking to recover a pair of saddlebags which "an old man had lost a day or two before, containing $100 in gold and silver, with some papers and other valuables." The saddlebags were never found. It was presumed that some one had found the money and thrown the other things away.

These men did not cross until evening. Then they all pi[t]ched in to swim over on horseback. They all made it safely except Smith who could not swim, neither could his horse. They both went under twice before he got loose from the horse. He went down with the current and went under again, [and would certainly have drowned but for] a bunch of willows in the main channel with a pile of drift wood which he happened to catch as he came to the surface. . . . The boys contrived to get ropes out to him and brought him to shore.[37]

A messenger had already been sent back by Hays urging General Somervell to send forward men to construct a bridge across the river. Accordingly, Somervell dispatched the companies of Captains J. B. Robertson and Isaac N. Mitchell to bridge the stream so that the army could cross to the western bank.[38] Upon approaching within a mile of the river the men discovered a vast sheet of water spread out before them, and if it had not been for the trees arising from it they might have concluded that they had struck an arm of the Gulf of Mexico rather than the Nueces. In many instances the mud was belly deep to their horses. Although it was a cold, cloudy, dismal day with a keen norther blowing full blast, the men attacked the task which had been assigned them. Colonel Cook, who had gone with the advance party, was of the opinion that the river could be crossed. So with that "go ahead" disposition which characterized many of his actions, he stripped to his underclothes and proceeded to swim the river alone. Two hours later he returned to report that a bridge had been constructed by the scouting party across the main channel and thus the army could cross on foot without swimming. Taking advantage of a drift, the men, using hatchets, felled trees from both banks into the stream so that their tops met and interlaced. Sizeable pieces of brush were then worked into the felled trees, followed later by smaller pieces, and finally by a layer of reed cane and long

[37] *Ibid.*, Dec. 3, 1842.
[38] McCutchan, Diary, ms., pp. 16–18. Brown, *History of Texas*, II, 236, says that Fisher's and Mitchell's companies were sent.

grass.[39] This causeway was so well constructed that even horses could cross it with safety.[40]

Cook now took the lead and the members of the two companies followed, each man for himself and leading his horse.

Often, [says McCutchan, one of the members] we were to our middles in mud and water, then to the knee, and again, with a sudden plunge, to our shoulders; but as far as I am aware, none were compelled to swim, until we had reached the bank of the main stream. Here finding at one or two trials that our horses could not cross on the bridge, we unpacked, unsaddled, carried our baggage over on the miniature construction, and consigned our horses to the flood.[41]

All the men gained the opposite bank in safety and moved a short distance up the river to a camp site which had been selected by Hays, about three-fourths of a mile up the river on an open flat with some prairie and excellent grass. Here they awaited the arrival of the main army, which did not come up until the next afternoon, the 5th. By the time it had crossed the river the sun was low on the western bank.

Since the crossing of the Nueces had required considerable exertion and labor, General Somervell decided to rest his army for a couple of days and await a report from Major Hays before resuming the march to Laredo. During this time the men, in small groups, occupied themselves drying their blankets, wiping and fixing their guns, or grooming their horses. All persons following the army, but who had not attached themselves officially to any component of it were ordered to "report themselves forthwith to the Captain of some company for duty."[42] On the 4th and 5th some of the best hunters killed several deer, "as we have nothing to eat but a little poor beef," recorded Adams. "Some of the men have none at all. We have had very little to eat for several days. Some of the men have a little coffee," which they purchased before leaving San Antonio; but most of the troops lacked the necessary cash for such purchases. "The Government furnished nothing but some poor beeves and they are wild stock or some that were taken

[39] Winkler (ed.), "Hendricks' Narrative," *Southwestern Historical Quarterly,* XXIII (1919–1920), 122; Brown, *History of Texas,* II, 236; Bell, *Narrative,* p. 15.

[40] Adams, "[Journal of an] Expedition Against the Southwest," Dec. 4, 1842, ms.

[41] McCutchan, Diary, ms., pp. 17–18.

[42] A. Somervell, General Order No. 53, Head Quarters, Camp Sauce, Decr 4, 1842, in "A Record Book of the General & Special Orders and Letters of the South Western Army," p. 41, ms.

from unloyal subjects. Some of the men have been without coffee for two or three weeks; the beef and venison that we get is very poor." The number of deer killed was not large, for they were very wild.[43] On the 5th Adams killed a "beautiful black and white, spotted Rab[b]it," which he cooked for breakfast, preserving the skin, ears, and feet, which he later sent to a Miss McDade by her brother, a member of Colonel Bennett's company, when he returned home. Some of the men employed themselves in cooking at different fires a hearty meal of wild turkey, venison, and beef with appetites that a sultan might have envied. Starting a fire required considerable skill. There were no matches, so the usual method was to take a piece of rag and rub powder into it, after which it was rammed into an empty gun and fired out, the flash igniting the powdered rag. Some of the men employed another method to get their fires started. They removed the flints from their guns, and with a piece of steel, made for this purpose, or a knife, struck sparks into a rag or some other inflammable substance, into which gun powder had been poured.

Two nights were passed at this encampment, which was called Camp San Ignacio. On the 5th General Somervell ordered the remaining beeves killed and barbecued, preparatory to a forced march upon the return of Captain Hays from Laredo where he had been sent two days before (on the 3rd). Several men in each mess remained up all night drying the meat so that when the order came to move forward it would not be necessary to make fires. On the night of the 5th Bogart's men camped out four miles ahead of the main army at a waterhole. The Lipans joined them in camp, and about midnight Colonel Flacco arrived with a letter from Hays to General Somervell, stating that he was thirty-five miles north of Laredo and had taken two Mexican spies.[44] Bogart, himself, received orders from Hays to move forward until he met the latter, which he did after going four miles and the two spy groups encamped the remainder of the night with the Lipans.

George Lord, some forty years later, claimed that on December 5 he overheard General Somervell remark that he had received a dispatch from President Houston to break up the expedition at all costs, and that Colonel Cook, being appraised of the instructions, replied, "Gen. we cannot break *up* this expedition, the men will mutinize, they are determined to cross the Río Grande and fight the enemy, but my advice is

[43] Adams, "[Journal of an] Expedition Against the Southwest," Dec. 5, 1842, ms.
[44] *Ibid.*, Dec. 6, 1842.

to fling every impediment in its way and let it break itself up."[45] The editor of the *Telegraph and Texas Register*[46] reported that an express rider from Washington, the temporary capital of the Republic, passed through LaGrange about December 2 with orders from the President to General Somervell. The purpose of these orders was not known, but it was currently reported in LaGrange that they would delay the march of the army.

Lord claims that this dispatch was kept secret from the command, except Colonel Cook, Colonel Bennett, Major Howard, and Judge Humphries. In a speech delivered in the United States Senate on August 1, 1854, Houston admitted that General Somervell returned from the Río Grande "in conformity with his [the President's] orders and marched his troops back again to Texas."[47] The writer has been unable to find the dispatch referred to by Lord, but this is no conclusive proof that it was not written, for many of the public records of the Republic were destroyed in the burning of the office of the Adjutant General in 1855, and of the state capitol in November 1881. Nor, on the other hand, can it be claimed by Houston's speech that he meant to say he specifically ordered the expedition back. He would not need to, for Somervell enjoyed wide discretionary authority in this respect. After the failure of the Somervell expedition and its off-shoot, the Mier expedition, became known in Texas, an editorial appeared in the *Telegraph and Texas Register* on January 18, 1843.

We have no disposition to censure Gen. Somervell [wrote the editor] for his conduct during this disgraceful campaign. He was doubtless acting under the orders of the President, and if he has violated those orders he is amenable to the laws of his country for his misconduct. If, however, he has obeyed those orders to the *letter*, upon his superiors rests the responsibility. The President has long since "prophecied" that such would be the result of this expedition. The *prophet* who had it in his power to direct the movements of this army might well *foretell* its fate. If any intelligent man had been previously told that the troops would be detained at Béxar several weeks after the time appointed for them to march to the Río Grande, and that during this vexatious delay, they would be in want of many of the necessaries of life, he would have *prophecied* that many would desert. If he had been told that on the arrival of

45 Affidavit of Geo[rge] Lord, dated Feb. 16, 1881, in Mrs. C. T. Traylor, "George Lord," *Frontier Times*, XV (1937–1938), 533–535.

46 Dec. 7, 1842.

47 U. S. Congress *Congressional Globe*, 1853–1855, Appendix, 1214–1218; see also *Writings of Sam Houston*, VI, 79.

the army at Laredo, the General would proclaim publicly that all who wished to leave the army could have free permission to return home, he would have *prophecied* that many would avail themselves of this opportunity to forsake the ranks, and thus the army would be weakened still further. If after this, he had been told that orders would be given for the troops to march home after the capture of the first inconsiderable town, and before they had fired a single shot at the enemy, and before any enemy had appeared capable of obstructing their progress, he would have *prophecied* that a portion of the troops would refuse to obey orders and thus a division of the army would follow as a natural consequence. We confess, when we examine carefully the conduct of General Somervell, we cannot discern what object he had in marching to the Río Grande. If, as it appears, his object was merely to march to Laredo or Guerrero, and then return without even exchanging a single shot with the enemy; so far as the honor and credit of the Republic is concerned, he might better have merely marched his army up the first hill west of Béxar, and then marched down again, and then disbanded his troops and gone home. If by this achievement he had not acquired as much real glory as the

> "French King, who, with forty thousand men
> Marched up a hill and then marched down agen,"

he certainly would have done less injury to the country and have gained more glory, than he has acquired by marching all the way to Guerrero and back again without capturing a single prisoner of note, or fighting one battle.

It is true that on November 5 Houston sent a personal letter to Charles Elliot, the British chargé d'affaires to Texas, requesting him to obtain permission from the British Foreign Office to act as the agent of Texas in securing peace with Mexico.[48] Yet, letters from the War Department, dated two weeks later, give no indication that the expedition was to be recalled.[49]

The main army passed another night on the west bank of the river, some of the men staying up all night to finish barbecuing the meat. Toward night of the second day that they were in camp a new norther blew up accompanied by a hard, dashing rain, thunder, and lightning. The night was so dark that the men seemed lost in a sea of blackness.

---

[48] Houston to Charles Elliot, Washington, Nov. 5, 1842 (Private), *Writings of Sam Houston*, III, 191–192; Ephraim D. Adams (ed.), *British Diplomatic Correspondence Concerning the Republic of Texas, 1836–1846,* pp. 131–132. Houston wrote: "You are aware of my intense anxiety for peace with Mexico."

[49] M. C. Hamilton to Alexander Somervell, Washington, Nov. 19, 1842, *Writings of Sam Houston*, III, 197–199; Houston to Gen. A. Somervell, Washington, Nov. 23, 1842, in *ibid.,* III, 201–202; M. C. Hamilton to Col. William G. Cooke, Dept. of War & Marine, Washington, Nov. 22, 1842, in Army Papers (Texas), ms.

The thunder rolled and shook the earth with its frightful discharges of electricity and the cold rain fell in torrents and soon penetrated their clothing. As a counterpart to the howling inferno, or possibly in an effort to soothe its madness, an incessant rattle or imitation of the tattoo was performed by the men's teeth involuntarily chattering the part of "bones" in a tolerably arranged musical concert, which kept perfect time with the strains of the wind whistling through the chaparral as the Texans hovered closely around smoldering fires. The wind howled, and the trees, both large and small, groaned under the strain. The horses neighed and became restless. About midnight a general stampede of the *caballada* took place. Dreadful confusion ensued. The night was as dark as pitch, and men, horses, and mules rushed madly about amid the flash of lightning. A thousand horses and mules tore through the camp, and men dodged left and right to avoid being trampled. In jumping to escape the on-rushing animals, the Reverend Edward Fontaine[50] (a great-grandson of Patrick Henry) fell backward into a clump of prickly pears securing quite a collection of barbs in the seat of his pants and elsewhere. During the succeeding days his captain, Dr. Jerome B. Robertson, spent his leisure hours extracting the needles from the unfortunate parson's body.[51] Toward morning

> All that vast host of golden nails
> That stay the floor of heaven[52]

looked down once more in all their brightness from amid scudding clouds. Soon the birds began to twitter as heralds of the dawn.

About daylight one of the sentinels hailed two approaching horsemen, who proved to be young Chief Flacco and the Lipan deaf-mute, bringing a note from Hays, who had stopped with his men and two prisoners about eighteen miles away, on account of having lamed his horse in the capture of two Mexican spies. From them it was learned that the scouting party had penetrated to Laredo, and that Hays had succeeded in running down and capturing two Mexican rancheros, one of whom had been severely wounded by the Indians.[53] From these

---

[50] For an excellent biographical sketch of Rev. Edward Fontaine, at one time confidential secretary to Lamar, see Professor S. W. Geiser's notes on him in *Southwestern Historical Quarterly*, XLVII (1943–1944), 181–183.

[51] Brown, *History of Texas*, II, 237.

[52] Therese Lindsey, "Stars," in *Blue Norther: Texas Poems*, p. 33.

[53] Brown, *Indian Wars and Pioneers of Texas*, p. 65. It is said that in the race to overtake the two Mexican horsemen, Flacco, the Lipan chief, led the field of some

enemy scouts it was understood that there was no Mexican force of importance on or near the Río Grande at Laredo, except a garrison of eighty regular soldiers under Colonel Calixto Bravo stationed in a small fort on the west bank of the river opposite the town. Hays reported that General Woll's troops were still at Presidio above and that Colonel Canales was below either at Guerrero or at some point between there and Matamoros. The commander of the main Mexican forces at this time, General Isidro Reyes, was encamped at Paso de Aguila so that he could operate effectively to protect both San Fernando and Presidio del Río Grande.[54] Hays believed that by forced marches the Texan army might take the small garrison at Laredo, and General Somervell decided to attempt it.

In preparation for a rapid descent upon Laredo, Somervell issued the following order to his men:

The attention of the army is directed to the following articles of the Rules and Articles for the Government of the armies of the Republic viz Art 42d "Any officer or soldier who shall without urgent necessity, without leave of his superior officers, quit his guard, platoon or division shall be punished according to the nature of his offence by the sentence of a Court Martial."

Art. 44th "Any officer or soldier who shall misbehave himself before the enemy, runaway or shamefully abandon any fort, post or guard which he or they may be commanded to defend, or speak words inducing others to do the same, or shall cast away his arms and ammunition, or who shall quit his post or colors to plunder or pillage; every such offender being duly convicted shall suffer death or such other punishment as shall be ordered by the sentence of a General Court Martial." These Articles will be vigorously enforced. They are essential as well to the security as to the honor of the Army. It is also ordered that all property captured from the enemy shall be equally distributed among the officers and soldiers share and share alike.[55]

---

twenty-five rangers, closely followed by Hays, on the horse that had been given him by Leonard W. Groce, and by Ben McCulloch on Old Pike.

[54] *Telegraph and Texas Register*, Feb. 1, 1843; Winkler (ed.), "Hendricks' Narrative," *Southwestern Historical Quarterly*, XXIII (1919–1920), 123; Isidro Reyes to His Excellency the Secretary of War and Marine, Head Quarters of the Army of the North, Passo de Aguila, Dec. 5, 1842, quoted from *el Diario del Gobierno* in the *Morning Star* (Houston), Jan. 31, 1843.

[55] A. Somervell, General Order No. 57, Head Quarters, Camp San Ignatio [San Ygnacio], Decm᷍ᵇ 6, 1842, in "A Record Book of the General & Special Orders and Letters of the South Western Army," pp. 46–47, ms.; except for the last sentence (probably intentionally omitted), General Order No. 57 is reproduced in John Hemphill, Acting Adjutant-General of the Texas Militia, to Anson Jones, Washington, Texas, Jan. 23, 1843, in Army Papers (Texas), ms.; and in State Department

Leaving a few men behind to round up the missing animals, the army moved forward at an early hour on the 6th through the cacti and the cochineal toward Laredo. The land became less desirable—more desolate in appearance. Often rabbits and deer could be seen scampering across the spreading plain of cacti and mesquite; and occasionally, wolves, catamounts, and panthers were frightened from cover. Wild horses, or mustangs, at a respectful distance gazed for an instant at their cousins in bondage, and then with a shrill snort galloped off, tossing their manes disdainfully, and halted awhile and "caracoled about like so many well-trained race-horses, and with erected ears, and open nostrils, and with their long and bushy manes and tails expanded to the wind. . . . outstripped the latter in its flight over the prairie,"[56] and were soon lost in the chaparral faraway to the west. Hays' company, out in front, encountered some wild cattle which they pursued; they were fortunate enough to kill four fat ones. These were, indeed, "a God send to us at the time," wrote a member of Bogart's company, since the beeves of the expedition were being driven along with the main army.[57] It was a cold, rainy morning, with a strong north wind blowing, and the Texans were approximately sixty miles from their immediate objective—Laredo. Unfortunately, during the night one of the captured spies effected his escape from Hays' camp, although it was thought that he would not go far as he had been badly wounded by three arrows of the Lipans while being captured. In view of his condition, he had not been as carefully guarded as he might have been. His guard, William Alsbury,[58] overcome by fatigue, had made a pillow of the prisoner's body and soon fell asleep. With great skill and daring the prisoner had gently placed the head of his slumbering guard upon a saddle and left. Hays was much exasperated by the carelessness of the guard. He determined to recapture the prisoner, if he could; so, taking a single companion, Ben McCulloch, he proceeded quickly in pursuit to the outskirts of Laredo

(Texas), Department of State Letterbook, Home Letters (1842–1846), ms., II, pp. 69–71.

[56] [Frederic Benjamin Page], *Prairiedom: Rambles and Scrambles in Texas or New Estremadura by a Suthron*, p. 97.

[57] Winkler (ed.), "Hendricks' Narrative," *Southwestern Historical Quarterly*, XXIII (1919–1920), 123; Adams, "[Journal of an] Expedition Against the Southwest," Dec. 6, 1842, ms.

[58] Winkler (ed.), "Hendricks' Narrative," *Southwestern Historical Quarterly*, XXIII (1919–1920), 123; Brown, *History of Texas*, II, 237; Adams, "[Journal of an] Expedition against the Southwest," Dec. 7, 1842, ms.

for the purpose of overtaking or intercepting the escaped prisoner; but he failed to come upon him. He later learned that the prisoner had preceded him to Laredo and given the alarm.

During the day the army made a good day's march of about twenty miles, and the site selected for a camp (San Ygnacio, on the Laredo road) was reached one hour after dark. The main army under Somervell encamped on the east (north) side of a small creek and Bogart's company on the west side. Water was "scarce and bad" and the country was so open and bare of timber that it was with difficulty the men could find sufficient wood with which to cook.[59] There was, by now, not one tent in the whole command. While the rain descended and the winds blew, the Texans passed the night huddled over a smoldering campfire, listening to the mournful howling of wolves in the distance, or the shrill scream of a panther. If the latter were near, it seemed for a moment unlike anything on earth, and if far off its cry sounded like the wailing of some terrible monster gasping for life. It was a miserable night for the stouthearted Texans; yet, the mess men set about preparing two day's rations, principally dried beef, in order not to make any fires after leaving this place.

On the morning of December 7 General Somervell ordered Colonel James R. Cook to take six companies of the best mounted men, make a forced march, cross the Río Grande, either above or below town, as he saw best, and cut off the retreat of the enemy garrison.[60] Meanwhile Somervell himself would proceed more leisurely with the main body of troops and arrive in sufficient time to render assistance if any were necessary from the Texas side of the river—thus attacking on both sides of the river simultaneously. If it was found impracticable to cross the river, the two spy companies after reaching the regular crossing below the town were "to march up under its eastern bank, near the margin of

---

[59] McCutchan, Diary, ms., pp. 17–18, 21. Adams, "[Journal of an] Expedition Against the Southwest," Dec. 6, 1842, ms., says, "we camped on a small creek where we got plenty of wood, water, & grass for our horses."

[60] There were two passable fords of the Río Grande in the vicinity of Laredo. One was the Paso de Jacinto (the Paso de los Indios), about two leagues above the town, and the other the Paso de Miguel de la Garza, three leagues below the town in the vicinity of "la Canada de los Abiones." H. E. Bolton (ed.), "Tienda de Cuervo's Ynspección of Laredo, 1757," *Quarterly of the Texas State Historical Association*, VI (1902–1902), 194 n. See also A. Somervell, General Order No. 55, Head Quarters, Camp San Ygnacio on the Laredo Road, Decr 6, 1842, in "A Record Book of the General & Special Orders and Letters of the South Western Army," pp. 42–44, ms.

the water, until . . . [they were] opposite the public square, where . . . [they] were to remain stationary until daylight, which was to be the signal for the whole army to enter the town."⁶¹ It was hoped that the small Mexican garrison after being cut off would surrender without a fight because of the odds against it. Thus one of the main objectives of the expedition would be achieved—a sufficient number of prisoners who could be exchanged for the Texans being held by the Mexican government. Among those sent forward were the companies of Hays and Bogart who now resumed the lead, with Hays in the vanguard. After four miles, Bogart's men reached Hays' camp of the previous evening, and there, thirty-five miles from Laredo, awaited the arrival of the regiment. Upon the regiment's coming up, "a very nervous and eloquent address" was delivered by Colonel Hemphill and a few orders were issued. In General Order No. 56 Somervell appealed to the troops for unity and a firm determination to punish the enemy severely wherever he might be found. In the light of subsequent accusations against Somervell for a lack of energy in the campaign, his address to the troops is of considerable significance.

Soldiers:
The first campaign for offensive operations against Mexico has commenced. Upon you has fallen the honor of first carrying the war into the enemy's country, and your valor and gallantry will prove that you merit the distinction of leading the van in the battles of the country.

Remember, though the recollection is painful, that for the last year a series of outrages have been inflicted upon us by the marauding border incursions of the enemy. Our Frontier Towns have been taken and sacked—our habitations desolated—our countrymen slaughtered—and but too many of our best citizens dragged into gloomy captivity.

We have lamented these calamities—let them now be avenged. Let us even turn them to profit, by teaching us to adopt that harmony in council, that unanimity in action and that subordination united with energy, the want of which has hitherto paralyzed all our efforts. They are as necessary to the safety of the soldier as they are to the honor of the country.

Soldiers: The petty successes of the enemy have rendered him confident. Let us pursue him to his retreats, and in his strong-holds punish his audacity. Let us teach him that we not only understand and appreciate the inestimable blessings of Liberty, but that our bravery is in proportion to our intelligence, and that we are determined to chastize the enemy wherever he may be

⁶¹ Winkler (ed.), "Hendricks' Narrative," *Southwestern Historical Quarterly*, XXIII (1919–1920), 124.

found. In battle let the enemy feel the fierceness of a just resentment. In victory be generous to the conquered.

You have encountered great fatigue in traversing the vast wilderness which separates you from the enemy. You have borne it with patience, and the General cannot refrain from expressing his satisfaction at the orderly conduct of the officers and soldiers on the campaign. Such soldierly behaviour and such patience and preserving energy teach him to rely on you with confidence in every peril which may be encountered. Repress every symptom of discord and insubordination. Be firm and united and you will be resistless. The enemy has been often conquered by an inferior force, and should he again be met, your stout hearts and good rifles will swell the number of your country's triumphs. Let us march then to battle and be assured that victory ever attends the deserving and the brave.[62]

After Somervell's address had been read, the troops proceeded eighteen miles and encamped for two or three hours at a waterhole. At this time the men had a bite to eat while they waited further orders from General Somervell.

After breakfasting and packing, the main body of Texans moved on rapidly at daylight, carrying only two days' provisions so as to facilitate the march. Most of the men were mounted, although some were now on foot. The first part of the day was cloudy, but towards noon the sun came out. Two miles[63] of marching brought Bogart's men to Hays' camp where they learned that the wounded prisoner had escaped two nights before. Alsbury was placed under arrest, and the expedition moved on. Actually, the escape probably did little harm, for the Mexican authorities on the Río Grande had already been apprised of the march of the Texan expedition. On December 1, Antonio Pérez, who had been ordered to Béxar by General Reyes to investigate the objective of the Texans assembling at that point, reached Presidio del Río Grande to inform Reyes that Somervell had begun his march for the frontier with a large force supported by one six-pounder. This report was confirmed by the other spies arriving later in the day, who, in addition, stated that the French flag at San Antonio had been insulted by the Texans, who had removed lead, flour, and other articles from the vice consul's home. This was "just punishment to those who have recognized the independence of those pirates," exclaimed Reyes in his official report. Consequently,

---

[62] A. Somervell, General Order No. 56, Head Quarters, Camp Nueces, Dec' 6, 1842, in "A Record Book of the General & Special Orders and Letters of the South Western Army," pp. 44–46, ms.

[63] Four miles, says Adams, "[Journal of an] Expedition Against the Southwest," Dec. 7, 1842, ms.

in order to give protection to either Presidio or San Fernando, Reyes established himself in the passage of los Adjuntos, and assured the Minister of War that no matter which place might be the point of attack his valiant troops would punish the audacity of the reckless adventurers.[64] Since the escaped Mexican ranchero had undoubtedly fled into the town and warned the inhabitants of the approach of the Texan force, it was believed that by now the Mexican soldiers had probably performed a precipitate retreat. During the halt, the men and animals were permitted to rest and take refreshments; however, few fires were made for fear the smoke would be seen by the enemy scouts.

Near sunset, the Texan army resumed its march towards Laredo, twelve miles distant, hoping to reach the town about daylight on the following morning. Major Hays, with the assistance of Ben McCulloch, maintained the scouting party out in front. It was now night. "The skies became clear and the stars shone forth in the glory of a beautiful night."[65] The command moved rapidly forward along the narrow cart trail, which bristled on each side with a dense mesquite chaparral described by a campaigner as an irregular, impenetrable mass of "scraggly, scrubby, crooked, infernally illegitimate and sin-begotten bushy trees loaded with millions of thornpins."[66] The army moved forward the best it could, guided by the light of the stars and the dim light of a pale moon, which made its appearance soon after sunset and seemed to career madly across the clouds, barely lighting up the sombre scene. Later, as the moon set and the darkness increased, various bodies of the army fell into confusion. However, the exhausted men and their horses stumbled along in the night. During the night one man was lost and nothing was ever heard of him afterwards. Five miles over broken ridges brought the army to a deep ravine of almost perpendicular banks, which the men were compelled to cross in single file, leading their horses.[67] Here a halt was ordered by Colonel Cook to permit the men, scattered over four to five miles, to catch up. After about two hours, the stragglers came up, and a forward movement of three or four miles was made before another halt was called. When the expedition arrived within approximately four miles of Laredo the road became more distinguishable, showing cart tracks made by wood haulers and as the

[64] Isidro Reyes to the Minister of War, Río Grande, Dec. 1, 1842, quoted from *El Diario del Gobierno* by *El Cosmopolita* (Mexico City), Dec. 14, 1842.

[65] Brown, *History of Texas*, II, 237.

[66] Quoted in Justin H. Smith, *The War with Mexico*, I, 148.

[67] Adams, "[Journal of an] Expedition Against the Southwest," Dec. 7, 1842, ms.

Texans proceeded, the road became plainer and plainer. When within two miles of the town, the force halted to await the return of the spies. The horses with their "rigging on" were tied out to graze, while the men tried to take a nap. It was 11 P.M., and the night was fairly dark.

Shortly after midnight, around 1 o'clock, Colonel Cook, with the four companies assigned him, commenced his advance towards the crossing. After proceeding a short distance, he left the main road and took a route through the chaparral over hills and through dry ravines full of rocks and pebbles to reach the river about one mile below town. A short time later, the march was interrupted when one of the Lipans was thrown from his horse and incurred a severe wound from his spear piercing his body. Within a quarter of a mile of the Río Grande, the vanguard rode into a deep barranca through which ran a small stream of water, communicating with the main river at the crossing immediately below. Dismounting, the men led their horses down this deep gully to the Río Grande shielded in their progress by a thirty foot bluff. Hays and McCulloch, who had preceded Cook to the river, had failed to find boats in which the men, arms, and ammunition could be crossed in dry condition. Swiming over they found a single perogue but the water at this point was so swift that it could not be managed. The bed of the river was so full of rocks and the water ran so swiftly that the Texans did not attempt to cross in the perogue for fear of losing their arms and being drowned.[68] The absence of boats for crossing had been reported to Cook and Somervell at 2 o'clock in the morning. Upon reaching the river, Colonel Cook made several unsuccessful attempts to cross; finally, however, he reported to Somervell that it was impossible to cross the river,[69] but that "he would occupy the ground between the town and the river, with the troops under his command."[70]

It was now four o'clock in the morning. The two spy companies were paraded, and it was determined to seize Laredo with the soldiers who

[68] *Ibid.*

[69] He apparently failed to find the ford, probably because he did not go far enough down the river. Soon after the founding of Laredo, the San Miguel de la Garza Crossing was described as "so easy that sheep and goats cross it; by means of which a direct road is open from this settlement to Coahuila and Texas and over which numerous travelers pass without any difficulty." Treviño (Archivo General, Historia, 56, Doc. 10, folio 3) quoted in Bolton (ed.), "Tienda de Cuervo's Ynspección of Laredo, 1757," *Quarterly of the Texas State Historical Association,* VI (1902–1903), 196 n.

[70] A. Somervell to G. W. Hill, Sec. of War and Marine, Feb. 1, 1843, *Morning Star* (Houston), Feb. 18, 1843.

were said to be there. Four men from each company were detailed to guard the horses and baggage, but "many more must have stayed there or somewhere else," reported Adams, "as only 80 men were with us as we went up."[71] Hays' and Bogart's companies now proceeded on foot along the river front between the edge of the water and the steep embankment. The river was low, and there was a considerably shoally beach, covered with sand and pebbles and, in places, with dark frowning rocks. Protected and concealed by the bluff under which Santa Anna had encamped his army in 1836, they took up a position a short distance from the public square where they halted until daylight wrapped in their blankets as it was rather cold. A little later, when they moved forward again, they rid themselves of all loose appendages and deposited them under the bank until their return. In the meantime, the remaining companies under Cook's authority rejoined the main body of troops which had advanced to within a short distance of the town.

[71] Adams, "[Journal of an] Expedition Against the Southwest," Dec. 7, 1842, ms.

CHAPTER TWENTY-ONE

The Capture and Plunder of Laredo

AN HOUR BEFORE daybreak, "after a night in the saddle with an occasional respite, during which the men were permitted to slumber, under arms, with rein in hand," the Texans at last found themselves drawn up in the form of a "Half Moon" before the town of Laredo. Their ranks extended in a semicircle along the east bank of the Río Bravo from above the town to the bank below. While they waited they could distinctly hear the dogs barking and roosters crowing in town. Excitement ran high among the men, despite their weariness and hunger from the long fatiguing march of the previous day and night, which climaxed a surprise move against Laredo lasting seventeen instead of the usual seven days. Ordered to maintain dead silence, the men were kept mounted throughout the remainder of the night, sitting like statues upon their horses awaiting the coming of day. With the coming and going of couriers, captains, and others from the vicinity of the general and "The mysterious whisperings" and secrecy surrounding the general's actions, the men near headquarters began to gain the impression that daylight would bring a fight. Soon the whisperings and rumors of impending action spread like a ripple from the vicinity of the general throughout the entire column drawn up before the town. Tensely the men awaited the dawn. While they longed "anxiously for a 'Side of Beef ribs,' a cup of coffee, and a good long nap on the natural couch formed of 'Mother Earth',"[1] a few of the toil-worn campaigners were anxious for a "little skirmish" by the way of earning their breakfast, if it could be obtained. This, however, could not be effected, as the garrison had been apprised of their advance and had withdrawn across the Paso de Jacinto,[2] near

---

[1] Joseph D. McCutchan, Diary, ms., p. 23.
[2] This crossing was so named because it had been discovered by Jacinto de León in 1746, nine years before the founding of Laredo. Herbert E. Bolton, *Texas in the Middle Eighteenth Century*, p. 298. Jacinto Pass is now, according to Virgil N. Lott and Mercurio Martinez, *Kingdom of Zapata*, p. 210, about a mile above Laredo.

Laredo, to the west bank of the river and no hostile movement was made by the Mexicans within the town.

With the first faint streaks of day, several persons from the ranchos on the opposite side of the river came down for water, but did not discover the Texans. A few minutes later, two women in a perogue started to cross to the Texan side of the river, but when about half way across discovered the Texan troops and turned back, although apparently without showing much alarm. As soon as it was fairly daylight the spy companies moved along between two pathways that led down to the river, when about this time a small boy came down on the Texan side of the river to water a mule,[3] but did not discover the Texans until he was almost at the water's edge and Colonel Ben McColloch was nearly at him. The boy was captured. He was very much surprised, but submitted very kindly and from him it was learned that there was no Mexican force in town. While the boy was being questioned, one or two women approaching the river, perhaps for water, suddenly discovered by the dim light of the morning the bristling ranks of armed men extending from right to left along the bank. Uttering a short, shrill scream, they turned and fled in the direction of the town. The boy was now turned loose to go about his business. If there had been any doubt previously of whether or not the Mexicans had been forewarned of the Texan advance, it now ceased to exist. The Texans quickly scrambled up the embankment and formed in lines at the head of several streets, but met no opposition. Much to their chagrin they found that the soldiers (one hundred in number) with most of the citizens had fled to parts unknown. The inhabitants who remained in the town began to assemble in groups on the western bank.

A little after sunrise the Texan vanguard under Captain Bell entered Laredo without the firing of a shot, only to find women, children, dogs, and a few old men lining the streets, doffing their hats and welcoming the invaders with cries of *"Buenos dias cabelleros! Nosotros son amigos de los Americanos!" "Buenos hombres!" "Buenos Americanos!"*[4] The

---

[3] Harvey Alexander Adams, "[Journal of an] Expedition Against the Southwest in 1842 and 1843," Dec. 7, 1842, ms., says a Mexican came down with two horses to water.

[4] John Henry Brown, *History of Texas, from 1685 to 1892*, II, 237–238. Translated: "Good morning, Gentlemen! We are friends of the Americans!" "Good men!" "Good Americans!" They did not say "friends" of the "Texans," but to the average Mexican a "Texian" was an "American," and they did not make any distinction between the two.

510

Mexicans appeared as joyous at seeing the Texans as if they had been receiving their own relatives, offering them cakes, *piloncillos*, and other things to eat.[5] As one narrator of the expedition recorded, "our belligerent feelings were turned into shame for ourselves" at seeing these poor defenceless and bewildered people; and yet, we all felt "badly humbugged."[6] Thus ended what some of the Texan volunteers in ridicule termed "the siege of Laredo." Hays' and Bogart's men repaired to the ravine for their horses and blankets.

In a little while Captain Bell brought Don Florencio Villareal, the alcalde, and two prominent citizens, who with great politeness and submission surrendered the town to General Somervell.[7] One member of the Mexican delegation, an old man, after shaking hands with several of the Texan officers, approached Flacco and extended a hand in greeting, but the Indian sternly drew himself up and levelled his spear and by other signs indicated he would rather kill on the spot than greet him as a friend.[8] During his stay at Laredo, Flacco would not speak to a single Mexican, and "appeared to be constantly watching for an opportunity to avenge the blood of his countrymen." The advance companies hoisted the Texan flag on one of the main steeples and had it flying fifteen minutes before General Somervell entered the town with the main force. The General paraded his army of about 730 men, including 40 on the sick list. Forewarned of the advance of the Texans, the Mexican garrison, under the command of Colonel Bravo, and many of the leading citizens had evacuated the town by crossing to the west bank, taking with them most of their goods and provisions of value. Their horses and mules, said to number a thousand head,[9] had also been driven off during the night, except for a few which were concealed in the houses, and the yokes of oxen had been run into the thick chaparral near the town. The lack of a sufficient number of available horses was a sad disappointment to many of the Texans whose mounts had

[5] McCutchan, Diary, ms., Dec. 10, 1842; Adams, "[Journal of an] Expedition Against the Southwest," Dec. 7, 1842, ms.

[6] Thomas J. Green, *Journal of the Texian Expedition Against Mier*, p. 55.

[7] Lucy A. Erath (ed.), "Memoirs of Major George Bernard Erath," *Southwestern Historical Quarterly*, XXVIII (1923–1924), 40; *Lamar Papers*, VI, 116; Seb S. Wilcox, "Laredo during the Texas Republic," *Southwestern Historical Quarterly*, XLII (1938–1939), 101, lists the following officials of Laredo at the beginning of 1842: Florencio Villareal, alcalde; Reyes Ortiz and Miguel Dovalina, aldermen; and Faustino Ramírez, justice of the peace.

[8] *Telegraph and Texas Register*, Jan. 11, 1843.

[9] Adams, "[Journal of an] Expedition Against the Southwest," Dec. 8, 1842, ms.

given out during the trip to Laredo and whose riders had been forced to make long marches, "packing their baggage and provisions on their shoulders." Many of them were inconvenienced by the loss of their blankets and clothes, often left behind with the pack animals; and "as the winter had set in with unusual severity, the absence of such indispensable comforts was keenly felt."[10] Added to this, the Texan army had consumed the last of its provisions by the time it reached Laredo, and the last of the beeves driven along with the expedition had been abandoned when the forced march had been started.

The Villa San Agustín de Laredo, commonly known as Laredo, had been established on May 15, 1755, by Don Tomás Sánchez de la Barrera y Gallardo, owner of a stock ranch opposite Dolores, acting under permission given by Don José Vasquez Borrego, a subordinate of General José de Escandón,[11] colonizer of the Colonia del Nuevo Santander (Saint Andrew's New Colony). Laredo, situated on a sandy bank about twenty feet above the water's edge, was one of the oldest towns upon the lower Río Grande. It was ideally located. A short distance to the north was El Paso de Jacinto and a few leagues to the south was El Paso de Miguel de la Garza, which after the founding of Laredo took popular precedence over the Presidio Crossing (or French Crossing as it was sometimes referred to after the visit of St. Denis) at San Juan Bautista (now Guerrero, Coahuila), and El Camino Real shifted southward to make Laredo the gateway between northern Mexico and San Antonio. Laredo had suffered a great deal in the past from attacks of Indians (particularly the fierce Comanches and Apaches, and thieving Lipans) and more recently from the activities of the revolutionists. The Río Grande had flooded the town during the spring rises of 1842 and caused considerable damage.[12] The place had not been prosperous for

[10] William Preston Stapp, *The Prisoners of Perote: Containing a Journal Kept by the Author Who Was Captured by the Mexicans, at Mier, December 25, 1842, and Released from Perote, May 16, 1844*, p. 24.

[11] I. J. Cox, "The Southwest Boundary of Texas," *Quarterly of the Texas State Historical Association*, VI (1902–1903), 91; Harold Schoen (comp.), *Monuments Erected by the State of Texas to Commemorate the Centenary of Texas Independence*, p. 90; Florence Johnson Scott, *Historical Heritage of the Lower Río Grande: A Historical Record of Spanish Exploration, Subjugation, and Colonization of the Lower Río Grande and the Activities of José Escandón, Count of Sierra Gorda together with the Development of Towns and Ranches under Spanish, Mexican and Texas Sovereignties, 1747–1848*, pp. 42–43.

[12] Wilcox, "Laredo during the Texas Republic," *Southwestern Historical Quarterly*, XLII (1938–1939), 101.

some time, and its population had declined since 1828, amounting in 1842 to fewer than two thousand inhabitants.[13] The town was little more than a heap of ruins, and scarcely a home in it could be called comfortable, even by the standards of that day. A desolate air enveloped the whole city, and there was "not a single tree to gladden the eye as the vegetation of this arid land . . . [consisted] of small mesquites and huisache with cactus scattered here and there."[14]

General M. B. Lamar, who commanded the occupation troops in the town in 1846, informed General Zachary Taylor that "seven hundred of its inhabitants had been killed within the last twenty years."[15] Its carefree people were fond of dancing, and little inclined to work. "The women [of Laredo], who are, as a general rule good looking," reported a traveler, "are ardently fond of luxury and leisure; they have rather loose ideas of morality, which cause the greater part of them to have shameful relations openly, especially with the officers, both because they are more numerous and spend their salary freely, and because they are more skillful in the art of seduction."[16] The only substantial work performed by the inhabitants was cattle raising, and occasionally the carrying on of a considerable and rather important trade with San Antonio, exchanging such items as beans, leather, *piloncillos*, shoes, saddles, mules, and horses for calico, tobacco, American hardware, and other commodities. But in 1842 the ranches were in a deplorable condition, and during the last few years the trade had suffered much from the freebooters. Even in normal times food supplies at Laredo were extremely scarce. The little corn that was cultivated by the inhabitants was planted near the city in tracts which were flooded by the river in times of high water. The scarcity of rain scarcely permitted planting in other places and the constant Indian danger discouraged farming at too great a distance from the protection of the town. Laredo customarily depended upon Candela and other places for its corn, flour, brown sugar, and *vino mescal*.

[13] *Ibid.*, pp. 83–107; Thomas W. Bell, *A Narrative of the Capture and Subsequent Sufferings of the Mier Prisoners in Mexico, Captured in the Cause of Texas, Dec. 26th, 1842 and Liberated Sept. 16, 1844*, p. 15; "Census of Laredo: List of Municipal Officers, Laredo, Dec. 14, 1846," in *Lamar Papers*, VI, 44–65.

[14] José María Sánchez, "A Trip to Texas in 1828," *Southwestern Historical Quarterly*, XXIX (1925–1926), 251.

[15] M. B. Lamar to Gen. Zachary Taylor, Laredo, Dec. 24, 1846, in *Lamar Papers*, VI, 69.

[16] Sánchez, "A Trip to Texas in 1828," *Southwestern Historical Quarterly*, XXIX (1925–1926), 251.

The alcalde, Don Florencio Villareal,[17] and other officials lost no time in placing the town at the disposal of the Texans, and Somervell accordingly levied a requisition upon the community for supplies of food, blankets, and clothing for his bedraggled and hungry army. The Texan army did not take up quarters in the town, but, guided by the local authorities, it passed through, leaving the plaza on the left, to encamp at a site selected by the town's officers. At a mile or a mile and a half above town Somervell pitched his camp upon a sand-bar to await the supplies of meat, bread, and other necessary items,[18] which had been so profusely promised by the Mexican officialdom, but which actually was delivered only in such "stinted quantities as their fears allowed them to bring in." About noon, eight or ten beeves were driven into camp and butchered, being practically the only supplies, besides two hundred pounds of flour and a small quantity of *piloncillo* and white sugar—"taken, not given"—to arrive during the day.[19] The beeves furnished scarcely sufficient meat for one day's rations.[20] A large portion of the town's provisions had been conveyed across the river or cached at a distance from the town. Quite a number of sacks of flour were found hidden in the chaparral two miles from Laredo. The Texans found a "worn and much travelled way going from town down the river which had been travelled with Mexican carts, but at 2½ or 3 miles from town the signs all died out as though they had scattered in every direction," and the Texans were unable to find out where the vehicles had gone or where the supposedly valuable articles might have been cached. After several hours they gave up the search.[21] A great number of the Texans were not willing to await the tedious operation of a requisition, and being fearful of losing an opportunity for self-profit went "into houses and stores and took a great many such things as they could lay hands upon and took them by force and carried them off by violence, breaking down doors, opening boxes, and trunks and taking off blankets wherever they could find them, even from the beds of women, leaving them to weep the fate of their unhappy lot." The lateness of the day and

[17] Wilcox, "Laredo during the Texas Republic," *Southwestern Historical Quarterly*, XLII (1938–1939), 101; Kathleen DaCamara, *Laredo on the Río Grande*, p. 17.

[18] Brown, *History of Texas*, II, 238.

[19] Adams, "[Journal of an] Expedition Against the Southwest," Dec. 8, 1842, ms.

[20] Green, *Journal of the Texian Expedition Against Mier*, p. 55; Brown, *History of Texas*, II, 238; Erath (ed.), "Memoirs of Major George Bernard Erath," *Southwestern Historical Quarterly*, XXVII (1923–1924), 41.

[21] Adams, "[Journal of an] Expedition Against the Southwest," Dec. 9, 1842, ms.

the order to move the camp were the only things that put a stop to this state of things.[22]

The army remained encamped above Laredo for about six hours while most of the Texans rested, slept, and permitted their horses to graze on the scanty supply of grass available in the vicinity. During this time the white flags of surrender of the Mexicans could be seen flying in every direction on the opposite side of the river. About two o'clock in the afternoon, as a result of the interposition of Colonel Cook and other officers, it was decided to move the army for the night to a better camp site for greater protection in the event of an attack; rumors were afloat that a Mexican force nearly equal to the Texan army was in the vicinity.[23] The army, eager to move, now retraced its steps down the river, past the town but not through it, following along a level road lined with shrubs. It had proceeded only a quarter of a mile when word came from the rear that the enemy was in sight on the opposite side of the river. The army was halted, but the clouds of dust which had been the cause of the alarm proved to be a few Texans returning from an excursion across the river earlier in the day to pick up horses—"this privilege having been granted by the Mexicans"—reported Hendricks, but not by General Somervell. After this flurry of excitement, the army proceeded on its march. The vegetation became more plentiful and the grass of a better quality. About an hour before sundown the army encamped. The camp site was on a high hill three miles immediately below Laredo and "within a few hundred yards of the river, from the western bank of which our position," recorded Hendricks, "would have been exposed to a cannonade had a Mexican force engaged us." The spot selected for the night, known as Camp Chacón after the adjacent stream of that name, was almost entirely surrounded by a deep ravine, from which it would have required a considerable force to dislodge the Texans. Immediately in front of their camp was a deep hollow, through which the expedition had recently passed, and on either side, especially the northern, "the rise was abrupt and steep, and the road in its passage had huge banks, bluffs, and caves on either hand, and through the hollow there ran a small stream called the Shackow [Chacón]."[24] Across the river the Mexican spies could see the flare of the Texan campfires.

[22] *Ibid.*, Dec. 8, 1842.   [23] Bell, *Narrative*, p. 16.

[24] E. W. Winkler (ed.), "Sterling Brown Hendricks' Narrative of the Somervell Expedition to the Rio Grande," *Southwestern Historical Quarterly*, XXIII (1919–1920), 126–127. See also J. D. Affleck, "History of John C. Hays," pt. I, p. 40. Affleck says that the Chacón was a small stream five miles below Laredo.

On the march through the hollow, one of Captain Cameron's men, DeBoyce by name, was killed almost instantly by the accidental discharge of a messmate's gun, the ball entering his heart.[25] The body was brought into camp and the deceased, being the first member of the expedition to lose his life, was accorded a soldier's burial. During the evening the beeves were killed, dressed, and quartered for cooking. Tripods and poles for suspending the meat over a fire were erected. In a few instances holes were dug in the ground and the meat roasted over live coals. In either case, men in fringed shirts stood by to guard and shift the roasting hunks of beef while their comrades hovered a short distance away silhouetted against the clear yellow glow of the campfires. As soon as the cooked meat was taken from the fire it was quickly cut into smaller pieces with bowie knives, and the hungry men standing around snatched hot pieces of it and tossed them from hand to hand as they made off to wait for them to cool before devouring them. During the evening a number of the men became intoxicated with mescal, marihuana, and *aguardiente* which they had found stored in some of the houses in Laredo.[26]

At night General Somervell placed picket guards about the camp and took other precautionary measures to insure the safety of his men. One picket was sent in the direction of Laredo to occupy a stand on the north side of the hollow, and a part of this picket was placed above and below in or near the same hollow. Sterling Brown Hendricks of Bogart's company had charge of this picket, and while he slept during the night with those of his men who were not on duty, "a diabolical wolf had the audacity to run over" him. The picket guard on the opposite side of the camp was commanded by Lieutenant Ben McCulloch of Hays' company. During the night one of the sentinels came very near firing on one of the Texans who had stayed rather late in Laredo and was unprepared to give the countersign.

Once more the men became suspicious of Somervell's action. The main road along the Río Grande was on the west side of the river, and

[25] John C. Duval, *The Adventures of Big-Foot Wallace: The Texas Ranger and Hunter*, p. 168; Stapp, *Prisoners of Perote*, p. 24; Memucan Hunt to Francis Moore, Jr., Editor of the *Telegraph*, Houston, dated Bexar, Jan. 8, 1843, in *Morning Star* (Houston), Jan. 17, 1843. Winkler (ed.), "Hendricks' Narrative," *Southwestern Historical Quarterly*, XXIII (1919–1920), 127, says that the boy was "shot dead by the accidental discharge of his own gun." Harvey A. Adams says he was accidentally shot, "the charge passing through his body just above the right nipple." Adams, "[Journal of an] Expedition Against the Southwest," Dec. 8, 1842, ms.

[26] Adams, "[Journal of an] Expedition Against the Southwest," Dec. 8, 1842, ms.

the crossing was at Laredo; hence his pointing the army in the direction of the San Antonio road seemed to indicate to many, who were already inclined to be critical of everything that the commanding officer did, that he intended to take the men home.

Mention has been made of a small number of Texans crossing the river after the occupation of Laredo. Without permission of their general, Thomas Jefferson Green and five others conducted a raid across the river upon the small town of Galveston early in the afternoon. Green (who had been denied a seat in the Senate of the Second Congress from Béxar County because he was not a resident citizen of the county when elected) subsequently tried to defend his conduct at Laredo by making the following statement in his bombastic history of the Mier expedition:

Feeling as others felt, that, if . . . [Somervell returned home] it would be a lasting disgrace upon our country and ourselves . . . without crossing into Mexico, I took five men with me, crossed the river to the small town of Galveston, planted the Texian banner in the name of our country, demanded of the alcalde five good mules, which the boys took, and recrossed the river to camp. This place was the military station of Colonel Bravo, who was then secreted in Laredo, while his troops were still at that place. Upon my return to camp, I informed the officers that I had been among Bravo's troops, expecting, of course, General Somervell would send and capture them; but his mind was in other ways intent.[27]

Thomas Jefferson Green, however, was known to have very little respect for authority. Born in Warren County, North Carolina, February 14, 1802, he was the ninth of twelve children born to Solomon and Fanny (Hawkins) Green. He was a student at the University of North Carolina in 1819, and in 1822 he received an appointment to West Point Military Academy but stayed only four months (July 1–October 30, 1822). In 1823 he represented Warren County in the House of Representatives of the North Carolina Legislature. Four years later, on January 8, 1830, he married Sarah A. Wharton of Nashville, Tennessee, and settled in Mississippi, and from there moved to a plantation near St. Marks, Florida, where his only child, Wharton J. Green, was born. Green served two years (1834–1835) in the territorial legislature of Florida. Following the death of his wife in March, 1835, the war in Texas attracted his attention. He organized the Texas Land Company in 1836 and moved to Texas, but abandoned his colonization project, obtained a brigadier general's commission in the Texan army from

[27] Green, *Journal of the Texian Expedition Against Mier*, pp. 55–56.

President Burnet on March 19, 1836, and returned to the United States to raise volunteers and to receive contributions and negotiate loans and contracts not to exceed fifty thousand dollars.[28] He again arrived in Texas on the steamer *Ocean* at Velasco on June 3, 1836, with some 230 volunteers from New Orleans. Finding a few Texans and recent arrivals from the United States dissatisfied with the new government's determination to send Santa Anna and his staff, then prisoners in Texas, to Vera Cruz, Green forced the Texan government to land the Mexican president and his officers from the scooner-of-war *Invincible* on which they had been placed preparatory to sailing to Mexico, and sought to have them court-martialled.

Late in the afternoon of June 3, Green ordered his own cabin on the *Ocean* to be prepared for the reception of the distinguished prisoner. Supper was served at half past six, and during the meal Green is alleged to have remarked that when he visited Mexico, he would expect Santa Anna to give him coffee in brighter metal than the tin plate in which Santa Anna was being served. Santa Anna is quoted as having replied, "Ah! yes, my dear General, I do long for this unfortunate war to be over, and then I want to see you in Mexico where I can reciprocate your kindness."[29]

Green often considered himself above being commanded by his superiors. In the summer of 1836 he "reached Gen. [Thomas J.] Rusk's Army" at Victoria, but, reported David Macomb, "refuses to be commanded by him therefore keeps aloof. He asserts that his commission is older than Gen. Rusk's. God help the work when the army of Texas is commanded by such a man. You are I presume aware that I know him thoroughly, for the last 8 or 9 years in Florida."[30]

[28] David G. Burnet to Gen. Thomas J. Green, March 19, 1836, William C. Binkley (ed.), *Official Correspondence of the Texan Revolution, 1835–1836*, I, 517–518.
[29] Mrs. Ina Kate (Hamon) Reinhardt, "The Public Career of Thomas Jefferson Green," ms., p. 29.
[30] David Macomb to James Morgan, Steam Saw Mill, San Jacinto, July 28, 1836, Binkley, *Official Correspondence of the Texan Revolution*, II, 897–899.
In the fall of 1836, he was elected to represent Béxar County in the House of Representatives of the First Congress of Texas, and in the Senate of the Second Congress; but shortly after his Senate term commenced, his seat was declared vacant and Juan N. Seguin was chosen in his place. *Handbook of Texas*, I, 728; [Elizabeth LeNoir Jennett], *Biographical Directory of the Texan Conventions and Congresses*, pp. 91–92.
On February 15, 1855, Sam Houston made the following remarks in the United

The Capture and Plunder of Laredo

Although the unauthorized raid across the disputed boundary of Texas upon an enemy town was allowed to go unpunished, it resulted in strict orders to the sentinels to prohibit the men thereafter leaving camp without orders from their company commanders. "Predatory warfare on unarmed citizens in the enemys territory was not among the objects contemplated" in the Somervell expedition to the Río Grande.[31] However, on the morning of the 9th this general order was not strictly enforced and many of the men and subordinate officers left camp "contrary to the orders and earnest request of every field officer and

States Senate concerning a pamphlet distributed among members of the Senate by Green:

> I will not offend respectable ears with an allusion to dark reminiscences connected with his [Green's] character and private life in Texas. From the time the lash was inflicted upon him by Jesse A. Bynum, in North Carolina, to the last act of swindling to which he resorted in Texas and Mexico, his notoriety has been unenviable. I am sorry that I have mentioned his name in the honorable Senate. He has obtruded it here. I would not advise any decent and respectable person to touch him with a fifteen-foot pole, unless he had gloves upon his hands of double thickness, and then he should cast away the pole to avoid the influence of the contaminating shock.

U. S. Congress, *Congressional Globe*, 1853–1855, pt. I, p. 742. "He is a man of infamous character," wrote Houston, "and has robbed Texas of many valuable lives by his cowardice, and has cost her thousands of money. . . . To let you know how he is estimated in Texas, I will tell you one fact. He ran for Congress, and I think there were some forty counties in the District. In them he only received forty-three votes. This was his standing in Texas where he was *well* known." Such was the ex-President's opinion of the man whom he had nominated in 1836 to be the senior brigadier general in the army of Texas, only to have the nomination rejected by the Texas Senate on December 20 and again on December 22. Sam Houston to Joseph Smith, Boston, Mass., dated Washington, March 26, 1856, in *Writings of Sam Houston*, VI, 301; E. W. Winkler (ed.), *Secret Journals of the Senate, Republic of Texas, 1836–1845*, pp. 35, 40. For Colonel William S. Fisher's review of Green's book on the Mier Expedition, see *Northern Standard* (Clarksville), Jan. 14, 1846.

[31] John Hemphill to Anson Jones, Washington, Texas, Jan. 23, 1843, in Army Papers (Texas), ms. Also see Sam Houston to Brigadier General A. Somervell, Executive Department, Washington, Oct. 3, 1842, in *Writings of Sam Houston*, III, 170–171; and General Order No. 57 issued by General A. Somervell and reproduced on page 470 of the same work. Guy M. Bryan to Rutherford B. Hayes, Peach Point, near Brazoria, Texas, Jan. 21, 1843, in E. W. Winkler (ed.), "The Bryan-Hayes Correspondence," *Southwestern Historical Quarterly*, XXV (1921–1922), pp. 103–105. See also A. Somervell, General Order No. 58, Head Quarters, Laredo, Decr 8, 1842, in "A Record Book of the General & Special Orders and Letters of the South Western Army," pp. 47–48, ms.

nearly all the company officers, [and] an immense majority of the privates," [32] for the purpose of entering Laredo. Others "obtained leave . . . to revisit Laredo, with no declared object beyond that of examining the place."[33] One small party of Texans decided to examine the calaboose. They rode up to the jail, and their leader representing himself as General Vasquez, demanded that the jailor release the prisoners. The jailor, however, did not recognize the Texan soldier from the Colorado as General Vasquez, and refused to open the door. Whereupon, he was driven from the prison and the door broken open, and all the convicts, about twenty in number, huddled around the Texans. They were told to give three cheers for Texas, which they did with great glee. They were then informed that they were on Texas soil and were free to go wherever they wished.[34] Three men went to the alcalde and threatened to hang him if he did not show them where he had hidden his silver. They cocked their guns and put a rope around his neck. The frightened official was about to submit to their demands when Major Henry Clay Davis, late of Kentucky and Texan commissary at the time, and McBeth, who had lived for some time in San Antonio, came upon them, and "for fear of being brought to trial for what they were about to do, the men slunk away."[35] When the alcalde informed Davis of what the men were about to do to him, the major became so incensed that he resigned his commission and declared that he was going home. Davis and McBeth took leave of the expedition ostensibly with the intention of returning home. Instead, however, it was reported, they "deserted to the Mexican army at San Fernando, 140 miles north," carrying to General Reyes letters from the alcalde at Laredo informing him of the movements of the Texan expedition. Suspecting treachery, General Reyes cast the deserters into the same prison as that occupied by Cornelius Van Ness, Thomas Hancock, Archibald Fitzgerald, and several other Texans. However, later, with the arrival of additional information from the alcalde at Laredo and from Colonel Bravo, they were released and given a ball by General Reyes, reported Green.[36]

[32] *Telegraph and Texas Register*, Jan. 18, 1842; see also Memucan Hunt to Francis Moore, Jr., Editor of the Telegraph, Houston, [dated:] Béxar, Jan, 8, 1843, *Morning Star* (Houston), Jan. 17, 1843.
[33] Stapp, *Prisoners of Perote*, p. 25.
[34] *Telegraph and Texas Register*, Jan. 4, 1843.
[35] Adams, "[Journal of an] Expedition Against the Southwest," Dec. 9, 1842, ms.
[36] *Ibid.*

Others on the Somervell expedition believed that this was not the case. Among them was Harvey Adams, who recorded:

It was said by some that Clay Davis went over to the Mexicans, but this was as bad as their steeling [*sic*] operations. I believe that it has been generally conceded that Clay Davis has always been a true friend of Texas. He said . . . that he would not have anything to do with men who would rob in their own country,

Laredo being within the claimed jurisdiction of Texas.[37]

Sooner or later, during the morning of the 9th, approximately one third of the members of the expedition re-entered Laredo and many of them pillaged the town "worse than ever," taking "what they pleased," from the Mexican families. Among the visitors to the town were those most destitute of clothing, blankets, and other necessary items. They made a "regular business of the matter, found out where the Commissary Stores were and ransacked them from top to bottom." Heavy doors, three or four inches in thickness, securely fastened, were broken down after several set-tos by heavy battering rams of square cypress beams twenty to twenty-five feet in length shouldered by three or four men who would take a running start and ram them against the doors. "Several squads of men were to be seen in different parts of the town walking through the streets with beams on their shoulders, making an assault on some door."[38] The commissary buildings were constructed of rock with very thick walls and a rock floor. After the largest of these was broken into there was "a general rush . . . by the men to see who would be foremost to capture any prize. . . . In the general rush the men would set their guns against the wall, others would knock them down and it is the greatest wonder that a number of them were not killed."[39] At this place, reported Adams, an immense quantity of paper and "shuck" cigarettes were found stored in large boxes, which were opened and their contents placed "in old shirts, rags, or pieces of cloth and carried off." Although General Somervell was, in the beginning, accused of winking at the robbing of the people of Laredo, "when it became too formidable then another face had to be put to it."[40]

---

[37] Green, *Journal of the Texian Expedition Against Mier*, pp. 141–142.
[38] Adams, "[Journal of an] Expedition Against the Southwest," Dec. 9, 1842, ms.
[39] *Ibid.*
[40] Harvey A. Adams, "Journal of the Expedition of Alexander, Against the Enemies of the South West, in the 2nd and 3rd Years of the Reign of *Sam*," 19th para-

The pillaging continued until about 2 P.M., when Somervell, being apprised of the extent and true nature of the depredations being carried on by some of the men of his command, assembled his officers in a council of war, where it was voted to restore the stolen property to the inhabitants of Laredo. He then sent an order into town for all the men to return to camp immediately. At the same time the captains were instructed to have their men turn in at the guard fire all articles which had been seized from the Mexicans and which were not considered necessary for the support of the army. In the meantime, while the order to return to camp was being carried into town, Somervell ordered a "guard placed out in the shape of a V, the open ends pointing to town so as to catch every one." The guard had orders to keep all returnees from town within the "V" until they arrived at the camp guard fire,

where there was a strong guard in circular form, placed so as to catch every man who came inside of these lines. Once arrived [at] camp every man was ordered to come forward and deposit whatever he had taken. There was no other alternative. But some who smelt the rat in time, who had valuable things, got outside the lines and hid their ill-gotten gains in the Schapparall [chaparral] until the things all blew over, and some staid out until the army moved on, and then followed in the wake of it.[41]

Upon their return to camp, the men came loaded with as various and motley an assortment of pillage as was ever brought within the line of a civilized force, including blankets, beds, bed-clothes, pillows and cushions nicely embroidered, cooking utensils of various designs, soap, candles, horses, mules and asses, beeves, veals and muttons, poultry of every genus of ornithology, honey, bread, flour, sugar, *piloncillos* and coffee, cigarettes, saddles and bridles, coats, hats, baby clothes, and every "specimen of male apparel known amongst the Mexicans, with miscellaneous decorations in use among the gentler sex, that our blushing muse forbids us to catalogue."[42] Bob Lott was reported to have gotten one hundred doubloons[43] out of a drawer in one of the Laredo homes. He also got three or four of the finest Mexican blankets, and turned down an offer of $75 for one of them.

---

graph, in Adams, "[Journal of an] Expedition Against the Southwest," Dec. 9, 1842, ms.

[41] *Ibid.*

[42] Stapp, *Prisoners of Perote*, p. 25; see also Adams, "[Journal of an] Expedition Against the Southwest," Dec. 9, 1842, ms.

[43] A doubloon was worth about eight dollars. Green (ed.), *Samuel Maverick, Texan*, p. 166 n.

He was one who went in for making the thing pay. [concluded Adams] One of these Blankets had the rising sun in the center and its rays terminated to its outer parts with brilliant colors of the rain-bow, and where it was white it was like driven snow. I was informed by the Mexican from whom it was taken that his Sister worked three years at Montclova making this blanket and it was the pride of her life. The Mexican cried while he was telling me about it.[44]

It was rumored that the Mexicans of Laredo lost four thousand dollars in silver plate to the rapacious Texans, but Adams believed that the inhabitants were not rich, and that if any quantity of valuable plate existed, it must have been removed from the town and hidden, as very few of the men found any plate and none in large quantities.

The body of "toll-takers," as they described themselves, came riding into camp, driving their livestock before them,

and with their bodies enwrapped to treble the ordinary dimensions of men, their persons hung about with all the variegated drapry of Jew clothes-pedlars, and horses panting under pyramidal burdens, as queerly assorted as a Carolina *moover*, looked more like a troop of equestrian harlequins, than brave and manly soldiers, who had crossed desert, bog, and river, to chastise the insolence of their country's foes, and avenge the manes [sic] of their butchered brethren.[45]

As the plunderers entered camp they encountered a reception far different from what they expected. Generally the emotions of those who had remained in camp varied from pity, mirth, and boisterous laughter to ridicule, shame, and indignation. This unbridled license on the part of a minority was generally condemned by both officers and privates, although the "strange cavalcade of masquers" sought to defend their conduct. They pretended to justify their disobedience of orders by claiming that the Mexican officials were not fulfilling General Somervell's requisition for provisions; and, that as they had become disgusted and dissatisfied with the general's failure to provide them with food, they had taken it upon themselves to look after their own needs. Likewise, it was argued that the general should have informed his men, "I have furnished you these ten beeves and these few sacks of flour; I can do no more, now look out for yourselves; here is a list of articles which you have a right by the usages of war to take, and, as Texians, it is expected you will take nothing else."[46] Such an argument lacked plausibility, for

[44] Adams, "[Journal of an] Expedition Against the Southwest," Dec. 9, 1842, ms.
[45] Stapp, *Prisoners of Perote*, p. 25.
[46] Green, *Journal of the Texian Expedition Against Mier*, pp. 56–57.

men who had no respect for authority and would ignore one order could not be expected to abide by another given by the same authority. Others contended that a precedent for their action had been set the previous evening when Green and others demanded and received five mules from the alcalde of Galveston, across the river, without being punished for their conduct. Little respect did these men have for their own word. They had all agreed to obey the orders of their officers; and yet, they ignored them whenever the rules and regulations seemed to impose any sort of restraint upon their conduct.

The order to turn in the loot at the guard fire brought a great deal of bitter criticism from the guilty. Many of them were quite indignant. Some declared that they had paid for the items they had secured; others sought to vindicate their pillage and unbridled license on the basis of "necessity," "retaliation," and "spoils of war." Had not Vasquez and Woll in their raids on San Antonio carried off valuable property? Among the property taken on these raids were twenty-nine yokes of oxen and several carts belonging to R. T. Higginbotham, a wagon and three or four yokes of oxen belonging to William Small, and other property belonging to M. Loscew, William Keen, J. B. Seer, Wilson I. Riddle, and other individuals.[47] Why should not the Mexicans of Laredo be made to pay for the losses of the Texans at San Antonio? Some of the soldiers voluntarily restored all they had taken that day and the day before but occasionally the captains found it necessary to seize the plunder from its present holders to insure its restitution. When collected the plunder made a pile the size of "a good large house, and no doubt every thing that could be concealed was taken care of by these men, whose conduct was indeed, most infamous."[48] Referring to the sacking of Laredo, an English visitor to Texas in 1843 wrote concerning those who took part in it, "These men were *loafers*—the dangerous and unprincipled set of people of whom General Houston is so anxious to free the country. One of the few respectable individuals who took part in the expedition told us, that they were heartily ashamed of being there, and for his own part, he felt 'dreadful[ly] small' on the occasion."[49]

[47] Memucan Hunt to Francis Moore, Jr., Béxar, Jan. 8, 1843, *Telegraph and Texas Register*, Jan. 18, 1843.

[48] Winkler (ed.), "Hendricks' Narrative," *Southwestern Historical Quarterly,* XXIII (1919–1920), 127–128.

[49] Mrs. [M. C.] Houstoun, *Texas and the Gulf of Mexico: or Yachting in the New World,* II, 165.

Less than four years later General Zachary Taylor had similar problems with the Texans in his army in northern Mexico.

In regard to your letter of the 24th, [he wrote to Dr. R. C. Wood in respect] to the outrages committed by the Texan volunteers on the Mexicans and others, I have not the power to remedy it or apply the corrective. I fear they are a lawless set—[50]

I agree with you in doubting the reorganization of the Texans, I feel but little interest in the matter; altho I expect if they could be made subordinate they would be the best, at any rate as good as any volunteer corps in service; but I fear they are & will continue too licentious to do much good.[51]

Many of the Texans who participated in the outrage at Laredo, after a little reflection, united in heartily condemning the plundering and aided in the restoration of the Mexican property. In the end, the general's order was as well carried out as possible. McCutchan's Diary[52] reflects the sentiments of the more thoughtful, stable members of the expedition.

Many were thoughtless in the act, but still the crime is the same. I was thankful that I had not gone to town on that day. For all who went—though many took no part in it—were considered as partially culpable. I do not accuse all—Oh, no! There were some whom I know—whom I had seen at home—whom I felt must be innocent, but I knew not who the guilty were. Sooner than I would have had that act to rest upon me, I would have laid my bones on the Enemies Soil, if it were but single handed, I had sought death. Here was a Town, on the soil claimed by Texas; its inhabitants, claiming to be Texians, and opened their doors to us, as to friends—had received the soldiers of Texas as deliverers, and yet, those inhabitants, were not safe in the possession of their private property. Suffice it to say, Texas must wear the stain, for the conduct of a few disorderly volunteers; who might have been restrained, had the officers have taken the proper course.

As the plunder was being collected, Somervell hastily penned a letter to the alcalde, apologizing for the misconduct of "some bad men belonging to the army."

Although the whole country from the Sabine to the Río Grande [he wrote] is considered by my Government as belonging to the Republic of Texas, yet

[50] Z. Taylor to [Dr. R. C. Wood, U. S. A., Fort Polk], Matamoros, México, June 30, 1846, William H. Samson (ed.), *Letters of Zachary Taylor from the Battle-Fields of the Mexican War*, pp. 18–22.
[51] Same to Same, Matamoros, Mexico, July 7, 1846, *ibid.*, pp. 22–25.
[52] p. 24.

having found the town of Laredo governed by authorities receiving their appointment under the Government and Laws of Mexico, I am willing for the present to recognize the right to exercise the authority confided to them.

Your rights, religion, customs and usages shall be respected.

I regret to learn that some bad men belonging to the army under my command have committed acts of outrage in your town. The army is composed of volunteers and is difficult to control. But I am proud to state to you that these acts have excited the indignation of a large portion of the Army and are utterly reprobated by myself and officers under my command. We will make you all the reparation in our power, by returning all such articles as are not essential to the Army.

You will come down with one or two men and take the articles back to town.[53]

The Mexicans came with carts and took back those things which the Texas command did not consider valuable to the progress of the expedition. The items retained were principally coffee, flour, saddles, soap, and sugar.

[53] A. Somervell, Gen.'l Com[man]d[in]g to the Alcalde of the town of Laredo, Head Quarters, Camp Chacón, Decr 9th, 1842, in Army Papers (Texas)), ms.; copy also in State Department (Texas), Department of State Letterbook, Home Letters, II (1842–1846), ms. See also Green, *Journal of the Texian Expedition Against Mier,* p. 58; Winkler (ed.), "Hendricks' Narrative," *Southwestern Historical Quarterly,* XXIII (1919–1920), 127–128.

CHAPTER TWENTY-TWO

The March to Guerrero

IN THE COUNCIL OF WAR which discussed the plunder of Laredo, the question of the future course of the expedition had also been considered, but "without being able to obtain a concurrence of feeling as to crossing the river."[1] The discussions revealed that some of the officers were in favor of crossing the Río Grande and carrying the war into Mexico by moving rapidly down the west bank of the river, inflicting punishment on the enemy and then quickly recrossing and heading for home before the Mexicans could rally their forces. In the afternoon of December 9, after the property had been restored to the citizens of Laredo, General Somervell ordered a resumption of the march down the east bank of the Río Grande. After proceeding several miles the head of the column was suddenly turned left into a dense and difficult growth of chaparral, in the direction of the settled area of Texas. At times during the march the men found it necessary to hew their way through the thick undergrowth with their heavy hack knives. To many of them, it now looked as if the expedition were headed for home without coming within striking distance of the enemy. It was believed by many that the general intended to return home immediately by way of San Patricio, "as it was currently reported and by some believed . . . that a Mexican force had marched on the upper route from Presidio and another from Matamoros below to intercept and cut us off," reported Hendricks. Some believed that the general was "trying to conceal himself in the chaperel without a possibility of being discovered by

---

[1] E. W. Winkler (ed.), "Sterling Brown Hendricks' Narrative of the Somervell Expedition to the Rio Grande," *Southwestern Historical Quarterly*, XXIII (1919–1920), 127–128. John Henry Brown, *History of Texas, from 1685 to 1892*, II, 238, contends that 13 out of 14 of the officers voted to cross the river, but Hendricks, who was critical of Somervell, admits that the council was unable to reach a decision on the question. Francis R. Lubbock in *Six Decades in Texas: or Memoirs of Francis Richard Lubbock*, p. 147, says eleven captains voted in favor of crossing the river and fighting.

the most scrutinizing enemy."[2] The guide told them that he would take them to water within four miles, but for several hours the expedition wound about through the prickly pear and thorn bushes, turning more and more in the direction of the San Antonio road, when about ten o'clock at night, "from exhaustion, sore shins, and disgust, all hands came to a halt, without water and without supper,"[3] having in their winding course traveled only seven miles. A camp was pitched upon a little mesquite flat without water. In spite of the severe cold weather, only a few fires were permitted. Half-dried beef was practically the only food available. Captain Cameron "refused to detail his quota of the guard, declaring he would furnish an army retreating from *nothing*, without effecting any thing, not one man for that purpose."[4] Although jokes were told, anecdotes related, and the usual forms of merriment were present, the mysterious and unaccountable conduct of General Somervell, who had not informed the men of his intention to go home, had given rise to considerable dissatisfaction among them and produced many loud murmurs and much bitter criticism. The men, many of whom had left their homes, their wives and children, and traveled over miles of prairie and swollen streams during the worst season of the year, were not content to sulk about in the chaparral like "a despicable hoard of cowards" when the enemy and his country were before them. Furthermore, some of the men were not too happy at Somervell's policy of arresting stragglers. Others were unhappy because of the lack of discipline and felt that little could now be accomplished. During the night their ridicule of the general's conduct and their manifestations of discontent reached Somervell's ears. The next morning Somervell informed a fellow officer that he had not slept a wink all night, for thinking of what should be done. Somervell's problem was a difficult one. To return home without engaging the Mexicans in battle would surely bring down upon his head great popular odium. To go on without provisions

---

[2] Thomas W. Bell, *A Narrative of the Capture and Subsequent Sufferings of the Mier Prisoners in Mexico, Captured in the Cause of Texas, Dec. 26th, 1842, and Liberated Sept. 16th, 1844,* p. 16.

[3] Thomas J. Green, *The Texian Expedition Against Mier,* p. 59. See also Winkler (ed.), "Hendricks' Narrative," *Southwestern Historical Quarterly,* XXIII (1919–1920), 128; William Preston Stapp, *The Prisoners of Perote: Containing a Journal Kept by the Author Who Was Captured by the Mexicans at Mier, December 25, 1842, and Released from Perote, May 16, 1844,* p. 26, says that the army halted at 8 P.M.

[4] Memucan Hunt to Francis Moore, Jr., Editor of the *Telegraph,* Houston, dated Béxar, Jan. 8, 1843, in *Morning Star* (Houston), Jan. 17, 1843.

of any kind and with a shortage of horses, depending upon the country and its inhabitants for subsistence, would likely end in disaster. Likewise, to linger long upon the Río Grande would allow the Mexicans an opportunity to rally an overwhelming force which might also be disastrous to the Texan army. While still in a state of uncertainty, Somervell arose in the morning to inform the troops that they would be conducted to water and after breakfast the officers would again hold a council.[5]

Early the next morning (Saturday, December 10) the army resumed its march, and, after going on a circuitous route five miles, two miles on the back track,[6] located a scanty supply of water in the Cañon de San Andres and halted for breakfast, remaining here two or three hours. The water was quite muddy and foul but was thankfully received by the thirsty Texans. As they had now proceeded some ten miles in a southeasterly direction from Laredo, Colonel Thomas Green, of Fayette County, who had been serving as brigade inspector under General Somervell, resigned in disgust and attached himself to Major Jack Hays' scouting party as a private. After breakfast, another council of war was held. Fourteen captains were present, and all but three committed themselves in favor of relentlessly pursuing the enemy into Mexico and engaging him in battle. But evidence of considerable discontent throughout the entire command was indicated by the desire of many of the men to return home. Seeing that a majority of the officers were in favor of carrying the war to the Mexicans and that some were opposed, General Somervell decided to refer the matter to the army itself. He now proceeded to order the captains to draw up their respective companies for review, and the council was adjourned.

After the company commanders had mustered their men and drawn them up under a hill in the open prairie to suit the general, Somervell addressed them, stating briefly the objects of the expedition; complained of the pillage of Laredo; proposed to march to Guerrero provided the men would be obedient to orders and refrain from pillage; and concluded by calling for volunteers to follow him or any other leader of their own choice across the Río Grande to achieve something to blot out the stain of the plundering of Laredo. Those in favor of entering the enemy's territory were requested to occupy the neighboring

[5] Green, *The Texian Expedition Against Mier*, pp. 59–60; Joseph D. McCutchan, Diary, ms., p. 26.

[6] Harvey Alexander Adams, "[Journal of an] Expedition Against the Southwest in 1842 and 1843," Dec. 10, 1842, ms.

hill (one of two Cerritos de Mendez) on his right; whereas, those who desired to return were to retain their positions. Out of 715 men in the camp, all but about 100 marched into line on the hill, "but the patriotism of 87 more oozed out by the next morning."[7] The following pledge was drafted and signed by the captains of the companies desiring to pursue the enemy:

Head Quarters
So. W. Army near Laredo
Decr 10th 1842

We the undersigned agree to cross the Río Grande for the purpose of waging war on Mexico. We also agree to be governed strictly by the Rules and Articles for the Government of the armies of this Republic, and especially to abstain from depredations on the property or disturbing the persons of unarmed citizens. And that all offenses of this kind shall be punished as the Articles of War direct. All property captured from the enemy shall be equally distributed between the officers and soldiers. The Commanding General shall make requisitions and give orders for whatever supplies be required by the Army. We also pledge ourselves to sustain the officers in all their efforts to enforce orders and the Rules and Regulations of the service generally.[8]

The some 500 "stout hearts and ready hands" who indicated their desire to invade the enemy's territory, each, according to Lieutenant Austin Bryan, "individually signed a written pledge [similar to the above] to obey their officers and refrain from plunder."[9]

One hundred and eighty-seven who ultimately decided to return home claimed that they had had enough or believed that nothing of significance could be accomplished by the expedition. The plundering of Laredo furnished a pretext for some, alleging that they could no longer serve in the same ranks with men who had been guilty of robbery. However, back in Texas some effort was made to discredit them for having abandoned the expedition, by saying that they returned "because the officers would make them respect [the] [pro]perty of private Citizens and not [permit them[10]] to commit plunder and rapine at their

[7] *Ibid.*

[8] Copy in John Hemphill to Anson Jones, Washington, Texas, Jan. 23, 1843, in Army Papers (Texas), ms.; copy also in State Department (Texas), Department of State Letterbook, Home Letters, II (1842–1846), ms., pp. 69–71.

[9] Guy M. Bryan to Rutherford B. Hayes, Peach Point, near Brazoria, Texas, Jan. 21, 1843, E. W. Winkler (ed.), "The Bryan-Hayes Correspondence," *Southwestern Historical Quarterly*, XXV (1921–1922), 103–107.

[10] Torn. Words supplied by the author.

own discretion." Their return, wrote H. F. Gillett, "amounts to no more
than dishonorable discharge."[11] Those who did not care to continue the
expedition were told that they were at liberty to go home and that a
competent officer would be placed in charge to conduct them to the
settled area where they could be disbanded. Those returning consisted
largely of the remainder of the drafted militiamen from Montgomery
and Washington counties, some of whose number had abandoned the
expedition at Béxar before it had gotten underway.[12] These men were
placed first under the command of Colonel Bennett, but shortly thereafter, on the same day, the order placing the men under Bennett was
cancelled and Lieutenant Colonel McCrocklin was designated to command the men on the homeward march. Leaving San Antonio on their
left, the men were to be marched by way of Gonzales to Washington
County, where they were to be given honorable discharges for their
term of service. Five prisoners were placed under the charge of Mc-
Crocklin, who was instructed to turn them over to the disposition of
the President of the Republic.[13] At this time Colonel Cook resigned

---

[11] H. F. Gillett to Ashbel Smith, Washington, Texas, Jan. 10, 1843, in Ashbel
Smith Papers, 1838–1842, ms.

[12] Telegraph and Texas Register, Jan. 18, 1843.

[13] A. Somervell, General Order No. 60, Head Quarters, Camp near Laredo,
Decemᵇ 10, 1842; A. Somervell, General Order No. 61, Head Quarters, Camp La
Ratama, Decʳ 10, 1842, in "A Record Book of the General & Special Orders and
Letters of the South Western Army," p. 49, ms. A. Somervell to G. W. Hill, Sec. of
War and Marine, Washington, Feb. 1, 1843, Morning Star (Houston), Feb. 18,
1843. Somervell reported that on December 8 he paraded an army of 683 men at
Laredo. Of these 185 returned under Colonels Bennett and McCrocklin; 189 re-
turned under Somervell on December 19; and 309 continued down the river as the
Mier expedition. Somervell reported that he "proposed to march to 'Guerrero,'
provided the officers and men would agree to comply with certain articles, the
more effectually to enforce order and subordination, and to protect the property
and persons of unarmed citizens." McCutchan (Diary, p. 26) says approximately
550 agreed to continue the expedition and 185 to return home. Green, The Texian
Expedition Against Mier, pp. 60–61, says that out of 740 men present about
200 indicated their desire to return home. This does not mean that all those
who indicated their desire to return home did so. The number 740 may indicate
that there were still men accompanying the expedition but unaffiliated with
it, besides those who had participated in the plunder of Laredo and had avoided
turning in their loot by disassociating themselves from the command thereafter.
From Laredo, say John H. Brown and Francis R. Lubbock, "two hundred of them,
under Capts. Jerome B. and E. S. C. Robertson, returned home." (John Henry
Brown, Indian Wars and Pioneers of Texas, p. 141; Lubbock, Six Decades in Texas,
p. 147). Stapp, Prisoners of Perote, p. 26, claims that nearly 500 wished to con-

the command to which he had been elected, stating, it is said, that "he was unwilling to remain in the responsible office . . . when such insubordination as he witnessed was sanctioned by his superiors; he . . . declared that he had witnessed Gen. Somervell laughing with indifference at the disobedience of his own orders, and that success could not attend an expedition thus conducted."[14] Several names, including that of Memucan Hunt, were mentioned to succeed him. However, he was persuaded to accept his former command and was re-elected by acclamation. The First Battalion of the Second Regiment was now dissolved and the companies that elected to continue the march down the Río Grande were attached to the First Regiment and permitted to draw for letter designations of H, I, and K.[15]

What was Somervell's object? Before going into a discussion of the motives underlying his conduct, it might be interesting to pause for a brief sketch of this general, who was hated by so many of the men whom he commanded. Somervell was born on June 11, 1796, in Maryland, and in 1817 moved to Louisiana to engage in business. From there he came to Texas in 1832 and was granted land in Austin's second colony; and in the following year he entered the mercantile business at San Felipe in partnership with James F. Perry. Somervell was at San Antonio in November 1835 and participated in the "Grass Fight." He was elected lieutenant colonel of the first regiment of Texas volunteers in March 1836 and fought in the battle of San Jacinto, after which he served as Secretary of War in President Burnet's cabinet from May 30 to August 8, 1836. Later he was elected senator to the First and Second Congresses to represent the district composed of the counties of Colorado and Austin. He was one of the trustees of Galveston University.[16] Soon after the adjournment of the Second Congress, Somervell moved to Fort Bend

---

tinue the expedition and so does Hunt to Moore, Jan. 8, 1843, *Morning Star* (Houston), Jan. 17, 1843. Winkler (ed.), "Hendricks' Narrative," *Southwestern Historical Quarterly*, XXIII (1919–1920), 129, reported that "out of seven hundred and thirty men, about two hundred and thirty were for returning."

[14] Memucan Hunt to Francis Moore, Jr., Editor of the *Telegraph*, Houston, dated Bexar, Jan. 8, 1843, *Morning Star* (Houston), Jan. 17, 1843.

[15] A. Somervell, General Order No. 62, Head Quarters, Camp San Ignacio, Decr 12, 1842, in "A Record Book of the General & Special Orders and Letters of the South Western Army," pp. 51–52, ms.

[16] Frank W. Johnson, *A History of Texas and Texans*, I, 349. "Proposed Charter of the Galveston University, in the Republic of Texas," W. L. McCalla, *Adventures in Texas, Chiefly in the Spring and Summer of 1840: with a Discussion of Comparative Character, Political, Religious and Moral*, Appendix I, p. 151.

County, and there on November 12, 1839, he was elected brigadier general of the First Brigade, Texas Militia.[17] According to Dr. John Washington Lockhart, who knew Somervell personally, "the General was an ordinary looking man, low of stature and inclined to be a bit fleshy; a man of good, general disposition, approachable by all; always in good humor, kind and generous. The young men liked him and with them he was always sociable,"[18] and was noted for his "fits" of loud laughter.[19] On at least one occasion he is known to have advanced money to pay the crew of the schooner *Watchman*, who had threatened to leave when their captain could not raise a small sum of money on a treasury order which had been given him for that purpose.[20] He was appointed collector of customs for the district of Matagorda (Port Calhoun) in April 1842, and unanimously confirmed by the Senate on December 14, 1842.[21] He served in the capacity of collector of customs, except when called to active military service, until his death in 1854. He lived close to the bay at Deckrow's Point.[22] In March and again in October 1842, Somervell was placed in charge of the troops which had assembled on the western frontier to repel the Mexican invaders. His latest instructions had placed him in command of the Southwestern Army of Operations with authority to lead it in an attack upon Mexico if certain conditions—adequate food, clothing, and munitions, and proper discipline—were met and if he thought such an attack might prove successful. He had violated his instructions on several occasions—by establishing his headquarters at San Antonio, by not enforcing discipline among his troops, and by leading an ill-equipped and poorly provisioned expedition in an attack upon an enemy state at some distance. Now, at the gateway to the enemy's country, he again disregarded his instructions. He informed the men that he would place his commission in their hands.

[17] Sam Houston Dixon and Louis Wiltz Kemp, *The Heroes of San Jacinto*, p. 126; *Writings of Sam Houston*, II, 493 n; *National Cyclopaedia of American Biography*, V, 244.

[18] Mrs. Jonnie Lockhart Wallis and Laurance L. Hill, *Sixty Years on the Brazos: The Life and Letters of Dr. John Washington Lockhart, 1824–1900*, p. 186.

[19] Rena Maverick Green (ed.), *Samuel Maverick, Texan, 1803–1870: A Collection of Letters, Journals and Memoirs*, p. 284.

[20] A. Somervell to D. G. Burnet, Velasco, Aug. 12, 1836, William C. Binkley (ed.), *Official Correspondence of the Texan Revolution, 1835–1836*, II, 925.

[21] E. W. Winkler (ed.), *Secret Journals of the Senate: Republic of Texas, 1836–1845*, p. 232.

[22] Rena Maverick Green (ed.), *Memoirs of Mary A. Maverick: Arranged by Mary A. Maverick and Her Son George Madison Maverick*, p. 87.

He surrendered to the men whom he commanded the commission which the President of Texas had given him. He would lead them if they desired or he would "cheerfully serve among the foremost in the ranks."[23] This play for popularity had its effect, although only momentarily. Somervell was immediately elected by acclamation, without a dissenting voice, to lead those who wished to continue the expedition against the enemy. He now became their "volunteer leader" instead of their appointed commanding officer. Possibly he felt it was proper to let the militiamen return home, since the militiamen who had been called out had either already deserted or were unhappy about continuing the expedition, believing, no doubt, as the President himself had believed back in the summer, that the militia could not be allowed and was not obligated to cross the boundary into a foreign country without authorization from Congress. Such a schism in his ranks would probably have jeopardized the expedition if it crossed into the enemy's country; and, yet, the majority were strongly determined to go forward. So with the drafted militiamen almost unanimously determined to go no farther, General Somervell would no longer have any troops of the First Brigade, Texas Militia, to command. What could be more humiliating than for a brigadier general, instead of leading his troops with their faces pointed in the direction of the enemy, to follow them home harassed by enemy cavalry. Not desiring to be caught in this undignified role and seeing himself without militiamen to command unless he were willing to risk bloodshed by enforcing discipline and obedience to orders, he made an impassioned appeal to the troops and left his future status and rank to the determination of those who wished to push forward aggressively. As a result, Somervell was elected to lead those who wished to continue the expedition against the enemy.

Following the division, each side made efforts to induce friends to return home or to continue with the main body and "partake of the toils and glories of combat," but with no results; each seemed inclined to follow his own council. The "homeward bound," under the command of Lieutenant Colonel McCrocklin, assisted by Colonel Bennett, were disgusted with the campaign and were anxious to return home by the shortest route possible.[24]

A council of officers was held by the invading force in which it was agreed that the reduced army would march down the river, capture

[23] Green, *The Texian Expedition Against Mier*, p. 60.

[24] A. Somervell to G. W. Hill, Secretary of War and Marine, Washington, Feb. 1, 1843, *Morning Star* (Houston), Feb. 18, 1843.

Reveilla, or Guerrero as it was called, and continue on to Mier and Camargo, unless intercepted and defeated by a superior force. All of these towns were on the west side of the Río Grande, and at one time or another had been visited by some of the men in the expedition. The decision to cross the river did not seem a rash one, for only eighteen months before a smaller body of Texans had revealed the weakness of the Mexican government's control of its northern frontier. If so small a force as Jordan's could meet with such success and from the vicinity of Saltillo fight its way out of Mexico after being abandoned by its Mexican friends, a larger expedition composed entirely of Texans, it was reasoned, might be even more successful.[25]

It was considered advisable to proceed down the left bank of the river and obscure, as much as possible, the advance of the expedition from the enemy on the opposite bank by keeping some distance from the river. There was no doubt concerning the hasty preparations being made by the Mexican authorities to contain the invading force, and probably by this time news of the capture of Laredo had reached crowded garrisons below, at Matamoros and beyond, as well as above, at San Fernando. In the meantime, while the expedition lay at the watering place, it was overtaken by Captain Peter H. Bell, aide-de-camp to General Somervell, who had been dispatched the evening before to Laredo to inform the alcalde that the plunder taken by the Texans had been collected and awaited his orders. Captain Bell reported that he had difficulty in leaving Laredo, and was only able to do so when the alcalde escorted him personally to the suburbs. Bell declared that "the whole of the western bank of the Río Grande was lined at that place [Laredo] with rancheros armed and infuriated at the conduct of our men the day before."[26] Both groups of Texans now marched down the valley in which the division had been effected to encamp for their last night together some three miles below on the Arroyo de Dolores, a small stream at what came to be known as Camp La Retama. Here they found better water and grass for their horses. In all they had traveled about fifteen miles during the day.

Early on Sunday morning, December 11, the two divisions separated —Bennett's and McCrocklin's men (187 in all) directing their course homeward, and General Somervell's setting their face in a southerly di-

[25] Juan Nepo[muceno] Molano and Luis Lopez to Mariano Arista, Palmillas, Oct. 12, 1840, *Austin City Gazette*, Dec. 16, 1840.

[26] Winkler (ed.), "Hendricks' Narrative," *Southwestern Historical Quarterly*, XXIII (1919–1920), 128.

rection so as to strike the Río Grande sixty miles below Laredo, opposite Guerrero, a small, sleepy Mexican town situated a short distance from the west bank of the river.

Bennett was ordered to proceed by the most direct and practicable route to Gonzales and there disband his command. The main company under Colonel Bennett was commanded by Captain E. Sterling C. Robertson.[27] Ultimately, about the middle of January 1843, Colonel Bennett's men, numbering about 150 of the Montgomery County drafted militiamen, arrived in Montgomery.[28]

Somervell's small army—now only approximately two-thirds its size when it left the Medina three weeks before—was "full of spirit and fire, and ready for action under any circumstances."[29] The cold weather of the last two days continued, making riding very disagreeable. Keeping east of the settlements in the neighborhood of the old Rancho de Dolores, ten leagues southeast of Laredo and about two hundred yards from the junction of the Arroyo de Dolores and the Río Grande; past the Carolitas Ranch, the San Francisco Hills, the ranches San Ygnacio, Ramireño (five miles below San Ygnacio on the Arroyo del Burro), and Salmoneño; they proceeded along the north bank of the river so as to conceal their advance as much as possible from the watchful eyes of enemy scouts. It was a circuitous route through a wilderness, covered thick with thorny cactus and tough mesquites in all their devilish growth, lasting almost four days. Some of the men wondered if their commander had become panicky and was trying to conceal himself in the chaparral to prevent observation by any spies or scouts of the enemy.[30]

Back in Texas the press kept the public informed of the progress of the Texan expedition. As the army moved from Laredo toward Guerrero, the *Telegraph and Texas Register*[31] pointed out that there was "a fine high dry road" leading to the latter place, and that its

inhabitants were not prepared for defence .... The sudden and unexpected appearance of our army, [it continued] has spread terror and consternation throughout the whole country, and it is thought Guerrero, Mier, Comargo and Rhinosa will be captured in rapid succession. There is no large body

[27] John D. Affleck, "History of John C. Hays," ms., pt. I, p. 291; Adams, "[Journal of an] Expedition Against the Southwest," Dec. 11, 1842, ms.

[28] *Telegraph and Texas Register*, Jan. 18, 1843.

[29] McCutchan, Diary, ms., p. 27.

[30] Bell, *Narrative*, p. 16.

[31] Jan. 4, 1843.

of central troops at either of these towns. The army of Gen. Somervell is somewhat less than seven*teen* hundred men; but the news of his success will probably induce hundreds of our daring youth to flock to his standard, and in a few weeks his army may be augmented to two or three thousand men. He is evidently making rapid marches towards Matamoros, and as there are only three or four hundred Mexican troops at that city, it may soon follow the fate of Laredo.

The first night Somervell's small army came to a salt water hole, twenty miles from the point of division, but succeded in getting fresh water. The only forage available for their horses was the dry mesquite grass, which afforded but slight sustenance. On the night of the 12th an excellent camp site was found on a small ravine eighteen miles from their last but; "provisions were alarmingly scarce";[32] grass likewise was scanty and the water was bad. Among the early travelers in this area, the Río Grande Valley was often referred to as "the desert of death." Many of the messes were without meat until the hunters who had gone out on the 12th—some with permission and others without permission[33] —returned on the night of the 13th with considerable quantities of venison, turkey, and fine beeves.[34] There were hundreds of wild horses and cattle in this area. That night the Texans camped at a small creek of salt water, having made eighteen miles through a rolling country. They found several holes of fresh water, but the water was not very good. For the past three days as the expedition ranged along down the river, the men could see a line of mountains beyond it, looking like a long low cloud on the western horizon, and as Guerrero was approached the mountains became more conspicuous. Mountains lay before them, to the left and to the right of the expedition at a distance of some hundred miles. The tortuous route was continued through bogs, and mesquite thickets, and along the edge of several pretty lakes. Lacerated and bleeding hands, faces, and legs, and tattered pantaloons and sore shins plainly explained why the men did not think very highly of the cunning military tactics of their "elected" commander. Sticking into their flesh and torturing them most horribly were the spines of the most prickly of all thorny plants—the cactus—better known to them as the omnipresent

[32] McCutchan, Diary, ms., p. 28; Bell, *Narrative*, pp. 16–17; I. J. Cox, "The Southwest Boundary of Texas," *Quarterly of the Texas State Historical Association*, VI (1902–1903), 90–91.

[33] Stapp, *Prisoners of Perote*, p. 27.

[34] Steaks carved from the breast of the turkey were very highly regarded by the frontiersmen.

and infernal prickly pear. On the following night, the 14th, man and horse fared a little better, as the army encamped in a beautiful valley where a plentiful supply of grass of the best quality could be had and meat and "tolerable water" were available in abundance.[35] The site selected for the camp, however, showed signs of fires and of having been an old camping ground. During the night some of the men discovered a peculiar inability to sleep while others indicated their restlessness by turning and twisting as they slept, for a general apprehension prevailed throughout the camp that the enemy was hovering in the vicinity. If Mexican spies were in the neighborhood, the army was not molested, and dawn brought relief to the minds of the worried. On the 15th the troops passed "through quite a handsome valley, occasionally though rendered valueless by the number of gullies, fizures, and ravines into which it had, in many places, been cut and carved, by long drouths, and sudden rains."[36] The Texan scouts reported signs of a sizable concentration of Mexican troops in the vicinity of Guerrero, sixty miles below Laredo. Hays' company being in advance took two prisoners—an old man and his son, who were herding approximately fifteen hundred to two thousand sheep and goats. The captives agreed to pilot the Texans to the ford at which time it was agreed they would be freed. Captain Ben McCulloch, a member of Hays' company, was sent ahead with ten men and one of the captives to look for a point along the river where the army might cross, but "owing to the ignorance of his guide did not reach the river near . . . [Guerrero] until after the greater part of the army had crossed."[37] When eventually set loose, the captives did not leave the Texans.

Suddenly, about mid-morning, the army turned west, and at noon halted on the east bank of the Río Bravo (Río Grande), the "Bold River of the North," opposite the mouth of the Río Salado, a small, rapid, clear stream emptying into the Río Bravo some six miles southeast of the town of Guerrero, twelve leagues below Dolores, and a hundred miles by water above Mier.[38] Brown with mud, the swollen Río Grande flowed swiftly at their feet. Above Guerrero, the Río Grande was "a continued series of shoals, rocks, and rapids."[39] As the Texans

[35] McCutchan, Diary, ms., p. 28; Winkler (ed.), "Hendricks' Narrative," *Southwestern Historical Quarterly*, XXIII (1919–1920), 129.
[36] McCutchan, Diary, ms., p. 28.
[37] Bell, *Narrative*, pp. 16–17.
[38] Guerrero was some 54–55 miles from Laredo by land.
[39] John Russell Bartlett, *Personal Narrative of Explorations and Incidents in*

neared the river, several ranches off to their right, belonging to a small settlement dating from 1770 and known as Carrizo,[40] were discovered, and in a short time the Texans came to several large flocks of sheep guarded by shepherds. The shepherds were seized and questioned. A number of lambs were lassoed and taken along for the invaders' supper, ere the flocks were scattered and driven off by the natives. The herdsmen revealed that there were no Mexican forces at Guerrero, for General Canales, it was said, had marched all troops for the relief of Laredo.

Texas, New Mexico, California, Sonora, and Chihuahua, Connected with the United States and Mexican Boundary Commission During the Years 1850, '51, '52, and '53, II, 509.

[40] Now known as Zapata, Texas. Frank C. Pierce, *A Brief History of the Lower Río Grande Valley,* p. 134.

CHAPTER TWENTY-THREE

The Capture of Guerrero

AT THE MOUTH of the Salado was an excellent ford and a good road led from it to Guerrero on its southern bank (where the head of the defeated Federalist Antonio Zapata had been displayed in 1840, by order of General Arista, as a warning to those who contested the Centralist authority[1]). Here situated on the Mexican side, at the confluence of the Salado and Río Grande, was a village of the Carrizo Indian tribe, whose members had constantly opposed the Centralists.[2] Guerrero then called Reveilla had been founded in October 1750. In 1828 the town was renamed in honor of Vicente Guerra, a ranchman from the province of Coahuila who had recommended to Escandón the settling of families in that area. The town was built upon the northern bank of the Salado at approximately six miles from the Río Grande and some fifty-four miles below Laredo.[3] Guerrero was approximately the size of Béxar.

[1] Morning Star (Houston), Jan. 7, 1843; Telegraph and Texas Register, Jan. 11, 1843; Maverick Diary, in Samuel Augustus Maverick, Papers, ms., Oct. 7, 1842.

[2] Telegraph and Texas Register, Jan. 4, 1843; "When a Handful of Americans Invade Mexico," reprinted from the Hidalgo News in the Frontier Times, VI (1928–1929), 246–248; Lamar Papers, VI, 105–106.

[3] Joseph D. McCutchan, Diary, ms., p. 28; Morning Star (Houston), Jan. 7, 1843; William Preston Stapp, The Prisoners of Perote: Containing a Journal Kept by the Author Who Was Captured by the Mexicans at Mier, December 25, 1842, and Released from Perote, May 16, 1844, p. 29; Thomas J. Green, Journal of the Texian Expedition Against Mier, p. 61; John Henry Brown, History of Texas, from 1685 to 1892, II, 239; E. W. Winkler (ed.), "Sterling Brown Hendricks' Narrative of the Somervell Expedition to the Río Grande," Southwestern Historical Quarterly, XXIII (1919–1920), 130; Memucan Hunt to Francis Moore, Jr., Houston, dated Béxar, Jan. 8, 1843, Morning Star (Houston), Jan. 17, 1843; Florence Johnson Scott, Historical Heritage of the Lower Río Grande: A Historical Record of Spanish Exploration, Subjugation and Colonization of the Lower Río Grande Valley and the Activities of José Escandón, Count of Sierra Gorda together with the Development of Towns and Ranches under Spanish, Mexican and Texas Sovereignties, 1748–1848, p. 32; Frank C. Pierce, A Brief History of the Lower Río Grande Valley, pp. 18, 135.

Instead of covering the distance from Laredo to Guerrero by a rapid march of two days down the west bank of the Río Bravo del Norte, the Texan army had spent seven days in indecision and toilsome marching over a difficult terrain. Although somewhat bewildered by the zig-zagged march of the Texans, the Mexican authorities soon fathomed the military maneuver, which "the tattered pantaloons and sore shins of . . . [the Texans] too plainly told them was an unpardonable piece of stupidity and a cruel waste of time."[4] The delay was used to advantage by the Mexican authorities in rounding up an army to defend Mexican homes and the national honor. Centralists and Federalists for the time being forgot their differences and rallied to the defense of their country.

Holding themselves back so as to avoid being seen, the Texans sought to use the herdsmen as a decoy to engage the Mexicans and Indians whom they saw on the opposite bank in conversation while others in the expedition proceeded to attempt to cross the river. However, upon the sudden arrival of the Texans at the river opposite their village, some of the Carrizo Indians, a few of whom had fought with the Mexicans in the battle of the Coleto in March 1836, became greatly alarmed and rushed off toward the town of Guerrero at full speed. Others took refuge in the hills, and could be seen later perched upon their tops half a mile below where the Texans crossed. It became readily apparent then that if Mexican troops were stationed at Guerrero an hour or two would bring them to the defense of the crossing, which even a small force might suc-cessfully hold against the limited means available to the Texans for transporting persons and baggage.[5] If the Texans were to cross at this point, the west bank would have to be occupied at once to facilitate their crossing; but to get across was not any easy matter. All the boats had been removed, and for a while it seemed as if the Texan advance had been stymied, but soon a dugout was discovered secreted in the bushes near the water's edge on the eastern bank not far from the crossing. So without waiting for orders to occupy the west bank, Thomas Jefferson Green and Captain Charles K. Reese, of the Brazoria company, took the initiative, jumped into the canoe,[6] and crossed to the opposite side. There they hoisted the Texas banner, seized a larger dugout, which

---

[4] Green, *The Texian Expedition Against Mier*, pp. 61–62.

[5] *Ibid.*, p. 62; Winkler (ed.), "Hendricks' Narrative," *Southwestern Historical Quarterly*, XXIII (1919–1920), 130.

[6] Dugout or pirogue.

would hold twelve to fifteen men including baggage,[7] and returned with it and the canoe to the troops waiting on the east bank. Thereupon, Major Hays effected a passage for his men, transporting six or seven men at a time in the small canoe and a few more in the larger one. "We had to sit in the bottom of the canoe each with his rifle across his knees and were not allowed to touch the gunwales" for fear of upsetting "the frail craft."[8] In this way the rangers were paddled across the river by one man and landed on the Mexican side. The horses were driven into the water and forced to swim across. The smaller craft was of very little use to the men in crossing the river, it "being very clumsy and hard to manage owing to its irregular shape and the swiftness of the current."[9] In front of the Texans and about two hundred yards from the western bank of the river rose a considerable hill on whose top were the homes of the Mexicans and Indians who had fled. Between the base of the hill and the river, enclosed by a fence, lay a Mexican farm, whose corn crop had just been pulled and piled on the ground. "On this corn the men at once, and very imprudently, turned their horses, leaving them to feed and take care of themselves."[10] The side of the hill nearest the Texans was scarred with pits, caverns, bluffs, and ditches formed by time and the washing rains. Thick brush and undergrowth covered the side of the hill, and near the houses were several brush fences. A road led from the river to the top of the hill and beyond. At the top of the hill a small ravine extended along each side of the road at a distance of some twenty or twenty-five yards from the road. On top of one of the houses on the hill, Hays posted a sentinel.

While the men belonging to the companies of Hays and Bogart were in the process of crossing with their baggage and swimming their horses, Captain Bogart and Green mounted to reconnoitre in the direction of the town. About two miles down the road the two Texans ascended a hill only to encounter at the top, at sixty yards distance, an advance group of Mexican cavalrymen on their way toward the crossing. The mutual surprise, as might be supposed, was great, but the pause was only momentary. "Green and Bogart, wheeling their horses about, came

[7] Harvey Alexander Adams, "[Journal of an] Expedition Against the Southwest in 1842 and 1843," Dec. 14, 1842, ms.

[8] Adele B. Looscan (ed.), "Journal of Lewis Birdsall Harris," *Southwestern Historical Quarterly*, XXV (1921–1922), 190.

[9] Adams, "[Journal of an] Expedition Against the Southwest," Dec. 14, 1842, ms.

[10] Winkler (ed.), "Hendricks' Narrative," *Southwestern Historical Quarterly*, XXIII (1919–1920), 130.

thundering down the road, with the whole Mexican squadron in pursuit, shouting *Karahho* (God damn you) with a vengeance."[11] They had not gone far when Green's horse fell, but was soon back on his feet. As the race continued for a half a mile, the two Texans, in spite of spurs and lash, found themselves hard pressed, and the Mexican cavalry having drawn so close that the rancheros could be heard cocking their *escopetas*, although they did not fire because of the speed of their horses under whip and spur. Green, being upon the slowest of the two horses, soon realized he was falling behind Bogart and would probably be captured if he did not, by some quick thinking, outwit the Mexicans. Suddenly remembering the blood-red silk flag which he carried in his hat, he decided to unfurl it while he skimmed along over the hard surface of the road toward the crossing. Both hands were full—one carrying his rifle and the other guiding his horse—so he thrust a corner of the flag between his teeth and as Canales' *defensores* saw it streaming back over his shoulder, flapping in the breeze, they broke off the pursuit at a half a mile from the river, fearing that they were running into an ambush. The enemy now spread out along each side of the road, and gradually inching his way forward, took command of a small hill, his rear being concealed by a knoll which made it impossible to estimate his numbers. From this vantage point Canales' *defensores*, whom the Texans learned later comprised approximately three hundred men,[12] watched the movements of the invaders from a respectful distance.[13]

In the meantime, Green and Bogart "came rushing down under the bank of the river ordering the men to Parade! Parade!"[14] There was confusion confounded among the men. One order was to parade on horseback; another to parade on foot. Amid the excitement it was soon realized that the former was impossible since the horses were "scattered to the 4 winds" and their blankets, saddles, and bridles were in a similar scattered condition.[15] Consequently, the men were paraded on foot.

At the first appearance of dust kicked up by the pursuing Mexican cavalry, the sentinel on the housetop had given the alarm. At the time,

[11] *Ibid.*, p. 131; see also Adams, "[Journal of an] Expedition Against the Southwest," Dec. 14, 1842, ms.

[12] John Henry Brown, *Indian Wars and Pioneers of Texas*, p. 573, mistakenly says that Canales had 700 rancheros.

[13] Winkler (ed.), "Hendricks' Narrative," *Southwestern Historical Quarterly*, XXIII (1919–1920), 131; McCutchan, Diary, ms., pp. 28–29; Stapp, *Prisoners of Perote*, pp. 28–29; Green, *The Texian Expedition Against Mier*, pp. 62–63.

[14] Adams, "[Journal of an] Expedition Against the Southwest," Dec. 14, 1842, ms.

[15] *Ibid.*

Major Hays was in the midst of ferrying the two spy companies across the river. During the three hours that the expedition had been in the process of crossing, only seventy-five men had reached the western bank. This number included forty-five of Bogart's company and half of Hays' rangers. The sudden alarm caused considerable confusion among the Texans. Hays at once dispatched a special messenger to General Somervell urging him to rush re-enforcements to his assistance, while he sought to maintain the bridgehead on the west bank. General Somervell promised assistance, and immediately began issuing orders; but the capacity of the canoes was very limited and it would take time to transfer any sizable number of men to the west bank. While the men were busily crossing as rapidly as possible in the order which they had maintained on the march, Ben McCulloch, who had been sent to reconnoitre Guerrero before the main army reached the east bank of the river opposite the Indian village and who had become lost, arrived upon the scene at the crossing with his party of ten men.[16]

Those who crossed the river found themselves caught between the second bank and the water itself, but were free to maneuver at discretion, entirely screened from the enemy's view. Because of the dire need for ferry boats to expedite the crossing of the river, Captain Lowrey and his company of about fifty men, among the first to cross after the two ranger companies, was dispatched down the west side of the Río Grande, protected by the second bank, to the mouth of the Salado with orders to reconnoitre along its banks for additional boats. The reconnaissance party succeeded in locating two ferry boats which were brought around by water to the point of crossing. They greatly facilitated the later stage of "jumping" the river. In the meantime,[17] apprehensive that the overwhelming odds of the Mexican cavalry might prove disastrous to his small band, Hays disposed his men in a scattered manner, with orders to present themselves by showing their heads above the bank, peering at the foe as though merely curious, and then, disappearing temporarily, to repeat the process at other places, far distant from their original positions. The object was to make the Mexicans believe that the Texan force was greater than it actually was. In this

[16] Stapp, *Prisoners of Perote*, p. 28; Thomas W. Bell, *A Narrative of the Capture and Subsequent Sufferings of the Mier Prisoners in Mexico, Captured in the Cause of Texas, Dec. 26th, 1842 and Liberated Sept. 16th, 1844*, p. 17.

[17] Looscan (ed.), "Journal of Lewis Birdsall Harris," *Southwestern Historical Quarterly*, XXV (1921–1922), 191.

effort to deceive the enemy, the Texans were successful. Meanwhile, the Mexicans were practicing a different version of the same deception. They appeared to be approaching in vast numbers when they first came into view, but changed their course to the right, taking up a position on a high ridge in full view. Their line, which appeared to be a half mile long, filed to the left and came down the ridge toward the Texans at the river, until the troops lost themselves in the valley and were hidden from view by the timber. The Mexicans would then file to the left and follow the course of the valley, hiding their movements from the view of the Texans, until they once again reached the point where they had first come into view. The Mexicans kept repeating this evolution of arms from 2 P.M. until it began to get dark. At first the Texans believed there were thousands upon thousands of them, but finally with the aid of a good field glass they "could tell when the same colored horse and rider came around and by counting them ascertained that there were 483 men acting as cavalry. If there were any infantry we did not see them," reported Adams. "But we began to understand the ruse which was played upon us so adroitly."[18]

After sufficient re-enforcements had crossed the river, a portion of the Texans under the leadership of Colonel Cook boldly ascended the bank and formed on the hill nearer the enemy and at some distance from the river.[19] Captain Cameron's men took position on the hill beside Bogart's. It was now about an hour before sundown. Thomas J. Green raised his blood red flag on top of one of the Carrizo or Careese Indian huts and two or three other flags or banners were raised at other points.[20] The enemy retained his position, making showy and brilliant maneuvers before the Texans, keeping them on the *qui vive*; but not venturing to attack their position. Toward nightfall, when it became evident from the deployment of the Texan force that the Mexican position could only be held at the risk of an engagement, Canales' cavalry retreated, leaving the Texans in possession of the field without the discharge of a single shot. Apparently the Mexicans failed to realize the decided advantage in numbers they had over the Texans when they first contacted them west of the Río Grande. A number of the Texans begged Somervell for permission to attack the enemy, but he refused to

[18] Adams, "[Journal of an] Expedition Against the Southwest," Dec. 14, 1842, ms.
[19] Looscan (ed.), "Journal of Lewis Birdsall Harris," *Southwestern Historical Quarterly*, XXV (1921–1922), 191.
[20] Adams "[Journal of an] Expedition Against the Southwest," Dec. 14, 1842, ms.

grant their request, adducing the lateness of the hour and the lack of acquaintance with the terrain as reasons for the refusal.[21]

An order was issued not to cross any more men that night,[22] but the crossing of the river by the men of the regiment continued until midnight. Even then, it was impossible to get all of the men across. General Somervell, therefore, found it necessary to divide his force for the night, leaving sixty men to guard some of the horses on the east side of the river. The division took place in spite of the fact he had received intelligence that approximately three thousand Mexican troops were fifteen miles up the river. This decision, which in the opinion of many of the men jeopardized the fate of the Texan army unnecessarily, cannot be completely excused on the basis of lack of adequate transportation facilities for crossing the river, which, at this point, was slightly over three hundred yards wide. However, the danger of losing some of the horses which would have to swim the river was at least a partial justification for delaying crossing them until morning. Hence, the necessity of retaining a guard for them on the east bank. Subsequent evidence proved that the report of a large enemy force in the immediate vicinity was false, but at the time Somervell had no justification for disbelieving it; and, therefore, it was his duty as a soldier and commanding officer, to take all necessary precautions to insure the safety of his army. Sentinels were placed about both camps, and Order No. 63 was issued on the west bank of the river to all officers and soldiers prohibiting them "from leaving the Encampment without a written permission signed by a captain and countersigned by a field officer and the sentinels were strictly enjoined to permit no one to pass the lines without such "written permission."[23] The men on the Mexican side of the river were instructed to remain at their posts, while one man was detailed from each mess to prepare supper, making the fires under the bluff or second bluff of the river. Other mess men were detailed to kill eighty sheep, twice as many goats, and a number of hogs and fowls. There was plenty of corn in ricks, fodder, and grass for the horses of the whole command for the first two days.

[21] Winkler (ed.), "Hendricks' Narrative," *Southwestern Historical Quarterly*, XXIII (1919–1920), 131.

[22] Adams, "[Journal of an] Expedition Against the Southwest," Dec. 14, 1842, ms.

[23] John Hemphill, Act[g] Adj[t] Genl of the Texas Militia, to the Hon. Anson Jones, Sec[y] of State, Washington, Texas, Jan. 23, 1843, State Department (Texas), Department of State, Letterbook, Home Letters, II (1842–1846), 67–71, ms. The order was dated West Branch of the Río Grande (near Guerrero), Decr 15th, 1842.

Throughout the night the men slept upon their arms, ready to spring up at a moment's notice. There was no alarm during the night, nor did the enemy approach in force. At daylight the remainder of the regiment and horses began crossing over with speed. A large number of sheep and goats from a herd on the Mexican side of the river was butchered. While breakfast was being prepared, some of the Texan spies came in to report that the Mexicans were still concentrating and that a party of them was advancing toward the Texan position. Immediately the Texan companies on the Mexican side of the river were paraded under arms, but more careful investigation showed that those approaching were carrying a white flag, apparently desiring a parley.[24]

An hour after sunrise, the alcalde of Guerrero, a Frenchman by birth,[25] accompanied by one or two other officials, arrived at the Texan outposts under a flag of truce and asked for the Texan commander. Being brought before General Somervell, the Mexican authorities offered to place the town at the disposal of the Texan commander and to comply, as far as possible, with any requisition he might make. Although the alcalde offered to furnish lodging in the town for the Texan army, he implored General Somervell to prevent a pillage of the town and its inhabitants, as it was rumored among the Mexican population that the Texans intended to burn the town and put its inhabitants to the sword. No doubt they had heard of the "sack" of Laredo. Somervell promised to keep the Texans from pillaging the town, provided the modest requisition of five days' provisions for twelve hundred men[26] and other necessary supplies, including shoes and hats for those in need, one hundred head of horses and mules, saddles, fifty blankets, and other items, was furnished. It was agreed that the supplies would be delivered at a point selected by the Mexicans on the road along the north bank of the Salado one mile from Guerrero.

In the meantime, while Somervell conversed, through his interpreter, Hammeken, with the Mexican officials and the Texan rear-guard completed its crossing of the river, the main army was busily preparing something to eat. Practically the only food available was mutton and corn. From the flock which the Texans appropriated in the vicinity, about one hundred and fifty sheep were selected, killed, skinned, and the better cuts cooked. Late in the afternoon the Texans were ready to

[24] Adams, "[Journal of an] Expedition Against the Southwest," Dec. 15, 1842, ms.

[25] Brown, *Indian Wars and Pioneers of Texas*, p. 573, says the alcalde of Guerrero was accompanied by a Frenchman who spoke English well.

[26] Adams, "[Journal of an] Expedition Against the Southwest," Dec. 15, 1842, ms.

547

advance upon Guerrero. The heavy mist which had fallen throughout most of the day now turned into an incessant rain.

About nightfall they reached the point on the Salado which had been appointed for the delivery of the articles requisitioned and which was intended to serve as their place for encampment during the night. The location aroused the suspicions of the Texans, who knew that the Mexican troops who had only recently evacuated Guerrero were encamped two miles beyond. The Mexicans retreated farther, as the Texans established themselves near the town and sent out reconnaissance parties.[27] Not only had the site for the delivery of the supplies been selected by the Mexicans, but it was on a gentle slope, "perfectly barren and destitute of timber either for firewood or protection in case of attack." The only protection was provided by a few bushes, growing here and there, and the limited number of cypress trees along the Salado. "The Salado, a small river, flowed immediately in front of us," wrote Hendricks, and on its bank the articles demanded of the Mexicans had been deposited in meager quantities and of second-hand quality. Among the items brought were hats, shoes, saddles, flour, corn, and *piloncillos*. Many were rejected because of their poor quality and ridiculously small quantity.[28] "Beyond this stream," said Hendricks, "and not more than two hundred yards from where we stood, and immediately in front of us, lay a range of hills, from which we could have been swept by artillery in every direction, without any possibility of our replying as the river was not fordable." Most of the men who were acquainted with Mexican promises and perfidy refused to go to the place selected by the enemy. They were wet and tired, and in an ungovernable mood. They "cursed the whol[e] roteen [*sic*] of officers, who would place any reliance in Mexican promises."[29]

Everything about the site raised Somervell's suspicion. The men were

[27] Guy M. Bryan to Rutherford B. Hayes, Peach Point, near Brazoria, Texas, Jan. 21, 1843, E. W. Winkler (ed.), "The Bryan-Hayes Correspondence," *Southwestern Historical Quarterly*, XXV (1921–1922), 103–107.

[28] Winkler (ed.), "Hendricks' Narrative," *Southwestern Historical Quarterly*, XXIII (1919–1920), 133. See also Adams, "[Journal of an] Expedition Against the Southwest," Dec. 15, 1842, ms.; McCutchan, Diary, ms., p. 31; Stapp, *Prisoners of Perote*, p. 28. Somervell later reported, "I refused to encamp . . . the troops in town, although accommodations were tendered for that purpose." A. Somervell to G. W. Hill, Sec. of War and Marine, Washington, Feb. 1, 1843, *Morning Star* (Houston), Feb. 18, 1843.

[29] Adams, "[Journal of an] Expedition Against the Southwest," Dec. 15, 1842, ms.

ordered not to unsaddle their horses without permission, and a company of men was paraded to guard the men killing beeves. After an hour of uncertainty in this location, Somervell ordered the troops moved up the river about three hundred yards to a point where they were somewhat protected by a rising knoll and numerous ravines and gullies.[30] Some of the outlying hills and valleys had patches of timber, but there was no grass of consequence in the whole area; so the horses were tied to the few scattered huisache bushes and each was fed three pints of corn. It was after dark when the Texans reached the new site and pitched their camp upon "a bleak, barren, rocky hill" near the bank of the Salado opposite the falls. The height of the falls was about twenty feet over a solid bed of sandstone. From their camp they could hear the roar of another falls "between our camp and the south of the River."[31] Across the river in the distance could be seen a ranch and several houses belonging to Mexicans. At this point General Somervell again issued orders prohibiting any officer or soldier from leaving the encampment "without written permission signed by a Captain and countersigned by a Field Officer." The sentinels were strictly enjoined to permit no one to pass the lines without such a written permission.[32] Having no opportunity to stretch the few tents they possessed, the men lay upon the wet ground exposed to the cold winds and pitiless rain, "which increased on the next day to a violent storm," and continued until noon. All ravines, ditches, and gullies overflowed; and the water rushed through the mountain gorges carrying rocks of immense size, demolishing trees and every movable object in its pathway. Occasionally during the night, sleet and snow fell, but melted soon after striking the ground. Trees for firewood and tent poles were not available, and the officers and men, exposed to the severities of the night, slept but little as they shivered, squatted together here and there in small groups and cat-napped while the ice-cold north wind whipped through their wet clothes. General Somervell found an old stump which he set afire and a number of the men huddled around it.[33]

[30] Harvey A. Adams says they moved up the river one-half mile. *Ibid.*, Dec. 15, 1842.

[31] *Ibid.*

[32] John Hemphill, Acting Adjutant General of the Texas Militia, to Anson Jones, Washington, Texas, Jan. 23, 1843, State Department (Texas), Department of State Letterbook, Home Letters, II (1842–1846), 67–71.

[33] Sidney S. Callender to John H. Brown, 994 Magazine Street, New Orleans, June 2, 1886, John Henry Brown Papers, 1835–1872, ms.

The night was very cold [recorded McCutchan], the rain continued to fall; we had no shelter, no fires, and but little to eat; our arms were wet; not one gun of the army perhaps, would have fired clear; and one twelve Pounder, on the opposite side of the river, well managed, would have created dreadful execution among the men, ere they could have retired! Indeed our position was miserable, dreadful, and perrilous [*sic*]! In that situation the Texan army passed the night, within one mile of a town where good, safe, and comfortable quarters could have been secured.[34]

Apparently the Mexican cavalry had evacuated the town and the vicinity for the Texan scouts failed to contact it, and the rain had obliterated the tracks of the horses. Somervell considered it unwise to quarter his troops in the town, however, for fear they would injure the inhabitants. During the night a number of the officers in the expedition visited the town, and brought back loot of various kinds, among "which were several of the finest mules we had met with, elegantly and richly caparisoned."[35] They claimed that these were gifts from the villagers, and they may well have been. The Mexicans no doubt were seeking to conciliate their visitors and avert a complete pillage of their town. For this purpose, the terrified citizenry donated a varied assortment of articles.

The next morning, December 16, in the midst of rain, the articles which had been furnished by the town of Guerrero were distributed. The requisition had called for coffee, sugar, blankets, shoes, corn, and other articles needed by the troops, including one hundred horses. The alcalde, an official who acts as mayor, judge, and *paterfamilias* in a Mexican town, had profusely and energetically promised to comply with the request, but the fulfillment of the requisition had been quite unsatisfactory. The alcalde had sent out only about ten pounds each of sugar and coffee, eight or ten pairs of shoes, six or eight "well worn" and "very aged" hats, a few old worn-out blankets, a number of worn-out saddles, a few beeves, and less than a quart of corn for each horse.[36] No horses had been sent. The fulfillment of the requisition was an insult to the Texan army; and "the very insufficient quantity of rations [was]

[34] McCutchan, Diary, ms., p. 31. See also A. Somervell to G. W. Hill, Sec. of War and Marine, Washington, Feb. 1, 1843, *Morning Star* (Houston), Feb. 18, 1843; *Telegraph and Texas Register*, Feb. 22, 1843.

[35] Stapp, *Prisoners of Perote*, p. 29.

[36] McCutchan, Diary, ms., p. 32; Green, *The Texian Expedition Against Mier*, p. 64; Winkler (ed.), "Hendricks' Narrative," *Southwestern Historical Quarterly*, XXIII (1919–1920), 133; Stapp, *Prisoners of Perote*, p. 29. Stapp says two days' provisions were supplied.

more calculated to make men mad than to allay their hunger."[37] Especially was this true when the Texans could see that the land along the river was apparently very fertile and had been cultivated with care and was productive of such crops as corn, oats, beans, potatoes, and other foods.

Instead of seizing the town and whatever useful stores were available in it, General Somervell, much to the astonishment and chagrin of his men, ordered a retreat. He was forced to return the expedition to the river, "where the horses could be fed, and shelter and wood procured."[38] The Texan guns were wet and needed to be dried. The troops, with stiffened limbs, were marched rapidly through the rain toward the river. In order to facilitate crossing the river, a detail was ordered to take down six large flat-bottom boats (chalanas) which had been found near the falls of the Salado, seven miles above its junction with the Río Bravo and adjacent to the Texan camp. Several of these boats carried large quantities of delftware and a large number of sugar kettles which the Texans pitched into the river.[39] Each of the vessels was capable of carrying from eight to ten horses.

The river had risen considerable during the night and "was way up its banks, rushing along in mad career."[40] For this and other reasons, only a few of the Texans were able to cross before night descended. At this point the wind shifted to the north, the weather became very cold, and soon it began to sleet. The horses were tied up to trees or bushes without food, and "a good number of them froze to death by the trees where they were tied."[41] During the day (the 16th) the Río Grande had risen two feet, but in the course of the night it fell ten inches. A majority of the men encamped on the west bank where they passed "a wet,

[37] Green, *Journal of the Texian Expedition Against Mier,* p. 64.

[38] A. Somervell to G. W. Hill, Sec. of War and Marine, Washington, Feb. 1, 1843, *Morning Star* (Houston), Feb. 18, 1843.

[39] William H. Emory, *Report on the United States and Mexican Boundary Survey, Made under the Direction of the Secretary of the Interior,* I, 67; Lucy A. Erath (ed.), "Memoirs of Major George Bernard Erath," *Southwestern Historical Quarterly,* XXVII (1923–1924), 42–43; Memucan Hunt to Francis Moore, Jr., Editor of the *Telegraph,* Houston, dated Béxar, Jan. 8, 1843, *Morning Star* (Houston), Jan. 17, 1843, says four large flat-boats were carried down; Adams "[Journal of an] Expedition Against the Southwest," Dec. 16, 1842, ms., says six trading boats were found.

[40] Sidney S. Callender to John H. Brown, 994 Magazine St., New Orleans, June 2, 1886, John Henry Brown Papers, 1835–1872, ms.

[41] Adams, "[Journal of an] Expedition Against the Southwest," Dec. 16, 1842, ms.

cold, and miserable night, without outposts or sentries, and but little wood,"[42] by which to warm and dry. The damp weather made it difficult to set on fire the rails obtained from nearby fences. The men sought protection under the banks of the river, in adjacent hedges, and in the huts of the Carrizo Indians on the hill. Those of Adams' mess, along with Colonel Hemphill, sought protection in one of the huts which was about forty by twenty feet, half underground, built of stone and covered with earth. There were six or eight loop holes in it.[43] About 10 P.M. two Mexican carts arrived from Guerrero with provisions of flour and *piloncillo* which had to be stored in the hut. The cart men were nearly frozen. They were placed under guard until the next morning when they were liberated. The Mexicans declared there would be a better place down the river to furnish the supplies the Texans demanded.

The next morning some of the Texans went into Guerrero on their own hook to get horses and other articles, but the Mexicans would not sell them anything, it was reported, but gave them a *piloncillo* apiece, a handful of cigars, and some bread. They came away very much disappointed.[44] During the day while the main body of the Texan army was occupied in crossing the Río Grande, Captain Hays and Bogart, with seventy men, were retained on the western side of the river to secure compliance with the requisition which had been made upon the town for one hundred horses to mount the horseless Texans. By night the whole army, except the two spy companies, had been transferred to the opposite shore in spite of the rain. By morning the river had again risen, this time full to the banks. Word came that the Mexican authorities found it impossible to comply with the request for horses. About the same time, it was alleged, Somervell "received a pre-emptory order from General Houston to return and not to advance any further into Mexico."[45] However, no definite proof of such an order has been found. Strong sentiment against the command now developed among the Texans, in their camp near what was later known as the town of Zapata (since flooded by the waters from the Falcon Dam), and at one time "it looked as though there would be a general revolt, but better councils prevailed."[46] However, it was only with great difficulty that sufficient

[42] McCutchan, Diary, ms., p. 32.
[43] Adams, "[Journal of an] Expedition Against the Southwest," Dec. 16, 1842, ms.
[44] *Ibid.*, Dec. 17, 1842.
[45] Looscan (ed.), "Journal of Lewis Birdsall Harris," *Southwestern Historical Quarterly,* XXV (1921–1922), 190.
[46] *Ibid.*

discipline was restored to parade a guard.[47] The men were vehement in their desire not to return home without fighting the enemy. The men on foot and those whose horses had been weakened or injured since leaving the Medina did not relish treading on foot the many miles back to their homes.

On the morning of the 7th, previous to our taking possession of Laredo, [wrote Hunt] Acting Adjutant-General Hemphill read an order from Gen. Somervell, which assured the troops that of the property taken from the enemy, there should be an equal distribution. I regret to state, however, that Gen. Somervell forfeited this pledge so far as related to the horses and mules which had been brought into camp. In some instances Captains of companies would allow their men to detach themselves in small numbers and acquire for their purposes any number of horses and mules they could find; other officers denied their men this privilege, saying that all property thus acquired, should be procured by regular details of men, and equally divided between officers and men; [but, when we commenced to retreat from before Guerrero] Gen. Somervell failed altogether to conform to his pledge. The Captains, consequently, who had been most particular in requiring and enforcing discipline and subordination from their men in not allowing parties to leave camp, acquired no horses or mules to supply those of their companies whose horses were unfit for service.[48]

In order to appease the discontented and possibly to "satisfy the men in following him home," General Somervell now dispatched Adjutant General Hemphill at 10 A.M. across the river with an order to the spy companies to enter Guerrero, and to demand, in lieu of the one hundred horses, five thousand dollars to be paid at once. If this demand should not be complied with, Hays was authorized to inform the alcalde that the Texan general would forthwith seize Guerrero. Because of the danger apprehended from this step, only thirty-five of Bogart's company, including officers, and seventeen of Hays' volunteered to follow their leaders into the town. About one-fourth of the men refused to participate in the plan. It has been said that "some . . . were out on special duty, but many staid back through fear and cowardice."[49]

[47] Stapp, *Prisoners of Perote*, p. 30; A. Somervell to G. W. Hill, Sec. of War and Marine, Washington, Feb. 1, 1843, *Morning Star* (Houston), Feb. 18, 1843.

[48] Memucan Hunt to Francis Moore, Jr., Editor of the *Telegraph*, Houston, dated Bexar, Jan. 8, 1843, *Morning Star* (Houston), Jan. 17, 1843.

[49] Winkler (ed.), "Hendricks' Narrative," *Southwestern Historical Quarterly*, XXIII (1919–1920), 134; see also Adams, "[Journal of an] Expedition Against the Southwest," Dec. 18, 1842, ms.

Guerrero was a fine-looking, well-constructed town, situated on the
north bank of the Salado and contained an estimated population of
fifteen hundred to two thousand inhabitants. Its houses were built of
stone and possessed flat roofs. Each house was surrounded by a wall.
The streets and two public squares were well laid off and presented an
appearance of "elegance and neatness."

There is one cathedral in the place, [wrote one of the Texan visitors] and
several large public buildings. The inhabitants have fine gardens and throughout the place there are numerous groves of orange trees, that give it a most
luxurient and smiling appearance. . . . There are two strong forts in the place,
and every house is a kind of fortification. Had they known how to fight, few,
if any of us, would ever have returned to our friends, with thoughts and
dreams of Mexico.[50]

While the small band of Texans were on their mission to Guerrero,
General Somervell posted ninety men to cover their retreat if Canales
should cause trouble.

As Captain Hays led his small band into Guerrero "fear and timidity
seemed to seize the whole population." Not the slightest opposition was
offered to their entrance, although the Texans saw not less than four
hundred Mexicans in the place. Many had fled the city shortly after the
arrival of the Texans on the Río Grande two days before. Hays communicated General Somervell's new request to the alcalde. The alcalde
promised to do everything possible to secure the amount of money required. Hays impressed upon him the necessity of an immediate compliance with the order. In the meantime while the alcalde summoned
his council by ringing the large and small bells of the cathedral, Hays
formed his men in open order around three sides of the main (Church)
square, with his men fronting the center. The Texan flag was unfurled
and flown at the upper end of the line of troops. Sentinels were mounted
on some of the houses where they could watch in every direction for
the return of Canales' cavalry or other hostile force. The citizenry, who
seemed as meek as lambs, brought out several sacks of corn to feed the
Texans' horses. The corn was poured upon the flag stones in the public
square. Each man stayed by the side of his horse ready to mount it at a
moment's notice. The *señoritas* voluntarily brought "los Texianos"
piloncillos, pan (bread), *tortillas,* and cigars and cigarettes as a treat.
"The people, especially the male portion, looked daggers at us," re-

[50] Winkler (ed.), "Hendricks' Narrative," *Southwestern Historical Quarterly,*
XXIII (1919–1920), 134–135.

ported Adams, "but the women appeared to look kindly upon us as they were the principal ones who gave us anything to eat."[51]

While the money was being collected, the alcalde's beautiful daughter, the finest dressed woman some of the Texans had ever seen, came into the room and remained there near her father most of the time the Texans were in occupation of the town. At the end of an hour and a half the alcalde reported that all he could raise was $381. The Mexican officials explained that their own troops had been quartered upon the town and had plundered the inhabitants of nearly all they had. Hays refused to accept the $381 counted out on the marble table in the front room of the alcalde's house and appeared to be highly incensed at the failure of the Mexicans to raise the sum demanded. The silver was now placed in a thick buckskin saddle wallet, and the alcalde was arrested and compelled to accompany Hays for the purpose of explaining to General Somervell his failure to fulfil the requisition that had been demanded. At 3 P.M. Hays withdrew his troops from Guerrero. A frenchman accompanied the group.[52] At this point the accounts of what transpired differ widely. One account says that upon the alcalde's arrival at the Texan headquarters east of the river, he explained to General Somervell with great protestations that the rancheros had driven off all the horses in the neighborhood; and that since the men of wealth had fled the town leaving behind the poor, it was not within his power to furnish the whole of the $5,000 which had been demanded, but that he was willing to pay all that he had been able to raise, which he held up tied in a handkerchief.[53] The Texan general "instantly flew into a rage, and cursing the Mexican alcalde most unmercifully, ordered him to . . . [return] to Gurrero with his money, and never let him see or hear

[51] Adams, "[Journal of an] Expedition Against the Southwest," Dec. 18, 1842, ms.

[52] *Ibid.*

[53] Although some accounts report as much as $700 being raised, the only eye witness report that I have been able to locate in which the exact amount is given is the one by Harvey A. Adams, who claims he was stationed on guard duty in front of the alcalde's house and saw the Mexican dollars counted out, and that the sum was only $381. *Ibid.* Winkler (ed.), "Hendricks' Narrative," *Southwestern Historical Quarterly*, XXIII (1919–1920), 134, and Memucan Hunt to Dr. Francis Moore, Bexar, Jan. 8, 1843, *Morning Star* (Houston), Jan. 17, 1843, both say that $700 was offered. Green, *The Texian Expedition Against Mier*, p. 65, says Hays was offered $380; and Stapp, *Prisoners of Perote*, p. 30, reports he was offered $173; Erath (ed.), "Memoirs of Major George Bernard Erath," *Southwestern Historical Quarterly*, XXVII (1923–1924), 42, says "more than two hundred dollars," were offered.

of him again."[54] Another version is that when Hays reached the crossing, he called loudly to General Somervell, naming the amount of money offered. "The General said if that is all they can do, tell them to take it back with them." The Texans who had gone into town were surprised at the reply of their general, but as orders now came for them to cross immediately, they began to do so. By the time they had gotten across it was getting very dark. Adams, whose account I have followed here, says, "five or six of Hays men remained" at the Indian hut on the west side "with the men who brought the money. The money was never allowed to go back."[55]

In levying the original requisition and later the money contribution upon the town of Guerrero, Somervell had threatened to turn five hundred men loose upon the town to sack it if his demands had not been complied with; but, now that his troops were on the east bank of the Río Bravo, he relinquished the hope of obtaining horses and money from the inhabitants of Guerrero by threats or otherwise and directed his attention toward returning home.

By the morning of December 19 all the Texans had crossed to the east side of the river. Their camp was approximately six hundred yards from the river. There was no grass for their horses, but they did have a scanty supply of corn from the ranches above and below the camp. Seeing that his men were more disorderly than ever and that it was impossible to enforce obedience,[56] Somervell concluded that to stay longer upon the Río Grande, especially in the vicinity of the two important Mexican military posts of San Fernando and Matamoros, might prove disastrous to the expedition. His personal friends were aware of his intentions and the impending order to return to Gonzales; and, consequently, availed themselves of the "opportunity of collecting mules, horses, mares, and colts, which they profited by."[57] In order to delay as long as possible the Mexican force, which was no doubt collecting in the vicinity, General Somervell, on the previous night, had ordered the fleet of boats sunk; but, some of those to whom the order had been given,

[54] Winkler (ed.), "Hendricks' Narrative," *Southwestern Historical Quarterly,* XXIII (1919–1920), 135.

[55] Adams, "[Journal of an] Expedition Against the Southwest," Dec. 18, 1842, ms.

[56] Guy M. Bryan to Rutherford B. Hayes, Peach Point near Brazoria, Texas, Jan. 21, 1843, Winkler (ed.), "The Bryan-Hayes Correspondence," *Southwestern Historical Quarterly,* XXV (1921–1922), 103–105.

[57] Green, *The Texian Expedition Against Mier,* p. 66.

believing the General's object was to destroy all means of carrying the war against the enemy, merely moved the boats a few miles below, and left the general under the impression that his order had been carried out.[58] The seeds of another schism and division of the army were germinating. On the morning of the 19th an order was issued for the troops to begin the march at 10 o'clock for the settled area of Texas, by way of the junction of the Frio and Nueces rivers, and thence to Gonzales where they were to be disbanded.[59] Although many of the men had expected such an order, it's announcement proved disheartening to a large majority of them. The men, it is said, "became perfectly wild," and called their general all sorts of names, some unprintable. They had long wanted to engage the Mexican army and some had hoped to seize and plunder Mexican towns both for personal gain and in retaliation for the destruction and loss of property and lives at San Antonio, Victoria, Harrisburg, and Goliad by the Mexican invading army of '36 and later raiding expeditions. Some preferred a "grave in the desolate wilds of a western prairie" to returning home without meeting the enemy.[60] Others questioned Somervell's motives, and presumed he had "gained sufficient *honor* and glory, by taking two defenceless towns," and was now "determined to return home with a *whole body*, and a *Hat full* of glory, while it was yet time. He thought," declared McCutchan, " 'Now is the time, before it is everlastingly too late!' He could see if we stayed thare much longer, we would *have* to *fight*—and that would have been far from congenial with his nice sense of feeling."[61] "He got awfully scared," said Harvey Adams.[62]

[58] *Ibid.*, p. 66. In an affidavit, dated May 7, 1881, J. J. Humphreys, a member of the expedition, reports that Green, Fisher, he and others were told by General Somervell to take the boats and go ahead, wishing that he (Somervell), too, could go. Mrs. C. T. Traylor, "George Lord," *Frontier Times*, XVI (1938–1939), 536.

[59] "Order No. 64. Head Quarters, Camp opposite the mouth of the Salado, East Bank of the Río Grande [Dec. 19, 1842]," in A. Somervell to G. W. Hill, Sec. of War and Marine, Washington, Feb. 1, 1843, *Morning Star* (Houston), Feb. 18, 1843; John Hemphill to Anson Jones, Washington, Jan. 23, 1843, Army Papers (Texas), ms.; also copy in State Department (Texas), Department of State Letterbook, Home Letters, II (1842–1846), 69–71; M. C. Hamilton to Anson Jones, Department of War and Marine, Washington, Dec. 24, 1844 (being "Special Report of the Secretary of War and Marine"), in Texas Congress, *Journals of the Ninth Congress of the Republic of Texas*, Appendix, p. 75.

[60] McCutchan, Diary, ms., p. 83.

[61] *Ibid.*, pp. 132–133.

[62] Adams, "[Journal of an] Expedition Against the Southwest," Dec. 18, 1842, ms.

Being in charge of the expedition, General Somervell probably felt, more than anyone else, the responsibility for the welfare and safety of his men. In his report to the Secretary of War, he stated that "having been eleven days on the river, and knowing the various positions and bodies of the enemy's troops, I was satisfied that they were concentrating in such numbers as to render a longer stay an act of imprudence."[63] Furthermore, Somervell had failed to solve satisfactorily the all important problem of discipline; and, too, the expedition was in great need of food, clothing, and munitions, but the order to return on the 19th, declared Somervell, "was from no apprehension of the scarcity of the stores of subsistence" but out of regard to the safety of his men due to the concentration of the Mexican forces along this section of the Río Grande frontier. The several problems mentioned above had never been solved, and there is reason to believe that the Administration never expected them to be solved. From the beginning, very little energy had been shown by the commanding officer in prosecuting the campaign which, no doubt, was instituted as a political move to appease western demands for an invasion of Mexico and to reveal to the uncontrollable hotheads the utter futility of sustaining an attack on Mexico without adequate equipment, supplies, and discipline. During their eleven days upon the Río Grande many of the men had reached the conclusion that there was very little possibility of accomplishing their original objectives. "There was little harmony among the many filibustering men in the command, who were continually stirring up strife, which caused almost a mutiny in camp at times. . . . Every officer [was] seeking military fame and trammeling each other to the Generalship."[64] Yet, so much dissatisfaction developed from the general order to return home, that a few of the "more hot headed . . . determined to separate from the command and cross the river, and as they expressed it, rake down the settlements on the Mexican side and bring in as many cattle and horses

---

[63] Report of Brig.-Gen. A. Somervell to the Hon. G. W. Hill, Sec. of War and Marine, Washington, Feb. 1, 1843, in Texas Congress, *Journals of the Ninth Congress of the Republic of Texas*, Appendix, p. 75. "We ascertained from some spies," recorded Adams, "that the enemy were concentrating troops from Procedia [Presidio] and all the interior towns to attack us. Canales and Ampudia from Matamoros were moving up also." Adams, "[Journal of an] Expedition Against the Southwest," Dec. 18, 1842, ms.

[64] Adams, "[Journal of an] Expedition Against the Southwest," Dec. 18, 1842, ms.

as they could manage."[65] Five captains and most of the men under them forthwith refused to obey the order. The five captains were Fisher, Eastland (anxious to avenge the death of his cousin, Nicholas Mosby Dawson), Cameron, Ryon, and Pierson,[66] who were supported not only by a majority of their own men, but also by a large number of officers and privates from other companies. Bogart's men, while twelve of the company were out trying to mount themselves with better horses, voted by a majority of two to return; and when the vote was protested be-

[65] Looscan (ed.), "Journal of Lewis Birdsall Harris," *Southwestern Historical Quarterly*, XXV (1921–1922), 190.

[66] Captain William M. Eastland, born in Kentucky, March 21, 1806, and reared and educated in Tennessee, was encouraged by General Edward Burleson to come to Texas in 1834 to engage in the timber business. He settled at LaGrange; fought in the battle of San Jacinto; and in 1837 succeeded Captain M. Andrews in command of the rangers, but when he attempted to exercise rigid discipline, his men, "marched out, stacked their arms, told him to go to hell and they would go home." Eastland, however, yielded gracefully and maintained the respect of his men. In 1839 he served as captain of one of three companies of volunteers organized in the upper settlements of the Colorado for an expedition against the Comanches. Eastland went to the relief of San Antonio in September 1842, at the head of a company, but arrived too late to fight the Mexicans. He stayed on in San Antonio after Woll's retreat and joined the Somervell expedition. Sam Houston Dixon and Louis Wiltz Kemp, *The Heroes of San Jacinto*, pp. 208–209; Walter Prescott Webb, *The Texas Rangers*, pp. 42–44.

William M. Ryon (1808–1875) was born in Kentucky, and came to Texas in 1837. Clarence R. Wharton, *History of Fort Bend County*, p. 117.

John Goodloe Warren Pierson, son of John and Elizabeth (Goodloe) Pierson, Jr., was born in Union County, Kentucky, February 15, 1795. He was descendant of Scotch-English parents, his grandfather, Robert Pierson, having immigrated to America in 1774. In 1814 he married Purity Pennington, who gave birth to three children. After the death of his wife, Pierson came to Texas in 1824 with his brother James Tilman Pierson. In Texas, he married Elizabeth Montgomery, who likewise bore him three children. In 1833 he was made surveyor general of the Nashville Colony by Sterling C. Robertson. Upon the death of his second wife, he married a third time, in 1835, this time a widow, Mrs. Narcissa Slatter, daughter of Peter Cartwright. This marriage netted three more children. Pierson represented the Municipality of Viesca (name changed to Milam County, Dec. 27, 1835) in the Consultation. Early in March 1836, he was appointed aide-de-camp to organize the militia of the Municipality of Milam. In 1836, after the murder of the Rev. J. W. Parker family by Indians, Pierson moved from Navasota Creek to Grimes County, where he died on May 7, 1849, at the age of fifty-four. Edmund Pierson, "Goodloe Warren Pierson," ms.; Marjorie Rogers, "Old Viesca," *Frontier Times* VIII (1930–1931), 489–492; William C. Binkley (ed.), *Official Correspondence of the Texan Revolution*, I, 40, 491; H. P. N. Gammel (ed.), *Laws of Texas*, I, 1002–1003.

cause of the absences, Bogart refused to delay or reconsider on the ground that circumstances did not permit delaying.[67] Twenty of Bogart's men joined Colonel Fisher's expedition.

The decision of whether to return home or to repudiate Somervell's authority and continue down the river was a difficult one for more than one volunteer. John Fenn of Fort Bend County asked Lieutenant Shipman, "John, which way shall we go?"

"We are good soldiers," was the ready reply, "and must obey orders," but when the test came and his captain and a majority of the company went with those who were going into Mexico, Shipman went, too.

John Fenn also turned his horse to follow, but Robert Herndon took hold of his bridle and said, "Come, John, you are young, go back with me," and he yielded.[68] Two others, William Sullivan and a man named Woodson of Fort Bend, came back with Fenn.

It was reported that Fisher desired to take his men far enough down the river to enable them "to procure horses for those of his company who were on foot, or whose horses were unable to carry them, and [to obtain] a necessary supply of food to take them into the settlements"[69]— a distance of "nearly three hundred miles . . . most[ly] through an uninhabited country where nothing could be obtained for sustenance but game."[70] When the necessary horses and supplies had been obtained, he declared, he would be willing to return home. Fisher expected, at the most, not to be delayed more than a day or two in getting back to Washington County from whence he had marched with his men.

Since leaving Laredo, several of the officers had been hoping to proceed down the river as far as Camargo, and, after capturing that place, to cross the river and return home by way of San Patricio.[71] Having entered the army and marched to the Río Grande "with the expectation of meeting the enemy in battle, and having been thus far disappointed," said Thomas W. Bell, "it was thought not at all improper to remain a

[67] Adams, "[Journal of an] Expedition Against the Southwest," Dec. 19, 1842, ms.

[68] A. J. Sowell, *History of Fort Bend County, Containing Biographical Sketches of Many Noted Characters*, p. 104.

[69] Memucan Hunt to Francis Moore, Jr., Editor of the *Telegraph*, Houston, dated Bexar, Jan. 8, 1843, *Morning Star* (Houston), Jan. 17, 1843; see also Erath (ed.), "Memoirs of George Bernard Erath," *Southwestern Historical Quarterly*, XXVII (1923–1924), p. 43; McCutchan's Diary, p. 133.

[70] Bell, *Narrative*, p. 17.

[71] *Morning Star*, Jan. 7, 1843.

while longer, and at some favorable opportunity give the tawny sons of Montezuma undeniable proofs of what they might expect to receive at the hands of Texans; wielding the fatal rifle and urged by resentment of their wrongs to use them with unerring skillfulness."[72] When they struck at Laredo and Guerrero the Texans had found the Mexican center weak, for their main forces were at Matamoros and Presidio del Río Grande; but, reported *El Semanario* of Monterey, their successes "swelled them with pride" until they made the mistake of thinking they could rob Mier, too.[73]

Later writing from prison in Matamoros, Major J. D. Cocke, whose statements were endorsed by John R. Baker, Israel Canfield, and all the captains, sought to defend their "imputed rashness" in detaching themselves from General Somervell's command by alleging they

were mainly promoted by disgust and mortification at the fact that the frontier of our country had been three times invaded, and our habitations as repeatedly desolated, and yet no blow of vengeance or retaliation had been struck by Texas. We crossed the river to stir up the whirlwind of war about the dwellings of the enemy. . . . We were more afraid of being branded on our return as recreants, than we were of the worst possible results to be apprehended from such disobedience; and, moreover, we were not supplied with a sufficiency of provisions to take us home from Guerrero, and this fact operated upon many of the men who were willing, had the case been otherwise to have returned. It was stamped at the time as unofficer-like conduct in Gen. S. to presume to march the command home without adequate supplies and horses—many of the men being on foot and others with weak horses, utterly unable to perform the trip—when, too, we were surrounded by an abundant commissariat department [Mexico].[74]

Realizing that a division of the force at this point might jeopardize the march home by making the smaller units more vulnerable to an attack by enemy cavalry, Memucan Hunt, a former minister to the United States and Secretary of the Navy, and now a member of Captain

---

[72] Bell, *Narrative*, p. 17.

[73] *El Semanario*, (Monterey), Dec. 29, 1842, quoted in *Diario del Gobierno* (Mexico City), Jan. 13, 1843.

[74] Major J. D. Cocke to ———, Matamoros, Jan. 12, 1843, reprinted from the *New Orleans Bulletin* in the *Morning Star* (Houston), March 4 and 7, 1843. The letter was endorsed by Edwin [Ewen] Cameron, John R. Baker, Claudius Buster, William M. Eastland, J. G. W. Pierson, Charles K. Reese, William Ryon, and Israel Canfield, who were described as "captains."

Fisher's Company, sought to avoid a division by requesting, in person, that a council of officers be called to talk the matter over. The council met, and when it looked as if nothing would be accomplished, Hunt ventured to suggest to General Somervell that the whole force continue its march down the river for a day or two longer so as "to enable the officers and men on foot to be mounted on horses which would take them to their homes, and secure as little division as possible on our return." General Somervell, however, refused to alter his order. Captain Fisher then asked if the general would permit the men to choose their own officers as high as brigade general, which meant that Somervell would have to stand for re-election to the command of the expedition if he wished to lead it. This the general refused to sanction, and no election was held. Thereupon, Fisher, representing several of his fellow officers, requested permission to separate from the expedition with the idea of continuing the march down the river. Somervell refused to accede to the request; whereupon, three hundred and five dissatisfied officers and men withdrew from the command to carry on a private war of their own.[75] Discipline had completely collapsed. Memucan Hunt[76] and Captain Edward W. Smith of Harrison County were the only men to withdraw from Captain Fisher's company. They joined Captain Sims' company of Bastrop. Many of the men who elected to return home gave a part or all of their ammunition to those who preferred to follow Fisher.[77]

Here we find the beginnings of the famous Mier Expedition, many of whose members lived to regret their insubordination but always blamed General Somervell for their subsequent misfortunes. Writing from prison in Matamoros, one of the Mier men suggested that Texas should reward the general for his "hasty retreat" from the Río Grande by giving him an office in Béxar "to take care of the women of that place, so as to prevent the Mexicans violating them."[78] For their imprisonment, James D.

[75] Memucan Hunt to Francis Moore, Jr., Editor of the *Telegraph*, Houston, dated Bexar, Jan. 8, 1843, *Morning Star* (Houston), Jan. 17, 1843; McCutchan, Diary, ms., p. 32; Green, *The Texian Expedition Against Mier*, p. 66. Green says 304 separated from Somervell's command.

[76] [Frederic Benjamin Page], *Prairiedom: Rambles and Scrambles in Texas or New Estremadura by a Suthron*, p. 105.

[77] "I divided all my ammunition," wrote Harris, "with two boys 16 or 17 years old," one named Robert H. Beale and the other John C. C. Hill. Looscan (ed.), "Journal of Lewis Birdsall Harris," *Southwestern Historical Quarterly*, XXV (1921–1922), 190.

[78] Quoted from the *Texas Times* (Galveston), Feb. 4, 1843, by the *New Orleans Picayune*, Feb. 8, 1843.

McCutchan blamed Somervell: ". . . his weak heart, and old woman's Soul, that is to be attributed, the unfortunate termination of that illfated [Mier] Expedition."[79]

The responsibility for the failure to outfit an effective offensive expedition against Mexico may not be attributed to any single leader, but rather to the financial weakness of the Republic and to disobedience among the militiamen and volunteers constituting the army. Just as in the case of the failure at Corpus Christi and the fiasco at the Hondo, the unsuccessful efforts on the Río Grande resulted from the utter refusal of many of the Texans "to submit to a moderate degree of restraint, obedience and self-denial."[80] Disobedience of orders was a

[79] McCutchan, Diary, ms., p. 83.

[80] Marmaduke, "A Volunteer Army; What One Is and What It May Be," *Morning Star* (Houston), March 25, 1843. "Marmaduke" declared that the Texas military system needed to be reformed, and suggested that the reformation

must originate mainly where the evil exists—in the ranks—from the concerted and earnest influence of the cool, clear-headed, and intelligent, over the rash, stupid, and ignorant. . . . My main theme is that the volunteers of a Texas General ought to obey him. . . . To volunteers . . . I would say, beware of the noisy stump orator who thunders forth his disorganizing harangues with the tongue of a lyon [*sic*] and the brains of an ass, the disturber who is ever declaiming on the commander's faults and his own untried merits. Beware of the vain boaster who without ever having seen a battle fought or learned the simplest evolution aspires to the command of men more experienced; but above all others, beware of him who electioneers by appealing to your basest passions—by alluring you to plunder and outrage, for every word of the empty swaggerer portends disaster and disgrace. Any Texian force which may hereafter invade Mexico, and goes with the full intention of indulging in pillage is sure of defeat. However well ordered it may be at first, its discipline will be irretrievably lost once the mania for "raking down" fully possesses it. The soldier who is bent on seeking and securing plunder cannot and will not attend to his duty; so soon as the taint becomes general, discipline, vigilance, and unity of action are gone; and the enemy has only to watch, and he will soon, find an opportunity of cutting up the marauders in detail or of surprising and crushing them en mass.

In re "Col. Marmaduke," see William J. Mitchell to Gen. M. Lamar, Milledgeville [Ga.], Jan. 31, 1838, *Lamar Papers*, V, 172. Describing the Texas soldier, Carl, Prince of Solms-Braunfels, wrote:

. . . the American is warlike by nature. He shoulders a gun and, taking sufficient ammunition along departs from his home a soldier. Thus gangs and bands of troops rise up. They choose their own officers, but do not obey them. Of course such positions are hardly desirable, for even though elected, nevertheless, the officer, if he tries to secure respect and order, exposes himself to being shot by his own men. . . . A more undisciplined soldier cannot be found than such a bunch of American volunteers.

Carl, Prince of Solms-Braunfels, *Texas, 1844–1845*, pp. 86–87.

thing not peculiar to Texans. It seems to have been a characteristic of the American frontiersman to be impatient of discipline. "The natural turbulence and independence of the frontiersman," says Professor Webb, "made obedience distasteful to him. . . . The leader had to *emerge* from the group, and all that the state could do was to confirm and legalize a fact. . . . The price of failure at any time was death to his prestige and supremacy."[81] Somervell was partly to blame for the breakup of the expedition, but the responsibility for the failure to outfit an effective offensive operation against Mexico can scarcely be attributed to any single person.

[81] Webb, *The Texas Rangers,* p. 79.

CHAPTER TWENTY-FOUR

Somervell Marches Home

AFTER THE WITHDRAWAL of Fisher and the others who did not care to return home immediately, the rest of the Texas army, numbering 189 officers and men, being mostly the remainder of the drafted militia, the staff officers, and a part of the Houston volunteers, began their march for Gonzales at 1 P.M., December 19. Among those returning with Somervell were Colonel John Hemphill, acting adjutant general; Colonel James R. Cook, acting inspector general and colonel of the First Regiment; Colonel William G. Cooke, acting quartermaster general; Lieutenant Colonel George T. Howard and Major D. Murphree, both of the First Regiment; and Captain Peter H. Bell, aide-de-camp to General Somervell. The following companies returned:[1]

Captain	Commanding Officers	Non-Commissioned Officers and Privates	Aggregate
1. Bogart, Samuel	3	36	39
2. Sims, Bartlett	2	16	18
3. McNeill, John Shelby	3	25	28
4. Lowrey, James P.	2	17	19
5. Barrett, W. M.	3	65	68
6. Mitchell, Isaac N.	1	12	13

[1] "Abstract of the Muster-Rolls of the Companies comprising the Army on the South-Western Frontier, commanded by Brigadier [General] Somervell, that marched from Guerrero in obedience to Order No. 64," in Texas Congress, *Journals of the House of Representatives of the Ninth Congress of the Republic of Texas*, Appendix, p. 75; Memucan Hunt to Francis Moore, Jr., Editor of the *Telegraph*, Houston, dated Bexar, Jan. 8, 1843, *Telegraph and Texas Register*, Jan. 18, 1843. Other officers returning were Lts. Thomas S. Lubbock, John P. Borden, Moses A. Bryan, John Henry Brown, Captain James A. Sylvester, and Memucan Hunt and Ed[ward] Levin. Francis R. Lubbock, *Six Decades or Memoirs of Francis Richard Lubbock*,

It is reported that Clark L. Owen's company returned, as well as most of the men belonging to Hays' company. Although Hays did not reach San Antonio with Somervell; yet, he is reported by the general as being among those returning.[2] Hays left the Río Grande with General Somervell; however, several of his rangers, including Ben McCulloch, volunteered to join Fisher's command and were permitted to stay and perform scouting duty for those who insisted on pushing down the river towards Mier.[3] After Hays had gone a hundred miles from the Río Grande, he discovered that "his fine clay bank horse, a present from Tennessee," had gotten loose and headed for the Río Grande. Mounting another horse, Hays trailed him, finally locating him in a stable of a Mexican ranch on the river where he had kept him while the Texan army had camped before Guerrero. Hays slipped in at night and took his horse from the stable without being discovered by the Mexicans who had returned to the ranch. Hays reached San Antonio about a week after General Somervell.[4]

---

p. 147. According to M. C. Hamilton's report, the muster roll for W. M. Barrett's Company "appears to have been made out, at the date the men were mustered into service, though it was returned as a 'discharge roll.' It embraces," he said, "the whole period from the 1st of October, 1842, to 1st January, 1843, and bears date 24th November, 1842." M. C. Hamilton, Acting Secretary, to Anson Jones, Department of War and Marine, Washington, Dec. 24, 1844, in Texas Congress, *Journals of the Ninth Congress of the Republic of Texas*, Appendix, p. 69.

[2] A. Somervell to G. W. Hill, Secretary of War and Marine, Washington, Feb. 1, 1843, *Telegraph and Texas Register*, Feb. 22, 1843.

[3] J. D. Affleck, "History of John C. Hays," pt. II, pp. 296–299, says that Hays headed the scouting party for Colonel Fisher, and that on the 23rd of December he determined to abandon the enterprize, which he did the next day, alleging that his presence was required at San Antonio now that Somervell was giving up the expedition, and there was "the necessity of resuming his independent command at that place, based on such a contingency, in compliance with orders from the Secretary of War." He advised Colonel Fisher and his men, continued Affleck, to abandon their objective, as a large Mexican force was being concentrated to oppose them. The truth is that it was Ben McCulloch, and not Hays, who commanded the scouting party, which is proof that Hays was not along. Hays had a reputation for obedience of orders, and it is not likely that he would have disobeyed Somervell. Also, it is improbable that he would have been so foolish as to get involved in Fisher's expedition, when he only had to reflect back three years to the mess Reuben Ross and his men had gotten themselves into by running off to Mexico without governmental approval.

[4] Adele B. Looscan (ed.), "Journal of Lewis Birdsall Harris," *Southwestern Historical Quarterly*, XXV (1921–1922), 193.

Somervell's intention was to march to Gonzales and there disband the troops. The men had not gone far, however, before all was confusion in the order of march, and on the return trip the men became "as disgusted and demoralized a set as you ever saw," recorded Harris.[5] Since it could not be agreed which was the proper route to follow, a number of the men became mutinous and refused to recognize General Somervell as their commander, substituting in his place Flacco, the able Indian chief.[6] The command now split, first into two units with the larger one being under General Somervell. The other, under Captain Bogart, followed in the rear. Ultimately another division of the force ocurred when between fifty and sixty men under Colonel Cook "unintentionally" became detached from Somervell's command and proceeded by themselves for several days.[7] Part of Hays' spy company found leadership under Flacco when Hays returned to the Río Grande in search of his horse.

The main unit of returning Texans traveled about fifteen miles the first afternoon. During the two succeeding days Somervell made short marches to enable the men, who had no provisions of any kind and were dependent upon the game of the area, to procure a necessary supply of beef from among the vast numbers of Mexican cattle running in the woods east of the Río Grande. The afternoon the men headed for home was somewhat foggy, and one of the units, of which Harvey A. Adams was a member, wound about in the chaparral, scarcely knowing where it was going. At night it camped four hundred yards from a small stream called the Tuscosa.[8] On the 20th this unit crossed several creeks that were overflowed and got wet mid-side to their horses. The route pursued by Bogart's company was described as "horrible." At 2 p.m. the company camped one mile northeast of the Tuscosa in a mesquite flat to graze their horses and to collect cattle for beef.[9] The next day they slaughtered several of the beeves that had been collected and an effort

[5] Ibid., pp. 190–191.
[6] William Preston Stapp, The Prisoners of Perote: Containing a Journal Kept by the Author Who Was Captured by the Mexicans, at Mier, December 25, 1842, and Released from Perote, May 16, 1844, p. 30.
[7] Memucan Hunt to Francis Moore, Jr., Editor of the Telegraph, Houston, dated Béxar, Jan. 8, 1843, Morning Star (Houston), Jan. 17, 1843.
[8] Harvey Alexander Adams, "[Journal of an] Expedition Against the Southwest in 1842 and 1843," Dec. 19, 1842, ms.
[9] Ibid., Dec. 20, 1842.

was made to dry the meat, but the weather was so unfavorable, they ended by barbecuing it.

During the afternoon of the 19th, and throughout the 20th and 21st, small bands of Texans from the several units scoured the surrounding countryside in search of Mexican horses belonging to some of the ranches in the vicinity. On the 21st Adams and two others, while out hunting, came across a drove of horses, which they pursued "into the shades of night," losing the horses as well as themselves. By firing off their guns at intervals and traveling late at night, they were able, with the aid of signal guns fired from the camp, to come in. Much to their astonishment the signals were directly opposite to where they supposed their camp was located; so they pondered for some time whether to go in or camp out until daylight, fearing that the signals might be those of a decoy.[10] There was risk either way; so after consultation they decided to go in, and much to their joy they entered their own camp at 10 P.M.

On the 22nd Somervell began a more rapid march for the settled area of Texas, but mud, prickly pear, and mesquite slowed the progress of the forlorn campaigners. The Indian guide "got bewildered in the dense chapperel" which they encountered and through which the Texans sought to hack their way with *machetes*.[11] "The sun was obscured," reported one of the returnees, "and the chapperal was so thick that one could not tell in what direction he was going. Our line had to go in single file and we found that when night came we had come around very nearly" to the point from which we had started that morning.[12] Thus the men became scattered, straggling along aimlessly in small groups through almost impenetrable thickets of chaparral and cactus, without order or discipline, and leaving considerable portions of their clothing and "occasionally an eye"[13] hanging to the thorny bushes. At night they camped without a guard. Late on the 23rd Bogart's unit came up with that of Colonel Cook and a part of Hays'.[14]

There was neither road nor path to guide the men through this wilder-

[10] *Ibid.*, Dec. 21, 1842.

[11] Machetes (*ma-che-tes*), a kind of long, heavy knife, similar to those used in cutting down Indian corn.

[12] Looscan (ed.), "Journal of Lewis Birdsall Harris," *Southwestern Historical Quarterly*, XXV (1921–1922), 191.

[13] Adams, "[Journal of an] Expedition Against the Southwest," Dec. 23, 1842, ms.

[14] *Ibid.*

ness. "In this desert wild we were doomed to wander for many days," wrote Hendricks, who was among those returning, "exposed to every evil, and suffering a thousand perplexing anxieties."[15] During most of the time the weather was cloudy, wet, and intensely cold. Provisions gave out, and the men ate rabbits, hawks, roots, herbs, and a few even ate the roasted skin of deer they had killed some time before.[16] One mess of nine killed and ate a yearling colt.[17] On another occasion when one of the men shot a sand-hill crane at a distance of one hundred and thirty yards, his companions made it into soup in order "to make it go as far as possible." More than one man cooked his cowhide "aparaho" or large pouch commonly used for carrying provisions. Traveling in rather large groups, the men found it almost impossible to find game near enough for a shot. However, on one occasion several of the men in a party of four got a shot at a buck, and

as it fell, [said Harris] we—being in a hurry, as we were some distance in the rear of the line—each gathered a leg of the deer and skinned down to the back, and as each one let go to get in position to take out the entrails the deer jumped up and ran, the skin flapping as it ran. "Ha! Ha!" [exclaimed one of the men] "that's the Devil sure." In fact, [continued Harris] we were all so startled and it was such a strange occurrence that for a few moments we stood and looked at each other in dumb amazement,[18]

but one of the men, who was determined not to be so easily cheated out of his venison steaks, took up his rifle and trailed the bleeding deer. Going a short distance, he soon located the deer lying down, and a quick shot ensured that a few men, at least, would have venison for supper.

The troopers who had been most negligent in laying in a supply of jerked meat when the opportunity afforded and had made the least effort to hunt and kill game, were the most persistent and troublesome beggars. Men got lost, and both men and horses were worn down by fatigue; nevertheless, they struggled on.

---

[15] E. W. Winkler (ed.), "Sterling Brown Hendricks' Narrative of the Somervell Expedition to the Rio Grande," *Southwestern Historical Quarterly*, XXIII (1919–1920), 138; see also Adams, "[Journal of an] Expedition Against the Southwest," Dec. 19–20, 1842, ms.

[16] Winkler (ed.), "Hendricks' Narrative," *Southwestern Historical Quarterly*, XXIII (1919–1920), 139.

[17] Looscan (ed.), "Journal of Lewis Birdsall Harris," *Southwestern Historical Quarterly*, XXV (1921–1922), 191.

[18] *Ibid.*

At the same time that Somervell pulled out determined to reach home before his men starved to death, Bogart's men, having cooked part of the meat they had butchered, resumed their march. Their intention, too, was to cross the Nueces at the mouth of the Río Frio. Their course was through a flat mesquite country. After proceeding about twenty-five miles, they made camp in a low flat, where there was a fairly good supply of grass, but only two or three mud puddles as a source of water. The north wind laid at dusk, and a heavy frost was the result. Their guide was a tall French-Canadian, who possessed a small compass and claimed to be a botanist, for he was always discanting on some plant they passed.[19]

After making about thirty miles on the 23rd Bogart's company came up with a part of Hays' and Colonel Cook's men, some fifty men in all, but did not join them. The units had plenty of good grass for their horses that night, but the next morning the several parties each went its own way, each asserting that the routes of the others were wrong. During the day, Bogart's men were able to make only twelve miles through the dense thickets by hewing and hacking their way with the heavy knives they carried. Late in the evening they emerged into an open flat which appeared familiar to them.[20] The next day being Sunday, the men decided to rest and give their famished horses an opportunity to graze. During the afternoon they resumed their march. The weather was foggy and a light drizzling rain commenced to fall toward night. Wild cattle were seen, but none of the men could get close enough to shoot one, although their meat supply was practically nil. The following morning, about ten or eleven o'clock, as they were preparing to break camp, they were startled by the booming of cannon, which not only told them that their comrades under Fisher were engaging the Mexicans in battle, but that they themselves had made very little progress toward home, being only an estimated day's journey from Mier.[21] "Our Boys were wild with joy," recorded Adams, and wanted Captain Bogart to lead them to the relief of their comrades on the

[19] Adams, "[Journal of an] Expedition Against the Southwest," Dec. 22, 1842, ms.

[20] *Ibid.*, Dec. 23–24, 1842.

[21] *Ibid.*, Dec. 25, 1842. Adams mistakenly reports hearing the Mexican cannon fire on Sunday, Dec. 25, 1842, between the hours of ten and eleven in the morning. No cannon were fired at that time. Winkler (ed.), "Hendricks' Narrative," *Southwestern Historical Quarterly*, XXIII (1919–1920), 138, mentions hearing the cannon on December 26. Hendricks was also a member of Bogart's unit.

river. Upon some reflection and consultation, however, it was determined to continue the march homeward. After much ridicule from the
men, a probable justified display of ill-tempers, and a bawling out by
the captain, the French-Canadian was relieved of his responsibilities as
guide for having led the company on such "a wild goose chase," and
Bogart himself assumed the responsibility of acting as guide. The line
of march was then taken up in the opposite direction, with their backs
to the river. Soon a light rain began to fall. "Our route," recorded
Adams, was "through the worst thickets and mud, over high hills and
low valleys. . . . The men who pretended to be Guides have been lost
ever since we left the Río Grande on the 19th. . . . The Guides are not
certain which is [the] right course to take."[22] The next day the fog and
mist lifted enough for a brief period to permit the men a glimpse of the
sun for the third time in eight days. On the 27th the chaparral was as
thick as ever; the horses became weaker, and a few had to be abandoned. Some of the men began to talk of having to kill the others for
food unless they were able to shoot wild cattle or game. During the day
two of the men killed deer. On the 28th the company arrived at a small
creek and rested two hours. Here they struck Colonel Cook's trail; and,
after proceeding along it for a mile came up with another portion of the
regiment. The men were practically out of meat, although hunters had
been out all the way since leaving the Río Grande. Game was scarce
and wild. The men probably were no better hunters than they were
guides. In those days a good hunter usually developed an excellent
sense of direction.

After several days, the men under Somervell succeeded in getting out
of the chaparral, and at last arrived in sight of the "Pilot Knobs," a
group of hills in the vicinity of the Nueces, where "eternal desolation
seemed to brood and slumber upon their gloomy tops."[23] The men under
the general's immediate command were scattered for miles. There was
neither order nor discipline. The guard at night had been abolished
during the march. Both men and horses were worn down with fatigue,
and the former were without provisions. On December 29 Somervell
struck the Nueces within four miles of the Laredo crossing, and moved
up the river, where he was joined by Colonel Cook and his men and
preparations were made to cross by forming a temporary bridge over

[22] Adams, "[Journal of an] Expedition Against the Southwest," Dec. 26, 1842,
ms.

[23] Winkler (ed.), "Hendricks' Narrative," *Southwestern Historical Quarterly*,
XXIII (1919–1920), 121, 138.

which the men might pass. December 30 and 31 were spent in crossing the Nueces, and in traversing a marsh two miles wide on the other side, which, itself, required the better portion of a day. With Cook's men taking the lead, the Texans carried their baggage over on a log or on several logs lashed together to form a raft and swam their horses across the river. None of the men or horses were lost in crossing the stream, but fifty horses, including General Somervell's, were lost in the bog. Toward night, December 31, the men struck high land and encamped. Some of the men now killed their horses for food, of which the general partook. The next morning the army resumed its march, and about 1 P.M., after tramping eight or ten miles, it reached the Laredo road and was officially disbanded: "The exultation was boisterous, and the shout proceeded from one end of our line to the other," said Hendricks, "those in the rear catching it up, until, like one vast halleluha, it seemed to shake both earth and sky."[24] With joy, they recognized the road, the country, and the signs of their march out. With renewed energy and vigor the men pressed forward to the Frio and thence to the San Miguel, having to foot it most of the way because of the jaded condition of their horses. When a party of nine men of Captain Lowrey's company reached the Atascosa about sundown in the afternoon and were in the process of encamping for the night, the men heard wild turkeys flying into the nearby trees to roost. Each man started out to get a turkey, and did not return to the camp site until each had obtained one. They then built a good fire, and soon each man had his turkey on a stick in the ground before the fire. Without salt or seasoning of any kind, the turkeys were roasted, and "as a piece became cooked," reported Harris, "we cut it off and found it very palatable, . . . and I think there was no time during that night that you might not have seen someone eating turkey, and by morning there were nine turkey skeletons resting around the camp."[25]

In the meantime, on the 29th, Bogart's men reached a lagoon emptying into the Nueces, and followed it for a mile on its south side, and the following day proceeded up along its shore for nearly three miles before they could cross it, and even then they had considerable difficulty in doing so. Three miles beyond the lagoon, the company struck the

[24] *Ibid.*, p. 139. See also A. Somervell, General Order No. 65, Head Quarters, Camp East Bank Nueces, Janᵧ 1, 1843, in "A Record Book of the General & Special Orders and Letters of the South Western Army," p. 50, ms.

[25] Looscan (ed.), "Journal of Lewis Birdsall Harris," *Southwestern Historical Quarterly*, XXV (1921–1922), 192.

trail of that portion of the regiment they had left the previous evening.[26] Pursuing the trail, for they had now begun to learn that independence did not always pay, they nooned it at Cook's camp of the night before, three miles from where Bogart had struck the trail. Bogart's men spent the afternoon and night at this spot, knowing that the men of the regiment were half a mile ahead "preparing to cross the Nueces, and were felling timber, collecting brush and driftwood to form a bridge." Somervell and Cook crossed their men late that afternoon, and Bogart's men broke camp early the next morning, entered the river bottom, and after a half mile arrived at the crossing where they took advantage of the labor of their comrades of the day before. They rummaged through the rawhide kyacks (saddle packs), for carrying provisions, that Cook's men had discarded, so famished where they for what meat they might find. Adams says he found a lump of tallow about the size of two fists which he prized more than gold, and that he even "cut off some of the thick parts of the Rawhide thinking that it might be roasted and prevent starvation."

At the river the men stripped their horses and swam them across; after which each man shouldered his saddle, blankets, guns, and coffee pot and carried them across the improvised bridge. Across the Nueces, the Texans still had much work in store for themselves before they reached dry land two miles away. In traversing this two mile distance they found it necessary to cross ten or twelve sloughs of the worst kind. At times the men were to their arm pits in water and mud; some of the horses were so feeble they could not make it through the sloughs; so ropes of hair or rawhide were placed around them and they were pulled across. Sometimes it was necessary to roll a horse over "a time or two, wait till they . . . rested, help them up, and go to the next one," and then to the next, and the next "through the whole batch of them." It was nearly night when man and horse reached dry land.

We never dared to ride, [reported Adams] but walked, waded and swam during the entire day. We were wet to the skin. There was plenty of mesquite wood where we camped; so we built a rousing fire, and dried ourselves. . . . [Our mess of five men] had nothing to eat but that piece of tallow and the Rawhide. The last we roasted and tried to eat, but it was a poor substitute to appease hunger.

---

[26] The account in this and the following paragraph is drawn from Adams, "[Journal of an] Expedition Against the Southwest," Dec. 30, 1842, ms.

Some of Cook's men were encamped in the vicinity and were killing their horses and mules to eat and dry.

Two of their party [continued Adams] had been out all day on the hunt and came in, just as our fire was burned to coals, with a fine Deer hung on a pole. I was delegated to beg them for a portion for ourselves. After a long time and using every argument [that I knew] one of the men cut-off the head with very little neck, skin and all, and threw it at me. I took it with many thanks. We rolled it into the coals, hide, hair, and all, just as it was and it was the sweetest morsel that 5 men ever tasted. This [was] all we had to eat for 3 days.

On New Year's day they traveled eight miles to the Laredo road and one half mile farther to encamp in a valley. Two men from one of the messes spent all afternoon hunting for game, but returned without any. Deer were seen, but they were too wild and the chaparral was too dense. About sunset one of the men succeeded in killing a Mexican hawk perched on a thorn bush at a distance of eighty yards. The hawk was carried into camp, cleaned, cut up, and placed in the largest coffee pot with a piece of the badly worn tallow that had been found on the bank of the Nueces. The pot was then filled with water. Pebbles were added for seasoning, and a new delicacy—known as "Rock-hawk soup" —had been created.

It was a very poor hawk and required a good deal of boiling. After it was cooked it tasted very well, but about the time we were getting through with it, [reported Adams, the men in the mess] commenced one after another getting sick and to heave up Jonah at a fearful rate. All began to think they were poisoned. Some thought it was the tallow, others that it was the bird. Of all the sick fellows not one died, but they did vomit their insides nearly out. This Trial ended the Rock-hawk soup business.[27]

The next day they roasted some more rawhide and some cactus, which they tried to eat, "but it was no *go-he.*"

At 9 o'clock on the morning of the 3rd, one of Bogart's men came into camp with a deer, but by the time it was divided among forty men, there was "only a bite apiece."[28] After some delay and a scanty breakfast of venison, they resumed march along the Laredo road, and by nightfall had covered about fifteen miles, camping at one of the spots they had encamped in going out. The next morning they enjoyed a light breakfast

[27] *Ibid.,* Jan. 1, 1843.
[28] *Ibid.,* Jan. 3, 1843.

of sage tea, and traveled during the day quite empty.[29] Their objective was to reach Calaveras' Ranch on the San Antonio River where they hoped to find ample provisions, but late in the afternoon they came to an abandoned ranch, where they met a detail driving cattle to meet them.

When Colonel Cook and his men, who were in advance of the main body of troops, crossed the Nueces, they took a lower route than the one pursued by Somervell, and upon reaching the Medina, two of the men, Badger, of Harris County, and Young of the Spy Company, drove back several beeves to the starving men under Somervell. Badger and Young met the army at the old, uninhabited rancho on the Laredo road thirty miles below San Antonio. With great dexterity the cattle were slaughtered and prepared for cooking. At last the hungry men had "a glorious feast, and spent nearly the whole evening and night in roasting and eating. Indeed, the only misfortune was that many of the men made themselves sick by eating too much," too rapidly, and were troubled by diarrhea and vomiting.[30] Here they were overtaken by two men who had escaped from Mier.[31] Many of the men were weakened by the lack of food and the strenuous marches, mostly on foot, slept until a late hour the next day; and finally when the march was renewed men fainted throughout the day "from fatigue and starvation." "Runners were sent back on the trail to urge them forward," stating "that plenty of beef would be on hand to meet them that evening if they would only hold out to travel a few miles. That night each mess of seven men was given one-half of a large beef, which it placed on a spit and barbecued whole. While one side was cooking the men were cutting and eating from the other. They kept turning and eating all night but those who ate hastily usually got sick and ejected all; whereas, those who took their time had no trouble. By late evening most of the several parties had been reunited at this point, in the sense that they met here. A few of the first arrivals had gone on to San Antonio.[32]

Flacco was offered a reward by General Somervell and others to go back to the Nueces and bring in some horses left there. Accompanied by the Lipan deaf mute, several other Lipans, two Mexicans (one of whom was named Rivas), an Apache named Luis, and several Anglo-Texans, he returned to the vicinity of the Nueces and is reported to have

[29] *Ibid.*, Jan. 4, 1843.
[30] *Ibid.*
[31] John Henry Brown, "Autobiography," ms.
[32] Adams, "[Journal of an] Expedition Against the Southwest," Jan. 5, 1843, ms.

rounded up fifty horses. Accounts of what happened next vary. Apparently while driving the horses back to the Texan settlements, the Lipan deaf mute was taken sick and he and Flacco stopped on the Medina while the white men went on. According to several accounts, the next morning two of the white men, Tom Thernon [Thurmond?] and another named James B. Ravis [Reavis], who lived on the Trinity, were missing, and a few days later they were seen in Seguin with Flacco's horses."[33] On the other hand, John Henry Brown asserted that Flacco and the deaf-mute were "basely murdered by Rivas and the Mexican, who drove the horses into Eastern Texas and Louisiana and sold them."[34] In any case, not long thereafter, James O. Rice in his escape from Mier to Texas discovered the bodies of the two Indians about twenty miles west of San Antonio near the Medina. Upon investigation, the Indians were found to have been murdered.[35]

On January 3, Somervell's party, including Memucan Hunt, arrived at the Medina.[36] On the 5th, leaving the camp rather late in the morning, a party of seven from Bogart's company headed for Flores' Ranch, six miles northwest of present Floresville, on the San Antonio River eighteen miles away. Since the river was at flood stage and it was late in the afternoon when they reached it, they decided to wait until morning to swim it. In the meantime, they gathered and ate pecans which they found in great abundance near the river. The scenery here was very

---

[33] Noah Smithwick, *The Evolution of a State*, pp. 221–224. See also *Lamar Papers*, VI, 297; *Telegraph and Texas Register*, March 29, 1843.

[34] John Henry Brown, *Indian Wars and Pioneers of Texas*, pp. 573–574; see also John D. Affleck, "John C. Hays," pt. II, pp. 299–300.

[35] In order to forestall, if possible, an indiscriminate revenge being taken by the Lipans upon the settlers, it was made to appear that Flacco and his companions had been murdered by Mexican bandits, and reports were even circulated that near their bodies were found six dead Cherokees, indicating that they had died in battle fighting the tribe's irreconcilable enemy. The Lipans, it was thought, never knew the truth, but shortly after the unhappy incident, the remnant of their band left the settlement for the Rio Grande country, after Flacco's father and a part of the tribe had gone to the Medina to investigate the deaths. Smithwick, *The Evolution of a State*, pp. 221–224; Carl C. Rister, *The Southwestern Frontier, 1865–1881*, p. 36. *Telegraph and Texas Register*, March 29, 1843. According to Brown the Lipans "became the implacable enemies of their former allies and subsequently committed many killings and depredations on the Western frontier." Brown, *Indian Wars and Pioneers of Texas*, p. 574.

[36] Memucan Hunt to Francis Moore, Jr., Béxar, Jan. 8, 1843, *Telegraph and Texas Register*, Jan. 18, 1843.

beautiful, with high bluffs along the river. The next morning they crossed the San Antonio and proceeded up the river in a northwest direction to the ranch, where they obtained the first so-called bread they had had since December 13. At the ranch were two Mexican women and three teenage "*señoritas.*" The Texans were welcomed and given the best hospitality the accommodations could afford. The seven men were fed *tortillas* to their heart's (stomach's) content, which required two hours of eating. One of the women knelt upon goat skins spread upon a dirt floor, and with a metate ground water-soaked corn for two hours, which the young ladies patted and rolled out into thin cakes. The other woman baked them on a gridiron hung over a fire made on the earthen floor. The only pay the Texans could offer, were pieces of jerked beef and a cow hide, for they had nothing else with which to pay. After eating, the Texans headed up the east bank of the San Antonio River, picking up thirty head of cattle which they drove to the old dilapidated mission of Espada, two miles below the San Juan Mission.[37] At the Espada Mission some of the cattle were butchered and the meat dried for the continuance of their homeward journey. The hides were exchanged in San Antonio for other necessities they would need. On the 8th they moved up to Mission Concepción and went into San Antonio to receive their discharge from the "Army of the Southwest,"[38] after which they proceeded toward home living off the generosity of the settlers.

The first group of returnees, including some of Captain Sims' men, reached San Antonio on January 4 and obtained there the first bread that they had had in twenty days. Bogart and some of his men arrived at Béxar during the evening of the 4th, and General Somervell[39] arrived two days later—the same day that Dr. R. Watson of Houston and Hensley of Washington County, along with other members of the escaped

---

[37] Adams, "[Journal of an]Expedition Against the Southwest," Jan. 6, 1843, ms.
[38] *Ibid.*, Jan. 8, 1843.
[39] Somervell rested at San Antonio for a few days before reporting to the President and Secretary of War at Washington-on-the-Brazos, the new seat of government. Afterwards he resumed his duties as collector of customs at Port Calhoun, and after annexation was reappointed to that position and held it until his mysterious death in 1854. "The statement that he started in a small boat from Lavaca to Saluria, carrying a considerable amount of money, has been accepted as authentic. The boat never reached Saluria, and a search for him was made, the boat was found floating with the bottom side up and his body lashed to the timbers of the boat. He was doubtless robbed and murdered, as the money was never discovered." Sam Houston Dixon and Louis Wiltz Kemp, *The Heroes of San Jacinto*, p. 126.

camp guard at Mier began to reach San Antonio,[40] while Sidney S. Callender, Michael Cronican, under whom Callender had served in the revolution, and other members from the same camp guard, led by St. Clair, reached San Patricio.[41] By January 8, reported Hunt, "the whole number who left the Río Grande with Gen. S[omervell] have either arrived in town [San Antonio] or its vicinity."[42] Most of the legally appointed officers returned from the Río Grande with General Somervell.

Before a full report of the campaign could be made known, a joint resolution was presented in the House of Representatives, sitting at Washington-on-the-Brazos, and voted on January 13, 1843, expressing thanks on behalf of Congress to General Somervell and "the brave and chivalrous troops under his command for their gallant descent upon the frontier of Mexico and for the capture of Laredo."[43]

[40] Memucan Hunt to Francis Moore, Jr., Béxar, Jan. 8, 1843, *Telegraph and Texas Register*, Jan. 18, 1843; Winkler (ed.), "Hendricks' Narrative," *Southwestern Historical Quarterly*, XXIII (1919–1920), 139.

[41] Sidney S. Callender to John H. Brown, 994 Magazine St., New Orleans, June 2, 1886, John Henry Brown Papers, 1835–1872, ms.

[42] Memucan Hunt to Francis Moore, Jr., Béxar, Jan. 8, 1843, *Telegraph and Texas Register*, Jan. 18, 1843. *The Civilian and Galveston Gazette*, Jan. 18, 1843, reported Somervell arriving at Gonzales with 200 men, but the editor seems to be mistaken about his figures. Somervell discharged the men at San Antonio, and after a few days proceeded to Washington-on-the-Brazos by way of Gonzales.

[43] "Resolution Proposing a Vote of Thanks to the Army for the Capture of Laredo," in Texas Congress, Bills, 7th Congress of Texas, ms.

Epilogue

ON MARCH 5, 1842, a month after the adjournment of the regular session of the Sixth Congress at Austin, troops of the Mexican army under the command of General Rafael Vasquez seized San Antonio, while other Mexican troops surprised and captured Goliad and Refugio. This assault upon the frontier settlements east of the Nueces caused great excitement in Texas, and was followed by a sequence of events which made the year 1842 the most exciting in the frontier history of the Republic since the spring of 1836. President Lamar's aggressive policy towards Mexico, as represented by the ill-fated Santa Fé expedition and the treaty pledging naval assistance to Yucatán, appears to have been the immediate cause for the retaliatory expedition against the outlying settlements of Texas. Nevertheless, although Mexico frequently talked of renewing her effort to subjugate Texas, the Vasquez campaign in Texas was neither such an attempt nor the vanguard of a larger force to enter Texas for that purpose. The seizure of Goliad, Refugio, and San Antonio must be regarded as a warning to persons outside Texas that Mexico still considered Texas a part of the Mexican nation over which she expected to restore her authority. It was a warning to Texans that they could expect retaliation for any aggression beyond the ancient boundaries of the province of Texas, and that Mexico would condone neither smuggling from Texas nor the extension of Anglo-American settlements beyond the Nueces. Texans might even conclude that periodic raiding parties would be dispatched into Texas from troop concentrations to be established along the Río Grande.

The recent clandestine operations of Philip Dimitt and others below the Nueces were regarded with great apprehension in Mexico; such bold aggressiveness on the part of Texans in the direction of the upper

579

and lower Río Grande settlements needed to be halted. Santa Anna's bombastic threat of February 18, 1842, to James Hamilton, published at home and abroad, was designed to frighten those individuals who might be considering making Texas their home, and to reiterate that Mexico felt that the war in Texas was not yet over. At the same time such an enunciation might have the effect of dampening the sentiment for annexation of Texas in the United States. The Vasquez invasion was designed to accomplish these same ends.

The Mexican troops in the spring of 1842 only stayed in Texas a few days, and withdrew almost as fast as they had entered, without being either pursued or attacked. The effects of their incursion, however, were many. Texans, particularly in the west and south, and at Houston and Galveston, clamored vehemently for retaliation against the Mexican frontier and for a forcible release of the Texan Santa Fé prisoners. The invasion disrupted the planting of corn in Texas, the mainstay of the frontiersmen, and made life more difficult and insecure. It caused many Anglo-Texans to abandon the frontier perimeter from Austin to Refugio; discouraged individuals and families from coming to Texas to settle; strengthened the anti-annexation sentiment in the United States; and intensified the western frontiersman's demands for protection.

In his second administration, as in his first, President Houston sought to pursue a policy of leaving Mexico alone. His policy was one of defense against raiding parties or against any full-scale attack that the Mexican government might launch, but he believed that Mexico was torn by too much dissension at home to offer a serious threat to Texas unless provoked. Texas needed peace to increase her population and her economic strength, and as she grew she would become less susceptible to attack by Mexico. Houston did, however, take advantage of the invasion to order removal of the national archives and the seat of government from Austin.

In the United States there was great excitement at the news of the invasion, and many men were willing to emigrate immediately to Texas as volunteers, as in the days of 1835–1836; but as news was received of the Mexican withdrawal, many of these would-be volunteers changed their minds and stayed at home. However, among certain individuals and groups in Texas and within the United States, there was the hope of using the Mexican raid as an excuse to invade Mexico in order to force the recognition of Texas independence, to force the release of citizens of both Texas and the United States languishing in Mexican dungeons, and to extend the boundary claimed for Texas, with the ulti-

580

mate hope that a large segment of Mexican territory, including Texas, might be added to the United States. More than one individual in Texas and in the United States believed that a campaign against Mexico would afford an opportunity for adventure and glory, for personal gain and employment, and for the spread of Anglo-Saxon culture and influence through territorial expansion or the reformation of Mexican political, economic, and social life.

The official reaction in Texas to the Vasquez occupation of San Antonio was, at first, simply to repel the invader. But, as there was considerable popular clamor from the inhabitants of the western counties for a campaign of retaliation against Mexico, President Houston, with tongue in cheek, issued orders to Brigadier General Alexander Somervell of the First Brigade, Texas Militia, to march the troops assembled in the west to cross the Río Grande and attack the settlements of northern Mexico, if the troops were found to be of sufficient strength and discipline. When the troops at San Antonio refused to submit to Somervell's command, they were disbanded.

The demand in the west for an army of invasion continued, and Houston soon found it expedient to issue a call for assembling such an army, which, when properly formed, would be marched under orders of the Texan government against Mexico, supported by the Texan militia. Houston believed that he must not only assent to the demand for an invasion of Mexico, but that he must seize the initiative from those who talked boldly of marching against Mexico with or without orders. He wished to forestall such a rash move by a group of "hot-heads." An attack upon northern Mexico could only infuriate Mexico and bring other raiding expeditions against Texas. There was even a possibility that such an attack would so provoke the Mexicans as to make them forget their local differences and unite to repel an enemy that might threaten their very existence as a nation. It might so strengthen the central government of Mexico as to enable it to launch a full-scale campaign to subjugate its rebellious province. Private, unofficial expeditions could embarrass the administration and endanger the public interests.

Houston knew very well that financial support for a campaign against Mexico could not be had from a bankrupt citizenry and a depleted national treasury, and that foreign assistance in a material and financial way was most uncertain. Furthermore, he had serious doubts about developing and maintaining discipline in any volunteer army that could be raised. He certainly had no intentions of letting an army start for Mexico unless it was properly commanded, equipped, supplied, and

581

disciplined, and of sufficient size to justify the expectation that it would be successful. He had little hope that such an army could be assembled. However, he felt that he must prove to the critics at home that no expedition could be launched with a hope of success. At the same time, Houston realized that if the effort to launch an announced expedition against Mexico should fail the enemy might be encouraged to more bold and aggressive action against Texas. However, if the attempt to raise the expedition could be arranged so as to show the critics of his Mexican policy that a campaign against Mexico was impractical and, at the same time, to warn Mexico that any attack upon Texas could lead to a possible invasion of its own northern frontier, then the effort might not be totally in vain. It must be realized that if Houston's efforts in the spring and summer of 1842, which on the surface seemed quite sincere but which were regarded by some individuals as the machinations of a Talleyrand, had been successful, Houston would then, indeed, have become entangled in his own web.

When news of the Vasquez seizure of San Antonio reached him, Houston relied upon volunteers and hastily assmbled militiamen to defend the country and expel the enemy. Later, he openly toyed with the idea of using the militia in an offensive operation against Mexico to wring from her peace and the recognition of Texas independence. However, before sending the militia on offensive operations, he wanted Congress' authorization for such usage; yet when Congress authorized the usage of militia beyond the borders of the Republic, he raised constitutional objections. He needled Congress about its failure to provide real financial support for a campaign; and, yet, he knew all along that Texas could neither borrow money from abroad nor raise sufficient revenue at home to support an offensive campaign against Mexico. Houston seems to have desired to appear to do all (in his own way) that was possible to meet the demands of those who supported forceful action against Mexico, but in the end, when the plans failed—as he knew they would—he was not unhappy.

The expeditionary force that he recruited, composed largely of volunteers from the United States, had virtually disbanded for lack of provisions, pay, and discipline before the remnant of the army was attacked near Lipantitlán by a superior Mexican force led by Antonio Canales and Cayetano Montero, who recognized the weakness of the Texan army south of the Nueces.

Having failed to launch a campaign in July, Houston gave the malcontents further pre-occupation at home by developing plans late in July for assembling an expedition on the Cíbolo in the vicinity of San Antonio. The period for the troops to rendezvous had been set for August 1842, but none had assembled by the time General Adrián Woll surprised and seized San Antonio on September 11. The orders for Woll's campaign in Texas had been issued in June before the collapse of the Texan expeditionary force on the lower Nueces, and seem to have been designed to harass Texas and to force her to give up any thought of offensive operations against the Mexican frontier, to determine to what extent the Texans might be assembling in the Gonzales-Seguin or San Antonio area, and to reiterate to the world that Mexico still regarded Texas to be a part of her national domain. At least the campaign gave Santa Anna an opportunity to strengthen himself politically at home by satisfying the people in Mexico of his sincerity and determination to carry on hostilities against Texas, but permitted him to postpone any formidable invasion of Texas until Yucatán had been subdued. He might thus for a while get around his long vaunted boast of resubjugating Texas, a boast which many observers in and outside of Mexico believed he had no intention of carrying out anyway.

Woll met with more resistance at San Antonio than his predecessor had in the spring. A brief skirmish on the 11th, followed by the battle of Salado Creek and the Dawson massacre on the 18th, with significant losses on both sides, resulted in Woll's hasty retreat and added to the burning desire of many Texans to march forthwith to the Río Grande, to retaliate upon the settlements of nothern Mexico, and to seize prisoners to exchange for the ones Woll had carried into Mexico.

Houston again designated Somervell to command the troops assembling in the west to repel the enemy; and, in time, authorized Somervell to lead the volunteers that Vice-President Edward Burleson, without prior consultation with or approval of the President, had called to meet at San Antonio by October 25 for an attack upon the Río Grande settlements. Houston was not sure that the proposed expedition would get off, but if it did he wanted the men to be led by a dependable authorized field commander and to march under the flag of the Republic, which would afford them protection under the rules of international law. When discipline broke down and the Somervell expedition fell apart, some three hundred of its members refused to return home from the vicinity of Guerrero, Mexico, and chose to go on as freebooters. They went down the Río Grande to Mier without authorization and without the protection of their nation's flag, and were to suffer horribly for their refusal to obey Somervell's orders to return home. The Mier expedition and its significance in the frontier history of Texas and Mexico will constitute the third book of this series on the Texas-Mexican frontier during the days of the Texas Republic

APPENDICES

APPENDIX A

Muster Rolls of Certain Select Frontier Forces, 1842

Muster Roll of Captain [Samuel] Bogart's Company of the Army of the Republic of Texas [Enlisted in Washington County] from the Eleventh day of March 1842, to the Fourth day of May 1842, Muster into Service for the Term of three Months[1]

1. Bogart, Samuel	Capt.
2. Chambless, ——	1st Lt.
3. Little, E. D.	2nd Lt.
4. Niman, Thomas	1st Sergt.
5. Day, Henry	2nd Sergt.
6. Charles, Rufus	3rd Sergt.
7. Ashmore, John	[Privates]

8. Ayers, F. W.
9. Bailey, Thomas
10. Ben[n]ett, Samuel
11. Bogart, C. H.
12. Browning, Jackson
13. Calvert, N. H.
14. Chapple [Chappell], George
15. Chapple [Chappell], N. J.
16. Deen, W. B.
17. Demoss, G. W.
18. Dobson, Trimmier
19. Edney, N. J.
20. Edney, William

21. Ferrell, John
22. Foster, J. W.
23. Gilliland, Thomas
24. Harber, George W.
25. Hardeman, William
26. Hargrove, William
27. McDade, James W.
28. McDade, John
29. Marshall, Joseph
30. Medews [Meadows?], Donal[d]
31. Michel, John
32. Middleton, Thomas
33. Ravill, B. F.
34. Reynolds[2] [Rennels], H. A.
35. Stephens, J. M.
36. Stephens, John
37. Stephens, Thomas
38. Stribling, James
39. Tremmer, John

Muster Roll of James H. Gillespie's Company of Volunteers, Vasquez Campaign, 1842[3]

Allen, George
Allen, Isaac
Alley, George

Anderson, Franklin
Anderson, Richard
Avant, John

[1] In Militia Rolls (Texas), ms.

[2] Opposite the name "H. A. Reynolds" is written "H. A. Rennels."

[3] In Army Papers (Texas), ms. The names have been rearranged in alphabetical order. The bracketed material is from Frank Brown, "Annals of Travis County and of the City of Austin," IX, 12–13. Brown gives a partial list, plus these additional

Barber, James
Bartlett, Marshall
Blakey, Everett
Brite, John
Brite, Thomas
Bryce, J. W.
Burke, Nicholas
Burleson, John
Burleson, Jonathan
Burnett, D. D.
Cannon, William R.
Clements, Nathan
Clifton, Josiah
Coffman, E. G.
Conlee [Conley], Preston
Conlee, S. B.
Coulter, M. W.
Dalrymple, W. C.
Davis, Jonathan
Dunbar, William
Fentress, Lemmel
Fort, W. D.
Gage, Shirley
Gamble, George A.
Gammell, William
Garrett, W. H.
Glasscock, Thomas
Halton, W. S.
Hancock, L. S.
Hemphill, ——
Hemphill, [Neill]
Herror, John
Highsmith, Samuel
Hill, A. W.
Hill, W. P[eyton]
Holderman, A. S.
Huling, M[arcus] B.
Jenkins, John
Jobe, E. H.
Jobe, E. L.

Jobe, P[hilip] W.
Leftwick, Addison
Luther, Samuel
McDaniel, John
McMilion, Malley
Miliner, Logan
Moppin, Garnett
Murchison, Aaron
Nichols, Lewis
Owen, Robert
Owen, William
Pace, Robert
Patton, J. M.
Perry, Rufus
Philips, Cornelius
Philips, Henry
Raper, M. B.
Reding, Wm. R.
Reed, J. W.
Reed, Robert
Rogers, Jonathan
Rogers, M. M.
Saterthwait, S.
Simpson, James
Sims, Bartlett
Smith, James
Smithson, E. C.
Stone, John [B.]
Strickland, C. W.
Strother, C.
Sullivan, L. P.
Tatum, Willis
Warwick, B. F.
Weeks, Joseph
Whitaker, J. W.
White, Hamilton
Woods, W. H.
Yates, John C.
Yoast, F.

---

names which have not been verified as members of the company: James Edminston, "Buck" Billingsley, George Neill, John Taney, ——— Weyman, F. Wells, Goodloe Miller, John D. Nash, Wayne Barton, Pleasant A. Barnhill, and James Casner.

Roster of Captain Washington D. Miller's Company,
[March 11, 1842][4]

Officers

Miller, Washington D.	Captain	Knoop, John	4th Sergt.
Cheek, Noah	1st Lieut.	Strawn, William G.	1st Corpl.
Wright, Ben	2d Lieut.	Freeman, Thomas	2d Corpl.
Parkerson, Millard M.	1st Sergt.	Rice, Robert	3d Corpl.
Murchison, Daniel	2d Sergt.	Anderson, Nathan B.	4th Sergt.
Hall, John	3d Sergt.	Stedman, John	Musician

Privates

Anderson, Charles S.
Bee, Hamilton P.
Bell, William
Birt, Samuel P.
Bratton, George
Brothers, John
Browning, C. C.
Burckle, Christian G.
Callender, Sidney S.
Charlton, John
Cherry, William
Cole, James
Cronican, M.
Cummings, Stephen
Custard, William
Dalrymple, John
Davis, Stephen
Dowling, Josiah
Ellis, Richard
Evison, William
Farley, M.
Haas, Winterlin
Henry, John R.
Howland, E. P.
Latto, William
Mallon, N. R.

Matthews, James H.
Mayfield, James S.
Murchison, Alexander
Palmer, Thomas
Powell, William F.
Raymond, James H.
Rice, Lorenzo D.
Ricks, George W.
Schlitter, Bartolome
Seigers, Edward
Smith, Donald
Taylor, John
Thaen, Isaac M.
Thomas, David
Thomas, William D.
Tussy, Henry
Twiefel, Tobias
Veith, T. S.
Wahrenberger, John
Wallace, William A. A.
Ward, Thomas
Wells, Moses
Welsh, James
Wesson, James M.
Yost, J.

[4] From Brown, "Annals of Travis County," IX, 11–12, based on a roster found in the Washington D. Miller Papers, 1833–1860, ms., in 1874 by Miller's brother, L. K. Miller. The names of the privates have been rearranged in alphabetical order.

The Galveston Artillery Company Membership
1842[5]

List of Officers

Howe, John	Captain	Denny, W. G.	Secretary
Crawford, A. C.	1st Lieut.	Frankland, C.	Treasurer
Nordman, L. E.	2d Lieut.	Lynch, E. O.	Standard Bearer

Honorary Members

Beaumont, Maj[or] J. K.
Borden, Gail, Jr.
Cock[e], Major J. H.
Jackson, Col. A. M.
Jones, John B.
Jones, Dr. Levi
Love, Col. James

McKinney, T. F.
Menard, Col. M. B.
Millard, Col. Henry
Mills, Col. J. H.
Seafield, Lt. Col. Charles
Shelby, A. B.
Williams, Samuel M.

Sergeants

Barnard, E. L.
Denny, William G.

Joseph, Thomas L.
Mead, William F.

Corporals

Dean, Alexander
Robinson, S. S.

Se——[illegible], John A.
Street, Parker G.

Privates

Ball, George
Bennett, John H.
Berry, Albert
Blossom, J. H.
Bryant, C[harles] C.
Bush, John T.
Caplin, Charles
Close, H.
Davie, John P.
Dunn, J. G.[,] M.D.
Follett, Alonzo
Garcia, M[acino]
Geisendorff, F. W.
Hall, Ambrose
Hall, William
Hartshorn, Benjamin J.

Hartwell, J. R.
Herdman [Henderson?], James
Lange, Leeder
Magill, John H.
Messina, S.
Montier, David
Montier, Timothy
Mugins, H.
O'Brian, John
Oliphant, James
Parker, N. B.
Shepherd, B. A.
Sherwood, M. B.
Throp, William
Tronson, John
Trumball, Marcus

[5] Galveston Artillery Company, *The Charter and Constitution of the Galveston Artillery Company, Organized Sept. 13th, 1840*, p. 8. William G. Denny's name appears twice in this list: first as secretary and again as one of the sergeants. The names have been rearranged in alphabetical order.

Galveston Fusileers
March 10, 1842[6]

Officers

Swingle, A.	Captain	Howard, Robert H.	3d Sergt.
Cole, James P.	1st Lieut.	Hopkins, Math	4th Sergt.
Farish, Oscar	2d Lieut.	Banks, William J.	1st Corpl.
Merriman, F. B.	3d Lieut.	Smith, Henry M.	2d Corpl.
Baumelein, Dr. C. T.	Surgeon	Groesbeck, J. D.	3d Corpl.
Bryant, Charles G.	Orderly Sergt.	Dyer, Isadore	4th Corpl.
Berger, J. P.	2d Sergt.		

Privates

Barr, William E.
Bates, Thomas
Beatson, Robert
Blakeman, Elijah
Blue, Uriah
Brown, Henry
Butler, Jonas
Byrne, William C.
Cody, A. J.
Cooke, W. M.
Darrough, John L.
Davis, John
De Young, John
Geisendorf, F. M.
Grant, J. C.
Halsey, R. M.
Hancock, Jesse
Hannay, R. M.
Hinton, Samuel
Hoffman, Charles
Hoofmeister, H. H.
Hopkins, Thomas J.
James, Alfred F.
Johnson, William
Jones, Gustave
Jones, James A.
Kelly, Peter
Ketchum, J. D.

Kneeland, J. W.
Lawrence, Charles
Mansy, John
Matson, J. W.
Metz, George
Myers, L. S.
Nye, Alvin
Padget, James
Peacock, John
Powell, Charles
Rains, George C.
Reed, John W.
Reed, Richmond W.
Rigley, John
Serbon, G. G.
Shaw, J. C.
Southwick, Stephen
Stephens, J. C.
Sweeney, William R.
Sydnor, John S.
Teal, S. B.
Van Sickle, Stephen
Walton, John H.
Whiteman, Thomas
Williamson, Marcus
Wilson, W. B.
Winfrey, Phillip

[6] Ben C. Stuart, "Early Galveston Military Companies, 1839–1901," ms., pp. 8–10; also, Militia Rolls (Texas), ms. The latter list seems to be incomplete. It omits all officers and a number of the privates who are listed by Stuart; it shows Jesse Hammett instead of Jesse Hancock, J. Pidgley instead of John Rigley; and M. L. Shuffler. The names of the privates have been rearranged in alphabetical order.

Original List of Members of the Galveston Hussar Cavalry Company, March 11–12, 1842[7]

Potter, H. N.	Captain	Hartfield, A[sa]
Coles, B. L.	1st Lieut.	Levie, George
Primrose, M.	2d Lieut.	Magers, A[lonzo] G.
Smith, Thomas S.	Orderly Sergt.	Oliphant, J. N.
Adcock, E. M.		Pollock, John
Allen, R. A.		Sasse, Jacob
Arnold, H[enry]		Sellers, John
Davis, William		Tyler, William A.
Dedrick, Fred		Wheeler, A. [C.]
Gainer, John		Wild, Samuel

We whose names are hereunto subscribed pledge ourselves to join the Galveston Hussars at Richmond on the Brazos and do hereby enroll ourselves for the space of two months or during the war and are to furnish our own horses and equipped [*sic*].

Goodman, Hiram	Kerley, John
Goodman, L. C.	Tougale, M.
Goodman, Stephen	Whitehead, E.
Harrison, J. S.	

[Others who receipted for Jenks' rifles on March 11, 1842, and agreed to mount themselves and be ready to march to the frontier were]

Gray, P. W.	Sergeant, Daniel
Marston, J. Daniel	Wheeler, J. O.

Muster Roll of Captain John P. Gill's Company of Mounted Volunteers Commanded by Colonel Clark L. Owen Called into the Service of the Republic of Texas on the Twentieth day of March 1842, [Discharged June 20, 1842; in actual service six weeks][8]

Officers

1. John P. Gill	Capt.
2. Tho[ma]s Blackwell	1st Lieut.
3. Ben[jamin] F. Hill	2d Lieut.
1. R. M. Forbes	1st Sergt.

[7] Minutes of a meeting aboard the Steam-Boat *Dayton*, March 11, 1842, signed by B. L. Coles, chairman, and George Levie, Secretary. Galveston Hussar Cavalry Company, Papers, 1842, ms. The names have been rearranged in alphabetical order.

[8] In Militia Rolls (Texas), ms. The names of the privates have been rearranged in alphabetical order.

2. Fred Vogh	2d Sergt.
3. Ja[me]s C. Wilson	3d Sergt.
4. J. S. McNeal	4th Sergt.
1. W. C. C. Lynch	1st Corpl.
2. Ja[me]s Lonis	2d Corpl.
3. John F. Hanson	3d Corpl.
4. J. S. Bostick	4th Corpl.

Privates

1. Anderson, Jas. S.
2. Armstrong, George
3. Bell, James H.
4. Brigham, S. B.
5. Brown, R. R.
6. Bryan, William J.
7. Burns, William
8. Carson, William J.
9. Champin, R.
10. Corleit, E.
11. Crowley, James
12. Daggett, N. W.
13. Dale, Elisha
14. Davis, Edward
15. Dockrill, Jarvis
16. Doss, S. W.
17. Drinan, W. J.
18. Durnet, S. J.
19. Easley, Frank S.
20. Felton, B. F.
21. Fisk, Francis
22. Flack, C. P.
23. Fulkenson, Abe
24. Gautir, Peter W.
25. George, Joseph J.
26. Hammeken, George L.
27. Harris, John W.
28. Harvey, John
29. Hawkins, J. T.
30. Henderson, James
31. Henrie, D. D.
32. Hill, Jordan
33. Hill, Robert H.
34. Hinkle, Samuel
35. Hoskins, John N.
36. Jack, William H.
37. James, Thomas D.

38. Jameson, C.
39. Jarvis, George
40. Johnson, Thomas D.
41. Jolim, J. S.
42. Lamar, M. B.
43. Leonard, Washington
44. Lipscomb, S. S.
45. Loyd, Joseph
46. Lusk, William
47. McGreel, Peter
48. McMasters, William
49. McNeel, D. B.
50. McNeel, Pinckney
51. McNeel, Pleasant D.
52. Martin, Larkin
53. Melburn, Ben
54. Melton, John
55. Mills, D. G.
56. Mimms, Lumbard
57. Murray, ——
58. O'Connor, Thomas J.
59. Oldham, ——
60. Outersides, William
61. Page, Harrison
62. Parkman, Curtis
63. Patton, Charles F.
64. Pease, E. M.
65. Phar, Augustus
66. Potter, Reuben M.
67. Purcell, Edward
68. Quinan, George
69. Robinson, Tod
70. Short, Jordan N.
71. Sinnickson, J. J.
72. Smilcir, John
73. Smith, Francis
74. Spencer, Winfield S.

75. Swenny, John Jr.
76. Swenny, Jordan
77. Swett, James R.
78. Terry, William J.
79. Towns, R. J.
80. Walcot, H. N.

81. Walnut, John
82. Webber, Charles W.
83. Weems, James E.
84. Westall, Henson G.
85. Williams, Edward
86. Wilson, James

Muster Roll of Captain Albert C. Horton's Company of Volunteers, Commanded by Colonel Clark L. Owen, Called into the Service of the Republic of Texas on the Sixth Day of March 1842– April 13, 1842[9]

Officers

[Horton, Albert C.]	Captain
Hannam, A. B.	1st Lieut.
Lann, James W.	2d Lieut.
Belknap, James T.	1st Orderly Sergt.

Privates

Attwell, James
Bauer, C.
Bridges, Thomas
Cayce, John
Delass, W[illia]m. L.
Denison, James
Dennis, Tho[ma]s M.
Dunley, C. C.
Filosola, Peter
Greer, Felix
Hailey, Robert
Hayden, David
Hendrick, Ben[jamin] F.
Herbert, C. C.
Jacques, Gideon
Johnson, Francis
Kincheloe, L.
Lawson, Albert

Love, Frank
Loverin, W[illia]m H.
McCamley, John W.
McFarland, James
Martin, J. F.
Maynard, W[illia]m J.
Noble, ——
Phillips, William J.
Plunkett, John
Ringo, ——   joined March 6
Royall, W[illia]m R.
Schenck, Jacob   joined March 6
Sheppard, Dillon J.
Sheppard, James G.
Stewart, Thomas
Stewart, W. W.
Vanslyke, Andrew M.
Wallach, W. D. (Price's Co.)

The time only while actually in the field is here specified. The men were permitted to return to their homes on the 13th April but with orders to hold themselves in readiness for actual service at the shortest notice.

[9] In Militia Rolls (Texas), ms. The names of the privates have been rearranged in alphabetical order. William H. Lonerin's and W. D. Wallach's services are shown as being audited in Captain John T. Price's Company.

Muster Roll of Captain John S. Menefee's Company of Volunteers, Commanded by Colonel Clark L. Owen, Called into the Service of the Republic of Texas on the Sixth day of March 1842 [and discharged June 6, 1842][10]

Officers

1. Menefee, John S.	Captain
2. Usher, Patrick	1st Lieut.
3. Birdwell, William	2d Lieut.
1. McNutt, Nicholas	1st Sergt.
2. Menefee, George	2d Sergt.
3. Turner, Edwin W.	3d Sergt.
4. Keizer, William	4th Sergt.

Privates

1. Alexander, Mathews
2. Allen, Daniel
3. Banks, J. B.
4. Billings, George R.
5. Brown, Ja[me]s M.
6. Carl, Daniel
7. Caruthers, James
8. Clare, A. M.
9. Clare, Daniel A.
10. Coleman, David
11. Creanor, Charles M.
12. Dorsheimer, Andrew
13. Douglas, Thadeus
14. Douglass, Augustine
15. Dowess, Isaac
16. Dunlap, Andrew J.
17. Dunlap, William
18. Edwards, William C.
19. Estill, W. R.
20. Ewen, Albert
21. Ferrill, McAmy
22. Fine, Levi
23. Gray, James
24. Harrison, Charles G.
25. Haynes, Thomas N.
26. Jenkins, Bradford S.
27. Jones, Johnson
28. Kitchen, Henry
29. McHenry, John
30. McPeters, Thomas
31. Mayes, William
32. Mills, Edward L.
33. Mosier, A.
34. Rockefellow, Peter
35. Royster, Thomas F.
36. Rozier, John P.
37. Scott, Andrew
38. Simons, Joseph
39. Simons, Mavrick
40. Stone, James J.
41. Tilley, John P.
42. Trayon, Geo[rge] W.
43. Turner, Robert W.
44. Turner, Stephen R.
45. Weldy, Samuel
46. Wells, Francis F.
47. Wheeler, G. O.
48. White, Benj[amin] J.
49. White, Francis M.
50. White, John T.
51. Wickham, Asa
52. Wickham, John R.
53. Youngblood, Jesse

[10] In Militia Rolls (Texas), ms. The names of the privates have been rearranged in alphabetical order.

Muster Roll of Captain John Rugeley's Company of Volunteers Commanded by Colonel Clark L. Owen, Called into the Service of the Republic of Texas on the 6th day of March 1842 [and discharged about April 13, 1842][11]

Officers

[Rugeley, John]	Captain
Hardeman, Monroe	1st Lieut.
——	2d Lieut.
Wright, Franklin	Orderly Sergt.
not now known	1st Sergt.
not now known	2d Sergt.
not now known	3rd Sergt.
not now known	4th Sergt.
not now known	1st Corpl.
not now known	2d Corpl.
not now known	3rd Corpl.
not now known	4th Corpl.

Privates

Anderson, James D.
Cage, Ben
Davis, Terry
Duncan, John
Eagan, Gabriel
Graves, Jerome B.
Hardeman, John
Hardeman, Owen
Hill, ——
Howell, Thomas
Jackson, ——
January, Henry
Lacy, William D.

Lee, Partilla
Lilley, J. W.
Lokey, ——
Moore, John
Natherly, Thomas
Robinson, Thomas
Rugeley, Rowland
Shrock, J. H. H.
Slade, H. C.
Smith, Thomas
Thompson, Eli
Watkins, William

[11] In Militia Rolls (Texas), ms. Apparently this roll was made out several years after the service reported was rendered. The names of the privates have been rearranged in alphabetical order.

Muster Roll of Captain John M. Smith's Company of Volunteers,
Commanded by Colonel Clark L. Owen, Called into the Service
of the Republic of Texas on the Sixth day of March 1842,
to June 6, 1842[12]

Officers

Smith, John M.   Captain
Baker, John R.   1st Lieut.
Brey, Ferd[inand]   Orderly Sergt.

Privates

Adams, Thomas   Hart, Patrick
Anderson, George   Hefferman [Hefferon], John
Bass, A. W.   Johnson, Charles
Bennett, Elijah   Johnson, Isaac
Bennett, James   Mills, Lawson
Brennan, John   Mills, John
Canfield, Israel   Quinn, Patrick
Cardwell, C.   Reed, William
Cardwell, William   Walker, Andrew
Dodge, Joseph   Weeks, Henry D.
Ferguson, H.   Whaling [Whalen], Henry

Muster Roll of Captain Lafayette Ward's Company of Texas Volunteers,
Commanded by Colonel Clark L. Owen, Called into the Service
of the Republic of Texas on the 6th day of March 1842
[and discharged on June 6, 1842][13]

Officers

Ward, Lafayette   Captain
Rogers, John A., Jr.   1st Lieut.
Hensley, William R.   2d Lieut.
Kerr, James   1st Sergt.
Baker, Abram   2d Sergt.
Cooper, Campbell   3rd Sergt.
Pearce, Benjamin B.   4th Sergt.

[12] In Militia Rolls (Texas), ms. The names of the privates have been rearranged
in alphabetical order.
[13] In Militia Rolls (Texas), ms. The names of the privates have been rearranged
in alphabetical order.

Allen, James L.	Mills, James
Alley, William	Nail, William
Barry, Joseph	O'Neill, James
Beard, Samuel	Peacock, James
Bracken, Will[ia]m	Pearce, Theodore
Calahan, John	Reynolds, Isham
Coleman, Young	Rogers, F. A.
Cox, Nathaniel G.	Rogers, H. A.
Dexter, James W.	Rogers, S. C. A.
Ely, John N.	Ryon, William
Evans, Joseph	Stapp, D. M.
Ewers, John J.	Stapp, Oliver H.
Goodman, C. C.	Stapp, Walter
Guthrie, William	Stern, Isaac
Hall, G. W.	Swan, Robert
Hensely, Alen	Thompson, N. B.
Jones, Johnston (name also on	Walton, George
John S. Menefee's Roll)	Ward, Russell
Jourdan, William	White, D. N.
Lettick, G. W.	White, James G.
Looney, Henry P.	White, Peter
McAvoy, Patrick	Williams, Alexander
McCullough, Samuel	Williams, Joshua
McPeters, James	Williams, Neal
Milby, Robert	

Muster Roll of Captain S. S. S. Ballowe's Company in Service of the Republic of Texas[14]

No.	Names	Rank	Date of Entering Service	Term of Service entered for	Arms & equipment & by whom furnished
1. S. S. S. Ballowe		Captain		six months	sword, pistol, etc.
2. A. Hawk		1st Lieut.		" "	" " "
3. S. H. Dill		2nd Lieut.		" "	" " "
4. G. H. Burk		3rd "		" "	" & Rifle
1. D. L. Carney		1st Serg.		six months	Musket
2. J. E. Selby		2nd "		" "	"
3. W. M. Berryhill		3rd "		" "	"
4. James Gorman		4th "		" "	"

[14] In Militia Rolls (Texas), ms. The names of the privates have been rearranged in alphabetical order.

5. Alexander, E. G.	Private	six months		Musket
6. Birmingham, Z.	"	"	"	"
7. Brister, R. E.	"	"	"	"
8. Brodie, J. H.	"	"	"	Rifle & accoutrement
9. Brown, T. R.	"	"	"	Musket
10. Conlon, W. T.	"	"	"	"
11. Cowin, T. H.	"	"	"	"
12. Cummings, W.	"	"	"	"
13. Deadmore, J. D.[,] M.D.	"	"	"	"
14. Dolton, O.	"	"	"	"
15. Fitzgerald, G.	"	"	"	"
16. Fogg, W. P.	"	"	"	"
17. Francis, W. H.	"	"	"	"
18. Graham, W. A.	"	"	"	"
19. Grey, J. D.	"	"	"	"
20. Hunter, R.	"	"	"	"
21. Huntsman, W. C.	"	"	"	"
22. Kennard, W.	"	"	"	"
23. Kersey, Thos P.	"	"	"	"
24. Lockheart, W. B.	"	"	"	"
25. McNeill, A. G.	"	"	"	"
26. Mars, N. T.	"	"	"	"
27. Mitchell, E. H.	"	"	"	"
28. Mitchell, J. R.	"	"	"	"
29. Murray, A.	"	"	"	"
30. Secrest, J. M.	"	"	"	"
31. Sumner, E. B.	"	"	"	Rifle & accoutrements
32. Wallace, A.	"	"	"	Musket
33. West, J. S.	"	"	"	"
34. Wood, Peter[,] M.D.	"	"	"	"
35. Wren, T. W.	"	"	"	"
36. Youree, W. P.[,] M.D.	"	"	"	"

May 7th 1842
City of Galveston
Republic of Texas

I certify on honor that the above is a correct Muster Roll of the Compan[y of Union] Guards under my command in service of the Republic of Texas and that the [remarks] set opposite the name of each officer & soldier are just.

S. S. S. Ballowe
Captain Comdg. the Company

1842
Galveston
Republic of Texas

I do hereby certify that I have this day mustered & minutely inspected the Company of "Union Guards" under Command of Captain S. S. S. Ballowe & that they all agreed to enter the service of the Republic of Texas to serve for six months to be [subject] to the orders of the Commanding Officer & the Rules & Articles of War, & to [give tr]ue allegiance to the Constitution & Laws of this Republic during [their] period of service.

W. J. Mills, Major
Texas Army
Inspecting & Mustering Officer

Muster Roll of the San Antonio Comp[y]
Capt. C. Johnson, [September 1842][15]

No.	Names		Remarks
1.	C[hauncey] Johnson	Capt.[16]	
2.	A[rchibald] Fitzgerald	1st Lt.	Killed at the break of the Salado 25th Feb. 1843.
3.	William Bugg[17]	2nd do	
4.	R[obert] S. Neighbors[18]	1st Sgt.	
5.	James L. Trueheart[19]	2nd do	
6.	John Lee	3rd do	
7.	N. Harbert[20]	4th do	
8.	Allen, Isaac[21]	Privates[22]	
9.	Alsbury, H. A[lexander][23]		
10.	Beck, Truman B.		

[15] Compiled by A. Neill and D. C. Ogden, Austin, November, 1850. In Militia Rolls (Texas), ms. Unless otherwise specified the bracketed material comes from General Adrián Woll's report to the Minister of War and Marine, dated San Antonio, Texas, September 12, 1842, and reproduced in translation in Joseph Milton Nance (trans. and ed.), Brigadier General Adrián Woll's Report of His Expedition into Texas in 1842," *Southwestern Historical Quarterly*, LVIII (1954–1955), 533. Other information given in the following notes is drawn from Rena Maverick Green (ed.), *Samuel Maverick, Texan, 1803–1870: A Collection of Letters, Journals and Memoirs*, pp. 173–175; Frederick C. Chabot (ed.), *The Perote Prisoners: Being the Diary of James L. Trueheart Printed for the First Time Together With an Historical Introduction*, pp. 101–102; *Diario del Gobierno*, Oct. 22, 1842; *Telegraph and Texas Register*, Nov. 2 and 30, 1842; William E. Jones and Others to the American Officers and Citizens, San Antonio, September 14, 1842, copy in Waddy Thompson Papers. Captured, but freed within a few days, were Bryan Callaghan, Joseph McClelland, John S. Johnson (boy), Antonio Menchaca, another boy, and five Mexican residents of San Antonio.

[16] Woll lists Johnson's rank as "colonel." Johnson was a watchmaker by trade.

[17] William Bugg, John Lee, Truman Beck, Edward Brown, and John Perry were all farmers.

[18] Woll shows Neighbors as "quartermaster general."

[19] Woll lists Trueheart as "district secretary."

[20] Woll shows the name as N. Herbert. His first name was apparently Nathaniel; he was a carpenter.

[21] Isaac Allen was a tailor by trade; James H. Brown was a farrier; John Dalrymple and John Lehmann, clerks: Augustus Elley, a miner; John Forester and George C. Hatch, laborers; Francis McKay, a physician; Joseph C. Morgan, Marcus L. B. Rapier, and John Young, carpenters; Duncan C. Ogden, John Riddle, and John Twohig, merchants; John Smith, a mason; and Samuel Stone, a hatter.

[22] The names of the privates have been rearranged in alphabetical order.

[23] Woll shows the name as "Alexander Alsbury." Alsbury was a physician.

11. Booker, S.[24]   Accidentally shot by a Mexican
                                      soldier.

12. Brown, Edward
13. Brown, James H.
14. Colquhoun, L.[25]
15. Crews, J[oseph] A.[26]   Died in Perote Hospital of the epi-
                                      demic.
16. Cunningham, J[ohn] R.[27]   Died in the Leona River, Septem-
                                      ber 1842.
17. Dalrymple, John   Escaped from Perote Castle 2nd
                                      July 1843.

18. Davis, D[avid] J.[28]
19. Elley, A[ugustus]

20. Forester, John   Escaped 2nd July 1843 from Pe-
                                      rote Castle.

21. Glenn, S[imon]
22. Gray, F. S. [29]   Died in Perote Hospital of the epi-
                                      demic.

23. Hancock, Thomas

24. Hatch, George C.   Escaped 7th May 1843 from Pe-
                                      rote Castle.
25. Hutchinson, A[nderson][30]   Liberated by Genl. Santa Anna to
                                      Gen. Thompson.
26. Jackson, Riley   Died in Perote Castle.

[24] Woll lists S. Booker as a "surgeon."

[25] Colquhoun's first name is given in some sources as "Ludovic."

[26] Woll's report lists the name as "José A. Cruz, clerk." Anglo-Americans among the prisoners give the name as "Crews." E. W. Winkler (ed.), "The Béxar and Dawson Prisoners," *Quarterly of the Texas State Historical Association*, XIII (1909–1910), 312–313, 137–320; W[illia]m F. Wilson to Dear Brother, Castle of Perota, April 22, 1844, and W[illia]m F. Wilson to [Col. A. Turner], Republic of Mexico, Castle of Perota, July 29, 1844, in "Two Letters from a Mier Prisoner," in *ibid.*, II (1898–1899), 233–236; William E. Jones and Others to the American Officers and Citizens, San Antonio, Sept. 14, 1842, in Waddy Thompson Papers, 1824–1843, ms. Cruz was a clerk of the court.

[27] Woll lists Cunningham as a "lawyer."

[28] The name is given as J. J. Davis in *Telegraph and Texas Register*, Nov. 2, 1842; and in J. D. Affleck, "History of John C. Hays," pt. I, p. 251; but as David J. Davis in William E. Jones and Others to the American Officers and Citizens, San Antonio, September 11, 1842, in Samuel A. Maverick Papers, ms. Davis, whose first name is given in still other sources as "DeWitt," was a laborer.

[29] French Strother Gray is listed by Woll as "colonel and lawyer." He was assistant district attorney.

[30] Woll lists Hutchinson as "district judge."

No.	Names	Remarks
27.	Jones, William E.[31]	Liberated by Genl. Santa Anna to Genl. Thompson.
28.	Lehman[n], John	
29.	Leslie, A. F.	
30.	McKay, Francis	
31.	Maverick, Samuel A.[32]	Liberated by Genl. Santa Anna to Genl. Thompson.
32.	Morgan, David[33]	Escaped the 7th of May 1843, from Perote Castle.
33.	Morgan, J[oseph] C.	
34.	Neill, Andrew[34]	Escaped in December '42 from San Juan Tetiohuaca.
35.	Nobles, S. A.[35]	
36.	Nowell, Samuel[36]	Liberated by Col. José Mª Carrasco.
37.	O'Phelan, William H.[37]	Liberated to the English minister by Genl. Santa Anna.
38.	Ogden, D. C. [38]	Released by Genl. Santa Anna.
39.	Perry John	
40.	Peterson, C[ornelius] W.[39]	
41.	Rapier, M[arcus] L. B.	
42.	Riddle, John	Liberated to the English minister by Genl. Santa Anna.
43.	Riddle, Wilson [Irwin][40]	Liberated to the English minister by Genl. Santa Anna.

[31] Woll shows Jones to be a "lawyer." Jones was a member of congress.

[32] Woll lists Maverick as a "lawyer." Maverick was also a member of congress.

[33] He is listed by Woll as "Davis Morgan," but by the *Telegraph and Texas Register*, Nov. 2, 1842, as "David Morgan." He was a merchant by trade.

[34] Neill is listed by Woll as a "lawyer and physician."

[35] Nobles is listed by Woll as "S. Nobles," but in the *Telegraph and Texas Register*, Nov. 2, 1842, as "S. R. Nobles," and in Thomas J. Green, *Journal of the Texian Expedition Against Mier*, p. 448, as "S. L. Nobles." Still other sources give the name as "S. J. Nobles."

[36] This name was probably "Norvell" rather than "Nowell."

[37] Woll simply shows "William O'phelan." O'Phelan was a traveler.

[38] Ogden's first name is given in some sources as "Duncan."

[39] Woll lists Peterson as a "lawyer." He was the district attorney.

[40] Woll shows the name as "W. J. Riddle," and so does William E. Jones and Others to the American Officers and Citizens, San Antonio, September 11, 1842, Samuel A. Maverick Papers, ms., but in the *Telegraph and Texas Register*, Nov. 2, 1842, it is given as "W. C. Riddle." Riddle was a merchant.

44. Robinson, James W.[41]

Liberated by Genl. Santa Anna Feby 1843.

45. Schaeffer, George[42]
46. Smith, John
47. Stone, Samuel
48. Trapnall, J[ohn] C.[43]

Died in Perote Hospital in the epidemic.

49. Twohig, John

Escaped 2nd July 1843 from Perote Castle.

50. Van Ness, George
51. Voss, [Johann] George [Andreas][44]
52. Young, John

---

[41] Shown on the Woll list as a "lawyer."

[42] Shown as "George P. Schaeffer" by Woll and the *Telegraph and Texas Register,* Nov. 2, 1842; but as "George P. Schaffer" by William E. Jones and Others to the American Officers and Citizens, San Antonio, September 11, 1842, in Samuel A. Maverick Papers, ms.

[43] Shown by Woll as "John Trapnell, lawyer."

[44] Woll shows the name as "Johann G. Andreas Voss," but in the *Telegraph and Texas Register,* Nov. 2, 1842, and in William E. Jones and Others to the American Officers and Citizens, San Antonio, September 11, 1842, in Samuel A. Maverick Papers, ms., it is "George Voss." Voss was a merchant.

Muster Roll of Captain Alexander Stevenson's Company [of] "Missouri Invincibles" in the Service of the Republic of Texas for Six Months[45]

No.	Name	Rank	Date of Entering Service of the Republic of Texas	Term of Service Entered For	Arms & Equipment & by whom Furnished
1.	Alexander Stevenson	Capt.			Furnished by themselves Sword, pistols, &c
2.	William Thacher	1st Lt.			" "
3.	Francis Gleason	2d Lt.			" "
					" "
1.	Isaac Hill	1st Sgt.			
2.	James Johnson	2d "			
3.	Loren G. Jeffries	3d "			
4.	Samuel Johnson	4th "			
1.	Jacob A. Earhart	1st Cpl.			
2.	Rufus Good[e]now	2d "			
3.	Jesse Morris	3d "			
4.	Andrew Addison	4th "			
1.	John Frye	Ensign			
1.	Adams, James	Private			
2.	Barton, George	"			
3.	Chase, William M.	"			
4.	Conley, John A.	"			
5.	Davis, John O.	"			
6.	Day, Thomas A.	"			
7.	Dougherty, Patrick R.	"			
8.	Downe, James A.	"			
9.	Ellis, William	"			
10.	Fitzsimmons, William	"			
11.	Fuller, William M.	"			
12.	Gray, James	"			
13.	Grosjean, John C.	"			
14.	Hamilton, Mirabeau	"			
15.	Hancock, Francis	"			
16.	Hatch, Eber	"			
17.	Hawes, John B.	"			
18.	Hervey, Edward M.	"			
19.	Higerson, John	"			

[45] In Militia Rolls (Texas), ms. The names of the privates have been rearranged in alphabetical order.

20. Hogan, Thomas H.	Private	
21. Hunt, Thomas C.	"	
22. Jeffres, William	"	
23. Johnson, James	"	
24. Kent, Thomas	"	
25. Lake, Storm	"	
26. Larget, John	"	
27. Larkey, David M.	"	
28. Lawrence, John	"	
29. McBride, Patrick H.	"	
30. McDonough, Martin	"	
31. Mann, William H.	"	
32. Mellan, James	"	
33. Miller, Marcus A. G.	"	
34. Morgan, George	"	
35. Morris, William	"	
36. Mullan, Thomas	"	
37. Murphy, George W.	"	
38. Murphy, James Mc.	"	Seventy-five muskets and
39. Muselman, John	"	accoutrements furnished
40. Neville, Frederick A.	"	for the use of the com-
41. Otto, John	"	pany by Colonel Wash-
42. Palmer, John	"	ington
43. Rowen, Edmund M.	"	
44. Rowen, Stephen E.	"	
45. Rutgers, Edward	"	
46. Sandusky, John S.	"	
47. Shepherd, William	"	
48. Slocum, George W.	"	
49. Stapp, William P.	"	
50. Strong, Ralph	"	
51. Underwood, Benjamin	"	
52. Vass, James	"	
53. Watkins, [John H.][46]	"	
54. Wheeler, Tobias	"	
55. Winters, John	"	
56. Work, Thomas	"	

(Continued on next page)

[46] See Public Debt Papers (Texas), ms. for John H. Watkins, for service in Captain Alexander Stevenson's Company of "Missouri Invincibles."

May 25th 1842
City of Galveston
Republic of Texas

I certify on honor that the above is a correct Muster Roll of the Company of Missouri Invincibles under my command in the service of the Republic of Texas, & that the Remarks set opposite the name of each officer & soldier are accurate & just.

Alexander Stevenson
Captain Commanding the Company

May 25th 1842
City of Galveston
Republic of Texas

I hereby certify that I have this day mustered & minutely inspected the Company of "Missouri Invincibles" under command of Captain Alexander Stevenson, & that they all agreed to enter the service of the Republic of Texas to serve for six months, to be obedient to the orders of the Commanding Officer, & the Rules & Articles of War, and to bear true allegiance to the Constitution & Laws of this Republic during their period of service.

W. J. Mills, Major Texas Army
Inspecting & Mustering Officer

Muster Roll of Captain Walter Hickey's Company "Natchez Mustangs" in Service of the Republic of Texas [for six months service][47]

No.	Name	Rank	Remarks
1.	Walter Hickey	Capt.	Furnished themselves sword, pistol, &c.
2.	James Monroe	1st Lt.	" " " "
3.	John Dixon	2d Lt.	" " " "
4.	D. G. Renner	3d Lt.	" " " "
1.	Samuel Hamlet	Orderly Sgt.	Musket & accoutrements
2.	P. N. Hitchcock	2d Sgt.	
3.	William Fletcher	3d "	
4.	Charles Goosoneaux	4th "	

[47] In Militia Rolls (Texas), ms. The names of the privates have been rearranged in alphabetical order.

5. James Young	5th Sgt.	
1. James Russel	1st Cpl.	Fifteen muskets fur-
2. Martin Fitzgerald	2d "	nished by Mr. Ryan; fif-
3. Samuel Yates	3d "	teen muskets & ten rifles
4. John Sternes	4th "	by Capt. Hickey & also
1. Boss, George A.	Private	accoutrements.
2. Bover, Isaac	"	
3. Cole, R. F.	"	
4. Connelly, James	"	
5. Conway, John	"	
6. Corbin, J. W.	"	
7. Crawley, ——	"	Deserted
8. Cronanbolt, Lewis	"	
9. Davis, Edward	"	
.0. Davis, John	"	
.1. Dedman, E. C.	"	
.2. Duncan, Robert	"	
.3. Ferriman, Campbell	"	
.4. Flores, F. B.	"	
.5. Hackstaff, John	"	
.6. Hamrick, W. M.	"	
.7. Hickey, E.	"	
.8. Hopson, W. J.	"	
.9. Howard, R. R.	"	
:0. Johnson, Nat. M.	"	
:1. Joy, William B.	"	
:2. Kirby, L. D.	"	
:3. Knowles, L. S.	"	
:4. Lumley, Thomas	"	
:5. M'Collum, Thomas	"	
:6. M'Cormick, Thomas	"	
:7. M'Cosky, Alfred	"	
:8. M'Donald, M. J.	"	
:9. M'Murray, Charles H.	"	
:0. Minthurn, Walter De	"	
:1. Mire, William	"	
:2. Monteith, Abraham	"	
:3. Moore, Thomas	"	
:4. Mulhausen, Francis	"	
:5. Pawling, Benjamin M.	"	
:6. Perkey, S. H.	"	
:7. Perrot, William	"	
:8. Phillips, Thomas	"	
:9. Rodgers, ——	"	Deserted

No.	Name	Rank	Remarks
40.	Rodham, Charles	Private	
41.	Sanders, A. H.	"	
42.	Sanders, T. F.	"	
43.	Warren, James M.	"	
44.	Williams, Henry	"	

[Endorsed on back:] May 24th City of Galveston
Republic of Texas

I do hereby certify that the foregoing "Muster Roll" exhibits a correct statement of the Company of "Natchez Mustangs" under my command, in the service of the Republic of Texas, & that the Remarks set opposite the name of each officer & soldier are accurate & just.

Walter Hickey
Captain Commanding the Company

May 24th 1842   City of Galveston
Republic of Texas

I do hereby certify that I have this day mustered & minutely inspected the Company of "Natchez Mustangs" under command of Captain Walter Hickey, & that they all agreed to enter the service of the Republic of Texas to serve for six months, to be obedient to the orders of the Commanding Officer, & the Rules & Articles of War, & to bear true allegiance to the Constitution & Laws of this Republic during their period of service.

W. J. Mills, Major Texas Army
Inspecting & Mustering Officer

[also on back in column:]   Capn Hickey's men
Anderson
Farley
Herren
Alston
Sanders

Muster Roll of Captain H. H. Brower's Company for
May 15, 1842 [Company A][48]

Name	Rank	Name	Rank
Brower, H. H.	Captain	McElwy	Private
Moore, W. P.	1st Lieut.	McGuigan	"
Work, G. C.	2nd Lieut.	McInis	"
Sullivan, I.	1st Sergt.	McNair	"
Baugher, William	2nd Sergt.	Mar[c]ks, [John]	"
Byington, G[eorge]	3rd Sergt.	Marshall	"
Boyle, I. H.	4th Sergt.	Martin, 1st	"
Mongar, J. T.	5th Sergt.	Martin, 2nd	"
Flaherty, I.	1st Corpl.	Mongeon	"
Osbourne, J.	2nd Corpl.	Morall	"
Shattuck, H.	3rd Corpl.	Newitt	"
Scott, J.	4th Corpl.	O'Daniel	"
Allen, [C. A.]	Private	O'[M]eara	"
Babcock, [Jeremiah]	"	Peters	"
Beach	"	Pettis	"
Brown	"	Philips, A.	"
Carr	"	Philips, G.	"
Clark	"	Plitt	"
Cook	"	Riley	"
Davis	"	Roarke	"
Frieher	"	Sherrod	"
Hulse, [David]	"	Thornton	"
Kelley	"	Williams, T.	"
Kerman	"	Williams, W.	"
Kieff	"	Wright	"
Kirk	"		

Men were equipped with rifles, muskets, pistols, Bowie knives, bayonets, cartridge boxes, clothing, powder, and balls.

Remarks: Shirts, pants and shoes wanted. On hand 8 kegs bbg. powder—no coffee or sugar on hand. Four of the muskets will not bear inspection, nor have I means of repairing them.

H. H. Brower

[48] Frederick C. Chabot, *Corpus Christi and Lipantitlán,* pp. 33–34. Chabot says that the Muster Roll of Captain H. H. Brower's company "A" shows 52 names, but he only lists 51, and omits the given names of most of the privates. Brower's Roll is not in the Texas State Archives. The names of the privates have been rearranged in alphabetical order.

Muster Roll of Captain Jack R. Everett's Company of Mobile, Alabama, Volunteers in the Service of the Republic of Texas for Six Months [Company B][49]

No.	Name	Rank	Date of Enrollment	Remarks
1.	John R. Everett	Capt.	April 1842	Discharged Oct. 2 '42
2.	E. S[L?] Ratcliff	1st Lt.	"	" "
3.	Thomas P. Mills	2d Lt.	"	" "
1.	J. W. Thompson	1st Sgt.	"	" "
2.	N. H. Birmingham	2d "	"	" "
3.	D. D. Donaldson	3d "	"	Deserted July 25th
4.	A. L. Rowen	4th "	"	" "
1.	W. B. Sayre	1st Cpl.	"	" Aug. 10
2.	I. N. Fleeson	2d "	"	Disch. Oct. 2
3.	J. H. Marsh	3d "	"	Deserted July 25
4.	W. B. Fleeson	4th "	"	Disch. Oct. 2
1.	Anderson, Peter	Private	"	" "
2.	Beaumont, W. D.	"	"	Deserted about Aug. 15
3.	Boon, Thomas W.	"	"	Discharged Oct. 2
4.	Brackenridge, R.	"	"	" "
5.	Briggs, W. R.	"	"	Honbly disch. by Sec. War Aug. 19
6.	Carr, John	"	"	Honbly disch. by Sec. War Aug. 19
7.	Cassedy, Bernard			
8.	Cassedy, James	"	"	Discharged Oct. 2
9.	Chapin, Eli P.	"	"	Disch. Oct. 2
10.	Cochran, Peter	"	"	Discharged Oct. 2
11.	Cooper, Thomas	"	"	Honbly disch. by Sec. War & Mar. Aug. 19
12.	Croghan [Croggan], Samuel	"	"	Disch. Oct. 2
13.	Eaton, Pearl	"	"	Discharged Oct. 2
14.	Ensminger, Daniel	"	"	" "
15.	Everett, C. E.	"	"	" "
16.	Furman, A.	"	"	" "
17.	Gallaher, Charles	"	"	" "
18.	Glasscock, J. A.	"	"	" "
19.	Hagle, George	"	"	" "
20.	Heath, J. P.	"	"	" "
21.	Hoffer, John	"	"	" "
22.	Hopkins, F.	"	"	Died August 1842
23.	Hudson, C. B.	"	"	Discharged Oct. 2
24.	Hugo, Simon	"	"	" "
25.	Jackson, W. T.	"	"	" "
26.	Janerette, Thomas D.	"	"	" "

[49] In Militia Rolls (Texas), ms. The names of the privates have been rearranged in alphabetical order.

27. Johnston, J. P.	Private	April 1842	Deserted Aug. 1842
28. Loper, M.	"	"	Discharged Oct. 2
29. McFearson, W.	"	"	Honbly disch. by Sec. War & Mar. Aug. 19
30. McNair, G. L.	"	"	Discharged Oct. 2
31. Minton, S. F.	"	"	" "
32. Mosely, W. A.	"	"	" "
33. Nelson, W. A.	"	"	Dicharged Oct. 2, 1842
34. Odair, John	"	"	Honbly disch. by Sec. War & Mar. Aug. 19
35. Peterson, Charles	"	"	Discharged Oct. 2
36. Peterson, Oliver	"	"	Honbly disch. by Sec. War & Mar. Aug. 19
37. Porter, Asa	"	"	Discharged Oct. 2
38. Rover, T. F.	"	"	" "
39. Smith, J. C.	"	"	" "
40. Studley, F. W.	"	"	Discharged Oct. 2, 1842
41. Terrell, Richard	"	"	Discharged Oct. 2
42. Terry, S. P.	"	"	" "
43. Thrall, Eli	"	"	" "
44. Toomer, W. A.	"	"	Dishonorably discharged Aug. 1842
45. Vabler, W. D.	"	"	Discharged Oct. 2
46. Vandergriff, Earl	"	"	" "
47. Wallis, John	"	"	" "
48. Williamson, George	"	"	Discharged from inability

Recapitulation

Captain	1	Corporals	4
1st Lt.	1	Privates	47
2d Lt.	1	Total	55
Sergeants	4	Aggregate	58

Republic of Texas
Galveston
April 1st 1842

I certify on honor that the foregoing is a correct Muster Roll of the Company of Troops under my command in the service of the Republic of Texas, and that the remarks set opposite the names to be accurate and just.

J. R. Everett
Captain Commanding the Company

On the 19th Aug 1842 Bernard Cassedy came to the Department & reported himself a private of the above company, several members of the Company came forward [to say] that he came from the United States and had been with them since that time and that his name had been omitted through mistake, whereupon he received an honorable discharge from the Sec'y of War & Marine.

Robert Oliver
Chf Clk of War & Marine

[endorsed: Filed by Capt. Everett, Sept. 1, 1851]

Roll of Augustus Williams' Company C, Tennessee Volunteers Reported Present for Duty, La Panticlen [Lipantitlán], July 3, 1842[50]

Macbeth, John	1st Lieut.	Meader	Private
George, Phillip B.	2nd Sergt.	Miller	"
Caythart, C. G.	1st Corpl.	Miller, 2d	"
Hanks, Thomas	3rd Corpl.	Mitchell	"
Baggett	Private	Peel	"
Bell	"	Steel	"
Ford	"	Taylor	"
Frazier	"	Tolefero	"
Gordon	"	Tracey (sick)	"
Gray	"	Turnage	"
Johnson	"	Veneman	"

Detached from service, absent, or furloughed:

Williams, A.	Captain	Echols	Private
Wallace, A.	Orderly Sergt.	Gray	"
Ragsdale, E. B.	3rd Corpl.	Sorrels	"

Absent without leave or deserted:

O'Conner, Hugh	2nd Lieut.	Moseley, I.	Private
Shelton, John	2nd Sergt.	Pain, Govan	"
King, Samuel B.	3rd Sergt.	Peck, Ruluff	"
Gall, Fred B.	4th Sergt.	Richardson, John	"
Cochran, R.	1st Corpl.	Ross, David K.	"
Peeples, William	3rd Corpl.	Runnells, James A.	"
Riley, John	4th Corpl.	Sick, Thomas	"
Crawford, William H.	Private	Sneed, Thomas	"
Davis, I. C.	"	Turnage, Walker	"
Dyson, G. E.	"	Wray, John	"
Kirksey, John	"	White, Z.	"
MacCaslin, A. M.	"	Windborn, David	"
McMahan, James	"	Zeeland, A.	"

[signed:]

John MacBeth, 1st Lt.

Phillip B. George, 2nd Sergt.

[50] In Chabot, *Corpus Christi and Lipantitlán*, p. 34. This roll is incomplete. The original muster roll has not been found. The names of the privates have been rearranged in alphabetical order.

Muster Roll of Captain J. M. Allen's Company [of] "Galveston Invincibles" Mustered into Service of the Republic of Texas for Six Months [Company D][51]

No.	Name	Rank	Date of Entering Service of the Republic of Texas	Term of Service Entered For	Arms & Equipment & by whom Furnished
1.	John M. Allen	Capt.	1842 April 8	Six months	Furnished by themselves Sword, pistol, &c
2.	J. N. Taylor	1st Lt.	"	"	" "
3.	E. T. Fox	2d Lt.	"	"	" "
1.	W. C. Ogilvie	Orderly Sgt.	"	"	Furnished by Government Musket, cartridge box, belts
2.	M. R. Edwards	2d Sgt.	"	"	" " "
3.	J. Eyler	3d "	"	"	" " "
4.	J. L. Provost	4th "	"	"	" " "
1.	W. H. Flood	1st Cpl.	"	"	" " "
2.	J. A. Dast	2d "	"	"	" " "
3.	W. Ross	3d "	"	"	" " "
4.	J. B. McClasky	4th "	"	"	" " "
1.	Begiet, Henry	Private	"	"	" " "
2.	Burns, M.	"	"	"	" " "
3.	Colt, G.	"	"	"	" " "
4.	Conwell, C.	"	"	"	" " "
5.	Emblem, J.	"	"	"	" " "
6.	Gandie, I.	"	"	"	" " "
7.	Glass, H. J.	"	"	"	" " "
8.	Gray, J. L.	"	"	"	" " "
9.	Hay, A.	"	"	"	" " "
10.	Heiser, P.	"	"	"	" " "
11.	Hunter, E. J.	"	"	"	" " "
12.	Jeffreys, F. N.	"	"	"	" " "
13.	Lesilinetzsky, W.	"	"	"	" " "
14.	Mills, G.	"	"	"	" " "
15.	Moore, Henry	"	"	"	" " "
16.	Osborne, J. A.	"	"	"	" " "

[51] In Militia Rolls (Texas), ms. The names of the privates have been rearranged in alphabetical order.

No.	Name	Rank	Date of Entering Service of the Republic of Texas	Term of Service Entered For	Arms & Equipment & by whom Furnished
17. Pearson, J.		Private	1842 April 8	Six months	Furnished by Government Musket, cartridge box, belts
18. Pettigue, T. D.		"	"	"	" " "
19. Ramsey, A.[,] M.D.		"	"	"	" " "
20. Reavis, J. B.		"	"	"	" " "
21. Reid, S. C.		"	"	"	" " "
22. Shutz, J.		"	"	"	" " "
23. Smith, B. E.		"	"	"	" " "
24. Spencer, A.		"	"	"	" " "
25. Williamson, W.		"	"	"	" " "
26. Wright, J. F.		"	"	"	" " "

April 8th 1842
Galveston, Texas

I certify on honor that the above is a correct Muster Roll Company of Galveston Invincibles under my command & that the arms set opposite the name of each officer & Private are accurate & just.

J. M. Allen
Captain Commanding the Company

April 8, 1842
Republic of Texas
City of Galveston

I certify that I have this day inspected the above Company of "Galveston Invincibles," under command of Captain John M. Allen & that they all agreed to enter the service of the Republic to serve for six months.

W. J. Miles, Quarter Master
4th R. T. M. Inspecting
& Mustering Officer.

Muster Roll of Captain H. W. Allen's Company [of] "Mississippi Guards" in Service of the Republic of Texas [Company E][52]

No.	Name	Rank	Date of Entering Service of the Republic of Texas	Term of Service Entered For	Arms & Equipment & by whom Furnished	Remarks
1.	H. W. Allen	Capt.	1842 April 9	Six months	Furnished by themselves Sword, pistol, &c	Grand Gulf, Miss.
2.	Jonas Leaman	1st Lt.	"	"	"	
3.	D. W. Fields	2nd Lt.	"	"	"	
4.	W. B. Williams	3rd Lt.	"	"	"	
1.	A. W. D. Limsden	Ensign	"	"	"	
2.	L. A. Williams	Orderly Sgt.	"	"	Musket, pistols, knife	
3.	W. C. Parke	2nd Sgt.	"	"	" "	
4.	R. Hackett	3rd Sgt.	"	"	" "	
5.	B. W. Rummy	4th Sgt.	"	"	" "	
1.	D. F. Burney	1st Cpl.	"	"	Rifle, pistols, knife	Entered Capt. Williams' Co.
2.	A. Wallace	2nd Cpl.	"	"	" "	"
3.	N. Stansbury	3rd Cpl.	"	"	" "	"
4.	T. D. Evans	4th Cpl.	"	"	" "	"
1.	Allen, J. A.	Private	"	"	" "	"
2.	Barnes, J. T.	"	"	"	Rifle	"
3.	Bradley, W.	"	"	"	Musket	
4.	Butler, J. M.	"	"	"	"	"
5.	Clarke, J. J.	"	"	"	"	
6.	Cocke, B.	"	"	"	Rifle	
7.	Eckols, W. L.	"	"	"	"	"
8.	Fontleroy, T. W.	"	"	"	Musket	
9.	Frazer, S.	"	"	"	Rifle	
10.	Gilmore, W. D.	"	"	"	"	"
11.	Gray, J.	"	"	"	"	"
12.	Hays, W.	"	"	"	Musket	"
13.	Howard, W. R.	"	"	"	"	

[52] In Militia Rolls (Texas), ms. The names of the privates have been rearranged in alphabetical order.

No.	Name	Rank	Date of Entering Service of the Republic of Texas	Term of Service Entered For	Arms & Equipment & by whom Furnished	Remarks
14.	Hubbard, D.	Private	1842 April 9	Six months	Musket	
15.	Irwin, A.	"	"	"	Rifle	
16.	James, O.	"	"	"	"	
17.	Lambertson, R.	"	"	"	"	Entered Capt. Williams Co.
18.	Lee, Lot	"	"	"	"	
19.	Lewis, G.	"	"	"	"	
20.	Michon, E.	"	"	"	Musket	
21.	Moon, J. A.	"	"	"	Rifle	
22.	Morgan, W. S.	"	"	"	Musket	
23.	Moss, J. J.	"	"	"	Rifle	"
24.	Postell, J.	"	"	"	Musket	
25.	Ragsdale, E. B.	"	"	"	Rifle	"
26.	Terry, G. W.	"	"	"	"	"
27.	Wharton, J.	"	"	"	"	

April 9th 1842
Houston, Tex

I certify on honor that the above is a correct Muster Roll of the Company of Mississippi Volunteer Guards under my command and that the "Remarks" set opposite the name of each officer & Private are accurate & just.

H. W. Allen
Captain Commanding the Company

April 25th 1842
Republic of Texas
City of Galveston

I certify that I have this day inspected th above Company of Mississippi Guards unde Command of Captain H. W. Allen & tha they all agreed to enter the service of th Republic of Texas to serve for six months.

W. J. Miles, Quarter Master
4th Regt. T. M.
Inspecting & Mustering
Officer

Muster Roll of Captain John J. B. Hoxey's Company of Georgia Volunteers Mustered into the Service of the Republic of Texas for Six Months, Galveston April 23d 1842
[Company F][53]

No.	Name	Rank	Arms & Equipment & by whom furnished to the soldiers
1.	John J. B. Hoxey	Capt.	Furnished by themselves Sword, pistols, &c
2.	William R. Shivers	1st Lt.	" "
3.	Thomas Y. Redd	2d Lt.	" "
1.	B. M. Mimms	Orderly Sgt.	Musket & accountrement
2.	E. L. Burns	2d "	Shot gun "
3.	A. English	3d "	Rifle & equipments
4.	D. Y. Thorn	4th "	Musket, cart. box
5.	P. K. Edgar	5th "	" "
1.	John M. Traywick	1st Cpl.	" "
2.	A. F. Lawrence	2d "	Rifle & accountrement
3.	Thomas Hoxey junr.	3d "	" & pistol
4.	P. W. Clayton	4th "	" "
1.	Arnold, J. B.	Private	" & accountrement
2.	Baker, W. H.	"	" "
3.	Berry, F. H.	"	Musket, cart. box, pistol
4.	Blalock, W. H.	"	" & pistol
5.	Broome, A. D.	"	Shot gun
6.	Brown, James H.	"	Musket, cart. box, pistol
7.	Cade, J. B.	"	Musket, c. box
8.	Calhoun, Thomas	"	Shot gun, c. box
9.	Carter, George W.	"	Musket, c. box
10.	Cross, Way	"	Musket, c. box
11.	Ernest, Benjamin N.	"	
12.	Erwin, John	"	Musket & bowie knife
13.	Goolsbee, John F.	"	Rifle & equipments
14.	Gordon, George W.	"	Musket & c. box
15.	Hindy, S.	"	Shot gun
16.	Holt, James L.	"	Musket, c. box
17.	Humphries, J. C.	"	
18.	Johnson, A. C.	"	Musket, c. box
19.	Lee, Andrew	"	" "
20.	Lee, P. H.	"	Shot gun

[53] In Militia Rolls (Texas), ms. The names of the privates have been rearranged in alphabetical order.

No.	Name	Rank	Arms & Equipment & by whom furnished to the soldiers
21.	Lewis, Charles S.	Private	Musket, c. box
22.	Moore, N. J.	"	Musket, c. box, pistol
23.	Reid, W. T.	"	" "
24.	Richardson, J. E.	"	" "
25.	Stewart, Augustus	"	Shot gun "
26.	Taylor, A. J.	"	Rifle "
27.	Tennille, Joseph P.	"	Musket "
28.	Wellborn, Jackson	"	" "
29.	Willers, William	"	Shot gun "
30.	Williamson, R. M. D.	"	" "
31.	Yarborough, P.	"	" "

April 23d 1842
Galveston, Texas

I certify on honor that the above is a correct Muster Roll of the Company of Georgia Volunteers under my command, & that the "Remarks" &c set opposite the name of each officer & Private are accurate & just.

Jno. J. B. Hoxey
Captain Commanding the Company

April 23d 1842
Republic of Texas
City of Galveston

I certify that I have this day inspected the above Company of Georgia Voluteers under the command of Captain John J. B. Hoxey, & that they all agreed to enter into the service of the Republic of Texas to serve for six months.

W. J. Mills, Quarter Master 4th
Regiment Texas Militia
Inspecting & Mustering Officer

Recapitulation of the Company

Captain	1	Commissioned officers	3
1st Lt.	1	Total non-commissioned	
2d Lt.	1	and privates	37
Sergts.	5	Aggregate	40
Corporals	4		
Privates	28		

618

Muster Roll of Captain T. N. Wood's Company of Alabama
Volunteers Mustered into the Service of the Republic of
Texas for Six Months, Galveston, April 23, 1842
[Company G][54]

No.	Name	Rank	Arms & Equipment Furnished to the Soldier
1. Thomas N. Wood	Capt.	Sword &c furnished themselves
2. J. H. Sims	1st Lt.	" " "
3. Jesse Price	2d Lt.	" " "
4. B. Quinn	3d Lt.	" " "
1. A. W. Starr	Orderly Sgt.	Sword, pistols, knife
2. Mark T. Lyon	2d "	Rifle, pistol, knife
3. Thomas O. Meek	3d "	Yager, pistol
4. James Mabe	4th "	Rifle, bowie knife
1. Jackson Lee	1st Cpl.	Yager
2. John L. Jones	2d "	Shot gun, k[nife], pistol
3. William Daniels	3d "	Rifle, pistols
4. William Hampton	4th "	" , pistol
1. Bagley, Edward F.	Private	" , "
2. Ball, Henry	"	" , bowie [knife], pistol
3. Barter, James L.	"	
4. Bonner, John	"	Small shot gun
5. Braneka, Henry	"	
6. Chamberlayne, R. K.	"	
7. Climer, Andrew	"	Musket, bowie [knife]
8. Conway, Thomas	"	Rifle, " "
9. Cooper, Jackson A.	"	Double barrel gun
10. Fitzsimons, John T.	"	Rifle
11. Haiggler, Thomas L.	"	Rifle
12. Hamer, Frederick D.	"	Musket, pistol
13. Haslett, David	"	Small shot gun
14. Jackson, William W.	"	Musket
15. Johnson, Charles H.	"	" broken
16. Johnson, Lawrence W.	"	Small shot gun, 2 pistols
17. Jordan, Leroy G.	"	Rifle, cutlass
18. Kendricks, Silas	"	Rifle
19. Kircheville, Andrew J.	"	Rifle, 1 pistol
20. Malone, Simon	"	Musket
21. Norwood, Daniel M.	"	Rifle, 1 pistol

[54] In Militia Rolls (Texas), ms. The names of the privates have been rearranged in alphabetical order.

No.	Name	Rank	Arms & Equipment Furnished to the Soldier
22.	Perry, John S.	Private	Yager, 1 pistol
23.	Phelps, John	"	Double barrell gun
24.	Porter, Samuel T.	"	Musket, bowie [knife]
25.	Ragan, Giles C.	"	Musket, 2 pistols
26.	Ray, Constantine	"	Rifle, bowie [knife], 2 pistols
27.	Rooks, Dennis	"	Shot gun, 2 pistols
28.	Shackleford, Richard	"	Rifle, bowie [knife]
29.	Tann, William H.	"	Musket
30.	Tully, Thomas J.	"	" damaged
31.	Turner, W. C.	"	Rifle
32.	Weaver, Jacob	"	Musket
33.	Wilkie, James	"	Musket
34.	Word, Jackson	"	Yager, 1 pistol

April 23d 1842
Galveston, Texas

I certify on honor that the above is a correct Muster Roll of the Company of Alabama Volunteers under my command, & that the "Remarks" set opposite the names of the officers & men are accurate & just.

Thos. Newton Wood
Captain Commanding the Company

April 23, 1842
Republic of Texas
City of Galveston

I certify that I have this day inspected th above Company of Alabama Volunteers un der command of Captain T. N. Wood & th they, all agreed to enter the service of th Republic of Texas to serve for six months.

W. J. Mills, Quarter Master 4th
Regt. T. M.
Inspecting & Mustering Officer

APPENDIX B

Captain Nicholas M. Dawson's Company, September 18, 1842[1]

Killed		Native State
1. Dawson, Nicholas Mosby	(Captain)	Kentucky
2. Alexander, Jerome B.	(Lieutenant)	Kentucky
3. Eastland, Robert Moore	(Lieutenant)	Tennessee
4. Adams, ——[2]		

[1] List of men of Dawson's Company killed near Salado Creek, reported by "a gentleman at La Grange," *Telegraph and Texas Register*, Nov. 2, 1842. The native state of the individual listed is based upon information given in the *Civilian and Galveston Gazette*, Nov. 2, 1842. See also Harold Schoen (comp.), *Monuments Erected by the State of Texas to Commemorate the Centenary of Texas Independence*, p. 93; Leonie Rummel Weyand and Houston Wade, *An Early History of Fayette County*, pp. 155–156, 310. Samuel A. Maverick recorded in his diary under date of October 4, 1842, at San Fernando de Agua Verde that the San Antonio prisoners were joined by the ten Dawson men who had not been wounded. He reports Dawson's Company having consisted of 53 men. Green (ed.), *Samuel Maverick, Texan*, p. 177. The *Civilian and Galveston Gazette*, Nov. 2, 1842, lists 42 killed, wounded, and prisoners of Dawson's Company, and says there were in addition six men from the Cuero settlement and Mr. Maverick's Negro, thus making a total of 49. The *Telegraph and Texas Register*, Nov. 2, 1842, carries a list of the Dawson men killed based upon a "letter of Mr. Baldwin enclosing a copy of a letter of a gentleman from La Grange under date of October 25, 1842," which lists 33 persons killed. We are positive that 15 men (including 5 wounded) were taken prisoners, and that 2 men escaped from Dawson's battlefield. Carved on the tomb of the Dawson and Mier men on Monument Hill overlooking LaGrange, Texas, are the names of 54 men believed to have comprised Dawson's Company. Five of these names were not in the early published or recorded listings of the Dawson men: Zed Barclay (Barkley), John Beard, Thomas D. James, Richard McGee, Norman Miles Wells. Thomas D. James is reported to have effected his escape from the battlefield, but the writer has been unable to confirm this fact. L. A. Duewall, *The Story of Monument Hill*, pp. 32–33. The monument on the court house grounds in La-Grange, Texas, erected to the memory of the Dawson Men, was corrected by the State of Texas in 1936 to read, "Captain Nicholas Mosby Dawson and 36 other volunteers were killed near Salado Creek, in Béxar County, Texas." William Moses Jones, *Texas History Carved in Stone*, p. 82. On the shaft of the monument erected in 1936 on Monument Hill, near LaGrange, in honor of the men of the Mier Expedition of 1842, and of Captain Nicholas Mosby Dawson's Company of September 1842, the name of Winfield S. Lowe has been added to make 55 names. See Schoen (ed.), *Monuments Erected by the State of Texas*, p. 93. Houston Wade, who did a great deal of research on the men of the Mier Expedition and of the Dawson Company, shows only 50 names for the latter. Weyand and Wade, *An Early History of Fayette County*, pp. 155–156, 310.

[2] *Civilian and Galveston Gazette*, Nov. 2, 1842, lists "Adams" as a prisoner, but all other accounts say that he died in battle. He does not appear on the listing in the *Telegraph and Texas Register*, Nov. 2, 1842.

Killed	Native State
5. Alley, James	
6. Barkley, Robert	Tennessee
7. Berry, David [W.]	Virginia
8. Brookfield, Francis E.[3]	New York
9. Butler, [Thomas][4]	Tennessee
10. Church, T. J[ohn]	Tennessee
11. Cummings, John[5]	Maine
12. Dancer, John	Tennessee
13. Dickerson, Lewis W.[6]	Tennessee
14. Farris, Lew	
15. Field, Charles S.[7]	New York
16. Forest, J. N.	
17. Gar[e]y, Elijah	
18. Griffin, Joe[8]	
19. Hall, Harvey [W.]	Tennessee
20. Hill, George A.	Mississippi
21. Jones, Asa	Alabama
22. Jones, John F.	Alabama
23. Leftwich, ——	
24. Lewis, Patrick[9]	
25. Linn, William[10]	
26. Low[e], W[infield] [S.]	

[3] *Civilian and Galveston Gazette,* Nov. 2, 1842, gives this name as "Frank W. Brookfield," but several other sources give it as listed here.

[4] *Telegraph and Texas Register,* Nov. 2, 1842, simply lists the name as "Mr. Butler," but the *Civilian and Galveston Gazette,* Nov. 2, 1842, gives it as "Thomas Butler."

[5] *Telegraph and Texas Register,* Nov. 2, 1842, lists "J. Cummings" and also a "John Cummings," but all other sources mention only "John Cummings," so the writer has excluded "J. Cummings."

[6] *Telegraph and Texas Register,* Nov. 2, 1842, shows the name as "L. W. Dickinson," and the tomb on Monument Hill, near LaGrange, shows him listed as "Lieutenant Dickerson." Jones, *Texas History Carved in Stone,* pp. 83–85.

[7] *Civilian and Galveston Gazette,* Nov. 2, 1842, gives the name as "Charles F. Field."

[8] Joe Griffin, Negro slave of Samuel A. Maverick, is mentioned in the *Civilian and Galveston Gazette,* Nov. 2, 1842, but his name is not given.

[9] This name is reported in James L. Trueheart Diary as being furnished by John Bradley. Chabot (ed.), *The Perote Prisoners,* pp. 111–112.

[10] Both the *Civilian and Galveston Gazette,* Nov. 2, 1842, and the *Telegraph and Texas Register,* Nov. 2, 1842, show William Linn as a prisoner, but he does not show up on the various lists of prisoners made by the Mexicans, or by the Texans who were prisoners. The *Telegraph and Texas Register* lists John MacCredae (McGrady) as being killed. He was among the prisoners taken.

27. Pendleton, John W[esley]	Missouri
28. Rice, Thomas[11]	
29. Savage, William	
30. Scallons, Elam	Tennessee
31. Scallons, John W[esley][12]	Tennessee
32. Simms, Thomas S.	Tennessee
33. Slack, Richard	Delaware
34. Trimble, Edward	Missouri
35. Veach, John	
36. Woods, Zadoc[k]	Tennessee

Prisoners[13]

	Native State	Occupation
1. Barkley, Richard A.	Tennessee	saddler
2. Bradley, John	New York	
3. Coltrin, William	Missouri	painter
4. Faison, Nathaniel W.	Tennessee	merchant
5. Kornegay, David Smith	North Carolina	farmer
6. Manton, Edward T.	New York	farmer
7. Morrell, Allen H. (boy)	Tennessee	
8. Robinson, Joseph C.	Missouri	farmer
9. Shaw, Joseph	Indiana	farmer
10. Trimble, William James		farmer

Prisoners-Wounded

1. Harrell, Milvern	Missouri
2. Higgerson, John	Ireland
3. MacCredae, John	Scotland
4. Patterson, W. D.	
5. Woods, Norman B.	Missouri

Escaped

1. Miller, Alsey S.
2. Woods, Henry Gonzalvo

[11] The name is listed in the *Telegraph and Texas Register*, Nov. 2, 1842, as "Mr. Price."

[12] The surname is listed in the *Telegraph and Texas Register* as "Scallions."

[13] Reported in *Civilian and Galveston Gazette*, Nov. 2, 1842. See also Nance (ed.), "Brigadier General Adrián Woll's Report of His Expedition into Texas in 1842," *Southwestern Historical Quarterly*, LVIII (1954–1955), 546; Schoen (ed.), *Monuments Erected by the State of Texas*, p. 93; Weyand and Wade, *An Early History of Fayette County*, pp. 155–156.

APPENDIX C

Troops Mustered Near San Antonio for the Somervell Expedition, November 1842[1]

Captain William M. Barrett's Co., 1st Reg^t of South Western Army
Col. Jos[eph] L. Bennett—From Octr 1st 1842 to Jany 1st 1843[2]

Names	Rank	Time	Date of Enlistment	Pay Due
W[illia]m M. Barrett	Capt.	90 days	Octr 1st 1842	
Isaac McGam	1st Lieut.		" " "	
Andrew Boyer	2nd Lieut.		" " "	
James Clark	1st Sergt.		" " "	
William Oliphant	2nd Do		" " "	
Joshua Robbins	3rd Do		" " "	
J. E. Payton	4th Do		[Oct.] 27th	
Thomas Lamb	1st Corpl.		Octr 1st 1842	

[1] Before the Somervell expedition could begin its march to the Río Grande, the companies that marched to the southwestern frontier and those that were formed there underwent several reorganizations. There were some transfers from one unit to another; and there were a number of desertions. The muster rolls reproduced here seem to be the only ones in existence today. They were the basis for the payment of claims for military service. All are copies or later certifications of company membership, and all are in manuscript. A few are in more than one copy and occasionally show slight variations in the spelling of names and in the listing of other detail, either because of carelessness in copying or because they were not always from a common source. The original rolls (or copies) which were forwarded by Somervell in November 1842, to Department of War and Marine seem not to have survived the fire that destroyed the Adjutant-General's Office in the early days of statehood.

The muster rolls for Captain William M. Eastland's Company, Captain William Ryon's Company, and Major John C. Hays' Spy Company for the period of the Somervell expedition have not been located. Rolls for Eastland's and Ryon's companies, as constituted on the Mier expedition, are available and will be reproduced in volume three of this work, but owing to the reorganization of the companies that went into the formation of the Mier expedition, it would be misleading to reproduce them here as rolls of the Somervell expedition.

While the general format of each muster roll has been preserved, the names of the men have been arranged in alphabetical order. The names at the end of a roll were additions to the rolls as originally drawn and have not been integrated into the main alphabetical listing but have been alphabetized within themselves.

[2] Copy in Sam S. Smith Collection, ms., and in Public Debt Papers (Texas), ms., of Andrew B. Hanna.

624

Henry Ford	2nd Corpl.	Octr 1st 1842
J. D. Murphy	3d Do	" " "
George Hunter	4th Do	" " "
Bird, W[illia]m	Private	" " "
Brown, Richard	"	" " "
Campbell, J. K.	"	" " "
Colvin, John	"	" " "
Crab, Lowery	"	" " "
Crowson, John	"	" " "
Curvin, Thomas	"	" " "
Darlin, Hugh	"	" " "
Davis, Madison	"	" " "
Dillard, W[illia]m M.	"	" " "
Ford, Craner	"	" " "
Fuller, Daniel	"	" " "
Gammon, J. G.	"	" " "
Goodman, G. C.	"	" " "
Gray, Michael	"	" " "
Gray, Pleasant	"	" " "
Hale, Harrison	"	" " "
Hamilton, John	"	" " "
Hampton, Hugh	"	" " "
Heath,, S. P.	"	[Oct.] 27th
Heath, W[illia]m	"	Octr 1st 1842
Hightower, R. D.	"	" " "
Hill, O. H. P.	"	" " "
Hobbs, P. H.	"	" " "
Holderfield, B.	"	" " "
Hunter, S. P.	"	" " "
Hunter, W[illia]m	"	" " "
Jourdon, John	"	" " "
Lauderdale, S. J.	"	" " "
Loler, Levi	"	" " "
McAdams, Geo[rge]	"	" " "
McBride, W[illia]m M.	"	" " "
McColum, T. J.	"	" " "
Nieley [Nealy?], John	"	" " "
Peetree, Peter	"	" " "
Pickern, Joseph	"	" " "
Plumer, L. T. M.	"	" " "
Randolph, P[erry]	"	" " "
Rector, W[illia]m	"	" " "
Roberts, Allen	"	" " "
Rockley, Wilson	"	" " "
Rorr, W[illia]m C.	"	" " "
Smith, Jackson	"	" " "

Names	Rank	Time	Date of Enlistment	Pay Due
Smith, S. R.	Private		Octr 1st 1842	
Steel, H.	"		" " "	
Templeton, A. W.	"		" " "	
Tippet, W[illia]m	"		" " "	
Visor, M. D.	"		" " "	
Visor, W. J.	"		" " "	
Walker, O. M. P.	"		" " "	
Walker, Robert	"		" " "	
Wells, Cretonden	"		" " "	
Wilson, James	"		" " "	
Withersby, W. A. D.	"		" " "	
Young, Pleasant	"		" " "	
Perkins, Aloni	"		" " "	

Mustered into service November 10th 1842 by Jos[eph] L. Bennett

Capt. Samuel Bogart's Co., 1st Reg^t South Western Army—Col. Ja[me]s R. Cook—From Septr 25th 1842 to Novr 15th 1843[3]

Names	Rank		Time	Date of Enlistment	Pay due
Samuel Bogart	R	Capt.		Sept. 25th 1842	
John M. Dickson	R	1st Lieut.		" " "	
S. B. Hendricks	R	2nd Do		" " "	
J. D. Giddings	R	1st Sergt.		" " "	
John Ashmore	R	2nd Do		" " "	
W. B. Cody		3d Do		" " "	
Rufus Charles	R	1st Corpl.		" " "	
Henry Day	R	2nd Corpl.		" " "	
Thomas Bailey	R	3d Corpl.		" " "	
Adams, H. A.	R	Private		" " "	
Atkinson, John	R	"		" " "	
Ayres, F. W.	R	"		Oct. 1st 1842	
Ayres, William P.	R	"		Oct. 1st 1842	
Barker, T. S.	R	"		" 1st 1842	
Bates, W[illia]m	R	"		" 1st 1842	

[3] Copy in Sam S. Smith Collection, ms. The letter "R" preceding the rank of the individual is written in pencil and indicates that the individual returned from the Río Grande with Somervell.

Bell, T[homas] W.	Private	Sept. 25th 1842
Bennett, S. G.	"	" " "
Brookshire, A. S.	R "	Oct. 1st 1842
Brown, W[illia]m (on furlough)	"	Oct. 17th 1842
Campbell, John	R "	" " "
Chamberlain, B. W.	"	Sept. 25th 1842
Cheek, B. S.	R "	" " "
Clemmons, L. C.	R "	" " "
Crawford, C. W.	"	" " "
Crawford, J. W.	"	Sept. 25th 1842
Dean, W. B.	"	Oct. 17th 1842
Dobson, T.	R "	" " "
Edney, N. J.	R "	" " "
Foster, J. W.	"	" " "
Gilleland, W[illia]m	"	" " "
Harbour, G. W.	R "	" " "
Kemp, E. H.	R "	" " "
Kinne, James	R "	Oct. 1st 1842
Knight, James	R "	" " "
Kuykendall, ——	"	Sept. 25th 1842
McDade, John A.	"	Oct. 17th 1842
McIntire, W[illia]m	R "	Sept. 25th 1842
Marshall, J. T.	"	" " "
Middleton, T. W.	"	Oct. 17th 1842
Mitchell, John	"	Sept. 25th 1842
Payne, John	"	Oct. 25th 1842
Price, Williamson	R "	Oct 17th 1842
Rutledge, T. P.	"	Sept. 25th 1842
Santy, W. A.	R "	Oct. 1st 1842
Sherwood, John E.	"	Sept. 25th 1842
Smith, T. J.	R "	Oct. 17th 1842
Stephens, John M.	"	Sept. 25th 1842
Stevenson, J. B.	R "	" " "
Stubling, J. A.	R "	" " "
Temple, W. A.	R "	" " "
Trimmier, John	R "	" " "
Trimmier, Tho[ma]s	"	Sept. 25th 1842
Walker, Edward	R "	Oct. 1st 1842
Woodward, W. H.	R "	Sept. 25th 1842
Young, Charles	R "	Oct. 1st 1842

Muster Roll dated Nov[r] 10th 1842
    Mustered by Ja[me]s R. Cook—Nov[r] 15th 1842
[added in pencil:]
H. H. Helfer	R
Tho[ma]s Hood	R
John Ivy	R
Dan R. Jones	R

Capt. William Bowen's Co., 1st Reg^t of South Western Army—Col. Jos[eph] L. Bennett—From Octr 1st 1842 to Jany 1st 1843[4]

Names	Rank	Time	Date of Enlistment	Pay due
[William Bowen]	[Capt.]	3 mos.	Oct. 1st 1842	
Richard S. Willis	1st Lieut.		[Oct.] 27th	
William McCoy	2nd Lieut.		Oct. 1st 1842	
Franklin Brigance	1st Sergt.		" " "	
G[eorge] W. Seaton	3d Sergt.		" " "	
Biggum [Benjamin] White	4th Sergt.		" " "	
M. L. Kinnard	1st Corpl.		" " "	
John Roan	2nd Corpl.		" " "	
T. K. Hadley	3d Corpl.		" " "	
Harry Brigance	4th Corpl.		" " "	
Arnold, Benjamin	Private		" " "	
Bader, E.	"		" " "	
Bird, Daniel	"		[Oct.] 27th	
Bowen, Adam R.	"		" "	
Brown, C. A.	"		Oct. 1st 1842	
Carter, Giles	"		" " "	
Carter, John	"		" " "	
Cummins, William	"		" " "	
Edwards, Eren	"		" " "	
Ellington, A. M.	"		[Oct.] 27th	
Ellington, Thomas	"		Oct. 1st 1842	
English, Levi	"		[Oct.] 27th	
Foller, J. B.	"		Oct. 1st 1842	
Foller, J[onathan] E.	"		" " "	
Fuqua, Henry	"		" " "	
Gilbert, John	"		" " "	
Gilbert, Joseph	"		" " "	
Gilbert, Robert	"		" " "	
Gilbert, Thomas	"		[Oct.] 27th	
Gower, George	"		Oct. 1st 1842	
Goodbre[a]d, Philip	"		" " "	
Grace, Morgan	"		" " "	
Gray, W. J.	"		" " "	
Hobbs, Robert	"		" " "	
Jackson, Joseph	"		" " "	
Jones, Peter	"		" " "	
Larison, Thomas	"		" " "	
Lloyd, Peter	"		" " "	
McGowan, Samuel	"		" " "	

[4] Copy in Sam S. Smith Collection, ms., and in Militia Rolls (Texas), ms., dated Adjutant General's Office, Austin, Texas, August 18, 1851, and certified by Captain William Bowen.

McGowan, William C.	Private	Oct. 1st 1842	
McGuffin, Samuel	"	" " "	
McKissack, McI. D.	"	" " "	
Mann, James E.	"	" " "	
Norad, William	"	" " "	
Ray, Robert	"	" " "	
Ringold, Thomas	"	[Oct.] 27th	
Robertson, E. P.	"	Oct. 1st 1842	
Sanders, Drury	"	[Oct.] 27th	
Sa[u]nders, Leonidas	"	Oct. 1st 1842	
Scott, J[ohn] A.	"	" " "	
Smith, William W.	"	" " "	
Stephens, J. B.	"	" " "	
Tumlinston [Tumlinson], John	"	" " "	
Vincent, Adam	"	" " "	
Walker, Joel	"	" " "	
Walker, Lewis	"	" " "	
West, Martin	"	[Oct.] 27th	
White, William	"	Oct. 1st 1842	
Zuber, William P.	"	" " "	

Mustered into service November 10th 1842 by Jos[eph] L. Bennett

Capt. Ewen Cameron's Co., 1st Reg^t of South Western Army— Col. Ja[me]s R. Cook[5]

Names	Rank	Time	Date of Enlistment	Pay due
E. Cameron	Capt.		Novr 12th 1842	
J. R. Baker	1st Lieut.		" " "	
A. A. Lee	2nd Do		" " "	
I. Canfield	Sergt.		" " "	
Adams, J.	Private		" " "	
Anderson, Geo[rge]	"		" " "	
Arthur, F.	"		" " "	
Bobo, L.	"		" " "	
Bray, F.	"		" " "	
Brennan, J.	"		" " "	
Brown, [H.]	"		" " "	
Callaghan, J^n	[in pencil:] Wounded at Salado. Since dead.			
Canty, J.	Private		Novr 12th 1842	
Cash, J. L.	"		" " "	
Chaves, A.	"		" " "	

[5] Copy in Sam S. Smith Collection, ms.

Names	Rank	Time	Date of Enlistment	Pay due
DeBow, S.	Private		Novr 12th 1842	
Dillon, J. T.	"		" " "	
Downs, Geo[rge] [N.]	"		" " "	
Egrey, C.	"		" " "	
Glasscock, J[ames] [A.]	"		" " "	
Harper, J.	"		" " "	
LaForge, A. B.	"		" " "	
Lewis, G[ideon]	"		" " "	
Lord, G[eorge]	"		" " "	
McClellan, S[amuel]	"		" " "	
McGrue, J.	"		" " "	
McKinnell, A[lexander]	"		" " "	
McMichen, J[ames] M.	"		" " "	
Maher, P[atrick]	"		" " "	
Mills, John	"		" " "	
Mills, Lawson	"		" " "	
Moody, J.	"		" " "	
Morehead, J. T.	"		" " "	
Murray, T.	"		" " "	
Neill [Nealy?], J.	"		" " "	
Parker, W. T.	"		" " "	
Ripley, W[illia]m	"		" " "	
Snook, J.	"		" " "	
Tatem, Tho[ma]s	"		" " "	
Thompson, W[illia]m	"		" " "	
Tower, I.	"		" " "	
Turner, R. W.	"		" " "	
Van Horn, W[illia]m H.	"		" " "	
Walker, A.	"		" " "	
Ward, W[illia]m	"		" " "	
Weeks, H. D.	"		" " "	
Wells, J. L.	"		" " "	
Whalen, H[enr]y	"		" " "	
Wheeler, T.	"		" " "	
White, A. E.	"		" " "	
White, F.	"		" " "	
Wilkinson, Ja[me]s	"		" " "	
Wilkinson, M.	"		" " "	
Cocke, J. D.	"		" " "	
Johnson, James	"		" " "	
Simmons, W[illia]m	"		" " "	

Muster Roll dated November 20th 1842
Mustered by Ja[me]s R. Cooke—same date

Capt. P. H. Coe's Co., 1st Reg[t] South Western Army— Col. Ja[me]s R. Cook[6]

Names	Rank	Time	Date of Enlistment	Pay due
P. H. Coe	Capt.		Oct. 17 1842	
R. D. Heek	1st Lieut.		" " "	
J. H. Tom	2nd Do		" " "	
H. C. McIntire	1st Sergt.		" " "	
John B. Duprey	2nd Do		" " "	
A. M. Tardy	3d Do		" " "	
Stewart Pipkin	4th Do		" " "	
W. P. Darby	1st Corpl.		" " "	
G. M. Buckman	2nd Do		" " "	
Borin, James	Private		" " "	
Borin, Mathew	"		" " "	
Bridgman, J. C.	"		" " "	
Clemmons, L.	"		" " "	
Cole, William A.	"		" " "	
Culbirth, Benjamin	"		" " "	
Ellis, John	"		" " "	
Ervin, Jordin A.	"		" " "	
Farral, Jesse	"		" " "	
Fuller, Ralph	"		" " "	
Graham, Joshua (A[cting] Q[uarter] M[aster])			" " "	
Greer, G. D.	Private		" " "	
Harrel[l], John	"		" " "	
Helfer, H. H.	"		" " "	
Herington, John	"		" " "	
Higgins, Thompson	"		" " "	
Higgins, W[illia]m A.	"		" " "	
Johnson, Jesse H.	"		" " "	
Lee, Nelson	"		" " "	
Leekin, Jeremiah	"		" " "	
Mitchel[l], J. W.	"		" " "	
Mory, Nelson	"		" " "	
Mullen, Peter	"		" " "	
Odum, R. P.	"		" " "	
Pepkin, W[illia]m	"		" " "	
Ransom, Thomas	"		" " "	
Tandy, W[illia]m M.	"		" " "	
Tarver, B. E.	"		" " "	
Tom, Alford	"		" " "	
Tom. Charles	"		" " "	

[6] Ibid.

Names	Rank	Time	Date of Enlistment	Pay due
West, George	Private		Oct. 17 1842	
Whitehead, Richard	"		" " "	
Winn, William	"		" " "	
Ervin, Thomas	"		" " "	
Evans, Wister	"		" " "	
Guinn, George	"		" " "	
Hackworth, W. W.	"		" " "	
Owcn, M. T.	"		" " "	
Pennington, Elijah	"		" " "	
Pennington, Elisha	"		" " "	
Pucket, R. R.	"		" " "	

Muster Roll dated November 20th 1842
Mustered by Ja[me]s R. Cook same date

Capt. William S. Fisher's Co.—2nd Reg^t South Western Army Col. Commanding[7]

Names	Rank	Time	Date of Enlistment	Pay due
William S. Fisher	Capt.			
Warren Wilkinson	1st Lieut.			
Claudius Buster	2nd Do			
A. C. Hyde	1st Sergt.			
W[illia]m A. Jackson	2nd Do			
Tho[ma]s Smith	3d Do			
W[illia]m Mitchell	4th Do			
Armstrong, James [C.]	Private			
Arnett, J. H.	"			
Biggs, S. W.	"			
Bonnell, G. W.	"			
Brenham, R. F.	"			
Burrus, A. F.	"			
Bush, George [W.]	"			
Calvert, James [H.]	"			
Connell, W[illia]m	"			
Crawford, R. M.	"			
Davis, Campbell	"			

[7] *Ibid.*

632

Edwards, L[eonidas]	Private
Hackstaff, S. L.	"
Harrison, W[illia]m H.	"
Hensley, Charles	"
Hensley, William	"
Humphrey, Benj[ami]n	"
Jones, John E.	"
Keene, Richard	"
Lester, Elias	"
Lock[er]man, Stanley	"
Matson, James	"
Millen, W. E.	"
Moore, L. P.	"
Ogden, J. M.	"
Ransom, Thomas	"
Shannon, John	"
Shaw, Jonathan	"
Simpson, James	"
Smith, Gabriel	"
Toops, John	"
Vaugh[a]n, J. L.	"
Webb, Tho[ma]s H.	"
Wilkinson, L.	"
Willis, J. W.	"
Wills, Benten	"

Muster Roll dated Nov[r] 9th 1842
Mustered by Ja[me]s R. Cook Nov[r] 15th 1842

Capt. M. G. McGuffin's Comp[y] Discharges Somervell Expedition 1842[8]

Names	Rank	Length of Service
M. G. McGuffin	Capt.	3 months
Alexander McBride	1st Lieut.	2 "
R. B. Martin	Ensign	2 "
Joseph I. [Q?] Worsham	Asst. Comm[y]	3 "
Sam[ue]l G. Clepper	Orderly Sergt.	3 "
W. H. Fowler	Aide or Clerk Co.	2 "
Bell, W[illia]m W.	Private	2 "
Fowler, Samuel	"	2 "
Gay, Geo[rge]	"	2 "
Henderson, F. K.	"	3 "
Mathews, James R.	"	Proof
Morris, John	"	2 months
Neal, Lewis	"	3 "
Pace, Richard E.	"	2 "
Pilkinton, Clinch	"	3 "
Shannon, Owen	"	2 "
Stewart, Cha[rle]s B.	"	2 "
Stewart, David	"	2 "
Tager, Richard	"	2 "
Uzzell, Elisha	"	2 "
Wade, J. M.	"	2 "
Weekly, George W.	"	2 "

Capt. John S. McNeel's [McNeill's] Co., 1st Reg[t] South Western Army[9]

Names	Rank	Time	Date of Enlistment
McNeel [McNeill], J. S.	R Capt.		Oct. 2nd 1842
M. A. Bryan	R 1st Lieut.		" " "
J. Sweeney	R 2nd Do		" " "
C. A. Clarke	1st Sergt.		" " "
O. C. Phelps	2nd Do		" " "
E. Dale	R 3d Do		" " "
K. K. Koontz	R 4th Do		" " "

[8] "Captain M. G. McGuffin's Comp[y] Discharges," [Somervell Expedition, 1842], Army Papers (Texas), ms.

[9] Copy in Sam S. Smith Collection, ms. The letter "R" preceding the rank of the individual is written in pencil and indicates that the individual returned from the Río Grande with Somervell.

Name		Rank	Date
Alexander, J. R.		Private	Oct. 2nd 1842
Anderson, J. S.	R	"	" " "
Austin, J.		"	" " "
Beesley, D. H. E.		"	" " "
Bell, J. H.	R	"	" " "
Bennet, C. H.		"	" " "
Berry, J.		"	" " "
Colville, T.		"	" " "
Dockrell, J.	R	"	" " "
Douglass, F. W.		"	" " "
Ernest, H.	R	"	" " "
Erwin, J.		"	" " "
Este, H. D.		"	" " "
Estis, J. B.	R	"	" " "
Fisk, F. G.	R	"	" " "
Fulkerson, A. H.	R	"	" " "
Hammekin, G. L.	R	"	" " "
Harvey, J.		"	" " "
Hueser, J. A.	R	"	" " "
Lewis, A. J.		"	" " "
Loonis, J.	R	"	" " "
Lusk, W. H.	R	"	" " "
Lynch, W. C. C.	R	"	" " "
Lyons, S. C.		"	" " "
McGinnis, J.	R	"	" " "
McNeel, D. B.	R	"	" " "
Miller, W.		"	" " "
Munson, M. S.	R	"	" " "
Norris, J. L.		"	" " "
Owens, J.		"	" " "
Pharr, A.	R	"	" " "
Phelps, V. H.		"	" " "
Reese, C. R.		"	" " "
Reese, W. E.		"	" " "
Scoby, A. W.		"	" " "
Scott, J.	R	"	" " "
Sinnickson, J. J.		"	" " "
Susemiski, J.	R	"	" " "
Susemiski, N. F.	R	"	" " "
Terry, W. T.	R	"	" " "
Walnut, J.	R	"	" " "
Ward, J.	R	"	" " "
Warren, T.		"	" " "
West, G.		"	" " "
Wilson, J. C.		"	" " "
Pullam, E. P.	R	"	" " "

Muster Roll dated November 20th 1842. Mustered by Ja[me]s R. Cook

Capt. Levi Manning's Co., 1st Reg[t] S. W. Army—Col. Jos[eph] L. Bennett—From Oct. 1st 1842 to Jan[y] 1st 1843[10]

Names	Rank	Time	Date of Enlistment	Pay due
Alsobrook, W[illia]m	Private	90 days	Oct. 1st 1842	
Ambrose, M.	1st Sergt.		Oct. 27th	
Ammons, Jesse	Private		Oct. 1st 1842	
Angling, Abram	3d Sergt.		" " "	
Do , Elija[h]	Private		" " "	
Do , John	"		" " "	
Baker, W. E.	"		" " "	
Boss, G. A.	"		" " "	
Bradl[e]y, John	"		" " "	
Brown, J. T.	"		" " "	
Clary, David	"		" " "	
Do , F. R.	"		" " "	
Dunham, R. H.	1st Lieut.		" " "	
Eubank, J. T.	Private		" " "	
Garan, Dan	"		" " "	
Grimes, Jacob	"		" " "	
Grubbs, F.	"		" " "	
Hannon, John	"		" " "	
Hedenberg, A. D.	"		" " "	
James, W[illia]m	"		" " "	
Jones, G. S.	4th Sergt.		" " "	
Levering, Henry	Private		" " "	
Loftis, G. W.	"		" " "	
Manning, Levi	Captain		" " "	
Miller, W[illia]m	Private		" " "	
Morris, W[illia]m	"		" " "	
Newton, Benj[ami]n	"		Nov. 27th 1842	
Owen, Anthony	"		Oct. 1st 1842	
Pinkney, T. S.	2nd Lieut.		" " "	
Raper, Dan[ie]l	Private		" " "	
Roberts, Tho[ma]s	"		" " "	
Shannon, John	"		" " "	
Slater, S. L.	"		" " "	
Smith, John	"		" " "	
Taylor, Nathan	"		" " "	
Tucker, Ed[ward]	"		" " "	
Vandirre, John	"		" " "	
Vaughn, John	"		" " "	
Votan, Brien	"		" " "	
Votan, Elija[h]	"		" " "	
White, J. W.	"		" " "	

Muster Roll dated Nov[r] 10th 1842
Mustered by Jos[eph] L. Bennett same date

[10] Copy in Sam S. Smith Collection, ms.; also see Public Debt Papers (Texas), ms., of John McGinley, and Army Papers (Texas), ms.

Capt. Isaac N. Mitchell's Co., 1st Reg^t of South Western Army— Col. James R. Cook—From Novr 11th 1842[11]

Names	Rank	Time	Date of Enlistment	Pay due
I. N. Mitchell	R Capt.		Novr 11th 1842	
J. H. Evetts	1st Lt.		" " "	
Alvin Nye	2nd Lt.		" " "	
J. H. Brown	R 1st Sergt.		" " "	
Bridger, Henry	Private		" " "	
Brown, J. D.	"		" " "	
Clark, E.	"		" " "	
Clark, G. W.	"		" " "	
Coates, William	"		" " "	
Cox, N. G.	"		" " "	
Ellis, W. L.	R "		" " "	
Greenwood, B. C.	R "		" " "	
Hancock, Francis	"		" " "	
Hopson, William	"		" " "	
Johnson, Robert	"		" " "	
Linn, Edward	R "		" " "	
Livergood, J. H.	"		" " "	
Millican, J.	"		" " "	
Millican, J. H.	"		" " "	
Millican, L.	R "		" " "	
Overton, D.	"		" " "	
Phillips, W. M.	R "		" " "	
Powell, W. S.	R "		" " "	
Price, J.	"		" " "	
Rector, L.	"		" " "	
Rountree, M. C.	R "		" " "	
Scott, Jonathan	R "		" " "	
Stapp, O. H.	R "		" " "	
Stapp, W. P.	"		" " "	
Stapp, W. W.	R "		" " "	
Stuterville, J. C.	R "		" " "	
Vandyke, W.	"		" " "	
Vess, William	"		" " "	
Walker, W.	"		" " "	
Walton, G. W.	"		" " "	
Young, James	"		" " "	
Young, W[illia]m	"		" " "	
Zumwalt, I. K.	"		" " "	
Ewes, John	"		" " "	
Smith, John P.	"		" " "	

Enlisted at La Baca & Washington   Date of Muster Roll—Novr 11th 1842
Mustered by Ja[me]s R. Cook—Novr 21st 1842

[11] Copy in Sam S. Smith Collection, ms. The letter "R" preceding the rank of the individual is written in pencil and indicates that the individual returned from the Río Grande with Somervell.

Capt. Clark L. Owen's Co. (I), 1st Reg[t] Volunteers—Col. James R. Cook—From ———— to ————[12]

Names	Rank	Time	Date of Enlistment	Pay due
Clark L. Owen	Capt.		Octr 19th 1842	
John T. Price	1st Lieut.		" " "	
John P. Borden	2nd Lieut.		" " "	
George Guthrie	1st Sergt.		" " "	
William Guthrie	2nd Sergt.		" " "	
James A. Sylvester	3d Sergt.		" " "	
James Peacock	4th Sergt.		" " "	
Alexander, Mathew	Private		" " "	
Bass, James	"		" " "	
Bray, Ferdinand	"		" " "	
Coleman, David	"		" " "	
Cooper, Campbell	"		" " "	
Creamer, Charles M.	"		" " "	
Deison, Gustavus	"		" " "	
Donnelly, C. C.	"		" " "	
Dunlap, Andrew J.	"		" " "	
Edwards, C. W.	"		" " "	
Edwards, W. C.	"		" " "	
Elliott, Jacob	"		" " "	
Ferrell, McAmy	"		" " "	
Friar, D. B.	"		" " "	
Friar, Edward	"		" " "	
Gleeson [Gleason], C. K.	"		" " "	
Gray, James W.	"		" " "	
Hall, George H.	"		" " "	
Heard, Stephen R.	"		" " "	
Hope, Thomas	"		" " "	
Hyland, Henry	"		" " "	
Lee, Lot	"		" " "	
McDonald, Daniel	"		" " "	
McNutt, Nicholas	"		" " "	
Martin, W[illia]m J.	"		" " "	
Menafee, [Menefee], Thomas	"		" " "	
Miller, Henry	"		" " "	
Moser [Mosier], Adam	"		" " "	
Pearce, Benjamin	"		" " "	
Porter, Asa	"		" " "	
Rockfeller, Peter	"		" " "	
Rogers, John A.	"		" " "	
Rogers, Joseph H.	"		" " "	

[12] Copy in Sam S. Smith Collection, ms.

Rozier, John T.	Private	Octr 19th 1842
Simons, Joseph T.	"	" " "
Smith, Leroy H.	"	" " "
Thurmond, Alfred [S.]	"	" " "
Trahern, George W.	"	" " "
Turnbull, James	"	" " "
Usher, Patrick	"	" " "
White, John T.	"	" " "
Willoughby, Robert	"	" " "
Woodson, Benjamin	"	" " "
Youngblood, Jesse	"	" " "

Muster Roll dated November 23rd 1842
Mustered by R. H. Dunham

Muster Roll of Capt. E. S. C. Robertson's Company D of the 2nd Regiment 1st Brigade Army of the Republic of Texas, Commanded by Lt. Col. J. L. McCrocklin from the 17th day of October 1842 (when last mustered) to the 10th day of November 1842. [Enrolled:] Oct. 17, 1842, at Independence[13]

No.	Names	Class	Remarks
1.	Allen, W. W.	2	AWOL
2.	Ashmore, John	1	AWOL
3.	Blakey, T. W.	1	present in person
4.	Carr, A. C.	2	AWOL
5.	Chappell, Robert	1	AWOL
6.	Clampet, Francis	1	personated by J. Bratton
7.	Clon, J. J.	2	AWOL
8.	Cockerill, John C.	2	AWOL
9.	Comes, M. N.	1	personated by George Elgin
10.	Conn, Hugh	2	AWOL
11.	Cooper, Thomas	1	present in person
12.	Covington, Charles	1	AWOL
13.	Dallas, Walter R.	2	present in person
14.	Dallas, William A.	2	AWOL
15.	Daniels, J. R.	2	AWOL
16.	Dix, John Sr.	2	AWOL

[13] Copy in Militia Rolls (Texas), ms.; also in Army Papers (Texas), ms., and in Sam S. Smith Collection, ms. The latter does not show the names of those listed "AWOL."

No.	Names	Class	Remarks
17.	Dix, John Sr. [sic]	2	AWOL
18.	Dobson, Tremere [Trimmier]	2	AWOL
19.	Duncan, George J.	2	present in person
20.	Dunham, Solomon	1	AWOL
21.	Edney, Newton	1	AWOL
22.	Farmer, Willis	2	AWOL
23.	Fleury, A. B.	1	AWOL
24.	Gee, Richard	1	present
25.	Hackworth, W.	1	present & transferred to Co. A
26.	Hale, Mason	2	AWOL
27.	Hox[e]y, Asa	2	personated by John Carter; transferred to Bennett's Reg^t
28.	Irion, Van R.	2	present
29.	Isbel, William	2	AWOL
30.	Ivy, John	1	present
31.	Jacobs, J. J.	1	personated by H. Williams
32.	Laroque, J. E.	1	AWOL
33.	Lee, Joel	1	personated by W. D. Houton [Houghton]
34.	Louis, W. L.	1	AWOL
35.	McDowell, G. A.	2	AWOL
36.	McDowell, Jonathan	1	AWOL
37.	Marsh, Shubal	2	AWOL
38.	Miller, Jacob	2	AWOL
39.	Milligin, Creed T.	2	AWOL
40.	Nelson, ——	2	AWOL
41.	Nevil, ——	1	AWOL
42.	Niles, J. W. J.	2	AWOL
43.	Norris, J. M.	2	present
44.	Page, Jefferson	1	AWOL
45.	Park, Moses	1	personated by J. Sneath
46.	Perkins, G. W.	1	AWOL
47.	Pierce, Carl	2	AWOL
48.	Pierce, Horatio	1	present
49.	Quin, Edmund	1	AWOL
50.	Rainey, Clement	1	AWOL
51.	Redding, ——	1	AWOL
52.	Rhodes, J[ohn] A.	1	AWOL
53.	Rice, J. P.	1	present
54.	Robinson, E.	1	AWOL
55.	Root, J. B.	2	personated by G. B. Harris
56.	Sanders, B. F.	1	AWOL
57.	Seward, John	2	AWOL
58.	Seward, Samuel	2	AWOL
59.	Shaw, Lot	2	personated by T. A. Thompson
60.	Smith, William	1	present

61. Taylor, Edw[ar]d W.	1	personated by H. Taylor
62. Waller, ——	2	AWOL
63. Whitesides, E. S.	2	present
64. Whitesides, G. W.	2	present
65. Willie, James	1	promoted adjutant
66. Willingham, Marion	1	AWOL
67. Wilson, W. C.	2	AWOL
68. Wyatt, B.	2	AWOL

Names of commissioned, non-commissioned officers, musicians, artificers, and privates present

1. E. S. [C.] Robertson	captain
2. G. W. Whitesides	1st lt. on furlough
3. W. R. Dallas	2nd lt.
4. William Smith	orderly sergeant
5. Richard Gee	2nd sergeant

1. Barnhill, P. A.	[privates]
2. Blakey, T. W.	
3. Boswell, R. B.	
4. Bratten, Joseph	detailed sergeant major
5. Clark, David	
6. Collette, John	
7. Cooper, Thomas	
8. Cuthbert, Benjamin	
9. Daniel, J.	
10. Duncan, G. J.	
11. Dunn, James	
12. Elgin, George	detailed
13. Finney, Robert	
14. Fuqua, S.	
15. Gentry, J. R.	
16. Gentry, T.	
17. Gentry, W. M.	
18. Greesham [Gresham], E. H.	
19. Harris, G. B.	
20. Houton [Houghton], W. D.	detailed to the Adjutant General's Office
21. Houston, A. D.	
22. Ivy, John	
23. Jackson, H. M.	
24. Karner, John	volunteer
25. Love, H.	
26. Lyon, P.	
27. McCaleb, Alson	
28. McCaleb, W. B.	
29. McFall, Samuel [C.]	
30. Norris, J. M.	detailed colour bearer
31. Oldham, T. S.	

641

32. Oldham, William
33. Osborn, J. M.
34. Pierce, H.
35. Re[a]vis, J. B.
36. Redden, J. J.
37. Rice, J. G.
38. Rice, J. P.
39. Rice, S.   on furlough
40. Ritchie, William
41. Roberts, C. M.
42. Smith, John   subs[titute] for Moses Park
43. Spence, A.
44. Taylor, H.
45. Thompson, T. A.
46. Welch, Robert C.   AWOL
47. Whitesides, E. S.
48. Williams, A. B.
49. Williams, H.   subs[titute] for J. J. Jacobs
50. Williams, J.
51. Williams, S.

I certify on honor that this muster roll exhibits the true state of Captain E. S. C. Robertson's Company D of the first Regiment of 2nd Brigade T. M. for the period herein mentioned; that that "Remarks" set opposite the name of each officer and soldier, are accurate and just; and that the "recapitulation" exhibits in every particular the true state of the company.   Date Novr 11th 1842
Station Camp Hope   (signed) E. S. C. Robertson
             Commanding the Company

I certify on honor, that I have carefully examined this Muster Roll and that I have this twentieth day of November 1842 mustered and minutely inspected the above named company of the First Regiment of the South Western Army.
          Jas. R. Cook
       Inspector and Mustering Officer

        Recapitulation
1 captain, 1 2nd lt., 2 sargts., 32 privates—34 total—36 aggregate
    extra duty 8 " 42 44
    sick   6 " 48 50
    furlough 4 " 52 53 [54?]

I, E. S. C. Robertson, Captain Commanding late Company D 1st Regiment 1st Brigade of the South Western Army of Texas certify, that the above and foregoing Roll is a correct copy of the original Roll on file in the Adjutant General's Office and that this copy is made out by me, as captain as aforesaid and countersigned by John Hemphill Adjutant General of the late South Western Army, to serve as a duplicate discharge, by which all of the members of said company who have lost their discharges and have not presented any claim before the 1st day of Sept. 1850, for said service may secure their pay for a tour of three months service according to their respective rank as given in this Roll and as Captain as aforesaid request that the

Auditor and Comptroller will proceed to audit and issue certificates of pay to all those who may not have presented their claims and hold said pay certificates subject to the order of the parties or their Legal Representatives. Given at the City of Austin this

30th day of August 1851
E. Sterling C. Robertson
Capt. Comp. D. 1st Reg^t
1st Brig^e S. W. Army

and I do further certify that all officers and soldiers marked Present on the above muster roll and not furloughed served either a three months tour or composed a part of the Mier Expedition.

Sept. 1st 1851
E. Sterling C. Robertson

Approved
  John Hemphill
    late Act^g Adj^t Genl
    S. W. Army

Capt. Jerome B. Robertson's Co., 1st Reg^t of South Western Army[14]

Names	Rank	Time	Date of Enlistment	Pay due
J. B. Robertson	Capt.		Octr 17th 1842	
J. A. Doak	1st Lieut.		″ ″ ″	
J. D. McKutchion [McCutchan]	2nd Lieut.		″ ″ ″	
F. W. T. Harrison	1st Sergt.		″ ″ ″	
D. B. Patterson	2nd Sergt.		″ ″ ″	
J. Hamilton	3d Sergt.		″ ″ ″	
F. T. Duffoe	4th Sergt.		″ ″ ″	
D. R. Hal[l]owell	1st Corpl.		″ ″ ″	
N. S. Outlaw	2nd Corpl.		″ ″ ″	
J. Cunningham	3d Corpl.		″ ″ ″	
J. C. Robertson	4th Corpl.		″ ″ ″	
Barney, D. F.	Private		″ ″ ″	
Berry, J. B.	″		″ ″ ″	
Brown, J. H.	″		″ ″ ″	
Brown, L.	″		″ ″ ″	
Brown, W. A.	″		″ ″ ″	
Cam[p]bell, ——	″		″ ″ ″	
Chamberlain, H.	″		″ ″ ″	
Chapman, A.	″		″ ″ ″	
Clark, D. H.	″		″ ″ ″	
Collins, J. M.	″		″ ″ ″	

[14] Copy in Sam S. Smith Collection, ms.

Names	Rank	Time	Date of Enlistment	Pay due
Cook, J[ames] R.	Private		Octr 17th 1842	
Cook, L. D.	"		" " "	
Cook, W. D.	"		" " "	
Davis, ——	"		" " "	
Early, T.	"		" " "	
Edwards, L.	"		" " "	
Forquhar, A.	"		" " "	
Franklin, J. R.	"		" " "	
Goodman, S.	"		" " "	
Harbour, C. [?]	"		" " "	
Herrington, J.	"		" " "	
Hood, T.	"		" " "	
Kign, D.	"		" " "	
Lahn, J.	"		" " "	
Lott, R. A.	"		" " "	
Lusk, P. H.	"		" " "	
McClusky, ——	"		" " "	
McInnkins, W[illia]m	"		" " "	
McMath, W. F.	"		" " "	
Moon, J.	"		" " "	
Nelson, T. [K.]	"		" " "	
Perry, S. W.	"		" " "	
Ridins, G. B.	"		" " "	
?Seben, E.	"		" " "	
Sensebaugh, T. J.	"		" " "	
Strickland, ——	"		" " "	
Waller, ——	"		" " "	
?Waltis, M.	"		" " "	
Williamson, ——	"		" " "	
Witherspoon, J.	"		" " "	
Wooldridge, T.	"		" " "	
Ferman, A.	"		" " "	
Finney, R.	"		" " "	

24 absent without leave

Muster Roll dated Novr 21st 1842
Mustered into service by R. H. Dunham

Capt. Bartlett Sims' Co.—Reg^t South Western Army—Col. Ja[me]s R. Cook—From Octr 26th to Novr 21st 1842[15]

Names		Rank	Time	Date of Enlistment
Bartlett Sims	R	Capt.		Oct. 26th 1842
George Allen	R	1st Lieut.		" " "
Mark M. Rogers		2nd Do		" " "
L. P. Sullivan	R	1st Sergt.		" " "
G. M. Moppen		2nd Do		" " "
Edward Turner		3d Do		" " "
Alley, George W.		Private		" " "
Anderson, Francis	R	"		" " "
Barber, James		"		" " "
Bissell, Theodore		"		" " "
Bo[w]man, P. F.		"		" " "
Brite, Thomas	R	"		" " "
Buckman, Oliver		"		" " "
Clark, Henry W.		"		" " "
Clopton, W[illia]m A.		"		" " "
Coffman, E. G.		"		" " "
Davies, William		"		" " "
Dunbar, William		"		" " "
Dunn, J. G.	R	"		" " "
Dunn, Tho[ma]s	R	"		" " "
Fort, W. D.	R	"		" " "
Gibson, W[illia]m		"		" " "
Hancock, G. D.	R	"		" " "
Herrens, John H.	R	"		" " "
Holderman, A. S.		"		" " "
Holton, W. S.		"		" " "
Hudson, David		"		" " "
Love, Robert	R	"		" " "
Nichols, Q. J.	R	"		" " "
Rogers, Silas L.	R	"		" " "
Sargent, Carter		"		" " "
Do , William		"		" " "
Smith, Donal[d]		"		" " "
Stephens, J. S.		"		" " "
Tanney, John		"		" " "
Ury, James		"		" " "
Warnock, B. F.	R	"		" " "
Williams, Levi		"		" " "

Muster Roll dated Novr 21st 1842
Mustered by Ja[me]s R. Cook same date

[added in pencil]:

Hunt, M. M.	R
Moppen, Garritt	R
Smith, E. H.	R

[15] *Ibid.* The letter "R" preceding the rank of the individual is written in pencil and indicates that the individual returned from the Río Grande with Somervell.

Capt. Gard[i]ner Smith's Co., Reg[t] South Western Army—Col. Ja[me]s R. Cook—From ——— to Nov[r] 12th 1842[16]

Names		Rank	Time	Date of Enlistment
Gard[i]ner Smith		Capt.		
Tho[ma]s S. Lubbock		1st Lieut.		
Eph[raim] M. Haines	R	2nd Do		
Lewis B. Harris	R	1st Sergt.		
James Pierpont		2nd Do		
Henry Kuykendall	R	3d Do		
Joseph Baker	R	4th Do		
George Ingram	R	1st Corpl.		
James Munroe		2nd Do		
William Wilson		3d Do		
Antonio Erhart		4th Do		
Allen, David		Private		
Atwood, W[illia]m		"		
Badger, James D.	R	"		
Benzano, Edw[ar]d		"		
Brann, James	R	"		
Bryan[t], Barney		"		
Callender, S[idney] [S.]		"		
Cochran, John	R	"		
Cocke, James D.		"		
Copeland, Willis		"		
Cronican, Michael		"		
Davis, Daniel		"		
Doughterty, ———	R	"		
Evans, W[illia]m G.		"		
Ewing, John	R	"		
Floyt, John T.		"		
Gattis, D. H.		"		
Higgins, W[illia]m G.	R	"		
James, Madison		"		
Lindsey, Charles	R	"		
Loftis, Charles		"		
Lowery, James P.	R	"		[penciled in:] Capt.
McCauley, Malcolm		"		
Maltby, T. D.		"		
Miner, Joel	R	"		
Moore, James		"		
Needham, W[illia]m		"		
Pennington, James		"		
Pierpont, W[illia]m		"		
Pilley, [M.] Robert		"		

[16]*Ibid.*

Raymond, Daddy [*sic*]   Private
Rice, Sanford   "
Roberts, Henry H.   "
Southmazd, John A.   R   "
Sweezy, John   "
Toliver, George W.   "

Muster Roll dated Novr 12th 1842
  Mustered by Ja[me]s R. Cook Novr 20th 1842

[added in pencil]:
  Drumond [?], James   R
  Jones, Eben C.   R
  Waring, Tho[ma]s   R
  Wilson, W. N.   R

Capt. Richard Williams' Co., 1st Reg^t S. W. Army— Col. Jos[eph] L. Bennett[17]

Names	Rank	Time	Date of Enlistment	Pay due
Richard Williams	Capt.	3 mos.	Octr 1st 1842	
W[illia]m R. Marsh	1st Lieut.		" " "	
Almerene Lacy	2nd Do		" " "	
Nutes Elkins	1st Sergt.		" " "	
Jesse Johnson	2nd Do		" " "	
John Redding	3d Do		" " "	
Robert Redding	4th Do		" " "	
James Winters	1st Corpl.		" " "	
Jackson Crouch	2nd Do		" " "	
J. L. Ridgeway	3d Do		" " "	
Tho[ma]s M. Bizzell	4th Do		" " "	
Alphin, S[amuel] G.	Private		" " "	
Alston, H[enry]	"		" " "	
Baker, J[ohn]	"		" " "	
Click, G. W.	"		" " "	
Cude, James	"		" " "	
Daniels, B.	"		" " "	
Day, Larkin	"		" " "	
Elkins, James	"		" " "	
Franks, B.	"		" " "	

[17] Copy in Sam S. Smith Collection, ms.; see also "Capt. R. Williams' Company Discharges," [Somervell Expedition, 1842], Army Papers (Texas), ms.

Names	Rank	Time	Date of Enlistment	Pay due
Hollis, D[avid]	Private		Oct' 1st 1842	
Houston, D[avid]	"		" " "	
Hulone, W[illia]m	"		" " "	
Irvin, B. F.	"		" " "	
Irvin, Peter	"		" " "	
Kellet, T[homas] J.	"		" " "	
Kelton, R[obert]	"		" " "	
Langhum, B. B.	"		" " "	
Langhum, Cha[rle]s	"		" " "	
Long, J. H.	"		" " "	
McCreary, J.	"		" " "	
McGary, W[illia]m	"		" " "	
Morrow, A. M.	"		" " "	
O'Bannon, J.	"		" " "	
Owens, P. W.	"		" " "	
Park, J[ohn]	"		" " "	
Roark, J[ohn] A.	"		" " "	
Robison, Daniel	"		" " "	
Russell, J.	"		" " "	
Sellers, W. [Henry]	"		" " "	
Shepperd, Jacob	"		" " "	
Slaymen, James	"		" " "	
Smith, Jesse	"		" " "	
Tabor, Hudson	"		" " "	
Tolbert, E[lijah]	"		" " "	
Ware, William	"		" " "	
Whitehead, Henry	"		" " "	
Winters, B[enjamin]	"		" " "	
Do , G. F.	"		" " "	
Do , Willis	"		" " "	
Wood, J. H.	"		" " "	
Do , W. H.	"		" " "	
Young, Geo[rge]	"		" " "	
Dockery, M.	"		" " "	

Muster Roll dated November 10th 1842
Mustered by —— same date

Capt. Zac[c]heus Wilson's Co., 1st Reg[t] of South Western Army, Col. Jos[eph] L. Bennett—From Oct[r] 1st 1842 to Jan[y] 1st 1843[18]

Names	Rank	Time	Date of Enlistment	Pay due
Zac[c]heus Wilson	Capt.	3 mos.	Oct. 1st 1842	
A. Hanna	1st Lieut.		" " "	
A. Vaughn	2nd Lieut.		" " "	
J. Lee	1st Sergt.		" " "	
J. Dean	2nd Do		[Oct.] 27th	
John Rector	3d Do		Oct. 1st 1842	
J. M. Fowler	4th Do		" " "	
T. P. Plaster	1st Corpl.		" " "	
N. G. Bynum	2nd Do		" " "	
J. N. Jones	3d Do		" " "	
John McMillion	4th Do		" " "	
Alexander, C. C.	Private		" " "	
Brimberry, Alford	"		" " "	
Brimberry, Samuel	"		" " "	
Burch, John	"		" " "	
Copeland, Richard	"		" " "	
Cummings, W.	"		" " "	
French, B.	"		" " "	
Gray, William	"		" " "	
Hill, Charles	"		" " "	
Hill, Samuel	"		[Oct.] 27th	
Jones, C. C.	"		Oct. 1st 1842	
Jones, James	"		" " "	
King, R. B.	"		" " "	
Kirby, George	"		" " "	
Kirby, John	"		" " "	
Martin, John	"		" " "	
Middleton, W. B.	"		" " "	
Poe, George	"		" " "	
Preston, S. S.	"		" " "	
Ramsdale, D.	"		" " "	
Reason, James (Blacksmith)	"		" " "	
Reaves, S. P.	"		" " "	
Rock, Charles	"		" " "	
Shaw, G. C.	"		" " "	
Stringfield, M. R.	"		[Oct.] 27th	
White, Headley	"		Oct. 1st 1842	
Wright, Calvin	"		" " "	

Mustered November 10th 1842 by Jos[eph] L. Bennett

[18] Copy in Sam S. Smith Collection, ms

Capt. Israel Worsham's Co. Discharges Somervell Expedition 1842[19]

Names	Rank	Length of Service
Irsael Worsham	Capt.	3 months
Thomas B. Rankin	1st Lieut.	Do
Hezekiah S. Arnold	2nd "	2 months

[19] "Captain Israel Worsham's Company Discharges," [Somervell Expedition, 1842], Army Papers (Texas), ms.

BIBLIOGRAPHY

A. *Primary Sources*

    1. PUBLIC DOCUMENTS
        a. MANUSCRIPTS
        b. PRINTED MATERIAL
    2. PRIVATE PAPERS, LETTERS, AND MEMOIRS
        a. MANUSCRIPTS AND TYPESCRIPTS
        b. PRINTED MATERIAL
    3. MAPS
    4. NEWSPAPERS

B. *Secondary Sources*

    1. MANUSCRIPTS AND TYPESCRIPTS
    2. PRINTED MATERIAL
        a. BOOKS
        b. ARTICLES AND PERIODICALS

BIBLIOGRAPHY

A. *Primary Sources*

1. PUBLIC DOCUMENTS

a. MANUSCRIPTS

Alabama. Military State Register. *See* Military State Register (Alabama).
Arista, Mariano. "Proceso institutido contra los extranjeros Victor Lupín y Benito Watman acusados de haber tomado armas contra el gobierno de la Republica. Marzo 26 de 1840." Archivo de la Secretaría de Gobierno, Saltillo, Coahuila, Vol. XLI, Exp. Núm. 1360, Legájo Núm. 34 (1839–1842). Transcript in Archives Collection, University of Texas Library.
Army Papers (Texas). Texas State Archives.
Barker, [Eugene C.]. Transcripts from Archivo de la Secretaría de Relaciones Asuntos Varios Comercio. *See* Relaciones Exteriores Asuntos Varios Comercio...
—. Transcripts from Archivo de la Secretaría de Relaciones Exteriores Reseñas Politicas. *See* Relaciones Exteriores Reseñas Politicas...
Bills. *See* Texas Congress. Bills...
City Records (Matamoros), Vols. 1–57 (1811–1859). Photostats in Archives Collection, University of Texas Library.
Claim Papers (Texas). *See* Miscellaneous Claim Papers (Texas).
Comptroller's Military Service Records (Texas). Texas State Archives.
Congressional Papers (Texas). *See* Texas Congress. Congressional Papers.
Consular Correspondence (Texas), 1838–1875. Texas State Archives.
Consular Dispatches (United States), 1837–1848 (Matamoros). Microfilm in Archives Collection, University of Texas Library.
Consular Letters (Texas), 1835–1844. Microfilm in Archives Collection, University of Texas Library.
Correspondence and Reports of American Agents and Others in Texas, 1836–1845. *See* Smith, Justin H. "Transcripts"...
Domestic Correspondence (Texas), 1835–1846. Texas State Archives.
Domestic Correspondence (Texas), undated. Texas State Archives.
Executive Documents (Texas). *See* Record of Executive Documents...; Executive Records...

Executive Records, of the Second Term of General Sam Houston's Administration of the Government of Texas, December 1841–December 1844. Texas State Archives.

"Expediente sobre la creación de una junta patriotica en esta capital para colectar donativos para la guerra de Téjas, Julio 30 de 1842." Archivo de la Secretaría de Gobierno, Saltillo, Coahuila, Exp. Núm. 1360 (1842), Legájo Núm. 34 (1839–1842). Photostat in Archives Collection, University of Texas Library.

Foreign Letters (Texas). *See* State Department (Texas). Foreign Letters, 1842–1844.

Fort Bend County Probate Court. *See* Records of the Probate Court, Fort Bend County, Texas.

Galveston, Texas. *See* Records of the Proceedings . . . at Galveston . . .

Galveston Hussar Cavalry Company. Papers, 1842. Rosenberg Library, Galveston, Texas.

General Land Office Records (Texas). General Land Office, Austin, Texas.

Hussar Company. *See* Galveston Hussar Cavalry Company.

"Journal A, Records of the City of San Antonio." *See* San Antonio.

Land Office Records (Texas). *See* General Land Office Records (Texas).

Legation Records (Texas). *See* State Department (Texas). Legation Records, May 1839–Aug. 1844.

"Manuscript Record Book Containing the Minutes of the Citizens Committee for the Defense of Galveston, 1842." (Title on cover: "Record of Jury Certificates issued by the Clerk of the District Court as per His Certificates of File.") Minutes in the handwriting of Gail Borden, Jr. Rosenberg Library, Galveston, Texas.

Matamoros City Records. *See* City Records (Matamoros).

Memorials and Petitions (Texas). Texas State Archives.

Messages of the Presidents. *See* Texas Congress. Congressional Papers; Executive Records . . .

Military State Register (Alabama). Military Division, Alabama State Department of Archives and History.

Militia Rolls (Texas). Texas State Archives.

Miscellaneous Claim Papers (Texas). Texas State Archives.

Muster Rolls (Rangers). *See* Texas Rangers.

Petitions. *See* Memorials and Petitions (Texas).

President (Texas). *See* Executive Records . . .; Proclamations of the Presidents (Texas); Record of Executive Documents . . .

Proclamations of the Presidents (Texas). Texas State Archives.

Public Debt Papers (Texas). Texas State Archives.

Rangers (Texas). *See* Texas Rangers.

Receipt Rolls (Rangers). *See* Texas Rangers.

"Record Book of the General & Special Orders and Letters of the South Western Army, November 1842[–January 1843], A." Manuscript Division, New York Public Library.

Record of Executive Documents from the 10th December 1838 to the 14th December 1841. Texas State Archives.

Record of the Proceedings and Acts of the Commissioners to Conduct the Fortifications at Galveston Under the Act Entitled an Act for the Protection of the Sea Coast [January 14, 1843], March 3, 1843–Aug. 2, 1843. Title on cover: "Record of Jury Certificates issued by the Clerk of the District Court as per His Certificates of File." Records are in the handwriting of Gail Borden, Jr. Rosenberg Library, Galveston, Texas.

Records of the Probate Court, Fort Bend County, Texas. County Courthouse, Richmond, Texas.

"Relaciones Exteriores Asuntos Varios Comercio Estados Unidos, 1825–1849," Barker Transcripts from the Archivo de la Secretaría. Archives Collection, University of Texas Library.

"Relaciones Exteriores Reseñas Politicas, 1841–1842. Estados Unidos 1842," Barker Transcripts from the Archivo de la Secretaría. Archives Collection, University of Texas Library.

Republic of Texas Papers. *See* Texas Republic Papers, 1835–1846.

San Antonio. "Journal A, Records of the City of San Antonio." Typescript in Archives Collection, University of Texas Library.

Smith, Justin H. "Transcripts," Vol. V. Latin American Collection, University of Texas Library.

Somervell, A. *See* "Record Book of the General & Special Orders and Letters of the South Western Army, November 1842[–January 1843], A."

State Department (Texas). Foreign Letters, 1842–1844. Texas State Archives.

—. Legation Records, May 1839–Aug. 1844. Microfilm copy in Texas A&M University Library, from original in Texas State Archives.

—. Department of State Letterbook, No. I (November 1836–January 1842). Texas State Archives.

—. Department of State Letterbook, Home Letters, II (1842–1846). Texas State Archives.

—. State Department Records, Book 3. Texas State Archives.

Texas. Army Papers. *See* Army Papers (Texas).

—. Claim Papers. *See* Miscellaneous Claim Papers (Texas).

—. Comptroller's Military Service Records. *See* Comptroller's Military Service Records (Texas).

—. Consular Correspondence. *See* Consular Correspondence (Texas), 1838–1875.

—. Consular Letters. *See* Consular Letters (Texas), 1835–1844.

—. Domestic Correspondence. *See* Domestic Correspondence (Texas), 1835–1846.

—. Executive Documents. *See* Record of Executive Documents . . .; Executive Record . . .; Proclamations of the President (Texas).

—. General Land Office. *See* General Land Office (Texas).

—. Memorials and Petitions. *See* Memorials and Petitions (Texas).
—. Militia Rolls. *See* Militia Rolls (Texas); Texas Rangers.
—. Presidential Records. *See* Executive Records . . . ; Proclamations of
 the President (Texas); Record of Executive Documents . . .
—. Public Debt Papers. *See* Public Debt Papers (Texas).
Texas Congress. Bills, 7th Congress of Texas. Texas State Archives.
—. Congressional Papers. Texas State Archives.
Texas Rangers. Muster Rolls, 1830–1860. Texas State Archives.
—. Receipt Rolls, 1830–1860. Texas State Archives.
Texas Republic Papers, 1835–1846. Archives Collection, University of
 Texas Library.
Texas State Department. *See* State Department (Texas).
United States Consular Dispatches. *See* Consular Dispatches (United
 States).

b. PRINTED MATERIAL

Adams, Ephraim D. (ed.). *British Diplomatic Correspondence Concerning the Republic of Texas, 1836–1846.* Austin, Texas: Texas State
 Historical Association, 1917.
—. (ed.). "Correspondence from the British Archives Concerning Texas,
 1837–1848," in *Quarterly of the Texas State Historical Association,*
 XV–XXI (1911–1918).
Ampudia, Pedro de. *El General Comandante de las armas á los habitantes
 de Tamaulipas.* [Text begins]: "Compatriotas. Los perfidos cuanto
 ingratos tejanos reunidos en masa se abanzan hacia esta plaza con la
 decidida intención de atacarnos, y de elevar la guerra y la devastación
 del pais hasta donde puedan." [Dated and signed at end:] Matamoros,
 Abril 17 de 1842. Pedro de Ampudia. [At end:] Impreso por Antonio
 Castañeda en la 1ª Calle de Michoacán. [Matamoros: 1842]. Broadside. Copy in Archives Collection, University of Texas Library.
Andrade, Juan José. *Documentos que públíca sobre la Evacuación de la
 ciudad de San Antonio de Béjar del Departamento de Téjas a sus compatriotas.* Monterey: Imprenta de Nivel, 1836.
Arista, Mariano. "To Mr. Mirabeau Lamar, Lampazos [Mexico], April
 21, 1841 (confidential)," in *Quarterly of the Texas State Historical
 Association,* VII (1903–1904), 173–174.
Binkley, William C. (ed.). *Official Correspondence of the Texan Revolution, 1835–1836.* 2 vols. New York: D. Appleton & Company, Inc.,
 1936.
Bolton, H. E. (ed.). "Tienda de Cuervo's Ynspección of Laredo, 1757,"
 in *Quarterly of the Texas State Historical Association,* VI (1902–
 1903), 187–203.
Brandt, Mrs. B. *See* Taylor, Virginia H.
Burleson, Edward. *To the Public* [being an Address of General Edward
 Burleson to his "Fellow-Citizens of Texas!"] dated April 6, 1842; followed by a letter from him to Brigadier General A. Somerville (*i.e.,*

Somervell) and Somervell's reply, both dated San Antonio, March 31, 1842; and ending with Burleson's address disbanding the volunteers under his command, dated Alamo, San Antonio de Béxar, April 2, 1842 [Houston? *Telegraph* Office? 1842]. Broadside. Copy in Southern Historical Collection, University of North Carolina Library, Chapel Hill, North Carolina.

Castañeda, Carlos E. (trans.). *The Mexican Side of the Texan Revolution [1836]: By the Chief Mexican Participants* . . . Translated with Notes by Carlos E. Castañeda. Dallas, Texas: P. L. Turner Co., 1928.

Chalmers, John G. *See* Texas Treasury Department. *Annual Report of Treasurer* . . .

Chapman, W[illiam] W. *Report of exploration of the Rio Grande, made by H. Love, in the Keel-Boat Major Babbitt. . . . Navigation of the River, Military Posts, Soil, Products, etc.* (In *The Coast Depot and Shipping Port of the Valley of the Rio Grande* . . . New York: Pudney & Russell, printers, 1850. pp. 15–23.)

Civilian [and Galveston Gazette]—Extra, Monday, March 21, 1842. Address from the committee of safety of Matagorda "To the Citizens (of) the Eastern Counties," telling of the approach of the Mexican army and appealing for help, signed by M. Talbott, Chief Justice, Chairman, and eight others, and dated Matagorda, March 19, 1842. Text begins, "The following reached us this morning by Mr. S. Mussina, who left Matagorda at noon on Saturday . . . ." [Galveston, Texas: *Civilian and Galveston Gazette* Office, 1842]. Broadside. Copy in Thomas W. Streeter Collection, Yale University Library.

Coast Depot and Shipping Port of the Valley of the Rio Grande, and the Provinces of Mexico Tributary Thereto, with the Government Map of that Region of Country, published in 1850, together with the Report of the Explorations of the Rio Grande, The. New York: Pudney & Russell, printers, 1850.

Committee of Vigilance. *See* Houston Committee of Vigilance.

Congress (Texas). *See* Texas Congress.

Connor, Seymour V. (ed.). *Texas Treasury Papers: Letters Received in the Treasury Department of the Republic of Texas, 1836–1846.* 3 vols. Austin: Texas State Library, 1955.

Emory, William H. *Report on the United States and Mexican Boundary Survey, Made under the Direction of the Secretary of the Interior.* 3 vols. Washington, D. C.: Cornelius Wendell, printer, 1857.

Eve, Joseph. *See* Nance, Joseph Milton (ed.).

Everett, Edward. "Report on Indians on Mexican Territory," in Secretary E. Everett, "Transmitting Correspondence with Mexican Minister Relative to the Encroachment of the Indians of the United States upon the Territories of Mexico." *U. S. Senate Executive Documents* no. 14 (Serial No. 660, Vol. III), 32nd Congress, 2nd Session.

Galveston Artillery Company. *The Charter and Constitution of the Galveston Artillery Company, Organized Sept. 13th, 1840.* [Galveston, Texas]: Printed by S. Bangs, *Galveston Chronicle* Office [1842?]. 8

pp. Copies in Rosenberg Library, Galveston, Texas, and Barker Texas History Center, University of Texas Library.

Gammel, H. P. N. (ed.). *Laws of Texas.* 10 vols. Austin, Texas: The Gammel Book Co., 1898.

Garrison, George P. (ed.). *Diplomatic Correspondence of Texas,* in *Annual Report of the American Historical Association,* 1907, Vol. II; 1908, Vol. II, pts. 1–2. Washington, D.C.; Government Printing Office, 1908–1911. This work will be cited in the present study as "1907, I," "1908, II," and "1908, III."

General Orders. See Jackson, Alden A. M.; Texas War Department.

Harris County. *See* Houston Committee of Vigilance.

Hockley, George W. [Proclamation of George W. Hockley, Secretary of War and Navy, dated Austin, March 7, 1842, beginning:] "The force of the enemy at Bexar and Goliad is ascertained: it should not create alarm or panic. . . ." [Austin, Texas: *Austin City Gazette* Office, 1842]. Broadside. Copy in Texas State Archives.

—. *See also* Texas War Department. *Report of the Secretary of War and Marine . . .*

Houston, Sam. *Address of the President of the Republic to the People of Texas,* [Executive Department, City of Houston, April 14, 1842]. [Houston, Texas:] Houstonian Press, [1842]. 8 pp. Copy in Barker Texas History Center, University of Texas Library.

—. *Letter of Gen. Houston to Santa Anna, together with the letter of the latter written at Orozimbo, in 1836, and the Veto Message of President Houston, delivered to the First Congress at Columbia.* Houston, Texas: Telegraph Power Press, [1842]. 8 pp. Copy in Barker Texas History Center, University of Texas Library.

—. *By the President of the Republic of Texas. A Proclamation.* [Calling the regular session of the Seventh Congress to meet at Washington, Texas, instead of at Austin, on December 5, 1842. Dated at end: November 21, 1842, and signed:] By the President, Sam Houston, Anson Jones, Secretary of State. [Washington, Texas: *Texian and Brazos Farmer* Office, 1842]. 4 page folder printed on page [1]. Copy in Rosenberg Library, Galveston, Texas.

—. *By the President of the Republic of Texas. A Proclamation.* [Calling for special session of Congress to meet at Houston on June 27, 1842. Dated at end, Houston, May 24, 1842, and signed:] Sam Houston. By the President: Anson Jones, Secretary of State. [Houston, Texas: 1842]. 4 page folder printed on p. [1]. Photostat in Barker Texas History Center, University of Texas Library.

—. *President's Message. Printed by order of the House of Representatives.* Houston, Texas: Telegraph Power Press, [1842]. 4 pp. Copy in Masonic Grand Lodge of Texas Library, Waco, Texas.

—. *Veto Message of the President of the Republic of Texas to the Bill "Authorizing Offensive War Against Mexico and for Other Purposes."* [Dated:] Executive Department, City of Houston, July 22d, 1842.

Bibliography

Houston, Texas: Telegraph Press [1842]. 4 pp. Copy in Houston Public Library, Houston Texas.

Houston Committee of Vigilance. [Report of Public Meeting beginning:] "At a large meeting of the citizens of Harris County, assembled at the Court House this afternoon, in pursuance of a call from the Committee of Vigilance and Safety. . . . Houston City, March 15, 1842." [Headed] *The Houstonian.* Extra. March 15, 5 o'clock P.M. [Signed:] Barnard E. Bee, Chairman. J. W. Pitkin, Secretary. [Following it is a short letter from Houston to the committee dated: Houston City, March 15, 1842.] [Houston: *Houstonian* Office, 1842]. Broadside. Copy in Texas State Archives.

Houstonian Extra, The. March 15, [1842,] 11 o'clock A.M. [Text begins:] "The Austin mail arrived this morning. . . ." [Publishes a report on the progress of the Mexican invasion followed by an order from Sam Houston, to Brig. Gen. E. Morehouse, dated March 15, 1842, an order from Morehouse to his troops of the same date, and a proclamation of George W. Hockley to the public dated March 7, 1842.] [Houston, Texas: *Houstonian* Office, 1842]. Broadside. Copy in Texas State Archives.

Jackson, Alden A. M. *Attention Head-Quarters, 4th Regiment, 2d Brigade, Texas Militia, Galveston, Oct. 23, 1842, Order No. 30.* [Text begins:] "In obedience to a special order of this date from Col. George W. Hockley, commanding on Galveston Island, this Regiment will be mustered into the service of the Republic on Tuesday the 25th inst. . . . " [At end:] By order of Alden A. M. Jackson, Col. Commanding. C. G. Bryant, Act. Adj. [Galveston: 1842]. Broadside. Copy in Texas State Archives.

Jones, Anson. *Memoranda and Official Correspondence Relating to the Republic of Texas, Its History and Annexation—Including a Brief Autobiography of the Author.* New York: D. Appleton & Company, Inc., 1859.

Laws Passed by the Sixth Congress of the Republic of Texas: Published by Authority. Austin, Texas: S. Whiting, Public Printer, 1842.

Manning, William R. (ed.). *Diplomatic Correspondence of the United States: Inter-American Affairs,* Vol. 8. Washington, D.C.: Government Printing Office, 1937.

Milam Guards (Houston). *Constitution and By-Laws of the Milam Guards: Established August, 1838.* Houston, Texas: Telegraph Power Press, 1839. 11 pp. Copy in Barker Texas History Center, University of Texas Library.

Nance, Joseph Milton (trans. and ed.). "Brigadier General Adrián Woll's Report of his Expedition into Texas in 1842," in *Southwestern Historical Quarterly,* LVIII (1954–1955), 523–552.

—. (ed.). "A Letter Book of Joseph Eve, United States Chargé d'Affaires to Texas," in *Southwestern Historical Quarterly,* XLIII (1939–1940), 196–221, 365–377, 486–510; XLIV (1940–1941), 96–116.

659

Santa Anna, Antonio López de. *Manifesto Relative to His Operations in the Texas Campaign and His Capture,* translated by Carlos E. Castañeda, in *The Mexican Side of the Texas Revolution [1836]: By the Chief Mexican Participants.* . . . Dallas, Texas: P. L. Turner Co., 1928.

Smither, Harriet (ed.). *Journals of the Fourth Congress of the Republic of Texas.* 3 vols. in 1. Austin, Texas: Von Boeckmann-Jones Co., 1931.

—. *Journals of the Sixth Congress of the Republic of Texas.* 3 vols. Austin, Texas: Von Boeckmann-Jones Co., 1940–1945.

Somervell, A. [Form of army orders beginning:] "Captain —— In accordance with an order from the Executive, dated Houston, March 22d, 1842, giving me instructions to cross the Río Grande, should the forces in the field justify such a movement; you are authorized to raise all the men you can, for the campaign; . . ." [Signed at end:] A. Somervell, General 1st Brigade, T. M., G. H. Harrison, Acting Brigade Major. [n. p.: 1842]. Broadside. Copy in Texas State Archives.

Taylor, Virginia H., and Mrs. B. Brandt (eds.). *Texas Treasury Papers: Letters Received in the Treasury Department of the Republic of Texas, 1836–1846.* Vol. IV, *Supplement and Letters Received from the Military Departments.* Austin, Texas: Texas State Library, 1956.

Texas Congress. *Appendix to the Journals. See* Texas Congress . . . *Journals.*

—. *Journals of the House of Representatives of the Seventh Congress of the Republic of Texas, convened at Washington, on the 14th November 1842.* Washington, Texas: Thomas Johnson, Public Printer, 1843.

—. *Journals of the House of Representatives of the Eighth Congress of the Republic of Texas.* Houston: Cruger & Moore, Public Printers, 1844.

—. *Journals of the House of Representatives of the Ninth Congress of the Republic of Texas.* Washington, Texas: Miller and Cushney, Public Printers, 1845.

—. *Journals of the Ninth Congress of the Republic of Texas.* Appendix. Washington, Texas: Miller & Cushney, Public Printers, 1845.

—. *Journals of the Senate of the Republic of Texas: Sixth Congress, 1841–1842.* Austin: S. Whiting, Public Printer, 1842.

—, House of Representatives. *Report on [sic] the Finance Committee.* [Austin, Texas: *Austin City Gazette* Office, 1842]. 15 pp. Copy in Houston Public Library, Houston, Texas.

—, House of Representatives. *Report of Majority of Military Committee, July 4, 1842.* Printed by Order of the House of Representatives. Houston: Telegraph Press, [1842]. Copy in Texas Masonic Grand Lodge Library, Waco, Texas.

—, Senate. *Secret Journals. See* Winkler, E. W. (ed.) *Secret Journals of the Senate* . . .

Texas State Constitutional Convention. *See* Weeks, William F. *Debates of the Texas Convention.*

Texas Treasury Department. *Annual Report of Treasurer of the Republic of Texas, for 1841. By order of the House of Representatives.* Austin,

Texas: S. Whiting, Public Printer, 1842. 10 pp. Copy in Houston Public Library, Houston, Texas.

—. *See also* Connor, Seymour V. (ed.). *Texas Treasury Papers* . . . ; Taylor, Virginia H. and Mrs. B. Brandt (eds.). *Texas Treasury Papers . . . Supplement.*

Texas War Department. *Report of the Secretary of War and Marine* [George W. Hockley], [June 23, 1842]. Printed by order of the House of Representatives. Houston, Texas: Telegraph Power Press, [1842]. 3 pp. Copy in Texas Masonic Grand Lodge, Waco, Texas.

—. *See also* Hockley, George W. [Proclamation . . .].

To Arms! To Arms! Texians!! Arrangements entered into by the citizens of Austin, with reference to the approach of the Mexicans; and the latest information from the West of the Invading Army. [Dated:] Gazette Office, Half-past 10 o'clock, Mond[ay] morn[ing] [March 7, 1842]. [Austin, Texas: *Austin City Gazette* Office, 1842]. Broadside. Copy in General Land Office, Austin, Texas.

Travis Guards (Austin). *Constitution and By-Laws of the Travis Guards: Adopted March First, 1840.* Austin, Texas: Cruger and Bonnell's Print, 1840. 16 pp. Copy in Barker Texas History Center, University of Texas Library.

Treasury Department (Texas). *See* Connor, Seymour V. (ed.). *Texas Treasury Papers* . . . ; Taylor, Virginia H. and Mrs. B. Brandt (eds.). *Texas Treasury Papers . . . Supplement*; Texas Treasury Department.

United States Congress. *Congressional Globe,* 1841–1843, 1853–1855. Washington, D. C.: Printed at the *Globe* Office for the Editors, 1840–1844, 1853–1855.

—. *Senate Executive Documents,* 31st Congress, 1st Session, vol. III, no. 32 (serial no. 558). [Washington, D. C.:] Union Office, [1850].

—. *Senate Executive Documents,* 32nd Congress, 2nd Session, Vol. III, no. 14 (Serial no. 660). [No imprint].

United States State Department. *See* Everett, Edward. "Report . . ."

Weeks, William F. *Debates of the Texas Convention.* Houston: [Telegraph and Texas Register Press], 1846.

Winkler, E. W. (ed.). *Secret Journals of the Senate: Republic of Texas, 1836–1845.* [Austin, Texas]: Austin Printing Co., 1911.

[Woll, Adrián]. *Expedición hecha en Téjas, por una parte de la Division del Cuerpo de Egército del Norte.* Monterey: Impreso por Francisco Molina, 1842.

Woll, Adrián. *See also* Nance, Joseph Milton (trans. and ed.).

2. Private Papers, Letters, and Memoirs

a. MANUSCRIPTS AND TYPESCRIPTS

Adams, Harvey Alexander. "[Journal of an] Expedition Against the Southwest in 1842 and 1843." Typescript in Archives Collection, University of Texas Library, of original diary in possession of Miss Ophelia Gilmore of Austin.

Allen, John Melville. Papers, 1835–1847. Rosenberg Library, Galveston, Texas.

Autograph Collection, 1808–1921, Containing Signatures and Letters of Eminent Men of Texas and the United States. Rosenberg Library, Galveston, Texas.

Barrett, Don Carlos. Papers, 1800–1897. Typescript in Archives Collection, University of Texas Library.

Billingsley, Jesse. Papers, 1835–1889. Archives Collection, University of Texas Library.

Brown, John Henry. "Autobiography." Archives Collection, University of Texas Library.

—. Papers 1835–1872. Archives Collection, University of Texas Library.

Bryan, Guy Morrison. Papers. Archives Collection, University of Texas Library.

Bryan, John A. Papers, 1841–1872. Archives Collection, University of Texas Library.

Bryan, Moses A. Papers, 1821–1888. Archives Collection, University of Texas Library.

Burleson, Edward, Papers, 1821–1875. Archives Collection, University of Texas Library.

Burleson, Jonathan. Papers, 1839–1867. Archives Collection, University of Texas Library.

Burnet, David G. Papers, 1821–1869. Rosenberg Library, Galveston, Texas.

—. Papers, 1830–1890. Archives Collection, University of Texas Library.

Cartwright, Mathew. Papers, 1821–1859. Archives Collection, University of Texas Library.

Chalk, Whitfield. "Reminiscences of Whitfield Chalk." Round Rock, [Texas]: March 4, [c1900]. 20 pp. Rosenberg Library, Galveston, Texas.

Clark, James. Papers, 1827–1845. Archives Collection, University of Texas Library.

Dancy, John W. Diary. Archives Collection, University of Texas Library.

Dimitt, Philip. Papers. Texas State Archives.

Duerr, Christian Friedrich. Diary, March 21, 1839–Dec. 31, 1844. Typed copy in Archives Collection, University of Texas Library, from original in the Library of Baylor University, Waco, Texas.

Fisher, George. Papers, 1835–1856. Texas State Archives.

Ford, John S. "Memoirs." Archives Collection, University of Texas Library.

—. Papers, 1815–1860. Archives Collection, University of Texas Library.

Fowler, Littleton. Papers, Feb. 9, 1841–Dec. 10, 1843. Archives Collection, University of Texas Library.

Franklin, Ben C. Papers, 1805–1889. Archives Collection, University of Texas Library.

662

Bibliography

Goodman, H. H. Papers, 1838–1844. Archives Collection, University of Texas Library.

Gray, Milly R. "Diary of Mrs. Milly R. (Mrs. William Fairfax) Gray, December 1, 1832–February 12, 1840." Typescript in Rosenberg Library, Galveston, Texas.

Grover, George W. Papers. Rosenberg Library, Galveston, Texas.

—. "Scrap Book." Rosenberg Library, Galveston, Texas.

Houston, Sam. Unpublished Correspondence, 1842. Archives Collection, University of Texas Library.

Hunt, Memucan. Papers. Texas State Archives.

Hunt, Mrs. Memucan. Diary. Typescript. 50 pp. Texas State Archives.

Jenkins, John H. Sr. "Personal Reminiscences of Texas History Relating to Bastrop County, 1828–1847, as Dictated to his Daughter-in-law, Mrs. Emma Holmes Jenkins of Bastrop, Texas." Typescript in Archives Collection, University of Texas Library.

Jones, Anson. Diaries. Archives Collection, University of Texas Library.

McCutchan, Joseph D. Diary. Rosenberg Library, Galveston, Texas.

McLeod, Hugh D. Papers. Texas State Archives.

Manton, Edward. Papers, 1818–1891. Photostats in Archives Collection, University of Texas Library.

Maverick, Samuel Augustus. Diary. See Maverick, Samuel Augustus. Papers.

—. Diaries, Miscellaneous, 1829–1843. See Maverick, Samuel Augustus. Papers.

—. Papers. Archives Collection, University of Texas Library.

Menefee, John S. Papers, 1831–1859. Archives Collection, University of Texas Library.

Menefee, William C. Papers, 1831–1895. Archives Collection, University of Texas Library.

Miller, Washington D. Papers, 1833–1860. Texas State Archives.

—. Papers. Hardin-Simmons University Library.

Morgan, James. Papers, 1841–1845. Rosenberg Library, Galveston, Texas.

Perry, James F. Papers. Transcripts in Archives Collection, University of Texas Library.

Pierson, Edmund. "Goodloe Warren Pierson." Manuscript in possession of Miss Irene Windel, Bryan, Texas.

Reding, William R. Papers, 1837–1874. Archives Collection, University of Texas Library.

—, and A. W. Tunnard. Papers, Jan.–June 1840, 1845. Archives Collection, University of Texas Library.

Rusk, Thomas J. Papers. Archives Collection. University of Texas Library.

Seguin, Juan N. Papers. Texas State Archives.

Sherman, Sidney. Papers. Rosenberg Library, Galveston, Texas.

Smith, Ashbel. Papers, 1838–1842. Archives Collection, University of Texas Library.

Smith, Henry. Papers, 1822–1846. Archives Collection, University of Texas Library.
Smith, Sam S. Collection. Archives Collection, University of Texas Library.
Sterne, Adolphus. Papers. Texas State Archives.
Thompson, Waddy. Papers, 1824–1848. Archives Collection, University of Texas Library.
Tunnard, A. W. *See* Reding, William R.
Van Zandt, Isaac. Papers, 1839–1843. Transcripts in Archives Collection, University of Texas Library.
Wade, Houston. Papers. Texas State Archives.
Wagner, H. R. Manuscript Collection. Yale University Library.
Woodhouse, Matthew P. Papers. Texas State Archives.

b. PRINTED MATERIAL

[Anonymous.] "A Leaf from Memory: Scene of the Battle-Field of Salado, by an Old Texian," in *Texas Almanac for 1860*, Galveston, Texas: Richardson and Co., [1860?], pp. 72–74.
Austin City Gazette—Extra, [March 7, 1842]. [Austin, Texas: *Austin City Gazette* Office, 1842].
Barker, E. C. *See* Williams, Amelia.
Barnes, Charles M. (comp.). *Antonio Menchaca Memoirs*. Yanoguana Society *Publications*, II. San Antonio, Texas: Artes Gráficas, 1937.
Bartlett, John Russell. *Personal Narrative of Explorations and Incidents in Texas, New Mexico, California, Sonora, and Chihuahua, Connected with the United States and Mexican Boundary Commission During the Years 1850, '51, '52, and '53.* 2 vols. New York: D. Appleton & Company, Inc., 1854.
Bell, Thomas W. *A Narrative of the Capture and Subsequent Sufferings of the Mier Prisoners in Mexico, Captured in the Cause of Texas, Dec. 26th, 1842 and Liberated Sept. 16th, 1844.* DeSoto County, Mississippi: R. Morris & Co., 1845.
Black, Reading W. *See* Moore, Ike (ed.).
Bollaert, William. "Arrival in Texas in 1842, and Cruise of the Lafitte," in *Coburn's United Service Magazine*, November 1846, pp. 341–355.
—. *See also* Hollon, W. Eugene and Ruth Lapham Butler (eds.).
Breese, Samuel. *See* Morse, Sidney E.
Bryan, Guy M. *See* Winkler, E. W.
Burnet, David G. *Reply to the Report of the Committee on the Santa Fé Expedition.* Houston, Texas: Telegraph Press, [1842]. 7 pp. Copy in Barker Texas History Center, University of Texas Library.
Butler, Ruth Lapham. *See* Hollon, W. Eugene.
Carl, Prince of Solms-Braunfels. *Texas, 1844–1845.* Houston, Texas: Anson Jones Press, 1936.
Chabot, Frederick C. (ed.). *The Perote Prisoners: Being the Diary of James L. Trueheart Printed for the First Time Together with an Historical Introduction.* San Antonio, Texas: The Naylor Company, 1924.

664

Bibliography

Crane, William Carey. *Life and Select Literary Remains of Sam Houston of Texas*. Philadelphia: J. B. Lippincott & Co., 1884.

Croffut, W. A. (ed.). *Fifty Years in Camp and Field: Diary of Major General Ethan Allen Hitchcock*. New York: G. P. Putnam's Sons, 1909.

Dresel, Gustav. *See* Freund, Max (trans. and ed.).

Dedimus, Henry. *New Orleans as I Found It*. New York: Harper & Brothers, 1845.

Erath, George B. *See* Erath, Lucy A. (ed.).

Erath, Lucy A. (ed.). "Memoirs of Major George Barnard Erath," in *Southwestern Historical Quarterly*, XXVII (1923–1924), 27–51, 140–163.

[Folsom, George]. *Mexico in 1842: A Description of the Country, Its Natural and Political Features; with a Sketch of Its History Brought Down to the Present Year. To Which Is Added, an Account of Texas and Yucatán; and of the Santa Fé Expedition*. New York: Charles J. Folsom, 1842.

Freund, Max (trans. and ed.). *Gustav Dresel's Houston Journal: Adventures in North America and Texas, 1837–1841*. Austin: University of Texas Press, 1954.

Green, Rena Maverick (ed.). *Memoirs of Mary A. Maverick: Arranged by Mary A. Maverick and Her Son George Madison Maverick*. San Antonio, Texas: Alamo Printing Company, 1921.

—. (ed.). *Samuel Maverick, Texan, 1803–1870: A Collection of Letters, Journals and Memoirs*. San Antonio, Texas: [privately printed (H. Wolff, printer, N. Y.)], 1952 [*i.e.* 1953].

— (ed.). *See also* Swisher, John M.

Green, Thomas J. *Journal of the Texian Expedition Against Mier*. New York: Harper & Brothers, 1845.

Green, Wharton J[ackson]. *Recollections and Reflections: An Auto[biography] of Half a Century and More*. n.p.: Presses of Edwards and Broughton Printing Co., 1906.

Gulick, Charles Adams, Jr., and Others (eds.). *The Papers of Mirabeau Buonaparte Lamar*. 6 vols. Austin, Texas: A. C. Baldwin & Sons, 1921–1927.

Harris, Lewis Birdsall. *See* Looscan, Adele B. (ed.).

Hayes, Rutherford B. *See* Winkler, E. W. (ed.).

Hendricks, Sterling Brown. *See* Winkler, E. W. (ed.).

Hitchcock, Ethan Allen. *See* Croffut, W. A. (ed.).

Hollon, W. Eugene, and Ruth Lapham Butler (eds.). *William Bollaert's Texas*. Norman: University of Oklahoma Press, 1956.

Houston, Sam. *See* Crane, William Carey; Williams, Amelia and E. C. Barker (eds.).

Houstonian. Extra, The. March 15, 11 o'clock A.M., [1842]. [Houston: *Houstonian* Office, 1842]. Broadside. Texas State Archives.

Houstoun, Mrs. [M. C.]. *Texas and the Gulf of Mexico: or Yachting in the New World*. 2 vols. London: John Murray, Albermarle St., 1844.

Attack and Counterattack

Jenkins, John Holland. *See* Jenkins, John Holland, III (ed.).
Jenkins, John Holland, III (ed.). *Recollections of Early Texas: The Memoirs of John Holland Jenkins.* Austin: University of Texas Press, 1958.
Lamar, Mirabeau Buonaparte. *See* Gulick, Charles Adams, Jr., and Others (eds.).
Linn, John J. *Reminiscences of Fifty Years in Texas.* New York: D. & J. Sadlier & Co., 1883. Austin, Texas: The Steck Company, 1935, (facsimile reproduction of the original, including title-page of New York edition of 1883).
Looscan, Adele B. (ed.). "Journal of Lewis Birdsall Harris," in *Southwestern Historical Quarterly,* XXV (1921–1922), 63–71, 131–146, 185–197.
Lubbock, Francis R. *Six Decades in Texas: or Memoirs of Francis Richard Lubbock.* Austin, Texas: Ben C. Jones & Co., 1900.
McCaleb, Walter Flavins (ed.). *See* Reagan, John H.
McCalla, W. L. *Adventures in Texas, Chiefly in the Spring and Summer of 1840: with a Discussion of Comparative Character, Political, Religious and Moral.* Philadelphia: 1841.
McClintock, William A. "Journal of a Trip through Texas and Northern Mexico in 1846–1847," in *Southwestern Historical Quarterly,* XXXIV (1930–1931), 20–37, 141–158, 231–256.
McNair, George L., *Texian Campaign of 1842.* [New Orleans: 1942]. Broadsheet. Copy in Archivo General de la Secretaría de Relaciones Exteriores, Mexico City, Mexico.
Maverick, Mary A. *See* Green, Rena Maverick (ed.).
Maverick, Samuel. *See* Green, Rena Maverick (ed.).
Mayer, Brantz. *Mexico: As It Was and As It Is.* 3rd ed. Baltimore: William Taylor & Co., 1846.
Menchaca, Antonio. *Memoirs. See* Barnes, Charles M. (comp.)
Moore, E. W. *To the People of Texas: An Appeal in Vindication of His Conduct of the Navy.* Galveston, Texas: [*Civilian and Galveston Gazette* Office], 1843.
Moore, Ike (ed.). *The Life and Diary of Reading W. Black: A History of Early Uvalde.* Uvalde, Texas: Private printing for the El Progreso Club. [The Calithump Press, Austin, Texas], 1934.
Morrell, Z[enos] N. *Flowers and Fruits in the Wilderness: or Forty-Six Years in Texas and Two Winters in Honduras.* 4th ed. rev. Dallas, Texas: W. G. Scarff & Co., Publishers, 1886.
[Page, Frederic Benjamin]. *Prairiedom: Rambles and Scrambles in Texas or New Estremadura by a Suthron.* New York: Paine & Durgess, 1845.
Reagan, John H. *Memoirs with Special Reference to Secession and the Civil War* . . . ed. by Walter Flavins McCaleb. New York: The Neale Publishing Co., 1906.
Reid, John C. *Reid's Tramp, or a Journal of* . . . *Travel Through Texas, New Mexico, Arizona, Sonora, and California.* Selma, Alabama; J. Hardy & Co., 1858.

666

Bibliography

Roemer, Ferdinand. *Texas with Particular Reference to German Immigration and the Physical Appearance of the Country Described through Personal Observation* [1845–1847]. Translated from the German by Oswald Mueller. San Antonio, Texas: Standard Printing Co., 1935.

Samson, William H. (ed.). *Letters of Zachary Taylor from the Battle-Fields of the Mexican War.* Rochester, New York: The Genesee Press, 1908.

Sánchez, José María. "A Trip to Texas in 1828," translated by Carlos E. Castañeda, in *Southwestern Historical Quarterly*, XXIX (1925–1926), 249–288.

Seguin, Juan N. *Personal Memoirs of Juan N. Seguin: from the Year 1834 to the Retreat of General Woll from the City of San Antonio in 1842.* San Antonio, Texas: Ledger Book and Job Office, 1858.

Smither, Harriet (ed.). "Diary of Adolphus Sterne," in *Southwestern Historical Quarterly*, XXX–XXXVIII (1926–1935).

Solms-Braunfels, Prince Carl of. *See* Carl, Prince of Solms Braunfels.

Spellman, L. U. (ed.). "Letters of the 'Dawson Men' from Perote Prison, Mexico, 1842–1843," in *Southwestern Historical Quarterly*, XXXVIII (1934–1935), 246–269.

Stapp, William Preston. *The Prisoners of Perote: Containing a Journal Kept by the Author Who Was Captured by the Mexicans, at Mier, December 25, 1842, and Released from Perote, May 16, 1844.* Philadelphia: G. B. Zieber and Company, 1845.

Sterne, Adolphus. *See* Smither, Harriet (ed.).

Swisher, John M. *The Swisher Memoirs*, ed. by Rena Maverick Green. San Antonio, Texas: The Segmund Press, Inc., 1932.

Taylor, Zachary. *See* Samson, William H. (ed.).

To Arms! To Arms! Texians!! Arrangements entered into by the Citizens of Austin, with reference to the approach of the Mexicans; and the latest information from the West of the Invading Army. [Austin City] Gazette Office, Half-past 10 o'clock, Mon[day] morn[ing], [March 7, 1842]. Broadside, General Land Office, Austin, Texas.

Trueheart, James L. *See* Chabot, Frederick C. (ed.).

Voice from the West!!!, A. [Text begins:] "Fellow Citizens:—The Piteous cries, and dying groans of our imprisoned and slaughtered countrymen, come to our ears in every breeze that sweeps over the Western prairies; . . . [A plea for vengeance against the Mexicans for the capture of the Santa Fé expedition, signed "A Citizen"]. [Austin, Texas: *Austin City Gazette* Office, 1842]. Broadside. Copy (incomplete) in Texas Masonic Grand Lodge, Waco, Texas.

Williams, Amelia W., and Eugene C. Barker (eds.). *The Writings of Sam Houston, 1813–1863.* 8 vols. Austin: University of Texas Press, 1938–1943.

Winkler, E. W. (ed.). "The Bexar and Dawson Prisoners," in *Quarterly of the Texas State Historical Association*, XIII (1909–1910), 292–

324. The original copy of the Anderson Hutchinson diary printed in Winkler's article is located in the Texas State Archives.
— (ed.). "The Bryan-Hayes Correspondence," in *Southwestern Historical Quarterly*, XXV–XXX (1921–1927).
— (ed.). *Manuscript Letters and Documents of Early Texians, 1821–1845*. Austin, Texas: The Steck Company 1937.
— (ed.). "Sterling Brown Hendricks' Narrative of the Somervell Expedition to the Río Grande," in *Southwestern Historical Quarterly*, XXIII (1919–1920), 114–140.

3. MAPS

Arrowsmith, John. *Map of Texas: Compiled from surveys in the Land Office of Texas and Other Official Surveys.* London: Published by John Arrowsmith, 1841. Used as frontispiece in William Kennedy, *The Rise, Progress, and Prospects of the Republic of Texas.* 2 vols. London: R. Hastings, 1841.

Austin, Stephen F. *See* Castañeda, Carlos E., and Early Martin, Jr.

Blake, J. Edmond. "Map of the Country in the Vicinity of San Antonio de Bexar," 1845. Original in the National Archives, Washington, D. C.

Castañeda, Carlos E., and Early Martin, Jr. *Three Manuscript Maps of Texas by Stephen F. Austin; with Biographical and Bibliographical Notes.* Austin, Texas: Privately printed, 1930.

Central America Including Texas, California, and the Northern States of Mexico [1842]. [London:] published by the Society for Diffusion of Useful Knowledge by Chapman & Hall, 186 Strand, 1842. Original in Archives Collection, University of Texas Library.

Coast of Texas: From documents furnished by W. Kennedy, Esq., H.M. Consul at Galveston, The. London: Published according to Act of Parliament at the Hydrographic Office of the Admiralty, August 20, 1844. Original in Texas State Archives.

Emory, William H. *Map of Texas and the Countries Adjacent: Compiled in the Bureau of the Corps of Topographical Engineers from the best authorities for the State Department* . . . [Washington, D. C.:] Published by order of the United States Senate, 1844. Original in Texas State Archives.

García y Cubas, Antonio. *Atlas geográfico estadistico é histórico de la republica Mexicana.* Mexico City: J. M. Fernández de Lara, 1858.

Hooker, W. "Map of the State of Coahuila and Texas." Published as frontispiece in Mary Austin Holley, *Texas.* Austin, Texas: The Steck Company, 1935.

Ikin, Arthur. "Map of Texas." J. & C. Walker, Lithographers. Published as frontispiece in Arthur Ikin, *Texas: Its History, Topography, Agriculture, Commerce, and General Statistics.* London: Sherwood, Gilbert, and Piper, 1848.

Mapa de los Estados Unidos Méjicanos arreghida a la distribucion que en diversos de . . . ha hecho del territorio el Congreso general Méjicano. Paris: Publicado por Rosa, 1837.

Mexico & Guatimala [sic] with the Republic of Texas. Edinburgh: W. Lizars, [1836?]. Copy in Texas State Archives.

Morse. Sidney E., and Samuel Breese. *Texas [1844].* New York: 1844. Original in Texas State Archives.

New Map of Texas, 1841. n. p.: Day & Haghe Lithographers to the Queen, [1841]. Original in Texas State Archives.

[Page, Frederic Benjamin]. "Mexico." Published as frontispiece in [Frederic Benjamin Page], *Prairiedom: Rambles and Scrambles in Texas or New Estremadura by a Suthron.* New York: Paine & Burgess, 1845.

Rieves, S. L. "Travis County, Texas, 1840: Showing Militia Beats." Map was prepared for Mrs. David C. Gracy, Gracy-Travis County Abstract Company, Austin, Texas, by S. L. Rieves, March 5, 1939. [Austin, Texas: 1939]. Original in Texas State Archives.

United States Geological Survey. *Brackettville [Texas] Quadrangle,* May 1897 ed. Reprinted in U.S. Dept. of the Interior, *Geological Survey.* Washington, D.C.: Government Printing Office, 1932.

—. *Cline [Texas] Quadrangle.* Reprinted in U.S. Dept. of the Interior, *Geological Survey.* Washington, D.C.: Government Printing Office, 1949.

—. *Uvalde [Texas] Quadrangle,* Feb. 1898 ed. Reprinted in U.S. Dept. of Interior *Geological Survey.* Washington, D.C.: Government Printing Office, 1931.

U. S. Soil Survey. "Dimmit County, Texas." U.S. Dept. of Agriculture, *Soil Survey.* 1938, no. 4 (issued April 1943).

—. "Southwest Texas." U.S. Department of Agriculture, *Field Operations of the Bureau of Soils,* 1911, no. 28.

—. "Zavala County, Texas." U.S. Department of Agriculture, *Soil Survey,* 1934, no. 21 (issued June 1940).

Williams, C. S. *Map of Texas from the Most Recent Authorities [1845].* Philadelphia: C. S. Williams, 1845. Original in Texas State Archives.

Wyld, James. *Wyld's Map of Texas, 1840.* London: Published by James Wyld, Geographer to the Queen, Charing Cross East, 1840. Original in Archives Collection, University of Texas Library.

Yeager, B. E. *A New Map of Texas with the Contiguous American & Mexican States: Compiled from the Latest Authorities.* Galveston, Texas: E. Yeager, 1840. Original in National Archives, Washington, D.C.

4. Newspapers

El Ancla (Matamoros), January 4–August 30, 1841.
Anti-Slavery Standard (New York), April 21, 1842.
Austin City Gazette, 1839–1842.
Boletín del Gobierno (Mexico City), July 19–27, 1840.
Boletín Oficial (Mexico City), September 1–October 3, 1846.

Civilian and Galveston Gazette (Galveston), 1838–1843.
Colorado Gazette and Advertiser (Matagorda), 1839–1842.
Commercial Bulletin (New Orleans), March 17, 1842.
El Cosmopolita (Mexico City), December 19, 1835–July 1843.
Daily Bulletin (Austin), November 27, 1841–January 18, 1842.
Daily Texian (Austin), December 18, 1841; January 11, 13, 18, 1842.
Dallas Morning News, June 16, 1907.
Diario del Gobierno (Mexico City), 1835–1846.
Gaceta de Gobierno de Tamaulipas (Ciudad Victoria), February 1, 1840–July 20, 1844.
Gaceta de Tampico, July–December 1839; September 28, 1842.
Galveston Daily Advertiser, April 4, 1842.
Galveston Daily News, February 1 and October 18, 1896.
Guadalupe Gazette-Bulletin (Seguin), Historical Centennial Edition, April 30, 1936.
El Honor Nacional (Matamoros), December 27, 1841.
Houstonian (Houston), September 20, 1842.
El Latigo de Téjas (Matamoros), 1843–1844.
Morning Star (Houston), 1839–1845.
New Orleans Bee, 1841–1843.
New Orleans Picayune, 1841–1843.
Niles' Weekly Register (Baltimore), 1811–1849.
Northern Standard (Clarksville), 1842–1845.
Philadelphia Public Ledger, April 4 and June 14, 1842.
El Provisional (Matamoros), October 14, 1842.
Seguin Enterprise, July 22, 1938.
The State Times (Austin), July 26, 1856.
Telegraph and Texas Register (Houston), 1835–1846.
The Texas Democrat (Austin), December 16, 1846.
Texas National Register (Washington), December 7, 1844–October 9, 1845.
Wetumpka Argus (Wetumpka, Alabama), September 21, 1842.

B. *Secondary Sources*

1. Manuscripts and Typescripts

Adams, Allen F. "The Leader of the Volunteer Grays: The Life of William G. Cooke, 1808–1847." Masters' thesis, Southwest Texas State Teachers College, 1940.

Affleck, J. D. "History of John C. Hays," Pts. I–II. Typescript in Archives Collection, University of Texas Library.

Barker, Bernice. "The Texan Expedition to the Rio Grande in 1842." Masters' thesis, University of Texas, 1929.

Boerner, Gerald. "Austin, 1836–1877." 61 pp. Typescript in Texas State Archives.

Bridges, Jim L. "The History of Fort Bend County, 1822–1861." Masters' thesis, University of Texas, 1939.

Bibliography

Brown, Alma Howell. "The Consular Service of the Republic of Texas." Masters' thesis, University of Texas, 1928.

Brown, Frank. "Annals of Travis County and of the City of Austin." 13 vols. Typescript in Texas State Archives.

Crane, Robert Edmund Lee, Jr. "The Administration of the Customs Service of the Republic of Texas." Masters' thesis, University of Texas, 1939.

—. "The History of the Revenue Service and the Commerce of the Republic of Texas." Ph.D. dissertation, University of Texas, 1950.

Crawford, Polly Pearl. "The Beginnings of Spanish Settlements in the Lower Río Grande Valley." Masters' thesis, University of Texas, 1925.

Dyer, J. O. "Historical Notes of Galveston." Rosenberg Library, Galveston, Texas.

Fox, Neal B. "A Correlated Study-Unit of a Diary of the Expedition Against the Southwest, 1842–1843." Masters' thesis, Southwest Texas State Teachers College, 1947.

"Galveston Artillery Company." Typescript in Rosenberg Library, Galveston, Texas.

"Galveston Sketches." Typescript in Texas State Archives.

Gambrell, Thomas DeWitt. "The Army of the Republic of Texas." Masters' thesis, University of Texas, 1937.

Gore, Walter Reece. "The Life of Henry Laurence Kinney." Masters' thesis, University of Texas, 1948.

Grover, Walter E. "A Historical Sketch of Galveston Island West of the City Limits." Rosenberg Library, Galveston, Texas.

Highsmith, Kige. "Biographical Sketch of Jesse Billingsley." In Jesse Billingsley Papers, Archives Collection, University of Texas Library.

Hill, Laurance L. See Wallis, Mrs. Jonnie Lockhart.

Huson, Hobart. "Iron Men: A History of the Republic of the Río Grande and the Federalist War in Northern Mexico." [1940]. One of the Sextuplicate typed copies of the original MS. Archives Collection, University of Texas Library.

Luker, Julia Eugenia. "The Diplomatic Relations between Texas and Mexico, 1836–1842." Masters' thesis, University of Texas, 1920.

Moore, Robert Lee. "History of Refugio County." Masters' thesis, University of Texas, 1937.

Neal, B. Fox. "A Correlated Study-Unit of a Diary of the Expedition Against the Southwest, 1842–1843." Masters' thesis, Southwest Texas State Teachers College, 1947.

Reinhardt, Mrs. Ina Kate (Hamon), "The Public Career of Thomas Jefferson Green in Texas." Masters' thesis, University of Texas, 1939.

Stuart, Ben C. "Early Galveston Military Companies, 1839–1901." 70 pp. Rosenberg Library, Galveston, Texas.

—. "Ephraim McLean." 72 pp. Rosenberg Library, Galveston, Texas.

—. "Texas Fighters and Frontier Rangers." Archives Collection, University of Texas Library.

2. Printed Material

a. books

Adams, E. D. *British Interests and Activities in Texas 1838–1846*. Baltimore: Johns Hopkins Press, 1910.

Alcarez, Ramón, and Others. *Apunta de la historia de la guerra entre Mexico y los Estados Unidos*. Mexico City: 1848.

Aldrich, Armistead Albert. *The History of Houston County, Texas: Together with Biographical Sketches of Many Pioneers and Later Citizens of Said County, Who Have Made Notable Contributions to Its Development and Progress*. San Antonio, Texas: The Naylor Company, 1943.

Alessio Robles, Vito. *Coahuila y Texas desde la consumación de la independencia hasta el tratado de paz de Guadalupe Hidalgo*. 2 vols. Mexico City: 1945–1946.

[Anonymous]. *A History of the San Antonio Quartermaster Depot*. [San Antonio, Texas?]: 1943.

Baker, D. W. C. (comp.). *A Texas Scrap-Book: Made Up of the History, Biography, and Miscellany of Texas and Its People*. New York: A. S. Barnes & Co., [1875].

Bancroft, Hubert Howe. *History of Mexico*. 6 vols. San Francisco: The History Co., 1886–1887.

—. *History of Texas and the North Mexican States*. 2 vols. San Francisco: A. L. Bancroft and Company, 1889.

Barker, Eugene C. (ed.). *Texas History for High Schools and Colleges*. Dallas, Texas: Turner Company, 1929.

Bartholomew, Ed Ellsworth. *The Houston Story: A Chronicle of the City of Houston and the Texas Frontier from the Battle of San Jacinto to the War Between the States, 1836–1865*. Houston, Texas: The Frontier Press of Texas, 1951.

Bayard, Ralph F. *Lone-Star Vanguard: The Catholic Re-occupation of Texas, 1838–1848*. Saint Louis, Missouri: The Vincentian Press, 1945.

Binkley, William C. *The Expansionist Movement in Texas, 1836–1850*. Berkeley: University of California Press, 1925.

Biographical Directory of the American Congress, 1774–1927. [Washington, D.C.]: Government Printing Office, 1928.

Bishop, Curtis, and Bascom Giles. *Lots of Land*. Austin, Texas: The Steck Company, 1949.

Bolton, Herbert E. *Texas in the Middle Eighteenth Century*. Berkeley: University of California Press, 1915.

Brown, John Henry. *History of Texas, from 1685 to 1892*. 2 vols. Saint Louis, Missouri: L. E. Daniell, [1892–1893].

—. *Indian Wars and Pioneers of Texas*. Austin, Texas: L. E. Daniell, [189–?].

Bustamante, Carlos María. *Apuntes para la historia del gobierno del general D. Antonio López de Santa-Anna*. Mexico City: 1845.

672

Bibliography

Callcott, Wilfrid Hardy. *Santa Anna: The Story of an Enigma Who Once Was Mexico*. Norman: University of Oklahoma Press, 1936.

Carreño, Alberto M. (ed.). *Jefes del ejército méxicano en 1847: biografías de generals de division y de coronels del ejército méxicano por fines del año de 1847* [Fly leaf says to the end of "1840"]. Mexico City: Imprenta y Folotipia de la Secretaría de Fomento, 1914.

Carroll, H. Bailey. *See* Webb, Walter Prescott.

— and Milton R. Gutsch (comps. and eds.). *Texas History Theses: A Check List of the Theses and Dissertations Relating to Texas History Accepted at The University of Texas, 1893–1951*. Austin: The Texas Historical Association, 1955.

Castañeda, Carlos Eduardo, and Frederick C. Chabot. *Early Texas Album: Fifty Illustrations with Notes*. Austin, Texas: 1929.

— and Jack Autry Dabbs (eds.). *Guide to the Latin American Manuscripts in the University of Texas Library*. Cambridge, Massachusetts: Harvard University Press, 1939.

Chabot, Frederick C. *The Alamo: Altar of Texas Liberty*. n.p.: 1931.

—. *Corpus Christi and Lipantitlán*. San Antonio, Texas: Artes Gráficas, 1942.

—. *Indians and Missions*. San Antonio, Texas: Naylor Printing Co., 1930.

—. *San Fernando: the Villa Capital of the Province of Texas, with Illustrations, and with an Account of the Present San Fernando Cathedral and other Landmarks, as well as of the Settlers Themselves*. San Antonio, Texas: Naylor Printing Co., 1930.

—. *With the Makers of San Antonio*. San Antonio, Texas: Artes Gráficas, 1937.

—. *See also* Castañeda, Carlos Eduardo.

Clemens, Jeremiah. *Mustang Gray: A Romance*. Philadelphia: 1858.

Conrad, Howard Louis. *Nathaniel J. Brown: Biographical Sketch and Reminiscences of a Noted Pioneer*. Chicago: Byron S. Palmer Printing Company, 1892.

Corpus Christi: A History and Guide. [Corpus Christi, Texas]: Corpus Christi Caller-Times, 1942.

Cravens, John Nathan. *James Harper Starr: Financier of the Republic of Texas*. Austin, Texas: The Daughters of the Republic of Texas, 1950.

Dabbs, Jack Autry. *See* Castañeda, Carlos Eduardo.

Daniell, L. E. *Personnel of the Texas State Government*. San Antonio, Texas: Maverick Printing House, 1892.

DeCamara, Kathleen. *Laredo on the Río Grande*. San Antonio, Texas: The Naylor Company, 1949.

DeRyee, William, and R. E. Moore. *The Texas Album of the Eighth Legislature*. Austin, Texas: Miner, Lambert and Perry, 1860.

DeShields, James T. *Border Wars of Texas: being an Authentic and Popular Account, in Chronological Order, of the Long and Bitter Conflict Waged between Savage Indian Tribes and the Pioneer Settlers of Texas*. Tioga, Texas: The Herald Company, 1912.

673

Dictionary of American Biography. 22 vols. New York: Charles Scribner's Sons, 1928–1958.

Dixon, Sam Houston, and Louis Wiltz Kemp. *The Heroes of San Jacinto.* Houston, Texas: Anson Jones Press, 1932.

Donecker, Frances. *See* Steen, Ralph W.

Duewall, L. A. *The Story of Monument Hill.* LaGrange, Texas: The LaGrange Journal, 1955.

Duval, John C. *The Adventures of Big-Foot Wallace: The Texas Ranger and Hunter.* [Macon, Georgia]: J. W. Burke and Co., 1870.

Dyer, Joseph O. *The Early History of Galveston.* Centenary ed. [Galveston, Texas: Oscar Springer, printer], 1916.

Elliott, Claude (comp. and ed.). *Theses on Texas History: A Check List of Theses and Dissertations in Texas History Produced in the Departments of History of Eighteen Texas Graduate Schools and Thirty-Three Graduate Schools Outside of Texas, 1907–1952.* Austin: The Texas State Historical Association, 1955.

Ford, John Salmon. *See* Oates, Stephen B. (ed.).

Frost, J. *The Mexican War and Its Warriors: Comprising a Complete History of All the Operations of the American Armies in Mexico: With Biographical Sketches and Anecdotes of the Most Distinguished Officers in the Regular Army and Volunteer Force.* New Haven and Philadelphia: H. Mansfield, [1848?].

Fuess, Claude Moore. *Daniel Webster.* 2 vols. Boston: Little, Brown, & Company, 1930.

Fulmore, Z. T. *The History and Geography of Texas as Told in County Names.* Austin, Texas: The Steck Company, 1915.

Gambrell, Herbert Pickens. *Anson Jones: the Last President of Texas.* Garden City, New York: Doubleday & Company, Inc. 1948.

—. *Mirabeau Buonaparte Lamar: Troubadour and Crusader.* Dallas, Texas: Southwest Press, 1934.

Garst, [Doris] Shannon. *Big Foot Wallace of the Texas Rangers.* New York: Julian Messner, Inc., 1951.

Giles, Bascom. *See* Bishop, Curtis.

Greer, James Kimmins. *Colonel Jack Hays: Texas Frontier Leader and California Builder.* New York: E. P. Dutton & Company, Inc., 1952.

Gutsch, Milton R. *See* Carroll, H. Bailey.

Handy, Mary Olivia. *History of Fort Sam Houston.* San Antonio, Texas: The Naylor Company, 1951.

Henderson, Harry McCorry. *Colonel Jack Hays, Texas Ranger.* San Antonio, Texas: The Naylor Company, 1954.

Heusinger, Edward W. *A Chronology of Events in San Antonio: being a Concise History of the City, Year by Year, from the Beginning of Its Establishment to the End of the First Half of the Twentieth Century.* San Antonio, Texas: Standard Printing Co., 1951.

Hill, Jim Dan. *The Texas Navy: in Forgotten Battles and Shirtsleeve Diplomacy.* Chicago, Illinois: University of Chicago Press, 1937.

Bibliography

Hogan, William Ransom. *The Texas Republic: A Social and Economic History.* Norman: University of Oklahoma Press, 1946.

House, Boyce. *City of Flaming Adventure: The Chronicle of San Antonio.* San Antonio, Texas: The Naylor Company, 1949.

Houston: A History and Guide. Compiled by Workers of the Writer's Program of the Work Projects Administration in Texas. *American Guide Series.* Houston, Texas: The Anson Jones Press, 1942.

Huson, Hobart. *District Judges of Refugio County.* Refugio, Texas: Refugio Timely Remarks, 1941.

Jack Hays: The Intrepid Texas Ranger. [Bandera, Texas: Frontier Times, n.d.].

James, Marquis. *The Raven: A Biography of Sam Houston.* Indianapolis, Indiana: The Bobbs-Merrill Co., 1929.

[Jennett, Elizabeth LeNoir]. *Biographical Directory of the Texan Conventions and Congresses.* Austin, Texas: Book Exchange, Inc., 1941.

Johnson, Frank W. *A History of Texas and Texans.* 5 vols. Chicago and New York: The American Historical Society, 1914.

Johnston, William Preston. *The Life of Gen. Albert Sidney Johnston: Embracing His Services in the Armies of the United States, the Republic of Texas, and the Confederate States.* New York: D. Appleton & Company, Inc., 1879.

Jones, William Moses. *Texas History Carved in Stone.* Houston: Monument Publishing Co., 1958.

Kemp, Louis Wiltz. *See* Dixon, Sam Houston; Kilman, Ed.

Kennedy, William. *Texas: The Rise, Progress, and Prospects of the Republic of Texas.* 2 vols. London: R. Hastings, 1841.

Kilman, Ed, and Lou W. Kemp. *Texas Musketeers: Stories of Early Texas Battles and Their Heroes.* Richmond, Virginia; Atlanta, Georgia, [etc.]: Johnson Publishing Co., 1935.

Lester, Charles Edwards. *Sam Houston and His Republic.* New York: Burgess, Stringer & Company, 1846.

[Lester, Charles Edwards]. *The Life of Sam Houston, The Hunter, Patriot, and Statesman of Texas: The Only Authentic Memoir of Him Ever Published.* Philadelphia: Davis, Porter & Coates, 1866.

—. *The Life of Sam Houston: The Only Authentic Memoir of Him Ever Published.* New York: J. C. Derby, 1855.

Lindsey, Theresa. "Stars," in *Blue Norther: Texas Poems.* New York: H. Vinal, 1925.

Lott, Virgil N., and Mercurio Martinez. *Kingdom of Zapata.* San Antonio, Texas: The Naylor Company, 1953.

Lotto, F. *Fayette County: Her History and Her People.* Schulenburg, Texas: Sticker Steam Press, 1902.

McCampbell, Coleman. *Saga of a Frontier Seaport.* Dallas, Texas: Southwest Press, 1934.

—. *Texas Seaport: The Story of the Growth of Corpus Christi and the Coastal Bend Area.* New York: Exposition Press, 1952.

Attack and Counterattack

McMaster, John B. *A History of the People of the United States, from the Revolution to the Civil War.* 8 vols. New York: D. Appleton & Company, Inc., 1883–1913.

Madray, Mrs. I. C. *A History of Bee County: with Some Brief Sketches about Men and Events in Adjoining Counties.* Beeville, Texas: Beeville Publishing Co., 1939.

Martinez, Mercurio. See Lott, Virgil N.

Nance, Joseph Milton. *After San Jacinto: The Texas-Mexican Frontier, 1836–1841.* Austin: University of Texas Press, 1963.

National Cyclopaedia of American Biography. 43 vols. New York: James T. White & Co., 1898–1961.

Oates, Stephen B. (ed.). *Rip Ford's Texas: By John Salmon Ford.* Austin, Texas: University of Texas Press, 1963.

Paddock, B[uckley] B. *A History of Central and Western Texas: compiled from Historical Data Supplied by Commercial Clubs, Individuals, and Other Authentic Sources.* 2 vols. Chicago: The Lewis Publishing Company, 1911.

Pearson, Newcomb. *The Alamo City.* San Antonio, Texas: P. Newcomb, 1926.

Peral, Miguel Angel. *Diccionario biográphico mexicano.* Mexico City: Editorial P. A. C., 1944.

Pierce, Frank C. *A Brief History of the Lower Río Grande Valley.* Menasha, Wisconsin: George Banta Publishing Co., 1917.

Pierer, Heinrich August. *Universal-Lexikon der Gergangenheit und gegenwart oder Neuestes encyclopädisches wörterbuch der wissenschaften, künste und Gewerbe.* 20 vols. New York: L. W. Schmidt, 1865.

Prieto, Alejandro. *Historia, geografía y estadistica del Estado de Tamaulipas.* Mexico City: 1873.

Rader, Jesse L. *South of Forty: From the Mississippi to the Río Grande.* Norman: University of Oklahoma Press, 1947.

Raines, C. W. *A Bibliography of Texas: Being a Descriptive List of Books, Pamphlets, and Documents Relating to Texas in Print and Manuscript since 1536, including a Complete Collation of the Laws; with an Introductory Essay on the Materials of Early Texas History.* Austin, Texas: The Gammel Book Co., 1896.

Ray, Worth S. *Austin Colony Pioneers: including the History of Bastrop, Fayette, Grimes, Montgomery and Washington Counties, Texas and their earliest Settlers.* Austin, Texas: 1949.

Red, William S. *A History of the Presbyterian Church in Texas.* Austin, Texas: The Steck Company, 1936.

Reid, Samuel C., Jr., *The Scouting Expeditions of McCulloch's Texas Rangers.* Austin, Texas: The Steck Company, 1935.

Rister, Carl C. *The Southwestern Frontier, 1865–1881.* Cleveland, Ohio: The Arthur H. Clark Co., 1928.

Riva Palacio, Vicente. *Mexico á través de los siglos.* 5 vols. [Mexico City: Publicaciónes Herrerias, 1939?].

676

Bibliography

Rivera Cambas, Manuel. *Los gobernantes de México*. 2 vols. Mexico City: Imprenta de J. M. Aguilar Ortiz, [1872]–1873.

Rives, George L. *The United States and Mexico, 1821–1848*. 2 vols. New York: Charles Scribner's Sons, 1913.

Robinson, Fay[ette]. *Mexico and Her Military Chieftains: from the Revolution of Hidalgo to the Present Time*. Hartford, Connecticut: S. Andrus & Son, 1851.

Rose, Victor M. *The Life and Services of Gen. Ben McCulloch*. Philadelphia: Pictorial Bureau of the Press, 1888.

Saldivar, Gabriel. *Historia compendiada de Tamaulipas*. Mexico City: [Editorial Beatriz de Silva], 1945.

Schmitz, Joseph William. *Texan Statecraft, 1836–1845*. San Antonio, Texas: The Naylor Company, 1941.

Schoen, Harold (comp.). *Monuments Erected by the State of Texas to Commemorate the Centenary of Texas Independence*. Austin, Texas: Commission of Control for Texas Centennial Celebration, 1938.

Scott, Florence Johnson. *Historical Heritage of the Lower Río Grande: A Historical Record of Spanish Exploration, Subjugation and Colonization of the Lower Río Grande Valley and the Activities of José Escandón, Count of Sierra Gorda together with the Development of Towns and Ranches under Spanish, Mexican and Texas Sovereignties, 1747–1848*. San Antonio, Texas: The Naylor Company, 1937.

Siegel, Stanley. *A Political History of the Texas Republic, 1836–1845*. Austin: University of Texas Press, 1956.

Smith, Justin H. *The Annexation of Texas*. Corrected ed. New York: Barnes & Noble, Inc., 1941.

—. *The War with Mexico*. 2 vols. New York: The Macmillan Company, 1919.

Smithwick, Noah. *The Evolution of a State*. Austin, Texas: Gammel Book Company, 1900.

Sowell, A. J. *Early Settlers and Indian Fighters of Southwest Texas*. Austin, Texas: Ben C. Jones & Co., Printers, 1900.

—. *History of Fort Bend County: Containing Biographical Sketches of Many Noted Characters*. Houston, Texas: W. H. Coyle & Co., 1904.

Steen, Ralph W., and Frances Donecker. *Our Texas*. Rev. ed. Austin, Texas: The Steck Company, 1954.

Streeter, Thomas W. *Bibliography of Texas*. 3 parts. Cambridge, Massachusetts: Harvard University Press, 1955–1960.

Taylor, Paul S. *An American-Mexican Frontier: Nueces County, Texas*. Chapel Hill: University of North Carolina Press, 1934.

Thrall, H. S. *A Pictorial History of Texas: from the Earliest Visits of European Adventurers to A. D. 1879*. Rev. and enl. Nashville, Tennessee: 1889.

Vapereau, Gustave. *Dictionnaire Universel des Contemporains: Contenant Toutes les Personnes Notables de la France et des Pays Etrangers*. 3rd ed. Paris: Librairie de L. Hachette, 1865.

677

Vestal, Stanley. *Big Foot Wallace.* Boston: Houghton Mifflin Company, 1942.

Wade, Houston. *See* Weyand, Leonie Rummel.

Wallis, Mrs. Jonnie Lockhart, and Laurance L. Hill. *Sixty Years on the Brazos: The Life and Letters of Dr. John Washington Lockhart, 1824–1900.* Los Angeles, California: [Press of Dunn Bros.], 1930.

Waugh, Julia Nott. *Castro-Ville and Henry Castro, Empresario.* San Antonio: Standard Printing Company, 1934.

Webb, Walter Prescott. *The Texas Rangers.* Boston: Houghton Mifflin Company, 1935.

—. "The Texas Rangers," in Eugene C. Barker (ed.), *Texas History for High Schools and Colleges.* Dallas, Texas: Turner Company, 1929. pp. 592–598.

— and H. Bailey Carroll (eds.). *The Handbook of Texas.* 2 vols. Austin: The Texas State Historical Association, 1952.

Wells, Tom Henderson. *Commodore Moore and the Texas Navy.* Austin: University of Texas Press, 1960.

Weyand, Leonie Rummel, and Houston Wade. *An Early History of Fayette County.* [LaGrange, Texas: *LaGrange Journal* Plant, 1936].

Wharton, Clarence R. *History of Fort Bend County.* San Antonio, Texas: The Naylor Company, 1939.

Wilbarger, J. W. *Indian Depredations in Texas.* 2nd ed. Austin, Texas: Hutching's Printing House, 1890.

Wooten, Dudley G. (ed.). *A Comprehensive History of Texas, 1685 to 1897.* 2 vols. Dallas, Texas: W. G. Scarff, 1898.

Wortham, Louis J. *A History of Texas.* 5 vols. Fort Worth, Texas: Wortham-Molyneaux, 1924.

Yoakum, H. *History of Texas from Its First Settlement in 1685 to Its Annexation to the United States in 1846.* 2 vols. New York: J. S. Redfield, 1855.

b. ARTICLES AND PERIODICALS

Barton, Henry W. "The Problem of Command in the Army of the Republic of Texas," *Southwestern Historical Quarterly,* LXII (1958–1959), 299–311.

Binkley, William Campbell. "The Last Stage of Texan Military Operations Against Mexico, 1843," *Southwestern Historical Quarterly,* XXII (1918–1919), 260–271.

Blount, Lois Foster. "A Brief Study of Thomas J. Rusk: Based on His Letters to His Brother, David, 1835–1856," *Southwestern Historical Quarterly,* XXXIV, (1930–1931), 181–202, 271–292.

Brown, Alma H. "Consular Service of the Republic of Texas," *Southwestern Historical Quarterly,* XXXIII (1929–1930), 299–314.

Bugbee, Lester G. "The Old Three Hundred," *Quarterly of the Texas State Historical Association,* I (1897–1898), 108–117.

Bibliography

Christian, A. K. "Mirabeau Buonaparte Lamar," *Southwestern Historical Quarterly*, XXIII (1919–1920), 153–170, 231–270; XXIV (1920–1921), 39–80, 85–139, 195–234, 317–324.

Cox, I. J., "The Southwest Boundary of Texas," *Quarterly of the Texas State Historical Association*, VI (1902–1903), 81–102.

Coyner, C. Luther. "Peter Hansbrough Bell," *Quarterly of the Texas State Historical Association*, III (1899–1900), 49–53.

Crimmins, M. L. "John W. Smith: the Last Messenger from the Alamo and the First Mayor of San Antonio," *Southwestern Historical Quarterly*, LIV (1950–1951), 344–346.

DeShields, James T. "Jack Hays: Famous Texas Ranger," in *The American Home Journal*, June 1906.

Dienst, Alex. "The Navy of the Republic of Texas," *Quarterly of the Texas State Historical Association*, XII (1908–1909), 165–203, 249–275; XIII (1909–1910), 1–43, 85–127.

Ellis, Anna. "Dawson Massacre Anniversary to See Unveiling of Memorial," *San Antonio Express*, Sept. 15, 1935.

Frontier Times (Bandera, Grand Prairie), October 1923–December 1954.

Graf, Leroy P. "Colonizing Projects in Texas South of the Nueces, 1820–1845," *Southwestern Historical Quarterly*, L (1946–1947), 431–448.

"Jack Hays and His Men," in *The Texas Democrat*, December 16, 1846.

Lindsey, Therese. "Stars," in *Blue Norther: Texas Poems*. New York: H. Vinal, 1925.

Lockhart, John W. "Darkest Days in Texas," *Galveston Daily News*, March 26, 1893.

Looscan, Adele B. "Harris County, 1822–1845," in *Southwestern Historical Quarterly*, XVIII (1914–1915), 195–207, 261–286, 399–409; XIX (1915–1916), 37–64.

McCampbell, Coleman. "Colonel Kinney's Romance with Daniel Webster's Daughter," *Crystal Reflector* (Corpus Christi), June 1939.

Marshall, Thomas M. "Diplomatic Relations of Texas and the United States, 1839–1843," *Quarterly of the Texas State Historical Association*, XV (1911–1912), 267–293.

Nance, Joseph Milton. "Adrián Woll: Frenchman in the Mexican Military Service," *New Mexico Historical Review*, XXXIII (1957–1958), 177–186.

Newsom, W. L. "The Postal System of the Republic of Texas," *Southwestern Historical Quarterly*, XX (1916–1917), 103–131.

Quarterly of the Texas State Historical Association. See Southwestern Historical Quarterly.

Ramsdell, Charles. "Introduction to Seguin," *San Antonio Express Magazine*, Sept. 18, 1949.

—. "Old England in Béxar," in *San Antonio Express*, Sept. 18, 1949.

Rogers, Marjorie. "Old Viesca," *Frontier Times*, VIII (1930–1931), 489–492.

Schoen, Harold. "The Free Negro in the Republic of Texas," *Southwestern Historical Quarterly,* XXXIX (1935–1936), 292–308; XL (1936–1937), 26–34, 85–113, 169–199, 267–289.

Southwestern Historical Quarterly. Vols. I–LXVII. Austin, Texas: Texas State Historical Association, 1897–1964.

Spell, Lota M. "Samuel Bangs: The First Printer in Texas," *Southwestern Historical Quarterly,* XXXV (1931–1932), 267–278.

Terrell, Alexander W. "The City of Austin from 1839 to 1865," *Quarterly of the Texas State Historical Association,* XIV (1910–1911), 113–128.

Tilloson, Cyrus. "Lipantitlán," *Frontier Times,* XXV (1947–1948), 27–29.

Traylor, Mrs. C. T. "George Lord," *Frontier Times,* XVI (1938–1939), 533–535.

Warren, Harry. "Col. William G. Cooke," *Quarterly of the Texas State Historical Association,* IX (1905–1906), 210–219.

Weinert, Willie Mae. "Colonel Andrew Neill," in *Seguin Enterprise,* July 22, 1938.

Wilcox, Seb S. "Laredo During the Texas Republic," *Southwestern Historical Quarterly,* XLII (1938–1939), 83–107.

Williams, Amelia. "A Critical Study of the Siege of the Alamo and of the Personnel of Its Defenders," *Southwestern Historical Quarterly,* XXXVI (1932–1933), 251–287; XXXVII (1933–1934), 1–44, 79–115, 157–184, 237–312.

Zuber, W. P. "The Escape of Rose from the Alamo," *Quarterly of the Texas State Historical Association,* V (1901–1902), 1–11.

INDEX

INDEX

Aberdeen, George H. G. (Lord): on Texan blockade, 124; states British policy on military aid in Texas-Mexican conflict, 128–129; opposition of, to tripartite mediation, 131; mention of, 139

Acenis, France: 471 n

acequias, San Antonio: 453

Achlin, Christopher ("Kit") B.: 350, 394

Ackland, Kit. SEE Achlin, Christopher ("Kit") B.

Adams, ——: in Dawson's company, 621

Adams, Andrew L.: and Vasquez raid, 18, 21, 34, 36; mention of, 36 n, 350; in battle of Salado Creek, 362

Adams, Harvey Alexander: biographical sketch of, 343 n; mention of, 366, 433, 476, 487, 552, 567; on Dawson massacre, 367; on visit of Green (T. J.), 431; on scout duty, 433; wood carving made by, 460–461; records notes on *papyrus*, 494; as member of Bogart's (S.) company, 626

Adams, J.: 629

Adams, James: 604

Adams, Thomas: 597

Adams, William: and Vasquez raid, 18, 21, 36; sells horse to Maverick (S. A.), 20; biographical sketch of, 36 n; mention of, 350, 352–353; in battle of Salado Creek, 362

Adcock, ——: on Mexican invasion, 42

Adcock, E. M.: 592

Addicks, Thomas H. O'S.: 284, 383 n

Addington, Henry: 131

adjutant-general, Texas: Hemphill (J.) named, 441; Cooke (W. G.) named, 441 n; burning of office of, 498, 624 n

Adkins, William L.: 26 n

Affleck, J. D.: 29 n

Agatón. SEE Quinoñes, Agatón

agents, Mexican: reports from, 229

—, Texan: sending abroad of, 82; warning against, 133; in United States, 133–135; expenses of, 135; instructions to, 145

Agua Dulce: Texan forces near, 229, 239, 245; Mexican forces at, 241; Las Motas de, 242, 248

Agua Nueva, Mexico: cavalry from, 51; Mexican troops at, 240

aguardiente: 516

Agua Verde Creek: 333

Aguila, Mexico: 129

Aguila, Paso de: 449, 501

Aguilar, Ana: 318 n

Alabama: mention of, 36 n, 133, 167, 192, 271, 622; volunteers from, 133, 134, 167–168, 170, 173, 176, 619

—, House of Representatives: 167

Alameda County, California: 12

Alamo: mention of, 22 n, 29, 32 n, 304 n, 309, 317, 353, 355, 376, 460; Mexican troops stationed in, 317; Texan volunteers meet in front of, 406; Burleson (E.) at, 434; location of, 450; description of, 450–451; defacing of, 460

Alamo (Mexico), battle of: 481

Alamo plaza: 307, 451

Alarm Bell of the West: 22, 49, 94

Alazán Creek: Texan prisoners at, 328

alcalde of Brazoria: 64 n

— of Guerrero, Mexico: and Somervell expedition, 547, 554–555, 555–556, 547

— of Laredo, Texas: and Somervell expedition, 511, 520, 525, 535

Alcantro, battle of: 481

Aldama, Mexico: battalion of, 309–310

Alexander, C. C.: 649

Alexander, E. G.: 599
Alexander, J. M.: 441
Alexander, J. R.: 635
Alexander, Jerome B.: in Dawson fight, 374, 374 n, 621
Alexander, Mathews: 595, 638
Alexandria, Louisiana: volunteers at, 288
Allee, Alfred. SEE Lee, Alfred A.
Allen, Augustus C.: mention of, 90; on Mexican forces at San Antonio, 337; in battle of Salado Creek, 361
Allen, C. A.: 203 n, 609
Allen, Daniel: 595
Allen, David: 646
Allen, George: 587, 645
Allen, Henry W.: company under, 170, 172, 246, 278, 615; mention of, 202 n
Allen, Isaac: 203 n, 587, 600
Allen, J. A.: 615
Allen, J. M.: company under, 172, 204 n, 613; return of, to Galveston for supplies, 191; efforts of, to obtain French artillerists for army, 192
Allen, James L.: 598
Allen, R. A.: 592
Allen, W. W.: 639
Alley, George W.: 587, 645
Alley, James: 622
Alley, William: 598
Alphin, Samuel G.: 647
Alsbury, ——: 218
Alsbury, Mrs.: goes with Texan prisoners, 329
Alsbury, H. Alexander: 600
Alsbury, William: 502, 505
Alsobrook, William: 636
Alston, ——: 608
Alston, Henry: 647
Alton: transports volunteers, 171
Alvarado, Mexico: *Washington* at, 43
Alvarez, Juan: uprising of, 309
Ambrose, M.: 636
American Eagle (Memphis): 148, 216
Ammons, Jesse: 636
ammunition: mention of, 44, 70, 72–75, 80, 385, 406, 484, 562, 609; shortage of, 56, 57, 146, 466–467; seized from Austin arsenal, 96; at San Luis Potosí, 105
Amoladeras Crossing: 314, 314 n
Ampudia, Pedro de: commands troops at Matamoros, 63, 229, 230; mention of, 237, 558 n; named counsellor, 340; as

commandant of Tamaulipas, 340; report on expected arrival of, 382; departs from Matamoros, 482 n
Anderson, ——: 608
Anderson, Charles S.: 589
Anderson, Francis: 645
Anderson, Franklin: 587
Anderson, George: 597, 629
Anderson, James D.: 596
Anderson, James S.: 593, 635
Anderson, Jinny: 457
Anderson, John D.: 14
Anderson, Kenneth L.: 263
Anderson, Nathan B.: 589
Anderson, Peter: 610
Anderson, Richard: 587
Andrade, Juan José: 310, 451
Andrews, John D.: heads Houston committee of vigilance and safety, 82
Andrews, M.: 559 n
Andrews, Stephen P.: at Galveston, 83; as agent to United States, 83, 146
Angling, Abram: 636
Angling, Elijah: 636
Angling, John: 636
Anglo-Americans. SEE Anglo-Texans
Anglo-Saxon race: 107, 143
Anglo-Texans: mention of, 9, 43; at San Antonio, 12, 18, 305; flee San Antonio, 34, 35, 224, 305, 306, 322, 431; and Seguin (J. N.), 37; at Corpus Christi, 43, 115 n; return of, to San Antonio, 223; at Matamoros, 238; and defense of San Antonio, 305, 306; lawlessness of, 418 n; frontier abandoned by, 580
annexation to United States, Texas: interest in, 126; effects of Mexican invasion on, 151; opposition to, in United States, 215, 580
Anti-Quaker (Austin): 49, 94
Apache Indians: mention of, 446, 446 n–447 n, 494 n; attacks of, upon Laredo, 512, 513. SEE ALSO Lipan Indians
Apalachicola, Florida: 171
aparajos: 488
Aransas, Texas: sea expedition to, 79; mention of, 86, 246; location of, 175
Aransas Bay: 45, 46, 175
Aransas Pass: 85, 86
Aransas River: 41, 86, 176
Aranzazu, Fort: 175
Aranzazu River: 41, 86, 176
Arceneiga, Miss: 457

navy, 120; moves volunteers to Live
Oak Point, 174
Boyle, I. H.: 609
Bracken, William: 598
Bradley, ——: 203 n
Bradley, John: at San Antonio, 18; bio-
graphical sketch, 18 n–19 n; mention of,
21; at Capote Farm, 35; letters of, 224;
at San Fernando, 333; Elliot (W.) fur-
nishes horse to, 385; military service of,
623, 636
Bradley, Mrs. John: 18, 20
Bradley, W.: 615
Braneka, Henry: 619
Brann, James: 646
Brashear, W. C.: 162 n
Bratten, Joseph: 639, 641
Bratton, George: 589
Bratton, J. SEE Bratten, Joseph
Bravo, Calixto: mention of, 16, 520; in
Vasquez raid, 30; makes surpise attack
on Indians, 52; and Woll raid, 337;
commands garrison opposite Laredo,
501, 511
Bravo, Nicolás: rumors of invasion of
Texas by, 42; as acting president, 298
Bray, Ferdinand: 597, 629, 638
Brazoria, Municipality of. SEE Brazoria,
Texas
Brazoria, Texas: mention of, 15 n, 64 n,
71, 175 n, 305; and Mexican invasion,
59; plans for convention at, 156; militia
at, 194; volunteers from, 480, 541
Brazoria County, Texas: militia of, 114;
194, 409, 410; mention of, 163, 175 n,
198, 258–259, 445, 461; vote of, on
"war bill," 257
Brazos County, Texas: vote of, on "war
bill," 257; troops from, 410. SEE ALSO
Navasota County
Brazos River: volunteers west of, 74, 96 n,
411; mention of, 77, 95, 114, 213, 243,
257, 286, 337, 417, 421, 592; wreck of
Columbus at, 115 n; recession of frontier to, 418; flood of, 435
Brazos Santiago: sloop *Washington* at,
43; Texan plans for capturing, 86; failure of *Lafitte* to visit, 110; mention of,
117; troops reported at, 482
Brazos valley: 162, 421
bread: mention of, 40, 66, 272, 472, 522,
554, 577; provision for, 171; report on,
172; shortage of, 439, 465

Breckenridge, R.: 610
Brenham, Richard Fox: 64 n, 293, 632
Brennan, John: 597, 629
Brey, Ferdinand. SEE Bray, Ferdinand
Bridger, Henry: 637
bridges: lack of, at San Antonio, 453
Bridges, Thomas: 594
Bridgman, J. C.: 631
bridles: 60, 522
Brigade, First (Southwestern Army): 444
—, First (Texas Militia): 114, 412, 533
—, Second (Southwestern Army): 444,
532
Brigance, Franklin: 628
Brigance, Harry: 628
Briggs, E. A.: 63
Briggs, W. R.: 610
Brigham, Asa: 64, 64 n
Brigham, S. B.: 593
Brilliante: at Galveston, 117
Brimberry, Alford: 649
Brimberry, Samuel: 649
Briscoe, G. C.: 253 n
Brister, R. E.: 599
Britain. SEE Great Britain
Brite, John: 588
Brite, Thomas: 588, 645
Brodie, J. H.: 599
Brookfield, Francis E.: 622
Brookfield, Frank W. SEE Brookfield,
Francis E.
Brookshire, A. S.: 627
Broome, A. D.: 617
Brothers, John: 589
Brower, H. H.: 178 n, 246, 609
Brower, John S.: in U. S., 137, 150
Brown, ——: 609
Brown, C. A.: 628
Brown, Caleb S.: 348
Brown, Edward: 601
Brown, George William: at Galveston
public meeting, 71; Houston's (S.) let-
ter to, 108; health of, 109 n
Brown, H.: 629
Brown, H. H. SEE Brower, H. H.
Brown, Henry: 591
Brown, J. D.: 637
Brown, J. H.: 637, 643
Brown, James H.: 601, 617
Brown, James M.: 427, 595
Brown, John Henry: and Vasquez raid,
23, 25, 29 n, 33; on Texan vote to re-
treat, 29 n; mention of, 348, 360, 360 n;

caballada: 44, 400, 500. See also horses, Mexican
Cabezos, Blas: commands spy unit, 240
cacti: 343, 491, 502, 513
Caddo Indians: in Vasquez's (R.) army, 27, 30, 51
Cade, J. B.: 617
Cage, Ben: 596
Cahawba, Alabama: 178
Cairns, W. J.: killing of, by Mexicans, 42, 43, 86, 208
caissons: at arsenal, 96, 227
Calahan, John: 598
Calaveras, ———: 52–53
Calaveras' Ranch: 52, 224, 575
Caldwell, John: 100, 368
Caldwell, Mathew: assembles volunteers, 36; and Woll raid, 336, 342, 346, 356–378, 380, 382, 385, 388, 389, 390, 392–395, 396–397, 398, 399–404, 479; mention of, 336, 345, 386 n, 422, 447; warns of the march of Pérez (A.), 338; commands Texas volunteer army, 343, 347, 350, 392; spirit of, 344, 399; biographical sketch of, 347–348; at battle of Salado Creek, 349–350, 356, 358, 362, 364, 378, 382; inability of, to aid Dawson (N. H.), 368; and lack of discipline in army, 396, 401–402; address of, to troops, 398; and failure to pursue Woll (A.), 399–404; death of, 402; route of, 479
Caldwell, Texas: militia at, 195
Calhoun, Thomas: 617
Calhoun, Texas. See Port Calhoun, Texas
calico: trade in, 208, 513
California: 20 n, 386 n
Callaghan, ———: 23, 318
Callaghan, Bryan: as Woll prisoner, 323 n, 328, 353, 600 n
Callaghan, Jn: 629
Callahan, James H.: commands company of volunteers at San Antonio, 23, 24; Minute Men under, buy lots in Seguin, 336; mention of, 348
Callender, Sidney S.: mention of, 488 n, 578; military service of, 589, 646
Calvert, James H.: 632
Calvert, N. H.: 587
Calvillo, Cavalry of Explorers from: 51
Calvillo Rancho. See Calaveras' Ranch
Calvo, Michael: 11
Camargo, Mexico: *defensores* of, 7, 44;

Mexican forces move from, 7, 239, 240, 252–253; mention of, 44, 112 n, 202, 238, 471 n, 536; depredations of Indians against, 110, 230; plans for attack on, 484, 534, 560
Cameron, Ewen: at Corpus Christi, 43; escape of, 43, 87; commands company on Nueces, 205, 247; in battle of Lipantitlán, 253; biographical sketch of, 253 n; ranger company of, 276, 286; voted thanks at Victoria, 283; proposed expedition of, against Mexico, 287; *Telegraph* praises courage of, 287; and pursuit of Woll, 348, 361, 399; mention of, 445, 462 n, 516, 545; on Somervell expedition, 478–479, 528, 559, 561 n, 629
Camino Real, El: 512
Campbell, ———: 242, 286, 643
Campbell, J. K.: 625
Campbell, Mrs. James: 19
Campbell, John: 627
Camp Boggy: 489
Camp Chacón: 515
Camp Cooke: 449, 470, 473, 474
Campechano (Schooner): 129
Camp Everitt: 186
Camp Hope: 447, 478, 642
Camp Howard: 480
Camp La Retama: 535
Camp León: 424
Camp Murphree: 487
Camp Nueces, Mexico: 181
Camp Rocky: 413, 436
Camp San Ignacio. See Camp San Ygnacio
Camp, San Ygnacio: 497, 503
Camp Williams: 186
Canada de los Abiones: 503 n
Canales, Antonio: mention of, 237, 241, 263, 277, 297, 543, 558 n, 582; at Corpus Christi, 238; and Aubrey-Kinney Rancho, 238; and battle of Lipantitlán, 239, 240, 245–246, 247, 251–252, 252–253; as commandant of the Villas del Norte, 240; at Guerrero, 501, 539, 545, 554
Canary Islands: 243
Candela, Mexico: 513
Candelaria, Andrea: 455
Canfield, Israel: imprisonment of, 561; criticizes Somervell (A.), 561 n; military service of, 597, 629
cannister: 57
cannon, Mexican: mention of, 240, 242,

Index

394, 570; use of, against Texans, 249; abandoned by Gougales, 341; at Arroyo Hondo, 391; report of, 481
—, Texan: removal of, from San Antonio, 29, 32; captured by Vasquez (R.), 32; mention of, 34, 79–80, 239, 411, 505; ammunition for, 57; at Austin, 68; on Santa Fé expedition, 68 n; at Galveston, 72, 75, 425–426; sent to San Antonio, 94, 444, 473, 479, 480; at Corpus Christi, 192; taken to Gonzales, 228; location of, 241; for Somervell expedition, 444, 473, 479, 480
Cannon, William R.: 588
canoes: use of, in crossing Río Grande, 240, 332; mention of, 311, 436, 541
Cañon de San Andres: 529
Cañon Ford: 329, 386, 479
canteens: 172, 272
Cantero, José María: 324 n
Cantú, José: 52–53
Canty, J.: 629
Capitol Hill, Austin: fort on, 68
Caplin, Charles: 590
Capote Farm: 21, 35, 36
Capote Hills: location of, 21
caps, coon skin: 174
—, percussion: mention of, 23 n, 304; shortage of, 57, 436; at Washington-on-the-Brazos, 467
Carbajal, Bruno: 324 n
Carbajal, Manuel: 29 n, 352
Cárdenas, Jesús: 237
Cardwell, C.: 597
Cardwell, William: 597
Careese Indian. SEE Carrizo Indians
Carl, Daniel: 595
Carlos, Francisco: 229
Carlos Rancho: location of, 223; Mexicans at, 223, 286; Texan army at, 276; report of Mexican soldiers at, 339
Carmen, Campeche: Moore (E. W.) at, 118
Carney, D. L.: 598
Carolitas Ranch: 536
Carr, ——: 609
Carr, A. C.: 639
Carr, John: 610
Carrasco, José María: enters Texan lines, 26, 28; as aide-de-camp to Vasquez (R.), 30; mention of, 51, 313, 319, 322, 326, 357, 367–368, 602; as quartermaster to Woll's (A.) army, 311, 319;

takes horse from Maverick (S. A.), 328; in Dawson (N. W.) fight, 363, 372, 380; reports heavy death toll of Mexicans, 380; appraises the situation at the Arroyo Hondo, 396, 402
carretas: 313, 402
Carrizo, Texas: 471 n, 538–539, 552
Carrizo Indians: join with Mexicans, 223; mention of, 470 n, 540, 552
Carson, William J.: 593
Carter, George W.: 617
Carter, Giles: 628
Carter, John: 628, 640
cartment: impressment of, 470
cartouche boxes. SEE cartridge boxes
cartridge boxes: need for, 57; mention of, 74, 609, 613, 617–618; report on, 172; receipt of, 213
cartridges: molded by women, 75
carts: mention of, 20, 35, 384, 390, 514, 526; abandoned by Woll (A.), 431–432; impressment of, 470; bring supplies to Texans, 552
Cartwright, Peter: 559 n
Caruthers, James: 595
Casa Blanca, Texas: 39, 241
Casares, Laureno: 251 n
Casey, Thomas: as commander at Corpus Christi, 178, 179, 180–181, 182
Cassedy, Bernard: 610
Cassedy, James: 610
Cash, J. L.: 629
Casner, James: 588 n
Castañeda, Francisco: commands presidial companies, 316, 358; pursues Hayes (J. C.), 355; order to, to attack Texans, 356
Castleman, John: 394 n
Castro (Lipan Chief): mention of, 41, 193; at Austin, 67; claims of, for pay, 224; with Texan army, 226
Castro, Henri: 214
Castroville, Texas: 386, 389
casualties, Mexican: in Dawson fight, 373; Brown (J.H.) reports on, 378; Woll (A.) reports on, 378–379; Hunt (M.) reports on, 379; Caldwell (J.) reports on, 380
—, Texan: in Dawson fight, 373; Arrangoiz (F. de) reports on, 377 n; Brown (J. H.) reports on, 378; Caldwell (M.) reports on, 378; Woll's (A.) report on,

693

701

Index

Fullinwider, Peter H.: 275
Fuqua, Henry: 628
Fuqua, S.: 641
Furman, A.: 610
"fusees": description of, 78
Fusileers. SEE Galveston Fusileers

Gage, Shirley: 588
Gainer, John: 592
Gaines, Edmund P.: 140
Galán, Norverto: 7, 40
Galban, Damacio: 15
Galbreath, Thomas: 377 n
Gall, Fred B.: 612
Gallaher, Charles: 610
Galveston, Mexico: raid against, 517, 524
—, Texas: mention of, 40 n, 44 n, 59, 70–
71, 73–74, 77–79, 108, 120, 123, 125,
237, 269, 300 n, 341, 387 n, 592, 617;
and Vasquez raid, 57, 72, 76; sends
commissioners to U.S., 57; volunteers
at, 62, 111, 138, 162–163, 167–168,
169, 170, 171, 174, 178, 192, 193, 239,
246, 278; arsenal at, 68 n, 467; Merchants Exchange at, 70; public meeting
at, 70–71, 153, 161–162; defenses of,
72, 76, 410, 411, 414–415, 425–426;
militia at, 72, 194, 246; support for war
effort in, 75, 111, 163, 410; formation of
Fusileers at, 78; Houston (S.) at, 80;
supplies from U.S. at, 83, 213; "War
Party" at, 83; and sea expedition, 85;
ships at, 88, 117, 118, 119, 123–124,
293; death of McLean (E. W.) at,
115 n; foreign naval vessels at, 117,
123–124; Mexican threat to blockade,
117; Moore (E. W.) at, 118, 120, 121,
183; British consul at, 151; conditions
in, 152, 171, 174, 221; and army on
Nueces, 183; desertions at, 204; dissatisfaction at, 218; disobedience of
citizens in, 221; rumors at, of Mexican
advances, 276 n, 425; Mexican ships at,
293, 299; and Woll raid, 410; *Texas
Times* at, 419; storm at, 410, 415, 425
Galveston Artillery Company: organization of, 77; Fusileers combine with, 78;
members of, 590
Galveston Coast Guard: votes to sell
liquor, 76; operation of, 77; and fitting
out of *Lafitte*, 78; commanded by Wade
(J.), 79; equipment of, 80; poem dedi-

cated to, 84–85; return of, 87; inspection of, 167; mention of, 411
Galveston County, Texas: mention of, 156,
198, 258–259; and "war bill," 257
Galveston Daily Advertiser: Yates (A. J.)
as publisher of, 71; mention of, 163; on
invading Mexico, 163
Galveston Fusileers: organized at Galveston, 77–78; combines with Galveston
Artillery Company, 78; equipment of,
80; at Deckrow's, 85; at Lamar, 87;
division of, 87; return of, to Galveston,
87; inspection of, 167; roster of, 591
Galveston Guards: organization of, 77;
inspection of, 167
Galveston Hussar Cavalry: formation of,
77–78; in Second Brigade, T. M., 78;
ordered to San Felipe, 78; equipment
of, 78; members of, 592
Galveston Invincibles: return of, to Galveston, 203; flag of, 250 n–251 n; mention of, 613; commanded by Allen
(J. M.), 613–614
Galveston Island: fort at east end of, 72;
restrictions on leaving, 80; Cruger (N.)
at, 134; U.S. citizens on, 140; troops on,
167; artillery sent to, 411; fear of attack
on, 424; flight of persons from, 424
Galveston Times: on government, 218
Galveston University: 532
Galveston Vedettes. SEE Galveston Coast
Guards
Gambier, Ohio: 149
Gamble, George A.: 588
gambling: in Texan army, 202; at San
Antonio, 303; mention of, 456
Gammell, William: 588
Gammon, J. G.: 625
Gandie, I.: 613
Garan, Dan: 636
García, Francisco: uprising of, 309
García, José: 324 n
García, José María: 12
García, Macino: 590
García, Miguel: 324 n
Garcitas, Rancho de: 240
Garey, Elijah: 622
Gardinier, Aaron A.: 177 n
Garita, La. SEE Powder House, 588
Garrett, W. H.: 588
Garrido, Juan: 319
Garza family: 471 n
Garza, Pedro. SEE Garza, Refugio de la

705

Index

Goodman, L. C.: 592

Goodman, S.: 644

Goodman, Stephen: 592

Goodman, William B.: visit of, to Mexican camp, 44; in charge of commissary, 189, 205; reports disorder among Texan troops, 276–277

Goolsbee, John F.: 617

Goosoneaux, Charles: 606

Gordon, G. W.: 203 n, 612, 617

Gorman, James: 598

Gougales, ——: 340, 341

Government Plaza, San Antonio. SEE Plaza de Constitución, San Antonio

Gower, George: 628

Grace, Morgan: 628

Graham, Joshua: 631

Graham, W. A.: 599

Grand Gulf, Mississippi: Jaques and Browning at, 15 n; volunteers from, 170; mention of, 615

grand jury: 305

Grangenito: 240

Grant, J. C.: 591

Grant, James: 97, 196

Granville, —— (slave): 18, 20

grape shot: 57

grapes: 303 n, 450

grass: mention of, 20, 314; lack of, 157

"Grass Fight": Somervell (A.) in, 98 n, 532

Graves, Jerome B.: 596

Gravesend, England: *Montezuma* sails from, 128

Gray, ——: 612

Gray, French Strother: appeals to citizens of Gonzales for aid, 25; capture of, by Woll (A.), 323; military service of, 601

Gray, J. L.: 613

Gray, James: 595, 604, 615

Gray, James W.: 638

Gray, Michael: 625

Gray, P. W.: 592

Gray, Pleasant: 625

Gray, W. J.: 628

Gray, William: 649

Great Britain: mention of, 18 n, 123; mediation of, 81 n, 132, 264–265, 267, 434; sends naval vessel to Galveston, 117; interference with commerce of, 124; U.S. relations with, 130, 138; Texan treaties with, 130, 131; and Mexican invasion, 151; return of Ken-

nedy (W.) to, 169 n; misrepresentation of Texas in, 214

Green, Fanny Hawkins: 517

Green, John, Jr.: 56–57, 70

Green, Solomon: 517

Green, Thomas: commands troops, 67, 93–94, 389; accompanies Burleson (E.), 93–94; as brigade major, 442, 529; and raising of troops, 473

Green, Thomas Jefferson: and Burleson (E.), 100, 102–103, 417; mention of, 113, 301 n, 406, 472, 557 n; disruptive actions of, 157, 431; and Houston (S.), 157; demands offensive action against Mexico, 157; at Columbus, 417; biographical sketch of, 517–518; and Somervell expedition, 517, 518, 524, 541, 542, 562; crosses Río Grande, 517, 524, 541, 542; insubordination of, 517, 518, 524, 541, 542; conference of, with Santa Anna, 518

Green, Wharton J.: 301 n

Greens and Wigrams: shipyard of, 127

Greenwood, B. C.: 637

Greer, Felix: 594

Greer, G. D.: 631

Greer, John A.: as president pro tempore of Senate, 197, 258; and "war bill," 258, 259

Greesham, E. H. SEE Gresham, E. H.

Gresham, E. H.: 641

Grey, J. D.: 599

Griffin, Joe (slave): mention of, 18, 457; accompanies Maverick (S. A.) to San Antonio, 305; death of, 369; in Dawson fight, 372, 622

Grimes, Jacob: 636

Grimes County, Texas: 412, 559 n

grist mill: 533, 539

Groce, Leonard W.: 427, 501 n

Groesbeck, J. D.: 591

Grosjean, John C.: 604

Grubbs, F.: 636

Guadalajara, Mexico: 309

Guadaloupe: equipment of, 12; construction of, in England, 127, 128; at Vera Cruz, 129

Guadalupe River: mention of, 21, 28–29, 33, 35, 68, 156, 333, 336, 352–353, 407, 447, 479; volunteers from, 28 n, 96; description of, 35; settlements on, 63, 229, 307, 421; Texan troops on, 91, 335, 364; thieving party from, 188, 225; val-

707

Henderson, James W. ("Smokey"): 446
Hendrick, Benjamin F.: 594
Hendricks, Sterling Brown: commands picket guard, 516; on Somervell expedition, 527, 532 n, 587
Henrie, D. D.: 593
Henry, John R.: 589
Henry, Patrick: 500
Hensley, ——: 577
Hensley, Alen: 598
Hensley, Charles: 633
Hensley, William: 633
Hensley, William R.: 597
Herbert, C. C.: 594
Herbert, Nathaniel. SEE Harbert, Nathaniel
Herbert, P. Walter: speech of, 157
Herdman, James. SEE Henderson, James
herdsmen. SEE rancheros
Hermitage: 12, 267
Hernández, José: 324 n
Herington, John: 631
Hernández, Juan: 319 n
Herndon, John H.: 442
Herndon, Robert: 560
Herren, ——: 608
Herrens, John H.: 645
Herrera, Francisco: 352, 353, 358
Herrington, J.: 644
Herror, John: 588
Hervey, Edward M.: 604
Hibernia. SEE San Patricio, Texas
Hickey, E.: 607
Hickey, Walter: 152, 173, 277, 606
Hickory Point: 412
Higerson, John: 604
Higgerson, John: 623
Higginbotham, R. T.: 524
Higginbotham, Roderick F.: 453 n
Higginbotham, Thomas: 439
Higginbotham's Mill: 433, 439, 443
Higgins, Thompson: 631
Higgins, William A.: 631
Higgins, William G.: 646
Highsmith, Benjamin F.: as courier, 33; and Seguin (J. N.), 52–53; on Somervell expedition, 394
Highsmith, Samuel: 33, 34, 588
Hightower, R. D.: 625
Hill, ——: 596
Hill, A. W.: 588
Hill, Benjamin F.: 592
Hill, Charles: 649

Hill, George: 338
Hill, George A.: 622
Hill, H. B.: 64
Hill, Isaac: 604
Hill, John Christopher Columbus: 562 n
Hill, Jordan: 593
Hill, O. H. P.: 625
Hill, Robert H.: 593
Hill, Samuel: 649
Hill, W. Peyton: 588
Hinkle, Samuel: 593
Hinton, Samuel: 591
Hitchcock, Captain: 171
Hitchcock, Ethan Allen: 209
Hitchcock, L. M.: commands *Borden*, 79
Hitchcock, P. N.: 606
Hobbs, P. H.: 625
Hobbs, Robert: 628
Hockley, George W.: as Secretary of War and Marine, 11–12, 413–414; on finances of War Department, 11–12; and Vasquez raid, 26, 55, 56–57, 65, 66, 92, 94, 95; and militia, 55, 97, 424; proclaims martial law at Austin, 65; organizes spies, 66; and Burleson (E.), 92; sends cannon to San Antonio, 94; and archives war, 95, 137; and defense of Galveston Island, 100 n, 411, 424, 425; serves as escort for Santa Anna (A. L. de), 106 n; and Moore (E. W.), 120; mention of, 162 n, 183; named engineer for Port of Galveston, 414
Hoffer, John: 610
Hoffman, Charles: 591
Hogan, Thomas H.: 605
hogs: 36, 100, 439, 546
Holden, Joshua: 64
Holderfield, B.: 625
Holderman, A. S.: 588, 645
Holliday, John J.: 293
Holliday, M. E.: 138
Hollis, David: 648
Holly Springs, Mississippi: 152
Holt, James L.: 617
Holton, W. S.: 645
honey: 487, 522
Hondo, Arroyo: Texas spies on, 17; mention of, 315, 330, 390, 431, 563; Woll (A.) prisoners on, 330; Woll (A.), retreats across, 390–392; fight at, 394; Texans discontinue pursuit at, 398
Hood, Thomas: 627, 644
Hoofmeister, H. H.: 591

Hope, Thomas: 638
Hope, Camp: 447, 478, 642
Hopkins, Frank: 203 n, 610
Hopkins, Math: 591
Hopkins, Thomas J.: 591
Hopson, W. J.: 607
Hopson, William: 637
horses: capture of, by Texans, 4–5, 35, 44, 464, 511, 553; mention of, 20, 29, 39, 60, 115 n, 239, 281, 311, 349, 353, 403, 406, 416, 427, 432, 454, 509, 511, 522, 550, 554, 567–569; scarcity of, 39; and Mexican raids, 39, 49, 64; capture of, by Lipans, 41; capture of, by Mexicans, 43, 104, 223, 224; contribution of, 72, 75, 76; impressment of, 81, 276, 547, 552; need for, 147, 342, 562; restoration of, to Mexican traders, 206; during Woll raid, 313, 318, 324, 355; of Texan prisoners, 328; lost by Woll (A.), 332, 388, 431, 433; and Somervell expedition, 433, 447, 466, 472, 474, 479, 487; trade in, 513; loss of, by Texans, 551, 571, 574
—, pack: 272, 439, 484–485
—, wild: mention of, 314, 537; hunting of, 454, 492; large herds of, 493; description of, 502
Horton, Albert C.: 45, 339, 446, 594
Hoskins, John N.: 593
Hospital, Perote: 601, 603
Houghton, William D.: 293, 445, 640–641
House of Representatives, Alabama: 167
House of Representatives, Texas. SEE Congress, Texas
houses: description of, 35; contribution of, 75, 76; mention of, 322
Houston, A. D.: 641
Houston, David: 648
Houston, Sam: and army, 3, 73, 80–81, 83–84, 97, 117, 156, 170, 171, 182, 251, 289, 309, 399–400, 412; policy of, toward Mexico, 3, 6, 11, 71, 73, 81, 82, 88, 92, 97, 104, 105, 106 n, 107–109, 123, 124, 135–137, 154, 158–160, 261–262, 263–264, 265, 267, 269–270, 270–271, 284, 410, 580, 581–582; defense policy of, 3–4, 71, 72–73, 80–82, 92, 97, 104, 105, 107–109, 117, 124, 135–137, 154, 164, 182–183, 280, 289, 399–400, 410, 580, 581–582; mention of, 5, 12–13, 53, 64, 191, 257, 342 n, 387 n, 417–419, 441 n, 524; and Vasquez raid,

6, 11, 70–71, 72–73, 80; attacks on, 22 n, 71, 101–103, 183, 216, 217, 218, 265, 266, 267; at Galveston, 70–72, 200, 218; call to arms by, 73, 83–84, 137, 242, 289, 409; and army at Lipantitlán, 80, 81, 82, 83–84, 89, 97, 153, 196; and blockade of Mexico, 88, 294; and Johnston (A. S.), 89, 160–161; and Burleson (E.), 99, 101–103, 156; and foreign governments, 117, 499; and navy, 118, 119, 120, 122, 123, 164; enemies of, 154, 183, 197; support for, 158, 161; and "war bill," 184–185, 198–199, 261–262, 263–264, 267; and Congress, 184–185, 198–199, 200, 257, 261–262, 263–264, 267, 269; attitude of, toward marauders, 188; drinking by, 188–189; and archives war, 199–200; at Houston, 200, 422; orders release of Mexican traders, 206; description of, 215–216, 219–220; officials appointed by, 218, 280; and colonization, 231; and Woll raid, 399–400; at Washington-on-the-Brazos, 412, 422; and Somervell expedition, 423, 428, 440–441, 483, 497, 552; and Indians, 432; and Green (T. J.), 518 n–519 n
Houston, Texas: Houston (S.) at, 6, 80, 81; mention of, 42, 56, 64 n, 73, 77, 183, 222, 330, 343 n, 439, 577; and Vasquez raid, 57, 61–62, 69, 96 n; volunteers from, 61–62, 70, 77, 111, 410, 411–412, 413, 435; troops at, 61–62, 70, 73, 77, 410; arms at, 73, 288, 411; "War Party" at, 83; Van Ness (G.) at, 105; Somervell (A.) at, 115; Moore (E. W.) at, 122; mayor of, 192; militia at, 194; Hays, (J. C.) at, 280; and Mexican spies, 302; and Woll raid, 409, 410, 411, 465; artillery from, sent to Galveston, 411
Houston Artillery Company: 68 n
Houston County: militia in, 194; and "war bill," 257; mention of, 259
Houstonian: 70
Houston Street, San Antonio: 366 n
Houstoun, Mrs. M. C.: on Houston (S.), 219
Houton, W. D.: SEE Houghton, W. D.
Howard, George Thomas: mention of, 11, 445; illness of, 100 n; reports enemy soldiers at Carlos Rancho, 339; and Somervell expedition, 442, 498, 565

Index

rankawa Indians; Lipan Indians; Mescaleros; Tahuacano Indians; Tonkawa Indians; Waco Indians

Indios, Paso de los: 503 n, 509, 512

Infantry, Fourth Regiment of (Army of the North): 240, 242, 251

—, Seventh Regiment of (Army of the North): 237

—, Sixth Regiment of (Army of the North): 50

—, Twelfth Regiment of (Army of the North): 50

Inge, Fort: 313

Ingram, George: 646

Innes, George B.: 646

inspector general (Texas), acting: 266

—, acting assistant: 193–194

invasion, French: 298

—, of Mexico: mention of, 6, 424, 440; Mexican preparations against, 10, 229, 448–449; *Telegraph and Texas Register* on, 109; Texan plans for, 117, 144, 166, 289, 291, 295, 412, 428; Houston (S.) on, 144, 163, 262, 289, 412; purpose of, 144; requirements for, 145; and U.S., 145, 157, 580; public approval of, 153, 154, 155–156, 163, 265, 287–288, 406, 417, 427, 434, 581; objections to, 154, 268; publicity of, 166; volunteers for, 229; and Eve (J.), 293. SEE ALSO Somervell expedition

—, of Texas: reports of, 6–7, 92, 223–224, 276, 288, 293, 295, 337, 339, 429; difficulties of, 8; Mexican preparations for, 9; failure of, 59; resentment about, 59; size of force in, 76, 229; effects of, on Mexico, 151; effects of, on Texas, 153–154, 300; mention of, 213. SEE ALSO Vasquez campaign; Woll campaign

Invincible: 518

Ireland: 19 n

Irion, Van R.: 640

Irish colony: 208

iron: 472

Irvin, B. F.: 648

Irvin, Peter: 648

Irwin, A.: 616

Isbel, William: 640

Ivy, John: 641

Ivy, John: 627

Ivy, John: 640

jacales: 451

Jacinto, El Paso de: 503 n, 509, 512

Jack, William H.: military service of, 71, 593; at Galveston meeting, 163; as member of Senate, 198; and "war bill," 258, 259

jack rabbits: 314

Jackson, ——: 305, 485 n, 596

Jackson, Colonel: 246

Jackson, Alden A. M.: commands militia, 57, 70, 72, 424; and defenses of Galveston, 72; and fitting out of ships, 80; mention of, 590

Jackson, Andrew: mention of, 12, 16, 206; visit of Santa Anna (A. L. de) to, 106 n; on "war bill," 267–268

Jackson, H. M.: 641

Jackson, Joseph: 628

Jackson, Riley: 601

Jackson, W. T.: 610

Jackson, William A.: 632

Jackson, William W.: 619

Jackson, Mississippi: 150

Jackson County: militia from, 44, 195, 290; volunteers from, 45, 290; mention of, 177 n, 445

Jacobs, J. J.: 640, 642

Jacques, Gideon: 594

Jalisco, Mexico: 27 n, 236

James, Alfred F.: 591

James, Madison: 646

James, O.: 616

James, Thomas D.: 593, 621 n

James, William: 636

Jameson, C.: 593

Janerette, Thomas D.: 610

January, Henry: 596

Jaques, William B.: on Béxar County Committee of Safety, 14; biographical sketch of, 14 n–15 n; at San Antonio, 18; and Vasquez raid, 27, 28 n, 35, 47, 48; furnishes supplies for troops, 23; at Capote Farm, 35; home, of, burned, 48; mention of, 34 n, 385

Jaques, Mrs. William B: mention of, 15 n, 33–34, 323, 386; flees San Antonio, 18; buries money, 34

Jaques and Browning: 15 n

Jarvis, George: 593

Jaso, Candelario: 324 n

Jasper, Texas: militia in, 195

Jasper County: militia in, 195

javelinas: 314

713

714

88, 110; mention of, 111; transfer of supplies to army by, 191; to transport troops, 410
LaForge, A. B.: 630
La Garita. SEE Powder House
LaGrange, Texas: mention of, 25 n, 305, 326, 364, 368, 375, 498, 559 n, 621 n; Hays (J. C.) dispatches courier to, 33; militia at, 194, 436; Lockmar (A.) at, 224; public meeting at, 337; and Pérez's (A.) march, 338; heavy rains at, 341; volunteers from, 385, 389, 436; Burleson (E.) at, 420–421, 421 n
Laguna de Términos: 118
Laguna Espantosa: 314 n, 331
Laguna Madre: Texan cannon at, 241
Lahn, J.: 644
Laird, John: shipyard of, 127
Lake, Storm: 605
Lake Espantosa. SEE Laguna Espantosa
Lake Lipantitlán: 185 n, 186
Lamar, Mirabeau Buonaparte: mention of, 3, 5, 13, 71, 73, 106 n, 133, 163, 244, 382, 386 n, 441 n; expenditures of, 5; and Vasquez raid, 45; administration of, 67, 478 n; and location of capital, 200; challenged to duel by Hunt (M.), 266; at San Antonio, 457; on Laredo, 513; military service of, 593
Lamar, Texas: Fusileers stationed at, 87; customhouse at, 175; hasty Texan retreat from, 276, 286; mention of, 276–277
Lamar County, Texas: militia in, 195; and "war bill," 257
Lamb, Thomas: 624
Lamberson, R. SEE Lamberston, R.
Lamberston, R.: 203 n, 616
Lampazos, Mexico: 27, 449, 481 n
La Nava, Mexico: Texan prisoners at, 332; corn at, 482
land, public: sale of, 136; decline in value of, 221
land office: papers of, 65–66
land scrip: value of, 264
lands, Cherokee: 136–137, 274
Lange, Leeder: 590
Langhum, B. B.: 648
Langhum, Charles: 648
Lann, James W.: 594
La Panticlen. SEE Lipantitlán
La Parita Creek: 488, 490–491
La Pita-Presidio road: 313

Laredo, Texas: mention of, 10, 236, 502, 516, 525, 536–537, 560; García (J. M.) at, 12; and Vasquez (R.) campaign, 50; depredations of Indians against, 110, 512; Texan attack on, 112, 483, 506—510; Mexican garrison at, 481, 504, 509–510; and Somervell (A.) expedition, 483, 500, 501, 502–503, 503–504, 506–508, 508–509, 509–510, 510–511, 514–515, 519–524, 525, 527, 535, 578; officials of, 511 n; flood damage to, 512; description of, 512–513; lack of prosperity of, 512–513; population of, 513; trade of, with San Antonio, 513; looting of, by Texans, 514–515, 519–524, 525, 527; Mexican defense of, 539, 561
Laredo, Villa San Augustín de. SEE Laredo, Texas
Laredo crossing of Nueces: 571
Laredo road: 484, 486, 490, 572, 574, 575
La Retama, Camp: 535
Larget, John: 605
Larison, Thomas: 628
Larkey, David M.: 605
Laroque, J. E.: 640
La Rosita: Mexican army at, 241
Las Moras Creek: 313
Las Motas de Agua Dulce: 242
Las Rucias: 15 n
Latham, F. S.: 148, 216, 273
Latham, James: 225
La Trinidad Creek: 241
Latto, William: 589
Lauderdale, S. J.: 625
Lauderdale, Tennessee: 467 n
Lavaca River: volunteers from, 21, 23–24, 338, 348, 389, 437, 444; mention of, 45, 115 n, 337, 343, 445, 577 n
law, Mexican: 37
lawlessness: on Texan frontier, 4–5, 211–212, 418
Lawrence, A. F.: 617
Lawrence, Charles: 591
Lawrence, John: 605
Lawson, Albert: 594
lawyers: 193, 602 n–603 n
Lea, Martin A.: 134
lead: mention of, 23 n, 61, 78, 288 n, 304; contraband trade in, 119; report on, 172; contribution of, to Texas cause, 213; procuring of, 337, 470–471, 472,

Lockhart, J.: 427
Lockhart, John Washington: 533
Lockheart, W. B.: 599
Lockman, Stanley. SEE Lockerman, Stanley
Lockmar, Anton: 224
Lockmar, Antonio. SEE Lockmar, Anton
Loftis, Charles: 646
Loftis, G. W.: 636
Logan County, Kentucky: 174 n
Lokey, ———: 596
Loler, Levi: 625
lomerío de San Saba: 315
London, England: raising of Texas loan in, 106; mention of, 124, 127
Lonerin, William H. SEE Loverin, William H.
lone star flag. SEE flag, Texan
Long, J. H.: 648
Long, J. M.: 93, 222
Lonis, James: 593
Lookout Tower. SEE Powder House
Looncy, Henry P.: 598
Loonis, J.: 635
looting: of San Antonio by Mexican troops, 31; of Laredo, by Texans, 461, 522–523, 524
Loper, M.: 611
Lord, George: 497, 630
Lords of the Treasury, England: permit *Montezuma* to sail, 128
Loscew, M.: 524
Los Olmos Creek: 240, 241
Los Patricios Creek: 241
Los Presenos Creek: 241
Lothrop, J. T. K.: 121
Lott, Bob. SEE Lott, R. A.
Lott, R. A.: 522, 644
Lough Fergus Farm, Scotland: 18 n
Louis, W. L.: 640
Louisiana: mention of, 64 n, 88 n, 532, 576; volunteers from, 133, 437
Louisville, Kentucky: 146, 148
Love, Frank: 594
Love, H.: 641
Love, James: at Galveston public meeting, 71, 72, 163; on Galveston committee of vigilance, 71; and Houston (S.), 218; mention of, 590
Love, Robert: 645
Loverin, William H.: 594
Lowe, John: 361
Lowe, Winfield S.: 621 n, 622

Lowery, James P. SEE Lowrey, James P.
Lowrey, James P.: 544, 565, 572, 646
Loyalist Look Out: 181
Loyd, Joseph: 593
Lubbock, Francis R.: 527 n, 531 n
Lubbock, Thomas S.: 417, 445, 463 n, 565 n, 646
Luckie, Samuel H.: 350, 389, 390
Luis (Apache): 494 n, 575
lumber: cargo of, 85
lumbering: 559 n
Lumley, Thomas: 607
Lusk, P. H.: 644
Lusk, William H.: 593, 635
Luther, Samuel: 588
Lynch, E. O.: 590
Lynch, W. C. C.: 593, 635
Lynchburg, Texas: 74
Lyon, Mark T.: 619
Lyon, P.: 641
Lyons, S. C.: 635

Mabe, James: 619
machetes: 568
Macomb, David: 518
Madison Parish, Louisiana: 175 n
Madley, John: 14
Magers, Alonzo G.: 592
Magill, John H.: 590
maguey: ropes made from, 494
Maher, Patrick: 630
Mahler farm: 348
mails. SEE postal service, Texas
Maine: 622
Main Plaza. SEE Plaza de Constitución, San Antonio
major general, militia: office of, 274; election of, 274–275
Mallon, Nathan R.: 304, 336, 589
Malone, Simon: 619
Maltby, T. D.: 646
Manero, Victores: 378
Manga de Clavo, Mexico: 298
manifest destiny: 143
Manley, A. P.: 26 n
Mann, James E.: 629
Mann, William H.: 605
Manning, Levi: 636
Mansy, John: 591
Manton, Edward T.: 333, 375, 623
manufactures, British: 126
marauders: on Texas frontier, 5–6, 24,

Index

Zuñiga. SEE La Bahía del Espíritu Santo, Texas

Nuestra Señora del Refugio: 41, 86, 223

Nuevo León, Mexico: auxiliaries in, 9–10; Comanche attack upon, 230; mention of, 311

Nuevo Santander, Colonia del: 512

nullification controversy, South Carolina: 106 n

Nye, Alvin: 591, 637

oats: 551

O'Bannon, J.: 648

O'Brian, John: 590

Ocean: brings volunteers, 518

Ochula Lake: Texan camp near, 190

O'Conner, Hugh. SEE O'Connor, Hugh

O'Connor, Hugh: 178 n, 203, 245, 612

O'Connor, Thomas J.: 593

Odair, John: 611

O'Daniel, ——: 609

Odd Fellows' Hall: Senate meets at, 197

Odin, John M.: 351

Odum, R. P.: 631

Ogden, D. C. SEE Ogden, Duncan C.

Ogden, Duncan C.: Seguin's (J. N.) debt to, 11; and Vasquez raid, 23, 26, 30, 33, 56; as Woll (A.) prisoner, 602

Ogden, James M.: 64 n, 633

Ogilvie, W. C.: 613

Ohio: 20 n, 343 n

Ohio Statesman-Extra (Columbus): 59

Old Capitol building, Houston: 197

Old Franklin. SEE Franklin, Texas

Oldham, ——: 593

Oldham, T. S.: 641

Oldham, William: 642

"Old Paint." SEE Caldwell, Mathew

"Old Pike": 494, 501 n

"Old Sam." SEE Houston, Sam

Old San Antonio Road: 512

"Old Three Hundred": 477 n

Oliphant, J. N.: 592

Oliphant, James: 590

Oliphant, William: 624

Oliver, Robert: 444 n, 611

Olmos Creek: 240, 241

O'Meara, ——: 609

O'Neal, James R.: 141–142

O'Neill, James: 598

O'Phelan, William H.: 328, 602

ordnance, Texan: depletion of, 143

Ortiz, Guillermo: 324 n

Ortiz, Reyes: 511 n

Osborn, J. M.: 642

Osborne, J. A.: 613

Osbourne, J.: 609

Oso, Rincón del: 63–64, 229

Oso River: 208

Otto, John: 605

Outersides, William: 593

Outlaw, N. S.: 643

overcoats: 355

Overton, D.: 637

Owen, Anthony: 636

Owen, Clark L.: mention of, 40 n, 47, 187, 253, 422, 445, 592, 594–597; at Goliad, 44; as leader of Texan troops, 44–45, 86, 112 n, 177; and land-sea expedition, 86; Burleson (E.) receives report from, 99; Williams (A.) instructed to report to, 177; biographical sketch of, 177 n; in Sixth Congress, 177 n; relinquishes command to Casey (T.), 178–179; reports Mexican advance upon Corpus Christi, 242; to collect beeves, 244; commands ranger company at Victoria, 280, 295, 340; ordered to collect ammunition, 291; and Houston (S.), 295; and Somervell expedition, 478, 566, 638

Owen, James D.: 40 n, 283, 340

Owen, M. T.: 632

Owen, Robert: 588

Owen, William: 588

Owens, J.: 635

Owens, P. W.: 648

Ownsby, James P.: 187–188

oxen: mention of, 32, 341, 347, 349, 383 n, 479; hides of, 35; sale of, 76; impressment of, 276, 470; driven off from Laredo, 511; Mexican seizure of, 524

oystering: 86

Pace, Richard E.: 634

Pace, Robert: 588

Padget, James: 591

Page, Frederic Benjamin: 452

Page, Harrison: 593

Page, Jefferson: 640

Pain, Govan: 203 n, 612

paixhan guns: 129, 150

Pajaritos Creek: 53

Pakenham, Richard: sends Hamilton's (J.) letter to Santa Anna (A. L. de), 106; attitude of, toward Texas, 131; on

727

Texan Santa Fé expedition, 131; and mediation, 131; mention of, 602
Palacios, Eulalio: 42
Palmer, John: 605
Palmer, Thomas: 589
Palo Blanco: 241
Panic of 1837: effects of, on Texas, 5–6; U.S. recovery from, 212
pañola. SEE "cold flour"
Panola County, Texas. SEE Harrison County, Texas
pantaloons: mention of, 60, 80, 609; shortage of, 465, 476
Panther: taken as prize, 86
panthers: 502–503
papyrus: made from Maguey plant, 494
Parez, Antonio: 304
Paris, France: 308
Paris, Texas: militia at, 195
Parita Creek: 488, 490–491
Park, John: 648
Park, Moses: 640, 642
Parke, W. C.: 615
Parker, J. W.: 559 n
Parker, N. B.: 590
Parker, W. T.: 630
Parkersburg, Virginia: 138
Parkerson, Millard M.: 589
Parkman, Curtis: 593
Paso Cavallo: location of, 74–75; mention of, 84; Texan expedition crosses bar at, 85; customhouse near, 115 n
Paso de Aguila: 449, 501
Paso de Jacinto: 503 n, 509, 512
Paso del Gobernador: 286
Paso de los Indios: 503 n, 509, 512
Paso de Miguel de la Garza: 503 n, 512
Paso de Santa Cruz: 241
Patricios Creek: 241
patrols, military: 90
Patterson, D. B.: 643
Patterson, W. D.: 404–405, 623
Patton, ——: 23
Patton, Charles F.: 593
Patton, J. M.: 588
Patton, William H.: 24, 52, 106 n
Pavón, Francisco González: 481
Pawling, Benjamin M.: 607
Paxton, James: 300 n
Payne, B. Owen: 288
Payne, John: 627
Payton, J. E.: 624
Peach Creek: 338, 386 n

Peacock, ——: 23
Peacock, James: 598, 638
Peacock, John: 591
Pearce, Benjamin B.: 597, 638
Pearce, Theodore: 598
Pearson, J.: 614
Pearson, William H.: 462 n
peasants, German: 420
—, Irish: 420
Pease, Elisha Marshall: 593
pecans: 313, 461, 463, 576
Pecan Street, Austin, Texas: 96
Peck, Ruluff: 203 n, 612
Pedraza, M. Gómez: 309
Peel, ——: 612
Peel, Robert: 125, 131
Peeples, William: 612
Peetree, Peter: 625
pelados: 409
Pembroke: 127 n
Pendleton, John Wesley: 623
Pennington, Elijah: 632
Pennington, Elisha: 632
Pennington, James: 646
Pennington, Purity: 559 n
Pennsylvania: 19 n, 441 n
Peoples, William: 203 n
Pepkin, William: 631
Pérez, Antonio: in San Antonio, 10, 431, 505; mention of, 326; pursues Hays (J. C.), 355; reports march of Somervell expedition, 505; at Presidio del Río Grande, 505
Perkins, Aloni: 626
Perkins, G. W.: 640
Perky, S. H.: 607
perogue: 507, 510
Perote Castle, Mexico: 601–603
Perrot, William: 607
Perry, Cicero Rufus: 368
Perry, Hurd ("Dutch"): 394 n
Perry, James F.: 169, 532
Perry, John: 602
Perry, John S.: 620
Perry, Rufus: 588
Perry, S. W.: 644
Perry County, Alabama: 175
Peters, ——: 609
Peterson, C. W. SEE Peterson, Cornelius W.
Peterson, Charles: 320, 323, 611
Peterson, Cornelius W.: 602
Peterson, Oliver: 611

powder: mention of, 23 n, 61, 288 n, 304, 609; and Vasquez raid, 29, 46; capture of, 46, 250; Mexican trade in, 119; report on, 172; contribution of, 213; Hays (J. C.) obtains, 337; sent to Galveston, 411; shortage of, 436, 465, 467, 470
powder flasks: report on, 172
powder horns: 74, 155
Powder House, San Antonio: location of, 32, 451; Texan spies near, 346–347; description of, 346 n; Hays (J. C.) approach to, 354–355
Powell, Charles: 591
Powell, Samuel G.: 333
Powell, W. S.: 637
Powell, William F.: 589
Power, —— (of New York): as reported owner of *Mary Elizabeth*, 119
Power, Charles: 125
Power, James: 86, 175, 179
Power and Hewetson Colony: 86
Presbyterian Church, Galveston: 425
—, Houston: House of Representatives meets at, 198
Presenos Creek: 241
President, Texas: election of, 5, 99
—, United States: 218
President's Hill, Austin: 68
presidial company, Béxar: 344–345
—, Laredo: 344–345
presidials: 7, 9, 352
Presidio Crossing, Río Grande: 403, 486, 512
Presidio del Río Grande: Texan spies on, 15; Vasquez (R.) at, 49; Woll (A.) at, 54, 311, 403; mention of, 155, 313, 333, 449, 474 n, 558 n; route from San Antonio to, 165; Texan prisoners at, 323 n, 329, 332, 463 n; Reyes (I.) at, 377, 501, 506; Seguin (J. N.) at, 385; Texan commissioners at, 432; Mexican troops at, 463, 481, 561; provisions at, 464; proposed attack on, 483; Cherokees near, 484
Presidio del San Miguel Lipantitlán. See Lipantitlán, Texas
Presidio-La Pita road: 313
Presidio road: 26, 307, 330, 386, 473, 479, 484, 486–487
press, in Texas: irresponsibility of, 166
Preston, S. S.: 649
Price, J.: 637
Price, Jesse: 619

Price, John T.: 253, 594 n, 638
Price, Williamson: 627
prickly pear: 313, 331, 343, 350, 449, 493, 537
Prigo: volunteers sent in, 183
Primrose, M.: 592
prisoners, Dawson: taking of, 334, 385; treatment of, 373–374 383 n; on affair at Arroyo Hondo, 397–398
—, Mexican: at San Jacinto, 310; capture of, by Hays (J. C.), 335, 388, 500; capture of, at Corpus Christi, 340; reveal information about Woll's (A.) army, 347, 382; taken to Caldwell's (M.) camp, 388; release of, 433
—, San Antonio: address of, to the people of Texas, 320, 326–328; capture of, 321, 322; treatment of, 325; removal of, to Mexico, 328, 330, 334, 406, 441 n, 463, 474 n
—, Santa Fé: mention of, 10, 580; Caldwell (M.) as, 400; return of, 408
privateers: 117, 119
private property, Texan: seized by Mexican army, 35, 37; impressment of, 92, 418
prizes: adjudication of, 79
proclamations, Texan: 135
—, Mexican: mention of, 7, 269; distribution of, in Texas, 37, 40, 41, 44, 86; of Woll (A.) to troops, 404
Progreso: capture of, by Texas navy, 118; transports supplies for Mexican army, 119
Providence, Rhode Island: 343 n
Provisional Government, Texas: 20 n
provisions: mention of, 20, 73–75, 80, 406; requisition of, 23, 547; contribution of, 76, 213, 514; from United States citizens, 213; shortage of, 512; in Laredo, 512, 514
Provost, J. L.: 613
public credit, Texas: decline of, 199
public opinion: on invasion of Mexico, 267
Public Plaza. See Plaza de Constitución, San Antonio
public records, Texas: loss of, 48; disposition of, at Austin, 65–66
Pucket, R. R.: 632
Pulaski, Tennessee: 19 n
Pullam, E. P.: 635
pumpkins: 420
Purcell, Edward: 593

731

Reed, Robert: 588
Reed, William: 597
Reed and Company, James: 137
Reese, C. R.: 635
Reese, Charles K.: 541, 561 n
Reese, W. E.: 635
reform, retrenchment and: 425
Refugio, Texas: Mexican attack on, ordered by Mexico, 7, 41, 579; mention of, 44, 59, 93, 242, 580; Texan sea expedition sends express to, 86
Refugio, Mission of: 41, 86, 223
Refugio County, Texas: mention of, 175, 340; requisition of cattle in, 189; and militia draft, 194; chief justice of, 340 n
Regenearador: 129
Regiment, First, First Brigade (Southwestern Army): 444
—, First, Second Brigade (Southwestern Army): 444
—, Fourth, Second Battalion (Army of the North): 240, 242, 251
—, Seventh, First Battalion (Army of the North): 250
—, Seventh, Third Company (Army of the North): 250
Reid, S. C.: 614
Reid, W. T.: 618
Reilly, Michael: 189
Reily, James: 129; on U.S. Indians on frontier, 139; on protection of U.S. citizens, 139–140
Reinosa, Mexico: mention of, 39, 536; offensive operations against, 112; recruitment of Indians at, 237; auxiliaries from, 240, 242
Rennels, H. A.: 587
Renner, D. G.: 606
Republic of the Río Grande: 333
Retama, Camp La: 535
retrenchment and reform: 425
Retrieve: seizure of, by Texas, 174; transports volunteers, 174
Reveilla, Mexico. SEE Guerrero, Mexico
revenue cutter: 79
revolution, Texas: effects of, on frontier, 3–4; mention of, 343, 441 n
Reyes, Isidro: commands Army of the North, 236, 239, 299, 310; address of, to troops, 239; orders of, to Montero (C.), 240; foreign negotiations with, 294; as governor and commandant general of the Department of Puebla, 299;

and Woll (A.) raid, 312, 377, 404; Texan flag forwarded to, 321; and Woll (A.) prisoners, 329, 332; mention of, 329, 354, 505–506; and defense against Texans, 448–449, 482; as Minister of War, 448 n; at San Fernando, 481; at Lampazos, 481 n, 482 n; at Paso de Aguila, 501; and Texan deserters, 520
Reynolds, H. A. SEE Rennels, H. A.
Reynolds, Isham: 598
Reynolds, James A.: 205
Rhea, ———: murder of, 339
Rhinosa, Mexico. SEE Reinosa, Mexico
Rhodes, John A.: 640
Rice, ———: 336
Rice, J. G.: 640, 642
Rice, James O.: 576
Rice, Lorenzo D.: 589
Rice, Robert: 589
Rice, S.: 642
Rice, Sanford: 647
Rice, Thomas: 623
Richardson, J. E.: 618
Richardson, John: 203 n, 612
Richmond, Texas: and Vasquez raid, 63; mention of, 77, 435, 592; militia at, 194
Ricks, George W.: 589
Riddle, John: 322, 602
Riddle, Sarah Elizabeth: 19
Riddle, W. C.: SEE Riddle, Wilson Irwin
Riddle, W. J.: SEE Riddle, Wilson Irwin
Riddle, Wilson Irwin: as merchant, 11, 19 n; at San Antonio, 11, 18, 19 n; biographical sketch of, 19 n; loss of property of, in Mexican raids, 19 n, 524; capture of, 19 n, 322; furnishes supplies for troops, 23; as Woll (A.) prisoner, 322, 602
Riddle, Mrs. Wilson I.: 19
Riddle, Wilson J.: SEE Riddle, Wilson Irwin
Ridgeway, J. L.: 647
Ridins, G. B.: 644
rifles: capture of, by Mexicans, 43, 223, 250; mention of, 60, 74, 80, 95, 155, 342, 484, 609, 615, 617–619; contribution of, 75; report on, 172
Rigley, John: 591
Riley, ———: 609
Riley, John: 203n, 612
Rincón de la Cerda: 250
Rincón del Oso: 63–64, 229
Ringo, ———: 594

Index

Ringold, Thomas: 629
Río Bravo del Norte. SEE Río Grande
Río Frio: mention of, 16, 315, 557, 570, 572; Texan prisoners at, 331; in flood, 480; Somervell expedition crosses, 491
Río Grande: as boundary of Texas, 4, 525; Mexican authority north of, 4, 97, 110; mention of, 6–7, 10, 37, 41, 43, 47, 49, 94, 116, 145, 157 n, 182, 192, 200–201, 208, 214, 221, 223, 226, 236, 238, 243, 267, 280, 290–291, 293, 295, 300, 304, 307, 328, 351, 354, 412, 417, 422, 429, 447, 458, 476, 481, 484, 486, 506, 512, 516, 534, 536, 538, 540, 562, 566, 571, 624 n; Mexican military forces along, 9, 15, 230, 240, 339, 449, 535; Texas plans attack along, 64, 85, 93, 96, 97, 101, 105, 107, 155, 158, 165, 229, 408, 420–421; Vasquez's (R.) army crosses, 100; Mexican traders on, 207; Woll (A.) raid from, 229 n, 230, 240, 331, 403; Texan spy companies near, 273; Fort Duncan on, 313; Woll (A.) prisoners at, 331, 332; driving off of cattle to, 430; closing of roads to, 433; Somervell expedition on, 497, 503, 507, 515, 529, 541, 542; conditions on, 537; in flood, 551; settlements along, 580
Río Grande, Presidial Cavalry from: 50
Río Grande City, Texas: 471 n
Río Grande Company (Mexican): 391
Río Hondo. SEE Hondo Arroyo
Río Salado. SEE Salado Creek; Salado River (Mexico)
Río Seco: Fort Lincoln on, 313; Woll (A.) prisoners at, 330; mention of, 479
Ripley, William: 630
Ritchie, William: 642
Rivas, ———. SEE Reavis, James B.
road, Austin–San Antonio: 366 n
—, Gonzales–San Antonio: 32 n, 352
—, La Bahía: 32 n, 433
—, Laredo: 484, 486, 490, 572, 574, 575
—, Matamoros: 185
—, Medina: 433
—, Pittman: 366 n
—, Presidio del Río Grande: 26, 307, 330, 386, 473, 479, 484, 486–487
—, Presidio–La Pita: 313
—, San Antonio: 512, 528
—, San Antonio–Monclova: 332
—, San Marcos: 377
—, Seguin–San Antonio: 32, 343, 359

—, Uvalde–San Antonio: 313
roads: across west Texas, 313; on Galveston Island, 426
Roan, John: 628
Roark, John A.: 648
Roarke, ———: 609
robbers: 13, 211–212, 461. SEE ALSO marauders
Robbins, Joshua: 624
Roberts, Allen: 625
Roberts, C. M.: 642
Roberts, Henry H.: 647
Roberts, Thomas: 636
Roberston, E. P.: 629
Robertson, Elijah Sterling Clack: mention of, 445, 463 n, 485 n, 559 n, 642–643; on Somervell expedition, 478, 531 n, 641
Robertson, J. C.: 643
Robertson, Jerome B.: as brigade inspector, 442; mention of, 445, 500; on Somervell expedition, 478, 495, 531 n, 643
Robertson County, Texas: mention of, 114, 176; militia in, 195, 290, 410; and "war bill," 257; volunteers from, 290, 410
Robespierre, Maximilien: 158
Robinson, ———: 286
Robinson, E.: 640
Robinson, James W.: flees San Antonio, 19; biographical sketch of, 20 n; as Woll (A.) prisoner, 20 n, 323, 603; death of, 20 n; gun of, kills Van Ness (C.), 29 n, 224; purchase of horse for, 333
Robinson, Joseph C.: 590, 623
Robinson, Thomas: 596
Robinson, Tod: and "war bill," 257; military service of, 593
Robison, Daniel: 648
Rock, Charles: 649
Rockefellow, Peter. SEE Rockefeller, Peter
Rockfeller, Peter: 595, 638
Rockley, Wilson: 625
Rocky, Camp: 413, 436
Rocky Mountains: 292 n–293 n
Rodgers, ———: 607
Rodgers, J. D.: 427
Rodham, Charles: 608
Rodríquez, Ambrosio: 33, 52, 55, 324 n
Rodríquez, Basilio: 324 n
Rodríguez y Taylor, Marina: 333
Roemer, Ferdinand: 456–457
Rogers, F. A.: 598
Rogers, H. A.: 598

Sargent, Carter: 645
Sargent, William: 645
Sasse, Jacob: 592
Saterthwait, S.: 588
Saunders, Leonidas: 629
Savage, William: 623
Savannah, Georgia: 146
Savariego, Manuel: ordered to invade
   Texas, 7; Mexicans leagued with, 223;
   Indians join command of, 237
saw mill: near San Juan Capistrano, 439
Sayre, W. B.: 610
Scallions, Elam. SEE Scallons, Elam
Scallions, John W. SEE Scallons, John
   Wesley
Scallions, John Wesley. SEE Scallons, John
   Wesley
Scallons, Elam: 374, 623
Scallons, John Wesley: 623
Schaeffer, George P.: 603
Schaffer, George P. SEE Schaeffer, George
   P.
Schenck, Jacob: 594
Schlitter, Bartolome: 589
Schmidt & Company: 119
Scoby, A. W.: 635
Scotland: 253 n
Scott, ——: 67
Scott, Captain: 204 n
Scott, Andrew: 595
Scott, George W.: 70
Scott, J.: 609, 635
Scott, James W.: 53
Scott, John A.: 629
Scott, Jonathan: 637
Scott, William F.: 178 n
Scott, Winfield: 308
scouts, Mexican: 33, 352. SEE ALSO spies,
   Mexican
—, Texan: from Austin, 68; increasing ac-
   tivity of, 383; reports from, 538; pursuit
   of, by Mexican troops, 542–543. SEE
   ALSO spies, Texan; spy company, Texan
screech owls: 489
Scurry, Thomas: 467 n
Se—— (illegible), John A.: 590
Seafield, Charles: 590
Seaton, George W.: 628
Seben, E.: 644
Seco Creek. SEE Río Seco
Second Battalion, Fourth Regiment, Army
   of the North: 242, 251

Second Battalion of the Fourth Regiment
   of infantry, Army of the North: 240
Second Company of Auxiliaries, Reinosa:
   251
Second Regiment, First Brigade of Militia,
   Texas: 412
Second Regiment of Cavalry. SEE army,
   Texas: Second Regiment of cavalry of
Secrest, J. M.: 599
Secrest, Washington H.: 411
secret agent, Mexican: 105
Secretary of State, Texas: 133
Secretary of the Treasury, Texas: 64 n, 67,
   133
Secretary of War and Marine, Texas:
   Hockley (G. W.) as, 11–12, 413–414;
   Austin Vigilance Committee to, 65;
   mention of, 74, 558; Somervell (A.) as,
   88 n, 532; militia draft prepared by,
   193; Hunt (M.) declines office of, 266;
   and Hays (J. C.), 280, 335; Hamilton
   (M. C.) as, 414, 466–468, 479. SEE
   ALSO War and Marine, Texas Department of
Seegar, William: 121
Seer, J. B.: 524
Seguin, Erasmo: mention of, 53; cattle
   stolen from, 204; follows Woll's (A.)
   army, 384
Seguin, Juan Nepomuceno: at trial of
   González (J. M.), 10 n; as mayor of
   San Antonio, 11, 53; visits Mexico in
   1841, 11; and Vasquez raid, 11, 12, 18,
   38, 52; and defense of San Antonio, 12;
   mention of, 29 n, 304 n, 305, 326, 346,
   384, 518 n; and Santa Fé expedition,
   37; and Arista's (M.) proclamation, 37;
   and Burleson (E.), 52; hostility at San
   Antonio toward, 52; attacks on, 53, 100;
   military service of, to Texas, 53; biographical sketch of, 53–54; seeks asylum
   in Mexico, 53, 54; and Woll raid, 54,
   313, 317, 319 n, 352–353, 357–358;
   visit of, to San Antonio, 282; and Goodman, 319 n; warning of, to Mexicans of
   San Antonio, 385; regrets leaving Texas,
   385; return of, to San Antonio, 431
Seguin, Texas: mention of, 12, 22, 33, 35,
   301–302, 338, 413, 441 n, 576; history
   of, 15 n, 335–336; and Vasquez raid, 15,
   18, 21, 23, 25, 33, 34, 35, 68, 69; refugees at, 21; Anglo-Texans escape to,
   322; and Woll raid, 322, 336, 337, 339,

Index

Smilcir, John: 593
Smith, ——: 436, 495
Smith, Ashbel: Jones (A.) to, 80; mission of, to Britain, 81 n, 128; at Galveston, 81 n; and Saligny (A. de), 123, 139; goes to France, 130–131; at New York, 262; Hockley (G. W.) to, 414 n
Smith, B. E.: 614
Smith, Donald: 589, 645
Smith, E. H.: 645
Smith, Edward W.: 562
Smith, Erastus ("Deaf"): 310, 367, 411
Smith, Mrs. Erastus: 461
Smith, Francis: 593
Smith, French: 24
Smith, Gabriel: 633
Smith, Gardiner: 413, 445, 478, 646
Smith, Henry: 221
Smith, Henry M.: 591
Smith, J. C.: 611
Smith, Jackson: 625
Smith, James: 588
Smith, Jesse: 648
Smith, John: 603, 636, 642
Smith, John M.: 45, 597
Smith, John P.: 637
Smith, John W.: and Seguin (J. N.), 54; rumored to have joined Mexicans, 70; as assistant quartermaster, 99; as mayor of San Antonio, 223, 304; letters of, 224; and Woll raid, 304, 322, 326, 336, 349, 389 n, 429; biographical sketch of, 304 n, 336 n; as senator from Béxar, 304 n, 336 n; death of, 304 n
Smith, Joseph: 418
Smith, Joseph F.: 205, 207
Smith, Leroy H.: 639
Smith, N. O.: 417
Smith, S. R.: 626
Smith, T. J.: 627
Smith, Thomas: 596, 632
Smith, Thomas S.: 592
Smith, Walter: 133, 137, 150
Smith, William: 640–641
Smith, William H.: 20 n
Smith, William W.: 629
Smither, Robert: 444 n
Smithers, Launcelot: biographical sketch of, 30 n; murder of, 30 n, 339, 352–353; as mayor pro tempore of San Antonio, 30 n; and Vasquez raid, 30; as clerk, 36 n
Smithson, E. C.: 588

smuggling: 126, 214–215
snakes: 315
Sneath, J.: 640
Sneed, Richard: 203 n
Sneed, Thomas: 612
Snelling, John O.: 26 n
Snively, Jacob: as quartermaster general, 66; as acting assistant inspector general of militia, 195; reports stolen property, 203 n; supplies requested of, 466
Snodgrass, William: 43, 86
Snook, J.: 630
Soledad Street, San Antonio: 19 n, 326
Solórzano, Joaquín: 309
Somervell, Alexander: commands troops following Vasquez raid, 56, 81, 88, 90, 98, 100, 111–112, 114–115, 182; biographical sketch of, 88 n, 532–533; and Houston (S.), 90, 182, 417, 423, 497; cited for bravery, 98 n; and Green (T. J.), 100; mention of, 157 n, 421, 429, 442, 446, 455, 461, 464, 467, 471–472, 581; authorized to cross the Río Grande, 112; as collector of customs, 115, 577 n; commands troops following Woll raid, 415, 416, 417, 422, 423, 428, 437, 440–441, 447, 458, 462, 463, 468–469; orders to, 422, 423, 468–469, 497; polls army on deposing Houston (S.), 423; Telegraph and Texas Register on, 428, 498; protection of private property by, 436; and Bogart (S.), 447; criticism of, 458, 498, 516–517, 528, 557, 561; caliber of troops under, 462; and deserters, 472, 501; leads expedition to Río Grande, 480, 489, 494–577 passim; and Hays (J. C.), 449, 495; and looting, 501, 519, 522, 525–526; captures Laredo, 503–508, 511, 514, 519, 522, 525–526, 527; defense of, 533–534, 557–558; capture of Guerrero by, 544, 545–546, 549, 551, 553, 555–556; and Flacco, 575; death of, 577 n
Somervell expedition: McCulloch (B.) serves as scout on, 386 n; mention of, 407, 583; description of soldiers on, 439, 485–486; organizing of, 443; army units in, 444, 532, 533; size of, 483, 531 n; equipping of, 484; march of 484, 486, 487–490, 492, 497, 502, 527; in the bogs of the Atascosa, 487–490; illness on, 492; food supply for, 493, 496; at Nueces, 495–496; captures Laredo,

503–508, 511, 514, 519, 522, 525–526, 527; discontent of troops in, 528, 536, 548–549; lack of discipline in, 528, 562–564; and invasion of Mexico, 530; Green (T. J.) on, 531 n; McCutchan (J. D.) on, 531 n; Somervell (A.) on, 531 n; capture of Guerrero by, 544, 545–546, 549, 551, 553, 555–556; march home of, 552, 557, 567–584; and Mier expedition, 552, 561–562, 562–564

Sorrells, James: 26 n

Sorrels, ———: 612

Soto, ———: 408 n

Soto, Mrs. Jesusa: 20

Soto La Marina, Mexico: 308

South American Association. SEE Mexican and South American Association, 124

South Carolina: 133, 441 n

Southmazd, John A.: 647

Southwestern Army. SEE Somervell expedition

Southwestern Army of Operations. SEE Somervell expedition

southwestern frontier: ranger companies for, 274

Southwick, Stephen: 591

Sowell, Andrew: 351

Spain: 29 n

Spaniards: 119, 298

Spence, A.: 642

Spencer, (son of J. C.), 141

Spencer, A.: 614

Spencer, J. C.: 141

Spencer, Winfield S.: 593

spies, Mexican: capture of, 100, 497; execution of, 100; at Corpus Christi, 286; traders as, 299; report made by, 315–316; for Woll (A.), 315–316; report about, 328, 423, 433, 497; kill Texans, 389; escape of, 502; mention of, 515, 538. SEE ALSO scouts, Mexican

—, Texan: and Vasquez raid, 15, 24, 26–27, 49, 59, 100; toward Río Grande, 15, 431–432; pursuit of, 24; capture of, 26–27, 49; report about, 26–27, 433; near Victoria, 59; on Vasquez's (R.) army, 100; on Mexican Río Grande defenses, 238; and Woll raid, 245, 286, 296, 306, 307, 335, 336, 339, 340, 344, 345, 346, 364–365, 368; at Corpus Christi, 286; from Victoria, 286, 339; near San Antonio, 306, 307, 335, 344; need for, 335; from Goliad, 339; on Nueces, 340, 432;

mutinous condition in, 345; reorganization of, 346; for Dawson (N. M.), 364–365; for Billingsley (J.), 368; and Somervell expedition, 431–432, 433, 506; for Bogart (S.), 431, 432; inadequate corps of, 431–432; led by Mexican guide, 433; army awaits return of, 506. SEE ALSO scouts, Texan; spy company, Texan

Springfield, Massachusetts: 68

spurs: made of silver, 456; making of, 466

spy camp: removal of, 476

spy company, Texan: on frontier, 91; proposed formation of, 157, 188, 447; number of men in, 189; mention of, 575

standard, Texan. SEE flag, Texan

Stansbury, N.: 615

Stapp, ———: 531 n–532 n

Stapp, D. M.: 598

Stapp, Elijah: 247 n

Stapp, Nancy Shannon: 247 n

Stapp, Oliver H.: 598, 637

Stapp, W. W.: 637

Stapp, Walter: 598

Stapp, William Preston: 247 n, 605, 637

Starr, A. W.: 619

State, Texas Secretary of: 133

steamship, iron: 73, 127

Stedman, John: 589

Steel, ———: 612

Steel, H.: 626

Stephens, J. B.: 629

Stephens, J. C.: 87, 591

Stephens, J. M.: SEE Stephens, John M.

Stephens, John M.: 587, 627

Stephens, J. S.: 645

Stephens, Thomas: 587

Stern, Isaac: 598

Sterne, Adolphus: on depression, 221; on condition of the mails, 225; prophesies Mexican invasion, 341; on frontier conditions, 418

Sternes, John: 607

Stevenson, Alexander: 173, 191, 277, 604

Stevenson, E. W.: 461

Stevenson, J. B.: 627

Stewart, Augustus: 618

Stewart, Charles B.: 634

Stewart, David: 634

Stewart, James: 594

Stewart, W. W.: 594

Stickney, ———: 67

Stiff, Jesse: 114–115

744

Index

warships, Mexican: built in U.S., 117; built in England, 117; fear of, 424
"War Song of Texas": 370–371
Warwick, B. F.: 588
Washington, Lewis M. H.: agent to U.S., 134, 153; at Mobile, 150; troops under, 191, 246; at New Orleans, 191, 218; at Corpus Christi, 193; mention of, 196, 279
Washington: cruises of, 43, 79, 177; command of, 79; at Galveston, 79; at Corpus Christi, 87; privateering acts of, 119; transports provisions, 177
Washington, Arkansas: 59
Washington, D.C.: Santa Anna (A. L. de) goes to, 160 n; news of Texan invasion at, 139, 325; and Texas–U.S. treaty, 265; mention of, 386 n
Washington County, Mississippi: 149
Washington County, Texas: volunteers from, 63, 290, 407, 435, 437, 472, 476, 587; militia of, 114, 195, 290, 407, 409, 412, 435, 437, 444, 472, 531, 587; and "war bill," 257; mention of, 259, 445, 469, 477, 531, 560, 577
Washington-on-the-Brazos, Texas: mention of, 64 n, 418, 423, 441 n, 466, 578 n; and Vasquez raid, 342; volunteers from, 342; troops at, 412; government at, 417, 421, 422, 434; *Weekly Texian* at, 419; Congress at, 421, 434; Houston (S.) at, 422 n, 498; contributions to army from, 427; no ammunition at, 469; militia at, 531
Washita Mountains: 115 n
Watchman: 533
water: 44, 157, 165
Waterloo. SEE Austin, Texas
Watkins, John H.: 605
Watkins, William: 596
Watrous, J. C.: 57, 72, 83, 159
Watson, R.: 577
Weaver, Jacob: 620
Weaver, L. G.: 444 n
Webb, James: and "war bill," 257–258; mention of, 442 n
Webb, Thomas H.: 633
Webb, Walter P.: 281, 564
Webb County, Texas: 313
Webber, Charles W.: 594
Webster, Daniel: on Indians' Southwestern frontier, 139; negotiations of, 139; to Thompson (W.), 233–235; to Boca-

negra (J. M.), 233–235
Webster, Julia: 210 n
Webster-Ashburton Treaty: 130
Weekly, George W.: 634
Weekly Texian (Austin): 26
Weeks, Henry D.: 597, 630
Weeks, Joseph: 588
Weems, James E.: 594
Welch, Aristides: 148
Welch, Robert C.: 642
Weldy, Samuel: 595
Wellborn, Jackson: 618
wells: Somervell expedition digs, 490
Wells, ——: 43, 86, 87
Wells, Cretonden: 626
Wells, F.: 588 n
Wells, Francis F.: 595
Wells, Francis W.: 338
Wells, J. L.: 630
Wells, J. M.: 189, 346
Wells, Lysander: 100 n
Wells, Moses: 589
Wells, Norman Miles: 621 n
Welsh, James: 589
Wesson, James M.: 589
West, George: 632, 635
West, J. S.: 599
West, Martin: 629
Westall, Henson G.: 594
Western Advocate (Austin): 419
West Point Military Academy: 517
Weyman, ——: 588 n
Whalen, Henry: 360, 597, 630
Whaling, Henry. SEE Whalen, Henry
Wharton: outfitting of, 71, 75, 80; condition of, 75, 88, 121, 122; and Houston (S.), 80; dispatch of, to Sisal, 118; at New Orleans, 121, 424; at Galveston, 121
Wharton, J.: 616
Wharton, Sarah A.: 517
Wharton County, Texas: 477 n
Wheatons, Mrs.: 435
Wheeler, A. C.: 592
Wheeler, G. O.: 595
Wheeler, J. O.: 592
Wheeler, T.: 630
Wheeler, Tobias: 605
Whitaker, ——: 48–49
Whitaker, J. W.: 588
White, ——: 43
White, A. E.: 630
White, Alvin: 205

747